W9-CEV-497

DISCARD

NTC's AMERICAN IDIOMS DICTIONARY

DATE DUE

OCT 0 6 2010	

BRODART, CO. Cat. No. 23-221-003

NTC's AMERICAN IDIOMS DICTIONARY

The Most Practical Reference for the Everyday Expressions of Contemporary American English

THIRD EDITION

Richard A. Spears, Ph.D.

NTC Publishing Group

Library of Congress Cataloging-in-Publication Data

Spears, Richard A.
NTC's American idioms dictionary / Richard A. Spears — 3rd ed.
p. cm.
Includes index.
ISBN 0-8442-0273-8 (hard) — ISBN 0-8442-0274-6 (soft)
1. English language—United States—Idioms—Dictionaries.
2. Figures of speech—Dictionaries. 3. Americanisms—Dictionaries.
I. Title: American idioms dictionary. II. Title.
PE2839 .S64 2000
423'.1—dc21 99-58402

Cover design by Nick Panos
Interior design by Terry Stone

Published by NTC Publishing Group
A division of NTC/Contemporary Publishing Group, Inc.
4255 West Touhy Avenue, Lincolnwood (Chicago), Illinois 60712-1975 U.S.A.
Copyright © 2000 by NTC/Contemporary Publishing Group, Inc.
All rights reserved. No part of this book may be reproduced, stored in a retrieval system, or transmitted in any form or by any means, electronic, mechanical, photocopying, recording, or otherwise, without the prior written permission of NTC/Contemporary Publishing Group, Inc.
Printed in the United States of America
International Standard Book Number: 0-8442-0273-8 (hardbound)
0-8442-0274-6 (softbound)
02 03 04 05 LB 19 18 17 16 15 14 13 12 11 10 9 8 7 6 5 4 3 2
AUSTIN COMMUNITY COLLEGE
LIBRARY SERVICES

Contents

To the User vii

Terms and Symbols ix

About This Dictionary xi

Dictionary 1

Phrase-Finder Index 447

Appendix 621

To the User

All languages have phrases or sentences that cannot be understood literally. Even if you know the meaning of all the words in a phrase and understand all the grammar of the phrase completely, the meaning of the phrase may still be confusing. Many proverbs, informal phrases, and common sayings offer this kind of problem. A phrase or sentence of this type is said to be idiomatic. This dictionary is a collection of the idiomatic phrases and sentences that occur frequently in American English. The third edition contains more than one thousand idiomatic expressions not listed in the second edition and a number of new features that provide additional convenience and simplicity.

Using the Dictionary

1. Start by looking up the complete phrase that you are seeking in the dictionary. Each expression is alphabetized under the first word of the phrase, except the words *a*, *an*, and *the*. After the first word, entry heads are alphabetized letter by letter. For example, **in so many words** will be found in the section dealing with the letter *i*. Entry phrases are never inverted or reordered like **so many words, in**; **words, in so many**; or **many words, in so**. Initial articles—*a*, *an*, and *the*—are not alphabetized and appear in a different typeface in the entry. In the entry heads, the words *someone* or *one* stand for persons, and *something* stands for things. These and other generic expressions appear in a different typeface.
2. If you do not find the phrase you want, or if you cannot decide exactly what the phrase is, look up any major word in the phrase in the Phrase-Finder Index, which begins on page 447. There you will find all the phrases that contain the key word you have looked up. Pick out the phrase you want and look it up in the dictionary.
3. An entry head may have one or more alternate forms. The entry head and its alternates are printed in **boldface type**, and the alternate forms are preceded by "AND." Two or more alternate forms are separated by a semicolon (;).
4. Many of the entry phrases have more than one major sense. These senses are numbered with boldface numerals.

5. Individual numbered senses may have additional forms that appear in **boldface type**, in which case the AND and the additional form(s) follow the numeral.
6. The boldface entry head (together with any alternate forms) is usually followed by a definition or explanation. Explanations are enclosed in angle brackets (< and >), and explain or describe the entry head rather than define it. Definitions take the form of words, phrases, or sentences that are semantic equivalents of the entry head. Alternate definitions and restatements of the definitions are separated by a semicolon (;). These additional definitions are usually given to show slight differences in meaning or interpretation. Sometimes an alternate definition is given when the vocabulary of the first definition is difficult.
7. Some entries include instructions to look up some other phrase. For example:

   scarcer than hen's teeth Go to (as) scarce as hen's teeth.
8. A definition or explanation may be followed by comments in parentheses. These comments tell about some of the variations of the phrase, explain what it refers to, give other useful information, or indicate cross-referencing.
9. Some definitions are preceded by additional information in square brackets. This information makes the definition clearer by supplying information about the typical grammatical context in which the phrase is found.
10. Sometimes the numbered senses refer only to people or things, but not both, even though the entry head indicates both *someone or something*. In such cases, the numeral is followed by "[with *someone*]" or "[with *something*]."
11. Examples are introduced by a □ or a [T] and are in *italic type*. The [T] introduces an example containing two elements that have been transposed, such as a particle and the object of a verb. This is typically found with phrasal verbs.
12. Some entry heads stand for two or more idiomatic expressions. Parentheses are used to show which parts of the phrase may or may not be present. For example: **(all) set to do something** stands for **all set to do something** and **set to do something**.

Terms and Symbols

[....] enclose a partial entry that is followed by an instruction about where to find the whole entry or a comment. For instance, [heart stands still] Go to one's **heart stands still**.

<....> enclose a description of or explanation about an entry head rather than a definition. For instance, Finders keepers(, losers weepers). <a phrase said when something is found.>

□ (a box) marks the beginning of an example.

[T] (a box containing a "T") marks the beginning of an example in which two elements of the phrase, usually a particle and an object, are transposed.

AND indicates that an entry head has variant forms that are the same or similar in meaning as the entry head. One or more variant forms are preceded by AND.

entry block is the body of an entry starting with a boldface word or phrase type and running to the next boldface word or phrase.

entry head is the first phrase or word, in boldface type, of an **entry block**; the phrase or word that the definition explains.

go to means to turn to the **entry head** indicated.

see also means to consult the **entry head** indicated for additional information or to find expressions similar in form or meaning to the **entry head** containing the **see also** instruction.

Type Styles

Entry heads are printed in **boldface type**, e.g., **Join the club!**

Variable parts of an entry are printed in condensed type, e.g., **just the same (to** someone**)**.

Entry heads being referred to as cross-references are printed in sans serif type, e.g., get the short end of the stick.

Variable parts of cross-references are printed in light condensed type, e.g., ease off (on someone or something).

Words or phrases that are mentioned but are not entries are printed in *italic type*, e.g., (Preceded by *be* or *seem*).

Examples are printed in *italic type*, e.g., □ *The cashier was not allowed to leave the bank until the manager balanced the books.*

Definitions, descriptions, and comments are printed in roman type, e.g., a very active and energetic person who always succeeds.

Words or phrases being emphasized in examples are printed in roman type, e.g., □ *And stop hiding* your *head in the sand. All of us will die somehow, whether we smoke or not.*

The articles *a*, *an*, and *the* appear in roman type at the beginning of an entry head, and these words are ignored in the process of alphabetizing, e.g., a **babe in the woods**, which is found under *B*, not under *T*.

About This Dictionary

NTC's American Idioms Dictionary is designed for easy use by lifelong speakers of English, as well as the new-to-English speaker or learner. The dictionary uses 14,000 examples to illustrate the meanings of approximately 8,500 idiomatic forms in 7,500 entry blocks. An appendix includes 500 irreversible binomial and trinomial phrases. The dictionary contains a unique Phrase-Finder Index that allows the user to identify and look up any expression in the dictionary from a single key word.

This is a dictionary of form and meaning. It focuses on the user's need to know the meaning, usage, and appropriate contexts for each idiomatic phrase. Specialized knowledge of English lexical and sentential semantics and English grammar is not used in indexing, defining, or explaining the idiomatic expressions.

English is a highly variable language. American English has differences that correlate with geographical location, the level and register of use, and other differences that relate to characteristics of the speaker. To include examples that would represent all kinds of American English as spoken by all kinds of speakers is not possible. The kind of American English used in the dictionary is generally what one would expect to hear used by educated, polite individuals representative of the traditional American home, family, and community. It is widely used in the United States and understood by English speakers throughout the country.

Idioms or idiomatic expressions are often defined as "set phrases" or "fixed phrases." The number of idiomatic expressions that are totally invariant is really quite small, however, even when the English proverbs are included in this category. Most such phrases can vary the choice of noun or pronoun and most select from a wide variety of verb tense and aspect patterns. Adjectives and some adverbs can be added at will to idiomatic phrases. Furthermore, the new-to-English user is faced with the difficulty of isolating an idiomatic expression from the rest of the sentence and determining where to find it in a dictionary of idioms. If the user fails to extract the essential idiomatic expression, the likelihood of finding it in *any* dictionary is reduced considerably.

In dictionaries that list each idiomatic expression under a "key word," there may be some difficulty in deciding what the "key word" is. In phrases such as **on the button** or **in the cards**, the key word, the only noun in the phrase, is easy to determine if one has correctly isolated the phrase from the sentence in which it was found. In phrases that have more than one noun, such as **all hours of the day and night** or **A bird in the hand is worth two in the bush**, deciding on a "key word" may be more difficult. It is even more difficult when the only noun in the phrase is one of the variable words, such as with **go around with her old friends**, **go around with Jim**, and **go around with no one at all**, which are examples of **go around with someone**.

This dictionary uses the Phrase-Finder Index to get around the problems users face with trying to isolate the complete idiom and trying to predict its location in the dictionary. Simply look up *any* major word—noun, verb, adjective, or adverb—in the Phrase-Finder index, and you will find the form of the entry head that contains the definition you seek.

Another important feature for the learner is the use of object placeholders indicating human and nonhuman. Typical dictionary entries for idiomatic phrases—especially for phrasal verbs, prepositional verbs, and phrasal prepositional verbs—omit direct objects, as in **put on hold**, **bail out**, or **see through**. This dictionary uses the stand-in forms such as someone, something, some amount, or somewhere for variable objects and other variable forms. These stand-in forms are in condensed type.

All of that information is vital to learners of English, although it seems to come perfectly naturally to lifelong English speakers. For example, there is a big difference between **put someone on hold** and **put something on hold**, or between **bail someone out** and **bail something out**. There is also a great difference between **see something through** and **see through something**. These differences may never be revealed if the entry heads are just **put on hold**, **bail out**, and **see through**, with no object indicated.

Many idioms have optional parts. In fact, a phrase may seem opaque simply because it is really just an ellipsis of a longer, less opaque phrase. This dictionary shows as full a form of an idiom as possible with the frequently omitted parts in parentheses. For example: **back down**

(from someone or something**)**, **be all eyes (and ears)**, and **(every) once in a while**.

The dictionary includes numerous irreversible binomials and trinomials—sequences of two or three words that are in a fixed order, such as *fast and furious*, but not *furious and fast*. These sequences are listed in the Appendix, beginning on page 621, and those that require explanation are cross-referenced to entries in the dictionary.

The compiler has included idiomatic phrases drawn from or suggested by Anne Bertram in *NTC's Dictionary of Proverbs and Clichés*, *NTC's Dictionary of Euphemisms*, and *NTC's Dictionary of Folksy, Regional, and Rural Sayings* and Elizabeth Kirkpatrick in *NTC's English Idioms Dictionary*.

A

[a] <Entries beginning with *a*, *an*, or *the* are alphabetized under the second word in the entry. That means that **a bed of roses** will appear in the *B*s.>

an **A for effort** recognition for having tried to do something even if it was not successful. □ *The plan didn't work, but I'll give you an A for effort for trying so hard.* □ *Bobby played his violin in the concert and got an A for effort. It sounded terrible.*

(a little) new to (all) this an apologetic way of saying that one is experiencing something new or participating in something new and is therefore ineffective or inept. □ *I'm sorry I'm slow. I'm a little new to all this.* □ *She's new to this. She needs practice.*

abide by something to follow the rules of something; to obey someone's orders. □ *John felt that he had to abide by his father's wishes.* □ *All drivers are expected to abide by the rules of the road.*

able to breathe (easily) again AND **able to breathe (freely) again** able to relax and recover from a busy or stressful time; able to catch one's breath. (Also literal. *Able to* can be replaced with *can*.) □ *Now that the lion has been caught, we'll be able to breathe freely again.* □ *Now that the annual sale is over, the sales staff will be able to breathe again.* □ *Final exams are over, so I can breathe easily again.*

able to breathe (freely) again Go to able to breathe (easily) again.

able to do something **blindfolded** AND **able to** do something **standing on** one's **head** able to do something easily and quickly, possibly without even looking. (Informal. *Able to* can be replaced with *can*.) □ *Bill boasted that he could pass his driver's test blindfolded.* □ *Mary is very good with computers. She can program blindfolded.* □ *Dr. Jones is a great surgeon. He can take out an appendix standing on his head.*

able to do something **standing on** one's **head** Go to **able to** do something **blindfolded**.

able to do something **with** one's **eyes closed** able to do something very easily, even without having to think about it or look at it. (Also literal. Also with *can*. Always affirmative.) □ *It's easy. I can do it with my eyes closed.* □ *I can clean the house with my eyes closed! It's easy!*

able to fog a mirror alive, even if just barely. (Usually jocular. Refers to the use of a small mirror placed under one's nose to tell if one is breathing or not.) □ *Look, I don't need an athlete to do this job. Anybody able to fog a mirror will do fine!* □ *I'm so tired this morning, I feel like I'm hardly able to fog a mirror.*

able to make something able to attend an event. (Also literal. Informal. *Able to* can be replaced with *can*.) □ *I don't think I'll be able to make your party, but thanks for asking me.* □ *We are having another one next month. We hope you can make it then.*

able to take a joke to be able to accept ridicule good-naturedly; to be the object or butt of a joke willingly. (*Able to* can be replaced with *can*.) □ *Let's play a trick on Bill and see if he's able to take a joke.* □ *Better not tease Ann. She can't take a joke.*

able to take just so much able to endure only a limited amount of discomfort. (*Able to* can be replaced with *can*.) □ *Please stop hurting my feelings. I'm able to* *take just so much before I get angry.* □ *I can take just so much.*

able to take something able to endure something; able to endure abuse. (Often in the negative. *Able to* can be replaced with *can.* See also the previous entry.) □ *Stop yelling like that. I'm not able to take it anymore.* □ *Go ahead, hit me again. I can take it.*

above and beyond (something**)** more than is required. □ *Her efforts were above and beyond. We appreciate her time.* □ *All this extra time is above and beyond her regular hours.*

(above and) beyond the call of duty in addition to what is required; more than is required in one's job. □ *We didn't expect the police officer to drive us home. That was above and beyond the call of duty.* □ *The English teacher helped students after school every day, even though it was beyond the call of duty.*

above average higher or better than the average. □ *Max's grades are always above average.* □ *His intelligence is clearly above average.*

above par better than average or normal. □ *His work is above par, so he should get paid better.* □ *Your chances of winning the game are a little above par.*

above reproach not deserving of blame or criticism. □ *Some politicians behave as though they are above reproach.* □ *You must accept your punishment. You are not above reproach.*

above suspicion honest enough that no one would suspect you; to be in a position where you could not be suspected. □ *The general is a fine old man, completely above suspicion.* □ *Mary was at work at the time of the accident, so she's above suspicion.*

aboveboard AND **honest and aboveboard; open and aboveboard** in the open; visible to the public; honest. (Especially with *keep,* as in the examples below.) □ *Don't keep it a secret. Let's make sure that everything is aboveboard.* □ *You can do whatever you wish, as long as you keep it honest and aboveboard.* □ *The inspector had to make sure that everything was open and aboveboard.*

absent without leave AND **AWOL** absent from a military unit without permission; absent from anything without permission. (*AWOL* is an abbreviation. This is a serious offense in the military.) □ *The soldier was taken away by the military police because he was absent without leave.* □ *John was AWOL from school and got into a lot of trouble with his parents.*

according to all accounts AND **by all accounts** from all the reports; everyone is saying. □ *According to all accounts, the police were on the scene immediately.* □ *According to all accounts, the meeting broke up over a very minor matter.* □ *By all accounts, it was a very poor performance.*

according to Hoyle according to the rules; in keeping with the way it is normally done. (Refers to the rules for playing games. Edmond Hoyle wrote a book about games. This expression is usually used for something other than games.) □ *That's wrong. According to Hoyle, this is the way to do it.* □ *The carpenter said, "This is the way to drive a nail, according to Hoyle."*

according to one's **own lights** according to the way one believes; according to the way one's conscience or inclinations lead one. (Rarely used informally.) □ *People must act on this matter according to their own lights.* □ *John may have been wrong, but he did what he did according to his own lights.*

according to someone or something as said or indicated by someone or something. □ *According to the weather forecast, this should be a beautiful day.* □ *According to my father, this is a very good car to buy.* □ *It's too cold to go for a walk, according to the thermometer.*

according to something in proportion to something. □ *You will get paid according to the number of hours that you work.* □ *The doctor charges patients according to their ability to pay.*

accustomed to someone or something used to or comfortable with someone or something; accepting of someone or something as common and usual. □ *We were accustomed to wearing shoes.* □ *They aren't accustomed to paying a visit without bringing a gift.* □ *I'll never become accustomed to you.*

[ace in the hole] Go to someone's **ace in the hole**.

an **aching heart** the feeling of distress because of love that is lost or has faded away, described as being in the heart, where love is said to reside. □ *I try to tell my aching heart that I don't love him.* □ *There is no medicine for an aching heart.*

acid test a test whose findings are beyond doubt or dispute. (Refers to a chemical test that shows whether a metal is gold.) □ *Her new husband seems generous, but the acid test will be if he lets her mother stay with them.* □ *The senator isn't very popular just now, but the acid test will be if he gets reelected.*

acknowledge receipt (of something**)** to inform the sender that what was sent was received. (Commonly used in business correspondence.) □ *In a letter to a shoe company, Mary wrote, "I'm happy to acknowledge receipt of four dozen pairs of shoes."* □ *John acknowledged receipt of the bill.* □ *The package hasn't arrived, so I'm unable to acknowledge receipt.*

acknowledge someone **to be right** to admit or state that someone is correct about something. □ *Mary acknowledged Bill to be right about the name of the store.* □ *Bill said that the car was useless, and the mechanic acknowledged him to be right.*

acquire a taste for something to develop a liking for food, drink, or something else; to learn to like something. □ *One acquires a taste for fine wines.* □ *Many people are never able to acquire a taste for foreign food.* □ *Mary acquired a taste for art when she was very young.*

across the board equally for everyone or everything. □ *The school board raised the pay of all the teachers across the board.* □ *Congress cut the budget by reducing the money for each department 10 percent across the board.*

act as someone to perform in the capacity of someone, temporarily or permanently. □ *I'll act as your supervisor until Mrs. Brown returns from vacation.* □ *This is Mr. Smith. He'll act as manager from now on.*

act high-and-mighty to act proud and powerful. (Informal.) □ *Why does the doctor always have to act so high-and-mighty?* □ *If Sally wouldn't act so high-and-mighty, she'd have more friends.*

an **act of faith** an act or deed demonstrating religious faith; an act or deed showing trust in someone or something. □ *He lit candles in church as an act of faith.* □ *For him to trust you with his safety was a real act of faith.*

an **act of God** an occurrence (usually an accident) for which no human is responsible; a dramatic act of nature such as a storm, an earthquake, or a windstorm. □ *My insurance company wouldn't pay for the damage because it was an act of God.* □ *The thief tried to convince the judge that the diamonds were in his pocket due to an act of God.*

an **act of war** an international act of violence for which war is considered a suitable response; any hostile act between two people. □ *To bomb a ship is an act of war.* □ *Can spying be considered an act of war?* □ *"You just broke my stereo," yelled John. "That's an act of war!"*

act one's **age** to behave more maturely; to act as grown-up as one really is. (This is frequently said to a child.) □ *Come on, John, act your age. Stop throwing rocks.* □ *Mary! Stop picking on your little brother. Act your age!*

act something **out** to perform an imaginary event as if one were in a play. □ *Bill always acted his anger out by shouting and pounding his fists.* 🅃 *The psychiatrist asked Bill to act out the way he felt about getting fired.*

act up to misbehave; to run or act badly. □ *John, why do you always have to act up when your father and I take you out to eat?* □ *My arthritis is acting up. It really hurts.*

☐ *My car is acting up. I could hardly get it started this morning.*

Actions speak louder than words. It is better to do something about a problem than just talk about it. (Proverb.) ☐ *Mary kept promising to get a job. John finally looked her in the eye and said, "Actions speak louder than words!"* ☐ *After listening to the senator promising to cut federal spending, Ann wrote a simple note saying, "Actions speak louder than words."*

add fuel to the fire AND **add fuel to the flame** to make a problem worse; to say or do something that makes a bad situation worse; to make an angry person even more angry. (Also literal.) ☐ *To spank a crying child just adds fuel to the fire.* ☐ *Bill was shouting angrily, and Bob tried to get him to stop by laughing at him. Of course, that was just adding fuel to the flame.*

add fuel to the flame Go to add fuel to the fire.

add insult to injury to make a bad situation worse; to hurt the feelings of a person who has already been hurt. ☐ *First, the basement flooded, and then, to add insult to injury, a pipe burst in the kitchen.* ☐ *My car barely started this morning, and to add insult to injury, I got a flat tire in the driveway.*

add up (to something**)** **1.** to total up to a particular amount. ☐ *The bill added up to $200.* ☐ *These groceries will add up to almost sixty dollars.* ☐ *These numbers just won't add up.* **2.** to mean something; to signify or represent something; to result in something. ☐ *All this adds up to trouble!* ☐ *I don't understand. What does all this add up to?* ☐ *If you think about it carefully, these facts add up perfectly.*

address someone **as** something **1.** to talk to or write to a person, using a particular title. ☐ *They addressed Abraham Lincoln as "Mr. President."* ☐ *A physician is usually addressed as "Doctor."* **2.** to treat a person you are talking with in a particular manner. ☐ *You should address him as your equal.* ☐ *Do not address me as your superior.*

advanced in years Go to up in years.

advise against something to suggest that something not be done. ☐ *I advised against quitting work early.* ☐ *Lisa always advises against hasty actions.*

advise someone **against** doing something to supply someone with a suggestion of not doing something. ☐ *I advised Bill against quitting his job.* ☐ *Lisa advised Tom against doing it.*

an **affinity for** someone or something a strong preference for something; a strong liking for something. ☐ *Cats have an affinity for seafood.* ☐ *Mary's affinity for classical music accounts for her large collection of recordings.*

afraid of one's **own shadow** easily frightened; always frightened, timid, or suspicious. ☐ *After Tom was robbed, he was even afraid of his own shadow.* ☐ *Jane has always been a shy child. She has been afraid of her own shadow since she was three.*

after a fashion in a manner that is just barely adequate; poorly. ☐ *He thanked me—after a fashion—for my help.* ☐ *Oh, yes, I can swim, after a fashion.*

after all **1.** anyway; in spite of what had been decided. (Often refers to a change in plans or a reversal of plans.) ☐ *Mary had planned to go to the bank first, but she came here after all.* ☐ *It looks like Tom will go to law school after all.* **2.** remember; consider the fact that. ☐ *Don't punish Tommy! After all, he's only three years old!* ☐ *After all, we really didn't hurt anyone!*

after all is said and done when everything is settled or concluded; finally. (See also when all is said and done.) ☐ *After all was said and done, it was a lovely party.* ☐ *After all is said and done, it will turn out just as I said.*

after hours after the regular closing time; after any normal or regular time, such as one's bedtime. ☐ *John was arrested in a bar after hours.* ☐ *The soldier was caught sneaking into the barracks after hours.* ☐ *John got a job sweeping floors in the bank after hours.*

after the fact after something has happened; after something, especially a crime, has taken place. (Primarily a legal phrase.) ☐ *John is always making excuses after the fact.* ☐ *Remember to lock your car whenever you leave it. If it's stolen, there is nothing you can do after the fact.*

after the fashion of someone or something in the manner or style of someone or something. (See also **after a fashion.**) ☐ *She walks down the street after the fashion of a grand lady.* ☐ *The church was built after the fashion of an English cathedral.*

again and again repeatedly; again and even more. ☐ *I like going to the beach, and I will go back again and again.* ☐ *He knocked on the door again and again until I finally answered.*

against someone's **will** without a person's consent or agreement. ☐ *You cannot force me to come with you against my will!* ☐ *Against their will, the men were made to stand up against the wall and be searched.*

against the clock in a race with time; in a great hurry to get something done before a particular time. (See also **race against time.**) ☐ *Bill set a new track record, running against the clock. He lost the actual race, however.* ☐ *In a race against the clock, they rushed the special medicine to the hospital.*

ahead of one's **time** having ideas or attitudes that are too advanced to be acceptable to or appreciated by the society in which one is living. ☐ *People buy that artist's work now, but his paintings were laughed at when he was alive. He was ahead of his time.* ☐ *Mary's grandmother was ahead of her time in wanting to study medicine.*

ahead of schedule having done something before the time listed on the schedule. ☐ *I want to be able to finish the job ahead of schedule.* ☐ *We don't have to rush because we are ahead of schedule.*

ahead of the game being early; having an advantage over a situation; having done more than necessary. (Informal or slang.) ☐ *Whenever we go to a movie, we show up ahead of the game and have to wait.* ☐ *Bill has to study math very hard to keep ahead of the game.* ☐ *Bob does extra work so he's always ahead of the game.*

ahead of time beforehand; before the announced time. ☐ *If you show up ahead of time, you will have to wait.* ☐ *Be there ahead of time if you want to get a good seat.*

aid and abet someone to help someone; to incite someone to do something that is wrong. ☐ *He was scolded for aiding and abetting the boys who were fighting.* ☐ *It's illegal to aid and abet a thief.*

aim to do something to mean to do something; to intend to do something in the future. (Folksy.) ☐ *I aim to paint the house as soon as I can find a brush.* ☐ *He aims to take a few days off and go fishing.*

Ain't it the truth? Isn't that just the way it is?; I agree with you completely. (Informal.) ☐ *A: Things aren't the way they used to be in the good old days. B: Ain't it the truth?* ☐ *A: You just can't buy good shoes anymore. B: Ain't it the truth?*

air one's **dirty linen in public** AND **wash** one's **dirty linen in public** to discuss private or embarrassing matters in public, especially when quarreling. (This *linen* refers to sheets and tablecloths or other soiled cloth.) ☐ *John's mother had asked him repeatedly not to air the family's dirty linen in public.* ☐ *Mr. and Mrs. Johnson are arguing again. Why must they always air their dirty linen in public?* ☐ *Jean will talk to anyone about her financial problems. Why does she wash her dirty linen in public?*

air one's **grievances** to complain; to make a public complaint. ☐ *I know how you feel, John, but it isn't necessary to air your grievances over and over.* ☐ *I know you're busy, sir, but I must air my grievances. This matter is very serious.*

air something **out** to freshen up something by placing it in the open air; to freshen a room by letting air move through it. ☐ *It's so stale in here. Mary, please open a window and air this place out.* ☐ *Please take this pillow outside and air it out.* 🅃 *I'll have to air out the car. Someone has been smoking in it.*

alive and kicking AND **alive and well** well and healthy. (Informal.) □ *JANE: How is Bill? MARY: Oh, he's alive and kicking.* □ *The last time I saw Tom, he was alive and well.*

alive and well Go to alive and kicking.

alive with someone or something covered with, filled with, or active with people or things. □ *Look! Ants everywhere. The floor is alive with ants!* □ *When we got to the ballroom, the place was alive with dancing.* □ *The campground was alive with campers from all over the country.*

all and sundry everyone; one and all. (Folksy.) □ *Cold drinks were served to all and sundry.* □ *All and sundry came to the village fair.*

all around Robin Hood's barn going somewhere not by a direct route; going way out of the way [to get somewhere]; by a long and circuitous route. □ *We had to go all around Robin Hood's barn to get to the little town.* □ *She walked all around Robin Hood's barn looking for a shop that sold Finnish glassware.*

all at once 1. suddenly. □ *All at once the chair broke, and Bob fell to the floor.* □ *All at once she tripped on a stone.* **2.** all at the same time. □ *The entire group spoke all at once.* □ *They were trying to cook dinner, clean house, and paint the closet all at once.*

(all) at sea (about something**)** confused; lost and bewildered. □ *Mary is all at sea about getting married.* □ *When it comes to higher math, John is totally at sea.*

(all) balled up troubled; confused; in a mess. (Slang.) □ *Look at you! You're really all balled up!* □ *John is all balled up because his car was stolen.* □ *Of course this typewriter won't work. It's all balled up.*

(all) beer and skittles all fun and pleasure; easy and pleasant. (Skittles is the game of ninepins, a game similar to bowling.) □ *Life isn't all beer and skittles, you know!* □ *For Sam, college was beer and skittles. He wasted a lot of time and money.*

all better now improved; cured. (Folksy or juvenile.) □ *My leg was sore, but it's all better now.* □ *I fell off my tricycle and bumped my knee. Mommy kissed it, and it's all better now.*

all day long throughout the day; during the entire day. □ *We waited for you at the station all day long.* □ *I can't keep smiling all day long.*

all dressed up dressed in one's best clothes; dressed formally. □ *We're all dressed up to go out to dinner.* □ *I really hate to get all dressed up just to go somewhere to eat.*

all for something very much in favor of something. (*For* is usually emphasized.) □ *Bill is all for stopping off to get ice cream.* □ *Mary suggested that they sell their house. They weren't all for it, but they did it anyway.*

(all) for the best good in spite of the way it seems now; better than you think. (Often said when someone dies after a serious illness.) □ *I'm very sorry to hear of the death of your aunt. Perhaps it's for the best.* □ *I didn't get into the college I wanted, but I couldn't afford it anyway. It's probably all for the best.*

all gone used up; finished; over with. □ *Oh, the strawberry jelly is all gone.* □ *We used to have wonderful parties, but those days are all gone.*

all in tired; exhausted; all tuckered out. □ *I just walked all the way from town. I'm all in.* □ *"What a day!" said Sally. "I'm all in."*

all in a day's work part of what is expected; typical or normal. (Also literal.) □ *I don't particularly like to cook, but it's all in a day's work.* □ *Putting up with rude customers isn't pleasant, but it's all in a day's work.* □ *Cleaning up after other people is all in a day's work for a chambermaid.*

all in all considering everything that has happened; in summary and in spite of any unpleasantness. □ *All in all, it was a very good party.* □ *All in all, I'm glad that I visited New York City.*

all in good time at some future time; in **good time**; soon. (This phrase is used to encourage people to be patient and wait quietly.) ☐ *When will the baby be born? All in good time.* ☐ *MARY: I'm starved! When will Bill get here with the pizza? TOM: All in good time, Mary, all in good time.*

(all) in one breath spoken rapidly, usually while one is very excited. (Also literal.) ☐ *Ann said all in one breath, "Hurry, quick! The parade is coming!"* ☐ *Jane was in a play, and she was so excited that she said her whole speech in one breath.* ☐ *Tom can say the alphabet all in one breath.*

all in one piece safely; without damage. (Informal.) ☐ *Her son come home from school all in one piece, even though he had been in a fight.* ☐ *The package was handled carelessly, but the vase inside arrived all in one piece.*

(all) in the family restricted to one's own family, as with private or embarrassing information. (Especially with *keep.*) ☐ *Don't tell anyone else. Please keep it all in the family.* ☐ *He only told his brother because he wanted it to remain in the family.*

(all) joking aside AND **(all) kidding aside** being serious for a moment; in all seriousness. ☐ *I know I laugh at him but, joking aside, he's a very clever scientist.* ☐ *I know I threatened to leave and go round the world, but, joking aside, I need a vacation.*

(all) kidding aside Go to (all) joking aside.

all kinds of someone or something a great number of people or things; a great amount of something, especially money. (Informal. Also literal, meaning "all types.") ☐ *There were all kinds of people there, probably thousands.* ☐ *The Smith family has all kinds of money.*

all manner of someone or something all types of people or things. ☐ *We saw all manner of people there. They came from every country in the world.* ☐ *They were selling all manner of things in the country store.*

all night long throughout the whole night. ☐ *I couldn't sleep all night long.* ☐ *John was sick all night long.*

all of a sudden suddenly. ☐ *All of a sudden, lightning struck the tree we were sitting under.* ☐ *I felt a sharp pain in my side all of a sudden.*

all or nothing 1. everything or nothing at all. ☐ *Sally would not accept only part of the money. She wanted all or nothing.* ☐ *I can't bargain over trifles. I will have to have all or nothing.* **2.** time to choose to do something or not to do it. ☐ *It was all or nothing. Tim had to jump off the truck or risk drowning when the truck went into the water.* ☐ *Jane stood at the door of the airplane and checked her parachute. It was all or nothing now. She had to jump or be looked upon as a coward.*

an **all-out effort** a very good and thorough effort. (See also make an all-out effort.) ☐ *We need an all-out effort to get this job done on time.* ☐ *The government began an all-out effort to reduce the federal budget.*

all-out war total war, as opposed to small, warlike acts or threats of war. ☐ *We are now concerned about all-out war in the Middle East.* ☐ *Threats of all-out war caused many tourists to leave the country immediately.*

all over 1. finished; dead. (Compare this with (all) over with.) ☐ *Dinner is all over. I'm sorry you didn't get any.* ☐ *It's all over. He's dead now.* **2.** everywhere. (See also all over the earth.) ☐ *Oh, I just itch all over.* ☐ *She's spreading the rumor all over.*

(all) over again starting over completely again; going through something completely yet another time. ☐ *Do I have to go through this all over again?* ☐ *Please start over again for those who came in late.*

all over but the shouting essentially decided and concluded. (An elaboration of all over, which means "finished.") ☐ *The last goal was made just as the final whistle sounded. Tom said, "Well, it's all over but the shouting."* ☐ *Tom worked hard in college and graduated last month. When he got his diploma, he said, "It's all over but the shouting."*

all over the earth AND **all over the world** everywhere. ☐ *Grass grows all over the earth.* ☐ *It's the same way all over the world.*

all over the place everywhere; in all parts of a particular location. ☐ *Tom, stop leaving your dirty clothes all over the place.* ☐ *We keep finding this kind of problem all over the place.*

all over the world Go to **all over the earth**.

all over town 1. everywhere in town. ☐ *Our dog got loose and ran all over town.* ☐ *Jane looked all over town for a dress to wear to the party.* **2.** known to everyone. ☐ *Now keep this a secret. I don't want it all over town.* ☐ *In a short time the secret was known all over town.*

(all) over with finished. (See also **all over**.) ☐ *His problems are all over with now.* ☐ *After dinner is all over with, we can play cards.*

all right 1. well, good, or okay, but not excellent. (Informal. This phrase has all the uses that *okay* has.) ☐ *I was a little sick, but now I'm all right.* ☐ *His work is all right, but nothing to brag about.* ☐ *All right, it's time to go.* **2.** beyond a doubt; as the evidence shows. ☐ *The dog's dead all right. It hasn't moved at all.* ☐ *The train's late all right. It hasn't been late in months.* **3.** hooray. (An exclamation of joy or encouragement.) ☐ *The Bears won! All right!* ☐ *All right! That's the way to do it!*

All right for you! That's it for you!; That's the last chance for you! (Juvenile and informal. Usually said by a child who is angry with a playmate.) ☐ *All right for you, John. See if I ever play with you again.* ☐ *All right for you! I'm telling your mother what you did.*

all right with someone agreeable to someone. ☐ *If you want to ruin your life and marry Tom, it's all right with me.* ☐ *I'll see if it's all right with my father.*

all set ready to begin; okay. (See also **(all) set to** do something.) ☐ *TOM: Is everything all right? JANE: Yes, we are all set.* ☐ *We are ready to leave now. Are you all set?*

(all) set to do something prepared or ready to do something. (See also **all set**.) ☐ *Are you set to cook the steaks?* ☐ *Yes, the fire is ready, and I'm all set to start.*

(all) shot to hell totally ruined. (Informal. Use caution with *hell*.) ☐ *My car is all shot to hell and can't be depended on.* ☐ *This knife is shot to hell. I need a sharper one.*

(all) skin and bones Go to **nothing but skin and bones**.

all sweetness and light very sweet, innocent, and helpful. (Perhaps insincerely so.) ☐ *She was mad at first, but after a while, she was all sweetness and light.* ☐ *At the reception, the whole family was all sweetness and light, but they argued and fought after the guests left.*

all systems (are) go everything is ready. (Informal. Originally said when preparing to launch a rocket.) ☐ *The rocket is ready to blast off—all systems are go.* ☐ *TOM: Are you guys ready to start playing? BILL: Sure, Tom, all systems go.*

all talk (and no action) talking about doing something, but never actually doing it. ☐ *The car needs washing, but Bill is all talk and no action on this matter.* ☐ *Bill keeps saying he'll get a job soon, but he's all talk and no action.* ☐ *Bill won't do it. He's just all talk.*

All that glitters is not gold. Many attractive and alluring things have no value. (Proverb.) ☐ *The used car looked fine but didn't run well at all. "Ah, yes," thought Bill, "all that glitters is not gold."* ☐ *When Mary was disappointed about losing Tom, Jane reminded her, "All that glitters is not gold."*

all the livelong day throughout the whole day. (Folksy.) ☐ *They kept at their work all the livelong day.* ☐ *Bob just sat by the creek fishing, all the livelong day.*

all the rage in current fashion. ☐ *A new dance called the "floppy disc" is all the rage.* ☐ *Wearing a rope instead of a belt is all the rage these days.*

all the same AND **just the same** nevertheless; anyhow. ☐ *They were told not to* *bring presents, but they brought them all the same.* □ *His parents said no, but John went out just the same.*

all the same (to someone**)** AND **just the same (to** someone**)** of no consequence to someone; immaterial to someone. □ *It's all the same to me whether we win or lose.* □ *If it's just the same to you, I'd rather walk than ride.* □ *If it's all the same, I'd rather you didn't smoke.*

all the time 1. throughout a specific period of time. □ *Bill was stealing money for the last two years, and Tom knew it all the time.* □ *Throughout December and January, Jane had two jobs all the time.* **2.** at all times; continuously. □ *Your blood keeps flowing all the time.* □ *That electric motor runs all the time.* **3.** repeatedly; habitually. □ *She keeps a handkerchief in her hand all the time.* □ *She hums softly all the time.*

all the way from the beginning to the end; the entire distance, from start to finish. (See also go all the way (with someone).) □ *The ladder reaches all the way to the top of the house.* □ *I walked all the way home.*

all thumbs awkward and clumsy, especially with one's hands. □ *Poor Bob can't play the piano at all. He's all thumbs.* □ *Mary is all thumbs when it comes to gardening.*

all told totaled up; including all parts. □ *All told, he earned about $700 last week.* □ *All told, he has many fine characteristics.*

all to the good for the best; for one's benefit. □ *He missed the train, but it was all to the good because the train had a wreck.* □ *It was all to the good that he died without suffering.*

(all) tuckered out tired out; worn out. (Folksy.) □ *Poor John worked so hard that he's all tuckered out.* □ *Look at that little baby sleeping. She's really tuckered out.*

all walks of life all social, economic, and ethnic groups. □ *We saw people there from all walks of life.* □ *The people who came to the art exhibit represented all walks of life.*

(all) well and good good; desirable. □ *It's well and good that you're here on time. I was afraid you'd be late again.* □ *It's all well and good that you're passing English, but what about math and science?*

all wet mistaken; wrongheaded; on the wrong track. (Also literal.) □ *It's not that way, John. You're all wet.* □ *If you think that prices will come down, you're all wet.*

all wool and a yard wide genuine; genuinely warmhearted and friendly. (Informal and folksy. Refers to cloth that is 100 percent wool and exactly one yard wide.) □ *Old Bob is a true gentleman—all wool and a yard wide.* □ *The banker, hardly all wool and a yard wide, wouldn't give us a loan.*

All work and no play makes Jack a dull boy. One should have recreation as well as work. (Proverb. *Jack* does not refer to anyone in particular. The phrase can be used for persons of either sex.) □ *Stop reading that book and go out and play! All work and no play makes Jack a dull boy.* □ *The doctor told Mr. Jones to stop working on weekends and start playing golf, because all work and no play makes Jack a dull boy.*

(all) worked up (about something**)** Go to (all) worked up (over something).

(all) worked up (over something**)** AND **(all) worked up (about** something**)** excited and agitated about something. (See also get worked up (over something).) □ *Tom is all worked up over the threat of a new war.* □ *Don't get all worked up about something that you can't do anything about.* □ *Bill is all worked up again. It's bad for his health.*

(all) year round throughout all the seasons of the year; during the entire year. □ *The public swimming pool is enclosed so that it can be used all year round.* □ *In the South they can grow flowers all year round.*

allow for someone or something **1.** to plan on having enough of something (such as food, space, etc.) for someone. □ *Mary is bringing Bill on the picnic, so be sure to allow for him when buying the food.* □ *Allow for an extra person when setting the table tonight.* **2.** to plan on the possibility of something. □ *Allow for a few rainy days on your vacation.* □ *Be sure to allow for future growth when you plant the rosebushes.*

All's well that ends well. An event that has a good ending is considered good, even if some things went wrong along the way. (Proverb. This is the name of a play by Shakespeare.) □ *I'm glad you finally got here, even though your car had a flat tire on the way. Oh, well. All's well that ends well.* □ *The groom was late for the wedding, but everything worked out all right. All's well that ends well.*

the **almighty dollar** the U.S. dollar, worshiped as a god; money, viewed as more important and powerful than anything else. □ *Bill was a slave to the almighty dollar.* □ *It's the almighty dollar that drives the whole country.*

almost lost it having been so angry or distraught as to nearly lose one's temper, composure, or control. (Also literal. Informal.) □ *I was so mad, I almost lost it.* □ *When he saw the dent in his fender, he almost lost it.*

along in years Go to up in years.

along with someone or something in addition to someone or something; together with someone or something. □ *Jane went to the mall along with David.* □ *I ate some chocolates along with some fruit.*

alongside (of) someone or something as compared to a person or a thing. (Also literal. Informal. The things being compared need not be beside one another.) □ *Our car looks quite small alongside of theirs.* □ *My power of concentration is quite limited alongside of yours.*

alpha and omega both the beginning and the end; the essentials, from the beginning to the end; everything, from the beginning to the end. (Refers to the first and last letters of the Greek alphabet.) □ *He was forced to learn the alpha and omega of corporate law in order to even talk to the lawyers.* □ *He loved her deeply; she was his alpha and omega.*

amount to something [for someone or something] to be or to become valuable or successful. □ *Most parents hope that their children will amount to something.* □ *I put $200 in the bank, and I hope it will amount to something in twenty years.*

amount to the same thing AND **come to the same thing** to be the same as something; to have the same effect as something. □ *Borrowing can be the same as stealing. If the owner does not know what you have borrowed, it amounts to the same thing.* □ *Beer, wine. They come to the same thing if you drink and drive.*

[an] <Entries beginning with *a*, *an*, or *the* are alphabetized under the **second** word in the entry. That means that **a bed of roses** will appear in the *B*s.>

and change [some number of dollars] plus between 1 and 99 cents more. □ *The book cost $12.49. That's twelve dollars and change.* □ *Subway fare is now one dollar and change.*

and so forth continuing talking in the same way; and so on. □ *She told me everything about her kids and so on and so forth.* □ *I heard about problems at work and so forth.*

and something **to spare** AND **with** something **to spare** with extra left over; with more than is needed. (With *something, time, room, money, plenty, etc.*) □ *I had as much flour as I needed with something to spare.* □ *Fred said he should have enough cash to last the week—with money to spare.*

and so on continuing on in the same way [without saying all the details]; continuing to talk, saying more and more. □ *He told me about all his health problems, including his arthritis and so on.* □ *I need some help getting ready for dinner, setting the table, and so on.*

and the like and similar things or people. □ *I eat hamburgers, hot dogs, and the like.* □ *I bought shirts, pants, socks, and the like.*

and then some and even more; more than has been mentioned. (Folksy.) □ *John is going to have to run like a deer and then some to win this race.* □ *The cook put the* *amount of salt called for into the soup and then some.*

and what have you and so on; and other similar things. ☐ *Their garage is full of bikes, sleds, old boots, and what have you.* ☐ *The merchant sells writing paper, pens, string, and what have you.*

angry enough to chew nails Go to mad enough to chew nails.

another country heard from <a catch phrase said when someone makes a comment or interrupts.> ☐ *Jane and Bill were discussing business when Bob interrupted to offer an opinion. "Another country heard from," said Jane.* ☐ *In the middle of the discussion, the baby started crying. "Another country heard from," said Tom.*

(another) nail in someone's or something's **coffin** something that will harm or destroy someone or something. ☐ *Every word of criticism that Bob said about the boss was a nail in his coffin.* ☐ *Losing the export order was the final nail in the company's coffin.*

answer for someone or something [with *something*] to assume responsibility for something. (Also literal.) ☐ *John had to answer for the theft of the bicycle since it was found at his house.* ☐ *Someday we'll all have to answer for our wrongdoings.*

answer someone's **purpose** AND **serve** someone's **purpose** to fit or suit someone's purpose. ☐ *This piece of wood will answer my purpose quite nicely.* ☐ *The new car serves our purpose perfectly.*

answer the door [after hearing the doorbell or a knock] to go to the door to see who is there. ☐ *Would you please answer the door? I am busy.* ☐ *I wish someone would answer the door. I can't wait all day.*

answer to someone to explain to someone; to justify one's actions to someone. (Usually with *have to.*) ☐ *If John cannot behave properly, he'll have to answer to me.* ☐ *The car thief will have to answer to the judge.*

any number of someone or something a large number; a sufficiently large number. (Used when the exact number is not important.) ☐ *Any number of people can vouch for my honesty.* ☐ *I can give you any number of reasons why I should join the army.* ☐ *I ate there any number of times and never became ill.*

Any port in a storm. When one is in difficulties one must accept any way out, whether one likes the solution or not. (Proverb.) ☐ *I don't want to live with my parents, but it's a case of any port in a storm. I can't find an apartment.* ☐ *He hates his job, but he can't get another. Any port in a storm, you know.*

appear as something to act a certain part in a play, opera, etc. ☐ *Madame Smith-Franklin appeared as Carmen at the City Opera last season.* ☐ *The actor refused to appear as a villain in the play.*

appear out of nowhere to appear suddenly, without warning. (Almost the same as come out of nowhere.) ☐ *A huge bear appeared out of nowhere and roared and threatened us.* ☐ *A butler appeared out of nowhere and took our coats.*

the **apple of** someone's **eye** someone's favorite person or thing; a boyfriend or a girlfriend. ☐ *Tom is the apple of Mary's eye. She thinks he's great.* ☐ *John's new stereo is the apple of his eye.*

apples and oranges a pair of people or things representing two entities that are not similar. ☐ *You can't talk about Fred and Ted in the same breath! They're apples and oranges.* ☐ *Talking about her current book and her previous best-seller is like comparing apples and oranges.*

arguing for the sake of arguing AND **arguing for the sake of argument** simply arguing to be difficult or contrary. ☐ *You are just arguing for the sake of arguing. You don't even know what the issue is.* ☐ *He is annoying, because he is always arguing for the sake of argument.*

arguing for the sake of argument Go to arguing for the sake of arguing.

arm in arm linked or hooked together by the arms. ☐ *The two lovers walked arm in arm down the street.* ☐ *Arm in arm, the line of dancers kicked high, and the audience roared its approval.*

armed and dangerous said of an armed person who is suspected of a crime and has not been captured and who is likely to resist arrest. (This is a warning to police officers.) □ *Max is at large, presumed to be armed and dangerous.* □ *The suspect has killed once and is armed and dangerous.*

armed to the teeth heavily armed with deadly weapons. □ *The bank robber was armed to the teeth when he was caught.* □ *There are too many guns around. The entire country is armed to the teeth.*

(a)round the clock continuously for twenty-four hours at a time; all day and all night. □ *The priceless jewels were guarded around the clock.* □ *Grandfather was so sick that he had to have nurses round the clock.*

(a)round-the-clock constant; day and night. (Adjective.) □ *Grandfather required around-the-clock care.* □ *I tuned into the around-the-clock news station.*

arrange something **with** someone **1.** AND **arrange to** do something **with** someone to plan an event so as to include another person or persons. □ *Jane arranged a meeting with Ann.* □ *Bill arranged to go to the station with Tom and Mary.* **2.** to get someone's consent for something. □ *Mary arranged the entire affair with her employer.* □ *The new mother arranged the christening with the pastor.*

arrange to do something **with** someone Go to arrange something with someone.

arrive in a body Go to come in a body.

arrive on the scene Go to come on the scene.

as a duck takes to water easily and naturally. (Informal.) □ *She took to singing just as a duck takes to water.* □ *The baby adapted to bottle-feeding as a duck takes to water.*

as a (general) rule usually; almost always. □ *He can be found in his office as a general rule.* □ *As a general rule, Jane plays golf on Wednesdays.* □ *As a rule, things tend to get less busy after supper time.*

as a last resort as the last choice; if everything else fails. □ *Call the doctor at home only as a last resort.* □ *As a last resort, she will perform surgery.*

as alike as (two) peas in a pod very similar. (Compare this with like (two) peas in a pod.) □ *The twins are as alike as two peas in a pod.* □ *These two books are as alike as peas in a pod.*

as a matter of course normally; as a normal procedure. □ *The nurse takes your temperature as a matter of course.* □ *You are expected to make your own bed as a matter of course.*

as a matter of fact actually; in addition to what has been said; in reference to what has been said. (See also matter-of-fact.) □ *As a matter of fact, John came into the room while you were talking about him.* □ *I'm not a poor worker. As a matter of fact, I'm very efficient.*

as an aside as a comment; as a comment that is not supposed to be heard by everyone. □ *At the wedding, Tom said as an aside, "The bride doesn't look well."* □ *At the ballet, Billy said as an aside to his mother, "I hope the dancers fall off the stage!"*

as a result of something because of something that has happened. □ *As a result of the accident, Tom couldn't walk for six months.* □ *We couldn't afford to borrow money for a house as a result of the rise in interest rates.*

as a token (of something**)** symbolic of something, especially of gratitude; as a memento of something. □ *He gave me a rose as a token of the time we spent together.* □ *Here, take this $100 as a token of my appreciation.* □ *I can't thank you enough. Please accept this money as a token.*

(as) awkward as a cow on a crutch AND **(as) awkward as a cow on roller skates** very awkward. □ *When Lulu was pregnant, she was awkward as a cow on a crutch.* □ *Tom will never be a gymnast. He's as awkward as a cow on roller skates!*

(as) awkward as a cow on roller skates Go to (as) awkward as a cow on a crutch.

(as) bad as all that as bad as reported; as bad as it seems. (Usually expressed in the negative.) □ *Come on! Nothing could be as bad as all that.* □ *Stop crying. It can't be as bad as all that.*

(as) bald as a baby's backside Go to (as) bald as a coot.

(as) bald as a coot AND **(as) bald as a baby's backside** completely bald. □ *If Tom's hair keeps receding like that, he'll be bald as a coot by the time he's thirty.* □ *FRED: Now, I'll admit my hair is thinning a little on the top, but— JANE: Thinning? You're not thinning, you're as bald as a baby's backside!*

(as) baleful as death promising evil; very threatening. □ *The wind's moan was as baleful as death.* □ *His voice sounded baleful as death.*

(as) big as all outdoors very big, usually referring to a space of some kind. (Folksy.) □ *You should see Bob's living room. It's as big as all outdoors.* □ *The new movie theater is as big as all outdoors.*

(as) big as life AND **(as) big as life and twice as ugly** an exaggerated way of saying that a person or a thing appeared in a particular place. (Folksy. The second phrase is slang.) □ *The little child just stood there as big as life and laughed very hard.* □ *I opened the door, and there was Tom as big as life.* □ *I came home and found this cat in my chair, as big as life and twice as ugly.*

(as) big as life and twice as ugly Go to (as) big as life.

(as) black as a skillet black. □ *I don't want to go down to the cellar. It's as black as a skillet down there.* □ *The bruise turned black as a skillet.*

(as) black as a stack of black cats very black. □ *I'm scared to go into that closet. It's as black as a stack of black cats in there.* □ *Her hair was black as a stack of black cats.*

(as) black as a sweep extremely dirty. (The *sweep* is a chimney sweep.) □ *After playing in the mud all morning, the children were as black as sweeps.* □ *When Jane came in from working on her car, Alan told her, "Wash before you come to the dinner table. You're black as a sweep!"*

(as) black as coal completely black. □ *Mark's eyes were as black as coal.* □ *The stranger's clothes were all black as coal.*

(as) black as night very dark and black. □ *The ink in this pen is black as night.* □ *During the eclipse, my room was as black as night.*

(as) black as one **is painted** as evil as described. (Usually negative.) □ *The landlord is not as black as he is painted. He seems quite generous.* □ *Young people are rarely black as they are painted in the media.*

(as) black as pitch very black; very dark. □ *The night was as black as pitch.* □ *The rocks seemed black as pitch against the silver sand.*

(as) black as the ace of spades very black. (Refers to playing cards.) □ *The car was long and shiny and black as the ace of spades.* □ *Jill's shoes are black as the ace of spades.*

(as) blind as a bat with imperfect sight; blind. □ *My grandmother is as blind as a bat.* □ *I'm getting blind as a bat. I can hardly read this page.*

(as) bold as brass very bold; bold to the point of rudeness. □ *Lisa marched into the manager's office, bold as brass, and demanded her money back.* □ *The tiny kitten, as bold as brass, began eating the dog's food right in front of the dog's nose.*

(as) bright as a button intelligent; quick-minded. (Usually used to describe children.) □ *Why, Mrs. Green, your little girl is as bright as a button.* □ *You can't fool Mandy. She may be only six years old, but she's bright as a button.*

(as) bright as a new pin bright and clean; shiny. □ *After Nora cleaned the house, it was as bright as a new pin.* □ *My kitchen floor is bright as a new pin since I started using this new floor wax.*

(as) broad as a barn door very broad. □ *Jim's backside is as broad as a barn door.*

☐ *The weight-lifter's chest was broad as a barn door.*

(as) busy as a beaver AND **(as) busy as a bee** very busy. ☐ *I don't have time to talk to you. I'm as busy as a beaver.* ☐ *You don't look busy as a beaver to me.* ☐ *Whenever there is a holiday, we are all as busy as bees getting things ready.*

(as) busy as a bee Go to (as) busy as a beaver.

(as) busy as a cat on a hot tin roof full of lively activity; very busy. ☐ *I'm afraid I can't go to lunch with you on Saturday; I'll be busy as a cat on a hot tin roof, between working overtime and the two parties I have to go to.* ☐ *Jerry's three part-time jobs kept him as busy as a cat on a hot tin roof.*

(as) busy as a hibernating bear not busy at all. ☐ *TOM: I can't go with you. I'm busy. JANE: Yeah. You're as busy as a hibernating bear.* ☐ *He lounged on the sofa all day, busy as a hibernating bear.*

(as) busy as a one-armed paperhanger very busy. ☐ *My boss keeps me as busy as a one-armed paperhanger.* ☐ *I've got plenty of work. I'm busy as a one-armed paperhanger.*

(as) busy as Grand Central Station very busy; crowded with customers or other people. (Refers to Grand Central Station in New York City.) ☐ *This house is as busy as Grand Central Station.* ☐ *When the tourist season starts, this store is busy as Grand Central Station.*

(as) busy as popcorn on a skillet very active. ☐ *She rushed around, as busy as popcorn on a skillet.* ☐ *Prying into other folks' business kept him busy as popcorn on a skillet.*

(as) calm as a toad in the sun very calm and content. ☐ *She smiled, as calm as a toad in the sun.* ☐ *Nothing ruffles him. He's calm as a toad in the sun.*

(as) clean as a hound's tooth very clean. (*Clean* can mean "innocent," as in the first example.) ☐ *John had faith that he would not be convicted for the robbery, since he had been clean as a hound's tooth since getting out of prison.* ☐ *After his mother scrubbed him thoroughly, James was as clean as a hound's tooth.*

(as) clean as a whistle very clean. ☐ *The wound isn't infected. It's clean as a whistle.* ☐ *I thought the car would be filthy, but it was as clean as a whistle.*

(as) clear as a bell very clear and easy to hear. ☐ *I fixed the radio, so now all the stations come in clear as a bell.* ☐ *Through the wall, I could hear the neighbors talking, just as clear as a bell.*

(as) clear as crystal 1. very clear; transparent. ☐ *The stream was as clear as crystal.* ☐ *She cleaned the windowpane until it was clear as crystal.* **2.** very clear; easy to understand. ☐ *The explanation was as clear as crystal.* ☐ *Her lecture was not clear as crystal, but at least it was not dull.*

(as) clear as mud not understandable. (Informal.) ☐ *Your explanation is as clear as mud.* ☐ *This doesn't make sense. It's clear as mud.*

(as) clear as vodka 1. very clear. ☐ *The weather is as clear as vodka.* ☐ *The river wasn't exactly as clear as vodka because it had just rained.* **2.** very understandable. ☐ *Everything he said is as clear as vodka.* ☐ *I understand what John said, but everything you say is clear as vodka.*

(as) close as two coats of paint close and intimate. ☐ *When Tom and Mary were kids, they were as close as two coats of paint.* ☐ *All their lives, the cousins were close as two coats of paint.*

(as) cocky as the king of spades boastful; overly proud. (Refers to playing cards.) ☐ *He'd challenge anyone to a fight. He's as cocky as the king of spades.* ☐ *She strutted in, cocky as the king of spades.*

(as) cold as a witch's caress AND **(as) cold as a witch's tit** very cold; chilling. (Use caution with *tit.*) ☐ *The wind was as cold as a witch's caress.* ☐ *She gave me a look as cold as a witch's caress.*

(as) cold as a witch's tit Go to (as) cold as a witch's caress.

(as) cold as marble Very cold indeed. (Used to describe a person who is either physically or emotionally cold.) ☐ *Raymond took Joanna's hand. It was cold as marble.* ☐ *No one ever got a smile out of Caroline, who was as cold as marble.*

(as) comfortable as an old shoe very comfortable; very comforting and familiar. ☐ *This old house is fine. It's as comfortable as an old shoe.* ☐ *That's a great tradition—comfortable as an old shoe.*

(as) common as an old shoe low class; uncouth. ☐ *That trashy girl is just as common as an old shoe.* ☐ *Jim may have money, but he's common as an old shoe.*

(as) common as dirt vulgar; ill-mannered. ☐ *FRED: Did you notice Mr. Jones blowing his nose into the linen napkin at dinner? ELLEN: I'm not surprised. Everyone knows that the Joneses are as common as dirt.* ☐ *Despite Jane's efforts to imitate the manners of the upper class, the town's leading families still considered her common as dirt.*

(as) conceited as a barber's cat very conceited; vain. ☐ *Ever since he won that award, he's been as conceited as a barber's cat.* ☐ *She's stuck up all right—conceited as a barber's cat.*

(as) cool as a cucumber calm and not agitated; with one's wits about one. (Informal.) ☐ *The captain remained as cool as a cucumber as the passengers boarded the lifeboats.* ☐ *During the fire the homeowner was cool as a cucumber.*

(as) crazy as a betsy bug loony. ☐ *TOM: Susan says she's really the Queen of England. BILL: She's crazy as a betsy bug.* ☐ *Ever since his wife left him, Joe's been acting as crazy as a betsy bug.*

(as) crazy as a loon very silly; completely insane. (Folksy.) ☐ *If you think you can get away with that, you're as crazy as a loon.* ☐ *Poor old John is crazy as a loon.*

(as) crazy as a peach-orchard boar loony. ☐ *What's wrong with Jim? He's acting as crazy as a peach-orchard boar.* ☐ *Mary's been standing out on the street corner telling everybody the world's about to end. Poor thing—she's crazy as a peach-orchard boar.*

(as) crooked as a barrel of fishhooks AND **(as) crooked as a fishhook** dishonest. ☐ *Don't play cards with him. He's as crooked as a barrel of fishhooks.* ☐ *After Jane cheated a few folks, word got around that she was crooked as a fishhook.*

(as) crooked as a dog's hind leg dishonest. ☐ *Don't trust John. He's as crooked as a dog's hind leg.* ☐ *Mary says all politicians are crooked as a dog's hind leg.*

(as) crooked as a fishhook Go to (as) crooked as a barrel of fishhooks.

(as) dead as a dodo dead; no longer in existence. (Informal.) ☐ *Yes, Adolf Hitler is really dead—as dead as a dodo.* ☐ *That silly old idea is dead as a dodo.*

(as) dead as a doornail dead. (Informal.) ☐ *This fish is as dead as a doornail.* ☐ *John kept twisting the chicken's neck even though it was dead as a doornail.*

(as) deaf as a post very deaf; profoundly deaf. ☐ *He can't hear a thing you say. He's as deaf as a post.* ☐ *Our old dog is deaf as a post and he can't see much either.*

(as) different as night and day completely different. ☐ *Although Bobby and Billy are twins, they are as different as night and day.* ☐ *Birds and bats appear to be similar, but they are different as night and day.*

(as) drunk as a lord AND **(as) drunk as a skunk** very drunk. ☐ *He came home drunk as a lord again.* ☐ *She was as drunk as a lord by the time they left here.*

(as) drunk as a skunk Go to (as) drunk as a lord.

(as) dry as a bone completely dry. ☐ *During the drought, the soil was as dry as a bone.* ☐ *The dog's water dish was dry as a bone.*

(as) dry as dust 1. very dry. ☐ *The bread is as dry as dust.* ☐ *When the leaves are dry as dust, they break into powder easily.* **2.** very dull; very boring. ☐ *This book is as dry as dust. I am going to stop reading it.* ☐ *Her lecture was dry as dust—just like her subject.*

(as) dull as dishwater AND **(as) dull as ditchwater** very uninteresting. □ *I'm not surprised that he can't find a partner. He's as dull as dishwater.* □ *Mr. Black's speech was as dull as dishwater.*

(as) dull as ditchwater Go to (as) dull as dishwater.

(as) easy as ABC very easy. □ *Making apple pie is as easy as ABC.* □ *Calculus is easy as ABC.*

(as) easy as (apple) pie very easy. (Informal.) □ *Mountain climbing is as easy as pie.* □ *Making a simple dress out of cotton cloth is easy as pie.*

(as) easy as duck soup very easy; requiring no effort. (Informal. When a duck is cooked, it releases a lot of fat and juices, making a "soup" without effort.) □ *Finding your way to the shopping center is easy as duck soup.* □ *Getting Bob to eat fried chicken is as easy as duck soup.*

(as) easy as falling off a log AND **(as) easy as rolling off a log** very easy. (Folksy.) □ *Passing that exam was as easy as falling off a log.* □ *Getting out of jail was easy as rolling off a log.*

(as) easy as rolling off a log Go to (as) easy as falling off a log.

(as) exciting as watching (the) paint dry very, very dull. □ *This book is about as exciting as watching paint dry.* □ *Listening to you is exciting as watching the paint dry.*

(as) far as anyone knows AND **so far as anyone knows** to the limits of anyone's knowledge. (Informal. The *anyone* can be replaced with a more specific noun or pronoun.) □ *As far as anyone knows, this is the last of the great herds of buffalo.* □ *Far as I know, this is the best one.* □ *These are the only keys to the house so far as anyone knows.*

as far as it goes as much as something does, covers, or accomplishes. (Usually said of something that is inadequate.) □ *Your plan is fine as far as it goes. It doesn't seem to take care of everything, though.* □ *As far as it goes, this law is a good one. It should require stiffer penalties, however.*

as far as possible AND **so far as possible** as much as possible; to whatever degree is possible. □ *We must try, as far as possible, to get people to stop smoking in buses.* □ *As far as possible, the police will issue tickets to all speeding drivers.* □ *I'll follow your instructions so far as possible.*

(as) far as someone or something **is concerned** AND **so far as** someone or something **is concerned 1.** [with *someone*] for all that someone cares; if someone is to make the decision. □ *You can take your old dog and leave as far as I'm concerned.* □ *Far as I'm concerned, you can get out and never come back.* □ *So far as I'm concerned, you're okay.* **2.** [with *something*] having to do with something; pertaining to something; as for something. □ *This bill? As far as that's concerned, the committee will have to take care of it.* □ *As far as the roof's concerned, it will just have to last another year.*

(as) fat as a pig exceptionally fat; grotesquely fat. □ *If I don't stop eating this cake, I'll be fat as a pig!* □ *You really ought to go on a diet; you're as fat as a pig.*

(as) fit as a fiddle healthy and physically fit. □ *Mary is as fit as a fiddle.* □ *Tom used to be fit as a fiddle. Look at him now!*

(as) flat as a board very flat. (Also used to describe someone's chest or abdomen, referring to well-developed abdominal muscles or to small or absent breasts or pectoral development—in either sex.) □ *Jane was flat as a board until she was sixteen, when she suddenly blossomed.* □ *The terrain in that part of the country is as flat as a board.*

(as) flat as a pancake very flat. (Informal.) □ *The punctured tire was as flat as a pancake.* □ *Bobby squashed the ant flat as a pancake.*

as for someone or something **1.** AND **as to** someone or something regarding someone or something. □ *As for the mayor, he can pay for his own dinner.* □ *As for you, Bobby, there will be no dessert tonight.* □ *As for this chair, there is nothing to do but throw it away.* □ *As to your idea about building a new house, forget it.* **2.** [with *someone*] quoting someone; speaking for someone. ☐ *As for me, I prefer vegetables to meat.* ☐ *As for Tom, he refuses to attend the concert.*

(as) free as a bird carefree; completely free. ☐ *Jane is always happy and free as a bird.* ☐ *The convict escaped from jail and was as free as a bird for two days.* ☐ *In the summer I feel free as a bird.*

(as) free as (the) air completely free; without obligations or responsibilities. ☐ *The day I got out of the army, I felt as free as air.* ☐ *No, I'm not married. I don't even have a girlfriend. I'm free as the air.*

(as) fresh as a daisy very fresh; fresh and alert. ☐ *The morning dew was as fresh as a daisy.* ☐ *Sally was fresh as a daisy and cheerful as could be.*

(as) full as a tick AND **(as) tight as a tick** very full of food or drink. (Informal. Refers to a tick that has filled itself full of blood.) ☐ *Little Billy ate and ate until he was as tight as a tick.* ☐ *Our cat drank the cream until he became full as a tick.*

(as) funny as a barrel of monkeys AND **more fun than a barrel of monkeys** very funny. (Almost the same as **as much fun as a barrel of monkeys.**) ☐ *Todd was as funny as a barrel of monkeys.* ☐ *The entire evening was funny as a barrel of monkeys.* ☐ *The party was more fun than a barrel of monkeys.*

(as) funny as a crutch not funny at all. ☐ *Your trick is about as funny as a crutch. Nobody thought it was funny.* ☐ *The well-dressed lady slipped and fell in the gutter, which was funny as a crutch.*

(as) gaudy as a butterfly gaudy; colorful. ☐ *Marie looked as gaudy as a butterfly in her new dress.* ☐ *Michael's scarf is gaudy as a butterfly.*

(as) gentle as a lamb very gentle. (Used to describe people.) ☐ *Don't be afraid of Mr. Smith. He may look fierce, but he's as gentle as a lamb.* ☐ *Lisa was gentle as a lamb when dealing with children.*

(as) good as done the same as being done; almost done. (Other past participles can replace *done* in this phrase: *cooked, dead, finished, painted, typed,* etc.) ☐ *This job is as good as done. It'll just take another second.* ☐ *Yes, sir, if you hire me to paint your house, it's as good as painted.* ☐ *When I hand my secretary a letter to be typed, I know that it's as good as typed right then and there.*

(as) good as gold genuine; authentic. ☐ *Mary's promise is as good as gold.* ☐ *Yes, this diamond is genuine—good as gold.*

as good as one's word obedient to one's promise; dependable in keeping one's promises. ☐ *He was as good as his word. He lent me the books as promised.* ☐ *She said she would baby-sit and she was as good as her word.*

(as) graceful as a swan very graceful. ☐ *The boat glided out onto the lake as graceful as a swan.* ☐ *Jane is graceful as a swan.*

(as) gruff as a bear gruff; curt and unsociable. ☐ *I hate to ask Erica questions; she's always gruff as a bear.* ☐ *I'm always as gruff as a bear before I've had my first cup of coffee.*

(as) happy as a clam happy and content. (Note the variation in the examples. Sometimes with additional phrases, such as *in butter sauce* or *at high tide.*) ☐ *Tom sat there smiling, as happy as a clam.* ☐ *There they all sat, eating corn on the cob and looking happy as clams.*

(as) happy as a lark visibly happy and cheerful. (Note the variation in the examples.) ☐ *Sally walked along whistling, as happy as a lark.* ☐ *The children danced and sang, happy as larks.*

(as) happy as can be very happy. ☐ *We are both as happy as can be.* ☐ *Bob was happy as can be when he won the lottery.*

(as) hard as a rock AND **(as) hard as stone** very hard. ☐ *This cake is as hard as a rock!* ☐ *I can't drive a nail into this wood. It's hard as stone.*

(as) hard as nails very hard; cold and cruel. (Refers to the nails that are used with a hammer.) ☐ *The old loaf of bread was dried out and became as hard as nails.* ☐ *Ann was unpleasant and hard as nails.*

(as) hard as stone Go to (as) hard as a rock.

(as) high as a kite AND **(as) high as the sky 1.** very high. □ *The tree grew as high as a kite.* □ *Our pet bird got outside and flew up high as the sky.* **2.** drunk or drugged. □ *Bill drank beer until he got as high as a kite.* □ *The thieves were high as the sky on drugs.*

(as) high as the sky Go to (as) high as a kite.

(as) hoarse as a crow hoarse. □ *After shouting at the team all afternoon, the coach was as hoarse as a crow.* □ *JILL: Has Bob got a cold? JANE: No, he's always hoarse as a crow.*

(as) hot as fire very hot; burning hot. □ *I'm afraid Betsy has a high fever. Her forehead is hot as fire.* □ *In the summertime, the concrete sidewalks feel as hot as fire.*

(as) hot as hell very hot. (Informal. Use caution with *hell.*) □ *It's as hot as hell outside. It must be near 100 degrees.* □ *I hate to get into a car that has been parked in the sun. It's hot as hell.*

(as) hungry as a bear very hungry. (Informal.) □ *I'm as hungry as a bear. I could eat anything!* □ *Whenever I jog, I get hungry as a bear.*

(as) hungry as a hunter very hungry. □ *Is there anything to eat? I've been out hoeing my garden all morning, and I'm as hungry as a hunter!* □ *We'd better have a big meal ready by the time Tommy gets home; he's always hungry as a hunter after soccer practice.*

as I expected Go to (just) as I expected.

(as) innocent as a lamb guiltless; naive. □ *"Hey! You can't throw me in jail," cried the robber. "I'm innocent as a lamb."* □ *Look at the baby, as innocent as a lamb.*

as it were as one might say. (Sometimes used to qualify an assertion that may not sound reasonable.) □ *He carefully constructed, as it were, a huge sandwich.* □ *The Franklins live in a small, as it were, exquisite house.*

(as) large as life in person; actually, and sometimes surprisingly, present at a place. □ *I thought Jack was away, but there he was as large as life.* □ *Jean was not expected to appear, but she turned up large as life.*

(as) light as a feather of little weight. □ *Sally dieted until she was as light as a feather.* □ *Of course I can lift the box. It's light as a feather.*

(as) likely as not probably; with an even chance either way. □ *He will as likely as not arrive without warning.* □ *Likely as not, the game will be canceled.*

as long as 1. AND **so long as** since; because. □ *As long as you're going to the bakery, please buy some fresh bread.* □ *So long as you're here, please stay for dinner.* **2.** AND **so long as** if; only if. □ *You may have dessert so long as you eat all your vegetables.* □ *You can go out this evening as long as you promise to be home by midnight.* **3.** for a specified length of time. □ *You may stay out as long as you like.* □ *I didn't go to school as long as Bill did.* **4.** [in comparisons] of equal length. □ *Is this one as long as that one?* □ *This snake is as long as a car!*

as luck would have it by good or bad luck; as it turned out; by chance. □ *As luck would have it, we had a flat tire.* □ *As luck would have it, the check came in the mail today.*

(as) mad as a hatter 1. crazy. (From the crazy character called the Hatter in Lewis Carroll's *Alice's Adventures in Wonderland.*) □ *Poor old John is as mad as a hatter.* □ *All these screaming children are driving me mad as a hatter.* **2.** angry. (This is a misunderstanding of *mad* in the first sense. Folksy. The first *as* can be omitted.) □ *You make me so angry! I'm as mad as a hatter.* □ *John can't control his temper. He's always mad as a hatter.*

(as) mad as a hornet angry. □ *You make me so angry. I'm as mad as a hornet.* □ *Jane can get mad as a hornet when somebody criticizes her.*

(as) mad as a March hare crazy. (From the name of a character in Lewis Carroll's

Alice's Adventures in Wonderland.) □ *Sally is getting as mad as a March hare.* □ *My Uncle Bill is mad as a March hare.*

(as) mad as a wet hen angry. (Folksy.) □ *Bob was screaming and shouting—as mad as a wet hen.* □ *What you said made Mary mad as a wet hen.*

(as) mad as hell very angry. (Informal. Use caution with *hell.*) □ *He made his wife as mad as hell.* □ *Those terrorists make me mad as hell.*

(as) meek as a lamb meek; quiet and docile. □ *Only an hour after their argument, Joe went to Elizabeth and, meek as a lamb, asked her to forgive him.* □ *Betsy terrorizes the other children, but she's as meek as a lamb around her elders.*

(as) merry as a cricket cheerful. (Old-fashioned.) □ *Mary is as merry as a cricket whenever she has company come to call.* □ *George is such a pleasant companion; he's usually merry as a cricket.*

(as) merry as the day is long very happy and carefree. □ *The little children are as merry as the day is long.* □ *Only on vacation are we merry as the day is long.*

as much fun as a barrel of monkeys a great deal of fun. (Almost the same as (as) funny as a barrel of monkeys.) □ *Roger is as much fun as a barrel of monkeys.* □ *The circus was as much fun as a barrel of monkeys.*

(as) naked as a jaybird naked. □ *"Billy," called Mrs. Franklin, "get back in the house and get some clothes on. You're as naked as a jaybird."* □ *Tom had to get naked as a jaybird for the doctor to examine him.*

(as) neat as a pin neat and orderly. □ *Brad is such a good housekeeper; his apartment is always as neat as a pin.* □ *Joanne certainly is well-organized. Her desk is neat as a pin.*

(as) nutty as a fruitcake silly; crazy. (Slang. A fruitcake usually has lots of nuts in it.) □ *Whenever John goes to a party, he gets as nutty as a fruitcake.* □ *Sally has been acting as nutty as a fruitcake lately.*

(as) old as the hills very old. □ *The children think their mother's as old as the hills, but she's only forty.* □ *That song's not new. It's old as the hills.*

as one as if a group were one person. (Especially with *act, move,* or *speak.*) □ *All the dancers moved as one.* □ *The chorus spoke as one.*

(as) pale as a ghost Go to (as) white as a ghost.

(as) pale as death extremely pale. (The reference to death gives this phrase ominous connotations.) □ *Rita was as pale as death when she came out of the doctor's office.* □ *What's the matter? You're pale as death!*

(as) patient as Job very patient. (Refers to a character in the Bible.) □ *If you want to teach young children, you must be as patient as Job.* □ *The director who is working with that temperamental actor must have the patience of Job.*

(as) phony as a three-dollar bill phony; bogus. □ *This guy's as phony as a three-dollar bill.* □ *The whole deal stinks. It's as phony as a three-dollar bill.*

(as) plain as a pikestaff obvious; very clear. □ *JILL: Why does the Senator always vote for measures that would help the tobacco industry? JANE: It's as plain as a pikestaff—because there are a lot of tobacco growers in his district, and he wants them to vote for him.* □ *FRED: I have a suspicion that Marcia is upset with me. ALAN: A suspicion? Come on, Fred, that's been plain as a pikestaff for quite some time!*

(as) plain as day 1. very plain and simple. □ *Although his face was as plain as day, his smile made him look interesting and friendly.* □ *Our house is plain as day, but it's comfortable.* **2.** clear and understandable. □ *The lecture was as plain as day. No one had to ask questions.* □ *His statement was plain as day.*

(as) plain as the nose on one's **face** obvious; clearly evident. (Informal.) □ *What do you mean you don't understand? It's as plain as the nose on your face.* □ *Your guilt is plain as the nose on your face.*

(as) pleased as punch very pleased; very pleased with oneself. (Refers to the character Punch in [English] Punch and Judy puppet shows. *Punch* is sometimes capitalized.) □ *Wally was as pleased as punch when he won the prize.* □ *She seems pleased as punch, but she knows she doesn't deserve the award.*

(as) poor as a church mouse very poor. □ *My aunt is as poor as a church mouse.* □ *The Browns are poor as church mice.*

(as) pretty as a picture very pretty. □ *Sweet little Mary is as pretty as a picture.* □ *Their new house is pretty as a picture.*

(as) proud as a peacock very proud; haughty. □ *John is so arrogant. He's as proud as a peacock.* □ *The new father was proud as a peacock.*

(as) pure as the driven snow pure and virginal. (Often used ironically.) □ *JILL: Sue must have gone to bed with every man in town. JANE: And I always thought she was as pure as the driven snow.* □ *Robert was notoriously promiscuous, but tried to convince all his girlfriends that he was pure as the driven snow.*

(as) queer as a three-dollar bill very strange. □ *Today I saw a woman pushing a lawn mower down the street and singing to it as she went. I thought she was queer as a three-dollar bill.* □ *JILL: In all the years I've known him, Mike has never had a suit and he goes barefoot. FRED: That's because he's as queer as a three-dollar bill.*

(as) quick as a flash Go to (as) quick as a wink.

(as) quick as a wink AND **(as) quick as a flash** very quickly. □ *As quick as a wink, the thief took the lady's purse.* □ *I'll finish this work quick as a wink.* □ *The dog grabbed the meat as quick as a flash.* □ *The summer days went by quick as a flash.*

(as) quick as greased lightning very quickly; very fast. (Folksy. See also like greased lightning.) □ *Jane can really run. She's as quick as greased lightning.* □ *Quick as greased lightning, the thief stole my wallet.*

(as) quiet as a mouse very quiet; shy and silent. (Informal. Often used with children.) □ *Don't yell; whisper. Be as quiet as a mouse.* □ *Mary hardly ever says anything. She's quiet as a mouse.*

(as) quiet as the grave very quiet; silent. □ *The house is as quiet as the grave when the children are at school.* □ *This town is quiet as the grave now that the offices have closed.*

(as) red as a cherry bright red. (Somewhat old-fashioned.) □ *When the children came in from ice-skating, Clara's nose was as red as a cherry.* □ *When Lester proposed marriage, Nancy blushed as red as a cherry.*

(as) red as a poppy bright red. (Usually used to describe someone blushing.) □ *You must be embarrassed—you're as red as a poppy!* □ *When her boss praised her in front of the whole office, Emily turned red as a poppy.*

(as) red as a rose intensely red. □ *Bill blushed as red as a rose when we teased him.*

(as) red as a ruby deep red. (Often used to describe a person's lips.) □ *Linda has a beautiful face, with big blue eyes and lips as red as rubies.*

(as) red as blood completely red; deep red. (The reference to blood gives this expression sinister connotations.) □ *The magician's cape was lined with satin as red as blood.* □ *I want to have my car painted red as blood.*

(as) regular as clockwork dependably regular. (Informal.) □ *She comes into this store every day, as regular as clockwork.* □ *Our tulips come up every year, regular as clockwork.*

(as) right as rain correct; genuine. (Folksy.) □ *Your answer is as right as rain.* □ *John is very dependable. He's right as rain.*

(as) scarce as hens' teeth AND **scarcer than hens' teeth** very scarce or nonexistent. (An exaggeration. Chickens don't have teeth.) □ *I've never seen one of those. They're as scarce as hens' teeth.* □ *I was* *told that the part needed for my car is scarcer than hens' teeth, and it would take a long time to find one.*

(as) sharp as a razor 1. very sharp. ☐ *The penknife is sharp as a razor.* ☐ *The carving knife will have to be as sharp as a razor to cut through this meat.* **2.** very sharp-witted or intelligent. ☐ *The old man's senile, but his wife is as sharp as a razor.* ☐ *Don't say too much in front of the child. She's as sharp as a razor.*

(as) sharp as a tack intellectually bright. ☐ *Melissa doesn't say very much, but she's sharp as a tack.* ☐ *Sue can figure things out from even the slightest hint. She's as sharp as a tack.*

(as) sick as a dog very sick; sick and vomiting. ☐ *We've never been so ill. The whole family was sick as dogs.* ☐ *Sally was as sick as a dog and couldn't go to the party.*

(as) silent as the dead AND **(as) silent as the grave** completely silent. (Has ominous connotations because of the reference to death. Usually used to promise someone that you will be silent and therefore not betray a secret.) ☐ *I knew something was wrong as soon as I entered the classroom; everyone was silent as the dead.* ☐ *Jessica is as silent as the grave on the subject of her first marriage.* ☐ *If you tell me what Katy said about me, I promise to be as silent as the grave.*

(as) silent as the grave Go to (as) silent as the dead.

(as) silly as a goose very foolish. ☐ *Edith is as silly as a goose. She thinks that reading aloud to her houseplants will help them grow.* ☐ *JILL: The ad in the newspaper said this lotion would make my hair grow faster, but I've been using it for a whole month and my hair is still the same length. JANE: You're as silly as a goose! Do you believe everything you read in newspaper ads?*

(as) slick as a whistle quickly and cleanly; quickly and skillfully. ☐ *Tom took a broom and a mop and cleaned the place up as slick as a whistle.* ☐ *Slick as a whistle, Sally pulled off the bandage.*

(as) slippery as an eel devious; undependable. ☐ *Tom can't be trusted. He's as slippery as an eel.* ☐ *It's hard to catch Joe in his office because he's slippery as an eel.*

(as) slow as molasses in January AND **slower than molasses in January** slow. ☐ *Can't you get dressed any faster? I declare, you're as slow as molasses in January.* ☐ *The traffic on the way to the concert was slower than molasses in January.*

(as) sly as a fox smart and clever. ☐ *My nephew is as sly as a fox.* ☐ *You have to be sly as a fox to outwit me.*

(as) smooth as glass smooth and shiny. (Often used to describe calm bodies of water.) ☐ *The bay is as smooth as glass, so we should have a pleasant boat trip.* ☐ *Eugene polished the floor until it was smooth as glass.*

(as) smooth as silk very smooth. ☐ *This pudding is smooth as silk.* ☐ *Your skin is as smooth as silk.*

(as) snug as a bug in a rug cozy and snug. (Informal. The kind of thing said when putting a child to bed.) ☐ *Let's pull up the covers. There you are, Bobby, as snug as a bug in a rug.* ☐ *What a lovely little house! I know I'll be snug as a bug in a rug.*

(as) sober as a judge 1. very formal, somber, or stuffy. ☐ *You certainly look gloomy, Bill. You're sober as a judge.* ☐ *Tom's as sober as a judge. I think he's angry.* **2.** not drunk; alert and completely sober. ☐ *John's drunk? No, he's as sober as a judge.* ☐ *You should be sober as a judge when you drive a car.*

(as) soft as a baby's bottom very soft and smooth to the touch. ☐ *This cloth is as soft as a baby's bottom.* ☐ *No, Bob doesn't shave yet. His cheeks are soft as a baby's bottom.*

(as) soft as down soft to the touch. (Refers to the softness of goose or duck down.) ☐ *The kitten's fur was as soft as down.* ☐ *The baby's skin was soft as down.*

(as) soft as silk very soft. ☐ *This fabric is as soft as silk.* ☐ *Your touch is soft as silk.*

(as) soft as velvet very soft to the touch. ☐ *The horse's nose felt as soft as velvet.* ☐

This lotion will make your skin soft as velvet.

(as) solid as a rock very solid; dependable. □ *Jean has been lifting weights every day, and her arm muscles are solid as a rock.* □ *This company builds typewriters that are as solid as a rock.*

as soon as at the moment that; at the time that; when. □ *I fell asleep as soon as I lay down.* □ *John ate dinner as soon as he came home.*

(as) soon as possible at the earliest time. □ *I'm leaving now. I'll be there as soon as possible.* □ *Please pay me as soon as possible.*

(as) sound as a dollar 1. very secure and dependable. □ *This investment is as sound as a dollar.* □ *I wouldn't put my money in a bank that isn't sound as a dollar.* **2.** sturdy and well-constructed. □ *This house is as sound as a dollar.* □ *The garage is still sound as a dollar. Why tear it down?*

(as) sour as vinegar sour and disagreeable. □ *The old man greeted us ill-naturedly, his face as sour as vinegar.* □ *JILL: Is Mary in a bad mood today? JANE: Yes, sour as vinegar.*

(as) steady as a rock very steady and unmovable; very stable. □ *His hand was steady as a rock as he pulled the trigger of the revolver.* □ *You must remain as steady as a rock when you are arguing with your supervisor.*

(as) stiff as a poker rigid and inflexible; stiff and awkward. (Usually used to describe people.) □ *This guy's dead. He's cold and as stiff as a poker.* □ *John is not a very good dancer; he's stiff as a poker.*

(as) still as death immobile; completely still. (The reference to death gives this expression ominous connotations.) □ *George sat as still as death all afternoon.* □ *When the storm was over, everything was suddenly still as death.*

(as) straight as an arrow 1. [of something] very straight. □ *The road to my house is as straight as an arrow, so it should be very easy to follow.* **2.** [of someone] honest or forthright. (*Straight* here means "honest.") □ *Tom is straight as an arrow. I'd trust him with anything.*

(as) strong as a horse [of someone] very strong. □ *JILL: My car broke down; it's sitting out on the street. JANE: Get Linda to help you push it; she's as strong as a horse.* □ *The athlete was strong as a horse. He could lift his own weight with just one hand.*

(as) strong as a lion very strong. □ *See if you can get Melissa to help us move our furniture. She's as strong as a lion.* □ *The football player was strong as a lion.*

(as) strong as an ox very strong. □ *Tom lifts weights and is as strong as an ox.* □ *Now that Ann has recovered from her illness, she's strong as an ox.*

(as) stubborn as a mule very stubborn. □ *My husband is as stubborn as a mule.* □ *Our cat is stubborn as a mule.*

as such the way something is; as someone or something is. □ *I cannot accept your manuscript as such. It needs revisions.* □ *You are new here, and as such, I will have to train you.*

(as) sure as death sure; very certain. □ *As political tension increased, it became more and more apparent that war was coming, as sure as death.* □ *JILL: Is the company definitely going to lay people off? JANE: Sure as death.*

(as) sweet as honey AND **(as) sweet as sugar 1.** very sweet. □ *These little cakes are as sweet as honey.* □ *This fruit juice is as sweet as honey.* **2.** charming; very nice and friendly. □ *She is as sweet as honey whenever she talks to me.* □ *He seems sweet as honey, but he is really mean.*

(as) sweet as sugar Go to (as) sweet as honey.

(as) swift as an arrow very fast. □ *The new intercity train is swift as an arrow.* □ *My week of vacation sped by as swift as an arrow.*

(as) swift as the wind very fast. □ *This new car is as swift as the wind.* □ *Joe ran swift as the wind, trying to get home in time.*

(as) swift as thought extremely fast. ☐ *Thanks to modern communication devices, news can now travel almost as swift as thought.* ☐ *You won't have to wait for me long; I'll be there, swift as thought.*

as the crow flies straight across the land, as opposed to distances measured on a road, river, etc. (Folksy.) ☐ *It's twenty miles to town on the highway, but only ten miles as the crow flies.* ☐ *Our house is only a few miles from the lake as the crow flies.*

(as) thick as pea soup [of a liquid or fog] very thick. (Informal.) ☐ *This fog is as thick as pea soup.* ☐ *Wow, this coffee is strong! It's thick as pea soup.*

(as) thick as thieves very close-knit; friendly; allied. ☐ *Mary, Tom, and Sally are as thick as thieves. They go everywhere together.* ☐ *Those two families are thick as thieves.*

(as) tight as a drum 1. stretched tight. ☐ *Julia stretched the upholstery fabric over the seat of the chair until it was as tight as a drum.* **2.** sealed tight. ☐ *Now that I've caulked all the windows, the house should be tight as a drum.* **3.** very stingy. ☐ *He won't contribute a cent. He's as tight as a drum.*

(as) tight as a tick Go to **(as) full as a tick**.

(as) tight as Dick's hatband very tight. ☐ *I've got to lose some weight. My belt is as tight as Dick's hatband.* ☐ *This window is stuck tight as Dick's hatband.*

as to someone or something Go to **as for** someone or something.

(as) tough as an old boot 1. very tough. ☐ *This meat is tough as an old boot.* ☐ *Bob couldn't eat the steak. It was as tough as an old boot.* **2.** very strong; not easily moved by feelings such as pity. ☐ *Margaret is never off work. She's as tough as an old boot.* ☐ *Don't expect sympathy from the boss. She's tough as an old boot.*

(as) true as steel very loyal and dependable. ☐ *Through all my troubles, my husband has been as true as steel.* ☐ *Pedro was a staunch friend, true as steel.*

(as) ugly as a toad very ugly. ☐ *Maria may be a beautiful woman, but when she was a child she was as ugly as a toad.* ☐ *The shopkeeper was ugly as a toad, but he was kind and generous, and everyone loved him.*

(as) ugly as sin very ugly. ☐ *The new building is as ugly as sin.* ☐ *The old woman is ugly as sin, but she dresses beautifully.*

as usual as is the normal or typical situation. ☐ *John ordered eggs for breakfast as usual.* ☐ *He stood quietly as usual, waiting for the bus to come.*

(as) warm as toast very warm and cozy. ☐ *The baby will be warm as toast in that blanket.* ☐ *We were as warm as toast by the side of the fire.*

(as) weak as a baby [of someone] physically very weak. ☐ *Six weeks of illness left the athlete as weak as a baby.* ☐ *Hot, humid weather like this always makes me feel weak as a baby.*

(as) weak as a kitten weak; weak and sickly. ☐ *John is as weak as a kitten because he doesn't eat well.* ☐ *Oh! Suddenly I feel weak as a kitten.*

as well also; in addition. ☐ *Could I have some more potatoes as well?* ☐ *I'm feeling tired, and dizzy as well.*

as well as 1. in addition to someone or something. ☐ *Mary and Jane are coming to the party, as well as Tom.* ☐ *I'm studying biology and chemistry, as well as history.* **2.** to the same high degree as someone or something; as much as. ☐ *Mary's parents treated me as well as they treated her.* ☐ *I did as well as you on the test.*

(as) white as a ghost AND **(as) pale as a ghost** [of a person] very pale. ☐ *His face is as white as a ghost.* ☐ *He turned pale as a ghost when he saw his injured leg.*

(as) white as a sheet very pale. ☐ *Jane was white as a sheet for weeks after her illness.* ☐ *Mary went as white as a sheet when she heard the news.*

(as) white as the driven snow very white. ☐ *I like my bed sheets to be as white as the driven snow.* ☐ *We have a new kitten whose fur is white as the driven snow.*

(as) wise as an owl very wise. ☐ *Grandfather is as wise as an owl.* ☐ *My goal is to be wise as an owl.*

(as) wise as Solomon very wise. (Refers to a character in the Bible.) ☐ *If you are in trouble, get Chris to advise you. He's as wise as Solomon.* ☐ *This is a difficult problem. You'd need to be as wise as Solomon to be able to solve it.*

aside from someone or something not including someone or something. ☐ *Aside from a small bank account, I have no money at all.* ☐ *Aside from Mary, I have no friends.*

ask for something to do something that will cause trouble. (Also literal.) ☐ *Don't talk to me that way! You're really asking for it.* ☐ *Anyone who acts like that is just asking for a good talking to.*

ask for the moon to ask for too much; to make great demands. ☐ *When you're trying to get a job, it's unwise to ask for the moon.* ☐ *Please lend me the money. I'm not asking for the moon!*

ask for trouble AND **look for trouble** to seem to be trying to get into trouble; to do something that would cause trouble; to do or say something that will cause trouble. ☐ *Stop talking to me that way, John. You're just asking for trouble.* ☐ *The guard asked me to leave unless I was looking for trouble.* ☐ *Anybody who threatens a police officer is just asking for trouble.* ☐ *You're looking for trouble if you ask the boss for a raise.*

ask someone **out** to ask a person for a date. ☐ *Mary hopes that John will ask her out.* Ⓣ *John doesn't want to ask out his best friend's girl.*

asleep at the switch not attending to one's job; failing to do one's duty at the proper time. (Also literal.) ☐ *The guard was asleep at the switch when the robber broke in.* ☐ *If I hadn't been asleep at the switch, I'd have seen the stolen car.*

assault and battery a violent attack [upon someone] followed by a beating. (A criminal charge.) ☐ *Max was charged with two counts of assault and battery.* ☐ *Dave does not go out at night because he does not want to be a victim of assault and battery.*

assault the ears [for sound or speech] to be very loud or persistent. ☐ *That loud music assaults the ears!* ☐ *I can't hear with all that talk assaulting my ears.*

assemble a case (against someone**)** Go to **build a case (against** someone**)**.

assume liability to accept the responsibility for paying a cost. ☐ *Mr. Smith assumed liability for his son's student loans.* ☐ *The store assumed liability for the injured customer's hospital bill.*

at all without distinguishing; without qualification. (See the examples for word order variations.) ☐ *It really wasn't very cold at all.* ☐ *It really wasn't at all cold.* ☐ *Tom will eat anything at all.* ☐ *Jane isn't at all hungry.* ☐ *Grandma was always ready to go anywhere at all.*

at all costs AND **at any cost** regardless of the difficulty or cost; no matter what. ☐ *I intend to have that car at all costs.* ☐ *I'll get there by six o'clock at all costs.* ☐ *Mary was going to get that job at any cost.*

at all times constantly; continuously. ☐ *You must keep your passport handy at all times when you are traveling in a foreign country.* ☐ *When you're in a crowd, you must watch your child at all times.*

at a loss (for words) unable to speak; speechless; befuddled. ☐ *I was so surprised that I was at a loss for words.* ☐ *Tom was terribly confused—really at a loss.*

at an early date soon; some day soon. ☐ *The note said, "Please call me at an early date."* ☐ *You're expected to return the form to the office at an early date.*

at any cost Go to **at all costs**.

at any rate anyway. (Informal. Frequently used as an introduction to a conclusion or a final statement.) ☐ *At any rate, we had a nice time at your party. We are grateful that you asked us.* ☐ *It's not much, at any rate, but it's the best we can do.*

at a premium at a high price; priced high because of something special. ☐ *Sally bought the shoes at a premium because they were of very high quality.* ☐ *This model of car is selling at a premium because so many people want to buy it.*

at a set time at a particular time; at an assigned time. □ *Each person has to show up at a set time.* □ *Do I have to be there at a set time, or can I come whenever I want?*

at a sitting at one time; during one period. (Refers to an activity that takes place while a person is seated.) □ *The restaurant could feed only sixty people at a sitting.* □ *I can read about 300 pages at a sitting.*

at a snail's pace very slowly. □ *When you watch a clock, time seems to move at a snail's pace.* □ *You always eat at a snail's pace. I'm tired of waiting for you.*

at a stretch continuously; without stopping. □ *We all had to do eight hours of duty at a stretch.* □ *The baby doesn't sleep for more than three hours at a stretch.*

at bay at a distance. □ *I have to keep the bill collectors at bay until I get my check.* □ *The wolves will not remain at bay for very long.*

at best AND **at most** in the best view; in the most positive judgment; as the best one can say. □ *I believe her to be totally negligent. Her actions were careless at best.* □ *At best we found their visit pleasantly short.* □ *The dinner was not at all pleasant. At best the food was not burned.* □ *At most she was careless, but not criminal.* □ *We found their visit pleasingly short at most.*

at close range very near; in close proximity. (Usually used in regard to shooting.) □ *The hunter fired at the deer at close range.* □ *The powder burns tell us that the gun was fired at close range.*

at cross-purposes with opposing purposes; with goals that interfere with each other. □ *We are arguing at cross-purposes. We aren't even discussing the same thing.* □ *Bill and Tom are working at cross-purposes. They'll never get the job done right.*

at death's door near death. (Euphemistic.) □ *I was so ill that I was at death's door.* □ *The family dog was at death's door for three days, and then it finally died.*

at ease relaxed and comfortable. □ *I don't feel at ease driving when there is a lot of traffic.* □ *Mary is most at ease when she's near the sea.*

at every turn everywhere; everywhere one looks. □ *There is a new problem at every turn.* □ *Life holds new adventures at every turn.*

at face value from outward appearance; from what something first appears to be. (From the value printed on the "face" of a coin or bank note.) □ *Don't just accept her offer at face value. Think of the implications.* □ *Joan tends to take people at face value and so she is always getting hurt.*

at first initially; at the beginning. □ *He was shy at first. Then he became more friendly.* □ *At first we chose the red one. Later we switched to the blue one.*

at first blush Go to **at first glance.**

at first glance AND **at first blush** when first examined; at an early stage. □ *At first glance, the problem appeared quite simple. Later we learned just how complex it really was.* □ *He appeared quite healthy at first glance.* □ *At first blush, she appeared to be quite old.*

(at) full blast using full power; as loudly as possible. □ *The neighbors had their televisions on at full blast.* □ *The car radio was on full blast. We couldn't hear what the driver was saying.*

at full speed AND **at full tilt** as fast as possible. □ *The motor was running at full speed.* □ *John finished his running at full speed.* □ *Things are now operating at full tilt.*

at full tilt Go to **at full speed.**

at half-mast halfway up or down. (Primarily referring to flags. Can be used for things other than flags as a joke.) □ *The flag was flying at half-mast because the general had died.* □ *Americans fly flags at half-mast on Memorial Day.* □ *The little boy ran out of the house with his pants at half-mast.*

at hand close by. (Used with both time and distance. See also **close at hand; near at hand.**) □ *I don't happen to have your ap-*

plication at hand at the moment. □ *With the holiday season at hand, everyone is very excited.*

at hazard risked; in danger; at risk. □ *He is not willing to have much of his money at hazard in the stock market.* □ *Your entire life is at hazard unless you wear a helmet when you ride your bicycle.*

at home at or in one's dwelling. □ *Is Mary at home, or is she still at work?* □ *What time will she be at home?*

at home with someone or something comfortable with someone or something; comfortable doing something. (Also literal. See also **feel at home**.) □ *Tom is very much at home with my parents.* □ *Sally seems to be very much at home with her car.* □ *Mary seems to be at home with her job.*

at it again doing something again. (Informal.) □ *I asked Tom to stop playing his trumpet, but he's at it again.* □ *They are at it again. Why are they always fighting?*

at large 1. free; uncaptured. (Usually said of criminals running loose.) □ *At noon the day after the robbery, the thieves were still at large.* □ *There is a murderer at large in the city.* **2.** in general; according to a general sample. □ *Truck drivers at large don't like the new law.* □ *Students at large felt that the rule was too strict.* **3.** representing the whole group rather than its subsections. (Always refers to a special kind of elective office.) □ *He ran for representative at large.* □ *She represented shareholders at large on the governing board.*

at last Go to at (long) last.

at least 1. no less than; no fewer than. □ *There were at least four people there that I knew.* □ *I want to spend at least three weeks in Mexico.* **2.** anyway; in spite of difficulties. □ *At least we had a good evening, even though the afternoon was rainy.* □ *At least we came away with some of our money left.*

at leisure 1. resting; not working. □ *What do you usually do when you are at leisure?* □ *During the summer when you are at leisure, you ought to play golf.* **2.** AND **at one's leisure** at one's convenience. □ *Choose one or the other at your leisure.* □ *Please drop by at your leisure.*

at length 1. after some time; finally. □ *At length, the roses bloomed and the tomatoes ripened.* □ *And at length, the wizard spoke.* **2.** AND **at some length** for quite a long time. □ *He spoke on and on at some length.* □ *He described the history of his village at length.*

at liberty free; unrestrained. □ *The criminal was set at liberty by the judge.* □ *You're at liberty to go anywhere you wish.* □ *I'm not at liberty to discuss the matter.*

at loggerheads (with someone**)** in opposition; at an impasse; in a quarrel. □ *Mr. and Mrs. Franklin have been at loggerheads for years.* □ *The two political parties were at loggerheads during the entire legislative session.* □ *She was at loggerheads with him for years.*

at (long) last after a long wait; finally. □ *At last the hostages were released.* □ *Sally earned her diploma at long last.*

at loose ends restless and unsettled; unemployed. □ *Just before school starts, all the children are at loose ends.* □ *When Tom is home on the weekends, he's always at loose ends.* □ *Jane has been at loose ends ever since she lost her job.*

at most Go to at best.

at night during the night. □ *Most people sleep at night.* □ *Mary studies at night.*

at odds (with someone**)** in opposition to someone; at loggerheads (with someone). □ *Mary is always at odds with her father about how late she can stay out.* □ *John and his father are always at odds too.*

at once immediately; at this very moment. □ *John, come here at once!* □ *Bring me my coffee at once!* □ *Shall I do it at once or wait until morning?*

at one fell swoop AND **in one fell swoop** in a single incident; as a single event. (This phrase preserves the old word *fell,* meaning "terrible" or "deadly.") □ *The party guests ate up all the snacks at one fell swoop.* □ *When the stock market crashed,* *many large fortunes were wiped out in one fell swoop.*

at one's **best** in the best of health; displaying the most civilized behavior. (Often in the negative.) □ *I'm not at my best when I'm angry.* □ *He's at his best after a good nap.*

at one's **leisure** Go to at leisure.

at one's **wit's end** at the limits of one's mental resources. □ *I'm at my wit's end with this problem. I cannot figure it out.* □ *Tom could do no more. He was at his wit's end.*

at peace 1. peaceful; relaxed; happy. □ *I am always at peace when I sit in my rocking chair.* □ *When the warm breeze is blowing, I am at peace.* **2.** dead. □ *It was a long illness, but she is at peace now.* □ *At last, Uncle Tom is at peace.*

at play [at this moment] involved in playing. □ *The children are at play, and I am doing household chores.* □ *Whether I am at work or at play, I try to be pleasant to people.*

at present now; at this point in time. □ *We are not able to do any more at present.* □ *We may be able to lend you money next week, but not at present.*

at random without sequence or order. □ *Sally picked four names at random from the telephone book.* □ *The gunman walked into the crowded restaurant and fired at random.* □ *Jane will read almost anything. She selects four novels at random at the library each week and reads them all.*

at regular intervals at points that are equal in distance apart. □ *You will find service stations at regular intervals along the highway.* □ *There are streetlights at regular intervals on the main street of town.*

at rest not moving; not active. □ *After the hectic day, the office was finally at rest by midnight.* □ *Do not remove your seat belt until the plane is at rest.*

at risk in a situation where there is risk or hazard; in danger. □ *I refuse to put my family's welfare at risk by quitting my job.* □ *Your whole future is at risk if you don't stop smoking.*

at sea on the sea; away on a voyage on the ocean. (See also (all) at sea (about something).) □ *The ship is at sea now, and you can't disembark.* □ *I spent many happy days at sea on my cruise.*

at sea (about something**)** Go to (all) at sea (about something).

at sea level located at the bottom of the sea. □ *It is easier to breathe at sea level than in the mountains.* □ *Boats on the ocean are at sea level, but those on rivers are not.*

at sixes and sevens disorderly; lost and bewildered; at loose ends. □ *Mrs. Smith is at sixes and sevens since the death of her husband.* □ *Bill is always at sixes and sevens when he's home by himself.*

at some length Go to at length.

at someone's **beck and call** ready to obey someone. □ *What makes you think I wait around here at your beck and call? I live here too, you know!* □ *It was a fine hotel. There were dozens of maids and waiters at our beck and call.*

at someone's **doorstep** AND **on** someone's **doorstep** in someone's care; as someone's responsibility. □ *Why do you always have to lay your problems at my doorstep?* □ *I shall put this issue on someone else's doorstep.* □ *I don't want it on my doorstep.*

at someone's **earliest convenience** as soon as it is easy or convenient for someone. (This is also a polite way of saying *immediately.*) □ *Please stop by my office at your earliest convenience.* □ *Bill, please have the oil changed at your earliest convenience.*

at someone's **mercy** Go to at the mercy of someone.

at someone's **request** due to someone's request; on being asked by someone. □ *At his mother's request, Tom stopped playing the saxophone.* □ *At the request of the police officer, Bill pulled his car over to the side of the road.*

at someone's **service** ready to help someone in any way. □ *The count greeted me warmly and said, "Welcome to my home. Just let me know what you need. I'm at* *your service."* □ *The desk clerk said, "Good morning, madam. We are always at your service."*

at some time **sharp** exactly at a named time. □ *You must be here at noon sharp.* □ *The plane is expected to arrive at seven forty-five sharp.*

at stake to be won or lost; at risk; hanging in the balance. □ *That's a very risky investment. How much money is at stake?* □ *I have everything at stake on this wager.*

at that rate in that manner; at that speed. (See also **at this rate**.) □ *If things keep progressing at that rate, we'll be rich by next year.* □ *At that rate we'll never get the money that is owed us.*

at the appointed time at the announced or assigned time. □ *The cab pulled up in the driveway at the appointed time.* □ *We all met at the hotel at the appointed time.*

at the bottom of the hour on the half hour; the opposite of **at the top of the hour**. (Typically heard on television or the radio. Refers to the minute hand on a clock.) □ *Hear the news on WNAG at the bottom of the hour.* □ *We will have an interview with Harry Smith at the bottom of the hour.*

at the bottom of the ladder at the lowest level of pay and status. □ *Most people start work at the bottom of the ladder.* □ *When Ann got fired, she had to start all over again at the bottom of the ladder.*

at the break of dawn Go to at the crack of dawn.

at the crack of dawn AND **at the break of dawn** at the time of the earliest light of the day. □ *Jane was always up at the crack of dawn.* □ *The birds start singing at the break of dawn.*

at the drop of a hat immediately and without urging. □ *John was always ready to go fishing at the drop of a hat.* □ *If you need help, just call on me. I can come at the drop of a hat.*

at the eleventh hour at the last possible moment. (See also **eleventh-hour decision**.) □ *She always turned her term papers in at the eleventh hour.* □ *We don't worry about death until the eleventh hour.*

at the end of nowhere at a remote place; at some distance from civilization. □ *They live way out in the country at the end of nowhere.* □ *The police will never find us here at the end of nowhere.*

at the end of one's **rope** AND **at the end of** one's **tether** at the limits of one's endurance. □ *I'm at the end of my rope! I just can't go on this way!* □ *These kids are driving me out of my mind. I'm at the end of my tether.*

at the end of one's **tether** Go to at the end of one's rope.

at the end of the day when everything else has been taken into consideration. (Also literal.) □ *At the end of the day you will have to decide where you want to live.* □ *The committee interviewed many applicants for the post, but at the end of the day made no appointment.*

at the expense of someone or something to the detriment of someone or something; to the harm of someone or something. □ *He had a good laugh at the expense of his brother.* □ *He took a job in a better place at the expense of a larger income.*

at the forefront (of something**)** AND **in the forefront (of** something**)** the most important place; the place of greatest activity. □ *I interviewed Max Brown, the director who is in the forefront of the movie industry.* □ *The university I go to is at the forefront of computer technology.*

at the height of something at the most intense or forceful aspect of something. □ *At the height of his career, Tom was known around the world.* □ *At the height of the party, there were 50 people present.*

at the helm (of something**)** in the position of being in control of something. (Also literal for ships and boats.) □ *The president is at the helm of the company.* □ *Things will go well with Anne at the helm.*

at the last gasp at the very last; at the last chance; at the last minute. (Refers to someone's last breath before death.) □ *She finally showed up at the last gasp,* *bringing the papers that were needed.* ☐ *We got there at the last gasp, just before our names were called.*

at the last minute at the last possible chance. (Compare this with **at the eleventh hour.**) ☐ *Please don't make reservations at the last minute.* ☐ *Why do you ask all your questions at the last minute?*

at the latest no later than. ☐ *Please pay this bill in ten days at the latest.* ☐ *I'll be home by midnight at the latest.*

at the mercy of someone AND **at** someone's **mercy** under the control of someone; without defense against someone. ☐ *We were left at the mercy of the arresting officer.* ☐ *Mrs. Franklin wanted Mr. Franklin at her mercy.*

at the outset at the beginning. (See also **from the outset.**) ☐ *It seemed like a very simple problem at the outset.* ☐ *At the outset, they were very happy. Then they had money problems.*

at the point of doing something Go to **on the point of** doing something.

at the present time AND **at this point (in time)** now; at present. (Used often as a wordy replacement for *now.*) ☐ *We don't know the location of the stolen car at the present time.* ☐ *The tomatoes are doing nicely at the present time.* ☐ *At this point in time, we feel very sad about his death.* ☐ *Yes, it's sad, but there is nothing we can do at this point.*

at the rear of something located at the back part of something. ☐ *I keep my tools at the rear of my garage.* ☐ *There's a creek at the rear of my property.*

at the same time nevertheless; however. (Also literal.) ☐ *Bill was able to make the car payment. At the same time, he was very angry about the bill.* ☐ *We agree to your demands. At the same time, we object strongly to your methods.*

at the top of one's **lungs** Go to **at the top of one's voice.**

at the top of one's **voice** AND **at the top of** one's **lungs** with a very loud voice. ☐ *Bill called to Mary at the top of his voice.* ☐ *How can I work when you're all talking at the top of your lungs?*

at the top of the hour at the exact beginning of the hour. (Typically heard on television or the radio. See also **at the bottom of the hour.** Refers to the minute hand on a clock.) ☐ *Every class in my school starts at the top of the hour.* ☐ *Our next newscast will be at the top of the hour.*

at the (very) outside at the very most. ☐ *The car repairs will cost $300 at the outside.* ☐ *I'll be there in three weeks at the outside.*

at (the) worst in the worst view; in the most negative judgment; as the worst one can say about something. ☐ *At worst, Tom can be seen as greedy.* ☐ *Ann will receive a ticket for careless driving, at the worst.*

at the zenith of something at the highest point of something; at the pinnacle of something. ☐ *At the zenith of his career, the teacher died suddenly.* ☐ *The scientist was at the zenith of her career when she made her discovery.*

at this juncture at this point in time; at this pause. ☐ *There is little more that I can say at this juncture.* ☐ *We can, if you wish, at this juncture, request a change in venue.*

at this point (in time) Go to **at the present time.**

at this rate at this speed. (Compare this with **at any rate** and **at that rate.**) ☐ *Hurry up! We'll never get there at this rate.* ☐ *At this rate, all the food will be gone before we get there.*

at this stage Go to **at this stage of the game.**

at this stage of the game AND **at this stage** at the current point in some event; currently. (The first phrase is informal.) ☐ *We'll have to wait and see. There isn't much we can do at this stage of the game.* ☐ *At this stage, we are better off not calling the doctor.*

at times sometimes; occasionally. ☐ *I feel quite sad at times.* ☐ *At times, I wish I had never come here.*

at will whenever one wants; freely. (Compare this with **at liberty.**) □ *You're free to come and go at will.* □ *The soldiers were told to fire their guns at will.* □ *You can eat anything you want at will.*

at work 1. working (at something); busy (with something). □ *Tom is at work on his project. He'll be finished in a minute.* □ *Don't disturb me when I'm busy at work.* **2.** at one's place of work. □ *I'm sorry to call you at work, but this is important.* □ *She's at work now. She'll be home at supper time.*

at worst Go to **at (the) worst.**

attached to someone or something fond of something or something. □ *John is really attached to his old-fashioned ideas.* □ *I'm really attached to this old house.*

attract someone's **attention** to cause someone to take notice; to get someone's attention. □ *I called and waved to attract Ann's attention.* □ *A small yellow flower attracted my attention.*

augur well for someone or something to indicate or predict good things for someone or something. (Usually in the negative.) □ *This latest message does not augur well for the hostages.* □ *I am afraid that this does not augur well for the outcome of the election.*

avail oneself **of** something to help oneself by making use of something that is available. □ *We availed ourselves of Tom's goodwill and let him repair the fence.* □ *The campers availed themselves of the first chance in a week to take a shower.*

avenue of escape the pathway or route along which someone or something escapes. □ *The open window was the bird's only avenue of escape from the house.* □ *Bill saw that his one avenue of escape was through the back door.*

avoid someone or something **like the plague** to avoid someone or something totally. (Informal.) □ *What's wrong with Bob? Everyone avoids him like the plague.* □ *I don't like opera. I avoid it like the plague.*

away from one's **desk** not available for a telephone conversation; not available to be seen. (Sometimes said by the person who answers a telephone in an office. It means that the person whom the caller wants is not immediately available due to personal or business reasons.) □ *I'm sorry, but Ann is away from her desk just now. Can you come back later?* □ *Tom is away from his desk, but if you leave your number, he will call you right back.*

awkward as a cow on a crutch Go to **(as) awkward as a cow on a crutch.**

awkward as a cow on roller skates Go to **(as) awkward as a cow on roller skates.**

AWOL Go to **absent without leave.**

B

a **babe in the woods** a naive or innocent person; an inexperienced person. □ *Bill is a babe in the woods when it comes to dealing with plumbers.* □ *As a painter, Mary is fine, but she's a babe in the woods as a musician.*

back and fill to act indecisively; to change one's direction repeatedly; to reverse one's course. (Originally nautical, referring to alternately filling the sails with wind and releasing the wind.) □ *The president spent most of his speech backing and filling on the question of taxation.* □ *The other candidate was backing and filling on every issue, depending on whom she was addressing.*

back and forth backwards and forwards; first one way and then another way. (Compare this with **to and fro**.) □ *The young man was pacing back and forth in the hospital waiting room.* □ *The pendulum on the clock swung back and forth.*

back down (from someone or something**)** AND **back off (from** someone or something**)** to yield to a person or a thing; to fail to carry through on a threat. □ *Jane backed down from her position on the budget.* □ *It's probably better to back down from someone than to have an argument.* □ *John agreed that it was probably better to back down than to risk getting shot.* □ *Bill doesn't like to back off from a fight.* □ *Sometimes it's better to back off than to get hurt.*

back East to or from the eastern United States, often the northeastern or New England states. (See also **down South**, **out West**, and **up North**. This is used even by people who have never been in the East.) □ *Sally felt that she had to get back East for a few days.* □ *Tom went to school back East, but his brother attended college in the Midwest.*

back in circulation 1. [for a thing to be] available to the public again. (Said especially of things that are said to circulate, such as money, library books, and magazines.) □ *I've heard that gold coins are back in circulation in Europe.* □ *I would like to read* War and Peace. *Is it back in circulation, or is it still checked out?* **2.** [for a person to be] socially active again; dating again after a divorce or breakup with one's lover. (Informal.) □ *Now that Bill is a free man, he's back in circulation.* □ *Tom was in the hospital for a month, but now he's back in circulation.*

back off (from someone or something**)** Go to **back down (from** someone or something**)**.

back of the beyond the most remote place; somewhere very remote. (Informal.) □ *John hardly ever comes to the city. He lives at the back of the beyond.* □ *Mary likes lively entertainment, but her husband likes to vacation in the back of the beyond.*

back order something [for a merchant] to order something that is not in stock and then make delivery to the customer when the goods become available. (The merchant may hold your money until the order is filled.) □ *The store didn't have the replacement part for my vacuum cleaner, so the manager back ordered it for me.* □ *The shop had to back order some of the items on my list.*

back out (of something**)** to withdraw from something you have agreed to do; to break an agreement. (Also literal.) □ *The buyer tried to back out of the sale, but the seller wouldn't permit it.* □ *Please don't* *back out of our date.* □ *Mary backed out at the last minute.*

back someone or something **up** to support someone or something; to concur with someone. (Also literal.) □ *Please back me up in this argument.* 🅃 *I would like you to back up John in this discussion.*

back the wrong horse to support someone or something that cannot win or succeed. (Also literal, as in horse racing.) □ *I don't want to back the wrong horse, but it seems to me that Jed is the better candidate.* □ *Fred backed the wrong horse in the budget hearings.*

back-to-back 1. adjacent and touching backs. □ *They started the duel by standing back-to-back.* □ *Two people who stand back-to-back can manage to see in all directions.* **2.** following immediately. (Said of things or events.) □ *The doctor had appointments set up back-to-back all day long.* □ *I have three lecture courses back-to-back every day of the week.*

back to square one back to the beginning. (Also literal with a board game. See also the following entry.) □ *Negotiations have broken down, and it's back to square one.* □ *We lost the appeal of the court case, so it's back to square one.*

back to the drawing board time to start over again; it is time to plan something over again. (Also literal. Note the variation in the examples.) □ *It didn't work. Back to the drawing board.* □ *I flunked English this semester. Well, back to the old drawing board.*

back to the salt mines time to return to work, school, or something else that might be unpleasant. (As if the speaker were a slave who works in the salt mines.) □ *It's eight o'clock. Time to go to work! Back to the salt mines.* □ *School starts in the fall, and then it's back to the salt mines again.*

bad as all that Go to **(as) bad as all that.**

bad blood (between people**)** unpleasant feelings or animosity between people. □ *There is bad blood between Fred and Jim. They cannot be civil to one another.* □ *There is no bad blood between us. I don't know why we should quarrel.*

bad-mouth someone or something to say bad things about someone or something. (Slang.) □ *Mr. Smith was always bad-mouthing Mrs. Smith. They didn't get along.* □ *John bad-mouths his car constantly because it doesn't run.*

bag and baggage AND **part and parcel** with one's luggage; with all one's possessions. (Informal. See also **part and parcel (of** something**)**.) □ *Sally showed up at our door bag and baggage one Sunday morning.* □ *All right, if you won't pay the rent, out with you, bag and baggage!* □ *Get all your stuff—part and parcel—out of here!*

bag of tricks a collection of special techniques or methods. □ *What have you got in your bag of tricks that could help me with this problem?* □ *Here comes Mother with her bag of tricks. I'm sure she can help us.*

bail out (of something**) 1.** to jump out of an airplane (with a parachute). □ *John still remembers the first time he bailed out of a plane.* □ *When we get to 8,000 feet, we'll all bail out and drift down together. We'll open our parachutes at 2,000 feet.* **2.** to abandon a situation; to get out of something. (Informal.) □ *John got tired of school, so he just bailed out.* □ *Please stay, Bill. You've been with us too long to bail out now.*

bail someone or something **out 1.** [with *someone*] to deposit a sum of money that allows someone to get out of jail while waiting for a trial. □ *John was in jail. I had to go down to the police station to bail him out.* 🅃 *You kids are always getting into trouble. Do you really expect me to bail out the whole gang of you every time you have a problem?* **2.** [with *something*] to remove water from the bottom of a boat by dipping or scooping. □ *Tom has to bail the boat out before we get in.* 🅃 *You should always bail out a boat before using it.* **3.** to rescue someone or something from trouble or difficulty. □ *The proposed law was in trouble, but Todd bailed it out at the last minute.* □ *I was going to be late with my* *report, but my roommate lent a hand and bailed me out at the last minute.*

bait and switch a deceptive merchandising practice where one product is advertised to get people's attention [the bait], but pressure is applied to get the customer to purchase a more expensive item. ☐ *Walter described the appliance store as bait and switch, since they never seemed to have in stock the bargains that they advertised.* ☐ *Max accused the merchant of bait and switch and stalked out of the store.*

balance the accounts 1. AND **balance the books** to determine through accounting that accounts are in balance, that all money is accounted for. ☐ *Jane was up all night balancing the accounts.* ☐ *The cashier was not allowed to leave the bank until the manager balanced the books.* **2.** to get even [with someone]. ☐ *Tom hit Bob. Bob balanced the accounts by breaking Tom's toy car.* ☐ *Once we have balanced the accounts, we can shake hands and be friends again.*

balance the books Go to balance the accounts.

bald as a baby's backside Go to (as) bald as a baby's backside.

bald as a coot Go to (as) bald as a coot.

baleful as death Go to (as) baleful as death.

ball and chain a person's special burden; a job. (Usually considered slang. Prisoners are sometimes fettered with a chain attached to a leg on one end and a heavy metal ball on the other.) ☐ *Tom wanted to quit his job. He said he was tired of that old ball and chain.* ☐ *Mr. Franklin always referred to his wife as his ball and chain.*

ball of fire a very active and energetic person who always succeeds. (Usually considered slang.) ☐ *Sally is a real ball of fire—she works late every night.* ☐ *Ann is no ball of fire, but she does get the job done.*

balled up Go to (all) balled up.

the **balls of** one's **feet** the bottom part of the feet just under the toes. ☐ *Mary got blisters on the balls of her feet from playing tennis.* ☐ *The dancer balanced on the balls of his feet.*

bang one's **head against a brick wall** Go to beat one's head against the wall.

bank on something to count on something; to rely on something. ☐ *The weather service said it wouldn't rain, but I wouldn't bank on it.* ☐ *My word is to be trusted. You can bank on it.*

baptism of fire a first experience of something, usually something difficult or unpleasant. ☐ *My son's just had his first visit to the dentist. He stood up to the baptism of fire very well.* ☐ *Mary's had her baptism of fire as a teacher. She was assigned to the worst class in the school.*

the **bare** something the smallest amount of something possible. ☐ *Bob did the bare minimum of work to pass the class.* ☐ *Food, clothing, and shelter are the bare necessities of life.*

bargain for something AND **bargain on** something to plan for something; to expect something. (Also literal. Informal.) ☐ *We knew it would be difficult, but we didn't bargain for this kind of trouble.* ☐ *I bargained on an easier time of it than this.*

bargain on something Go to bargain for something.

barge in (on someone or something**)** to break in on someone or something; to interrupt someone or something. ☐ *Oh! I'm sorry. I didn't mean to barge in on you.* ☐ *They barged in on the church service and caused a commotion.* ☐ *You can't just barge in like that!*

[bark is worse than one's **bite]** Go to One's bark is worse than one's bite.

bark up the wrong tree to make the wrong choice; to ask the wrong person; to follow the wrong course. (Refers to a hunting dog's error.) ☐ *If you think I'm the guilty person, you're barking up the wrong tree.* ☐ *The baseball players blamed their bad record on the pitcher, but they were barking up the wrong tree.*

base one's **opinion on** something to make a judgment or form an opinion from something. □ *You must not base your opinion on one bad experience.* □ *I base my opinion on many years of studying the problem.*

batten down the hatches to prepare for difficult times. (A nautical expression, meaning, literally, to seal the hatches against the arrival of a storm.) □ *Here comes that contentious Mrs. Jones. Batten down the hatches!* □ *Batten down the hatches, Congress is in session again.*

battle something **out** to argue something to a conclusion; to fight something to a conclusion. □ *The Senate and the House disagree on the bill, so they will have to battle a compromise out.* 🅃 *The two young toughs went into the alley to battle out their disagreement.*

bawl someone **out** to scold someone in a loud voice. □ *The teacher bawled the student out for arriving late.* 🅃 *Teachers don't usually bawl out students.*

[be] <For phrases that can begin with *be, become,* or *seem like,* consult some other word in the phrase in the Phrase-Finder Index.>

be about something to be busy doing something, especially doing one's business. □ *It's eight o'clock, and it's time I was about my homework.* □ *Good-bye, Jane. I must be about my business.*

be a heartbeat away from something [for someone] to be the next ruler upon the final heartbeat of the current ruler. (Especially in reference to U.S. presidential succession.) □ *The vice president is just a heartbeat away from being president.* □ *The prince was only a heartbeat away from being king.*

be-all and (the) end-all Go to the be-all and (the) end-all.

the **be-all and (the) end-all** something that is the very best or most important; something so good that it will end the search for something better. □ *Finishing the building of his boat became the be-all and end-all of Roger's existence.* □ *Sally is the be-all and the end-all of Don's life.*

be all ears listening eagerly and carefully. (See also the following entry.) □ *Well, hurry up and tell me. I'm all ears.* □ *Be careful what you say. The children are all ears.*

be all eyes (and ears) to be alert for something to happen; to wait eagerly for something to happen or for someone or something to appear. (See also the previous entry.) □ *There they were, sitting at the table, all eyes. The birthday cake was soon to be served.* □ *Nothing can escape my notice. I'm all eyes and ears.*

be all things to all men AND **be all things to all people** [for someone or something] to be liked or used by all people; [for someone or something] to be everything that is wanted by all people. □ *You simply can't be all things to all people.* □ *The candidate set out to be all things to all men and came off looking very wishy-washy.*

be all things to all people Go to be all things to all men.

be a million miles away to be distracted and daydreaming; not to be paying attention. (Also literal.) □ *You were a million miles away while I was talking to you.* □ *Most of the class was a million miles away in the hot spring afternoon.*

be a new one on someone to be something one has not heard before and that one is not ready to believe. (Informal. The *someone* is often *me.*) □ *Jack's poverty is a new one on me. He always seems to have plenty of money.* □ *The city's difficulties are a new one on me.*

be curtains for someone or something to be the death, end, or ruin of someone or something. (Informal. From the lowering or closing of the curtains at the end of a stage performance.) □ *If the car hadn't swerved, it would have been curtains for the pedestrians.* □ *If they can't get into the export market, it's curtains for the whole company.*

be death on something to be very harmful to something. (Informal or slang.) □ *The salt they put on the roads in the winter is*

death on cars. □ *That teacher is death on slow learners.*

(be) easier said than done said of a task that is easier to talk about than to do. □ *Yes, we must find a cure for cancer, but it's easier said than done.* □ *Finding a good job is easier said than done.*

be flying high 1. to be very successful in one's ambitions; to obtain an important or powerful position. (Also literal. Often with the implication that this will not last very long.) □ *The government is flying high just now, but wait until the budget is announced.* □ *He's flying high these days, but he comes from a very poor family.* **2.** to be in a state of euphoria. (From good news, success, or drugs.) □ *Wow! Todd is really flying high. Did he discover a gold mine?* □ *Sally is flying high. What's she on?*

be friends with someone to be a friend of someone. □ *Sally is friends with Bill.* □ *Mary and Bill are friends with one another.*

be from Missouri to require proof; to have to be shown [something]. (Also literal. From the nickname for the state of Missouri, the "Show Me" State.) □ *You'll have to prove it to me. I'm from Missouri.* □ *She's from Missouri and has to be shown.*

be game to be ready for action; to be agreeable to participating in something. □ *"I'm game," David replied when I suggested we go bowling.* □ *We're going to the park to play football. Are you game?*

be into something to be interested in something; to be involved in something. (Slang.) □ *Did you hear? Tom is into skydiving!* □ *Too many people are into drugs.*

be off 1. to be spoiled; to be running incorrectly, as with a mechanical device. □ *Oh! I'm afraid that this meat is off. Don't eat it.* □ *I don't have the exact time. My watch is off.* **2.** to leave; to depart. □ *Well, I must be off. Good-bye.* □ *The train leaves in an hour, so I must be off.*

be off on the wrong foot AND **be off to a bad start** to have started something with negative factors. (Literal in reference to marching. See also **get** **wrong foot; get off to a bad sta** **on the wrong foot.**) □ *I'm sorry* *to a bad start. I tried to be frie* *hope that we won't be off to a b* *after our little argument.*

be off to a bad start Go to **be off** **wrong foot.**

be of service (to someone**)** to help so one; to serve someone. (A phrase oft used by salesclerks. See also **be at** som one's **service.**) □ *Good morning, madam. May I be of service to you?* □ *Welcome to the Warwick Hotel. Can I be of service?*

be of the persuasion that something is so to hold a belief that something is true or is in existence. □ *Anne is of the persuasion that supports that candidate for mayor.* □ *The paranoid was of the persuasion that aliens lived among us.*

be reluctant to do something to be unwilling to do something. □ *David was reluctant to admit his mistakes.* □ *The witness was reluctant to testify and was ordered to do so by the judge.*

be sick to vomit. (Euphemistic. Also with *get,* as in the examples. Also literal, meaning "to suffer from an illness.") □ *Mommy, Billy just got sick on the floor.* □ *Oh, excuse me! I think I'm going to be sick.* □ *Bob was sick all over the carpet.*

be so Go to **be too.**

be swimming in something to be engulfed by an excess of something, as if it were a flood. (Also literal.) □ *The war-torn city was swimming in blood.* □ *I am just swimming in paperwork.*

be that as it may even if what you say is true. □ *I am sorry to hear that, but, be that as it may, you still must carry out your responsibilities.* □ *Be that as it may, I still cannot help you.*

be the case to be true; to be an actual situation. □ *I think Bill is a vegetarian, and if that is the case, we should not serve him meat.* □ *Susie believes trees can talk, but that is not the case.*

be the death of me (yet) [these kinds of problems will] be my ruin, death, or

downfall. □ *This cold will be the death of me.* □ *All these problems will be the death of me yet.*

[b]e the last straw AND **be the straw that broke the camel's back** to be the final thing.; to be the last little burden or problem that causes everything to collapse. (From the image of a camel being loaded down with much weight, one straw at a time. Finally, at some point, when one is adding straw after straw, one straw will finally be too much and the camel's back will break.) □ *When Sally came down sick, that was the straw that broke the camel's back.* □ *When she showed up late, that was the straw that broke the camel's back.*

be the spit and image of someone AND **be the spitting image of** someone to look very much like someone; to resemble someone very closely. (Folksy. The second version is a frequent error.) □ *John is the spit and image of his father.* □ *I'm not the spit and image of anyone.* □ *At first, I thought you were saying* spitting *image.*

be the spitting image of someone Go to be the spit and image of someone.

be the straw that broke the camel's back Go to be the last straw.

be to do something to be obliged to do something; to be expected or directed to do something. □ *Am I to clean up the entire kitchen by myself?* □ *John is to take the money to the bank.*

be too AND **be so** to be something (despite anything to the contrary). (An emphatic form of *is, am, are, was, were.* See also do too, have too.) □ *MOTHER: Billy, you aren't old enough to be up this late. BILLY: I am too!* □ *I was so! I was there exactly when I said I would be!*

be used to doing something Go to be used to something.

be used to something AND **be used to** doing something accustomed to something; comfortable with something because it is familiar. □ *We are used to cooking our own food.* □ *I lived in Alaska so long that I am used to the cold.*

be with someone to be on someone's side; to be allied with someone. (Also literal.) □ *Keep on trying, John. We are all with you.* □ *I'm with you in your efforts to win reelection.*

bear a grudge (against someone**)** AND **have a grudge (against** someone**); hold a grudge (against** someone**)** to have an old resentment for someone; to be continually angry at someone. (See also nurse a grudge (against someone).) □ *She bears a grudge against the judge who sentenced her.* □ *I have a grudge against my landlord for overcharging me.* □ *How long can a person hold a grudge? Let's be friends.*

bear fruit to yield results; to give results. (Also literal for fruit-bearing plants and trees.) □ *I hope your new plan bears fruit.* □ *We've had many good ideas, but none of them has borne fruit.*

bear in mind that something is so to remember that something is so; to consider that something is so. (See also keep someone or something in mind.) □ *Bear in mind that the trip will be expensive.* □ *I asked the teacher to bear in mind that I am just a beginner.*

bear one's **cross** AND **carry** one's **cross** to carry or bear one's burden; to endure one's difficulties. (This is a Christian biblical theme. It is always used figuratively except in the biblical context.) □ *It's a very bad disease, but I'll bear my cross.* □ *I can't help you with it. You'll just have to carry your cross.*

bear someone or something **in mind** Go to keep someone or something in mind.

bear something **out** to demonstrate or prove that something is right. □ *I hope that the facts will bear your story out.* 🅃 *I'm sure that the facts will bear out my story.*

bear the brunt (of something**)** to withstand the worst part or the strongest part of something, such as an attack. □ *I had to bear the brunt of her screaming and yelling.* □ *Why don't you talk with her the next time? I'm tired of bearing the brunt.*

bear watching to need watching; to deserve observation or monitoring. □ *This problem will bear watching.* □ *This is a*

very serious disease, and it will bear watching for further developments.

bear with someone or something to be patient with someone or something; to endure someone or something. □ *Please bear with me while I fill out this form.* □ *Please bear with my old car. It'll get us there sooner or later.*

beard the lion in his den to face an adversary on the adversary's home ground. □ *I went to the tax collector's office to beard the lion in his den.* □ *He said he hadn't wanted to come to my home, but it was better to beard the lion in his den.*

beat about the bush Go to beat around the bush.

beat a dead horse to continue fighting a battle that has been won; to continue to argue a point that is settled. (A dead horse will not run no matter how hard it is beaten.) □ *Stop arguing! You have won your point. You are just beating a dead horse.* □ *Oh, be quiet. Stop beating a dead horse.*

beat a (hasty) retreat to retreat or withdraw very quickly. □ *We went out into the cold weather, but beat a retreat to the warmth of our fire.* □ *The dog beat a hasty retreat to its own yard.*

beat a path to someone's **door** [for people] to come to someone in great numbers. (So many people will wish to come and see you that they will wear down a pathway to your door.) □ *I have a product so good that everyone is beating a path to my door.* □ *If you really become famous, people will beat a path to your door.*

beat around the bush AND **beat about the bush** to avoid answering a question; to stall; to waste time. □ *Stop beating around the bush and answer my question.* □ *Let's stop beating about the bush and discuss this matter.*

beat one's **brains out (to** do something**)** to work very hard (to do something). (Informal or slang.) □ *I beat my brains out to solve the problem.* □ *That's the last time I'll beat my brains out trying to cook a nice dinner for you.*

beat one's **head against the wall** AND **bang** one's **head against a brick wall** to waste one's time trying to accomplish something that is completely hopeless. □ *You're wasting your time trying to fix up this house. You're just beating your head against the wall.* □ *You're banging your head against a brick wall trying to get that dog to behave properly.*

beat someone **down (to size)** AND **knock** someone **down (to size)** to make a person more humble, possibly by beating. (See also **cut** someone **down (to size)**.) □ *If you keep acting so arrogant, someone is going to beat you down to size.* □ *It's time someone knocked you down to size.* □ *I'll try to be more thoughtful. I don't want anyone to beat me down.*

beat someone **to the draw** Go to **beat** someone **to the punch**.

beat someone **to the punch** AND **beat** someone **to the draw** to do something before someone else does it. □ *I wanted to have the first new car, but Sally beat me to the punch.* □ *I planned to write a book about computers, but someone else beat me to the draw.*

beat someone **up** to harm or subdue a person by beating and striking. □ *The robber beat me up and took my money.* 🅃 *I really want to beat up that robber.*

beat something **into** someone's **head** to force someone to learn something, possibly through violence. (This can be a threat of violence and should not be used casually.) □ *I studied for hours. I have never beat so much stuff into my head in such a short time.* □ *You're going to learn this math if I have to beat it into your head.*

[beat the band] Go to to beat the band.

beat the clock to do something before a deadline; to finish before the time is up. □ *Sam beat the clock, arriving a few minutes before the doors were locked.* □ *They were afraid they would be late and hurried in order to beat the clock.*

beat the gun to manage to do something before the ending signal. (Originally from sports, referring to making a goal in the last seconds of a game. See also jump the gun.) □ *The ball beat the gun and dropped through the hoop just in time.* □ *Tom tried to beat the gun, but he was one second too slow.*

beat the living daylights out of someone AND **beat the stuffing out of** someone; **beat the tar out of** someone; **whale the tar out of** someone to beat or spank someone, probably a child. (Folksy. These are all threats to do violence and should not be used casually.) □ *If you do that again, I'll beat the living daylights out of you.* □ *The last time Bobby put the cat in the refrigerator, his mother beat the living daylights out of him.* □ *If you continue to act that way, I'll beat the tar out of you.* □ *He wouldn't stop, so I beat the stuffing out of him.* □ *He threatened to whale the tar out of each of them.*

beat the pants off someone **1.** to beat someone severely. (Informal. Refers to physical violence, not the removal of someone's pants.) □ *The thugs beat the pants off their victim.* □ *If you do that again, I'll beat the pants off you.* **2.** to win out over someone. (Informal. This has nothing to do with violence or removing pants.) □ *In the footrace, Sally beat the pants off Jane.* □ *Tom beats the pants off Bob when it comes to writing poetry.*

beat the rap to escape conviction and punishment (for a crime). (Slang, especially criminal slang.) □ *He was charged with drunk driving, but he beat the rap.* □ *The police hauled Tom in and charged him with a crime. His lawyer helped him beat the rap.*

beat the stuffing out of someone Go to beat the living daylights out of someone.

beat the tar out of someone Go to beat the living daylights out of someone.

Beauty is only skin-deep. Looks are only superficial. (Proverb.) □ *BOB: Isn't Jane lovely? TOM: Yes, but beauty is only skin-deep.* □ *I know that she looks like a million dollars, but beauty is only skin-deep.*

becoming on someone complimentary to someone; enhancing one's good looks. (Refers to clothing and other personal ornaments.) □ *The dress you wore last night is not becoming on you.* □ *That color is becoming on you.*

becoming to someone complimentary to someone; enhancing one's good looks. (Refers to hairstyle and things that add to one's good looks. See also becoming on someone.) □ *Your new fur coat is becoming to you.* □ *That hairstyle is very becoming to you.*

a **bed of roses** a situation or way of life that is always happy and comfortable. □ *Living with Pat can't be a bed of roses, but her husband is always smiling.* □ *Being the boss isn't exactly a bed of roses. There are so many problems to take care of.*

beef something **up** to make something stronger; to supplement something. (Informal or slang.) □ *The government decided to beef the army up by buying hundreds of new tanks.* T *Okay, let's beef up the opening song. Please, everyone, sing louder!*

[been had] Go to have been had.

beer and skittles Go to (all) beer and skittles.

before long soon. □ *Billy will be grown-up before long.* □ *Before long, we'll be without any money if we keep spending so much.*

before you can say Jack Robinson almost immediately. (Often found in children's stories.) □ *And before you could say Jack Robinson, the bird flew away.* □ *I'll catch a plane and be there before you can say Jack Robinson.*

before you know it almost immediately. □ *I'll be there before you know it.* □ *If you keep spending money like that, you'll be broke before you know it.*

beg off (on something**)** to ask to be released from something; to refuse an invitation. □ *I'm sorry. I'll have to beg off on your invitation.* □ *I have an important meeting, so I'll have to beg off.*

beg the question 1. to carry on a false argument where one assumes as proved the very point that is being argued, or more generally, to evade a principled discussion of the issue at hand. (Essentially a criticism of someone's line of argument.) ☐ *Stop talking in circles. You're begging the question.* ☐ *A: Why do two lines that are equidistant from one another never meet? B: Because they are parallel. A: You are begging the question.* **2.** to invite the (following) question. (This erroneous reinterpretation of **beg the question** is becoming increasingly popular and widespread.) ☐ *His complaints beg the question: Didn't he cause all of his problems himself?*

beg to differ (with someone**)** to disagree with someone; to state one's disagreement with someone in a polite way. (Usually used in a statement made to the person being disagreed with.) ☐ *I beg to differ with you, but you have stated everything exactly backwards.* ☐ *If I may beg to differ, you have not expressed things as well as you seem to think.*

beggar description to defy description; to be unable to be described. ☐ *The house was a mess. The place beggared description.* ☐ *Our reaction to the proposal beggars description. We were deeply disturbed for days.*

Beggars can't be choosers. One should not criticize something one gets for free. (Proverb.) ☐ *I don't like the old hat that you gave me, but beggars can't be choosers.* ☐ *It doesn't matter whether people like the free food or not. Beggars can't be choosers.*

begin to see daylight to begin to foresee the end of a long task. (Also literal. See also see the light (at the end of the tunnel).) ☐ *I've been working on my thesis for two years, and at last I'm beginning to see daylight.* ☐ *I've been so busy. Only in the last week have I begun to see daylight.*

begin to see the light to begin to understand (something). (Also literal.) ☐ *My algebra class is hard for me, but I'm beginning to see the light.* ☐ *I was totally confused, but I began to see the light after your explanation.*

beginning of the end the start of the final phase of something or of someone's death. ☐ *When he stopped coughing and remained still, I knew it was the beginning of the end.* ☐ *The enormous federal deficit marked the beginning of the end as far as our standard of living is concerned.*

behind closed doors in secret; away from observers, reporters, or intruders. (Refers to being in a private room with the doors closed.) ☐ *They held the meeting behind closed doors, as the law allowed.* ☐ *Every important issue was decided behind closed doors.*

behind in something AND **behind on** something late with something; late in doing something. ☐ *I'm behind in my car payments.* ☐ *She's behind on her work.*

behind on something Go to **behind in** something.

behind schedule having failed to do something by the time listed on the schedule. ☐ *We have to hurry and finish soon because we are behind schedule.* ☐ *The project is behind schedule. Very late, in fact.*

behind someone's **back** in secret; without someone's knowledge. ☐ *Please don't talk about me behind my back.* ☐ *She sold the car behind his back.*

behind the eight ball in a difficult or awkward position. (Informal. Refers to billiards, a game played with numbered balls.) ☐ *Bob broke his wife's crystal vase and is really behind the eight ball.* ☐ *I ran over the neighbor's lawn with my car, so I'm really behind the eight ball.*

behind the scenes privately; out of public view. ☐ *The people who worked behind the scenes are the real heroes of this project.* ☐ *I worked behind the scenes in the play.* ☐ *We don't usually thank the people who are behind the scenes.*

behind the times old-fashioned. ☐ *Sarah is a bit behind the times. Her clothes are quite old-fashioned.* ☐ *Our legislature is a bit behind the times.*

Behind you! Watch out behind you!; There is danger behind you! ☐ *Behind you! That car almost hit you.* ☐ *There are snakes everywhere! Behind you! Look out!*

belabor the point to spend too much time on a point of discussion. ☐ *I don't want* *to belabor the point, but the sooner we get these things settled, the better.* □ *If the speaker would agree not to belabor the point further, I will place it on the agenda for the next meeting.*

believe it or not to choose to believe something or not. (Indicating that an assertion may be hard to believe.) □ *Believe it or not, I just got home from work.* □ *I'm over fifty years old, believe it or not.*

bell, book, and candle symbols of witchcraft. □ *Look, I can't work miracles! Do you expect me to show up at your house with bell, book, and candle, and make everything right? You have to take charge of your own destiny!* □ *On the top shelf of the tiny used-book store, Jim saw a bell, book, and candle sitting in a row, and he knew he was going to find some very interesting reading material.*

below average lower or worse than average. □ *Tom's strength is below average for a child his size.* □ *Dad asked why my grades are below average.*

below par not as good as average or normal. □ *I feel a little below par today. I think I am getting a cold.* □ *His work is below par, and he is paid too much money.*

belt something **out** to sing or play a song loudly and with spirit. □ *When she's playing the piano, she really belts the music out.* 🅃 *She really knows how to belt out a song.*

bend over backwards (to do something**)** Go to fall over backwards (to do something).

bend someone's **ear** to talk to someone, perhaps annoyingly. □ *Tom is over there, bending Jane's ear about something.* □ *I'm sorry. I didn't mean to bend your ear for an hour.*

bent on doing something determined to do something. □ *Jane was bent on having her own apartment.* □ *Her mother was bent on keeping her at home.*

beside oneself **(with** something**)** in an extreme state of some emotion. (Preceded by *be* or *seem.*) □ *I was beside myself with joy.* □ *Sarah could not speak. She was beside herself with anger.* □ *I laughed so hard I was beside myself.*

beside the point AND **beside the question** irrelevant; of no importance. □ *That's very interesting, but beside the point.* □ *That's beside the point. You're evading the issue.* □ *Your observation is beside the question.*

beside the question Go to beside the point.

best bib and tucker one's best clothing. (Folksy.) □ *I always wear my best bib and tucker on Sundays.* □ *Put on your best bib and tucker, and let's go to the city.*

the **best-laid plans of mice and men** AND the **best-laid schemes of mice and men** the best thought-out plans of anyone. □ *If a little rain can ruin the best-laid plans of mice and men, think what an earthquake might do!* □ *The best-laid schemes of mice and men are often disturbed by any small matter.*

the **best-laid schemes of mice and men** Go to the best-laid plans of mice and men.

the **best part of** something almost all of something; a large part of something; the major part of something. □ *The discussion took the best part of an hour.* □ *The best part of the meeting was taken up by budgetary matters.*

bet one's **bottom dollar** AND **bet** one's **life** to be quite certain (about something). (Both are informal and folksy. A *bottom dollar* is the last dollar.) □ *I'll be there. You bet your bottom dollar.* □ *I bet my bottom dollar you can't swim across the pool.* □ *You bet your life I can't swim that far.* □ *I bet my life on it.*

bet one's **life** Go to bet one's bottom dollar.

[better half] Go to one's better half.

better late than never better to do something late than not at all. □ *I wish you had come here sooner, but better late than never.* □ *She bought a house when she was quite old. Better late than never.*

better off (doing something**)** AND **better off (if** something **were done)** in a better position if something were done. □ *She'd be better off selling her house.* □ *They are better off flying to Detroit.* □ *They would* *be better off if they flew to Detroit.* ☐ *I'm better off now.*

better off (if one **were** somewhere else**)** Go to better off (somewhere).

better off (if something **were done)** Go to better off (doing something).

better off (somewhere) AND **better off (if** one **were** somewhere else**)** in a better position somewhere else. ☐ *They would be better off in Florida.* ☐ *We'd all be better off if we were in Florida.* ☐ *I know I'd be better off.*

between a rock and a hard place AND **between the devil and the deep blue sea** in a very difficult position; facing a hard decision. (Informal.) ☐ *I couldn't make up my mind. I was caught between a rock and a hard place.* ☐ *He had a dilemma on his hands. He was clearly between the devil and the deep blue sea.*

between life and death in a position where living or dying is an even possibility. (Especially with *caught* or *hovering*.) ☐ *And there I was on the operating table, hovering between life and death.* ☐ *The mountain climber hung by his rope, caught between life and death.*

between the devil and the deep blue sea Go to between a rock and a hard place.

between you, me, and the lamppost confidentially, just between you and me. ☐ *Just between you, me, and the lamppost, Fred is leaving school.* ☐ *Now don't tell anyone else. This is just between you, me, and the lamppost.*

betwixt and between 1. between (people or things). ☐ *I liked the soup and the dessert and all that came betwixt and between.* ☐ *I sat betwixt and between all the actors who weren't on stage.* **2.** undecided. ☐ *I wish she would choose. She has been betwixt and between for three weeks.* ☐ *Tom is so betwixt and between about getting married. I don't think he's ready.*

beyond a reasonable doubt almost without any doubt. (A legal phrase.) ☐ *The jury decided beyond a reasonable doubt that she had committed the crime.* ☐ *She was also found guilty beyond a reasonable doubt.*

beyond measure more than can be measured; in a very large amount. ☐ *They brought in hams, turkeys, and roasts, and then they brought vegetables and salads beyond measure.* ☐ *They thanked all of us beyond measure.*

beyond one's **depth 1.** in water that is too deep. (See also in over one's head.) ☐ *Sally swam out beyond her depth.* ☐ *Jane swam out to get her even though it was beyond her depth, too.* **2.** beyond one's understanding or capabilities. ☐ *I'm working beyond my depth in algebra class.* ☐ *Poor John was involved in a problem that seemed really beyond his depth.*

beyond one's **means** more than one can afford. (See also live beyond one's means.) ☐ *I'm sorry, but this house is beyond our means. Please show us a cheaper one.* ☐ *They felt that a Caribbean cruise is beyond their means.*

beyond the call of duty Go to (above and) beyond the call of duty.

beyond the pale unacceptable; outlawed; over the top. ☐ *Your behavior is simply beyond the pale.* ☐ *Because of Tom's rudeness, he's considered beyond the pale and is never asked to parties anymore.*

beyond the shadow of a doubt completely without doubt. (Said of a fact, not a person. See also beyond a reasonable doubt.) ☐ *We accepted her story as true beyond the shadow of a doubt.* ☐ *Please assure us that you are certain of the facts beyond the shadow of a doubt.*

beyond words more than one can say. (Especially with *grateful, shocked,* and *thankful.*) ☐ *Sally was thankful beyond words.* ☐ *I don't know how to thank you. I'm grateful beyond words.*

bid adieu to someone or something AND **bid** someone or something **adieu** to say good-bye to someone or something. (This *adieu* is French for *good-bye* and should not be confused with *ado.*) ☐ *Now it's time to bid adieu to all of you gathered here.* ☐ *He silently bid adieu to his favorite hat as the wind carried it down the street.*

bid someone or something **adieu** Go to bid adieu to someone or something.

bide one's **time** to wait patiently. ☐ *I've been biding my time for years, just waiting for a chance like this.* ☐ *He's not the type just to sit there and bide his time. He wants some action.*

big and bold [of things] large and capable of getting attention. ☐ *The lettering on the book's cover was big and bold, and it got lots of attention, but the price was too high.* ☐ *She wore a brightly colored dress. The pattern was big and bold and the skirt was very full.*

big as all outdoors Go to (as) big as all outdoors.

big as life Go to (as) big as life.

big as life and twice as ugly Go to (as) big as life.

a **big frog in a small pond** an important person in the midst of a less important setting. (Preceded by *be, become, seem like,* or *act like.*) ☐ *I'd rather be a big frog in a small pond than the opposite.* ☐ *The trouble with Tom is that he's a big frog in a small pond. He needs more competition.*

the **big moment** AND the **moment everyone has been waiting for** the special time that everyone has been waiting for. ☐ *The big moment has come. I will now announce the winner.* ☐ *This is the big moment that you all have been waiting for!*

big of someone generous of someone; kind or forgiving of someone. (Sometimes sarcastic.) ☐ *He gave me some of his apple. That was very big of him.* ☐ *It was big of Sally to come over and apologize like that.*

binge and purge to overeat and then vomit, over and over. (A symptom of the condition called bulimia.) ☐ *She had binged and purged a number of times before she finally sought help from a doctor.* ☐ *Terry had been bingeing and purging for a number of years and was very, very thin.*

A **bird in the hand is worth two in the bush.** Something you already have is better than something you might get. ☐ *Bill has offered to buy my car for $4,000. Someone else might pay more, but a bird in the hand is worth two in the bush.* ☐ *I might be able to find a better price, but a bird in the hand is worth two in the bush.*

the **birds and the bees** human reproduction. (A euphemistic way of referring to human sex and reproduction.) ☐ *My father tried to teach me about the birds and the bees.* ☐ *He's twenty years old and doesn't understand about the birds and the bees.*

a **bird's-eye view 1.** a view seen from high above. (Refers to the height of a flying bird.) ☐ *We got a bird's-eye view of Cleveland as the plane began its descent.* ☐ *From the top of the tower you get a splendid bird's-eye view of the village.* **2.** a brief survey of something; a hasty look at something. (Refers to the smallness of a bird's eye.) ☐ *The course provides a bird's-eye view of the works of Mozart, but it doesn't deal with them in enough detail for your purpose.* ☐ *All you need is a bird's-eye view of the events of World War II to pass the test.*

Birds of a feather flock together. People of the same type seem to gather together. (Proverb.) ☐ *Bob and Tom are just alike. They like each other's company because birds of a feather flock together.* ☐ *When Mary joined a club for redheaded people, she said, "Birds of a feather flock together."*

bite off more than one **can chew** to take (on) more than one can deal with; to be overconfident. (This is used literally for food and figuratively for other things, especially difficult projects.) ☐ *Billy, stop biting off more than you can chew. You're going to choke on your food someday.* ☐ *Ann is exhausted again. She's always biting off more than she can chew.*

bite one's **nails** to be nervous or anxious; to bite one's nails from nervousness or anxiety. (Used both literally and figuratively.) ☐ *I spent all afternoon biting my nails, worrying about you.* ☐ *We've all been biting our nails from worry.*

bite one's **tongue** to struggle not to say something that you really want to say. (Used literally only to refer to an accidental biting of one's tongue.) □ *I had to bite my tongue to keep from telling her what I really thought.* □ *I sat through that whole conversation biting my tongue.*

bite someone's **head off** to speak sharply and angrily to someone. □ *There was no need to bite Mary's head off just because she was five minutes late.* □ *The boss has been biting everybody's head off since his accident.*

bite the bullet to put up with or endure (something). (Informal or slang.) □ *I didn't want to go to the doctor, but I bit the bullet and went.* □ *John, you just have to bite the bullet and do what you're told.*

bite the dust to fall to defeat; to die. (Typically heard in movies about the old western frontier.) □ *A bullet hit the sheriff in the chest, and he bit the dust.* □ *Poor old Bill bit the dust while mowing the lawn. They buried him yesterday.*

bite the hand that feeds one to harm someone who does good things for you. (Literal in reference to a dog, cat, or other animal.) □ *I'm your mother! How can you bite the hand that feeds you?* □ *She can hardly expect much when she bites the hand that feeds her.*

a **bitter pill to swallow** an unpleasant fact that has to be accepted. □ *It was a bitter pill for her brother to swallow when she married his enemy.* □ *We found his deception a bitter pill to swallow.*

black-and-blue bruised; showing signs of having been physically harmed. (Also literal.) □ *The child was black-and-blue after having been struck.* □ *She was black-and-blue all over after falling out of the tree.*

black as a skillet Go to (as) black as a skillet.

black as a stack of black cats Go to (as) black as a stack of black cats.

black as a sweep Go to (as) black as a sweep.

black as coal Go to (as) black as coal.

black as night Go to (as) black as night.

black as one **is painted** Go to (as) black as one is painted.

black as pitch Go to (as) black as pitch.

black as the ace of spades Go to (as) black as the ace of spades.

black out to faint or pass out. □ *Sally blacked out just before the crash.* □ *I was so frightened that I blacked out for a minute.*

the **black sheep of the family** the worst member of the family. □ *Mary is the black sheep of the family. She's always in trouble with the police.* □ *He keeps making a nuisance of himself. What do you expect from the black sheep of the family?*

blast off [for a rocket] to shoot into the sky. □ *What time does the rocket blast off?* □ *It won't blast off today. It has been canceled.*

blaze a trail (in something) to create and develop a new area of study or development. (Literal in reference to creating and marking a trail.) □ *In the area of conservation, Wright and Walters blazed a trail in the use of technology to preserve topsoil.* □ *Professor Williams blazed a trail in the study of physics.*

bleep something **out** to replace a word or phrase in a radio or television broadcast with some sort of musical tone. (This is sometimes done to prevent a bad word or other information from being broadcast.) □ *He tried to say the word on television, but they bleeped it out.* 🅃 *They tried to bleep out the whole sentence.*

a **blessing in disguise** something that turns out to be fortunate and advantageous after seeming to be the opposite at first. □ *Our missing the train was a blessing in disguise. It was involved in a crash.* □ *It was a blessing in disguise that I didn't get the job. I was offered a better one the next day.*

blind as a bat Go to (as) blind as a bat.

the **blind leading the blind** having to do with a situation where people who don't know how to do something try to explain it to other people. □ *Tom doesn't know anything about cars, but he's trying to* *teach Sally how to change the oil. It's a case of the blind leading the blind.* □ *When I tried to show Mary how to use a computer, it was the blind leading the blind.*

Blood is thicker than water. Go to Blood runs thicker than water.

Blood runs thicker than water. AND **Blood is thicker than water.** People who are related have stronger obligations to each other than to people outside the family and are expected to endure family problems. (Proverb.) □ *My friends invited me to go camping on Saturday, but I have to go to my cousin's wedding instead. Blood is thicker than water, after all.* □ *If you ever need help, don't ask your friends. Come home and ask us, your family. Blood is thicker than water.*

blood, sweat, and tears the signs of great personal effort. □ *There will be much blood, sweat, and tears before we have completed this project.* □ *After years of blood, sweat, and tears, Timmy finally earned a college degree.*

bloody but unbowed [one's head] showing signs of a struggle, but not bowed in defeat. □ *Liz emerged from the struggle, her head bloody but unbowed.* □ *We are bloody but unbowed and will fight to the last.*

blow a fuse 1. to burn out a fuse. □ *The microwave oven blew a fuse, so we had no power.* □ *You'll blow a fuse if you use too many appliances at once.* **2.** Go to blow a gasket.

blow a gasket AND **blow a fuse; blow** one's **cork; blow** one's **top; blow** one's **stack** to become very angry; to lose one's temper. (Slang.) □ *I was so mad I almost blew a gasket.* □ *I've never heard such a thing. I'm going to blow a fuse.* □ *I blew my cork when he hit me.* □ *I was so mad I could have blown my top.* □ *I makes me so mad I could blow my stack.*

blow-by-blow account AND **blow-by-blow description** a detailed description (of an event) given as the event takes place. (This referred originally to boxing or other combat.) □ *I want to listen to a blow-by-blow account of the prizefight.* □ *The lawyer got the witness to give a blow-by-blow description of the argument.*

blow-by-blow description Go to blow-by-blow account.

blow hot and cold to be changeable or uncertain (about something). □ *He keeps blowing hot and cold on the question of moving to the country.* □ *He blows hot and cold about this. I wish he'd make up his mind.*

blow off steam Go to let off steam.

blow one's **cookies** Go to blow one's lunch.

blow one's **cool** Go to lose one's cool.

blow one's **cork** Go to blow a gasket.

blow one's **lines** Go to fluff one's lines.

blow one's **lunch** AND **blow** one's **cookies** to vomit. (Slang.) □ *The accident was so horrible I almost blew my lunch.* □ *Don't run so hard, or you'll blow your cookies.*

blow one's **nose** to drive mucus and other material from the nose using air pressure from the lungs. □ *Excuse me, I have to blow my nose.* □ *Bill blew his nose into his handkerchief.*

blow one's **own horn** Go to toot one's own horn.

blow one's **stack** Go to blow a gasket.

blow one's **top** Go to blow a gasket.

blow over to go away without causing harm. □ *If we are lucky, the storm will blow over.* □ *Given time, all this controversy will blow over.*

blow someone or something **away 1.** to kill or destroy someone or something. (Also literal. Slang.) □ *He drew his gun and blew the thief away.* 🆃 *His bad attitude blew away the whole deal.* **2.** [with *someone*] to overcome someone emotionally. □ *The bad news really blew me away.* □ *Your news just blew me away! How exciting!*

blow someone or something **off 1.** [with *something*] to neglect or bumble something. (Slang.) □ *He would do better in school if he didn't blow his math class off.* 🆃 *He blew off his homework.* **2.** [with *someone*] to deceive or cheat someone. (Slang.) □ *She really blew me off on the question of* *grades. She was really failing all the time.* 🅃 *She blew off the teacher by cheating on the test.*

blow someone or something **to smithereens** to explode someone or something into tiny pieces. ☐ *The bomb blew the ancient church to smithereens.* ☐ *The mortar blew the entire squad to smithereens.*

blow someone's **cover** to reveal someone's true identity or purpose. ☐ *The spy was very careful not to blow her cover.* ☐ *I tried to disguise myself, but my dog recognized me and blew my cover.*

blow someone's **mind 1.** to destroy the function of one's brain. (Slang.) ☐ *It was a terrible experience. It nearly blew my mind.* ☐ *She blew her mind on drugs.* **2.** to overwhelm someone; to excite someone. (Slang.) ☐ *It was so beautiful, it nearly blew my mind.* ☐ *The music was so wild. It blew my mind.*

blow something to ruin or waste something. ☐ *I had a chance to do it, but I blew it.* ☐ *He blew the whole five dollars on candy.*

blow something **out of all proportion** to cause something to be unrealistically proportioned relative to something else. (The *all* can be left out.) ☐ *The press has blown this issue out of all proportion.* ☐ *Let's be reasonable. Don't blow this thing out of proportion.*

blow the lid off (something**)** to reveal something, especially wrongdoing; to make wrongdoing public. ☐ *The police blew the lid off the smuggling ring.* ☐ *The government is glad that they blew the lid off.*

blow the whistle (on someone**)** to report someone's wrongdoing to someone (such as the police) who can stop the wrongdoing. ☐ *The citizens' group blew the whistle on the street gangs by calling the police.* ☐ *The gangs were getting very bad. It was definitely time to blow the whistle.*

blow up to fall apart or get ruined. ☐ *The whole project blew up. It will have to be canceled.* ☐ *All my planning was blown up this afternoon.*

blow up (at someone**)** to get angry at someone; to lose one's temper and yell at someone. ☐ *I'm sorry. I didn't mean to blow up.* ☐ *You'd blow up, too, if you'd had a day like mine.*

blow up in someone's **face 1.** to blow up or explode suddenly. (Also literal.) ☐ *The bomb blew up in the terrorist's face.* ☐ *The firecracker blew up in his face and injured him.* **2.** [for something] to get ruined while someone is working on it. (Also literal.) ☐ *All my plans blew up in my face.* ☐ *It is terrible for your life to get ruined and blow up in your face.*

blue around the gills Go to pale around the gills.

blue blood the blood [heredity] of a noble family; aristocratic ancestry. ☐ *The earl refuses to allow anyone who is not of blue blood to marry his son.* ☐ *Although Mary's family is poor, she has blue blood in her veins.*

bog down to slow down; to become stuck. ☐ *The project bogged down because of so much red tape.* ☐ *We bog down every year at this time because many of our workers go on vacation.*

boggle someone's **mind** to confuse someone; to overwhelm someone; to **blow** someone's **mind**. ☐ *The size of the house boggles my mind.* ☐ *She said that his arrogance boggled her mind.*

boil down to something to reduce to something; to come down to something; to be essentially something. (Also literal.) ☐ *It all boils down to whether you wish to buy a car.* ☐ *It boils down to a question of good health.*

boil something **down** to summarize something; to make information more concise. (Also literal in reference to liquids.) ☐ *I don't have time to listen to the whole story. Please boil it down for me.* 🅃 *Please boil down the report so I can read it on the plane.*

bold as brass Go to (as) bold as brass.

bone of contention the subject or point of an argument; an unsettled point of disagreement. ☐ *We've fought for so long that we've forgotten what the bone of contention is.* ☐ *The question of a fence* *between the houses has become quite a bone of contention.*

bone up (on something**)** to study something thoroughly; to review the facts about something. □ *I have to bone up on the state driving laws because I have to take my driving test tomorrow.* □ *I take mine next month, so I'll have to bone up, too.*

boot someone **out** Go to kick someone out.

bore someone **stiff** AND **bore** someone **to death** to bore someone very much. (*Stiff* is an old slang word meaning "dead.") □ *The play bored me stiff.* □ *The lecture bored everyone to death.*

bore someone **to death** Go to bore someone stiff.

bored silly AND **bored stiff; bored to distraction; bored to tears** very bored; completely bored. (Usually an exaggeration.) □ *I was bored silly at the lecture.* □ *The dull speaker left me bored to distraction.* □ *I am bored to tears. Let's go home.*

bored stiff Go to bored silly.

bored to death very bored. □ *The children were bored to death.* □ *I've never been so bored to death in my life.*

bored to distraction Go to bored silly.

bored to tears Go to bored silly.

born and bred Go to born and raised.

born and raised AND **born and bred** born and nurtured through childhood, usually in a specific place. □ *She was born and raised in a small town in western Montana.* □ *Freddy was born and bred on a farm and had no love for city life.*

born out of wedlock born to an unmarried mother. □ *The child was born out of wedlock.* □ *In the city many children are born out of wedlock.*

born with a silver spoon in one's **mouth** born with many advantages; born to a wealthy family. □ *Sally was born with a silver spoon in her mouth.* □ *I'm glad I was not born with a silver spoon in my mouth.*

borrow trouble to worry needlessly; to make trouble for oneself. □ *Worrying too much about death is just borrowing trouble.* □ *Do not get involved with politics. That's borrowing trouble.*

boss someone **around** to give orders to someone; to keep telling someone what to do. □ *Stop bossing me around. I'm not your employee.* 🆃 *Captain Smith bosses around the whole crew. That's his job.*

bottle something **up 1.** to constrict something as if it were put in a bottle. □ *The patrol boats bottled the other boats up at the locks on the river.* 🆃 *The police bottled up the traffic while they searched the cars for the thieves.* **2.** to hold one's feelings within; to keep from saying something that one feels strongly about. □ *Let's talk about it, John. You shouldn't bottle it up.* 🆃 *Don't bottle up your problems. It's better to talk them out.*

the **bottom line 1.** the last figure on a financial balance sheet representing net profit or loss. □ *What's the bottom line? How much do I owe you?* □ *Don't tell me all those figures! Just tell me the bottom line.* **2.** the result; the final outcome. □ *I know about all the problems, but what is the bottom line? What will happen?* □ *The bottom line is that you have to go to the meeting because no one else can.*

bottom out to reach the lowest point. □ *The price of wheat bottomed out last week. Now it's rising again.* □ *My interest in school bottomed out in my junior year, so I quit and got a job.*

Bottoms up! Everyone should drink now! (Said at the end of a drinking toast.) □ *Here's to the bride and groom. Bottoms up!* □ *Bottoms up! Drink hearty!*

bound and determined determined. □ *We were bound and determined to get there on time.* □ *I'm bound and determined that this won't happen again.*

bound for somewhere on the way to somewhere; planning to go to somewhere. □ *I'm bound for Mexico. In fact, I'm leaving this afternoon.* □ *I'm bound for the bank. Do you want to go, too?*

bound hand and foot with hands and feet tied up. □ *The robbers left us bound hand*

and foot. ☐ *We remained bound hand and foot until the maid found us and untied us.*

bound to (do something**)** to be certain to do something. ☐ *They are bound to come home soon. They always come home early.* ☐ *Oh, yes. They are bound to.*

bow and scrape to be very humble and subservient. ☐ *Please don't bow and scrape. We are all equal here.* ☐ *The salesclerk came in, bowing and scraping, and asked if he could help us.*

bow out to quit and depart; to resign; to retire. ☐ *I've done all that I can do. Now is the time to bow out.* ☐ *Most workers bow out at the normal retirement age.*

bowl someone **over** to surprise or overwhelm someone. (Also literal.) ☐ *The news bowled me over.* ☐ *The details of the proposed project bowled everyone over.*

Boys will be boys. That's the kind of thing that boys seem to do.; That's the kind of silly behavior that boys and men exhibit. (Proverb.) ☐ *They really messed up the living room, but boys will be boys.* ☐ *Boys will be boys, but they can be trained.*

brain someone to strike a person on the skull as if to knock out the person's brains. ☐ *I thought he was going to brain me, but he only hit me on the shoulder.* ☐ *If you don't do it, I'll brain you.*

[bread and butter] Go to someone's bread and butter.

bread-and-butter letter a letter or note written to follow up on a visit; a thank-you note. ☐ *When I got back from the sales meeting, I took two days to write bread-and-butter letters to the people I met.* ☐ *I got sort of a bread-and-butter letter from my nephew, who wants to visit me next summer.*

bread and water the most minimal meal possible; a prison meal. (Also literal. Refers to the stereotypical prison meal.) ☐ *Max knew that if he got in trouble again it would be at least a year on bread and water.* ☐ *This dinner is terrible again. I would rather have bread and water! Why don't we ever have pizza?*

break a code to figure out a code; to decipher a code. ☐ *The intelligence agents finally broke the enemy's code.* ☐ *When they broke the code, they were able to decipher messages.*

break a habit AND **break the habit; break** one's **habit** to end a habit. ☐ *I was not able to break the habit of snoring.* ☐ *It's hard to break a habit that you have had for a long time.*

break a law AND **break the law** to fail to obey a law; to act contrary to a law. ☐ *Lisa broke the law when she drove the wrong way on a one-way street.* ☐ *If you never break the law, you will never get arrested.*

Break a leg! Good luck! (Also literal. Theatrical slang. This is said to actors before a performance instead of *Good luck.*) ☐ *Before the play, John said to Mary, "Break a leg!"* ☐ *Saying "Break a leg!" before a performance is an old theatrical tradition.*

break a record to surpass a previously set high record of achievement by setting a new one. ☐ *The athlete broke all the school records in swimming.* ☐ *The record was broken after thirty years.*

break camp to close down a campsite; to pack up and move on. ☐ *Early this morning we broke camp and moved on northward.* ☐ *Okay, everyone. It's time to break camp. Take those tents down and fold them neatly.*

break down 1. [for something] to fall apart; [for something] to stop operating. (See also **break** someone or something **down.**) ☐ *The air-conditioning broke down, and we got very warm.* ☐ *The car broke down in the parking lot.* **2.** [for one] to lose control of one's emotions; [for one] to have a nervous collapse. ☐ *He couldn't keep going. He finally broke down and wept.* ☐ *I was afraid I'd break down.*

break even for income to equal expenses. (This implies that money was not earned or lost.) ☐ *Unfortunately my business just managed to break even last year.* ☐ *I made a bad investment, but I broke even.*

break ground (for something**)** to start digging the foundation for a building. ☐ *The* *president of the company came to break ground for the new building.* ☐ *This was the third building this year for which this company has broken ground.* ☐ *When will they break ground?*

Break it up! Stop fighting!; Stop it! (Said to two or more people causing a disturbance.) ☐ *All right! Break it up, you guys!* ☐ *Stop your talking! Break it up and get back to work.*

break loose (from someone or something**)** to get away from a person or a thing that is holding one. (Compare this with **cut loose (from** someone or something**)**.) ☐ *The criminal broke loose from the police officer.* ☐ *It's hard to break loose from home.* ☐ *I was twenty years old before I could break loose.*

break new ground to begin to do something that no one else has done; to pioneer (in an enterprise). (See also **break ground (for** something**)**.) ☐ *Dr. Anderson was breaking new ground in cancer research.* ☐ *They were breaking new ground in consumer electronics.*

break off (with someone**)** to end a friendship with someone, especially a boyfriend or a girlfriend. ☐ *Tom has finally broken off with Mary.* ☐ *I knew it couldn't last. He was bound to break off.*

break one's **back (to** do something**)** Go to **break** one's **neck (to** do something**)**.

break one's **habit** Go to **break a habit**.

break one's **neck (to** do something**)** AND **break** one's **back (to** do something**)** to work very hard to do something. ☐ *I broke my neck to get here on time.* ☐ *That's the last time I'll break my neck to help you.* ☐ *There is no point in breaking your back. Take your time.*

break one's **word** not to do what one said one would do; not to keep one's promise. (The opposite of **keep** one's **word**.) ☐ *Don't say you'll visit your grandmother if you can't go. She hates people who break their word.* ☐ *If you break your word, she won't trust you again.*

break out 1. to burst forth suddenly, as with a fire, a riot, giggling, shouting, etc. ☐ *A fire broke out in the belfry.* ☐ *A round of giggling broke out when the teacher tripped.* ☐ *A riot almost broke out when the police came.* **2.** [for one's face] to erupt in pimples. ☐ *Bob's face has started breaking out badly.* ☐ *My face breaks out when I eat a lot of chocolate.*

break out in a cold sweat to perspire from fever, fear, or anxiety; to begin to sweat profusely or suddenly. ☐ *I was so frightened I broke out in a cold sweat.* ☐ *The patient broke out in a cold sweat.*

break out (in something**)** to erupt with something such as a rash, a cold sweat, or pimples. ☐ *After being in the woods, I broke out in a rash. I think it's poison ivy.* ☐ *I hate to break out like that.* ☐ *When I eat chocolate, I break out in pimples.* ☐ *I was so frightened I broke out in a cold sweat.* ☐ *The patient broke out in a cold sweat.*

break (out) in(to) tears to start crying suddenly. ☐ *I was so sad that I broke out into tears.* ☐ *I always break into tears at a funeral.* ☐ *It's hard not to break out in tears under those circumstances.*

break out (of something**)** to escape from something, often by destructive means. (Especially from prison, but also in figurative senses.) ☐ *The convicts plotted to break out of prison.* ☐ *You don't have the guts to break out of jail!* ☐ *Don finally broke out of the depression that had held him captive for so long.* ☐ *The lion broke out of its cage.*

break someone or something **down 1.** [with *someone*] to force someone to give up and tell secrets or agree to do something. ☐ *After threats of torture, they broke the spy down.* 🅃 *They broke down the agent by threatening violence.* **2.** [with *something*] to tear something down; to destroy something. ☐ *They used an ax to break the door down.* 🅃 *We broke down the wall with big hammers.*

break someone or something **in 1.** [with *someone*] to train someone to do a job; to supervise a new person learning a new job. ☐ *It takes time to break a new worker in.* 🅃 *Are they hard to break in?* 🅃 *I have to* *break in a new worker.* **2.** [with *something*] to make something fit by wearing or using it. Ⓣ *I'll be glad when I've finished breaking in these shoes.* □ *Yes, it takes time to break them in.* Ⓣ *They are easy to break in, though.* □ *The car will run better after I break it in.*

break someone or something **up 1.** [with *someone*] to cause a person to laugh, perhaps at an inappropriate time. (Informal.) □ *John told a joke that really broke Mary up.* Ⓣ *The comedian's job was to break up the audience by telling jokes.* **2.** [with *something*] to destroy something. □ *The storm broke the docks up on the lake.* Ⓣ *The police broke up the gambling ring.* **3.** [with *something*] to put an end to something. □ *The police broke the fight up.* Ⓣ *Walter's parents broke up the party at three in the morning.*

break someone's **fall** to cushion a falling person; to lessen the impact of a falling person. □ *When the little boy fell out of the window, the bushes broke his fall.* □ *The old lady slipped on the ice, but a snowbank broke her fall.*

break someone's **heart** to cause someone emotional pain. □ *It just broke my heart when Tom ran away from home.* □ *Sally broke John's heart when she refused to marry him.*

break something **down (for** someone**)** to explain something to someone in simple terms or in an orderly fashion. □ *She doesn't understand. You will have to break it down for her.* □ *I can help. This is a confusing question. Let me break it down for you.*

break something **down (into** something**)** to divide something into smaller parts; to divide something into its component parts. □ *Please break this paragraph down into sentences.* Ⓣ *The chemist broke down the compound into a number of elements.* □ *Walter broke the project down into five tasks and assigned them to various people.*

break something **to pieces** to shatter something. (Informal.) □ *I broke my crystal vase to pieces.* □ *I dropped a glass and broke it to pieces.*

break something **to** someone to tell bad news to someone. □ *I hated to break the news to Dad about his car.* □ *Bill broke it to his employees gently.*

break the back of something to end the domination of something; to reduce the power of something. □ *The government has worked for years to break the back of organized crime.* □ *This new medicine should break the back of the epidemic.*

break the bank to use up all one's money. (As in casino gambling where a gambler wins more money than the house has on hand.) □ *It will hardly break the bank if we go out to dinner just once.* □ *Buying a new dress at that price won't break the bank.*

break the habit Go to break a habit.

break the ice to initiate social interchanges and conversation; to get something started. (Also literal.) □ *Tom is so outgoing. He's always the first one to break the ice at parties.* □ *It's hard to break the ice at formal events.* □ *Sally broke the ice by bidding $20,000 for the painting.*

break the law Go to break a law.

break the news (to someone**)** to tell someone some important news, usually bad news. □ *The doctor had to break the news to Jane about her husband's cancer.* □ *I hope that the doctor broke the news gently.*

break through (something) to overcome something nonphysical, such as a barrier caused by law, regulation, prejudice, attitude, etc. (Also literal.) □ *Tom was able to break through racial barriers.* □ *The scientists broke through the mystery surrounding the disease and found the cause.*

break up (with someone**)** to end a love affair or a romance. □ *Tom finally broke up with Mary.* □ *I thought they would break up. He has been so moody lately.*

breaking and entering the crime of forcing one's way into a place. (A criminal charge.) □ *Max was charged with four counts of breaking and entering.* □ *It was not an act of breaking and entering. The thief just opened the door and walked right in.*

a **breath of fresh air 1.** air that is not stale or smelly. (This is the literal sense.) □ *I feel faint. I think I need a breath of fresh air.* □ *You look ill, John. What you need is a breath of fresh air.* **2.** air that is not (figuratively) contaminated with unpleasant people or situations. (This is a sarcastic version of sense 1.) □ *You people are disgusting. I have to get out of here and get a breath of fresh air.* □ *I believe I'll go get a breath of fresh air. The intellectual atmosphere in here is stifling.* **3.** a new, fresh, and imaginative approach (to something). (Usually with *like*.) □ *Sally, with all her wonderful ideas, is a breath of fresh air.* □ *New furniture in this room is like a breath of fresh air.*

breathe down someone's **neck 1.** to keep close watch on someone; to watch someone's activities. (Also literal. Refers to standing very close behind a person.) □ *I can't work with you breathing down my neck all the time. Go away.* □ *I will get through my life without your help. Stop breathing down my neck.* **2.** to try to hurry someone along; to make someone get something done on time. (The subject does not have to be a person. See the second example.) □ *I have to finish my taxes today. The tax collector is breathing down my neck.* □ *I have a deadline breathing down my neck.*

breathe easy to assume a relaxed state after a stressful period. (Also literal.) □ *After all this is over, I'll be able to breathe easy again.* □ *He won't be able to breathe easy until he pays off his debts.*

breathe one's **last** to die; to breathe one's last breath in the process of dying. □ *Mrs. Smith breathed her last this morning.* □ *I'll keep running every day until I breathe my last.*

brew a plot to plot something; to make a plot. □ *The children brewed an evil plot to get revenge on their teacher.* □ *We brewed a plot so that we would not have to help with dinner.*

bricks and mortar buildings. (The buildings referred to can be constructed out of anything.) □ *The new president of the college preferred to invest in new faculty members rather than bricks and mortar.* □ *Sometimes people are happy to donate millions of dollars for bricks and mortar, but they never think of the additional cost of annual maintenance.*

bright and early very early. □ *Yes, I'll be there bright and early.* □ *I want to see you here on time tomorrow, bright and early, or you're fired!*

bright as a button Go to (as) bright as a button.

bright as a new pin Go to (as) bright as a new pin.

bright-eyed and bushy-tailed very cheerful and eager. (Refers to the twinkling eyes and quick, energetic movements of a squirrel.) □ *She appeared at the top of the stairs, bright-eyed and bushy-tailed, ready to start the day.* □ *I am awake, but I am hardly bright-eyed and bushy-tailed.*

brimming with something **1.** full of some kind of happy behavior. □ *The volunteer worker was brimming with goodwill.* □ *The giggling children were brimming with joy.* **2.** full to the point of overflowing. □ *Tom's glass was brimming with milk.* □ *The pool was brimming with water.*

bring down the curtain (on something**)** Go to ring down the curtain (on something).

bring down the house to excite a theatrical audience to laughter or applause or both. □ *Her performance didn't bring down the house—it emptied it.* 🅃 *This is a great joke. The last time I told it, it brought the house down.*

bring home the bacon to earn a salary. (Folksy.) □ *I've got to get to work if I'm going to bring home the bacon.* □ *Go out and get a job so you can bring home the bacon.*

bring people or other creatures **out in droves** to lure or draw out someone or some creature in great number. □ *The availability of free drinks brought people out in droves.* □ *The fresh grass sprouts brought the deer out in droves.*

bring someone **around 1.** to bring someone for a visit; to bring someone for someone (else) to meet. □ *Please bring your wife* *around sometime. I'd love to meet her.* □ *You've just got to bring the doctor around for dinner.* **2.** to bring someone to consciousness. □ *The doctor brought Tom around with smelling salts.* □ *The boxer was knocked out, but the doctor brought him around.* **3.** to persuade someone (to accept something); to manage to get someone to agree (to something). □ *The last debate brought a lot of voters around to our candidate.* □ *I knew I could bring her around if I just had enough time to talk to her.*

bring someone or something **up 1.** to mention a person or a thing. □ *I'm sorry. I won't bring him up again.* 🅃 *Please don't bring up that matter again.* 🅃 *Please don't bring up John Jones's name again.* **2.** to raise a child or an animal. □ *Her uncle brought her up.* 🅃 *It's difficult to bring up a pet monkey.*

bring someone or something **up-to-date** to make someone or something more modern. (See also **bring** someone **up-to-date (on** someone or something).) □ *Let's buy some new furniture and bring this room up-to-date.* □ *John tried to bring himself up-to-date by changing his hairstyle, but he still looked like the same old John.*

bring someone **to** to bring someone to consciousness; to wake someone up. (See also **bring** someone **around; come to.**) □ *The nurse brought the patient to.* □ *She's hurt! Come on, help me bring her to.*

bring someone **up-to-date (on** someone or something**)** to tell someone the news about something. □ *Please bring me up-to-date on the Middle East situation.* □ *Please bring me up-to-date on John. I want to hear all the news.* □ *And bring me up-to-date, too.*

bring something **about** to make something happen. □ *Is she clever enough to bring it about?* 🅃 *Oh, yes, she can bring about anything she wants.*

bring something **crashing down (around one)** to destroy something that one has built; to destroy something that one has a special interest in. □ *She brought her whole life crashing down around her.* □ *Bob's low grade in English brought everything crashing down when his parents grounded him.*

bring something **home to** someone to cause someone to realize the truth of something. □ *Seeing the starving refugees on television really brings home the tragedy of their situation.* □ *It wasn't until she failed her test that the importance of studying was brought home to her.*

bring something **into question** to question something; to raise a question about something. □ *It was necessary to bring your part in this matter into question.* □ *The city council brought the building project into question.*

bring something **off** to make something happen; to produce a great event. □ *She managed to bring the party off with no difficulty.* 🅃 *She brought off a similar party last season.*

bring something **to a head** to cause something to come to the point when a decision has to be made or an action taken. □ *The latest disagreement between management and the union has brought matters to a head. There will be an all-out strike now.* □ *It's a relief that things have been brought to a head. The disputes have been going on for months.*

bring something **to light** to make something known; to discover something. □ *The scientists brought their findings to light.* □ *We must bring this new evidence to light.*

bring something **to** someone's **attention** to make someone aware of something; to mention or show something to someone. □ *I would like to bring this problem to your attention.* □ *If there is something I should know about, please bring it to my attention.*

bring up the rear to move along behind everyone else; to be at the end of the line. (Originally referred to marching soldiers.) □ *Here comes John, bringing up the rear.* □ *Hurry up, Tom! Why are you always bringing up the rear?*

broad as a barn door Go to (as) broad as a barn door.

broad in the beam with wide hips or large buttocks. (From a nautical expression for a wide ship.) □ *I am getting a little broad in the beam. It's time to go on a diet.* □ *John is just naturally broad in the beam.*

[brother's keeper] Go to one's **brother's keeper.**

brush up (on something**)** to review something, especially a school subject. □ *I think I should brush up on my Spanish before I go to Mexico.* □ *I've heard you speak Spanish. You need to do more than brush up.*

buck for something to aim, try, or strike for a goal. (Originally referred to trying to get a higher military rank.) □ *Bill acts that way because he's bucking for corporal.* □ *Tom is bucking for a larger office.*

buck up cheer up. □ *Buck up, old friend! Things can't be all that bad.* □ *I know I have to buck up. Life must go on.*

buckle down (to something**)** to settle down to something; to begin to work seriously at something. □ *If you don't buckle down to your job, you'll be fired.* □ *You had better buckle down and get busy.*

bug out to leave; to pack up and get out. (Slang.) □ *It's time to bug out. Let's get out of here.* □ *I just got a call from headquarters. They say to bug out immediately.*

bug someone to irritate someone; to bother someone. (Slang.) □ *Go away! Stop bugging me!* □ *Leave me alone. Go bug someone else.*

build a case (against someone**)** AND **assemble a case (against** someone**); gather a case (against** someone**)** to put together the evidence needed to make a legal or disciplinary case against someone. □ *The police easily built a case against the drunken driver.* □ *As soon as we gather the case against her, we will arrest her.*

build a fire under someone to do something to make someone else start doing something. (Informal.) □ *The teacher built a fire under the students, and they really started working.* □ *Somebody built a fire under Bill, so he finally went out and got a job.*

build castles in Spain Go to **build castles in the air.**

build castles in the air AND **build castles in Spain** to daydream; to make plans that can never come true. □ *Ann spends most of her time building castles in Spain.* □ *I really like to sit on the porch in the evening, just building castles in the air.*

build (someone or something**) up 1.** to make someone or something stronger or bigger. □ *Tom is eating lots of fresh fruits and vegetables to build himself up for basketball.* □ *Tom needs to build up.* □ *Tom needs to build himself up.* 🅃 *The farmer built up his stone fences where they had weakened.* **2.** to advertise, praise, or promote someone or something. 🅃 *Theatrical agents work very hard to build up their clients.* 🅃 *An advertising agency can build up a product so much that everyone will want it.*

build something **to order** to build something especially for the customer who ordered it. (See also **make** something **to order.**) □ *Our new car was built to order just for us.* □ *My company builds computers to order. No two are alike.*

build up to something to lead up to something; to work up to something. □ *You could tell by the way she was talking that she was building up to something.* □ *The sky was building up to a storm.*

a **bull in a china shop** a very clumsy or wild person around breakable things; a thoughtless or tactless person. (*China* is fine crockery.) □ *Look at Bill, as awkward as a bull in a china shop.* □ *Get that big dog out of my garden. It's like a bull in a china shop.* □ *Bob is so rude, a regular bull in a china shop.*

bump into someone AND **run into** someone to chance on someone; to meet someone by chance. (Also literal.) □ *Guess who I bumped into downtown today?* □ *I ran into Bob Jones yesterday.*

bump someone **off** AND **knock** someone **off** to kill someone. (Slang, especially criminal slang.) □ *They tried to bump her off,* *but she was too clever and got away.* 🅃 *The crooks bumped off the witness to the crime.* □ *They tried to knock them all off.*

a **bundle of nerves** someone who is very nervous and anxious. □ *Mary was a bundle of nerves until she heard that she passed the test.* □ *You always seem to be such a bundle of nerves.*

burn one's **bridges (behind** one) **1.** to make decisions that cannot be changed in the future. □ *If you drop out of school now, you'll be burning your bridges behind you.* □ *You're too young to burn your bridges that way.* **2.** to be unpleasant in a situation that you are leaving, ensuring that you'll never be welcome to return. □ *If you get mad and quit your job, you'll be burning your bridges behind you.* □ *No sense burning your bridges. Be polite and leave quietly.* **3.** to cut off the way back to where you came from, making it impossible to retreat. □ *The army, which had burned its bridges behind it, couldn't go back.* □ *By blowing up the road, the spies had burned their bridges behind them.*

burn one's **bridges in front of** one to create future problems for oneself. (A play on **burn** one's **bridges (behind** one).) □ *I made a mistake again. I always seem to burn my bridges in front of me.* □ *I accidentally insulted a math teacher whom I will have to take a course from next semester. I am burning my bridges in front of me.*

burn (oneself**) out** to do something so long and so intensely that one gets sick and tired of doing it and can no longer do it well. □ *I burned myself out as an opera singer. I just cannot do it anymore.* □ *Tom burned himself out playing golf. He can't stand it anymore.* □ *Tom burned out too young.*

burn out [for electrical or mechanical devices] to break down and become useless. □ *I hope the light bulb in the ceiling doesn't burn out. I can't reach it.* 🅃 *The motor burned out.*

burn someone **at the stake 1.** to set fire to a person tied to a post (as a form of execution). □ *They used to burn witches at the stake.* □ *Look, officer, I only ran a stop sign. What are you going to do, burn me at the stake?* **2.** to chastise or denounce someone severely, but without violence. □ *Stop yelling. I made a simple mistake, and you're burning me at the stake for it.* □ *Sally only spilled her milk. There is no need to shout. Don't burn her at the stake for it.*

burn someone **in effigy** to burn a dummy or other figure that represents a hated person. (See also **hang** someone **in effigy**.) □ *For the third day in a row, they burned the king in effigy.* □ *Until they have burned you in effigy, you can't really be considered a famous leader.*

burn someone or something **to a crisp** to burn someone or something totally or very badly. □ *The flames burned him to a crisp.* □ *The cook burned the meat to a crisp.*

burn someone **up** to make someone very angry. (Informal.) □ *People like that just burn me up!* □ *It burns me up to hear you talk that way.* 🅃 *His answers really burned up the committee members.*

burn the candle at both ends to work very hard and stay up very late at night. □ *No wonder Mary is ill. She has been burning the candle at both ends for a long time.* □ *You can't keep on burning the candle at both ends.*

burn the midnight oil to stay up working, especially studying, late at night. (Refers to working by the light of an oil lamp.) □ *I have to go home and burn the midnight oil tonight.* □ *If you burn the midnight oil night after night, you'll probably become ill.*

burn with a low blue flame to be very angry. (Refers to the imaginary heat caused by extreme anger. A blue flame is a hot flame.) □ *By the time she showed up three hours late, I was burning with a low blue flame.* □ *Whenever Ann gets mad, she just presses her lips together and burns with a low blue flame.*

burned to a cinder burned very badly. (Not necessarily literal.) □ *I stayed out in the sun too long, and I am burned to a cinder.* □ *This toast is burnt to a cinder.*

burned up very angry. □ *I've never been so burned up in my life.* □ *I'm really burned up at Bob.*

burst at the seams [for someone] to "explode" (figuratively) with pride or laughter. (Also literal with things.) □ *Tom nearly burst at the seams with pride.* □ *We laughed so hard we just about burst at the seams.*

burst in on someone or something [for someone] to enter a room, interrupting someone or some activity. (Often without knocking or seeking permission to enter.) □ *Tom burst in on his sister and her boyfriend while they were kissing.* □ *I must ask you not to burst in on a board meeting again. Whatever it is can wait.*

burst into flames to catch fire suddenly; to ignite all at once. □ *Suddenly, the car burst into flames.* □ *It was so hot in the forest fire that a few trees literally burst into flames.*

burst into tears AND **burst out crying** to begin to cry suddenly. (See also **break (out) in(to) tears**.) □ *After the last notes of her song, the audience burst into tears, such was its beauty and tenderness.* □ *The brother and sister burst into tears on hearing of the death of their dog.* □ *Some people find themselves bursting out crying for no reason at all.*

burst onto the scene to appear suddenly in a location. □ *When Charles burst onto the scene, no one was prepared for the news he brought.* □ *The police suddenly burst onto the scene and arrested everyone present.*

burst out crying Go to **burst into tears**.

burst out laughing to begin to laugh suddenly. □ *The entire audience burst out laughing at exactly the wrong time, and so did the actors.* □ *Every time I think of you sitting there with a lap full of noodle soup, I burst out laughing.*

burst someone's **bubble** to destroy someone's illusion or delusion; to destroy someone's fantasy. □ *I hate to burst your bubble, but Columbus did not discover Canada.* □ *Even if I am completely wrong, please don't burst my bubble.*

burst with joy to be full to the bursting point with happiness. (See also **burst at the seams**.) □ *When I got my grades, I could have burst with joy.* □ *Joe was not exactly bursting with joy when he got the news.*

burst with pride to be full to the bursting point with pride. (See also **burst at the seams**.) □ *My parents were bursting with pride when I graduated from college.* □ *I almost burst with pride when I was chosen to go up in the space shuttle.*

bury one's **head in the sand** AND **hide** one's **head in the sand** to ignore or hide from obvious signs of danger. (Refers to an ostrich, which we picture with its head stuck into the sand or the ground.) □ *Stop burying your head in the sand. Look at the statistics on smoking and cancer.* □ *And stop hiding your head in the sand. All of us will die somehow, whether we smoke or not.*

bury the hatchet to stop fighting or arguing; to end old resentments. □ *All right, you two. Calm down and bury the hatchet.* □ *I wish Mr. and Mrs. Franklin would bury the hatchet. They argue all the time.*

business as usual having things go along as usual. □ *Right after the flood, it was business as usual in all the stores.* □ *Please, everyone, business as usual. Let's get back to work.*

the **business end of** something the part or end of something that actually does the work or carries out the procedure. □ *Keep away from the business end of the electric drill to avoid getting hurt.* □ *Don't point the business end of that gun at anyone. It might go off.*

a **busman's holiday** leisure time spent doing something similar to what one does at work. □ *Tutoring students in the evening is too much of a busman's holiday for our English teacher.* □ *It's a bit of a busman's holiday to ask her to be wardrobe mistress for our amateur production in the summer. She's a professional dressmaker.*

bust a gut (to do something**)** to work very hard; to strain oneself to do something. (Slang. *Gut* is considered impolite in some circumstances. *Bust* is an informal form of *burst*.) □ *I don't intend to bust a gut to get there on time.* □ *I busted a gut to get there the last time, and I was the first one there.*

busy as a beaver Go to (as) busy as a beaver.

busy as a beaver (building a new dam) Go to (as) busy as a beaver (building a new dam).

busy as a bee Go to (as) busy as a beaver.

busy as a cat on a hot tin roof Go to (as) busy as a cat on a hot tin roof.

busy as a hibernating bear Go to (as) busy as a hibernating bear.

busy as a one-armed paperhanger Go to (as) busy as a one-armed paperhanger.

busy as Grand Central Station Go to (as) busy as Grand Central Station.

busy as popcorn on a skillet Go to (as) busy as popcorn on a skillet.

but for someone or something if it were not for someone or something. □ *But for the railing, I'd have fallen down the stairs.* □ *But for the children, Mrs. Smith would have left her husband years ago.*

butt in (on someone or something**)** to interrupt someone or something. □ *Pardon me for butting in on your conversation, but this is important.* □ *John butted in on Tom and Jane to tell them that the mail had come.* □ *That's a strange reason to butt in. What was in the mail?*

butter someone **up** to praise and flatter someone, usually with the intention of requesting a favor. □ *I believe my landlady prefers for me to butter her up rather than getting the rent on time.* 🅃 *If I butter up the teacher, will he give me a good grade?*

button one's **lip** to get quiet and stay quiet. (Often used with children.) □ *All right now, let's button our lips and listen to the story.* □ *Button your lip, Tom! I'll tell you when you can talk.*

buy a pig in a poke to purchase or accept something without having seen or examined it. (*Poke* means "bag." Compare this with **buy** something **sight unseen.**) □ *Buying a car without test-driving it is like buying a pig in a poke.* □ *He bought a pig in a poke when he ordered a diamond ring by mail.*

buy someone **off** to bribe someone; to win someone over by gifts or favors. □ *It's not hard to buy politicians off.* 🅃 *They bought off the whole city council with campaign contributions.*

buy something to believe someone; to accept something to be a fact. (Also literal. Informal.) □ *It may be true, but I don't buy it.* □ *I just don't buy the idea that you can swim that far.*

buy something **for a song** to buy something cheaply. □ *No one else wanted it, so I bought it for a song.* □ *I could buy this house for a song, because it's so ugly.*

buy something **on credit** to purchase something now and pay for it later (plus interest). (See also **sell** something **on credit.**) □ *Almost everyone who buys a house buys it on credit.* □ *I didn't have any cash with me, so I used my credit card and bought a new coat on credit.*

buy something **sight unseen** to buy something without seeing it first. (Compare this with **buy a pig in a poke.**) □ *I bought this land sight unseen. I didn't know it was so rocky.* □ *It isn't usually safe to buy something sight unseen.*

buy something **to go** AND **get** something **to go; have** something **to go; order** something **to go** to purchase food to take out; to make a purchase of cooked food to be taken elsewhere to be eaten. □ *Let's stop here and buy six hamburgers to go.* □ *I didn't thaw anything for dinner. Let's stop off on the way home and get something to go.* □ *No, I don't want to sit at a table. I'll just have a cup of coffee to go.*

by a hair('s breadth) AND **by a whisker** just barely; by a very small distance. (The *whisker* phrase is folksy.) □ *I just missed getting on the plane by a hair's breadth.* □ *I made it by a hair!* □ *The arrow missed the deer by a whisker.*

by all accounts Go to according to all accounts.

by all appearances apparently; according to what one sees. □ *She is, by all appearances, ready to resume work.* □ *By all appearances, we ought to be approaching the airport.*

by all means certainly; yes; absolutely. (Compare this with **by any means**.) □ *I will attempt to get there by all means.* □ *BOB: Can you come to dinner tomorrow? JANE: By all means. I'd love to.*

by all means of something using every possible manner of something to do something. □ *People will be arriving by all means of transportation.* □ *The surgeon performed the operation by all means of instruments.*

by a mile by a great distance. (Also literal. An exaggeration in this case.) □ *You missed the target by a mile.* □ *Your estimate of the budget deficit was off by a mile.*

by and by after a period of time has passed. (Most often seen in children's stories.) □ *By and by the bears returned home, and can you guess what they found?* □ *And by and by the little boy became a tall and handsome prince.*

by and large generally; usually. (Originally a nautical expression.) □ *I find that, by and large, people tend to do what they are told to do.* □ *By and large, rosebushes need lots of care.*

by any means by any way possible. □ *I need to get there soon by any means.* □ *I must win this contest by any means, fair or unfair.* □ *It cannot be done by any means.*

by a show of hands a vote expressed by people raising their hands. □ *We were asked to vote for the candidates for captain by a show of hands.* □ *Bob wanted us to vote on paper, not by a show of hands, so that we could have a secret ballot.*

by a whisker Go to **by a hair('s breadth)**.

by chance accidentally; randomly; without planning. □ *I found this book by chance at a book sale.* □ *We met by chance in a class in college.*

by check by using a check. □ *He paid for the book by check.* □ *You will be paid by check.*

by choice due to conscious choice; on purpose. □ *I do this kind of thing by choice. No one makes me do it.* □ *I didn't go to this college by choice. It was the closest one to home.*

by coincidence by an accidental and strange similarity; by an unplanned pair of similar events or occurrences. □ *We just happened to be in the same place at the same time by coincidence.* □ *By coincidence, the circus was in town when I was there. I'm glad because I love circuses.*

by day AND **by night** during the day; during the night. □ *By day, Mary worked in an office; by night, she took classes.* □ *Dave slept by day and worked by night.*

by dint of something because of something; due to the efforts of something. (*Dint* is an old word meaning "force," and it is never used except in this phrase.) □ *They got the building finished on time by dint of hard work and good organization.* □ *By dint of much studying, John got through college.*

by fits and starts irregularly; unevenly; with much stopping and starting. □ *Somehow, they got the job done by fits and starts.* □ *By fits and starts, the old car finally got us to town.*

by guess and by golly by luck; with the help of God. (Folksy. *Golly* is a disguise of *God*.) □ *They managed to get the shed built by guess and by golly.* □ *I lost my ruler and had to install the new floor tile by guess and by golly.*

by herself **1.** with no one else present; alone. □ *She hates to go to strange places by herself.* □ *She sat by herself at a table big enough for six people.* **2.** with the help of no one else. □ *She can do it by herself.* □ *Susan is unable to get there by herself.*

by himself **1.** alone; with no one else present. □ *He is home by himself tonight.* □ *He hates to eat by himself. It makes him feel lonely.* **2.** with the help of no one else. □ *Can he do it by himself?* □ *The two-year-old boy can get dressed by himself.*

by hook or (by) crook by any means, legal or illegal. (Folksy.) ☐ *I'll get the job done by hook or by crook.* ☐ *I must have that house. I intend to get it by hook or crook.*

by itself with the help of nothing else; without the addition of anything else. ☐ *Will this be enough by itself?* ☐ *Can the dog get out of the house by itself?*

by leaps and bounds rapidly; by large movements forward. ☐ *Our garden is growing by leaps and bounds.* ☐ *The profits of my company are increasing by leaps and bounds.*

by means of something using something; with the use of something. ☐ *I opened the bottle by means of a bottle opener.* ☐ *I was able to afford a car by means of a loan.*

by mistake in error; accidentally. ☐ *I'm sorry. I came into the wrong room by mistake.* ☐ *I chose the wrong road by mistake. Now we are lost.*

by myself 1. with no one else present; alone. ☐ *I sat at the table by myself.* ☐ *I will not be at the party. I will be at home by myself tonight.* **2.** without the help of anyone else. ☐ *I did it all by myself.* ☐ *Do you think I can eat this whole pie by myself?*

by night Go to **by day**.

by no means absolutely not; certainly not. ☐ *I'm by no means angry with you.* ☐ *BOB: Did you put this box here? TOM: By no means. I didn't do it, I'm sure.*

by oneself **1.** with no one else present; alone. ☐ *Must one sit by oneself or may one join another group?* ☐ *One just hates eating by oneself, doesn't one?* **2.** with the help of no one else. ☐ *One is expected to do it by oneself.* ☐ *Can one do this by oneself?*

by ourselves 1. with no one else present; alone. ☐ *Do we have to sit here by ourselves? Can't we sit with Mary and Max?* ☐ *We like to eat by ourselves, so we can talk about private matters.* **2.** with the help of no one else. ☐ *We can do it by ourselves.* ☐ *Can we lift this by ourselves, or do we need some help?*

by return mail by a subsequent mailing (back to the sender). (A phrase indicating that an answer is expected soon, by mail.) ☐ *Since this bill is overdue, would you kindly send us your check by return mail?* ☐ *I answered your request by return mail over a year ago. Please check your records.*

by shank's mare by foot. (*Shank* refers to the shank of the leg. Folksy. See also **go** (somewhere) **by shank's mare.**) ☐ *My car isn't working, so I'll have to travel by shank's mare.* ☐ *I'm sore because I've been getting around by shank's mare.*

by the each; per. (Used to show a unit of measure, but not the rate of a measure.) ☐ *Lettuce is sold by the head.* ☐ *Gas is sold by the gallon.*

by the book Go to **by the numbers**.

by the day one day at a time. ☐ *I don't know when I'll have to leave town, so I rent this room by the day.* ☐ *Sally is in such distress. She manages to live only by the day.*

by the dozen twelve at a time; in a group of twelve. (Almost the same as the following entry.) ☐ *I purchase socks by the dozen.* ☐ *Eggs are usually sold by the dozen.* ☐ *Around here we have problems by the dozen.*

by the dozens many; by some large, indefinite number. (Similar to but less than *hundreds.* Almost the same as the previous entry.) ☐ *Just then people began showing up by the dozens.* ☐ *I baked cakes and pies by the dozens.*

by the handful in measurements equal to a handful; lots. ☐ *Billy is eating candy by the handful.* ☐ *People began leaving by the handful at midnight.*

by the hour at each hour; after each hour. ☐ *It kept growing darker by the hour.* ☐ *I have to take this medicine by the hour.* ☐ *The illness is getting worse by the hour.*

by the month one month at a time. ☐ *Not many apartments are rented by the month.* ☐ *I needed a car for a short while, so I rented one by the month.*

by themselves 1. with help from no one else. ☐ *Do you think they can do it by* *themselves?* □ *Mike and Max cannot lift the piano by themselves.* **2.** with no one else present; alone. □ *They are sitting there by themselves. Let's sit with them.* □ *They enjoy spending the evening at home by themselves.*

by the nape of the neck by the back of the neck. (Mostly found in real or mock threats.) □ *He grabbed me by the nape of the neck and told me not to turn around if I valued my life. I stood very still.* □ *If you do that again, I'll pick you up by the nape of the neck and throw you out the door.*

by the numbers AND **by the book** according to the rules. (Informal.) □ *He always plays the game by the numbers. He never cheats.* □ *I want all my people to go by the numbers. This place is totally honest.* □ *We always go by the book in matters like this.*

by the same token in the same way; reciprocally. □ *Tom must be good when he comes here, and, by the same token, I expect you to behave properly when you go to his house.* □ *The mayor votes for his friend's causes. By the same token, the friend votes for the mayor's causes.*

by the seat of one's **pants** by sheer luck and very little skill. (Informal. Especially with *to fly.*) □ *I got through school by the seat of my pants.* □ *The jungle pilot spent most of his days flying by the seat of his pants.*

by the skin of one's **teeth** just barely; by an amount equal to the thickness of the (imaginary) skin on one's teeth. (Informal or slang.) □ *I got through that class by the skin of my teeth.* □ *I got to the airport late and missed the plane by the skin of my teeth.*

by the sweat of one's **brow** by one's efforts; by one's hard work. □ *Tom raised these vegetables by the sweat of his brow.* □ *Sally polished the car by the sweat of her brow.*

by the way incidentally; in addition; while I think of it. □ *By the way, I'm not going to the bank today.* □ *Oh, by the way, your shoes need polishing.*

by the week one week at a time. □ *I plan my schedules by the week.* □ *Where can I rent a room by the week?*

by the year one year at a time. □ *Most apartments are available by the year.* □ *We budget by the year.*

by virtue of something because of something; due to something. □ *She's permitted to vote by virtue of her age.* □ *They are members of the club by virtue of their great wealth.*

by way of something **1.** passing through something; via something. □ *He came home by way of Toledo.* □ *She went to the bank by way of the drugstore.* **2.** in illustration; as an example. □ *By way of illustration, the professor drew a picture on the board.* □ *He read them a passage from Shakespeare by way of example.*

by word of mouth by speaking rather than writing. □ *I learned about it by word of mouth.* □ *I need it in writing. I don't trust things I hear about by word of mouth.*

by yourself 1. with no one else present; alone. □ *Do you want to sit here by yourself, or can I sit here too?* □ *Don't sit at home by yourself. Come to the movie with me.* **2.** with the help of no one else. □ *Can you really do this by yourself?* □ *Bill, can you lift this by yourself?*

by yourselves 1. with no one else present; alone. □ *Are you two going to sit here by yourselves all evening?* □ *Don't sit home by yourselves. Come to the party.* **2.** with the help of no one else. □ *Can you do this by yourselves?* □ *Can all of you get to the meeting by yourselves?*

C

call a meeting to ask that people assemble for a meeting; to request that a meeting be held. □ *The mayor called a meeting to discuss the problem.* □ *I'll be calling a meeting of the town council to discuss the new building project.*

call a spade a spade to call something by its right name; to speak frankly about something, even if it is unpleasant. □ *Well, I believe it's time to call a spade a spade. We are just avoiding the issue.* □ *Let's call a spade a spade. The man is a liar.*

call for someone or something **1.** to arrive to collect or pick up a person or a thing. (Used especially when you are to pick someone up and are acting as an escort.) □ *I will call for you about eight this evening.* □ *The messenger will call for your reply in the morning.* **2.** to need, require, or demand something or the services of someone. □ *The recipe calls for two cups of flour.* □ *This job calls for someone with good eyesight.*

call it a day to quit work and go home; to say that a day's work has been completed. □ *I'm tired. Let's call it a day.* □ *The boss was mad because Tom called it a day at noon and went home.*

call it a night to end what one is doing at night and go [home] to bed. □ *At midnight, I called it a night and went to bed.* □ *Guest after guest called it a night, and at last we were alone.*

call it quits to quit; to resign from something; to announce that one is quitting. (Informal.) □ *Okay! I've had enough! I'm calling it quits.* □ *Time to go home, John. Let's call it quits.*

call of nature the need to go to the lavatory. (Humorous.) □ *Stop the car here! I have to answer the call of nature.* □ *There was no break in the agenda to take account of the call of nature.*

call on someone to visit someone. □ *I have to call on my aunt this Sunday.* □ *Bill called on his brother in the hospital.*

call out (to someone**)** to shout to someone. □ *Mike called out to Tom that there was a telephone call for him.* □ *I heard someone call out, but I could see no one.*

call someone **down** to reprimand a person; to **bawl** someone **out.** □ *The teacher had to call Sally down in front of everybody.* □ *"I wish you wouldn't call me down in public," cried Sally.*

call someone **names** to call a person unpleasant or insulting names. (Usually viewed as a juvenile act.) □ *Mommy! John is calling me names again!* □ *We'll never get anywhere by calling one another names.*

call someone **on the carpet** to reprimand a person. (The phrase presents images of a person called into the boss's carpeted office for a reprimand.) □ *One more error like that and the boss will call you on the carpet.* □ *I'm sorry it went wrong. I really hope he doesn't call me on the carpet again.*

call someone or something **in** to call on the special talents, abilities, or power of someone or something. □ *They had to call a new doctor in.* [T] *Yes, they had to call in a specialist.* [T] *They had to call in a huge tractor to move the boulder.*

call someone or something **into question** to cause someone or something to be evaluated; to examine or reexamine the qualifications or value of someone or something. □ *Because of her poor record, we were forced to call Dr. Jones into question.* □ *We called Dr. Jones's qualifications into question.* □ *They called the whole project into question.* T *I cannot call into question the entire medical profession.*

call someone or something **off 1.** to call a halt to an attack by someone or something. □ *Please call your dog off. It's trying to bite me!* T *Okay, you can call off the police. I surrender.* T *It's time to call off the manhunt. The criminal has given himself up.* **2.** [with *something*] to cancel an event. □ *It's too late to call the party off. The first guests have already arrived.* T *Because of rain, they called off the baseball game.*

call someone or something **up 1.** to call a person, business, or office on the telephone. □ *Mary called the company up and ordered a new supply of medicine.* T *Tom called up Mary.* **2.** [with *something*] to summon information from a computer. T *John used a computer to call up the information.* T *With a few strokes on the computer keyboard, Sally called up the figures she was looking for.*

call someone's **bluff** to demonstrate that a person is or is not being deceptive, usually by demanding that the person prove a claim or carry out a threat. □ *All right, I'll call your bluff. Show me you can do it!* □ *Tom said, "I've got a gun here in my pocket, and I'll shoot if you come any closer!" "Go ahead," said Bill, calling his bluff.*

call the dogs off to stop threatening, chasing, or hounding (a person). (Also literal. Informal. Note the variation in the examples.) □ *All right, I surrender. You can call your dogs off.* T *Tell the sheriff to call off the dogs. We caught the robber.* T *Please call off your dogs!*

call the meeting to order to start a meeting officially; to announce that the meeting has started. □ *The president called the meeting to order shortly after noon.* □ *We cannot do anything until someone calls the meeting to order.*

call (the) roll AND **take (the) roll** to call the names of people on the rolls, expecting them to reply if they are present. □ *After I call the roll, please open your books to page 12.* □ *I will take roll, and then we will do arithmetic.*

call the shots AND **call the tune** to make the decisions; to decide what is to be done. (Informal.) □ *Sally always wants to call the shots, and Mary doesn't like to be bossed around. They don't get along well.* □ *Sally always wants to call the tune.* □ *Look here, friend, I'm calling the shots. You just be quiet.*

call the tune Go to call the shots.

calm as a toad in the sun Go to (as) calm as a toad in the sun.

the **calm before the storm** Go to the lull before the storm.

can take it to the bank able to depend on the truthfulness of my statement: it is not counterfeit or bogus; to be able to bank on something. □ *Believe me. What I am telling you is the truth. You can take it to the bank.* □ *This information is as good as gold. You can take it to the bank.*

Can you imagine? Can you believe that?; Imagine that! □ *She wore jeans to the dance. Can you imagine?* □ *Billy was eating the houseplant! Can you imagine?*

cancel something **out** to destroy the effect of something; to balance something. T *This last payment cancels out my debt.* □ *Yes, your last payment cancels it out.* T *Bob's two good grades canceled out his two failing grades.*

cannot help doing something not able to refrain from doing something; not able not to do something. □ *Anne is such a good cook, I can't help eating everything she makes.* □ *Since John loves to shop, he can't help spending money.*

cannot stomach someone or something Go to not able to stomach someone or something.

[can't] Go to the expressions listed at not able, as well as those listed below.

can't carry a tune [to be] unable to sing a simple melody; lacking musical ability.

(Almost always negative. Also with *cannot.*) ☐ *I wish that Tom wouldn't try to sing. He can't carry a tune.* ☐ *Listen to poor old John. He really cannot carry a tune.*

can't do anything with someone or something not [to be] able to manage or control someone or something. (Also with *cannot.*) ☐ *Bill is such a problem. I can't do anything with him.* ☐ *My hair is such a mess. I just can't do anything with it.*

can't help but do something [to be] unable to choose any but one course of action. (Also with *cannot.*) ☐ *Her parents live nearby, so she can't help but go there on holidays.* ☐ *Bob is a tennis fan and can't help but travel to Wimbledon each year.*

can't hold a candle to someone not [to be] equal to someone; unable to measure up to someone. (Also with *cannot.*) ☐ *Mary can't hold a candle to Ann when it comes to auto racing.* ☐ *As for singing, John can't hold a candle to Jane.*

can't make heads or tails (out) of someone or something [to be] unable to understand someone or something. (Also with *cannot.*) ☐ *John is so strange. I can't make heads or tails of him.* ☐ *Do this report again. I can't make heads or tails out of it.*

can't see beyond the end of one's **nose** [to be] unaware of the things that might happen in the future; not farsighted; self-centered. (Also with *cannot.*) ☐ *John is a very poor planner. He can't see beyond the end of his nose.* ☐ *Ann can't see beyond the end of her nose. She is very self-centered.*

can't see one's **hand in front of** one's **face** [to be] unable to see very far, usually due to darkness or fog. (Also with *cannot.*) ☐ *It was so dark that I couldn't see my hand in front of my face.* ☐ *Bob said that the fog was so thick he couldn't see his hand in front of his face.*

can't stand (the sight of) someone or something AND **can't stomach** someone or something [to be] unable to tolerate someone or something; disliking someone or something extremely. (Also with *cannot.*) ☐ *I can't stand the sight of cooked carrots.* ☐ *Mr. Jones can't stand the sight of blood.* ☐ *None of us can stand this place.* ☐ *Nobody can stand Tom when he smokes a cigar.* ☐ *I can't stomach your foul language.* ☐ *I just can't stomach Mr. Smith.*

can't stomach someone or something Go to **can't stand (the sight of)** someone or something.

can't wait (for something **to happen)** [to be very eager and] to be unable to endure the wait for something to happen. ☐ *I am so anxious for my birthday to come. I just can't wait.* ☐ *Tom can't wait for Mary to arrive.*

can't wait (to do something**)** [to be very eager and] unable to endure the wait until it is possible to do something. ☐ *I'm glad it's almost summertime—I just can't wait to go swimming!* ☐ *Jimmy can't wait to go to school tomorrow.*

cap and gown the academic cap or mortarboard and the robe worn in academic ceremonies. ☐ *We all had to rent cap and gown for graduation.* ☐ *I appeared wearing my cap and gown, but I had shorts on underneath because it gets so hot at that time of year.*

capable of doing something having the ability to do something. ☐ *Do you think Tom is capable of lifting 200 pounds?* ☐ *No one I know is capable of such a crime!*

a **card** an entertaining and clever person who says or does funny things. (Preceded by *be, become, seem like,* or *act like.*) ☐ *He is such a card. Always making jokes.* ☐ *Mary is a card, and someone is going to have to deal with her!*

the **cards are stacked against** one luck is against one. (Informal. Refers to playing cards. See also **have the cards stacked against** one; **stack the cards (against** someone or something**)**.) ☐ *I have the worst luck. The cards are stacked against me all the time.* ☐ *How can I accomplish anything when the cards are stacked against me?*

carried away excited or moved to (extreme) action (by someone or something). ☐ *The crowd got carried away and did a lot of damage to the park.* ☐ *I know* *that planning a party is fun, but don't get carried away.*

carry (a lot of) weight (with someone or something**)** to be very influential with someone or some group of people. □ *Your argument does not carry a lot of weight with me.* □ *The senator's testimony carried a lot of weight with the council.* □ *Her opinion carries weight with most of the members.*

carry a secret to one's **grave** Go to carry a secret to the grave.

carry a secret to the grave AND **carry a secret to** one's **grave** to avoid telling a secret, even to the day of one's death. □ *John carried our secret to his grave.* □ *Trust me, I will carry your secret to the grave!*

carry a torch (for someone**)** to be in love with someone who is not in love with you; to brood over a hopeless love affair. (Also with *the.*) □ *John is carrying a torch for Jane.* □ *Is John still carrying a torch?* □ *Yes, he'll carry the torch for months.*

carry coals to Newcastle to do something unnecessary; to do something that is redundant or duplicative. (Newcastle is an English town from which coal was shipped to other parts of England.) □ *Taking food to a farmer is like carrying coals to Newcastle.* □ *Mr. Smith is so rich he doesn't need any more money. To give him money is like carrying coals to Newcastle.*

carry on (about someone or something**)** to make a great fuss over someone or something; to cry and become out of control about someone or something. (Note the variation in the examples below.) □ *Billy, stop carrying on about your tummy ache like that.* □ *Billy, you must stop carrying on so.* □ *The child carried on endlessly about his mother.*

carry one's **cross** Go to bear one's cross.

carry one's **(own) weight** AND **pull** one's **(own) weight** to do one's share; to earn one's keep. □ *Tom, you must be more helpful around the house. We all have to carry our own weight.* □ *Bill, I'm afraid that you can't work here anymore. You just haven't been carrying your weight.* □ *If you would just pull your weight, we would finish this by noon.*

carry on somehow to manage to continue somehow, in spite of problems. □ *Even though we did not have a lot of money, we managed to carry on somehow.* □ *Don't worry about us. We will carry on somehow.*

carry on without someone or something to manage to continue without someone or something. □ *I don't know how we will be able to carry on without you.* □ *We can't carry on without a leader!*

carry on (with someone or something**) 1.** [with *something*] to continue with something. □ *Can I please carry on with my work now?* □ *Yes, please carry on.* **2.** [with *someone*] to behave improperly with someone; to be affectionate in public. □ *Look at Jane carrying on with Tom. They ought to be ashamed.* □ *Jane, stop carrying on like that!*

carry over to extend into another time period or location. □ *I don't like for bills to carry over into the next month.* □ *Please do not let the paragraph carry over.*

carry something **off** to make a planned event—especially a joke or deception—work out successfully. (Also literal, meaning to take something away. See also **pull** something **off.**) □ *It was a huge party, but the hostess carried it off beautifully.* 🅃 *The magician carried off the trick with great skill.*

carry something **out** to perform a task; to perform an assignment. (Also literal meaning to remove something.) □ *"This is a very important job," said Jane. "Do you think you can carry it out?"* 🅃 *The students didn't carry out their assignments.*

carry something **over** to let something like a bill extend into another period of time; to extend to another location. □ *We'll carry the amount of money due over into the next month.* 🅃 *Yes, please carry over the balance.* □ *We'll have to carry this paragraph over to the next page.*

carry the ball 1. to be the player holding the ball, especially in football when a goal is made. (Sports.) □ *It was the fullback* *carrying the ball.* ☐ *Yes, Tom always carries the ball.* **2.** to be in charge; to make sure that a job gets done. (See also **drop the ball.**) ☐ *We need someone who knows how to get the job done. Hey, Sally! Why don't you carry the ball for us?* ☐ *John can't carry the ball. He isn't organized enough.*

carry the day AND **win the day** to be successful; to win a competition, argument, etc. (Originally meaning to win a battle.) ☐ *Our team didn't play well at first, but we won the day in the end.* ☐ *Hard work won the day and James passed his exams.*

carry the torch 1. to uphold a set of goals; to lead or participate in a (figurative) crusade. ☐ *The battle was over, but John continued to carry the torch.* ☐ *If Jane hadn't carried the torch, no one would have followed, and the whole thing would have failed.* **2.** Go to **carry a torch (for** someone**).**

carry the weight of the world on one's **shoulders** to appear to be burdened by all the problems in the whole world. ☐ *Look at Tom. He appears to be carrying the weight of the world on his shoulders.* ☐ *Cheer up, Tom! You don't need to carry the weight of the world on your shoulders.*

carry through (on something**)** Go to **follow through (on** something**).**

a **case in point** an example of what one is talking about. ☐ *Now, as a case in point, let's look at nineteenth-century England.* ☐ *Fireworks can be dangerous. For a case in point, look what happened to Bob Smith last week.*

a **case of mistaken identity** the incorrect identification of someone. ☐ *It is simply a case of mistaken identity.* ☐ *I am not the criminal you want to arrest. This is a case of mistaken identity.*

cash-and-carry a method of buying and selling goods at the retail level where the buyer pays cash for the goods and carries the goods away. (As opposed to paying on credit or having something delivered.) ☐ *Sorry, we don't accept credit cards. This is strictly cash-and-carry.* ☐ *I bought the chair cash-and-carry before I realized that there was no way to get it home.*

cash in one's **chips** to die. (Also literal. Slang. From an expression used in gambling, chiefly poker.) ☐ *Bob cashed in his chips yesterday.* ☐ *I'm too young to cash in my chips.*

cash in (on something**)** to earn a lot of money at something; to make a profit at something. (See also **cash** something **in.**) ☐ *This is a good year for farming, and you can cash in on it if you're smart.* ☐ *It's too late to cash in on that particular clothing fad.*

cash on the barrelhead money paid for something when it is purchased; money paid at the time of sale. (Folksy. See also **cash-and-carry.**) ☐ *I don't extend credit. It's cash on the barrelhead only.* ☐ *I paid $12,000 for this car—cash on the barrelhead.*

cash or credit [a purchase made] either by paying cash or by putting the charges on a credit account. ☐ *When Fred had all his purchases assembled on the counter, the clerk asked, "Cash or credit?"* ☐ *That store does not give you a choice of cash or credit. They want cash only.*

cash something **in** to exchange something with cash value for the amount of money it is worth. ☐ *I should have cashed my bonds in years ago.* 🅃 *It's time to cash in your U.S. savings bonds.* 🅃 *I need to cash in an insurance policy.*

cast about for someone or something Go to **cast around for** someone or something.

cast around for someone or something AND **cast about for** someone or something to seek someone or something; to seek a thought or an idea. (Refers to a type of person rather than a specific person.) ☐ *John is casting around for a new cook. The old one quit.* ☐ *Bob is casting about for a new car.* ☐ *Mary cast about for a way to win the contest.*

cast aspersions on someone to make a rude and insulting remark. ☐ *I resent your casting aspersions on my brother and his ability!* ☐ *It is rude to cast aspersions on people in general.*

cast doubt(s) (on someone or something**)** to cause someone or something to be doubted. ☐ *The police cast doubt on my story.* ☐ *How can they cast doubt? They haven't looked into it yet.* ☐ *The city council cast doubt on John and his plan.* ☐ *They are always casting doubts.*

cast in the same mold very similar. ☐ *The two sisters are cast in the same mold—equally mean.* ☐ *All the members of the family are cast in the same mold and they all end up in prison.*

cast one's **lot in with** someone to join in with someone and accept whatever happens. ☐ *Mary cast her lot with the group going to Spain. They had a wonderful time.* 🅃 *I decided to cast in my lot with the home team this year.*

cast (one's**) pearls before swine** to waste something good on someone who doesn't care about it. (From a biblical quotation.) ☐ *To sing for them is to cast pearls before swine.* ☐ *To serve them French cuisine is like casting one's pearls before swine.*

cast one's **vote** to vote; to place one's ballot in the ballot box. ☐ *The citizens cast their votes for president.* ☐ *The wait in line to cast one's vote was almost an hour.*

cast the first stone to make the first criticism; to be the first to attack. (From a biblical quotation.) ☐ *Well, I don't want to be the one to cast the first stone, but she sang horribly.* ☐ *John always casts the first stone. Does he think he's perfect?*

Cat got your tongue? Why do you not speak?; Speak up and answer my question! (Folksy.) ☐ *Answer me! What's the matter, cat got your tongue?* ☐ *Why don't you speak up? Cat got your tongue?*

catch-as-catch-can the best one can do with whatever is available. ☐ *We went hitchhiking for a week and lived catch-as-catch-can.* ☐ *There were ten children in our family, and every meal was catch-as-catch-can.*

catch a whiff of something Go to **get a whiff of** something.

catch cold AND **take cold** to contract a cold (the disease). ☐ *Please close the window, or we'll all catch cold.* ☐ *I take cold every year at this time.*

catch fire to begin to burn; to ignite. ☐ *If the wood were not so wet, it would catch fire more easily.* ☐ *The curtains blew against the flame of the candle and caught fire.*

catch forty winks AND **catch some Zs; take forty winks** to take a nap; to get some sleep. (Informal. See also **forty winks**.) ☐ *I'll just catch forty winks before getting ready for the party.* ☐ *Tom always tries to catch some Zs before going out for a late evening.* ☐ *I think I'll go to bed and take forty winks. See you in the morning.* ☐ *Why don't you go take forty winks and call me in about an hour?*

catch hell Go to **get the devil**.

catch it to get into trouble and receive punishment. (Informal. See also **get the devil**.) ☐ *I know I'm going to catch it when I get home.* ☐ *Bob hit Billy in the face. He really caught it from the teacher.*

catch one **off** one's **guard** Go to **catch** someone **off guard**.

catch one's **breath** to resume one's normal breathing after exertion; to return to normal after being busy or very active. ☐ *I don't have time to catch my breath.* ☐ *I ran so fast that it took ten minutes to catch my breath.*

catch one's **death (of cold)** AND **take** one's **death of cold** to contract a cold; to catch a serious cold. (See also **catch cold**.) ☐ *If I go out in this weather, I'll catch my death of cold.* ☐ *Dress up warm or you'll take your death of cold.* ☐ *Put on your raincoat or you'll catch your death.*

catch one **with** one's **pants down** to catch someone doing something, especially something that ought to be done in secret or in private. (Informal. Use with caution. This refers to having one's pants down in the bathroom.) ☐ *John couldn't convince them he was innocent. They caught him with his pants down.* ☐ *Did you hear that John took the camera? The store owner caught him with his pants down.*

catch (on) fire to ignite and burn with flames. ☐ *Keep your coat away from the flames, or it will catch fire.* ☐ *Lightning struck the prairie, and the grass caught on fire.*

catch on (to someone or something**)** to figure someone or something out; to solve a puzzle; to see through an act of deception. ☐ *Mary caught on to Bob and his tricks.* ☐ *Ann caught on to the woman's dishonest plan.* ☐ *The woman thought that Ann wouldn't catch on.*

catch sight of someone or something to see someone or something briefly; to get a glimpse of someone or something. ☐ *I caught sight of the rocket just before it flew out of sight.* ☐ *Ann caught sight of the robber as he ran out of the bank.*

catch someone **in the act (of** doing something**)** to catch a person doing something illegal or private. (See also **in the act (of** doing something**)**.) ☐ *They know who set the fire. They caught someone in the act.* ☐ *I caught Tom in the act of stealing a car.*

catch someone **napping** to find someone unprepared. (Informal. Literally, to discover someone "asleep.") ☐ *The enemy soldiers caught our army napping.* ☐ *The thieves caught the security guard napping.*

catch someone **off balance** to catch a person who is not prepared; to surprise someone. ☐ *Sorry I acted so flustered. You caught me off balance.* ☐ *The robbers caught Ann off balance and stole her purse.*

catch someone **off guard** AND **catch** one **off** one's **guard** to catch a person at a time of carelessness. (Compare this with **catch** someone **off-balance**.) ☐ *Tom caught Ann off guard and frightened her.* ☐ *She caught me off my guard, and I told the location of the jewels.*

catch someone **red-handed** to catch a person in the act of doing something wrong. (See also **caught red-handed**.) ☐ *Tom was stealing the car when the police drove by and caught him red-handed.* ☐ *Mary tried to cash a forged check at the bank, and the teller caught her red-handed.*

catch someone's **eye** AND **get** someone's **eye** **1.** to establish eye contact with someone. (Also with *have,* as in the example.) ☐ *Tom got Mary's eye and waved to her.* ☐ *When Tom had her eye, he smiled at her.* **2.** to appear and attract someone's interest. ☐ *A small red car passing by caught my eye.* ☐ *One of the books on the top shelf caught my eye, and I took it down to look at it.*

catch some Zs Go to catch forty winks.

catch the devil Go to get the devil.

catch up (to someone or something**)** AND **catch up (with** someone or something**)** to move faster in order to reach someone or something ahead, moving in the same direction. ☐ *The red car caught up with the blue one.* ☐ *Bill caught up with Ann, and they walked to the bank together.* ☐ *He had to run to catch up to her.*

catch up (with someone or something**)** Go to catch up (to someone or something).

caught in the act seen doing something illegal or private. ☐ *Tom was caught in the act.* ☐ *She's guilty. She was caught in the act.*

caught in the cross fire Go to caught in the middle.

caught in the middle AND **caught in the cross fire** caught between two arguing people or groups, making it difficult to remain neutral. (Both are also literal.) ☐ *The cook and the dishwasher were having an argument, and Tom got caught in the middle. All he wanted was his dinner.* ☐ *Mr. and Mrs. Smith tried to draw me into their argument. I don't like being caught in the middle.* ☐ *Bill and Ann were arguing, and poor Bobby, their son, was caught in the cross fire.*

caught red-handed caught in the act of doing something wrong. ☐ *Tom was caught red-handed.* ☐ *Many car thieves are caught red-handed.*

caught short to be without something you need, especially money. ☐ *I needed eggs for my cake, but I was caught short.* ☐ *Bob had to borrow money from John to pay for the meal. Bob is caught short quite often.*

caught unaware(s) surprised and unprepared. ☐ *Sorry. You startled me when you* *came up behind me. I was caught unaware.* □ *The clerk was caught unawares, and the robber emptied out the cash register before the clerk could sound the alarm.*

cause a commotion Go to cause a stir.

cause a stir AND **cause a commotion** to cause people to become agitated; to cause trouble in a group of people; to shock or alarm people. (Notice the example with quite.) □ *When Bob appeared without his evening jacket, it caused a stir in the dining room.* □ *The dog ran through the church and caused quite a commotion.*

cause (some) eyebrows to raise to shock people; to surprise and dismay people. (See also raise some eyebrows.) □ *John caused eyebrows to raise when he married a poor girl from Toledo.* □ *If you want to cause some eyebrows to raise, just start singing as you walk down the street.*

cause (some) tongues to wag to cause people to gossip; to give people something to gossip about. □ *The way John was looking at Mary will surely cause some tongues to wag.* □ *The way Mary was dressed will also cause tongues to wag.*

cave in (to someone or something**)** [for someone] to yield and give in to someone else or to something. (Also literal in reference to the collapse of caves, tunnels, ceilings, etc.) □ *Mr. Franklin always caves in to Mrs. Franklin.* □ *It's easier to cave in than to go on fighting.* □ *Tom caved in to the pressure of work.*

cease and desist to stop doing something and stay stopped. (A legal phrase.) □ *The judge ordered the merchant to cease and desist the deceptive practices.* □ *When they were ordered to cease and desist, they finally stopped.*

chalk something **up to** something to recognize something as the cause of something else. □ *We chalked her bad behavior up to her recent illness.* 🅃 *I had to chalk up the loss to experience.* 🅃 *I chalked up my defeat to my impatience.*

champ at the bit AND **chomp at the bit** to be ready and anxious to do something. (Originally said about horses.) □ *The kids were champing at the bit to get into the swimming pool.* □ *The dogs were champing at the bit to begin the hunt.*

chance something to risk doing something; to try doing something. □ *I don't usually ride horses, but this time I will chance it.* □ *Bob didn't have reservations, but he went to the airport anyway, chancing a cancellation.*

chance (up)on someone or something to find someone or something by chance. □ *I just happened to chance upon this excellent restaurant down by the river. The food is superb.* □ *We were exploring a small Kentucky town when we chanced on an old man who turned out to be my great-uncle.*

change hands [for something] to be sold or passed from owner to owner. □ *How many times has this house changed hands in the last ten years?* □ *We built this house in 1920, and it has never changed hands.*

change horses in the middle of the stream to make major changes in an activity that has already begun; to choose someone or something else after it is too late. □ *I'm already baking a cherry pie. I can't bake an apple pie. It's too late to change horses in the middle of the stream.* □ *The house is half-built. It's too late to hire a different architect. You can't change horses in the middle of the stream.*

a **change of pace** an addition of some variety in one's life. □ *Going to the beach on the weekend will be a change of pace.* □ *The doctor says I need a change of pace.*

a **change of scenery** a move to a different place, where the scenery is different or where things in general are different. □ *I thought I would go to the country for a change of scenery.* □ *A change of scenery would help me relax and organize my life.*

change someone's **mind** to cause a person to think differently (about someone or something). □ *Tom thought Mary was unkind, but an evening out with her changed his mind.* □ *I can change my mind if I want to. I don't have to stick with an idea.*

change someone's **tune** to change the manner of a person, usually from bad to good, or from rude to pleasant. □ *The teller was most unpleasant until she learned that I'm a bank director. Then she changed her tune.* □ *"I will help change your tune by fining you $150," said the judge to the rude defendant.*

change the subject to begin talking about something different. □ *They changed the subject suddenly when the person whom they had been discussing entered the room.* □ *We'll change the subject if we are embarrassing you.*

chapter and verse detailed, in reference to sources of information. (A reference to the method of referring to biblical text.) □ *He gave chapter and verse for his reasons for disputing that Shakespeare had written the play.* □ *The suspect gave chapter and verse of his associate's activities.*

charge someone or something **up 1.** [with *someone*] to get someone excited and enthusiastic. 🅃 *The speaker charged up the crowd to go out and raise money.* □ *Mrs. Smith tried to charge her husband up about getting a job.* **2.** [with *something*] to restore a charge to an electrical storage battery. (Also without *up.*) 🅃 *They charged up the battery overnight.* □ *My car charges the battery whenever the engine runs.*

charged up 1. [of someone] excited; enthusiastic □ *The crowd was really charged up.* □ *Tom is so tired that he cannot get charged up about anything.* **2.** [of something] full of electrical power. (Also without *up.*) □ *The battery is completely charged up.* □ *If the battery isn't charged, the car won't start.*

charm the pants off (of) someone to use charming behavior to persuade someone to do something. (Use with caution.) □ *She is so nice. She just charms the pants off of you.* □ *He will try to charm the pants off you, but you can still refuse to take the job if you don't want to do it.*

cheat on someone to commit adultery; to be unfaithful to one's lover. □ *"Have you been cheating on me?" cried Mrs. Franklin.* □ *"No, I haven't been cheating on you," said Mr. Franklin.*

check in (on someone or something**)** Go to **look in (on** someone or something**)**.

check into something Go to **look into** something.

check out to be verified or authenticated. □ *I spent all afternoon working with my checkbook, trying to get the figures to check out.* □ *The police wouldn't believe that I am who I say I am until they made a few telephone calls to see if my story checked out.*

checks and balances a system where power is kept in control and balance among the various branches of government. □ *The newspaper editor claimed that the system of checks and balances built into our Constitution has been subverted by party politics.* □ *We depend on checks and balances in government to keep despots from seizing control of the government.*

cheek by jowl side by side; close together. □ *The pedestrians had to walk cheek by jowl along the narrow streets.* □ *The two families lived cheek by jowl in one house.*

cheer someone **on** to give words or shouts of encouragement to someone who is trying to do something. □ *John was leading in the race, and the whole crowd was cheering him on.* □ *Sally was doing so well in her performance that I wanted to cheer her on.*

cheer someone **up** to make a sad person happy. □ *When Bill was sick, Ann tried to cheer him up by reading to him.* 🅃 *Interest rates went up, and that cheered up all the bankers.*

cheer up to become more happy. □ *Things are bad for you now, but you'll cheer up when they get better.* □ *Cheer up, Tom! Things can't be that bad.*

cheesed off bored; depressed; annoyed. □ *He was cheesed off with his job.* □ *She was cheesed off when she missed the bus.*

chew someone **out** AND **eat** someone **out** to scold someone; to bawl someone out thoroughly. (Informal. Used much in the military.) □ *The sergeant chewed the corporal out; then the corporal chewed the* *private out.* 🆃 *The boss is always chewing out somebody.* 🆃 *The coach ate out the entire football team because of their poor playing.*

chew the fat AND **chew the rag** to have a chat with someone; to talk very informally with one's close friends. (Informal.) □ *Hi, old buddy! Come in and let's chew the fat.* □ *They usually just sat around and chewed the rag. They never did get much done.*

chew the rag Go to chew the fat.

chicken out (of something**)** to withdraw from something due to fear or cowardice. (Informal.) □ *Jane was going to go parachuting with us, but she chickened out at the last minute.* □ *I'd never chicken out of parachute jumping, because I'd never agree to do it in the first place!*

The **chickens have come home to roost.** All the problems have returned to the person who caused them and that person must now solve them or take the blame. (Literal for chickens whose home is a chicken house. See also come home (to roost).) □ *You took on too much credit card debt and now you are broke. The chickens have finally come home to roost.* □ *Your car broke down because you never changed the oil. The chickens have come home to roost.*

child's play something very easy to do. □ *The test was child's play to her.* □ *Finding the right street was child's play with a map.*

chilled to the bone very cold. □ *I was chilled to the bone in that snowstorm.* □ *The children were chilled to the bone in the unheated room.*

chime in (with something**)** to add one's voice to something; to add something to the discussion, usually by interrupting. □ *Billy chimed in by reminding us to come to dinner.* □ *Everyone chimed in on the final chorus of the song.*

chink in one's **armor** a special weakness that provides a means for attacking or impressing someone otherwise invulnerable. □ *His love for his child is the chink in his armor.* □ *Jane's insecurity is a chink in her armor.*

chip in (on something**)** AND **chip in** something **on** something**; chip** something **in (on** something**)** to contribute a small amount of money to a fund that will be used to buy something. □ *Would you care to chip in on a gift for the teacher?* □ *Yes, I'd be happy to chip in.* □ *Could you chip in a dollar on the gift, please?*

chip in something **on** something Go to chip in (on something).

a **chip off the old block** a person (usually a male) who behaves in the same way as his father or resembles his father. (Usually informal.) □ *John looks like his father—a real chip off the old block.* □ *Bill Jones, Jr., is a chip off the old block. He's a banker just like his father.*

chip something **in (on** something**)** Go to chip in (on something).

chips and dip potato chips, or some other kind of crisply fried substance, and a sauce or dressing to dip them into before eating them. □ *There were tons of chips and dip and all kinds of cold pop available for everyone.*

chisel someone **out of** something to cheat someone to get money or belongings. □ *The company tried to chisel the government out of taxes it owed.* □ *Bill chiseled his little sister out of her allowance.*

choke someone **up** to make a person become overemotional and speechless; to make a person begin to cry. (Informal.) □ *The sight of all those smiling people choked Bob up, and he couldn't go on speaking.* 🆃 *The funeral procession choked up the whole family.*

choke something **off** to stifle something; to force something to an end. □ *The car ran over the hose and choked the water off.* 🆃 *The president choked off the debate.*

chomp at the bit Go to champ at the bit.

choose up sides to form into two opposing teams by having a leader or captain take turns choosing players. □ *Let's choose up sides and play baseball.* □ *When*

I choose up sides, all the best players don't end up on the same team.

claim a life [for something] to take the life of someone. □ *The killer tornado claimed the lives of six people at the trailer park.* □ *The athlete's life was claimed in a skiing accident.*

clam up to shut up; to refuse to talk; to close one's mouth (as tightly as a clam closes its shell). (Slang.) □ *You talk too much, John. Clam up!* □ *When they tried to question her, she clammed up.*

clamp down (on someone or something**)** to become strict with someone; to become strict about something. (Also literal.) □ *Because Bob's grades were getting worse, his parents clamped down on him.* □ *The police have clamped down on speeders in this town.* □ *Things have already gone too far. It's too late to clamp down.*

clap eyes on someone or something to see someone or something, perhaps for the first time; to **set eyes on someone or something**. (Informal.) □ *I wish she had never clapped eyes on her fiancé.* □ *I haven't clapped eyes on a red squirrel for years.*

clean as a hound's tooth Go to (as) clean as a hound's tooth.

clean as a whistle Go to (as) clean as a whistle.

clean out (of something**)** Go to fresh out (of something).

clean up to make a great profit. (Also literal. Informal.) □ *John won at the races and really cleaned up.* □ *Ann cleaned up by taking a job selling encyclopedias.*

clean up one's **act** to reform one's conduct; to improve one's performance. (Informal. Originally referred to polishing one's stage performance.) 🅃 *Since Sally cleaned her act up, she has become very productive.* □ *If you don't clean up your act, you'll be sent home.*

clear as a bell Go to (as) clear as a bell.

clear as crystal Go to (as) clear as crystal.

clear as mud Go to (as) clear as mud.

clear as vodka Go to (as) clear as vodka.

clear of something without touching something; away from something. □ *Please stand clear of the doors while the train is moving.* □ *Make sure the dog moves clear of the driveway before backing the car up.*

clear out to get out (of a place); to leave. □ *All right, you people, clear out of here now.* □ *I knew right then that it was time to clear out.*

clear sailing progress made without any difficulty; an easy situation. □ *Once you've passed that exam, it will be clear sailing.* □ *Working there was not all clear sailing. The boss had a very bad temper.*

clear someone's **name** to prove that someone is not guilty of a crime or misdeed. □ *I was accused of theft, but I cleared my name.* □ *The student was accused of cheating, but her name was cleared.*

clear something **up 1.** to explain something; to solve a mystery. □ *I think that we can clear this matter up without calling in the police.* 🅃 *First we have to clear up the problem of the missing jewels.* **2.** to cure a disease or a medical condition. (Especially facial pimples.) □ *There is no medicine that will clear pimples up.* 🅃 *The doctor will give you something to clear up your cold.*

clear the air to get rid of doubts or hard feelings. (Also literal. Sometimes this is said about an argument or other unpleasantness.) □ *All right, let's discuss this frankly. It'll be better if we clear the air.* □ *Mr. and Mrs. Brown always seem to have to clear the air with a big argument before they can be sociable.*

clear the decks get out of the way; get out of this area. (From a naval expression, "Clear the decks for action!" urging seaman to prepare for battle or other action.) □ *Clear the decks! Here comes the teacher.* □ *Clear the decks and take your seats.*

clear the table to remove the dishes and other eating utensils from the table after a meal. (The opposite of **set the table**.) □ *Will you please help clear the table?* □ *After you clear the table, we'll play cards.*

clear up 1. [for a problem] to become solved. ☐ *This matter won't clear up by itself.* ☐ *The confusion cleared up very quickly when I explained.* **2.** [for a disease] to cure itself or run its course. ☐ *I told you your pimples would clear up without special medicine.* ☐ *My rash cleared up in a week.*

climb on the bandwagon to join others in supporting someone or something. (See also get on the bandwagon, jump on the bandwagon.) ☐ *Come join us! Climb on the bandwagon and support Senator Smith!* ☐ *Look at all those people climbing on the bandwagon! They don't know what they are getting into!*

climb the wall(s) to do something desperate when one is extremely anxious, bored, or excited. (Informal or slang.) ☐ *I'm so upset I could climb the wall.* ☐ *The meeting was so long and the speaker so boring that most of the audience wanted to climb the wall.*

clip someone's **wings** to restrain someone; to reduce or put an end to a teenager's privileges. (Informal.) ☐ *You had better learn to get home on time, or I will clip your wings.* ☐ *My mother clipped my wings. I can't go out tonight.*

cloak-and-dagger involving secrecy and plotting. ☐ *A great deal of cloak-and-dagger stuff goes on in political circles.* ☐ *A lot of cloak-and-dagger activity was involved in the appointment of the director.*

close as two coats of paint Go to (as) close as two coats of paint.

close at hand within reach; handy. (See also at hand.) ☐ *I'm sorry, but your letter isn't close at hand. Please remind me what you said in it.* ☐ *When you're cooking, you should keep all the ingredients close at hand.*

close enough for government work fairly close or accurate. (Jocular.) ☐ *I can do math pretty well. Close enough for government work anyway.* ☐ *This isn't quite right, but it's close enough for government work.*

close in (on someone or something**)** to overwhelm or surround someone or something. ☐ *My problems are closing in on me.* ☐ *The wolves closed in on the elk.* ☐ *They howled as they closed in.*

close one's **eyes to** something to ignore something; to pretend that something is not really happening. ☐ *You can't close your eyes to hunger in the world.* ☐ *I just closed my eyes to the problem and pretended that it wasn't there.*

close ranks to move closer together in a military formation. (See also close ranks (behind someone or something); close ranks (with someone).) ☐ *The soldiers closed ranks and marched on the enemy.* ☐ *All right! Stop that talking and close ranks.*

close ranks (behind someone or something**)** to support someone or something; to back someone or something. ☐ *We will close ranks behind the candidate.* ☐ *She needs our help. Let's close ranks behind her and give her the support she needs.*

close ranks (with someone**)** to join with someone. ☐ *We can fight this menace only if we close ranks.* ☐ *Let's all close ranks with Ann and adopt her suggestions.*

close something **down** AND **shut** something **down** to make something stop operating; to put something out of business. ☐ *The police closed the factory down.* 🅃 *The manager shut down the factory for the holidays.* 🅃 *The city council closed down the amusement park.*

close the books (on someone or something**)** to put an end to a matter that concerns someone or something. (*The books* here refers to financial accounting records.) ☐ *It's time to close the books on the Franklin case.* ☐ *Yes, let's close the books on Mr. Franklin.* ☐ *You closed the books too soon. Here is some new information.*

close the door on someone or something Go to shut the door on someone or something.

close to home AND **where** one **lives** affecting one personally and intimately. (Informal.) ☐ *Her remarks were a bit too close to home. I was afraid she was discussing me!* ☐ *She's got me figured out all right. She knows where I live.* ☐ *Every criticism she made of the performance hit a little too close to home for my comfort. I* *didn't know I was so bad!* ☐ *When you go through an experience like that and see the horror of a hurricane face to face, that sort of gets you where you live!*

close to someone fond of someone; very good friends with someone. ☐ *Tom is very close to Mary. They may get married.* ☐ *Mr. Smith isn't exactly close to Mrs. Smith.*

close up shop to quit working, for the day or forever. (Informal.) ☐ *It's five o'clock. Time to close up shop.* ☐ *I can't make any money in this town. The time has come to close up shop and move to another town.*

closefisted (with money) Go to tightfisted (with money).

cloud up 1. [for the sky] to get cloudy, as if it were going to rain. ☐ *All of a sudden it clouded up and began to rain.* ☐ *It usually clouds up at sunset.* **2.** [for someone] to grow very sad, as if to cry. (See also turn on the waterworks.) ☐ *The baby clouded up and let out a howl.* ☐ *Whenever Mary got homesick, she'd cloud up. She really wanted to go home.*

clue someone **in (on** something**)** to inform someone of something. (Informal.) ☐ *Please clue me in on what's going on.* ☐ *Yes, clue her in.*

clutch at straws to continue to seek solutions, ideas, or hopes that are insubstantial. ☐ *When you talk of inheriting money, you are just clutching at straws.* ☐ *That is not a real solution to the problem. You are just clutching at straws.*

The **coast is clear.** There is no visible danger. ☐ *I'm going to stay hidden here until the coast is clear.* ☐ *You can come out of your hiding place now. The coast is clear.*

coast-to-coast from the Atlantic to the Pacific Oceans (in the continental U.S.A.); all the land between the Atlantic and Pacific Oceans. ☐ *My voice was once heard on a coast-to-coast radio broadcast.* ☐ *Our car made the coast-to-coast trip in eighty hours.*

coat and tie [for men] a jacket or sports coat and necktie. (A standard of dress between casual and a suit.) ☐ *My brother was not wearing a coat and tie, and they would not admit him into the restaurant.* ☐ *I always carry a coat and tie in my car just in case I have to dress up a little for something.*

cock-and-bull story a silly, made-up story; a story that is a lie. ☐ *Don't give me that cock-and-bull story.* ☐ *I asked for an explanation, and all I got was your ridiculous cock-and-bull story!*

cock of the walk someone who acts more important than others in a group. ☐ *The deputy manager was cock of the walk until the new manager arrived.* ☐ *He loved acting cock of the walk and ordering everyone about.*

cocky as the king of spades Go to (as) cocky as the king of spades.

coffee and Danish a cup of coffee and a Danish sweet roll. ☐ *A few of us like to have coffee and Danish before we start work.* ☐ *Coffee and Danish is not my idea of a good breakfast!*

coffee-table book a book that is more suitable for display than for reading, typically, an illustrated book left on the coffee table for visitors to examine. ☐ *This book is more of a coffee-table book than an art book. I prefer something more scholarly.* ☐ *We purchased a coffee-table book for Jan's birthday.*

coffee, tea, or milk a choice of beverage. (Originally used by airline personnel when offering something to drink to the passengers.) ☐ *She asked me if I wanted coffee, tea, or milk, and I chose just plain water.* ☐ *Would you prefer coffee, tea, or milk to go with your meal?*

cold as a witch's caress Go to (as) cold as a witch's caress.

cold as a witch's tit Go to (as) cold as a witch's tit.

cold as marble Go to (as) cold as marble.

cold comfort no comfort or consolation at all. ☐ *She knows there are others worse off than she is, but that's cold comfort.* ☐ *It was cold comfort to the student that others had failed as badly as he did.*

a **cold fish** a person who is distant and unfeeling. (Informal or slang. Preceded by *be, become, seem like,* or *act like.*) □ *Bob is so dull—a real cold fish.* □ *She hardly ever speaks to anyone. She's a cold fish.*

cold, hard cash cash, not checks or promises. (Informal.) □ *I want to be paid in cold, hard cash, and I want to be paid now!* □ *Pay me now! Cash on the barrelhead—cold, hard cash.*

come about 1. to happen. □ *How did this come about?* □ *This came about due to the severe weather.* **2.** [for a sailboat] to turn. □ *Look how easily this boat comes about.* □ *Now, practice making the boat come about.*

come a cropper to have a misfortune; to fail. (From an expression meaning to fall off one's horse.) □ *Bob invested all his money in the stock market just before it fell. Boy, did he come a cropper.* □ *Jane was out all night before she took her tests. She really came a cropper.*

come across someone or something AND **run across** someone or something to find someone or something; to discover someone or something. □ *John came across a book he had been looking for.* □ *Where did you run across that lovely skirt?*

Come again. 1. Come back.; Return some other time. □ *I'm so glad you enjoyed our party. Please come again sometime.* □ *The store clerk gave me my change and my purchase and said, "Thank you. Come again."* **2.** Say it again. I did not hear you. (Folksy. Usually **Come again?**) □ *TOM: Hello, Grandfather. GRANDFATHER: Come again? You'll have to talk louder.* □ *The farmer looked at me and said, "Come again?"*

Come and get it! Dinner is ready. Come and eat it! (Folksy.) □ *A shout was heard from the kitchen, "Come and get it!"* □ *No one says "Come and get it!" at a formal dinner.*

come and gone already arrived and already departed. □ *No, Joy is not here. She's come and gone.* □ *Sorry, you are too late for your appointment. The doctor has come and gone.*

come apart at the seams suddenly to lose one's emotional self-control. (Informal. From the literal sense referring to something falling apart. See also **burst at the seams; fall apart at the seams.**) □ *Bill was so upset that he almost came apart at the seams.* □ *I couldn't take anymore. I just came apart at the seams.*

come (a)round 1. finally to agree or consent (to something). □ *I thought he'd never agree, but in the end he came around.* □ *She came round only after we argued for an hour.* **2.** to return to consciousness; to wake up. □ *He came around after we threw cold water in his face.* □ *The boxer was knocked out, but came round in a few seconds.*

come as no surprise not to be surprising [for someone] to learn [something]. □ *It will come as no surprise for you to learn that the company is losing money this year.* □ *It came as no surprise that the president had been lying.*

come away empty-handed to return without anything. (See also **go away empty-handed.**) □ *All right, go gambling. Don't come away empty-handed, though.* □ *Go to the bank and ask for the loan again. This time don't come away empty-handed.*

come by something **1.** to travel by a specific carrier, such as a plane, a boat, or a car. □ *We came by train. It's more relaxing.* □ *Next time, we'll come by plane. It's faster.* **2.** to find or get something. □ *How did you come by that haircut?* □ *Where did you come by that new shirt?*

come by something **honestly 1.** to get something honestly. □ *Don't worry. I came by this watch honestly.* □ *I have a feeling she didn't come by it honestly.* **2.** to inherit something—a character trait—from one's parents. □ *I know I'm mean. I came by it honestly, though.* □ *She came by her kindness honestly.*

come clean (with someone**)** to be completely honest with someone; to confess (everything) to someone. □ *The lawyer said, "I can help you only if you come clean* *with me." ☐ All right, I'll come clean. Here is the whole story.*

come down [for something] to descend (to someone) through inheritance. ☐ *All my silverware came down to me from my great-grandmother.* ☐ *The antique furniture came down through my mother's family.*

come down hard on someone or something to attack vigorously; to scold someone severely. ☐ *Tom's parents really came down hard on him for coming home late.* 🅃 *Yes, they came down on him hard.*

come down in the world to lose one's social position or financial standing. ☐ *Mr. Jones has really come down in the world since he lost his job.* ☐ *If I were unemployed, I'm sure I'd come down in the world, too.*

come down to earth to become realistic; to become alert to what is going on around one. (Informal.) ☐ *You have very good ideas, John, but you must come down to earth. We can't possibly afford any of your suggestions.* ☐ *Pay attention to what is going on. Come down to earth and join the discussion.*

come down to something to be reduced to something; to amount to no more than something. (Informal. Similar to **boil down to** something.) ☐ *It comes down to whether you want to go to the movies or stay at home and watch television.* ☐ *It came down to either getting a job or going back to college.*

come down with something to become ill with some disease. ☐ *I'm afraid I'm coming down with a cold.* ☐ *I'll probably come down with pneumonia.*

come from far and wide to come from many different places. ☐ *Everyone was there. They came from far and wide.* ☐ *We have foods that come from far and wide.*

come from nowhere to come as a surprise with no warning. ☐ *The dogs came from nowhere and attacked my cat.* ☐ *The whole set of problems came from nowhere. There was no way we could have foreseen them.*

come full circle to return to the original position or state of affairs. ☐ *The family sold the house generations ago, but things have come full circle and one of their descendants lives there now.* ☐ *The employer's power was reduced by the unions at one point, but matters have come full circle again.*

come hell or high water no matter what happens. (Informal. Use caution with *hell*.) ☐ *I'll be there tomorrow, come hell or high water.* ☐ *Come hell or high water, I intend to have my own home.*

come home (to roost) [for a problem] to return to cause trouble [for someone]. (See also **The chickens have come home to roost.**) ☐ *As I feared, all my problems came home to roost.* ☐ *Yes, problems all come home eventually.*

come home to someone to become apparent to someone; to be realized by someone. ☐ *The truth of the matter suddenly came home to me.* ☐ *It all came home to me while I was taking a bath. Suddenly I understood everything.*

come in a body AND **arrive in a body** to arrive as a group. ☐ *All the guests came in a body.* ☐ *Things become very busy when everyone arrives in a body.*

come in for something AND **fall in for** something to receive something; to acquire something. ☐ *Billy came in for a good bawling-out when he arrived home.* ☐ *Mary came in for a tremendous amount of money when her aunt died.* ☐ *Sally fell in for a lot of trouble when she bought a used car.*

come in handy to be useful or convenient. (Informal.) ☐ *A small television set in the bedroom would come in handy.* ☐ *A good hammer always comes in handy.* ☐ *A nice cool drink would come in handy about now.*

come in out of the rain to become alert and sensible; to **come down to earth**. (Also literal. See also **not know enough to come in out of the rain.**) ☐ *Pay attention, Sally! Come in out of the rain!* ☐ *Bill will fail if he doesn't come in out of the rain and study.*

come into its own Go to come into one's own.

come into one's **own** AND **come into its own 1.** [for one] to achieve one's proper recognition. □ *Sally finally came into her own.* □ *After years of trying, she finally came into her own.* **2.** [for something] to achieve its proper recognition. □ *The idea of an electric car finally came into its own.* □ *Film as an art medium finally came into its own.*

come into something to inherit something. (Also literal. See also **come in for** something, which is very close in meaning.) □ *Jane came into a small fortune when her aunt died.* □ *Mary came into a house and a new car when her rich uncle died.*

come of age to reach an age when one is old enough to own property, get married, and sign legal contracts. □ *When Jane comes of age, she will buy her own car.* □ *Sally, who came of age last month, entered into an agreement to purchase a house.*

come off to happen; to take place. (Also literal referring to something that becomes disconnected. Informal.) □ *What time does this party come off?* □ *How did your speech come off?* □ *It came off very well.*

Come off it! Tell the truth!; Be serious! (Slang.) □ *Come off it, Bill! I don't believe you!* □ *Come on, Jane. Come off it! That can't be true.*

come off second-best to win second place or worse; to lose out to someone else. □ *John came off second-best in the race.* □ *Why do I always come off second-best in an argument with you?*

come on to hurry up; to follow (someone). □ *Come on! I'm in a hurry.* □ *If you don't come on, we'll miss the train.*

come on like gangbusters to approach people in a wild and exciting manner; to seem very active and pushy when approaching people. □ *Why is she so unpolished? She comes on like gangbusters and frightens people away.* □ *The people in this town come on like gangbusters and they seem very rude at first.*

come on somehow to appear as having certain characteristics to other people. (Informal. Especially with *strong,* which means "intensely." See also the previous entry.) □ *Jane comes on like a very unpleasant person.* □ *She really comes on strong.* □ *John doesn't care how he comes on.*

come on the scene AND **arrive on the scene** to appear in a certain area or place. (Used in particular in police reports or dramatizations of police reports.) □ *What time did the picnickers come on the scene?* □ *The witness arrived on the scene at about 7:13 in the evening.*

come out 1. to become; to turn out. (Also literal.) □ *We'll just have to wait and see how things come out.* □ *I'm baking a cake. I hope it comes out okay.* **2.** to be presented to the public; to be released to the public. □ *My new book came out last month.* □ *Mary Ann Smith came out last fall at a lovely party.* **3.** Go to **come out (of the closet).**

come out ahead to end up with a profit; to improve one's situation. (Compare this with **break even.**) □ *I hope you come out ahead with your investments.* □ *It took a lot of money to buy the house, but I think I'll come out ahead.*

come out for someone or something to announce one's support for someone or something. □ *I'm coming out for Senator Brown's reelection.* □ *All the employees came out for a longer workweek.*

come out in the wash to work out all right. (Informal. This means that problems or difficulties will go away as dirt goes away in the process of washing.) □ *Don't worry about that problem. It'll all come out in the wash.* □ *This trouble will go away. It'll come out in the wash.*

come out of left field [for a problem or dilemma] to come from an unexpected place. □ *This new problem came out of left field. We were really surprised.* □ *Your remarks came out of left field. I can't understand your complaint.*

come out of nowhere to appear suddenly. (Almost the same as **appear out of**

nowhere.) ☐ *Suddenly, a truck came out of nowhere.* ☐ *Without warning, the storm came out of nowhere.*

come out of one's **shell** to become more friendly; to be more sociable. (Refers to a turtle that sticks its head and legs out of its shell when it feels safe.) ☐ *Ann, you should come out of your shell and spend more time with your friends.* ☐ *Come out of your shell, Tom. Go out and make some friends.*

come out of the blue to appear suddenly as if falling from the sky. (*The blue* refers to the blue sky.) ☐ *This idea came out of the blue, and I think it is a good one.* ☐ *Sally showed up at the party even though no one told her where it was. She just came out of the blue.*

come out (of the closet) 1. to reveal one's secret interests. ☐ *Tom Brown came out of the closet and admitted that he likes to knit.* ☐ *It's time that all of you lovers of chamber music came out of the closet and attended our concerts.* **2.** to reveal that one is a homosexual. (See also **come out**.) ☐ *Tom surprised his parents when he came out of the closet.* ☐ *It was difficult for him to come out of the closet.*

come out with something to say something; to announce something. ☐ *Sometimes Jane comes out with the most interesting comments.* ☐ *Jane came out with a long string of curse words.*

come over 1. to join this party or side; to change sides or affiliation. ☐ *Tom was formerly an enemy spy, but last year he came over.* ☐ *I thought that Bill was a Republican. When did he come over?* **2.** to come for a visit. ☐ *See if Ann wants to come over.* ☐ *I can't come over. I'm busy.*

come someone's **way** to come to someone. ☐ *I wish a large sum of money would come my way.* ☐ *I hope that no bad luck comes my way.*

come through 1. to do what one is expected to do, especially under difficult conditions. ☐ *You can depend on Jane. She'll always come through.* ☐ *We thought that there would be no food, but Tom came through at the last minute with everything we needed.* **2.** [for something] to be approved; [for something] to gain approval. ☐ *Our mortgage loan application finally came through!* ☐ *Your papers came through, and you can be sure that the matter has been taken care of.*

come through something **with flying colors** to survive something quite well. (See also **with flying colors**.) ☐ *Todd came through the test with flying colors.* ☐ *Mr. Franklin came through the operation with flying colors.*

come to to become conscious; to wake up. ☐ *We threw a little cold water in his face, and he came to immediately.* ☐ *Come to, John! You act as if you were in a daze.*

come to a bad end to have a disaster, perhaps one that is deserved or expected; to die an unfortunate death. ☐ *My old car came to a bad end. Its engine burned up.* ☐ *The evil merchant came to a bad end.*

come to a dead end to come to an absolute stopping point. ☐ *The building project came to a dead end.* ☐ *The street came to a dead end.* ☐ *We were driving along and came to a dead end.*

come to a head to come to a crucial point; to come to a point when a problem must be solved. ☐ *Remember my problem with my neighbors? Well, last night the whole thing came to a head.* ☐ *The battle between the two factions of the city council came to a head yesterday.*

come to an end to stop; to finish. ☐ *The party came to an end at midnight.* ☐ *Her life came to an end late yesterday.*

come to an untimely end to come to an early death. ☐ *Poor Mr. Jones came to an untimely end in a car accident.* ☐ *Cancer caused Mrs. Smith to come to an untimely end.*

come to a pretty pass to develop into a bad, unfortunate, or difficult situation. ☐ *Things have come to a pretty pass when people have to beg in the streets.* ☐ *When parents are afraid of their children, things have come to a pretty pass.*

come to a standstill to stop, temporarily or permanently. ☐ *The building project* *came to a standstill because the workers went on strike.* ☐ *The party came to a standstill until the lights were turned on again.*

come to a stop [for someone or something] to stop moving or happening. ☐ *The bus finally came to a stop so I could get off.* ☐ *The loud noise finally came to a stop.*

come to blows (over something**)** [for people] to become increasingly angry and begin to fight about something, usually by striking blows, or verbally. ☐ *They got excited about the accident, but they never actually came to blows over it.* ☐ *Yes, they aren't the kind of people who come to blows.*

come to grief to fail; to have trouble or grief. ☐ *The artist wept when her canvas came to grief.* ☐ *The wedding party came to grief when the bride passed out.*

come to grips with something to face something; to comprehend something. ☐ *He found it difficult to come to grips with his grandmother's death.* ☐ *Many students have a hard time coming to grips with algebra.*

come to life to become alive or lively. (Usually used in a figurative sense.) ☐ *The party came to life about midnight.* ☐ *As the anesthetic wore off, the patient came to life.*

come to light to become known. ☐ *Some interesting facts about your past have just come to light.* ☐ *If too many bad things come to light, you may lose your job.*

come to mind [for a thought or idea] to enter into one's consciousness. (Compare this with **cross** someone's **mind.**) ☐ *Do I know a good barber? No one comes to mind right now.* ☐ *Another idea comes to mind. Why not cut your own hair?*

come to naught Go to come to nothing.

come to nothing AND **come to naught** to amount to nothing; to be worthless. ☐ *So all my hard work comes to nothing.* ☐ *Yes, the whole project comes to naught.*

come to one's **senses** to wake up; to become conscious; to start thinking clearly. ☐ *John, come to your senses. You're being quite stupid.* ☐ *In the morning I don't come to my senses until I have had two cups of coffee.*

come to pass to happen. (Formal.) ☐ *When did all of this come to pass?* ☐ *When will this event come to pass?*

come to rest to stop moving. ☐ *When the car comes to rest, you can get in.* ☐ *The leaf fell and came to rest at my feet.*

come to terms with someone or something **1.** to come to an agreement with someone. ☐ *I finally came to terms with my lawyer about his fee.* ☐ *Bob, you have to come to terms with your father's wishes.* **2.** to learn to accept someone or something. (See also **come to grips with** something.) ☐ *She had to come to terms with the loss of her sight.* ☐ *It's time you came to terms with your boss and her unreasonable demands.*

come to the fore to become prominent; to become important. ☐ *The question of salary has now come to the fore.* ☐ *Since his great showing in court, my lawyer has really come to the fore in city politics.*

come to the point AND **get to the point** to get to the important part (of something). ☐ *He has been talking a long time. I wish he would come to the point.* ☐ *Quit wasting time! Get to the point!* ☐ *We are talking about money, Bob! Come on, get to the point.*

come to the same thing Go to amount to the same thing.

come to think of it I just remembered [something]. ☐ *Come to think of it, I know someone who can help.* ☐ *I have a screwdriver in the trunk of my car, come to think of it.*

come true [for a dream or a wish] actually to happen. ☐ *When I got married, all my dreams came true.* ☐ *Coming to the big city was like having my wish come true.*

come unglued to lose emotional control; to have a mental breakdown; to break out into tears or laughter. (Slang.) ☐ *When Sally heard the joke, she almost came unglued.* ☐ *When the bank took away my car, I came unglued and cried and cried.*

come up to happen unexpectedly. (Also literal.) □ *I'm sorry, I cannot come to your party. Something has come up.* □ *The storm came up so quickly that I almost got blown away.*

come up in the world to improve one's status or situation in life. □ *Since Mary got her new job, she has really come up in the world.* □ *A good education helped my brother come up in the world.*

come up smelling like roses to end up looking good or respectable after being involved in some difficult or notorious affair. □ *It was a nasty political campaign, but both candidates came up smelling like roses.* □ *I was not surprised that my congressional representative came up smelling like roses after his colleagues investigated him.*

come up with someone or something to find or supply someone or something. □ *I came up with a date at the last minute.* □ *My mom is always able to come up with a snack for me in the afternoon.* □ *I don't have the tool you need, but I'll see if I can come up with something.*

come what may no matter what might happen. □ *I'll be home for the holidays, come what may.* □ *Come what may, the mail will get delivered.*

come within an ace of doing something Go to come within an inch of doing something.

come within an inch of doing something AND **come within an ace of** doing something almost to do something; to come very close to doing something. □ *I came within an inch of going into the army.* □ *I came within an inch of falling off the roof.* □ *She came within an ace of buying the house.*

come with the territory to be expected under circumstances like this. (Refers to the details and difficulties attendant to something like the assignment of a specific sales territory to a salesperson. When one accepts the assignment, one accepts the problems.) □ *There is a lot of paperwork in this job. Oh, well, I guess it comes with the territory.* □ *There are problems, but that comes with the territory.*

comfortable as an old shoe Go to (as) comfortable as an old shoe.

commit something **to memory** to memorize something. □ *We all committed the Gettysburg Address to memory.* 🅃 *I committed to memory the whole list of names and numbers.*

common as an old shoe Go to (as) common as an old shoe.

common as dirt Go to (as) common as dirt.

con someone **out of** something to trick someone out of money or something of value. (Slang.) □ *Anne conned her little sister out of her allowance.* □ *Dave conned me out of my autographed baseball.*

conceited as a barber's cat Go to (as) conceited as a barber's cat.

confide in someone to tell secrets or personal matters to someone. □ *Sally always confided in her sister Ann.* □ *She didn't feel that she could confide in her mother.*

conk out 1. [for someone] to collapse as from exhaustion. (Slang.) □ *I was so tired I just went home and conked out.* □ *I was afraid I would conk out while I was driving.* **2.** [for something] to break down; to quit running. (Slang.) □ *My car conked out finally.* □ *I hope my computer doesn't conk out.*

conspicuous by one's **absence** to have one's absence (from an event) noticed. □ *We missed you last night. You were conspicuous by your absence.* □ *How could the bride's father miss the wedding? He was certainly conspicuous by his absence.*

contradiction in terms a statement containing a seeming contradiction. □ *A wealthy pauper is a contradiction in terms.* □ *A straight-talking politician may seem a contradiction in terms.*

contrary to something in spite of something; regardless of something. □ *Contrary to what you might think, I am neat and tidy.* □ *Contrary to public opinion, my uncle is well and healthy.*

control the purse strings to be in charge of the money in a business or a household. □ *I control the purse strings at our house.* □ *Mr. Williams is the treasurer. He controls the purse strings.*

cook someone's **goose** to damage or ruin someone. □ *I cooked my own goose by not showing up on time.* □ *Sally cooked Bob's goose for treating her the way he did.*

cook something **to perfection** to cook something perfectly. □ *John cooked my steak to perfection.* □ *The entire dinner was cooked to perfection!*

cook something **up** to plot something; to improvise something. (Also literal.) □ *Mary cooked an interesting party up at the last minute.* 🅃 *Let me see if I can cook up a way to get you some money.*

cook the accounts to cheat in bookkeeping; to make the accounts appear to balance when they do not. □ *Jane was sent to jail for cooking the accounts of her mother's store.* □ *It's hard to tell whether she really cooked the accounts or just didn't know how to add.*

cooking with gas doing things the right way. (Also literal. Informal. From an advertising slogan.) □ *That's great. Now you're cooking with gas.* □ *Things are moving along nicely with the project. The entire staff is really cooking with gas.*

cool as a cucumber Go to (as) cool as a cucumber.

cool down Go to cool off.

Cool it! Calm down!; Take it easy! (Slang.) □ *Don't get mad, Bob. Cool it!* □ *Cool it, you guys! No fighting around here.*

cool off AND **cool down 1.** to lose or reduce heat. □ *I wish my soup would cool off. I'm hungry.* □ *It'll cool down this evening, after dusk.* **2.** to let one's anger die away. □ *I'm sorry I got angry. I'll cool off in a minute.* □ *Cool off, Tom. There is no sense getting so excited.* **3.** to let one's passion or love die away. □ *TED: Is Bob still in love with Jane? BILL: No, he's cooled off a lot.* □ *TED: I thought that they were both cooling down.*

cool one's **heels** to wait (for someone). (Informal.) □ *I spent all afternoon cooling my heels in the waiting room while the doctor talked on the telephone.* □ *All right. If you can't behave properly, just sit down here and cool your heels until I call you.*

cool someone **down** AND **cool** someone **off 1.** to reduce someone's anger. (Also literal.) □ *I just stared at him while he was yelling. I knew that would cool him down.* □ *The coach talked to them for a long time. That cooled them off.* **2.** to reduce someone's passion or love. □ *When she slapped him, that really cooled him down.* □ *Dating Mary was too intense, so Bill cooled himself off by dating Sally for a while.*

cool someone **off** Go to **cool** someone **down**.

cop a plea to plead guilty to a crime in hopes of receiving a lighter punishment. (Slang, especially criminal slang.) □ *The robber copped a plea and got only two years in jail.* □ *When you cop a plea, it saves the court system a lot of money.*

cop out to get out of a difficult situation; to sneak out of a difficult situation. (Slang.) □ *At the last minute she copped out on us.* □ *Things were going badly for Senator Phillips, so he copped out by resigning.*

a **copycat** a person who copies or mimics what someone else does. (Usually juvenile. Can be preceded by *be, become, seem like,* or *act like.*) □ *Sally wore a pink dress just like Mary's. Mary called Sally a copycat.* □ *Bill is such a copycat. He bought a coat just like mine.*

cost an arm and a leg to cost too much. □ *It cost an arm and a leg, so I didn't buy it.* □ *Why should a little plastic part cost an arm and a leg?*

cost a pretty penny to cost a lot of money. □ *I'll bet that diamond cost a pretty penny.* □ *You can be sure that house cost a pretty penny. It has seven bathrooms.*

cough something **up** to produce something unwillingly (that someone has requested). (Also literal. Informal.) □ *All right, Bill. Cough the stolen diamonds up or else.* □ *Okay, okay. I'll cough them up.* 🅃 *Bill had to cough up forty dollars to pay for the broken window.*

Could be better. satisfactory, but capable of improvement. □ *The pie's okay, but could be better.* □ *Q: How do you feel? A: Could be better.*

Could be worse. satisfactory, but not as bad as it could be. □ *Q: How are things? A: Could be worse.* □ *Things could be worse, and in a little while, they probably will be.*

could do with someone or something to want or need someone or something; to benefit from someone or something. (Compare this with **go for** someone or something.) □ *I could do with a nice cool drink right now.* □ *I could do with some help on this project.* □ *This house could do with some cleaning up.* □ *They said they could do with John to help them finish faster.* □ *My car could do with a bigger engine.*

couldn't be better completely satisfactory. □ *I feeling great and couldn't be better.* □ *We had a wonderful time and our vacation couldn't have been better.*

couldn't be happier totally happy. □ *We are delighted. Couldn't be happier.* □ *They both couldn't be happier since they got married.*

could(n't) care less unable to care at all. (Informal. **Could care less** is almost slang.) □ *John couldn't care less whether he goes to the party or not.* □ *So she won first place. I couldn't care less.* □ *I could care less if I live or die.*

count noses to count people. □ *I'll tell you how many people are here after I count noses.* □ *Everyone is here. Let's count noses so we can order hamburgers.*

count one's **chickens before they hatch** to plan how to utilize good results before they have occurred. (Frequently used in the negative.) □ *You're way ahead of yourself. Don't count your chickens before they hatch.* □ *You may be disappointed if you count your chickens before they hatch.*

count on someone or something to rely on someone or something. □ *Can I count on you to be there at noon?* □ *I want to buy a car I can count on in winter weather.*

count someone **in (on** something**)** to include someone in something. (Compare this with **count** someone **out (for** something**)**.) □ *If you're looking for a group to go mountain climbing, count me in on it.* 🅃 *I would like to count in your entire family, but there isn't enough room.* □ *Please count me in.*

count someone **out (for** something**)** to exclude someone from something. (Compare this with **count** someone **in (on** something**)**.) □ *Please count me out for the party next Saturday. I have other plans.* □ *You should count the whole family out. We are going to the beach for the weekend.*

a **couple of** two; two or three; a few; some; not many. □ *Bill grabbed a couple of beers from the refrigerator.* □ *I hung a couple of pictures on the wall.*

course of action the procedures or sequence of actions that someone will follow to accomplish a goal. □ *I plan to take a course of action that will produce the best results.* □ *The committee planned a course of action that would reduce costs and eliminate employees.*

cover a lot of ground AND **cover a lot of territory 1.** to travel over a great distance; to investigate a wide expanse of land. □ *The prospectors covered a lot of ground, looking for gold.* □ *My car can cover a lot of ground in one day.* **2.** to deal with much information and many facts. □ *The history lecture covered a lot of ground today.* □ *Mr. and Mrs. Franklin always cover a lot of ground when they argue.*

cover a lot of territory Go to cover a lot of ground.

cover for someone **1.** to make excuses for someone; to conceal someone's errors. □ *If I miss class, please cover for me.* □ *If you're late, I'll cover for you.* **2.** to handle someone else's work. □ *Dr. Johnson's partner agreed to cover for him during his vacation.* □ *I'm on duty this afternoon. Will you please cover for me? I have a doctor's appointment.*

cover someone's **tracks (up)** to conceal one's trail; to conceal one's past activities. □

She was able to cover her tracks up so that they couldn't find her. 🅃 *It's easy to cover up your tracks if you aren't well known.* ☐ *The robber failed to cover his tracks.*

cover something **up** to conceal something. (Also literal.) 🅃 *They covered up the truth about the crime.* ☐ *We'll cover this little matter up and make up a story for the press.*

cover the territory Go to cover the waterfront.

cover the waterfront AND **cover the territory** to deal with many things, much space, or much information from many points of view. (Informal.) ☐ *That lecture really covered the waterfront. I could hardly follow it.* ☐ *Why can't she stick to the point? She has to cover the territory every time she talks.*

cozy up (to someone**)** to be extra friendly with someone, perhaps in hope of special favors in return. (Informal or slang.) ☐ *Look at that lawyer cozying up to the judge!* ☐ *Lawyers who cozy up like that usually get into big trouble.*

crack a book to open a book to study. (Slang. Almost always in the negative.) ☐ *I passed that test with an A, and I didn't even crack a book.* ☐ *If you think you can get through college without cracking a book, you're wrong.*

crack a joke to tell a joke. (Informal.) ☐ *She's never serious. She's always cracking jokes.* ☐ *As long as she's cracking jokes, she's okay.*

crack a smile to smile a little, perhaps reluctantly. (Informal.) ☐ *She cracked a smile, so I knew she was kidding.* ☐ *The soldier cracked a smile at the wrong time and had to march for an hour as punishment.*

crack down (on someone or something**)** to be hard on someone or something; to enforce a rule or law more strenuously. ☐ *They are cracking down on speeding around here.* ☐ *It's about time they cracked down.*

crack open a bottle to open a bottle; to remove the cork or seal from a bottle, usually a bottle of an alcoholic drink. ☐ *They cracked open a bottle to celebrate her arrival.* ☐ *Let's crack open a bottle of champagne and celebrate.*

crack someone or something **up 1.** [with *something*] to crash something; to destroy something (in an accident). ☐ *The driver cracked the car up in an accident.* 🅃 *The pilot cracked up the plane.* **2.** [with *someone*] to make someone laugh. ☐ *She told a joke that really cracked us up.* 🅃 *I cracked up my history class with a silly remark.*

crack something **wide open** to expose and reveal some great wrongdoing. (Also literal.) ☐ *The police cracked the drug ring wide open.* ☐ *The newspaper story cracked the trouble at city hall wide open.*

crack up 1. [for a plane, boat, car, etc.] to crash. ☐ *The plane cracked up in the storm.* ☐ *The boat cracked up on the rocks.* **2.** [for someone] to break out in laughter. ☐ *The audience really cracked up during the second act.* ☐ *The class cracked up when I told my joke, but the teacher didn't like it.* **3.** to go crazy. (Slang.) ☐ *The mayor cracked up after only a year in office.* ☐ *I was afraid the mayor would crack up because of too much work.*

cramp someone's **style** to limit someone in some way. ☐ *I hope this doesn't cramp your style, but could you please not hum while you work?* ☐ *To ask him to keep regular hours would really be cramping his style.*

crank something **out** to produce something; to make something in a casual and mechanical way. (Slang.) ☐ *John can crank a lot of work out in a single day.* 🅃 *That factory keeps cranking out cars even though no one buys them.*

crash and burn to fail spectacularly. (Also literal, as with a car or a plane.) ☐ *Poor Chuck really crashed and burned when he made his presentation at the sales meeting.* ☐ *Mary just knew that the whole project would crash and burn if she didn't keep a close watch on it.*

crazy about someone or something AND **crazy for** someone or something**; mad about** someone or something; **mad for** someone or something; **nuts about** someone or something very fond of someone or something. (Slang.) ☐ *Ann is crazy about John.* ☐ *He's crazy about her, too.* ☐ *I'm mad about their new song.* ☐ *Our whole family is nuts about homemade ice cream.*

crazy as a betsy bug Go to (as) crazy as a betsy bug.

crazy as a loon Go to (as) crazy as a loon.

crazy as a peach-orchard boar Go to (as) crazy as a peach-orchard boar.

crazy for someone or something Go to crazy about someone or something.

the **cream of the crop** the best of all. ☐ *This particular car is the cream of the crop.* ☐ *The kids are very bright. They are the cream of the crop.*

create an uproar AND **make an uproar** to cause an outburst or sensation. (Especially with *such.*) ☐ *The dog got into church and made an uproar.* ☐ *Her poodle created an uproar in the restaurant.* ☐ *Why did you make such an uproar?*

create a scene Go to make a scene.

create a stink (about something**)** AND **make a stink (about** something**); raise a stink (about** something**)** to make a major issue out of something; to make much over something; to make a lot of complaints and criticisms about something. (Slang. Compare this with make a federal case out of something.) ☐ *Tom created a stink about Bob's remarks.* ☐ *Why did he make a stink about that?* ☐ *Tom is always trying to raise a stink.*

creature comforts things that make people comfortable. ☐ *The hotel room was sparse, but all the creature comforts were there.* ☐ *The entire country of Adonia seemed to lack the expected creature comforts.*

a **credit to** someone or something someone or something that is of value or benefit. (Preceded by *be, become,* or *seem like.*) ☐ *I always want to be a credit to my school.* ☐ *John is not what you would call a credit to his family.*

a **crick in** one's **back** a twisted or cramped place in the back that causes pain. ☐ *I can't move! I've got a crick in my back!* ☐ *I had a crick in my back all night and I couldn't sleep.*

a **crick in** one's **neck** a twisted place or a cramp in the neck that causes pain. ☐ *I got a crick in my neck from sleeping in a draft.* ☐ *When I read on the plane, I get a crick in my neck.*

crooked as a barrel of fishhooks Go to (as) crooked as a barrel of fishhooks.

crooked as a dog's hind leg Go to (as) crooked as a dog's hind leg.

crooked as a fishhook Go to (as) crooked as a fishhook.

cross a bridge before one **comes to it** to worry excessively about something before it happens. (Note the variation in the examples.) ☐ *There is no sense in crossing that bridge before you come to it.* ☐ *She's always crossing bridges before coming to them. She needs to learn to relax.*

cross a bridge when one **comes to it** to deal with a problem only when one is faced with the problem. (Note the variation in the examples.) ☐ *Please wait and cross that bridge when you come to it.* ☐ *He shouldn't worry about it now. He can cross that bridge when he comes to it.*

cross-examine someone to ask someone questions in great detail; to question a suspect or a witness at great length. ☐ *The police cross-examined the suspect for three hours.* ☐ *The lawyer plans to cross-examine the witness tomorrow morning.*

cross one's **fingers** Go to keep one's fingers crossed (for someone or something).

cross one's **heart (and hope to die)** to pledge or vow that the truth is being told. ☐ *It's true, cross my heart and hope to die.* ☐ *It's really true—cross my heart.*

cross someone's **mind** Go to pass through someone's mind.

cross someone's **palm with silver** to give money to someone in payment for a service. (A fortune-teller might ask for a potential customer to cross her palm with silver. Used in that sense or jocularly for something like tipping a porter.) □ *I crossed his palm with silver, but he still stood there.* □ *You will find that things happen much faster in hotels if you cross the staff's palms with silver fairly often.*

cross someone **up** to give someone trouble; to defy or betray someone. (Also without *up*.) □ *You really crossed me up when you told Tom what I said.* □ *Please don't cross me up again.*

cross swords (with someone**) (on** something**)** to enter into an argument with someone. □ *I don't want to cross swords with Tom on this matter.* □ *The last time we crossed swords, we had a terrible time.*

cross the Rubicon to do something that inevitably commits one to following a certain course of action. (The crossing of the River Rubicon by Julius Caesar inevitably involved him in a war with the senate in 49 B.C.) □ *Jane crossed the Rubicon by signing the contract.* □ *Find another job before you cross the Rubicon and resign from this one.*

crushed by something demoralized; with hurt feelings. (Also literal.) □ *The whole family was completely crushed by the news.* □ *I was just crushed by your attitude. I thought we were friends.*

the **crux of the matter** the central issue of the matter. (*Crux* is an old word meaning "cross.") □ *All right, this is the crux of the matter.* □ *It's about time that we looked at the crux of the matter.*

cry before one **is hurt** to cry or complain before one is injured. □ *Bill always cries before he's hurt.* □ *There is no point in crying before one is hurt.*

cry bloody murder to scream as if something very serious has happened. (See also scream bloody murder.) □ *Now that Bill is really hurt, he's crying bloody murder.* □ *There is no point in crying bloody murder about the bill if you aren't going to pay it.*

cry crocodile tears Go to shed crocodile tears.

cry one's **eyes out** to cry very hard. □ *When we heard the news, we cried our eyes out with joy.* □ *She cried her eyes out after his death.*

cry over spilled milk to be unhappy about something that cannot be undone. (Also literal.) □ *I'm sorry that you broke your bicycle, Tom. But there is nothing that can be done now. Don't cry over spilled milk.* □ *Ann is always crying over spilled milk.*

cry wolf to cry or complain about something when nothing is really wrong. □ *Pay no attention. She's just crying wolf again.* □ *Don't cry wolf too often. No one will come.*

crying need for someone or something a definite or desperate need for someone or something. □ *There is a crying need for someone to come in and straighten things out.* □ *All the people in that area have a crying need for better housing.*

a **crying shame** a very unfortunate situation; a real shame. □ *It's a crying shame that people cannot afford adequate housing.* □ *That everyone could not attend the concert was a crying shame.*

cue someone **in 1.** to give someone a cue; to indicate to someone that the time has come. □ *Now, cue the orchestra director in.* 🅃 *All right, cue in the announcer.* **2.** to tell someone what is going on. (Informal. Almost the same as clue someone in (on something).) □ *I want to know what's going on. Cue me in.* 🅃 *Cue in the general about the troop movement.*

curdle someone's **blood** to frighten or disgust someone severely. □ *The story was scary enough to curdle your blood.* □ *The terrible scream was enough to curdle my blood.*

Curiosity killed the cat. It is dangerous to be curious. (Proverb.) □ *Don't ask so many questions, Billy. Curiosity killed the cat.* □ *Curiosity killed the cat. Mind your own business.*

curl someone's **hair** AND **make** someone's **hair curl** to frighten or alarm someone; to shock someone with sight, sound, or taste. (Also literal.) □ *Don't ever sneak up on me like that again. You really curled my* *hair.* □ *The horror film made my hair curl.*

curl up and die to retreat and die. □ *When I heard you say that, I could have curled up and died.* □ *No, it wasn't an illness. She just curled up and died.*

curry favor (with someone**)** to try to win favor from someone. □ *The lawyer tried to curry favor with the judge.* □ *It's silly to curry favor. Just be yourself.*

cut a big swath Go to cut a wide swath.

a **cut above** someone or something a measure or degree better than someone or something else. (Especially with *average,* as in the examples.) □ *Your shirt is beautiful, but mine is a cut above yours.* □ *John isn't the best mechanic in town, but he's a cut above average.*

cut across something to reach beyond something; to embrace a wide variety; to slice across a figurative boundary or barrier. (Also literal.) □ *His teaching cut across all human cultures and races.* □ *This rule cuts across all social barriers.*

cut a fine figure to look good; to look elegant. (Formal. Usually said of a male.) □ *Tom really cuts a fine figure on the dance floor.* □ *Bill cuts a fine figure since he bought some new clothes.*

cut-and-dried fixed; determined beforehand; usual and uninteresting. □ *I find your writing quite boring. It's too cut-and-dried.* □ *The lecture was, as usual, cut-and-dried. It was the same thing we've heard for years.*

cut and paste 1. to cut something out of paper with scissors and paste it onto something else. □ *The teacher told the little children that it was time to cut and paste, and they all ran to the worktables.* □ *Mary made a tiny house by cutting and pasting little strips of paper.* **2.** something trivial, simple, or childish. □ *I hate this job. It's nothing but cut and paste.* □ *I don't mind doing things that have to be done, but I hate to waste my time on cut and paste.*

cut and run to get free and run away. (Slang. As in cutting loose the rope on a ship's or boat's anchor and sailing away in a hurry.) □ *Max decided to cut and run when he heard the police sirens.* □ *As soon as I finish what I am doing here, I'm going to cut and run. I've got to get home by six o'clock.*

cut a wide swath AND **cut a big swath** to seem important; to attract a lot of attention. □ *In social matters, Mrs. Smith cuts a wide swath.* □ *Bob cuts a big swath whenever he appears in his military uniform.*

cut back (on something**)** to reduce one's use of something; to use less of something. □ *The government has to cut back on its spending.* □ *It's very difficult for the government to cut back.*

cut both ways to affect both sides of an issue equally. □ *Remember that your suggestion that costs should be shared cuts both ways. You will have to pay as well.* □ *If our side cannot take along supporters to the game, then yours cannot either. The rule has to cut both ways.*

cut class to skip going to class. (Informal.) □ *If Mary keeps cutting classes, she'll fail the course.* □ *I can't cut that class. I've missed too many already.*

cut corners to reduce efforts or expenditures; to do things poorly or incompletely. □ *You cannot cut corners when you are dealing with public safety.* □ *Don't cut corners, Sally. Let's do the job right.*

cut from the same cloth AND **made from the same mold** sharing a lot of similarities; seeming to have been created, reared, or fashioned in the same way. □ *She and her brother are cut from the same cloth. They both tell lies all the time.* □ *They are made from the same mold and even sound alike on the telephone.*

Cut it out! Stop doing that! □ *That's enough! Cut it out!* □ *Stop doing that. It hurts! Cut it out!*

cut loose (from someone or something**)** to break away from someone or something; to break ties with someone or something; to act in a free manner. (Also literal. Compare this with **break loose (from** someone or something**)**.) □ *Jane is finding it* *hard to cut loose from her family.* □ *Cutting loose is part of growing up.* □ *When those farm boys get to town, they really cut loose from convention.* □ *They sure are wild when they cut loose.*

cut loose (with something**)** Go to **let go (with** something**)**.

cut no ice (with someone**)** to fail to change the mind of someone; to have no influence on someone. (Informal.) □ *What you just said will cut no ice with the manager.* □ *All that may be true, but it cuts no ice with me.* □ *That idea cuts no ice. It won't help at all.* □ *It cuts no ice that your mother is the mayor.*

cut off to stop by itself or oneself. (Informal.) □ *The machine got hot and cut off.* □ *Bob cut off in midsentence.*

cut off one's **nose to spite** one's **face** to harm oneself while trying to harm another person. (Note the variation in the examples.) □ *Billy loves the zoo, but he refused to go with his mother because he was mad at her. He cut off his nose to spite his face.* □ *Find a better way to be angry. It is silly to cut your nose off to spite your face.*

cut one's **eyeteeth on** something to have done something since one was very young; to have much experience at something. (Folksy.) □ *Do I know about cars? I cut my eyeteeth on cars.* □ *I cut my eyeteeth on Bach. I can whistle everything he wrote.*

cut one's **losses** to reduce someone's losses of money, goods, or other things of value. □ *I sold the stock as it went down, thus cutting my losses.* □ *He cut his losses by putting better locks on the doors. There were fewer robberies.* □ *The mayor's reputation suffered because of the scandal. He finally resigned to cut his losses.*

cut one's **(own) throat** [for someone] to experience certain failure; to do damage to oneself. (Also literal. Informal.) □ *If I were to run for office, I'd just be cutting my throat.* □ *Judges who take bribes are cutting their own throats.*

cut out for something well-suited for something; with a talent for something. (Compare this with **cut out to be** something.) □ *Tom was not cut out for banking.* □ *Sally was cut out for the medical profession.*

cut out the deadwood to remove unproductive persons from employment. (Also literal as in pruning away dead branches or deadwood.) □ *This company would be more profitable if management would cut out the deadwood.* □ *When we cut out the deadwood, all our departments will run more smoothly.*

cut out to be something well-suited for a particular role or a particular occupation. (Compare this with **cut out for** something.) □ *Tom was not cut out to be a banker.* □ *Sally was cut out to be a doctor.*

cut (someone**) a check** to write a check; to have a computer print a check. □ *We will cut a check for the balance due you later this afternoon.* □ *We will cut you a check as soon as possible.*

cut someone **dead** to ignore someone totally. □ *Joan was just about to speak to James when he cut her dead.* □ *Jean cut her former husband dead.*

cut someone **down (to size)** AND **take** someone **down (to size)** to make a person humble; to put one in one's place. (See also **beat** someone **down (to size)**.) □ *John's remarks really cut me down to size.* □ *Jane is too conceited. I think her new boss will take her down to size.* □ *The boss's angry stare will really cut her down.*

cut someone **in** to give someone a share of something. (Informal or slang.) □ *Shall we cut Bill in on this deal?* □ *I don't think we should cut anybody in.* 🆃 *Pretty soon we'll have to cut in the whole town.*

cut someone **off without a penny** to end someone's allowance; to fail to leave someone money in one's will. □ *Mr. and Mrs. Franklin cut their son off without a penny after he quit school.* 🆃 *They cut off both of their sons without a penny.* 🆃 *We learned, when Uncle Sam's will was read, that he cut off his own flesh and blood without a penny.*

cut someone or something **to the bone 1.** to slice flesh or meat deep to the bone. □ *The knife cut John to the bone. He had to* *be sewed up.* ☐ *Cut each slice of ham to the bone. Then each slice will be as big as possible.* **2.** [with *something*] to cut down severely (on something). ☐ *We cut our expenses to the bone and are still losing money.* ☐ *Congress had to cut the budget to the bone in order to balance it.*

cut someone or something **up** to criticize someone or something severely. (Also literal. Slang.) ☐ *Jane is such a gossip. She was really cutting Mrs. Jones up.* 🅃 *The professor really cut up my essay.*

cut someone **to the quick** to hurt someone's feelings very badly. ☐ *Your criticism cut me to the quick.* ☐ *Tom's sharp words to Mary cut her to the quick.*

cut teeth [for a baby or young person] to grow teeth. ☐ *Billy is cranky because he's cutting teeth.* ☐ *Ann cut her first tooth this week.*

cut the ground out from under someone to destroy the foundation of someone's plans or someone's argument. ☐ *The politician cut the ground out from under his opponent.* 🅃 *Congress cut out the ground from under the president.*

cut to the chase to get to the important matters. ☐ *Let's stop all this chatter and cut to the chase.* ☐ *I like the way you cut to the chase and don't waste my time.*

cut up to act wildly; to show off and be troublesome; to act like a clown. (Slang. See also **cut** someone or something **up**.) ☐ *Tom, Billy! Stop cutting up, or I'll send you to the principal's office.* ☐ *If you spent more time studying than cutting up, you'd get better grades.*

D

[daily dozen] Go to one's **daily dozen.**

the **daily grind** [someone's] everyday work routine. (Informal.) ☐ *I'm getting very tired of the daily grind.* ☐ *When my vacation was over, I had to go back to the daily grind.*

damn someone or something **with faint praise** to criticize someone or something indirectly by not praising enthusiastically. ☐ *The critic did not say that he disliked the play, but he damned it with faint praise.* ☐ *Mrs. Brown is very proud of her son's achievements, but damns her daughter's with faint praise.*

dance to another tune to shift to a different kind of behavior; to change one's behavior or attitude. (See also **change** someone's **tune; sing a different tune.**) ☐ *After being yelled at, Ann danced to another tune.* ☐ *A stern talking-to will make her dance to another tune.*

dance with death to attempt to do something that is very risky. ☐ *The crossing of the border into Adonia was like dancing with death.* ☐ *You are dancing with death in your effort to cross that narrow ledge.*

dare someone **(to** do something**)** to challenge someone to do something. ☐ *Sally dared Jane to race her to the corner.* ☐ *You wouldn't do that, would you? I dare you.*

dark horse someone or something whose abilities, plans, or feelings are little known to others. (From horse racing.) ☐ *It's difficult to predict who will win the prize—there are two or three dark horses in the tournament.* ☐ *Everyone was surprised at the results of the election. The dark horse won.*

darken someone's **door** [for an unwelcome person] to come to someone's door seeking entry. (As if the unwelcome visitor were casting a shadow on the door. Formal or jocular.) ☐ *Who is this who has come to darken my door?* ☐ *Is that you, John, darkening my door again? I thought you were out of town.* ☐ *The heroine of the drama told the villain never to darken her door again.* ☐ *She touched the back of her hand to her forehead and said, "Go, and never darken my door again!"*

dart in and out [for something moving] to dart quickly between two things, or into a number of things, and move away again. ☐ *On the highway, a small car was darting in and out of the two right lanes of traffic.* ☐ *A small bird darted in and out of the bush, probably going into a nest inside.*

dash cold water on something Go to **pour cold water on** something.

dash something **off** to send something off, usually quickly. ☐ *I'll dash a quick note off to Aunt Mary.* 🅃 *Ann just dashed off a message to her parents.*

date back (to sometime**)** to extend back to a particular time; to have been alive at a particular time in the past. ☐ *My late grandmother dated back to the Civil War.* ☐ *This record dates back to the sixties.* ☐ *How far do you date back?*

Davy Jones's locker the bottom of the sea, especially when it is a grave. (From the seamen's name for the evil spirit of the sea. See also **go to Davy Jones's locker.**) ☐ *They were going to sail around the world, but ended up in Davy Jones's locker.* ☐ *Most of the gold from that trading ship is in Davy Jones's locker.*

dawn on someone to occur to someone; to cross someone's **mind.** ☐ *It just dawned on me that I forgot my books.* ☐ *When will it dawn on him that his audience is bored?*

day after day every day; daily; all the time. ☐ *He wears the same clothes day after day.* ☐ *She visits her husband in the hospital day after day.*

day and night AND **night and day** all the time; around the clock. ☐ *The nurse was with her day and night.* ☐ *The house is guarded night and day.*

day in and day out AND **day in, day out** on every day; for each day. ☐ *She smokes day in and day out.* ☐ *They eat nothing but vegetables, day in, day out.*

day in, day out Go to day in and day out.

day-to-day daily; everyday; common. ☐ *They update their accounts on a day-to-day basis.* ☐ *Just wear your regular day-to-day clothing.*

daylight robbery the practice of blatantly or grossly overcharging. ☐ *It's daylight robbery to charge that amount of money for a hotel room!* ☐ *The cost of renting a car at that place is daylight robbery.*

[days are numbered] Go to one's days are numbered.

days running AND **weeks running; months running; years running** days in a series; months in a series; etc. (Follows a number.) ☐ *I had a bad cold for 5 days running.* ☐ *For two years running, I brought work home from the office every night.*

dead ahead straight ahead; directly ahead. ☐ *Look out! There is a cow in the road dead ahead.* ☐ *The farmer said that the town we wanted was dead ahead.*

dead and buried gone forever. (Refers literally to persons and figuratively to ideas and other things.) ☐ *Now that memories of Uncle Bill are dead and buried, we can throw away his old boots.* ☐ *That kind of thinking is dead and buried.*

dead and gone dead and buried, and probably forgotten. ☐ *John is dead and gone. There is no reason to fear him anymore.* ☐ *Her husband is dead and gone, but she is getting along fine.*

dead as a dodo Go to (as) dead as a dodo.

dead as a doornail Go to (as) dead as a doornail.

a **dead duck** someone or something that is failed, finished, or nearly dead. ☐ *He missed the exam. He's a dead duck.* ☐ *Yes, John's a dead duck. He drove his car into a tree.*

dead in someone's or something's **tracks** stopped exactly where someone or something is at the moment. (This does not usually have anything to do with death. The phrase is often used with *stop*.) ☐ *Her unkind words stopped me dead in my tracks.* ☐ *When I heard the rattlesnake, I stopped dead in my tracks.* ☐ *The project came to a halt dead in its tracks.*

dead letter 1. a piece of mail that is returned to the post office as both undeliverable and unreturnable. ☐ *At the end of the year, the post office usually has bushels of dead letters.* ☐ *Some of the dead letters are opened to see if there is an address inside.* **2.** an issue, law, or matter that is no longer important or that no longer has force or power. (Usually **a dead letter.** Could also be used for a person.) ☐ *His point about the need for education reform is a dead letter. It is being done now.* ☐ *This point of law is a dead letter since the last Supreme Court ruling on this matter.*

a **dead loss** a total loss. ☐ *My investment was a dead loss.* ☐ *This car is a dead loss. It was a waste of money.*

dead on its feet AND **dead on** one's **feet** exhausted; worn out; no longer useful. ☐ *Ann is so tired. She's really dead on her feet.* ☐ *He can't teach well anymore. He's dead on his feet.* ☐ *This inefficient company is dead on its feet.*

dead on one's **feet** Go to dead on its feet.

dead set against someone or something totally opposed to someone or something. (See also one's **heart is (dead) set against** something.) ☐ *I'm dead set against the new tax* *proposal.* ☐ *Everyone is dead set against the mayor.*

dead to the world tired; exhausted; sleeping soundly. (Compare this with **dead on** one's **feet.**) ☐ *I've had such a hard day. I'm really dead to the world.* ☐ *Look at her sleep. She's dead to the world.*

deaf and dumb unable to hear or speak. (Used without any intended malice, but no longer considered polite. Sometimes euphemized as "hearing and speech impaired.") ☐ *Fred objected to being called deaf and dumb.* ☐ *Aunt Clara—she was deaf and dumb, you know—lived to be over 100.*

deaf as a post Go to **(as) deaf as a post.**

deal in something to buy and sell something. ☐ *My uncle is a stockbroker. He deals in stocks and bonds.* ☐ *My aunt deals in antiques.*

death and taxes death, which is inevitable, and the payment of taxes, which is unavoidable. (A saying that emphasizes the rigor with which taxes are collected.) ☐ *There is nothing as certain on this old planet as death and taxes.* ☐ *Max said he could get out of anything except death and taxes.*

death on someone or something **1.** very effective in acting against someone or something. ☐ *This road is terribly bumpy. It's death on tires.* ☐ *The sergeant is death on lazy soldiers.* **2.** [with *something*] accurate or deadly at doing something requiring skill or great effort. ☐ *John is death on curve balls. He's our best pitcher.* ☐ *The boxing champ is really death on those fast punches.*

decide in favor of someone or something to determine that someone or something is the winner. ☐ *The judge decided in favor of the defendant.* ☐ *I decided in favor of the red one.*

deem it (to be) necessary AND **deem that it is necessary** to believe that something is necessary. ☐ *Mary deemed that it was necessary to leave town that night.* ☐ *Lisa deemed it necessary to go home.*

deem that it is necessary Go to **deem it (to be) necessary.**

deep-six someone or something to get rid of someone or something; to dispose of someone or something. (Slang. To bury someone or something six feet deep, the standard depth for a grave.) ☐ *Take this horrible food out and deep-six it.* ☐ *That guy is a pain. Deep-six him so the cops will never find him.*

[deepest sympathy] Go to one's **deepest sympathy.**

a **den of iniquity** a place filled with wickedness. ☐ *The town was a den of iniquity and vice was everywhere.* ☐ *Police raided the gambling house, calling it a den of iniquity.*

desert a sinking ship AND **leave a sinking ship** to leave a place, a person, or a situation when things become difficult or unpleasant. (Rats are said to be the first to leave a ship that is sinking.) ☐ *I hate to be the one to desert a sinking ship, but I can't stand it around here anymore.* ☐ *There goes Tom. Wouldn't you know he'd leave a sinking ship rather than stay around and try to help?*

devil-may-care attitude AND **devil-may-care manner** a very casual attitude; a worry-free or carefree attitude. ☐ *You must get rid of your devil-may-care attitude if you want to succeed.* ☐ *She acts so thoughtlessly with her devil-may-care manner.*

devil-may-care manner Go to **devil-may-care attitude.**

a **devil of a job** AND the **devil's own job** the most difficult task. (Informal.) ☐ *We had a devil of a job fixing the car.* ☐ *It was the devil's own job finding a hotel with vacancies.*

the **devil's own job** Go to **devil of a job.**

a **diamond in the rough** a valuable or potentially excellent person or thing hidden by an unpolished or rough exterior. ☐ *Ann looks like a stupid woman, but she's a fine person—a real diamond in the rough.* ☐ *That piece of property is a dia-*

mond in the rough. Someday it will be valuable.

die a natural death 1. [for someone] to die by disease or old age rather than by violence or foul play. □ *I hope to live to 100 and die a natural death.* □ *The police say she didn't die a natural death, and they are investigating.* **2.** [for something] to fade away or die down. □ *I expect that all this excitement about computers will die a natural death.* □ *Most fads die a natural death.*

die in one's **boots** AND **die with** one's **boots on** to go down fighting; to die in some fashion other than in bed; to die fighting. (A cliché popularized by western movies. The villains of these movies said they preferred death by gunshot or hanging to dying in bed. See also go down fighting.) □ *I won't let him get me. I'll die in my boots.* □ *He may give me a hard time, but I won't be overcome. I'll fight him and die with my boots on.*

The **die is cast.** some process is past the point of no return. (This *die* is one of a pair of dice. This *cast* means "thrown.") □ *After that speech favoring reform of the education system, the die is cast. This is now a campaign issue.* □ *The die is cast. There is no turning back on this point.*

die laughing 1. to meet one's death laughing—in good spirits, revenge, or irony. □ *Sally is such an optimist that she'll probably die laughing.* □ *Bob tried to poison his rich aunt, who then died laughing because she had taken Bob out of her will.* **2.** to laugh very long and hard. (Informal.) □ *The joke was so funny that I almost died laughing.* □ *The play was meant to be funny, but the audience didn't exactly die laughing.*

die of a broken heart 1. to die of emotional distress. □ *I was not surprised to hear of her death. They say she died of a broken heart.* □ *In the movie, the heroine appeared to die of a broken heart, but the audience knew she was poisoned.* **2.** to suffer from emotional distress, especially from a failed romance. □ *Tom and Mary broke off their romance and both died of broken hearts.* □ *Please don't leave me. I know I'll die of a broken heart.*

die of boredom to suffer from boredom; to be very bored. □ *No one has ever really died of boredom.* □ *We sat there and listened politely, even though we almost died of boredom.*

die on someone **1.** [for someone] to die while in someone's care. □ *The ambulance driver didn't want his patient to die on him.* □ *"Come on, don't die on me!" cried the emergency room doctor.* **2.** [for something, such as a car engine] to stop running while one is using it. □ *My car just died on me.* □ *His computer keeps dying on him.*

die on the vine Go to wither on the vine.

die with one's **boots on** Go to die in one's boots.

different as night and day Go to (as) different as night and day.

dig in 1. to eat a meal; to begin eating a meal. (Informal. See also Come and get it!) □ *Dinner's ready, Tom. Sit down and dig in.* □ *The cowboy helped himself to some beans and dug in.* **2.** to apply oneself to a task; to tackle (something) vigorously. □ *Sally looked at the big job ahead of her. Then she rolled up her sleeves and dug in.* □ *"Tom," hollered Mrs. Smith, "you get to that pile of homework and dig in this very minute."*

dig one's **heels in** to refuse to alter one's course of action or opinions; to be obstinate or determined. □ *The student dug her heels in and refused to obey the instructions.* □ *I'm digging in my heels. I'm not going back.*

dig one's **own grave** to be responsible for one's own downfall or ruin. □ *The manager tried to get rid of his assistant, but he dug his own grave. He got fired himself for trying.* □ *The committee has dug its own grave with the new tax bill.*

dig some dirt up on someone to find out something bad about someone. (Informal.) □ *If you don't stop trying to dig some dirt up on me, I'll get a lawyer and sue you.* T *The citizens' group dug up* *some dirt on the mayor and used it against her at election time.*

dig someone or something to understand something; to relate to a person or a thing. (Slang.) □ *I really dig Tom. He's a special guy.* □ *I really dig rock music.*

dig someone or something **up** to go to great effort to find someone or something. (There is an implication that the thing or person dug up is not the most desirable, but is all that could be found.) □ *Mary dug a date up for the dance next Friday.* 🅃 *I dug up a recipe for roast pork with pineapple.* 🅃 *I dug up a carpenter who doesn't charge very much.*

dig something **out** to work hard to locate something and bring it forth. (Also literal.) □ *They dug the contract out of the file cabinet.* □ *I dug this old suit out of a box in the attic.* 🅃 *I dug out an old dress and wore it to the fifties party.*

a **dime a dozen** abundant; cheap and common. (Also literal.) □ *People who can write good books are not a dime a dozen.* □ *Romantic movies are a dime a dozen.*

dine out Go to eat (a meal) out.

dip in(to something**)** to take or borrow from a supply of something, especially a supply of money. (Also literal.) □ *I had to dip into my savings account to pay for the car.* □ *I hate to dip in like that.* □ *She put out her hand and dipped into the chocolate box.*

dirt cheap extremely cheap. (Informal.) □ *Buy some more of those plums. They're dirt cheap.* □ *In Italy, the peaches are dirt cheap.*

dirty old man an older man who is excessively interested in sex. □ *Tell your daughter to stay away from him. He's a dirty old man and might attack her.* □ *There were several dirty old men looking at pornographic magazines in the park.*

dirty one's **hands** Go to **get** one's **hands dirty**.

dirty work 1. unpleasant or uninteresting work. □ *My boss does all the traveling. I get all the dirty work to do.* □ *She's tired of doing all the dirty work at the office.* **2.** dishonest or underhanded actions; treachery. □ *She knew there was some dirty work going on when she saw her opponents whispering together.* □ *The company seems respectable enough, but there's a lot of dirty work that goes on.*

divide and conquer to cause the enemy to split into two or more warring factions, and then move in to conquer all of them. □ *Mary thought she could divide and conquer the board of directors, but they had survived such tactics many times, and her efforts failed.* □ *Sam led his men to divide and conquer the enemy platoon, and his strategy succeeded.*

divide something **fifty-fifty** AND **split** something **fifty-fifty** to divide something into two equal parts. (Informal. Each *fifty* means 50 percent.) □ *Tommy and Billy divided the candy fifty-fifty.* □ *The robbers split the money fifty-fifty.*

do a double take to react with surprise; to have to look twice to make sure that one really saw correctly. (Informal.) □ *When the boy led a goat into the park, everyone did a double take.* □ *When the nurse saw that the man had six toes, she did a double take.*

do a flip-flop (on something**)** AND **do an about-face** to make a sudden reversal of opinion. (Informal or slang.) □ *Without warning, the government did a flip-flop on taxation.* □ *It had done an about-face on the question of deductions last year.*

do a job on someone or something **1.** to damage someone or something; to mess up someone or something. (Informal or slang.) □ *The robbers really did a job on the bank guard. They beat him when they robbed the bank.* □ *The puppy did a job on my shoes. They are all chewed to pieces.* **2.** [with *something*] to defecate on something. (Informal and euphemistic. Note the variation in the second example.) □ *The puppy did a job on the living-room carpet.* □ *It's supposed to do its job on the newspapers in the basement.*

do a land-office business to do a large amount of business in a short period of time. □ *The ice cream shop always does a* *land-office business on a hot day.* □ *The tax collector's office did a land-office business on the day that taxes were due.*

do an about-face Go to do a flip-flop (on something).

do an errand Go to run an errand.

do a number on someone or something to damage or harm someone or something. (Slang.) □ *The teacher did a number on the whole class. That test was terrible.* □ *Tom did a number on Mary when he went out with Ann.*

do a snow job on someone to deceive or confuse someone. (Informal or slang.) □ *Tom did a snow job on the teacher when he said that he was sick yesterday.* □ *I hate it when someone does a snow job on me. I find it harder and harder to trust people.*

do away with someone or something **1.** [with *someone*] to kill someone; to dispose of someone or something. □ *The crooks did away with the witness.* □ *I was there, too. I hope they don't try to do away with me.* **2.** [with *something*] to get rid of something; to dispose of something. □ *This chemical will do away with the stain in your sink.* □ *The time has come to do away with that old building.*

do credit to someone AND **do** someone **credit** to add to the reputation of someone. □ *Your new job really does credit to you.* □ *Yes, it really does you credit.*

Do I need to paint you a picture? It is so very simple, so why do you require more explanation to understand it? □ *What is so difficult? Do I need to paint you a picture?* □ *I've explained it every way I can. Do I need to paint you a picture?*

do justice to something **1.** to do something well; to represent or portray something accurately. □ *Sally did justice to the contract negotiations.* □ *This photograph doesn't do justice to the beauty of the mountains.* **2.** to eat or drink a great deal. □ *Bill always does justice to the turkey on Thanksgiving.* □ *The party didn't do justice to the roast pig. There were nearly ten pounds left over.*

do not have a care in the world being free and casual; being unworried and carefree. (*Do not have* can be replaced with *be without.*) □ *I really feel good today—as if I didn't have a care in the world.* □ *Ann always acts as if she doesn't have a care in the world.*

do not have a leg to stand on [for an argument or a case] to have no support. (Informal. *Do not have* can be replaced with *be without.*) □ *You may think you're in the right, but you don't have a leg to stand on.* □ *My lawyer said I didn't have a leg to stand on, so I shouldn't sue the company.*

do not have all one's **marbles** do not have all one's mental capacities. (Also literal. Informal.) □ *John acts as if he doesn't have all his marbles.* □ *I'm afraid that I don't have all my marbles all the time.*

do one's **bit** Go to do one's part.

do one's **duty** to do one's job; to do what is expected of one. □ *Please don't thank me. I'm just doing my duty.* □ *Soldiers who fight in wars are doing their duty.*

do oneself **proud** [for one] to make oneself proud. (Folksy. See also **do credit to** someone.) □ *Well, Bill really did himself proud in the horse race.* □ *You did yourself proud by raising that fine-looking, prizewinning hog.*

do one's **(level) best** to do (something) as well as one can. □ *Just do your level best. That's all we can ask of you.* □ *Tom isn't doing his best. We may have to replace him.*

do one's **(own) thing** to do what one likes or what one pleases. (Informal or slang.) □ *Tom doesn't like being told what to do. He prefers to do his own thing.* □ *When you do your thing, you have no one but yourself to blame if things don't work out.*

do one's **part** AND **do** one's **bit** to do one's share of the work; to do whatever one can do to help. □ *All people everywhere must do their part to help get things under control.* □ *I always try to do my bit. How can I help this time?*

do or die to do something or die trying. (Refers to an attitude adopted when one must do something whether one wants to or not. Occurs as a noun or an adjective.) □ *It was do or die. There was no turning back now.* □ *He simply had to get to the airport on time. It was a case of do or die.*

do so Go to **do too**.

do somehow **by** someone to treat someone in a particular manner. (Informal. Do not confuse this with a passive construction. The *someone* is not the actor but the object.) □ *Tom did all right by Ann when he brought her red roses.* □ *I did badly by Tom. I fired him.*

do someone **a good turn** to do something that is helpful to someone. □ *My neighbor did me a good turn by lending me his car.* □ *The teacher did me a good turn when he told me to work harder.*

do someone **a kindness** to do a kind deed for a person. □ *My neighbor did me a kindness when he cut my grass.* □ *I am always happy to have the opportunity of doing someone a kindness.*

do someone **credit** Go to **do credit to** someone.

do someone **damage** to harm someone. (Informal.) □ *I hope she doesn't plan to do me damage.* □ *They did us damage by telling the whole story to the newspapers.*

do someone **good** to benefit someone. (Informal.) □ *A nice hot bath really does me good.* □ *A few years in the army would do you good.*

do someone **one better** Go to **go** someone **one better**.

do someone or something **in 1.** [with *someone*] to make someone tired. □ *That tennis game really did me in.* □ *Yes, hard activity will do you in.* **2.** [with *someone*] to cheat someone; to **take** someone **in**. □ *The crooks did the widow in.* 🅃 *They did in the widow by talking her into giving them all the money in her bank account.* **3.** [with *someone*] to kill someone. 🅃 *The crooks did in the bank guard.* 🅃 *They'll probably do in the witnesses soon.* **4.** [with *something*] to destroy something. 🅃 *The huge waves totally did in the seaside community.* □ *The fire did the wooden building in.*

do someone or something **over** AND **make** someone or something **over 1.** [with *someone*] to buy a new wardrobe for someone; to redo someone's hair. (See also **make a fuss (over** someone or something**)**.) □ *Sally's mother did Sally over for the play tryouts.* □ *It's very expensive to do a person over completely.* □ *The designer did Sally over completely.* **2.** [with *something*] to rebuild, redesign, or redecorate something. □ *We did our living room over for the holidays.* 🅃 *We made over the family room because it was looking shabby.*

do someone **out of** something to cheat someone out of something. (Informal or slang.) □ *They did the widow out of her life savings.* □ *I won't let anyone do me out of anything. I'm a very cautious and suspicious person.*

do someone's **bidding** to do what is requested by someone. □ *The servant grumbled but did his employer's bidding.* □ *Am I expected to do your bidding whenever you ask?*

do someone's **heart good** to make someone feel good emotionally. (Also literal. Informal.) □ *It does my heart good to hear you talk that way.* □ *When she sent me a get-well card, it really did my heart good.*

do something **by hand** to do something with one's hands rather than with a machine. □ *The computer was broken so I had to do the calculations by hand.* □ *All this tiny stitching was done by hand. Machines cannot do this kind of work.*

do something **fair and square** to do something fairly. (Folksy. See also **fair and square**.) □ *He always plays the game fair and square.* □ *I try to treat all people fair and square.*

do something **for a living** to do some kind of work to earn enough money to live. □ *John paints houses for a living.* □ *What do you do for a living?*

do something **hands down** to do something easily and without opposition. □ *The mayor won the election hands down.* □

She was the choice of the people hands down.

do something **in a heartbeat** to do something almost immediately. ☐ *If I had the money, I would go back to college in a heartbeat.* ☐ *Just tell me that you need me and I'll come there in a heartbeat.*

do something **in person** to appear somewhere and do something oneself rather than sending someone else or doing it over the telephone, or by mail. ☐ *I know the money should be in his account. I saw him put it there in person.* ☐ *The famous actor came to the hospital and greeted each patient in person.*

do something **in public** to do something where anyone looking could see it. ☐ *You should dress neatly when you appear in public.* ☐ *I wish that you wouldn't talk to me so rudely in public.* ☐ *Bob, you must behave properly in public.*

do something **in secret** to do something privately or secretly. ☐ *Why do you always do things like that in secret?* ☐ *There is no need to count your money in secret.*

do something **in vain** to do something with no result; to do something that fails. ☐ *They rushed her to the hospital, but they did it in vain.* ☐ *We tried in vain to get her there on time.*

do something **on the fly** to do something while one is moving; to do something (to something that is in motion). (Slang. This has nothing to do with actual flight.) ☐ *We can't stop the machine to oil it now. You'll have to do it on the fly.* ☐ *We will have to find the break in the film on the fly—while we are showing it.*

do something **on the run** to do something while one is moving hurriedly; to do something while one is going rapidly from one place to another. (Informal.) ☐ *I was very busy today and had to eat on the run.* ☐ *I didn't have time to meet with Bill, but I was able to talk to him on the run.*

do something **on the sly** to do something slyly or sneakily. (Informal.) ☐ *He was seeing Mrs. Smith on the sly.* ☐ *She was supposed to be losing weight, but she was snacking on the sly.*

do something **over (again)** to redo something; to repeat the doing of something. ☐ *This isn't right. You'll have to do it over again.* ☐ *The teacher made me do my paper over.*

do something **the hard way 1.** to accomplish something in the most difficult manner, rather than by an easier way. ☐ *I made it to this job the hard way. I came up through the ranks.* ☐ *She did it the hard way. She had no help from her parents.* **2.** to do something the wrong way. ☐ *No, you can't pound in nails like that. You're doing it the hard way.* ☐ *I'm sorry. I learn things the hard way.*

do something **to excess** to do too much of something; to consume too much of something. ☐ *Anne often drinks to excess at parties.* ☐ *John smokes to excess when he works.*

do something **up** to repair or redecorate something. ☐ *If we're going to sell the house, we'll have to do it up.* 🅃 *I'm going to do up the kitchen.*

do something **up brown** to do something just right. (Folksy. Refers to cooking something until it has just the right amount of brownish color.) ☐ *Of course I can do it right. I'll really do it up brown.* ☐ *Come on, Bob. Let's do it right this time. I know you can do it up brown.*

do something **with a vengeance** to do something with vigor; to do something energetically as if one were angry with it. (Folksy.) ☐ *Bob is building that fence with a vengeance.* ☐ *Mary is really weeding her garden with a vengeance.*

do the dishes to wash and dry dishes, glasses, cups, knives, forks, etc., after a meal. ☐ *Bill, you cannot go out and play until you've done the dishes.* ☐ *Why am I always the one who has to do the dishes?*

do the honors to act as host or hostess and serve one's guests by pouring drinks, slicing meat, making (drinking) toasts, etc. ☐ *All the guests were seated, and a huge, juicy turkey sat on the table. Jane Thomas turned to her husband and said, "Bob, will* *you do the honors?" Mr. Jones smiled and began slicing thick slices of meat from the turkey.* □ *The mayor stood up and addressed the people who were still eating their salads. "I'm delighted to do the honors this evening and propose a toast to your friend and mine, Bill Jones. Bill, good luck and best wishes in your new job in Washington." And everyone sipped a bit of wine.*

do the trick to do exactly what needs to be done. (Folksy.) □ *Push it just a little more to the left. There, that does the trick.* □ *If you lend me five dollars, I'll have enough to do the trick.*

do too AND **do so** to do something (despite anything to the contrary). (An emphatic way of saying *do.* See also **be too, have too.**) □ *BOB: You don't have your money with you. BILL: I do too!* □ *He does so! I saw him put it in his pocket.* □ *She did too. I saw her do it.*

do without (someone or something) to manage to get through life without someone or something that you want or need. □ *I guess I'll just have to do without a car.* □ *I don't know how I can do without.* □ *The boss can't do without a secretary.*

Do you read me? Do you understand what I am telling you? (Typically asked of someone receiving a radio communication, such as from an airplane or an airport control tower. Also used as an emphatic way of asking if one is understood.) □ *This is Delta heavy 54. Do you read me?* □ *I have said no twenty times already! The answer is still no! Do you read me?*

dog and pony show a display, demonstration, or exhibition of something—such as something one is selling. (Refers to a circus act where trained dogs leap onto and off of trained ponies, in exactly the same sequence each time the show is performed.) □ *Gary was there with his dog and pony show, trying to sell his ideas to whomever would listen to him.* □ *Don't you get tired of running through the same old dog and pony show, week after week?*

dog-eat-dog a situation in which one has to act ruthlessly in order to survive or succeed; ruthless competition. □ *It is dog-eat-dog in the world of business these days.* □ *Universities are not quiet peaceful places. It's dog-eat-dog to get a promotion.*

dog in the manger one who prevents other people from doing or having what one does not wish them to do or have. (From one of Aesop's fables in which a dog—which cannot eat hay—lay in the hayrack [manger] and prevented the other animals from eating the hay.) □ *Jane is a real dog in the manger. She cannot drive, but she will not lend anyone her car.* □ *If Martin were not such a dog in the manger, he would let his brother have that dinner jacket he never wears.*

dollar for dollar considering the amount of money involved; considering the cost. (Informal. Often seen in advertising.) □ *Dollar for dollar, you cannot buy a better car.* □ *Dollar for dollar, this laundry detergent washes cleaner and brighter than any other product on the market.*

done in tired; exhausted; terminated; killed. □ *I am really done in after all that exercise.* □ *The project was done in by a vote of the board.* □ *The witness was afraid he would be done in by the mobsters.*

done to a T AND **done to a turn** cooked just right. (Folksy. See also **fit** someone **to a T; suit** someone **to a T.**) □ *Yummy! This meat is done to a T.* □ *I like it done to a turn, not too done and not too raw.*

done to a turn Go to **done to a T.**

Don't hold your breath. Do not stop breathing (while waiting a long time for something to happen). (Informal.) □ *You think he'll get a job? Ha! Don't hold your breath.* □ *I'll finish building the fence as soon as I have time, but don't hold your breath.*

Don't let it go any further. AND **Don't let it out of this room.** Don't tell this secret to anyone else. (Also literal.) □ *This is a strict secret. Don't let it go any further.* □ *I'll tell you what you what to know, but don't let it go any further.*

Don't let it out of this room Go to **Don't let it go any further.**

Don't let someone or something **get you down.** Do not allow yourself to be overcome by someone or something. ☐ *Don't let their constant teasing get you down.* ☐ *Don't let Tom get you down. He's not always unpleasant.*

Don't quit your day job. You are not very good at what you are doing, so don't quit your regular job in hopes that you can support yourself doing this. ☐ *I saw your comedy act at the nightclub. Don't quit your day job!* ☐ *So, you laid the bricks in this wall. Well, don't quit your day job.*

doomed to failure certain to fail, usually because of some obvious flaw. ☐ *This project was doomed to failure from the very beginning.* ☐ *The play is doomed to failure because there is not a good story line.*

door-to-door 1. having to do with movement from one door to another or from one house to another. (See also **from door to door.**) ☐ *John is a door-to-door salesman.* ☐ *We spent two weeks making a door-to-door survey.* **2.** by moving from one door to another or one house to another. ☐ *Anne is selling books door-to-door.* ☐ *We went door-to-door, collecting money.*

a **dose of** one's **own medicine** the same kind of treatment that one gives to other people. (Often with *get* or *have.*) ☐ *Sally never is very friendly. Someone is going to give her a dose of her own medicine someday.* ☐ *He didn't like getting a dose of his own medicine.*

double back (on someone or something**)** [for a person or animal] to reverse motion, moving toward someone or something rather than away from someone or something. ☐ *The deer doubled back on the hunter.* ☐ *The robber doubled back on the police, and they lost track of him.* ☐ *He doubled back on his trail.*

double-cross someone to betray someone by doing the opposite of what was promised; to betray a person by not doing what was promised. (Slang. Originally criminal slang.) ☐ *If you double-cross me again, I'll kill you.* ☐ *Tom is mad at Jane because she double-crossed him on the sale of his car.*

double in brass to serve two purposes; to be useful for two different things. (Refers to a musician who can play a trumpet or trombone, etc., in addition to some other instrument.) ☐ *The English teacher also doubles in brass as the football coach.* ☐ *The drummer doubles in brass as a violinist.*

double up (with someone**)** to share something with someone. ☐ *We don't have enough books. Tom, will you double up with Jane?* ☐ *When we get more books, we won't have to double up anymore.* ☐ *We'll share hotel rooms to save money. Tom and Bill will double up.*

doubting Thomas someone who will not easily believe something without strong proof or evidence. (From the Bible.) ☐ *Mary won't believe that I have a dog until she sees him. She's such a doubting Thomas.* ☐ *This school is full of doubting Thomases. They want to see Jimmy's new bike with their own eyes.*

down-and-dirty sneaky, unfair, low-down, and nasty. (Slang.) ☐ *The boys played a real down-and-dirty trick on the teacher.* ☐ *A political campaign provides a lot of down-and-dirty speeches that only confuse the voters.*

down-and-out having no money or means of support. ☐ *There are many young people down-and-out in Los Angeles just now.* ☐ *John gambled away all his fortune and is now completely down-and-out.*

down-at-the-heels shabby; poorly dressed. (Refers to shoes that are worn down at the heels.) ☐ *The hobo was really down-at-the-heels.* ☐ *Tom's house needs paint. It looks down-at-the-heels.*

down by some amount having a score that is lower, by the specified amount, than someone else's score or the other team's score. ☐ *At halftime, the home team was down by 14 points.* ☐ *Down by one run, the team scored two runs in the ninth inning and won the game.*

down for the count finished for the time being. (From boxing, where a fallen fighter remains down [resting] until the last count, or even beyond.) □ *After the professor rebuked me in class, I knew I was down for the count.* □ *I am down for the count, but I'll try again tomorrow.*

down in the dumps sad or depressed. (Informal.) □ *I've been down in the dumps for the past few days.* □ *Try to cheer Jane up. She's down in the dumps for some reason.*

down in the mouth sad-faced; depressed and unsmiling. □ *Since her dog died, Barbara has been down in the mouth.* □ *Bob has been down in the mouth since the car wreck.*

down on one's **luck** without any money; unlucky. (Euphemistic for *broke.*) □ *Can you lend me twenty dollars? I've been down on my luck lately.* □ *The gambler had to get a job because he had been down on his luck and didn't earn enough money to live on.*

down on someone or something against someone or something; negative about someone or something. □ *I've been down on red meat lately. It's better to eat chicken or fish.* □ *The teacher was down on Tom because he's always talking in class.*

down South to or in the southeastern United States. (See also **back East; out West; up North.**) □ *I used to live down South.* □ *We are going down South for the winter.*

down the drain lost forever; wasted. (Also literal. Informal.) □ *I just hate to see all that money go down the drain.* □ *Well, there goes the whole project, right down the drain.*

down the hatch [to] swallow (something). (Informal or slang. Sometimes said when someone takes a drink of alcohol.) □ *Come on, Billy. Eat your dinner. Down the hatch!* □ *John raised his glass of beer and said, "Down the hatch."*

down the street a short distance away on this same street. □ *Sally lives just down the street.* □ *There is a drugstore down the street. It's very convenient.*

down the tubes ruined; wasted. (Slang.) □ *His political career went down the tubes after the scandal. He's lost his job.* □ *The business went down the tubes.*

down-to-earth 1. direct, frank, and honest. □ *You can depend on Ann. She's very down-to-earth.* □ *It's good that she's down-to-earth and will give us a frank response.* **2.** practical; not theoretical; not fanciful. □ *Her ideas for the boutique are always very down-to-earth.* □ *The committee's plans for the village are anything but down-to-earth.*

down to the last detail considering all of the details. □ *Jean planned the party very carefully, down to the last detail.* □ *Mary wanted to be in charge of everything right down to the last detail.*

down to the wire at the very last minute; up to the very last instant. (Refers to a wire that marks the end of a horse race.) □ *I have to turn this in tomorrow, and I'll be working down to the wire.* □ *When we get down to the wire, we'll know better what to do.*

down with some disease ill; sick at home. (Can be said about many diseases.) □ *Tom isn't here. He's down with a cold.* □ *Sally is down with the flu.* □ *The whole office has come down with something.*

downhill all the way easy all the way. (Informal.) □ *Don't worry about your algebra course. It's downhill all the way.* □ *The mayor said that the job of mayor is easy—in fact, downhill all the way.*

downhill from here on easy from this point on. (Informal.) □ *The worst part is over. It's downhill from here on.* □ *The painful part of this procedure is over. It's downhill from here on.*

drag one's **feet** to act very slowly, often deliberately. □ *The government is dragging its feet on this bill because it costs too much.* □ *If the planning department had not dragged their feet, the building would have been built by now.*

a **drag (on** someone**)** a burden to someone; a bore. (Slang. Preceded by *be, become, seem like,* or *act like.*) □ *Mr. Franklin* *seems like a drag on Mrs. Franklin.* □ *Yes, I'd expect him to be a drag.*

draw a bead on someone or something to aim at someone or something; to pick out someone or something for special treatment. (Informal.) □ *Ann wants a new car, and she has drawn a bead on a red convertible.* □ *Jane wants to get married, and she has drawn a bead on Tom.*

draw a blank 1. to get no response; to find nothing. □ *I asked him about Tom's financial problems, and I just drew a blank.* □ *We looked in the files for an hour, but we drew a blank.* **2.** to fail to remember (something). □ *I tried to remember her telephone number, but I could only draw a blank.* □ *It was a very hard test with just one question to answer, and I drew a blank.*

draw a line between something **and** something **else** AND **draw the line between** something **and** something **else** to separate two things; to distinguish or differentiate between two things. (See also **draw the line (at** something**)**.) □ *It's necessary to draw a line between bumping into people and striking them.* □ *It's very hard to draw the line between slamming a door and just closing it loudly.*

draw blood 1. to make a wound that bleeds. □ *The dog chased me and bit me hard, but it didn't draw blood.* □ *The boxer landed just one punch and drew blood immediately.* **2.** to anger or insult a person. □ *Sally screamed out a terrible insult at Tom. Judging by the look on his face, she really drew blood.* □ *Tom started yelling and cursing, trying to insult Sally. He wouldn't be satisfied until he had drawn blood, too.*

draw interest 1. to appear interesting and get (someone's) attention. (Note the variation in the examples below.) □ *This kind of event isn't likely to draw a lot of interest.* □ *What kind of thing will draw interest?* **2.** [for money] to earn interest while on deposit. □ *Put your money in the bank so it will draw interest.* □ *The cash value of some insurance policies also draws interest.*

draw lots AND **draw straws** to choose from a group of things to determine who will do something. (Typically, to choose a straw from a bundle of straws. The person with the shortest straw is selected.) □ *We drew lots to decide who would wash the dishes.* □ *The players drew straws to determine who would go first.*

draw someone or something **out 1.** [with *someone*] to coax someone to speak or answer; to bring someone into a conversation or other social interaction. □ *Jane is usually very shy with older men, but Tom really drew her out last evening.* 🅃 *John drew out Mr. Smith on the question of tax increases.* **2.** [with *something*] to make something longer in length or time. 🅃 *Jane drew out the conversation for more than twenty minutes.* □ *Bill drew the taffy candy out into a long string.*

draw (someone's**) fire (away from** someone or something**)** to make oneself a target in order to protect someone or something. (Refers to gunfire.) □ *The mother bird drew fire away from her chicks.* □ *The hen drew the hunter's fire away from her nest.* □ *Birds draw fire by flapping their wings to get attention.* □ *The president drew fire away from Congress by proposing a compromise.*

draw something **to a close** to make something end. □ *It is now time to draw this evening to a close.* □ *What a lovely vacation. It's a shame that we must draw it to a close.*

draw something **up** to put something into writing; to prepare a written document; to put plans on paper. (Used especially with legal documents prepared by a lawyer.) □ *You should draw a will up as soon as you can.* 🅃 *I went to see my lawyer this morning about drawing up a will.* 🅃 *The architect is drawing up plans for the new city hall.*

draw straws Go to draw lots.

draw the line (at something**)** to set a limit at something; to decide when a limit has been reached. (See also **hold the line (at** someone or something**)**.) □ *You can make as much noise as you want, but I draw the* *line at fighting.* □ *It's hard to keep young people under control, but you have to draw the line somewhere.*

draw the line between something **and** something **else** Go to **draw a line between** something **and** something **else.**

draw to a close to end; to come to an end. □ *This evening is drawing to a close.* □ *It's a shame that our vacation is drawing to a close.*

drawn and quartered dealt with very severely. (Refers to a practice of torturing someone guilty of treason, usually a male, by disemboweling and dividing the body into four parts.) □ *Todd was practically drawn and quartered for losing the Wilson contract.* □ *You were much too harsh with Jean. No matter what she did, she didn't need to be drawn and quartered for it!*

a **dream come true** a wish or a dream that has become real. □ *Going to Hawaii is like a dream come true.* □ *Having you for a friend is a dream come true.*

Dream on. What you are expecting or wanting to happen is nothing but fantasy, so enjoy yourself and create as many fantasies as you want. □ *You want to get promoted to general manager? Dream on.* □ *You, an opera singer? Dream on.*

dredge something **up** Go to **rake** something **up.**

dress someone **down** to bawl someone out; to give someone a good scolding. (Primarily military.) □ *The sergeant dressed the soldier down severely.* □ *I know they'll dress me down when I get home.*

dressed to kill dressed in fancy or stylish clothes. (Slang.) □ *Wow, look at Sally! She's really dressed to kill.* □ *A person doesn't go to church dressed to kill.*

dressed to the nines dressed very well. (What *nines* means is not known.) □ *Tom showed up at the dance dressed to the nines.* □ *Sally is even dressed to the nines at the office.*

dribs and drabs in small irregular quantities. (Especially with *in* and *by.*) □ *The checks for the charity are coming in in dribs and drabs.* □ *The members of the orchestra arrived by dribs and drabs.* □ *All her fortune was spent in dribs and drabs on silly things—like clothes and fine wines.*

drink to excess to drink too much alcohol; to drink alcohol continually. □ *Mr. Franklin drinks to excess.* □ *Some people drink to excess only at parties.*

drive a hard bargain to work hard to negotiate prices or agreements in one's own favor. (Informal.) □ *I saved $200 by driving a hard bargain when I bought my new car.* □ *All right, sir, you drive a hard bargain. I'll sell you this car for $12,450.* □ *You drive a hard bargain, Jane, but I'll sign the contract.*

drive at something to be making a point; to be approaching the making of a point. □ *I do not understand what you are telling me. What are you driving at?* □ *She was driving at how important it is to get an education.*

drive someone **crazy** AND **drive** someone **mad 1.** to make someone insane. □ *He's so strange that he actually drove his wife crazy.* □ *Doctor, there are little green people following me around trying to drive me mad.* **2.** to annoy or irritate someone. □ *This itch is driving me crazy.* □ *All these telephone calls are driving me mad.*

drive someone **mad** Go to **drive** someone **crazy.**

drive someone **out (of office)** Go to **force** someone **out (of office).**

drive someone **to the wall** Go to **force** someone **to the wall.**

drive someone **up the wall 1.** to make someone insane. (Slang.) □ *Mr. Franklin drove his wife up the wall.* □ *All my problems will drive me up the wall someday.* **2.** to annoy or irritate someone. (Slang.) □ *Stop whistling that tune. You're driving me up the wall.* □ *All his talk about moving to California nearly drove me up the wall.*

drive something **home** to make something clearly understood. (Also literal.) □ *Why do I always have to shout at you to drive something home?* 🅃 *Sometimes you have to be forceful to drive home a point.*

drive something **into the ground** Go to run something into the ground.

driving force (behind someone or something**)** a person or a thing that motivates or directs someone or something. □ *Money is the driving force behind most businesses.* □ *Ambition is the driving force behind Tom.* □ *Love can also be a driving force.*

drop a bomb(shell) AND **explode a bombshell; drop a brick** to announce shocking or startling news. (Also literal for *bomb* and *brick*. Informal or slang.) □ *They really dropped a bombshell when they announced that the mayor had cancer.* □ *Friday is a good day to drop a bomb like that. It gives the business world the weekend to recover.* □ *They must speak very carefully when they explode a bombshell like that.* □ *They really dropped a brick when they told the cause of her illness.*

drop a brick Go to drop a bomb(shell).

drop around (sometime**)** AND **drop by (**sometime**)** to come and visit at some future time. (Similar to drop in (on someone).) □ *Nice to see you, Mary. You and Bob must drop around sometime.* □ *Please do drop around when you're out driving.* □ *We'd love to have you drop by.*

drop by (sometime**)** Go to drop around (sometime).

drop by the wayside Go to fall by the wayside.

drop dead 1. to die suddenly. □ *I understand that Tom Anderson dropped dead at his desk yesterday.* □ *No one knows why Uncle Bob suddenly dropped dead.* **2.** Go away and stop bothering me. (Rude slang.) □ *If you think I'm going to put up with your rudeness all afternoon, you can just drop dead!* □ *Drop dead! I'm not your slave!*

drop everything to stop doing whatever one is doing. □ *Drop everything and go outside. The house is on fire.* □ *Do you expect me to drop everything and come and pick you up at school?*

drop in one's **tracks** to stop or collapse from exhaustion; to die suddenly. □ *If I keep working this way, I'll drop in my tracks.* □ *Uncle Bob was working in the garden and dropped in his tracks. We are all sorry that he's dead.*

drop in (on someone**)** AND **drop in (to say hello)** to pay someone a casual visit, perhaps a surprise visit. □ *I hate to drop in on people when they aren't expecting me.* □ *You're welcome to drop in at any time.* □ *We won't stay a minute. We just dropped in to say hello.*

a **drop in the bucket** Go to a drop in the ocean.

a **drop in the ocean** AND a **drop in the bucket** just a little bit; not enough of something to make a difference. □ *But one dollar isn't enough! That's just a drop in the ocean.* □ *At this point your help is nothing more than a drop in the ocean. I need far more help than twenty people could give.* □ *I won't accept your offer. It's just a drop in the bucket.*

drop in (to say hello) Go to drop in (on someone).

drop names to mention the names of important or famous people as if they were personal friends. □ *Mary always tries to impress people by dropping the names of well-known film stars.* □ *Bill's such a snob. Leave it to him to drop the names of all the local gentry.*

drop off (to sleep) to go to sleep without difficulty; to fall asleep. □ *I sat in the warm room for five minutes, and then I dropped off to sleep.* □ *After I've eaten dinner, I can drop off with no trouble at all.*

drop out (of something**)** to stop being a member of something; to stop attending or participating in something. (Also literal.) □ *I'm working part time so that I won't have to drop out of college.* □ *I don't want to drop out at this time.*

drop someone to stop being friends with someone, especially with one's boyfriend or girlfriend. □ *Bob finally dropped Jane. I don't know what he saw in her.* □ *I'm surprised that she didn't drop him first.*

drop someone **a few lines** Go to drop someone a line.

drop someone **a line** AND **drop** someone **a few lines** to write a letter or a note to someone. (*Line* refers to lines of writing.) □ *I dropped Aunt Jane a line last Thanksgiving.* □ *She usually drops me a few lines around the first of the year.*

drop someone's **name** to mention the name of an important or famous person as if the person were a personal friend. □ *Mary always tries to impress people by dropping a well-known movie star's name.* □ *Joan is such a snob. Leave it to her to drop some social leader's name.*

drop the ball to make a blunder; to fail in some way. (Refers to dropping the ball in a ball game.) □ *Everything was going fine in the election until my campaign manager dropped the ball.* □ *You can't trust John to do the job right. He's always dropping the ball.*

drop the other shoe to do the deed that completes something; to do the expected remaining part of something. (Refers to the removal of shoes at bedtime. One shoe is dropped, and then the process is completed when the second shoe drops.) □ *Mr. Franklin has left his wife. Soon he'll drop the other shoe and divorce her.* □ *Tommy has just failed three classes in school. We expect him to drop the other shoe and quit altogether any day now.*

drop the subject to stop talking about whatever is being talked about. □ *This is a disgusting conversation. Let's drop the subject.* □ *He had heard enough about my operation, so I just dropped the subject.*

drown one's **sorrows** Go to drown one's troubles.

drown one's **troubles** AND **drown** one's **sorrows** to try to forget one's problems by drinking a lot of alcohol. (Informal.) □ *Bill is in the bar, drowning his troubles.* □ *Jane is at home, drowning her sorrows.*

drown someone or something **out** to make so much noise that someone or something cannot be heard. □ *I can't hear what you said. The radio drowned you out.* 🅃 *We couldn't hear all the concert because the airplanes drowned out the quiet parts.*

drug on the market on the market in great abundance; a glut on the market. □ *Right now, small computers are a drug on the market.* □ *Ten years ago, small transistor radios were a drug on the market.*

drum some business up to stimulate people to buy what you are selling. □ *I need to do something to drum some business up.* 🅃 *A little bit of advertising would drum up some business.*

drum someone **out of** something to expel or send someone away from something, especially in a formal or public fashion. (From the military use of drums on such occasions.) □ *The officer was drummed out of the regiment for misconduct.* □ *I heard that he was drummed out of the country club for cheating on his golf score.*

drum something **into** someone**('s head)** to make someone learn something through persistent repetition. □ *Yes, I know that. They drummed it into me as a child.* □ *Now I'm drumming it into my own children.* □ *I will drum it into their heads day and night.*

drunk and disorderly a criminal charge for public drunkenness accompanied by bad or offensive behavior. □ *The judge fined Max for being drunk and disorderly.* □ *In addition to being convicted for driving while intoxicated, Max was found guilty of being drunk and disorderly.*

drunk as a lord Go to (as) drunk as a lord.

drunk as a skunk Go to (as) drunk as a lord.

dry as a bone Go to (as) dry as a bone.

dry as dust Go to (as) dry as dust.

dry run an attempt; a rehearsal. □ *We had better have a dry run for the official ceremony tomorrow.* □ *The children will need a dry run before their procession in the pageant.*

dry someone **out** to help a drunk person get sober. □ *We had to call the doctor to help dry Mr. Franklin out.* 🅃 *It takes time to* *dry out someone who has been drinking for a week.*

dry up to become silent; to stop talking. (Also literal. Informal.) □ *The young lecturer was so nervous that he forgot what he was going to say and dried up.* □ *Actors have a fear of drying up on stage.* □ *Oh, dry up! I'm sick of listening to you.*

duck and cover 1. to dodge something, such as an issue or a difficult question, and attempt to shield oneself against similar issues or questions. (Refers to ducking down and taking cover to protect oneself.) □ *The candidate's first reaction to the question was to duck and cover.* □ *The debaters were ducking and covering throughout the evening.* **2.** dodging something, such as an issue or a difficult question, and attempting to shield oneself against similar issues or questions. (Typically **duck-and-cover**.) □ *These politicians are experts at duck-and-cover.* □ *When in doubt, turn to duck-and-cover.*

dull as dishwater Go to (as) dull as dishwater.

dull as ditchwater Go to (as) dull as dishwater.

Dutch auction an auction or sale that starts off with a high asking price that is then reduced until a buyer is found. □ *Dutch auctions are rare—most auctioneers start with a lower price than they hope to obtain.* □ *My real estate agent advised me to ask a reasonable price for my house rather than get involved with a Dutch auction.*

Dutch courage unusual or artificial courage arising from the influence of alcohol. □ *It was Dutch courage that made the football fan attack the policeman.* □ *It will take a bit of Dutch courage to make an after-dinner speech.*

Dutch treat a social occasion where one pays for oneself. (See also **go Dutch**.) □ *"It's nice of you to ask me out to dinner," she said, "but could we make it a Dutch treat?"* □ *The office outing is always a Dutch treat.*

Dutch uncle a man who gives frank and direct advice to someone in the manner of a parent or relative. □ *I would not have to lecture you like a Dutch uncle if you were not so extravagant.* □ *He acts more like a Dutch uncle than a husband. He's forever telling her what to do in public.*

duty bound (to do something**)** forced by a sense of duty and honor to do something. □ *Good evening, madam. I'm duty bound to inform you that we have arrested your husband.* □ *No one made me say that. I was duty bound.*

dyed-in-the-wool permanent; indelible; stubborn. (Usually said of a person.) □ *My uncle was a dyed-in-the-wool farmer. He wouldn't change for anything.* □ *Sally is a dyed-in-the-wool socialist.*

dying to do something very anxious to do something. □ *I'm just dying to go sailing in your new boat.* □ *After a long hot day like this one, I'm just dying for a cool drink of water.*

E

an **eager beaver** someone who is very enthusiastic; someone who works very hard. □ *New volunteers are always eager beavers.* □ *The young assistant gets to work very early. She's a real eager beaver.*

an **eagle eye** careful attention; an intently watchful eye. (From the sharp eyesight of the eagle.) □ *The students wrote their essays under the eagle eye of the headmaster.* □ *The umpire kept his eagle eye on the tennis match.*

early bird someone who gets up or arrives early or starts something very promptly, especially someone who gains an advantage of some kind by so doing. (See also The **early bird gets the worm.**) □ *The members of the Smith family are all early birds. They caught the first bus to town.* □ *I was an early bird and got the best selection of flowers.*

The **early bird gets the worm.** The early person will get the reward or benefit. □ *Don't be late again! Don't you know that the early bird gets the worm?* □ *I'll be there before the sun is up. After all, the early bird gets the worm.*

early on early; at an early stage. □ *We recognized the problem early on, but we waited too long to do something about it.* □ *This doesn't surprise me. I knew about it early on.*

Early to bed, early to rise(, makes a man healthy, wealthy, and wise). Going to bed early and getting up early is good for you. (Proverb. Sometimes said to explain why a person is going to bed early. The last part of the saying is sometimes left out.) □ *Tom left the party at ten o'clock, saying, "Early to bed, early to rise, makes a man healthy, wealthy, and wise."* □ *I always get up at dawn. After all, early to bed, early to rise.*

earn one's **keep** to help out with chores in return for food and a place to live; to earn one's pay by doing what is expected. □ *I earn my keep at college by shoveling snow in the winter.* □ *Tom hardly earns his keep around here. He should be fired.*

[ears are red] Go to one's **ears are red.**

[ears are ringing] Go to one's **ears are ringing.**

ease off (on someone or something**)** AND **ease up (on** someone or something**)** to reduce the urgency with which one deals with someone or something; to put less pressure on someone or something. □ *Ease off on John. He has been yelled at enough today.* □ *Yes, please ease off. I can't stand any more.* □ *Tell them to ease up on the horses. They are getting tired.* □ *Tell them to ease up now! They are making the horses work too hard.*

ease up (on someone or something**)** Go to **ease off (on** someone or something**)**.

easier said than done Go to **(be) easier said than done.**

easy as ABC Go to **(as) easy as ABC.**

easy as (apple) pie Go to **(as) easy as (apple) pie.**

easy as duck soup Go to **(as) easy as duck soup.**

easy as falling off a log Go to **(as) easy as falling off a log.**

easy as rolling off a log Go to **(as) easy as falling off a log.**

easy come, easy go <a phrase used when accepting the loss of something that re-

quired only a small amount of effort to get in the first place.> □ *Ann found twenty dollars in the morning and spent it foolishly at noon. "Easy come, easy go," she said.* □ *John spends his money as fast as he can earn it. With John it's easy come, easy go.*

Easy does it. Act with care. (Informal.) □ *Be careful with that glass vase. Easy does it!* □ *Now, now, Tom. Don't get angry. Easy does it.*

easy to come by easily found; easily purchased; readily available. □ *Please be careful with that phonograph record. It was not easy to come by.* □ *A good dictionary is very easy to come by.*

eat (a meal) out AND **dine out** to eat a meal at a restaurant. □ *I like to eat a meal out every now and then.* □ *Yes, it's good to eat out and try different kinds of food.* □ *It costs a lot of money to dine out often.*

eat and run to eat a meal or a snack and then leave. □ *Well, I hate to eat and run but I have to take care of some errands.* □ *I don't invite John to dinner anymore because he always has some excuse to eat and run.*

eat away at someone or something **1.** to remove parts, bit by bit. □ *John's disease was eating away at him.* □ *The acid in the rain slowly ate away at the stone wall.* **2.** [with *someone*] to bother or worry someone. □ *Her failure to pass the exam was eating away at her.* □ *Fear of appearing in court was eating away at Tom.*

eat high on the hog to eat good or expensive food. (Folksy. Compare this with **live high on the hog**. Note the *so* in the second example. See also **live high off the hog**.) □ *The Smith family has been eating pretty high on the hog since they had a good corn harvest.* □ *John would have more money to spend on clothing if he didn't eat so high on the hog.*

eat humble pie 1. to act very humbly when one is shown to be wrong. □ *I think I'm right, but if I'm wrong, I'll eat humble pie.* □ *You think you're so smart. I hope you have to eat humble pie.* **2.** to accept insults and humiliation. □ *John, stand up for your rights. You don't have to eat humble pie all the time.* □ *Beth seems quite happy to eat humble pie. She should stand up for her rights.*

eat like a bird to eat only small amounts of food; to peck at one's food. □ *Jane is very slim because she eats like a bird.* □ *Bill is trying to lose weight by eating like a bird.*

eat like a horse to eat large amounts of food. (Informal.) □ *No wonder he's so fat. He eats like a horse.* □ *John works like a horse and eats like a horse, so he never gets fat.*

eat one's **cake and have it too** Go to **have** one's **cake and eat it too.**

eat one's **hat** <a phrase telling the kind of thing that one would do if a very unlikely event really happens.> (Informal. Always used with an *if*-clause.) □ *If we get there on time, I'll eat my hat.* □ *I'll eat my hat if you get a raise.* □ *He said he'd eat his hat if she got elected.*

eat one's **heart out 1.** to be very sad (about someone or something). □ *Bill spent a lot of time eating his heart out after his divorce.* □ *Sally ate her heart out when she had to sell her house.* **2.** to be envious (of someone or something). (Informal.) □ *Do you like my new watch? Well, eat your heart out. It was the last one in the store.* □ *Don't eat your heart out about my new car. Go get one of your own.*

eat one's **words** to have to take back one's statements; to confess that one's predictions were wrong. □ *You shouldn't say that to me. I'll make you eat your words.* □ *John was wrong about the election and had to eat his words.*

eat out of someone's **hands** to do what someone else wants; to obey someone eagerly. (Often with *have*.) □ *Just wait! I'll have everyone eating out of my hands. They'll do whatever I ask.* □ *The president has Congress eating out of his hands.* □ *A lot of people are eating out of his hands.*

eat someone **out** Go to **chew** someone **out**.

eat someone **out of house and home** to eat a lot of food (in someone's home); to eat all the food in the house. □ *Billy has a huge appetite. He almost eats us out of house and home.* □ *When the kids come home from college, they always eat us out of house and home.*

eat something **up** to enjoy, absorb, or appreciate. (Also literal. Informal.) □ *The audience loved the comedian. They ate his act up and demanded more.* 🅃 *The children ate up Grandfather's stories. They listened to him for hours.*

ebb and flow to decrease and then increase, as with tides; a decrease followed by an increase, as with tides. □ *The fortunes of the major political parties tend to ebb and flow over time.* □ *The ebb and flow of democracy through history is a fascinating subject.*

edge someone **out** to remove a person from a job, office, or position, usually by beating the person in competition. □ *The vice president edged the president out during the last election.* 🅃 *Tom edged out Bob as the new cook at the restaurant.*

egg someone **on** to encourage, urge, or dare someone to continue doing something, usually something unwise. □ *John wouldn't have done the dangerous experiment if his brother hadn't egged him on.* □ *The two boys kept throwing stones because the other children were egging them on.*

either feast or famine either too much (of something) or not enough (of something). (Also without *either*.) □ *This month is very dry, and last month it rained almost every day. Our weather is either feast or famine.* □ *Sometimes we are busy, and sometimes we have nothing to do. It's feast or famine.*

elbow someone **out (of** something**)** to force or pressure someone out of something, such as an office, post, or status. (Also literal when attempting to use one's elbows to move the person beside oneself away.) □ *The old head of the company was elbowed out of office by a young vice president.* □ *They tried to elbow me out, but I held on to what was mine.*

eleventh-hour decision a decision made at the last possible minute. (See also **at the eleventh hour**.) □ *Eleventh-hour decisions are seldom satisfactory.* □ *The president's eleventh-hour decision was made in a great hurry, but it turned out to be correct.*

an **end in itself** for its own sake; toward its own ends; toward no purpose but its own. □ *For Bob, art is an end in itself. He doesn't hope to make any money from it.* □ *Learning is an end in itself. Knowledge does not have to have a practical application.*

the **end of the line** Go to the **end of the road**.

the **end of the road** AND the **end of the line** the end; the end of the whole process; death. (*Line* originally referred to railroad tracks.) □ *Our house is at the end of the road.* □ *We rode the train to the end of the line.* □ *When we reach the end of the road on this project, we'll get paid.* □ *You've come to the end of the line. I'll not lend you another penny.* □ *When I reach the end of the road, I wish to be buried in a quiet place, near some trees.*

end something **up** to bring something to an end. (Informal. Also without *up*.) □ *I want you to end your game up and come in for dinner.* 🅃 *We can't end up the game until someone scores.*

end up by doing something to conclude something by doing something. (Compare this with **end up** doing something.) □ *We ended up by going back to my house.* □ *They danced until midnight and ended up by having pizza in the front room.*

end up doing something AND **wind up** doing something to have to do something that one had not planned to do. (Compare this with **end up by** doing something.) □ *We ended up going back to my house after all.* □ *Todd wound up inviting everyone to his house, even though he planned to spend the evening at home alone.*

end up (somehow**)** to end something at a particular place, in a particular state, or by having to do something. (Compare this with **end up by** doing something.) □ *I ended up having to pay for everyone's dinner.* □ *After paying for dinner, I ended up* *broke.* □ *We all ended up at my house.* □ *After playing in the rain, we all ended up with colds.*

end up somewhere AND **wind up** somewhere to finish at a certain place. □ *If you don't get straightened out, you'll end up in jail.* □ *I fell and hurt myself, and I wound up in the hospital.*

end up with the short end of the stick Go to get the short end of the stick.

engage in small talk to talk only about minor matters rather than important or personal matters. □ *All the people at the party were engaging in small talk.* □ *They chatted about the weather and otherwise engaged in small talk.*

Enjoy your meal. <a polite phrase said by a waiter or waitress when delivering food to the table.> □ *There you go. Enjoy your meal.* □ *Do you have the medium steak? Enjoy your meal.*

Enough is enough. That is enough, and there should be no more. □ *Stop asking for money! Enough is enough!* □ *I've heard all the complaining from you that I can take. Stop! Enough is enough!*

enough to go (a)round a supply adequate to serve everyone. (Informal.) □ *Don't take too much. There's not enough to go around.* □ *I cooked some extra potatoes, so there should be enough to go around.*

enter one's **mind** to come to one's mind; [for an idea or memory] to come into one's consciousness. □ *Leave you behind? The thought never even entered my mind.* □ *A very interesting idea just entered my mind. What if I ran for Congress?*

enter the fray Go to join the fray.

equal to someone or something able to handle or deal with someone or something. (Also literal.) □ *I'm afraid that I'm not equal to Mrs. Smith's problem right now. Please ask her to come back later.* □ *That's a very difficult task, but I'm sure Bill is equal to it.*

escape someone's **notice** to go unnoticed; to be overlooked. (Usually a way to point out that someone has failed to see or respond to something.) □ *I suppose my earlier request escaped your notice, so I'm writing again.* □ *I'm sorry. Your letter escaped my notice.*

even in the best of times even when things are good; even when things are going well. □ *It is hard to get high-quality leather even in the best of times.* □ *John had difficulty getting a loan even in the best of times because of his poor credit record.*

even steven even (with someone or something). (Informal or slang. Preceded by *be* or *seem*.) □ *Bill hit Tom; then Tom hit Bill. Now they are even steven.* □ *Mary paid Ann the $100 she owed her. Ann said, "Good, we are even steven."*

ever and anon now and then; occasionally. (Literary and archaic.) □ *Ever and anon the princess would pay a visit to the sorcerer in the small walled garden directly behind the castle.* □ *We eat swan ever and anon, but not when we can get wild boar.*

Every cloud has a silver lining. There is something good in every bad thing. (Proverb.) □ *Jane was upset when she saw that all her flowers had died from the frost. But when she saw that the weeds had died too, she said, "Every cloud has a silver lining."* □ *Sally had a sore throat and had to stay home from school. When she learned she missed a math test, she said, "Every cloud has a silver lining."*

Every dog has his day Go to Every dog has its day.

Every dog has its day. AND **Every dog has his day.** Everyone will get a chance. (Proverb.) □ *Don't worry, you'll get chosen for the team. Every dog has its day.* □ *You may become famous someday. Every dog has his day.*

every inch a something AND **every inch the** something completely; in every way. □ *Mary is every inch the schoolteacher.* □ *Her father is every inch a gentleman.*

every inch the something Go to every inch a something.

every last one every one; every single one. (Informal.) □ *You must eat all your peas!*

Every last one! □ *Each of you—every last one—has to take some medicine.*

every living soul every person. (Informal.) □ *I expect every living soul to be there and be there on time.* □ *This is the kind of problem that affects every living soul.*

every minute counts AND **every moment counts** time is very important. □ *Doctor, please try to get here quickly. Every minute counts.* □ *When you take a test, you must work rapidly because every minute counts.* □ *When you're trying to meet a deadline, every moment counts.*

every moment counts Go to every minute counts.

every nook and cranny every small, out-of-the-way place where something can be hidden. □ *We looked for the tickets in every nook and cranny. They were lost. There was no doubt.* □ *The decorator had placed flowers in every nook and cranny.*

(every) now and again Go to (every) now and then.

(every) now and then AND **(every) now and again; (every) once in a while** occasionally; infrequently. □ *We eat lamb every now and then.* □ *We eat pork now and then.* □ *I read a novel every now and again.* □ *We don't go to the movies except maybe every now and then.* □ *I drink coffee every once in a while.* □ *I drink tea once in a while.*

(every) once in a while Go to (every) now and then.

every other person or thing every second person or thing; alternating. □ *The magician turned every other card over.* □ *Every other table had an ashtray on it.*

every time one **turns around** frequently; at every turn; with annoying frequency. (Informal.) □ *Somebody asks me for money every time I turn around.* □ *Something goes wrong with Bill's car every time he turns around.*

(every) Tom, Dick, and Harry everyone, without discrimination; ordinary people. (Not necessarily males.) □ *The golf club is very exclusive. They don't let any Tom, Dick, and Harry join.* □ *Mary's sending out very few invitations. She doesn't want every Tom, Dick, and Harry turning up.*

every which way in all directions. (Folksy.) □ *The children were all running every which way.* □ *The wind scattered the leaves every which way.*

everything but the kitchen sink almost everything one can think of. □ *When Sally went off to college, she took everything but the kitchen sink.* □ *John orders everything but the kitchen sink when he goes out to dinner, especially if someone else is paying for it.*

everything from A to Z Go to everything from soup to nuts.

everything from soup to nuts AND **everything from A to Z** almost everything one can think of. □ *For dinner we had everything from soup to nuts.* □ *In college I studied everything from soup to nuts.* □ *She mentioned everything from A to Z.*

everything humanly possible everything that is in the range of human powers. □ *The rescuers did everything humanly possible to find the lost campers.* □ *The doctor tried everything humanly possible to save the patient.*

Everything's coming up roses. Everything is really just excellent. □ *Life is wonderful. Everything is coming up roses.* □ *Q: How are things going? A: Everything's coming up roses.*

the **exception that proves the rule** <a saying identifying an exception to a rule or guideline as emphasizing the existence of the rule.> □ *Sixth-graders do not have to wear school uniforms, but they're the exception that proves the rule.* □ *The youngest dog is allowed in the house. He's the exception that proves the rule.*

exchange more than some number of **words with** someone to say hardly anything to someone. (Always negated.) □ *I know Tom was there, but I am sure that I didn't exchange more than three words with him before he left.* □ *We hardly exchanged more than two words the whole evening.* □

Sally and Liz didn't have enough time to exchange more than five words.

exciting as watching (the) paint dry Go to (as) exciting as watching (the) paint dry.

excuse oneself to make polite apologies or explanations before leaving a place. □ *Please excuse me. I must leave.* □ *I will have to excuse myself from this meeting since I have a vested interest in the outcome.*

excuse someone **1.** to forgive someone. (Usually with *me*. Said when interrupting or when some other minor offense has been committed. There are many mannerly uses of this expression.) □ *John came in late and said, "Excuse me, please."* □ *John said "excuse me" when he interrupted our conversation.* □ *When John made a strange noise at the table, he said quietly, "Excuse me."* □ *John suddenly left the room saying, "Excuse me. I'll be right back."* **2.** to permit someone to leave; to permit someone to remain away from an event. □ *The coach excused John from practice yesterday.* □ *The teacher excused John, and he ran quickly from the room.*

expecting (a child) pregnant. (Euphemism.) □ *Tommy's mother is expecting a child.* □ *Oh, I didn't know she was expecting.*

expense is no object Go to money is no object.

explain oneself **1.** to explain what one has said or done or what one thinks or feels. (Formal and polite.) □ *Please take a moment to explain yourself. I'm sure we are interested in your ideas.* □ *Yes, if you give me a moment to explain myself, I think you'll agree with my idea.* **2.** to give an explanation or excuse for something wrong that one may have done. (Usually said in anger.) □ *Young man! Come in here and explain yourself this instant.* □ *Why did you do that, Tom Smith? You had better explain yourself, and it had better be good.*

explain something **away** to give a good explanation for something; to explain something so that it seems less important; to make excuses for something. □ *This is a very serious matter, and you cannot just explain it away.* 🅃 *John couldn't explain away his low grades.*

explode a bombshell Go to drop a bomb(shell).

express one's **anger** to allow a release or expression of anger, such as through angry words. □ *Don't keep your emotions inside of you. You have to learn to express your anger.* □ *Bob expresses his anger by yelling at people.*

extend credit (to someone**)** AND **extend** someone **credit** to allow someone to purchase something on credit. □ *I'm sorry, Mr. Smith, but because of your poor record of payment, we are no longer able to extend credit to you.* □ *Look at this letter, Jane. The store won't extend credit anymore.* □ *We are unable to extend that company credit any longer.*

extend one's **sympathy (to** someone**)** to express sympathy to someone. (A very polite and formal way to tell someone that you are sorry about a misfortune.) □ *Please permit me to extend my sympathy to you and your children. I'm very sorry to hear of the death of your husband.* □ *Let's extend our sympathy to Bill Jones, who is in the hospital with a broken leg. We should send him some flowers.*

extend someone **credit** Go to extend credit (to someone).

extenuating circumstances special circumstances that account for an irregular or improper way of doing something. □ *Mary was permitted to arrive late because of extenuating circumstances.* □ *Due to extenuating circumstances, the class will not meet today.*

the **eye of the storm** the center of a problem; the center of a commotion or a disturbance. □ *Tom, finding himself at the eye of the storm, tried to blame someone else for the problem.* □ *The manager's office was known as the eye of the storm since all the major problems ended up there.*

eyeball-to-eyeball person to person; face to face. □ *The discussions will have to be* *eyeball-to-eyeball to be effective.* □ *Telephone conversations are a waste of time. We need to talk eyeball-to-eyeball.*

[eyes are bigger than one's **stomach]** Go to One's eyes are bigger than one's stomach.

F

face someone **down** to overcome someone by being bold; to disconcert someone by displaying great confidence. □ *The teacher faced the angry student down without saying anything.* 🅃 *The mayor couldn't face down the entire city council.*

face the music to receive punishment; to accept the unpleasant results of one's actions. □ *Mary broke a dining-room window and had to face the music when her father got home.* □ *After failing a math test, Tom had to go home and face the music.*

face-to-face 1. in person; in the same location. (Said only of people. An adverb.) □ *Let's talk about this face-to-face. I don't like talking over the telephone.* □ *Many people prefer to talk face-to-face.* **2.** facing one another; in the same location. □ *I prefer to have a face-to-face meeting.* □ *They work better on a face-to-face basis.*

the **facts of life 1.** the facts of sex and reproduction, especially human reproduction. (See also birds and the bees.) □ *My parents told me the facts of life when I was nine years old.* □ *Bill learned the facts of life from his classmates.* **2.** the truth about the unpleasant ways that the world works. □ *Mary really learned the facts of life when she got her first job.* □ *Tom couldn't accept the facts of life in business, so he quit.*

fair and impartial fair and unbiased. (Usually referring to some aspect of the legal system, such as a jury, a hearing, or a judge.) □ *Gary felt that he had not received a fair and impartial hearing.* □ *We demand that all of our judges be fair and impartial in every instance.*

fair and square completely fair(ly). □ *She won the game fair and square.* □ *The division of the money should be fair and square.*

fair game someone or something that it is quite permissible to attack. □ *I don't like seeing articles exposing people's private lives, but politicians are fair game.* □ *Journalists always regard movie stars as fair game.*

fair-haired boy a favored person. (Not necessarily young or male.) □ *The teacher's fair-haired boy always does well on tests.* □ *The supervisor's son was the fair-haired boy on the construction site.*

[fair share] Go to one's fair share.

fair to middling only fair or okay; a little better than acceptable. (Folksy.) □ *I don't feel sick, just fair to middling.* □ *The play wasn't really good. It was just fair to middling.*

fair-weather friend someone who is your friend only when things are going well for you. (This person will desert you when things go badly for you. Compare this with A friend in need is a friend indeed.) □ *Bill wouldn't help me with my homework. He's just a fair-weather friend.* □ *A fair-weather friend isn't much help in an emergency.*

fall afoul of someone or something AND **run afoul of** someone or something to get into a situation where one is opposed to someone or something; to get into trouble with someone or something. □ *Dan fell afoul of the law at an early age.* □ *I hope that you will avoid falling afoul of the district manager. She can be a formidable enemy.* □ *I hope I don't run afoul of your sister. She doesn't like me.*

fall (all) over oneself to behave awkwardly and eagerly when doing something. (See also **fall over backwards (to** do something**).**) □ *Tom fell all over himself trying to make Jane feel at home.* □ *I fall over myself when I'm doing something that makes me nervous.*

fall all over someone to give a lot of attention, affection, or praise to someone. (Informal.) □ *My aunt falls all over me whenever she comes to visit.* □ *I hate for someone to fall all over me. It embarrasses me.*

fall apart at the seams [for something] to break into pieces; to fall apart; [for material that is sewn together] to separate at the seams. (Literal for cloth, otherwise figurative. See also **come apart at the seams.**) □ *My new jacket fell apart at the seams.* □ *This old car is about ready to fall apart at the seams.*

fall asleep to go to sleep. □ *The baby cried and cried and finally fell asleep.* □ *Tom fell asleep in class yesterday.*

fall back on someone or something to turn to someone or something for help. (Also literal.) □ *Bill fell back on his brother for help.* □ *John ran out of ink and had to fall back on his pencil.*

fall between two stools to come somewhere between two possibilities and so fail to meet the requirements of either. □ *The material is not suitable for an academic book or for a popular one. It falls between two stools.* □ *He tries to be both teacher and friend, but falls between two stools.*

fall by the wayside AND **drop by the wayside** to give up and quit before the end (of something). (Refers to being too exhausted to finish a footrace.) □ *John fell by the wayside and didn't finish college.* □ *Many people start out to train for a career in medicine, but some of them drop by the wayside.* □ *All of her projects fall by the wayside when she tires of them.*

fall down on the job to fail to do something properly; to fail to do one's job adequately. (Also literal referring to an accident while one is working.) □ *The team kept losing because the coach was falling down on the job.* □ *Tom was fired because he fell down on the job.*

fall flat (on its face) Go to **fall flat (on** one's **face).**

fall flat (on one's **face)** AND **fall flat (on its face)** to be completely unsuccessful. (Informal.) □ *I fell flat on my face when I tried to give my speech.* □ *The play fell flat on its face.* □ *My jokes fall flat most of the time.*

fall for someone or something **1.** [with *someone*] to fall in love with someone. □ *Tom fell for Ann after only two dates. He wants to marry her.* □ *Some men always fall for women with blond hair.* **2.** [with *something*] to be deceived by something. □ *I can't believe you fell for that old trick.* □ *Jane didn't fall for Ann's story.*

fall from grace to cease to be held in favor, especially because of some wrong or foolish action. □ *He was the teacher's pet until he fell from grace by failing the history test.* □ *Mary was the favorite grandchild until she fell from grace by running away from home.*

fall head over heels to fall down, perhaps turning over or rolling. (Also literal.) □ *Fred tripped on the rug and fell head over heels into the center of the room.* □ *Slow down or you will fall down—head over heels.*

fall head over heels in love (with someone**)** to fall deeply in love with someone, perhaps suddenly. □ *Roger fell head over heels in love with Maggie, and they were married within the month.* □ *Very few people actually fall head over heels in love with each other.* □ *She fell head over heels in love and thought she was dreaming.*

fall ill to become ill. □ *Tom fell ill just before he was to perform.* □ *We both fell ill after eating the baked fish.*

fall in to line up in a row, standing shoulder to shoulder. (Also literal, meaning "to collapse." Usually refers to people in scouting or the military. Compare this with **fall in(to) line** and **fall out.**) □ *The Boy Scouts were told to fall in behind the scoutmaster.* □ *The soldiers fell in quickly.*

fall in for something Go to **come in for** something.

fall in love (with someone**)** to develop the emotion of love for someone. ☐ *Tom fell in love with Mary, but she only wanted to be friends.* ☐ *John is too young to really fall in love.*

fall into a trap AND **fall into the trap; fall into** someone's **trap** to become caught in someone's scheme; to be deceived into doing or thinking something. (Also literal.) ☐ *We fell into a trap by asking for an explanation.* ☐ *I fell into his trap when I agreed to drive him home.* ☐ *We fell into the trap of thinking he was honest.*

fall in(to) line 1. to line up with each person (except the first person) standing behind someone. (Compare this with **fall in.**) ☐ *The teacher told the students to fall in line for lunch.* ☐ *Hungry students fall into line very quickly.* **2.** to conform; to **fall in(to) place.** ☐ *All the parts of the problem finally fell into line.* ☐ *Bill's behavior began to fall in line.*

fall in(to) place to fit together; to become organized. ☐ *After we heard the whole story, things began to fall in place.* ☐ *When you get older, the different parts of your life begin to fall into place.*

fall into someone's **trap** Go to **fall into a trap.**

fall into the trap Go to **fall into a trap.**

fall in with someone or something **1.** [with *someone*] to meet someone by accident; to join with someone. ☐ *John has fallen in with a strange group of people.* ☐ *We fell in with some people from our hometown when we went on vacation.* **2.** to agree with someone or something. ☐ *Bill was not able to fall in with our ideas about painting the house red.* ☐ *Bob fell in with Mary's plans to move to Texas.*

fall off to decline or diminish. ☐ *Business falls off during the summer months.* ☐ *My interest in school fell off when I became twenty.*

fall on deaf ears [for talk or ideas] to be ignored by the persons they were intended for. ☐ *Her pleas for mercy fell on deaf ears.* ☐ *All of Sally's good advice fell on deaf ears. Walter had made up his own mind.*

fall out 1. to happen; to result. ☐ *As things fell out, we had a wonderful trip.* ☐ *What fell out of our discussion was a decision to continue.* **2.** to leave one's place in a formation when dismissed. (Usually in scouting or the military. The opposite of **fall in.**) ☐ *The scouts fell out and ran to the campfire.* ☐ *All the soldiers fell out and talked among themselves.*

fall out (with someone **about** something**)** Go to **fall out (with** someone **over** something**).**

fall out (with someone **over** something**)** AND **fall out (with** someone **about** something**)** to quarrel or disagree about something. ☐ *Bill fell out with Sally over the question of buying a new car.* ☐ *Bill fell out with John about who would sleep on the bottom bunk.* ☐ *They are always arguing. They fall out about once a week.*

fall over backwards (to do something**)** AND **bend over backwards (to** do something**); lean over backwards (to** do something**)** to do everything possible to please someone. (Informal. See also **fall (all) over** oneself.) ☐ *The taxi driver fell over backwards to be helpful.* ☐ *The teacher bent over backwards to help the students understand.* ☐ *The principal said that it was not necessary to bend over backwards.* ☐ *You don't have to lean over backwards to get me to help. Just ask.*

fall short (of something**) 1.** to lack something; to lack enough of something. ☐ *We fell short of money at the end of the month.* ☐ *When baking a cake, the cook fell short of eggs and had to go to the store for more.* **2.** to fail to achieve a goal. ☐ *We fell short of our goal of collecting a thousand dollars.* ☐ *Ann ran a fast race, but fell short of the record.*

fall through not to happen; to come to nothing. (Informal.) ☐ *Our plans fell through, and we won't be going to Texas after all.* ☐ *The party fell through at the last minute.*

fall to to begin (to do something). (Compare this with **turn to.**) ☐ *The hungry children took their knives and forks and fell* *to.* □ *The carpenter unpacked his saw and hammer and fell to.* □ *The boys wanted to fight, so the coach put boxing gloves on them and told them to fall to.* □ *John fell to and cleaned up his room after he got yelled at.*

fall to someone **to** do something to become the responsibility of someone. □ *It always falls to me to apologize first.* □ *Why does it fall to me to answer the telephone every time it rings?*

fall (up)on someone or something **1.** to attack someone or something. (Also literal.) □ *The cat fell upon the mouse and killed it.* □ *The children fell on the birthday cake and ate it all.* **2.** [with *someone*] [for a task] to become the duty of someone. □ *The task of telling Mother about the broken vase fell upon Jane.* □ *The job of cleaning up the spill fell upon Tom.*

familiar with someone or something having a good knowledge of someone or something. □ *Are you familiar with changing a flat tire?* □ *I'm can't speak German fluently, but I'm somewhat familiar with the language.*

Familiarity breeds contempt. Knowing a person closely for a long time leads to bad feelings. (Proverb.) □ *Bill and his brothers are always fighting. As they say: "Familiarity breeds contempt."* □ *Mary and John were good friends for many years. Finally they got into a big argument and became enemies. That just shows that familiarity breeds contempt.*

a **fan of** someone a follower of someone; someone who idolized someone. (Preceded by *be, become, seem like,* or *act like.*) □ *My mother is still a fan of the Beatles.* □ *I'm a great fan of the mayor of the town.*

fan the flames (of something**)** to make something more intense; to make a situation worse. □ *The riot fanned the flames of racial hatred even more.* □ *The hostility in the school is bad enough without anyone fanning the flames.*

far and away the best unquestionably the best. □ *This soap is far and away the best.* □ *Sally is good, but Ann is far and away the best.*

far as anyone knows Go to (as) far as anyone knows.

far as something **is concerned** Go to (as) far as something is concerned.

a **faraway look** AND a **far-off look** an appearance on one's face of having one's mind in another place. □ *Dave had a faraway look in his eyes, so I touched him to get his attention.* □ *Katherine's face had a far-off look indicating that she was daydreaming.*

far be it from me to do something it is not really my place to do something. (Always with *but,* as in the examples below.) □ *Far be it from me to tell you what to do, but I think you should buy the book.* □ *Far be it from me to attempt to advise you, but you're making a big mistake.*

a **far cry from** something a thing that is very different from something else. (Informal.) □ *What you did was a far cry from what you said you were going to do.* □ *The song they played was a far cry from what I call music.*

far from it not it at all; not at all. □ *Do I think you need a new car? Far from it. The old one is fine.* □ *BILL: Does this hat look strange? TOM: Far from it. It looks good.*

far into the night late into the night; late. □ *She sat up and read far into the night.* □ *The party went on far into the night.*

a **far-off look** Go to a far-away look.

far out 1. far from the center of things; far from town. □ *The Smiths live sort of far out.* □ *The restaurant is nice, but too far out.* **2.** strange. (Slang.) □ *Ann acts pretty far out sometimes.* □ *The whole group of people seemed pretty far out.*

farm someone or something **out 1.** [with *someone*] to send someone (somewhere) for care or development. □ *When my mother died, they farmed me out to my aunt and uncle.* 🅃 *The team manager farmed out the baseball player to the minor leagues until he improved.* **2.** [with *something*] to send something (elsewhere) to be dealt with. □ *Bill farmed his chores out to his* *brothers and sisters and went to a movie.* 🅃 *I farmed out various parts of the work to different people.*

fast and furious very rapidly and with unrestrained energy. □ *Her work in the kitchen was fast and furious, and it looked lovely when she finished.* □ *Everything was going so fast and furious at the store during the Christmas rush that we never had time to eat lunch.*

faster and faster at an increasing rate of speed; fast and then even faster. □ *The car went faster and faster and I was afraid we would crash.* □ *The cost of education goes up faster and faster every year.*

fat and happy well-fed and content. □ *Since all the employees were fat and happy, there was little incentive to improve productivity.* □ *You look fat and happy. Has life been treating you well?*

fat as a pig Go to **(as) fat as a pig.**

fat chance very little likelihood. (Informal.) □ *Fat chance he has of getting a promotion.* □ *You think she'll lend you the money? Fat chance!*

favor someone or something **with** something to provide someone or something with something beneficial or special. □ *Mary favored us with a song.* □ *Nature favored Bill with curly hair.*

feast one's **eyes (on** someone or something**)** to look at someone or something with pleasure, envy, or admiration. □ *Just feast your eyes on that beautiful, juicy steak!* □ *Yes, feast your eyes. You won't see one like that again for a long time.*

a **feather in** one's **cap** an honor; a reward for something. □ *Getting a new client was really a feather in my cap.* □ *John earned a feather in his cap by getting an A in physics.*

feather one's **(own) nest 1.** to decorate and furnish one's home in style and comfort. (Birds line their nests with feathers to make them warm and comfortable.) □ *Mr. and Mrs. Simpson have feathered their nest quite comfortably.* □ *It costs a great deal of money to feather one's nest these days.* **2.** to use power and prestige to provide for oneself selfishly. (Said especially of politicians who use their offices to make money for themselves.) □ *The mayor seemed to be helping people, but she was really feathering her own nest.* □ *The building contractor used a lot of public money to feather his nest.*

fed up (to somewhere**) (with** someone or something**)** bored with or disgusted with someone or something. (Informal. The *somewhere* can be *here, the teeth, the gills,* or other places.) □ *I'm fed up with Tom and his silly tricks.* □ *I'm fed up to here with high taxes.* □ *They are fed up to the teeth with screaming children.* □ *I'm really fed up!*

feed one's **face** to eat; to eat a regular meal. (Slang.) □ *Come on, everyone. It's time to feed your faces.* □ *Bill, if you keep feeding your face all the time, you'll get fat.*

feed someone **a line** Go to **give** someone **a line.**

feed the kitty to contribute money to a special, voluntary collection. (See also **pass the hat.**) □ *Please feed the kitty. Make a contribution to help sick children.* □ *Come on, Bill. Feed the kitty. You can afford a dollar for a good cause.*

feel a glow of something a feeling of contentment, happiness, satisfaction, peace, etc. □ *Anne felt a glow of happiness as she held her new baby.* □ *Sitting by the lake, the lovers felt a warm glow of contentment.*

feel at home to feel as if one belongs; to feel as if one were in one's home; to feel accepted. (See also **at home with** someone or something.) □ *I liked my dormitory room. I really felt at home there.* □ *We will do whatever we can to make you feel at home.*

feel dragged out to feel exhausted. (Informal.) □ *What a day! I really feel dragged out.* □ *If he runs too much, he ends up feeling dragged out.*

feel fit to feel well and healthy. □ *If you want to feel fit, you must eat the proper food and get enough rest.* □ *I hope I still feel fit when I get old.*

feel free (to do something**)** to feel like one is permitted to do something or take something. □ *Please feel free to stay for dinner.* □ *If you see something you want in the refrigerator, please feel free.*

feel it beneath one **(to** do something**)** to feel that one would be lowering oneself to do something. □ *Ann feels it beneath her to carry her own luggage.* □ *I would do it, but I feel it beneath me.*

feel like a million (dollars) to feel well and healthy, both physically and mentally. □ *A quick swim in the morning makes me feel like a million dollars.* □ *What a beautiful day! It makes you feel like a million.*

feel like a new person to feel refreshed and renewed, especially after getting well or getting dressed up. □ *I bought a new suit, and now I feel like a new person.* □ *Bob felt like a new person when he got out of the hospital.*

feel like doing something **1.** to want to do something; to be in the mood to do something. □ *Do you feel like stopping work to eat something?* □ *I feel like going on a vacation.* **2.** to feel well enough to do something. □ *I believe I'm getting well. I feel like getting out of bed.* □ *I don't feel like going to the party. I have a headache.*

feel like (having) something to want to have something or do something. □ *I feel like having a nice cool drink.* □ *I feel like a nice swim.*

feel one's **gorge rise** to sense that one is getting very angry. □ *I felt my gorge rise and I knew I was going to lose my temper.* □ *Bob could feel his gorge rise as he read his tax bill.*

feel on top of the world to feel very good, as if one were ruling the world. □ *I feel on top of the world this morning.* □ *I do not actually feel on top of the world, but I have felt worse.*

feel out of place to feel that one does not belong in a place. □ *I feel out of place at formal dances.* □ *Bob and Ann felt out of place at the picnic, so they went home.*

feel put-upon to feel taken advantage of or exploited. □ *Bill refused to help because he felt put-upon.* □ *Sally's mother felt put-upon, but she took each of the children home after the birthday party.*

feel someone **out** to try to find out how someone feels (about something). (Informal. This does not involve touching anyone.) □ *Sally tried to feel Tom out on whether he'd make a contribution.* 🅃 *The students felt out their parents to find out what they thought about the proposed party.*

feel something **in** one's **bones** AND **know** something **in** one's **bones** to sense something; to have an intuition about something. □ *The train will be late. I feel it in my bones.* □ *I failed the test. I know it in my bones.*

feel the pinch to experience hardship because of having too little money. □ *The Smiths used to go abroad every year, but now that he's retired, they're really feeling the pinch.* □ *You're bound to feel the pinch a bit when you're a student.*

feel up to something to feel well enough or prepared enough to do something. (Often in the negative.) □ *I don't feel up to jogging today.* □ *Aunt Mary didn't feel up to making the visit.* □ *Do you feel up to going out today?*

feeling no pain drunk. □ *Bob's on his eighth beer and feeling no pain.* □ *At midnight when we were all feeling no pain, the landlord comes up and tells us to be quiet.*

fence someone **in** to restrict someone in some way. (Also literal. See also **hem** someone or something **in.**) □ *I don't want to fence you in, but you have to get home earlier at night.* □ *Don't try to fence me in. I need a lot of freedom.*

fend for oneself Go to **shift for** oneself.

ferret something **out of** someone or something to remove or retrieve something from someone or something, usually with cunning and persistence. (In the case of *someone*, the thing being ferreted out would be information.) □ *I tried very hard, but I couldn't ferret the information out of the clerk.* □ *I had to ferret out the answer from a book in the library.*

few and far between very few; few and widely scattered. (Informal.) ☐ *Get some gasoline now. Service stations on this highway are few and far between.* ☐ *Some people think that good movies are few and far between.*

a **few cards short of a deck** Go to a few cards shy of a full deck.

a **few cards shy of a full deck** AND a **few cards short of a deck; two bricks shy of a load** [of someone] not very smart or clever. ☐ *Bob's nice, but he's a few cards shy of a full deck.* ☐ *You twit! You're two bricks shy of a load!*

fiddle about (with someone or something**)** Go to fiddle around (with someone or something).

fiddle around (with someone or something**)** AND **fiddle about (with** someone or something**) 1.** [with *someone*] to tease, annoy, or play with someone; to waste someone's time. (See also mess around (with someone or something).) ☐ *All right, stop fiddling around with me and tell me how much you will give me for my car.* ☐ *Now it's time for all of you to quit fiddling around and get to work.* ☐ *Tom, you have to stop spending your time fiddling about with your friends. It's time to get serious with your studies.* **2.** [with *something*] to play with something; to tinker with something ineptly. ☐ *My brother is outside fiddling around with his car engine.* ☐ *He should stop fiddling around and go out and get a job.* ☐ *Stop fiddling about with that stick. You're going to hurt someone.*

fiddle while Rome burns to do nothing or something trivial while knowing that something disastrous is happening. (From a legend that the emperor Nero played the lyre while Rome was burning.) ☐ *The lobbyists don't seem to be doing anything to stop this tax bill. They're fiddling while Rome burns.* ☐ *The doctor should have sent for an ambulance right away instead of examining the woman. In fact, he was just fiddling while Rome burned.*

field questions to answer a series of questions, especially from reporters. ☐ *After her speech, Jane fielded questions from reporters.* ☐ *The president's press agents field questions from the newspaper.*

fight against time to hurry to meet a deadline or to do something quickly. ☐ *The ambulance sped through the city to reach the accident, fighting against time.* ☐ *All the students fought against time to complete the test.*

fight someone or something **hammer and tongs** AND **fight** someone or something **tooth and nail; go at it hammer and tongs; go at it tooth and nail** to fight against someone or something energetically and with great determination. ☐ *They fought against the robber tooth and nail.* ☐ *The dogs were fighting each other hammer and tongs.* ☐ *The mayor fought the new law hammer and tongs.* ☐ *We'll fight this zoning ordinance tooth and nail.*

fight someone or something **tooth and nail** Go to fight someone or something hammer and tongs.

a **fighting chance** a good possibility of success, especially if every effort is made. (See also sporting chance.) ☐ *They have at least a fighting chance of winning the race.* ☐ *The patient could die, but he has a fighting chance since the operation.*

figure in something [for a person] to play a role in something. ☐ *Tom figures in our plans for a new building.* ☐ *I don't wish to figure in your future.*

figure on something to plan on something; to make arrangements for something. (Informal.) ☐ *We figured on twenty guests at our party.* ☐ *I didn't figure on so much trouble.*

figure someone or something **out** to understand someone or something; to find an explanation for someone or something. ☐ *It's hard to figure John out. I don't know what he means.* 🅃 *I can't figure out this recipe.*

fill someone **in (on** someone or something**)** to inform someone about someone or something. ☐ *Please fill me in on what is happening in Washington.* ☐ *Please fill me in on Ann. How is she doing?* ☐ *Sit down,* *and I'll fill you in.* 🅃 *Later, I'll fill in everyone else.*

fill someone's **shoes** to take the place of some other person and do that person's work satisfactorily. (Refers to the notion of taking on someone else's problems by wearing the other person's shoes.) □ *I don't know how we'll be able to do without you. No one can fill your shoes.* □ *It'll be difficult to fill Jane's shoes. She did her job very well.*

fill the bill AND **fit the bill** to be exactly the thing that is needed. □ *Ah, this steak is great. It really fills the bill.* □ *I think that this book will fit the bill just right.*

filled to the brim filled all the way full; filled up to the top edge. □ *I like my coffee cup filled to the brim.* □ *If the glass is filled to the brim, I can't drink without spilling the contents.*

a **final fling** the last act or period of enjoyment before a change in one's circumstances or life-style. □ *You might as well have a final fling before the baby's born.* □ *Mary's going out with her girlfriends for a final fling. She's getting married next week.*

find a happy medium Go to strike a happy medium.

find fault (with someone or something**)** to find things wrong with someone or something. □ *We were unable to find fault with the meal.* □ *Sally's father was always finding fault with her.* □ *Some people are always finding fault.*

find it in one's **heart (to** do something**)** to have the courage or compassion to do something. □ *She couldn't find it in her heart to refuse to come home to him.* □ *I can't do it! I can't find it in my heart.*

find its **way** somewhere [for something] to end up in a place. (This expression avoids accusing someone of moving the thing to the place.) □ *The money found its way into the mayor's pocket.* □ *The secret plans found their way into the enemy's hands.*

find oneself to discover what one's talents and preferences are. □ *Bill did better in school after he found himself.* □ *John tried a number of different jobs. He finally found himself when he became a cook.*

find one's **feet** to become used to a new situation or experience. □ *She was lonely when she first left home, but she is finding her feet now.* □ *It takes time to learn the office routine, but you will gradually find your feet.*

find one's **own level** to find the position or rank to which one is best suited. (As water "seeks its own level.") □ *You cannot force clerks to be ambitious. They will all find their own level.* □ *The new student is happier in the beginning class. It was just a question of letting her find her own level.*

find one's **tongue** to be able to talk. (Informal.) □ *Tom was speechless for a moment. Then he found his tongue.* □ *Ann was unable to find her tongue. She sat there in silence.*

find one's **way (around)** to be able to move about an area satisfactorily. □ *I can go downtown by myself. I can find my way around.* □ *I know the area well enough to find my way.* □ *He can find his way around when it comes to car engines.*

find one's **way** somewhere to discover the route to a place. □ *Mr. Smith found his way to the museum.* □ *Can you find your way home?*

find someone **guilty** AND **find** someone **innocent** to decide guilt or innocence and deliver a verdict in a court of law. □ *The judge found the defendant not guilty by reason of insanity.* □ *The jury found the defendant innocent.*

find someone **innocent** Go to find someone guilty.

find someone or something **out 1.** [with *something*] to discover facts about someone or something; to learn a fact. □ *I found something out that you might be interested in.* 🅃 *We found out that the Smiths are going to sell their house.* **2.** [with *someone*] to discover something bad about someone. □ *John thought he could get away with smoking, but his mother found him out.* □ *Jane was taking a two-hour lunch period until the manager found her out.*

find (something) **out the hard way** Go to learn (something) the hard way.

Finders keepers(, losers weepers). <a phrase said when something is found.> (The person who finds something gets to keep it. The person who loses it can only be sorry.) □ *John lost a quarter in the dining room yesterday. Ann found the quarter there today. Ann claimed that since she found it, it was hers. She said, "Finders keepers, losers weepers."* □ *John said, "I'll say finders keepers when I find something of yours!"*

fine and dandy all right; okay; really fine. □ *Everything is fine and dandy at work. No special problems at the present time.* □ *I feel fine and dandy. The new medicine seems to be working.*

a **fine how-de-do** Go to a fine how-do-you-do.

a **fine how-do-you-do** AND a **fine how-de-do** a predicament. □ *What a mess! This is a fine how-do-you-do!* □ *Here's a fine how-de-do!*

a **fine kettle of fish** a real mess; an unsatisfactory situation. □ *The dog has eaten the steak we were going to have for dinner. This is a fine kettle of fish!* □ *This is a fine kettle of fish. It's below freezing outside, and the furnace won't work.*

the **fine print** Go to the small print.

a **fine state of affairs** Go to a pretty state of affairs.

fire a gun to shoot a gun; to discharge a gun. □ *The police caught the robber who had fired the gun.* □ *Jane fired the gun and hit the target.*

fire away at someone or something **1.** to shoot at someone or something. □ *The hunters fired away at the ducks.* □ *On television, somebody is always firing away at somebody else.* **2.** [with *someone*] to ask many questions of someone; to criticize someone severely. □ *When it came time for questions, the reporters began firing away at the mayor.* □ *Members of the opposite party are always firing away at the president.*

firing on all cylinders AND **hitting on all cylinders** working at full strength; making every possible effort. (Refers to an internal combustion engine.) □ *The team is firing on all cylinders under the new coach.* □ *The factory is hitting on all cylinders to finish the orders on time.*

first and foremost first and most important. □ *First and foremost, I think you should work harder on your biology.* □ *Have this in mind first and foremost: Keep smiling!*

first and ten [in football] the first down [of four] with ten yards needed to earn another first down. □ *It is first and ten on the forty-yard line, and Army has the ball.* □ *There will be no first and ten on the last play because there was a flag on the play.*

First come, first served. The first people to arrive will be served first. □ *They ran out of tickets before we got there. It was first come, first served, but we didn't know that.* □ *Please line up and take your turn. It's first come, first served.*

first of all the very first thing; before anything else. □ *First of all, put your name on this piece of paper.* □ *First of all, we'll try to find a place to live.*

first off first; the first thing. (Almost the same as first of all.) □ *He ordered soup first off.* □ *First off, we'll find a place to live.*

first thing (in the morning) before anything else in the morning. □ *Please call me first thing in the morning. I can't help you now.* □ *I'll do that first thing.*

first things first the most important things must be taken care of first. □ *It's more important to get a job than to buy new clothes. First things first!* □ *Do your homework now. Go out and play later. First things first.*

fish for a compliment to try to get someone to pay you a compliment. (Informal.) □ *When she showed me her new dress, I could tell that she was fishing for a compliment.* □ *Tom was certainly fishing for a compliment when he modeled his fancy haircut for his friends.*

fish for something to try to get information (from someone). (Also literal.) □ *The lawyer was fishing for evidence.* □ *The teacher spent a lot of time fishing for the right answer from the students.*

fish in troubled waters to involve oneself in a difficult, confused, or dangerous situation, especially in order to gain an advantage. □ *Frank is fishing in troubled waters by buying more shares of that company. They are supposed to be in financial difficulties.* □ *The company could make more money by selling armaments abroad, but they would be fishing in troubled waters.*

fish or cut bait either do the task you are supposed to be doing or quit and let someone else do it. □ *Mary is doing much better on the job since her manager told her to fish or cut bait.* □ *The boss told Tom, "Quit wasting time! Fish or cut bait!"*

fit and trim slim and in good physical shape. □ *Jean tried to keep herself fit and trim at all times.* □ *For some people, keeping fit and trim requires time, effort, and self-discipline.*

fit as a fiddle Go to (as) fit as a fiddle.

fit for a king totally suitable. □ *What a delicious meal. It was fit for a king.* □ *Our room at the hotel was fit for a king.*

fit in someone Go to **fit** someone **in(to** something).

fit in (with someone or something**)** to be comfortable with someone or something; to be in accord or harmony with someone or something. □ *I really feel as if I fit in with that group of people.* □ *It's good that you fit in.* □ *This chair doesn't fit in with the style of furniture in my house.* □ *I won't buy it if it doesn't fit in.*

fit like a glove to fit very well; to fit tightly or snugly. □ *My new shoes fit like a glove.* □ *My new coat is quite snug. It fits like a glove.*

fit someone **in(to** something**)** AND **fit in** someone to manage to put someone into a schedule. □ *The doctor is busy, but I can fit you into the schedule.* □ *Yes, here's an opening in the schedule. I can fit you in.*

fit someone or something **out (with** something**)** to provide or furnish someone or something with something. □ *They fitted the camper out with everything they needed.* □ *They fitted them out for only $140.* □ *He fitted his car out with lots of chrome.*

fit someone **to a T 1.** Go to **suit** someone **to a T. 2.** [for something] to fit a person very well. □ *His new jacket fits him to a T.* □ *My new shoes fit me to a T.*

fit the bill Go to fill the bill.

fit to be tied very angry and excited. (Folksy. To be so angry that one has to be restrained with ropes.) □ *If I'm not home on time, my parents will be fit to be tied.* □ *When Ann saw the bill, she was fit to be tied.*

fit to kill dressed up to look very fancy or sexy. (Folksy.) □ *Mary put on her best clothes and looked fit to kill.* □ *John looked fit to kill in his tuxedo.*

fix someone's **wagon** to punish someone; to get even with someone; to plot against someone. (Informal.) □ *If you ever do that again, I'll fix your wagon!* □ *Tommy! You clean up your room this instant, or I'll fix your wagon!* □ *He reported me to the boss, but I fixed his wagon. I knocked his lunch on the floor.*

fix someone **up (with** someone or something**) 1.** [with *something*] to supply a person with something. (Informal.) □ *The usher fixed us up with seats at the front of the theater.* 🅃 *We fixed up the visitors with a cold drink.* **2.** [with *someone*] AND **line** someone **up with** someone to supply a person with a date or a companion. (Informal.) □ *They lined John up with my cousin, Jane.* □ *John didn't want us to fix him up.* 🅃 *We fixed up Bob with a date.*

fizzle out to die out; to come to a stop shortly after starting; to fail. □ *It started to rain, and the fire fizzled out.* □ *The car started in the cold weather, but it fizzled out before we got very far.* □ *My attempt to run for mayor fizzled out.* □ *She started off her job very well, but fizzled out after about a month.*

flare up [for emotions or a chronic disease] to grow intense suddenly. (Refers to a fire, suddenly burning brighter or with more vigor.) ☐ *Just when we thought we had put the fire out, it flared up again.* ☐ *Mr. Jones always flares up whenever anyone mentions taxes.* ☐ *My hay fever usually flares up in August.*

a **flash in the pan** someone or something that draws a lot of attention for a very brief time. (Refers to a small grease fire in a frying pan. Informal.) ☐ *I'm afraid that my success as a painter was just a flash in the pan.* ☐ *Tom had hoped to be a singer, but his career was only a flash in the pan.*

flat as a board Go to (as) flat as a board.

flat as a pancake Go to (as) flat as a pancake.

flat broke completely broke; with no money at all. (Informal.) ☐ *I spent my last dollar, and I'm flat broke.* ☐ *The bank closed its doors to the public. It was flat broke!*

flat out 1. clearly and definitely; holding nothing back. (Informal.) ☐ *I told her flat out that I didn't like her.* ☐ *They reported flat out that the operation was a failure.* **2.** at top speed, with the accelerator pedal flat on the floor. (Slang.) ☐ *How fast will this car go flat out?* ☐ *This car will hit about 110 miles per hour flat out.*

Flattery will get you nowhere. You can praise me, but I'm not going to give you what you want. ☐ *I am glad to hear that I am beautiful and talented, but flattery will get you nowhere.* ☐ *Flattery will get you nowhere, but that doesn't mean you should stop flattering me!*

flesh and blood 1. a living human body, especially with reference to its natural limitations; a human being. ☐ *This cold weather is more than flesh and blood can stand.* ☐ *Carrying 300 pounds is beyond mere flesh and blood.* **2.** the quality of being alive. ☐ *The paintings of this artist are lifeless. They lack flesh and blood.* ☐ *This play needs flesh and blood, not the mumbling of intensely dull actors.* **3.** one's own relatives; one's own kin. ☐ *That's no way to treat one's own flesh and blood.* ☐ *I want to leave my money to my own flesh and blood.* ☐ *Grandmother was happier living with her flesh and blood.*

flesh something **out** to make something more detailed, bigger, or fuller. (As if one were adding flesh to a skeleton.) ☐ *This is basically a good outline. Now you'll have to flesh it out.* 🅃 *The play was good, except that the author needed to flesh out the third act. It was too short.*

flight of fancy an idea or suggestion that is out of touch with reality or possibility. ☐ *What is the point in indulging in flights of fancy about foreign vacations when you cannot even afford the rent?* ☐ *We are tired of her flights of fancy about marrying a millionaire.*

fling oneself **at** someone Go to **throw** oneself **at** someone.

flip one's **lid** Go to **flip** one's **wig**.

flip one's **wig** AND **flip** one's **lid** to suddenly become angry, crazy, or enthusiastic. (Slang.) ☐ *Whenever anyone mentions taxes, Mr. Jones absolutely flips his wig.* ☐ *Stop whistling. You're going to make me flip my lid.* ☐ *When I saw that brand-new car and learned it was mine, I just flipped my wig.*

flirt with the idea of doing something to think about doing something; to toy with an idea; to consider something, but not too seriously. ☐ *I flirted with the idea of going to Europe for two weeks.* ☐ *Jane flirted with the idea of quitting her job.*

float a loan to get a loan; to arrange for a loan. ☐ *I couldn't afford to pay cash for the car, so I floated a loan.* ☐ *They needed money, so they had to float a loan.*

flora and fauna plants and animals. (Latin.) ☐ *The magazine story described the flora and fauna of Panama.* ☐ *We went for a hike in the Finnish wilderness hoping to learn all about the local flora and fauna.*

flotsam and jetsam worthless matter; worthless encumbrances. (Refers to the floating wreckage of a ship and its cargo or to floating cargo deliberately cast overboard to stabilize a ship in a rough sea.) ☐ *His mind is burdened with the flotsam* *and jetsam of many years of poor instruction and lax study habits.* ☐ *Your report would be better if you could get rid of a lot of the flotsam and jetsam and clean up the grammar a bit.*

fluff one's **lines** AND **blow** one's **lines; muff** one's **lines** to speak one's speech badly or forget one's lines when one is in a play. (Informal.) ☐ *The actress fluffed her lines badly in the last act.* ☐ *I was in a play once, and I muffed my lines over and over.* ☐ *It's okay to blow your lines in rehearsal.*

flunk out to fail a course; to fail out of school. ☐ *Tom didn't study, and he finally flunked out.* ☐ *Bill is about to flunk out of geometry.*

flunk someone **out** to cause someone to leave school by giving a failing grade. ☐ *The teacher flunked Tom out.* 🅃 *The professor wanted to flunk out the whole class.*

flush with something **1.** even with something; sharing a surface with something. ☐ *The edge of the sink is flush with the counter.* ☐ *The wood flooring is flush with the carpet so people won't trip.* **2.** having lots of something. ☐ *Our garden is flush with fresh vegetables.* ☐ *The committee was flush with helpful ideas.*

fly-by-night irresponsible; untrustworthy. (Refers to a person who sneaks away secretly in the night.) ☐ *The carpenter we hired was a fly-by-night worker who did a very bad job.* ☐ *You shouldn't deal with a fly-by-night merchant.*

fly in the face of someone or something AND **fly in the teeth of** someone or something to disregard, defy, or show disrespect for someone or something. ☐ *John loves to fly in the face of tradition.* ☐ *Ann made it a practice to fly in the face of standard procedures.* ☐ *John finds great pleasure in flying in the teeth of his father.*

a **fly in the ointment** a small, unpleasant matter that spoils something; a drawback. ☐ *We enjoyed the play, but the fly in the ointment was not being able to find our car afterward.* ☐ *It sounds like a good idea, but there must be a fly in the ointment somewhere.*

fly in the teeth of someone or something Go to **fly in the face of** someone or something.

fly into the face of danger to take great risks; to threaten or challenge danger, as if danger were a person. (This may refer to flying, as in an airplane, but not necessarily.) ☐ *John plans to go bungee-jumping this weekend. He really likes flying into the face of danger.* ☐ *Willard was not exactly the type to fly into the face of danger, but tonight was an exception, and he ordered enchiladas.*

fly off the handle to lose one's temper. (Informal.) ☐ *Every time anyone mentions taxes, Mrs. Brown flies off the handle.* ☐ *If she keeps flying off the handle like that, she'll have a heart attack.*

fly the coop to escape; to get out or get away. (Informal. Refers to a chicken escaping from a chicken coop.) ☐ *I couldn't stand the party, so I flew the coop.* ☐ *The prisoner flew the coop at the first opportunity.*

foam at the mouth to be very angry. (Informal. Related to a "mad dog"—a dog with rabies—which foams at the mouth.) ☐ *Bob was raving—foaming at the mouth. I've never seen anyone so angry.* ☐ *Bill foamed at the mouth in anger.*

fob something **off (on** someone**)** to trick someone into accepting something that is worthless. (Informal.) ☐ *The car dealer fobbed a car off on Tom.* 🅃 *He also fobbed off a bad car on Jane.* ☐ *Some car dealers are always trying to fob something off.*

foist something **(off) on** someone to force someone to take something that they don't want. ☐ *Bill tried to foist the task of washing dishes off on his sister.* ☐ *The city council foisted the new garbage dump on the poorest neighborhood in the city.*

fold one's **hands** to bring one's hands together, palm to palm, with the fingers interlocking; to grasp one's hands together, palm to palm, perpendicular to one another. ☐ *Please fold your hands and put them on the table while the teacher reads you a story.* ☐ *Sue folded her hands to pray.*

fold something **up** to put an end to something; to close something such as a business or some other enterprise. (Refers to folding something closed.) □ *Mr. Jones was going broke, so he folded his business up.* 🅃 *The producer decided to fold up the play early. It was losing money.*

fold, spindle, or mutilate to harm or disfigure a machine-readable document, such as a computer punch card. (Such a document, if folded, placed on a bill spike, or otherwise punctured, would no longer be machine-readable. Now rarely seen on a bill but the expression is sometimes used in a figurative sense.) □ *At the bottom of the bill, it said "do not fold, spindle, or mutilate," and Jane, in her anger, did all three.* □ *Look here, chum, if you don't want to get folded, spindled, or mutilated, you had better do what you are told!*

fold up to close up; to end. (Alluding to something that folds closed or collapses along its folds.) □ *The play folded up after two days.* □ *It's time to fold up and go home.*

follow in someone's **footsteps** Go to **follow in** someone's **tracks**.

follow in someone's **tracks** AND **follow in** someone's **footsteps** to follow someone's example; to assume someone else's role or occupation. □ *The vice president was following in the president's footsteps when he called for budget cuts.* □ *She followed in her father's footsteps and went into medicine.*

follow one's **heart** to act according to one's feelings; to obey one's sympathetic or compassionate inclinations. □ *I couldn't decide what to do, so I just followed my heart.* □ *I trust that you will follow your heart in this matter.*

follow one's **nose 1.** to go straight ahead, the direction that one's nose is pointing. (Folksy.) □ *The town that you want is straight ahead on this highway. Just follow your nose.* □ *The chief's office is right around the corner. Turn left and follow your nose.* **2.** to follow an odor to its source. (Informal.) □ *The kitchen is at the back of the building. Just follow your nose.* □ *There was a bad smell in the basement—probably a dead mouse. I followed my nose until I found it.*

follow orders to do as one has been instructed. □ *You have to learn to follow orders if you want to be a marine.* □ *I didn't do anything wrong. I was only following orders.*

follow someone or something **up 1.** [with *something*] to add more information or detail to something; to follow something through. □ *Bill had to follow my suggestion up.* 🅃 *The police followed up my story.* **2.** [with *someone*] to review someone's work and check it over. □ *The person who follows you up will make sure you're doing the right thing.* 🅃 *When I followed up Mary, I found errors in her work.*

follow someone's **lead** to do as someone else does; to accept someone's guidance; to follow someone's direction. □ *Just follow my lead and you will not get lost.* □ *John followed his father's lead and became a lawyer.*

follow suit to follow in the same pattern; to follow someone else's example. (From card games.) □ *Mary went to work for a bank, and Jane followed suit. Now they are both head cashiers.* □ *The Smiths went out to dinner, but the Browns didn't follow suit. They stayed home.*

follow the crowd to do what everyone else is doing. □ *I am an independent thinker. I could never just follow the crowd.* □ *When in doubt, I follow the crowd. At least I don't stand out like a fool.*

follow through (on something**)** AND **carry through (on** something**)** to complete a task; to see a task through to its completion. □ *You must follow through on the things that you start.* □ *Don't start the job if you can't follow through.* □ *Ask Sally to carry through on her project.*

follow up (on someone or something**)** to find out more about someone or something. □ *Please follow up on Mr. Brown and his activities.* □ *Bill, Mr. Smith has a complaint. Would you please follow up on it?*

☐ *We can take care of that when we follow up.*

follow up (on something**)** to check (on something) and do what needs to be done. ☐ *I will follow up on this matter and make sure it is settled.* ☐ *There is a problem with the bank account. Will you please follow up?*

fond of someone or something to like someone or something. ☐ *I'm fond of chocolate.* ☐ *Mary isn't fond of me, but I'm fond of her.*

food for thought something to think about. ☐ *I don't like your idea very much, but it's food for thought.* ☐ *Your lecture was very good. It contained much food for thought.*

A **fool and his money are soon parted.** A person who acts unwisely with money soon loses it. (Often said about a person who has just lost a sum of money because of poor judgment.) ☐ *When Bill lost a $400 bet on a horse race, Mary said, "A fool and his money are soon parted."* ☐ *When John bought a cheap used car that fell apart the next day, he said, "Oh, well, a fool and his money are soon parted."*

fool around (with someone or something**)** to fiddle, play, or mess with someone or something; to waste time with someone or something. (Informal.) ☐ *John is out fooling around with his friends again.* ☐ *That child spends most of his time fooling around.* ☐ *Please don't fool around with the light switch. You'll break it.* ☐ *There are lots of interesting things in here, but you must leave them alone. Don't fool around.*

fools rush in (where angels fear to tread) people with little experience or knowledge often get involved in difficult or delicate situations that wiser people would avoid. (Proverb.) ☐ *I wouldn't ask Jean about her divorce, but Kate did. Fools rush in, as they say.* ☐ *Only the newest member of the committee questioned the chairman's decision. Fools rush in where angels fear to tread.*

foot the bill to pay the bill; to pay (for something). ☐ *Let's go out and eat. I'll foot the bill.* ☐ *If the bank goes broke, don't worry. The government will foot the bill.*

footloose and fancy-free without responsibilities or commitments. ☐ *All the rest of them have wives, but John is footloose and fancy-free.* ☐ *Mary never stays long in any job. She likes being footloose and fancy-free.*

for a lark AND **on a lark** for a joke; as something done for fun. ☐ *For a lark, I wore a clown's wig to school.* ☐ *On a lark, I skipped school and drove to the beach.*

for all I care I don't care if (something happens). (Informal.) ☐ *For all I care, the whole city council can go to the devil.* ☐ *They can all starve for all I care.*

for all I know according to the information I have; I think; probably. (Informal.) ☐ *For all I know, the mayor has resigned already.* ☐ *She may have gone to town for all I know.*

for all intents and purposes virtually; practically speaking; in effect. (Sometimes this expression has very little meaning.) ☐ *He entered the room, looking for all intents and purposes as if he would burst into song.* ☐ *She said that for all intents and purposes she had completed her assignment.*

for all it's worth AND **for what(ever) it's worth** if it has any value. ☐ *My idea—for all it's worth—is to offer them only $300.* ☐ *Here is my thinking, for whatever it's worth.* ☐ *Ask her to give us her opinion, for what it's worth.*

for all practical purposes as might be reasonably expected; essentially. ☐ *For all practical purposes, this is simply a matter of right and wrong.* ☐ *This should be considered final, for all practical purposes.*

for all something in spite of something; even with so much of something. ☐ *For all her complaining, she still seems to be a happy person.* ☐ *For all my aches and pains, I'm still rather healthy.*

for all the world 1. exactly; precisely. (Especially with *look*.) ☐ *She sat there looking for all the world as if she was going to cry.* ☐ *It started out seeming for all the* *world like a beautiful day. Then a storm came up.* **2.** everything. (Usually in the negative.) □ *I wouldn't give up my baby for all the world.* □ *They wouldn't sell their property for all the world.*

for better or for worse under any conditions; no matter what happens. □ *I married you for better or for worse.* □ *For better or for worse, I'm going to quit my job.*

for chicken feed AND **for peanuts** for nearly nothing; for very little money. (Informal.) □ *Bob doesn't get paid much. He works for chicken feed.* □ *You can buy an old car for chicken feed.* □ *I won't do that kind of work for peanuts!*

For crying out loud! For heaven's sake!; I am amazed! (An exclamation of surprise and mild shock.) □ *For crying out loud! I didn't expect to see you here.* □ *For crying out loud! What a time to call someone on the telephone.*

for days on end for many days. □ *We kept on traveling for days on end.* □ *Doctor, I've had this pain for days on end.*

for fear of something out of fear of something; because of fear of something. □ *He doesn't drive for fear of an accident.* □ *They lock their doors for fear of being robbed.*

for free for no charge or cost; free of any cost. □ *They let us into the movie for free.* □ *I will let you have a sample of the candy for free.*

for good forever; permanently. □ *I finally left home for good.* □ *They tried to repair it many times before they fixed it for good.*

for good measure as extra; (adding) a little more to make sure there is enough. □ *When I bought a pound of nails, the clerk threw in a few extra nails for good measure.* □ *I always put a little extra salt in the soup for good measure.*

for hours on end for many hours. □ *We sat and waited for the doctor for hours on end.* □ *We listened to the speaker for hours on end.*

for instance for example. □ *I've lived in many cities, for instance, Boston, Chicago, and Detroit.* □ *Jane is very generous. For instance, she volunteers her time and gives money to charities.*

for keeps forever; permanently. (Informal. See also **play for keeps**. Compare this with **for good**.) □ *When I get married, it'll be for keeps.* □ *We've moved around a lot. Now I think we'll stay here for keeps.*

for kicks for fun; just for entertainment; for no good reason. (Slang.) □ *They didn't mean any harm. They just did it for kicks.* □ *We drove over to the next town for kicks.*

for life for the remainder of one's life. □ *The accident caused me to become blind for life.* □ *She will stay in prison for life.*

for one's **(own) part** as far as one is concerned; from one's point of view. □ *For my own part, I wish to stay here.* □ *For her part, she prefers chocolate.*

for one's **(own) sake** for one's good or benefit; in honor of someone. □ *I have to earn a living for my family's sake.* □ *I did it for my mother's sake.* □ *I didn't do it for my own sake.*

for openers AND **for starters** to start with. (Informal.) □ *For openers, they played a song everyone knows.* □ *For starters, I'll serve a delicious soup.*

for peanuts Go to **for chicken feed**.

for real authentic; genuine; really. (Informal or slang.) □ *Is this diamond for real?* □ *Are you for real?* □ *Are we there for real?*

for safekeeping for the purpose of keeping someone or something safe. □ *I put my jewelry in the vault for safekeeping.* □ *I checked my fur coat at the entrance to the bar for safekeeping.*

for sale available for purchase; buyable. (Compare this with **on sale**.) □ *Is this item for sale?* □ *How long has this house been for sale?* □ *My car is for sale. Are you interested?*

for short in a short form. (Usually refers to names of people or things.) □ *My name is William. They call me Bill for short.* □ *Almost everyone who is named Robert is called Bob for short.*

for starters Go to **for openers**.

for sure certainly; surely. (Informal or slang.) ☐ *MARY: Do you like my new jacket? JANE: For sure.* ☐ *For sure, I want to go on the picnic.*

for that matter besides; in addition. ☐ *If you're hungry, take one of my doughnuts. For that matter, take two.* ☐ *I don't like this house. The roof leaks. For that matter, the whole place is falling apart.* ☐ *Tom is quite arrogant. So is his sister, for that matter.*

[for the asking] Go to one's for the asking.

for the best Go to (all) for the best.

for the better better; an improvement. (See also take a turn for the better.) ☐ *A change of government would be for the better.* ☐ *A new winter coat would certainly be for the better.*

for the birds worthless; undesirable. (Slang.) ☐ *This television program is for the birds.* ☐ *Winter weather is for the birds.*

for the devil of it AND **for the heck of it; for the hell of it** just for fun; because it is slightly evil; for no good reason. (Informal. Use caution with *hell*.) ☐ *We filled their garage with leaves just for the devil of it.* ☐ *Tom tripped Bill for the heck of it.* ☐ *John picked a fight with Tom just for the hell of it.*

for the duration for the whole time that something continues; for the entire period of time required for something to be completed; for as long as something takes. ☐ *We are in this war for the duration.* ☐ *However long it takes, we'll wait. We are here for the duration.*

for the good of someone or something for the benefit, profit, or advantage of someone or something. ☐ *The president said the strict drug laws were for the good of the country.* ☐ *David took a second job for the good of his family.*

for the heck of it Go to for the devil of it.

for the hell of it Go to for the devil of it.

for the life of one even if one's life were threatened; even in exchange for one's life. (Informal. Always with a negative, and usually having to do with one's memory.) ☐ *For the life of me, I don't remember your name.* ☐ *She couldn't recall the correct numbers for the life of her.* ☐ *For the life of them, they couldn't remember the way home.*

for the moment AND **for the time being** for the present; for now; temporarily. ☐ *This will have to do for the moment.* ☐ *This is all right for the time being. It'll have to be improved next week, however.* ☐ *This good feeling will last only for the time being.* ☐ *This solution is satisfactory for the moment.*

for the most part mostly; in general. ☐ *For the most part, the class is enjoying geometry.* ☐ *I like working here for the most part.*

for the odds to be against one for things to be against one generally; for one's chances of success to be slim. ☐ *You can give it a try, but the odds are against you.* ☐ *I know the odds are against me, but I wish to run in the race anyway.*

for the record so that (one's own version of) the facts will be known; so there will be a record of a particular fact. (This often is said when there are reporters present.) ☐ *I'd like to say—for the record—that at no time have I ever accepted a bribe from anyone.* ☐ *For the record, I've never been able to get anything done around city hall without bribing someone.*

for the sake of someone or something for the good of someone or something; for the honor or recognition of someone or something. (Compare this with for one's own sake.) ☐ *I did it for the sake of all those people who helped me get through school.* ☐ *I'm investing in a house for the sake of my children.* ☐ *For the sake of honesty, Bill shared all the information he had.*

for the time being Go to for the moment.

for what(ever) it's worth Go to for all it's worth.

forbidden fruit someone or something that one finds attractive or desirable partly because having the person or thing is immoral or illegal. (From the fruit in the Garden of Eden that was forbidden to

Adam by God.) □ *Jim flirts with his sister-in-law only because she's forbidden fruit.* □ *The boy watches that program only when his parents are out. It's forbidden fruit.*

force someone or something **down** someone's **throat** Go to **shove** someone or something **down** someone's **throat.**

force someone **out (of office)** AND **drive** someone **out (of office)** to pressure someone to leave an elective office. □ *The city council forced the mayor out of office.* □ *Please resign immediately, or I'll have to drive you out.*

force someone's **hand** to force a person to reveal plans, strategies, or secrets. (Refers to a handful of cards in card playing.) □ *We didn't know what she was doing until Tom forced her hand.* □ *We couldn't plan our game until we forced the other team's hand in the last play.*

force someone **to the wall** AND **drive** someone **to the wall** to push someone to an extreme position; to put someone into an awkward position. □ *He wouldn't tell the truth until we forced him to the wall.* □ *They don't pay their bills until you drive them to the wall.*

a **force to be reckoned with** someone or something that is important and powerful and must not be ignored. □ *Walter is a force to be reckoned with. Be prepared to deal with him.* □ *The growing discontent with the political system is a powerful force to be reckoned with.*

fore and aft at the front and the back, usually of a boat or ship. □ *They had to attach new lights fore and aft because the old ones were not bright enough to meet the new regulations.* □ *The captain ordered a watch stationed fore and aft.*

a **foregone conclusion** a conclusion already reached; an inevitable result. □ *That the company was moving to California was a foregone conclusion.* □ *That the mayor will win reelection is a foregone conclusion.*

forever and a day Go to **forever and ever.**

forever and ever AND **forever and a day** forever. □ *I will love you forever and ever.* □ *This car won't keep running forever and ever. We'll have to get a new one sometime.* □ *We have enough money to last forever and a day.*

forget oneself to forget one's manners or training. (Said in formal situations alluding to belching, bad table manners, and, in the case of very young children, pants-wetting.) □ *Sorry, Mother, I forgot myself.* □ *John, we are going out to dinner tonight. Please don't forget yourself.*

forgive and forget to forgive someone (for something) and forget that it ever happened. □ *I'm sorry, John. Let's forgive and forget. What do you say?* □ *It was nothing. We'll just have to forgive and forget.*

fork money out (for something**)** to pay (perhaps unwillingly) for something. (Informal. Often mention is made of the amount of money. See the examples below.) □ *Do you think I'm going to fork twenty dollars out for that book?* □ *Forking money out to everyone is part of life in a busy economy.* 🅃 *I like that stereo, but I don't want to fork out a lot of money.*

fork something **over** to give something to someone. (Refers to handing over money. Slang. Usually used in a command.) □ *Now! Fork it over now!* 🅃 *Okay, Joe. Fork over that twenty dollars you owe me.*

form and substance meaningful content; structure and meaningful content. (See also **sum and substance.**) □ *The first act of the play was one screaming match after another. It lacked form and substance throughout.* □ *Jane's report was good. The teacher commented on the excellent form and substance of the paper.*

form an opinion to think up or decide on an opinion. (Note the variation in the examples.) □ *I don't know enough about the issue to form an opinion.* □ *Don't tell me how to think! I can form my own opinion.* □ *I don't form opinions without careful consideration.*

forty winks a short sleep; a nap. (Informal. See also **catch forty winks.**) □ *I had forty* *winks on the plane.* □ *If you're lucky you'll get forty winks while the children are out.*

foul one's **own nest** to harm one's own interests; to bring disadvantage upon oneself. □ *He tried to discredit a fellow senator with the president, but just succeeded in fouling his own nest.* □ *The boss really dislikes Mary. She certainly fouled her own nest when she spread those rumors about him.*

foul play illegal activity; bad practices. □ *The police investigating the death suspect foul play.* □ *Each student got an A on the test, and the teacher imagined it was the result of foul play.*

foul someone or something **up** to cause disorder and confusion for someone or something; to tangle up someone or something; to **mess** someone or something **up**. (Informal.) □ *Go away! Don't foul me up any more.* 🅃 *You've fouled up my whole day.* 🅃 *Watch out! You're going to foul up my kite strings.* 🅃 *Stay off the field. You're going to foul up the coach.*

foul up to do (something) badly; to mess something up. (Informal.) □ *At the last minute, he fouled up and failed the course.* □ *Take your time. Plan your moves, and don't foul up.*

fouled up messed up; in disorder. □ *My fishing line is all fouled up.* □ *The football team got fouled up and lost the game.*

fraught with danger [of something] full of something dangerous or unpleasant. □ *The spy's trip to Russia was fraught with danger.* □ *My escape from the kidnappers was fraught with danger.*

free and clear without encumbrance, particularly in regard to the ownership of something. □ *After the last payment, Jane owned the car free and clear.* □ *If you can't prove that you own the house and the land it stands on free and clear, you can't sell it.*

free and easy casual. □ *John is so free and easy. How can anyone be so relaxed?* □ *Now, take it easy. Just act free and easy. No one will know you're nervous.*

free as a bird Go to (as) free as a bird.

free as (the) air Go to (as) free as (the) air.

free-for-all a disorganized fight or contest involving everyone; a brawl. □ *The picnic turned into a free-for-all after midnight.* □ *The race started out in an organized manner, but ended up being a free-for-all.*

free translation a translation that is not completely accurate and not well thought out. □ *John gave a free translation of the sentence, which did not help us at all.* □ *Anne gave a very free translation of the poem.*

fresh as a daisy Go to (as) fresh as a daisy.

fresh out (of something**)** AND **clean out (of** something**)** just now having sold or used up the last of something. (Folksy.) □ *Sorry, I can't serve you scrambled eggs. We are fresh out of eggs.* □ *We are fresh out of nails. I sold the last box just ten minutes ago.* □ *Lettuce? Sorry. I'm fresh out.* □ *Sorry. We are clean out of dried beans.*

A **friend in need is a friend indeed.** A true friend is a person who will help you when you really need someone. (Compare this with fair-weather friend.) □ *When Bill helped me with geometry, I really learned the meaning of "A friend in need is a friend indeed."* □ *"A friend in need is a friend indeed" sounds silly until you need someone very badly.*

friend or foe a friend or an enemy. □ *I can't tell whether Jim is friend or foe.* □ *"Who goes there? Friend or foe?" asked the sentry.*

frighten one **out of** one's **wits** AND **scare** one **out of** one's **wits** to frighten one very badly. (See also frighten the wits out of someone.) □ *Oh! That loud noise scared me out of my wits.* □ *I'll give him a good scolding and frighten him out of his wits.*

frighten someone **to death** AND **scare** someone **to death** to frighten someone severely. (Also literal.) □ *The dentist always frightens me to death.* □ *She scared me to death when she screamed.*

frighten the (living) daylights out of someone Go to frighten the wits out of someone.

frighten the wits out of someone AND **frighten the (living) daylights out of** someone; **scare the (living) daylights out of** someone; **scare the wits out of** someone to frighten someone very badly. ☐ *We nearly had an accident. It frightened the living daylights out of me.* ☐ *The incident scared the wits out of me.*

frightened to death AND **scared to death** severely frightened. (Also literal.) ☐ *I don't want to go to the dentist today. I'm frightened to death.* ☐ *I'm frightened to death of dogs.* ☐ *She's scared to death she'll fail algebra.*

fritter something **away** to waste something little by little, especially time or money. (Folksy.) ☐ *Don't stand around and fritter the whole day away.* 🅃 *Stop frittering away my hard-earned money!*

from dawn to dusk during the period of the day when there is light; from the rising of the sun to the setting of the sun. ☐ *I have to work from dawn to dusk on the farm.* ☐ *The factory runs from dawn to dusk to produce hats and gloves.*

from day to day on a daily basis; one day at a time; occasionally. ☐ *We face this kind of problem from day to day.* ☐ *I'll have to check into this matter from day to day.* ☐ *When you're very poor, you live from day to day.*

from door to door moving from one door to another—typically, from one house to another. (See also **door-to-door.**) ☐ *Anne went from door to door, selling books, to earn money for college.* ☐ *The children went from door to door, saying "Trick or treat!" at each one.*

from far and near AND **from near and far** from all around, both close by and farther away. (Reversible, but with a preference for **from far and near.**) ☐ *All the young people from far and near gathered at the high school for the game.* ☐ *The eagles gathered from near and far at the river where the salmon were spawning.*

from hand to hand from one person to a series of other persons. ☐ *The book traveled from hand to hand until it got back to its owner.* ☐ *By the time the baby had been passed from hand to hand, it was crying.*

from head to toe from the top of one's head to one's feet; all over the body. (See also **from tip to toe.**) ☐ *She was decked out in flowers from head to toe.* ☐ *The huge parka covered the small child from head to toe, assuring that she would be well protected against the cold.*

from near and far Go to **from far and near.**

from overseas from a location on the other side of the Atlantic or Pacific Ocean, according to the point of view of someone located in the U.S. ☐ *The latest word from overseas is that the treaty has been signed.* ☐ *Is there any news from overseas about the war?*

from pillar to post from one place to a series of other places; (figuratively) from person to person, as with gossip. ☐ *My father was in the army, and we moved from pillar to post year after year.* ☐ *After I told one person my secret, it went quickly from pillar to post.*

from rags to riches from poverty to wealth; from modesty to elegance. ☐ *The princess used to be quite poor. She certainly moved from rags to riches.* ☐ *After I inherited the money, I went from rags to riches.*

from side to side moving first to one side and then to the other, repeatedly. ☐ *The pendulum of the clock swings from side to side.* ☐ *The singers swayed from side to side as they sang.*

from start to finish from the beginning to the end; throughout. ☐ *I disliked the whole business from start to finish.* ☐ *Mary caused problems from start to finish.*

from stem to stern from one end to another. (Refers to the front and back ends of a ship.) ☐ *Now, I have to clean the house from stem to stern.* ☐ *I polished my car carefully from stem to stern.*

from the bottom of one's **heart** sincerely. (Compare this with **with all** one's **heart and soul.**) ☐ *When I returned the lost kitten to Mrs. Brown, she thanked me from* *the bottom of her heart.* ☐ *Oh, thank you! I'm grateful from the bottom of my heart.*

from the cradle to the grave from birth to death; throughout one's life. ☐ *The government promised to take care of us from the cradle to the grave.* ☐ *You can feel secure and well protected from the cradle to the grave.*

from the ground up from the beginning; from start to finish. (Refers to the building of a house or other building.) ☐ *We must plan our sales campaign carefully from the ground up.* ☐ *Sorry, but you'll have to start all over again from the ground up.*

from the heart from a deep and sincere emotional source. ☐ *I know that your kind words come from the heart.* ☐ *We don't want your gift unless it comes from the heart.*

from the horse's mouth Go to (straight) from the horse's mouth.

from the old school holding attitudes or ideas that were popular and important in the past, but which are no longer considered relevant or in line with modern trends. ☐ *Grammar was not taught much in my son's school, but fortunately he had a teacher from the old school.* ☐ *Aunt Jane is from the old school. She never goes out without wearing a hat and gloves.*

from the outset from the beginning. ☐ *We had problems with this machine from the outset.* ☐ *We knew about the unfriendly judge from the outset of our trial.*

from the top from the beginning of something, such as a song or a script. ☐ *Okay, let's try it again from the top.* ☐ *Play it from the top one more time.*

from the word *go* from the beginning. (Informal.) ☐ *I knew about the problem from the word* go. ☐ *She was failing the class from the word* go.

from this day forward Go to from this day on.

from this day on AND **from this day forward** from today into the future. (Formal.) ☐ *We'll live in love and peace from this day on.* ☐ *I'll treasure your gift from this day forward.*

from time to time occasionally. ☐ *We have pizza from time to time.* ☐ *From time to time, a visitor comes to our door.*

from tip to toe from the top to the bottom. (Not necessarily of a person. See also from head to toe.) ☐ *She is wearing all new clothes from tip to toe.* ☐ *The house needs to be cleaned thoroughly from tip to toe.*

from top to bottom from the highest point to the lowest point; throughout. (Compare this with from stem to stern.) ☐ *I have to clean the house from top to bottom today.* ☐ *We need to replace our elected officials from top to bottom.*

from way back from far in the past; from an earlier time. (Informal.) ☐ *Grandfather comes from way back.* ☐ *This antique clock is from way back.*

fruit(s) of one's **labor(s)** the results of one's work. ☐ *We displayed the fruits of our labor at the convention.* ☐ *What have you accomplished? Where is the fruit of your labors?*

full as a tick Go to (as) full as a tick.

full blast Go to (at) full blast.

full of beans Go to full of hot air.

full of bull Go to full of hot air.

full of hot air AND **full of beans; full of bull; full of it; full of prunes** full of nonsense; talking nonsense. (Slang.) ☐ *Oh, shut up, Mary. You're full of hot air.* ☐ *Don't pay any attention to Bill. He's full of beans.* ☐ *My English professor is full of bull.* ☐ *You're full of it.* ☐ *She doesn't know what she's talking about. She's just full of prunes.*

full of it Go to full of hot air.

full of Old Nick Go to full of the devil.

full of oneself conceited; self-important. ☐ *Mary is very unpopular because she's so full of herself.* ☐ *She doesn't care about other people's feelings. She's too full of herself.*

full of prunes Go to full of hot air.

full of the devil AND **full of Old Nick** always making mischief. (Informal. *Old Nick* is another name for the devil.) ☐ *Tom is a lot of fun, but he's sure full of the devil.* ☐ *I've never seen a child get into so much mischief. He's really full of Old Nick.*

full steam ahead forward at the greatest speed possible; with as much energy and enthusiasm as possible. (From an instruction given to engineers on steamships.) ☐ *It will have to be full steam ahead for everybody if the factory gets this order.* ☐ *It's going to be full steam ahead for me this year. I take my final exams.*

fun and games playing around; doing worthless things. (Informal.) ☐ *All right, Bill, the fun and games are over. It's time to get down to work.* ☐ *This isn't a serious course. It's nothing but fun and games.*

funny as a barrel of monkeys Go to (as) funny as a barrel of monkeys.

funny as a crutch Go to (as) funny as a crutch.

funny business trickery or deception; illegal activity. ☐ *From the silence as she entered the room, the teacher knew there was some funny business going on.* ☐ *There's some funny business going on at the warehouse. Stock keeps disappearing.*

funny ha-ha amusing; comical. (Informal. Compare this with **funny peculiar**.) ☐ *I didn't mean that Mrs. Peters is funny ha-ha. She's weird—funny peculiar, in fact.* ☐ *Mike thinks his jokes are funny ha-ha, but we laugh because they are so silly.*

funny peculiar odd; eccentric. (Informal. Compare this with **funny ha-ha**.) ☐ *I didn't mean that Mary is funny ha-ha. She's weird—funny peculiar, in fact.* ☐ *His face is sort of funny—funny peculiar, that is.*

G

gain ground to make progress; to advance; to become more important or popular. □ *Our new product is gaining ground against that of our competitor.* □ *Since the government announced the new policies, the stock market is gaining ground.*

The **game is up.** AND The **jig is up.** The deception is over.; The illegal activity has come to an end. □ *When the police were waiting for them inside the bank vault, the would-be robbers knew that the game was up.* □ *"The jig is up!" said the cop as he grabbed the shoulder of the pickpocket.*

a **game that two can play** a manner of competing that two competitors can use; a strategy that competing sides can both use. (Also literal.) □ *The mayor shouted at the city council, "Politics is a game that two can play."* □ *"Flattery is a game that two can play," said John as he returned Mary's compliment.*

gang up (on someone**)** to form into a group and attack someone. (Usually a physical attack, but it can also be a verbal attack.) □ *We can't win against the robber unless we gang up on him.* □ *All right, you guys, don't gang up on me. Play fair!*

a **gas** [someone or something] wild or funny. □ *You should have been at Susan's party last night. It was a gas.* □ *That movie was such a gas. I haven't laughed so hard in ages.*

gas up to fill up one's gasoline tank with gasoline. (Informal.) □ *I have to stop at the next service station and gas up.* □ *The next time you gas up, try some of the gasoline with alcohol in it.*

gather a case (against someone**)** Go to build a case (against someone).

gaudy as a butterfly Go to (as) gaudy as a butterfly.

gear (oneself**) up (for** something**)** to prepare for something; to get into shape for something. □ *We are gearing up for a very busy summer season.* □ *We are not ready yet. We have to gear up.* □ *Tom is gearing himself up for his exams.*

gear something **to** someone or something to cause something to match something else or some group of people; to create or adapt something for a specific purpose. □ *Tim geared his speech to his audience.* □ *The newspaper geared its language to a fourth-grade reading level.*

generous to a fault too generous; overly generous. □ *My favorite uncle is generous to a fault.* □ *Sally—always generous to a fault—gave away her sandwiches.*

gentle as a lamb Go to (as) gentle as a lamb.

get a bang out of someone or something Go to get a charge out of someone or something.

get a bee in one's **bonnet** to get an idea or a thought that remains in one's mind; to get an obsession. (Also with *have*. See the note at get a big send-off. See also put a bee in someone's bonnet.) □ *I have a bee in my bonnet that you'd be a good manager.* □ *I got a bee in my bonnet about swimming. I couldn't stop wanting to go swimming.*

get a big send-off to receive or enjoy a happy celebration before departing. (Note: *Get* can be replaced with *have*. Note the variation in the examples. *Get* usually means "to become, to acquire, or to cause." *Have* usually means "to possess, to be, or to have resulted in."

See also **give** someone **a big send-off.**) ☐ *I had a wonderful send-off before I left.* ☐ *John got a fine send-off as he left for Europe.*

get a black eye 1. to get a bruise near the eye from being struck. (The area around the eye is darkened, not black. Also with *have.* See the note at **get a big send-off.**) ☐ *I got a black eye from walking into a door.* ☐ *I have a black eye where John hit me.* **2.** to have one's character or reputation harmed. ☐ *Mary got a black eye because of her complaining.* ☐ *The whole group now has a black eye.*

get a break to have good fortune; to receive a bit of luck. (Often with *lucky, nice,* etc. Also with *have.* See the note at **get a big send-off.**) ☐ *Mary is going to get a break.* ☐ *I wish I'd get a lucky break.* ☐ *Why don't I have a lucky break when I need one?* ☐ *She's got a lucky break and doesn't even know it.*

get a bright idea for a clever thought or idea to occur (to someone). (Also with *have.* See the note at **get a big send-off.**) ☐ *Now and then I get a bright idea.* ☐ *John hardly ever gets a bright idea.* ☐ *Listen here! I have a bright idea!*

get a charge out of someone or something AND **get a bang out of** someone or something; **get a kick out of** someone or something to receive special pleasure from someone or something. (Informal.) ☐ *Tom is really funny. I always get a kick out of his jokes.* ☐ *Bill really got a bang out of the present we gave him.* ☐ *Mary got a charge out of Bob's visit.*

get a charley horse to develop a cramp in the arm or leg, usually from strain. (Also with *have.* See the note at **get a big send-off.**) ☐ *Don't work too hard or you'll get a charley horse.* ☐ *Poor Tom is always getting a charley horse in his leg.* ☐ *Sally can't play. She has a charley horse.*

get a checkup to have a physical examination by a physician. (Also with *have.* See the note at **get a big send-off.**) ☐ *She got a checkup yesterday.* ☐ *I going to have a checkup in the morning. I hope I'm okay.*

get a clean bill of health [for someone] to be pronounced healthy by a physician. (Also with *have.* See the note at **get a big send-off.**) ☐ *Sally got a clean bill of health from the doctor.* ☐ *Now that Sally has a clean bill of health, she can go back to work.*

get a crush on someone to become infatuated with someone. (Also with *have.* See the note at **get a big send-off.**) ☐ *Mary thinks she's getting a crush on Bill.* ☐ *Sally says she'll never get a crush on anyone again.* ☐ *John has a crush on Mary.*

get a dirty look from someone to get frowned at by someone. ☐ *I stopped whistling when I got a dirty look from Ann.* ☐ *I got a dirty look from the teacher. I don't know why.*

get a feel for something Go to **get the feel of** something.

get a fix on something **1.** to find out the exact location of something. (Also with *have.* See the note at **get a big send-off.** See also **give** someone **a fix on** something.) ☐ *I can't get a fix on your location. Where are you?* ☐ *We are trying to get a fix on your radio transmission.* ☐ *I have a fix on them now.* **2.** to begin to understand the direction of a discussion. ☐ *I can't quite get a fix on what you're trying to say.* ☐ *I can't get a fix on where you're going with this argument.*

get a foothold (somewhere**)** AND **get a toehold (**somewhere**)** an initial position of support; a starting point. ☐ *It's difficult to get a foothold in the education market when schools are laying off teachers.* ☐ *Max's father helped him get a toehold in the textile industry.*

get a free hand (with someone or something**)** to be granted complete control over something. (Also with *have.* See the note at **get a big send-off.** See also **give** someone **a free hand (with** something**)**.) ☐ *I didn't get a free hand with the last project.* ☐ *John was in charge then, but he didn't have a free hand either.* ☐ *I demand to have a free hand with my own child!*

get a frog in one's **throat** to get soreness or something else in one's throat that prevents one from talking well. (This often leads to one clearing one's throat. Also with *have*. See the note at **get a big send-off**.) □ *The speaker got a frog in his throat and had to stop talking for a while.* □ *Excuse me. I have a frog in my throat.*

get after someone to remind, scold, or nag someone (to do something). (Informal. See also **keep after** someone.) □ *John hasn't taken out the garbage. I'll have to get after him.* □ *Mary's mother will get after her if she doesn't do the dishes.*

get a grasp of something to understand something. (Also with *good*, *solid*, and *sound*, as in the examples. Also with *have*. See the note at **get a big send-off**.) □ *Try to get a grasp of the basic rules.* □ *You don't have a good grasp of the principles yet.* □ *John was unable to get a solid grasp of the methods used in his work, and we had to let him go.*

get a handle on something Go to **have a handle on** something.

get a hand with something to receive assistance with something. (Also with *have*. See the note at **get a big send-off**.) □ *Mary would really like to get a hand with that. It's too much for one person.* □ *I'd like to have a hand with this.*

get ahead of oneself [for someone] to do or say something sooner than it ought to be done so that the proper explanation or preparations have not been made. □ *I have to stick to my notes or I will get ahead of myself in my lecture.* □ *When he bought a new little bicycle before the baby was born, he was getting ahead of himself.*

get a head start (on someone or something**)** **1.** [with *someone*] to start (something) earlier than someone else. (Also with *have*. See the note at **get a big send-off**.) □ *Bill always gets there first because he gets a head start on everybody else.* □ *I'm doing well in my class because I have a head start.* **2.** [with *something*] to start something earlier (than someone else). □ *I was able to get a head start on my reading during the holidays.* □ *If I hadn't had a head start, I'd be behind in my reading.*

get (a)hold of someone or something **1.** [with *someone*] to make contact with someone; to call someone on the telephone. (See also **get** one's **hands on** someone or something; **get in touch (with** someone**)**. Also with *have*. See the note at **get a big send-off**.) □ *I'll try to get hold of you in the morning.* □ *It's very hard to get hold of John. He's so busy.* **2.** [with *something*] to obtain something. □ *I'm trying to get hold of a glass jar. I need it for school.* □ *Does anyone know where I can get hold of a spare tire?* □ *I have hold of a very large piece of land.* **3.** Go to **take (a)hold of** someone or something.

get a hurry on AND **get a move on** to start to hurry. (Informal.) □ *We are going to leave in five minutes, Jane. Get a hurry on!* □ *Mary! Get a move on! We can't wait all day.*

get a jump(start) Go to **get a start**.

get a kick out of someone or something Go to **get a charge out of** someone or something.

get a licking AND **take a licking** to get a spanking; to get beat in a fight. (Folksy.) □ *Billy, you had better get in here if you don't want to get a licking.* □ *Bob took a real licking in the stock market.* □ *Tom took a licking in the fight he was in.*

Get a life! Don't act so stupid!; Get a purpose for existing! (Slang. Usually rude.) □ *Hey, stupid! You want to get run over? Get a life!* □ *You worthless jerk! Get a life!*

get a line on someone or something to get an idea on how to locate someone or something; to find out about someone who can help find someone or something. (Also with *have*. See the note at **get a big send-off**.) □ *I got a line on a book that might help explain what you want to know.* □ *Sally has a line on someone who could help you fix up your apartment.*

get (all) dolled up to dress (oneself) up. □ *I have to get all dolled up for the dance tonight.* □ *I just love to get dolled up in my best clothes.*

get a load off one's **feet** AND **take a load off** one's **feet** to sit down; to enjoy the results of sitting down. (Informal.) □ *Come in, John. Sit down and take a load off your* *feet.* □ *Yes, I need to get a load off my feet. I'm really tired.*

get a load off one's **mind** to say what one is thinking; to talk about what is troubling one; to **speak** one's **mind.** (Informal.) □ *He sure talked a long time. I guess he had to get a load off his mind.* □ *You aren't going to like what I'm going to say, but I have to get a load off my mind.*

get a load of someone or something look at someone or something. (Informal or slang.) □ *Get a load of that guy. Have you ever seen such arrogance?* □ *Get a load of that car. It's got real wire wheels.*

get along (in years) to grow older. □ *Grandfather is getting along in years.* □ *Yes, he's really getting along.*

get along (on a shoestring) to be able to afford to live on very little money. □ *For the last two years, we have had to get along on a shoestring.* □ *With so little money, it's hard to get along.*

get along (without (someone or something**))** to manage without someone or something; to do without someone or something. □ *I don't think I can get along without my secretary.* □ *My secretary just quit, and I don't think I will be able to get along.* □ *I like steak, but I can't afford it. I guess I'll have to get along without.*

get along (with someone or something**)** Go to **get on (with** someone or something**).**

get a lot of mileage out of something to get a lot of use from something, as if it were a car. □ *Bob always got a lot of mileage out of one joke.* □ *I got a lot of mileage out of my TV before it broke down.*

get a lump in one's **throat** to have the feeling of something in one's throat—as if one were going to cry. (Also with *have.* See the note at **get a big send-off.**) □ *Whenever they play the national anthem, I get a lump in my throat.* □ *I have a lump in my throat because I'm frightened.*

get a move on Go to **get a hurry on.**

get an earful to hear or listen to a great amount of discussion, criticism, or complaint. □ *She was really mad about something, and I sure got an earful.* □ *Sue was standing around the corner while Jim and Mary were arguing and got an earful.*

get an eyeful (of someone or something**)** to see everything; to see a shocking or surprising sight. □ *The office door opened for a minute and I got an eyeful of the interior.* □ *Mary got an eyeful of the company's extravagant spending when she peeked into the conference room.*

get an in (with someone**)** to develop a way to request a special favor from someone; to gain influence with someone. (The *in* is a noun. Also with *have.* See the note at **get a big send-off.**) □ *Did you get an in with the mayor? I have to ask him a favor.* □ *Sorry, I don't have an in, but I know someone who does.*

get another guess coming Go to **get another think coming.**

get another think coming AND **get another guess coming** to have to rethink something because one was wrong the first time. (Folksy. *Think* is a noun here. Also with *have.* See the note at **get a big send-off.**) □ *She's quite wrong. She's got another think coming if she wants to walk in here like that.* □ *You have another guess coming if you think you can treat me like that!*

get ants in one's **pants** to become nervous and agitated. (Refers to the agitation caused by ants crawling into one's pants. Slang. Also with *have.* See the note at **get a big send-off.**) □ *I always get ants in my pants before a test.* □ *I wonder if all actors get ants in their pants before they go on stage.*

get a rain check (on something**)** AND **take a rain check (on** something**) 1.** to accept a piece of paper allowing one to see an event—which has been canceled—at a later time. (Originally said of sporting events that had to be canceled because of rain. Also with have. See the note at **get a big send-off.**) □ *The game was canceled because of the storm, but we all got rain checks on it.* □ *I didn't take a rain check because I'm leaving town for a month.* **2.** to accept (or request) a reissuance of an invitation at a later date.

(Said to someone who has invited you to something that you cannot attend now, but would like to attend at a later time.) ☐ *We would love to come to your house, but we are busy next Saturday. Could we take a rain check on your kind invitation?* ☐ *Oh, yes. You have a rain check that's good anytime you can come by and visit.* **3.** to accept a piece of paper that allows one to purchase an item on sale at a later date. (Stores issue these pieces of paper when they run out of specially priced sale merchandise.) ☐ *The store was all out of the shampoo they advertised, but I got a rain check.* ☐ *Yes, you should always take a rain check so you can get it at the sale price later when they have more.*

get a raw deal to receive unfair or bad treatment. (Slang. Also with *have*. See the note at **get a big send-off**. See also **give** someone **a raw deal**.) ☐ *Mary got a raw deal on her traffic ticket. She was innocent, but she had to pay a big fine.* ☐ *I bought a used TV that worked for two days and then quit. I sure got a raw deal.* ☐ *You sure had a raw deal.*

get a reputation (as a something**)** to become recognized for being something. (Can be a good or a bad reputation. Also with *have*. See the note at **get a big send-off**.) ☐ *You'll get a reputation as a cheater.* ☐ *She once had a reputation as a singer.* ☐ *Behave yourself, or you'll get a reputation.* ☐ *Unfortunately, Tom's got a reputation.*

get a reputation (for doing something**)** to become recognized for doing something. (Often a bad reputation, as in the examples. Also with *have*. See the note at **get a big send-off**.) ☐ *You'll get a reputation for cheating.* ☐ *I don't want to get a reputation.* ☐ *He's got a bad reputation.* ☐ *I have a reputation for being honest.*

get a rise out of someone to get a reaction from someone, usually anger or laughter. (Informal.) ☐ *Mary really liked my joke. I knew I could get a rise out of her.* ☐ *I got a rise out of him by telling him to go home.*

get a rough idea (about something**)** AND **get a rough idea (of** something**)** to receive a general idea; to receive an estimate. (Also with *have*. See the note at **get a big send-off**.) ☐ *I need to get a rough idea of how many people will be there.* ☐ *I don't need to know exactly. Just get a rough idea.* ☐ *Judy has got a rough idea about who'll be there.* ☐ *I have a rough idea. That's good enough.*

get a rough idea (of something**)** Go to **get a rough idea (about** something**)**.

get around to be experienced; to know a lot about life. (Informal. Use with caution—especially with females—since this can also refer to sexual experience. See also **have been around**.) ☐ *That's a hard question. I'll ask Jane. She gets around.* ☐ *John knows a lot about New York City. He gets around.*

get around to doing something to find time to do something; to do something after a long delay. (Compare this with **get (around) to** something.) ☐ *I finally got around to buying a new coat.* ☐ *It takes Sally years to get around to visiting her aunt.* ☐ *I finally got around to doing the breakfast dishes.*

get (around) to something to manage to deal with someone or something after a delay. (Compare this with **get around to** doing something.) ☐ *It was noon before I got around to the breakfast dishes.* ☐ *The doctor was not able to get to John, even though John waited for three hours.* ☐ *I can't get around to you until tomorrow.*

get a run for one's **money 1.** to receive what one deserves, expects, or wants. (See also **give** one **a run for** one's **money**.) ☐ *I get a run for my money at a high school football game.* ☐ *I get a run for my money in the stock market.* **2.** to receive a challenge. ☐ *Bob got a run for his money when he tried to convince Mary to go to college.* ☐ *Bill got a run for his money playing cards with John.*

get a shellacking AND **take a shellacking 1.** to receive a beating. (Informal.) ☐ *The boxer took a shellacking and lost the fight.* ☐ *I got a shellacking when I broke the window.* **2.** to be beaten—as in sports. (Informal.) ☐ *Our team played well, but got* *a shellacking anyway.* ☐ *I practiced my tennis game so I wouldn't take a shellacking in the tournament.*

get a slap on the wrist to get a light punishment (for doing something wrong). (Also with *have*. See the note at **get a big send-off**. See also **give** someone **a slap on the wrist**.) ☐ *He created quite a disturbance, but he only got a slap on the wrist.* ☐ *I thought I'd get a slap on the wrist for speeding, but I got fined $200.* ☐ *She had a slap on the wrist about that before.*

get a start 1. AND **get a jump(start)** to receive help starting one's car. ☐ *My car is stalled. I need to get a start.* ☐ *I got my car going. I got a jump from John.* **2.** to receive training or a big opportunity in beginning one's career. (The same as **get** one's **start**. Also with *have*. See the note at **get a big send-off**.) ☐ *She got a start in show business in Cincinnati.* ☐ *She had a start when she was only four.*

get a taste of one's **own medicine** [for one] to receive difficulties of the same kind that one has been causing other people. (Also with *have*. See the note at **get a big send-off**. See also **dose of** one's **own medicine**.) ☐ *Now you see how it feels to have someone call you names! You are getting a taste of your own medicine!* ☐ *John, who is often rude and abrupt with people, was devastated when the teacher treated him rudely. He doesn't like having a taste of his own medicine.*

get a thing about someone or something to develop strong likes or dislikes about someone or something. (Also with *have*. See the note at **get a big send-off**.) ☐ *I have a thing about celery. I can't stand it.* ☐ *John can't get enough celery. He's got a thing about it.* ☐ *John has a thing about Mary. He thinks he's in love.*

get a toehold (somewhere**)** Go to **get a foothold** (somewhere).

get a tongue-lashing to receive a severe scolding. (Folksy. Also with *have*. See the note at **get a big send-off**. See also **give** someone **a tongue-lashing**.) ☐ *I really got a tongue-lashing when I got home.* ☐ *Ted will have a tongue-lashing at home.* ☐ *I never had a tongue-lashing like that before.*

get at someone or something **1.** to attack or strike someone or something. (Compare this with **go at** someone or something. Also with *have*.) ☐ *The cat jumped over the wall to get at the mouse.* ☐ *Ok, you guys. There he is. Have at him!* **2.** [with *something*] to eat food; to gobble up food. (Informal. Also with *have*.) ☐ *I can't wait to get at that cake.* ☐ *Dinner's ready. Sit down and have at it.* **3.** [with *someone*] to find a way to irritate someone; to manage to wound someone, physically or emotionally. ☐ *Mr. Smith found a way to get at his wife.* ☐ *John kept trying to get at his teacher.* **4.** [with *something*] to explain or try to explain something; to hint at something. ☐ *We spent a long time trying to get at the answer.* ☐ *I can't understand what you're trying to get at.* **5.** [with *something*] to begin to do something; to **get (around) to** something. ☐ *I won't be able to get at it until the weekend.* ☐ *I'll get at it first thing in the morning.*

get at the heart of the matter Go to **get to the heart of the matter**.

get away (from it all) to get away from one's work or daily routine; to go on a vacation. ☐ *I just love the summer when I can take time off and get away from it all.* ☐ *Yes, that's the best time to get away.*

get away with something to do something bad and not get punished or found out. ☐ *Tom did it again and didn't get punished. He's always getting away with murder.* ☐ *Just because she's so popular, she thinks she can get away with anything.* ☐ *You'll never get away with it.*

get a whiff of something AND **catch a whiff of** something to learn about someone almost accidentally. (Also literal.) ☐ *The boss got a whiff of the problems in the accounting department.* ☐ *No one will get a whiff of your trouble with the police. I'll see to that.*

get a word in edgeways Go to **get a word in edgewise**.

get a word in edgewise AND **get a word in edgeways** to manage to say something when other people are talking and ignoring you. (Often in the negative.) □ *It was such an exciting conversation that I could hardly get a word in edgewise.* □ *Mary talks so fast that nobody can get a word in edgeways.*

get back (at someone**)** AND **have back at** someone to repay one for a bad deed; to **get even (with** someone**)**. (**Have back at** someone is informal or folksy. Compare this with **have at** someone or something at **get at** someone or something.) □ *Tom called me a jerk, but I'll get back at him.* □ *I don't know how I'll get back, but I will.* □ *Just wait. I'll have back at you!*

get back into circulation to start being social with people again after a period of being by oneself; to start dating again, especially after a divorce or breakup with a lover. □ *Sally is anxious to get back into circulation after the nasty divorce she went through.* □ *Todd could not bring himself to get back into circulation after the death of his wife.*

get back into harness to return to one's workplace, such as after a vacation or a period of illness. (Refers to harnessing a horse so it can return to work.) □ *I am not at all anxious to get back into harness after spending two weeks in Mexico.* □ *Tom was eager to get back into harness after his illness.*

get back on one's **feet** to become independent again; to become able to **get around** again. (Note the variations with *own* and *two* in the examples.) □ *He was sick for a while, but now he's getting back on his feet.* □ *My parents helped a lot when I lost my job. I'm glad I'm back on my own feet now.* □ *It feels great to be back on my own two feet again.*

get back (to someone**)** to continue talking with someone (at a later time); to find out information and tell it to a person (at a later time). □ *I don't have the answer to that question right now. Let me find out and get back to you.* □ *Okay. Please try to get back early tomorrow.*

get better to improve. □ *I had a bad cold, but it's getting better.* □ *Business was bad last week, but it's getting better.* □ *I'm sorry you're ill. I hope you get better.*

get busy to start working; to work harder or faster. □ *The boss is coming. You'd better get busy.* □ *I've got to get busy and clean this house up.* □ *Come on, everybody. Let's get busy and get this job done.*

get butterflies in one's **stomach** to get a nervous feeling in one's stomach. (Informal. Also with *have.* See the note at **get a big send-off.** See also **give** one **butterflies in** one's **stomach.**) □ *Whenever I have to go on stage, I get butterflies in my stomach.* □ *She always has butterflies in her stomach before a test.*

get by (on something**)** to manage on the least amount of money, supplies, goods, etc. (Compare this with **get along (on a shoestring).**) □ *We don't have much money. Can we get by on love?* □ *I'll get by as long as I have you.* □ *We don't have very much food, but we'll get by for the weekend.*

get by (with something**) 1.** to satisfy the minimum requirements. □ *I was failing geometry, but managed to get by with a D.* □ *I took the bar exam and just barely got by.* **2.** to do something bad and not get caught or punished; to **get away with** something. □ *Tom cheated on the test and got by with it.* □ *Maybe you can get by like that once or twice, but you'll get caught.*

get carried away to be overcome by emotion or enthusiasm (in one's thinking or actions). (Also literal when someone or something is transported away.) □ *Calm down, Jane. Don't get carried away.* □ *Here, Bill. Take this money and go to the candy store, but don't get carried away.*

get close (to someone or something**) 1.** [with *someone*] to be close friends with someone; to get to know someone well. □ *I would really like to get close to Jane, but she's so unfriendly.* □ *We talked for hours and hours, but I never felt that we were getting close.* □ *It's very hard to get next to someone who won't talk to you.* **2.** [with *something*] to almost equal something; to be almost as good as something. (Often in the negative.) □ *I practiced and practiced, but my bowling couldn't get close to*

Mary's. □ *Her performance was so good that I couldn't get close.*

get cold feet AND **have cold feet** to become timid or frightened; to have one's feet seem to freeze with fear. □ *I usually get cold feet when I have to speak in public.* □ *John got cold feet and wouldn't run in the race.*

get cracking to get moving; to **get busy.** (Folksy.) □ *Let's go. Come on, get cracking!* □ *Move it! We don't have all day. Let's get cracking!* □ *We'll never get finished if you don't get cracking.*

get credit (for something**)** to receive praise or recognition for one's role in something. (Especially with *a lot of, much,* etc., as in the examples below.) □ *Mary should get a lot of credit for the team's success.* □ *Each of the team captains should get credit.*

get down to brass tacks to begin to talk about important things; to **get down to business.** □ *Let's get down to brass tacks. We've wasted too much time chatting.* □ *Don't you think that it's about time to get down to brass tacks?*

get down to business AND **get down to work** to begin to get serious; to begin to negotiate or conduct business. □ *All right, everyone. Let's get down to business. There has been enough playing around.* □ *When the president and vice president arrive, we can get down to business.* □ *They're here. Let's get down to work.*

get down to cases to begin to discuss specific matters; to **get down to business.** □ *When we've finished the general discussion, we'll get down to cases.* □ *Now that everyone is here, we can get down to cases.*

get down to (doing) something to begin doing some kind of work in earnest. □ *I have to get down to my typing.* □ *John, you get in here this minute and get down to that homework!*

get down to the facts to begin to talk about things that matter; to get to the truth. □ *The judge told the lawyer that the time had come to get down to the facts.* □ *Let's get down to the facts, Mrs. Brown. Where were you on the night of January 16?*

get down to the nitty-gritty to **get down to the facts;** to **get down to cases.** (Slang.) □ *Stop fooling around. Get down to the nitty-gritty.* □ *Let's stop wasting time. We have to get down to the nitty-gritty.*

get down to work Go to **get down to business.**

get even (with someone**)** to repay someone's bad deed; to **get back (at** someone**).** □ *Bill hit Bob, and Bob got even with Bill by hitting him back.* □ *Some people always have to get even.*

get fresh (with someone**)** to become overly bold or impertinent with someone. □ *When I tried to kiss Mary, she slapped me and shouted, "Don't get fresh with me!"* □ *I can't stand people who get fresh.*

get goose bumps AND **get goose pimples** [for one's skin] to feel prickly or become bumpy due to cold, fear, or excitement. (Also with *have.* See the note at **get a big send-off.**) □ *When he sings, I get goose bumps.* □ *I never get goose pimples.* □ *That really scared her. Now she's got goose pimples.*

get goose pimples Go to **get goose bumps.**

get gray hair(s) to have one's hair turn gray from stress or frustration. (Also with *have.* See the note at **get a big send-off.**) □ *I'm getting gray hair because I have three teenage boys.* □ *Oh, Tom, stop it! I'm going to get gray hairs.* □ *I have gray hairs from raising four kids.*

get hell Go to **get the devil.**

get in on something to become associated with something, such as an organization or an idea; to find out or be told about special plans. (Also with *be,* as in the final example.) □ *There is a party upstairs, and I want to get in on it.* □ *I want to get in on your club's activities.* □ *Mary and Jane know a secret, and I want to get in on it.* □ *I'm happy to be in on your celebration.* □ *There is going to be a surprise party, and I'm in on it.*

get in (on the ground floor) to become associated with something at its start. (Refers to getting into an elevator at the lowest level when it is not yet crowded.) ☐ *If you move fast, you can still get in on the ground floor.* ☐ *A new business is starting up, and I want to get in early.*

get in someone's **hair** [for someone] to bother or irritate someone. (Also literal.) ☐ *Billy is always getting in his mother's hair.* ☐ *I wish you'd stop getting in my hair.*

get into a jam Go to get into a mess.

get into a mess AND **get into a jam** to get into difficulty or confusion. (Informal. Compare this with **get out of a mess.**) ☐ *Try to keep from getting into a mess.* ☐ *"Hello, Mom," said John on the telephone. "I'm at the police station. I got into a jam."*

get into an argument (with someone**)** to begin to argue with someone. ☐ *Let's try to discuss this calmly. I don't want to get into an argument with you.* ☐ *Tom got into an argument with John.* ☐ *Tom and John got into an argument.* ☐ *Let's not get into an argument.*

get into full swing AND **get into high gear** to move into the peak of activity; to start moving fast or efficiently. (Informal.) ☐ *In the summer months, things really get into full swing around here.* ☐ *We go skiing in the mountains each winter. Things get into high gear there in November.*

get into high gear Go to **get into full swing.**

get in(to) hot water to get into trouble or difficulty; to get involved in something that is complicated or troublesome. ☐ *When you start trying to build your own computer, you are getting into hot water.* ☐ *When Fred was caught cheating on his exam, he got into hot water.*

get into the act to try to be part of whatever is going on. (Refers to someone trying to get on stage and participate in a performance.) ☐ *I can do this by myself. There is no need for you to get into the act.* ☐ *Everyone wants to get into the act. Please let us do it. We don't need your help!*

get into the swing of things to join into the routine or the activities. ☐ *Come on, Bill. Try to get into the swing of things.* ☐ *John just couldn't seem to get into the swing of things.*

get in touch (with someone**)** to communicate with someone; to telephone or write to someone. (See also **keep in touch (with** someone**).**) ☐ *I have to get in touch with John and ask him to come over for a visit.* ☐ *Yes, you must try to get in touch.*

get involved (with someone**)** to become associated with someone. (Sometimes romantically involved.) ☐ *Sally is getting involved with Bill. They've been seeing a lot of each other.* ☐ *I hope they don't get too involved.* ☐ *He didn't want his son involved with the gangs.*

get it Go to **get** something.

get it (all) together to become fit or organized; to organize one's thinking; to become relaxed and rational. (Slang. Also with *have*. See the note at **get a big send-off.**) ☐ *Bill seems to be acting more normal now. I think he's getting it all together.* ☐ *I hope he gets it together soon. His life is a mess.* ☐ *When Jane has it all together, she really makes sense.* ☐ *Sally is a lovely person. She really has it together.*

get it in the neck to receive something bad, such as punishment or criticism. (Slang. Compare this with **get it.**) ☐ *I don't know why I should get it in the neck. I didn't break the window.* ☐ *Bill got it in the neck for being late.*

get lost 1. to become lost; to lose one's way. ☐ *We got lost on the way home.* ☐ *Follow the path, or you might get lost.* **2.** Go away!; Stop being an annoyance! (Slang. Always a command.) ☐ *Stop bothering me. Get lost!* ☐ *Get lost! I don't need your help.* ☐ *Stop following me. Get lost!*

get mad (at someone or something**) 1.** to become angry at someone or something. ☐ *Don't get mad at me. I didn't do it.* ☐ *I got mad at my car. It won't start.* ☐ *I get mad every time I think about it.* **2.** [with *something*] to muster all one's physical and mental resources in order to do something. (Informal or slang.) ☐ *Come on, Bill. If you're going to lift your end of the piano, you're going to have to get mad* *at it.* □ *The sergeant keep yelling, "Work, work! Push, push! Come on, you guys, get mad!"*

get married to become united as husband and wife. □ *Bill and Sally got married when they were in college.* □ *We got married in Texas just after we graduated from college.*

get mixed-up to get confused. □ *I get mixed-up easily whenever I take a test.* □ *Sorry, I didn't say the right thing. I got mixed-up.*

get nowhere fast not to make progress; to get nowhere. (Informal or slang.) □ *I can't seem to make any progress. No matter what I do, I'm just getting nowhere fast.* □ *Come on. Speed up this car. We're getting nowhere fast.*

get off 1. to escape or avoid punishment (for doing something wrong). (Also literal meaning to disembark.) □ *It was a serious crime, but Mary got off with a light sentence.* □ *I was afraid that the robber was going to get off completely.* **2.** to start off (on a friendship). (See also **get off on the wrong foot**. Compare this with **get along (with** someone**)**.) □ *Tom and Bill had never met before. They seemed to get off all right, though.* □ *I'm glad they got off so well.* **3.** to leave; to depart. □ *The plane did not get off on time.* □ *We have to get off early in the morning before the traffic gets heavy.*

get off easy AND **get off lightly** to receive very little punishment (for doing something wrong). (See also **get a slap on the wrist**.) □ *It was a serious crime, but Mary got off easy.* □ *Billy's punishment was very light. Considering what he did, he got off lightly.*

Get off it! Don't talk nonsense!; Don't talk like that! (Usually a command.) □ *Get off it, Tom! You don't know that for a fact.* □ *Oh, get off it! You sound so conceited!*

get off lightly Go to **get off easy**.

get off on the wrong foot AND **get off to a bad start** to start something (such as a friendship) with negative factors. (Also literal. See also **get off; be off on the wrong foot; be off to a bad start; start off on the wrong foot**.) □ *Bill and Tom got off on the wrong foot. They had a minor car accident just before they were introduced.* □ *Let's work hard to be friends. I hate to get off on the wrong foot.* □ *Bill is getting off to a bad start in geometry. He failed the first test.*

get off scot-free Go to **go scot-free**.

Get off someone's **back!** Go to **Get off** someone's **case!**

Get off someone's **case!** AND **Get off** someone's **back!; Get off** someone's **tail!** Leave someone alone!; Stop picking on someone! (Slang. Usually a command.) □ *I'm tired of your criticism, Bill. Get off my case!* □ *Quit picking on her. Get off her back!* □ *Leave me alone! Get off my tail!*

Get off someone's **tail!** Go to **Get off** someone's **case!**

get off the hook to free oneself from an obligation. □ *They have asked you to lead the parade, and I don't think you can get off the hook.* □ *I couldn't get off the hook no matter how much I pleaded.*

get off to a bad start Go to **get off on the wrong foot**.

get off to a flying start to have a very successful beginning to something. □ *The new business got off to a flying start with those export orders.* □ *We shall need a large donation from the local citizens if the charity is to get off to a flying start.*

get off your high horse to become less haughty. □ *You should get off your high horse and pay attention more to what people think.* □ *If she would get off her high horse and try to be human, everyone would like her better.*

get one's **act together** to get oneself organized, especially mentally. (Slang. Originally from theatrical use. Also with *have*. See the note at **get a big send-off**.) □ *I'm so confused about life. I have to get my act together.* □ *Bill Smith had a hard time getting his act together after his mother's death.* □ *Mary really has her act together. She handles herself very well.*

get one's **bearings** to determine where one is; to determine how one is oriented to one's immediate environment. (Also with *have*. See the note at **get a big send-off**.) □ *After he fell, it took Ted a few minutes to get his bearings.* □ *I don't have my bearings yet. Wait a minute.*

get one's **comeuppance** to get a reprimand; to get the punishment one deserves. (Folksy.) □ *Tom is always insulting people, but he finally got his comeuppance. Bill hit him.* □ *I hope I don't get my comeuppance like that.*

get one's **ducks in a row** to get something into order or into line; to put one's affairs in order; to get things ready. (Informal. Also with *have*. See the note at **get a big send-off**. Refers to a mother duck leading a row of ducklings.) □ *Jane is organized. She really has all her ducks in a row.* □ *You can't hope to go into a company and sell something until you get your ducks in a row.* □ *As soon as you people get your ducks in a row, we'll leave.*

get (oneself) **into a stew (over** someone or something**)** to be worried or upset about someone or something. □ *Please don't get yourself into a stew over Walter.* □ *Liz is the kind of person who gets into a stew over someone else's business.*

get one's **feet on the ground** AND **have** one's **feet on the ground** to get firmly established or reestablished. (Also literal.) □ *He's new at the job, but soon he'll get his feet on the ground.* □ *Her productivity will improve after she gets her feet on the ground again.*

get one's **feet wet** to begin something; to have one's first experience of something. (Also literal. Informal. Also with *have*. See the note at **get a big send-off**.) □ *Of course he can't do the job right. He's hardly got his feet wet yet.* □ *I'm looking forward to learning to drive. I can't wait to get behind the steering wheel and get my feet wet.* □ *I've only been at this job for a month, and I don't have my feet wet yet.*

get one's **fill of** someone or something to receive enough of someone or something. (Also with *have*. See the note at **get a big send-off**.) □ *You'll soon get your fill of Tom. He can be quite a pest.* □ *I can never get my fill of shrimp. I love it.* □ *Three weeks of visiting grandchildren is enough. I've had my fill of them.*

get one's **fingers burned** to have a bad experience. (Also literal. Also with *have*. See the note at **get a big send-off**.) □ *I had my fingers burned the last time I did this.* □ *I tried that once before and got my fingers burned. I won't try it again.* □ *If you go swimming and get your fingers burned, you won't want to swim again.*

get one's **foot in the door** to achieve a favorable position (for further action); to take the first step in a process. (Refers to people selling things from door to door who block the door with a foot so it cannot be closed on them. Also with *have*. See the note at **get a big send-off**.) □ *I think I could get the job if I could only get my foot in the door.* □ *It pays to get your foot in the door. Try to get an appointment with the boss.* □ *I have a better chance now that I have my foot in the door.*

get one's **hands dirty** AND **dirty** one's **hands; soil** one's **hands** to become involved with something illegal; to do a shameful thing; to do something that is beneath one. (Also literal.) □ *The mayor would never get his hands dirty by giving away political favors.* □ *I will not dirty my hands by breaking the law.* □ *Sally felt that to talk to the hobo was to soil her hands.*

get one's **hands on** someone or something AND **lay** one's **hands on** someone or something to get (a)hold of someone or something; to get someone or something in one's grasp. (Informal. Sometimes said in anger, as if one may wish to do harm.) □ *Just wait until I get my hands on Tom. I'll really give him something to think about.* □ *When I lay my hands on my book again, I'll never lend it to anyone.*

get one's **head above water** to get ahead of one's problems; to catch up with one's work or responsibilities. (Also literal. Also with *have*. See the note at **get a big send-off**.) □ *I can't seem to get my head above water. Work just keeps piling up.* □ *I'll be glad when I have my head above water.*

get one's **hooks into** someone or something to grasp someone or something; to acquire someone or something; to get someone or something in one's grasp. (Slang. Said of someone who is grasping and acquisitive and who will not let go easily. Usually said about a person or about something that is small enough to grasp in one's hand.) □ *I want to get my hooks into a copy of that book.* □ *She can't wait until she gets her hooks into George.*

get one's **just deserts** to get what one deserves. □ *I feel better now that Jane got her just deserts. She really insulted me.* □ *Bill got back exactly the treatment that he gave out. He got his just deserts.*

get one's **just reward(s)** to get something as bad as one deserves. □ *The criminal who was sent to prison got his just rewards.* □ *I am sure that when he died, he got his just reward.*

get one's **knuckles rapped** to receive punishment. (Also literal. Also with *have.* See the note at **get a big send-off.**) □ *I got my knuckles rapped for whispering too much.* □ *You will have your knuckles rapped if you are not careful.*

get one's **money's worth** to get everything that has been paid for; to get the best quality for the money paid. (Also with *have.* See the note at **get a big send-off.**) □ *Weigh that package of meat before you buy it. Be sure you're getting your money's worth.* □ *I didn't get my money's worth with my new camera, so I took it back.* □ *I will stay here and watch the movie over and over until I get my money's worth.*

get one's **nose out of** someone's **business** to stop interfering in someone else's business; to mind one's own business. (See also **keep** one's **nose out of** someone's **business.**) □ *Go away! Get your nose out of my business!* □ *Bob just can't seem to get his nose out of other people's business.*

get one's **(own) way (with** someone or something**)** to have someone or something follow one's plans; to control someone or something. (Also with *have.* See the note at **get a big send-off.**) □ *The mayor got his way with the city council.* □ *He seldom gets his own way.* □ *How often do you have your way with your own money?* □ *Parents usually have their way with their children.*

get one's **say** to be able to state one's position; to be able to say what one thinks. (Also with *have.* See the note at **get a big send-off.** See also **have a voice (in** something**).**) □ *I want to have my say on this matter.* □ *He got his say, and then he was happy.*

get one's **sea legs** to become accustomed to the movement of a ship at sea; to be able to walk steadily on the constantly rolling and pitching decks of a ship. (Also with *have.* See the note at **get a big send-off.**) □ *Jean was a little awkward at first, but in a few days she got her sea legs and was fine.* □ *You may feel a little sick until you get your sea legs.* □ *I will feel better when I have my sea legs.*

get one's **second wind 1.** for one's breathing to become stabilized after exerting oneself for a short time. (Also with *have.* See the note at **get a big send-off.**) □ *John was having a hard time running until he got his second wind.* □ *Bill had to quit the race because he never got his second wind.* □ *"At last," thought Ann, "I have my second wind. Now I can really swim fast."* **2.** to become more active or productive (after starting off slowly). □ *I usually get my second wind early in the afternoon.* □ *Mary is a better worker now that she has her second wind.*

get one's **start** to receive the first major opportunity of one's career. □ *I had my start in painting when I was thirty.* □ *She helped me get my start by recommending me to the manager.*

get one's **teeth into** something to start on something seriously, especially a difficult task. (Informal. See also **sink** one's **teeth into** something.) □ *Come on, Bill. You have to get your teeth into your biology.* □ *I can't wait to get my teeth into this problem.*

get one's **walking papers** to get fired. (Informal. See also **give** one one's **walking papers.**) □ *Well, I'm through. I got my walking papers today.* □ *They are closing down* *my department. I guess I'll get my walking papers soon.*

get one's **wires crossed** to get confused about something. (Informal. As if one's brain were an electrical circuit. Also with *have.* See the note at **get a big send-off.**) □ *You don't know what you are talking about. You really have your wires crossed!* □ *Joan got her wires crossed about who arrived first. It was Bob, not Gary.*

get one's **wits about** one to pull oneself together for action; to set one's mind to work, especially in a time of stress. (Also with *have.* See the note at **get a big send-off.**) □ *Let me get my wits about me so I can figure this out.* □ *I don't have my wits about me at this time of the morning.*

get on someone to pester someone (about something); to pressure someone. (Also literal.) □ *John is supposed to empty the trash every day. He didn't do it, so I will have to get on him.* □ *It's time to get on Bill about his homework. He's falling behind.*

get on someone's **nerves** to irritate someone. □ *Please stop whistling. It's getting on my nerves.* □ *All this arguing is getting on their nerves.*

get on the bandwagon AND **jump on the bandwagon** to join the popular side (of an issue); to take a popular position. □ *You really should get on the bandwagon. Everyone else is.* □ *Jane has always had her own ideas about things. She's not the kind of person to jump on the bandwagon.*

get on the good side of someone to get in someone's favor. □ *You had better behave properly if you want to get on the good side of Mary.* □ *If you want to get on the good side of your teacher, you must do your homework.*

get on (with someone or something**)** AND **get along (with** someone or something**) 1.** [with *someone*] to be friends with someone; to have a good relationship with someone. (The friendship is always assumed to be good unless it is stated to be otherwise.) □ *How do you get on with John?* □ *I get along with John just fine.* □ *We get along.* □ *I don't get on with John.* □ *We don't get along.* **2.** [with *something*] to continue with something. □ *I must get on with my work.* □ *Now that the crisis is over, I'll get on with my life.*

get out from under someone or something **1.** [with *someone*] to get free of someone's control. □ *Mary wanted to get out from under her mother.* □ *We started our own business because we needed to get out from under our employer.* **2.** [with *something*] to get free of a burdensome problem. □ *I can't go out tonight until I get out from under this pile of homework.* □ *There is so much work to do! I don't know when I'll ever get out from under it.*

get out of a jam to get free from a problem or a bad situation. □ *Would you lend me five dollars? I need it to get out of a jam.* □ *I need some help getting out of a jam.*

get out of a mess to get free of a bad situation. (Informal. Also with *this, such a,* etc. See the examples. Compare this with **get into a mess.**) □ *How can anyone get out of a mess like this?* □ *Please help me get out of this mess!*

get out of someone's way AND **get out of the way** to move out of the path or route. □ *Will you please get out of the way?* □ *The dog got out of Jane's way just before she stepped on it.*

get out of the way Go to get out of someone's way.

get out of the wrong side of the bed Go to get up on the wrong side of the bed.

get out while the getting is good to leave a place while it is still possible to do so; to withdraw from a place, position, or some organization at an opportune time. □ *The party was getting noisy enough that one of the neighbors was bound to call the police, so we left. We always get out while the getting is good.* □ *Everyone at my office was being required to do more and more work. I decided to get out while the getting was good. I quit.*

get over someone or something to recover from someone or something. □ *Now that Bob has left me, I have to learn to get over him.* □ *It was a horrible shock. I don't know* *when I'll get over it.* □ *It was a serious illness. It took two weeks to get over it.*

get physical (with someone**)** **1.** to use physical force against someone. □ *The coach got in trouble for getting physical with some members of the team.* □ *When the suspect wouldn't cooperate, the police were forced to get physical.* **2.** to touch someone in lovemaking. □ *I've heard that Bill tends to get physical with his dates.* □ *I don't care if he gets physical—within reason.*

get ready (to do something**)** to prepare to do something. □ *Get ready to jump!* □ *It's time to get ready to go to work.* □ *It's time to get ready.*

get religion to become serious (about something), usually after a powerful experience; to develop a strong religious belief. (Folksy. Also with *have*. See the note at **get a big send-off.**) □ *I've always had religion. I don't need a crisis to make me get it.* □ *When I had an automobile accident, I really got religion. Now I'm a very safe driver.* □ *Soldiers often say they got religion in the midst of a battle.*

get rid of someone or something to get free of someone or something; to dispose of or destroy someone or something. □ *I'm trying to get rid of Mr. Smith. He's bothering me.* □ *I'll be happy when I get rid of my old car.*

get right on something to do something immediately. □ *I know it has to be done today. I'll get right on it.* □ *Please get right on these reports as soon as possible.*

get rolling to get started. (Informal.) □ *Come on. It's time to leave. Let's get rolling!* □ *Bill, it's 6:30. Time to get up and get rolling!*

get second thoughts about someone or something to have new doubts about someone or something. (Also with *have*. See the note at **get a big send-off.**) □ *I'm beginning to get second thoughts about Tom.* □ *Tom is getting second thoughts about it, too.* □ *We now have second thoughts about going to Canada.*

get set get ready; get organized. (Also with *be*, as in the examples below.) □ *We are going to start. Please get set.* □ *We are set. Let's go.* □ *Hurry up and get set!*

get sick **1.** to become ill (perhaps with vomiting). □ *I got sick and couldn't go to school.* □ *My whole family got sick with the flu.* **2.** to vomit. (A euphemism.) □ *Mommy, the dog just got sick on the carpet.* □ *Bill got sick in the hallway.*

get sidetracked to become diverted from one's task; to start off on a second task before the first one is finished. □ *I'm sorry the work is not completed. I got sidetracked.* □ *Pay attention to what you are doing and don't get sidetracked.*

get someone **down** to depress someone; to make someone sad. □ *Try not to let all your problems get you down.* □ *She is very cheerful and practically nothing gets her down.*

get (someone**) off the hook** to free someone from an obligation. (Informal. When *someone* is omitted, this refers to oneself.) □ *Thanks for getting me off the hook. I didn't want to attend that meeting.* □ *I couldn't get off the hook by myself.*

get someone or something **across** Go to put someone or something **across.**

get someone or something **down** **1.** [with *something*] to manage to swallow something, especially something large or unpleasant. □ *The pill was huge, but I got it down.* □ *It was the worst food I have ever had, but I got it down somehow.* **2.** [with *someone*] to depress a person; to make a person very sad. (Also with *have*. See the note at **get a big send-off.**) □ *My dog ran away, and it really got me down.* □ *Oh, that's too bad. Don't let it get you down.* □ *All my troubles really have me down.*

get someone or something **out of** one's **head** Go to **get** someone or something **out of one's mind.**

get someone or something **out of** one's **mind** AND **get** someone or something **out of** one's **head** to manage to forget someone or something; to stop thinking about or wanting someone or something. (Almost the same as **put** someone or something **out of one's mind.**) □ *I can't get him out of my mind.* □ *Mary couldn't get the song out of* *her mind.* ☐ *Get that silly idea out of your head!*

get someone or something **out of the way** to remove someone or something out of the path or route. ☐ *Get your big feet out of my way!* ☐ *Please get your child out of the way!*

get someone **out of a jam** to free someone from a problem or a bad situation. (Informal. Compare this with **in a jam.**) ☐ *I like John. He got me out of a jam once.* ☐ *I would be glad to help get you out of a jam.*

get someone **over a barrel** AND **get** someone **under** one's **thumb** [for someone] to be put **at the mercy of** someone; to get control over someone. (Informal. Also with *have.* See the note at **get a big send-off.**) ☐ *He got me over a barrel, and I had to do what he said.* ☐ *Ann will do exactly what I say. I've got her over a barrel.* ☐ *All right, John. You've got me under your thumb. What do you want me to do?*

get someone's **back up** Go to **get** someone's **dander up.**

get someone's **dander up** AND **get** someone's **back up; get** someone's **hackles up; get** someone's **Irish up** to make someone get angry. (Informal. Also with *have.* See the note at **get a big send-off.**) ☐ *Now, don't get your dander up. Calm down.* ☐ *I insulted him and really got his hackles up.* ☐ *Bob had his Irish up all day yesterday. I don't know what was wrong.* ☐ *She really got her back up when I asked her for money.* ☐ *Now, now, don't get your hackles up. I didn't mean any harm.*

get someone's **ear** to get someone to listen (to you). (Also with *have.* See the note at **get a big send-off.** Compare this with **bend** someone's **ear.**) ☐ *He got my ear and talked for an hour.* ☐ *While I have your ear, I'd like to tell you about something I'm selling.*

get someone's **eye** Go to **catch** someone's **eye.**

get someone's **goat** to irritate someone; to annoy and arouse someone to anger. (Also with *have.* See the note at **get a big send-off.**) ☐ *I'm sorry. I didn't mean to get your goat.* ☐ *Jean got Sally's goat and Sally made quite a fuss about it.* ☐ *Tom really had her goat for a while.*

get someone's **hackles up** Go to **get** someone's **dander up.**

get someone's **Irish up** Go to **get** someone's **dander up.**

get someone's **number 1.** to find out someone's telephone number. (Also with *have.* See the note at **get a big send-off.**) ☐ *As soon as I get Mary's number, I'll call her.* ☐ *I have her number. Do you want me to write it down for you?* **2.** to find out about a person; to learn the key to understanding a person. (Informal.) ☐ *I'm going to get your number if I can. You're a real puzzle.* ☐ *I've got Tom's number. He's ambitious.*

get someone **under** one's **thumb** Go to **get** someone **over a barrel.**

get something AND **get it 1.** to receive punishment. (Also literal meaning to receive something or to contract a disease.) ☐ *Bill broke the window, and he's really going to get a scolding.* ☐ *John got it for arriving late at school.* **2.** to receive the meaning of a joke; to understand something. ☐ *John told a joke, but I didn't get it.* ☐ *Bob laughed very hard, but Mary didn't get it.*

get something **across (to** someone**)** to convey information to someone; to teach someone. ☐ *I'm trying to get this across to you. Please pay attention.* ☐ *I'll keep trying until I get it across.*

get something **into** someone's **thick head** Go to **get** something **through** someone's **thick skull.**

get something **off** one's **chest** to tell something that has been bothering you. (Also with *have.* See the note at **get a big send-off.**) ☐ *I have to get this off my chest. I broke your window with a stone.* ☐ *I knew I'd feel better when I had that off my chest.*

get something **off (the ground)** to get something started. (Also literal.) ☐ *I can relax after I get this project off the ground.* ☐ *You'll have a lot of free time when you get the project off.*

get something **on** someone to learn something potentially damaging to someone. (Also with *have*. See the note at **get a big send-off.**) □ *Tom is always trying to get something on me. I can't imagine why.* □ *If he has something on you, he'll have you over a barrel.* □ *If he gets something on you, you ought to get something on him.*

get something **out in the open** to make something public; to stop hiding a fact or a secret. □ *We had better get this out in the open before the press gets wind of it.* □ *I'll feel better when it's out in the open. I can't stand all of this secrecy.*

get something **out of** one's **system 1.** to get something like food or medicine out of one's body, usually through natural elimination. □ *He'll be more active once he gets the medicine out of his system.* □ *My baby, Mary, ate applesauce and has been crying for three hours. She'll stop when she gets the applesauce out of her system.* **2.** to be rid of the desire to do something; to do something that you have been wanting to do so that you aren't bothered by wanting to do it anymore. □ *I bought a new car. I've been wanting to for a long time. I'm glad I finally got that out of my system.* □ *I can't get it out of my system! I want to go back to school and earn a degree.*

get something **out of** something to get some kind of benefit from something. □ *I didn't get anything out of the lecture.* □ *I'm always able to get something helpful out of our conversations.*

get something **over (with)** to complete something, especially something you have dreaded. (Also with *have*. See the note at **get a big send-off.**) □ *Oh, please hurry and get it over with. It hurts.* □ *Please get it over.* □ *When I have this over with, I can relax.*

get something **sewed up** AND **get** something **wrapped up** to have something settled or finished. (See also **wrap** something **up.** Also with *have*. See the note at **get a big send-off.**) □ *I'll take the contract to the mayor tomorrow morning. I'll get the whole deal sewed up by noon.* □ *Don't worry about the car loan. I'll have it sewed up in time to make the purchase.* □ *I'll get the loan wrapped up, and you'll have the car this week.*

get something **straight** to understand something clearly. (Informal. Also with *have*. See the note at **get a big send-off.**) □ *Now get this straight. You're going to fail history.* □ *Let me get this straight. I'm supposed to go there in the morning?* □ *Let me make sure I have this straight.*

get something **through** someone's **thick skull** AND **get** something **into** someone's **thick head** to manage to get someone, including oneself, to understand something. (Informal.) □ *He can't seem to get it through his thick skull.* □ *If I could get this into my thick head once, I'd remember it.*

get something **to go** Go to **buy** something **to go.**

get something **under** one's **belt 1.** to eat or drink something. (This means the food goes into one's stomach and is under one's belt. Informal. Also with *have*. See the note at **get a big send-off.**) □ *I'd feel a lot better if I had a cool drink under my belt.* □ *Come in out of the cold and get a nice warm meal under your belt.* **2.** to learn something well; to assimilate some information. □ *I have to study tonight. I have to get a lot of algebra under my belt.* □ *Now that I have my lessons under my belt, I can rest easy.*

get something **under way** to get something started. (Also with *have*. See the note at **get a big send-off.**) □ *The time has come to get this meeting under way.* □ *Now that the president has the meeting under way, I can relax.*

get something **wrapped up** Go to **get** something **sewed up.**

get stars in one's **eyes** to be obsessed with show business; to be stage-struck. (Also with *have*. See the note at **get a big send-off.**) □ *Many young people get stars in their eyes at this age.* □ *Ann has stars in her eyes. She wants to go to Hollywood.*

get the advantage of someone AND **get the advantage over** someone**; get the edge on** someone**; get the edge over** someone to achieve a position superior to someone else. (The word *the* can be replaced with *an*. Also with *have*. See the note at **get a big send-off**. See also **take advantage of** someone or something.) ☐ *Toward the end of the race, I got the advantage over Mary.* ☐ *She'd had an advantage over me since the start of the competition.* ☐ *I got an edge on Sally, too, and she came in second.* ☐ *It's speed that counts. You can have the edge over everyone, but if you don't have speed, you lose.*

get the advantage over someone Go to **get the advantage of** someone.

get the air to be ignored or sent away. (See also **give** someone **the air**.) ☐ *Whenever I get around Tom, I end up getting the air.* ☐ *I hate to get the air. It makes me feel unwanted.*

get the ax Go to get the sack.

get the ball rolling AND **set the ball rolling; start the ball rolling** to start something; to get some process going. (Informal. Also with *have*. See the note at **get a big send-off**.) ☐ *If I could just get the ball rolling, then other people would help.* ☐ *Who else would start the ball rolling?* ☐ *I had the ball rolling, but no one helped me with the project.* ☐ *Ann set the ball rolling, but didn't follow through.*

get the benefit of the doubt to receive a judgment in your favor when the evidence is neither for you nor against you. (Also with *have*. See the note at **get a big send-off**. See also **give** someone **the benefit of the doubt**.) ☐ *In my math course, I was right between a B and an A. I got the benefit of the doubt—an A.* ☐ *I thought I should have had the benefit of the doubt, but the judge made me pay a fine.*

get the best of someone Go to **get the better of** someone.

get the better of someone AND **get the best of** someone to win out over someone in a competition or bargain. (Also with *have*. See the note at **get a big send-off**.) ☐ *Bill got the best of John in the boxing match.* ☐ *I tried to get the better of John, but he won anyway.* ☐ *I set out to have the better of Sally, but I didn't have enough skill.*

get the blues to become sad or depressed. (Also with *have*. See the note at **get a big send-off**.) ☐ *You'll have to excuse Bill. He has the blues tonight.* ☐ *I get the blues every time I hear that song.*

get the boot to be sent away (from somewhere); to be dismissed from one's employment; to be kicked out (of a place). (Slang. See also **get the sack; give** someone **the boot**.) ☐ *I guess I wasn't dressed well enough to go in there. I got the boot.* ☐ *I'll work harder at my job today. I nearly got the boot yesterday.*

get the brush-off to be ignored or sent away; to be rejected. (Slang.) ☐ *Don't talk to Tom. You'll just get the brush-off.* ☐ *I went up to her and asked for a date, but I got the brush-off.*

get the cold shoulder to be ignored; to be rejected. (Informal. See also **give** someone **the cold shoulder**.) ☐ *If you invite her to a party, you'll just get the cold shoulder.* ☐ *I thought that Sally and I were friends, but lately I've been getting the cold shoulder.*

get the creeps AND **get the willies** to become frightened; to become uneasy. (Slang. Also with *have*. See the note at **get a big send-off**.) ☐ *I get the creeps when I see that old house.* ☐ *I really had the willies when I went down into the basement.*

get the day off to have a day free from working. (Also with *have*. See the note at **get a big send-off**. See also **take the day off**.) ☐ *The next time I get a day off, we'll go to the zoo.* ☐ *I have the day off. Let's go to the zoo.*

get the devil AND **catch hell; catch the devil; get hell** to receive a severe scolding. (Informal. Use caution with *hell*.) ☐ *Bill is always getting the devil about something.* ☐ *I'm late. If I don't get home soon, I'll catch hell!* ☐ *I caught the devil yesterday for being late.*

get the drift of something to understand the general idea of something. ☐ *I knew enough German to get the drift of this article.* ☐ *I don't get the drift of what you're trying to tell me.*

get the edge on someone Go to get the advantage of someone.

get the edge over someone Go to get the advantage of someone.

get the facts straight to get a good understanding of the facts; to make sure that all the facts are accurate and properly stated. □ *Ask a lot of questions and get all of the facts straight.* □ *Please be sure you get the facts straight before you make a decision.*

get the feel of something AND **get a feel for** something [for someone] to learn the way something feels (when it is used). (Also with *have*. See the note at **get a big send-off**. See also **have the feel of** something.) □ *I haven't yet got the feel of this bat. I hope I don't strike out.* □ *I can drive better now that I have the feel of this car's steering.*

get the final word Go to **get the last word**.

get the floor to receive official permission to address the audience. (Also with *have*. See the note at **get a big send-off**.) □ *When I get the floor, I'll make a short speech.* □ *The last time you had the floor, you talked for an hour.*

get the gate to be sent away; to be rejected. (Slang. See also **give** someone **the gate**.) □ *I thought he liked me, but I got the gate.* □ *I was afraid I'd get the gate, and I was right.*

get the glad hand to receive an overly friendly welcome; to receive insincere attention. (Informal.) □ *Whenever I go into that store, I get the glad hand.* □ *I hate to go to a party and get the glad hand.*

get the go-ahead AND **get the green light** to receive a signal to start or continue. (Also with *have*. See the note at **get a big send-off**. See also **give** someone **the go-ahead**.) □ *We have to wait here until we have the go-ahead.* □ *I hope we get the green light on our project soon.*

get the go-by to be ignored or passed by. (Slang.) □ *It was my turn, but I got the go-by.* □ *Tom stood on the road for fifteen minutes trying to get a ride, but all he could get was the go-by.*

get the goods on someone to find out something potentially damaging or embarrassing about someone. (Slang. Also with *have*. See the note at **get a big send-off**.) □ *John beat me unfairly in tennis, but I'll get even. I'll get the goods on him and his cheating.* □ *The authorities have the goods on Mr. Smith. He has been selling worthless land again.*

get the green light Go to **get the go-ahead**.

get the hang of something to learn how to do something; to learn how something works. (Informal. Also with *have*. See the note at **get a big send-off**.) □ *As soon as I get the hang of this computer, I'll be able to work faster.* □ *Now that I have the hang of starting the car in cold weather, I won't have to get up so early.*

get the hard sell to receive considerable pressure to buy or accept (something). (Informal.) □ *I won't go to that store again. I really got the hard sell.* □ *You'll probably get the hard sell if you go to a used-car dealer.*

get the high sign to receive a prearranged signal. (Often refers to a hand signal or some other visual signal.) □ *When I got the high sign, I pulled cautiously out into the roadway.* □ *The train's engineer got the high sign and began to move the train out of the station.*

get the inside track to get the advantage (over someone) because of special connections, special knowledge, or favoritism. (The inside track is the shortest track in an oval race track that is divided into tracks. Also with *have*. See the note at **get a big send-off**.) □ *If I could get the inside track, I could win the contract.* □ *The boss likes me. Since I have the inside track, I'll probably be the new office manager.*

get the jump on someone to do something before someone; to get ahead of someone. (Also with *have*. See the note at **get a big send-off**.) □ *I got the jump on Tom and got a place in line ahead of him.* □ *We'll have to work hard to get the contract, because they have the jump on us.*

get the last laugh to laugh at or ridicule someone who has laughed at or ridiculed you; to put someone in the same bad position that you were once in; to **turn the tables (on someone)**. (Also with *have*. See the note at **get a big send-off**. See also **He who laughs last, laughs longest.**) □ *John laughed when I got a D on the final exam. I got the last laugh, though. He failed the course.* □ *Mr. Smith said I was foolish when I bought an old building. I had the last laugh when I sold it a month later for twice what I paid for it.*

get the last word AND **get the final word** to get to make the final point (in an argument); to get to make the final decision (in some matter). (Also with *have*. See the note at **get a big send-off**.) □ *The boss gets the last word in hiring.* □ *Why do you always have to have the final word in an argument?*

get the lead out AND **shake the lead out** to hurry; to move faster. (Slang. This means to get the lead weights out of your pants so you can move faster.) □ *Come on, you guys. Get the lead out!* □ *If you're going to sell cars, you're going to have to shake the lead out.*

get the low-down (on someone or something**)** to receive the full story about someone or something. (Slang. Also with *have*. See the note at **get a big send-off**. See also **give** someone **the low-down (on** someone or something**)**.) □ *I need to get the low-down on John. Is he still an accountant?* □ *Sally wants to get the low-down on the new expressway. Please tell her all about it.* □ *Now I have the low-down on the princess!*

get the message Go to get the word.

get the nod to get chosen. (Informal. Also with *have*. See the note at **get a big send-off**.) □ *The manager is going to pick the new sales manager. I think Ann will get the nod.* □ *I had the nod for captain of the team, but I decided not to do it.*

get the (old) heave-ho to get thrown out (of a place); to get dismissed (from one's employment). (Informal. From nautical use, where sailors used *heave-ho* to coordinate hard physical labor. One sailor called "Heave-ho," and all the sailors would pull at the same time on the *ho*. Also with *have*. See the note at **get a big send-off**. See also **give** someone or something **the (old) heave-ho**.) □ *I went there to buy a record album, but I got the old heave-ho. That's right. They threw me out!* □ *They fired a number of people today, but I didn't get the heave-ho.* □ *John had the old heave-ho last week. Now he's unemployed.*

get the once-over to receive a quick visual examination. (Note the variations in the examples. See also **give** someone **the once-over**.) □ *Every time John walks by I get the once-over. Does he like me?* □ *I went to the doctor yesterday, but I only had a once-over.* □ *I wanted a complete examination, not just a once-over.*

get the picture to understand the whole situation. (Informal or slang.) □ *Okay, Bob. That's the whole explanation. You get the picture?* □ *Yes, I got the picture.*

get the red-carpet treatment to receive very special treatment; to receive royal treatment. (This refers—sometimes literally—to the rolling out of a clean red carpet for someone to walk on. Also with *have*. See the note at **get a big send-off**. See also **give** someone **the red-carpet treatment; roll out the red carpet for someone.**) □ *I love to go to fancy stores where I get the red-carpet treatment.* □ *The queen expects to get the red-carpet treatment wherever she goes.*

get the runaround to receive a series of excuses, delays, and referrals. □ *You'll get the runaround if you ask to see the manager.* □ *I hate it when I get the runaround.*

get the sack AND **get the ax** to get fired; to be dismissed (from one's employment). (Slang. See also **give** someone **the ax.**) □ *I got the sack yesterday. Now I have to find a new job.* □ *I tried to work harder, but I got the ax anyway.*

get the shock of one's **life** to receive a serious (emotional) shock. (Also with *have*. See the note at **get a big send-off**.) □ *I opened the telegram and got the shock of* *my life.* ☐ *I had the shock of my life when I won $5,000.*

get the short end of the stick AND **end up with the short end of the stick** to end up with less (than someone else); to end up cheated or deceived. (Also with *have.* See the note at **get a big send-off.**) ☐ *Why do I always get the short end of the stick? I want my fair share!* ☐ *She's unhappy because she has the short end of the stick again.* ☐ *I hate to end up with the short end of the stick.*

get the show on the road to get (something) started. (Slang.) ☐ *Hurry up, you guys. Let's get the show on the road.* ☐ *If you don't get the show on the road right now, we'll never finish today.*

get the slip [for someone] to elude or escape (someone). (Slang.) ☐ *We followed her for two blocks, and then got the slip.* ☐ *The police got the slip, and the criminal got away.*

get the third degree to be questioned in great detail for a long period. (Slang. See also **give** someone **the third degree.**) ☐ *Why is it I get the third degree from you every time I come home late?* ☐ *Poor Sally spent all night at the police station getting the third degree.*

get the upper hand (on someone**)** to get into a position superior to someone; to **get the advantage of** someone. (Also with *have.* See the note at **get a big send-off.**) ☐ *John is always trying to get the upper hand on someone.* ☐ *He never ends up having the upper hand, though.*

get the willies Go to **get the creeps.**

get the word AND **get the message** to receive an explanation; to receive the final and authoritative explanation. ☐ *I'm sorry, I didn't get the word. I didn't know the matter had been settled.* ☐ *Now that I have gotten the message, I can be more effective in answering questions.*

get the works to receive a lot of something. (Slang. *The works* can be a lot of food, good treatment, bad treatment, etc. See also **give** someone **the works.**) ☐ *BILL: Shall we order a snack or a big meal? JANE: I'm hungry. Let's get the works.* ☐ *But, your honor. I shouldn't get the works. I only drove too fast!*

get the worst of something to experience the worst aspects of something. (Also with *have.* See the note at **get a big send-off.**) ☐ *No matter what happens at the office, I seem to get the worst of it.* ☐ *He always gets the worst of the bargain.* ☐ *I got to choose which one I wanted, but I still got the worst of the two.*

get through something **1.** to finish something; to work one's way through something. (Compare this with **get through with** something.) ☐ *If I read fast, I can get through this book in an hour.* ☐ *I don't think I can get through all this work by quitting time.* **2.** to survive something; to **go through** something. ☐ *This is a busy day. I don't know how I'll get through it.* ☐ *Sally hopes to get through college in three years.*

get through (to someone**) 1.** to reach someone; to manage to communicate to someone. ☐ *I called her on the telephone time after time, but I couldn't get through to her.* ☐ *I tried every kind of communication, but I couldn't get through.* **2.** to pass through (something). ☐ *The crowd was so thick that I couldn't get through to him.* ☐ *I tried, but I couldn't get through. The crowd was too heavy.* **3.** to make someone understand something; to **get** something **through** someone's **thick skull.** ☐ *Why don't you try to understand me? What do I have to do to get through to you?* ☐ *Can anybody get through, or are you just stubborn?* ☐ *Ann is still too sick to understand what I'm saying. Maybe I can get through to her tomorrow.*

get through with something to get finished with something. (Compare this with **get through** something.) ☐ *You can use this pencil when I get through with it.* ☐ *Can I have the salt when you get through with it?*

get time off to receive a period of time that is free from employment. (Compare this with **get the day off.** See also **take time off.** Also with *have.* See the note at **get a big send-off.**) ☐ *I'll have to get time off for jury duty.* ☐ *I got time off to go downtown* *and shop.* □ *I don't have time off from work very often.*

get time off for good behavior to have one's prison sentence shortened because of good behavior. (Also with *have.* See the note at **get a big send-off.**) □ *Bob will get out of jail tomorrow rather than next week. He got time off for good behavior.* □ *I know I will have time off for good behavior.*

get time to catch one's **breath** to find enough time to relax or behave normally. (Also literal. Also with *have.* See the note at **get a big send-off.**) □ *When things slow down around here, I'll get time to catch my breath.* □ *Sally was so busy she didn't even have time to catch her breath.*

get to first base (with someone or something**)** AND **reach first base (with** someone or something**)** to make a major advance with someone or something. (Informal. *First base* refers to baseball.) □ *I wish I could get to first base with this business deal.* □ *John adores Sally, but he can't even reach first base with her. She won't even speak to him.* □ *He smiles and acts friendly, but he can't get to first base.*

get to one's **feet** to stand up. □ *On a signal from the director, the singers got to their feet.* □ *I was so weak, I could hardly get to my feet.*

get to someone to affect someone emotionally in a bad way; to bother someone. □ *Working with abandoned children eventually got to David, and he had to transfer to another department.* □ *Nothing gets to me like seeing people litter.*

get to the bottom of something to get an understanding of the causes of something. (Also literal.) □ *We must get to the bottom of this problem immediately.* □ *There is clearly something wrong here, and I want to get to the bottom of it.*

get to the heart of the matter AND **get at the heart of the matter** to get to the essentials of a matter. □ *We have to stop wasting time and get to the heart of the matter.* □ *You've been very helpful. You really seem to be able to get to the heart of the matter.*

get to the point Go to come to the point.

get to the root of the problem to gain an understanding of the causes or basis of a problem and propose a solution; to **get to the bottom of** something. □ *It will take a little more study to get to the root of the problem.* □ *Let's stop avoiding the issue and get to the root of the problem.*

get tough (with someone**)** to become firm with someone; to use physical force against someone. (Compare this with **get physical (with** someone**).**) □ *The teacher had to get tough with the class because the students were acting badly.* □ *I've tried to get you to behave, but it looks like I'll have to get tough.*

get two strikes against one to get a number of things against one; to be in a position where success is unlikely. (From baseball where one is "out" after three strikes. Also with *have.* See the note at **get a big send-off.**) □ *Poor Bob got two strikes against him when he tried to explain where he was last night.* □ *I can't win. I've got two strikes against me before I start.*

get under someone's **skin** to bother or irritate someone. (Informal.) □ *John is so annoying. He really gets under my skin.* □ *I know he's bothersome, but don't let him get under your skin.*

get under way to start going; to start. (The word *get* can be replaced with *be.* Compare this with **get** something **under way.**) □ *The ship is leaving soon. It's about to get under way.* □ *Let us get our journey under way.* □ *I'm glad our project is under way.*

get-up-and-go energy; motivation. □ *I must be getting old. I just don't have my old get-up-and-go.* □ *A good breakfast will give you lots of get-up-and-go.*

get up enough nerve (to do something**)** to get brave enough to do something. □ *I could never get up enough nerve to sing in public.* □ *I'd do it if I could get up enough nerve, but I'm shy.*

get up on the wrong side of the bed AND **get out of the wrong side of the bed** to get up in the morning in a bad mood. □ *What's wrong with you? Did you get up* *on the wrong side of the bed today?* □ *Excuse me for being grouchy. I got out of the wrong side of the bed.*

get used to someone or something to become accustomed to someone or something. □ *I got used to being short many years ago.* □ *John is nice, but I really can't get used to him. He talks too much.*

get well to become healthy again. □ *Ann had a cold for a week, and then she got well.* □ *Hurry up and get well!*

get wet to become soaked with water. (See also **all wet**.) □ *Get out of the rain or you'll get wet.* □ *Don't get wet, or you'll catch a cold.*

get what's coming to one to get what one deserves. (See also **give** one **what's coming to** one.) □ *If you cheat, you'll get in trouble. You'll get what's coming to you.* □ *Billy got what was coming to him.*

get wind of something to hear about something; to receive information about something. (Informal.) □ *I just got wind of your marriage. Congratulations.* □ *Wait until the boss gets wind of this. Somebody is going to get in trouble.*

get wise (to someone or something**)** to find out about someone or something; to see through the deception of someone or something. (Informal or slang.) □ *Watch out, John. Your friends are getting wise to your tricks.* □ *John's friends are getting wise. He had better watch out.*

get with something **1.** to become alert. (Slang. Usually with *it*.) □ *Hey, stupid. Get with it!* □ *Wake up, Bill. Get with what's going on!* **2.** to get up to date on something. (Slang. Usually with *it*.) □ *You're too old-fashioned, Mary. Get with it!* □ *Tom just couldn't get with the newest dance fad.*

get worked up (about something**)** Go to **get worked up (over** something**)**.

get worked up (over something**)** AND **get worked up (about** something**)** to get excited or emotionally distressed about something. (See also **all worked up (over** something**)**.) □ *Please don't get worked up over this matter.* □ *They get worked up about these things very easily.* □ *I try not to get worked up.*

a **ghost of a chance** even the slightest chance; even the most insubstantial chance. □ *She can't do it. She doesn't have a ghost of a chance.* □ *There is just a ghost of a chance that I'll be there on time.*

gild the lily to add ornament or decoration to something that is pleasing in its original state; to attempt to improve something that is already fine the way it is. (Often refers to flattery or exaggeration.) □ *Your house has lovely brickwork. Don't paint it. That would be gilding the lily.* □ *Oh, Sally. You're beautiful the way you are. You don't need makeup. You would be gilding the lily.*

gird (up) one's **loins** to get ready; to prepare oneself (for something). □ *Well, I guess I had better gird up my loins and go to work.* □ *Somebody has to do something about the problem. Why don't you gird your loins and do something?*

give a blank check to someone Go to **give** someone **a blank check**.

give a good account of oneself to do (something) well or thoroughly. □ *John gave a good account of himself when he gave his speech last night.* □ *Mary was not hungry, and she didn't give a good account of herself at dinner.*

give-and-take flexibility; willingness to compromise. □ *Don't expect any give-and-take when you are negotiating with Roger.* □ *There was no question of give-and-take in the contract talks. They would not budge on their demands one little bit.*

give (an) ear to someone or something AND **give** one's **ear to** someone or something to listen to someone or to what someone is saying. (Compare this with **get** someone's **ear**.) □ *I gave an ear to Mary so she could tell me her problems.* □ *She wouldn't give her ear to my story.* □ *He gave ear to the man's request.*

give as good as one **gets** to give as much as one receives; to pay someone back **in kind**. (Usually in the present tense.) □ *John can take care of himself in a fight. He can give as good as he gets.* □ *Sally usu-*

ally wins a formal debate. She gives as good as she gets.

give birth to someone or some creature to bring a baby or other offspring into the world through birth. □ *Mary gave birth to a lovely baby girl.* □ *The raccoon gave birth to 6 little raccoons.*

give birth to something to give rise to or start something. □ *The composer gave birth to a new kind of music.* □ *They gave birth to a new view of language.*

give carte blanche to someone Go to **give** someone **carte blanche.**

give chase (to someone or something**)** to chase someone or something. □ *The dogs gave chase to the fox.* □ *A mouse ran by, but the cat was too tired to give chase.* □ *The police gave chase to the robber.*

give credence to something to believe something; to consider something believable. □ *He tells lies. Don't give credence to what he says.* □ *Please don't give credence to Mary. She doesn't know what she's talking about.*

give credit where credit is due to give credit to someone who deserves it; to acknowledge or thank someone who deserves it. □ *We must give credit where credit is due. Thank you very much, Sally.* □ *Let's give credit where credit is due. Mary is the one who wrote the report, not Jane.*

give free rein to someone AND **give** someone **free rein** to allow someone to be completely in charge (of something). (See also **get a free hand (with** someone or something**).**) □ *The boss gave the manager free rein with the new project.* □ *The principal gave free rein to Mrs. Brown in her classes.*

give ground to retreat (literally or figuratively). □ *When I argue with Mary, she never gives ground.* □ *I approached the barking dog, but it wouldn't give ground.*

give her the gun Go to **give it the gun.**

give in (to someone or something**)** to yield to someone or something; to give up to someone or something. □ *He argued and argued and finally gave in to my demands.* □ *I thought he'd never give in.*

Give it a rest. Stop talking and give your mouth a rest. (Informal.) □ *Shut up, Bob! Give it a rest!* □ *Give it a rest. You talk too much.*

give it the gun AND **give her the gun** to make a motor or engine run faster; to rev up an engine. (Informal or slang. The *her* is often pronounced "er.") □ *BILL:* □ *How fast will this thing go? BOB: I'll give it the gun and see.* □ *Hurry up, driver. Give 'er the gun. I've got to get there immediately.*

Give it time. Be patient.; In time, things will change for the better or for the worse. □ *Things will get better. Don't worry. Give it time.* □ *Of course, things will improve. Give it time.*

give it to someone **(straight)** to tell something to someone clearly and directly. (Informal.) □ *Come on, give it to me straight. I want to know exactly what happened.* □ *Quit wasting time, and tell me. Give it to me straight.*

Give it up. Give up.; Stop trying. □ *It's no use trying any more. Give it up.* □ *You will never get this car to start. Give it up.*

give of oneself to be generous with one's time and concern. □ *Tom is very good with children because he gives of himself.* □ *If you want to have more friends, you have to learn to give of yourself.*

Give one **an inch, and** one **will take a mile.** A person who is granted a little of something (such as a reprieve or lenience) will want more. (Proverb.) □ *I told John he could turn in his paper one day late, but he turned it in three days late. Give him an inch, and he'll take a mile.* □ *First we let John borrow our car for a day. Now he wants to go on a two-week vacation. If you give him an inch, he'll take a mile.*

give one **a run for** one's **money 1.** to give one what one deserves, expects, or wants. (See also **get a run for one's money.**) □ *High school football gives me a run for my money.* □ *I invest in the stock market, and that really gives me a run for my money.*

2. give one a challenge. ☐ *That was some argument. Bill gave John a run for his money.* ☐ *Tom likes to play cards with Mary because she always gives him a run for his money.*

give one **butterflies in** one's **stomach** to cause someone to have a nervous stomach. (See also **get butterflies in** one's **stomach.**) ☐ *Tests give me butterflies in my stomach.* ☐ *It was not frightening enough to give me butterflies in my stomach, but it made me a little apprehensive.*

give one one's **freedom** to set someone free; to divorce someone. ☐ *Mrs. Brown wanted to give her husband his freedom.* ☐ *Well, Tom, I hate to break it to you this way, but I have decided to give you your freedom.*

give one one's **walking papers** to fire someone; to **give** someone **the sack.** (Informal. See also **get** one's **walking papers.**) ☐ *Tom has proved unsatisfactory. I decided to give him his walking papers.* ☐ *We might even give Sally her walking papers, too.*

give one's **ear to** someone or something Go to **give (an) ear to** someone or something.

give one **what's coming to** one to give one what one deserves, either a punishment or a reward. (See also **get what's coming to one.**) ☐ *I'm here to be paid. Give me what's coming to me.* ☐ *Thank you. I will see that you get what's coming to you.*

give out to wear out; to become exhausted and stop. ☐ *The old lady's heart finally gave out.* ☐ *Our television set gave out right in the middle of my favorite program.* ☐ *Bill gave out in the middle of the race.*

give out with something to utter or say something. (Informal. Also with *have.* See the examples below.) ☐ *Suddenly, the dog gave out with a horrible growl.* ☐ *At that point, John gave out with a comment about how boring it all was.* ☐ *Come on, tell me. Have out with it!*

give rise to something to cause something. ☐ *The bad performance gave rise to many complaints.* ☐ *The new law gave rise to violence in the cities.*

give someone **a bang** AND **give** someone **a charge; give** someone **a kick** to give someone a bit of excitement. (Informal.) ☐ *John always gives me a bang.* ☐ *The whole afternoon, with all its silliness, gave me a charge anyway.*

give someone **a big send-off** to see someone off on a journey with celebration and encouragement. (See also **get a big send-off.**) ☐ *When I left for college, all my brothers and sisters came to the airport to give me a big send-off.* ☐ *When the sailors left, everyone went down to the docks and gave them a big send-off.*

give someone **a black eye 1.** to hit someone near the eye so that a dark bruise appears. ☐ *John became angry and gave me a black eye.* ☐ *The door began to swing closed as I approached and it gave me a black eye.* **2.** to harm the character or reputation of someone. (See also **get a black eye**) ☐ *The constant complaining gave the whole group a black eye.* ☐ *His behavior gave him a black eye with the manager.*

give someone **a blank check** AND **give a blank check to** someone to give someone freedom or permission to act as one wishes or thinks necessary. (Refers to a signed bank check with the amount left blank.) ☐ *He's been given a blank check with regard to reorganizing the work force.* ☐ *The manager has been given no instructions about how to train the staff. The owner just gave him a blank check.* ☐ *Jean gave the decorator a blank check and said she wanted the whole house done.*

give someone **a break** to give someone a chance; to give someone another chance or a second chance. ☐ *I'm sorry. Don't send me home. Give me a break!* ☐ *They gave me a nice break. They didn't send me home.*

give someone **a bright idea** to give someone a clever thought or idea. ☐ *That gives me a bright idea!* ☐ *Thank you for giving me a bright idea.*

give someone **a bum steer** to give someone misleading instructions or guidance; to make a misleading suggestion. (Slang. *Bum* = false; phony. *Steer* = guidance, as in the steering of a car.) □ *Max gave Ted a bum steer and Ted ended up in the wrong town.* □ *Someone gave me a bum steer and I paid far more than I needed to for a used car.*

give someone **a buzz** Go to **give** someone **a ring.**

give someone **a charge** Go to **give** someone **a bang.**

give someone **a clean bill of health** [for a doctor] to pronounce someone well and healthy. □ *The doctor gave Sally a clean bill of health.* □ *I had hoped to be given a clean bill of health, but there was something wrong with my blood test results.*

give someone **a dirty look** [for a person] to frown or make an angry face at someone. □ *Ann gave me a dirty look.* □ *I gave her a dirty look back.*

give someone **a fair shake** to give someone fair treatment. □ *He's unpleasant, but we have to give him a fair shake.* □ *We give all our people a fair shake.*

give someone **a fix on** something to tell someone the location of something. (See also **get a fix on** something.) □ *Please give me a fix on your location.* □ *If you give the tower a fix on where you are, they can advise you on runway selection.*

give someone **a free hand (with** something**)** to give someone complete control over something. (See also **get a free hand (with** someone or something**)**.) □ *They gave me a free hand with the project.* □ *I feel proud that they gave me a free hand. That means that they trust my judgment.*

give someone **a (good) dressing-down** a scolding. □ *After that dressing-down I won't be late again.* □ *The boss gave Fred a real dressing-down for breaking the machine.*

give someone **a hand (for** something**)** to applaud someone for something. □ *After she sang, they gave her a nice hand.* □ *Come on, give them a hand. They did very well.*

give someone **a hand (with** someone or something**)** to help someone with someone or something, often with the hands. □ *Will somebody please give me a hand with this?* □ *Can you give me a hand with the baby?*

give someone **a hard time** to give someone unnecessary difficulty. □ *Please don't give me a hard time.* □ *The clerk gave me a hard time, so I walked out.*

give someone **a head start (on** someone or something**)** **1.** [with *someone*] to allow someone to start (something) earlier than someone else. □ *They gave Bill a head start on everyone else, so he arrived early.* □ *Please give me a head start on Charles. He is too fast!* **2.** [with *something*] to allow someone to start something earlier (than someone else). □ *We'll give you a head start on the project.* □ *I need a head start on the test because I lost my glasses.*

give someone **a kick** Go to **give** someone **a bang.**

give someone **a licking** to beat someone. □ *Bill give Tom a licking in a fight.* □ *I'll give you a good licking if you don't leave me alone.*

give someone **a line** AND **feed** someone **a line** to lead someone on; to deceive someone with false talk. □ *Don't pay any attention to John. He gives everybody a line.* □ *He's always feeding us a line.*

give someone **an earful 1.** to scold someone. □ *I was so mad at her! I really gave her an earful.* □ *When I find that little jerk I'm going to give him an earful.* **2.** to tell someone a lot of gossip; to give someone a lot of information. □ *I just talked to Margaret. Boy did she give me an earful.* □ *She always gives me an earful. Otherwise I'd never know what's going on.*

give someone **a pain** to annoy or bother someone. (Slang.) □ *Here comes Sally. Oh, she gives me a pain.* □ *She's such a pest. She really gives me a pain.*

give someone **a pat on the back** Go to **pat** someone **on the back.**

give someone **a piece of** one's **mind** to bawl someone out; to **tell** someone **off; to rebuke someone.** □ *I've had enough from John. I'm going to give him a piece of my mind.*

☐ *Sally, stop it, or I'll give you a piece of my mind.*

give someone **a rain check (on** something**)** **1.** to give someone a piece of paper allowing admission to an event—which has been canceled—at a later time. ☐ *The game was canceled because of the rain, but they gave everyone rain checks.* ☐ *They were not able to show the film, so everyone was given a rain check.* **2.** to tell someone that an invitation to a social event will be reissued at a later date. ☐ *We couldn't go to the Smiths' party, so they gave us a rain check.* ☐ *We are sorry we cannot attend, but we would love for you to give us a rain check on another date.* **3.** to issue a piece of paper that allows one to purchase an item on sale at a later date. ☐ *If you have no more of the sale shampoo, will you give me a rain check on it, please?* ☐ *Can I have a rain check on this item? You don't have enough of it in stock.*

give someone **a raw deal** to treat someone unfairly or badly. (See also **get a raw deal**.) ☐ *The judge gave Mary a raw deal.* ☐ *The students think that the teacher gave them a raw deal.*

give someone **a reputation (as a** something**)** to cause someone to be known for being something. ☐ *That evening gave him a reputation as a flirt.* ☐ *Yes, it gave him a reputation.*

give someone **a reputation (for** doing something**)** to cause someone to be known for doing something. ☐ *Her excellent parties gave Jane a reputation for entertaining well.* ☐ *You had better be careful or your behavior will give you a reputation.*

give someone **a ring** AND **give** someone **a buzz** to call someone on the telephone. (Informal.) ☐ *Nice talking to you. Give me a ring sometime.* ☐ *Give me a buzz when you're in town.*

give someone **a rough idea (about** something**)** AND **give** someone **a rough idea (of** something**)** to give someone a general idea or an estimate about something. ☐ *I don't need to know exactly. Just give me a rough idea about how big it should be.* ☐ *Let me give you a rough idea about my plan.*

give someone **a rough idea (of** something**)** Go to **give** someone **a rough idea (about** something**)**.

give someone **a shellacking** **1.** to beat someone. (See also **get a shellacking**.) ☐ *My dad gave me a shellacking when I broke his fishing rod.* ☐ *If you do that again, I will give you a shellacking.* **2.** to beat someone (in a contest). ☐ *The other team gave us a shellacking.* ☐ *The Bears gave the Packers a shellacking.*

give someone **a slap on the wrist** AND **slap** someone **on the wrist; slap** someone's **wrist** to give someone a light punishment (for doing something wrong). (See also **get a slap on the wrist**.) ☐ *The judge gave her a slap on the wrist for speeding.* ☐ *The judge should have done more than slap her wrist.* ☐ *They should do more than just slap his wrist.*

give someone **a start** **1.** to help start someone's car. ☐ *John gave me a start when my car was stalled.* ☐ *Won't someone please give me a start?* **2.** to give someone training or a big opportunity in beginning one's career. ☐ *No one gave me a start in the theater, and I eventually gave up trying.* ☐ *My career began when my father gave me a start in his act.* **3.** to startle someone; to make someone jerk or jump from a sudden fright. (Often with *quite*.) ☐ *The thunderclap gave me quite a start.* ☐ *I didn't mean to give you a start. I should have knocked before I entered.*

give someone **a swelled head** to make someone conceited. ☐ *Fame gave John a swelled head.* ☐ *Don't let this success give you a swelled head.*

give someone **a tongue-lashing** to give someone a severe scolding. (Folksy. See also **get a tongue-lashing**.) ☐ *I gave Bill a real tongue-lashing when he got home late.* ☐ *I will give you a real tongue-lashing if you ever do that again.*

give someone **carte blanche** AND **give carte blanche to** someone to give someone freedom or permission to act as one wishes or thinks necessary. (Almost the same as **give** someone **a blank check**.) ☐ *He's been given carte blanche with the re-*

organization of the work force. ☐ *The manager has been given no instructions about how to train the staff. The owner just gave him carte blanche.* ☐ *Jean gave carte blanche to the decorator and said she wanted the whole house done.*

give someone **credit (for** something**)** to praise or recognize someone for doing something. ☐ *The coach gave Mary a lot of credit.* ☐ *The director gave John much credit for his fine performance.*

give someone **free rein** Go to **give free rein to** someone.

give someone **goose bumps** AND **give** someone **goose pimples** to cause someone to have prickly or bumpy skin owing to excitement or fear. ☐ *It was a scary movie and it gave me goose bumps.* ☐ *I hate being in that old house. It gives me goose pimples.*

give someone **goose pimples** Go to **give** someone **goose bumps.**

give someone **gray hair(s)** to cause someone's hair to turn gray from stress or frustration. (Usually an expression of fear that one's hair will turn gray.) ☐ *My three teenage boys are giving me gray hair.* ☐ *Your behavior is giving me gray hairs.*

give someone **hell** Go to **give** someone **the devil.**

give someone or something **a wide berth** to keep a reasonable distance from someone or something; to **steer clear (of** someone or something**)**. (Originally referred to sailing ships.) ☐ *The dog we are approaching is very mean. Better give it a wide berth.* ☐ *Give Mary a wide berth. She's in a very bad mood.*

give someone or something **the (old) heave-ho** to throw someone or something out; to get rid of someone or something; to fire someone. (Informal. See also **get the (old) heave-ho.**) ☐ *We gave Jane the old heave-ho today.* ☐ *John was behaving badly at our party, so my father gave him the heave-ho.* ☐ *This chair is completely worn out. Shall I give it the old heave-ho?*

give someone **pause** to cause someone to stop and think. ☐ *When I see a golden sunrise, it gives me pause.* ☐ *Witnessing an accident is likely to give all of us pause.*

give someone **some skin** [for two people] to touch two hands together in a special greeting, like a handshake. (Slang. One hand may be slapped down on top of the other, or they may be slapped together palm to palm with the arms held vertically. Usually said as a command.) ☐ *Hey, Bob, give me some skin!* ☐ *Come over here, you guys. I want you to meet my brother and give him some skin!*

give someone **the air** to ignore someone; to dismiss someone. (See also **get the air.**) ☐ *Tom always gives me the air. Is there something wrong with me?* ☐ *Why is she giving him the air? What did he do?*

give someone **the ax** AND **give** someone **the sack** to fire someone; to terminate someone's employment. (See also **get the sack.**) ☐ *I gave Tom the sack, and he has to find a new job.* ☐ *I had to give three people the ax yesterday. We are having to reduce our office staff.*

give someone **the benefit of the doubt** to make a judgment in someone's favor when the evidence is neither for nor against the person. (See also **get the benefit of the doubt.**) ☐ *I'm glad the teacher gave me the benefit of the doubt.* ☐ *Please, judge. Give me the benefit of the doubt.*

give someone **the boot** to dismiss someone; to kick someone out (of a place). (Slang. See also **get the boot.**) ☐ *You had better behave, or they'll give you the boot.* ☐ *I will give him the boot if he doesn't straighten up.*

give someone **the brush-off** to send someone away; to reject someone. (Slang.) ☐ *Tom wouldn't talk to her. He just gave her the brush-off.* ☐ *Please don't give me the brush-off!*

give someone **the bum's rush** to hurry someone into leaving; to usher someone out of a place quickly. (As someone might quickly escort a vagrant from a fancy restaurant.) ☐ *The young customer in the jewelry store was being given the bum's rush, so he pulled out an enormous roll of bills and the clerk became much* *more helpful.* □ *The doorman gave Bill the bum's rush at the restaurant because Bill did not have a tie on.*

give someone **the business** to harass someone; to give someone a bad time. (Informal.) □ *The people in that office can't answer your question. They just give you the business.* □ *I'll get rid of her. I'll give her the business.*

give someone **the cold shoulder** to ignore someone; to reject someone. (Informal. See also **get the cold shoulder.**) □ *She gave me the cold shoulder when I asked her to the party.* □ *Sally has been giving me the cold shoulder.*

give someone **the creeps** AND **give** someone **the willies** to make someone uneasy; to frighten someone. (Informal. See also **get the creeps.**) □ *That old house gives me the creeps.* □ *That strange old man gives him the willies.*

give someone **the devil** AND **give** someone **hell** to scold someone severely. (Informal. Use caution with *hell.*) □ *I'm going to give Bill hell when he gets home. He's late again.* □ *Bill, why do I always have to give you the devil?*

give someone **the eye** to look at someone in a way that communicates romantic interest. (Informal. See also **catch** someone's **eye.**) □ *Ann gave John the eye. It really surprised him.* □ *Tom kept giving Sally the eye. She finally left.*

give someone **the gate** to send someone away; to reject someone. (Slang. See also **get the gate.**) □ *Not only was he not friendly, he gave me the gate.* □ *He was rude, so we gave him the gate.*

give someone **the glad hand** to give someone an overly friendly welcome; to give someone insincere attention. (Informal.) □ *Here comes Tom. Watch him give us the glad hand and leave.* □ *These politicians give you the glad hand and ignore you after they are elected.*

give someone **the go-ahead** AND **give** someone **the green light** to give someone the signal to start or continue. (See also **get the go-ahead.**) □ *It's time to start work. Give everybody the go-ahead.* □ *They gave us the green light to start.*

give someone **the go-by** to pass by or ignore someone. (Slang.) □ *I could see that Tom wanted a ride, but I gave him the go-by.* □ *There was no reason to give the me go-by!*

give someone **the green light** Go to **give** someone **the go-ahead.**

give someone **the hard sell** to put pressure on someone to buy or accept (something). (Informal.) □ *They gave me the hard sell, but I still wouldn't buy the car.* □ *The clerk gave the customer the hard sell.*

give someone **the high sign** to give someone a prearranged signal. □ *As the robber walked past me, I gave the police officer a high sign. Then the officer arrested the robber.* □ *Things got started when I gave the conductor the high sign.*

give someone **the low-down (on** someone or something**)** to tell someone the full story about someone or something. (Slang. See also **get the low-down (on** someone or something**).**) □ *Please give Sally the low-down on the new expressway.* □ *I do not know what's going on. Please give me the low-down.*

give someone **the once-over** to visually examine someone quickly. (See also **get the once-over.**) □ *John gives me the once-over every time he walks by me.* □ *Why does he just give me the once-over? Why doesn't he say hello?*

give someone **the red-carpet treatment** to give someone very special treatment; to give someone royal treatment. (See also **get the red-carpet treatment.**) □ *We always give the queen the red-carpet treatment when she comes to visit.* □ *They never give me the red-carpet treatment.*

give someone **the runaround** to give someone a series of excuses, delays, and referrals. □ *If you ask to see the manager, they'll give you the runaround.* □ *Stop giving me the runaround!*

give someone **the sack** Go to **give** someone **the ax.**

give someone **the shirt off** one's **back** to be very generous or solicitous to someone. □ *Tom really likes Bill. He'd give Bill the shirt off his back.* □ *John is so friendly that he'd give anyone the shirt off his back.*

give someone **the slip** to escape from or elude someone. (Slang.) □ *We followed her for two blocks, and then she gave us the slip.* □ *Max gave Lefty the slip.*

give someone **the third degree** to question someone in great detail for a long period. (Slang. See also **get the third degree.**) □ *The police gave Sally the third degree.* □ *Stop giving me the third degree. I told you what I know.*

give someone **the willies** Go to **give** someone **the creeps.**

give someone **the works** to give someone the full amount or the full treatment. (Slang. See also **get the works.**) □ *The judge gave her the works for driving too fast.* □ *I want everything on my hamburger. Give me the works.*

give someone **tit for tat** to give someone something equal to what was given you; to exchange a series of things, one by one, with someone. (Informal.) □ *They gave me the same kind of difficulty that I gave them. They gave me tit for tat.* □ *He punched me, so I punched him. Every time he hit me, I hit him. I just gave him tit for tat.*

give someone **to understand** something to explain something to someone; to imply something to someone. (This may mislead someone, accidentally or intentionally.) □ *Mr. Smith gave Sally to understand that she should be home by midnight.* □ *The mayor gave the citizens to understand that there would be no tax increase. He didn't promise, though.*

give someone **what for** to scold someone. (Folksy.) □ *Billy's mother gave him what for because he didn't get home on time.* □ *I will really give you what for if you don't straighten up.*

give something **a lick and a promise** to do something poorly—quickly and carelessly. (Informal.) □ *John! You didn't clean your room! You just gave it a lick and a promise.* □ *This time, Tom, comb your hair. It looks as if you just gave it a lick and a promise.*

give something **a shot** AND **take a shot at** something to try something. □ *I have never dived before, but I will give it a shot.* □ *Tom decided to take a shot at writing a poem.*

give something **a whirl** make a try at doing something. □ *If at first you don't succeed, give it another whirl.* □ *John gave bowling a whirl last night.*

give something one's **best shot** to give a task one's best effort. □ *I gave the project my best shot.* □ *Sure, try it. Give it your best shot!*

give the bride away [for a bride's father] to accompany the bride to the groom in a wedding ceremony. □ *Mr. Brown is ill. Who'll give the bride away?* □ *In the traditional wedding ceremony, the bride's father gives the bride away.*

give the devil her due Go to **give the devil his due.**

give the devil his due AND **give the devil her due** to give your foe proper credit (for something). (This usually refers to a person who has been evil—like the devil.) □ *She's generally impossible, but I have to give the devil her due. She bakes a terrific cherry pie.* □ *John may cheat on his taxes and yell at his wife, but he keeps his car polished. I'll give the devil his due.*

give the game away to reveal a plan or strategy. (Informal.) □ *Now, all of you have to keep quiet. Please don't give the game away.* □ *If you keep giving out hints, you'll give the game away.*

give up the ghost to die; to release one's spirit. (Considered formal or humorous.) □ *The old man sighed, rolled over, and gave up the ghost.* □ *I'm too young to give up the ghost.*

give vent to something to express anger; to release one's anger, irritation, emotion, etc. (The *something* is usually anger, ire, irritation, etc.) □ *John gave vent to his anger by yelling at Sally.* □ *Bill couldn't* *give vent to his frustration because he had been warned to keep quiet.*

give voice to something to express a feeling or an opinion in words; to speak out about something. ☐ *The bird gave voice to its joy in the golden sunshine.* ☐ *All the people gave voice to their anger at Congress.*

a **given** a fact that is taken for granted; a fact that is assumed. ☐ *That Mary will go to college is a given. The question is what she is going to study.* ☐ *It is a given that the earth revolves around the sun.*

given to doing something likely to do something; inclined to do something habitually. ☐ *Mary is given to singing in the shower.* ☐ *Bob is given to shouting when things don't go his way.*

given to understand made to believe. ☐ *They were given to understand that there would be no tax increase, but after the election taxes went up.* ☐ *She was given to understand that she had to be home by midnight.*

gloss something **over** to cover up or conceal an error; to make something appear right by minimizing or concealing the flaws. ☐ *When I asked him not to gloss the flaws over, he got angry.* 🅃 *When Mr. Brown was selling me the car, he tried to gloss over its defects.*

glutton for punishment someone who seems to like doing or seeking out difficult, unpleasant, or badly paid tasks. ☐ *If you want to work for this charity, you'll have to be a glutton for punishment and work long hours for nothing.* ☐ *Jane must be a real glutton for punishment. She's typing Bill's manuscript free of charge, and he doesn't even thank her.*

gnash one's **teeth** to slash about with the teeth. ☐ *Bill clenched his fists and gnashed his teeth in anger.* ☐ *The wolf gnashed its teeth and chased after the deer.*

go about one's **business** to mind one's business; to move elsewhere and mind one's own business. ☐ *Leave me alone! Just go about your business!* ☐ *I have no more to say. I would be pleased if you would go about your business.*

go against the grain to go against the natural direction or inclination. (Refers to the grain of wood. See also **rub** someone('s **fur) the wrong way.**) ☐ *You can't expect me to help you cheat. That goes against the grain.* ☐ *Would it go against the grain for you to call in sick for me?*

go all out to use all one's resources; to be very thorough. (Informal. Compare this with **make an all-out effort.**) ☐ *Whenever they have a party, they really go all out.* ☐ *My cousin is coming for a visit, and she expects us to go all out.*

go all the way (with someone**)** AND **go to bed (with** someone**)** to have sexual intercourse with someone. (Euphemistic. Use with caution.) ☐ *If you go all the way, you stand a chance of getting pregnant.* ☐ *I've heard that they go to bed all the time.*

go along for the ride to accompany (someone) for the pleasure of riding along. ☐ *Join us. You can go along for the ride.* ☐ *I don't really need to go to the grocery store, but I'll go along for the ride.*

go a long way in doing something Go to **go a long way toward** doing something.

go a long way toward doing something AND **go a long way in** doing something almost to satisfy specific conditions; to be almost right. ☐ *This machine goes a long way toward meeting our needs.* ☐ *Your plan went a long way in helping us with our problem.*

go along (with someone or something**) 1.** [with *something*] to agree to something. (Also literal, meaning "to accompany someone.") ☐ *All right. I'll go along with your plan.* ☐ *I'm sure that John won't want to go along with it.* **2.** [with *someone*] to agree with someone. ☐ *I go along with Sally. I'm sure she's right.* ☐ *I can't go along with John. He doesn't know what he's talking about.*

go ape (over someone or something**)** to become very excited and enthusiastic about someone or something. (Slang.) ☐ *I really go ape over chocolate ice cream.* ☐ *Tom really goes ape over Mary.*

go (a)round in circles 1. to keep going over the same ideas or repeating the same actions, often resulting in confusion, without reaching a satisfactory decision or conclusion. □ *We're just going round in circles discussing the problems of the party. We need to consult someone else to get a new point of view.* □ *Fred's trying to find out what's happened but he's going round in circles. No one will tell him anything useful.* **2.** to be or act confused. (Informal.) □ *I'm so busy I'm going around in circles.* □ *I can't work anymore. I'm so tired that I'm going round in circles.*

go (a)round the bend 1. to go around a turn or a curve; to make a turn or a curve. □ *You'll see the house you're looking for as you go round the bend.* □ *John waved to his father until the car went round the bend.* **2.** to go crazy; to lose one's mind. (Informal.) □ *If I don't get some rest, I'll go round the bend.* □ *Poor Bob. He has been having trouble for a long time. He finally went around the bend.*

go around with someone Go to **hang around (with** someone**)**.

go astray to leave the proper path (literally or figuratively). □ *Stay right on the road. Don't go astray and get lost.* □ *Follow the rules I've given you and don't go astray. That'll keep you out of trouble.*

go at it hammer and tongs Go to **fight** someone or something **hammer and tongs.**

go at it tooth and nail Go to **fight** someone or something **hammer and tongs.**

go at someone or something to attack someone or something; to move or lunge toward someone or something. □ *The dog went at the visitor and almost bit him.* □ *He went at the door and tried to break it down.*

go away empty-handed to depart with nothing. (Compare this with **come away empty-handed.**) □ *I hate for you to go away empty-handed, but I cannot afford to contribute any money.* □ *They came hoping for some food, but they had to go away empty-handed.*

go AWOL to become absent without leave. (See also **absent without leave.**) □ *Private Smith went AWOL last Wednesday. Now he's in a military prison.* □ *Tom went AWOL once too often.*

go back on one's **word** to break a promise that one has made. □ *I hate to go back on my word, but I won't pay you $100 after all.* □ *Going back on your word makes you a liar.*

go bad to become rotten, undesirable, evil, etc. □ *I'm afraid that this milk has gone bad.* □ *Life used to be wonderful. Now it has gone bad.*

go bananas to go crazy or become silly. (Slang.) □ *Whenever I see Sally, I just go bananas! She's fantastic.* □ *This was a horrible day! I almost went bananas.*

go begging to be unwanted or unused. (As if an object were begging for an owner or a user.) □ *There is still food left. A whole lobster is going begging. Please eat some more.* □ *There are many excellent books in the library just going begging because people don't know they are there.*

go broke to completely run out of money and other assets. □ *This company is going to go broke if you don't stop spending money foolishly.* □ *I made some bad investments last year, and it looks as if I may go broke this year.*

go by the board to get ruined or lost. (This is a nautical expression meaning "to fall or be washed overboard.") □ *I hate to see good food go by the board. Please eat up so we won't have to throw it out.* □ *Your plan has gone by the board. The entire project has been canceled.*

go by the book to follow the rules exactly. (Refers to a book of rules.) □ *The judge of the contest went by the book and disqualified us in the first round.* □ *Everyone insisted that the chairman go by the book and rule against the questionable motion.*

go chase oneself to go away (and stop being a bother). (Slang.) □ *He was bothering me, so I told him to go chase himself.* □ *Get out, you pest! Go chase yourself!*

Go climb a tree! AND **Go fly a kite!; Go fry an egg!; Go jump in the lake!; Take a hike!; Take a walk!** Go away and stop bothering me! □ *Go away and stop both-*

ering me. Go climb a tree! ☐ *Go climb a tree! You are a pain in the neck.*

go cold turkey to stop (doing something) without tapering off. (Slang. Originally drug slang. Now concerned with breaking any habit.) ☐ *I had to stop smoking, so I went cold turkey. It's awful!* ☐ *When heroin addicts go cold turkey, they get terribly sick.*

go crazy to become crazy, disorientated, or frustrated. ☐ *It is so busy here that I think I will go crazy.* ☐ *Bob went crazy because his car got a flat tire.*

go down fighting to continue the struggle until one is completely defeated. ☐ *I won't give up easily. I'll go down fighting.* ☐ *Sally, who is very determined, went down fighting.*

go downhill [for something] to decline and grow worse and worse. (Also literal.) ☐ *This industry is going downhill. We lose money every year.* ☐ *As one gets older, one tends to go downhill.*

go down in history to be remembered as historically important. ☐ *Bill is so great. I'm sure that he'll go down in history.* ☐ *This is the greatest party of the century. I bet it'll go down in history.*

go Dutch to share the cost of a meal or some other event. (See also **Dutch treat**.) ☐ *JANE: Let's go out and eat. MARY: Okay, but let's go Dutch.* ☐ *It's getting expensive to have Sally for a friend. She never wants to go Dutch.*

go easy (on someone or something**) 1.** to be kind or gentle with someone or something. (See also **take it easy (on** someone or something**)**.) ☐ *Go easy on Tom. He just got out of the hospital.* ☐ *Go easy on the cat. It doesn't like to be roughed up.* ☐ *Okay, I'll go easy.* **2.** [with *something*] to use something sparingly. ☐ *Go easy on the mustard. That's all there is.* ☐ *When you make my sandwich, please go easy on the onions. I don't like them very well.*

go fifty-fifty (on something**)** to divide the cost of something in half with someone. ☐ *Todd and Jean decided to go fifty-fifty on dinner.* ☐ *The two brothers went fifty-fifty on a replacement for the broken lamp.*

Go fly a kite! Go to **Go climb a tree!**

go for broke to risk everything; to try as hard as possible. (Slang.) ☐ *Okay, this is my last chance. I'm going for broke.* ☐ *Look at Mary starting to move in the final hundred yards of the race! She is really going for broke.*

go for it to make a try for something; to decide to do something. (Slang.) ☐ *I have an offer of a new job. I think I'm going to go for it.* ☐ *Hey, great. Go for it!*

go for someone or something **1.** to desire someone or something. (Also literal meaning to go in someone's place. Usually with *could*, as in the examples.) ☐ *Look at that cute guy. I could really go for him.* ☐ *I could go for a nice cool glass of iced tea.* **2.** to attack someone or something; to lunge at someone or something. ☐ *The lion went for the antelope's throat.* ☐ *After the robber struck Bill, he went for John.* **3.** to reach for a weapon. ☐ *The robber went for his gun and the cop shot him.* ☐ *The hunter went for his knife, but it was too late. The bear was upon him.*

go from bad to worse to progress from a bad state to a worse state. ☐ *This is a terrible day. Things are going from bad to worse.* ☐ *My cold is awful. It went from bad to worse in just an hour.*

Go fry an egg! Go to **Go climb a tree!**

go great guns to go fast or energetically. (Folksy.) ☐ *I'm over my cold and going great guns.* ☐ *Business is great. We are going great guns selling ice cream.*

go haywire to go wrong; to malfunction; to break down. (Folksy.) ☐ *I was talking to Mary when suddenly the telephone went haywire. I haven't heard from her since.* ☐ *There we were, driving along, when the engine went haywire. It was two hours before the tow truck came.*

go hog-wild to behave wildly. (Folksy.) ☐ *Have a good time at the party, but don't go hog-wild.* ☐ *The teacher cannot control a class that is going hog-wild.*

go in a body to move in a group. ☐ *The whole team went in a body to talk to the* *coach.* □ *Each of us was afraid to go alone, so we went in a body.*

go in for something to take part in something; to enjoy (doing) something. □ *John doesn't go in for sports.* □ *None of them seems to go in for swimming.*

go in one ear and out the other [for something] to be heard and then forgotten. (See also in one ear and out (of) the other.) □ *Everything I say to you seems to go in one ear and out the other. Why don't you pay attention?* □ *I can't concentrate. Things people say to me just go in one ear and out the other.*

go into action AND **swing into action** to start doing something. □ *I usually get to work at 7:45, and I go into action at 8:00.* □ *When the ball is hit in my direction, you should see me swing into action.*

go into a nosedive AND **take a nosedive** **1.** [for an airplane] suddenly to dive toward the ground, nose first. □ *It was a bad day for flying, and I was afraid we'd go into a nosedive.* □ *The small plane took a nosedive. The pilot was able to bring it out at the last minute, so the plane didn't crash.* **2.** to go into a rapid emotional or financial decline, or a decline in health. (Informal.) □ *Our profits took a nosedive last year.* □ *After he broke his hip, Mr. Brown's health went into a nosedive, and he never recovered.*

go into a tailspin **1.** [for an airplane] to lose control and spin to the earth, nose first. □ *The plane shook and then suddenly went into a tailspin.* □ *The pilot was not able to bring the plane out of the tailspin, and it crashed into the sea.* **2.** [for someone] to become disoriented or panicked; [for someone's life] to fall apart. (Informal.) □ *Although John was a great success, his life went into a tailspin. It took him a year to get straightened out.* □ *After her father died, Mary's world fell apart, and she went into a tailspin.*

go into detail to give all the details; to present and discuss the details. □ *The clerk went into detail about the product with the customer.* □ *I just want a simple answer. Don't go into detail.*

go into effect AND **take effect** [for a law or a rule] to become effective; to start to function. □ *When does this new law go into effect?* □ *The new tax laws won't go into effect until next year.* □ *This law takes effect almost immediately.*

go into hiding to conceal oneself in a hidden place for a period of time. □ *The political dissident went into hiding.* □ *After robbing the bank, the bandits went into hiding for months.*

go into hock go into debt. □ *We will have to go into hock to buy a house.* □ *I go further into hock every time I use my credit card.*

go into one's **song and dance (about** something**)** to start giving one's explanations and excuses about something. (*One's* can be replaced by *the same old.*) □ *Please don't go into your song and dance about how you always tried to do what was right.* □ *John went into his song and dance about how he won the war all by himself.* □ *He always goes into the same old song and dance every time he makes a mistake.*

go into orbit to get very excited; to be in ecstasy. (Also literal. Slang.) □ *When I got a letter from my boyfriend in England, I almost went into orbit.* □ *Tom goes into orbit every time the football team scores.*

go into something to start something new. (Especially a new career, project, product line, etc. Compare this with be into something.) □ *I may quit selling and go into management.* □ *We are shifting production away from glass bottles, and we are going into vases and other decorative containers.* □ *After she graduated, she went into law.*

go it alone to do something by oneself. (Informal.) □ *Do you need help, or will you go it alone?* □ *I think I need a little more experience before I go it alone.*

Go jump in the lake! Go to Go climb a tree!

go like clockwork to progress with regularity and dependability. (Informal.) □ *The building project is progressing nicely. Everything is going like clockwork.* □ *The* *elaborate pageant was a great success. It went like clockwork from start to finish.*

go off [for something] to explode. ☐ *The fireworks didn't go off when they were supposed to.* ☐ *There was a bomb in the building, but it didn't go off.*

go off half-cocked to proceed without proper preparation; to speak (about something) without adequate knowledge. (Informal or slang.) ☐ *Don't pay any attention to what John says. He's always going off half-cocked.* ☐ *Get your facts straight before you make your presentation. There is nothing worse than going off half-cocked.*

go off on a tangent to go off suddenly in another direction; suddenly to change one's line of thought, course of action, etc. (A reference to geometry.) ☐ *Please stick to one subject and don't go off on a tangent.* ☐ *If Mary would settle down and deal with one subject she would be all right, but she keeps going off on tangents.*

go off the deep end AND **jump off the deep end** to become deeply involved (with someone or something) before one is ready; to follow one's emotions into a situation. (Informal. Refers to going into a swimming pool at the deep end—rather than the shallow end—and finding oneself **in deep water**. Applies especially to falling in love.) ☐ *Look at the way Bill is looking at Sally. I think he's about to go off the deep end.* ☐ *Now, John, I know you really want to go to Australia, but don't go jumping off the deep end. It isn't all perfect there.*

go on stop saying those things; not so; I don't believe you. (Also literal, meaning "to continue." Always as a command.) ☐ *Go on! You don't know what you're talking about!* ☐ *Oh, go on! You're just trying to flatter me.*

go on a binge to do too much of something. (Slang. Especially to drink too much.) ☐ *Jane went on a binge last night and is very sick this morning.* ☐ *Bill loves to spend money on clothes. He's out on a binge right now—buying everything in sight.*

go on a fishing expedition to attempt to discover information. (Also literal.) ☐ *We are going to have to go on a fishing expedition to try to find the facts.* ☐ *One lawyer went on a fishing expedition in court, and the other lawyer objected.*

go on and on to (seem to) last or go forever. (Folksy.) ☐ *You talk too much, Bob. You just go on and on.* ☐ *The road to their house is very boring. It goes on and on with nothing interesting to look at.*

go on an errand Go to run an errand.

go on a rampage to have a rampage. ☐ *The angry bull went on a rampage and broke the fence.* ☐ *My boss went on a rampage because the report wasn't finished.*

go on to a better land to die. (Euphemistic.) ☐ *After a long illness, Reggie went on to a better land.* ☐ *When I finally go on to a better land, I hope there is enough money for a proper funeral.*

go out (for something) to try out for something. (Usually refers to attempting to get onto a sports team. Also literal.) ☐ *Mary went out for the soccer team.* ☐ *Tom went out for baseball.* ☐ *He didn't go out last year.*

go out of fashion AND **go out of style** to become unfashionable; to become obsolete. ☐ *That kind of furniture went out of style years ago.* ☐ *I hope this kind of thing never goes out of fashion.*

go out of one's way (to do something) **1.** to travel an indirect route in order to do something. ☐ *I'll have to go out of my way to give you a ride home.* ☐ *I'll give you a ride even though I have to go out of my way.* **2.** to make an effort to do something; to endure and accept the bother of doing something. ☐ *We went out of our way to please the visitor.* ☐ *We appreciate anything you can do, but don't go out of your way.*

go out of style Go to go out of fashion.

go (out) on strike [for a group of people] to quit working at their jobs until certain demands are met. ☐ *If we don't have a contract by noon tomorrow, we'll go out on* *strike.* □ *The entire work force went on strike at noon today.*

go out (with someone**) 1.** to go out with someone for entertainment. □ *The Smiths went out with the Franklins to a movie.* □ *Those guys don't have much time to go out.* **2.** to go on a date with someone; to date someone regularly. □ *Is Bob still going out with Sally?* □ *No, they've stopped going out.*

go over to succeed; to be accepted. □ *His idea went over well.* □ *How did my joke go over?*

go over big with someone to be very much appreciated by someone. □ *Your jokes did not exactly go over big with my parents.* □ *We hope that the musical will go over big with the audience.*

go overboard to do too much; to be extravagant. (Also literal as on a ship.) □ *Look, Sally, let's have a nice party, but don't go overboard. It doesn't need to be fancy.* □ *Okay, you can buy a big comfortable car, but don't go overboard.*

go over like a lead balloon to fail; to go over badly. (Slang. See also go over with a bang.) □ *Your joke went over like a lead balloon.* □ *If that play was supposed to be a comedy, it went over like a lead balloon.* □ *Her suggestion went over like a lead balloon.*

go over someone**'s head** [for the intellectual content of something] to be too difficult for someone to understand. □ *All that talk about computers went over my head.* □ *I hope my lecture didn't go over the students' heads.*

go over something to review or explain something. (Also literal.) □ *The teacher went over the lesson.* □ *Will you please go over this form? I don't understand it.*

go over something **with a fine-tooth comb** AND **search** something **with a fine-tooth comb** to search through something very carefully. □ *I can't find my calculus book. I went over the whole place with a fine-tooth comb.* □ *I searched this place with a fine-tooth comb and didn't find my ring.*

go over with a bang to succeed spectacularly. (Informal. Compare this with go over like a lead balloon.) □ *The play was a success. It really went over with a bang.* □ *That's a great joke. It went over with a bang.*

go places to have a good future. (Informal.) □ *Sally shows great promise as a scholar. She's really going to go places.* □ *Tom is as good as we thought. He's certainly going places now.*

Go play in the traffic! Go to Take a long walk off a short pier.

go right through someone [for food] to pass through and out of the body very rapidly. (Informal. Use with caution.) □ *Those little apples go right through me, but I love them.* □ *I can't eat onions. They go right through me.*

go scot-free AND **get off scot-free** to go unpunished; to be acquitted of a crime. (This *scot* is an old word meaning "tax" or "tax burden.") □ *The thief went scot-free.* □ *Jane cheated on the test and got caught, but she got off scot-free.*

go sky-high to go very high, as with a price or a measurement. (Informal.) □ *Prices go sky-high whenever there is inflation.* □ *Oh, it's so hot. The temperature went sky-high about noon.*

go so far as to say something to put something into words; to risk saying something. □ *I think that Bob is dishonest, but I wouldn't go so far as to say he's a thief.* □ *Red meat may be harmful, but I can't go so far as to say it causes cancer.*

go someone **one better** AND **do** someone **one better** to do something superior to what someone else has done; to top someone. □ *That was a great joke, but I can go you one better.* □ *Your last song was beautifully sung, but Mary can do you one better.*

go (somewhere) **by shank's mare** to travel by foot; to go somewhere on foot. □ *The car wouldn't start so I had to go to work by shank's mare.* □ *We enjoy walking and go by shank's mare whenever we can.*

go stag to go to an event (which is meant for couples) without a member of the opposite sex. (Informal. Originally referred only to males.) □ *Is Tom going to take you, or are you going stag?* □ *Bob didn't want to go stag, so he took his sister to the party.*

go steady (with someone) to date someone on a regular basis. □ *Mary is going steady with John.* □ *Bill went steady for two years before he got married.*

go stir-crazy to become anxious because one is confined. (Slang. *Stir* is an old criminal word for "prison.") □ *If I stay around this house much longer, I'm going to go stir-crazy.* □ *John left school. He said he was going stir-crazy.*

go straight to begin to obey the law; to become law-abiding. (Also literal. Slang. Primarily criminal slang.) □ *When John got out of prison, he decided to go straight.* □ *I promised the teacher that I would go straight and that I would never cheat again.*

go the distance to do the whole amount; to play the entire game; to run the whole race. (Informal. Originally sports use.) □ *That horse runs fast. I hope it can go the distance.* □ *This is going to be a long, hard project. I hope I can go the distance.*

go the extra mile to try harder to please someone or to get the task done correctly; to do more than one is required to do to reach a goal. □ *I like doing business with that company. They always go the extra mile.* □ *My teacher goes the extra mile to help us.*

go the limit to do as much as possible. (Compare this with **go whole hog.**) □ *What do I want on my hamburger? Go the limit!* □ *Don't hold anything back. Go the limit.*

go through to be approved; to succeed in getting through the approval process. (See also **go through something.**) □ *I sent the board of directors a proposal. I hope it goes through.* □ *We all hope that the new law goes through.*

go through channels to proceed by consulting the proper persons or offices. (See also **work through channels.**) □ *If you want an answer to your questions, you'll have to go through channels.* □ *If you know the answers, why do I have to go through channels?*

go through something 1. to examine something. □ *Give me a day or two to go through this contract, and then I'll call you with advice.* □ *Don't go through it too fast. Read it carefully, or you might miss something.* **2.** to experience something; to endure something unpleasant; to **get through something.** □ *It was a terrible thing. I don't know how I went through it.* □ *It'll take four years to go through college.*

go through the changes to experience a rough period in one's life. (Slang.) □ *Sally's pretty upset. She's really going through the changes.* □ *Most teenagers spend their time going through the changes.*

go through the motions to make a feeble effort to do something; to do something insincerely. □ *Jane isn't doing her best. She's just going through the motions.* □ *Bill was supposed to be raking the yard, but he was just going through the motions.*

go through the roof to go very high; to reach a very high degree (of something). (Informal.) □ *It's so hot! The temperature is going through the roof.* □ *Mr. Brown got so angry he almost went through the roof.*

go through with something to decide to do something; to finish something. □ *We decided to go through with the new highway.* □ *I can't do it. I just can't go through with it.*

go to any length to do whatever is necessary. □ *I'll go to any length to secure this contract.* □ *I want to get a college degree, but I won't go to any length to get one.*

go to bat for someone to support or help someone. (Informal. From baseball. See **pinch-hit (for someone).**) □ *I tried to go to bat for Bill, but he said he didn't want any help.* □ *I heard them gossiping about Sally, so I went to bat for her.*

go to bed to go to where one's bed is, get into it, and go to sleep. □ *It's time for me to go to bed.* □ *I want to go to bed, but there is too much work to do.*

go to bed (with someone) Go to **go all the way (with someone)**.

go to bed with the chickens to go to bed at sundown; to go to bed very early (when the chickens do). □ *Of course I get enough sleep. I go to bed with the chickens.* □ *Mr. Brown goes to bed with the chickens and gets up with them, too.*

go to Davy Jones's locker to go to the bottom of the sea. (Thought of as a nautical expression.) □ *My camera fell overboard and went to Davy Jones's locker.* □ *My uncle was a sailor. He went to Davy Jones's locker during a terrible storm.*

go together 1. [for two things] to look, sound, or taste good together. □ *Do you think that this pink one and this purple one go together?* □ *Milk and grapefruit don't go together.* **2.** [for two people] to date each other regularly. □ *Bob and Ann have been going together for months.* □ *Tom and Jane want to go together, but they live too far apart.*

go to (hell) AND **go to (the devil)** to become ruined; to go away and stop bothering (someone). (Informal. Use caution with *hell.*) □ *This old house is just going to hell. It's falling apart everywhere.* □ *Leave me alone! Go to the devil!* □ *Oh, go to, yourself!*

go to hell in a handbasket to become totally worthless; to **go to (hell)**. (Informal. Use caution with *hell.* Not used as a command.) □ *The whole country is going to hell in a handbasket.* □ *Look at my lawn—full of weeds. It's going to hell in a handbasket.*

go too far to do more than is acceptable. (Also literal.) □ *I didn't mind at first, but now you've gone too far.* □ *If you go too far, I'll slap you.*

go to pieces 1. to break into pieces; to **fall apart**. □ *My old winter coat is going to pieces.* □ *I don't want to see a nice vase like that go to pieces.* **2.** to break out in tears; to break down mentally. □ *On hearing of the death, we just went to pieces.* □ *I couldn't talk about it any longer. I went to pieces.*

go to pot AND **go to the dogs** to go to ruin; to deteriorate. (Informal.) □ *My whole life seems to be going to pot.* □ *My lawn is going to pot. I had better weed it.* □ *The government is going to the dogs.*

go to rack and ruin AND **go to wrack and ruin** to go to ruin. (The words *rack* and *wrack* mean "wreckage" and are found only in this expression.) □ *That lovely old house on the corner is going to go to rack and ruin.* □ *My lawn is going to wrack and ruin.*

go to seed Go to **run to seed**.

go to someone's head to make someone conceited; to make someone overly proud. □ *You did a fine job, but don't let it go to your head.* □ *He let his success go to his head, and soon he became a complete failure.*

go to the bathroom 1. to go into a rest room, bathroom, or toilet. □ *BILL: Where is Bob? JANE: He went to the bathroom.* □ *John went to the bathroom to brush his teeth.* **2.** to eliminate bodily wastes through defecation and urination. □ *Mommy! The dog went to the bathroom on the carpet!* □ *Billy's in there going to the bathroom. Don't disturb him.*

go to (the devil) Go to **go to (hell)**.

go to the dogs Go to **go to pot**.

go to the expense (of doing something) to pay the (large) cost of doing something. □ *I hate to have to go to the expense of painting the house.* □ *It needs to be done, so you'll have to go to the expense.*

go to the lavatory to go somewhere and use a toilet. □ *Bob requested to leave the room to go to the lavatory.* □ *Please stop the car. I have to go to the lavatory.*

go to the limit to do as much as is possible to do. (Compare this with **go the limit**.) □ *Okay, we can't afford it, but we'll go to the limit.* □ *How far shall I go? Shall I go to the limit?*

go to the toilet to use a toilet for defecation or urination. □ *Jimmy washed his hands after he went to the toilet.* □ *Excuse me, I have to go to the toilet.*

go to the trouble (of doing something**)** AND **go to the trouble (to** do something**)** to endure the bother of doing something. □ *I really don't want to go to the trouble to cook.* □ *Should I go to the trouble of cooking something for her to eat?* □ *Don't go to the trouble. She can eat a sandwich.*

go to the trouble (to do something**)** Go to go to the trouble (of doing something).

go to the wall to be defeated; to fail in business. (Informal.) □ *We really went to the wall on that deal.* □ *The company went to the wall because of that contract. Now it's broke.*

go to town to work hard or fast. (Also literal. Informal.) □ *Look at all those ants working. They are really going to town.* □ *Come on, you guys. Let's go to town. We have to finish this job before noon.*

go to waste to be wasted; to be unused (and therefore thrown away). □ *Eat your potatoes! Don't let them go to waste.* □ *We shouldn't let all those nice flowers go to waste. Let's pick some.*

go to wrack and ruin Go to go to rack and ruin.

go under to fail. □ *The company was weak from the start, and it finally went under.* □ *Tom had a lot of trouble in school, and finally he went under.*

go under the knife to have a surgical operation. (Informal.) □ *Mary didn't want to go under the knife, but the doctor insisted.* □ *If I go under the knife, I want to be completely asleep.*

go up in flames AND **go up in smoke** to burn up. □ *The whole museum went up in flames.* □ *My paintings—my whole life's work—went up in flames.* □ *What a shame for all that to go up in smoke.*

go up in smoke Go to go up in flames.

go whole hog to do everything possible; to be extravagant. (Informal. Compare this with go the limit.) □ *Let's go whole hog. Order steak* and *lobster.* □ *Show some restraint. Don't go whole hog all the time.*

go window-shopping to go about looking at goods in store windows without actually buying anything. □ *The clerks usually go window-shopping in their lunch hour, looking for things to buy when they get paid.* □ *Joan said she was just going window-shopping, but she bought a new coat.*

go without (something**)** to manage to get along without something. (Compare this with do without (someone or something).) □ *I went without food for three days.* □ *Some people have to go without a lot longer than that.*

go with something **1.** to go well with something. □ *Milk doesn't go with grapefruit.* □ *Pink doesn't go with orange.* **2.** to choose something (over something else). (Informal.) □ *I think I'll go with the yellow one.* □ *We decided to go with the oak table rather than the walnut one.*

go with the flow [for someone] to proceed easily and cooperatively in the same manner that other people or processes are moving. (Informal.) □ *John is very easy to get along with. He just goes with the flow.* □ *I try to cooperate. I go with the flow where possible.*

go wrong to fail; [for something bad] to happen. □ *The project failed. I don't know what went wrong.* □ *I'm afraid that everything will go wrong.*

goes to show you [something] serves to prove a point to you. □ *It just goes to show you that too much sugar is bad for you.* □ *Of course you shouldn't have married her. It goes to show you that your parents are always right.*

goes without saying [something] is so obvious that it need not be said. □ *It goes without saying that you are to wear formal clothing to dinner each evening.* □ *Of course. That goes without saying.*

the **going** the condition of a path of travel or progress. □ *The going was rough through the mountains.* □ *I decided to sell my stock while the going was still good.*

the **going rate** the current rate. □ *The going interest rate for your account is 10 percent.* □ *Our babysitter charges us the going rate.*

a **gold mine of information** someone or something that is full of information. ☐ *Grandfather is a gold mine of information about World War I.* ☐ *The new encyclopedia is a positive gold mine of useful information.*

gone but not forgotten gone or dead but still remembered. ☐ *The good days we used to have together are gone, but not forgotten.* ☐ *Uncle Harry is gone but not forgotten. The stain where he spilled the wine is still visible in the parlor carpet.*

gone goose someone or something that has departed or run away. ☐ *Surely, the burglar is a gone goose by now.* ☐ *The child was a gone goose, and we did not know where to look for him.*

gone on died. (Euphemistic.) ☐ *My husband, Tom—he's gone on, you know—was a great one for golf.* ☐ *Let us remember those who have gone on before.*

gone to meet one's **Maker** died. (Euphemistic.) ☐ *Poor old Bob has gone to meet his Maker.* ☐ *After a long illness, Reggie went to meet his Maker.*

gone with the wind gone; mysteriously gone. (A phrase made famous by the Margaret Mitchell novel and film *Gone with the Wind*. The phrase is used to make *gone* have a stronger force.) ☐ *Everything we worked for was gone with the wind.* ☐ *Jean was nowhere to be found. She was gone with the wind.*

a **goner** dead or finished; as good as dead or nearly dead. (Informal. Preceded by *be, become, seem like,* or *act like.*) ☐ *The boy brought the sick fish back to the pet store to get his money back. "This one is a goner," he said.* ☐ *John thought he was a goner when his parachute didn't open.*

good and something very something. (The *something* can be *ready, mad, tired, worn-out,* etc.) ☐ *Now I'm good and mad, and I'm going to fight back.* ☐ *I'll be there when I'm good and ready.* ☐ *He'll go to bed when he's good and tired.*

good as done Go to (as) good as done.

good as gold Go to (as) good as gold.

good enough for someone or something adequate for someone or something. ☐ *This seat is good enough for me. I don't want to move.* ☐ *I'm happy. It's good enough for me.* ☐ *That table is good enough for my office.*

good-for-nothing 1. worthless. ☐ *Here comes that good-for-nothing boy now.* ☐ *Where is that good-for-nothing pen of mine?* **2.** a worthless person. ☐ *Tell that good-for-nothing to go home at once.* ☐ *Bob can't get a job. He's such a good-for-nothing.*

the **good old days** back in an earlier time, which everyone remembers as a better time, even if it really wasn't. ☐ *Back in the good old days, during WWII, they used real cactus needles in record players.* ☐ *The good old days didn't start until they had indoor bathrooms.*

good riddance (to bad rubbish) [it is] good to be rid (of worthless persons or things). ☐ *She slammed the door behind me and said, "Good riddance to bad rubbish!"* ☐ *"Good riddance to you, madam," thought I.*

good to go all ready to go; all checked and pronounced ready to go. ☐ *I've checked everything and we are good to go.* ☐ *Everything's good to go and we will start immediately.*

goof off to waste time. (Informal or slang.) ☐ *John is always goofing off.* ☐ *Quit goofing off and get to work!*

the **gospel truth** [of truth] undeniable. ☐ *The witness swore he was telling the gospel truth.* ☐ *I told my parents the gospel truth about how the vase broke.*

grab a bite (to eat) to get something to eat; to get food that can be eaten quickly. (Not usually done by grabbing.) ☐ *I need a few minutes to grab a bite to eat.* ☐ *Bob often tries to grab a bite between meetings.*

grace someone or something **with** one's **presence** to honor someone or something with one's presence. ☐ *"How nice of you to grace us with your presence," Mr. Wilson told Mary sarcastically as she entered the classroom late.* ☐ *The banquet was graced with the presence of the governor.*

graced with something made elegant by means of some ornament or decoration. ☐ *The altar was graced with lovely white flowers.* ☐ *The end of the beautiful day was graced with a beautiful sunset.*

graceful as a swan Go to (as) graceful as a swan.

a **grain of truth** even the smallest amount of truth. ☐ *The attorney was unable to find a grain of truth in the defendant's testimony.* ☐ *If there were a grain of truth to your statement, I would trust you.*

grasp at straws to depend on something that is useless; to make a futile attempt at something. ☐ *John couldn't answer the teacher's question. He was just grasping at straws.* ☐ *There I was, grasping at straws, with no one to help me.*

grate on someone**('s nerves)** to annoy someone; to bother someone. ☐ *My obnoxious brother is grating on my nerves.* ☐ *Your whining really grates on me.*

gray area an area of a subject or question that is difficult to put into a particular category because it is not clearly defined and may have connections or associations with more than one category. ☐ *The responsibility for social studies in the college is a gray area. Several departments are involved.* ☐ *Publicity is a gray area in that firm. It is shared between the marketing and design divisions.*

gray matter intelligence; brains; power of thought. (Brain tissue is grayish in color.) ☐ *Use your gray matter and think what will happen if the committee resigns.* ☐ *Surely they'll come up with an acceptable solution if they use a bit of gray matter.*

grease someone**'s palm** AND **oil** someone**'s palm** to bribe someone. (Slang.) ☐ *If you want to get something done around here, you have to grease someone's palm.* ☐ *I'd never oil a police officer's palm. That's illegal.*

a **great deal** much; a lot. ☐ *You can learn a great deal about nature by watching television.* ☐ *This is a serious problem and it worries me a great deal.*

the **greatest thing since sliced bread** the best thing there ever was. (Usually sarcastic.) ☐ *To hear her talk, you would think she had found the greatest thing since sliced bread.* ☐ *Todd thinks he is the greatest thing since sliced bread.*

Greek to me Go to (all) Greek to me.

green around the gills Go to pale around the gills.

green with envy envious; jealous. ☐ *When Sally saw me with Tom, she turned green with envy. She likes him a lot.* ☐ *I feel green with envy whenever I see you in your new car.*

grin and bear it to endure something unpleasant in good humor. ☐ *There is nothing you can do but grin and bear it.* ☐ *I hate having to work for rude people. I guess I have to grin and bear it.*

grind to a halt to slow to a stop; to run down. ☐ *By the end of the day, the factory had ground to a halt.* ☐ *The car ground to a halt, and we got out to stretch our legs.*

grip someone**'s attention** to attract and hold someone's attention. ☐ *The scary movie gripped my attention.* ☐ *The professor's interesting lecture gripped the attention of all the students.*

grist for someone**'s mill** something that can be put to good use or that can bring advantage or profit. ☐ *Some of the jobs that we are offered are more interesting than others, but each one is grist for my mill.* ☐ *The company is having to sell some tacky-looking dresses, but they are grist for their mill and keep the company in business.*

grit one**'s teeth** to grind one's teeth together in anger or determination. ☐ *I was so mad, all I could do was stand there and grit my teeth.* ☐ *All through the race, Sally was gritting her teeth. She was really determined.*

groan under the burden of something to suffer under the burden or domination of someone or something. ☐ *John groaned under the burden of his new responsibilities.* ☐ *The servant groaned under the burden of a cruel master.*

gross someone **out** to revolt someone; to make someone sick. (Slang.) □ *Oh, look at his face. Doesn't it gross you out?* 🅃 *That teacher is such a creep. He grosses out the whole class.*

ground someone to take away someone's privileges. (Informal. Usually said of a teenager.) □ *My father said that if I didn't get at least C's, he'd ground me.* □ *Guess what! He grounded me!*

grounded in fact based on facts. □ *This movie is grounded in fact.* □ *The stories in this book are all grounded in actual fact.*

grounds for something a basis or cause for legal action, such as a lawsuit. □ *Your negligence is grounds for a lawsuit.* □ *Is infidelity grounds for divorce in this state?*

grow on someone [for someone or something] to become commonplace and comfortable to a person. (The *someone* is usually *one, someone, a person,* etc., not a specific person.) □ *That music is strange, but it grows on you.* □ *I didn't think I could ever get used to this town, but after a while it grows on one.*

grow out of something to abandon something as one matures. (Also literal.) □ *I used to have a lot of allergies, but I grew out of them.* □ *She grew out of the habit of biting her nails.*

grow to do something to gradually begin to do certain things, using verbs such as *feel, know, like, need, respect, sense, suspect, think, want, wonder,* etc. □ *I grew to hate Bob over a period of years.* □ *As I grew to know Bob, I began to like him.*

gruff as a bear Go to (as) gruff as a bear.

grunt work work that is hard and thankless. □ *During the summer, I earned money doing grunt work.* □ *I did all of the grunt work on the project, but my boss got all of the credit.*

guard against someone or something to take care to avoid someone or something. □ *Try to guard against getting a cold.* □ *You should guard against pickpockets.*

guest of honor a guest who gets special attention from everyone; the person for whom a party, celebration, or ceremony is held. □ *Bob is the guest of honor, and many people will make speeches about him.* □ *The guest of honor sits at the front of the room on the dais.*

gulp for air to eagerly or desperately try to get air or a breath. □ *Tom gulped for air after trying to hold his breath for three minutes.* □ *Mary came up out of the water, gulping for air.*

gum something **up** AND **gum up the works** to make something inoperable; to ruin someone's plans. (Informal.) □ *Please, Bill, be careful and don't gum up the works.* □ *Tom sure gummed it up.* 🅃 *Tom sure gummed up the whole plan.*

gum up the works Go to gum something up.

gun for someone to be looking for someone, presumably to harm them. (Refers to a sheriff or outlaw seeking a person with the intention of shooting him. Originally from western and gangster movies.) □ *The coach is gunning for you. I think he's going to bawl you out.* □ *I've heard that the sheriff is gunning for me, so I'm getting out of town.*

gut feeling AND **gut reaction; gut response** a personal, intuitive feeling or response. □ *I have a gut feeling that something bad is going to happen.* □ *My gut reaction is that we should hire Susan for the job.*

gut reaction Go to gut feeling.

gut response Go to gut feeling.

gyp someone **out of** something to deceive someone in order to get something of value. □ *The salesclerk gypped me out of a dollar.* □ *The taxi driver tried to gyp me out of a fortune by driving all over town.*

H

hack something to endure something; to deal with something. (Slang. The *something* is usually *it.*) ☐ *I don't know if I can hack it.* ☐ *John works very hard, but he can't seem to hack it.*

had best do something ought to do something. (Informal. Almost the same as the following entry.) ☐ *You had best get that fixed right away.* ☐ *You had best be at school on time every day.*

had better do something ought to do something (or face the consequences). (Almost the same as the previous entry.) ☐ *I had better get home for dinner, or I'll get yelled at.* ☐ *You had better do your homework right now.*

had (just) as soon do something AND **would (just) as soon** do something would prefer to do something else; would be content to do something. (The *would* or *had* is usually *'d.* Also with *just,* as in the examples below.) ☐ *They want me to go into town. I'd as soon stay home.* ☐ *If you're cooking stew tonight, we'd as soon eat somewhere else.* ☐ *I would just as soon stay home as see a bad movie.* ☐ *If that's what we're having for dinner, I'd just as soon starve.*

(had) known it was coming Go to knew it was coming.

had rather do something AND **had sooner** do something would prefer to do something. (The *had* is usually expressed in a contraction, *'d.*) ☐ *I'd rather go to town than sit here all evening.* ☐ *They'd rather not.* ☐ *I'd sooner not make the trip.*

had sooner do something Go to **had rather** do something.

hail-fellow-well-met friendly to everyone; falsely friendly to everyone. (Usually said of males. See also **get the glad hand.**) ☐ *Yes, he's friendly, sort of hail-fellow-well-met.* ☐ *He's not a very sincere person. Hail-fellow-well-met—you know the type.* ☐ *What a pain he is. Good old Mr. Hail-fellow-well-met. What a phony!*

hail from somewhere [for someone] to come originally from somewhere. ☐ *I'm from Kansas. Where do you hail from?* ☐ *I hail from the Southwest.*

the **hair of the dog that bit** one a drink of liquor taken when one has a hangover; a drink of liquor taken when one is recovering from drinking too much liquor. (Informal.) ☐ *Oh, I'm miserable. I need some of the hair of the dog that bit me.* ☐ *That's some hangover you've got there, Bob. Here, drink this. It's some of the hair of the dog that bit you.*

hale and hearty well and healthy. ☐ *Doesn't Ann look hale and hearty?* ☐ *I don't feel hale and hearty. I'm really tired.*

Half a loaf is better than none. Having part of something is better than having nothing. (Proverb.) ☐ *When my raise was smaller than I wanted, Sally said, "Half a loaf is better than none."* ☐ *People who keep saying "Half a loaf is better than none" usually have as much as they need.*

half-and-half 1. a liquid that is half milk and half cream. ☐ *Harry would always pour half-and-half on his breakfast cereal in spite of what his doctor told him.* ☐ *There is less fat in half-and-half than there is in cream.* **2.** a substance composed half of one thing and half of another. ☐ *This coffee is half-and-half, so there isn't quite as much caffeine as in regular coffee.* ☐ *I* *can't decide between a chocolate sundae and a pineapple sundae, so make mine half-and-half.*

halfhearted (about someone or something**)** unenthusiastic about someone or something. □ *Ann was halfhearted about the choice of Sally for president.* □ *She didn't look halfhearted to me. She looked angry.*

ham something **up** to make a performance seem silly by showing off or exaggerating one's part. (Informal. A show-off actor is known as a *ham.*) □ *Come on, Bob. Don't ham it up!* 🅃 *The play was going fine until Bob got out there and hammed up his part.*

hammer away (at someone or something**)** to keep trying to accomplish something with someone or something. (Refers to repeated pounding with a hammer.) □ *John, you've got to keep hammering away at your geometry.* □ *They hammered away at the prisoner until he confessed.*

hammer something **home** to try extremely hard to make someone understand or realize something. □ *The teacher hammered the dates home.* 🅃 *I tried to hammer home to Anne the fact that she would have to get a job.* 🅃 *The boss hopes to hammer home the company's precarious financial position to the staff.*

hammer something **out 1.** to work hard at writing up an agreement; to work hard at writing something. (Literally to pound something flat with a hammer or mallet. This refers to hammering at the keys of a typewriter.) □ *I'm busy hammering my latest novel out.* 🅃 *The lawyers sat down to hammer out a contract.* **2.** to play something on the piano. □ *She hammered the song out loudly and without feeling.* 🅃 *Listen to John hammer out that song on the piano.*

hand in glove (with someone**)** very close to someone. □ *John is really hand in glove with Sally.* □ *The teacher and the principal work hand in glove.*

hand in hand 1. holding hands. □ *They walked down the street hand in hand.* □ *Bob and Mary sat there quietly, hand in hand.* **2.** together, one with the other. (Said of two things where the presence of one implies the other.) □ *Cookies and milk seem to go hand in hand.* □ *Teenagers and back talk go hand in hand.*

Hand it over. Give it to me. (Informal.) □ *It's mine. Hand it over!* □ *Come on. Give me the box of jewels. Hand it over!*

hand it to someone to give credit to someone. (Informal. Often with *have to* or *must.*) □ *I'll hand it to you. You did a fine job.* □ *We must hand it to Sally. She helped us a lot.*

hand-me-down something, such as an article of used clothing, that has been handed down from someone. (See also **hand** something **down (to** someone**)**.) □ *Why do I always have to wear my brother's hand-me-downs? I want some new clothes.* □ *This is a nice shirt. It doesn't look like a hand-me-down at all.*

hand over fist [for money and merchandise to be exchanged] very rapidly. □ *What a busy day. We took in money hand over fist.* □ *They were buying things hand over fist.*

hand over hand [moving] one hand after the other (again and again). □ *Sally pulled in the rope hand over hand.* □ *The man climbed the rope hand over hand.*

hand something **down (to** someone**) 1.** to give something to a younger person. (Either at death or during life. See also **hand-me-down.**) □ *John handed his old shirts down to his younger brother.* 🅃 *I hope my uncle will hand down his golf clubs to me when he dies.* **2.** to announce or deliver a (legal) verdict or indictment. 🅃 *The grand jury handed down seven indictments last week.* 🅃 *The jury handed down a guilty verdict.*

handle someone **with kid gloves** to be very careful with a touchy person. □ *Bill has become so sensitive. You really have to handle him with kid gloves.* □ *You don't have to handle me with kid gloves. I can take it.*

hands down without a doubt. (Usually regarding a choice or a winner.) □ *Jean was our choice for the new manager hands down.* □ *Todd won the race hands down.*

☐ *Sharon was the favorite librarian of all the people there hands down.*

Hands off! Do not touch [someone or something]! ☐ *Careful! Don't touch that wire. Hands off!* ☐ *The sign says, "Hands off!" and you had better do what it says.*

Hands up! AND **Stick 'em up!** Put your hands in the air! (Slang. Said by robbers and police officers. Hands that are in the air cannot reach or draw a weapon.) ☐ *All right, you, hands up!* ☐ *Stick 'em up! I got you covered.*

hang a left to turn to the left. (Slang. See also the following entry.) ☐ *Hang a left up at that light.* ☐ *Go three blocks and hang a left.*

hang a right to turn to the right. (Slang.) ☐ *At the next corner, hang a right.* ☐ *Hang a right at the stop sign.*

hang around (with someone**)** AND **go around with** someone to spend a lot of time with someone; to waste away time with someone. (See also run around with someone.) ☐ *John hangs around with Bill a lot.* ☐ *They've been going around with the Smiths.* ☐ *I've asked them all to stop hanging around.*

hang back to stay behind (the others); to hold back (from the others). ☐ *Walk with the group, Bob. Don't hang back. You'll get left behind.* ☐ *Three of the marchers hung back and talked to each other.*

hang by a hair AND **hang by a thread** to be in an uncertain position; to depend on something very insubstantial; to hang in the balance. (Informal.) ☐ *Your whole argument is hanging by a thread.* ☐ *John isn't failing geometry, but his passing grade is just hanging by a hair.*

hang by a thread Go to hang by a hair.

hang fire to delay or wait. ☐ *I think we should hang fire and wait for other information.* ☐ *Our plans have to hang fire until we get planning permission.*

hang in the balance to be in an undecided state; to be between two equal possibilities. ☐ *The prisoner stood before the judge with his life hanging in the balance.* ☐ *This whole issue will have to hang in the balance until Jane gets back from her vacation.*

hang in there to keep trying; to persevere. (Slang.) ☐ *I know things are tough, John, but hang in there.* ☐ *I know if I hang in there, things will come out okay.*

hang loose to relax; to remain calm. (Slang.) ☐ *I know I can pass this test if I just hang loose.* ☐ *Hang loose, Bob. Everything is going to be all right.*

hang one's **hat (up)** somewhere to take up residence somewhere. ☐ *George loves Dallas. He's decided to buy a house and hang his hat up there.* ☐ *Bill moves from place to place and never hangs his hat up anywhere.*

hang on someone's **coattails** Go to ride on someone's coattails.

hang on someone's **every word** to listen with complete attention to everything someone says. ☐ *He gave a great lecture. We hung on his every word.* ☐ *Look at the way John hangs on Mary's every word. He must be in love with her.*

hang on (to someone or something**)** AND **hold on (to** someone or something**)** to remember someone or something for a long time; to be affected very much by someone or something in the past. (Also literal meaning grasping or holding someone or something.) ☐ *That's a nice thought, Bob. Hang on to it.* ☐ *You've been holding on to those bad memories for too long. It's time to let them go.* ☐ *Yes, I can't keep hanging on.*

hang out (somewhere**)** to spend time somewhere; to waste time somewhere. ☐ *I wish you guys wouldn't hang out around the bowling alley.* ☐ *Why do you have to hang out near our house?*

hang out (with someone**)** to waste time in the company of someone. ☐ *I hope Bob isn't hanging out with the wrong people.* ☐ *He needs to spend more time studying and less time hanging out.*

hang someone **in effigy** to hang a dummy or some other figure of a hated person. (See also burn someone in effigy.) ☐ *They* *hanged the dictator in effigy.* □ *The angry mob hanged the president in effigy.*

hang tough to be firm in one's position; to stick to one's position. (Slang. Compare this with **hang in there.**) □ *I know that your parents don't want you to go out tonight, but hang tough. They may change their minds.* □ *Hang tough, Mary. You'll get your way!*

hang up to replace the telephone receiver; to terminate a telephone call. □ *If you have called a wrong number, you should apologize before you hang up.* □ *When you hear the busy signal, you're supposed to hang up.*

happen (up)on someone or something to meet someone, or find something unexpectedly. □ *I happened on this nice little restaurant on Elm Street yesterday.* □ *Mr. Simpson and I happened on one another in the bank last week.*

happy as a clam Go to (as) happy as a clam.

happy as a lark Go to (as) happy as a lark.

happy as can be Go to (as) happy as can be.

a **harbinger of things to come** AND a **portent of things to come;** a **sign of things to come;** a **taste of things to come** a sample of the events that are to occur in the future. □ *The first cuts in our budget are a harbinger of things to come.* □ *Today's visit from the auditors is a portent of things to come.*

hard-and-fast rigid or strict, especially when applied to rules, laws, or regulations. □ *The rule isn't hard-and-fast, but we expect you to obey it anyway.* □ *The company has a hard-and-fast rule about the use of radios, even in private offices.*

hard as a rock Go to (as) hard as a rock.

hard as nails Go to (as) hard as nails.

hard as stone Go to (as) hard as a rock.

a **hard nut to crack** AND a **tough nut to crack** difficult person or thing to deal with. (Informal.) □ *This problem is getting me down. It's a hard nut to crack.* □ *Tom sure is a hard nut to crack. I can't figure him out.* □ *He sure is a tough nut to crack.*

hard of hearing [of someone] unable to hear well; partially deaf. □ *Please speak loudly. I am hard of hearing.* □ *Tom is hard of hearing, but is not totally deaf.*

hard on someone's **heels** following someone very closely; following very closely to someone's heels. (Informal.) □ *I ran as fast as I could, but the dog was still hard on my heels.* □ *Here comes Sally, and John is hard on her heels.*

hard-pressed (to do something**)** Go to hard put (to do something).

hard put (to do something**)** AND **hard-pressed (to** do something**)** able to do something only with great difficulty. □ *I'm hard put to come up with enough money to pay the rent.* □ *I get hard put like that about once a month.*

hard up (for something**)** greatly in need of something. (Informal.) □ *Ann was hard up for cash to pay the bills.* □ *I was so hard up, I couldn't afford to buy food.*

hardly have time to breathe AND **scarcely have time to breathe** to be very busy. □ *This was such a busy day. I hardly had time to breathe.* □ *They made him work so hard that he hardly had time to breathe.*

hardly have time to think so busy that one can hardly think properly; very busy. □ *I've been so busy that I hardly have time to think.* □ *I hardly have time to think in the job that I do. We are just too busy.*

hark(en) back to something **1.** to have originated as something; to have started out as something. (*Harken* is an older word meaning "pay heed to.") □ *The word* ice-box *harks back to refrigerators that were cooled by ice.* □ *Our modern breakfast cereals hark back to the porridge and gruel of our ancestors.* **2.** to remind one of something. □ *Seeing a horse and buggy in the park harks back to the time when horses drew milk wagons.* □ *Sally says it harkens back to the time when everything was delivered by a horse-drawn wagon.*

harp on something to keep talking or complaining about something; to refer to something again and again. ☐ *Mary's always harping on being poor, but she has more than enough money.* ☐ *Jack has been harping on high taxes for years.*

hash something **over** to discuss something in great detail. (Informal.) ☐ *Okay, we can hash it over this afternoon.* 🅃 *Why don't you come to my office so we can hash over this contract?*

Haste makes waste. Time gained in doing something rapidly and carelessly will be lost when one has to do the thing over again correctly. (Proverb.) ☐ *Now, take your time. Haste makes waste.* ☐ *Haste makes waste, so be careful as you work.*

hat in hand Go to (with) hat in hand.

hate someone's **guts** to hate someone very much. (Informal and rude.) ☐ *Oh, Bob is terrible. I hate his guts!* ☐ *You may hate my guts for saying so, but I think you're getting gray hair.*

haul someone **in** to arrest someone; [for a police officer] to take someone to the police station. (Slang.) ☐ *The cop hauled the crook in.* 🅃 *They hauled in the suspects.* ☐ *The traffic officer said, "Do you want me to haul you in?"*

haul someone **over the coals** Go to rake someone over the coals.

haul up (somewhere) AND **pull up** (somewhere) to stop somewhere; to come to rest somewhere. ☐ *The car hauled up in front of the house.* ☐ *My hat blew away just as the bus pulled up.* ☐ *The attackers hauled up at the city gates.*

have a bad effect (on someone or something**)** to be bad for someone or something. ☐ *Aspirin has a bad effect on me.* ☐ *Cold weather has a bad effect on roses.*

have a ball have a really great time. (Slang. This *ball* is a formal, social dancing party.) ☐ *The picnic was fantastic. We had a ball!* ☐ *Hey, Mary! Have a ball at the party tonight!*

have a bee in one's **bonnet** to have an idea or a thought remain in one's mind; to have an obsession. ☐ *I have a bee in my bonnet that you'd be a good manager.* ☐ *I had a bee in my bonnet about swimming. I couldn't stop wanting to go swimming.*

have a big mouth to be a gossiper; to be a person who tells secrets. (Informal.) ☐ *Mary has a big mouth. She told Bob what I was getting him for his birthday.* ☐ *You shouldn't say things like that about people all the time. Everyone will say you have a big mouth.*

have a blowout 1. [for one's car tire] to burst. ☐ *I had a blowout on the way here. I nearly lost control of the car.* ☐ *If you have a blowout in one tire, you should check the other tires.* **2.** to have a big, wild party; to enjoy oneself at a big party. ☐ *Mary and Bill had quite a blowout at their house Friday night.* ☐ *Fred and Tom had quite a blowout last night.*

have a bone to pick (with someone**)** to have a disagreement to discuss with someone; to have something to argue about with someone. (See also bone of contention.) ☐ *Hey, Bill. I've got a bone to pick with you. Where is the money you owe me?* ☐ *I had a bone to pick with her, but she was so sweet that I forgot about it.* ☐ *You always have a bone to pick.*

have a brush with something to have a brief contact with something; to have a brief experience with something. (Especially with the law. Sometimes a *close* brush. Compare this with have a scrape (with someone or something).) ☐ *Ann had a close brush with the law. She was nearly arrested for speeding.* ☐ *When I was younger, I had a brush with scarlet fever, but I got over it.*

have a case (against someone**)** to have much evidence that can be used against someone. (See also build a case (against someone).) ☐ *Do the police have a case against John?* ☐ *No, they don't have a case.*

have a change of heart to change one's attitude or decision, usually from a negative to a positive position. ☐ *I had a change of heart at the last minute and gave the old lady some money.* ☐ *Since I talked to you last, I have had a change of heart. I now approve of your marrying Sam.*

have a chip on one's **shoulder** to be tempting someone else to an argument or a fight; to seem willing to instigate conflict. □ *Who are you mad at? You always seem to have a chip on your shoulder.* □ *John has had a chip on his shoulder ever since he got his speeding ticket.*

have a clean conscience (about someone or something**)** Go to **have a clear conscience (about** someone or something**)**.

have a clear conscience (about someone or something**)** AND **have a clean conscience (about** someone or something**)** to be free of guilt about someone or something. □ *I'm not sorry that John got the blame. I have a clean conscience about the whole affair.* □ *I have a clear conscience about John and his problems.* □ *I didn't do it. I have a clean conscience.* □ *She can't sleep at night because she doesn't have a clear conscience.*

have a close call Go to **have a close shave**.

have a close shave AND **have a close call** to have a narrow escape from something dangerous. (See also **have a brush with** something.) □ *What a close shave I had! I nearly fell off the roof when I was working there.* □ *I almost got struck by a speeding car. It was a close shave.*

have a clue (about something**)** to know anything about something; to have even a hint about something. (Usually negative.) □ *I don't have a clue about where to start looking for Jim.* □ *Why do you think I have a clue about Tom's disappearance?*

have a conniption (fit) to get angry or hysterical. (Folksy. See also **have a fit**.) □ *I got so mad I thought I was going to have a conniption.* □ *My father had a conniption fit when I got home this morning.*

have a crack at something Go to **have a try at** something.

have a familiar ring [for a story or an explanation] to sound familiar. □ *Your excuse has a familiar ring. Have you done this before?* □ *This term paper has a familiar ring. I think it has been copied.*

have a feeling about something Go to **have a feeling (that)**.

have a feeling (that) AND **have a feeling about** something to have a premonition that [something might happen]; to have an intuition about something. □ *I had a feeling that you might be dropping by this afternoon.* □ *I didn't have any facts to support it. I just had a feeling.*

have a field day to experience freedom from one's usual work schedule; to have a wild time. (Refers to a day when children are released from classes to take part in sports and athletic contests.) □ *The boss was gone and we had a field day today. No one got anything done.* □ *The air was fresh and clear, and everyone had a field day in the park during the lunch hour.*

have a finger in the pie AND **have** one's **finger in the pie** to have a role in something; to be involved in something. □ *Tess wants to have a finger in the pie. She doesn't think we can do it by ourselves.* □ *Sally always wants to have a finger in the pie.*

have a fit to be very angry. (Informal.) □ *The teacher had a fit when the dog ran through the classroom.* □ *John had a fit when he found his car had been damaged.*

have a foot in both camps to have an interest in or to support each of two opposing groups of people. □ *The shop steward had been promised a promotion and so had a foot in both camps during the strike—workers and management.* □ *Mr. Smith has a foot in both camps in the parent-teacher dispute. He teaches math, but he has a son at the school.*

have a frog in one's **throat** to have a feeling of hoarseness. □ *I cannot speak more clearly. I have a frog in my throat.* □ *I had a frog in my throat, and the telephone receptionist couldn't understand me.*

have a glass jaw to be susceptible to collapsing when struck on the head. (Informal. Said only of boxers who are frequently knocked down by a blow to the head.) □ *When the prizefighter was knocked out in his third fight, the newspapers said he had a glass jaw.* □ *Once a* *fighter has a glass jaw, he's finished as a boxer.*

have a go (at something**)** to make a try at something. (See also **take a try at** something.) ☐ *I've never fished before, but I'd like to have a go at it.* ☐ *Great, have a go right now. Take my fishing pole and give it a try.*

have a good command of something to know something well. ☐ *Bill has a good command of French.* ☐ *Jane has a good command of economic theory.*

have a good head on one's **shoulders** to have common sense; to be sensible and intelligent. ☐ *Mary doesn't do well in school, but she's got a good head on her shoulders.* ☐ *John has a good head on his shoulders and can be depended on to give good advice.*

have a (good) mind to do something to be tempted to do something; to be on the verge of doing something that one has thought about. ☐ *I have a good mind to tell her just exactly what I think of her.* ☐ *She had a mind to leave the room right then and there.*

have a good thing going to have something arranged for one's benefit. (Informal.) ☐ *Sally paints pictures and sells them at art fairs. She has a good thing going, and she makes good money.* ☐ *John inherited a fortune and doesn't have to work for a living anymore. He's got a good thing going.*

have a green thumb to have the ability to grow plants well. ☐ *Just look at Mr. Simpson's garden. He has a green thumb.* ☐ *My mother has a green thumb when it comes to houseplants.*

have a grudge (against someone**)** Go to bear a grudge (against someone).

have a hand in something to play a part in (doing) something. ☐ *I had a hand in the picnic plans.* ☐ *I want to have a hand in any revision of the script.*

have a handle on something AND **get a handle on** something to have or get control of something; to have or get an understanding of something. ☐ *Get a handle on your temper and calm down.* ☐ *The police chief had a handle on the potential riot situation.*

have a hard time to experience unnecessary difficulties. ☐ *I get a hard time every time I come to this store.* ☐ *I never have a hard time at the store across the street.*

have a head for something have the mental capacity for something. ☐ *Jane has a good head for directions and never gets lost.* ☐ *Bill doesn't have a head for figures and should never become an accountant.*

have a heart to be compassionate; to be generous and forgiving. ☐ *Oh, have a heart! Give me some help!* ☐ *If Ann had a heart, she'd have made us feel more welcome.*

have a heart of gold to be generous, sincere, and friendly. ☐ *Mary is such a lovely person. She has a heart of gold.* ☐ *You think Tom stole your watch? Impossible! He has a heart of gold.*

have a heart of stone to be cold and unfriendly. ☐ *Sally has a heart of stone. She never even smiles.* ☐ *The villain in the play had a heart of stone. He was an ideal villain.*

have a heart-to-heart (talk) to have a sincere and intimate talk. ☐ *I had a heart-to-heart talk with my father before I went off to college.* ☐ *I have a problem, John. Let's sit down and have a heart-to-heart.*

have a hold on someone to have a strong and secure influence on someone. ☐ *The strange religion seemed to have a strong hold on its followers.* ☐ *The drug has a hold on the minds of those who use it.*

have a hunch about something Go to have a hunch (that).

have a hunch (that) something will happen AND **have a hunch about** something to have an idea about what did, will, or should happen; to have a feeling that something will or should happen. ☐ *I had a hunch that you would be here when I arrived.* ☐ *I have a hunch about the way things will happen.*

have a keen interest in something to have a strong interest in something; to be very interested in something. □ *Tom had always had a keen interest in music, so he started a band.* □ *The children have a keen interest in having a pet, so I bought them a cat.*

have a look for someone or something Go to **take a look for** someone or something.

have a lot going (for one) to have many things working to one's benefit. □ *Jane is so lucky. She has a lot going for her.* □ *She has a good job and a nice family. She has a lot going.*

have a lot of promise to be very promising; to have a good future ahead. □ *Sally is quite young, but she has a lot of promise.* □ *This bush is small, but it has a lot of promise.*

have a lot on one's **mind** to have many things to worry about; to be preoccupied. □ *I'm sorry that I'm so grouchy. I have a lot on my mind.* □ *He forgot to go to his appointment because he had a lot on his mind.*

have a low boiling point to anger easily. (Informal.) □ *Be nice to John. He's upset and has a low boiling point.* □ *Mr. Jones sure has a low boiling point. I hardly said anything, and he got angry.*

have a mind like a steel trap to have a very sharp and agile mind; to have a mind capable of fast, incisive thought. □ *Sally can handle the questioning. She has a mind like a steel trap.* □ *If I had a mind like a steel trap, I wouldn't have so much trouble concentrating.*

have an accident 1. to experience something that was not foreseen or intended. □ *Traffic is very bad. I almost had an accident.* □ *Drive carefully. Try to avoid having an accident.* **2.** to lose control of the bowels or the bladder. (Euphemistic. Usually said of a young child.) □ *"Oh, Ann," cried Mother. "It looks like you've had an accident!"* □ *Mother asked Billy to go to the bathroom before they left so that he wouldn't have an accident in the car.*

have an ace up one's **sleeve** to have a secret or concealed means of accomplishing something. (Refers to being prepared to cheat in a card game.) □ *I think that Liz has an ace up her sleeve and will surprise us with success at the last minute.* □ *I have done all I can do. I have no idea what to do next. I don't have an ace up my sleeve, and I can't work miracles.*

have an ax to grind (with someone**)** to have something to complain about. (Informal.) □ *Tom, I need to talk to you. I have an ax to grind with you.* □ *Bill and Bob went into the other room to argue. They had an ax to grind.*

have an ear for something to have the ability to learn music or languages. □ *Bill doesn't have an ear for music. He can't carry a tune.* □ *Mary has a good ear for languages.*

have a near miss to nearly crash or collide. □ *The airplanes—flying much too close—had a near miss.* □ *I had a near miss while driving over here.*

have an eye for someone or something to have a taste or an inclination for someone or something. □ *Bob has an eye for beauty.* □ *He has an eye for color.* □ *Ann has an eye for well-dressed men.*

have an eye on someone or something AND **keep an eye on** someone or something to keep watch on someone or something; to keep track of someone or something. (The *an* can be replaced by *one's*.) □ *I have my eye on the apple tree. When the apples ripen, I'll harvest them.* □ *Please keep an eye on the baby.* □ *Will you please keep your eye on my house while I'm on vacation?*

have an eye out (for someone or something**)** AND **keep an eye out (for** someone or something**)** to watch for the arrival or appearance of someone or something. (The *an* can be replaced by *one's*.) □ *Please try to have an eye out for the bus.* □ *Keep an eye out for rain.* □ *Have your eye out for a raincoat on sale.* □ *Okay. I'll keep my eye out.*

have an in (with someone**)** to have a way to request a special favor from someone; to have influence with someone. □ *Do you have an in with the mayor? I have to* *ask him a favor.* ☐ *Sorry, I don't have an in, but I know someone who does.*

have an itch for something to have a desire for something. ☐ *I have an itch for a nice cool glass of lemonade.* ☐ *Who besides me has an itch for pizza?*

have an itching palm Go to have an itchy palm.

have an itch to do something to have a desire to do something. ☐ *I have an itch to see a movie tonight.* ☐ *Tom has an itch to go swimming.*

have an itchy palm AND **have an itching palm** to be in need of a tip; to tend to ask for tips. (As if placing money in the palm would stop the itching.) ☐ *All the waiters at that restaurant have itchy palms.* ☐ *The cabdriver was troubled by an itching palm. Since he refused to carry my bags, I gave him nothing.*

have a nose for something to have the talent for finding something. ☐ *Police dogs have a good nose for drugs.* ☐ *The reporter has a nose for news.*

have an out to have an excuse; to have a means of avoiding something. (Refers to a way out or means of escape. Informal. The *out* is a noun.) ☐ *He's very clever. No matter what happens, he always has an out.* ☐ *I agreed to go to a party that I don't want to go to now. I'm looking for an out.*

have a one-track mind to have a mind that thinks entirely or almost entirely about one subject, often sex. ☐ *Adolescent boys often have one-track minds. All they're interested in is the opposite sex.* ☐ *Bob has a one-track mind. He can only talk about football.*

have a passion for someone or something to have a strong feeling of need or desire for someone, something, or some activity. ☐ *Mary has a great passion for chocolate.* ☐ *John has a passion for fishing, so he fishes as often as he can.*

have a peep AND **take a peep** to look quickly, sometimes through a small hole. ☐ *Have a peep into the refrigerator and see if we need any milk.* ☐ *I took a peep at the comet through the telescope.*

have a penchant for doing something to have a taste, desire, or inclination for doing something. ☐ *John has a penchant for eating fattening foods.* ☐ *Ann has a penchant for buying clothes.*

have a pick-me-up to eat or drink something stimulating. (The *have* can be replaced with *need, want,* etc. The *me* does not change.) ☐ *I'd like to have a pick-me-up. I think I'll have a bottle of pop.* ☐ *You look tired. You need a pick-me-up.*

have a price on one's **head** to be wanted by the authorities, who have offered a reward for one's capture. (Informal or folksy. Usually limited to western and gangster movies.) ☐ *We captured a thief who had a price on his head, and the sheriff gave us the reward.* ☐ *The crook was so mean, he turned in his own brother, who had a price on his head.*

have a right to do something AND **have the right to** do something to have the freedom to do something; to possess legal or moral permission or license to do something. ☐ *You don't have the right to enter my home without my permission.* ☐ *I have a right to grow anything I want on my farmland.*

have a rough time (of it) to experience a difficult period. ☐ *Since his wife died, Mr. Brown has been having a rough time of it.* ☐ *Be nice to Bob. He's been having a rough time.*

have arrived to reach a position of power, authority, or prominence. ☐ *Jane saw her picture on the cover of the magazine and felt that she had finally arrived.* ☐ *When I got an office with a window, I knew that I had arrived.*

have a run-in with someone to have an unpleasant and troublesome encounter with someone. ☐ *I had a run-in with Anne at the party, so I left early.* ☐ *David had a small run-in with the law last night.*

have a run of bad luck to have bad luck repeatedly; to have bad things happen a number of times. ☐ *I have had a run of bad luck, and I have no more money to spend.* ☐ *The company had a run of bad luck over the last few years.*

have a run of something to have a continuous series of events. □ *The city had a run of serious crimes that angered the citizens.* □ *We had a run of very hot days last July.*

have a say (in something**)** Go to **have a voice (in** something**)**.

have a score to settle (with someone**)** to have a problem to clear up with someone; to have to get even with someone about something. (See also **settle a score with** someone.) □ *I have a score to settle with John.* □ *John and I have a score to settle.*

have a scrape (with someone or something**)** to come into contact with someone or something; to have a small battle with someone or something. (Compare this with **have a brush with** something.) □ *I had a scrape with the county sheriff.* □ *John and Bill had a scrape, but they are friends again now.*

have a screw loose to act silly or crazy. (Slang.) □ *John is such a clown. He acts as if he has a screw loose.* □ *What's the matter with you? Do you have a screw loose or something?*

have a shot at something Go to **have a try at** something.

have a smoke to smoke a cigarette, cigar, or pipe. (The *have* can be replaced with *need, want,* etc.) □ *Can I have a smoke? I'm very nervous.* □ *Do you have a cigarette? I need a smoke.*

have a snowball's chance in hell to have no chance at all; to have a chance no greater than that of a snowball in hell. (A snowball would melt in hell and have no chance of surviving. Use caution with *hell.*) □ *He has a snowball's chance in hell of passing the test.* □ *You don't have a snowball's chance in hell of her agreeing to marry you.*

have a soft spot in one's **heart for** someone or something to be fond of someone or something. □ *John has a soft spot in his heart for Mary.* □ *I have a soft spot in my heart for chocolate cake.*

have a spaz to get angry or hysterical; to have a **conniption (fit)**. (Slang.) □ *Relax, Bob. Don't have a spaz.* □ *My father had a spaz when I came in late last night.*

have a stroke to experience sudden unconsciousness or paralysis due to an interruption in the blood supply to the brain. (Also used as an exaggeration. See the last two examples below.) □ *The patient who received an artificial heart had a stroke two days after the operation.* □ *My great-uncle Bill—who is very old—had a stroke last May.* □ *Calm down, Bob. You're going to have a stroke.* □ *My father almost had a stroke when I came home at three o'clock this morning.*

have a sweet tooth to desire to eat many sweet foods—especially candy and pastries. □ *I have a sweet tooth, and if I don't watch it, I'll really get fat.* □ *John eats candy all the time. He must have a sweet tooth.*

have a taste for something a desire for a particular food, drink, or experience. □ *The Smiths have a taste for adventure and take exotic vacations.* □ *When she was pregnant, Mary often had a taste for pickles.*

have a thing going (with someone**)** AND **have** something **going (with** someone**)** to have a romance or a love affair with someone. (Informal.) □ *John and Mary have a thing going.* □ *Bill has a thing going with Ann.* □ *They have something going.*

have a try at something AND **have a shot at** something; **have a crack at** something to take a turn at trying to do something. (The expressions with *shot* and *crack* are more colloquial than the main entry phrase. See also the variants at **take a try at** something.) □ *You don't seem to be having a lot of luck with this. Can I have a try at it?* □ *Let Sally have a shot at it.* □ *If you let me have a crack at it, maybe I can be successful.*

have at someone or something Go to **get at** someone or something.

have a vested interest in something to have a personal or biased interest, often financial, in something. □ *Margaret has a vested interest in wanting her father to sell the family firm. She has shares in it and* *would make a large profit.* □ *Jack has a vested interest in keeping the village traffic-free.*

have a voice (in something**)** AND **have a say (in** something**)** to have a part in making a decision. □ *I'd like to have a voice in choosing the carpet.* □ *John wanted to have a say in the issue also.* □ *He says he seldom gets to have a say.*

have a way with someone or something to handle or deal well with someone or something. □ *John has a way with hamburger. It's always delicious.* □ *Mother has a way with Father. She'll get him to paint the house.*

have a weakness for someone or something to be unable to resist someone or something; to be fond of someone or something; to be (figuratively) powerless against someone or something. (Compare this with **have a soft spot in one's heart for** someone or something.) □ *I have a weakness for chocolate.* □ *John has a weakness for Mary. I think he's in love.*

have a whale of a time to have an exciting time; to have a big time. (Slang. *Whale* is a way of saying *big.*) □ *We had a whale of a time at Sally's birthday party.* □ *Enjoy your vacation! I hope you have a whale of a time.*

have a word with someone to speak to someone, usually privately. □ *The manager asked to have a word with me when I was not busy.* □ *John, could I have a word with you? We need to discuss something.*

have back at someone Go to **get back (at** someone**)**.

have bats in one's **belfry** to be slightly crazy. □ *Poor old Tom has bats in his belfry.* □ *Don't act so silly, John. People will think you have bats in your belfry.*

have bearing on something to apply to something; to affect or influence something. □ *The worker's opinion has no bearing on the boss's decision.* □ *Does this information have any bearing on the question?*

have been around to be experienced in life. (Informal. Use with caution—especially with females—since this can also refer to sexual experience. See also **get around.**) □ *Ask Sally about how the government works. She's been around.* □ *They all know a lot about life. They've been around.*

have been had to have been mistreated; to have been been cheated or dealt with badly. (Informal or slang.) □ *They were cheated out of a thousand dollars. They've really been had.* □ *Look what they did to my car. Boy, have I been had.*

have been through the mill have been badly treated; have become exhausted. (Informal.) □ *This has been a rough day. I've really been through the mill.* □ *This old car is banged up, and it hardly runs. It's been through the mill.*

have been to hell and back to have survived a great deal of trouble. □ *What a terrible day! I feel like I have been to hell and back.* □ *After a day of shopping, I feel like I have been to hell and back.*

have bigger fish to fry Go to **have other fish to fry.**

have broad shoulders to have the ability to take on unpleasant responsibilities; to have the ability to accept criticism or rebuke. (Refers to the apparent strength of broad shoulders to support a heavy burden.) □ *No need to apologize to me. I can take it. I have broad shoulders.* □ *Karen may have broad shoulders, but she can't endure endless criticism.*

have clean hands to be guiltless. (Refers to the blood on the hands of a murderer.) □ *Don't look at me. I have clean hands.* □ *The police took him in, but let him go again because he had clean hands.*

have cold feet Go to **get cold feet.**

have come a long way to have accomplished much; to have advanced much. (Also literal.) □ *My, how famous you are. You've come a long way.* □ *Tom has come a long way in a short time.*

have contact with someone a link to someone resulting in communication. (Also literal.) □ *I have had no contact with Bill* *since he left town.* ☐ *Tom had contact with a known criminal last month.*

have designs on someone or something to have plans for someone or something. ☐ *Mrs. Brown has designs on my apple tree. I think she's going to cut off the part that hangs over her fence.* ☐ *Mary has designs on Bill. I think she'll try to date him.*

have dibs on something to reserve something for oneself; to claim something for oneself. (Informal. See also **put** (one's) **dibs on** something.) ☐ *I have dibs on the last piece of cake.* ☐ *John has dibs on the last piece again. It isn't fair.*

have egg on one's **face** to be embarrassed because of an error that is obvious to everyone. (Also literal.) ☐ *Bob has egg on his face because he wore jeans to the party and everyone else wore formal clothing.* ☐ *John was completely wrong about the weather for the picnic. It snowed! Now he has egg on his face.*

have eyes bigger than one's **stomach** to have a desire for more food than one could possibly eat. (See also one's **eyes are bigger then** one's **stomach.**) ☐ *I know I have eyes bigger than my stomach, so I won't take a lot of food.* ☐ *Todd has eyes bigger than his stomach.*

have eyes in the back of one's **head** to seem to be able to sense what is going on outside of one's vision. ☐ *My teacher seems to have eyes in the back of her head.* ☐ *My teacher doesn't need to have eyes in the back of his head. He watches us very carefully.*

have feet of clay [for a strong person] to have a defect of character. ☐ *All human beings have feet of clay. No one is perfect.* ☐ *Sally was popular and successful. She was nearly fifty before she learned that she, too, had feet of clay.*

have foot-in-mouth disease to embarrass oneself through a silly blunder. (Informal. This is a parody on *foot-and-mouth disease* or *hoof-and-mouth disease,* which affects cattle and deer. See also **put** one's **foot in** one's **mouth.**) ☐ *I'm sorry I keep saying stupid things. I guess I have foot-in-mouth disease.* ☐ *Yes, you really have foot-in-mouth disease tonight.*

have growing pains 1. [for a child] to have pains—which are attributed to growth—in the muscles and joints. ☐ *The doctor said that all Mary had were growing pains and that nothing was really wrong.* ☐ *Not everyone has growing pains.* **2.** [for an organization] to have difficulties in its growth. ☐ *The banker apologized for losing my check and said the bank was having growing pains.* ☐ *Governments have terrible growing pains.*

have had enough to have had as much of something as is needed or will be tolerated. (Compare this with **have had it (up to here).**) ☐ *Stop yelling at me. I've had enough.* ☐ *No more potatoes, please. I've had enough.* ☐ *I'm leaving you, Bill. I've had enough!*

have had its day to be no longer useful or successful. ☐ *Streetcars have had their day in most American cities.* ☐ *Some people think that radio has had its day, but others prefer it to television.*

have had it (up to here) to have reached the end of one's endurance or tolerance. (Informal.) ☐ *Okay, I've had it. You kids go to bed this instant.* ☐ *We've all had it with you, John. Get out!* ☐ *I've had it. I've got to go to bed before I drop dead.* ☐ *Tom is disgusted. He said that he has had it up to here.*

have half a mind to do something Go to **have half a notion to** do something.

have half a notion to do something AND **have half a mind to** do something to have almost decided to do something, especially something unpleasant. (Informal.) ☐ *I have half a mind to go off and leave you here.* ☐ *The cook had half a notion to serve cold chicken.*

have hell to pay Go to **have the devil to pay.**

Have I got something **for you!** Would you believe that I have something really exciting for you? (Informal.) ☐ *Have I got something for you! Wait'll you hear about it!* ☐ *Have I got something for you! You're gonna love it.*

Have I made myself clear? Do you understand exactly what I am telling you? (Indicates anger or dominance.) □ *I don't intend to warn you again. Have I made myself clear?* □ *I do not want you to go there! Have I made myself clear?*

have it all over someone or something to be much better than someone or something. □ *This cake has it all over that one.* □ *My car has it all over yours.* □ *Sally can really run. She has it all over Bill.*

have it both ways to have both of two incompatible things. (Also literal. See also **have** one's **cake and eat it too.**) □ *John wants the security of marriage and the freedom of being single. He wants to have it both ways.* □ *John thinks he can have it both ways—the wisdom of age and the vigor of youth.*

have it in for someone to **have** something **against** someone; to plan to scold or punish someone. □ *Don't go near Bob. He has it in for you.* □ *Billy! You had better go home. Your mom really has it in for you.*

have method in one's **madness** to have a purpose in what one is doing, even though it seems to be mad. □ *What I'm doing may look strange, but there is method in my madness.* □ *Wait until she finishes; then you'll see that there is method in her madness.*

have mixed feelings (about someone or something**)** to be uncertain about someone or something. □ *I have mixed feelings about Bob. Sometimes I think he likes me; other times I don't.* □ *I have mixed feelings about my trip to England. I love the people, but the climate upsets me.* □ *Yes, I also have mixed feelings.*

have money to burn to have lots of money; to have more money than one needs. (See also **Money burns a hole in** someone's **pocket.**) □ *Look at the way Tom buys things. You'd think he had money to burn.* □ *If I had money to burn, I'd just put it in the bank.*

have more important fish to fry Go to have other fish to fry.

(have) never had it so good have never had so much good fortune. (Informal.) □ *No, I'm not complaining. I've never had it so good.* □ *Mary is pleased with her new job. She's never had it so good.*

have no business doing something to be wrong to do something; to be extremely unwise to do something. □ *You have no business bursting in on me like that!* □ *You have no business spending money like that!*

have none of something to tolerate or endure no amount of something. □ *I'll have none of your talk about quitting school.* □ *We'll have none of your gossip.* □ *I wish to have none of the sweet potatoes, please.*

have no staying power to lack endurance; not to be able to last. □ *Sally can swim fast for a short distance, but she has no staying power.* □ *That horse can race fairly well, but it has no staying power.*

have nothing on someone or something **1.** [with *someone*] to lack evidence against someone. (Informal.) □ *The police had nothing on Bob, so they let him loose.* □ *You've got nothing on me! Let me go!* **2.** to have no information about someone or something. □ *The dictionary had nothing on the word I looked up.* □ *The librarian said that the library has nothing on the Jones brothers.*

have nothing to do with someone or something **1.** not to be related to or concerned with someone or something. □ *Your wants and needs have nothing to do with my wants and needs.* □ *Waterloo? That has nothing to do with water!* **2.** to avoid being associated with someone or something. □ *She will have nothing to do with me anymore.* □ *I have nothing to do with computers after I found out how hard they are to operate.*

have one foot in the grave to be near death, either because of old age or because of illness. □ *Fred's uncle is ninety. He has one foot in the grave and may not live another two months.* □ *Terry has one foot in the grave and will perish unless he receives treatment soon.*

have one for the road to have a drink just before leaving. □ *I think I'll have one for the road, bartender.* □ *Forget having one for the road if you are driving.*

have one's **back to the wall** to be in a defensive position. (Informal. See also **push** someone **to the wall.**) ☐ *He'll have to give in. He has his back to the wall.* ☐ *How can I bargain when I've got my back to the wall?*

have one's **cake and eat it too** AND **eat** one's **cake and have it too** to enjoy both having something and using it up; to **have it both ways.** (Usually stated in the negative.) ☐ *Tom wants to have his cake and eat it too. It can't be done.* ☐ *Don't buy a car if you want to walk and stay healthy. You can't eat your cake and have it too.*

have one's **druthers** to get one's choice; to be permitted to have one's preference. (Folksy. The *druthers* is from *would rather.*) ☐ *If I had my druthers, I'd go to France.* ☐ *Tom said that if he had his druthers, he'd choose to stay home.*

have one's **ear to the ground** AND **keep** one's **ear to the ground** to listen carefully, hoping to get advance warning of something. (Refers to holding one's ear against the ground to listen for approaching horses or a train.) ☐ *John had his ear to the ground, hoping to find out about new ideas in computers.* ☐ *His boss told him to keep his ear to the ground so that he'd be the first to know of a new idea.*

have oneself something to select, use, or consume something. (Folksy. Also with nonreflexive pronouns, *me, him, her,* etc., as in the last example.) ☐ *He had himself a two-hour nap.* ☐ *I'll have myself one of those red ones.* ☐ *I think I'll have me a big, cold drink.*

have one's **feet on the ground** Go to get one's **feet on the ground.**

have one's **finger in the pie** Go to have a **finger in the pie.**

have one's **finger in too may pies** to be involved in too many things; to have too many tasks going to be able to do any of them well. ☐ *I'm too busy. I have my finger in too may pies.* ☐ *She never gets anything done because she has her finger in too many pies.*

have one's **hand in the till** to be stealing money from a company or an organization. (The *till* is a cash box or drawer.) ☐ *Mr. Jones had his hand in the till for years before he was caught.* ☐ *I think that the new clerk has her hand in the till. There is cash missing every morning.*

have one's **hands full (with** someone or something**)** to be busy or totally occupied with someone or something. (Literal when one cannot hold anything else in one's hands.) ☐ *I have my hands full with my three children.* ☐ *You have your hands full with the store.* ☐ *We both have our hands full.*

have one's **hands tied** to be prevented from doing something. (See also **tie** someone's **hands.**) ☐ *I can't help you. I was told not to, so I have my hands tied.* ☐ *John can help. He doesn't have his hands tied.*

have one's **head in the clouds** to be unaware of what is going on. ☐ *"Bob, do you have your head in the clouds?" said the teacher.* ☐ *She walks around all day with her head in the clouds. She must be in love.*

have one's **heart go out to** someone to have compassion for someone. ☐ *I can't have my heart go out to everyone.* ☐ *To have compassion is to have one's heart go out to those who are suffering.*

have one's **heart in the right place** to have good intentions, even if there are bad results. (See also one's **heart is in the right place.**) ☐ *I don't always do what is right, but my heart is in the right place.* ☐ *Good old Tom. His heart's in the right place.* ☐ *It doesn't matter if she lost the game. She has her heart in the right place.*

have one's **heart on** one's **sleeve** Go to **wear** one's **heart on** one's **sleeve.**

have one's **heart set against** something to be totally against something. (Also with *dead,* as in the example. See also **dead set against** someone or something; **set** one's **heart against** something.) ☐ *Jane has her heart dead set against going to Australia.* ☐ *John has his heart set against going to college.*

have one's **heart set on** something to be desiring and expecting something. ☐ *Jane has her heart set on going to London.* ☐ *Bob will be disappointed. He had his heart* *set on going to college this year.* □ *She had her heart set on it.*

have one's **heart stand still** <an expression said when one's heart (figuratively) stops beating because one is feeling strong emotions.> □ *I had my heart stand still once when I was overcome with joy.* □ *Lovers—at least the ones in love songs—usually have their hearts stand still.*

have one's **luck run out** for one's good luck to stop; for one's good fortune to come to an end. □ *I had my luck run out when I was in South America. I nearly starved.* □ *I hate to have my luck run out just when I need it.*

have one's **nose in a book** to be reading a book; to read books all the time. □ *Bob has his nose in a book every time I see him.* □ *His nose is always in a book. He never gets any exercise.*

have one's **nose in the air** to be conceited or aloof. (See also one's **nose is in the air**.) □ *Mary always seems to have her nose in the air.* □ *I wonder if she knows that she has her nose in the air.*

have one's **sights trained on** something Go to **train** one's **sights on** something.

have one's **words stick in** one's **throat** to be so overcome by emotion that one can hardly speak. □ *I sometimes have my words stick in my throat.* □ *John said that he never had his words stick in his throat.*

have one's **work cut out for** one to have a large and difficult task prepared for one. (See also one's **work is cut out for** one.) □ *They sure have their work cut out for them, and it's going to be hard.* □ *There is a lot for Bob to do. He has his work cut out for him.*

have other fish to fry AND **have bigger fish to fry; have more important fish to fry** to have other things to do; to have more important things to do. □ *I can't take time for your problem. I have other fish to fry.* □ *I won't waste time on your question. I have bigger fish to fry.*

have precedence over someone or something; AND **take precedence over** someone or something have the right to come before someone or something else. □ *Ambulances have precedence over regular cars at intersections.* □ *My manager's concerns take precedence over mine.*

have pull with someone to have influence with someone. (Slang. Also with *some, much, lots,* etc.) □ *Let's ask Ann to help us. She has pull with the mayor.* □ *Do you know anyone who has some pull with the bank president? I need a loan.*

have rocks in one's **head** to be silly or crazy. (Slang.) □ *John is a real nut. He has rocks in his head.* □ *I don't have rocks in my head—I'm just different.*

have second thoughts about someone or something to have doubts about someone or something. □ *I'm beginning to have second thoughts about Tom.* □ *We now have second thoughts about going to Canada.*

have seen better days to be worn or worn out. (Informal.) □ *This coat has seen better days. I need a new one.* □ *Oh, my old legs ache. I've seen better days, but everyone has to grow old.*

have so Go to **have too**.

have someone **dead to rights** to have proven someone unquestionably guilty. □ *The police burst in on the robbers while they were at work. They had the robbers dead to rights.* □ *All right, Tom! I've got you dead to rights! Get your hand out of the cookie jar.*

have someone **in** one's **pocket** to have control over someone. (Informal.) □ *Don't worry about the mayor. She'll cooperate. I've got her in my pocket.* □ *John will do just what I tell him. I've got him and his brother in my pocket.*

have someone **on the string** to have someone waiting for your decision. (Informal.) □ *Sally has John on the string. He has asked her to marry him, but she hasn't replied yet.* □ *Yes, it sounds like she has him on the string.*

have someone or something **in** one's **hands** to have control of or responsibility for someone or something. □ *You have the whole project in your hands.* □ *The boss* *put the whole project in your hands.* □ *I have to leave the baby in your hands while I go to the doctor.*

have someone or something **in tow** to lead, pull, or tow someone or something around. □ *Mrs. Smith has her son in tow.* □ *That car has a boat in tow.*

have someone or something **on** one's **hands** to be burdened with someone or something. □ *I run a record store. I sometimes have a large number of unwanted records on my hands.* □ *She the all the children on her hands today.*

have someone or something **on** one's **mind** to think often about someone or something; to be obsessed with someone or something. □ *Bill has chocolate on his mind.* □ *John has Mary on his mind every minute.*

have someone **over** to invite someone as a guest to one's house. □ *When can we have Aunt Jane over for dinner?* □ *I would love to have you over some time.*

have someone **pegged as** something Go to **peg** someone **as** something.

have someone's **blood on** one's **hands** to be responsible for someone's death; to be guilty of causing someone's death. (Also literal.) □ *The teenager's blood was on the policeman's hands.* □ *The king's blood was on the hands of the murderer who killed him.*

have someone's **hide** to scold or punish someone. (Refers to skinning an animal. Informal. Compare this with **skin** someone **alive.**) □ *If you ever do that again, I'll have your hide.* □ *He said he'd have my hide if I entered his garage again.*

have something against someone or something to possess something (such as prejudice or knowledge) that is harmful to someone or something. (Note the variation in the examples below.) □ *I have something against John. He was rude to me.* □ *Do you have something against North Americans?* □ *What do you have against me?* □ *I don't have anything against eating beef.*

have something **at hand** Go to **have** something **at** one's **fingertips.**

have something **at** one's **fingertips** AND **have** something **at hand** to have something within (one's) reach. (*Have* can be replaced with *keep.*) □ *I have a dictionary at my fingertips.* □ *I try to have everything I need at hand.* □ *I keep my medicine at my fingertips.*

have something **coming (to** one**)** to deserve punishment (for something). (Also literal. Informal.) □ *Bill broke a window, so he has a spanking coming to him.* □ *That's it, Bill. Now you've got it coming!*

have something **doing** AND **have** something **on** to have plans for a particular time. (Informal. Note the variation with *anything* in the examples below.) □ *BOB: Are you busy Saturday night? BILL: Yes, I've got something doing.* □ *I don't have anything doing Sunday night.* □ *I have something on almost every Saturday.*

have something **down pat** to have learned or memorized something perfectly. □ *I have practiced my speech until I have it down pat.* □ *Tom has his part in the play down pat. He won't make any mistakes.*

have something **going (for** oneself**)** [for someone] to have a beneficial scheme or operation going. (Informal.) □ *John really has something going for himself. He's a travel agent, and he gets to travel everywhere for free.* □ *I wish I could have something like that going.*

have something **going (with** someone**)** **1.** to have a business deal with someone. □ *Sally has a new business project going with Ann. They'll announce a new product in the spring.* □ *John and Tom work as stockbrokers. I've heard that they have a business deal going.* **2.** Go to **have a thing going (with** someone**).**

have something **hanging over** one's **head** to have something bothering or worrying one; to have a deadline worrying one. (Also literal. Informal.) □ *I keep worrying about getting drafted. I hate to have something like that hanging over my head.* □ *I have a history paper that is hanging over my head.*

have something **in common (with** someone or something**)** [for groups of people or things] to resemble one another in specific ways. □ *Bill and Bob both have red hair. They have that in common with each other.* □ *Bob and Mary have a lot in common. I can see why they like each other.*

have something **in hand** to have something in one's hand or close by. (Compare this with **have** something **at hand.**) □ *I have your letter of May tenth in hand.* □ *I have my pen in hand, and I'm ready to write.*

have something in mind to think of something in particular; to have an idea or image (of something) in one's mind. □ *BILL: I would like to purchase some boots. CLERK: Yes, sir. Did you have something in mind?* □ *I have something in mind, but I don't see it here. Good day.*

have something **in stock** to have merchandise available and ready for sale. □ *Do you have extra large sizes in stock?* □ *Of course, we have all sizes and colors in stock.*

have something **in store (for** someone**)** to have something planned for one's future. □ *Tom has a large inheritance in store for him when his uncle dies.* □ *I wish I had something like that in store.*

have something **made 1.** to hire someone to make something. □ *Isn't it a lovely coat? I had to have it made because I couldn't find one I liked in a store.* □ *We had the cake made at the bakery. Our oven isn't big enough for a cake that size.* **2.** to have achieved a successful state. (Slang. Usually with *it*.) □ *Mary really has it made. She inherited one million dollars.* □ *I wish I had it made like that.*

have something **on** Go to **have** something **doing.**

have something **on file** to have a written record of something in storage. □ *I'm sure I have your letter on file. I'll check again.* □ *We have your application on file somewhere.*

have something **on the ball** to have a particular amount of smartness or cleverness. (Slang.) □ *Both John and Mary have a lot on the ball. They should go far.* □ *I think I'd do better in school if I had more on the ball. I learn slowly.*

have something **on the brain** to be obsessed with something. (Slang.) □ *Bob has chocolate on the brain.* □ *Mary has money on the brain. She wants to earn as much as possible.*

have something **on the tip of** one's **tongue** to be on the verge of remembering a specific fact, such as someone's name; to have just forgotten a specific fact. (See also **on the tip of** one's **tongue.**) □ *Just give me a minute. I have her name on the tip of my tongue!* □ *I had her name on the tip of my tongue, but you made me forget it when you called.*

have something **out (with** someone**)** to settle a disagreement or a complaint. (Informal.) □ *John has been mad at Mary for a week. He finally had it out with her today.* □ *I'm glad we are having this out today.*

have something **stick in** one's **craw** to have something irritate or displease someone. (Folksy.) □ *I don't like to have Bill's words stick in my craw.* □ *He meant to have the problem stick in my craw and upset me.*

have something to do with something AND **[not] have anything to do with** something; **have nothing to do with** something to be associated with or related to something. □ *Does your dislike for Sally have something to do with the way she insulted you?* □ *My illness has something to do with my lungs.*

have something **to go** Go to **buy** something **to go.**

have something **to spare** to have more than enough of something. (Informal. See also **and** something **to spare.**) □ *Ask John for some firewood. He has firewood to spare.* □ *Do you have any candy to spare?*

have something up one's **sleeve** to have a secret or surprise plan or solution (to a problem). (Slang. Refers to cheating at cards by having a card hidden in one's sleeve.) □ *I've got something up my sleeve, and it should solve all your problems. I'll tell you what it is after I'm elected.* □ *The manager has something up her sleeve. She'll surprise us with it later.*

have sticky fingers to have a tendency to steal. (Slang.) □ *The clerk—who had sticky fingers—got fired.* □ *The little boy had sticky fingers and was always taking his father's small change.*

have the ball in one's **court** to be responsible for the next move in some process; to have to make a response to something that someone else has started. (Also literal.) □ *You have the ball in your court now. You have to answer the attorney's questions.* □ *There was no way that Liz could avoid acting. She had the ball in her court.*

have the best of both worlds to be in a situation where one can enjoy two different opportunities. □ *When Donna was a fellow at the university, she had the privileges of a professor and the freedom of a student. She definitely had the best of both worlds.* □ *Don hated to have to choose between retirement and continuing working. He wanted to do both so he could have the best of both worlds.*

have the cards stacked against one AND **have the deck stacked against** one to have one's chance at future success limited by factors over which one has no control; to have luck against one. □ *You can't get very far in life if you have the deck stacked against you.* □ *I can't seem to get ahead. I always have the cards stacked against*

have the courage of one's **convictions** to have enough courage and determination to carry out one's goals. □ *It's fine to have noble goals in life and to believe in great things. If you don't have the courage of your convictions, you'll never reach your goals.* □ *Jane was successful because she had the courage of her convictions.*

have the deck stacked against one Go to have the cards stacked against one.

have the devil to pay AND **have hell to pay** to have a great deal of trouble. (Informal. Use caution with *hell.*) □ *If you cheat on your income taxes, you'll have the devil to pay.* □ *I came home after three in the morning and had hell to pay.*

have the feel of something **1.** [for something] to feel like something (else). □ *This plastic has the feel of fine leather.* □ *The little car has the feel of a much larger one.* **2.** Go to **get the feel of** something.

have the gall to do something to have sufficient arrogance to do something. □ *I bet you don't have the gall to argue with the mayor.* □ *Only Jane has the gall to ask the boss for a second raise this month.*

have the gift of gab to have a great facility with language; to be able to use language very effectively. (Slang.) □ *My brother really has the gift of gab. He can convince anyone of anything.* □ *If I had the gift of gab like you do, I'd achieve more in life.*

have the makings of something to possess the qualities that are needed for something. □ *The young boy had the makings of a fine baseball player.* □ *My boss has all the makings of a prison warden.*

have the Midas touch to have the ability to be successful, especially the ability to make money easily. (From the name of a legendary king whose touch turned everything to gold.) □ *Bob is a merchant banker and really has the Midas touch.* □ *The poverty-stricken boy turned out to have the Midas touch and was a millionaire by the time he was twenty-five.*

have them rolling in the aisles to make an audience roll in the aisles with laughter. (Slang.) □ *I have the best jokes you've ever heard. I'll have them rolling in the aisles.* □ *What a great performance. We had them rolling in the aisles.*

have the patience of a saint to be very patient. (Refers to the "patience" that someone experiencing martyrdom might have.) □ *I don't know how she puts up with all those stupid questions. She has the patience of a saint.* □ *Hurry up, please. I am late and you are working too slow. I don't have the patience of a saint.*

have the presence of mind to do something to have the calmness and the ability to act sensibly in an emergency or difficult situation. □ *Jane had the presence of mind to phone the police when the child disap-*

peared. ☐ *The child had the presence of mind to take note of the car's license number.*

have the right-of-way to possess the legal right to occupy a particular space on a public roadway. (See also **yield the right-of-way.**) ☐ *I had a traffic accident yesterday, but it wasn't my fault. I had the right-of-way.* ☐ *Don't pull out onto a highway if you don't have the right-of-way.*

have the right to do something Go to **have a right to** do something.

have the shoe on the other foot to experience the opposite situation (from a previous situation). (Informal. Also with *be* instead of *have.* See the examples. See the proverb The **shoe is on the other foot.** Compare this with **in** someone else's **shoes.**) ☐ *I used to be a student, and now I'm the teacher. Now I have the shoe on the other foot.* ☐ *You were mean to me when you thought I was cheating. Now that I have caught you cheating, the shoe is on the other foot.*

have the time of one's **life** to have a very good time; to have the most exciting time in one's life. ☐ *What a great party! I had the time of my life.* ☐ *We went to Florida last winter and had the time of our lives.*

have the wherewithal (to do something**)** to have the means to do something, especially energy or money. ☐ *He has good ideas, but he doesn't have the wherewithal to carry them out.* ☐ *I could do a lot if only I had the wherewithal.*

have to do with someone or something to be associated with or related to someone or something. ☐ *This information only has to do with people who came in late.* ☐ *My illness has to do with my stomach.*

have to live with something to have to endure something. (See also **learn to live with** something.) ☐ *I have a slight limp in the leg that I broke last year. The doctor says I'll have to live with it.* ☐ *We don't like the new carpeting in the living room, but we'll have to live with it.*

have too AND **have so** to have done something (despite anything to the contrary). (This is an emphatic way of affirming that something has happened.) ☐ *BILL: You haven't made your bed. BOB: I have too!* ☐ *I have so turned in my paper! If you don't have it, you lost it!*

have too many irons in the fire to be doing too many things at once. ☐ *Tom had too many irons in the fire and missed some important deadlines.* ☐ *It's better if you don't have too many irons in the fire.*

have turned the corner to have passed a critical point in a process. (Also literal.) ☐ *The patient has turned the corner. She should begin to show improvement now.* ☐ *The project has turned the corner. The rest should be easy.*

have two strikes against one to have several things against one; to be in a position where success is unlikely. ☐ *Poor Bob had two strikes against him when he tried to explain where he was last night.* ☐ *I can't win. I have two strikes against me before I start.*

have what it takes to have the ability, courage, or stamina (to do something). ☐ *Bill has what it takes. He can swim for miles.* ☐ *Tom won't succeed. He doesn't have what it takes.*

Have you been keeping busy? <a vague greeting inquiry asking about how someone has been occupied.> (Really just a way to say hello and open a conversation.) ☐ *How are you? Have you been keeping busy?* ☐ *What've you been doing? Have you been keeping busy?*

hazard a guess to make a guess. ☐ *Even if you don't know, please hazard a guess.* ☐ *If you don't know the answer, hazard a guess.*

hazard an opinion to give an opinion. ☐ *Anne asked the attorney to hazard an opinion about the strength of her lawsuit.* ☐ *Don't feel like you have to hazard an opinion on something you know nothing about.*

He laughs best who laughs last Go to **He who laughs last, laughs longest.**

He who laughs last, laughs longest. AND **He laughs best who laughs last.** Whoever succeeds in making the last move or pulling the last trick has the most enjoyment. (Proverb.) □ *Bill had pulled many silly tricks on Tom. Finally Tom pulled a very funny trick on Bill and said, "He who laughs last, laughs longest."* □ *Bill pulled another, even bigger, trick on Tom and said, laughing, "He laughs best who laughs last."*

He who pays the piper calls the tune. The person who is paying for something has control over how the money is used. (Proverb.) □ *Fred's father is paying his way through college, and wants to help him choose his courses. He says that he who pays the piper calls the tune.* □ *The bride's parents should have a say in where the wedding is held since they're paying for it. He who pays the piper calls the tune.*

a **head** AND **per head** [for] a person; [for] an individual. (Also used for cattle.) □ *How much do you charge per head for dinner?* □ *It costs four dollars a head.*

head and shoulders above someone or something clearly superior to someone or something. (Often with *stand,* as in the example.) □ *This wine is head and shoulders above that one.* □ *John stands head and shoulders above Bob.*

head for someone or something to aim for or move toward someone or something. □ *She waved good-bye as she headed for the door.* □ *Ann came in and headed for her mother.*

head for the last roundup to reach the end of something. (Originally said of a dying cowboy.) □ *This ballpoint pen is headed for the last roundup. I have to get another one.* □ *I am so weak. I think I'm headed for the last roundup.*

head over heels in debt deeply in debt. □ *Finally, when she was head over heels in debt, she tore up her credit cards.* □ *I couldn't stand being head over heels in debt, so I always pay off my bills immediately.*

head over heels in love (with someone**)** very much in love with someone. (See also **fall head over heels in love (with** someone**)**.) □ *John is head over heels in love with Mary.* □ *They are head over heels in love with each other.* □ *They are head over heels in love.*

head someone or something **off** to prevent someone or something from arriving. □ *The doctors worked round the clock to head the epidemic off.* □ *Bill headed his mother off so that we had time to clean up the mess before she saw it.* 🅃 *The farmer headed off the herd of sheep before it ruined our picnic.*

head something **up** to serve as leader or head of something. □ *I had already agreed to head the fund-raising campaign up.* 🅃 *They asked me to head up the meeting.*

heads or tails the face of a coin or the other side of a coin. (Often used in an act of coin tossing, where one circumstance is valid if the front of a coin appears and another circumstance is valid if the other side appears.) □ *Jim looked at Jane as he flipped the coin into the air. "Heads or tails?" he asked.* □ *It doesn't matter whether the result of the toss is heads or tails. I won't like the outcome in any case.*

Heads up! Raise your head from work and look around you carefully for information, danger, or warnings that you need to see! □ *Heads up! Watch out for that door!* □ *Heads up! There is a car coming.*

heads will roll someone will get into severe trouble. (Informal.) □ *When the company's year-end results are known, heads will roll.* □ *Heads will roll when the principal sees the damaged classroom.*

hear a peep out of someone to get some sort of a response from someone; to hear the smallest word from someone. (Usually in the negative.) □ *I don't want to hear another peep out of you.* □ *I didn't know they were there. I didn't hear a peep out of them.*

hear of something to tolerate something; to permit something. (Usually negative.) □ *No, you cannot go to the movies! I won't hear of it!* □ *My mother wouldn't hear of my marrying Bill.*

hear someone **out** to listen to everything that someone has to say and to not interrupt or go away. □ *Please, hear me out.*

This is important. ☐ *He had a good idea, but the committee would not hear him out.*

heart and soul the central core [of someone or something]. (Also literal.) ☐ *My very heart and soul was made sad by her hurtful attitude.* ☐ *Now we are getting to the heart and soul of the matter.* ☐ *This feature is the heart and soul of my invention.*

[heart goes out to someone**]** Go to one's **heart goes out to** someone.

[heart is in one's **mouth]** Go to one's **heart is in** one's **mouth.**

[heart is in the right place] Go to one's **heart is in the right place.**

[heart is (dead) set against something**]** Go to one's **heart is (dead) set against** something.

[heart is set on something**]** Go to one's **heart is set on** something.

[heart misses a beat] Go to one's **heart misses a beat.**

[heart skips a beat] Go to one's **heart skips a beat.**

[heart stands still] Go to one's **heart stands still.**

heavy going difficult to do, understand, or make progress with. (Informal.) ☐ *Jim finds math heavy going.* ☐ *Talking to Mary is heavy going. She has nothing to say.*

hedge one's **bets** to reduce one's loss on a bet or on an investment by counterbalancing the loss in some way. (Slang.) ☐ *Bob bet Ann that the plane would be late. He usually hedges his bets. This time he called the airline and asked about the plane before he made the bet.* ☐ *John bought some stock and then bet Mary that the stock would go down in value in one year. He has hedged his bets perfectly. If the stock goes up, he sells it, pays off Mary, and still makes a profit. If it goes down, he reduces his loss by winning the bet he made with Mary.*

hell-bent for leather moving or behaving recklessly; riding a horse fast and recklessly. (Informal. Typically found in western movies.) ☐ *They took off after the horse thief, riding hell-bent for leather.* ☐ *Here comes the boss. She's not just angry; she's hell-bent for leather.*

hell on earth a very unpleasant situation, as if one were in hell. ☐ *That man made my life hell on earth!* ☐ *The whole time I was there was just hell on earth.*

help do something to assist [someone to] do something. ☐ *Bill can help load the truck.* ☐ *I am too tired to help mow the grass.* ☐ *Bill can help us load the truck.* ☐ *I am too tired to help you mow the grass.*

help oneself to take whatever one wants or needs. ☐ *Please have some candy. Help yourself.* ☐ *When you go to a cafeteria, you help yourself to the food.* ☐ *Bill helped himself to dessert.*

help (someone or something**) out (with** someone or something**)** to assist (someone or something) with a person or a thing. ☐ *Can you help me out with my geometry?* ☐ *Yes, I can help out.* 🅃 *Please help out my son with his geometry.* ☐ *Please help me out around the house.* 🅃 *We helped out the school with its fund-raising.*

hem and haw (around) to be uncertain about something; to be evasive; to say "ah" and "eh" when speaking—avoiding saying something meaningful. (Folksy.) ☐ *Stop hemming and hawing around. I want an answer.* ☐ *Don't just hem and haw around. Speak up. We want to hear what you think.*

hem someone or something **in** to trap or enclose someone or something. ☐ *The large city buildings hem me in.* 🅃 *Don't hem in the bird. Let it have a way to escape.*

the **here and now** the present, as opposed to the past or the future. ☐ *I don't care what's happening tomorrow or next week! I care about the here and now.* ☐ *The past is dead. Let's worry about the here and now.*

here and there at this place and that; from place to place. (Could imply a casual search. See also **here, there, and everywhere; hither and thither.**) ☐ *We find rare books in used-book stores here and there.*

□ *She didn't make a systematic search. She just looked here and there.*

Here goes nothing. I am beginning to do something that will probably fail or be poorly done. (Informal.) □ *Sally stood on the diving board and said, "Here goes nothing."* □ *As Ann walked onto the stage, she whispered, "Here goes nothing."*

Here (it) goes. Something is going to start.; I will start now.; I will do it now. (Informal or slang.) □ *I'm ready to start now. Here goes.* □ *Okay, it's my turn to kick the ball. Here it goes!*

here, there, and everywhere everywhere; at all points. (See also **hither, thither, and yon**. Compare this with **here and there**.) □ *Fred searched here, there, and everywhere, frantically looking for the lost check.* □ *She did not rest until she had been here, there, and everywhere, shopping for just the right gift.*

Here you go. AND **There you go.** Here is what you asked for. (Informal.) □ *"Here you go," said the waiter as he put the plate on the table.* □ *There you go. Here is your hamburger and your drink.*

Here's looking at you. Drink up. (A simple drinking toast.) □ *Here's look at you, Tom.* □ *Thanks for the drink. Here's looking at you.*

Here's mud in your eye. Drink up! (A simple and jocular drinking toast.) □ *Here's mud in your eye, Tom.* □ *Thanks for the drink. Here's mud in your eye.*

Here's to someone or something. <an expression used as a toast to someone or something to wish someone or something well.> □ *Here's to Jim and Mary! May they be very happy!* □ *Here's to your new job!*

hide-and-seek a guessing game where one has to find something or figure out something that is concealed or disguised. (Refers to a game where a person hides and another person tries to find the hidden person.) □ *I am tired of running up against a game of hide-and-seek every time I ask to see the financial records of this company.* □ *I have been trying to see the manager for two days. Where is she? I refuse to play hide-and-seek any longer. I want to see her now!*

hide one's **face in shame** to cover one's face because of shame or embarrassment. □ *Mary was so embarrassed. She could only hide her face in shame.* □ *When Tom broke Ann's crystal vase, he wanted to hide his face in shame.*

hide one's **head in the sand** Go to **bury** one's **head in the sand**.

hide one's **light under a bushel** to conceal one's good ideas or talents. (A biblical theme.) □ *Jane has some good ideas, but she doesn't speak very often. She hides her light under a bushel.* □ *Don't hide your light under a bushel. Share your gifts with other people.*

high and dry 1. safe; unbothered by difficulties; unscathed. (Refers to being safe from a flood.) □ *While the riot was going on, I was high and dry in my apartment.* □ *Liz came out of the argument high and dry.* **2.** abandoned; unsupported and helpless. (See also **leave** someone **high and dry**.) □ *Everyone else on the committee quit, leaving me high and dry.* □ *The company moved to Chicago, and I was left high and dry in Dallas.*

high-and-mighty self-important and arrogant. □ *I don't know why Albert is so high-and-mighty. He's no better than the rest of us.* □ *The boss acts high-and-mighty because he can fire us all.*

high as a kite Go to **(as) high as a kite**.

high man on the totem pole the person at the top of the hierarchy; the person in charge of an organization. (Informal. Compare this with **low man on the totem pole**.) □ *I don't want to talk to a secretary. I demand to talk to the high man on the totem pole.* □ *Who's in charge around here? Who's high man on the totem pole?*

high on something **1.** intoxicated with some drug. (Slang.) □ *He got thrown out of the movie because he was high on something.* □ *Bill was high on marijuana and was singing loudly.* **2.** enthusiastic about something. (Slang.) □ *Jane quit eating red meat. She's really high on fish, however.*

☐ *Bob is high on meditation. He sits and meditates for an hour each day.*

highflier a person who is ambitious or who is very likely to be successful. (Informal.) ☐ *Jack was one of the highfliers of our university year, and he is now in the foreign office.* ☐ *Tom is a highflier and has applied for the post of managing director.*

hightail it out of somewhere to run or ride a horse away from somewhere fast. (Folksy. Typically heard in western movies.) ☐ *Here comes the sheriff. We'd better hightail it out of here.* ☐ *Look at that guy go. He really hightailed it out of town.*

highways and byways [all the] roads; the major and minor roads and routes. (Both literal and figurative.) ☐ *I hope I meet you again some day on life's highways and byways.* ☐ *The city council voted to plant new trees along all the highways and byways of the town.*

hinge on something to depend on something. ☐ *This all hinges on how much risk you're willing to take.* ☐ *Whether we have the picnic hinges on the weather.*

hit a happy medium Go to strike a happy medium.

hit-and-miss AND **hit-or-miss** carelessly; aimlessly; without plan or direction. ☐ *There was no planning. It was just hit-and-miss.* ☐ *We handed out the free tickets hit-or-miss. Some people got one; others got five or six.*

hit-and-run an accident where the driver of a car strikes a person or another vehicle and speeds away without admitting to the deed or stopping to help. ☐ *Fred was injured in a hit-and-run accident.* ☐ *The state passed a law making any kind of hit-and-run accident a felony.*

hit a plateau to reach a higher level of activity, sales, production, output, etc., and then stop and remain unchanged. ☐ *When my sales hit a plateau, my boss gave me a pep talk.* ☐ *When production hit a plateau, the company built a new factory.*

hit a snag to run into a problem. (Informal.) ☐ *We've hit a snag with the building project.* ☐ *I stopped working on the roof when I hit a snag.*

hit a sour note Go to strike a sour note.

hit bottom to reach the lowest or worst point. ☐ *Our profits have hit bottom. This is our worst year ever.* ☐ *When my life hit bottom, I began to feel much better. I knew that if there was going to be any change, it would be for the better.*

hit home AND **strike home** to really make sense; [for a comment] to make a very good point. ☐ *Mary's criticism of my clothes hit home, so I changed.* ☐ *The teacher's comment struck home and the student vowed to work harder.*

hit it off (with someone**)** to quickly become good friends with someone. ☐ *Look how John hit it off with Mary.* ☐ *Yes, they really hit it off.*

hit one **close to home** Go to hit one where one lives.

hit one's **stride** Go to reach one's stride.

hit one **where** one **lives** AND **hit** one **close to home** to affect one personally and intimately. (Informal.) ☐ *Her comments really hit me where I live. Her words seemed to apply directly to me.* ☐ *I listened carefully and didn't think she hit close to home at all.*

hit-or-miss Go to hit-and-miss.

hit pay dirt to discover something of value. (Slang. Refers to discovering valuable ore.) ☐ *Sally tried a number of different jobs until she hit pay dirt.* ☐ *I tried to borrow money from a lot of different people. They all said no. Then when I went to the bank, I hit pay dirt.*

hit (someone**) below the belt** to do something unfair or unsporting to someone. (Informal. From boxing, where a blow below the belt line is not permitted.) ☐ *You really hit me below the belt when you told the boss about my tax problems.* ☐ *In business Bill is difficult to deal with. He hits below the belt.*

hit someone **hard** to affect someone's emotions strongly. (Also literal.) ☐ *The death* *of his friend hit John hard.* □ *The investor was hit hard by the falling stock prices.*

hit (someone) like a ton of bricks to surprise, startle, or shock someone. (Also literal. Informal.) □ *Suddenly, the truth hit me like a ton of bricks.* □ *The sudden tax increase hit like a ton of bricks. Everyone became angry.*

hit someone **(right) between the eyes** to become completely apparent; to surprise or impress someone. (Also literal. Informal.) □ *Suddenly, it hit me right between the eyes. John and Mary were in love.* □ *Then—as he was talking—the exact nature of the evil plan hit me between the eyes.*

hit someone **up (for** something**)** to ask someone for something. (Informal.) □ *John hit me up for a loan.* 🅃 *I told him to go hit up someone else.*

hit the books to begin to study; to study. (Slang.) □ *Well, time to hit the books.* □ *John, if you don't start hitting the books, you're going to fail.*

hit the bottle to drink alcohol to excess. (As if drinking directly from the bottle, that is, taking a *hit* from the bottle. Slang.) □ *Fred goes home and hits the bottle every night.* □ *Bill has been hitting the bottle a lot lately. I think he has a problem.*

hit the bricks to start walking; to go out into the streets. (Slang.) □ *If you want to get a job, you had better get out there and hit the bricks.* □ *I got fired today. The boss came by and told me to hit the bricks.*

hit the bull's-eye to achieve a goal perfectly. (Refers to hitting the center of a circular target. Informal.) □ *Your idea really hit the bull's-eye. Thank you!* □ *Jill has a lot of insight. She knows how to hit the bull's-eye in discussions.*

hit the ceiling to become very angry. (Also literal. Informal.) □ *My father hit the ceiling when I damaged the car.* □ *Our employer hit the ceiling when we lost an important contract.*

hit the hay AND **hit the sack** to go to bed and get some sleep. (Slang. Compare this with **sack out**.) □ *Look at the clock. It's time to hit the hay.* □ *I like to hit the sack before midnight.*

hit the high spots to do only the important, obvious, or good things. (Informal.) □ *I won't discuss the entire report. I'll just hit the high spots.* □ *First, let me hit the high spots; then I'll tell you about everything.*

hit the jackpot 1. to win at gambling. (Refers to the "jack" in playing cards.) □ *Bob hit the jackpot three times in one night.* □ *I've never hit the jackpot even once.* **2.** to have a success. □ *I hit the jackpot on a business deal.* □ *I really hit the jackpot in the library. I found just what I needed.*

hit the nail (right) on the head to do exactly the right thing; to do something in the most effective and efficient way; to identify the exact nature of something. (Also literal.) □ *You've spotted the flaw, Sally. You hit the nail on the head.* □ *Bob doesn't say much, but every now and then he hits the nail right on the head.*

hit the road to depart; to begin one's journey, especially on a road trip; to leave for home. □ *It's time to hit the road. I'll see you.* □ *We have to hit the road very early in the morning.*

hit the sack Go to **hit the hay**.

hit the skids to decline; to decrease in value. (Slang.) □ *Business usually hits the skids in the summer.* □ *Tom hit the skids after he lost his job.*

hit the spot to be exactly right; to be refreshing. (Informal.) □ *This cool drink really hits the spot.* □ *That was a delicious meal, dear. It hit the spot.*

hit (up)on something to discover or think up something. (Informal.) □ *Ann hit on the idea of baking lots of bread and freezing it.* □ *John hit upon a new way of planting corn.*

hitch a ride Go to **thumb a ride**.

hither and thither here and there. (Formal and archaic.) □ *The dog chased the poor bunny hither and thither, failing at every turn to capture it.* □ *Sharon searched* *hither and thither, hoping to find her lost Persian cat.*

hither, thither, and yon everywhere; here, there, and everywhere. (Formal and archaic.) □ *The prince looked hither, thither, and yon for the beautiful woman who had lost the glass slipper.* □ *The terrible wizard had sown the seeds of his evil vine hither, thither, and yon, and soon the evil, twisted plants began to sprout in all the land.*

hitting on all cylinders Go to firing on all cylinders.

a **hive of activity** the location where things are very busy. (Refers to the activity around a beehive.) □ *The hotel lobby was a hive of activity each morning.* □ *During the holidays, the shopping center is a hive of activity.*

hoarse as a crow Go to (as) hoarse as a crow.

Hobson's choice the choice between taking what is offered and getting nothing at all. (From the name of a stable owner in the seventeenth century who offered customers the hire of the horse nearest the door.) □ *We didn't really want that particular hotel, but it was a case of Hobson's choice. We booked very late and there was nothing else left.* □ *If you want a yellow car, it's Hobson's choice. The garage has only one.*

hoist by one's **own petard** AND **hoist with** one's **own petard** harmed or disadvantaged by an action of one's own that was meant to harm someone else. (From a line in Shakespeare's *Hamlet*.) □ *She intended to murder her brother but was hoist by her own petard when she ate the poisoned food intended for him.* □ *The vandals were hoist with their own petard when they tried to make an emergency call from the pay phone they had broken.*

hoist with one's **own petard** Go to hoist by one's own petard.

hold a grudge (against someone**)** Go to bear a grudge (against someone).

hold all the aces to be in a favorable position; to be in a controlling position. (Slang. Refers to having possession of all four aces in a card game.) □ *How can I advance in my job when my enemy holds all the aces?* □ *If I held all the aces, I'd be able to do great things.*

hold a meeting to meet; to have a meeting (of an organization). □ *We'll have to hold a meeting to make a decision.* □ *Our club held a meeting to talk about future projects.*

hold forth (on something**)** to speak at length. □ *I've never seen anyone who could hold forth so long.* □ *The professor held forth on economic theory for nearly an hour.*

hold no brief for someone or something not to care about someone or something; to dislike someone or something. □ *I hold no brief for bad typists.* □ *My father says he holds no brief for sweet potatoes.*

hold one's **breath** to stop doing something and wait until something special happens. (Also literal. Informal. Usually in the negative.) □ *BOB: The bus is going to come soon. BILL: Don't hold your breath until it does.* □ *I expect the mail to be delivered soon, but I'm not holding my breath.*

hold one's **end (of the bargain) up** to do one's part as agreed; to attend to one's responsibilities as agreed. □ *If you don't hold your end up, the whole project will fail.* 🅃 *Tom has to learn to cooperate. He must hold up his end of the bargain.*

hold one's **fire 1.** to refrain from shooting (a gun, etc.). □ *The sergeant told the soldiers to hold their fire.* □ *Please hold your fire until I get out of the way.* **2.** to postpone one's criticism or commentary. (Informal.) □ *Now, now, hold your fire until I've had a chance to explain.* □ *Hold your fire, Bill. You're too quick to complain.*

hold one's **ground** Go to stand one's ground.

hold one's **head up** to retain or display one's dignity. (Also literal.) □ *I've done nothing wrong. I can hold my head up in public.* 🅃 *I'm so embarrassed and ashamed. I'll never be able to hold up my head again.*

hold one's **own** to do as well as anyone else. ☐ *I can hold my own in a footrace any day.* ☐ *She was unable to hold her own, and she had to quit.*

hold one's **peace** to remain silent. ☐ *Bill was unable to hold his peace any longer. "Don't do it!" he cried.* ☐ *Quiet, John. Hold your peace for a little while longer.*

hold one's **temper** Go to keep one's temper.

hold one's **tongue** to refrain from speaking; to refrain from saying something unpleasant. (See also the fixed phrase Hold your tongue!) ☐ *I felt like scolding her, but I held my tongue.* ☐ *You must learn to hold your tongue, John. You can't talk to people that way.*

hold on (to someone or something**)** Go to hang on (to someone or something).

hold out for something to insist on getting something; to refuse to accept less than something. ☐ *The workers are holding out for a reasonable raise.* ☐ *The teachers are holding out for a reduction in class size.*

hold out the olive branch to offer to end a dispute and be friendly; to offer reconciliation. (The olive branch is a symbol of peace and reconciliation. A biblical reference.) ☐ *Jill was the first to hold out the olive branch after our argument.* ☐ *I always try to hold out the olive branch to someone I have hurt. Life is too short for a person to bear grudges for very long.*

hold someone **down** to try to keep someone from succeeding. (Also literal.) ☐ *I still think you're trying to hold him down.* 🅃 *I'm not trying to hold down my brother.*

hold someone **hostage** to keep someone as a hostage. ☐ *The terrorists planned to hold everyone hostage in the airplane.* ☐ *My neighbor was held hostage in his own home by a robber.*

hold someone **in high regard** to have very great respect for someone or something; to admire someone or something greatly. ☐ *We hold our employees in very high regard.* ☐ *I do not hold Bob's abilities in high regard.*

hold someone or something **in check** Go to keep someone or something in check.

hold someone or something **over** to retain someone or something (for a period of time). ☐ *The storm held John over for another day.* ☐ *The manager held the movie over for another week.*

hold someone or something **still** Go to keep someone or something still.

hold someone or something **up 1.** [with *someone*] to rob someone (figuratively or literally). ☐ *I don't eat at that restaurant any more. The food is too expensive. They really held me up the last time I ate there.* ☐ *That's the one who held me up at gunpoint.* 🅃 *The thug held up the old lady.* **2.** to detain someone or something; to make someone or something late. (Also literal meaning to keep someone or something upright.) ☐ *The traffic on the expressway held me up.* 🅃 *A storm in Boston held up our plane.*

hold someone or something **up (as an example)** to point out someone or something as a good example. (See also make an example of someone.) ☐ *I was embarrassed when the boss held me up as an example.* ☐ *I don't like for anyone to hold me up like that.* 🅃 *The teacher held up the leaf as an example of a typical compound leaf.*

hold someone's **attention** to keep someone's attention; to keep someone interested. ☐ *The boring teacher could not hold the students' attention.* ☐ *The mystery novel held my attention and I couldn't put it down.*

hold something **against** someone to blame something on someone; to bear a grudge against someone; to resent someone. (Also literal.) ☐ *Your brother is mean to me, but I can't hold it against you.* ☐ *You're holding something against me. What is it?*

hold still Go to keep still.

hold still for something Go to stand still for something.

hold the fort to take care of a place, such as a store or one's home. (Refers to defending a fort against attackers. Informal. From western movies.) ☐ *I'm going next door to visit Mrs. Jones. You stay here and hold the fort.* ☐ *You should open the store at eight o'clock and hold the fort until I get there at ten.*

hold the line (at someone or something**)** to limit the number of people or things; to limit (something) to someone or something. (See also **draw the line (at** something**)**.) ☐ *The room will seat fifty, but I think you should hold the line at forty.* ☐ *The Browns and the Smiths could be invited, but I think we ought to hold the line at the Browns.* ☐ *Okay, we'll hold the line.*

hold true [for something] to be true; [for something] to remain true. ☐ *Does this rule hold true all the time?* ☐ *Yes, it holds true no matter what.*

hold up to endure; to last a long time. ☐ *How long will this cloth hold up?* ☐ *I want my money back for this chair. It isn't holding up well.*

hold up (for someone or something**)** Go to **wait up (for** someone or something**)**.

hold up on something to delay doing something. ☐ *Please hold up on the project. We've run out of money.* ☐ *I have to hold up on my reading because I broke my glasses.*

hold with something to accept or agree with something. (Folksy. Usually in the negative.) ☐ *My father doesn't hold with fancy clothes.* ☐ *I don't hold with too many X rays.*

Hold your horses! Wait a minute and be reasonable!; Do not run off wildly! (Folksy. From western movies.) ☐ *Now, hold your horses, John. Be reasonable for a change.* ☐ *Don't get so mad. Just hold your horses.*

Hold your tongue! Be quiet!; Stop saying what you are saying! ☐ *Hold your tongue! I've heard enough of your insults.* ☐ *That's enough rudeness for today! Hold your tongue!*

a **hole in one 1.** an instance of hitting a golf ball into a hole in only one try. (From the game of golf.) ☐ *John made a hole in one yesterday.* ☐ *I've never gotten a hole in one.* **2.** an instance of succeeding the first time. ☐ *It worked the first time I tried it—a hole in one.* ☐ *Bob got a hole in one on that sale. A lady walked in the door, and he sold her a car in five minutes.*

hole up (somewhere**)** to hide somewhere; to live in hiding somewhere. (Slang. Typically in western or gangster movies.) ☐ *The old man is holed up in the mountains, waiting for the war to end.* ☐ *If we are going to hole up for the winter, we'll need lots of food.*

holier-than-thou excessively pious; acting as though one is more virtuous than other people. ☐ *Jack always adopts a holier-than-thou attitude to other people, but people say he has been in prison.* ☐ *Jane used to be holier-than-thou, but she is marrying Tom, who is a crook.*

home in (on someone or something**)** to aim exactly at something and move toward it. ☐ *The sheriff walked into the room and homed in on the horse thief.* ☐ *The plane homed in on the beacon at the airport.* ☐ *First, you must set your goal and then home in.*

honest and aboveboard Go to **aboveboard**.

Honest to God. Go to **Honest to goodness**.

Honest to goodness. AND **Honest to God.; Honest to Pete.** I speak the truth. (Some people may object to the use of *God* in this phrase.) ☐ *Did he really say that? Honest to goodness?* ☐ *Honest to Pete, I've been to the moon.* ☐ *I've been there, too—honest to God.*

Honest to Pete. Go to **Honest to goodness**.

The **honeymoon is over.** The early pleasant beginning has ended. ☐ *Okay, the honeymoon is over. It's time to settle down and do some hard work.* ☐ *I knew the honeymoon was over when they started yelling at me to work faster.*

honor someone's **check** to accept someone's personal check. ☐ *The clerk at the store wouldn't honor my check. I had to pay cash.* ☐ *The bank didn't honor your check when I tried to deposit it. Please give me cash.*

hooked (on something**) 1.** addicted to a drug or something similar. (Slang.) ☐ *Jenny is hooked on cocaine.* ☐ *She was not hooked on anything before that.* ☐ *John is hooked on coffee.* **2.** enthusiastic about something; supportive of something. ☐ *Mary is hooked on football. She never misses a game.* ☐ *Jane is so happy! She's hooked on life.*

hoot and holler to shout in disapproval; to call and shout one's displeasure. ☐ *After the umpire rendered his decision, the spectators hooted and hollered their thoughts on the matter.* ☐ *It's hard to play a good game of basketball when the fans are hooting and hollering at everything you do.*

a **hop, skip, and a jump** a short distance. (Also literal.) ☐ *Her house was just a hop, skip, and a jump away from mine, so we visited often.* ☐ *Our town is just a hop, skip, and a jump from a big city, so we get the advantages of both city and country life.*

Hop to it! Move fast!; Get started! (Slang.) ☐ *Come on, you guys, move it! Hop to it!* ☐ *Hop to it, Bill. You look like you're loafing.*

hope against (all) hope to have hope even when the situation appears to be hopeless. ☐ *We hope against all hope that she'll see the right thing to do and do it.* ☐ *There is little point in hoping against hope, except that it makes you feel better.*

hopeless at doing something incapable of doing something. ☐ *Tom is hopeless at cooking.* ☐ *Sally is hopeless at dusting. She hates it.*

hopped up 1. intoxicated with drugs or alcohol; stimulated by drugs or alcohol. (Slang.) ☐ *The old man was hopped up again. He was addicted to opium.* ☐ *John usually gets hopped up on the weekends.* **2.** excited; enthusiastic. (Slang.) ☐ *What are you hopped up about now? You're certainly cheery.* ☐ *I always get hopped up when I think of mountain climbing.*

horn in (on someone or something**) 1.** [with *someone*] to attempt to displace someone. (Informal.) ☐ *I'm going to ask Sally to the party. Don't you dare try to horn in on me!* ☐ *I wouldn't think of horning in.* **2.** [with *something*] to attempt to participate in something without invitation or consent. ☐ *Are you trying to horn in on my conversation with Sally?* ☐ *I hope you are not trying to horn in on our party.*

horse and buggy AND **horse and carriage** a carriage pulled by a horse, as opposed to a modern automobile. (A symbol of old-fashionedness or out-of-dateness. Particularly with *go out with*, as in the examples below.) ☐ *That kind of clothing went out with the horse and buggy.* ☐ *I thought suspenders went out with the horse and carriage, but I see them everywhere now.*

horse and carriage Go to horse and buggy.

horse around to play around; to waste time in frivolous activities. (Informal.) ☐ *Stop horsing around and get to work.* ☐ *The children were on the playground horsing around when the bell rang.*

a **horse of a different color** Go to a horse of another color.

a **horse of another color** AND a **horse of a different color** another matter altogether. ☐ *I was talking about trees, not bushes. Bushes are a horse of another color.* ☐ *Gambling is not the same as investing in the stock market. It's a horse of a different color.*

horse sense common sense; practical thinking. ☐ *Jack is no scholar but he has a lot of horse sense.* ☐ *Horse sense tells me I should not be involved in that project.*

hot and bothered 1. excited; anxious. (Informal.) ☐ *Now don't get hot and bothered. Take it easy.* ☐ *John is hot and bothered about the tax increase.* **2.** amorous; interested in romance or sex. (Informal and euphemistic. Use with caution.) ☐ *John gets hot and bothered whenever Mary comes into the room.* ☐ *The dog seems hot and bothered. I think it's that time of the year again.*

hot and heavy referring to serious passion or emotions. ☐ *Things were getting a little hot and heavy so Ellen asked to be taken home.* ☐ *The movie had one hot and heavy scene after another. Pretty soon it got to be a joke.*

hot as fire Go to (as) hot as fire.

hot as hell Go to (as) hot as hell.

hot on something enthusiastic about something; very much interested in something; knowledgeable about something. (Informal.) □ *Meg's hot on animal rights.* □ *Jean is hot on modern ballet just now.*

hot under the collar very angry. □ *The boss was really hot under the collar when you told him you lost the contract.* □ *I get hot under the collar every time I think about it.*

hotfoot it out of somewhere to run away from a place. (Folksy. Compare this with **high tail it out of** somewhere.) □ *Did you see Tom hotfoot it out of the office when the boss came in?* □ *Things are looking bad. I think we had better hotfoot it out of here.*

How goes it (with you)? Hello, how are you? (Informal.) □ *Hi, Mary. How goes it with you?* □ *How goes it, Bill?*

How's it going? How are you? (Informal.) □ *Hi, Bob. How's it going?* □ *How's it going? Everything all right?*

How's the world (been) treating you? How are you? □ *Hi, Jane, How's the world treating you?* □ *How's the world been treating you, Bill?*

a **hue and cry** a loud public protest or opposition. □ *There was a hue and cry when the city government tried to build houses on the playing field.* □ *The decision to close the local school started a real hue and cry.*

huff and puff to breathe very hard; to pant as one exerts effort. □ *John came up the stairs huffing and puffing.* □ *He huffed and puffed and finally got up the steep hill.*

hung up (on someone or something**)** obsessed with someone or something; devoted to someone or something. (Slang.) □ *John is really hung up on Mary.* □ *She's hung up, too. See how she smiles when he enters the room.*

hunger for something to have a strong desire for something. □ *All her life, Mary has had a hunger for affection.* □ *The prisoner was consumed with a hunger for freedom.*

hungry as a bear Go to (as) hungry as a bear.

hungry as a hunter Go to (as) hungry as a hunter.

hungry for something desiring something. □ *The orphan was hungry for the warmth of a family.* □ *Bill is hungry for knowledge and always studying.*

hunt-and-peck a slow "system" of typing where one searches for a letter and then presses it. (From the movement used by fowls when feeding.) □ *I never learned to type right. All I do is hunt-and-peck.* □ *I can't type. I just hunt-and-peck, but I get the job done—eventually.*

hunt high and low (for someone or something**)** AND **look high and low (for** someone or something**)**; **search high and low (for** someone or something**)** to look carefully in every possible place for someone or something. □ *We looked high and low for the right teacher.* □ *The Smiths are searching high and low for the home of their dreams.*

hunt someone or something **up** Go to **look** someone or something **up**.

hurl an insult (at someone**)** to direct an insult at someone; to say something insulting directly to someone. □ *Anne hurled an insult at Bob that made him very angry.* □ *If you two would stop hurling insults, we could have a serious discussion.*

a **hush fell over** someone or something a sudden silence enveloped something, someone, or a group. □ *As the conductor raised his arms, a hush fell over the audience.* □ *The coach shouted and a hush fell over the locker room.*

hush money money paid as a bribe to persuade someone to remain silent and not reveal certain information. □ *Bob gave his younger sister hush money so that she wouldn't tell Jane that he had gone to the movies with Sue.* □ *The crooks paid Fred hush money to keep their whereabouts secret.*

Hush your mouth! Please be quiet! (Not very polite.) □ *I've heard enough of that talk. Hush your mouth!* □ *Now, hush your mouth! You know you really should not talk about other people's problems like that!*

hustle and bustle confusion, hurry, and bother. □ *The hustle and bustle of the big city is especially annoying in the hot days of summer.* □ *Fred seems to enjoy the hustle and bustle of traffic during rush hour, so he is a very happy bus driver.*

I

I didn't catch your name. No one told me your name [or I have forgotten it]. (A carrying on of a conversation that has just started—if one hasn't been introduced properly—or simply finding out someone's name.) □ *I'm sorry, but I didn't catch your name.* □ *I'm Wally Ott. I didn't catch your name.*

I just have this feeling I have a premonition about this; I have a strange feeling about this. □ *I really don't know that something is wrong. I just have this feeling.* □ *I just have this feeling that she is not telling us the truth.*

if looks could kill <a catch phrase said when someone makes a frown at someone or when someone casts a dirty look.> □ *Did you see the way she looked at me? If looks could kill....* □ *If looks could kill. What a nasty glare.*

if not if that is not [the case]; if that is not so. □ *If not cleaned, the clock will stop running.* □ *He should be here at noon. If not, we will eat without him.*

if push comes to shove if the situation really becomes difficult; if matters escalate into a strong argument. (See also when push comes to shove.) □ *If push comes to shove, I am ready to be more aggressive.* □ *If push comes to shove, I am sure that our senator will help out.*

if so if that is [the case]; if that is so. □ *She might be late. If so, we will eat without her.* □ *She is supposed to be all right. If so, we have nothing to worry about.*

If the shoe fits, wear it. You should pay attention to advice or criticism if it applies to you. (Proverb.) □ *Some people here need to be quiet. If the shoe fits, wear it.* □ *This doesn't apply to everyone. If the shoe fits, wear it.*

if worst comes to worst in the worst possible situation; if things really get bad. □ *If worst comes to worst, we'll hire someone to help you.* □ *If worst comes to worst, I'll have to borrow some money.*

ill at ease uneasy; anxious. □ *I feel ill at ease about the interview.* □ *You look ill at ease. Please relax.*

ill-disposed to doing something not friendly; not favorable; not well disposed. □ *I am ill-disposed to doing hard labor.* □ *The police chief was ill-disposed to discussing the details of the case to the news reporters.*

I'll drink to that! I agree with that! (Informal. As if joining in with drinks following a toast.) □ *Great idea! I'll drink to that.* □ *That's a fine suggestion. I'll drink to that.*

ill-gotten gains money or other possessions acquired in a dishonest or illegal fashion. □ *Fred cheated at cards and is now living on his ill-gotten gains.* □ *Mary is also enjoying her ill-gotten gains. She deceived an old lady into leaving her money in her will.*

I'll (try to) catch you later. I will try to talk with you or meet with you at some future time. (Informal.) □ *I don't have time to talk to you now. I'll try to catch you later.* □ *Hi, I'm leaving. I'll catch you later.*

ill will hostile feelings or intentions. □ *I hope you do not have any ill will toward me because of our argument.* □ *Dave felt such ill will toward his family that he left his fortune to his best friend.*

I'm awful at names. Go to I'm terrible at names.

I'm damned if I do and damned if I don't. There are problems if I do something and problems if I don't do it. □ *I can't win. I'm damned if I do and damned if I don't* □ *No matter whether I go or stay, I am in trouble. I'm damned if I do and damned if I don't.*

(I'm) sorry. <an expression used to excuse oneself politely or apologize, especially when one has collided with someone, when one has offended someone, or to ask someone to repeat what has been said.> □ *"I'm sorry," I said to the woman I bumped into.* □ *I'm sorry, what did you say? I couldn't hear you.*

I'm terrible at names. AND **I'm awful at names.** I can't seem to remember anyone's name. (Said as an apology to someone whose name you have forgotten.) □ *I'm terrible at names. Please tell me yours again.* □ *Haven't we met already? I'm awful at names.*

Imagine that! Is that so?; How interesting and strange! (Said when one hears something that is interesting. Often sarcastic.) □ *Fell out of bed. Imagine that!* □ *She's late again. Imagine that!*

immediate occupancy [of an apartment or house] ready to be moved into at this moment. □ *This house is for immediate occupancy. You can move in today if you want.* □ *It's empty, so that means immediate occupancy.*

implicate someone **(in** something**)** to suggest that someone is involved in something. □ *The mayor was implicated in the murder.* □ *Jane's essay implicated her teacher in the cheating scandal.*

in a bad mood sad; depressed; grouchy; with low spirits. □ *He's in a bad mood. He may yell at you.* □ *Please try to cheer me up. I'm in a bad mood.*

in a bad way in a critical or bad state. (Can refer to health, finances, mood, etc.) □ *Mr. Smith is in a bad way. He may have to go to the hospital.* □ *My bank account is in a bad way. It needs some help from a millionaire.* □ *My life is in a bad way, and I'm depressed about it.*

in abeyance in reserve. □ *Until the judge determined that the evidence could be used in the trial, it was held in abeyance.* □ *I kept my opinion in abeyance.*

in a bind AND **in a jam** in a tight or difficult situation; stuck on a problem. (Note: *In* can be replaced with *into* to show movement toward or into the state described by *bind* or *jam.* Especially *get into.* See the examples below.) □ *I'm in a bind. I owe a lot of money.* □ *Whenever I get into a jam, I ask my supervisor for help.* □ *When things get busy around here, we get in a bind. We could use another helper.*

in accordance with something in agreement with; in conformity with. □ *In accordance with our discussion, I have prepared a contract.* □ *I did this in accordance with your request.*

in a (constant) state of flux Go to in flux.

in a coon's age AND **in a month of Sundays** in a very long time. (Folksy. Usually negative. The *coon* is a *raccoon.*) □ *How are you? I haven't seen you in a coon's age.* □ *I haven't had a piece of apple pie this good in a coon's age.* □ *John hasn't seen a movie in a month of Sundays.*

in addition (to something**)** additionally; further; moreover; as an additional thing or person. □ *In addition, I would like for you to sweep the kitchen floor.* □ *I put the books away, and in addition, I cleaned up my desk.*

in a dead heat [finishing a race] at exactly the same time; tied. □ *The two horses finished the race in a dead heat.* □ *They ended the contest in a dead heat.*

in advance [of something given, paid, or provided] before it is due. □ *The bill isn't due for a month, but I paid it in advance.* □ *I want my pay in advance.*

in a family way AND **in the family way** pregnant. (Informal.) □ *I've heard that Mrs. Smith is in a family way.* □ *Our dog is in the family way.*

in a fix in a bad situation. (Informal. *In* can be replaced with *into.* See **in a bind** and the examples below.) □ *I really got my-*

self into a fix. I owe a lot of money on my taxes. □ *John is in a fix because he lost his wallet.* □ *John got into a fix.*

in a flash quickly; immediately. (Informal.) □ *I'll be there in a flash.* □ *It happened in a flash. Suddenly my wallet was gone.*

in a fog preoccupied; not paying attention to what is going on around one; not alert. □ *Jane always seems to be in a fog.* □ *When I get up, I'm in a fog for an hour.*

in a fool's paradise in a condition of seeming happiness that will not last because it is based on false assumptions. □ *They think they can live on love alone, but they are living in a fool's paradise.* □ *The inhabitants of the island feel politically secure, but they are living in a fool's paradise. They could be invaded at any time.*

in agreement in harmony; agreeing. □ *The business partners were never in agreement about marketing strategies.* □ *Because the partners were not in agreement, the business failed.*

in a haze in a state of confusion. □ *After being hit in the head by the bat, Bill was in a haze.* □ *After surgery, I was in a haze until the anesthetic wore off.*

in a huff in an angry or offended manner. (Informal. *In* can be replaced with *into.* See in a bind and the examples below.) □ *He heard what we had to say, then left in a huff.* □ *She came in a huff and ordered us to bring her something to eat.* □ *She gets into a huff very easily.*

in a jam Go to in a bind.

in a jiffy very fast; very soon. (Slang.) □ *Just wait a minute. I'll be there in a jiffy.* □ *I'll be finished in a jiffy.*

in a lather flustered; excited and agitated. (*In* can be replaced with *into.* See in a bind and the examples below.) □ *Now, calm down. Don't be in a lather.* □ *I always get in a lather when I'm late.* □ *I get into a lather easily.*

in a little bit in a small amount of time; soon. □ *I will be there in a little bit. Please wait.* □ *In a little bit, we can go outside and play.*

in (all) good conscience having good motives; displaying motives that will not result in a guilty conscience. □ *In all good conscience, I could not recommend that you buy this car.* □ *In good conscience, she could not accept the reward. She had only been acting as any good citizen should.*

in all one's **born days** ever; in all one's life. (Folksy.) □ *I've never been so angry in all my born days.* □ *Have you ever heard such a thing in all your born days?*

in all probability very likely; almost certainly. □ *He'll be here on time in all probability.* □ *In all probability, they'll finish the work today.*

in a mad rush in a hurry; frantically. □ *I ran around all day today in a mad rush, looking for a present for Bill.* □ *Why are you always in a mad rush?*

in a month of Sundays Go to in a coon's age.

in and of itself itself; considering it alone. □ *The idea in and of itself is not bad, but the side issues introduce many difficulties.* □ *Her action, in and of itself, caused us no problem.*

in a nutshell in a few words; briefly; concisely. (Informal.) □ *I don't have time for the whole explanation. Please give it to me in a nutshell.* □ *Well, in a nutshell, we have to work late.*

in any case AND **in any event** no matter what happens. □ *I intend to be home by supper time, but in any case by eight o'clock.* □ *In any event, I'll see you this evening.*

in any event Go to in any case.

in a pinch in a situation where there is but one choice; in a situation where there is not time to locate another choice. □ *I don't care for this kind of paint, but it will do in a pinch.* □ *Tom is not the best choice around, but he will have to do in a pinch.*

in apple-pie order in very good order; very well organized. (Folksy. *In* can be replaced with *into.* See in a bind and the examples below.) □ *Please put everything in apple-pie order before you leave.* □ *I always put my desk in apple-pie order every* *evening.* □ *I've put my entire life into apple-pie order.*

in a (pretty) pickle AND **in a real pickle** in a mess; in trouble. (Informal. *In* can be replaced with *into.* See the note at **in a bind** and the examples below.) □ *John has gotten himself into a pickle. He has two dates for the party.* □ *Now we are in a real pickle. We are out of gas.*

in a quandary uncertain about what to do; confused. (*In* can be replaced with *into.* See the note at **in a bind** and the examples below.) □ *Mary was in a quandary about what college to go to.* □ *I couldn't decide what to do. I was in such a quandary.* □ *I got myself into a quandary.*

in a real pickle Go to **in a (pretty) pickle.**

in arrears overdue; late, especially in reference to bills and money. □ *This bill is three months in arrears. It must be paid immediately.* □ *I was in arrears on my car payments, so the bank threatened to take my car away.*

in a rut Go to **(stuck) in a rut.**

in a sense in a way; sort of. □ *In a sense, cars make life better.* □ *But, in a sense, they also make life worse.*

in a snit in a fit of anger or irritation. (Slang. *In* can be replaced with *into.* See the note at **in a bind** and the examples below.) □ *Mrs. Smith threw on her coat and left in a snit.* □ *Here comes John—in a snit again—as usual.* □ *Don't get into a snit.*

in a split second in just an instant. (Informal.) □ *The lightning struck, and in a split second the house burst into flames.* □ *Just wait. I'll be there in a split second.*

in a stage whisper in a loud whisper that everyone can hear. □ *John said in a stage whisper, "This play is boring."* □ *"When do we eat?" asked Billy in a stage whisper.*

in a stew (about someone or something**)** upset or bothered about someone or something. (Informal. *In* can be replaced with *into.* See **in a bind** and the examples below.) □ *I'm in such a stew about my dog. She ran away last night.* □ *Now, now. Don't be in a stew. She'll be back when she gets hungry.* □ *I hate to get into a stew about my friends.*

in a stupor in a dazed condition; in a condition in which one cannot concentrate or think. □ *The drunk driver walked away from the car accident in a stupor.* □ *In the morning, Mary remains in a stupor until she drinks coffee.*

in a (tight) spot caught in a problem; in a jam. (Informal. *In* can be replaced with *into.* See the note at **in a bind** and the examples below.) □ *Look, John, I'm in a tight spot. Can you lend me twenty dollars?* □ *I'm in a spot too. I need $300.* □ *I have never gotten into a tight spot.*

in a tizzy in an excited and confused condition. □ *John is in a tizzy because we're an hour late.* □ *Mary was in a tizzy when she couldn't find her keys.*

in at the kill Go to **in on the kill.**

in a vicious circle in a situation in which the solution of one problem leads to a second problem, and the solution of the second problem brings back the first problem, etc. (*In* can be replaced with *into.* See the note at **in a bind** and the examples below.) □ *Life is so strange. I seem to be in a vicious circle most of the time.* □ *I put lemon in my tea to make it sour, then sugar to make it sweet. I'm in a vicious circle.* □ *Don't let your life get into a vicious circle.*

in awe (of someone or something**)** fearful and respectful of someone or something. □ *Everyone in the country was in awe of the king and queen.* □ *I love my new car. In fact, I'm in awe of it.* □ *When I first saw the house, I just stood there in awe.*

in a word said simply; concisely said. □ *Mrs. Smith is—in a word—haughty.* □ *In a word, the play flopped.*

in a world of one's **own** aloof; detached; self-centered. (*In* can be replaced with *into.* See the note at **in a bind** and the examples below.) □ *John lives in a world of his own. He has very few friends.* □ *Mary walks around in a world of her own, but she's very intelligent.* □ *When she's thinking, she drifts into a world of her own.*

in bad faith without sincerity; with bad or dishonest intent; with duplicity. (Compare this with **in good faith.**) □ *It appears that you acted in bad faith and didn't live up to the terms of our agreement.* □ *If you do things in bad faith, you'll get a bad reputation.*

in bad sorts in a bad humor; in a bad mood. □ *Bill is in bad sorts today. He's very grouchy.* □ *I try to be extra nice to people when I'm in bad sorts.*

in bad taste AND **in poor taste** rude; vulgar; obscene. □ *Mrs. Franklin felt that your joke was in bad taste.* □ *We found the play to be in poor taste, so we walked out in the middle of the second act.*

in bad (with someone**)** having someone against you; having gotten into trouble with someone. (Informal. Compare this with **in good (with** someone**).**) □ *Sally is in bad with her parents for failing algebra.* □ *She's really in bad. She has real trouble.*

in behalf of someone AND **in** someone's **behalf; on behalf of** someone**; on** someone's **behalf; in** someone's **name** [doing something] as someone's agent; [doing something] in place of someone; for the benefit of someone. □ *I'm writing in behalf of Mr. Smith, who has applied for a job with your company.* □ *I'm calling on behalf of my client, who wishes to complain about your actions.* □ *I'm calling in her behalf.* □ *I'm acting on your behalf.*

in between located in the middle of two things, states, or possibilities. □ *It's not hot or cold. It's in between.* □ *A sandwich consists of two slices of bread with some other food in between.*

in black and white official, in writing or printing. (Said of something, such as an agreement or a statement, which has been recorded in writing. *In* can be replaced with *into.* See the note at **in a bind** and the examples below.) □ *I have it in black and white that I'm entitled to three weeks of vacation each year.* □ *It says right here in black and white that oak trees make acorns.* □ *Please put the agreement into black and white.*

in bloom with many flowers; at the peak of blooming. □ *The garden is beautiful when it is in bloom.* □ *The roses are in bloom and they smell so sweet!*

in blossom with many flowers opening; **in bloom.** □ *The peonies are in blossom early this spring.* □ *If the daffodils are in blossom, spring is on the way.*

in brief briefly; concisely. □ *The whole story, in brief, is that Bob failed algebra because he did not study.* □ *Please tell me in brief why you want this job.*

in broad daylight publicly visible in the daytime. □ *The thief stole the car in broad daylight.* □ *There they were, selling drugs in broad daylight.*

in bulk in large quantities or amounts, rather than smaller, more convenient quantities or amounts. □ *Jane always bought office supplies in bulk to save money.* □ *Dave purchased cereal in bulk because his family used so much of it.*

in cahoots (with someone**)** in conspiracy with someone; in league with someone. (Folksy.) □ *The mayor is in cahoots with the construction company that got the contract for the new building.* □ *Those two have been in cahoots before.*

in care of someone [to be delivered to someone] through someone or by way of someone. (Indicates that mail is to be delivered to a person at some other person's address.) □ *Bill Jones is living at his father's house. Address the letter to Bill in care of Mr. John Jones.* □ *Bill said, "Please send me my mail in care of my father at his address."*

in case in the event (that). □ *What do we do in case the building catches fire?* □ *We should close the windows just in case it rains.*

in case of something in the event of something. (Compare this with **in the case of** someone or something; **in case** something happens.) □ *Please leave the building at once in case of fire.* □ *Please take your raincoat in case of rain.*

in case something **happens** in the event that something takes place. (Compare this with **in case of** something.) □ *She carries an umbrella in case it rains.* □ *I have some aspirin in my office in case I get a headache.*

in character typical of someone's behavior. □ *For Tom to shout that way wasn't at all in character. He's usually quite pleasant.* □ *It was quite in character for Sally to walk away angry.*

in clover with good fortune; in a very good situation, especially financially. (Slang.) □ *If I get this contract, I'll be in clover for the rest of my life.* □ *I have very little money saved, so when I retire I won't exactly be in clover.*

in cold blood without feeling; with cruel intent. (Informal or slang. Frequently said of a crime, especially murder.) □ *The killer walked up and shot the woman in cold blood.* □ *How insulting! For a person to say something like that in cold blood is just horrible.*

in cold storage stored away for future use; in an out-of-the-way place. (Also literal.) □ *I have had this special gift in cold storage for an occasion such as this.* □ *Todd had been keeping himself in cold storage, trying to study for his exams.*

in concert (with someone**)** in cooperation with someone; with the aid of someone. □ *Mrs. Smith planned the party in concert with her sister.* □ *In concert they planned a lovely event.*

in condition AND **in shape** in good health; strong and healthy. (Used only with people. Compare this with **in good shape**. *In* can be replaced with *into.* See the note at **in a bind** and the examples below.) □ *Bob exercises frequently, so he's in condition.* □ *If I were in shape, I could run faster and farther.* □ *I'm not healthy. I have to try to get into shape.*

in consequence (of something**)** as a result of something; because of something. □ *In consequence of the storm, there was no electricity.* □ *The wind blew down the wires. In consequence, we had no electricity.*

in consideration of something in return for something; as a result of something. (Compare this with **out of consideration (for** someone or something**)**.) □ *In consideration of your many years of service, we are pleased to present you with this gold watch.* □ *In consideration of your efforts, here is a check for $3,000.*

in contempt (of court) disrespect for a judge or for courtroom procedures. □ *The bailiff ejected the lawyer who was held in contempt.* □ *The judge found the juror in contempt of court when she screamed at the attorney.*

in creation Go to on earth.

in custody of someone or something AND **in** someone's or something's **custody** the condition of being kept guarded by someone or some group. □ *The suspect was in the sheriff's custody awaiting a trial.* □ *The prisoner is in the custody of the state.*

in debt having debts; having much debt; owing money. □ *Mary is deeply in debt.* □ *I am in debt to the bank for my car loan.*

in deep 1. deeply involved. □ *John and Mary have been seeing each other for months now. They are really in deep.* □ *Bill loves the theater. He's definitely in deep. He tries out for all the plays and gets into many of them.* **2.** deeply in debt. □ *Bill owes a lot of money to the bank. He's really in deep.* □ *John is in deep with his stockbroker.*

in deep water in a dangerous or vulnerable situation; in a serious situation; in trouble. (Refers to swimming in or falling into water that is over one's head. See also **go off the deep end**. *In* can be replaced with *into.* See the note at **in a bind** and the examples below.) □ *John is having trouble with his taxes. He's in deep water.* □ *Bill is in deep water in algebra class. He's almost failing.* □ *He really got himself into deep water.*

in defiance (of someone or something**)** against someone's will or against instructions; in bold resistance to someone or someone's orders. □ *Jane spent the afternoon in the park, in defiance of her mother's instructions.* □ *She did it in defiance of her mother.* □ *She has done a number of things in defiance lately.*

in denial in a state of refusing to believe something that is true. □ *Mary was in denial about her illness and refused treatment.* □ *Tom doesn't think he's an alcoholic because he's still in denial.*

in detail with lots of details; giving all the details. □ *I explained the policy to the customer in detail.* □ *We planned the entire project in great detail.*

in disguise hidden behind a disguise; looking like something else. □ *Santa Claus was really the little child's father in disguise.* □ *What I thought was terrible turned out to be a blessing in disguise!*

in drag in the clothing of the opposite sex. (Usually refers to a man wearing women's clothing.) □ *The actor played the woman's part in drag.* □ *We all went to the costume party dressed in drag.*

in due course AND **in due time; in good time; in the course of time; in time** in a normal or expected amount of time. □ *The roses will bloom in due course.* □ *The vice president will become president in due course.* □ *I'll retire in due time.* □ *Just wait, my dear. All in good time.* □ *It'll all work out in the course of time.* □ *In time, things will improve.*

in due time Go to **in due course**.

in Dutch (with someone**)** in trouble with someone. (Informal. *In* can be replaced with *into.* See **in a bind** and the examples below.) □ *I'm in Dutch with my parents for my low grades.* □ *You're in Dutch quite a bit.* □ *Don't get into Dutch with anyone.*

in earnest sincerely. □ *This time I'll try in earnest.* □ *She spoke in earnest, and many people believed her.*

in effect 1. in existence; applicable. □ *A reduced rate at the hotel is in effect until the end of the year.* □ *The curfew is in effect for all minors.* **2.** producing a particular effect; effectively. □ *In effect, this new law will raise taxes for most people.* □ *This policy harms domestic manufacturers. In effect, all our clothing will be made in foreign countries.*

in essence basically; essentially. □ *I have lots of detailed advice for you, but in essence, I want you to do the best you can.* □ *In essence, lightning is just a giant spark of electricity.*

in exchange (for someone or something**)** in return for someone or something. □ *They gave us two of our prisoners in exchange for two of theirs.* □ *I gave him chocolate in exchange for some licorice.* □ *John gave Mary a book and got a sweater in exchange.*

in existence now existing; currently and actually being. □ *The tiger may not be in existence in a few decades.* □ *All the oil in existence will not last the world for another century.*

in fact in reality; really; actually. □ *I'm over forty. In fact, I'm forty-six.* □ *This is a very good computer. In fact, it's the best.*

in fashion fitting in well with the clothing that has been designed for a particular season of a particular year; fashionable. □ *I understand that long skirts are in fashion this year.* □ *I always want to find out what styles are in fashion so I can avoid them.*

in favor of someone Go to **in** someone's **favor**.

in favor (of someone or something**)** approving, supporting, or endorsing someone or something. (See also **in** someone's **favor**.) □ *Are you in favor of lower taxes?* □ *Of course, I'm in favor.*

in fear and trembling with anxiety or fear; with dread. □ *In fear and trembling, I went into the room to take the test.* □ *The witness left the courtroom in fear and trembling.*

in fine feather in good humor; in good health. (*In* can be replaced with *into.* See the note at **in a bind** and the examples below.) □ *Hello, John. You appear to be in fine feather.* □ *Of course I'm in fine feather. I get lots of sleep.* □ *Good food and lots of sleep put me into fine feather.*

in flight while flying. □ *A passenger became ill in flight and the pilot had to return to the airport.* □ *I really don't care to eat in flight. I am too nervous.*

in flux AND **in a (constant) state of flux** in constant change; changing. □ *I can't* *describe my job because it's in a constant state of flux.* □ *The price of gold is in flux.*

in force in a very large group. (See also **out in force**.) □ *The entire group arrived in force.* □ *The mosquitoes will attack in force this evening.*

in for something due to receive a surprise; due to receive punishment. (When the *something* is *it*, the *it* usually means punishment.) □ *I hope I'm not in for any surprises when I get home.* □ *Tommy, you broke my baseball bat. You're really in for it!*

in full swing in progress; operating or running without restraint. (*In* can be replaced with *into*. See the note at **in a bind** and the examples below.) □ *We can't leave now! The party is in full swing.* □ *Our program to help the starving people is in full swing. You should see results soon.* □ *Just wait until our project gets into full swing.*

in general referring to the entire class being discussed; speaking of the entire range of possibilities; in most situations or circumstances. □ *I like vegetables in general, but not beets.* □ *In general, I prefer a hotel room on a lower floor, but will take a higher room if it's special.*

in good condition Go to **in good shape**.

in good faith with good and honest intent; with sincerity. (Compare this with **in bad faith**.) □ *We are convinced you were acting in good faith, even though you made a serious error.* □ *I think you didn't sign the contract in good faith. You never intended to carry out our agreement.*

in good hands in the safe, competent care of someone. □ *Don't worry. Your children are in good hands. Sally is a good babysitter.* □ *Your car is in good hands. My mechanics are factory-trained.*

in good repair in good condition; operating well; well taken care of. (Usually said of a thing rather than a person.) □ *The house is in good repair and ought to attract a number of potential buyers.* □ *If the car were in good repair, it would run more smoothly.*

in good shape AND **in good condition** physically and functionally sound and sturdy. (Used for both people and things. Compare this with **in condition**. *In* can be replaced with *into*. See the note at **in a bind** and the examples below.) □ *This car isn't in good shape. I'd like to have one that's in better condition.* □ *Mary is in good condition. She works hard to keep healthy.* □ *You have to make an effort to get into good shape.*

in good spirits happy and cheerful; positive and looking toward the future, despite unhappy circumstances. □ *The patient is in good spirits and that will speed her recovery.* □ *Tom wasn't in very good spirits after he heard the bad news.*

in good time 1. quickly; in a short amount of time. □ *We traveled from Mexico to Texas in good time.* □ *I've never been able to make that trip in good time.* **2.** Go to **in due course**.

in good (with someone**)** in someone's favor; to **have pull with** someone. (Compare this with **in bad (with** someone**)**.) □ *I can ask Mary a favor. I'm in good with her.* □ *Well, I'm not in good with her.* □ *I don't know Mary. How do I go about getting in good?*

in great demand wanted by many people; eagerly sought after. □ *Liz is in great demand as a singer.* □ *Mary's paintings are in great demand.*

in great haste very fast; in a big hurry. □ *John always did his homework in great haste.* □ *Why not take time and do it right? Don't do everything in great haste.*

in hand controlled; under control. □ *I thought I had my destiny in hand, but then fate played a trick on me.* □ *Don't worry about me. I have everything in hand.*

in heat in a period of sexual excitement; in estrus. (*Estrus* is the period of time in which females are most willing to breed. This expression is usually used for animals. It has been used for humans in a joking sense. *In* can be replaced with *into*. See the note at **in a bind** and the examples below.) □ *She goes into heat every* *year at this time.* ☐ *When my dog is in heat, I have to keep her locked in the house.*

in heaven 1. in a state of absolute bliss or happiness. ☐ *Lisa was in heaven after winning the lottery.* ☐ *Resting in his hammock, John was simply in heaven.* **2.** dead. (A polite euphemism, and perhaps used more when speaking to children.) ☐ *Mary's daddy is in heaven. He was in a car accident.* ☐ *I am afraid that she is not just sleeping. She is in heaven.*

in high dudgeon feeling or exhibiting great resentment; taking great offense at something. (Often with *leave.*) ☐ *After the rude remarks, the person who was insulted left in high dudgeon.* ☐ *Dennis strode from the room in high dudgeon, and we knew he would get his revenge eventually.*

in high gear very fast and active. (Also literal. Informal. *In* can be replaced with *into.* See the note at in a bind and the examples below.) ☐ *Don't leave now. The party is just now in high gear.* ☐ *When Jane is in high gear, she's a superb athlete.* ☐ *When Jane moved into high gear, I knew she'd win the race.*

in hindsight Go to in retrospect.

in hock in debt. ☐ *After buying the luxury car, Bob was in hock for years.* ☐ *I am deeply in hock and have to pay off my debts.*

in honor of someone or something showing respect or admiration for someone or something. ☐ *Our club gave a party in honor of the club's president.* ☐ *I wrote a poem in honor of John and Mary's marriage.*

in hopes of something expecting something. (Also with *high,* as in the example.) ☐ *I was in hopes of getting there early.* ☐ *We are in high hopes that John and Mary will have a girl.*

in horror with intense shock or disgust. ☐ *Mike stepped back from the rattlesnake in horror.* ☐ *The jogger recoiled in horror when she came upon a body in the park.*

in hot water in trouble. (Slang. *In* can be replaced with *into.* See in a bind and the examples below.) ☐ *John got himself into hot water by being late.* ☐ *I'm in hot water at home for coming in late last night.* ☐ *I get into hot water a lot.*

in ink written or signed with a pen that uses ink. ☐ *You should write your report in ink.* ☐ *You must sign your checks in ink.*

in its entirety AND **in their entirety** in a state of completeness. ☐ *I watched the basketball game in its entirety.* ☐ *My friends and I ate the two large pizzas in their entirety.*

in its prime Go to in one's prime.

in jeopardy in danger; at risk; at hazard. ☐ *John puts himself in jeopardy every time he goes skydiving.* ☐ *I was in jeopardy when my car broke down on the deserted road.*

in (just) a minute Go to in (just) a second.

in (just) a second AND **in (just) a minute** in a very short period of time. ☐ *I'll be there in a second.* ☐ *I'll be with you in just a minute. I'm on the phone.*

in keeping (with something**)** AND **in line with** something in accord or harmony with something; following the rules of something. ☐ *In keeping with your instructions, I've canceled your order.* ☐ *I'm disappointed with your behavior. It really wasn't in keeping.* ☐ *It was not in line with the kind of behavior we expect here.*

in kind 1. in goods rather than in money. ☐ *The country doctor was usually paid in kind. He accepted two pigs as payment for an operation.* ☐ *Do you have to pay tax on payments made in kind?* **2.** similarly; [giving] something similar to what was received. ☐ *John punched Bill, and Bill gave it back in kind.* ☐ *She spoke rudely to me, so I spoke to her in kind.*

in labor [of a woman] experiencing the pains and exertion of childbirth. ☐ *Susan was in labor for nearly eight hours.* ☐ *As soon as she had been in labor for an hour, she went to the hospital.*

in league (with someone**)** in cooperation with someone; in a conspiracy with someone. ☐ *The mayor is in league with the city treasurer. They are misusing public* *money.* □ *Those two have been in league for years.*

in less than no time very quickly. □ *I'll be there in less than no time.* □ *Don't worry. This won't take long. It'll be over with in less than no time.*

in lieu of something in place of something; instead of something. (The word *lieu* occurs only in this phrase.) □ *They gave me roast beef in lieu of beefsteak.* □ *We gave money to charity in lieu of sending flowers to the funeral.*

in light of something because of certain knowledge; considering something. (As if knowledge or enlightenment were like light shone on ignorance.) □ *In light of what you have told us, I think we must abandon the project.* □ *In light of the clerk's rudeness, we didn't return to that shop.*

in limbo 1. a region on the border of hell. (In some Christian religions, there is a *limbo* set aside for souls that do not go to either heaven or hell. This sense is used only in this religious context. *In* can be replaced with *into.* See the note at **in a bind** and the examples below.) □ *The baby's soul was in limbo because she had not been baptized.* □ *Considering all things, getting into limbo is probably better than going to hell.* **2.** in a state of neglect; in a state of oblivion; in an indefinite state. □ *We'll have to leave the project in limbo for a month or two.* □ *After I got hit on the head, I was in limbo for about ten minutes.*

in line AND **on line** standing and waiting in a line of people. (*On line* is used typically by New Yorkers.) □ *I've been in line for an hour.* □ *Get in line if you want to buy a ticket.* □ *We waited on line to see the movie.*

in line with something Go to **in keeping (with** something**)**.

in love (with someone or something**)** feeling love for someone or something; experiencing a strong affectionate emotion for someone or something. □ *Mary was in love with her new car! It was perfect for her.* □ *John is deeply in love with Mary.* □ *Those two are really in love.*

in luck fortunate; lucky. □ *You want a red one? You're in luck. There is one red one left.* □ *I had an accident, but I was in luck. It was not serious.*

in many respects Go to **in some respects**.

in memory of someone to continue the good memories of someone; for the honor of a deceased person. □ *Many streets were renamed in memory of John F. Kennedy.* □ *We planted roses in memory of my deceased father.*

in midair in a point high in the air. □ *The planes crashed in midair.* □ *Extra fuel was released from the plane in midair.*

in mint condition in perfect condition. (Refers to the perfect state of a coin that has just been minted. *In* can be replaced with *into.* See the note at **in a bind** and the examples below.) □ *This is a fine car. It runs well and is in mint condition.* □ *We went through a house in mint condition and decided to buy it.* □ *We put our house into mint condition before we sold it.*

in name only nominally; not actual, only by terminology. □ *The president is head of the country in name only. Congress makes the laws.* □ *Mr. Smith is the boss of the Smith Company in name only. Mrs. Smith handles all the business affairs.*

in need [of someone] requiring basic things like food, clothing, and housing. □ *Please contribute some money for those who are in need.* □ *The charity works with old people who are in need.*

in need of something [of someone or some creature] requiring something. □ *We are in need of a new car.* □ *The company is in need of a larger building to hold all its employees.*

in neutral with the shift lever of a vehicle in the position where the motor is running but is not powering the wheels or other moving parts. □ *The car rolled down the hill because I'd left it in neutral and left the brake off.* □ *If you are moving and in neutral, you do not have control of your vehicle.*

in no mood to do something not to feel like doing something; to wish not to do something. ☐ *I'm in no mood to cook dinner tonight.* ☐ *Mother is in no mood to put up with our arguing.*

in nothing flat in exactly no time at all. (Informal.) ☐ *Of course I can get there in a hurry. I'll be there in nothing flat.* ☐ *We covered the distance between New York and Philadelphia in nothing flat.*

in no time (at all) very quickly. (Compare this with **in less than no time.**) ☐ *I'll be there in no time.* ☐ *It won't take long. I'll be finished in no time at all.*

in no uncertain terms in very specific and direct language. (*In* can be replaced with *into.* See the note at **in a bind** and the examples below.) ☐ *I was so mad. I told her in no uncertain terms to leave and never come back.* ☐ *I told him in no uncertain terms to stop it.* ☐ *He put his demands into no uncertain terms, and then they listened to him.*

in one breath Go to **(all) in one breath.**

in one ear and out (of) the other [for something to be] ignored; [for something to be] unheard or unheeded. (*In* can be replaced with *into.* See the explanation at **in a bind** and the examples. See also **go in one ear and out the other.**) ☐ *Bill just doesn't pay attention. Everything is in one ear and out the other.* ☐ *I told Billy to be home by dinnertime, but I am sure it's just in one ear and out the other.*

in one fell swoop Go to **at one fell swoop.**

in one's **birthday suit** naked; nude. (Informal. In the "clothes" in which one was born. *In* can be replaced with *into.* See the note at **in a bind** and the examples below.) ☐ *I've heard that John sleeps in his birthday suit.* ☐ *We used to go down to the river and swim in our birthday suits.* ☐ *You have to get into your birthday suit to bathe.*

in one's **blood** Go to **in the blood.**

in one's **book** according to one's own opinion. (Informal.) ☐ *He's okay in my book.* ☐ *In my book, this is the best that money can buy.*

in one's **cups** drunk. (Euphemistic.) ☐ *She doesn't make much sense when she's in her cups.* ☐ *The speaker—who was in his cups—could hardly be understood.*

in one's **element** in a natural or comfortable situation or environment. (Compare this with **out of** one's **element.** *In* can be replaced with *into.* See the note at **in a bind** and the examples below.) ☐ *Sally is in her element when she's working with algebra or calculus.* ☐ *Bob loves to work with color and texture. When he's painting, he's in his element.* ☐ *He's most comfortable when he can get into his element.*

in one's **glory** at one's happiest or best. ☐ *When I go to the beach on vacation, I'm in my glory.* ☐ *Sally is a good teacher. She's in her glory in the classroom.*

in one's **mind's eye** in one's mind. (Refers to visualizing something in one's mind.) ☐ *In my mind's eye, I can see trouble ahead.* ☐ *In her mind's eye, she could see a beautiful building beside the river. She decided to design such a building.*

in one's **opinion** according to one's belief or judgment. ☐ *In my opinion, that is a very ugly picture.* ☐ *That isn't a good idea in my opinion.*

in one's **(own) backyard** [figuratively] very close to one. (Also literal.) ☐ *That kind of thing is quite rare. Imagine it happening right in your backyard.* ☐ *You always think of something like that happening to someone else. You never expect to find it in your own backyard.*

in one's **(own) (best) interest(s)** to one's advantage; as a benefit to oneself. ☐ *It is not in your own interests to share your ideas with Jack. He will say that they are his.* ☐ *Jane thought it was in the best interest of her friend to tell his mother about his illness.*

in one's **prime** AND **in its prime** at one's or its peak or best time. (Compare this with **in the prime of life.**) ☐ *Our dog—which is in its prime—is very active.* ☐ *The program ended in its prime when we ran out of money.* ☐ *I could work long hours when I was in my prime.*

in one's **right mind** sane; rational and sensible. (Often in the negative.) □ *That was a stupid thing to do. You're not in your right mind.* □ *You can't be in your right mind! That sounds crazy!*

in one's **salad days** in one's youth. (Usually formal or literary. Comparing the greenness of a salad with the greenness, or freshness and inexperience, of youth.) □ *I recall the joys I experienced in the warm summer air in my salad days.* □ *In our salad days, we were apt to get into all sorts of mischief on the weekends.*

in one's **second childhood** [of an adult] interested in things or people that normally interest children. □ *My father bought himself a toy train, and my mother said he was in his second childhood.* □ *Whenever I go to the river and throw stones, I feel as if I'm in my second childhood.*

in one's **spare time** in one's extra time; in the time not reserved for doing something else. □ *I write novels in my spare time.* □ *I'll try to paint the house in my spare time.*

in one's **Sunday best** in one's best Sunday clothes; in the clothes one wears to church. (Folksy. See also Sunday-go-to-meeting clothes. *In* can be replaced with *into.* See the note at in a bind and the examples below.) □ *All the children were dressed up in their Sunday best.* □ *I like to be in my Sunday best whenever I go out.* □ *Let's get into our Sunday best and go out for dinner.*

in on the kill AND **in at the kill** present at the end of some activity, usually an activity with negative results. (Refers to being present when a hunted animal is put to death. Informal when used about any other activity.) □ *Congress was due to defeat the bill, and I went to Washington so I could be in on the kill.* □ *The judge will sentence the criminal today, and I'm going to be in at the kill.*

in orbit 1. [for something] to circle a heavenly body. (Planets, moons, and stars are heavenly bodies. *In* can be replaced with *into.* See the note at in a bind and the examples below.) □ *The moon is in orbit around the earth.* □ *They put the satellite into orbit.* **2.** ecstatic; thrilled; emotionally high. (Slang.) □ *Jane is in orbit about her new job.* □ *John went into orbit when he got the check in the mail.*

in order to do something for the purpose of doing something; as a means of doing something. □ *I went to college in order to further my education.* □ *I gave John three dollars in order to buy lunch.*

in other words said in another, simpler way. □ *BOB: Cease! Desist! BILL: In other words, you want me to stop?* □ *Our cash flow is negative, and our assets are worthless. In other words, we are broke.*

in over one's **head** having more difficulties than one can manage. (Informal. As if being in water that is too deep. See also in deep; in deep water.) □ *Calculus is very hard for me. I'm in over my head.* □ *Ann is too busy. She's really in over her head.*

in park [of an automobile transmission] having the gears locked so the automobile cannot move. □ *The driver stopped the car and placed it in park.* □ *You have to be in park in order to start this car.*

in part partly; to a lesser degree or extent. □ *I was not there, in part because of my disagreement about the purpose of the meeting. I also had a previous appointment.* □ *I hope to win, in part because I want the prize money.*

in particular specifically; especially. □ *I'm not going anywhere in particular.* □ *Of the three ideas, there is one I like in particular.*

in passing casually; as an aside. (See also mention someone or something in passing.) □ *I just heard your name in passing. I didn't hear more than that.* □ *The lecturer referred to George Washington in passing.*

in pencil written or signed with a pencil. □ *Why did you write your report in pencil?* □ *You can't sign a check in pencil!*

in perpetuity for an indefinitely long period of time; eternally. □ *My trust fund generates income in perpetuity.* □ *My family has owned this land for generations and will continue to do so in perpetuity.*

in person [with someone] actually present in a place rather than appearing in a film, on a television screen, on a telephone, or through a radio broadcast. □ *All the famous movie stars were there in person.* □ *You must appear in the office in person to collect the money that is due to you.*

in place 1. in (someone's or something's) proper place or location. (See also **out of place**. *In* can be replaced with *into*. See the note at **in a bind** and the examples below.) □ *The maid came into the room and put everything into place.* □ *It's good to see everything in place again.* **2.** proper. □ *Your remark was not in place.* □ *The presentation was quite in place and nicely done.*

in place of someone or something instead of someone or something. □ *John went in place of Mary.* □ *We had vegetables in place of meat.*

in plain English Go to **in plain language**.

in plain language AND **in plain English** in simple, clear, and straightforward language. (*In* can be replaced with *into*. See the note at **in a bind** and the examples below.) □ *That's too confusing. Please say it again in plain English.* □ *Tell me again in plain language.* □ *Please put it into plain language.*

in poor taste Go to **in bad taste**.

in practice 1. in an application (of a principle, etc.); in the actual doing of something. □ *Our policy is to be very particular, but in practice we don't care that much.* □ *The instructions say not to set it too high. In practice I always set it as high as possible.* **2.** well-rehearsed; well-practiced; well-exercised. □ *The swimmer was not in practice and almost drowned.* □ *I play the piano for a living, and I have to keep in practice.*

in print [of a book, magazine, newspaper, or other written material] available for sale from the publisher. (Compare this with **out of print**. See also **put** something **into print**.) □ *I think I can get that book for you. It's still in print.* □ *This is the only book in print on this subject.*

in private privately. □ *I'd like to speak to you in private.* □ *I enjoy spending the evening in private.*

in progress happening now; taking place at this time. □ *You can't go into that room. There is a meeting in progress.* □ *Please tell me about the work you have in progress.*

in proportion AND **out of proportion** showing the right or wrong proportion relative to something else. □ *That man's large head is out of proportion to his small body.* □ *The cartoonist drew the dog in proportion to its surroundings.*

in public in a place or way so that other people can see or know about something. □ *It's illegal to walk naked in public.* □ *John always tries to embarrass me whenever we're in public.*

in pursuit of something chasing after something. □ *Bill spends most of his time in pursuit of money.* □ *Every year Bob goes into the countryside in pursuit of butterflies.*

in quest of someone or something AND **in search of** someone or something seeking or hunting something; trying to find something. □ *They went into town in quest of a reasonably priced restaurant.* □ *Monday morning I'll go out in search of a job.*

in rags [dressing] in worn-out and torn clothing. □ *Oh, look at my clothing. I can't go to the party in rags!* □ *I think the new casual fashions make you look as if you're in rags.*

in reality viewing things realistically; really. □ *Jane dreamed it was snowing, but in reality, it was very warm.* □ *John looks happy, but in reality, he is miserable.*

in receipt of something in a state of having received something. □ *We are in receipt of your letter of request.* □ *When we are in receipt of your check for the full balance, we will mark your bill as paid.*

in recent memory the recent period of time in which things happened that can be remembered. □ *Never in recent memory has there been this much snow!* □

I haven't been this happy in recent memory!

in rehearsal a stage of development in the production of a play, opera, or concert, involving many rehearsals. ☐ *The play is in rehearsal now and will open next month.* ☐ *While the opera was still in rehearsal, the star developed a hatred for the director.*

in remission [of a serious disease] not as bad or seeming to be getting better. ☐ *While the disease was in remission, John got to leave the hospital.* ☐ *The doctor said my cancer was in remission.*

in retrospect AND **in hindsight** reconsidering the past with the knowledge one now has. ☐ *In retrospect, I would have gone to a better college.* ☐ *David realized, in hindsight, that he should have finished school.*

in return for (someone or something**)** by way of giving something back; as a way of paying someone back for something; as part of an exchange. ☐ *I helped Tom yesterday, and he helped me in return for my efforts.* ☐ *I paid $20 and received four tickets in return.*

in round figures Go to **in round numbers**.

in round numbers AND **in round figures** as an estimated number; a figure that has been rounded off. (*In* can be replaced with *into.* See the note at **in a bind** and the examples below.) ☐ *Please tell me in round numbers what it'll cost.* ☐ *I don't need the exact amount. Just give it to me in round figures.*

in ruin a state of having been destroyed. ☐ *The enemy army left the cities they attacked in ruin.* ☐ *The crops laid in ruin after the flood.*

in search of someone or something Go to **in quest of** someone or something.

in season 1. currently available for selling. (Some foods and other things are available only at certain seasons. Compare this with **out of season**. *In* can be replaced with *into,* especially when used with *come.* See the note at **in a bind** and the examples below.) ☐ *Oysters are available in season.* ☐ *Strawberries aren't in season in January.* ☐ *When do strawberries come into season?* **2.** legally able to be caught or hunted. ☐ *Catfish are in season all year round.* ☐ *When are salmon in season?*

in secret secretly. ☐ *They planned in secret to blow up the bridge.* ☐ *I will tell her in secret so no one else will hear.*

in session [of a court, congress, or other organization] operating or functioning. ☐ *Smoking is forbidden while the meeting is in session.* ☐ *The spectators must remain quiet while court is in session.*

in seventh heaven in a very happy state. ☐ *Ann was really in seventh heaven when she got a car of her own.* ☐ *I'd be in seventh heaven if I had a million dollars.*

in shambles in a messy state; destroyed. ☐ *After the earthquake, the town lay in shambles.* ☐ *The TV set was in shambles after John tried to fix it.*

in shape Go to **in condition**.

in short stated briefly. ☐ *At the end of the financial report, the board president said, "In short, we are okay."* ☐ *My remarks, in short, indicate that we are in good financial shape.*

in short order very quickly. ☐ *I can straighten out this mess in short order.* ☐ *The people came in and cleaned the place up in short order.*

in short supply scarce. (*In* can be replaced with *into.* See the note at **in a bind** and the examples below.) ☐ *Fresh vegetables are in short supply in the winter.* ☐ *Yellow cars are in short supply because everyone likes them and buys them.* ☐ *At this time of the year, fresh vegetables go into short supply.*

in sight able to be seen. ☐ *I hear birds, but there are none in sight.* ☐ *The locusts ate everything in sight.*

(in) single file lined up, one behind the other; in a line, one person or one thing wide. (*In* can be replaced with *into.* See the note at **in a bind** and the examples below.) ☐ *Have you ever seen ducks walking in single file?* ☐ *No, do they usually* *walk single file?* ☐ *Please march in single file.* ☐ *Please get into single file.*

in so many words exactly; explicitly; literally. ☐ *I told her in so many words to leave me alone.* ☐ *He said yes, but not in so many words.*

in some **neck of the woods** in some vicinity or neighborhood; in some remote place. (Folksy. The *some* is usually *this, that, your, their,* etc.) ☐ *I think that the Smiths live in your neck of the woods.* ☐ *What's happening over in that neck of the woods?*

in someone else's **place** Go to in someone else's shoes.

in someone else's **shoes** AND **in** someone else's **place** seeing or experiencing something from someone else's point of view. (See the note at in a bind and the examples. See also put oneself in someone else's place.) ☐ *You might feel different if you were in her shoes.* ☐ *Pretend you're in Tom's place, and then try to figure out why he acts the way he does.*

in someone's **behalf** Go to in behalf of someone.

in someone's **favor** **1.** to someone's advantage or credit. (Especially in sports scores, as in the examples below.) ☐ *The score was ten to twelve in our favor.* ☐ *At the end of the second half, the score was forty to three in the other team's favor.* **2.** liked by someone; approved of by someone. (*In* can be replaced with *into.* See the note at in a bind and the examples below.) ☐ *John might be able to help me. I hope I'm currently in his favor.* ☐ *My mother is mad at me. I'm certainly not in her favor.* ☐ *I'll try to get into her favor.* **3.** AND **in favor of** someone to someone, as when writing a check. (See also honor someone's check.) ☐ *Please make out a check for $300 in Tom's favor.* ☐ *I'm making out the check in favor of Mr. Brown.*

in someone's **name** **1.** Go to in behalf of someone. **2.** in someone's ownership; as someone's property. (*In* can be replaced with *into.* See the note at in a bind and the examples below.) ☐ *The house is in my name. I own all of it.* ☐ *I put the house into my husband's name.* ☐ *The car is in our names.*

in someone's or something's **custody** Go to in custody of someone or something.

in someone's **prayers** [of someone] remembered and called by name when someone prays. ☐ *I am sorry to hear of your sickness. You will be in our prayers.* ☐ *The whole family is in my prayers because they have suffered so much.*

in some respects AND **in many respects** with regard to some or many details. ☐ *In some respects, Anne's comments are similar to yours.* ☐ *The three proposals are quite different in many respects.*

in spite of someone or something regardless of someone or something; in defiance of someone or something. ☐ *In spite of what you said, I still like you.* ☐ *He went to the concert in spite of his parents.*

in step (with someone or something**)** **1.** [with *someone*] [marching or dancing] in cadence with another person; marching with the same rhythm as someone else. (*In* can be replaced with *into.* See the note at in a bind and the examples below.) ☐ *Please keep in step with Jane.* ☐ *You two, back there. You aren't in step.* ☐ *Get into step!* **2.** AND **in time** [with *something*] keeping in rhythm or cadence with music. ☐ *John, your marching isn't in step with the beat.* ☐ *I'm trying to play in time.* **3.** as up to date as someone or something. ☐ *Bob is not in step with the times.* ☐ *We try to keep in step.*

in stock readily available, as with goods in a store. ☐ *I'm sorry, I don't have that in stock. I'll have to order it for you.* ☐ *We have all our Christmas merchandise in stock now.*

in storage in a place where things are stored or kept. ☐ *Mary placed her winter clothes in storage during the summer.* ☐ *John's furniture is in storage while he is in the army.*

in style **1.** in fashion; fashionable. (Compare this with out of style. *In* can be replaced with *into,* especially with *come.* See the note at in a bind and the examples below.) ☐ *This old coat isn't in*

flesh? □ *I've wanted a color television for years, and now I've got one right here in the flesh.*

in the forefront (of something**)** Go to **at the forefront (of** something**)**.

in the gutter [for a person to be] in a low state; depraved. (Also literal. *In* can be replaced with *into.* See the note at **in a bind** and the examples below.) □ *You had better straighten out your life, or you'll end in the gutter.* □ *His bad habits put him into the gutter.*

in the hole in debt. (Informal. *In* can be replaced with *into* with *go.* See **in a bind** and the examples.) □ *I'm $200 in the hole.* □ *Our finances end in the hole every month.* □ *We went into the hole on that deal.*

in the hot seat Go to **on the hot seat**.

in the interest of someone or something as an advantage or benefit to someone or something; in order to advance or improve someone or something. (Formal.) □ *In the interest of health, people are asked not to smoke.* □ *The police imprisoned the suspects in the interest of public safety.*

in the interim (between things**)** in the meantime; in the time between the ending of something and the beginning of something else. □ *In the interim between her morning and afternoon classes, Susan rushed home to get a book she had forgotten.* □ *My favorite show starts in five minutes, but I'll talk to you in the interim.*

in their entirety Go to **in its entirety**.

in the know knowledgeable. (Informal. *In* can be replaced with *into.* See **in a bind** and the examples below.) □ *Let's ask Bob. He's in the know.* □ *I have no knowledge of how to work this machine. I think I can get into the know very quickly, though.*

in the lap of luxury in luxurious surroundings. (See the explanation at **in a bind** and the examples below.) □ *John lives in the lap of luxury because his family is very wealthy.* □ *When I retire, I'd like to live in the lap of luxury.*

in the last analysis Go to **in the final analysis**.

in the laundry with the clothes that are waiting to be washed. □ *Is my blue shirt clean or is it in the laundry?* □ *All my socks are in the laundry. What shall I do?*

in the limelight AND **in the spotlight** at the center of attention. (*In* can be replaced with *into.* See the note at **in a bind** and the examples. *Limelight* refers to an obsolete type of spotlight, and the word occurs only in this phrase.) □ *John will do almost anything to get himself into the limelight.* □ *I love being in the spotlight.* □ *All elected officials spend a lot of time in the limelight.*

in the line of duty as part of the expected (military or police) duties. □ *When soldiers fight people in a war, it's in the line of duty.* □ *Police officers have to do things they may not like in the line of duty.*

in the long run over a long period of time; ultimately. (Compare this with **in the short run**.) □ *We'd be better off in the long run buying one instead of renting one.* □ *In the long run, we'd be happier in the South.*

in the mainstream (of something**)** following the current trends or styles that are popular or are considered normal. □ *Bob is too old-fashioned to be in the mainstream of modern living.* □ *Max likes to make fun of people in the mainstream.*

in the market (for something**)** wanting to buy something. □ *I'm in the market for a video recorder.* □ *If you have a boat for sale, we're in the market.*

in the meantime the period of time between two things; the period of time between now and when something is supposed to happen. □ *The movie starts at 6:00. In the meantime, let's eat dinner.* □ *My flight was at 8:00. In the meantime, I played solitaire.*

in the middle of nowhere in a very remote place. (Informal. *In* can be replaced with *into.* See **in a bind** and the examples below.) □ *To get to my house, you have to drive into the middle of nowhere.* □ *We* *found a nice place to eat, but it's out in the middle of nowhere.*

in the money 1. wealthy. (Informal. See also on the money.) ☐ *John is really in the money. He's worth millions.* ☐ *If I am ever in the money, I'll be generous.* **2.** in the winning position in a race or contest. (Refers to winning the prize money.) ☐ *I knew when Jane came around the final turn that she was in the money.* ☐ *The horses coming in first, second, and third are said to be in the money.*

in the mood for something AND **in the mood to** do something having the proper state of mind for a particular situation or for doing something. ☐ *I'm not in the mood to see a movie tonight.* ☐ *Are you in the mood for pizza?*

in the mood to do something Go to in the mood for something.

in the near future in the time immediately ahead. (*In* can be replaced with *into.* See the note at in a bind and the examples below.) ☐ *I don't plan to go to Florida in the near future.* ☐ *Today's prices won't extend into the near future.* ☐ *What do you intend to do in the near future?*

in the neighborhood of something Go to (somewhere) in the neighborhood of something.

in the nick of time Go to in the (very) nick of time.

in the nude in a state of nudity. ☐ *Bill says he sleeps in the nude.* ☐ *All the little boys swam in the nude in the creek.*

in the offing happening at some time in the future. (See the note at in a bind and the examples below.) ☐ *There is a big investigation in the offing, but I don't know when.* ☐ *It's hard to tell what's in the offing if you don't keep track of things.*

in the open in the outdoors; in an area that is not closed in. ☐ *John's bike was stolen because he left it out in the open.* ☐ *Mary loves gardening because she loves to be in the open.*

in theory according to a theory; theoretically. ☐ *In theory, if I take my medicine regularly, I will get well.* ☐ *How things work in theory doesn't always match with how things work in reality.*

in the pink (of condition) in very good health; in very good condition, physically and emotionally. (Informal. *In* can be replaced with *into.* See in a bind and the examples below.) ☐ *The garden is lovely. All the flowers are in the pink of condition.* ☐ *Jane has to exercise hard to get into the pink of condition.* ☐ *I'd like to be in the pink, but I don't have the time.*

in the prime of life in the best and most productive and healthy period of life. (See also in one's prime. *In* can be replaced with *into.* See the note at in a bind and the examples below.) ☐ *The good health of one's youth can carry over into the prime of life.* ☐ *He was struck down by a heart attack in the prime of life.*

in the public eye publicly; visible to all; conspicuous. (*In* can be replaced with *into.* See the note at in a bind and the examples below.) ☐ *Elected officials find themselves constantly in the public eye.* ☐ *The mayor made it a practice to get into the public eye as much as possible.*

in the raw Go to in the altogether.

in the rear located in the space or area behind someone or something. ☐ *The waiter told me that the bathrooms were in the rear.* ☐ *All deliveries must be made in the rear.*

in the red in debt. (Compare this with in the black and out of the red. *In* can be replaced with *into.* See the note at in a bind and the examples below.) ☐ *My accounts are in the red at the end of every month.* ☐ *It's easy to get into the red if you don't pay close attention to the amount of money you spend.*

in there pitching trying very hard. (Informal.) ☐ *Bob is always in there pitching.* ☐ *Just stay in there pitching. You'll make some progress eventually.*

in the right on the moral or legal side of an issue; on the right side of an issue. (Compare this with in the wrong.) ☐ *I felt I was in the right, but the judge ruled against me.* ☐ *It's hard to argue with Jane. She always believes that she's in the right.*

in the right place at the right time in the location where something is to happen, exactly when it happens. (Usually about something good.) □ *I got a good deal on a car because I was in the right place at the right time.* □ *Unless you are in the right place at the right time, you won't get a chance to meet a movie star.*

in the running in competition; competing and having a chance to win. (Compare this with **out of the running**. *In* can be replaced with *into.* See the note at **in a bind** and the examples below.) □ *Is Tom still in the running? Does he still have a chance to be elected?* □ *I'm glad I didn't get into the running.*

in the same boat (as someone) in the same situation; having the same problem. (*In* can be replaced with *into.* See the explanation at **in a bind** and the examples below.) □ *TOM: I'm broke. Can you lend me twenty dollars? BILL: Sorry. I'm in the same boat.* □ *Jane and Mary are both in the same boat. They have been called for jury duty.* □ *I am in the same boat as Mary.*

in the same breath [stated or said] almost at the same time. □ *He told me I was lazy, but then in the same breath he said I was doing a good job.* □ *The teacher said that the students were working hard and, in the same breath, that they were not working hard enough.*

in the second place secondly; in addition. (Usually said after one has said **in the first place.**) □ *In the first place, you don't have enough money to buy one. In the second place, you don't need one.* □ *In the first place, I don't have the time. In the second place, I'm not interested.*

in the short run for the immediate future. (Compare this with **in the long run.**) □ *In the short run, we'd be better off saving our money.* □ *We decided to rent an apartment in the short run. We can buy a house later.*

in the soup in a bad situation. (Slang. *In* can be replaced with *into.* See **in a bind** and the examples below.) □ *Now I'm really in the soup. I broke Mrs. Franklin's window.* □ *I make a lot of mistakes. It's easy for me to get into the soup.*

in the spotlight Go to **in the limelight.**

in the swim of things involved in or participating in events or happenings. (The *in* can be replaced with *into.* See the explanation at **in a bind** and the examples. The opposite of **out of the swim of things.**) □ *I've been ill, but soon I'll be back in the swim of things.* □ *I can't wait to settle down and get into the swim of things.*

in the trust of someone under the responsibility or in the care of someone. □ *The state placed the orphan in the trust of the foster parents.* □ *Our bonds are left in the trust of our broker.*

in the twinkling of an eye very quickly. (A biblical reference.) □ *In the twinkling of an eye, the deer had disappeared into the forest.* □ *I gave Bill ten dollars and, in the twinkling of an eye, he spent it.*

in the unlikely event of something AND **in the unlikely event that something happens** if something—which probably will not happen—actually happens. (Compare this with **in the event of something.**) □ *In the unlikely event of my getting the job, I'll have to buy a car to get there every day.* □ *In the unlikely event of a fire, please walk quickly to an exit.*

in the unlikely event that something happens Go to **in the unlikely event of something.**

in the (very) nick of time just in time; at the last possible instant; just before it's too late. □ *The doctor arrived in the nick of time. The patient's life was saved.* □ *I reached the airport in the very nick of time.*

in the wake of something after something; as a result of some event. (Refers to the wake of a boat.) □ *We had no place to live in the wake of the fire.* □ *In the wake of the storm, there were many broken tree limbs.*

in the way of something as a kind of something; as a style of something. □ *What do you have in the way of leather shoes?* □ *We have nothing in the way of raincoats.* □

I've seen nothing in the way of nice weather in this part of the country.

in the wind about to happen. (Also literal.) ☐ *There are some major changes in the wind. Expect these changes to happen soon.* ☐ *There is something in the wind. We'll find out what it is soon.*

in the works being prepared; being planned; being done. (Informal.) ☐ *There are some new laws in the works that will affect all of us.* ☐ *I have some ideas in the works that you might be interested in.*

in the world Go to on earth.

in the worst way very much. (Also literal. Informal.) ☐ *I want a new car in the worst way.* ☐ *Bob wants to retire in the worst way.*

in the wrong on the wrong or illegal side of an issue; guilty or in error. (Compare this with **in the right**.) ☐ *I felt she was in the wrong, but the judge ruled in her favor.* ☐ *It's hard to argue with Jane. She always believes that everyone else is in the wrong.*

in the wrong place at the wrong time in the location where something is to happen exactly when it happens. (Usually about something bad.) ☐ *I always get into trouble. I'm just in the wrong place at the wrong time.* ☐ *It isn't my fault. I was just in the wrong place at the wrong time.*

the **in thing (to do)** the fashionable thing to do. ☐ *Eating low-fat food is the in thing to do.* ☐ *Bob is very old-fashioned. He never does the in thing.*

in this day and age presently; currently; nowadays. (Folksy.) ☐ *You don't expect people to be polite in this day and age.* ☐ *Young folks don't take care of their parents in this day and age.*

in time 1. Go to in due course. **2.** Go to in step (with someone or something). **3.** before the deadline; before the last minute. ☐ *Did you turn in your paper in time?* ☐ *I didn't go to Florida. I didn't get to the airport in time.*

in times past long ago; in previous times. ☐ *In times past, you would not have been able to wear casual clothing to work.* ☐ *In times past, the air always seemed fresher and cleaner.*

in top form 1. [of someone or some creature] in very good physical condition. ☐ *The runners are in top form, so this should be a good race.* ☐ *I'm not in top form, but I'm not a physical mess either.* **2.** able to make witty remarks and clever statements quickly and easily. ☐ *That was really funny, Bob. You are in top form tonight.*

in tow closely following; under someone's control. ☐ *The nanny walked into the park with three children in tow.* ☐ *The manager went to the meeting with her staff in tow.*

in transit while in the process of being transported. ☐ *Dave is in transit from London to Chicago.* ☐ *The new stereo is now in transit from the manufacturer.*

in triplicate [of a document] produced in three copies. ☐ *Mr. Smith asked me to type up his notes in triplicate.* ☐ *I completed each form in triplicate.*

in trouble 1. in danger; in difficulty; due for punishment. ☐ *If you don't be quiet, you're going to be in trouble.* ☐ *The company was in trouble for months, and then went bankrupt.* **2.** pregnant and unmarried. (Euphemistic.) ☐ *They had to get married. She was in trouble.* ☐ *She'll be in trouble before long, if she doesn't quit running around like that.*

in tune in a state where musical notes are at their proper intervals so that none are flat or sharp. (Compare this with **out of tune (with** someone or something**)**.) ☐ *Your piano is nicely in tune.* ☐ *The choir members all sang in tune.*

in tune with someone or something **1.** at the same or a harmonizing musical pitch. (*In* can be replaced with *into*. See the note at **in a bind** and the examples below.) ☐ *The violin isn't in tune with the piano.* ☐ *Bill, please get in tune with John.* **2.** [with *something*] keeping up with something. ☐ *Tom, your clothes are old-fashioned. You aren't in tune with the times.* ☐ *Come on, Sally. Get in tune with what's going on around you.*

in turn one at a time in sequence. □ *Each of us can read the book in turn.* □ *We cut the hair of every child in turn.*

in two shakes of a lamb's tail very quickly. □ *I'll be there in two shakes of a lamb's tail.* □ *In two shakes of a lamb's tail, the bird flew away.*

in unison 1. [of musical notes, instruments, or voices] having the same pitch. □ *This part of the piece is performed in unison.* □ *The twins sang in unison.* **2.** acting as one; together and at the same time. □ *In unison, all of the workers voted "yes" for the new contract.* □ *John and his wife responded to my question in unison.*

in view of something in consideration of something; because of something. □ *In view of the high cost of gasoline, I sold my car.* □ *I won't invite John to the meeting in view of his attitude.*

in with someone friends with someone; having influence with someone. □ *Are you in with John? I need to ask him for a favor.* □ *I've heard that the mayor is in with the county treasurer.*

inch along (something**)** to move slowly along something little by little. □ *The cat inched along the carpet toward the mouse.* □ *Traffic was inching along.*

inch by inch one inch at a time; little by little. □ *Traffic moved along inch by inch.* □ *Inch by inch, the snail moved across the stone.*

inclined to do something to tend to do something; to lean toward doing something. □ *Tom is inclined to tell jokes when he is with a group of people.* □ *I'm inclined to go to the beach tomorrow if it doesn't rain.*

incumbent upon someone **to** do something necessary for someone to do something. (*Upon* can be replaced with *on.*) □ *It's incumbent upon you to do the work.* □ *It was incumbent on me to make the presentation of the first prize.*

innocent as a lamb Go to (as) innocent as a lamb.

ins and outs of something the correct and successful way to do something; the special things that one needs to know to do something. □ *I don't understand the ins and outs of politics.* □ *Jane knows the ins and outs of working with computers.*

inside the box 1. as if bound by old, nonfunctional, or limiting structures, rules, or practices. (An adverb. Compare this with outside the box.) □ *If you keep your discussions inside the box, you will be bound by traditional limitations.* □ *Nothing can be accomplished inside the box to solve this problem. We have already tried every obvious solution.* **2.** bound by old, nonfunctional, or limiting structures, rules, or practices. (Usually **inside-the-box**. An adjective.) □ *You have some really inside-the-box ideas, Ralph. Why not be more creative?* □ *After some long, tedious, inside-the-box discussions, we arrived at the same old conclusion that we always arrive at.*

instrumental in doing something playing an important part in doing something. □ *John was instrumental in getting the contract to build the new building.* □ *Our senator was instrumental in defeating the bill.*

intent on doing something determined to do something. □ *The children were intent on making a snowman.* □ *The prisoner was intent on escaping.*

in(to) a jam in(to) a difficult situation. □ *Mary cannot keep track of the many times Dave got himself into a jam.* □ *I found myself in a jam when my car overheated on the highway.*

into being into existence. □ *The new law brought more problems into being.* □ *That idea came into being centuries ago.*

in(to) someone's **clutches** in the control of someone who has power or authority over someone else. □ *Snow White fell into the clutches of the evil witch.* □ *Once you're in my clutches, I'll ruin you.*

invasion of (someone's**) privacy** an intrusion that results in the loss of someone's privacy. □ *Your invasion of my privacy is not welcome!* □ *The athlete complained about the invasion of his privacy by the press.*

invest someone's **time in** something to put one's time, effort, or energy into a project. □ *Mary invests her time in charity work.* □ *I invested five weeks of my time building this model ship.*

invest someone **with** something to endow someone with something, such as power or privilege. □ *The Constitution invests the vice president with the authority to act on the president's behalf in certain conditions.* □ *The state has invested me with the authority to unite this couple in marriage.*

invest something **in** someone or something **1.** to put money, time, effort, etc., into some one or something, hoping for a return. □ *We will invest time and effort in Fred and make him into a movie star.* □ *Sharon invested a lot of money in the stock market.* **2.** to place power or authority under control of someone or something. □ *The Constitution has invested certain powers in the federal government and left the rest to the states.* □ *The law invests the power to arrest criminals in the sheriff's department.*

iron something **out** to solve a problem; to straighten out a problem; to smooth out a difficulty. (Also literal.) □ *The principal had to iron a classroom problem out.* [T] *I just have to iron out this little problem; then I'll be able to see you.*

issue a call for something to make a public invitation or request for something. □ *The prime minister issued a call for peace.* □ *The person who organized the writing contest issued a call for entries.*

It behooves one **to** do something. It is necessary for one to do something.; It is incumbent upon someone to do something. □ *It behooves me to report the crime.* □ *It behooves you to pay for the window that you broke.*

It never rains but it pours. A lot of bad things tend to happen at the same time. (Proverb.) □ *The car won't start, the stairs broke, and the dog died. It never rains but it pours.* □ *More bad news? It never rains but it pours.*

It (only) stands to reason. It is only reasonable to hold a certain opinion. □ *It stands to reason that most people will not buy a new car if they don't think they can pay for it.* □ *I think he will come back to pick up his check. It only stands to reason.*

It sucks. Go to That sucks.

It takes (some) getting used to. It is very unpleasant, but when it is gotten used to, it will not be so bothersome. (Said in recognition of the unpleasantness of something.) □ *I never ate duck's feet before. It takes some getting used to.* □ *These hot Mexican dishes seem impossible at first. They take some getting used to, I agree. But it's worth it.*

It'll never fly. It will never work!; It will never be approved! (Also literal. Refers to an evaluation of an unlikely-looking aircraft of some type.) □ *I have read your report and studied your proposal. It'll never fly.* □ *Your design for a new electric automobile is interesting, but it'll never fly!*

It's about time! It is almost too late!; I've been waiting a long time! (Informal. See also the following entry.) □ *So you finally got here! It's about time!* □ *They finally paid me my money. It's about time!*

It's (all) Greek to me. It is totally incomprehensible to me. □ *Can you explain what this paragraph in the lease means? Legal language is all Greek to me.* □ *I can't figure out this diagram of how to assemble my bicycle. It's all Greek to me.*

It's high time! It is past time [for someone or something]!; [Someone or something] is overdue! (Informal. See also the previous entry.) □ *It's high time that you got recognition for what you do!* □ *They sent me my check, and it's high time, too.*

It's not over till it's over. There is still hope for things to go the way I want until the entire event is over. (Proverb.) □ *They haven't won the game yet. It's not over till it's over.* □ *It looks bad for our side, but it's not over till it's over.*

It's no use (doing something**).** It is hopeless to do something.; It is pointless to do something. □ *It's no use trying to call on the telephone. The line is always busy.* □ *They tried and tried, but it was no use.*

J

a **jack-of-all-trades** someone who can do several different jobs instead of specializing in one. □ *John can do plumbing, carpentry, and roofing—a real jack-of-all-trades. He isn't very good at any of them.* □ *Take your car to a trained mechanic, not a jack-of-all-trades.*

jack someone **up** to motivate someone; to stimulate someone to do something. (Slang.) □ *The mail is late again today. We'll have to jack those people up at the post office.* [T] *I guess I'll have to jack up the carpenter again to repair my stairs.*

jack something **up 1.** to raise something up on a mechanical lifting device. □ *Now I have to jack the car up so I can change the tire.* [T] *Please jack up the car.* **2.** to raise the price of something. □ *The store keeps jacking prices up.* [T] *The grocery store jacked up the prices again last night.*

jazz something **up** to make something more exciting, colorful, or lively. (Slang. Said especially of music.) □ *When we play the music this time, let's jazz it up a bit.* [T] *I think we need to jazz up this room. It looks so drab.*

Jekyll and Hyde someone with both an evil and a good personality. (From the novel *The Strange Case of Dr. Jekyll and Mr. Hyde* by Robert Louis Stevenson.) □ *Bill thinks Mary is so soft and gentle, but she can be very cruel—she is a real Jekyll and Hyde.* □ *Jane doesn't know that Fred is a Jekyll and Hyde. She sees him only when he is being kind and generous, but he can be very cruel.*

The **jig is up.** Go to The **game is up.**

jockey for position to try to push or maneuver one's way into an advantageous position at the expense of others. □ *All the workers in the company are jockeying for position. They all want the manager's job.* □ *It is unpleasant working for a company where people are always jockeying for position.*

jog someone's **memory** to stimulate someone's memory to recall something. □ *Hearing the first part of the song I'd forgotten really jogged my memory.* □ *I tried to jog Bill's memory about our childhood antics.*

Johnny-come-lately someone who joins in (something) after it is under way. □ *Don't pay any attention to Sally. She's just a Johnny-come-lately and doesn't know what she's talking about.* □ *We've been here for thirty years. Why should some Johnny-come-lately tell us what to do?*

Johnny-on-the-spot someone who is in the right place at the right time. □ *Here I am, Johnny-on-the-spot. I told you I would be here at 12:20.* □ *Bill is late again. You can hardly call him Johnny-on-the-spot.*

join forces (with someone**)** to unite with someone. □ *We joined forces with the police to search for the lost child.* □ *The choirs joined forces to sing the song.*

join hands [for people] to hold hands so that each person is holding the hands of two other people; [for two people] to hold each other's hands. □ *Let us join hands and pray together.* □ *The dancers joined hands and formed a circle that moved to the left.*

Join the club! <an expression indicating that the person spoken to is in the same, or a similar, unfortunate state as the speaker.> (Informal.) □ *You don't have* *anyplace to stay? Join the club! Neither do we.* □ *Did you get fired too? Join the club!*

join the fray AND **jump into the fray; enter the fray** to join the fight or argument. □ *After listening to the argument, Mary decided to jump into the fray.* □ *Tom joined the fray and immediately got knocked down.*

joking aside Go to (all) joking aside.

jolt to a start AND **jolt to a stop** to start or stop moving suddenly, causing a jolt. □ *The truck jolted to a stop at the stop sign.* □ *The little car jolted to a quick start and threw the passenger back in his seat.*

jolt to a stop Go to jolt to a start.

judge one **on** one's **own merit(s)** to judge or evaluate one on one's own achievements and virtues, not someone else's. □ *Please judge me on my own merits, not on those of my family.* □ *You should judge Sally on her own merit. Forget that her mother is a famous opera star.*

judge something **on its own merit(s)** to judge or evaluate a thing on its own good points and usefulness. □ *You have to judge each painting on its own merits. Not every painting by a famous painter is superior.* □ *Each rose must be judged on its own merit.*

judging by something considering something; using something as an indication (of something else). □ *Judging by your wet clothing, it must be raining.* □ *Judging by the looks of this house, I would guess there has been a party here.*

juice and cookies trivial and uninteresting snacks or refreshments. (Also literal.) □ *The party was not much. They might as well have served juice and cookies.* □ *After juice and cookies, we all went back into the meeting room for another hour of talk, talk, talk.*

jump all over someone AND **jump down** someone's **throat; jump on** someone to scold someone severely. (Also literal. Slang.) □ *If I don't get home on time, my parents will jump all over me.* □ *Don't jump on me! I didn't do it!* □ *Please don't jump all over John. He wasn't the one who broke the window.* □ *Why are you jumping down my throat? I wasn't even in the house when it happened.*

jump at something to seize the opportunity to do something. (Usually with *it.* See also jump at the chance, from which this phrase comes.) □ *When I heard about John's chance to go to England, I knew he'd jump at it.* □ *If something you really want to do comes your way, jump at it.*

jump at the chance AND **jump at the opportunity; leap at the opportunity** to eagerly accept the opportunity to do something. □ *John jumped at the chance to go to England.* □ *I don't know why I didn't jump at the opportunity myself.* □ *I should have leaped at the chance.*

jump at the opportunity Go to jump at the chance.

jump bail AND **skip bail** to fail to appear in court for trial and give up one's bail bond. (Slang.) □ *Not only was Bob arrested for theft, he skipped bail and left town. He's in a lot of trouble.* □ *I thought only criminals jumped bail.*

jump down someone's **throat** Go to jump all over someone.

jump into the fray Go to join the fray.

jump off the deep end Go to go off the deep end.

jump on someone Go to jump all over someone.

jump on the bandwagon Go to get on the bandwagon.

jump out of one's **skin** to react strongly to a shock or a surprise. (Informal. Usually with *nearly, almost,* etc.) □ *Oh! You really scared me. I nearly jumped out of my skin.* □ *Bill was so startled he almost jumped out of his skin.*

jump the gun to start before the starting signal. (Originally used in sports contests that are started by firing a gun.) □ *We all had to start the race again because Jane jumped the gun.* □ *When we took the test, Tom jumped the gun and started early.*

jump the track 1. [for something] to fall or jump off the rails or guides. (Usually said about a train.) □ *The train jumped the track, causing many injuries to the passengers.* □ *The engine jumped the track, but the other cars stayed on.* **2.** to change suddenly from one thing, thought, plan, or activity to another. □ *The entire project jumped the track, and we finally had to give up.* □ *John's mind jumped the track while he was in the play, and he forgot his lines.*

jump through a hoop AND **jump through hoops** to do everything possible to obey or please someone; to **bend over backwards (to** do something**)**. (Informal. Trained animals jump through hoops.) □ *She expects us to jump through hoops for her.* □ *What do you want me to do—jump through a hoop?*

jump through hoops Go to jump through a hoop.

jump to conclusions AND **leap to conclusions** to judge or decide something without having all the facts; to reach unwarranted conclusions. □ *Now don't jump to conclusions. Wait until you hear what I have to say.* □ *Please find out all the facts so you won't leap to conclusions.*

jumping-off place Go to jumping-off point.

jumping-off point AND **jumping-off place** a point or place from which to begin something. □ *The local library is a logical jumping-off point for your research.* □ *The office job in that company would be a good jumping-off place for a job in advertising.*

The **jury is still out (on** someone or something**)**. A decision has not been reached on someone or something.; The people making the decision on someone or something have not yet decided. (Also literal.) □ *The jury is still out on Jane. We don't know what we are going to do about her.* □ *The jury is still out on the question of building a new parking lot.*

(just) as I expected I thought so; I knew it would be this way. □ *Just as I expected. The window was left open and it rained in.* □ *As I expected, he left work early again.*

(just) a stone's throw away (from something**)** Go to within a stone's throw (of something).

just in case (something happens**)** if (something happens). (Compare this with **in case** something **happens**.) □ *All right. I'll take the umbrella just in case it rains.* □ *I'll take along some aspirin, just in case.*

just one of those things just something that couldn't have been prevented; some unfortunate event caused by fate. □ *I'm sorry, too. It's not your fault. It's just one of those things.* □ *I feel terrible that I didn't pass the bar exam. I guess it was just one of those things.*

just so 1. in perfect order; neat and tidy. □ *Her hair is always just so.* □ *Their front yard is just so.* **2.** (Usually **Just so!**) Precisely right!; Quite right! □ *BILL: The letter should arrive tomorrow. TOM: Just so!* □ *JANE: We must always try our best. MARTIN: Just so!*

just the same Go to all the same.

just the same (to someone**)** Go to all the same (to someone).

just what the doctor ordered exactly what is required, especially for health or comfort. □ *That meal was delicious, Bob. Just what the doctor ordered.* □ *BOB: Would you like something to drink? MARY: Yes, a cold glass of water would be just what the doctor ordered.*

K

keel over [for a person] to fall over or fall down in a faint or in death. □ *Suddenly, Mr. Franklin keeled over. He had had a heart attack.* □ *It was so hot in the room that two people just keeled over.*

keen about someone or something Go to **keen on** someone or something.

keen on doing something willing or eager to do something. □ *Dave isn't very keen on going to the opera.* □ *The children are keen on swimming this afternoon. Shall I take them?*

keen on someone or something AND **keen about** someone or something to be enthusiastic about someone or something. □ *I'm not too keen on going to Denver.* □ *Sally is fairly keen about getting a new job.* □ *Mary isn't keen on her new boss.*

keep abreast (of something**)** to keep informed about something; to **keep up (with the times)**. (Also with *be* instead of *keep*, as in the examples below.) □ *I try to keep abreast of the financial markets.* □ *I believe that I'm abreast of foreign events.* □ *Yes, I try to keep abreast by reading the papers every day.*

keep a civil tongue (in one's **head)** to speak decently and politely. (Also with *have*. See the note at **keep a straight face**.) □ *Please, John. Don't talk like that. Keep a civil tongue in your head.* □ *John seems unable to keep a civil tongue.* □ *He'd be welcome here if he had a civil tongue in his head.*

keep a close rein on someone or something Go to **keep a tight rein on** someone or something.

keep after someone AND **keep at** someone; **keep on** someone; **stay after** someone to remind or nag someone over and over to do something. (See also **get after** someone.) □ *I'll keep after you until you do it!* □ *Mother stayed after Bill until he did the dishes.* □ *She kept at him until he dried them and put them away.* □ *She kept on him for forty minutes before he finally finished.*

keep an eye on someone or something Go to **have an eye on** someone or something.

keep an eye out (for someone or something**)** Go to **have an eye out (for** someone or something**)**.

keep a secret to know a secret and not tell anyone. □ *Please keep our little secret private.* □ *Do you know how to keep a secret?*

keep a stiff upper lip to be calm and unmoved by unsettling events. (Also with *have*. See the note at **keep a straight face**.) □ *John always keeps a stiff upper lip.* □ *Now, Billy, don't cry. Keep a stiff upper lip.* □ *Bill can take it. He has a stiff upper lip.*

keep a straight face to make one's face stay free from smiles or laughter. (Note: *Keep* can be replaced with *have*. *Keep* implies the exercise of effort, and *have* means that a state exists.) □ *It's hard to keep a straight face when someone tells a funny joke.* □ *I knew it was John who played the trick. He couldn't keep a straight face.* □ *John didn't have a straight face.*

keep a tight rein on someone or something AND **keep a close rein on** someone or something to watch and control someone or something diligently. □ *The office manager kept a tight rein on the staff.* □ *Mary keeps a close rein on her children.*

Keep at it! Keep doing what you are doing!; Keep trying! (Encouragement to keep working at something.) ☐ *The boss told me to keep at it every time he passed my desk.* ☐ *Keep at it, Tom! You can do it!*

keep at someone or something **1.** [with *someone*] Go to **keep after** someone. **2.** [with *something*] to continue doing something; to continue trying to do something. ☐ *John kept at his painting until the whole house was done.* ☐ *Keep at the job if you want to get it finished.*

keep body and soul together to feed, clothe, and house oneself. ☐ *I hardly have enough money to keep body and soul together.* ☐ *How the old man was able to keep body and soul together is beyond me.*

keep (close) watch (on someone or something**)** to monitor someone or something; to observe someone or something. ☐ *Keep close watch on Bill. I think he's loafing.* ☐ *Okay. I'll keep watch, but I think he's a good worker.*

keep (close) watch (over someone or something**)** to guard or care for someone or something. ☐ *I'm keeping watch over my children to make sure they have the things they need.* ☐ *I think that an angel is keeping close watch over her to make sure nothing bad happens to her.* ☐ *Angels don't have much to do except to keep watch.*

keep company (with someone**)** to spend much time with someone; to associate with or consort with someone. (Compare this with **keep** someone **company.**) ☐ *Bill has been keeping company with Ann for three months.* ☐ *Bob has been keeping company with a tough-looking bunch of boys.*

keep cool to stay calm and undisturbed. (Also literal. Informal or slang.) ☐ *Relax man, keep cool!* ☐ *If Sally could just keep cool before a race, she could probably win.*

keep from doing something to avoid doing something; to refrain from doing something. ☐ *How could I keep from crying? It was so sad!* ☐ *Try to keep from falling off the ladder.*

keep good time [for a clock or watch] to be accurate. (See also **keep time.**) ☐ *I have to return my watch to the store because it doesn't keep good time.* ☐ *My alarm clock really keeps good time.*

keep harping on something to continue to talk or complain about something; to keep raising a topic of conversation. (See also **harp on** something.) ☐ *Why do you keep harping on the same old complaint?* ☐ *You keep harping on my problems and ignore your own!*

keep house to manage a household. ☐ *I hate to keep house. I'd rather live in a tent than keep house.* ☐ *My grandmother kept house for nearly sixty years.*

keep in touch (with someone**)** AND **stay in touch (with** someone**)** to remain in friendly communication with someone. (See also **get in touch (with** someone**).**) ☐ *I try to keep in touch with my cousins.* ☐ *All our family tries to stay in touch.*

keep late hours to stay up or stay out until very late. (This can cause one to be late for appointments or responsibilities.) ☐ *I'm always tired because I keep late hours.* ☐ *If I didn't keep late hours, I wouldn't sleep so late in the morning.*

keep off (something**)** to stay off someone's land; not to trespass. ☐ *You had better keep off my property.* ☐ *The sign says "Keep off."*

keep on an even keel to remain cool and calm. (Originally nautical. See also **keep** something **on an even keel.**) ☐ *If Jane can keep on an even keel and not panic, she will be all right.* ☐ *Try to keep on an even keel and not get upset so easily.*

keep one's **cards close to** one's **chest** Go to **play** one's **cards close to the chest.**

keep one's **cards close to** one's **vest** Go to **play** one's **cards close to the chest.**

keep one's **chin up** to keep one's spirits high; to act brave and confident. (Informal.) ☐ *Keep your chin up, John. Things will get better.* ☐ *Just keep your chin up and tell the judge exactly what happened.*

keep one's **cool** to remain calm, even when provoked. (Informal.) ☐ *I have a hard* *time keeping my cool when someone is yelling at me.* □ *Whatever you do, try to keep your cool.*

keep one's **distance (from** someone or something**)** to maintain a respectful or cautious distance from someone or something. (The distance can be figurative or literal.) □ *Keep your distance from John. He's in a bad mood.* □ *Keep your distance from the fire.* □ *Okay. I'll tell Sally to keep her distance, too.*

keep one's **ear to the ground** Go to have one's **ear to the ground.**

keep one's **eye on the ball 1.** to watch or follow the ball carefully, especially when one is playing a ball game; to follow the details of a ball game very carefully. □ *John, if you can't keep your eye on the ball, I'll have to take you out of the game.* □ *"Keep your eye on the ball!" the coach roared at the players.* **2.** to remain alert to the events occurring around one. (Informal.) □ *If you want to get along in this office, you're going to have to keep your eye on the ball.* □ *Bill would do better in his classes if he would just keep his eye on the ball.*

keep one's **eyes open (for** someone or something**)** AND **keep** one's **eyes peeled (for** someone or something**)** to remain alert and watchful for someone or something. (The entries with *peeled* are informal. *Peel* refers to moving the eyelids back.) □ *I'm keeping my eyes open for a sale on winter coats.* □ *Please keep your eyes peeled for Mary. She's due to arrive here any time.* □ *Okay. I'll keep my eyes open.*

keep one's **eyes peeled (for** someone or something**)** Go to **keep** one's **eyes open (for** someone or something**).**

keep one's **feet on the ground** to remain firmly established. (See also **get** one's **feet on the ground.**) □ *Sally will have no trouble keeping her feet on the ground.* □ *If you can keep your feet on the ground, there should be no problem.*

keep one's **fingers crossed (for** someone or something**)** AND **cross** one's **fingers** to wish for luck for someone or something, often by crossing one's fingers; to hope for a good outcome for someone or something. □ *I hope you win the race Saturday. I'm keeping my fingers crossed for you.* □ *I'm trying out for a play. Keep your fingers crossed!*

keep one's **hand in (**something**)** to retain one's control of something. (See also **take a hand in** something.) □ *I want to keep my hand in the running of the business.* □ *Mrs. Johnson has retired from the library, but she still wants to keep her hand in.*

keep one's **hands off (**someone or something**)** to refrain from touching or handling someone or something. □ *I'm going to put these cookies here. You keep your hands off them.* □ *Get your hands off my book, and keep them off.*

keep one's **head** to remain calm and sensible when in an awkward situation that might cause a person to panic or go out of control. □ *She was very angry. We had to calm her down and encourage her to keep her head.* □ *Always try to keep your head when others are panicking.*

keep one's **head above water** to stay ahead of one's responsibilities; to remain financially solvent. (Also literal.) □ *Now that I have more space to work in, I can easily keep my head above water.* □ *While I was out of work, I could hardly keep my head above water.*

keep one's **mouth shut (about** someone or something**)** to keep quiet about someone or something; to keep a secret about someone or something. (Informal.) □ *They told me to keep my mouth shut about the boss or I'd be in big trouble.* □ *I think I'll keep my mouth shut.*

keep one's **nose clean** to keep out of trouble, especially trouble with the law. (Slang.) □ *I'm trying to keep my nose clean by staying away from those rough guys.* □ *John, if you don't learn how to keep your nose clean, you're going to end up in jail.*

keep one's **nose out of** someone's **business** to refrain from interfering in someone else's business. (See also **get** one's **nose out of** someone's **business.**) □ *Let John have his privacy, and keep your nose out of my* *business, too!* ☐ *Keep your nose out of my business!*

keep one's **nose to the grindstone** to keep busy continuously over a period of time. (See also **put** one's **nose to the grindstone.**) ☐ *The manager told me to keep my nose to the grindstone or be fired.* ☐ *Keep your nose to the grindstone, and you will prosper.*

keep one's **opinions to** oneself to stop mentioning one's own opinions, especially when they disagree with someone else's. ☐ *You ought to keep your opinions to yourself if you are going to be offensive.* ☐ *Please keep your rude opinions to yourself!*

keep one's **own counsel** to keep one's thoughts and plans to oneself; not to tell other people about one's thoughts and plans. ☐ *Jane is very quiet. She tends to keep her own counsel.* ☐ *I advise you to keep your own counsel.*

keep one's **place** to exhibit only the behavior appropriate to one's position or status in life. (Also literal.) ☐ *When I complained about the food, they told me to keep my place!* ☐ *I suggest you keep your place until you're in a position to change things.*

keep one's **temper** AND **hold** one's **temper** not to get angry; to hold back an expression of anger. (The opposite of **lose** one's **temper.**) ☐ *She should have learned to keep her temper when she was a child.* ☐ *Sally got thrown off the team because she couldn't hold her temper.*

keep one's **weather eye open** to watch for something (to happen); to be on the alert (for something); to be on guard. ☐ *Some trouble is brewing. Keep your weather eye open.* ☐ *Try to be more alert. Learn to keep your weather eye open.*

keep one's **wits about** one to keep one's mind operating in a time of stress. ☐ *If Jane hadn't kept her wits about her during the fire, things would have been much worse.* ☐ *I could hardly keep my wits about me.*

keep one's **word** to uphold one's promise. (The opposite of **break** one's **word.**) ☐ *I told her I'd be there to pick her up, and I intend to keep my word.* ☐ *Keeping one's word is necessary in the legal profession.*

keep on one's **toes** to stay alert and watchful. ☐ *If you want to be a success at this job, you will have to keep on your toes.* ☐ *Please keep on your toes and report anything strange that you see.*

keep on someone Go to **keep after** someone.

keep pace (with someone or something**)** to move at the same speed as someone or something; to **keep up (with** someone or something**).** ☐ *The black horse was having a hard time keeping pace with the brown one.* ☐ *Bill can't keep pace with the geometry class.* ☐ *You've just got to keep pace.*

keep quiet (about someone or something**)** AND **keep still (about** someone or something**)** not to reveal something about someone or something; to keep a secret about someone or something. ☐ *Please keep quiet about the missing money.* ☐ *Please keep still about Mr. Smith's illness.* ☐ *All right. I'll keep still.*

keep someone **company** to sit or stay with someone, especially someone who is lonely. ☐ *I kept my uncle company for a few hours.* ☐ *He was very grateful for someone to keep him company. He gets very lonely.*

keep someone **from** doing something to prevent someone from doing something. ☐ *I kept the child from falling in the lake by grabbing his collar.* ☐ *I try to keep myself from overeating, but I seem to fail frequently.*

keep someone **in line** to make certain that someone behaves properly. (Informal.) ☐ *It's very hard to keep Bill in line. He's sort of rowdy.* ☐ *The teacher had to struggle to keep the class in line.*

keep someone **in stitches** to cause someone to laugh loud and hard, over and over. (Informal. Also with *have.* See the note at **keep a straight face.**) ☐ *The comedian kept us in stitches for nearly an hour.* ☐ *The teacher kept the class in stitches, but the students didn't learn anything.* ☐ *She had us in stitches for ten minutes.*

keep someone **on tenterhooks** to keep someone anxious or in suspense. (Also with *have*. See the note at **keep a straight face**.) ☐ *Please tell me now. Don't keep me on tenterhooks any longer!* ☐ *Now that we have her on tenterhooks, shall we let her worry, or shall we tell her?*

keep someone or something **hanging in midair** Go to **leave** someone or something **hanging in midair**.

keep someone or something **in check** AND **hold** someone or something **in check** to keep someone or something under control; to restrain someone or something. ☐ *Hang on to this rope to keep the dog in check.* ☐ *I was so angry I could hardly hold myself in check.*

keep someone or something **in mind** AND **bear** someone or something **in mind** to remember and think about someone or something. ☐ *When you're driving a car, you must bear this in mind at all times: Keep your eyes on the road.* ☐ *As you leave home, keep your family in mind.*

keep someone or something **quiet** Go to **keep** someone or something **still**.

keep someone or something **still 1.** AND **keep** someone or something **quiet** to make someone or something silent or less noisy. ☐ *Can you please keep the baby quiet?* ☐ *Keep that stereo still!* **2.** [with *something*] AND **keep** something **quiet** to keep something a secret. (See also **keep quiet (about** someone or something**)**.) ☐ *I'm quitting my job, but my boss doesn't know yet. Please keep it quiet.* ☐ *Okay. I'll keep it still.* **3.** AND **hold** someone or something **still** to restrain or control someone or something so that the person or thing cannot move. (See also **keep still**.) ☐ *Please keep your foot still. It makes me nervous when you wiggle it.* ☐ *You have to hold the nail still if you want to hit it.*

keep someone or something **up 1.** [with *someone*] to prevent someone from going to bed; to keep someone awake. ☐ *Their party kept me up all night.* 🅃 *The noise kept up the entire household.* **2.** [with *something*] to continue doing something. ☐ *I don't know how long I can keep this up.* 🅃 *I can't keep up working this way much longer.*

keep someone **out in the cold** to prevent someone from being informed. (Also literal.) ☐ *Please don't keep me out in the cold. Tell me what's going on.* ☐ *Don't keep your supervisor out in the cold. Tell her what's going on.*

keep someone **posted** to keep someone informed (of what is happening); to keep someone up to date. ☐ *If the price of corn goes up, I need to know. Please keep me posted.* ☐ *Keep her posted about the patient's status.*

keep something **down** to keep food in one's stomach (without vomiting it up). ☐ *I don't know how I managed to keep the pill down.* ☐ *The food must have been spoiled. I couldn't keep it down.* ☐ *Sally is ill. She can't keep solid food down.*

keep something **on an even keel** to keep something in a steady and untroubled state. (See also **keep on an even keel**.) ☐ *The manager cannot keep the company on an even keel any longer.* ☐ *When the workers are unhappy, it is difficult to keep the factory on an even keel.*

keep something **quiet** Go to **keep** someone or something **still**.

keep something **to** oneself to keep something a secret. (Notice the use of *but* in the examples below.) ☐ *I'm quitting my job, but please keep that to yourself.* ☐ *Keep it to yourself, but I'm quitting my job.* ☐ *John is always gossiping. He can't keep anything to himself.*

keep something **under** one's **hat** to keep something a secret; to keep something in one's mind (only). (Informal. If the secret stays under your hat, it stays in your mind. Note the use of *but* in the examples below.) ☐ *Keep this under your hat, but I'm getting married.* ☐ *I'm getting married, but keep it under your hat.*

keep something **under wraps** to keep something concealed (until some future time). ☐ *We kept the plan under wraps until after the election.* ☐ *The automobile company kept the new model under wraps until most of the old models had been sold.*

keep still 1. AND **hold still** do not move. ☐ *Quit wiggling. Keep still!* ☐ *"Hold still.*

I can't examine your ear if you're moving," said the doctor. **2.** Go to **keep quiet (about** someone or something**)**.

keep still (about someone or something**)** Go to **keep quiet (about** someone or something**)**.

keep tab(s) (on someone or something**)** AND **keep track (of** someone or something**)** to monitor someone or something; to follow the activities of someone or something. □ *I'm supposed to keep track of my books.* □ *Try to keep tabs on everyone who works for you.* □ *It's hard to keep tabs when you have a lot of other work to do.* □ *I can't keep track of the money I earn. Maybe someone else is spending it.*

keep the ball rolling to cause something that is in progress to continue. (Also literal. See also **get the ball rolling**.) □ *Tom started the project, and we kept the ball rolling.* □ *Who will keep the ball rolling now that she is gone?*

keep the home fires burning to keep things going at one's home or other central location. (From a World War I song.) □ *My uncle kept the home fires burning when my sister and I went to school.* □ *The manager stays at the office and keeps the home fires burning while I'm out selling our products.*

keep the lid on something to restrain something; to keep something quiet. (Also literal. Informal.) □ *The politician worked hard to keep the lid on the scandal.* □ *The party was noisy because they weren't trying to keep the lid on it. It got louder and louder.*

keep the wolf from the door to maintain oneself at a minimal level; to keep from starving, freezing, etc. □ *I don't make a lot of money, just enough to keep the wolf from the door.* □ *We have a small amount of money saved, hardly enough to keep the wolf from the door.*

keep time 1. to maintain a musical rhythm. □ *Bob had to drop out of the band because he couldn't keep time.* □ *Since he can't keep time, he can't march and he can't play the drums.* **2.** to keep watch over the time in a game or an athletic contest. □ *Ann kept time at all the basketball games.* □ *Whoever keeps time has to watch the referee very carefully.* **3.** [for a clock or a watch] to keep track of time accurately. (See also **keep good time**.) □ *This watch doesn't keep time.* □ *My other watch kept time better.*

keep to oneself to remain solitary; to stay away from other people. □ *Ann tends to keep to herself. She doesn't have many friends.* □ *I try to keep to myself each morning so I can get some work done.*

keep track (of someone or something**)** Go to **keep tab(s) (on** someone or something**)**.

keep up an act AND **keep up** one's **act** to maintain a false front; to act in a special way that is different from one's natural behavior. □ *Most of the time John kept up an act. He was really not a friendly person.* □ *He works hard to keep up his act.*

keep up appearances to keep oneself looking calm or happy despite serious problems. □ *Even with all the trouble Dave was having at home, he still managed to keep up appearances.* □ *She was trained from childhood to keep up appearances no matter how bad she really felt.*

keep up one's **act** Go to **keep up an act**.

keep up (with someone or something**)** to keep pace **(with** someone or something**)**; to advance at the same rate as someone or something. (See the following two entries.) □ *You're running so fast that I cannot keep up with you.* □ *I don't make enough money to keep up with your spending.* □ *You don't even try to keep up.*

keep up (with the Joneses) to stay financially even with one's peers; to work hard to get the same amount of material goods that one's friends and neighbors have. □ *Mr. and Mrs. Brown bought a new car simply to keep up with the Joneses.* □ *Keeping up with the Joneses can take all your money.*

keep up (with the times) to stay in fashion; to keep up with the news; to be contemporary or modern. □ *I try to keep up with the times. I want to know what's going on.* □ *I bought a whole new wardrobe because I want to keep up with the times.*

☐ *Sally learns all the new dances. She likes to keep up.*

Keep your shirt on! Be patient! (Slang. Usually considered rude.) ☐ *Hey, keep your shirt on! I'll be with you in a minute.* ☐ *I'll bring you your hamburger when it's cooked. Just keep your shirt on, friend.*

keyed up anxious; tense and expectant. (Informal.) ☐ *I don't know why I'm so keyed up all the time. I can't even sleep.* ☐ *Ann gets keyed up before a test.*

kick a habit AND **kick the habit** to break a habit. (Slang.) ☐ *It's hard to kick a habit, but it can be done. I stopped biting my nails.* ☐ *I used to drink coffee every morning, but I kicked the habit.*

kick off 1. to start a football game by kicking the ball a great distance. ☐ *Tom kicked off in the last game. Now it's my turn.* ☐ *John tripped when he was kicking off.* **2.** AND **kick the bucket** to die. (Slang. Impolite.) ☐ *Don't say that George Washington "kicked off." Say that he "passed away."* ☐ *My cat kicked off last night. She was tough as a lion.* ☐ *When I kick the bucket, I want a huge funeral with lots of flowers and crying.*

kick oneself **(for** doing something**)** to regret doing something. (Informal.) ☐ *I could just kick myself for going off and not locking the car door. Now the car has been stolen.* ☐ *Don't kick yourself. It's insured.*

kick over Go to turn over.

kick someone or something **around 1.** to treat someone or something badly. (Also literal. Slang.) ☐ *I finally quit my job. My boss wouldn't stop kicking me around.* ☐ *Stop kicking my car around. It does everything I ask it.* **2.** [with *something*] to discuss an idea or a proposal. (Slang.) ☐ *That sounds like a good idea to me. Let's kick it around in our meeting tomorrow.* 🅃 *We kicked around John's idea for a while.*

kick someone **out** AND **boot** someone **out** to send someone away from a place. ☐ *I lived at home until I was eighteen and my father kicked me out.* 🅃 *He kicked out his own child?* 🅃 *Yes. He booted out my brother when he was twenty.*

kick something **in** to contribute some money (to a cause). (Literal meaning to break something in by kicking. Informal.) ☐ *John kicked five dollars in.* 🅃 *I'd be happy to kick in a dollar, but no more.*

kick something **off** to start something; to start off an event. (Also literal.) ☐ *They kicked the picnic off with a footrace.* 🅃 *We kicked off the party by singing rowdy songs.* 🅃 *That was a great way to kick off a weekend.*

kick the bucket Go to kick off.

kick the habit Go to kick a habit.

kick up to cause trouble or discomfort. ☐ *The ignition in my car is kicking up again. I will have to have it looked into.* ☐ *Aunt Jane's arthritis is kicking up. She needs to see the doctor again.*

kick up a fuss AND **kick up a row; kick up a storm** to become a nuisance; to misbehave and disturb (someone). (Informal. *Row* rhymes with *cow*. Note the variation in the examples.) ☐ *The customer kicked up such a fuss about the food that the manager came to apologize.* ☐ *I kicked up such a row that they kicked me out.* ☐ *Oh, what pain! My arthritis is kicking up a storm.*

kick up a row Go to kick up a fuss.

kick up a storm Go to kick up a fuss.

kick up one's **heels** to act frisky; to be lively and have fun. (Informal.) ☐ *I like to go to an old-fashioned square dance and really kick up my heels.* ☐ *For an old man, your uncle is really kicking up his heels.*

kid around (with someone**)** to tease and joke with someone. (Informal.) ☐ *I like to kid around with John. We are great friends.* ☐ *Yes, John and I used to kid around a lot.*

kidding aside Go to (all) joking aside.

kid('s) stuff a very easy task. (Informal.) ☐ *Climbing that hill is kid stuff.* ☐ *Driving an automatic car is kid's stuff.*

kill the fatted calf to prepare an elaborate banquet (in someone's honor). (From the biblical story recounting the return of the prodigal son. *Fatted* is older

English for *fattened.*) □ *When Bob got back from college, his parents killed the fatted calf and threw a great party.* □ *Sorry this meal isn't much, John. We didn't have time to kill the fatted calf.*

kill time to waste time. (Informal.) □ *Stop killing time. Get to work!* □ *We went over to the record shop just to kill time.*

kill two birds with one stone to solve two problems with one solution. □ *John learned the words to his part in the play while peeling potatoes. He was killing two birds with one stone.* □ *I have to cash a check and make a payment on my bank loan. I'll kill two birds with one stone by doing them both in one trip to the bank.*

killed outright killed immediately. □ *The driver was killed outright in the accident.* □ *Twenty people were killed outright in the explosion.*

a **kind of (a)** something a variety of something that is fairly close to the real thing, even though it is not exactly the real thing. (See also **sort of** something.) □ *I used a folded newspaper as a kind of hat to keep the rain off.* □ *Bill is serving as a kind of helper or assistant on this project.*

kind of something Go to **sort of** something.

a **kink in my neck** a twisted place or a cramp in the neck that causes pain. □ *I got a kink in my neck from sleeping in a draft.* □ *When I read on the plane, I get a kink in my neck.*

kiss and make up to forgive (someone) and be friends again. (Also literal.) □ *They were very angry, but in the end they kissed and made up.* □ *I'm sorry. Let's kiss and make up.*

kiss and tell to participate in something secret and private, and then tell other people about it. (Also literal.) □ *The project was supposed to be a secret between Jane and me, but she spread it all around. I didn't think she was the type to kiss and tell.* □ *I am willing to discuss it with you, but only if you promise not to kiss and tell.*

the **kiss of death** an act that puts an end to someone or something. (Informal.) □ *The mayor's veto was the kiss of death for the new law.* □ *Fainting on stage was the kiss of death for my acting career.*

kiss something **good-bye** to anticipate or experience the loss of something. □ *If you leave your camera on a park bench, you can kiss it good-bye.* □ *You kissed your wallet good-bye when you left it in the store.*

kit and caboodle the entire amount; everyone; everything. (Folksy. Often with *whole.*) □ *Everybody in the family was there—the whole kit and caboodle.* □ *The sheriff came and threw the crook out of town, kit and caboodle.*

kith and kin friends and relatives; people known to someone. (Older English. *Kith* means "acquaintances or neighbors" here.) □ *I was delighted to find all my kith and kin waiting for me at the airport to welcome me home.* □ *I sent cards to my kith and kin, telling them of my arrival.*

knee-high to a grasshopper not very tall; short and small, as a child. (Folksy.) □ *Hello, Billy. I haven't seen you since you were knee-high to a grasshopper.* □ *I have two grandchildren, both knee-high to a grasshopper.*

knew it was coming AND **(had) known it was coming** aware in advance that something was to happen. □ *I shouldn't act surprised. I knew it was coming.* □ *It's his own fault. He should have known it was coming.*

knit one's **brow** to wrinkle one's brow, especially by frowning. □ *The woman knit her brow and asked us what we wanted from her.* □ *While he read his book, John knit his brow occasionally. He must not have agreed with what he was reading.*

knock about (somewhere) to travel around; to act as a vagabond. (Informal.) □ *I'd like to take off a year and knock about Europe.* □ *If you're going to knock about, you should do it when you're young.*

knock-down-drag-out fight a serious fight; a serious argument. (Folksy.) □ *Boy, they really had a knock-down-drag-out fight.* □ *Stop calling each other names, or you're going to end up with a real knock-down-drag-out fight.*

knock it off to stop something; to cease something. (Slang.) □ *Shut up, you guys. Knock it off!* □ *Knock it off. I've heard enough of your music.*

knock off work to quit work (for the day). (Informal.) □ *It's time to knock off work.* □ *It's too early to knock off work.*

knock one **off** one's **feet** Go to **sweep** one **off** one's **feet**.

knock oneself **out (to** do something**)** to go to a great deal of trouble to do something. (Informal. As if one had worked oneself into unconsciousness.) □ *I knocked myself out to prepare this meal for you, and you won't even taste it!* □ *I don't know why I knock myself out to do these things for you. You are not at all appreciative.*

knock on wood <a phrase said to cancel out imaginary bad luck.> (The same as the British English "touch wood.") □ *My stereo has never given me any trouble—knock on wood.* □ *We plan to be in Florida by tomorrow evening—knock on wood.*

knock some heads together to scold some people; to get some people to do what they are supposed to be doing. (Also literal. Slang.) □ *If you kids don't quiet down and go to sleep, I'm going to come in your room and knock some heads together.* □ *The government is in a mess. We need to go to Washington and knock some heads together.*

knock someone **dead** to put on a stunning performance or display for someone. (Informal. *Someone* is often replaced by *'em* from *them.*) □ *This band is going to do great tonight. We're going to knock them dead.* □ *"See how your sister is all dressed up!" said Bill. "She's going to knock 'em dead."*

knock someone **down (to size)** Go to **beat** someone **down (to size)**.

knock someone **for a loop** Go to **throw** someone **for a loop**.

knock someone **off** Go to **bump** someone **off**.

knock someone or something **about** Go to **knock** someone or something **around**.

knock someone or something **around** AND **knock** someone or something **about** to mistreat someone or something physically. □ *They knocked my baggage around on the flight to Mexico.* □ *The tough guys knocked me around a little.* □ *They knocked my brother about a bit also.*

knock someone **out (cold) 1.** to knock someone unconscious. (Informal.) □ *The blow knocked the boxer out cold.* □ *The attacker knocked the old man out cold.* **2.** to overwhelm someone. (*Someone* includes *oneself.* See also **knock** oneself **out (to** do something**)**.) □ *The bad news really knocked me out.* □ *Her story was great. It just knocked me out cold!*

knock someone **over with a feather** to leave someone stunned or surprised by something extraordinary. (Folksy.) □ *I was so surprised you could have knocked me over with a feather.* □ *When she heard the news, you could have knocked her over with a feather.*

knock someone's **block off** to strike someone hard, especially in the head. (Slang. The *block* is the head.) □ *If you touch me again, I'll knock your block off.* □ *John punched Bob so hard that he almost knocked his block off.*

knock something **back** Go to **knock** something **down**.

knock something **down** AND **knock** something **back** to drink down a drink of something, especially something alcoholic. (Also literal. Slang.) □ *I don't see how he can knock that stuff down.* 🅃 *John knocked back two beers in ten minutes.*

knock something **off** to finish something, especially in haste or carelessly. (Also literal. Slang.) □ *I knocked it off with the help of Bob.* 🅃 *I knocked off the last chapter of my book in four hours.*

knock the props out from under someone to destroy someone's emotional, financial, or moral underpinnings; to destroy someone's confidence. □ *When you told Sally that she was due to be fired, you really knocked the props out from under her.* □ *I don't want to knock the props out* *from under you, but the bank is foreclosing on your mortgage.*

know (all) the tricks of the trade to possess the skills and knowledge necessary to do something. □ *Tom can repair car engines. He knows the tricks of the trade.* □ *If I knew all the tricks of the trade, I could be a better plumber.*

know a thing or two (about someone or something**)** to be well informed about someone or something; to know something unpleasant about someone or something. (Informal.) □ *I know a thing or two about cars.* □ *I know a thing or two about Mary that would really shock you.*

know a trick or two to know some special way of dealing with a problem. □ *I think I can handle all of this with no trouble. I know a trick or two.* □ *I may be a senior citizen, but I still know a trick or two. I think I can help you with this.*

know better (than to do something**)** to be wise enough, experienced enough, or well trained enough not to have done something wrong. □ *Mary should have known better than to accept a lift from a stranger.* □ *Children should know better than to play in the road.*

know-how knowledge and skill. (Informal.) □ *Peter doesn't have the know-how to mend that car.* □ *Mary hasn't the know-how to work the computer.*

know one's **ABCs** to know the alphabet; to know the most basic things (about something). □ *Bill can't do it. He doesn't even know his ABCs.* □ *You can't expect to a write letter when you don't even know your ABCs.*

know one's **onions** Go to **know** one's **stuff.**

know one's **place** to know the behavior appropriate to one's position or status in life. (See also **put** one **in** one's **place.**) □ *I know my place. I won't speak unless spoken to.* □ *People around here are expected to know their place. You have to follow all the rules.*

know one's **stuff** AND **know** one's **onions** to know what one is expected to know; to know what is needed. (Informal or slang. See also **know the score.**) □ *I know my stuff. I can do my job.* □ *She can't handle the assignment. She doesn't know her onions.*

know one's **way about** Go to **know** one's **way around.**

know one's **way around** AND **know** one's **way about** to know the techniques of getting something done, especially in a bureaucracy. (Also literal.) □ *Sally can get the job done. She knows her way around.* □ *Since Sally worked at city hall for a year, she really knows her way about.*

know someone **by sight** to know the name and recognize the face of someone. □ *I've never met the man, but I know him by sight.* □ *BOB: Have you ever met Mary? JANE: No, but I know her by sight.*

know someone or something **like a book** Go to **know** someone or something **like the palm of one's hand.**

know someone or something **like the back of** one's **hand** Go to **know** someone or something **like the palm of one's hand.**

know someone or something **like the palm of** one's **hand** AND **know** someone or something **like the back of** one's **hand; know** someone or something **like a book** to know someone or something very well. □ *Of course I know John. I know him like the back of my hand.* □ *I know him like a book.*

know something **backwards and forwards** AND **know** something **forwards and backwards** to know something very well; to know a passage of language so well that one could recite it backwards as well as forwards. □ *Of course I've memorized my speech. I know it backwards and forwards.* □ *Todd knows the skeletal structure of the frog backwards and forwards.*

know something **by heart** to know something perfectly; to have memorized something perfectly. □ *I know my speech by heart.* □ *I went over and over it until I knew it by heart.*

know something **forwards and backwards** Go to **know** something **backwards and forwards.**

know something **from memory** to have memorized something so that one does not have to consult a written version; to know something well from seeing it very often. (Almost the same as **know** something **by heart.**) □ *Mary didn't need the script because she knew the play from memory.* □ *The conductor went through the entire concert without music. He knew it from memory.*

know something **in** one's **bones** Go to **feel** something **in** one's **bones.**

know something **inside out** to know something thoroughly; to know about something thoroughly. (Informal.) □ *I know my geometry inside out.* □ *I studied and studied for my driver's test until I knew the rules inside out.*

know something **only too well** to know something very well; to know something from unpleasant experience. (Note the variation in the examples below.) □ *I know the problem only too well.* □ *I know only too well the kind of problem you must face.*

know the ropes to know how to do something. (Informal. See also **learn the ropes.**) □ *I can't do the job because I don't know the ropes.* □ *Ask Sally to do it. She knows the ropes.*

know the score AND **know what's what** to know the facts; to know the facts about life and its difficulties. (Also literal. Informal.) □ *Bob is so naive. He sure doesn't know the score.* □ *I know what you're trying to do. Oh, yes, I know what's what.*

know what's what Go to **know the score.**

know when one **is not wanted** to sense when one presence is not welcome; to know when one is not among friends. (Usually said when someone feels hurt by being ignored by people.) □ *I'm leaving this place! I know when I'm not wanted!* □ *She doesn't know when she's not wanted. Can't she tell she's out of place?*

know where all the bodies are buried to know all the secrets and intrigue; to know all the important details. □ *He is a good choice for president because he knows where all the bodies are buried.* □ *Since he knows where all the bodies are buried, he is the only one who can advise us.*

know whereof one **speaks** to know well the subject that one is speaking about. □ *You are wrong! You do not know whereof you speak.* □ *He simply doesn't know whereof he speaks.*

know where someone **stands (on** someone **or** something**)** to know what someone thinks or feels about someone or something. □ *I don't know where John stands on this issue.* □ *I don't even know where I stand.*

know which is which AND **tell which is which** to be able to distinguish one person or thing from another person or thing. □ *I have an old one and a new one, but I don't know which is which.* □ *I know that Bill and Bob are twins, but I can't tell which is which.*

know which side one's **bread is buttered on** to know what is most advantageous for one. □ *He'll do it if his boss tells him to. He knows which side his bread is buttered on.* □ *Since John knows which side his bread is buttered on, he'll be there on time.*

a **known fact** something that is generally recognized as a fact. □ *That grass is green is a known fact.* □ *It is a known fact that John was in Chicago on the night of the murder.*

known it was coming Go to **knew it was coming.**

a **known quantity** someone whose character, personality, and behavior are recognized and understood. □ *We need not worry about how John will behave. He is a known quantity.* □ *Lisa is a known quantity and I am sure she will not surprise us by voting with the opposition.*

knuckle down (to something**)** to get busy doing something; to get serious about one's work. (Informal.) □ *It's time you knuckled down to your studies.* □ *Sue must knuckle down if she wants to be successful at the office.*

knuckle under (to someone or something**)** to submit to someone or something; to yield or give in to someone or something. (Informal.) □ *You have to knuckle under to your boss if you expect to keep your job.* □ *I'm too stubborn to knuckle under.*

L

a **labor of love** a task that is either unpaid or badly paid and that one does simply for one's own satisfaction or pleasure or to please someone whom one likes or loves. ☐ *Jane made no money out of the biography she wrote. She was writing about the life of a friend and the book was a labor of love.* ☐ *Mary hates knitting, but she made a sweater for her boyfriend. What a labor of love.*

lace into someone or something AND **light into** someone or something to attack, devour, or scold someone or something. (Informal.) ☐ *We laced into a big meal of pork and beans.* ☐ *The bully punched John once, and then John really laced into him.* ☐ *John lit into him with both fists.* ☐ *My father really lit into me when I came in late. He yelled at me for ten minutes.*

laid-back relaxed and unperplexed by difficulties. (Slang.) ☐ *John is so laid-back. Nothing seems to disturb him.* ☐ *I wish I could be more laid-back. I get so tense.*

laid up immobilized for recuperation or repairs. (Said of people and things.) ☐ *I was laid up for two weeks after my accident.* ☐ *My car is laid up for repairs.* ☐ *I was laid up with the flu for a week.* ☐ *Todd was laid up for a month.*

the **land of Nod** sleep. (Humorous. Borrowed from the Bible, Gen. 4:16. From the fact that people sometimes nod when they are falling asleep.) ☐ *The baby is in the land of Nod.* ☐ *Look at the clock! It's time we were all in the land of Nod.*

land on both feet Go to land on one's feet.

land on one's **feet** AND **land on both feet** to recover satisfactorily from a trying situation or a setback. (Also literal. As if having fallen. Informal.) ☐ *Her first year was terrible, but she landed on both feet.* ☐ *It's going to be a hard day. I only hope I land on my feet.*

land up somehow **or** somewhere to finish somehow or somewhere; to come to be in a certain state or place at the end. (Usually in the wrong place or in a bad situation. See also **end up** somewhere.) ☐ *We set out for Denver but landed up in Salt Lake City.* ☐ *He's so extravagant that he landed up in debt.*

a **landslide victory** a victory by a large margin; a very substantial victory, particularly in an election. ☐ *The mayor won a landslide victory in the election.* ☐ *The younger man won a landslide victory in the presidential election.*

lap something **up** to believe something, especially something untrue. (Also literal. Informal.) ☐ *Did she believe it? She just lapped it up.* 🅃 *I can't imagine why she lapped up that ridiculous story.*

lapse into a coma to go into a coma. ☐ *The survivor of the crash lapsed into a coma.* ☐ *Aunt Mary lapsed into a coma and died.*

large as life Go to (as) large as life.

last but not least last in sequence, but not last in importance. (A cliché. Often said when introducing people.) ☐ *The speaker said, "And now, last but not least, I'd like to present Bill Smith, who will give us some final words."* ☐ *And last but not least, here is the loser of the race.*

a **last-ditch effort** a final effort; the last possible attempt. ☐ *I made one last-ditch effort to get her to stay.* ☐ *It was a last-ditch effort. I didn't expect it to work.*

the **last person** the most unlikely person of whom one could think in a particular situation; the most unlikely person to do something. (Also literal. Preceded by *be, become,* or *seem like.*) □ *Bob seems like the last person for Tom to insult. He's so hot-tempered.* □ *Mary was the last person to ask to chair the meeting—she's so shy.*

last will and testament Go to someone's **last will and testament.**

late in life when one is old. □ *She injured her hip running. She's exercising rather late in life.* □ *Isn't it sort of late in life to buy a house?*

late in the day far along in a project or activity; too late in a project or activity for action, decisions, etc., to be taken. □ *It was a bit late in the day for him to apologize.* □ *It's late in the day to try to change the plans.*

laugh all the way to the bank to be very happy about money that has been earned by doing something that other people might think is unfair. □ *He may not be in the nicest business, but he is doing well and can laugh all the way to the bank.* □ *She makes tons of money doing what no one else will do and laughs all the way to the bank.*

laugh out of the other side of one's **mouth** to change sharply from happiness to sadness. □ *Now that you know the truth, you'll laugh out of the other side of your mouth.* □ *He was so proud that he won the election. He's laughing out of the other side of his mouth since they recounted the ballots and found out that he lost.*

laugh something **off** to avoid or reject a serious problem by laughing at it. □ *Tom suffered an injury to his leg, but he laughed it off and kept playing ball.* Ⓣ *Mary just laughed off her bad experience.*

laugh something **out of court** to dismiss something as ridiculous. □ *The committee laughed the suggestion out of court.* □ *Bob's request for a large salary increase was laughed out of court.*

laugh up one's **sleeve** to laugh secretly; to laugh quietly to oneself. (Informal.) □ *Jane looked very serious, but I knew she was laughing up her sleeve.* □ *I told Sally that her dress was darling, but I was laughing up my sleeve because it was too small.*

launch forth (on something**)** Go to **set forth (on** something**); take off (on** something**).**

law unto oneself one who makes one's own laws or rules; one who sets one's own standards of behavior. □ *You can't get Bill to follow the rules. He's a law unto himself.* □ *Jane is a law unto herself. She's totally unwilling to cooperate.*

lay a finger on someone or something to touch someone or something, even slightly. (Usually in the negative. Compare this with **put** one's **finger on** something.) □ *Don't you dare lay a finger on my pencil. Go get your own!* □ *If you lay a finger on me, I'll scream.*

lay an egg [for someone] to give a bad performance. (Literal with birds and most reptiles. Informal.) □ *The cast of the play really laid an egg last night.* □ *I hope I don't lay an egg when it's my turn to sing.*

lay down one's **life (for** someone or something**)** to sacrifice one's life for someone or something. □ *Would you lay down your life for your country?* □ *There aren't many things for which I'd lay down my life.*

lay down on the job Go to **lie down on the job.**

lay down the law 1. to state firmly what the rules are (for something). □ *Before the meeting, the boss laid down the law. We all knew exactly what to do.* □ *The way she laid down the law means that I'll remember her rules.* **2.** to scold someone for misbehaving. (Informal.) □ *When the teacher caught us, he really laid down the law.* □ *Poor Bob. He really got it when his mother laid down the law.*

lay eyes on someone or something Go to **set eyes on** someone or something.

lay hold of someone or something to grasp someone or something with the hands. (Informal. Compare this with **get** one's **hands on** someone or something; **get (a)hold of** someone or something.) □ *Just wait till I lay hold of Bill!* □ *I can't wait to lay hold* *of that fishing pole. I'm ready to catch a huge fish.*

lay into someone or something to attack, consume, or scold someone or something. □ *Bob laid into the big plate of fried chicken.* □ *The bear laid into the hunter.* □ *My father really laid into me when I got home.*

lay it on thick AND **lay it on with a trowel; pour it on thick; spread it on thick** to exaggerate praise, excuses, or blame. □ *Sally was laying it on thick when she said that Tom was the best singer she had ever heard.* □ *After Bob finished making his excuses, Sally said that he was pouring it on thick.* □ *Bob always spreads it on thick.*

lay it on with a trowel Go to lay it on thick.

lay low Go to lie low.

lay off (someone or something**)** to leave someone or something alone; to stop bothering someone or something; to **take it easy (on** someone or something**)**. (Slang. See also **lay** someone **off.**) □ *Lay off Bill. He didn't mean any harm!* □ *Hey! I said lay off!* □ *Lay off the butter. Don't use it all up.*

the **lay of the land 1.** the arrangement of features on an area of land. □ *The surveyor mapped the lay of the land.* □ *The geologist studied the lay of the land, trying to determine if there was oil below.* **2.** the arrangement or organization of something other than land. □ *As soon as I get the lay of the land in my new job, things will go better.* □ *The company's corporate structure was complex, so understanding the lay of the land took time.*

lay one's **cards on the table** Go to **put** one's **cards on the table.**

lay one's **hands on** someone or something Go to **get** one's **hands on** someone or something.

lay over (somewhere**)** to pause somewhere during one's journey. (Compare this with **stop over (**somewhere**).**) □ *I had to lay over in San Antonio for a few hours before my plane left.* □ *I want a bus that goes straight through. I don't want to lay over.*

lay someone **away** to bury someone. □ *They laid my uncle away last week.* □ *They laid him away with a quiet ceremony.*

lay someone **off** to put an employee out of work, possibly temporarily. □ *They even laid the president off.* 🆃 *The computer factory laid off two thousand workers.*

lay someone **up** to cause someone to be ill in bed. □ *A broken leg laid me up for two months.* 🆃 *Flu laid up everyone at work for a week or more.*

lay something **by** Go to **put** something **by.**

lay something **in** to get something and store it for future use. □ *They laid a lot of food in for the holidays.* 🆃 *We always lay in a large supply of firewood each November.*

lay something **on** someone to direct blame, guilt, or verbal abuse at someone. (Also literal. Slang. See also **put the blame on** someone or something.) □ *Don't lay that stuff on me! It's not my fault.* □ *The boss is in the conference room laying a lot of anger on the sales staff.*

lay something **on the line** Go to **put** something **on the line.**

lay something **to rest** Go to **put** something **to rest.**

lay something **to waste** AND **lay waste to** something to destroy an area (literally or figuratively). □ *The invaders laid the village to waste.* □ *The kids came in and laid waste to my clean house.*

lay the blame on someone or something Go to **put the blame on** someone or something.

lay the finger on someone Go to **put the finger on** someone.

lay waste to something Go to **lay** something **to waste.**

lead a dog's life AND **live a dog's life** to lead a miserable life. □ *Poor Jane really leads a dog's life.* □ *I've been working so hard. I'm tired of living a dog's life.*

lead off to begin; to start (assuming that others will follow). □ *We were waiting for someone to start dancing. Finally, Bob and Jane led off.* □ *The hunter led off, and the dogs followed.* □ *The first baseman will* *lead off as the first batter in the baseball game.*

lead someone **by the nose** to force someone to go somewhere (with you); to lead someone by coercion. (Informal.) □ *John had to lead Tom by the nose to get him to the opera.* □ *I'll go, but you'll have to lead me by the nose.*

lead someone **down the garden path** to deceive someone. □ *Now, be honest with me. Don't lead me down the garden path.* □ *That cheater really led her down the garden path.*

lead someone **on a merry chase** to lead someone in a purposeless pursuit. □ *What a waste of time. You really led me on a merry chase.* □ *Jane led Bill on a merry chase trying to find an antique lamp.*

lead someone **to believe** something to imply something to someone; to cause someone to believe something untrue, without lying. □ *But you led me to believe that this watch was guaranteed!* □ *Did you lead her to believe that she was hired as a clerk?*

lead someone **to** do something to cause someone to do something. □ *This agent led me to purchase a worthless piece of land.* □ *My illness led me to quit my job.*

lead the life of Riley to live in luxury. (Informal. No one knows who Riley is.) □ *If I had a million dollars, I could live the life of Riley.* □ *The treasurer took our money to Mexico, where he lived the life of Riley until the police caught him.*

lead up to something to prepare the way for something. □ *His compliments were his way of leading up to asking for money.* □ *What were his actions leading up to?*

a **leading question** a question that suggests the kind of answer that the person who asks it wants to hear. □ *The mayor was angered by the reporter's leading questions.* □ *"Don't you think that the police are failing to stop crime?" is an example of a leading question.*

leaf through something Go to **thumb through** something.

leak something **(out)** AND **let** something **(get) out** to disclose special information to the press so that the resulting publicity will accomplish something. (Also literal. Usually said of government disclosures. Also used for accidental disclosures.) □ *Don't leak that information out.* □ *I don't want to be the one to leak it.* □ *They let it get out on purpose.*

lean on someone to try to make someone do something; to coerce someone to do something. (Also literal. Informal.) □ *If she refuses to do it, lean on her a bit.* □ *Don't lean on me! I don't have to do it if I don't want to.*

lean over backwards (to do something**)** Go to **fall over backwards (to** do something**)**.

lean toward doing something to tend toward doing something; to favor doing something. □ *The union is leaning toward accepting the proposal.* □ *My friends leaned toward swimming instead of shopping.*

leap at the opportunity Go to **jump at the chance**.

leap to conclusions Go to **jump to conclusions**.

learn something **by heart** to learn something so well that it can be written or recited without thinking; to memorize something. □ *The director told me to learn my speech by heart.* □ *I had to go over it many times before I learned it by heart.*

learn something **by rote** to learn something by memorizing without giving any thought to what is being learned. □ *I learned history by rote; then I couldn't pass the test that required me to think.* □ *If you learn things by rote, you'll never understand them.*

learn something **from the bottom up** to learn something thoroughly, from the very beginning; to learn all aspects of something, even the least important ones. □ *I learned my business from the bottom up.* □ *I started out sweeping the floors and learned everything from the bottom up.*

learn (something) **the hard way** AND **find** (something) **out the hard way** to learn something by experience, especially by an unpleasant experience. □ *She learned how to make investments the hard way.* □

I wish I didn't have to learn things the hard way. □ *I found out the hard way that it's difficult to work and go to school at the same time.* □ *Investing in real estate is tricky. I found that out the hard way.*

learn the ropes to learn how to do something; to learn how to work something. (Informal. See also **know the ropes; show** someone **the ropes.**) □ *I'll be able to do my job very well as soon as I learn the ropes.* □ *John is very slow to learn the ropes.*

learn to live with something to learn to adapt to something unpleasant or painful. (See also **have to live with** something.) □ *Finally the doctor told Marion that she was going to have to learn to live with her arthritis.* □ *The floor plan of the house we bought is not as handy as we had thought, but we will learn to live with it.*

least of all least; of smallest importance. (Informal.) □ *There were many things wrong with the new house. Least of all, the water faucets leaked.* □ *What a bad day. Many things went wrong, but least of all, I tore my shirt.*

leave a bad taste in someone's **mouth** [for someone or something] to leave a bad feeling or memory with someone. (Also literal. Informal.) □ *The whole business about the missing money left a bad taste in his mouth.* □ *It was a very nice party, but something about it left a bad taste in my mouth.* □ *I'm sorry that Bill was there. He always leaves a bad taste in my mouth.*

leave a lot to be desired to be lacking something important; to be inadequate. (A polite way of saying that something is bad.) □ *This report leaves a lot to be desired.* □ *I'm sorry to have to fire you, Mary, but your work leaves a lot to be desired.*

leave a sinking ship Go to desert a sinking ship.

leave no stone unturned to search in all possible places. (Refers to finding something under a rock.) □ *Don't worry. We'll find your stolen car. We'll leave no stone unturned.* □ *In searching for a nice place to live, we left no stone unturned.*

leave oneself **wide open for** something AND **leave** oneself **wide open to** something to invite criticism or joking about oneself; to fail to protect oneself from criticism or ridicule. □ *Yes, that was a harsh remark, Jane, but you left yourself wide open to it.* □ *I can't complain about your joke. I left myself wide open for it.*

leave oneself **wide open to** something Go to **leave** oneself **wide open for** something.

leave one's **mark on** someone [for someone like a teacher] to affect the behavior and performance of another person. □ *The wise professor left her mark on her students.* □ *My father left his mark on me, and I will always remember all his good advice.*

leave one **to** one's **fate** to abandon someone to whatever may happen—possibly death or some other unpleasant event. □ *We couldn't rescue the miners, and we were forced to leave them to their fate.* □ *Please don't try to help. Just go away and leave me to my fate.*

leave someone **flat 1.** to fail to entertain or stimulate someone. (Informal.) □ *Your joke left me flat.* □ *We listened carefully to his lecture, but it left us flat.* **2.** to leave someone without any money—**flat broke.** □ *Paying all my bills left me flat.* □ *The robber took all my money and left me flat.* **3.** to leave someone completely alone. □ *I was at the dance with Harry, but when he met Alice, he left me flat.* □ *They just walked off and left us flat.*

leave someone **for dead** to abandon someone as being dead. (The abandoned person may actually be alive.) □ *He looked so bad that they almost left him for dead.* □ *As the soldiers turned—leaving the enemy captain for dead—the captain fired at them.*

leave someone **high and dry 1.** to leave someone unsupported and unable to maneuver; to leave someone helpless. (Also literal. See also **high and dry.**) □ *All my workers quit and left me high and dry.* □ *All the children ran away and left Billy high and dry to take the blame for the broken window.* **2.** to leave someone **flat**

broke. □ *Mrs. Franklin took all the money out of the bank and left Mr. Franklin high and dry.* □ *Paying the bills always leaves me high and dry.*

leave someone **holding the bag** to leave someone to take all the blame; to leave someone appearing guilty. (Also literal. Informal.) □ *They all ran off and left me holding the bag. It wasn't even my fault.* □ *It was the mayor's fault, but he wasn't left holding the bag.*

leave someone **in peace** to stop bothering someone; to go away and leave someone alone. (Does not necessarily mean to go away from a person.) □ *Please go—leave me in peace.* □ *Can't you see that you're upsetting her? Leave her in peace.*

leave someone **in the lurch** to leave someone waiting for or anticipating your actions. □ *Where were you, John? You really left me in the lurch.* □ *I didn't mean to leave you in the lurch. I thought we had canceled our meeting.*

leave someone or something **hanging in midair** AND **keep** someone or something **hanging in midair** to suspend dealing with someone or something; to leave someone or something waiting to be finished or continued. (Also literal.) □ *She left her sentence hanging in midair.* □ *She left us hanging in midair when she paused.* □ *Tell me the rest of the story. Don't leave me hanging in midair.* □ *Don't leave the story hanging in midair.*

leave someone or something **in** one's **hands** to give one control of or responsibility for someone or something. □ *You left the whole project in my hands!* □ *I have to leave the care of baby in your hands while I go to the doctor.*

leave someone **out in the cold** to fail to inform someone; to exclude someone. (Also literal. Informal. Compare this with the previous entry.) □ *I don't know what's going on. They left me out in the cold.* □ *Tom wasn't invited. They left him out in the cold.*

leave something **on** to leave something running or operating. (Also literal in reference to wearing clothes.) □ *Please don't leave the light on.* □ *Ann went to school and left her radio on.*

leave something **open** to leave a date or time unscheduled. □ *I left something open on Friday, just in case we want to leave work early.* □ *Please leave an appointment open for Mrs. Wallace next week. She will be calling in to our office for an appointment.*

leave well enough alone Go to let well enough alone.

leave word (with someone**)** to leave a message with someone (who will pass the message on to someone else). □ *If you decide to go to the convention, please leave word with my secretary.* □ *Leave word before you go.* □ *I left word with your brother. Didn't he give you the message?*

left and right Go to right and left.

lend a hand (to someone**)** Go to lend (someone) a hand.

lend an ear (to someone**)** to listen to someone. □ *Lend an ear to John. Hear what he has to say.* □ *I'd be delighted to lend an ear. I find great wisdom in everything John has to say.*

lend color to something to provide an interesting accompaniment for something. □ *Your clever comments lent a great deal of color to the slide show of your vacation.* □ *The excellent master of ceremonies will lend color to an otherwise dry and uninteresting dance recital.*

lend oneself **or itself to** something [for someone or something] to be adaptable to something; [for someone or something] to be useful for something. □ *This room doesn't lend itself to bright colors.* □ *John doesn't lend himself to casual conversation.*

lend (someone) **a hand** AND **lend a hand (to** someone**)** to give someone some help, not necessarily with the hands. □ *Could you lend me a hand with this piano? I need to move it across the room.* □ *Could you lend a hand with this math assignment?* □ *I'd be happy to lend a hand.*

less than pleased displeased. □ *We were less than pleased to learn of your comments.* □ *Bill was less than pleased at the outcome of the election.*

the **lesser (of the two)** the smaller one (of two); the one having the least amount. □ *The last two pieces of pie were not quite the same size, and I chose the lesser of the two.* □ *Faced with a basket containing too much and one with too little, Tom chose the lesser.*

the **lesser of two evils** the less bad thing, of a pair of bad things. □ *I didn't like either politician, so I voted for the lesser of two evils.* □ *Given the options of going out with someone I don't like and staying home and watching a boring television program, I chose the lesser of the two evils and watched television.*

let alone someone or something not to mention or think of someone or something; not even to take someone or something into account. □ *Do I have a dollar? I don't even have a dime, let alone a dollar.* □ *I didn't invite John, let alone the rest of his family.*

Let bygones be bygones. One should forget the problems of the past. (Proverb.) □ *Okay, Sally, let bygones be bygones. Let's forgive and forget.* □ *Jane was unwilling to let bygones be bygones. She still won't speak to me.*

let go of someone or something to release someone or something. □ *Please let go of me!* □ *Don't let go of the steering wheel.*

let go (with something**)** AND **cut loose (with** something**); let loose (with** something**)** to shout something out or expel something; to shout or express something wildly. (Slang.) □ *The audience cut loose with a loud cheer.* □ *The whole team let go with a loud shout.* □ *John let loose with a horrendous belch.* □ *I wish you wouldn't let loose like that!*

let grass grow under one's **feet** to do nothing; to stand still. □ *Mary doesn't let the grass grow under her feet. She's always busy.* □ *Bob is too lazy. He's letting the grass grow under his feet.*

let her rip AND **let it roll** to go ahead and start something; let something begin. (Informal or slang. *Her* is usually *'er*.) □ *When Bill was ready for John to start the engine, he said, "Okay, John, let 'er rip."* □ *When Sally heard Bob say "Let 'er rip," she let the anchor go to the bottom of the lake.* □ *Let's go, Bill. Let it roll!*

let it all hang out to tell or reveal everything and hold back nothing (because one is relaxed or carefree). (Also literal. Slang.) □ *Sally has no secrets. She lets it all hang out all the time.* □ *Relax, John. Let it all hang out.*

Let it go. Forget it.; Stop worrying about it. □ *Don't get so angry about it. Let it go.* □ *Let it go. Stop fretting.*

let it roll Go to let her rip.

let loose (with something**)** Go to let go (with something).

let off steam AND **blow off steam** [for someone] to release excess energy or anger. (Also literal in the case of steam engines. Informal.) □ *Whenever John gets a little angry, he blows off steam.* □ *Don't worry about John. He's just letting off steam.*

let oneself **go** to become less constrained; to get excited and have a good time. □ *I love to dance and just let myself go.* □ *Let yourself go, John. Learn to enjoy life.*

let one's **emotions show** to be emotional, especially where it is not appropriate. □ *I'm sorry for the outburst. I didn't mean to let my emotions show.* □ *Please stop crying. You mustn't let your emotions show.*

let one's **hair down** to become more intimate and begin to speak frankly. (Also literal. Informal.) □ *Come on, Jane, let your hair down and tell me all about it.* 🅃 *I have a problem. Do you mind if I let down my hair?*

let out some kind of sound [for a living creature] to make some kind of a noise or sound. □ *Be quiet. Don't let out a sound!* □ *Suddenly, Jane let out a shriek.*

Let sleeping dogs lie. One should not search for trouble and one should leave well enough alone. (Proverb.) □ *Don't mention that problem with Tom again. It's almost forgotten. Let sleeping dogs lie.* □ *You'll never be able to reform Bill. Leave him alone. Let sleeping dogs lie.*

let someone **down** to disappoint someone; to fail someone. (Also literal.) □ *I'm sorry I let you down. Something came up, and I couldn't meet you.* □ *I don't want to let you down, but I can't support you in the election.*

let someone **go** to dismiss someone from employment; to fire someone. □ *John was not working out as well as we had hoped, and we had to let him go.* □ *They let a number of the older workers go and were faced with an age discrimination suit.*

let someone **have it (with both barrels)** to strike someone or attack someone verbally. (Refers to firing a shotgun. Informal. *With both barrels* intensifies the phrase. Refers to the firing a double-barreled shotgun.) □ *I really let Tom have it with both barrels. I told him he had better not do that again if he knows what's good for him.* □ *Bob let John have it—with both barrels.*

let someone **in on** something to tell someone the secret. (Informal. The *something* can be a *plan, arrangements, scheme, trick,* or anything else that might be kept a secret.) □ *Should we let John in on the secret?* □ *Please let me in on the plan.*

let someone **know (about** something**)** to tell someone something; to inform someone of something. □ *Please let me know about it soon.* □ *Will you be coming to the picnic? Please let me know.*

let someone **off easy** Go to **let** someone or something **off.**

let someone **off (the hook)** to release someone from a responsibility. □ *Please let me off the hook for Saturday. I have other plans.* □ *Okay, I'll let you off.*

let someone or something **off 1.** AND **let** someone **off easy** [with *someone*] to release or dismiss someone without punishment. (See also **get off easy.**) □ *The judge didn't let me off.* 🅃 *The judge let off Mary with a warning.* **2.** [with *someone*] to permit someone to disembark or leave a means of transportation. □ *The driver let Mary off the bus.* □ *"I can't let you off at this corner," said the driver.* **3.** [with *something*] to release something; to give something off. 🅃 *The engine was letting off some kind of smoke.* 🅃 *The flower let off a wonderful smell.*

let something **(get) out** Go to **leak** something **(out).**

let something **pass** to let something go unnoticed or unchallenged. □ *Bob let Bill's insult pass because he didn't want to argue.* □ *Don't worry, I'll let this little incident pass.*

let something **ride** to allow something to continue or remain as it is. (Informal.) □ *It isn't the best plan, but we'll let it ride.* □ *I disagree with you, but I'll let it ride.*

let something **slide** to neglect something. (Also literal. Informal.) □ *John let his lessons slide.* □ *Jane doesn't let her work slide.*

let something **slide by** Go to **let** something **slip by.**

let something **slip by** AND **let** something **slide by 1.** to forget or miss an important time or date. (Also literal.) □ *I'm sorry I just let your birthday slip by.* □ *I let it slide by accidentally.* **2.** to waste a period of time. □ *You wasted the whole day by letting it slip by.* □ *We were having fun, and we let the time slide by.*

let something **slip (out)** to tell a secret by accident. (Also literal.) □ *I didn't let it slip out on purpose. It was an accident.* □ *John let the plans slip when he was talking to Bill.*

Let the buyer beware. The person who buys something should investigate the goods or property thoroughly for damage or suitability. (Proverb.) □ *Be careful when buying things from street vendors. Let the buyer beware.* □ *It's the purchaser's job to make sure the goods are ok. Let the buyer beware.*

let the cat out of the bag AND **spill the beans** to reveal a secret or a surprise by accident. (Also literal.) □ *When Bill glanced at the door, he let the cat out of the bag. We knew then that he was expecting someone to arrive.* □ *We are planning a surprise party for Jane. Don't let the cat out* *of the bag.* □ *It's a secret. Try not to spill the beans.*

let the chance slip by to lose the opportunity (to do something). □ *When I was younger, I wanted to become a doctor, but I let the chance slip by.* □ *Don't let the chance slip by. Do it now!*

let things slide to ignore the things that one is supposed to do; to fall behind in the doing of one's work. (Also literal.) □ *I am afraid that I have let things slide while I was recovering from my operation.* □ *If I let things slide for even one day, I get hopelessly behind in my work.*

let up (on someone or something**)** to take the pressure off someone or something; to **take it easy (on** someone or something**).** □ *Please let up on me. I can't work any faster, and you're making me nervous.* □ *Let up on the project. You're working too hard.* □ *Yes, I guess I had better let up.*

let us do something we will do something [together]. (A gentle command. More formal than *let's*.) □ *Let us go in peace.* □ *Let us bow our heads in prayer.*

let well enough alone AND **leave well enough alone** to leave things as they are (and not try to improve them). □ *There isn't much more you can accomplish here. Why don't you just let well enough alone?* □ *This is as good as I can do. I'll stop and leave well enough alone.*

Let's do lunch. Let's have lunch together sometime. (Informal.) □ *Some time next week, let's do lunch.* □ *Can't talk to you now. Let's do lunch sometime.*

level something **at** someone to aim a remark at someone; to direct something at someone. □ *John leveled a sarcastic comment at his teacher.* □ *The editorial leveled its remarks at the mayor.*

level with someone to be honest with someone. (Slang.) □ *Come on, Bill. Level with me. Did you do it?* □ *I'm leveling with you. I wasn't even in town. I couldn't have done it.*

license to do something permission, right, or justification to do something. □ *You have no license to behave in that manner!* □ *Who granted you license to enter my house without knocking?*

a **lick of work** [not even] a bit of work. (Usually in the negative.) □ *I couldn't get her to do a lick of work all day long!* □ *The boys didn't do a lick of work while you were away.*

lick one's **chops** to show one's eagerness to do something, especially to eat something. (Refers to the licking of one's lips in expectation of eating. Some animals, but not people, really do lick their chops.) □ *We could tell from the way the boys were licking their chops that they really wanted a turn at riding the motorcycle.* □ *Fred started licking his chops when he smelled the turkey roasting in the oven.*

lick one's **lips** to show eagerness or pleasure about a future event. (Also literal. Informal. From the habit of people licking their lips when they are about to enjoy eating something.) □ *The children licked their lips at the sight of the cake.* □ *The author's readers were licking their lips in anticipation of her new novel.* □ *The journalist was licking his lips when he went off to interview the disgraced politician.*

lick something **into shape** AND **whip** something **into shape** to put something into good condition. (Informal.) □ *I have to lick this report into shape this morning.* □ *Let's all lend a hand and whip this house into shape. It's a mess.*

lie down on the job AND **lay down on the job** to do one's job poorly or not at all. (*Lay* is a common error for *lie*.) □ *Tom was fired because he was laying down on the job.* □ *You mean he was lying down on the job, don't you?* □ *Sorry, I was lying down on the job in English class.*

lie fallow 1. [for land] to remain unused. □ *Each year we let a different section of our farmland lie fallow.* □ *The land that is lying fallow this year will be cultivated next year.* **2.** [for a skill and talent] to remain unused and neglected. □ *You should not let your talent lie fallow. Practice the piano before you forget how to play it.* □ *His writing had lain fallow for so long that he could hardly write a proper sentence.*

lie in state [for a corpse] to be on display in a public place. □ *The dead leader lay in state for three days in the country's main city.* □ *While the king lay in state, many people walked by and paid their respects.*

lie in wait for someone or something to wait quietly in ambush for someone or something. □ *The lion lay in wait for the zebra.* □ *The robber was lying in wait for a victim.*

lie low AND **lay low** to keep quiet and not be noticed; to avoid being conspicuous. (Informal. *Lay* is a common error for *lie.*) □ *I suggest you lie low for a few days.* □ *The robber said that he would lay low for a short time after the robbery.*

lie through one's **teeth** to lie boldly. □ *I knew she was lying through her teeth, but I didn't want to say so just then.* □ *I'm not lying through my teeth! I never do!*

life is too short life is short and there is no point in wasting it on things like worry, hatred, vengeance, etc. □ *I am not going to spend any more time trying to get even with Wally. Life's too short.* □ *It's a waste of time worrying about money. Life is too short for that.*

the **life of the party** the type of person who is lively and helps make a party fun and exciting. □ *Bill is always the life of the party. Be sure to invite him.* □ *Bob isn't exactly the life of the party, but he's polite.*

Life's been good (to me). I am grateful that I am doing well in life. □ *I can't complain. Life's been good to me.* □ *I doing fine. Life's been good.*

lift a hand (against someone or something**)** AND **raise a hand (against** someone or something**)** to threaten (to strike) someone or something. (Often in the negative. The *a hand* can be replaced with *one's hand.*) □ *She's very peaceful. She wouldn't lift a hand against a fly.* □ *That's right. She wouldn't lift a hand.* □ *Would you raise your hand against your own brother?*

light as a feather Go to **(as) light as a feather.**

light into someone or something Go to **lace into** someone or something.

light out (for somewhere**)** to depart in haste for somewhere. (Informal.) □ *The bus pulled away and lit out for the next stop.* □ *It's time I lit out for home.* □ *I should have lit out ten minutes ago.*

light out (of somewhere**)** to depart somewhere in haste. (Informal.) □ *It's time I lit out of here. I'm late for my next appointment.* □ *Look at that horse go. He really lit out of the starting gate.*

Lightning never strikes twice (in the same place). It is extremely unlikely that the same misfortune will occur again in the same set of circumstances or to the same people. (Proverb.) □ *Ever since the fire, Jean has been afraid that her house will catch fire again, but they say that lightning never strikes twice.* □ *Supposedly lightning never strikes twice, but the Smiths' house has been robbed twice this year.*

like a bat out of hell with great speed and force. (Use caution with *hell.*) □ *Did you see her leave? She left like a bat out of hell.* □ *The car sped down the street like a bat out of hell.*

like a bolt out of the blue suddenly and without warning. (Refers to a bolt of lightning coming out of a clear blue sky. See also **out of a clear blue sky.**) □ *The news came to us like a bolt out of the blue.* □ *Like a bolt out of the blue, the boss came and fired us all.*

like a bump on a log unresponsive; immobile. □ *I spoke to him, but he just sat there like a bump on a log.* □ *Don't stand there like a bump on a log. Give me a hand!*

like a fish out of water appearing to be completely out of place; in a very awkward manner. □ *Vincent stood there in his rented tuxedo, looking like a fish out of water.* □ *Whenever I am with your friends, I feel like a fish out of water. What on earth do you see in them—or me?* □ *At a formal dance, John is like a fish out of water.*

like a house afire Go to **like a house on fire.**

like a house on fire AND **like a house afire** rapidly and with force. (Folksy.) □ *The truck came roaring down the road like a house on fire.* □ *The crowd burst through the gate like a house afire.*

(like) an open book like someone or something that is easy to understand. (Preceded by *be* or *seem.*) □ *Jane's an open book. I always know what she is going to do next.* □ *The committee's intentions are an open book. They want to save money.*

like a sitting duck AND **like sitting ducks** unguarded; unsuspecting and unaware. (The second phrase is the plural form. See also **be a sitting duck**.) □ *He was waiting there like a sitting duck—a perfect target for a mugger.* □ *The soldiers were standing at the top of the hill like sitting ducks. It's a wonder they weren't all killed.*

like a three-ring circus chaotic; exciting and busy. □ *Our household is like a three-ring circus on Monday mornings.* □ *This meeting is like a three-ring circus. Quiet down and listen!*

like crazy AND **like mad** furiously; very much, fast, many, or actively. (Slang.) □ *People are coming in here like crazy. There isn't enough room for them all.* □ *We sold ice cream like crazy. It was a very hot day.* □ *When she stubbed her toe, she started screaming like mad.*

like greased lightning very fast. (Folksy. Informal. See also **(as) quick as greased lightning**.) □ *He left the room like greased lightning.* □ *They fled the burning building like greased lightning.*

like it or lump it either accept it or **drop dead**. (Slang and fairly rude.) □ *I don't care whether you care for my attitude or not. You can just like it or lump it.* □ *This is all the food you get. Like it or lump it!*

Like it's such a big deal! It really isn't all that important! (Informal. Sarcastic.) □ *So I dropped the glass. Like it's such a big deal.* □ *Like it's such a big deal. Who cares?*

like lambs to the slaughter quietly and without seeming to realize or complain about the likely difficulties or dangers of a situation. □ *Young men fighting in World War I simply went like lambs to the slaughter.* □ *Our team went on the football field like lambs to the slaughter to meet the league-leaders.*

like looking for a needle in a haystack engaged in a hopeless search. □ *Trying to find a white dog in the snow is like looking for a needle in a haystack.* □ *I tried to find my lost contact lens on the beach, but it was like looking for a needle in a haystack.*

like mad Go to **like crazy**.

like nothing on earth 1. very untidy or very unattractive. (Informal.) □ *Joan arrived at the office looking like nothing on earth. She had fallen in the mud.* □ *Alice was like nothing on earth in that electric yellow dress.* **2.** very unusual; otherworldly. □ *The new car models look like nothing on earth this year.* □ *This cake is so good! It's like nothing on earth!*

like one of the family as if someone (or a pet) were a member of one's family. (Informal.) □ *We treat our dog like one of the family.* □ *We are very happy to have you stay with us, Bill. I hope you don't mind if we treat you like one of the family.*

like sitting ducks Go to **like a sitting duck**.

like to hear oneself **talk** [for someone] to enjoy one's talking more than other people enjoy listening to it. □ *I guess I don't really have anything to say. I just like to hear myself talk, I guess.* □ *There he goes again. He just likes to hear himself talk.*

like (two) peas in a pod very close or intimate. (Compare this with **as alike as (two) peas in a pod**.) □ *Yes, they're close. Like two peas in a pod.* □ *They're always together. Like peas in a pod.*

like water off a duck's back easily; without any apparent effect. □ *Insults rolled off John like water off a duck's back.* □ *The bullets had no effect on the steel door. They fell away like water off a duck's back.*

likely as not Go to **(as) likely as not**.

the **likes of** someone someone; anyone like someone. (Informal. Almost always in a negative sense.) □ *I don't like Bob. I* *wouldn't do anything for the likes of him.* ☐ *Nobody wants the likes of him around.*

the **line of least resistance** the course of action that will cause least trouble or effort. (Compare this with **path of least resistance.**) ☐ *Jane won't stand up for her rights. She always takes the line of least resistance.* ☐ *Joan never states her point of view. She takes the line of least resistance and agrees with everyone else.*

line one's **own pockets** to make money for oneself in a greedy or dishonest fashion. (Slang.) ☐ *When it was discovered that the sales manager was lining her own pockets with commissions, she was fired.* ☐ *If you line your pockets while in public office, you'll get in serious trouble.*

line someone or something **up with** something to position someone or something (or a group) in reference to other things. (See also **fix** someone **up (with** someone or something**).**) ☐ *Please line the chairs up with the floor tiles.* 🅃 *Line up this brick with the bricks below and at both sides. That's the way you lay bricks.* 🅃 *Line up the boys with the row of trees.*

line someone **up (for** something**)** to schedule someone for something; to arrange for someone to do or be something. ☐ *I lined gardeners up for the summer work on the gardens.* 🅃 *I lined up four of my best friends to serve as ushers at my wedding.*

line someone **up with** someone Go to **fix** someone **up with** someone.

the **lion's share (of** something**)** the larger share of something. ☐ *The elder boy always takes the lion's share of the food.* ☐ *Jim was supposed to divide the cake in two equal pieces but he took the lion's share.*

listen to reason to yield to a reasonable argument; to take the reasonable course. ☐ *Please listen to reason, and don't do something you'll regret.* ☐ *She got into trouble because she wouldn't listen to reason.*

litmus test a question or experiment that seeks to determine the state of one important factor. ☐ *His performance on the long exam served as a litmus test to determine whether he would go to college.* ☐ *The amount of white cells in my blood became the litmus test for diagnosing my disease.*

A **little bird told me.** learned from a mysterious or secret source. (Often given as an evasive answer to someone who asks how you learned something. Rude in some circumstances.) ☐ *"All right," said Mary, "where did you get that information?" John replied, "A little bird told me."* ☐ *A little bird told me where I might find you.*

a **little bit** a small amount; some. ☐ *Can I have a little bit of candy?* ☐ *I need a little bit of time to finish this essay.*

little by little slowly, a bit at a time. ☐ *Little by little, he began to understand what we were talking about.* ☐ *The snail crossed the stone little by little.*

A **little (hard) work never hurt anyone.** AND A **little (hard) work never killed anyone.** One should expect to do hard or difficult work and not avoid doing it. (Proverb.) ☐ *Go help your father with the yard work. A little hard work never hurt anyone.* ☐ *Go ahead. Bring me some more bricks. A little work never killed anyone.*

A **little (hard) work never killed anyone.** Go to A little (hard) work never hurt anyone.

A **little knowledge is a dangerous thing.** Incomplete knowledge can embarrass or harm someone or something. ☐ *The doctor said, "Just because you've had a course in first aid, you shouldn't have treated your own illness. A little knowledge is a dangerous thing."* ☐ *John thought he knew how to take care of the garden, but he killed all the flowers. A little knowledge is a dangerous thing.*

live a dog's life Go to lead a dog's life.

live a life of something to have a life of a certain quality or style. ☐ *The movie star lived a life of luxury.* ☐ *After Anne won the lottery, she lived the life of a queen.*

live and learn to increase one's knowledge by experience. (Also informal and folksy. Usually said when one is surprised to learn something.) ☐ *I didn't know that* *snakes could swim. Well, live and learn!* □ *John didn't know he should water his houseplants a little extra in the dry winter months. When they all died, he said, "Live and learn."*

live and let live not to interfere with other people's business or preferences. □ *I don't care what they do! Live and let live, I always say.* □ *Your parents are strict. Mine just live and let live.*

live beyond one's **means** to spend more money than one can afford. (Compare this with **live within** one's **means.**) □ *The Browns are deeply in debt because they are living beyond their means.* □ *I keep a budget so that I don't live beyond my means.*

live by one's **wits** to survive by being clever. □ *When you're in the kind of business I'm in, you have to live by your wits.* □ *John was orphaned at the age of ten and grew up living by his wits.*

live for the moment to live without planning for the future. □ *John has no health or life insurance. He lives only for the moment.* □ *When you're young, you tend to live for the moment and not plan for your future security.*

live from hand to mouth to live in poor circumstances. (Informal.) □ *When both my parents were out of work, we lived from hand to mouth.* □ *We lived from hand to mouth during the war. Things were very difficult.*

live happily ever after to live in happiness after a specific event. (Usually found at the end of fairy tales.) □ *The prince and the princess lived happily ever after.* □ *They went away from the horrible haunted castle and lived happily ever after.*

live high off the hog AND **live high on the hog** to live well and eat good food. (Folksy. Note the variation with *pretty.* See also **eat high on the hog.**) □ *After they discovered oil on their land, they lived pretty high on the hog.* □ *Looks like we're living high off the hog tonight. What's the occasion?*

live high on the hog Go to **live high off the hog.**

live in to live at the residence at which one works. (Said of servants.) □ *In order to be here early enough to prepare breakfast, the cook has to live in.* □ *Mr. Simpson has a valet, but he doesn't live in.*

live in an ivory tower to be aloof from the realities of living. (*Live* can be replaced by a number of expressions meaning "to dwell or spend time," as in the first example.) □ *If you didn't spend so much time in your ivory tower, you'd know what people really think!* □ *Many professors are said to live in ivory towers. They don't know what the real world is like.*

live it up to have an exciting time; to do what one pleases—regardless of cost—to please oneself. □ *At the party, John was really living it up.* □ *Come on! Have fun! Live it up!* □ *They spent a week in Mexico living it up and then came home broke.*

live off the fat of the land to grow one's own food; to live on stored-up resources or abundant resources. □ *If I had a million dollars, I'd invest it and live off the fat of the land.* □ *I'll be happy to retire soon and live off the fat of the land.* □ *Many farmers live off the fat of the land.*

live on borrowed time to live longer than circumstances warrant. □ *John has a terminal disease, and he's living on borrowed time.* □ *This project is living on borrowed time. It is overdue for completion.*

live out of a suitcase to live briefly in a place, never unpacking one's luggage. □ *I hate living out of a suitcase. For my next vacation, I want to go to just one place and stay there the whole time.* □ *We were living out of suitcases in a motel while they repaired the damage the fire caused to our house.*

live something **down** to overcome the shame or embarrassment of something. □ *You'll live it down someday.* 🅃 *Max will never be able to live down what happened at the party last night.*

live through something to endure something. □ *I thought I'd never be able to live through the lecture. It was so boring.* □ *I just can't live through another day like this.*

live up to one's **end of the bargain** to carry though on a bargain; to do as was promised in a bargain. ☐ *You can't quit now. You have to live up to your end of the bargain.* ☐ *Bob isn't living up to his end of the bargain, so I am going to sue him.*

live up to something to fulfill expectations; to satisfy a set of goals. (Often with *one's reputation, promise, word, standards,* etc.) ☐ *I hope I can live up to my reputation.* ☐ *The class lives up to its reputation of being exciting and interesting.* ☐ *He never lives up to his promises.* ☐ *She was unable to live up to her own high standards.*

live within one's **means** to spend no more money than one has. (Compare this with **live beyond** one's **means.**) ☐ *We have to struggle to live within our means, but we manage.* ☐ *John is unable to live within his means.*

loaded for bear 1. angry. (Slang and folksy.) ☐ *He left here in a rage. He was really loaded for bear.* ☐ *When I got home from work, I was really loaded for bear. What a horrible day!* **2.** drunk. (An elaboration of *loaded,* which means "drunk." Slang and folksy.) ☐ *By the end of the party, Bill was loaded for bear.* ☐ *The whole gang drank for an hour until they were loaded for bear.*

lock horns (with someone**)** to get into an argument with someone. (Informal.) ☐ *Let's settle this peacefully. I don't want to lock horns with the boss.* ☐ *The boss doesn't want to lock horns either.*

lock something **in** to make something, such as a rate of interest, permanent over a period of time. (Informal.) ☐ *We locked in an 11 percent rate on our mortgage.* ☐ *You should try to lock in a high percentage rate on your bonds.*

lock, stock, and barrel everything. ☐ *We had to move everything out of the house—lock, stock, and barrel.* ☐ *We lost everything—lock, stock, and barrel—in the fire.*

long and (the) short of it the whole story; all the necessary facts. ☐ *I was late and I missed my train, and that's the long and short of it.* ☐ *Soon after the big green frog turned into a handsome prince, Princess Ellen and her newfound love went to live happily ever after in a kingdom by the sea, and that's the long and the short of it.*

Long time no see. I have not seen you for a long time. (Informal.) ☐ *Hello, John. Long time no see.* ☐ *When John and Mary met on the street, they both said, "Long time no see."*

look as if butter wouldn't melt in one's **mouth** to appear to be cold and unfeeling (despite any information to the contrary). ☐ *Sally looks as if butter wouldn't melt in her mouth. She can be so cruel.* ☐ *What a sour face. He looks as if butter wouldn't melt in his mouth.*

look at someone **cross-eyed** to do something slightly provocative. (Informal.) ☐ *Bob is very excitable. He'd lose his temper if anyone so much as looked at him cross-eyed.* 🅃 *Don't even look cross-eyed at the boss this morning unless you want trouble.*

look daggers at someone to give someone a dirty look. (Compare this with **look at** someone **cross-eyed.**) ☐ *Tom must have been mad at Ann from the way he was looking daggers at her.* ☐ *Don't you dare look daggers at me! Don't even look cross-eyed at me!*

look down one's **nose at** someone or something Go to **look down on** someone or something.

look down on someone or something AND **look down** one's **nose at** someone or something to regard someone or something with contempt or displeasure. (Also literal.) ☐ *I think that John liked Mary, although he did seem to look down on her.* ☐ *Don't look down your nose at my car just because it's rusty and noisy.*

look for trouble Go to **ask for trouble.**

look forward to something to anticipate something with pleasure. ☐ *I'm really looking forward to your visit next week.* ☐ *We all look forward to your new book on gardening.*

look good on paper seems fine in theory, but not perhaps in practice; appears to be a good plan. ☐ *The plan looks good on paper, but it may not work.* ☐ *This looks good* *on paper. Let's hope it works in the real world.*

look high and low (for someone or something**)** Go to **hunt high and low (for** someone or something**)**.

look in (on someone or something**)** AND **check in (on** someone or something**)** to see to the welfare of someone or something; to visit someone or something. □ *I'll stop by your house and look in on things while you're on vacation.* □ *Yes, just look in and make sure nothing is wrong.* □ *I checked in on John yesterday. He's almost over his illness.* □ *He was glad I checked in.*

look into something AND **check into** something; **see into** something to investigate something. □ *I'll have to look into that matter.* □ *The police checked into her story.* □ *Don't worry about your problem. I'll see into it.*

look like a million dollars to look very good. □ *Oh, Sally, you look like a million dollars.* □ *Your new hairdo looks like a million dollars.*

look like death warmed over to look quite ill; to look as pale as a dead person. □ *Poor Tom had quite a shock. He looks like death warmed over.* □ *After her long ordeal with chemotherapy, she looked like death warmed over.*

look like something to give the appearance of predicting (something). □ *The sky looks like rain.* □ *No, it looks like snow.* □ *Oh, oh. This looks like trouble. Let's go.*

look like something **the cat dragged in** to look very shabby, worn, exhausted, or abused. (Also literal. Informal. Sometimes with *drug*.) □ *That new sofa of theirs looks like something the cat dragged in.* □ *Poor Dave looks like something the cat drug in. He must have been out late last night.*

look like the cat that swallowed the canary to appear as if one had just had a great success. □ *After the meeting John looked like the cat that swallowed the canary. I knew he must have been a success.* □ *What happened? You look like the cat that swallowed the canary.*

look on someone **as** something to view or think of someone as something. □ *I look on you as a very thoughtful person.* □ *Mary looked on Jane as a good friend.*

look out Go to **watch out**.

look out for someone or something Go to **watch out for** someone or something.

look someone **in the eye** Go to **look** someone **in the face**.

look someone **in the face** AND **look** someone **in the eye; stare** someone **in the face** to face someone directly. (Facing someone this way should assure sincerity.) □ *I don't believe you. Look me in the eye and say that.* □ *She looked him in the face and said she never wanted to see him again.* □ *I dare you to stare him in the face and say that!*

look someone or something **over** to examine someone or something carefully. □ *She looked him over and decided to hire him.* 🅃 *Please look over this report.*

look someone or something **up** AND **hunt** someone or something **up** to search for and find someone or something. □ *I don't know where the hammer is. I'll have to hunt it up.* □ *Ann looked the word up in the dictionary.* 🅃 *Would you please look up John? I need to talk to him.*

look the other way to ignore (something) on purpose. (Also literal.) □ *John could have prevented the problem, but he looked the other way.* □ *By looking the other way, he actually made the problem worse.*

look to one's **laurels** to take care not to lower or diminish one's reputation or position, especially in relation to that of someone else potentially better. □ *With the arrival of the new member of the football team, James will have to look to his laurels to remain as the highest scorer.* □ *The older members of the team will have to look to their laurels when young people join.*

look to someone or something **(for** something**)** to expect someone or something to supply something. □ *Children look to their parents for help.* □ *Tom looked to the bank for* *a loan.* ☐ *Most people who need to borrow money look to a bank.*

look under the hood to examine the engine of a car; to check the oil and water associated with the engine of a car. ☐ *I finished putting gas in. I need to look under the hood.* ☐ *Do you want me to look under the hood, sir?*

look up to someone to view someone with respect and admiration. ☐ *Bill really looks up to his father.* ☐ *Everyone in the class looked up to the teacher.*

loom large (on the horizon) to be of great importance, especially when referring to a possible problem, danger, or threat. (Also literal. A cliché.) ☐ *The exams were looming large on the horizon.* ☐ *Eviction was looming large when the students could not pay their rent.*

lord it over someone to dominate someone; to direct and control someone. ☐ *Mr. Smith seems to lord it over his wife.* ☐ *The boss lords it over everyone in the office.*

lose face to lose status; to become less respectable. ☐ *John is more afraid of losing face than losing money.* ☐ *Things will go better if you can explain to him where he was wrong, without making him lose face.*

lose ground to fall behind; to fall back. ☐ *She was recovering nicely yesterday, but she lost ground last night.* ☐ *We are losing ground in our fight against mosquitoes.*

lose heart to lose one's courage or confidence. ☐ *Now, don't lose heart. Keep trying.* ☐ *What a disappointment! It's enough to make one lose heart.*

lose one's **cool** AND **blow** one's **cool** to lose one's temper; to lose one's nerve. (Slang.) ☐ *Wow, he really lost his cool! What a tantrum!* ☐ *Whatever you do, don't blow your cool.*

lose oneself **(in** something**)** to become deeply involved in something (so that everything else is forgotten). ☐ *Jane has a tendency to lose herself in her work.* ☐ *I often lose myself in thought.* ☐ *Excuse me, I lost myself for a moment.*

lose one's **grip** to lose control of a situation. (Also literal.) ☐ *I can't seem to run things the way I used to. I'm losing my grip.* ☐ *They replaced the board of directors because it was losing its grip.*

lose one's **head (over** someone or something**)** to become confused or "crazy" about someone or something. (Literal in reference to execution by decapitation. Refers especially to emotional attachments.) ☐ *Don't lose your head over John. He isn't worth it.* ☐ *I'm sorry. I got upset and lost my head.*

lose one's **marbles** AND **lose** one's **mind** to go crazy; to go out of one's mind. (The first phrase is slang and can be literal. See also **not have all one's marbles**.) ☐ *What a silly thing to say! Have you lost your marbles?* ☐ *I can't seem to remember anything. I think I'm losing my mind.*

lose one's **mind** Go to **lose** one's **marbles**.

lose one's **reason** to lose one's power of reasoning, possibly in anger. ☐ *I was so confused that I almost lost my reason.* ☐ *Bob seems to have lost his reason when he struck John.*

lose one's **shirt** to lose all of one's assets (including one's shirt). (Also literal. Slang.) ☐ *I almost lost my shirt on that deal. I have to invest more wisely.* ☐ *No, I can't loan you $200. I just lost my shirt at the racetrack.*

lose one's **temper** to become angry. ☐ *Please don't lose your temper. It's not good for you.* ☐ *I'm sorry that I lost my temper.*

lose one's **touch (with** someone or something**)** to lose one's ability to handle someone or something. ☐ *I seem to have lost my touch with my children. They won't mind me anymore.* ☐ *We've both lost our touch as far as managing people goes.* ☐ *Tom said that he had lost his touch with the stock market.*

lose one's **train of thought** to forget what one was talking or thinking about. (See also **train of thought**.) ☐ *Excuse me, I lost my train of thought. What was I talking about?* ☐ *You made the speaker lose her train of thought.*

lose out (on something**)** Go to **miss out (on** something**)**.

lose out to someone or something to lose a competition to someone or something. □ *Our team lost out to the other team.* □ *Bill lost out to Sally in the contest.*

lose sleep (over someone or something**)** to worry about someone or something. (Literal when worry keeps one awake.) □ *I keep losing sleep over my son, who is in the army.* □ *Do you lose sleep over your investments?* □ *No, I don't lose sleep, and I never worry.*

lose touch (with someone or something**)** to lose contact with someone or something. (Compare this with **keep in touch (with** someone**)**.) □ *Poor Sally has lost touch with reality.* □ *I've lost touch with all my relatives.* □ *Jane didn't mean to lose touch, but she did.*

lose track (of someone or something**)** to forget where someone or something is; to lose or misplace someone or something. □ *I've lost track of the time.* □ *The mother lost track of her child and started calling her.* □ *When I get tired, I tend to lose track.*

lost-and-found an office or department that handles items that someone has lost that have been found by someone else. □ *The lost-and-found office had an enormous collection of umbrellas and four sets of false teeth!* □ *I found a book on the seat of the bus. I turned it in to the driver, who gave it to the lost-and-found office.*

lost and gone forever lost; permanently lost. □ *My poor doggy is lost and gone forever.* □ *My money fell out of my pocket, and I am sure that it is lost and gone forever.*

a **lost cause** a futile attempt; a hopeless matter. □ *Our campaign to have the new party on the ballot was a lost cause.* □ *Todd gave it up as a lost cause.*

lost in thought busy thinking. □ *I'm sorry, I didn't hear what you said. I was lost in thought.* □ *Bill—lost in thought as always—went into the wrong room.*

lost on someone having no effect on someone; wasted on someone. (Informal.) □ *The joke was lost on Jean. She didn't understand it.* □ *The humor of the situation was lost on Mary. She was too upset to see it.*

a **lot of** someone or something AND **lots of** people or things a large number of people or things; much of something. □ *I got a lot of presents for my birthday.* □ *I ate lots of cookies after dinner.*

lots of people or things Go to a **lot of** someone or something.

loud and clear clear and distinctly. (Originally said of radio reception that is heard clearly and distinctly.) □ *TOM: If I've told you once, I've told you a thousand times: Stop it! Do you hear me? BILL: Yes, loud and clear.* □ *I hear you loud and clear.*

louse something **up** to mess up or ruin something. (Slang.) □ *I've worked hard on this. Please don't louse it up.* 🅃 *You've loused up all my plans.*

lousy with something with something in abundance. (Slang.) □ *This place is lousy with cops.* □ *Our picnic table was lousy with ants.*

love at first sight love established when two people first see one another. □ *Bill was standing at the door when Ann opened it. It was love at first sight.* □ *It was love at first sight when they met, but it didn't last long.*

lovely weather for ducks rainy weather. □ *BOB: Not very nice out today, is it? BILL: It's lovely weather for ducks.* □ *I don't like this weather, but it's lovely weather for ducks.*

low man on the totem pole the least important person. (Compare this with **high man on the totem pole**.) □ *I was the last to find out because I'm low man on the totem pole.* □ *I can't be of any help. I'm low man on the totem pole.*

lower oneself **to** some level to bring oneself down to some lower level of behavior. (Also literal.) □ *I refuse to lower myself to your level.* □ *Has TV news lowered itself to the level of the tabloids?*

lower one's **sights** to set one's goals lower than they were. (Literal in reference to aiming a weapon.) □ *Even though you get* *frustrated, don't lower your sights.* ☐ *I shouldn't lower my sights. If I work hard, I can do what I want.*

lower one's **voice** to speak more softly. ☐ *Please lower your voice, or you'll disturb the people who are working.* ☐ *He wouldn't lower his voice, so everyone heard what he said.*

lower the boom on someone to scold or punish someone severely; to crack down on someone; to **throw the book at** someone. (Also literal. Informal.) ☐ *If Bob won't behave better, I'll have to lower the boom on him.* ☐ *The teacher lowered the boom on the whole class for misbehaving.*

luck out to get lucky (about something). (Slang.) ☐ *I won $100 in the lottery. I really lucked out.* ☐ *Bob lucked out when he got an easy teacher for geometry.*

[luck runs out] Go to one's **luck runs out.**

the **lull before the storm** AND the **calm before the storm** a quiet period just before a period of great activity or excitement. (Literal in reference to weather.) ☐ *It was very quiet in the cafeteria just before the students came in for lunch. It was the lull before the storm.* ☐ *In the brief calm before the storm, the clerks prepared themselves for the doors to open and bring in thousands of shoppers.*

lull someone **into a false sense of security** to lead someone into believing that all is well before attacking or doing someone bad. ☐ *We lulled the enemy into a false sense of security by pretending to retreat. Then we launched an attack.* ☐ *The boss lulled us into a false sense of security by saying that our jobs were safe and then let half the staff go.*

lull someone **to sleep** to cause someone to fall asleep. ☐ *The mother lulled her baby to sleep.* ☐ *The boring professor lulled the students to sleep.*

the **lunatic fringe** the more extreme members of a group. ☐ *Most of the members of that religious sect are quite reasonable, but Lisa belongs to the lunatic fringe.* ☐ *Many people try to avoid eating a lot of fat, but Mary is part of the lunatic fringe and will hardly eat anything.*

M

mad about someone or something Go to **crazy about** someone or something.

mad as a hatter Go to **(as) mad as a hatter.**

mad as a hornet Go to **(as) mad as a hornet.**

mad as a March hare Go to **(as) mad as a March hare.**

mad as a wet hen Go to **(as) mad as a wet hen.**

mad as hell Go to **(as) mad as hell.**

mad enough to chew nails AND **angry enough to chew nails** angry enough to bite through metal nails. □ *I am mad enough to chew nails! Who took my checkbook?* □ *Her sudden tirade made him angry enough to chew nails.*

mad for someone or something Go to **mad about** someone or something.

made for each other [for two people] to be very well suited romantically. □ *Bill and Jane were made for each other.* □ *Mr. and Mrs. Smith were not exactly made for each other. They really don't get along.*

made from the same mold Go to **cut from the same cloth.**

made to measure [of clothing] made especially to fit the measurements of a particular person. □ *Jack has his suits made to measure because he's rather large.* □ *Having clothes made to measure is rather expensive.*

made to order put together on request. (Compare this with **in stock.**) □ *This suit fits so well because it's made to order.* □ *His feet are so big that all his shoes have to be made to order.*

maiden voyage the first voyage of a ship or boat. □ *The liner sank on its maiden voyage.* □ *Jim is taking his yacht on its maiden voyage.*

main strength and awkwardness great force; brute force. (Folksy.) □ *They finally got the piano moved in to the living room by main strength and awkwardness.* □ *Lifting the table must be done carefully. This is not a job requiring main strength and awkwardness.*

make a bed AND **make** someone's **bed** to arrange neatly the sheets and blankets of a bed. □ *The hotel maid made our bed.* □ *Billy had to make his bed before he went to school.*

make a beeline for someone or something to head straight toward someone or something. (Refers to the way bees fly in a straight line. Informal.) □ *Billy came into the kitchen and made a beeline for the cookies.* □ *After the game, we all made a beeline for John, who was serving cold drinks.*

make a big deal about something Go to **make a federal case out of** something.

make a break for something **or** somewhere to move or run quickly to something or somewhere. (Informal.) □ *Before we could stop her, she made a break for the door and got away.* □ *The mouse got frightened and made a break for a hole in the wall.*

make a bundle AND **make a pile** to make a lot of money. (Slang.) □ *John really made a bundle on that deal.* □ *I'd like to make a pile and retire.*

make a check out (to someone**)** to write a check naming someone as payee. □

Please make a check out to John Jones. 🅃 *Do you want cash, or should I make out a check?*

make a clean breast of something to confess something; to **get something off** one's **chest**. ☐ *You'll feel better if you make a clean breast of it. Now tell us what happened.* ☐ *I was forced to make a clean breast of the whole affair.*

make a clean sweep to do something completely or thoroughly, with no exceptions. (Informal.) ☐ *The boss decided to fire everybody, so he made a clean sweep.* ☐ *They made a clean sweep through the neighborhood, repairing all the sidewalks.*

make a comeback to return to one's former (successful) career. (Informal.) ☐ *After ten years in retirement, the singer made a comeback.* ☐ *You're never too old to make a comeback.*

make a day of doing something AND **make a day of it** to spend the whole day doing something. ☐ *We went to the museum to see the new exhibit and then decided to make a day of it.* ☐ *They made a day of cleaning the attic.*

make a day of it Go to **make a day of** doing something.

make a dent in something to begin to consume or accomplish something. (Also literal. Informal.) ☐ *Bob, you've hardly made a dent in your dinner!* ☐ *There is a lot of rice left. We hardly made a dent in it all week.* ☐ *Get busy! You haven't even made a dent in your work.*

make a face to twist one's face into a strange expression in order to show one's dislike, ridicule, etc., or in order to make someone laugh. ☐ *The comedian made faces in order to amuse the children.* ☐ *Jane made a face when she was asked to work late.*

make a face (at someone**) 1.** to make a face at someone in ridicule. ☐ *Mother, Billy made a face at me!* ☐ *The teacher sent Jane to the principal for making a face in class.* **2.** to attempt to communicate to someone through facial gestures, usually an attempt to say "no" or "stop." ☐ *I started to tell John where I was last night, but Bill made a face so I didn't.* ☐ *John made a face at me as I was testifying, so I avoided telling everything.*

make a fast buck AND **make a quick buck** to make money with little effort. (Slang.) ☐ *Tom is always ready to make a fast buck.* ☐ *I made a quick buck selling used cars.*

make a federal case out of something AND **make a big deal about** something to exaggerate the seriousness of something. (The first entry head can be literal. Slang.) ☐ *Come on. It was nothing! Don't make a federal case out of it.* ☐ *I only stepped on your toe. Don't make a big deal about it.*

make a fool out of someone AND **make a monkey out of** someone to make someone look foolish. ☐ *John made a monkey out of himself while trying to make a fool out of Jim.* ☐ *John made a fool out of himself at the party.* ☐ *Are you trying to make a monkey out of me?*

make a friend AND **make friends** to establish a link of friendship with someone. ☐ *I have never found it difficult to make friends.* ☐ *Mary had to make new friends when she changed schools.*

make a fuss (over someone or something**)** AND **make over** someone or something **1.** to worry about or make a bother about someone or something. ☐ *Why do you fuss over a problem like that?* ☐ *Please don't make a fuss. Everything will be all right.* ☐ *Don't make over me so much!* **2.** to be very solicitous and helpful toward a person or a pet. ☐ *How can anyone make a fuss over a cat?* ☐ *Billy was embarrassed when his mother made a fuss over him.* **3.** to argue about someone or something. ☐ *Please don't make a fuss over who gets the last cookie.* ☐ *Please discuss it. Don't make a fuss over it!*

make a go of it to make something work out all right. (Informal.) ☐ *It's a tough situation, but Ann is trying to make a go of it.* ☐ *We don't like living here, but we have to make a go of it.*

make a great show of something to make something obvious; to do something in a showy fashion. □ *Ann made a great show of wiping up the drink that John spilled.* □ *Jane displayed her irritation at our late arrival by making a great show of serving the cold dinner.*

make a hit (with someone or something**)** to please someone. (Informal.) □ *The singer made a hit with the audience.* □ *She was afraid she wouldn't make a hit.* □ *John made a hit with my parents last evening.*

make a killing to have a great success, especially in making money. (Slang.) □ *John has got a job selling insurance. He's not exactly making a killing.* □ *Bill made a killing at the racetrack yesterday.*

make a laughingstock of oneself **or** something AND **make** oneself **or** something **a laughingstock** to make oneself a source of ridicule or laughter; to do something that invites ridicule. □ *Laura made herself a laughingstock by arriving at the fast-food restaurant in full evening dress.* □ *The board of directors made the company a laughingstock by hiring an ex-convict as president.*

make a living to earn enough money to live on. □ *I'll be glad when I get a job and can make a living.* □ *I can hardly make a living with the skills I have.*

make allowance(s) (for someone or something**)** **1.** to allow time, space, food, etc., for someone or something. □ *When planning the party, please make allowances for John and his family.* □ *I'm making allowance for ten extra guests.* **2.** to make excuses or explanations for someone or something; to take into consideration the negative effects of someone or something. □ *You're very late even when we make allowance for the weather.* □ *We have to make allowance for the age of the house when we judge its condition.*

make a long story short to bring a story to an end. (A formula that introduces a summary of a story or a joke.) □ *And—to make a long story short—I never got back the money that I lent him.* □ *If I can make a long story short, let me say that everything worked out fine.*

make a meal of something to eat only a large portion of one kind of food as an entire meal. □ *There were lots of salad makings, so we fixed a large salad and made a meal of it.* □ *We had tons of leftover turkey after the festival, so the next day we sat down and made a meal of it.*

make amends (for something**)** to do something as an act of restitution or to make up for some error, injury, or loss that one has caused. □ *After the argument, Jane later called her friend to make amends.* □ *After amends had been made, Jane took her friend to dinner.*

make a monkey out of someone Go to **make a fool out of** someone.

make a mountain out of a molehill to make a major issue out of a minor one; to exaggerate the importance of something. □ *Come on, don't make a mountain out of a molehill. It's not that important.* □ *Mary is always making mountains out of molehills.*

make an all-out effort to make a thorough and energetic effort. (See also **all-out effort**.) □ *Sally made an all-out effort to get to class on time.* □ *In my job, I have to make an all-out effort every day.*

make a name (for oneself**)** to become famous. □ *Sally wants to work hard and make a name for herself.* □ *It's hard to make a name without a lot of talent and hard work.*

make an appearance to appear; to appear in a performance. (Compare this with **put in an appearance**.) □ *We waited for thirty minutes for the professor to make an appearance, then we went home.* □ *The famous singing star made an appearance in Detroit last August.*

make an appointment (with someone**)** to schedule a meeting with someone. □ *I made an appointment with the doctor for late today.* □ *The professor wouldn't see me unless I made an appointment.*

make an example of someone to make a public issue out of someone's bad behavior. □ *The judge decided to make an example of John, so he fined him the full amount.* □ *The teacher made an example of Mary, who had disturbed the class constantly with her whispering.*

make an exception (for someone**)** to suspend a rule or practice for someone in a single instance. □ *Please make an exception just this once.* □ *The rule is a good one, and I will not make an exception for anyone.*

make an exhibition of oneself to embarrass oneself by showing off or doing something daring in public. (Sometimes under the influence of alcohol.) □ *You can be certain that Joan will have too much to drink and make an exhibition of herself.* □ *Sit down and be quiet. Stop making an exhibition of yourself.*

make a night of doing something to do something for the entire night. □ *We partied until three in the morning and then decided to make a night of it.* □ *Once or twice in the early spring we make a night of fishing.*

make an impression (on someone**)** to produce a memorable effect on someone. (Often with *good, bad,* or some other adjective.) □ *Tom made a bad impression on the banker.* □ *I'm afraid that you haven't made a very good impression on our visitors.* □ *You made quite an impression on my father.*

make an issue of someone or something Go to make a point of someone or something.

make a note of something to write something down. □ *Please make a note of this address.* □ *This is important. Make a note of it.*

make a nuisance of oneself to be a constant bother. □ *I'm sorry to make a nuisance of myself, but I do need an answer to my question.* □ *Stop making a nuisance of yourself and wait your turn.*

make an uproar Go to create an uproar.

make a pass at someone to flirt with someone; to make a romantic advance at someone. (This often has sexual implications. Compare this with make a play (for someone).) □ *I was shocked when Ann made a pass at me.* □ *I think Bob was making a pass at me, but he did it very subtly.*

make a pile Go to make a bundle.

make a pitch (for someone or something**)** to say something in support of someone or something; to attempt to promote, sell, or advance someone or something. (Informal.) □ *Bill is making a pitch for his friend's new product again.* □ *The theatrical agent came in and made a pitch for her client.* □ *Every time I turn on the television set, someone is making a pitch.*

make a play (for someone**)** to attempt to attract the romantic interest of someone. (Informal. Compare this with make a pass at someone.) □ *Ann made a play for Bill, but he wasn't interested in her.* □ *I knew he liked me, but I never thought he'd make a play.*

make a point to state an item of importance. (Also literal, as in sports and games.) □ *You made a point that we all should remember.* □ *He spoke for an hour without making a point.*

make a point of doing something to make an effort to do something. □ *Please make a point of mailing this letter. It's very important.* □ *The hostess made a point of thanking me for bringing flowers.*

make a point of someone or something AND **make an issue of** someone or something to turn someone or something into an important matter. □ *Please don't make a point of John's comment. It wasn't that important.* □ *I hope you make an issue of Tom's success and the reasons for it.* □ *Tom has a lot of problems. Please don't make an issue of him.*

make a practice of something AND **make** something **a practice** to turn something into a habitual activity. □ *Jane makes a practice of planting daisies every summer.* □ *Her mother also made it a practice.*

make a quick buck Go to make a fast buck.

make a reservation AND **make reservations** to reserve a seat, as in an airplane, restaurant, or theater in advance; to reserve a room, as in a hotel in advance. □ *Did you make a reservation or are we just going to chance getting a table?* □ *I made reservations for a flight at twelve noon.*

make arrangements (for someone or something**) 1.** to make plans for someone or something. □ *I'm making arrangements for the convention.* □ *It starts next week, and I hardly have time to make arrangements.* **2.** [with *someone*] to plan accommodations for someone. □ *John is coming for a visit next week. Please make arrangements for him at the hotel.* □ *I will make arrangements for everyone when I call the hotel.*

make a run for it to run fast to get away or get somewhere. (Informal. Compare this with make a break for something or somewhere.) □ *When the guard wasn't looking, the prisoner made a run for it.* □ *In the baseball game, the player on first base made a run for it, but he didn't make it to second base.*

make a scene AND **create a scene** to make a public display or disturbance. □ *When John found a fly in his drink, he started to create a scene.* □ *Oh, John, please don't make a scene. Just forget about it.*

make as if to do something to act as if one were about to do something. □ *The thief made as if to run away but changed his mind.* □ *Jane made as if to smack the child.*

make a silk purse out of a sow's ear to create something of value out of something of no value. (Often in the negative.) □ *Don't bother trying to fix up this old bicycle. You can't make a silk purse out of a sow's ear.* □ *My mother made a lovely jacket out of an old coat. She succeeded in making a silk purse out of a sow's ear.*

make a stink (about something**)** Go to create a stink (about something).

make away with someone or something AND **make off with** someone or something to take someone or something away; to make someone or something disappear. □ *The robber made away with the jewelry.* □ *The maid quickly made off with the children. We only saw them for a moment.*

make book on something to make or accept bets on something. (Slang.) □ *It looks as if it will rain, but I wouldn't make book on it.* □ *John's making book on the football game this Saturday.*

make (both) ends meet to manage to live on a small amount of money. (Also literal.) □ *It's hard these days to make ends meet.* □ *I have to work overtime to make both ends meet.*

make chin music to talk or chatter. (Slang.) □ *We sat around all evening making chin music.* □ *You were making chin music when you should have been listening.*

make cracks (about someone or something**)** to ridicule or make jokes about someone or something. (Informal.) □ *Please stop making cracks about my haircut. It's the new style.* □ *Some people can't help making cracks. They are just rude.*

make do (with someone or something**)** to do as well as possible with someone or something. □ *You'll have to make do with less money next year. The economy is very weak.* □ *We'll have to make do with John even though he's a slow worker.* □ *Yes, we'll have to make do.*

make eyes (at someone**)** to flirt with someone. □ *Tom spent all afternoon making eyes at Ann.* □ *How could they sit there in class making eyes?*

make fast work of someone or something Go to make short work of someone or something.

make for somewhere to run or travel to somewhere. (Slang, especially criminal slang.) □ *When I got out of class, I made for the gym.* □ *When he got out of jail, he made for Toledo.*

make free with someone or something **1.** [with *someone*] Go to take liberties with someone or something. **2.** [with *something*] to take advantage of or use something as if it were one's own. (Compare this with take liberties with someone or something.) □ *I wish you wouldn't come into my house and make free with my food and drink.* □

Please make free with my car while I'm gone.

make friends Go to **make a friend.**

make fun (of someone or something**)** to ridicule someone or something. ☐ *Please stop making fun of me. It hurts my feelings.* ☐ *Billy teases and makes fun a lot, but he means no harm.*

make good as something to succeed in a particular role. ☐ *I hope I make good as a teacher.* ☐ *John made good as a football player.*

make good (at something**)** to succeed at something. ☐ *Bob worked hard to make good at selling.* ☐ *Jane was determined to make good.*

make good money to earn a large amount of money. (Informal.) ☐ *Ann makes good money at her job.* ☐ *I don't know what she does, but she makes good money.*

make good on something **1.** to fulfill a promise. ☐ *Tom made good on his pledge to donate $1,000.* ☐ *Bill refused to make good on his promise.* **2.** to repay a debt. (See also **make** something **good.**) ☐ *I couldn't make good on my debts, and I got in a lot of trouble.* ☐ *If you don't make good on this bill, I'll have to take back your car.*

make good time to travel fast; to progress rapidly. ☐ *I am making good time. My report is almost finished.* ☐ *Now that we are clear of the city traffic, we can make good time.*

make hamburger out of someone or something AND **make mincemeat out of** someone or something to beat up or overcome someone or something. (Literal when referring to foodstuffs. Figurative with people. Slang.) ☐ *Stop acting silly, or I'll make hamburger out of you.* ☐ *Our team made mincemeat out of the other team.*

make it to succeed. (See also **make** something.) ☐ *I hope Bob's new business makes it.* ☐ *Donna wants to graduate this year. I hope she makes it.*

make it as far as something Go to **make it (until** something**).**

make it hot for someone to make things difficult for someone; to put someone under pressure. (Also literal. Slang.) ☐ *Maybe if we make it hot for them, they'll leave.* ☐ *John likes making it hot for people. He's sort of mean.*

make it one's **business to** do something to do something on one's own even if it means interfering in something that does not directly concern one. (As opposed to minding one's own business. See also **take it upon** oneself **to** do something.) ☐ *I know I doesn't concern me, but I made it my business to call city hall because someone had to.* ☐ *Jane made it her business to find out exactly what had happened to the old lady.*

make it to something Go to **make it (until** something**).**

make it (until something**)** AND **make it to** something**; make it as far as** something to endure until something; to last until some time. ☐ *I hope my car can make it to the next town.* ☐ *Do you think you can make it until we come to a stopping point?* ☐ *I made it as far as the first turn and decided to give up.*

make it worth someone's **while** to make something profitable enough for someone to do. (See also **worth** someone's **while.**) ☐ *If you deliver this parcel for me, I'll make it worth your while.* ☐ *The boss said he'd make it worth our while if we worked late.*

make life miserable for someone to make someone unhappy over a long period of time. ☐ *My shoes are tight, and they are making life miserable for me.* ☐ *Jane's boss is making life miserable for her.*

make light of something to treat something as if it were unimportant or humorous. ☐ *I wish you wouldn't make light of his problems. They're quite serious.* ☐ *I make light of my problems, and that makes me feel better.*

make little of someone or something to minimize someone or something; to **play** someone or something **down;** to belittle someone or something. ☐ *John made little of my efforts to collect money for charity.* ☐ *The* *neighbors made little of John and thought he would amount to nothing.*

make love (to someone**)** to share physical or emotional love (or both) with someone. (This phrase usually has a sexual meaning.) □ *Tom and Ann turned out the lights and made love.* □ *The actress refused to make love to the leading man on stage.*

make merry to have fun; to have an enjoyable time. □ *The guests certainly made merry at the wedding.* □ *The children were making merry in the backyard.*

make mincemeat out of someone or something Go to **make hamburger out of** someone or something.

make mischief to cause trouble. □ *Bob loves to make mischief and get other people into trouble.* □ *Don't believe what Mary says. She's just trying to make mischief.*

Make no bones about it. **Make no mistake (about it).**; Do not doubt it. (Folksy.) □ *This is the greatest cake I've ever eaten. Make no bones about it.* □ *Make no bones about it, Mary is a great singer.*

make no difference (to someone**)** not to matter to someone; for someone not to care (about something). □ *It makes no difference to me what you do.* □ *Do whatever you want. It really makes no difference.*

make no mistake (about it) without a doubt; certainly. (Informal.) □ *This car is a great buy. Make no mistake about it.* □ *We support your candidacy—make no mistake.*

make nothing of something to ignore something as if it had not happened; to think no more about something. (Often with *it*.) □ *My father caught me throwing the snowball, but he made nothing of it.* □ *I made nothing of the remark, even though it seemed quite rude.* □ *I saw him leave, but I made nothing of it.*

make off with someone or something Go to **make away with** someone or something.

make oneself **at home** to make oneself comfortable as if one were in one's own home. □ *Please come in and make yourself at home.* □ *I'm glad you're here. During your visit, just make yourself at home.*

make oneself **conspicuous** to attract attention to oneself. □ *Please don't make yourself conspicuous. It embarrasses me.* □ *Ann makes herself conspicuous by wearing brightly colored clothing.*

make oneself **heard** to speak loudly so that one will be heard above the noise. □ *I had to shout to make myself heard.* □ *He screamed to make himself heard over the sound of the plane's engines.*

make oneself **or** something **a laughingstock** Go to **make a laughingstock of** oneself **or** something.

make oneself **scarce** to go away. (Slang.) □ *Hey, kid, go away. Make yourself scarce.* □ *When there is work to be done, I make myself scarce.*

make (oneself**) up** to put makeup on oneself. □ *I have to make up now. I go on stage in ten minutes.* □ *I will make myself up. I don't need your help.*

make one's **mind up** to decide. □ *Please make your mind up. Which do you want?* Ⓣ *Would you help me make up my mind?*

make one's **way through** something Go to **pick** one's **way through** something.

make or break someone either to improve or ruin someone. □ *The army will either make or break him.* □ *It's a tough assignment, and it will either make or break her.*

make out (with someone or something**)** **1.** to manage to do (something) with someone or something. □ *I think I can make out with this hammer.* □ *If I can't make out with John, I'll have to ask for more help.* **2.** [with *someone*] to flirt with, kiss, or hug someone; to **make love (to** someone**)**. (Slang.) □ *Bob was trying to make out with Sally all evening.* □ *She didn't want to make out, so she left.*

make over someone or something Go to **make a fuss (over** someone or something**)**.

make overtures to give hints about something; to present or suggest ideas. □ *The company made overtures about hiring me.*

☐ *Tom is making overtures about inviting us to his country home next month.*

make peace (with someone**)** to end a quarrel with someone. (Compare this with **kiss and make up.**) ☐ *Don't you think it's time to make peace with your brother? There is no point in arguing anymore.* ☐ *Yes, it's time we made peace.*

make points (with someone**)** to gain favor with someone. (Slang.) ☐ *Tom is trying to make points with Ann. He wants to ask her out.* ☐ *He's trying to make points by smiling and telling her how nice she looks.*

make reservations Go to make a reservation.

make sense to be understandable to someone. ☐ *John doesn't make sense.* ☐ *What John says makes sense.*

make sense out of someone or something to understand or interpret someone or something. (Also with *some,* as in the second example.) ☐ *I can hardly make sense out of John.* ☐ *I'm trying to make some sense out of what John is saying.*

make short work of someone or something AND **make fast work of** someone or something to finish with someone or something quickly. ☐ *I made short work of Tom so I could leave the office to play golf.* ☐ *Billy made fast work of his dinner so he could go out and play.*

make someone **eat crow** to cause someone to retract a statement or admit an error. (Informal.) ☐ *Because Mary was completely wrong, we made her eat crow.* ☐ *They won't make me eat crow. They don't know I was wrong.*

make someone **look good** to cause someone to appear successful or competent (especially when this is not the case). (Also literal.) ☐ *John arranges all his affairs to make himself look good.* ☐ *The manager didn't like the quarterly report because it didn't make her look good.*

make someone **look ridiculous** to make someone look foolish (not funny). ☐ *This hat makes me look ridiculous.* ☐ *Please make me look good. Don't make me look ridiculous!*

make someone or something **available to** someone to supply someone with someone or something. ☐ *I made my car available to Bob.* ☐ *They made their maid available to us.*

make someone or something **over** Go to do someone or something **over.**

make someone's **bed** Go to make a bed; make the bed.

make someone's **blood boil** to make someone very angry. (Informal.) ☐ *It just makes my blood boil to think of the amount of food that gets wasted around here.* ☐ *Whenever I think of that dishonest mess, it makes my blood boil.*

make someone's **blood run cold** to shock or horrify someone. ☐ *The terrible story in the newspaper made my blood run cold.* ☐ *I could tell you things about prisons that would make your blood run cold.*

make someone's **flesh crawl** to cause someone's skin to feel funny or get goose pimples through fright. ☐ *Just to hear the story of the killings made my flesh crawl.* ☐ *The horror movie made our flesh crawl.*

make someone's **gorge rise** to cause someone to become very angry. ☐ *The unnecessary accident made my gorge rise.* ☐ *Getting his tax bill made Bob's gorge rise.*

make someone's **hair curl** Go to **curl** someone's **hair.**

make someone's **hair stand on end** to cause someone to be very frightened. (Literal if referring to the effects of a charge of static electricity. Informal.) ☐ *The horrible scream made my hair stand on end.* ☐ *The ghost story made our hair stand on end.*

make someone's **head spin** Go to make someone's **head swim.**

make someone's **head swim** AND **make** someone's **head spin 1.** to make someone dizzy or disoriented. ☐ *Riding in your car makes my head spin.* ☐ *Breathing the gas made my head swim.* **2.** to confuse or overwhelm someone. ☐ *All these numbers make my head swim.* ☐ *The physics lecture made my head spin.*

make someone sick to disgust someone. □ *I am really tired of your vile talk. You make me sick!* □ *She screamed at him that he made her sick and then she ran out of the house.*

make someone's **mouth water** to make someone hungry (for something). (Also literal for causing saliva to flow into someone's mouth. Informal.) □ *That beautiful salad makes my mouth water.* □ *Talking about food makes my mouth water.*

make someone's **position clear** to clarify where someone stands on an issue. □ *I don't think you understand what I said. Let me make my position clear.* □ *I can't tell whether you are in favor of or against the proposal. Please make your position clear.*

make someone **the scapegoat for** something to make someone take the blame for something. □ *They made Tom the scapegoat for the whole affair. It wasn't all his fault.* □ *Don't try to make me the scapegoat. I'll tell who really did it.*

make someone **up** to put makeup on someone. □ *She made herself up before leaving the house.* 🅃 *The crew made up the cast before the play.*

make something to attend an event. (See also make it.) □ *I hope you can make our party.* □ *I am sorry, but I won't be able to make it.*

make something **a practice** Go to make a practice of something.

make something **from scratch** to make something by starting with the basic ingredients. (Informal.) □ *We made the cake from scratch, using no prepared ingredients.* □ *I didn't have a ladder, so I made one from scratch.*

make something **good** AND **make** something **right** to replace or restore something. (Informal. See also set something right.) □ *I know I owe you some money, but don't worry, I'll make it good.* □ *I'm sorry I broke your window. I'll make it right, though.*

make something **out of nothing 1.** to make an issue of something of little importance. (See also make a mountain out of a molehill.) □ *Relax, John, you're making a big problem out of nothing.* □ *You have no evidence. You're making a case out of nothing.* **2.** to create something of value from nearly worthless parts. □ *My uncle—he sells sand—made a fortune out of nothing.* □ *My model airplane won the contest even though I made it out of nothing.*

make something **(out) of** something **1.** to make an interpretation of something. □ *Can you make anything out of this message? I don't understand it.* □ *I'm sorry, I can't make any sense out of it.* **2.** to interpret something negatively, possibly leading to a disagreement. (Informal. Compare this with make nothing of something.) □ *So, I'm wrong! You want to make something of it?* □ *The hostess made too much out of my absence.*

make something **right** Go to make something good.

make something **to order** to put something together only when someone requests it. (Usually said about clothing. See also build something to order.) □ *This store only makes suits to order.* □ *Our shirts fit perfectly because we make each one to order.*

make something **up 1.** to repay or redo something. 🅃 *Can I make up the test I missed?* 🅃 *Please make up the payment you missed.* □ *You can make it up.* **2.** to create a story or a lie. □ *That's not true! You just made it up!* □ *Bob made up a story about a tiny mouse and its friends.* **3.** to mix something up; to assemble something. □ *JOHN: Is my prescription ready? DRUGGIST: No, I haven't made it up yet.* 🅃 *I'll make up your prescription in a minute.*

make something **up out of whole cloth** to create a story or a lie from no facts at all. □ *I don't believe you. I think you made that up out of whole cloth.* 🅃 *Ann made up her explanation out of whole cloth. There was not a bit of truth in it.*

make something **up to** someone to repay someone; to make amends to someone. ☐ *I'm so sorry I've insulted you. How can I make it up to you?* ☐ *I'm sorry I broke our date. I'll make it up to you, I promise.*

make something **worth** someone's **while** to make something profitable enough for someone to do. ☐ *If you deliver this parcel for me, I'll make it worth your while.* ☐ *The boss said he'd make it worth our while if we worked late.*

make the bed AND **make** someone's **bed** to restore a bed to an unslept-in condition. ☐ *I make my bed every morning.* ☐ *The maid goes to all the rooms to make the beds.*

make the best of something to try to make a bad situation work out well. (Compare this with make the most of something.) ☐ *It's not good, but we'll have to make the best of it.* ☐ *Ann is clever enough to make the best of a bad situation.*

make the feathers fly Go to make the fur fly.

make the fur fly AND **make the feathers fly** to cause a fight or an argument; to create an uproar (about something). (Informal.) ☐ *When your mother gets home and sees what you've done, she'll really make the fur fly.* ☐ *When those two get together, they'll make the feathers fly. They hate each other.*

make the grade to be satisfactory; to be what is expected. (Informal.) ☐ *I'm sorry, but your work doesn't exactly make the grade.* ☐ *This meal doesn't just make the grade. It is excellent.*

make the most of something to make something appear as good as possible; to exploit something; to get as much out of something as is possible. (Compare this with make the best of something.) ☐ *Mary knows how to make the most of her talents.* ☐ *They designed the advertisements to make the most of the product's features.*

make the scene to appear somewhere, especially at a social event. (Slang.) ☐ *I hope I can make the scene Saturday night at the party.* ☐ *The big race is tomorrow. Man, I've got to make the scene. The whole world will be there!*

make time (for someone or something**)** to schedule time to see someone or do something. ☐ *I can make time for you tomorrow morning.* ☐ *I am very busy, but I can make time.* ☐ *You are going to have to start making time for balanced meals.*

make time (with someone**)** to flirt with, date, or hang around with someone. (Informal.) ☐ *I hear that Tom's been making time with Ann.* ☐ *I hear they've been making time for months.*

make up for lost time to do much of something; to do something fast. ☐ *Because we took so long eating lunch, we have to drive faster to make up for lost time. Otherwise we won't arrive on time.* ☐ *At the age of sixty, Bill learned to play golf. Now he plays it every day. He's making up for lost time.*

make up for someone or something to take the place of someone or something. ☐ *John can't play in the game Saturday, but I think I can make up for him.* ☐ *Do you think that this cat can make up for the one that ran away?*

make up (with someone**)** to reconcile with someone; to end a disagreement (with someone). ☐ *Bill and Max decided to make up.* ☐ *They made up with each other and are still very good friends.*

make use of someone or something to use or utilize someone or something. ☐ *If you make use of all your talents and skills, you should succeed.* ☐ *The technician makes good use of a number of special tools.*

make waves to make trouble or difficulties. (Also literal. Informal. Compare this with rock the boat.) ☐ *I don't want to make waves, but this just isn't right.* ☐ *Why do you always have to make waves? Can't you be constructive?*

make way to make progress; to move ahead. (Originally nautical. See also make way (for someone or something).) ☐ *Is this project making way?* ☐ *A sailboat can't make way if there is no wind.*

make way (for someone or something**)** to clear a path for someone or something. □ *Make way for the stretcher.* □ *Please make way for the nurse.* □ *Here comes the doctor—make way!*

man-about-town a fashionable man who leads a sophisticated life. □ *He prefers wine bars to pubs—quite a man-about-town.* □ *Jack's too much of a man-about-town to go to a football game.*

the **man in the street** the ordinary person. □ *Politicians rarely care what the man in the street thinks.* □ *The man in the street has little interest in literature.*

man to man AND **woman to woman** speaking frankly and directly, one person to another. □ *Let's discuss this man to man so we know what each other thinks.* □ *The two mothers discussed their child-raising problems woman to woman.*

Many hands make light work. A lot of help will make a chore seem easier. (Proverb.) □ *Let's all work together and get this finished. Many hands make light work.* □ *Many hands make light work, so please lend a hand.*

many is the time on many occasions. □ *Many is the time I wanted to complain, but I just kept quiet.* □ *Many is the time that we don't have enough to eat.*

march to (the beat of) a different drummer to believe in a different set of principles. □ *John is marching to a different drummer, and he doesn't come to our parties anymore.* □ *Since Sally started marching to the beat of a different drummer, she has had a lot of great new ideas.*

mark my word(s) remember what I'm telling you. □ *Mark my word, you'll regret this.* □ *This whole project will fail—mark my words.*

mark someone or something **down 1.** [with *someone*] to make a note about someone; to note a fact about someone. □ *I'm going to the party. Please mark me down.* □ *Mark me down, too.* **2.** [with *someone*] [for a teacher] to give someone a low score. □ *He'll mark you down for misspelled words.* 🅃 *I marked down Tom for bad spelling.* **3.** [with *something*] to lower the price of something. □ *Okay, we'll mark it down.* 🅃 *Let's mark down this price so it'll sell faster.*

mark something **up 1.** to mess something up with marks. 🅃 *Don't mark up your book!* □ *Who marked this book up?* **2.** to grade a paper and make lots of informative marks and comments on it. 🅃 *The teacher really marked up my term paper.* □ *Why did you mark my test up so much? I hardly made any errors.* **3.** to raise the price of something. □ *The grocery store seems to mark the price of food up every week.* 🅃 *They don't mark up the price of turkey at Thanksgiving.*

a **marvel to behold** someone or something quite exciting or wonderful to see. □ *Our new house is a marvel to behold.* □ *Mary's lovely new baby is a marvel to behold.*

a **match for** someone, something, or some creature someone, something, or some creature that is the equal of someone, something, or some other creature, especially in a contest. □ *My older brother is no match for me; he's much weaker.* □ *Your horse is a good match for mine in the race. Either one might win.*

matter-of-fact businesslike; unfeeling. (See also **as a matter of fact**.) □ *Don't expect a lot of sympathy from Ann. She's very matter-of-fact.* □ *Don't be so matter-of-fact. It hurts my feelings.*

a **matter of life and death** an issue of great urgency; a situation that will affect life or death. □ *We must find a doctor. It's a matter of life and death.* □ *A matter of life and death demands that I return home at once.*

a **matter of opinion** the matter of how good or bad someone or something is; a question about which there are different opinions. □ *It's a matter of opinion how good the company is. John thinks it's great and Fred thinks it's poor.* □ *How efficient the committee is is a matter of opinion.*

mean business to be very serious and determined about something. (Informal.) □ *Billy, get into this house and do your homework, and I mean business.* □ *We* *mean business when we say you must stop all this nonsense.*

mean for someone **to** do something to intend for someone to do something. □ *John meant for us to go with them to the zoo.* □ *John meant for Jane to do the dishes.*

mean nothing (to someone**) 1.** not to make sense to someone. □ *This sentence means nothing to me. It isn't clearly written.* □ *I'm sorry. This message means nothing.* **2.** [for someone] not to have feeling for (someone or something). □ *Do I mean nothing to you after all these years?* □ *Do all those years mean nothing?*

mean something **(to** someone**) 1.** to make sense to someone. (See also the preceding entry.) □ *Does this line mean anything to you?* □ *Yes, it means something.* **2.** for someone to have feeling for (someone or something). □ *You mean a lot to me.* □ *This job means a lot to Ann.*

mean to (do something**)** to plan or intend to do something. □ *Did you mean to do that?* □ *No, it was an accident. I didn't mean to.*

meant to be destined to exist. □ *Our love was meant to be!* □ *It was not meant to be.*

meant to be something destined or fated to be something. □ *Jane was meant to be a chemist.* □ *I was meant to be rich, but something didn't work right!*

measure up (to someone or something**)** to be equal to someone or something. □ *Ann is good, but she doesn't measure up to Mary.* □ *Tom measures up to the job.*

measure up (to someone's **expectations)** AND **measure up to** someone's **standards** to be as good as one expects. □ *This measures up to my standards quite nicely.* □ *This meal doesn't measure up to my expectations.*

measure up to someone's **standards** Go to measure up (to someone's expectations).

meat-and-potatoes basic, sturdy, and hearty. (Often refers to a robust person, usually a man, with simple tastes in food and other things.) □ *Fred was your meat-and-potatoes kind of guy. No creamy sauces for him.* □ *There is no point in trying to cook up something special for the Wilsons. They are strictly meat-and-potatoes.*

a **Mecca for** someone a place that is frequently visited by a particular group of people because it is important to them for some reason. (From the city of Mecca, the religious center of Islam.) □ *New York City is a Mecca for theatergoers.* □ *St. Andrews is a Mecca for golf enthusiasts because of its famous course.*

meek as a lamb Go to (as) meek as a lamb.

meet one's **death** AND **meet** one's **end** to experience something, especially death or problems. □ *After 20 years, my dog finally met his death when he got hit by a bus.* □ *The sky diver met his end when his parachute didn't open.*

meet one's **end** Go to meet one's death.

meet one's **match** to meet one's equal. □ *John played tennis with Bill yesterday, and it looks as if John has finally met his match.* □ *Listen to Jane and Mary argue. I always thought that Jane was loud, but she has finally met her match.*

meet one's **Waterloo** to meet one's final and insurmountable challenge. (Refers to Napoleon's defeat at Waterloo.) □ *The boss is being very hard on Bill. It seems that Bill has finally met his Waterloo.* □ *John was more than Sally could handle. She has finally met her Waterloo.*

meet someone **halfway** to offer to compromise with someone. (Also literal.) □ *No, I won't give in, but I'll meet you halfway.* □ *They settled the argument by agreeing to meet each other halfway.*

meet the requirements (for something**)** to fulfill the requirements for something. □ *Sally was unable to meet the requirements for the job.* □ *Jane met the requirements and was told to report to work the next day.*

a **meeting of minds** the establishment of agreement; complete agreement. □ *After a lot of discussion we finally reached a meeting of minds.* □ *We struggled to bring about a meeting of minds on the issues.*

melt in one's **mouth 1.** to taste very good. (Also can be literal.) ☐ *This cake is so good it'll melt in your mouth.* ☐ *John said that the food didn't exactly melt in his mouth.* **2.** [of meat] to be very, very tender. ☐ *My steak is so tender it could melt in my mouth.* ☐ *This fillet will melt in your mouth!*

mend (one's**) fences** to restore good relations (with someone). (Also literal.) ☐ *I think I had better get home and mend my fences. I had an argument with my daughter this morning.* ☐ *Sally called up her uncle to apologize and try to mend fences.*

mend one's **ways** to improve one's behavior. ☐ *John used to be very wild, but he's mended his ways.* ☐ *You'll have to mend your ways if you go out with Mary. She hates people to be late.*

mention someone or something **in passing** to mention someone or something casually; to mention someone or something while talking about someone or something else. ☐ *He just happened to mention in passing that the mayor had resigned.* ☐ *John mentioned in passing that he was nearly eighty years old.*

merry as a cricket Go to (as) merry as a cricket.

merry as the day is long Go to (as) merry as the day is long.

mess about (with someone or something**)** Go to mess around (with someone or something).

mess around (with someone or something**)** AND **mess about (with** someone or something**); monkey around (with** someone or something**); screw around (with** someone or something**)** to play with or waste time with someone or something. (Slang.) ☐ *Will you please stop messing around with that old car!* ☐ *Stop messing about! Get busy!* ☐ *Tom wastes a lot of time messing around with Bill.* ☐ *Don't monkey around with my computer!* ☐ *John is always screwing around with his stereo.*

mess someone or something **up 1.** [with *someone*] to rough someone up; to beat someone up. (Slang.) ☐ *The robbers threatened to mess Bob up if he didn't cooperate.* 🆃 *John messed up Bill a little, but no real harm was done.* **2.** [with *something*] to make something disorderly. ☐ *You really messed this place up!* 🆃 *Who messed up my bed?*

middle-of-the-road halfway between two extremes, especially political extremes. (Also literal.) ☐ *Jane is very left-wing, but her husband is politically middle-of-the-road.* ☐ *I don't want to vote for either the left-wing or the right-wing candidate. I prefer someone with more middle-of-the-road views.*

might and main great physical strength; great force. ☐ *The huge warrior, with all his might and main, could not break his way through the castle gates.* ☐ *The incredible might and main of the sea crushed the ship against the cliff.*

milestone in someone's **life** a very important event or point in one's life. (From the stone at the side of a road showing the distance to or from a place.) ☐ *Joan's wedding was a milestone in her mother's life.* ☐ *The birth of a child is a milestone in every parent's life.*

milk of human kindness natural kindness and sympathy shown to others. (From Shakespeare's play *Macbeth, I. v.*) ☐ *Mary is completely hard and selfish—she has no milk of human kindness in her.* ☐ *Roger is too full of the milk of human kindness and people take advantage of him.*

milk someone **for** something to pressure someone into giving information or money. ☐ *The reporter milked the mayor's aide for information.* ☐ *The thief milked me for $20.*

millstone about one's **neck** a continual burden or handicap. ☐ *This huge and expensive house is a millstone about my neck.* ☐ *Bill's inability to read is a millstone about his neck.*

mince (one's**) words** to lessen the force of one's statement by choosing weak or polite words; to be euphemistic. (Formal.) ☐ *I won't mince words. You did a rotten job.* ☐ *I'm not one to mince words, so I have to say that you behaved very badly.*

mind one's **own business** to attend only to the things that concern one. ☐ *Leave* *me alone, Bill. Mind your own business.* □ *I'd be fine if John would mind his own business.*

mind one's **p's and q's** to pay attention to small details of behavior, especially manners. □ *When we go to the mayor's reception, please mind your p's and q's.* □ *I always mind my p's and q's when I eat at a restaurant with white tablecloths.*

mind the store to take care of local matters. (Also literal. Informal.) □ *Please stay here in the office and mind the store while I go to the conference.* □ *I had to stay home and mind the store when Ann went to Boston.*

mind you <a phrase indicating that something should be taken into consideration.> □ *He's very well dressed, but mind you, he's got plenty of money to buy clothes.* □ *Lisa is unfriendly to me, but mind you, she's never very nice to anyone.*

mind your manners to be careful to use good manners. □ *Mind your manners while we visit Aunt Mary's house.* □ *Jimmy! Mind your manners!*

a **mine of information** someone or something that is full of information. □ *Grandfather is a mine of information about World War I.* □ *The new encyclopedia is a positive mine of useful information.*

the **minute** something happens the point in time at which an event happens. □ *I'll be inside the minute it rains.* □ *Call me the minute you get to town.*

a **miscarriage of justice** a wrong or mistaken decision, especially one made in a court of law. □ *Sentencing the old man on a charge of murder proved to be a miscarriage of justice.* □ *Punishing the student for cheating was a miscarriage of justice. He was innocent.*

misplace one's **trust (in** someone**)** to put trust in the wrong person; to put trust in someone who does not deserve it. □ *The writer misplaced his trust in his editor.* □ *The voters misplaced their trust in the corrupt politician.*

miss out (on something**)** AND **lose out (on** something**)** to fail to participate in something; to fail to take part in something. □ *I'm sorry I missed out on the ice cream.* □ *I lost out on it, too.* □ *We both missed out.*

miss (something) **by a mile** to fail to hit something by a great distance; to land wide of the mark. □ *Ann shot the arrow and missed the target by a mile.* □ *"Good grief, you missed by a mile," shouted Sally.*

miss the boat to miss out (on something); to be ignorant (of something). (Also literal. Slang.) □ *Pay attention, John, or you'll miss the boat.* □ *Tom really missed the boat when it came to making friends.*

miss the point to fail to understand the important part of something. (Also literal.) □ *I'm afraid you missed the point. Let me explain it again.* □ *You keep explaining, and I keep missing the point.*

[mission in life] Go to someone's mission in life.

mistake someone **for** someone **else** AND **mix** someone **up with** someone **else** to confuse someone with someone else; to think that one person is another person. □ *I'm sorry. I mistook you for John.* □ *Tom is always mistaking Bill for me. We don't look a thing alike, though.* □ *Try not to mix Bill up with Bob.*

mix and match 1. to assemble a limited number of items, usually clothing, in a number of different ways. □ *Alice was very good at mixing and matching her skirts, blouses, and sweaters so that she always could be attractively dressed on a limited budget.* □ *Gary always bought black, blue, and gray trousers and shirts so he could mix and match without too many bad combinations.* **2.** to select a number of items from an assortment, often in order to get a quantity discount. (As opposed to getting a quantity discount for buying a lot of only one item.) □ *The candles were 25 percent off, and you could mix and match colors, sizes, and length.* □ *I found a good sale on shirts. They were four for fifty dollars, and the store would let you mix and match.*

mix it up to argue or fight. (Also literal. Slang.) □ *First they were just talking, then suddenly one of them got mad and they really began to mix it up.* □ *Look at you, Bill! Your face is bleeding. Have you been mixing it up with John again?*

mix someone or something **up 1.** to confuse two things or two people with each other. □ *Please don't mix these ideas up. They are quite distinct.* 🅃 *I always mix up Bill and Bob.* □ *Why do you mix them up?* **2.** [with *someone*] to cause someone to be confused or puzzled. □ *I'm confused as it is. Don't mix me up anymore.* 🅃 *They mixed up my uncle by giving him too many things to remember.* **3.** [with *something*] to blend the ingredients of something; to assemble and mix the parts of something. (Usually refers to fluid matter such as paint, gasoline, or milk.) □ *The glue will be ready to use as soon as I mix it up.* 🅃 *Now, mix up the eggs, water, and salt; then add the mixture to the flour and sugar.*

mix someone **up with** someone **else** Go to **mistake** someone **for** someone **else.**

a **mixed bag** a varied collection of people or things. (Refers to a bag of game brought home after a day's hunting.) □ *The new students in my class are a mixed bag—some bright, some positively stupid.* □ *The furniture I bought is a mixed bag. Some of it is valuable and the rest is worthless.*

the **moment everyone has been waiting for** Go to the **big moment.**

the **moment of truth** the point at which someone has to face the reality or facts of a situation. □ *The moment of truth is here. Turn over your test papers and begin.* □ *Now for the moment of truth when we find out whether we have got permission or not.*

Money burns a hole in someone's **pocket.** Someone spends as much money as possible. (Proverb. See also **have money to burn.**) □ *Sally can't seem to save anything. Money burns a hole in her pocket.* □ *If money burns a hole in your pocket, you never have any for emergencies.*

Money is no object. AND **Expense is no object.** It does not matter how much something costs. □ *Please show me your finest automobile. Money is no object.* □ *I want the finest earrings you have. Don't worry about how much they cost because expense is no object.*

Money is the root of all evil. Money is the basic cause of all wrongdoing. (Proverb. The full version is *The love of money is the root of all evil.*) □ *Why do you work so hard to make money? It will just cause you trouble. Money is the root of all evil.* □ *Any thief in prison can tell you that money is the root of all evil.*

money talks money gives one power and influence to help get things done or get one's own way. (Informal.) □ *Don't worry. I have a way of getting things done. Money talks.* □ *I can't compete against rich old Mrs. Jones. She'll get her way because money talks.*

monkey around (with someone or something**)** Go to **mess around (with** someone or something**).**

monkey business playful or out of the ordinary activities; mischievous or illegal activities. □ *There's been some monkey business in connection with the bank's accounts.* □ *Bob left the company quite suddenly. I think there was some monkey business between him and the boss's wife.*

monkey suit a tuxedo. (Jocular. Possibly alluding to the fancy suit worn by an organ grinder's monkey.) □ *Do I have to wear a monkey suit to dinner?* □ *All the men except me wore monkey suits at dinner on the cruise.*

months running Go to **days running.**

mop the floor up with someone to overwhelm and physically subdue someone; to beat someone. (Slang. See also **wipe up the floor with** someone.) □ *Stop talking like that, or I'll mop the floor up with you!* 🅃 *Did you hear that? He threatened to mop up the floor with me!*

mope around to go about in a depressed state. (Informal.) □ *Since her dog ran away, Sally mopes around all day.* □ *Don't mope around. Cheer up!*

more and more an increasing amount; additional amounts. □ *As I learn more and more, I see how little I know.* □ *Dad seems to be smoking more and more lately.*

more dead than alive exhausted; in very bad condition; near death. (Almost always an exaggeration.) □ *We arrived at the top of the mountain more dead than alive.* □ *The marathon runners stumbled one by one over the finish line, more dead than alive.*

more fun than a barrel of monkeys Go to (as) funny as a barrel of monkeys.

more often than not usually. □ *These flowers will live through the winter more often than not.* □ *This kind of dog will grow up to be a good watchdog more often than not.*

more or less to some extent; approximately; sort of. □ *This one will do all right, more or less.* □ *We'll be there at eight, more or less.*

more someone or something **than** one **can shake a stick at** a lot; too many to count. (Folksy.) □ *There were more snakes than you could shake a stick at.* □ *There are lots of flowers in the field—more than one can shake a stick at.*

more than one **can bear** AND **more than** one **can take; more than** one **can stand** more of something, such as trouble or something bad, than a person can endure. □ *This news is more than I can bear!* □ *I've heard enough of this horrid music. It's more than I can stand.*

more than one **can stand** Go to more than one can bear.

more than one **can take** Go to more than one can bear.

more than someone **bargained for** more than one thought one would get. (Usually in reference to trouble or difficulty.) □ *When Betsy brought home the sweet little puppy for a companion, she got more than she bargained for. That animal has cost her hundreds of dollars in medical bills.* □ *I got more than I bargained for when I took this job.*

the **more the merrier** the more people there are, the happier they will be. □ *Of course you can have a ride with us! The more the merrier.* □ *The manager hired a new employee even though there's not enough work for all of us now. Oh, well, the more the merrier.*

more (to something**) than meets the eye** [there are] hidden values or facts in something. □ *There is more to that problem than meets the eye.* □ *What makes you think that there is more than meets the eye?*

the **morning after (the night before)** the morning after a night spent drinking, when one has a hangover. □ *Oh, I've got a headache. Talk about the morning after the night before!* □ *It looked like a case of the morning after the night before, and Frank asked for some aspirin.*

move heaven and earth to do something to make a major effort to do something. □ *"I'll move heaven and earth to be with you, Mary," said Bill.* □ *I had to move heaven and earth to get there on time.* □ *Your father and I had to move heaven and earth to pay for your braces and your college bills, and what thanks do we get?*

move in (on someone or something**) 1.** [with *someone*] to attempt to displace someone or take over someone's property, interests, or relationships. (Slang, especially criminal slang. Compare this with muscle in (on someone or something).) □ *Look here, pal, Sally's my girl. Are you trying to move in on me?* □ *It looks like the south-side gang is trying to move in. We'll have to teach them a lesson.* **2.** [with *someone*] to move into someone's household. □ *My mother-in-law moved in on us for two months.* □ *I wouldn't move in on you without an invitation.* **3.** to move closer to someone or something, especially with a camera. □ *Now, slowly move in on the cereal box. This will be a great advertisement.* □ *Hold the camera very steady and move in on the baby.*

move into something to get started in a new enterprise, job, etc. (Also literal.) □ *I moved into a new job last week. It's very* *exciting work.* □ *John moved into a new line of work, too.*

move up (in the world) to advance (oneself) and become successful. □ *The harder I work, the more I move up in the world.* □ *Keep your eye on John. He's really moving up.*

movers and shakers people who get things done; people who are productive and cause other people to be productive; people who create and produce. □ *The trouble with the ABC Company is that all the movers and shakers are leaving to take jobs elsewhere.* □ *It seems as if all the movers and shakers of the world are employed by a very small number of large firms.*

much ado about nothing a lot of excitement about nothing. (This is the title of a play by Shakespeare. Do not confuse *ado* with *adieu*.) □ *All the commotion about the new tax law turned out to be much ado about nothing.* □ *Your promises always turn out to be much ado about nothing.*

much in evidence very visible or evident. □ *John was much in evidence during the conference.* □ *Your influence is much in evidence. I appreciate your efforts.*

much sought after wanted or desired very much; highly desirable. □ *This kind of crystal is much sought after. It's very rare.* □ *Sally is a great singer. She's much sought after.*

muddy the water to make something less clear; to make matters confusing; to create difficulty where there was none before. (Also literal.) □ *Things were going along quite smoothly until you came along and muddied the water.* □ *The events of the past month have muddied the water as far as our proposed joint venture is concerned.*

muff one's **lines** Go to fluff one's lines.

mull something **over** to think about something; to ponder or worry about something. □ *That's an interesting idea, but I'll have to mull it over.* 🅃 *I'll mull over your suggestions and report to you next week.*

mum's the word don't spread the secret. □ *Don't tell anyone what I told you. Remember, mum's the word.* □ *Okay, mum's the word. Your secret is safe with me.*

murder on something very destructive or harmful to something. □ *Running a marathon is murder on your knees.* □ *This dry weather is murder on my crops.*

muscle in (on someone or something**)** to try forcefully to displace someone or take over someone's property, interests, or relationships. (Slang, especially criminal slang. Compare this with move in (on someone or something).) □ *Are you trying to muscle in on my scheme?* □ *If you try to muscle in, you'll be facing big trouble.*

a **must** something that you must do. (Informal. Preceded by *be, become,* or *seem like*.) □ *When you're in San Francisco, see the Golden Gate Bridge. It's a must.* □ *It's a must that you brush your teeth after every meal.*

muster (up) one's **courage** to build up one's courage; to call or bring forth one's courage. □ *I mustered my courage and dove from the high diving board.* □ *He had to muster up all his courage in order to attend the dance.*

my gut tells me (that) something is so my instincts tell me that something is so. (This refers to one's *gut reaction* or *gut response*, that is, the way someone feels about something.) □ *My gut tells me that her idea is a sound one.* □ *This looks good on paper, but my gut tells me that it is all wrong.*

my one and only one's spouse. (Informal. See also the one and only.) □ *Look at the time. I've got to get home to my one and only.* □ *You're my one and only. There is no one else for me.*

N

nail in someone's or something's **coffin** Go to **(another) nail in** someone's or something's **coffin.**

nail someone or something **down 1.** [with *someone*] to get a firm and final decision from someone (on something). (Also literal. Informal.) □ *I want you to find Bob and get an answer from him. Nail him down one way or the other.* 🅃 *Please nail down John on the question of signing the contract.* **2.** [with *something*] to get a firm and final decision (from someone) on something. (Informal.) 🅃 *Find Bob and nail down an answer.* □ *Let's get in touch with John and nail down this contract.*

naked as a jaybird Go to **(as) naked as a jaybird.**

the **naked eye** the human eye, unassisted by optics, such as a telescope, microscope, or spectacles. □ *I can't see the bird's markings with the naked eye.* □ *The scientist could see nothing in the liquid with the naked eye, but with the aid of a microscope, she identified the bacteria.* □ *That's how it appears to the naked eye.*

[name is mud] Go to one's **name is mud.**

the **name of the game** goal or purpose. (Slang.) □ *The name of the game is* sell. *You must sell, sell, sell if you want to make a living.* □ *Around here, the name of the game is look out for yourself.*

name someone **after** someone **else** AND **name** someone **for** someone **else** to give someone (usually a baby) the name of another person. □ *We named our baby after my aunt.* □ *My parents named me for my grandfather.*

name someone **for** someone **else** Go to **name** someone **after** someone **else.**

near at hand close or handy (to someone). (See also **at hand; close at hand.**) □ *Do you have a pencil near at hand?* □ *My dictionary isn't near at hand.*

neat as a pin Go to **(as) neat as a pin.**

neck and neck exactly even, especially in a race or a contest. (Informal.) □ *John and Tom finished the race neck and neck.* □ *Mary and Ann were neck and neck in the spelling contest. Their scores were tied.*

need something **like a hole in the head** not to need something at all. (Informal.) □ *I need a housecat like I need a hole in the head!* □ *She needs a car like she needs a hole in the head.*

need something **yesterday** to require something in a very big hurry. (Informal.) □ *Yes, I'm in a hurry! I need it yesterday!* □ *When do I need it? Now! Now! No, I need it yesterday!*

neither fish nor fowl not any recognizable thing; not any recognizable category. □ *The car that they drove up in was neither fish nor fowl. It must have been made out of spare parts.* □ *This proposal is neither fish nor fowl. I can't tell what you're proposing.*

neither here nor there of no consequence or meaning; irrelevant and immaterial. □ *Whether you go to the movie or stay at home is neither here nor there.* □ *Your comment—though interesting—is neither here nor there.*

neither hide nor hair no sign or indication (of someone or something). □ *We could find neither hide nor hair of him. I don't know where he is.* □ *There has been no one here—neither hide nor hair—for the last three days.*

never fear do not worry; have confidence. □ *I'll be there on time—never fear.* □ *I'll help you, never fear.*

never had it so good Go to (have) never had it so good.

never in one's **life** not in one's experience. □ *Never in my life have I been so insulted!* □ *He said that never in his life had he seen such an ugly painting.*

never mind forget it; pay no more attention (to something). □ *I wanted to talk to you, but never mind. It wasn't important.* □ *Never mind. I'm sorry to bother you.*

never would have guessed 1. never would have thought something to be the case. (Not used in other tenses.) □ *He was the one who did it? I never would have guessed.* □ *I never would have guessed that he wanted the job. He kept it a very good secret.* **2.** knew it all the time because it was so obvious. (Sarcastic. Not used in other tenses.) □ *I never would have guessed that he wanted the job. He only begged and begged for it.* □ *Now she wants to go back home? I never would have guessed! She has been homesick for days.*

new ball game Go to (whole) new ball game.

new blood Go to (some) new blood.

new hire a person who has recently been hired; a newly employed person. □ *Anne is our new hire who will begin work Tuesday.* □ *The accounting department is full of new hires.*

a **new lease on life** a renewed and revitalized outlook on life. □ *Getting the job offer was a new lease on life.* □ *When I got out of the hospital, I felt as if I had a new lease on life.*

new to (all) this Go to (a little) new to (all) this.

next-door neighbor the person living in the house or apartment closest to one's own. □ *My next-door neighbor came over to borrow a shovel.* □ *I will be visiting our next-door neighbor if you need me.*

next of kin someone's closest living relative or relatives. □ *The police notified the dead man's next of kin.* □ *My next of kin lives 800 miles away.*

next to nothing hardly anything; almost nothing. □ *This car's worth next to nothing. It's full of rust.* □ *I bought this antique chair for next to nothing.*

next to someone or something near to someone or something; adjacent to someone or something. □ *I live next to a bank.* □ *Please sit next to me.*

nice and some quality enough of some quality; adequately; sufficiently. □ *It is nice and cool this evening.* □ *I think your steak is nice and done now and probably overcooked.*

nickel and dime someone to charge someone many small amounts of money; to assess many small fees against someone. □ *We will not stay at that resort again. They nickel and dime you to death in that place. There is a charge for everything.* □ *Tuition at the university hasn't gone up in two years but other small fees have. They really nickel and dime you there.*

night and day Go to day and night.

a **night on the town** a night of celebrating (at one or more places in a town). □ *Did you enjoy your night on the town?* □ *After we got the contract signed, we celebrated with a night on the town.*

night owl someone who usually stays up very late. (Preceded by *be, become, seem like,* or *act like.*) □ *Anne's a real night owl. She never goes to bed before 2 A.M. and sleeps till noon.* □ *Jack's a night owl and is at his best after midnight.*

a **nine days' wonder** something that is of interest to people only for a short time. □ *Don't worry about the story about you in the newspaper. It'll be a nine days' wonder, and then people will forget.* □ *The elopement of Jack and Anne was a nine days' wonder. Now people never mention it.*

a **nine-to-five job** a job with regular and normal hours. □ *I wouldn't want a nine-to-five job. I like the freedom I have as my own boss.* □ *I used to work nights, but now I have a nine-to-five job.*

nip and tuck almost even; almost tied. (Informal.) ☐ *The horses ran nip and tuck for the first half of the race. Then my horse pulled ahead.* ☐ *In the football game last Saturday, both teams were nip and tuck throughout the game.*

nip something **in the bud** to put an end to something at an early stage. (Also literal.) ☐ *John is getting into bad habits, and it's best to nip them in the bud.* ☐ *There was trouble in the classroom, but the teacher nipped it in the bud.*

No big deal! Not a big problem! (Informal.) ☐ *It didn't hurt. No big deal!* ☐ *It isn't a problem. No big deal!*

no buts about it Go to no ifs, ands, or buts about it.

No can do. It can't be done.; I can't do it. (Slang.) ☐ *Sorry, John. No can do. I can't sell you this one. I've promised it to Mrs. Smith.* ☐ *BILL: Please fix this clock today. BOB: No can do. It'll take a week to get the parts.*

No comment. I have nothing to say on this matter. ☐ *Q: When did you stop beating your dog? A: No comment.* ☐ *Q: Georgie, did you chop down the cherry tree? A: No comment.*

no doubt surely; without a doubt; undoubtedly. ☐ *He will be here again tomorrow, no doubt.* ☐ *No doubt you will require a ride home?*

no end of something lots of something. (Informal.) ☐ *It was a wonderful banquet. They had no end of good food.* ☐ *Tom is a real problem. He's no end of trouble.*

no flies on someone someone is not slow; someone is not wasting time. (Refers to a person moving too fast to allow flies to light.) ☐ *Of course I work fast. I go as fast as I can. There are no flies on me.* ☐ *There are no flies on Robert. He does his work very fast and very well.*

no great shakes nothing important or worth noticing. (Slang.) ☐ *It's okay, but it's no great shakes.* ☐ *I like John, but he's no great shakes when it comes to sports.*

no hard feelings no anger or resentment. (Informal. *No* can be replaced with *any*.) ☐ *I hope you don't have any hard feelings.* ☐ *No, I have no hard feelings.*

No harm done. It is all right. No one or nothing has been harmed. (Informal.) ☐ *It's okay. No harm done.* ☐ *A: I am sorry I stepped on your toe. B: No harm done.*

no holds barred with no restraints. (Slang. From wrestling.) ☐ *I intend to argue it out with Mary, no holds barred.* ☐ *When Ann negotiates a contract, she goes in with no holds barred and comes out with a good contract.*

no ifs, ands, or buts about it AND **no buts about it** absolutely no discussion, dissension, or doubt about something. ☐ *I want you there exactly at eight, no ifs, ands, or buts about it.* ☐ *This is the best television set available for the money, no buts about it.*

no joke a serious matter. (Informal.) ☐ *It's no joke when you miss the last train.* ☐ *It's certainly no joke when you have to walk home.*

no kidding [spoken] honestly; [someone is] not joking or lying. (Slang.) ☐ *No kidding, you really got an A in geometry?* ☐ *I really did, no kidding.*

no laughing matter a serious matter. ☐ *Be serious. This is no laughing matter.* ☐ *This disease is no laughing matter. It's quite deadly.*

no love lost (between someone **and** someone **else)** no friendship wasted between someone and someone else (because they are enemies). ☐ *Ever since their big argument, there has been no love lost between Tom and Bill.* ☐ *You can tell by the way that Jane is acting toward Ann that there is no love lost.*

no matter what happens in any event; without regard to what happens (in the future). ☐ *We'll be there on time, no matter what.* ☐ *No matter what happens, we'll still be friends.*

No news is good news. If one has not had any information about someone or something for some time, it means that all is well, since one would have heard if anything bad or unfortunate had occurred.

(Proverb.) □ *I haven't heard from my son since he left for college, but I suppose no news is good news.* □ *I think Joan would have heard by now if she hadn't got the job. No news is good news.*

no point in something no purpose in doing something. □ *There is no point in locking the barn door now that the horse has been stolen.* □ *There's no point is crying over spilled milk.*

no problem Go to no sweat.

no skin off someone's **nose** Go to no skin off someone's teeth.

no skin off someone's **teeth** AND **no skin off** someone's **nose** no difficulty for someone; no concern of someone. □ *It's no skin off my nose if she wants to act that way.* □ *She said it was no skin off her teeth if we wanted to sell the house.*

no sooner said than done <an expression indicating that something has been done quickly and obediently.> □ *When Sally asked for someone to open the window, it was no sooner said than done.* □ *As Jane opened the window, she said, "No sooner said than done."*

no spring chicken not young (anymore). (Informal.) □ *I don't get around very well anymore. I'm no spring chicken, you know.* □ *Even though John is no spring chicken, he still plays tennis twice a week.*

no sweat AND **no problem** no difficulty; do not worry. (Slang.) □ *Of course I can have your car repaired by noon. No sweat.* □ *You'd like a red one? No problem.*

no trespassing do not enter. (Usually seen on a sign. Not usually spoken.) □ *The sign on the tree said, "No Trespassing." So we didn't go in.* □ *The angry farmer chased us out of the field shouting, "Get out! Don't you see the no trespassing sign?"*

no two ways about it no choice about it; no other interpretation of it. (Folksy. Note the form *there's* rather than *there are*.) □ *You have to go to the doctor whether you like it or not. There's no two ways about it.* □ *This letter means you're in trouble with the tax people. There's no two ways about it.*

no-win situation a situation where there is no correct or satisfactory solution. □ *The general was too weak to fight and too proud to surrender. It was a no-win situation.* □ *The huge dog my father gave us as a gift eats too much. If we get rid of the dog, my father will be insulted. If we keep it, we will go broke buying food for it. This is a classic no-win situation.*

no wonder [something is] not surprising. (Informal.) □ *No wonder the baby is crying. She's wet.* □ *It's no wonder that plant died. You watered it too much.*

nobody's fool a sensible and wise person who is not easily deceived. □ *Mary's nobody's fool. She knows Jack would try to cheat her.* □ *Anne looks as though she's not very bright, but she's nobody's fool.*

nod off to fall asleep, usually while sitting up. (Informal.) □ *Jack nodded off during the minister's sermon.* □ *Father always nods off after Sunday lunch.*

none of someone's **beeswax** none of someone's business (Slang.) □ *The answer to that question is none of your beeswax.* □ *It's none of your beeswax what I do with my spare time.*

none of someone's **business** not of someone's concern. (A gentle rebuke.) □ *Q: When are you going to leave for home? A: None of your business.* □ *How I manage to keep thin is none of your business.*

none other than someone the very person. □ *The new building was opened by none other than the mayor.* □ *Jack's wife turned out to be none other than my cousin.*

none the wiser not knowing any more. □ *I was none the wiser about the project after the lecture. It was a complete waste of time.* □ *Anne tried to explain the situation tactfully to Jack, but in the end, he was none the wiser.*

none the worse for wear no worse because of use or effort. □ *I lent my car to John. When I got it back, it was none the worse for wear.* □ *I had a hard day today, but I'm none the worse for wear.*

none too something not very something; not at all something. □ *The towels in the* *bathroom were none too clean.* □ *It was none too warm in their house.*

nose about Go to nose around.

nose around AND **nose about** to investigate; to check (into something). (Informal.) □ *I don't have an answer to your question, but I'll nose around and see what I can find out.* □ *I'll nose about, too. Who knows what we'll find out?*

nose in(to something**)** to move into something, front end first. □ *Slowly the car nosed into its parking place.* □ *You must nose in very carefully.*

[nose is in the air] Go to one's nose is in the air.

nose someone **out** to push someone away; to exclude someone. □ *Where I work someone is always trying to nose me out. I'd hate to lose my job.* 🅃 *John nosed out Bill from the team.*

not a bit none at all. □ *Am I unhappy? Not a bit.* □ *I don't want any mashed potatoes. Not a bit!*

[not able] Go to the expressions listed at can't as well as those listed below.

not able to call one's **time** one's **own** too busy; so busy as not to be in charge of one's own schedule. (Informal. *Not able to* is often expressed as *can't.*) □ *It's been so busy around here that I haven't been able to call my time my own.* □ *She can't call her time her own these days.*

not able to go on unable to continue (doing something—even living). (*Not able to* is often expressed as *can't.*) □ *I just can't go on this way.* □ *Before her death, she left a note saying she was not able to go on.*

not able to help something unable to prevent or control something. (*Not able to* is often expressed as *can't.*) □ *I'm sorry about being late. I wasn't able to help it.* □ *Bob can't help being boring.*

not able to make anything out of someone or something unable to understand someone or something. (*Not able to* is often expressed as *can't.* The *anything* may refer to something specific, as in the first example.) □ *I can't make sense out of what you just said.* □ *We were not able to make anything out of the message.*

not able to see the forest for the trees allowing many details of a situation to obscure the situation as a whole. (*Not able to* is often expressed as *can't.*) □ *The solution is obvious. You missed it because you can't see the forest for the trees.* □ *She suddenly realized that she hadn't been able to see the forest for the trees.*

not able to stomach someone or something AND **cannot stomach** someone or something not to be able to put up with someone or something; not to be able to tolerate or endure someone or something. □ *Jane cannot stomach violent movies.* □ *The unpopular student could not stomach a lot of ridicule.*

not able to wait to have to go to the bathroom urgently. (Also literal in a general sense. Informal.) □ *Mom, I can't wait.* □ *Driver, stop the bus! My little boy can't wait.*

not agree with someone [for food] to make someone ill; [for something one has eaten] to give one minor stomach distress. □ *Fried foods don't agree with Tom.* □ *I always have onions in my garden, but I never eat them. They just don't agree with me.*

not a living soul nobody. (Informal. See also not tell a (living) soul.) □ *No one was there—not a living soul.* □ *Not a living soul saw me leave.*

not all something **is cracked up to be** AND **not what** something **is cracked up to be** not as good as something is said to be. (Informal. Not always in the negative.) □ *This isn't a very good pen. It's not all it's cracked up to be.* □ *Is this one all it's cracked up to be?* □ *This restaurant isn't what it's cracked up to be.*

not all there not mentally adequate; crazy or silly. (Informal.) □ *Sometimes I think you're not all there.* □ *Be nice to Sally. She's not all there.*

not a moment to spare AND **without a moment to spare** just in time; with no extra time. □ *Hurry, hurry! There's not* *a moment to spare!* ☐ *I arrived without a moment to spare.*

not at all certainly not; absolutely not. ☐ *No, it doesn't bother me—not at all.* ☐ *I'm not complaining. Not me. Not at all.*

not bat an eyelid to show no signs of distress even when something bad happens or something shocking is said. ☐ *Sam didn't bat an eyelid when the mechanic told him how much the car repairs would cost.* ☐ *The pain of the broken arm must have hurt Sally terribly, but she did not bat an eyelid.*

not believe one's **eyes** not to believe what one is seeing; to be shocked or dumbfounded at what one is seeing. ☐ *I walked into the room and I couldn't believe my eyes. All the furniture had been stolen!* ☐ *When Jimmy opened his birthday present, he could hardly believe his eyes. Just what he wanted!*

not born yesterday experienced; knowledgeable in the ways of the world. ☐ *I know what's going on. I wasn't born yesterday.* ☐ *Sally knows the score. She wasn't born yesterday.*

not breathe a word (about someone or something**)** to keep a secret about someone or something. ☐ *Don't worry. I won't breathe a word about the problem.* ☐ *Please don't breathe a word about Bob and his problems.*

not breathe a word of it not to tell something (to anyone). ☐ *Don't worry. I won't breathe a word of it.* ☐ *Tom won't breathe a word of it.*

not buy something not accept something (to be true). (Also literal. Slang.) ☐ *You may think so, but I don't buy it.* ☐ *The police wouldn't buy his story.*

not by a long shot not by a great amount; not. (Informal.) ☐ *Did I win the race? Not by a long shot.* ☐ *Not by a long shot did she complete the assignment.*

not care two hoots (about someone or something**)** AND **not give two hoots (about** someone or something**); not give a hang (about** someone or something**); not give a hoot (about** someone or something**)** not to care at all about someone or something. (Folksy.) ☐ *I don't care two hoots about whether you go to the picnic or not.* ☐ *She doesn't give a hoot about me. Why should I care?* ☐ *I don't give a hang about it.*

not dry behind the ears Go to wet behind the ears.

not enough room to swing a cat not very much space. (Folksy.) ☐ *Their living room was very small. There wasn't enough room to swing a cat.* ☐ *How can you work in a small room like this? There's not enough room to swing a cat.*

not for a moment not at all; not even for a short amount of time; never. ☐ *I don't want you to leave. Not for a moment!* ☐ *I could not wish such a horrible punishment on anyone. Not for a moment!*

not for (anything in) the world AND **not for love nor money; not on your life** not for anything (no matter what its value). (Note the variation in the examples. The order of *love nor money* is fixed.) ☐ *I won't do it for love nor money.* ☐ *He said he wouldn't do it—not for the world.* ☐ *She said no, not for anything in the world.* ☐ *Me, go there? Not on your life!*

not for hire [of a taxi] not available to take new passengers. ☐ *The taxi was going to pick someone up at a nearby hotel and was not for hire.* ☐ *The taxi had a lighted sign that said it was not for hire.*

not for love nor money Go to not for (anything in) the world.

not for publication not to be talked about openly; secret. ☐ *Please tell no one about this. It's not for publication.* ☐ *This report is not for publication, so keep the results to yourself.*

not give a hang (about someone or something**)** Go to not care two hoots (about someone or something).

not give a hoot (about someone or something**)** Go to not care two hoots (about someone or something).

not give it another thought not to worry about something anymore. (A polite way of accepting someone's apology.) □ *It's okay. Please don't give it another thought.* □ *You should not give it another thought. No one was bothered at all.*

not give someone **the time of day** to ignore someone (usually out of dislike). (Informal.) □ *Mary won't speak to Sally. She won't give her the time of day.* □ *I couldn't get an appointment with Mr. Smith. He wouldn't even give me the time of day.*

not give two hoots (about someone or something**)** Go to **not care two hoots (about** someone or something**)**.

not half bad okay; pretty good. (Folksy.) □ *Say, this roast beef isn't half bad.* □ *Hey, Sally! You're not half bad!*

[not] have anything to do with something Go to **have** something **to do with** something.

not hold a candle to someone or something Go to **not hold a stick to** someone or something.

not hold a stick to someone or something AND **not hold a candle to** someone or something not to be nearly as good as someone or something. (Informal.) □ *Sally is much faster than Bob. Bob doesn't hold a stick to Sally.* □ *This TV doesn't hold a candle to that one. That one is much better.*

not hold water to make no sense; to be illogical. (Also literal. Informal. Said of ideas, arguments, etc., not people. It means that the idea has holes in it.) □ *Your argument doesn't hold water.* □ *This scheme won't work because it can't hold water.*

not hurt a flea not to harm anything or anyone, even a tiny insect. (Also with other forms of negation.) □ *Ted would not even hurt a flea. He could not have struck Bill.* □ *Ted would never hurt a flea, and he would not hit anyone as you claim.*

not in the same league with someone or something not anywhere nearly as good as someone or something. (Also literal.) □ *John isn't in the same league with Bob and his friends.* □ *This house isn't in the same league with our old one.*

not know beans (about someone or something**)** to know nothing about someone or something. (Slang.) □ *Bill doesn't know beans about flying an airplane.* □ *When it comes to flying, I don't know beans.* □ *She doesn't know beans about Bill.*

not know enough to come in out of the rain to be very stupid. □ *Bob is so stupid he doesn't know enough to come in out of the rain.* □ *You can't expect very much from somebody who doesn't know enough to come in out of the rain.*

not know from nothing to be stupid, innocent, and naive. (Slang. This *nothing* is not replaced with *something*. Usually with *don't*, as in the examples below.) □ *Old John—he don't know from nothing.* □ *What do you expect from somebody who don't know from nothing?*

not know if one **is coming or going** Go to **not know whether one is coming or going**.

not know one's **own strength** not to realize how destructive or harmful one's strength can be. (Present tense only.) □ *I didn't mean to hurt you. I guess I don't know my own strength.* □ *He might break the door down by accident. He doesn't know his own strength and could end up pushing too hard against the door.*

not know someone **from Adam** not to know someone at all. □ *I wouldn't recognize John if I saw him. I don't know him from Adam.* □ *What does she look like? I don't know her from Adam.*

not know the first thing about someone or something not to know anything about someone or something. □ *I don't know the first thing about flying an airplane.* □ *She doesn't know the first thing about John.*

not know where to turn AND **not know which way to turn** to have no idea about what to do (about something). □ *I was so confused I didn't know where to turn.* □ *We needed help, but we didn't know which way to turn.*

not know whether one **is coming or going** AND **not know if** one **is coming or going** to be very confused. □ *I'm so busy that I don't know if I'm coming or going.*

□ *You look as if you don't know whether you're coming or going.*

not know which way to turn Go to not know where to turn.

not let someone **catch** someone doing something AND **not want to catch** someone doing something to find someone doing something wrong. (The idea is that the person ought not to do the wrong thing again, not that the person simply avoid getting caught.) □ *How many times have I told you not to play ball in the house? Don't let me catch you doing that again.* □ *If I've told you once, I've told you a thousand times: Don't do that! I don't want to catch you doing it again!*

not lift a finger (to help someone**)** AND **not lift a hand (to help** someone**)** to do nothing to help someone. (The *someone* is *anyone* in the negative.) □ *They wouldn't lift a finger to help us.* □ *Can you imagine that they wouldn't lift a finger?* □ *Sally refused to lift a hand to help her own sister.*

not lift a hand (to help someone**)** Go to not lift a finger (to help someone).

not long for this world to be about to die. □ *Our dog is nearly twelve years old and not long for this world.* □ *I'm so tired. I think I'm not long for this world.*

not made of money [of a person] not having a lot of money; not having an unlimited supply of money. □ *I can't afford a car like that. I'm not made of money you know.* □ *There is only so much they can pay. They're not made of money.*

not miss a thing Go to not miss much.

not miss much 1. AND **not miss a thing** not to miss observing any part of what is going on. (Usually with *do* as in the examples below.) □ *Ted doesn't miss much. He is very alert.* □ *The puppy doesn't miss a thing. He sees every move you make.* **2.** not to miss experiencing something that really was not worth experiencing anyway. (Sarcastic. Usually with *do* as in the examples below.) □ *I missed the big sales meeting last week, but I understand I didn't miss much.* □ *BILL: I didn't see that new movie that is showing at the theater. TOM: You didn't miss much.*

not move a muscle to remain perfectly motionless. □ *Be quiet. Sit there and don't move a muscle.* □ *I was so tired I couldn't move a muscle.*

not on any account Go to on no account.

not one iota not even a tiny bit. □ *I won't give you any at all! Not one iota!* □ *I did not get one iota of encouragement from any of those people.*

not one's **place** not one's role to do something. □ *It was not my place to criticize my boss.* □ *It was Bill's place to ask the questions, not yours.*

not on your life Go to not for (anything in) the world.

not open one's **mouth** AND **not utter a word** not to say anything at all; not to tell something (to anyone). □ *Don't worry, I'll keep your secret. I won't even open my mouth.* □ *Have no fear. I won't utter a word.* □ *I don't know how they found out. I didn't even open my mouth.*

not see any objection (to something**)** Go to see no objection (to something).

not see farther than the end of one's **nose** AND **not see past the end of** one's **nose** not to care about what is not actually present or obvious; not to care about the future or about what is happening elsewhere or to other people. (Could be literal or an exaggeration in a heavy fog or in dim light.) □ *Mary can't see past the end of her nose. She doesn't care about what will happen in the future as long as she's comfortable now.* □ *Jack's been accused of not seeing farther than the end of his nose. He refuses to expand the company and look for new markets.*

not see past the end of one's **nose** Go to not see farther than the end of one's nose.

not set foot somewhere not to go somewhere. □ *I wouldn't set foot in John's room. I'm very angry at him.* □ *He never set foot here.*

not show one's **face** not to appear (somewhere). ☐ *After what she said, she had better not show her face around here again.* ☐ *If I don't say I'm sorry, I'll never be able to show my face again.*

not sleep a wink not to sleep at all. (Informal.) ☐ *I couldn't sleep a wink last night.* ☐ *Ann hasn't been able to sleep a wink for a week.*

not someone's **cup of tea** not something one prefers. ☐ *Playing cards isn't her cup of tea.* ☐ *Sorry, that's not my cup of tea.*

not take no for an answer not to accept someone's refusal. (Informal. A polite way of being insistent.) ☐ *Now, you must drop over and see us tomorrow. We won't take no for an answer.* ☐ *I had to go. They just wouldn't take no for an answer.*

not take stock in something Go to **take no stock in** something.

not tell a (living) soul not to reveal something to anyone. ☐ *You secret is safe with me. I won't tell a living soul.* ☐ *Promise you won't tell a soul, but I'm engaged.*

not up to scratch AND **not up to snuff** not adequate. (Informal. See also **up to snuff; up to scratch.**) ☐ *Sorry, your paper isn't up to scratch. Please do it over again.* ☐ *The performance was not up to snuff.*

not up to snuff Go to **not up to scratch.**

not utter a word Go to **not open** one's **mouth.**

not want to catch someone doing something Go to **not let** someone **catch** someone doing something.

not what something **is cracked up to be** Go to **not all** something **is cracked up to be.**

not with it not able to think clearly; not able to understand things. ☐ *Lisa's mother is not really with it anymore. She's going senile.* ☐ *Tom's not with it yet. He's only just come round from the anesthetic.*

not worth a dime AND **not worth a red cent** worthless. (Informal.) ☐ *This land is all swampy. It's not worth a dime.* ☐ *This pen I bought isn't worth a dime. It has no ink.* ☐ *It's not worth a red cent.*

not worth a hill of beans AND **not worth a plugged nickel** worthless. (Folksy.) ☐ *Your advice isn't worth a hill of beans.* ☐ *This old cow isn't worth a plugged nickel.*

not worth a plugged nickel Go to **not worth a hill of beans.**

not worth a red cent Go to **not worth a dime.**

not worth mentioning 1. not important enough to require a comment. ☐ *There are others, but they are not worth mentioning.* ☐ *A small number of books hint at the phenomenon, but they aren't worth mentioning.* **2.** [of an error or wrong] not worth apologizing for. ☐ *This isn't a problem at all. It's not worth mentioning.* ☐ *No need to apologize to me. No harm done. It's not worth mentioning.*

not worth one's **while** not worth bothering with; not worth spending time on. ☐ *It's not worth my while to discuss it with you.* ☐ *Don't bother trying to collect money from them. It isn't worth your while.*

not worth the trouble not important enough to require a comment. ☐ *Don't bother with it. It isn't worth the trouble.* ☐ *There is no point in trying to get the spot out of the carpet. It isn't worth the trouble.*

nothing but skin and bones AND **(all) skin and bones** very thin or emaciated. (Informal.) ☐ *Bill has lost so much weight. He's nothing but skin and bones.* ☐ *Look at Bill. He's just skin and bones.* ☐ *That old horse is all skin and bones. I won't ride it.*

nothing but something only something; just something. ☐ *Joan drinks nothing but milk.* ☐ *Fred buys nothing but expensive clothes.*

nothing doing no. (Informal.) ☐ *No, I won't do that. Nothing doing.* ☐ *BOB: Will you help me with this? BILL: Nothing doing.*

nothing down requiring no down payment. ☐ *You can have this car for nothing down and $140 a month.* ☐ *I bought a winter coat for nothing down and no payments due until February.*

nothing of the kind 1. no; absolutely not. □ *I didn't tear your jacket—nothing of the kind!* □ *Did I break your vase? Nothing of the kind!* **2.** nothing like that. □ *That's not true. We did nothing of the kind!* □ *She did nothing of the kind! She wasn't even there!*

nothing short of something more or less the same as something bad; as bad as something. □ *His behavior was nothing short of criminal.* □ *Climbing those mountains alone is nothing short of suicide.*

nothing to choose from no choice; no choice in the selection; not enough of something to make a choice. □ *I went to the store looking for new shoes, but there was nothing to choose from.* □ *By the time I got around to selecting a team of helpers, there was nothing to choose from.*

nothing to complain about all right. (Folksy. Said in answer to the question "How are you?") □ *Bob said he has nothing to complain about.* □ *BILL: How're you doing, Bob? BOB: Nothing to complain about, Bill. Yourself?*

nothing to it it is easy; no difficulty involved. □ *Driving a car is easy. There's nothing to it.* □ *Geometry is fun to learn. There's nothing to it.*

nothing to sneeze at not small or unimportant. (Informal.) □ *It's not a lot of money, but it's nothing to sneeze at.* □ *Our house isn't a mansion, but it's nothing to sneeze at.*

nothing to speak of not many; not much. (Informal.) □ *JOHN: What's happening around here? BILL: Nothing to speak of.* □ *MARY: Has there been any rain in the last week? SALLY: Nothing to speak of.*

nothing to write home about nothing exciting or interesting. (Folksy.) □ *I've been busy, but nothing to write home about.* □ *I had a dull week—nothing to write home about.*

Nothing ventured, nothing gained. You cannot achieve anything if you do not try. (Proverb.) □ *Come on, John. Give it a try. Nothing ventured, nothing gained.* □ *I felt as if I had to take the chance. Nothing ventured, nothing gained.*

now and again Go to **(every) now and then.**

now and then Go to **(every) now and then.**

Now hear this! Pay attention to what is going to be said! (In the manner of an announcement over the public address system, especially in the military.) □ *Now hear this! You have to turn off the television and go to bed!* □ *Now hear this! Now hear this! Everyone is ordered to abandon ship.*

now or never at this time and no other. □ *This is your only chance, John. It's now or never.* □ *I decided that it was now or never, and jumped.*

(Now), where was I? I was interrupted, so please help me remember what I was talking about. (The emphasis is on *was*.) □ *Now, where was I! I think I lost my place.* □ *Q: Where was I? A: You had just described the War of 1812.*

nowhere near not nearly. □ *We have nowhere near enough wood for the winter.* □ *They're nowhere near ready for the game.*

null and void canceled; worthless. □ *I tore the contract up, and the entire agreement became null and void.* □ *The judge declared the whole business null and void.*

[number is up] Go to **one's number is up.**

a **number of** things or people some things or people, in an indefinite amount. □ *I subscribe to a number of different magazines.* □ *A number of people are here now.*

nurse a grudge (against someone**)** to keep resenting and disliking someone over a period of time. (See also **bear a grudge (against** someone**)**.) □ *Sally is still nursing a grudge against Mary.* □ *How long can anyone nurse a grudge?*

nurse someone **back to health** [for anyone] to provide medical care that will restore someone to good health. □ *After my operation, my mother nursed me back to health.* □ *Lots of good food and loving care will help nurse you back to health.*

nuts about someone or something Go to **crazy about** someone or something.

the **nuts and bolts (of** something**)** the basic facts about something; the practical details of something. □ *Tom knows all about the nuts and bolts of the chemical process.* □ *Ann is familiar with the nuts and bolts of public relations.*

nutty as a fruitcake Go to **(as) nutty as a fruitcake.**

nuzzle up to someone or something to nestle against someone or something, especially if pressing with the nose or face. □ *The puppy nuzzled up to its mother.* □ *Tom nuzzled up to Jane and asked her for a kiss.*

O

occur to someone [for an idea or thought] to come into someone's mind. □ *It occurred to me that you might be hungry after your long journey.* □ *Would it ever occur to you that I want to be left alone?*

an **ocean of** someone or something Go to **oceans of** someone or something.

oceans of someone or something AND an **ocean of** someone or something a very large amount of something. □ *The naughty student was in oceans of trouble.* □ *After a week of vacation, there was an ocean of work to do.*

odd man out an unusual or atypical person or thing. □ *I'm odd man out because I'm not wearing a tie.* □ *You had better learn to work a computer unless you want to be odd man out.*

the **odd** something an extra or spare something. □ *The tailor repaired the odd loose button on my shirt.* □ *When I travel, I might buy the odd trinket or two, but I never spend much money.*

odds and ends small, miscellaneous things. □ *There were lots of odds and ends in the attic, but nothing of real value.* □ *I had the whole house cleaned up except for a few odds and ends that didn't seem to belong anywhere.*

odor of sanctity an atmosphere of excessive holiness or piety. □ *I hate their house. There's such an odor of sanctity, with Bibles and religious pictures everywhere.* □ *People are made nervous by Jane's odor of sanctity. She's always praying for people or doing good works and never has any fun.*

of age old enough to marry or to sign legal agreements. (See also **come of age**. Preceded by *be* or *seem*.) □ *Now that Mary is of age, she can buy her own car.* □ *When I'm of age, I'm going to get married and move to the city.*

of all the nerve how shocking; how dare (someone). (Informal. The speaker is exclaiming that someone is being very cheeky or rude.) □ *How dare you talk to me that way! Of all the nerve!* □ *Imagine anyone coming to a formal dance in jeans. Of all the nerve!*

of all things Can you imagine?; Imagine that! (Folksy.) □ *She wore jeans to the dance. Of all things!* □ *Billy, stop eating the houseplant! Of all things!*

of benefit (to someone**)** serving someone well; to the good of someone. □ *I can't believe that this proposal is of benefit to anyone.* □ *Oh, I'm sure it's of benefit.*

of interest (to someone**)** interesting to someone. □ *This is no longer of any interest.* □ *This is of little interest to me.*

of late lately. (Formal.) □ *Have you seen Sally of late?* □ *We haven't had an opportunity to eat out of late.*

of no avail Go to **to no avail**.

of one's **own accord** AND **of** one's **own free will** by one's own choice, without coercion. □ *I wish that Sally would choose to do it of her own accord.* □ *I'll have to order her to do it because she won't do it of her own free will.*

of one's **own free will** Go to **of** one's **own accord**.

of the first water [someone] of the finest quality. (From the system of grading pearls for quality.) □ *She is a very fine* *lady—a pearl of the first water.* ☐ *Tom is of the first water—a true gentleman.*

of the old school holding attitudes or ideas that were popular and important in the past, but which are no longer considered relevant or in line with modern trends. ☐ *Grammar was not much taught in my son's school, but fortunately he had a teacher of the old school.* ☐ *Aunt Jane is of the old school. She never goes out without wearing a hat and gloves.*

off again, on again Go to on again, off again.

off and on Go to on and off.

off and running started up and going. (Also literal, as in a footrace.) ☐ *The car was finally loaded by 9:30, and we were off and running.* ☐ *The construction of the building was going to take two years, but we were off and running, and it appeared we would finish on schedule.*

off base unrealistic; inexact; wrong. (Also literal in baseball.) ☐ *I'm afraid you're off base when you state that this problem will take care of itself.* ☐ *You're way off base!*

off campus not located on the grounds of a college or university. ☐ *Tom has an apartment off campus.* ☐ *The dean is off campus and cannot be reached.*

off-center not exactly in the center or middle. ☐ *The arrow hit the target a little off-center.* ☐ *The picture hanging over the chair is a little off-center.*

off chance slight possibility. ☐ *I need your phone number on the off chance I need more help.* ☐ *There's an off chance that we might be hiring next month.*

off-color 1. not the exact color (that one wants). ☐ *The book cover used to be red, but now it's a little off-color.* ☐ *The wall was painted off-color. I think it was meant to be orange.* **2.** in bad taste; rude, vulgar, or impolite. ☐ *That joke you told was off-color and embarrassed me.* ☐ *The night-club act was a bit off-color.*

off duty not working at one's job. (The opposite of on duty.) ☐ *I'm sorry, I can't talk to you until I'm off duty.* ☐ *The police officer couldn't help me because he was off duty.*

off like a shot away [from a place] very quickly. ☐ *He finished his dinner and was off like a shot.* ☐ *The thief grabbed the lady's purse and was off like a shot.*

off limits AND **out of bounds** forbidden. ☐ *This area is off limits. You can't go in there.* ☐ *Don't go there. It's out of bounds.* ☐ *That kind of behavior is off limits. Stop it!*

off one's **nut** Go to off one's rocker.

off one's **rocker** AND **off** one's **nut; off** one's **trolley** crazy; silly. (Slang.) ☐ *Sometimes, Bob, I think you're off your rocker.* ☐ *Good grief, John. You're off your nut.* ☐ *About this time of the day, I go off my trolley. I get so tired.*

off one's **trolley** Go to off one's rocker.

off season not in the busy time of the year. ☐ *We don't have much to do off season.* ☐ *Things are very quiet around here off season.*

off someone or something **goes** someone or something is leaving. (Said on the departure of someone or something.) ☐ *It's time to leave. Off I go.* ☐ *Sally looked at the airplane taking off and said, "Off it goes."*

off the air not broadcasting (a radio or television program). ☐ *The radio audience won't hear what you say when you're off the air.* ☐ *When the performers were off the air, the director told them how well they had done.*

off the (beaten) track in an unfamiliar place; on a route that is not often traveled. (See also off the track.) ☐ *Their home is in a quiet neighborhood, off the beaten track.* ☐ *We like to stop there and admire the scenery. It's off the track, but it's worth the trip.*

off-the-cuff spontaneous; without preparation or rehearsal. (Informal.) ☐ *Her remarks were off-the-cuff, but very sensible.* ☐ *I'm not very good at making speeches off-the-cuff.*

off the mark not quite exactly right. □ *Her answer was a little off the mark.* □ *You were off the mark when you said we would be a little late to the party. It was yesterday, in fact!*

off the record unofficial; informal. □ *This is off the record, but I disagree with the mayor on this matter.* □ *Although her comments were off the record, the newspaper published them anyway.*

off the subject not concerned with the subject being discussed. □ *I got off the subject and forgot what I was supposed to be talking about.* □ *The speaker was off the subject, telling about his vacation in Hawaii.*

off the top of one's **head** [to state something] quickly and without having to think or remember. (Informal.) □ *I can't think of the answer off the top of my head.* □ *Jane can tell you the correct amount off the top of her head.*

off the track 1. Go to off the (beaten) track. **2.** irrelevant and immaterial (comments). □ *I'm afraid you're off the track, John. Try again.* □ *I'm sorry. I was thinking about dinner, and I got off the track.*

off-the-wall odd; silly; unusual. (Slang.) □ *Why are you so off-the-wall today?* □ *This book is strange. It's really off-the-wall.*

off to a running start with a good, fast beginning, possibly a head start. □ *I got off to a running start in math this year.* □ *The horses got off to a running start.*

off to one side beside (something); (moved) slightly away from something. □ *Our garden has roses in the middle and a spruce tree off to one side.* □ *He took me off to one side to tell me the bad news.*

oil someone's **palm** Go to grease someone's palm.

old as the hills Go to (as) old as the hills.

old enough to be someone's **father** Go to old enough to be someone's mother.

old enough to be someone's **mother** AND **old enough to be** someone's **father** as old as someone's parents. (Also literal. Usually a way of saying that a person is too old.) □ *You can't go out with Bill. He's old enough to be your father!* □ *He married a woman who is old enough to be his mother.*

Old habits die hard. It's hard to stop doing things that are part of a habit, especially a habit that one is trying to break. (Proverb.) □ *A: My grandfather still uses hand signals when he turns right. B: Old habits die hard.* □ *Old habits die hard and bad one's last even longer.*

an **old hand at** doing something someone who is experienced at doing something. (Preceded by *be, become, seem like,* or *act like.*) □ *I'm an old hand at fixing clocks.* □ *He's an old hand at changing diapers.*

old hat old-fashioned; outmoded. (Informal. Preceded by *be, become,* or *seem.*) □ *That's a silly idea. It's old hat.* □ *Nobody does that anymore. That's just old hat.*

[old stamping ground] Go to one's old stamping ground.

on a bias AND **on the bias** on a diagonal line; on a diagonal pathway or direction. (Usually with reference to cloth.) □ *The panels of the dress were cut on a bias.* □ *The seamstress sewed the fabric on the bias.*

on account [money paid or owed] on a debt. □ *I paid twelve dollars on account last month. Wasn't that enough?* □ *I still have $100 due on account.*

on active duty in battle or ready to go into battle. (Military.) □ *The soldier was on active duty for ten months.* □ *That was a long time to be on active duty.*

on a diet trying to lose weight by eating less food or specific foods. □ *I didn't eat any cake because I'm on a diet.* □ *I'm getting too heavy. I'll have to go on a diet.*

on a first-name basis (with someone**)** knowing someone very well; good friends with someone. □ *I'm on a first-name basis with John.* □ *John and I are on a first-name basis.*

on a fool's errand involved in a useless journey or task. □ *Bill went for an interview, but he was on a fool's errand. The job* *had already been filled.* ☐ *I was sent on a fool's errand to buy some flowers. I knew the shop would be closed by then.*

on again, off again AND **off again, on again** uncertain; indecisive. ☐ *I don't know about the picnic. It's on again, off again. It depends on the weather.* ☐ *Jane doesn't know if she's going to the picnic. She's off again, on again about it.*

on a lark Go to for a lark.

on all fours on one's hands and knees. ☐ *I dropped a contact lens and spent an hour on all fours looking for it.* ☐ *The baby can walk, but is on all fours most of the time anyway.*

on and off AND **off and on** occasionally; erratically; now and again. ☐ *I feel better off and on, but I'm not well yet.* ☐ *He only came to class on and off.*

on any account for any purpose; for any reason; no matter what. (Compare this with on no account.) ☐ *On any account, I'll be there on time.* ☐ *This doesn't make sense on any account.*

on approval for examination, with the privilege of return. ☐ *I ordered the merchandise on approval so I could send it back if I didn't like it.* ☐ *Sorry, you can't buy this on approval. All sales are final.*

on a shoestring with a very small amount of money. ☐ *We lived on a shoestring for years before I got a good job.* ☐ *John traveled to Florida on a shoestring.*

on a splurge an instance of extravagant spending. ☐ *Bob went on a splurge and bought a new car.* ☐ *Susan has been on another spending splurge! Look at that new furniture.*

on a waiting list [with one's name] on a list of people waiting for an opportunity to do something. (*A* can be replaced with *the*.) ☐ *I couldn't get a seat on the plane, but I got on a waiting list.* ☐ *There is no room for you, but we can put your name on the waiting list.*

on behalf of someone Go to in behalf of someone.

on bended knee with great humility. (The form *bended* is obsolescent and occurs now only in this phrase.) ☐ *Do you expect me to come to you on bended knee and ask you for forgiveness?* ☐ *The suitors came on bended knee and begged the attention of the princess.*

on board 1. aboard (on or in) a ship, bus, airplane, etc. ☐ *Is there a doctor on board? We have a sick passenger.* ☐ *When everyone is on board, we will leave.* **2.** employed by (someone); working with (someone). (Informal.) ☐ *Our company has a computer specialist on board to advise us about automation.* ☐ *Welcome to the company, Tom. We're all glad you're on board now.*

on Broadway located in the Broadway theater district of New York City; performed in the Broadway theater district. ☐ *Our musical is the best thing on Broadway!* ☐ *I want to be a star on Broadway someday.*

on call ready to serve when called. ☐ *I live a very hard life. I'm on call twenty hours a day.* ☐ *I'm sorry, but I can't go out tonight. I'm on call at the hospital.*

on campus located or being on the grounds of a college or university. ☐ *Do you live on campus or off campus?* ☐ *I don't think that Lisa is on campus right now.*

on cloud nine very happy. (Informal.) ☐ *When I got my promotion, I was on cloud nine.* ☐ *When the check came, I was on cloud nine for days.*

on consignment [of goods] having been placed in a store for sale, without transferring the title of the goods to the operator of the store. ☐ *The artist placed his work in a gallery on consignment.* ☐ *I will attempt to sell your clothing on consignment.*

on credit using credit; buying something using credit. ☐ *I tried to buy a new suit on credit, but I was refused.* ☐ *The Smiths buy everything on credit and are very much in debt.*

on dead center 1. at the exact center of something. (*Dead* means "exact" here.) ☐ *The arrow hit the target on dead cen-*

ter. ☐ *When you put the flowers on the table, put them on dead center.* **2.** exactly correct. ☐ *Mary is quite observant. Her analysis is on dead center.* ☐ *My view isn't on dead center, but it's sensible.*

on deck 1. on the deck of a boat or a ship. ☐ *Everyone except the cook was on deck when the storm hit.* ☐ *Just pull up the anchor and leave it on deck.* **2.** ready (to do something); ready to be next (at something). ☐ *Ann, get on deck. You're next.* ☐ *Who's on deck now?*

on duty at work; currently doing one's work. (The opposite of **off duty**.) ☐ *I can't help you now, but I'll be on duty in about an hour.* ☐ *Who is on duty here? I need some help.*

on earth AND **in creation; in the world** really; indeed; in fact. (Used as an intensifier after *who, what, when, where, how, nothing, nowhere.*) ☐ *What on earth do you mean?* ☐ *How in creation do you expect me to do that?* ☐ *Who in the world do you think you are?* ☐ *When on earth do you expect me to do this?*

on easy street in luxury. (Slang.) ☐ *If I had a million dollars, I'd be on easy street.* ☐ *Everyone has problems, even people who live on easy street.*

on edge 1. on (something's own) edge. ☐ *Can you stand a dime on edge?* ☐ *You should store your records on edge, not flat.* **2.** nervous. ☐ *I have really been on edge lately.* ☐ *Why are you so on edge?*

on fire burning; being burned with flames. ☐ *Help! My car is on fire!* ☐ *That house on the corner is on fire!*

on foot by walking. ☐ *My bicycle is broken, so I'll have to travel on foot.* ☐ *You can't expect me to get there on foot! It's twelve miles!*

on good terms (with someone**)** friendly with someone. ☐ *I'm on good terms with Ann. I'll ask her to help.* ☐ *We're on good terms now. Last week we were not.*

on hold 1. waiting; temporarily halted. (See also **put** someone or something **on hold**.) ☐ *The building project is on hold while we try to find money to complete it.* ☐ *We put our plans on hold until we finished school.* **2.** left waiting on a telephone line. ☐ *I hate to call up someone and then end up on hold.* ☐ *I waited on hold for ten minutes when I called city hall.*

on horseback on the back of a horse. ☐ *Anne rode on horseback across the field.* ☐ *Because they loved horses, the couple decided to marry on horseback.*

on impact Go to (up)on impact.

on impulse after having had an impulse or sudden thought. ☐ *On impulse, Bob decided to buy a car.* ☐ *I didn't need a cellular telephone. I just bought it on impulse.*

on in years Go to up in years.

on land on the soil; on the land and not at sea. ☐ *The flight was rough and I feel better now that I am back on land.* ☐ *When I am at sea, I feel more relaxed than when I am on land.*

on line 1. Go to in line. **2.** connected to a remote computer. ☐ *As soon as I get on line, I can check the balance of your account.* ☐ *I was on line for an hour before I found out what I wanted to know.*

on location a place, located in a place distant from the movie studio, where a movie is filmed. ☐ *This movie was shot on location in Ontario.* ☐ *The actress went on location in Spain for her latest film.*

on medication taking medicine for a current medical problem. ☐ *I can't drive the car since I am on medication.* ☐ *He is on medication and hopes to be well soon.*

on no account AND **not on any account** for no reason; absolutely not. ☐ *On no account will I lend you the money.* ☐ *Will I say I'm sorry? Not on any account.*

on occasion occasionally. ☐ *We go out for dinner on occasion.* ☐ *I enjoy going to a movie on occasion.*

on one's **best behavior** being as polite as possible. ☐ *When we went out, the children were on their best behavior.* ☐ *I try to be on my best behavior all the time.*

on one's **feet 1.** standing up. ☐ *Get on your feet. They are playing the national an-*

them. □ *I've been on my feet all day, and they hurt.* **2.** well and healthy, especially after an illness. □ *I hope to be back on my feet next week.* □ *I can help out as soon as I'm back on my feet.*

on (one's) **guard** cautious; watchful. □ *Be on guard. There are pickpockets around here.* □ *You had better be on your guard.*

on one's **honor** on one's solemn oath; sincerely. □ *On my honor, I'll be there on time.* □ *He promised on his honor that he'd pay me back next week.*

on one's **mind** occupying one's thoughts; currently being thought about. □ *You've been on my mind all day.* □ *Do you have something on your mind? You look so serious.*

on one's **own** by oneself. □ *Did you do this on your own, or did you have help?* □ *I have to learn to do this kind of thing on my own.*

on one's **own time** not while one is at work. □ *The boss made me write the report on my own time. That's not fair.* □ *Please make your personal telephone calls on your own time.*

on one's **person** [of something] carried with one. □ *Always carry identification on your person.* □ *I'm sorry, I don't have any money on my person.*

on one's **toes** alert. (Also literal. See also **step on** someone's **toes.**) □ *You have to be on your toes if you want to be in this business.* □ *My boss keeps me on my toes.*

on one's **way to** doing something Go to **on the way to** doing something.

on order ordered with delivery expected. □ *Your car is on order. It'll be here in a few weeks.* □ *I don't have the part in stock, but it's on order.*

on par (with someone or something**)** equal to someone or something. □ *Your effort is simply not on par with what's expected from you.* □ *These two reports are right on par.*

on patrol Go to **(out) on patrol.**

on pins and needles anxious; in suspense. (See also **pins and needles.**) □ *I've been on pins and needles all day, waiting for you to call with the news.* □ *We were on pins and needles until we heard that your plane landed safely.*

on probation 1. serving a period of probation. □ *While Anne was on probation, she reported to the police regularly.* □ *John was on probation for a year.* **2.** serving a trial period. □ *All new members are on probation for a year.* □ *I was on probation in my job for a full year before it became permanent.*

on purpose intentionally; in a way that is meant or intended; not an accident. □ *The bully stepped on my foot on purpose.* □ *Jealously, Jimmy destroyed Billy's sand castle on purpose.*

on sale offered for sale at a special low price. □ *I won't buy anything that's not on sale.* □ *I need a new coat, but I want to find a nice one on sale.*

on schedule at the expected or desired time. □ *The plane came in right on schedule.* □ *Things have to happen on schedule in a theatrical performance.*

on second thought having given something more thought; having reconsidered something. □ *On second thought, maybe you should sell your house and move into an apartment.* □ *On second thought, let's not go to a movie.*

on someone's **account** because of someone. □ *Don't do it on my account.* □ *They were late on Jane's account.*

on someone's **back** Go to **on** someone's **case.**

on someone's **behalf** Go to **in behalf of** someone.

on someone's **case** AND **on** someone's **back** constantly criticizing someone. (Slang. See also **Get off** someone's **case!**) □ *I'm tired of your being on my case all the time.* □ *It seems as if someone is always on his back.*

on someone's **doorstep** Go to **at** someone's **doorstep.**

on someone's **head** on someone's own self. (Usually with *blame.*) □ *All the blame fell* *on their heads.* ☐ *I don't think that all the criticism should be on my head.*

on someone's or something's **last legs** [for someone or something] to be almost worn out or finished. (Informal.) ☐ *This building is on its last legs. It should be torn down.* ☐ *I feel as if I'm on my last legs. I'm really tired.*

on someone's **say-so** on someone's authority; with someone's permission. ☐ *I can't do it on your say-so. I'll have to get a written request.* ☐ *BILL: I canceled the contract with the ABC Company. BOB: On whose say-so?*

on someone's **shoulders** on someone's own self. (Also literal. Usually with *responsibility*.) ☐ *Why should all the responsibility fall on my shoulders?* ☐ *She carries a tremendous amount of responsibility on her shoulders.*

on someone's **way (**somewhere**)** Go to on the way (somewhere).

on speaking terms (with someone**)** on friendly terms with someone. (Often in the negative. Compare this with on good terms (with someone).) ☐ *I'm not on speaking terms with Mary. We had a serious disagreement.* ☐ *We're not on speaking terms.*

on standby waiting for one's turn, especially describing the status of travelers who wait near a train, plane, or bus, hoping that a seat will become available. ☐ *The passenger waited on standby for an available seat.* ☐ *The agent was able to seat all of the passengers on standby.*

on target on schedule; exactly as predicted. ☐ *Your estimate of the cost was right on target.* ☐ *My prediction was not on target.*

on the air broadcasting (a radio or television program). ☐ *The radio station came back on the air shortly after the storm.* ☐ *We were on the air for two hours.*

on the alert (for someone or something**)** watchful and attentive for someone or something. ☐ *Be on the alert for pickpockets.* ☐ *You should be on the alert when you cross the street in heavy traffic.*

on the average generally; usually. ☐ *On the average, you can expect about a 10 percent failure rate.* ☐ *This report looks okay, on the average.*

on the ball alert, effective, and efficient. (Slang.) ☐ *Sally has a lot on the ball.* ☐ *You've got to be on the ball if you want to succeed in this business.*

on the beam exactly right; thinking along the correct lines. (Informal.) ☐ *That's the right idea. Now you're on the beam!* ☐ *She's not on the beam yet. Explain it to her again.*

on the bench 1. directing a session of court. (Also literal. Said of a judge.) ☐ *I have to go to court tomorrow. Who's on the bench?* ☐ *It doesn't matter who's on the bench. You'll get a fair hearing.* **2.** sitting, waiting for a chance to play in a game. (In sports, such as basketball, football, soccer, etc.) ☐ *Bill is on the bench now. I hope he gets to play.* ☐ *John played during the first quarter, but now he's on the bench.*

on the bias Go to on a bias.

on the blink Go to on the fritz.

on the block 1. on a city block. ☐ *John is the biggest kid on the block.* ☐ *We had a party on the block last weekend.* **2.** on sale at auction; on the auction block. ☐ *We couldn't afford to keep up the house, so it was put on the block to pay the taxes.* ☐ *That's the finest painting I've ever seen on the block.*

on the borderline in an uncertain position between two statuses; undecided. (Also literal.) ☐ *Bill was on the borderline between an A and a B in biology.* ☐ *Jane was on the borderline of joining the navy.*

on the button exactly right; in exactly the right place; at exactly the right time. (Also literal. Informal.) ☐ *That's it! You're right on the button.* ☐ *He got here at one o'clock on the button.*

on the contrary as the opposite. (Compare this with to the contrary.) ☐ *I'm not ill. On the contrary, I'm very healthy.* ☐ *She's not in a bad mood. On the contrary, she's as happy as a lark.*

on the defensive overly ready to defend oneself. ☐ *John goes on the defensive when his athletic ability is questioned.* ☐ *The child was on the defensive when questioned about cheating.*

on the dot at exactly the right time. (Also literal. Informal. Compare this with **at** sometime **sharp.**) ☐ *I'll be there at noon on the dot.* ☐ *I expect to see you here at eight o'clock on the dot.*

on the double very fast. (Informal.) ☐ *Okay, you guys. Get over here on the double.* ☐ *Get yourself into this house on the double.*

on the eve of something just before something, possibly the evening before something. ☐ *John decided to leave school on the eve of his graduation.* ☐ *The team held a party on the eve of the tournament.*

on the face of it superficially; from the way it looks. ☐ *This looks like a serious problem on the face of it. It probably is minor, however.* ☐ *On the face of it, it seems worthless.*

on the fence (about something**)** undecided. (Informal.) ☐ *Ann is on the fence about going to Mexico.* ☐ *I wouldn't be on the fence. I'd love to go.*

on the fritz AND **on the blink** not operating; not operating correctly. (Slang.) ☐ *This vacuum cleaner is on the fritz. Let's get it fixed.* ☐ *How long has it been on the blink?*

on the go busy; moving about busily. (Informal.) ☐ *I'm usually on the go all day long.* ☐ *I hate being on the go all the time.*

on the heels of something soon after something. (Informal.) ☐ *There was a rainstorm on the heels of the windstorm.* ☐ *The team held a victory celebration on the heels of their winning season.*

on the horizon soon to happen. (Also literal. See also **in the offing.**) ☐ *Do you know what's on the horizon?* ☐ *Who can tell what's on the horizon?*

on the horns of a dilemma bothered by having to decide between two things, people, etc. ☐ *Mary found herself on the horns of a dilemma. She didn't know which to choose.* ☐ *I make up my mind easily. I'm not on the horns of a dilemma very often.*

on the hot seat AND **in the hot seat** in a difficult position; subject to much criticism. (Slang.) ☐ *I was really in the hot seat for a while.* ☐ *Now that John is on the hot seat, no one is paying any attention to what I do.*

on the hour at each hour on the hour mark. ☐ *I have to take this medicine every hour on the hour.* ☐ *I expect to see you there on the hour, not one minute before and not one minute after.*

on the house [something that is] given away free by a merchant. (Also literal. Informal.) ☐ *"Here," said the waiter, "have a cup of coffee on the house."* ☐ *I went to a restaurant last night. I was the 10,000th customer, so my dinner was on the house.*

on the job working; doing what one is expected to do. ☐ *I'm always on the job when I should be.* ☐ *I can depend on my furnace to be on the job day and night.*

on the level Go to **(strictly) on the level.**

on the lookout (for someone or something**)** watchful for someone or something. ☐ *Be on the lookout for signs of a storm.* ☐ *I'm on the lookout for John, who is due here any minute.* ☐ *Okay, you remain on the lookout for another hour.*

on the loose running around free. (Informal.) ☐ *Look out! There is a bear on the loose from the zoo.* ☐ *Most kids enjoy being on the loose when they go to college.*

on the make 1. building or developing; being made. (Informal.) ☐ *There is a company that is on the make.* ☐ *That was a very good sales strategy, John. You're a real-estate agent on the make.* **2.** making sexual advances; seeking sexual activities. (Slang.) ☐ *It seems like Bill is always on the make.* ☐ *He should meet Sally, who is also on the make.*

on the market available for sale; offered for sale. (Compare this with **on the block.**) ☐ *I had to put my car on the mar-*

ket. □ *This is the finest home computer on the market.*

on the mend getting well; healing. □ *My cold was terrible, but I'm on the mend now.* □ *What you need is some hot chicken soup. Then you'll really be on the mend.*

on the money AND **on the nose** in exactly the right place; in exactly the right amount (of money). (Also literal. Slang.) □ *That's a good answer, Bob. You're right on the money.* □ *This project is going to be finished right on the nose.*

on the move moving; happening busily. □ *What a busy day. Things are really on the move at the store.* □ *When all the buffalo were on the move across the plains, it must have been very exciting.*

on the nose Go to **on the money.**

on the off-chance because of a slight possibility that something may happen, might be the case; just in case. □ *I went to the theater on the off-chance that there were tickets for the show left.* □ *We didn't think we would get into the stadium, but we went anyway on the off-chance.*

on (the) one hand from one point of view; as one side (of an issue). □ *On one hand, I really ought to support my team. On the other hand, I don't have to time to attend all the games.* □ *On the one hand, I need Ann's help. On the other hand, she and I don't get along very well.*

on the other hand from another point of view; as the other side (of an issue). See the examples for **on (the) one hand.**

on the point of doing something AND **at the point of** doing something ready to start doing something. (Compare this with **on the verge (of** doing something**).**) □ *I was just on the point of going out the door.* □ *We were almost at the point of buying a new car.*

on the QT quietly; secretly. (Informal.) □ *The company president was making payments to his wife on the QT.* □ *The mayor accepted a bribe on the QT.*

on the right track following the right set of assumptions. (Refers to following the right trail.) □ *Tom is on the right track and will solve the mystery soon.* □ *You are on the right track to find the answer.*

on the rocks 1. in a state of destruction or wreckage. (Refers to a ship stranded on the rocks.) □ *I hear their marriage is on the rocks.* □ *The company is on the rocks and may not survive.* **2.** [poured] onto ice cubes in a glass. □ *Joan prefers her drinks on the rocks.* □ *Could I have a scotch on the rocks?*

on the spot 1. at exactly the right place; at exactly the right time. (Also literal. Informal. See also **Johnny-on-the-spot.**) □ *It's noon, and I'm glad you're all here on the spot. Now we can begin.* □ *I expect you to be on the spot when and where trouble arises.* **2.** in trouble; in a difficult situation. (Informal. Compare this with **on the hot seat.**) □ *There is a problem in the department I manage, and I'm really on the spot.* □ *I hate to be on the spot when it's not my fault.*

on the spur of the moment suddenly; spontaneously. □ *We decided to go on the spur of the moment.* □ *I had to leave town on the spur of the moment.*

on the strength of something because of the support of something, such as a promise or evidence; due to something. □ *On the strength of your comment, I decided to give John another chance.* □ *On the strength of my testimony, my case was dismissed.*

on the take accepting bribes. (Slang.) □ *I don't believe that the mayor is on the take.* □ *The county clerk has been on the take for years.*

on the tip of one's **tongue** about to be said; almost remembered. (Also literal. See also **have** something **on the tip of** one's **tongue.**) □ *It's right on the tip of my tongue. I'll think of it in a second.* □ *The answer was on the tip of my tongue, but Ann said it first.*

on the track of someone or something Go to **on the trail of** someone or something.

on the trail of someone or something AND **on the track of** someone or something seeking someone or something; about to find someone or something. □ *I'm on the trail of a new can opener that is supposed to be easier to use.* □ *I spent all morning on the track of the new secretary, who got lost on the way to work.*

on the up-and-up Go to **(strictly) on the up-and-up.**

on the verge (of doing something**)** just about to do something, usually something important. (Compare this with **on the point of** doing something.) □ *I'm on the verge of opening a shoe store.* □ *Tom was on the verge of quitting school when he became interested in physics.* □ *I haven't done it yet, but I'm on the verge.*

on the wagon not drinking alcohol; no longer drinking alcohol. (Also literal.) □ *None for me, thanks. I'm on the wagon.* □ *Look at John. I don't think he's on the wagon anymore.*

on the warpath angry and upset (at someone). (Informal.) □ *Oh, oh. Here comes Mrs. Smith. She's on the warpath again.* □ *Why are you always on the warpath? What's wrong?*

on the way (somewhere**)** AND **on** someone's **way (**somewhere**)** along the route to somewhere. □ *She's now on the way to San Francisco.* □ *Yes, she's on the way.*

on the way to doing something AND **on** one's **way to** doing something in the process of doing something. □ *You're on the way to becoming a very good carpenter.* □ *She's on her way to becoming a first-class sculptor.*

on the whole generally; considering everything. □ *On the whole, this was a very good day.* □ *Your work—on the whole—is quite good.*

on the wing while flying; while in flight. (Refers to birds, fowl, etc., not people or planes.) □ *There is nothing as pretty as a bird on the wing.* □ *The hawk caught the sparrow on the wing.*

on the wrong track going the wrong way; following the wrong set of assumptions. (Also literal.) □ *You'll never get the right answer. You're on the wrong track.* □ *They won't get it figured out because they are on the wrong track.*

on thin ice in a risky situation. (Also literal.) □ *If you try that you'll really be on thin ice. That's too risky.* □ *If you don't want to find yourself on thin ice, you must be sure of your facts.*

on time at the scheduled time; at the predicted time. □ *The plane landed right on time.* □ *We'll have to hurry to get there on time.*

on tiptoe standing or walking on the front part of the feet (the balls of the feet) with no weight put on the heels. (This is done to gain height or to walk quietly.) □ *I had to stand on tiptoe in order to see over the fence.* □ *I came in late and walked on tiptoe so I wouldn't wake anybody up.*

on top victorious over something; famous or notorious for something. (Also literal.) □ *I have to study day and night to keep on top.* □ *Bill is on top in his field.*

on top of something **1.** up-to-date on something; knowing about the current state of something. (Informal.) □ *Ask Mary. She's on top of this issue.* □ *This issue is constantly changing. She has to pay attention to it to stay on top of things.* **2.** in addition to something. □ *Jane told Bill he was dull. On top of that, she said he was unfriendly.* □ *On top of being dull, he's unfriendly.*

on top of the world Go to **(feel) on top of the world; (sitting) on top of the world.**

on trial being tried in court. □ *My sister is on trial today, so I have to go to court.* □ *They placed the suspected thief on trial.*

on vacation away, taking a vacation; on holiday. □ *Where are you going on vacation this year?* □ *I'll be away on vacation for three weeks.*

on view visible; on public display. □ *The painting will be on view at the museum.* □ *I'll pull the shades so that we won't be on view.*

once and for all finally and irreversibly. □ *I want to get this problem settled once and for all.* □ *I told him once and for all that he has to start studying.*

once in a blue moon very rarely. ☐ *I seldom go to a movie—maybe once in a blue moon.* ☐ *I don't go into the city except once in a blue moon.*

once-in-a-lifetime chance a chance that will never occur again in one's lifetime. ☐ *This is a once-in-a-lifetime chance. Don't miss it.* ☐ *She offered me a once-in-a-lifetime chance, but I turned it down.*

once in a while Go to (every) now and then.

once-over-lightly 1. a quick and careless treatment. (A noun. Said of an act of cleaning, studying, examination, or appraisal.) ☐ *Bill gave his geometry the once-over-lightly and then quit studying.* ☐ *Ann, you didn't wash the dishes properly. They only got a once-over-lightly.* **2.** cursory; in a quick and careless manner. (An adverb.) ☐ *Tom studied geometry once-over-lightly.* ☐ *Ann washed the dishes once-over-lightly.*

once upon a time once in the past. (A formula used to begin a fairy tale.) ☐ *Once upon a time, there were three bears.* ☐ *Once upon a time, I had a puppy of my own.*

one and all everyone. ☐ *"Good morning to one and all," said Jane as she walked through the outer office.* ☐ *Let's hope that this turns out to be a wonderful party for one and all.*

the **one and only** the famous and talented (person). (Used in theatrical introductions. See also my one and only.) ☐ *And now—the one and only—Jane Smith!* ☐ *Let's have a big hand for the one and only Bob Jones!*

one and the same the very same person or thing. ☐ *John Jones and J. Jones are one and the same.* ☐ *Men's socks and men's stockings are almost one and the same.*

one at a time Go to one by one.

one by one AND **one at a time** the first one, then the next one, then the next one, etc.; one at a time; each in turn. ☐ *I have to deal with problems one by one. I can't handle them all at once.* ☐ *Okay, just take things one at a time.* ☐ *The children came into the room one by one.* ☐ *Fred peeled potatoes one by one, hating every minute of it.*

one for the (record) books a record-breaking act. ☐ *What a dive! That's one for the record books.* ☐ *I've never heard such a funny joke. That's really one for the books.*

One good turn deserves another. A good deed should be repaid with another good deed. (Proverb.) ☐ *If he does you a favor, you should do him a favor. One good turn deserves another.* ☐ *Glad to help you out. One good turn deserves another.*

one in a hundred Go to one in a thousand.

one in a million Go to one in a thousand.

one in a thousand AND **one in a hundred; one in a million** unique; one of a very few. ☐ *He's a great guy. He's one in million.* ☐ *Mary's one in a hundred—such a hard worker.*

one jump ahead (of someone or something**)** AND **one move ahead (of** someone or something**)** one step in advance of someone or something. ☐ *Try to stay one jump ahead of the customer.* ☐ *If you're one move ahead, you're well prepared to deal with problems. Then, nothing is a surprise.*

one little bit any at all; at all. (Also literal.) ☐ *Jean could not be persuaded to change her mind one little bit.* ☐ *I don't want to hear anything more about it. Not even one little bit.*

One man's meat is another man's poison. One person's preference may be disliked by another person. (Proverb.) ☐ *John just loves his new fur hat, but I think it is horrible. Oh, well, one man's meat is another man's poison.* ☐ *The neighbors are very fond of their dog even though it's ugly, loud, and smelly. I guess one man's meat is another man's poison.*

One man's trash is another man's treasure. Something that one person considers worthless may be considered valuable by someone else. (Proverb.) ☐ *Q: Why would anyone want to hang a picture like that on the wall? A: One man's trash is another man's treasure.* ☐ *A: Bob's un-*

cle is always going through people's garbage, looking for old stuff. B: One man's trash is another man's treasure.

one move ahead (of someone or something**)** Go to one jump ahead (of someone or something).

one-night stand an activity lasting one night. (Informal. Refers to either a musical performance or a period of sexual activity.) □ *Our band has played a lot of one-night stands.* □ *What we want is an engagement for a week, not just a one-night stand.*

one of these days someday; in some situation like this one. □ *One of these days, someone is going to steal your purse if you don't take better care of it.* □ *You're going to get in trouble one of these days.*

one sandwich short of a picnic not very smart; lacking sufficient intelligence. (Jocular.) □ *Poor Bob just isn't too bright. He's one sandwich short of a picnic.* □ *She not stupid. Just one sandwich short of a picnic.*

One thing leads to another. One event sets things up for another event and so on. (As an explanation of how little problems lead to big problems.) □ *I kept spending more and more money until I was broke. You know how one thing leads to another.* □ *He bought a car, then a house, then a boat. One thing leads to another.*

one thing or person **after another** a series of things or people that seems without limit. □ *It's just one problem after another.* □ *One customer after another has been buying shoes today!*

one to a customer each person can have or receive only one. (Refers to sales restrictions where each customer is permitted to buy only one.) □ *"Only one to a customer!" said the chef as he handed out the hamburgers.* □ *Is it one to a customer, or can I take two now?*

one up (on someone**)** ahead of someone; with an advantage over someone. □ *Tom is one up on Sally because he got a job and she didn't.* □ *Yes, it sounds like Tom is one up.*

one way or another somehow. □ *I'll do it one way or another.* □ *One way or another, I'll get through school.*

One's **bark is worse than** one's **bite.** One may threaten, but not do much damage. (Proverb.) □ *Don't worry about Bob. He won't hurt you. His bark is worse than his bite.* □ *She may scream and yell, but have no fear. Her bark is worse than her bite.*

one's **better half** one's spouse. (Usually refers to a wife.) □ *I think we'd like to come for dinner, but I'll have to ask my better half.* □ *I have to go home now to my better half. We are going out tonight.*

one's **brother's keeper** someone responsible for someone else. (Preceded by *be, become, seem like,* or *act like.*) □ *I can't force these kids to go to school and get an education so they can get jobs. I am not my brother's keeper.* □ *You can't expect me to be my brother's keeper. Each of us should be responsible!*

one's **daily dozen** physical exercises done every day. (Informal.) □ *My brother always feels better after his daily dozen.* □ *She would rather do her daily dozen than go on a diet.*

one's **days are numbered** one faces death or dismissal. □ *If I don't get this contract, my days are numbered at this company.* □ *Uncle Tom has a terminal disease. His days are numbered.*

one's **deepest sympathy** one's very sincere sympathy. □ *I am so sorry about the death of your father. You have my deepest sympathy.* □ *She sent her deepest sympathy to the family.*

one's **ears are red** one's ears are red from embarrassment. (Also used figuratively.) □ *I'm so embarrassed. Wow, are my ears red!* □ *My ears are red! I can't believe I said that.*

one's **ears are ringing** one hears a ringing sound because of exposure to an explosion, very loud music, or some other very loud sound. □ *After the explosion, my ears* *were ringing for hours.* □ *My ears are ringing because I have a cold.*

oneself **again** healthy again; calm again; restored. (Preceded by *be, become, seem like,* or *act like.*) □ *After such a long illness, it's good to be myself again.* □ *I'm sorry that I lost my temper. I think I'm myself again now.*

One's **eyes are bigger than** one's **stomach.** One has taken more food than one can eat. □ *I can't eat all this. I'm afraid that my eyes were bigger than my stomach.* □ *Try to take less food. Your eyes are bigger than your stomach at every meal.*

one's **fair share** a share of something that is equal to what others get or in proportion to what is deserved. □ *Let him take more. He didn't get his fair share.* □ *I want my fair share. You cheated me! Give me some more!*

one's **for the asking** one's property if one asks for it. □ *I have a cherry pie here. A slice is yours for the asking if you want it.* □ *Uncle Mac said we could have his old car if we wanted it. It was ours for the asking.*

one's **heart goes out to** someone one feels compassion for someone. □ *My heart goes out to those starving children I see on television.* □ *We are so sorry. Our hearts go out to you.*

one's **heart is (dead) set against** something one is totally against something. □ *Jane's heart is set against going there.* □ *We are dead set against it.*

one's **heart is in** one's **mouth** one feels strongly emotional (about someone or something). □ *"Gosh, Mary," said John, "my heart is in my mouth whenever I see you."* □ *My heart is in my mouth whenever I hear the national anthem.* □ *It was a touching scene. My heart was in my mouth the whole time.*

one's **heart is in the right place** one has good intentions, even if the results are bad. (See also **have** one's **heart in the right place.**) □ *She gave it a good try. Her heart was in the right place.* □ *He is awkward, but his heart is in the right place.*

one's **heart is set on** something one desires and expects something. □ *Jane's heart is set on going to London.* □ *My heart is set on returning home.*

one's **heart misses a beat** AND one's **heart skips a beat** one's heart is fluttering or palpitating. □ *Whenever I'm near you, my heart skips a beat.* □ *When the racehorse fell, my heart missed a beat.*

one's **heart skips a beat** Go to one's **heart misses a beat.**

one's **heart stands still** one's heart (figuratively) stops beating because of strong emotions. □ *When I first saw you, my heart stood still.* □ *My heart will stand still until you answer.*

one's **luck runs out** one's good luck stops. □ *My luck ran out, so I had to come home.* □ *She will quit gambling when her luck runs out.*

one's **name is mud** one is in trouble or humiliated. (Slang.) □ *If I can't get this contract signed, my name will be mud.* □ *His name is mud ever since he broke the crystal vase.*

one's **nose is in the air** one is acting conceited or aloof. (Note the variation with *always.* See also **have** one's **nose in the air.**) □ *Mary's nose is always in the air.* □ *Her mother's nose was always in the air, too.*

one's **number is up** one's time to die—or to suffer some other unpleasantness—has come. (Informal.) □ *John is worried. He thinks his number is up.* □ *When my number is up, I hope it all goes fast.*

one's **old stamping ground** the place where one was raised or where one has spent a lot of time. (Folksy. There are variants with *stomping* and *grounds.*) □ *Ann should know about that place. It's near her old stamping ground.* □ *I can't wait to get back to my old stomping grounds.*

one's **way of life** one's lifestyle; one's pattern of living. □ *That kind of thing just doesn't fit into my way of life.* □ *Our way of life includes contributing to worthy causes.*

one's **work is cut out for** one one's task is prepared for one; one has a lot of work to do. (See also **have** one's **work cut out for** one.) ☐ *This is a big job. My work is cut out for me.* ☐ *The new president's work is cut out for him.*

only have eyes for someone to be loyal to only one person, in the context of romance. ☐ *Oh, Jane! I only have eyes for you!* ☐ *Don't waste any time on Tom. He only has eyes for Ann.*

onto someone or something having discovered the truth about someone or something. (Informal.) ☐ *The police are onto John's plot.* ☐ *Yes, they are onto him, and they are onto the plot.*

open a conversation to start a conversation. (See also **strike up a conversation.**) ☐ *I tried to open a conversation with him, but he had nothing to say.* ☐ *She opened a conversation with an inquiry into my health, which got me talking about my favorite subject.*

open and aboveboard Go to **aboveboard.**

an **open-and-shut case** something, usually a legal matter, that is simple and straightforward without complications. ☐ *The murder trial was an open-and-shut case. The defendant was caught with the murder weapon.* ☐ *Jack's death was an open-and-shut case of suicide. He left a suicide note.*

an **open book** someone or something that is easy to understand. ☐ *Jane's an open book. I always know what she is going to do next.* ☐ *The council is an open book. It wants to save money.*

open fire (on someone**)** to start (doing something, such as asking questions or criticizing). (Refers to starting to shoot at someone.) ☐ *The reporters opened fire on the mayor.* ☐ *When the reporters opened fire, the mayor was smiling, but not for long.*

open for business [of a shop, store, restaurant, etc.] operating and ready to do business. ☐ *The store is now open for business and invites you to come in.* ☐ *The construction will be finished in March, and we will be open for business in April.*

open one's **heart (to** someone**)** to reveal one's inmost thoughts to someone. ☐ *I always open my heart to my spouse when I have a problem.* ☐ *It's a good idea to open your heart every now and then.*

open Pandora's box to uncover a lot of unsuspected problems. ☐ *When I asked Jane about her problems, I didn't know I had opened Pandora's box.* ☐ *You should be cautious with people who are upset. You don't want to open Pandora's box.*

open season (on someone or something**) 1.** [with *something*] unrestricted hunting of a particular game animal. ☐ *It's always open season on rabbits around here.* ☐ *Is it ever open season on deer?* **2.** [with *someone*] a time when everyone is criticizing someone. (Informal. See also **open fire (on** someone**).**) ☐ *It seems as if it's always open season on politicians.* ☐ *At the news conference, it was open season on the mayor.*

open secret something that is supposed to be secret but is known to a great many people. ☐ *Their engagement is an open secret. Only their friends are supposed to know, but in fact, the whole town knows.* ☐ *It's an open secret that Max is looking for a new job.*

open someone's **eyes (to** something**) 1.** to become aware of something. ☐ *He finally opened his eyes to what was going on.* ☐ *It was a long time before he opened his eyes and realized what had been happening.* **2.** to cause someone else to be aware of something. ☐ *I opened his eyes to what was happening at the office.* ☐ *Why can't I make you understand? What do I have to do to open your eyes to the problem?*

open something **up 1.** to unwrap something; to open something. ☐ *Yes, I want to open my presents up.* [T] *I can't wait to open up my presents.* [T] *Open up this door!* **2.** to begin examining or discussing something. ☐ *Do you really want to open it up now?* [T] *Now is the time to open up the question of taxes.* **3.** to reveal the possibilities of something; to reveal an opportunity. ☐ *Your letter opened new possibilities up.* 🅃 *Your comments opened up a whole new train of thought.* **4.** to start the use of something, such as land, a building, a business, etc. ☐ *They opened the coastal lands up to cotton planting.* 🅃 *We opened up a new store last March.* **5.** to make a vehicle go as fast as possible. (Informal.) ☐ *We took the new car out on the highway and opened it up.* 🅃 *I've never really opened up this truck. I don't know how fast it'll go.* **6.** to make something less congested. ☐ *They opened the yard up by cutting out a lot of old shrubbery.* 🅃 *We opened up the room by taking the piano out.*

open the door to something to permit or allow something to become a possibility. (Also literal.) ☐ *Your policy opens the door to cheating.* ☐ *Your statement opens the door to John's candidacy.*

open to something agreeable to hear or learn about new ideas and suggestions. ☐ *The store owner was open to suggestions from her employees.* ☐ *We are always open to new ideas.*

open up 1. open your door. (A command.) ☐ *I want in. Open up!* ☐ *Open up! This is the police.* **2.** to become available. ☐ *A new job is opening up at my office.* ☐ *Let me know if any other opportunities open up.* **3.** to go as fast as possible. ☐ *I can't get this car to open up. Must be something wrong with the engine.* ☐ *Faster, Tom! Open up! Let's go!* **4.** to become clear, uncluttered, or open. ☐ *As we drove along, the forest opened up, and we entered into a grassy plain.* ☐ *The sky opened up, and the sun shone.*

open (up) a can of worms to uncover a set of problems; to create unnecessary complications. (Informal. *Can of worms* means "mess." Also with various modifiers such as *new, whole, another,* as in the examples. Compare this with open Pandora's box.) ☐ *Now you are opening a whole new can of worms.* ☐ *How about cleaning up this mess before you open up a new can of worms?*

open up (on someone or something**)** to attack someone or something; to fire a gun or other weapon at someone or something. ☐ *The sergeant told the soldiers to open up on the enemy position.* ☐ *"Okay, you guys," shouted the sergeant. "Open up!"*

open up (to someone**)** AND **open up (with** someone**)** to talk frankly, truthfully, or intimately. ☐ *Finally Sally opened up to her sister and told her what the problem was.* ☐ *Bill wouldn't open up with me. He's still keeping quiet.* ☐ *At last, Sally opened up and told everything.*

open up (with someone**)** Go to open up (to someone).

open with something to start out with something. (Usually said of a performance of some type.) ☐ *We'll open with a love song and then go on to something faster.* ☐ *The play opened with an exciting first act, and then it became very boring.*

opening gambit an opening movement or statement that is made to secure a position that is to one's advantage. ☐ *The rebel army's opening gambit was to bomb the city's business district.* ☐ *The prosecution's opening gambit was to call a witness who linked the defendant to the scene of the crime.*

the **opposite sex** [from the point of view of a female] males; [from the point of view of a male] females. (Also with *member of,* as in the example.) ☐ *Ann is crazy about the opposite sex.* ☐ *Bill is very shy when he's introduced to the opposite sex.* ☐ *Do members of the opposite sex make you nervous?*

or else or suffer the consequences. ☐ *Do what I tell you, or else.* ☐ *Don't be late for work, or else!*

or words to that effect or with other words that have about the same meaning. ☐ *She told me I ought to read more carefully—or words to that effect.* ☐ *I was instructed to go to the devil, or words to that effect.*

the **order of the day** something necessary or usual; an overriding necessity. ☐ *Warm clothes are the order of the day when camping in the winter.* ☐ *Going to* *bed early was the order of the day when we were young.*

order someone **about** AND **order** someone **around** to give commands to someone. □ *I don't like for someone to order me about.* □ *Don't order me around!*

order someone **around** Go to order someone about.

order something **to go** Go to buy something to go.

the **other side of the tracks** the poorer section of town or the richer section of town, depending on perspective. (Also literal. Usually refers to the wrong side of the tracks.) □ *He is from a wealthy family and I am from a very humble background, but he is the first boy I have met from the other side of the tracks, and I want to marry him.* □ *I hear he is dating someone from the other side of the tracks.*

other things being equal if things stay the way they are now; if there were no complications by other factors. □ *Other things being equal, we should have no trouble getting your order to you on time.* □ *I anticipate no problems, other things being equal.*

the **other way round** the reverse; the opposite. □ *No, it won't fit that way. Try it the other way round.* □ *It doesn't make any sense like that. It belongs the other way round.*

An **ounce of prevention is worth a pound of cure.** It is easier and better to prevent something bad than to deal with the results. □ *When you ride in a car, buckle your seat belt. An ounce of prevention is worth a pound of cure.* □ *Every child should be vaccinated against polio. An ounce of prevention is worth a pound of cure.*

out and about able to go out and travel around. □ *Beth has been ill, but now she's out and about.* □ *As soon as I feel better, I'll be able to get out and about.*

an **out-and-out** something a complete or absolute something; an indisputable something. (Informal. The *something* must always be a specific thing.) □ *If he said that, he told you an out-and-out lie!* □ *You're an out-and-out liar!*

out cold AND **out like a light** unconscious. □ *I fell and hit my head. I was out cold for about a minute.* □ *Tom fainted! He's out like a light!*

out from under (something**)** free and clear of something; no longer bearing a (figurative) burden. □ *I'll feel much better when I'm out from under this project.* □ *Now that I'm out from under, I can relax.*

out front in the front of one's house. □ *Our mailbox is out front.* □ *We have a spruce tree out front and a maple tree in the back.*

out in force appearing in great numbers. (See also in force.) □ *What a night! The mosquitoes are out in force.* □ *The police were out in force over the holiday weekend.*

out in left field offbeat; unusual and eccentric. (Literal in reference to a baseball field. Informal. See also come out of left field.) □ *Sally is a lot of fun, but she's sort of out in left field.* □ *What a strange idea. It's really out in left field.*

out like a light Go to out cold.

out of a clear blue sky AND **out of the blue** suddenly; without warning. (See also like a bolt out of the blue.) □ *Then, out of a clear blue sky, he told me he was leaving.* □ *Mary appeared on my doorstep out of the blue.*

out of (all) proportion of an exaggerated proportion; of an unrealistic proportion compared to something else; (figuratively) lopsided. □ *This problem has grown out of all proportion.* □ *Yes, this thing is way out of proportion.*

out of bounds 1. outside the boundaries of the playing area. (In various sports.) □ *The ball went out of bounds, but the referee didn't notice.* □ *The play ended when Sally ran out of bounds.* **2.** unreasonable. (Informal.) □ *Your demands are totally out of bounds.* □ *Your request for money is out of bounds.* **3.** Go to off limits.

out of breath breathing fast and hard. □ *I ran so much that I got out of breath.* □

Mary gets out of breath when she climbs stairs.

out of character 1. unlike one's usual behavior. ☐ *Ann's remark was quite out of character.* ☐ *It was out of character for Ann to act so stubborn.* **2.** inappropriate for the character that an actor is playing. ☐ *Bill went out of character when the audience started giggling.* ☐ *Bill played the part so well that it was hard for him to get out of character after the performance.*

out of circulation 1. no longer available for use or lending. (Usually said of library materials.) ☐ *I'm sorry, but the book you want is temporarily out of circulation.* ☐ *How long will it be out of circulation?* **2.** not interacting socially with other people. (Informal.) ☐ *I don't know what's happening because I've been out of circulation for a while.* ☐ *My cold has kept me out of circulation for a few weeks.*

out of commission 1. [for a ship] to be not currently in use or under command. ☐ *This vessel will remain out of commission for another month.* ☐ *The ship has been out of commission since repairs began.* **2.** broken, unserviceable, or inoperable. ☐ *My watch is out of commission and is running slow.* ☐ *I can't run in the marathon because my knees are out of commission.*

out of condition Go to out of shape.

out of consideration (for someone or something) with consideration for someone or something; with kind regard for someone or something. ☐ *Out of consideration for your past efforts, I will do what you ask.* ☐ *They let me do it out of consideration. It was very thoughtful of them.*

out of control AND **out of hand** uncontrollable; wild and unruly. ☐ *The party got out of control about midnight, and the neighbors called the police.* ☐ *We tried to keep things from getting out of hand.*

out of courtesy (to someone) in order to be polite to someone; out of consideration for someone. ☐ *We invited Mary's brother out of courtesy to her.* ☐ *They invited me out of courtesy.*

out-of-date old-fashioned; out of style; obsolete. (See also go out of style.) ☐ *Isn't that suit sort of out-of-date?* ☐ *All my clothes are out-of-date.*

out of earshot too far from the source of a sound to hear the sound. ☐ *I was out of earshot and could not hear the conversation.* ☐ *Mary waited until her children were out of earshot before mentioning the party to Bill.*

out of fashion Go to out of style.

out of favor (with someone) no longer desirable or preferred by someone. ☐ *I can't ask John to help. I'm out of favor with him.* ☐ *That kind of thing has been out of favor for years.*

out of gas 1. having no gasoline (in a car, truck, etc.). ☐ *We can't go any farther. We're out of gas.* ☐ *This car will be completely out of gas in a few more miles.* **2.** tired; exhausted; worn out. (Informal.) ☐ *What a day! I've been working since morning, and I'm really out of gas.* ☐ *This electric clock is out of gas. I'll have to get a new one.*

out of hand 1. Go to out of control. **2.** immediately and without consulting anyone; without delay. ☐ *I can't answer that out of hand. I'll check with the manager and call you back.* ☐ *The offer was so good that I accepted it out of hand.*

out of it Go to out to lunch.

out of keeping (with something) not following the rules of something; out of accord with something. (Compare this with in keeping (with something).) ☐ *The length of this report is out of keeping with your request.* ☐ *I didn't even read it because it was so much out of keeping.*

out of kilter 1. out of balance; crooked or tilted. (Slang.) ☐ *John, your tie is sort of out of kilter. Let me fix it.* ☐ *Please straighten the picture on the wall. It's out of kilter.* **2.** malfunctioning; on the fritz. (Slang.) ☐ *My furnace is out of kilter. I have to call someone to fix it.* ☐ *This computer is out of kilter. It doesn't work.*

out of line 1. Go to out of line (with something). **2.** improper. ☐ *I'm afraid that your* *behavior was quite out of line. I do not wish to speak further about this matter.* □ *Bill, that remark was out of line. Please be more respectful.*

out of line (with something**) 1.** not properly lined up in a line of things. □ *I told you not to get out of line. Now, get back in line.* □ *One of those books on the shelf is out of line with the others. Please fix it.* **2.** unreasonable when compared to something (else). □ *The cost of this meal is out of line with what other restaurants charge.* □ *Your request is out of line.*

out of luck without good luck; having bad fortune. (Informal.) □ *If you wanted some ice cream, you're out of luck.* □ *I was out of luck. I got there too late to get a seat.*

out of necessity because of necessity; due to need. □ *I bought this hat out of necessity. I needed one, and this was all there was.* □ *We sold our car out of necessity.*

out of one's **element** not in a natural or comfortable situation. (Compare this with in one's element.) □ *When it comes to computers, I'm out of my element.* □ *Sally's out of her element in math.*

out of one's **head** Go to out of one's mind.

out of one's **mind** AND **out of** one's **head; out of** one's **senses** silly and senseless; crazy; irrational. □ *Why did you do that? You must be out of your mind!* □ *Good grief, Tom! You have to be out of your head!* □ *She's acting as if she were out of her senses.*

out of one's **senses** Go to out of one's mind.

out of order 1. not in the correct order. □ *This book is out of order. Please put it in the right place on the shelf.* □ *You're out of order, John. Please get in line after Jane.* **2.** not following correct parliamentary procedure. □ *I was declared out of order by the president.* □ *Ann inquired, "Isn't a motion to table the question out of order at this time?"* **3.** not operating; broken. □ *The coffee machine is out of order. It takes your money and gives you no coffee.* □ *We will have to use the stairs. The elevator is out of order.*

out of place 1. not in a proper place. □ *The salt was out of place in the cupboard, so I couldn't find it.* □ *Billy, you're out of place. Please sit next to Tom.* **2.** improper and impertinent; out of line. □ *That kind of behavior is out of place in church.* □ *Your rude remark is quite out of place.*

out-of-pocket expenses the actual amount of money spent. (Refers to the money one person pays while doing something on someone else's behalf. One is usually paid back this money.) □ *My out-of-pocket expenses for the party were nearly $175.* □ *My employer usually pays all out-of-pocket expenses for a business trip.*

out of practice performing poorly due to a lack of practice. □ *I used to be able to play the piano extremely well, but now I'm out of practice.* □ *The baseball players lost the game because they were out of practice.*

out of print [for a book] to be no longer available for sale from the publisher. □ *The book you want is out of print, but perhaps I can find a used copy for you.* □ *It was published nearly ten years ago, so it's probably out of print.*

out of proportion Go to in proportion.

out of reach 1. not near enough to be reached or touched. □ *Place the cookies out of reach, or Bob will eat them all.* □ *The mouse ran behind the piano, out of reach. The cat just sat and waited for it.* **2.** unattainable. □ *I wanted to be president, but I'm afraid that such a goal is out of reach.* □ *I shall choose a goal that is not out of reach.*

out of season 1. not now available for sale. (The opposite of in season. Compare this with off season.) □ *Sorry, oysters are out of season. We don't have any.* □ *Watermelon is out of season in the winter.* **2.** not now legally able to be hunted or caught. □ *Are salmon out of season?* □ *I caught a trout out of season and had to pay a fine.*

out of service inoperable; not now operating. □ *Both elevators are out of service, so I had to use the stairs.* □ *The washroom is temporarily out of service.*

out of shape AND **out of condition** not in the best physical condition. □ *I get out of breath when I run because I'm out of shape.* □ *Keep exercising regularly, or you'll get out of condition.*

out of sight 1. not visible. (Especially with *get, keep,* or *stay.*) □ *The cat kept out of sight until the mouse came out.* □ *"Get out of sight, or they'll see you!" called John.* **2.** [for a price to be] very high. (Informal.) □ *I won't pay this bill. It's out of sight.* □ *The estimate was out of sight, so I didn't accept it.* **3.** figuratively stunning, unbelievable, or awesome. (Slang.) □ *Wow, this music is out of sight!* □ *What a wild party—out of sight!*

Out of sight, out of mind. If you do not see something, you will not think about it. (Proverb.) □ *When I go home, I put my schoolbooks away so I won't worry about doing my homework. After all, out of sight, out of mind.* □ *Jane dented the fender on her car. It's on the right side, so she doesn't have to look at it. Like they say, out of sight, out of mind.*

out of sorts not feeling well; grumpy and irritable. □ *I've been out of sorts for a day or two. I think I'm coming down with something.* □ *The baby is out of sorts. Maybe she's getting a tooth.*

out of spite with the desire to harm someone or something. □ *Jane told some evil gossip about Bill out of spite.* □ *That was not an accident! You did it out of spite.*

out of step (with someone or something**) 1.** AND **out of time (with** someone or something**)** [marching or dancing] out of cadence with someone else. □ *You're out of step with the music.* □ *Pay attention, Ann. You're out of time.* **2.** not as up-to-date as someone or something. □ *John is out of step with the times.* □ *Billy is out of step with the rest of the class.*

out of stock not immediately available in a store; [for goods] to be temporarily unavailable. □ *Those items are out of stock, but a new supply will be delivered on Thursday.* □ *I'm sorry, but the red ones are out of stock. Would a blue one do?*

out of style AND **out of fashion** not fashionable; old-fashioned; obsolete. □ *John's clothes are really out of style.* □ *He doesn't care if his clothes are out of fashion.*

out of the blue Go to out of a clear blue sky.

out of the corner of one's **eye** [seeing something] at a glance; glimpsing (something). □ *I saw someone do it out of the corner of my eye. It might have been Jane who did it.* □ *I only saw the accident out of the corner of my eye. I don't know who is at fault.*

out of the frying pan into the fire from a bad situation to a worse situation. (Often with *jump.*) □ *When I tried to argue about my fine for a traffic violation, the judge charged me with contempt of court. I really went out of the frying pan into the fire.* □ *I got deeply in debt. Then I really got out of the frying pan into the fire when I lost my job.*

out of the hole out of debt. (Also literal. Informal.) □ *I get paid next week, and then I can get out of the hole.* □ *I can't seem to get out of the hole. I keep spending more money than I earn.*

out of the ordinary unusual. □ *It was a good meal, but not out of the ordinary.* □ *Your report was nicely done, but nothing out of the ordinary.*

out of the question not possible; not permitted. □ *I'm sorry, but it's out of the question.* □ *You can't go to Florida this spring. We can't afford it. It's out of the question.*

out of the red out of debt. (Informal.) □ *This year our company is likely to get out of the red before fall.* □ *If we can cut down on expenses, we can get out of the red fairly soon.*

out of the running no longer being considered; eliminated from a contest. (Compare this with in the running.) □ *After the first part of the diving meet, three members of our team were out of the running.* □ *After the scandal was made public, I was no longer in the running. I pulled out of the election.*

out of the swim of things not in the middle of activity; not involved in things. (Informal. The opposite of **in the swim of things.**) □ *While I had my cold, I was out of the swim of things.* □ *I've been out of the swim of things for a few weeks. Please bring me up to date.*

out-of-the-way not on the regular route; following a different, more awkward, route. □ *They live on a quiet, out-of-the-way street.* □ *I know an out-of-the-way little restaurant on Maple Street.*

out of the woods past a critical phase; out of the unknown. (Informal.) □ *When the patient got out of the woods, everyone relaxed.* □ *I can give you a better prediction for your future health when you are out of the woods.*

out of thin air out of nowhere; out of nothing. (Informal.) □ *Suddenly—out of thin air—the messenger appeared.* □ *You just made that up out of thin air.*

out of this world wonderful; extraordinary. □ *This pie is just out of this world.* □ *Look at you! How lovely you look—simply out of this world.*

out of time (with someone or something**)** Go to **out of step (with** someone or something**).**

out of touch (with someone or something**) 1.** [with *someone*] no longer talking to or writing to someone; knowing no news of someone. □ *I've been out of touch with my brother for many years.* □ *We've been out of touch for quite some time.* **2.** [with *something*] not keeping up with the developments of something. □ *I've been out of touch with automobile mechanics for many years.* □ *I couldn't go back into mechanics because I've been out of touch for too long.*

out of town temporarily not in one's own town. □ *I'll be out of town next week. I'm going to a conference.* □ *I take care of Mary's cat when she's out of town.*

out of tune (with someone or something**) 1.** not in musical harmony with someone or something. (Compare this with **in tune.**) □ *The oboe is out of tune with the flute.* □ *The flute is out of tune with John.* □ *They are all out of tune.* **2.** not in (figurative) harmony or agreement. □ *Your proposal is out of tune with my ideas of what we should be doing.* □ *Your ideas and mine are out of tune.*

out of turn not at the proper time; not in the proper order. (See also **speak out of turn.**) □ *We were permitted to be served out of turn because we had to leave early.* □ *Bill tried to register out of turn and was sent away.*

out of w(h)ack 1. crazy; silly; irrational. (Slang.) □ *Why do you always act as if you're out of whack?* □ *I'm not out of wack. I'm eccentric.* **2.** out of adjustment; out of order. (Slang.) □ *I'm afraid that my watch is out of whack.* □ *The elevator is out of wack. We'll have to walk up.*

out of work unemployed, temporarily or permanently. □ *How long have you been out of work?* □ *My brother has been out of work for nearly a year.*

out on a limb in a dangerous position; taking a chance. (Also literal.) □ *I don't want to go out on a limb, but I think I'd agree to your request.* □ *She really went out on a limb when she agreed.*

out on bail out of jail because bail bond money has been paid. (The money will be forfeited if the person who is **out on bail** does not appear in court at the proper time. See also **jump bail.**) □ *Bob is out on bail waiting for his trial.* □ *The robber committed another crime while out on bail.*

out on parole out of jail but still under police supervision. □ *Bob got out on parole after serving only a few years of his sentence.* □ *He was out on parole because of good behavior.*

(out) on patrol away from a central location, watching over a distant area while moving through it. □ *Officer Smith is out on patrol and cannot see you now.* □ *The soldiers who are on patrol on this snowy night must be very cold.*

out on the town celebrating at one or more places in a town. (See also **night on the town.**) □ *I'm really tired. I was out* *on the town until dawn.* □ *We went out on the town to celebrate our wedding anniversary.*

out to lunch 1. eating lunch away from one's place of work or activity. □ *I'm sorry, but Sally Jones is out to lunch. May I take a message?* □ *She's been out to lunch for nearly two hours. When will she be back?* **2.** AND **out of it** not alert; giddy; uninformed. (Slang.) □ *Bill is really out of it. Why can't he pay attention?* □ *Don't be so out of it, John. Wake up!* □ *Ann is really out to lunch these days.*

out West in the western part of the United States. (See also back East, down South, up North.) □ *We lived out West for nearly ten years.* □ *Do they really ride horses out West?*

outgrow something **1.** to get too big for something. □ *Tom outgrew all his clothes in two months.* □ *The plant outgrew its pot.* **2.** to become too mature for something. □ *I outgrew my allergies.* □ *The boys will outgrow their toys.*

outguess someone to guess what someone else might do; to predict what someone might do. □ *I can't outguess Bill. I just have to wait and see what happens.* □ *Don't try to outguess John. He's too sharp and tricky.*

outside of something except for something; besides something. (Also literal.) □ *Outside of the cost of my laundry, I have practically no expenses.* □ *Outside of some new shoes, I don't need any new clothing.*

outside the box 1. as if not bound by old, nonfunctional, or limiting structures, rules, or practices. (An adverb. Compare this with inside the box.) □ *You need to move your discussions outside the box and get away from silly limitations.* □ *Nothing can be done outside the box in such a rigid intellectual environment.* **2.** not bound by old, nonfunctional, or limiting structures, rules, or practices. (Usually **outside-the-box**. An adjective.) □ *You have some really outside-the-box ideas, Ralph.* □ *After some long, outside-the-box discussions, we arrived at a creative solution.*

over again Go to (all) over again.

over and above something more than something; in addition to something. (Informal.) □ *I'll need another twenty dollars over and above the amount you have already given me.* □ *You've been eating too much food—over and above what is required for good nutrition. That's why you're gaining weight.*

over and done with finished. (Informal.) □ *I'm glad that's over and done with.* □ *Now that I have college over and done with, I can get a job.*

over and over (again) repeatedly. □ *She stamped her foot over and over again.* □ *Bill whistled the same song over and over.*

over my dead body not if I can stop you. (Slang. It means that you'll have to kill me to prevent me from keeping you from doing something.) □ *Over my dead body you'll sell this house!* □ *You want to quit college? Over my dead body!*

over someone's **head** too difficult or clever for someone to understand. (Also literal.) □ *The children have no idea what the new teacher is talking about. Her ideas are way over their heads.* □ *She enrolled in a physics course, but it turned out to be miles over her head.*

over the hill overage; too old to do something. (Informal.) □ *Now that Mary's forty, she thinks she's over the hill.* □ *My grandfather was over eighty before he felt as if he was over the hill.*

over the hump over the difficult part. (Informal.) □ *This is a difficult project, but we're over the hump now.* □ *I'm halfway through—over the hump—and it looks as if I may get finished after all.*

over the long haul for a relatively long period of time. □ *Over the long haul, it might be better to invest in stocks.* □ *Over the long haul, everything will turn out all right.*

over there Go to (way) over there.

over the short haul for the immediate future. □ *Over the short haul, you'd be better off to put your money in the bank.* □

Over the short haul, you may wish you had done something different. But things will work out all right.

over the top 1. having gained more than one's goal. □ *Our fund-raising campaign went over the top by $3,000.* □ *We didn't go over the top. We didn't even get half of what we set out to collect.* **2.** excessive; beyond the pale; overdone. □ *Her imitation of the president was over the top and completely offensive.* □ *This is not satire! It is cruel and over the top.*

over with Go to (all) over with.

owing to because of something; due to the fact of something. □ *Owing to the lateness of the evening, I must go home.* □ *We were late owing to the heavy traffic.*

own up (to something) to confess to something. □ *I know you broke the window. Come on and own up to it.* □ *The boy holding the baseball bat owned up. What else could he do?*

P

pack a punch Go to **pack a wallop**.

pack a wallop AND **pack a punch** to provide a burst of energy, power, or excitement. (Informal.) □ *Wow, this spicy food really packs a wallop.* □ *I put a special kind of gasoline in my car because I thought it would pack a punch. It didn't.*

a **pack of lies** a series of lies. □ *The thief told a pack of lies to cover up the crime.* □ *John listened to Bill's pack of lies about the fight and became very angry.*

pack them in to draw a lot of people. (Informal.) □ *It was a good night at the theater. The play really packed them in.* □ *The circus manager knew he could pack them in if he advertised the lion tamer.*

packed (in) like sardines packed very tightly. (Note the variation in the examples.) □ *It was terribly crowded there. We were packed in like sardines.* □ *The bus was full. The passengers were packed like sardines.* □ *They packed us in like sardines.*

pad the bill to put unnecessary items on a bill to make the total cost higher. (Informal.) □ *The plumber had padded the bill with things we didn't need.* □ *I was falsely accused of padding the bill.*

paddle one's **own canoe** to do (something) by oneself. (Also literal.) □ *I've been left to paddle my own canoe too many times.* □ *Sally isn't with us. She's off paddling her own canoe.*

a **pain in the neck** a bother; an annoyance. (Slang.) □ *This assignment is a pain in the neck.* □ *Your little brother is a pain in the neck.*

paint the town red to have a wild celebration during a **night on the town**. □ *Let's all go out and paint the town red!* □ *Oh, do I feel awful. I was out all last night, painting the town red.*

pal around (with someone**)** to be friends with someone; to be the companion of someone. □ *Bill likes to pal around with Mary, but it's nothing serious.* □ *Ann and Jane still like to pal around.*

pale around the gills AND **blue around the gills; green around the gills** looking sick. (Informal. The *around* can be replaced with *about*.) □ *John is looking a little pale around the gills. What's wrong?* □ *Oh, I feel a little green about the gills.*

pale as death Go to **(as) pale as death**.

palm something **off (on** someone**)** to try to get something accepted as good. □ *The crook palmed a fake $50 bill off on me.* □ *Bob palmed his research off as original work, but we all knew he plagiarized it.*

pan out Go to **turn out (all right)**.

paper over the cracks (in something**)** to try to hide faults or difficulties, often in a hasty or not very successful way. (Also literal when applying wallpaper.) □ *The politician tried to paper over the cracks in his party's economic policy.* □ *Tom tried to paper over the cracks in his relationship with the boss, but it was not possible.* □ *She didn't explain it. She just papered over the cracks.*

par for the course typical; about what one could expect. (This refers to golf courses, not school courses.) □ *So he went off and left you? Well that's about par for the course. He's no friend.* □ *I worked for days on this project, but it was rejected. That's par for the course around here.*

a **paradise (on earth)** a place on earth that is as lovely as paradise. ☐ *The retirement home was simply a paradise on earth.* ☐ *The beach where we went for our vacation was a paradise.*

Pardon my French. Excuse me for swearing or saying naughty words. (Informal.) ☐ *Pardon my French, but get that damn cat out of here!* ☐ *He slipped and fell on his butt, pardon my French.*

part and parcel (of something**)** part of something; an important part of something. (See also **bag and baggage.**) ☐ *This point is part and parcel of my whole argument.* ☐ *Get every part and parcel of this machine out of my living room.* ☐ *Come on! Move out—part and parcel!*

part company (with someone**)** to leave someone; to depart from someone. ☐ *Tom finally parted company with his brother.* ☐ *They parted company, and Tom got in his car and drove away.*

part someone's **hair** to come very close to someone. (Also literal. Informal. Usually an exaggeration.) ☐ *That plane flew so low that it nearly parted my hair.* ☐ *He punched at me and missed. He only parted my hair.*

partake of something to take something; to eat or drink something. (Formal.) ☐ *I don't usually partake of rich foods, but in this instance I'll make an exception.* ☐ *Good afternoon, Judge Smith, would you care to partake of some wine?*

partial to someone or something favoring or preferring someone or something. ☐ *The boys think their teacher is partial to female students.* ☐ *I am partial to vanilla ice cream.*

the **particulars of** something specific details about something. ☐ *My boss stressed the important particulars of the project.* ☐ *What are the particulars of your request?*

parting of the ways a point at which people separate and go their own ways. (Often with *come to a, arrive at a, reach a,* etc.) ☐ *Jane and Bob finally came to a parting of the ways.* ☐ *Bill and his parents reached a parting of the ways.*

the **party line** the official ideas and attitudes that are adopted by the leaders of a particular group and that the other members are expected to accept. (From *political party.*) ☐ *Tom has left the club. He refused to follow the party line.* ☐ *Many politicians agree with the party line without thinking.*

The **party's over.** A happy or fortunate time has come to an end. (Also literal. Informal.) ☐ *We go back to school tomorrow. The party's over.* ☐ *The staff hardly worked at all under the old management, but they'll find the party's over now.*

pass as someone or something AND **pass for** someone or something to succeed in being accepted as someone or something. ☐ *The spy was able to pass as a regular citizen.* ☐ *You could pass for your twin brother.* ☐ *The thief was arrested when he tried to pass as a priest.*

pass away AND **pass on** to die. (A euphemism.) ☐ *My aunt passed away last month.* ☐ *When I pass away, I want to have lots of flowers and a big funeral.* ☐ *When I pass on, I won't care about the funeral.*

pass for someone or something Go to **pass as** someone or something

pass muster to measure up to the required standards. (Folksy.) ☐ *I tried, but my efforts didn't pass muster.* ☐ *If you don't wear a suit, you won't pass muster at that fancy restaurant. They won't let you in.*

pass on Go to **pass away.**

pass out to faint; to lose consciousness. ☐ *Oh, look! Tom has passed out.* ☐ *When he got the news, he passed out.*

pass the buck to pass the blame (to someone else); to give the responsibility (to someone else). (Informal.) ☐ *Don't try to pass the buck! It's your fault, and everybody knows it.* ☐ *Some people try to pass the buck whenever they can.*

pass the hat to attempt to collect money for some (charitable) project. (Refers to a hat that is sometimes used to hold the collected cash.) ☐ *Bob is passing the hat to collect money to buy flowers for Ann.*

☐ *He's always passing the hat for something.*

pass the time to fill up time (by doing something). ☐ *I never know how to pass the time when I'm on vacation.* ☐ *What do you do to pass the time?*

pass the time of day (with someone**)** to chat or talk informally with someone. ☐ *I saw Mr. Brown in town yesterday. I stopped and passed the time of day with him.* ☐ *No, we didn't have a serious talk; we just passed the time of day.*

pass through someone's **mind** AND **cross** someone's **mind** to come to mind briefly; for an idea to occur to someone. (Compare this with **come to mind.**) ☐ *Let me tell you what just crossed my mind.* ☐ *As you were speaking, something passed through my mind that I'd like to discuss.*

passport to something something that allows something good to happen. ☐ *John's new girlfriend is his passport to happiness.* ☐ *Anne's new job is a passport to financial security.*

a **past master at** something someone proven to be extremely good or skillful at an activity. (Preceded by *be, become, seem like,* or *act like.*) ☐ *Mary is a past master at cooking omelets.* ☐ *Pam is a past master at the art of complaining.*

past someone's or something's **prime** beyond the most useful or productive period. ☐ *Joan was a wonderful singer, but she's past her prime now.* ☐ *This old car's past its prime. I'll need to get a new one.*

pat someone **on the back** AND **give** someone **a pat on the back** to congratulate someone; to encourage someone. (Also literal when the recipient is actually patted on the back.) ☐ *We patted Ann on the back for a good performance.* ☐ *When people do a good job, you should give them a pat on the back.*

patch someone or something **up 1.** [with *someone*] to doctor someone; to dress someone's wounds. (Informal.) ☐ *They patched John up in the emergency room.* 🅃 *I patched up Ann's cuts with bandages and sent her home.* **2.** [with *something*] to (figuratively) repair the damage done by an argument or disagreement. (Also literal.) ☐ *Mr. and Mrs. Smith are trying to patch things up.* 🅃 *We patched up our argument, then kissed and made up.*

the **path of least resistance** to do the easiest thing; to take the easiest route. (Often with *follow the* or *take the.* Compare this with **line of least resistance.**) ☐ *John will follow the path of least resistance.* ☐ *I like challenges. I won't usually take the path of least resistance.*

patient as Job Go to (as) patient as Job.

pave the way (for someone or something**)** to prepare (someone or something) for someone or something. ☐ *The public doesn't understand the metric system. We need to pave the way for its introduction.* ☐ *They are paving the way in the schools.*

pay a call on someone to visit someone. ☐ *Grandmother always paid us a call on Sundays.* ☐ *Let's pay a call on Mary at the hospital.*

pay a king's ransom (for something**)** to pay a great deal for something. (To pay an amount as large as one might have to pay to get back a king held for ransom.) ☐ *I would like to buy a nice watch, but I don't want to pay a king's ransom for it.* ☐ *It's a lovely house. I had to pay a king's ransom, but it is worth it.*

pay an arm and a leg (for something**)** AND **pay through the nose (for** something**)** to pay too much [money] for something. (Informal.) ☐ *I hate to have to pay an arm and a leg for a tank of gas.* ☐ *If you shop around, you won't have to pay an arm and a leg.* ☐ *Why should you pay through the nose?*

pay as you go 1. to pay costs as they occur; to pay for goods as they are bought (rather than charging them). (Literal when it means to pay for goods or services as you leave.) ☐ *You ought to pay as you go. Then you won't be in debt.* ☐ *If you pay as you go, you'll never spend too much money.* **2.** paying costs as they occur. (Usually **pay-as-you-go.**) ☐ *There is no charging allowed here. This store is strictly pay-as-you-go.* ☐ *I can't buy this* *then. I didn't know your policy was pay-as-you-go.*

pay attention (to someone or something**)** to be attentive to someone or something; to give one's attention or concentration to someone or something. ☐ *Pay attention to me!* ☐ *I'm paying attention!*

pay a visit to someone or something Go to **pay** (someone or something) **a visit.**

pay for something **1.** to pay out money for something. ☐ *Did you pay for the magazine, or shall I?* ☐ *No, I'll pay for it.* **2.** to be punished for something. ☐ *The criminal will pay for his crimes.* ☐ *I don't like what you did to me, and I'm going to see that you pay for it.*

pay homage to someone to praise, respect, and honor someone. ☐ *My parents taught me to pay homage to my elders.* ☐ *The widower paid homage to his dead wife by placing flowers on her grave.*

pay in advance to pay (for something) before it is received or delivered. ☐ *I want to make a special order. Will I have to pay in advance?* ☐ *Yes, please pay in advance.*

pay lip service (to something**)** to express loyalty, respect, or support for something insincerely. ☐ *You don't really care about politics. You're just paying lip service to the candidate.* ☐ *Don't sit here and pay lip service. Get busy!*

pay one's **debt (to society)** to serve a sentence for a crime, usually in prison. ☐ *The judge said that Mr. Simpson had to pay his debt to society.* ☐ *Mr. Brown paid his debt in state prison.*

pay one's **dues** to have earned one's right to something through hard work or suffering. (Literal when referring to paying the fees required to belong to an organization. Informal.) ☐ *He worked hard to get to where he is today. He paid his dues and did what he was told.* ☐ *I have every right to be here. I paid my dues!*

pay one's **last respects** to attend the wake or funeral of someone; to approach the coffin containing someone in a final act of respect. ☐ *I went to Bill's wake to pay my last respects.* ☐ *Everyone in town came to the mayor's funeral to pay their last respects.*

pay someone **a back-handed compliment** AND **pay** someone **a left-handed compliment** to give someone a false compliment that is really an insult. ☐ *John said that he had never seen me looking better. I think he was paying me a left-handed compliment.* ☐ *I'd prefer that someone insulted me directly. I hate it when someone pays me a back-handed compliment—unless it's a joke.*

pay someone **a compliment** to compliment someone. ☐ *Sally thanked me for paying her a compliment.* ☐ *When Tom did his job well, I paid him a compliment.*

pay someone **a left-handed compliment** Go to **pay** someone **a back-handed compliment.**

pay (someone or something**) a visit** AND **pay a visit to** someone or something to visit someone or something. ☐ *Bill paid a visit to his aunt in Seattle.* ☐ *Please pay a visit to our house whenever you are in town.*

pay someone or something **off 1.** [with *someone*] to pay someone a bribe (for a favor already done). (Compare this with **buy** someone **off.**) ☐ *The lawyer was put in prison for paying the judge off. The judge was imprisoned also.* 🆃 *The lawyer paid off the judge for deciding the case in the lawyer's favor.* **2.** to pay a debt; to pay a debtor; to pay the final payment for something bought on credit. ☐ *This month I'll pay the car off.* 🆃 *Did you pay off the plumber yet?*

pay someone **respect** to honor someone; to have and show respect for someone. ☐ *You really should pay your boss more respect.* ☐ *We have to pay our parents a lot of respect.*

pay someone's **(own) way** to pay the costs (of something) for someone. ☐ *I wanted to go to Florida this spring, but my parents say I have to pay my own way.* ☐ *My aunt is going to pay my way to Florida—only if I take her with me!*

pay the piper to face the results of one's actions; to receive punishment for something. (Also literal.) ☐ *You can put off* *paying your debts only so long. Eventually you'll have to pay the piper.* ☐ *You can't get away with that forever. You'll have to pay the piper someday.*

pay through the nose (for something**)** Go to **pay an arm and a leg (for** something**)**.

pay to do something to be beneficial to do something; to be profitable. ☐ *It doesn't pay to drive downtown when you can take the train.* ☐ *It pays to take an umbrella with you if it's supposed to rain.*

pay up Pay me now! (Slang.) ☐ *You owe me $200. Come on, pay up!* ☐ *If you don't pay up, I'll take you to court.*

peg away (at something**)** Go to **plug away (at** something**)**.

peg someone **as** something AND **have** someone **pegged as** something to think of someone in a certain way. ☐ *Susan pegged the new employee as a lazy worker.* ☐ *I had you pegged as an angry rebel before I got to know you.*

A **penny saved is a penny earned.** Money saved through thrift is the same as money earned by employment. (Sometimes used to explain stinginess.) ☐ *"I didn't want to pay that much for the book," said Mary. "After all, a penny saved is a penny earned."* ☐ *Bob put his money in a new bank that pays more interest than his old bank, saying, "A penny saved is a penny earned."*

penny-wise and pound-foolish <an expression meaning that it is foolish to lose a lot of money to save a little money.> (This is the British pound sterling.) ☐ *Sally shops very carefully to save a few cents on food, then charges the food to a charge card that costs a lot in annual interest. That's being penny-wise and pound-foolish.* ☐ *John drives thirty miles to buy gas for three cents a gallon less than it costs here. He's really penny-wise and pound-foolish.*

pep someone or something **up** to make someone or something more sprightly and active. ☐ *I need a bottle of pop to pep me up.* ☐ *The third act of this play needs something to pep it up. How about a few good jokes?*

per head Go to **a head**.

Perish the thought. Do not even consider thinking of something. (Formal.) ☐ *If you should become ill—perish the thought—I'd take care of you.* ☐ *I'm afraid that we need a new car. Perish the thought.*

perk someone or something **up** to make someone or something more cheery. ☐ *A nice cup of coffee would really perk me up.* 🅃 *Don't you think that new curtains would perk up this room?*

persist in doing something to continue, with determination, to do something. ☐ *John persists in thinking that he's always right.* ☐ *Tom persists in demanding that I agree to his terms.*

persist with something to continue the state of something; to extend an action or state. ☐ *Please do not persist with your demands that I agree to your terms.* ☐ *If you persist with this intrusion, I'm going to call the police.*

perspective on something a way of looking at a situation and determining what is important. ☐ *The jury did not have a good perspective on the crime since some of the evidence had to be ignored.* ☐ *Studying history gives one perspective on the present.*

[pet hate] Go to someone's **pet hate**.

[pet peeve] Go to someone's **pet peeve**.

peter out [for something] to die or dwindle away; [for something] to become exhausted gradually. (Informal.) ☐ *When the fire petered out, I went to bed.* ☐ *My money finally petered out, and I had to come home.*

phony as a three-dollar bill Go to **(as) phony as a three-dollar bill**.

pick a fight with someone Go to **pick a quarrel (with** someone**)**.

pick a lock to open a lock without a key; to open a lock without using a key. ☐ *The robber picked the lock with a nail file.* ☐ *The thief picked the lock on the safe and stole the money.*

pick and choose to choose very carefully from a number of possibilities; to be selective. □ *You must take what you are given. You cannot pick and choose.* □ *Meg is so beautiful. She can pick and choose from a whole range of boyfriends.*

pick a quarrel (with someone**)** AND **pick a fight with** someone to start an argument or fight with someone. □ *Are you trying to pick a quarrel with me?* □ *Max intended to pick a fight with Lefty.*

pick at someone or something **1.** to be very critical of someone or something; to **pick on** someone or something. (Informal.) □ *Why are you always picking at me?* □ *You always seem to be picking at your car.* **2.** [with *something*] to eat only little bits of something. □ *You're only picking at your food. Don't you feel well?* □ *Billy is only picking at his peas, and he usually eats all of them.*

pick holes in something AND **pick** something **to pieces** to criticize something severely; to find all the flaws or fallacies in an argument. (Also literal.) □ *The lawyer picked holes in the witness's story.* □ *They will pick holes in your argument.* □ *She picked my story to pieces.*

the **pick of** something the best of the group. □ *This playful puppy is the pick of the whole lot.* □ *These potatoes are the pick of the crop.*

pick one's **way through** something AND **make** one's **way through** something to work slowly and meticulously through written material. (Literal when referring to moving carefully through a route filled with obstacles.) □ *My teacher said he couldn't even pick his way through my report. It was just too confusing.* □ *I spent an hour picking my way through the state tax forms.*

pick on somebody your own size Go to pick on someone your own size.

pick on someone or something to criticize someone or something; to abuse someone or something. □ *Stop picking on me!* □ *Why are you always picking on your dog?* □ *Don't pick on our house. It's old, but we love it.*

pick on someone your own size AND **pick on somebody your own size** to abuse someone who is big enough to fight back. □ *Go pick on somebody your own size!* □ *Max should learn to pick on someone his own size.*

pick someone or something **off** to kill someone or something with a carefully aimed gunshot. (Also literal.) □ *The hunter picked the deer off with great skill.* 🅃 *The killer tried to pick off the police officer.*

pick someone or something **up 1.** [with *someone*] to go to a place in a car, bus, etc., and take on a person as a passenger. □ *Please come to my office and pick me up at noon.* 🅃 *I have to pick up Billy at school.* **2.** [with *someone*] to stop one's car, bus, etc., and offer someone a ride. □ *Don't ever pick a stranger up when you're out driving!* 🅃 *I picked up a hitchhiker today, and we had a nice chat.* **3.** [with *someone*] to attempt to become acquainted with someone for romantic or sexual purposes. (Informal.) □ *Who are you anyway? Are you trying to pick me up?* 🅃 *No, I never picked up anybody in my life!* **4.** [with *someone*] [for the police] to find and bring someone to the police station for questioning or arrest. □ *I tried to pick her up, but she heard me coming and got away.* 🅃 *Sergeant Jones, go pick up Sally Franklin and bring her in to be questioned about the jewel robbery.* **5.** [with *something*] to tidy up or clean up a room or some other place. □ *Let's pick this room up in a hurry.* 🅃 *I want you to pick up the entire house.* **6.** [with *something*] to find, purchase, or acquire something. □ *Where did you pick that up?* 🅃 *I picked up this tool at the hardware store.* **7.** [with *something*] to learn something. □ *I pick languages up easily.* 🅃 *I picked up a lot of knowledge about music from my brother.* 🅃 *I picked up an interesting melody from a movie.* **8.** [with *something*] to cause something to go faster, especially music. □ *All right, let's pick this piece up and get it moving faster.* □ *Okay, get moving. Pick it up!* **9.** [with *something*] to resume something. □ *Pick it up right where you stopped.* 🅃 *I'll have to pick up my work where I left off.* **10.** [with *something*] to receive radio signals; to bring something into view. □ *I can just pick it up with a powerful telescope.* 🅃 *I can hardly pick up a signal.* 🅃 *We can pick up a pretty good television picture where we live.* **11.** [with *something*] to find a trail or route. 🅃 *The dogs finally picked up the scent.* 🅃 *You should pick up Highway 80 in a few miles.*

pick someone's **brain(s)** to talk with someone to find out information about something. □ *I spent the afternoon with Donna, picking her brain for ideas to use in our celebration.* □ *Do you mind if I pick your brains? I need some fresh ideas.*

pick something **over** to sort through something; to rummage through something. □ *They picked all the records over.* 🅃 *The shoppers quickly picked over the sale merchandise.*

pick something **to pieces** Go to pick holes in something.

pick up 1. to tidy up. □ *When you finish playing, you have to pick up.* □ *Please pick up after yourself.* **2.** to get busy; to go faster. □ *Things usually pick up around here about 8:00.* □ *I hope things pick up a little later. It's boring here.*

pick up the check Go to pick up the tab.

pick up the tab AND **pick up the check** to intercept and pay the charges for a meal, entertainment, or other goods or services. (Meaning that the one who picks up the check pays the charges listed on it. Informal.) □ *Whenever we go out, my father picks up the tab.* □ *Order whatever you want. The company is picking up the check.*

picked over rejected; worn, dirty, or undesirable. □ *This merchandise looks worn and picked over. I don't want any of it.* □ *Everything in the store is picked over by the end of the month.*

the **picture of** something the perfect example of something; an exact image of something. □ *The young newlyweds were the picture of happiness.* □ *Our family is just the picture of love and joy.* □ *The doctor says I am the picture of health.*

pie in the sky a future reward after death, considered as a replacement for a reward not received on earth. □ *You expect to get rich from this scheme, but that's just pie in the sky.* □ *His promises are just pie in the sky! He is a liar if I ever saw one.*

piece of cake very easy. (Slang.) □ *No, it won't be any trouble. It's a piece of cake.* □ *It's easy! Look here—piece of cake.*

a **piece of the action** a share in a scheme or project; a degree of involvement. (Slang.) □ *If you guys are going to bet on the football game, I want a piece of the action, too.* □ *My brother wants in on it. Give him a piece of the action.*

a **piercing scream** a very loud and shrill scream. □ *Suddenly, there was a piercing scream from the next room.* □ *Bob heard Susan's piercing scream and ran to help her.*

pile in(to something**)** to climb into something or get into something roughly. □ *Okay, kids, pile in!* □ *The children piled into the car and slammed the door.*

pile out (of something**)** to get out of something roughly. □ *Okay, kids, pile out!* □ *The car door burst open, and the children piled out.*

pile something **up** to crash or wreck something. (Also literal meaning "to heap something up.") □ *Drive carefully if you don't want to pile the car up.* 🅃 *The driver piled up the car against a tree.*

pile up to crash or wreck. (Also literal.) □ *The car piled up against the tree.* □ *The bus piled up on the curve.*

a **pillar of strength** AND a **pillar of support;** a **tower of strength** someone or something that consistently provides moral, emotional, or financial support as does a pillar. □ *My parents are my pillars of support.* □ *The minister looked to God as her pillar of strength.* □ *Jack was a tower of strength during the time that his father was unemployed.*

a **pillar of support** Go to a pillar of strength.

pin one's **faith on** someone or something AND **pin** one's **hope(s) on** someone or something to put one's hope, trust, or faith in someone or something. □ *I'm pinning my faith on your efforts.* □ *Don't pin your hopes on Tom. He's not dependable.*

pin one's **hope(s) on** someone or something Go to **pin** one's **faith on** someone or something.

pin someone **down** to force someone to make a decision or choice. (See also **on pins and needles.**) □ *The doctor tried to pin Jane Smith down for her next appointment.* □ *I won't make up my mind for a week so don't try to pin me down now.*

pin someone **down (on** something**)** to force someone to explain or clarify something. (Also literal. Informal.) □ *Try to pin her down on the time.* 🅃 *Pin down Jane on exactly what she means.* □ *Please find out exactly how much it costs. Pin them down on the price.*

pin someone's **ears back** to scold someone severely; to beat someone. (Slang.) □ *Tom pinned my ears back because I insulted him.* □ *I got very mad at John and wanted to pin his ears back, but I didn't.*

pin something **on** someone to place the blame for something on someone. (Also literal. Slang.) □ *I didn't take the money. Don't try to pin it on me. I wasn't even there.* □ *The police managed to pin the crime on Bob.*

pinch-hit (for someone**)** to substitute for someone. (Originally from baseball, where it refers to a substitute batter.) □ *Will you pinch-hit for me at band practice?* □ *Sorry, I can't pinch-hit. I don't have the time.*

pins and needles a tingling feeling in some part of one's body, especially the arms and legs. (See also **on pins and needles.**) □ *I've got pins and needles in my legs.* □ *Mary gets pins and needles if she crosses her arms for long.*

pipe down to be quiet; to get quiet. (Slang.) □ *Okay, you guys, pipe down!* □ *I've heard enough out of you. Pipe down!*

a **pipe dream** a wish or an idea that is impossible to achieve or carry out. (From the dreams or visions induced by the smoking of an opium pipe.) □ *Going to the West Indies is a pipe dream. We'll never have enough money.* □ *Your hopes of winning a lot of money are just a silly pipe dream.*

pipe up with something to speak up and say something, especially with a high-pitched voice. □ *Billy piped up with a silly remark.* □ *Did I hear somebody pipe up with an insult?*

piping hot [of food] extremely hot. □ *On a cold day, I like to eat piping hot soup.* □ *Be careful! This coffee is piping hot!*

pique someone's **curiosity** AND **pique** someone's **interest** to arouse interest; to arouse curiosity. □ *The advertisement piqued my curiosity about the product.* □ *The professor tried to pique the students' interest in French literature.*

pique someone's **interest** Go to **pique** someone's **curiosity.**

pit someone or something **against** someone or something to set someone or something in opposition to someone or something. □ *The rules of the tournament pit their team against ours.* □ *John pitted Mary against Sally in the tennis match.* □ *In an interesting plowing match, Bill pitted himself against a small tractor.*

pitch a tent to erect a tent at a campsite. □ *The campers pitched their tent in a clearing in the woods.* □ *I pitched my tent next to a large oak tree.*

pitch-black very black; as black as pitch. □ *The hearse was pitch-black.* □ *The bandit rode on a pitch-black horse and wore black clothing.*

pitch camp to set up or arrange a campsite. □ *We pitched camp near the stream.* □ *Two campers went ahead of us to pitch camp while it was still light.*

pitch-dark very dark; as dark as pitch. □ *I couldn't see anything outside because it was pitch-dark.* □ *The room was pitch-dark, and I couldn't find the light switch!*

pitch in (and help) to get busy and help (with something). □ *Pick up a paintbrush and pitch in and help.* □ *Why don't some* *of you pitch in? We need all the help we can get.*

pitch someone **a curve (ball)** to surprise someone with an unexpected act or event. (Alluding to pitching a curve ball in baseball. It is the route of the ball that is curved, not the ball itself.) □ *You really pitched me a curve ball when you said I had done a poor job. I did my best.* □ *You asked Tom a hard question. You certainly pitched him a curve.*

the **pits** the worst possible. (Slang.) □ *John is such a boring person. He's the pits.* □ *This restaurant isn't the best, but it's not the pits either.*

place an order to submit an order. □ *My secretary placed an order for a new computer.* □ *I placed my order only yesterday.*

[place of business] Go to someone's place of business.

place someone to recall someone's name; to recall the details about a person that would help you identify the person. □ *I am sorry, I can't seem to place you. Could you tell me your name again?* □ *I can't place her. Did I meet her once before?*

place the blame on someone or something Go to put the blame on someone or something.

a **place to call** one's **own** Go to somewhere to hang (up) one's hat.

a **place to hang** one's **hat** Go to somewhere to hang (up) one's hat.

plain and simple Go to pure and simple.

plain as a pikestaff Go to (as) plain as a pikestaff.

plain as day Go to (as) plain as day.

plain as the nose on one's **face** Go to (as) plain as the nose on one's face.

play about (with someone or something**)** Go to play around (with someone or something).

play a joke on someone to make a joke that tricks someone. □ *The children played a joke on their teacher.* □ *I don't like it when you play jokes on me.*

play along with someone or something to agree to cooperate or conspire with someone or someone's plan; to pretend to agree to cooperate or conspire with someone or someone's plan. □ *I refused to play along with the treasurer when she outlined her plan.* □ *It might be wise to play along with the kidnappers, at least for a little while.* □ *I'll play along with your scheme until the others get here, but I don't like it.*

play around (with someone or something**)** AND **play about (with** someone or something**)** to engage in some amusing activity with someone or something; to tease someone or something. □ *Please don't play around with that vase. You'll break it.* □ *Don't play about with the parrot. It'll bite you.* □ *Bill and I were just playing around when we heard the sound of breaking glass.*

play a trick on someone to do a trick that affects someone. □ *Somebody played a trick on me by hiding my shoes.* □ *The little boys planned to play a trick on their teacher by turning up the heat in the classroom.*

play ball (with someone**)** to cooperate with someone. (Literal when referring to playing a ball game. Informal.) □ *Look, friend, if you play ball with me, everything will work out all right.* □ *Things would go better for you if you'd learn to play ball.*

play both ends (against the middle) [for one] to scheme in a way that pits two sides against each other (for one's own gain). (Informal.) □ *I told my brother that Mary doesn't like him. Then I told Mary that my brother doesn't like her. They broke up, so now I can have the car this weekend. I succeeded in playing both ends against the middle.* □ *If you try to play both ends, you're likely to get in trouble with both sides.*

play by ear Go to play something by ear.

a **play-by-play description** a description of an event given as the event is taking place. (Usually in reference to a sporting event.) □ *And now here is Bill Jones with a play-by-play description of the baseball game.* □ *John was giving me a play-by-play description of the argument going on next door.*

play cat and mouse (with someone**)** to alternate between kinds of behavior when dealing with someone, often in matters of pursuit. ☐ *The police played cat and mouse with the suspect until they had sufficient evidence to make an arrest.* ☐ *Tom had been playing cat and mouse with Ann. Finally she got tired of it and broke up with him.*

play dumb Go to play ignorant.

play fair to do something by the rules; to play something in a fair and just manner. ☐ *John won't play with Bill anymore because Bill doesn't play fair.* ☐ *You moved the golf ball with your foot! That's not playing fair!*

play fast and loose (with someone or something**)** to act carelessly, thoughtlessly, and irresponsibly. (Informal.) ☐ *I'm tired of your playing fast and loose with me. Leave me alone.* ☐ *Bob got fired for playing fast and loose with the company's money.* ☐ *If you play fast and loose like that, you can get into a lot of trouble.*

play first chair 1. to be the leader of a section of instruments in an orchestra or a band. ☐ *Sally learned to play the violin so well that she now plays first chair in the orchestra.* ☐ *I'm going to practice my flute so I can play first chair.* **2.** to act as a leader. ☐ *I need to get this job done. Who plays first chair around here?* ☐ *You're not the boss! You don't play first chair.*

play footsie (with someone**) 1.** to attract someone's attention by touching feet under the table; to flirt with someone. (Informal.) ☐ *Bill was trying to play footsie with Sally at the dinner table. The hostess was appalled.* ☐ *They shouldn't play footsie at a formal dinner.* **2.** to get involved with someone; to collaborate with someone. (Informal.) ☐ *The treasurer got fired for playing footsie with the vice president.* ☐ *When politicians play footsie, there is usually something illegal going on.*

play for keeps to take an action that is permanent or final. (Slang.) ☐ *Mary told me that Tom wants to marry me. I didn't know he wanted to play for keeps.* ☐ *I like to play cards and make money, but I don't like to play for keeps.*

play hard to get to be coy, shy, and fickle. (Usually refers to someone of the opposite sex.) ☐ *Why can't we go out? Why do you play hard to get?* ☐ *Sally annoys all the boys because she plays hard to get.*

play havoc with someone or something Go to raise havoc with someone or something.

play hob with someone or something Go to raise hob with someone or something.

play hooky not to go to school or to some important meeting. (Slang.) ☐ *Why aren't you in school? Are you playing hooky?* ☐ *I don't have time for the sales meeting today, so I think I'll just play hooky.*

play ignorant AND **play dumb** to pretend to be ignorant [of something]. ☐ *I played ignorant even though I knew about the surprise party.* ☐ *John played ignorant when I asked him if he knew who had been on the telephone.*

play innocent to pretend to be innocent and not concerned. ☐ *There is no need to play innocent. I know you broke the lamp!* ☐ *John is playing innocent, and he knows more than he is telling us.*

play into someone's **hands** [for a person one is scheming against] to come under one's control without realizing it. ☐ *John is doing exactly what I hoped he would. He's playing into my hands.* ☐ *John played into my hands by taking the coins he found in my desk. I caught him and had him arrested.*

play it cool to act calm and unconcerned. (Slang.) ☐ *No one will suspect anything if you play it cool.* ☐ *Don't get angry, Bob. Play it cool.*

play it safe to be or act safe; to avoid taking a risk. ☐ *You should play it safe and take your umbrella.* ☐ *If you have a cold or the flu, play it safe and go to bed.*

play one's **cards close to** one's **vest** Go to play one's cards close to the chest.

play one's **cards close to the chest** AND **play** one's **cards close to** one's **vest; keep** one's **cards close to** one's **chest;**

keep one's **cards close to** one's **vest** [for someone] to work or negotiate in a careful and private manner. (Literal when referring to concealing one's cards in a card game.) ☐ *It's hard to figure out what John is up to because he plays his cards close to his chest.* ☐ *Don't let them know what you're up to. Keep your cards close to your vest.*

play one's **cards right** AND **play** one's **cards well** to work or negotiate correctly and skillfully. (Also literal. Informal.) ☐ *If you play your cards right, you can get whatever you want.* ☐ *She didn't play her cards well, and she ended up with something less than what she wanted.*

play one's **cards well** Go to play one's cards right.

play one's **trump card** to use a special trick; to use one's most powerful or effective strategy or device. (Also literal. Informal.) ☐ *I won't play my trump card until I have tried everything else.* ☐ *I thought that the whole situation was hopeless until Mary played her trump card and solved the whole problem.*

play on something to have an effect on something; to manage something for a desired effect. ☐ *The clerk played on my sense of responsibility in trying to get me to buy the book.* ☐ *See if you can get her to confess by playing on her sense of guilt.*

play politics 1. to negotiate politically. ☐ *Everybody at city hall is playing politics as usual.* ☐ *If you're elected as a member of a political party, you'll have to play politics.* **2.** to allow politics to dominate in matters where principle should prevail. ☐ *Look, I came here to discuss this trial, not play politics.* ☐ *They're not making reasonable decisions. They're playing politics.*

play possum to pretend to be inactive, unobservant, asleep, or dead. (Folksy. The *possum* is an opossum.) ☐ *I knew that Bob wasn't asleep. He was just playing possum.* ☐ *I can't tell if this animal is dead or just playing possum.*

play second fiddle (to someone**)** to be in a subordinate position to someone. ☐ *I'm tired of playing second fiddle to John.* ☐ *I'm better trained than he, and I have more experience. I shouldn't play second fiddle.*

play someone **for** something to treat someone like (a) something. (Slang. Compare this with **take** someone **for** someone or something.) ☐ *Don't play me for a fool! I know what's going on.* ☐ *They played her for a jerk, but were they surprised!*

play someone **off against** someone else to scheme in a manner that pits two of your adversaries against one another. ☐ *Bill wanted to beat me up and so did Bob. I did some fast talking, and they ended up fighting with each other. I really played Bill off against Bob.* ☐ *The president played the House off against the Senate and ended up getting his own way.*

play someone or something **down** to lessen the effect or importance of someone or something. ☐ *John is a famous actor, but the director tried to play him down as just another member of the cast.* 🅃 *They tried to play down her earlier arrest.*

play someone or something **up** to make someone or something seem to be more important. ☐ *The director tried to play Ann up, but she was not really a star.* 🅃 *Try to play up the good qualities of our product.*

play something **by ear 1.** to be able to play a piece of music after just listening to it a few times, without looking at the notes. ☐ *I can play "Stardust" by ear.* ☐ *Some people can play Chopin's music by ear.* **2.** AND **play by ear** to play a musical instrument well, without formal training. ☐ *John can play the piano by ear.* ☐ *If I could play by ear, I wouldn't have to take lessons—or practice!* **3.** to improvise; to decide what to do after one is already involved in a situation. (Compare this with wing it.) ☐ *When we get into the meeting we'll have to play everything by ear.* ☐ *He never prepared his presentations. He always played things by ear.*

play (the) devil's advocate to put forward arguments against or objections to a proposition—which one may actually agree with—purely to test the validity of the proposition. (The devil's advocate was given the role of opposing the canonization of a saint in the medieval Church in order to prove that the grounds for canonization were sound.) ☐ *I agree with your plan. I'm just playing the devil's advocate so you'll know what the opposition will say.* ☐ *Mary offered to play devil's advocate and argue against our case so that we would find out any flaws in it.*

play the field to date many different people rather than going steady. (Informal. See also **go steady with** someone.) ☐ *When Tom told Ann good-bye, he said he wanted to play the field.* ☐ *He said he wanted to play the field while he was still young.*

play the fool to act in a silly manner in order to amuse other people. ☐ *The teacher told Tom to stop playing the fool and sit down.* ☐ *Fred likes playing the fool, but we didn't find him funny last night.*

play the market to invest in the stock market, perhaps recklessly. (Informal. As if it were a game or gambling.) ☐ *Would you rather put your money in the bank or play the market?* ☐ *I've learned my lesson playing the market. I lost a fortune.*

play to the gallery to perform in a manner that will get the strong approval of the audience; to perform in a manner that will get the approval of the ruder members of the audience. ☐ *John is a competent actor, but he has a tendency to play to the gallery.* ☐ *When he made the rude remark, he was just playing to the gallery.*

play tricks (on someone**)** to trick or confuse someone. ☐ *I thought I saw a camel over there. I guess my eyes are playing tricks on me.* ☐ *Please don't play tricks on your little brother. It makes him cry.*

play up to someone to try to gain someone's favor. ☐ *Bill is always playing up to the teacher.* ☐ *Ann played up to Bill as if she wanted him to marry her.*

play with fire to take a big risk. (Also literal. Informal.) ☐ *If you accuse her of stealing, you'll be playing with fire.* ☐ *I wouldn't try that if I were you—unless you like playing with fire.*

played out worn out; spent; exhausted. ☐ *This charcoal is just about played out.* ☐ *The batteries in this flashlight are almost played out.*

pleased as punch Go to (as) pleased as punch.

plenty of something lots of something; an abundance of something; enough of something. ☐ *I have plenty of candy. Do you want some?* ☐ *This project is giving me plenty of trouble.*

The **plot thickens.** Things are becoming more complicated or interesting. ☐ *The police assumed that the woman was murdered by her ex-husband, but he has an alibi. The plot thickens.* ☐ *John is supposed to be going out with Mary, but I saw him last night with Sally. The plot thickens.*

plow into someone or something to crash into someone or something; to bump hard into someone or something. (Also literal if one is running a plow into someone or something.) ☐ *The car plowed into the ditch.* ☐ *The runner plowed into another player.*

plow through something to work through something with determination. (Also literal.) ☐ *She plowed through the book to learn everything she could.* ☐ *Billy plowed through dinner and ran outside to play.*

pluck up one's **courage** to increase one's courage a bit. ☐ *Come on, Ann, make the dive. Pluck up your courage and do it.* ☐ *Pluck up your courage, Ann! You can do it!*

plug away (at something**)** AND **peg away (at** something**)** to keep trying something; to keep working at something. ☐ *John kept pegging away at the trumpet until he became pretty good at it.* ☐ *I'm not very good at it, but I keep plugging away.*

plug something **in** to place a plug into a receptacle. (*In* can be replaced with *into.*) ☐ *This television set won't work unless you plug it in!* 🅃 *Please plug in this lamp.*

plug something **up** to stop or fill up a hole, crack, or gap. ☐ *Take out the nail and plug the hole up with something.* 🅃 *You have to plug up the cracks to keep out the cold.*

plumb loco completely crazy. (Folksy.) □ *If you think you can stand up against Marshall Dillon, you're plumb loco.* □ *Bob is not just a little strange, he's plumb loco.*

poetic justice the appropriate but chance receiving of rewards or punishments by those deserving them. □ *It was poetic justice that Jane won the race after Mary tried to get her banned.* □ *The car thieves stole a car with no gas. That's poetic justice.*

the **point of no return** the halfway point; the point at which it is too late to turn back. (Often with *past.*) □ *The flight was past the point of no return, so we had to continue to our destination.* □ *The entire project is past the point of no return; we will have to continue with it.*

point of view a way of thinking about something; [someone's] viewpoint; an attitude or expression of self-interest. □ *From my point of view, all this talk is a waste of time.* □ *She has a strange point of view, but she has made some good observations about the problem.*

point someone or something **out** to select or indicate someone or something (from a group). □ *Everyone pointed the error out.* □ *She pointed the thief out to the police officer.* 🅃 *She pointed out the boy who took her purse.*

point something **up** to emphasize something; to demonstrate a fact. □ *I'd like to point your approach up by citing some authorities who agree with you.* 🅃 *This kind of incident points up the flaws in your system.*

point the finger at someone to blame someone; to identify someone as the guilty person. (See also **put the finger on** someone.) □ *Don't point the finger at me! I didn't take the money.* □ *The manager refused to point the finger at anyone in particular and said that everyone was sometimes guilty of being late.*

poised for something ready for something; in the right position and waiting for something. □ *The cat stared at the mouse, poised for action.* □ *The army was poised for battle.*

poised to do something ready to do something; in the right position to do something. □ *The cat is poised to jump on the mouse.* □ *The army is poised to attack at dawn.*

poke about AND **poke around** to look or search around. □ *I've been poking around in the library looking for some statistics.* □ *I don't mind if you look in my drawer for a paper clip, but please don't poke about.*

poke around Go to **poke about**.

poke fun (at someone**)** to make fun of someone; to ridicule someone. □ *Stop poking fun at me! It's not nice.* □ *Bob is always poking fun.*

poke one's **nose in(to** something**)** AND **stick** one's **nose in(to** something**)** to interfere with something; to be nosy about something. (Also literal.) □ *I wish you'd stop poking your nose into my business.* □ *She was too upset for me to stick my nose in and ask what was wrong.*

poles apart very different; far from coming to an agreement. (Preceded by *be, grow,* or *seem.*) □ *Mr. and Mrs. Jones don't get along well. They are poles apart.* □ *They'll never sign the contract because they are poles apart.*

polish something **off** to finish something off. □ *There is just a little bit of work left. It won't take any time to polish it off.* 🅃 *Bob polished off the rest of the pie.*

poop out to quit; to wear out and stop. (Slang.) □ *I'm so tired I could poop out right here.* □ *My car sounded as if it were going to poop out.*

pooped out [for a person or animal to be] exhausted. (Slang.) □ *The horse was pooped out and could run no more.* □ *I can't go on. I'm pooped out.*

poor as a church mouse Go to **(as) poor as a church mouse**.

poor but clean having little money but clean and of good habits, nonetheless. (Either extremely condescending or jocular. Some people would consider it offensive.) □ *My salary isn't very high, and I only have two color TV sets. Anyway, I'm poor but clean.* □ *When Fred uttered the phrase* poor but clean *in reference to some* *of the people working in the yard, Ellen went into a rage.*

pop off to make a wisecrack or smart-aleck remark. (Informal.) □ *If you pop off one more time, you'll have to stay after school.* □ *Bob keeps popping off at the worst times.*

pop one's **cork 1.** to suddenly become mentally disturbed; to go crazy. (Slang.) □ *I was so upset that I nearly popped my cork.* □ *They put him away because he popped his cork.* **2.** to become very angry. (Slang.) □ *My mother popped her cork when she heard about my grades.* □ *Calm down! Don't pop your cork.*

pop the question to ask someone to marry one. (Informal.) □ *I was surprised when he popped the question.* □ *I've been waiting for years for someone to pop the question.*

pop up 1. [for a baseball batter] to hit a baseball that goes upward rather than outward. □ *The catcher came to bat and popped up.* □ *I hope I don't pop up this time.* **2.** [for a baseball] to fly upward rather than outward. □ *The ball popped up and went foul.* □ *The ball will always pop up if you hit it in a certain way.* **3.** to arise suddenly; to appear without warning. □ *New problems keep popping up all the time.* □ *Billy popped up out of nowhere and scared his mother.*

a **portent of things to come** Go to a harbinger of things to come.

pose a question to ask a question; to imply the need for asking a question. □ *Genetic research poses many ethical questions.* □ *My interviewer posed a hypothetical question.*

pose as someone to pretend to be someone. □ *The impostor posed as the president of the company.* □ *My twin posed as me while I went on vacation.*

possessed by something under the control of something; obsessed with something. □ *She acted as if she were possessed by evil spirits.* □ *He was possessed by a powerful sense of guilt.*

possessed of something having something. (Formal.) □ *Bill was possessed of an enormous sense of self-worth.* □ *The Smiths were possessed of a great deal of fine ranch land.*

postage and handling charges for sending [something] through the mail and for wrapping and handling the item. (See also **shipping and handling**.) □ *The cost of the book was quite reasonable, but the postage and handling was outrageous.* □ *They did not charge postage and handling because I prepaid the order.*

the **pot calling the kettle black** [an instance of] someone with a fault accusing someone else of having the same fault. □ *Ann is always late, but she was rude enough to tell everyone when I was late. Now that's the pot calling the kettle black!* □ *You're calling me thoughtless? That's really a case of the pot calling the kettle black.*

pound a beat to walk a route. (Informal. Usually said of a police patrol officer.) □ *Officer Smith pounded the same beat for years and years.* □ *I don't want to pound a beat all my life.*

pound something **out 1.** to play something loudly on the piano. (Also literal. Slang. Compare this with **belt** something **out**.) □ *Don't pound the music out! Just play it.* 🅃 *Listen to her pound out that song.* **2.** to type something on a typewriter. (Slang.) □ *Please pound it out again. There are six errors.* 🅃 *It'll take just a few minutes to pound out this letter.*

pound the pavement to walk through the streets looking for a job. (Informal.) □ *I spent two months pounding the pavement after the factory I worked for closed.* □ *Hey, Bob. You'd better get busy pounding those nails unless you want to be out pounding the pavement.*

pour cold water on something AND **dash cold water on** something; **throw cold water on** something to discourage doing something; to reduce enthusiasm for something. □ *When my father said I couldn't have the car, he poured cold water on my plans.* □ *John threw cold water on the whole project by refusing to participate.* □ *I hate to dash cold water on your* *party, but you cannot use the house that night.*

pour it on thick Go to lay it on thick.

pour money down the drain to waste money; to spend money as if one were throwing it away. (Informal.) □ *What a waste! You're just pouring money down the drain.* □ *Don't buy any more of that low-quality merchandise. That's just throwing money down the drain.*

pour oil on troubled water(s) to calm things down. (If oil is poured onto rough seas during a storm, the water will become more calm.) □ *That was a good thing to say to John. It helped pour oil on troubled water. Now he looks happy.* □ *Bob is the kind of person who pours oil on troubled waters.*

pour one's **heart (out to** someone**)** to tell all one's hopes, fears, and feelings to someone. □ *She was so upset. She poured her heart out to Sally.* 🅃 *She sat there talking for over an hour—pouring out her heart.*

pouring rain very heavy rain. □ *The children's clothes were soaked after they played out in the pouring rain.* □ *I waited in the pouring rain for the next bus.*

the **power behind the throne** the person who controls the person who is apparently in charge. □ *Mr. Smith appears to run the shop, but his brother is the power behind the throne.* □ *They say that the vice president is the power behind the throne.*

the **powers that be** the people who are in authority. □ *The powers that be have decided to send back the immigrants.* □ *I have applied for a license, and the powers that be are considering my application.*

praise someone or something **to the skies** to give someone or something much praise. □ *He wasn't very good, but his friends praised him to the skies.* □ *They liked your pie. Everyone praised it to the skies.*

preach to the converted to praise or recommend something to someone who is already in favor of it. (Also literal.) □ *Mary was preaching to the converted when she tried to persuade Jean to become a feminist. She's been one for years.* □ *Bob found himself preaching to the converted when he was telling Jane the advantages of living in the country. She hates city life.*

precious few AND **precious little** very few; very little. (Informal. *Few* with things that are countable, otherwise, *little*.) □ *We get precious few tourists here in the winter.* □ *There's precious little food in the house and there is no money.*

precious little Go to precious few.

a **prelude to** something an act or event that comes before and signals another act or event. □ *Her rudeness to her boss was a prelude to her resignation.* □ *The invasion of Poland was a prelude to World War II.*

press one's **luck** Go to push one's luck.

press someone **to the wall** Go to push someone to the wall.

press the panic button Go to push the panic button.

pressed for time in a hurry. □ *I am sorry. I can't talk to you. I'm just too pressed for time.* □ *If you are pressed for time, you might want to stop for some food somewhere on the highway.*

pretty as a picture Go to (as) pretty as a picture.

Pretty is as pretty does. You should do pleasant things if you wish to be considered pleasant. (Proverb.) □ *Now, Sally. Let's be nice. Pretty is as pretty does.* □ *My great-aunt always used to say "pretty is as pretty does" to my sister.*

a **pretty state of affairs** AND a **fine state of affairs** an unpleasant state of affairs. (See also fine kettle of fish.) □ *This is a pretty state of affairs, and it's all your fault.* □ *What a fine state of affairs you've got us into.*

prevail (up)on someone to ask or beg someone (for a favor). □ *Can I prevail upon you to give me some help?* □ *Perhaps you could prevail on my brother for a loan.*

prick up one's **ears** to listen more closely. (Alluding to animals that move their ears about to hear better.) □ *At the sound of my voice on the telephone, my sister* *pricked up her ears.* □ *I pricked up my ears when I heard my name mentioned.*

pride and joy something or someone that one is very proud of. (Often in reference to a baby, a car, a house, etc.) □ *And this is our little pride and joy, Roger.* □ *Fred pulled up in his pride and joy and asked if I wanted a ride.*

Pride goes before a fall. Someone who behaves in an arrogant or vain way is likely to suffer misfortune. (Proverb. From the Bible.) □ *Bert was so busy admiring his reflection in a shop window that he stepped in a puddle. Pride goes before a fall.* □ *Jean was boasting about how well she thought she'd done on her final exams, but she failed them all. You know what they say. Pride goes before a fall.*

pride oneself **in** something Go to **pride** oneself **on** something.

pride oneself **on** something AND **pride** oneself **in** something to take special pride in something. □ *Ann prides herself on her apple pies.* □ *John prides himself in his ability to make people feel at ease.*

prime mover the force that sets something going; someone or something that starts something off. □ *The manager was the prime mover in getting the clerk fired.* □ *Discontent with his job was the prime mover in John's deciding to go to Alaska.*

privy to something uniquely knowledgeable about something. □ *The reporter became privy to the senator's evil plan.* □ *Why are you privy to this secret information?*

promise someone **the moon** Go to promise the moon (to someone).

promise the moon (to someone**)** AND **promise** someone **the moon** to make extravagant promises to someone. □ *Bill will promise you the moon, but he won't live up to his promises.* □ *My boss promised the moon, but only paid the minimum wage.*

prone to something likely to [do] something; apt to have something. □ *My boss is prone to fits of anger when my work isn't done.* □ *My sister is prone to sneezing because of her allergies.*

propose a toast to make a toast before drinking. □ *I'd like to propose a toast in honor of your birthday.* □ *At the wedding reception, the bride's father proposed a toast.*

proud as a peacock Go to (as) proud as a peacock.

prove to be someone or something to be shown to be someone or something; to be found to be someone or something. □ *Susan proved to be a good friend when she lent me some money.* □ *The food proved to be spoiled when I smelled it.*

provided that something is so on the condition that something is so. □ *I will come, provided that I am invited.* □ *I will help you, provided that you pay me.*

psyche out to go wild or crazy; to become irrational. (Slang. Pronounced as if it were spelled *sike*.) □ *I don't know what happened to me. Suddenly I psyched out and started yelling.* □ *Max nearly psyched out when he saw the bill.*

psyche someone **out 1.** to figure out someone psychologically. (Slang. Pronounced as if it were spelled *sike*.) □ *Don't try to psyche me out. Just be my friend.* 🅃 *I think I've psyched out my opponent so I can beat him.* **2.** to confuse someone; to cause someone to go crazy. (Slang. Pronounced as if it were spelled *sike*.) □ *All that bright light psyched me out. I couldn't think straight.* 🅃 *They psyched out the enemy soldiers, causing them to jump into the river.*

psyche someone **up** to cause someone to be enthusiastic about doing something. (Slang. Pronounced as if it were spelled *sike*.) 🅃 *The coach psyched up the team before the game.* □ *I need someone to psyche me up before I go on stage.*

psyched out confused and disoriented. (Slang. Pronounced as if it were spelled *siked*.) □ *What an upsetting day! I'm really psyched out.* □ *She is so psyched out she can't see straight.*

psyched up (for something**)** excited and enthusiastic. (Slang. Pronounced as if it were spelled *siked*.) □ *I can play a great* *tennis game if I'm psyched up.* □ *She is really psyched up for the game.*

publish or perish [for a professor] to publish many books or articles in scholarly journals or get released from a university or fall into disfavor in a university. (Also occurs as other parts of speech. See the examples below.) □ *Alice knew she would have to publish or perish if she took the teaching job.* □ *This is a major research university and publish or perish is the order of the day.* □ *When Jane heard that publish or perish was the rule at her university, she was afraid that she would not get any professors who were interested in her intellectual advancement.*

pull a boner to do something stupid or silly. (Slang.) □ *Boy, I really pulled a boner! I'm so dumb.* □ *If you pull a boner like that again, you're fired!*

pull a fast one to succeed in an act of deception. (Slang.) □ *She was pulling a fast one when she said she had a headache and went home.* □ *Don't try to pull a fast one with me! I know what you're doing.*

pull a gun (on someone**)** AND **pull a knife (on** someone**)** to bring out a gun or knife suddenly so that it is ready for use against someone. □ *I screamed when the mugger pulled a knife on me.* □ *The police shot the thief when he pulled a gun.*

pull a knife (on someone**)** Go to **pull a gun (on** someone**)**.

pull a stunt (on someone**)** AND **pull a trick (on** someone**)** to deceive someone. □ *Let's pull a trick on the teacher.* □ *Don't you dare pull a stunt like that!*

pull a trick (on someone**)** Go to **pull a stunt (on** someone**)**.

pull oneself **together** to become emotionally stabilized; to **regain** one's **composure**. □ *Now, calm down. Pull yourself together.* □ *I'll be all right as soon as I can pull myself together.*

pull oneself **up (by** one's **own bootstraps)** to achieve (something) through one's own efforts. □ *They simply don't have the resources to pull themselves up by their own bootstraps.* □ *If I could have pulled myself up, I'd have done it by now.*

pull one's **(own) weight** Go to **carry** one's **(own) weight**.

pull one's **punches 1.** [for a boxer] to strike with light blows to enable the other boxer to win. (Slang.) □ *Bill has been barred from the boxing ring for pulling his punches.* □ *"I never pulled my punches in my life!" cried Tom.* **2.** to hold back in one's criticism. (Slang. Usually in the negative. The *one's* can be replaced with *any*.) □ *I didn't pull any punches. I told her just what I thought of her.* □ *The teacher doesn't pull any punches when it comes to discipline.*

pull out all the stops to use all one's energy and effort in order to achieve something. (From the stops of a pipe organ. The more that are pulled out, the louder it gets.) □ *You'll have to pull out all the stops if you're going to pass the course.* □ *The doctors will pull out all the stops to save the child's life.*

pull rank (on someone**)** to assert one's rank, authority, or position over someone when making a request or giving an order. □ *Don't pull rank on me! I don't have to do what you say!* □ *When she couldn't get her way politely, she pulled rank and really got some action.*

pull someone or something **down 1.** [with *someone*] to degrade someone; to humiliate someone. (Also literal.) □ *I'm afraid that your friends are pulling you down. Your manners used to be much better.* □ *My bad habits are pulling me down.* 🅃 *There is no need to pull down everyone.* **2.** [with *something*] to earn a certain amount of money. (Slang.) 🅃 *She's able to pull down $400 a week.* 🅃 *I wish I could pull down a salary like that.* □ *How much is she pulling down?* **3.** [with *something*] to demolish something; to raze something. □ *Why do they want to pull it down? Why not remodel it?* 🅃 *They are going to pull down the old building today.* **4.** [with *something*] to lower or reduce the amount of something. □ *That last test pulled my grade down.* 🅃 *Let's see if we can pull down your temperature.*

pull someone's **leg** to kid, fool, or trick someone. (Informal.) □ *You don't mean that. You're just pulling my leg.* □ *Don't believe him. He's just pulling your leg.*

pull someone's or something's **teeth** to reduce the power of someone or something. (Also literal in the case of someone. Informal.) □ *The mayor tried to pull the teeth of the new law.* □ *The city council pulled the teeth of the new mayor.*

pull someone **through (**something**)** to help someone survive something. (Also literal.) □ *With the help of the doctor, we pulled her through her illness.* □ *With lots of encouragement, we pulled her through.*

pull something **off** to manage to make something happen. (Also literal. Slang. See also **carry** something **off.**) □ *Yes, I can pull it off.* 🅃 *Do you think you can pull off this deal?*

pull something on someone to play a trick on someone; to deceive someone with a trick. □ *You wouldn't pull a trick on me, would you?* □ *Who would pull something like that on an old lady?*

pull something **out of a hat** AND **pull** something **out of thin air** to produce something as if by magic. (Also literal.) □ *This is a serious problem, and we just can't pull a solution out of a hat.* □ *I'm sorry, but I don't have a pen. What do you want me to do, pull one out of thin air?*

pull something **out of thin air** Go to **pull** something **out of a hat.**

pull something **together** to organize something; to arrange something. (Compare this with **scrape** something **together.**) □ *How about a party? I'll see if I can pull something together for Friday night.* □ *This place is a mess. Please pull things together.*

pull strings to use influence (with someone to get something done). □ *I can get it done easily by pulling strings.* □ *Is it possible to get anything done around here without pulling strings?*

pull the plug (on someone or something**) 1.** to cause someone or something to end; to reduce the power or effectiveness of someone or something. (Informal.) □ *Jane pulled the plug on the whole project.* □ *The mayor was doing a fine job until the treasurer pulled the plug because there was no more money.* **2.** [with *someone*] to turn off someone's life support system in a hospital. (This results in the death of person whose life support has been terminated.) □ *They had to get a court order to pull the plug on their father.* □ *Fred signed a living will making it possible to pull the plug on him without a court order.*

pull the rug out (from under someone**)** to make someone ineffective. (Also literal.) □ *The treasurer pulled the rug out from under the mayor.* □ *Things were going along fine until the treasurer pulled the rug out.*

pull the wool over someone's **eyes** to deceive someone. □ *You can't pull the wool over my eyes. I know what's going on.* □ *Don't try to pull the wool over her eyes. She's too smart.*

pull through to get better; to recover from a serious illness or other problem. □ *She's very ill, but I think she'll pull through.* □ *Oh, I hope she pulls through.*

pull up (somewhere**)** Go to **haul up** (somewhere).

pull up stakes to move to another place. (Refers to pulling up tent stakes and moving to another campsite.) □ *I've been here long enough. It's time to pull up stakes.* □ *I hate the thought of having to pull up stakes.*

punch a hole in something to make a hole in something with something. □ *John punched a hole in the wall with his fist.* □ *Mary punched a hole in the paper with her pencil.*

pure and simple AND **plain and simple** absolutely; without further complication or elaboration. (Informal.) □ *I told you what you must do, and you must do it, pure and simple.* □ *Will you kindly explain to me what it is, pure and simple, that I am expected to do?* □ *Just tell me plain and simple, do you intend to go or don't you?* □ *I explained it to her plain and simple, but she still didn't understand.*

pure as the driven snow Go to **(as) pure as the driven snow.**

push off to go away. (Informal.) □ *We told the children to push off.* □ *Push off! We don't want you here.*

push one's **luck** AND **press** one's **luck** to expect continued good fortune; to expect to continue to escape bad luck. □ *You're okay so far, but don't push your luck.* □ *Bob pressed his luck too much and got into a lot of trouble.*

push someone **to the wall** AND **press** someone **to the wall** to force someone into a position where there is only one choice to make; to put someone in a defensive position. (Also literal.) □ *There was little else I could do. They pushed me to the wall.* □ *When we pressed him to the wall, he told us where the cookies were hidden.*

push the panic button AND **press the panic button** to panic; to become anxious or panicky. (Also literal. Slang.) □ *I do okay taking tests as long as I don't push the panic button.* □ *Whatever you do, don't press the panic button.*

pushing up daisies dead and buried. (Folksy.) □ *If you don't drive safely, you'll be pushing up daisies.* □ *We'll all be pushing up daisies in the long run.*

put a bee in someone's **bonnet** to give someone an idea (about something). (See also **get a bee in** one's **bonnet.**) □ *Somebody put a bee in my bonnet that we should go to a movie.* □ *Who put a bee in your bonnet?*

put a cap on something to put a limit on something (Also literal.) □ *We need to put a cap on spending on every department.* □ *The city put a cap on the amount each landlord could charge.*

put a hold on something place a restriction on something to show that it is reserved, delayed, or inactivated. □ *The bank put a hold on my credit card until I paid my bill.* □ *The committee agreed to put a hold on the troublesome piece of business.*

put all one's **eggs in one basket** to risk everything at once. (Also literal. Often negative.) □ *Don't put all your eggs in one basket. Then everything won't be lost if there is a catastrophe.* □ *John only applied to the one college he wanted to go to. He put all his eggs in one basket.*

put an end to something Go to **put a stop to** something.

put a spin on something to interpret an event to make it seem favorable or beneficial to oneself. □ *The mayor tried to put a positive spin on the damaging polls.* □ *The pundit's spin on the new legislation was highly critical.*

put a stop to something AND **put an end to** something to bring something to an end. □ *I want you to put a stop to all this bad behavior.* □ *Please put an end to this conversation.*

put ideas into someone's **head** to suggest something—usually something bad—to someone (who would not have thought of it otherwise). □ *Bill keeps getting into trouble. Please don't put ideas into his head.* □ *Bob would get along all right if other kids didn't put ideas into his head.*

put in a good word (for someone**)** to say something (to someone) in support of someone. □ *I hope you get the job. I'll put in a good word for you.* □ *Yes, I want the job. If you see the boss, please put in a good word.*

put in an appearance to appear (somewhere) for just a little while. (Compare this with **make an appearance.**) □ *I couldn't stay for the whole party, so I just put in an appearance and left.* □ *Even if you can't stay for the whole thing, at least put in an appearance.*

put off by someone or something distressed or repelled by someone or something. □ *I was really put off by your behavior.* □ *We were all put off by the unfairness of the rules.*

put on to pretend; to act as if something were true. □ *Ann wasn't really angry. She was just putting on.* □ *I can't believe she was just putting on. She really looked mad.*

put on a brave face to try to appear happy or satisfied when faced with misfortune or danger. □ *We've lost all our money, but* *we must put on a brave face for the sake of the children.* ☐ *Jim has lost his job and is worried, but he's putting on a brave face.*

put on a (brave) front Go to put up a (brave) front.

put on airs to act superior. ☐ *Stop putting on airs. You're just human like the rest of us.* ☐ *Ann is always putting on airs. You'd think she was a queen.*

put on an act to pretend that one is something other than what one is. (See also put on.) ☐ *Be yourself, Ann. Stop putting on an act.* ☐ *You don't have to put on an act. We accept you the way you are.*

put one **in** one's **place** to rebuke someone; to remind one of one's (lower) rank or station. ☐ *The boss put me in my place for criticizing her.* ☐ *Then her boss put her in her place for being rude.*

put one's **back (in)to** something **1.** to apply great physical effort to lift or move something. ☐ *All right, you guys. Put your backs into moving this piano.* ☐ *You can lift it if you put your back to it.* **2.** to apply a lot of mental or creative effort to doing something. ☐ *If we put our backs to it, we can bake twelve dozen cookies today.* ☐ *The artist put his back into finishing the picture on time.*

put one's **best foot forward** to act or appear at one's best; to try to make a good impression. ☐ *When you apply for a job, you should always put your best foot forward.* ☐ *I try to put my best foot forward whenever I meet someone for the first time.*

put one's **cards on the table** AND **lay** one's **cards on the table** to reveal everything; to be open and honest with someone. (Also literal. Informal.) ☐ *Come on, John, lay your cards on the table. Tell me what you really think.* ☐ *Why don't we both put our cards on the table?*

put (one's**) dibs on** something to lay a claim to something; to state one's claim to something. (Informal. See also have dibs on something.) ☐ *I put dibs on the last piece of cake.* ☐ *Mary put her dibs on the book you are reading. She gets it next.*

put oneself **in** someone else's **place** AND **put** oneself **in** someone else's **shoes** to allow oneself to see or experience something from someone else's point of view. (See also in someone else's place; in someone else's shoes.) ☐ *Put yourself in someone else's place, and see how it feels.* ☐ *I put myself in Tom's shoes and realized that I would have made exactly the same choice.*

put oneself **in** someone else's **shoes** Go to put oneself in someone else's place.

put one's **finger on** something to identify something as very important. (Also literal. Informal.) ☐ *Ann put her finger on the cause of the problem.* ☐ *Yes, she really put her finger on it.*

put one's **foot down (about** something**)** to become adamant about something. (Informal.) ☐ *Ann put her foot down about what kind of car she wanted.* ☐ *She doesn't put her foot down very often, but when she does, she really means it.*

put one's **foot in it** Go to put one's foot in one's mouth.

put one's **foot in** one's **mouth** AND **put** one's **foot in it; stick** one's **foot in** one's **mouth** to say something that you regret; to say something stupid, insulting, or hurtful. ☐ *When I told Ann that her hair was more beautiful than I had ever seen it, I really put my foot in my mouth. It was a wig.* ☐ *I put my foot in it by telling John's secret.*

put one's **hand(s) on** something to locate and acquire something. (Compare this with get one's hands on someone or something.) ☐ *I wish I could put my hands on a 1954 Chevrolet.* ☐ *If I could put my hands on that book, I could find the information I need.*

put one's **hand to the plow** to begin to do a big and important task; to undertake a major effort. (Also literal.) ☐ *If John would only put his hand to the plow, he could do an excellent job.* ☐ *You'll never accomplish anything if you don't put your hand to the plow.*

put one's **head on the block (for** someone or something**)** to take great risks for someone or something; to go to a lot of trouble or difficulty for someone or something; to attempt to gain favor for someone or something. (Also literal.) □ *I don't know why I should put my head on the block for Joan. What has she ever done for me?* □ *Sally tried to get me to put in a good word about her with the boss. You know, tell the boss what a great worker she is and how smart she is. The last time I put my head on the block for anyone, it all backfired, and when the person goofed up, I looked like an idiot!*

put one's **house in order** to put one's business or personal affairs into good order. (Also literal.) □ *There was some trouble at work and the manager was told to put his house in order.* □ *Every now and then, I have to put my house in order. Then life becomes more manageable.*

put one's **mind to** something to give one's complete attention to something. □ *I could finish this job tonight if I put my mind to it.* □ *Please put your mind to it and concentrate on getting it finished.*

put one's **nose to the grindstone** to keep busy doing one's work. (Also with *have* and *get,* as in the examples. See also **keep** one's **nose to the grindstone.**) □ *The boss told me to put my nose to the grindstone.* □ *I've had my nose to the grindstone ever since I started working here.* □ *If the other people in this office would get their noses to the grindstone, more work would get done.*

put one's **oar in** to give help; to interfere by giving advice; to **put** one's **two cents' worth in.** (Refers to adding one's efforts to rowing a boat.) □ *You don't need to put your oar in. I don't need your advice.* Ⓣ *I'm sorry. I shouldn't have put in my oar.*

put one's **shoulder to the wheel** to get busy. □ *You won't accomplish anything unless you put your shoulder to the wheel.* □ *I put my shoulder to the wheel and finished the job quickly.*

put one's **thinking cap on** to start thinking in a serious manner. (Usually used with children.) □ *It's time to put our thinking caps on, children.* Ⓣ *All right now, let's put on our thinking caps and do some arithmetic.*

put one's **two cents(' worth) in** to add one's comments (to something). (Informal.) Ⓣ *Can I put in my two cents' worth?* □ *Sure, go ahead—put your two cents in.*

put one **through** one's **paces** to make one demonstrate what one can do; to make one do one's job thoroughly. (See also **put** something **through its paces.**) □ *The boss really put me through my paces today. I'm tired.* □ *I tried out for a part in the play, and the director really put me through my paces.*

put on the dog to dress or entertain in an extravagant or showy manner. (Informal.) □ *The Smiths really put on the dog at their party last Saturday.* □ *They're always putting on the dog.*

put on the feed bag to eat a meal. (Literal with horses. Folksy and slang.) □ *It's noon—time to put on the feed bag.* □ *I didn't put on the feed bag until about eight o'clock last night.*

put out (about someone or something**)** irritated; bothered. □ *John behaved rudely at the party, and the hostess was quite put out.* □ *Liz was quite put out about the question.*

put out (some) feelers to attempt to find out something without being too obvious. (Refers to what an insect does to sense what is happening around it.) □ *I wanted to get a new job, so I put out some feelers.* □ *The manager was mean to everyone in the office, so everyone put out feelers in an attempt to find new jobs.*

put someone **away 1.** to kill someone. (Also literal. Slang.) □ *The gangster threatened to put me away if I told the police.* Ⓣ *They've put away witnesses in the past.* **2.** to bury someone. □ *My uncle died last week. They put him away on Saturday.* **3.** to have someone put into a mental institution. □ *My uncle became irrational, and they put him away.* Ⓣ *They put away my aunt the year before.*

put someone **down as** something bad to judge that someone is bad or undesirable in some way. (See also **put** someone or something **down.**) □ *He was so rude that I put him down as someone to be avoided.* □ *If* *you act silly all the time, people will put you down as a fool.*

put someone **down (for** something**)** to put someone's name on a list of people who volunteer to do something or give an amount of money. □ *Can I put you down for ten dollars?* □ *We're having a picnic, and you're invited. Everyone is bringing something. Can I put you down for potato salad?*

put someone **in the picture** to give someone all the necessary facts about something. (Literal for a painter or digital graphics artist.) □ *They put the police in the picture about how the accident happened.* □ *Would someone put me in the picture about what went on in my absence?*

put someone **off 1.** to avoid responding to someone; to delay a response to someone. □ *I keep asking her, but she just keeps putting me off.* □ *Don't put me off again. Answer me now!* **2.** to repel someone; to make someone feel uneasy. □ *Your bad attitude puts people off.*

put someone **on** to tease or deceive someone. (Slang.) □ *Oh, you're not serious. You're putting me on.* □ *Stop putting me on!*

put someone **on a pedestal** to respect, admire, or worship a person. □ *He has put her on a pedestal and thinks she can do no wrong.* □ *Don't put me on a pedestal. I'm only human.*

put someone **on the spot** to ask someone embarrassing questions; to demand that someone produce as expected. □ *Don't put me on the spot. I can't give you an answer.* □ *The boss put Bob on the spot and demanded that he do everything he had promised.*

put someone or something **across** AND **get** someone or something **across 1.** [with *someone*] to present someone in a good way or a good light. □ *I don't want Tom to make the speech. He doesn't put himself across well.* □ *I get myself across in situations like this. I'll do it.* **2.** to make a clear explanation of something; to explain oneself clearly. □ *The teacher got the idea across with the help of pictures.* □ *I'm taking a course in public speaking to help put myself across better.* **3.** [with *something*] to convince someone of something; to get a plan accepted. □ *After many weeks of trying, we were unable to put our plan across. They refused to accept it.* □ *We just couldn't get it across.*

put someone or something **at** someone's **disposal** to make someone or something available to someone; to offer someone or something to someone. □ *I'd be glad to help you if you need me. I put myself at your disposal.* □ *I put my car at my neighbor's disposal.*

put someone or something **down 1.** to belittle or degrade someone or something. (Slang.) □ *It's an old car, but that's no reason to put it down.* □ *Please stop putting me down all the time. It hurts my feelings.* 🅃 *You put down everything you don't understand!* **2.** [with *something*] to repress or (figuratively) crush something. 🅃 *The army was called to put down the rebellion.* □ *The police used tear gas to put the riot down.* **3.** [with *something*] to write something down. □ *I'll give you the address. Please put it down.* 🅃 *I'll put down the address in my address book.* **4.** [with *something*] to land an aircraft. □ *The pilot put the plane down exactly on time.* 🅃 *I can't put down this plane in the rain.* **5.** [with *something*] to take the life of an animal, such as a pet that is suffering. (This is usually done by a veterinarian.) □ *We had to put our dog down. She was suffering so.* □ *It's very difficult to put down one's pet.*

put someone or something **off 1.** [with *someone*] to divert or avoid someone. □ *I don't wish to see Mr. Brown now. Please put him off.* □ *I won't talk to reporters. Tell them something that will put them off.* 🅃 *Put off those annoying people.* **2.** [with *someone*] to upset or distress someone. □ *She always puts me off. She's so rude.* 🅃 *I try not to put off people.* **3.** [with *something*] to delay something; to postpone something. 🅃 *I had to put off my appointment with the doctor.* □ *It's raining, so we'll have to put the picnic off.*

put someone or something **on hold 1.** [with *someone*] to stop all activity or communication with someone. (See also **on hold.**) ☐ *John put Ann on hold and started dating Mary.* ☐ *"You can't just put me on hold!" cried Ann.* **2.** [with *someone*] to leave someone waiting on a telephone call. (See also **on hold.**) ☐ *Please don't put me on hold. I'll call back later when you aren't so busy.* ☐ *I'll have to put you on hold while I look up the information.* **3.** [with *something*] to postpone something; to stop the progress of something. (See also **on hold.**) ☐ *They put the project on hold until they got enough money to finish it.* ☐ *Sorry, but we must put your plan on hold.*

put someone or something **out 1.** [with *something*] to extinguish something. 🅃 *Put out the fire before you go to bed.* ☐ *My grandfather told me to put out the light and go to bed.* **2.** [with *someone*] to distress or inconvenience someone. ☐ *I'd like to have a ride home, but not if it puts you out.* 🅃 *Don't worry. It won't put out anybody.* **3.** [with *something*] to publish something. ☐ *They are putting the book out next month.* 🅃 *When did you put out the article?* **4.** [with *someone*] to make someone "out" in baseball. ☐ *The pitcher put the runner out.* 🅃 *I thought the catcher put out the runner.*

put someone or something **out of** one's **mind** to forget someone or something; to make an effort to stop thinking about someone or something. (Almost the same as **get** someone or something **out of** one's **mind.**) ☐ *Try to put it out of your mind.* ☐ *I can't seem to put him out of my mind.*

put someone or something **out to pasture** to retire someone or something. (Refers to a horse that is too old to work.) ☐ *Please don't put me out to pasture. I have lots of good years left.* ☐ *This car has reached the end of the line. It's time to put it out to pasture.*

put someone or something **to bed 1.** [with *someone*] to help someone—usually a child—get into a bed. ☐ *Come on, Billy, it's time for me to put you to bed.* ☐ *I want Grandpa to put me to bed.* **2.** [with *something*] to complete work on something and send it on to the next step in production, especially in publishing. ☐ *This edition is finished. Let's put it to bed.* ☐ *Finish the editing of this book and put it to bed.*

put someone or something **to sleep 1.** to kill someone or something. (Euphemistic.) ☐ *We had to put our dog to sleep.* ☐ *The robber said he'd put us to sleep forever if we didn't cooperate.* **2.** to cause someone or something to sleep, perhaps through drugs or anesthesia. ☐ *The doctor put the patient to sleep before the operation.* ☐ *I put the cat to sleep by stroking its tummy.* **3.** [with *someone*] to bore someone. ☐ *That dull lecture put me to sleep.* ☐ *Her long story almost put me to sleep.*

put someone or something **to the test** to see what someone or something can achieve. ☐ *I think I can jump that far, but no one has ever put me to the test.* ☐ *I'm going to put my car to the test right now, and see how fast it will go.*

put someone or something **up 1.** [with *someone*] to provide lodging for someone. ☐ *I hope I can find someone to put me up.* 🅃 *They were able to put up John for the night.* **2.** [with *something*] to preserve and store food by canning or freezing. ☐ *This year we'll put some strawberries up.* 🅃 *We put up a lot of food every year.* **3.** [with *something*] to offer something, such as an idea. ☐ *We need a better idea. Who'll put one up?* 🅃 *Let me put up a different idea.* **4.** [with *someone*] to run someone as a candidate. ☐ *I think you should put someone else up.* 🅃 *We're putting up Ann for treasurer.* **5.** [with *something*] to build a building, a sign, a fence, a wall, etc. ☐ *We'll put a garage up next month.* 🅃 *The city put up a fence next to our house.* **6.** [with *something*] to provide the money for something. ☐ *The government put the money up for the cost of construction.* 🅃 *Who will put up the money for my education?* **7.** [with *something*] to shape and arrange one's hair (with curlers, hairpins, etc.). ☐ *I can't go out because I just put my hair up.* 🅃 *I put up my hair every night.* **8.** [with *something*] to make a struggle, a fight, etc. (Usually *put up something,* and not *put* *something up.)* 🅃 *Did he put up a fight?* 🅃 *No, he only put up a bit of a struggle.*

put someone's **eye out** to puncture or harm someone's eye causing blindness. □ *Careful with that stick or you'll put your eye out.* □ *He fell and almost put his eye out!*

put someone's **nose out of joint** to offend someone; to cause someone to feel slighted or insulted. (Informal.) □ *I'm afraid I put his nose out of joint by not inviting him to the picnic.* □ *There is no reason to put your nose out of joint. I meant no harm.*

put someone **through the wringer** to give someone a difficult time. (Informal.) □ *They are really putting me through the wringer at school.* □ *The boss put Bob through the wringer over this contract.*

put someone **to bed with a shovel** to kill someone; to kill and bury someone. (Slang.) □ *That guy'd better be careful, or somebody's going to put him to bed with a shovel.* □ *"Watch out, wise guy," said the robber, "or I'll put you to bed with a shovel."*

put someone **to shame** to show someone up; to embarrass someone; to make someone ashamed. □ *Your excellent efforts put us all to shame.* □ *I put him to shame by telling everyone about his bad behavior.*

put someone **up to** something to cause someone to do something; to bribe someone to do something; to give someone the idea of doing something. □ *Who put you up to it?* □ *Nobody put me up to it. I thought it up myself.*

put someone **wise to** someone or something to inform someone about someone or something. (Informal.) □ *I put her wise to the way we do things around here.* □ *I didn't know she was taking money. Mary put me wise to her.*

put some teeth into something to increase the power of something. □ *The mayor tried to put some teeth into the new law.* □ *The statement is too weak. Put some teeth in to it.*

put something **by** AND **lay** something **by** to reserve a portion of something; to preserve and store something, such as food. (Folksy.) □ *I put some money by for a rainy day.* □ *I laid some eggs by for our use tomorrow.*

put something **down in black and white** to write down the terms of an agreement; to draw up a written contract; to put the details of something down on paper. (Refers to black ink and white paper.) □ *We agree on all the major points. Now, let's put it down in black and white.* □ *I think I understand what you are talking about, but we need to put it down in black and white.*

put something **down to** something AND **set** something **down to** something to explain something as being caused by something else. □ *I put his bad humor down to his illness.* □ *We set your failure down to your emotional upset.*

put something **forward** to state an idea; to advance an idea. (Also literal.) □ *Toward the end of the meeting, Sally put an idea forward.* □ *Now, I'd like to put something forward.* 🅃 *He put several suggestions forward.*

put something **in 1.** to submit something. (Also literal.) □ *In fact, I put the order in some time ago.* 🅃 *I put in a request for a new typewriter.* **2.** to spend an amount of time (doing something). □ *You put how much time in?* 🅃 *I put in four months on that project.*

put something **in mothballs** to put something in storage. (Also literal in reference to clothing. Often said of battleships.) □ *The navy put the old cruiser in mothballs and no one ever expected to see it again.* □ *Let's just put this small bicycle in mothballs until we hear of a child who can use it.*

put something **into practice** to start using a scheme or plan. □ *I hope we can put your idea into practice soon.* □ *The mayor hopes to put the new plan into practice after the next election.*

put something **into print** to have something printed and published. □ *It's true, but I never believed you'd put it into print.* □ *This is a very interesting story. I can't wait to put it into print.*

put something **into words** to state or utter a thought; to find a way to express a feeling with words. ☐ *I can hardly put my gratitude into words.* ☐ *John has a hard time putting his feelings into words.*

put something **off** to postpone something; to schedule something for a later time. ☐ *I have to put off our meeting until a later time.* ☐ *I put off a visit to the dentist as long as I could.*

put something **on** to place clothing onto one's body; to get into a piece of clothing. ☐ *I put on a heavy coat to go outside in the cold.* ☐ *Please put this on and see if it fits.*

put something **on ice** AND **put** something **on the back burner** to delay or postpone something; to put something on hold. (Also literal.) ☐ *I'm afraid that we'll have to put your project on ice for a while.* ☐ *Just put your idea on ice and keep it there till we get some money.*

put something **on paper** to write something down; to type or otherwise record something important. ☐ *You have a great idea for a novel. Now put it on paper.* ☐ *I'm sorry, I can't discuss your offer until I see something in writing. Put it on paper, and then we'll talk.*

put something **on the back burner** Go to **put** something **on ice.**

put something **on the cuff** to buy something on credit; to add to one's credit balance. ☐ *I'll take two of those, and please put them on the cuff.* ☐ *I'm sorry, Tom. We can't put anything more on the cuff.*

put something **on the line** AND **lay** something **on the line** to speak very firmly and directly about something. ☐ *She was very mad. She put it on the line, and we had no doubt about what she meant.* ☐ *All right, you kids. I'm going to lay it on the line. Don't ever do that again if you know what's good for you.*

put something **over** to accomplish something; to put something across. ☐ *This is a very hard thing to explain to a large audience. I hope I can put it over.* ☐ *This is a big request for money. I go before the board of directors this afternoon, and I hope I can put it over.*

put something **over (on** someone**)** to manage to trick or deceive someone. ☐ *They really put one over on me.* ☐ *It's easy to put something over if you plan carefully.*

put something **plainly** to state something firmly and explicitly. ☐ *To put it plainly, I want you out of this house immediately.* ☐ *Thank you. I think you've put your feelings quite plainly.*

put something **right** Go to **set** something **right.**

put something **straight** AND **set** something **straight** to clarify something; to straighten something out. ☐ *He has made such a mess of this report. It'll take hours to put it straight.* ☐ *I'm sorry I confused you. Let me set it straight.*

put something **through its paces** to demonstrate how well something operates; to demonstrate all the things something can do. (Compare this with **put** one **through** one's **paces.**) ☐ *I was down by the barn, watching Sally put her horse through its paces.* ☐ *This is an excellent can opener. Watch me put it through its paces.*

put something **together** to consider some facts and arrive at a conclusion. (Also literal.) ☐ *I couldn't put everything together to figure out the answer in time.* 🅃 *When I put together all the facts, I found the answer.*

put something **to (good) use** to use something. ☐ *This is a very nice present. I'm sure I'll put it to good use.* ☐ *I hope you can put these old clothes to use.*

put something **to rest** AND **lay** something **to rest** to put an end to a rumor; to finish dealing with something and forget about it. (Also literal.) ☐ *I've heard enough about Ann and her illness. I'd like to put the whole matter to rest.* ☐ *I'll be happy to lay it to rest, but will Jane?*

Put that in your pipe and smoke it! See how you like that!; It is final, and you have to live with it! ☐ *Well, I'm not going to do it, so put that in your pipe and smoke it!* ☐ *I'm sick of you, and I'm leaving. Put that in your pipe and smoke it!*

put the arm on someone to apply pressure to someone. (Slang.) ☐ *John's been* *putting the arm on Mary to get her to go out with him.* □ *John has been putting the arm on Bill to get him to cooperate.*

put the bite on someone AND **put the touch on** someone to try to get money from someone. (Slang.) □ *Tom put the bite on me for ten dollars.* □ *Bill put the touch on me, but I told him to drop dead.*

put the blame on someone or something AND **lay the blame on** someone or something; **place the blame on** someone or something to blame someone or something. □ *Don't put the blame on me. I didn't do it.* □ *We'll have to place the blame for the damage on the storm.*

put the cart before the horse to have things in the wrong order; to have things confused and mixed up. (Also with *have*.) □ *You're eating your dessert! You've put the cart before the horse.* □ *Slow down and get organized. Don't put the cart before the horse!* □ *John has the cart before the horse in most of his projects.*

put the clamps on (someone**)** to restrain or restrict someone. (Slang.) □ *Tom's parents put the clamps on him. They decided he was getting out of hand.* [T] *They got mad and put on the clamps.*

put the finger on someone AND **lay the finger on** someone to accuse someone; to identify someone as the one who did something. (Slang. See also point the finger at someone.) □ *Tom put the finger on John, and John is really mad.* □ *He'd better not lay the finger on me. I didn't do it.*

put the heat on (someone**)** AND **put the screws on (**someone**); put the squeeze on (**someone**)** to put pressure on someone (to do something); to coerce someone. (Slang.) □ *John wouldn't talk, so the police were putting the heat on him to confess.* □ *When they put the screws on, they can be very unpleasant.* □ *The police know how to put the squeeze on.*

put the kibosh on something to put an end to something; to veto something. (Slang.) □ *The mayor put the kibosh on the project.* □ *It's a great idea, and I'm sorry that I had to put the kibosh on it.*

put the screws on (someone**)** Go to put the heat on (someone).

put the skids on (something**)** to cause something to fail. (Slang.) □ *They put the skids on the project when they refused to give us any more money.* □ *That's the end of our great idea! Somebody put the skids on.*

put the squeeze on (someone**)** Go to put the heat on (someone).

put the touch on someone Go to put the bite on someone.

put to it in trouble or difficulty; hard up (for something such as money). (Slang.) □ *I'm in big trouble. I'm really put to it.* □ *John was put to it to get there on time.*

put two and two together to figure something out from the information available. (Also literal.) □ *Well, I put two and two together and came up with an idea of who did it.* □ *Don't worry. John won't figure it out. He can't put two and two together.*

put up a (brave) front AND **put on a (brave) front** to appear to be brave (even if one is not). □ *Mary is frightened, but she's putting up a brave front.* □ *If she weren't putting on a front, I'd be more frightened than I am.*

put upon by someone to be made use of to an unreasonable degree. (Typically passive.) □ *My mother was always put upon by her neighbors. She was too nice to refuse their requests for help.* □ *Jane feels put upon by her husband's parents.* □ *They're always coming to stay with her.*

Put up or shut up! 1. <a command to prove something or stop talking about it; to do something or stop promising to do it.> (Slang.) □ *I'm tired of your telling everyone how fast you can run. Now, do it! Put up or shut up!* □ *Now's your chance to show us that you can run as fast as you can talk. Put up or shut up!* **2.** <a command to bet money in support of what one advocates.> (See also Put your money where your mouth is!) □ *If you think that your horse is faster than mine, then make a bet. Put up or shut up!* □ *You think you can beat me at cards? Twenty bucks says you're wrong. Put up or shut up!*

put up with someone or something to endure someone or something. □ *I can't put up with you anymore. I'm leaving.* □ *She couldn't put up with the smell, so she opened the window.*

put weight on to gain weight; to grow fat. □ *I have to go on a diet because I've been putting on a little weight lately.* 🅃 *The doctor says I need to put on some weight.*

put words into someone's **mouth** to speak for another person without permission. □ *Stop putting words into my mouth. I can speak for myself.* □ *The lawyer was scolded for putting words into the witness's mouth.*

Put your money where your mouth is! <a command to stop talking big and make a bet.> □ *I'm tired of your bragging about your skill at betting. Put your money where your mouth is!* □ *You talk about betting, but you don't bet. Put your money where your mouth is!*

putty in someone's **hands** easily influenced by someone else; excessively willing to do what someone else wishes. □ *Bob's wife is putty in his hands. She never thinks for herself.* □ *Jane's putty in her mother's hands. She always does exactly what she is told.*

puzzle something **out** to figure something out; to try to figure something out. □ *I looked and looked at it, but I couldn't puzzle it out.* 🅃 *See if you can puzzle out this confusing mess.*

Q

quake in one's **boots** Go to shake in one's boots.

queer as a three-dollar bill Go to (as) queer as a three-dollar bill.

quick and dirty [done] fast and carelessly; [done] fast and cheaply. □ *I am not interested in a quick and dirty job. I want it done right.* □ *The contractor made a lot of money on quick and dirty projects that would never last very long.*

quick as a flash Go to (as) quick as a wink.

quick as a wink Go to (as) quick as a wink.

quick as greased lightning Go to (as) quick as greased lightning.

quick on the draw Go to quick on the trigger.

quick on the trigger AND **quick on the draw 1.** quick to draw a gun and shoot. (Informal.) □ *Some of the old cowboys were known to be quick on the trigger.* □ *Wyatt Earp was particularly quick on the draw.* **2.** quick to respond to anything. (Informal.) □ *John gets the right answer before anyone else. He's really quick on the trigger.* □ *Sally will probably win the quiz game. She's really quick on the draw.*

quick on the uptake quick to understand (something). □ *Just because I'm not quick on the uptake, it doesn't mean I'm stupid.* □ *Mary understands jokes before anyone else because she's so quick on the uptake.*

quiet as a mouse Go to (as) quiet as a mouse.

quiet as the grave Go to (as) quiet as the grave.

quite a bit AND **quite a few; quite a little; quite a lot; quite a number** much or many. □ *Do you need one? I have quite a few.* □ *I have quite a little—enough to spare some.* □ *How many? Oh, quite a number.*

quite a few Go to quite a bit.

quite a little Go to quite a bit.

quite a lot Go to quite a bit.

quite a number Go to quite a bit.

quite a something definitely [something]; a good example of [something]. □ *The captain of the swim team is quite a swimmer.* □ *That's quite a bruise you have there.*

quote a price to name or state in advance the charge for doing or supplying something. □ *The mechanic quoted a price of $100 to repair my car.* □ *The carpenter quoted a price for fixing up the stairs.*

R

race against time 1. a rush; rushing to beat a deadline. □ *We were in a race against time to beat the deadline.* □ *It was a race against time, but we made it.* **2.** to hurry to beat a deadline. □ *We had to race against time to finish before the deadline.* □ *You don't need to race against time. Take all the time you want.*

rack one's **brain(s)** to try very hard to think of something. (Informal.) □ *I racked my brains all afternoon, but couldn't remember where I put the book.* □ *Don't waste any more time racking your brain. Go borrow the book from the library.*

racked with pain suffering from severe pain. □ *My body was racked with pain, and I nearly passed out.* □ *I sat there racked with pain, waiting for the doctor.*

rail at someone **(about** something**)** to complain loudly or violently to someone about something. □ *Jane railed at the treasurer about not having received her check.* □ *I am not responsible for your problems. Don't rail at me!*

rain cats and dogs to rain very hard. □ *It's raining cats and dogs. Look at it pour!* □ *I'm not going out in that storm. It's raining cats and dogs.*

rain on someone's **parade** to ruin someone's planned event; to spoil someone's plans or scheme. (Informal.) □ *I hate to rain on your parade, but the guest of honor cannot come to the reception.* □ *The boss rained on our parade by making us all work overtime.*

rain or shine no matter whether it rains or the sun shines. □ *Don't worry. I'll be there rain or shine.* □ *We'll hold the picnic—rain or shine.*

rain something **out** [for the weather] to spoil something by raining. □ *Oh, the weather looks awful. I hope it doesn't rain the picnic out.* 🅃 *It's starting to sprinkle now. Do you think it will rain out the ball game?*

raise a hand (against someone or something**)** Go to **lift a hand (against** someone or something**)**.

raise (an) objection (to someone or something**)** to mention an objection about someone or something. □ *I hope your family won't raise an objection to my staying for dinner.* □ *I'm certain no one will raise objection. We are delighted to have you.*

raise a stink (about something**)** Go to **create a stink (about** something**)**.

raise cain (with someone or something**)** Go to **raise the devil (with** someone or something**)**.

raise havoc with someone or something AND **play havoc with** someone or something to create confusion or disruption for or among someone or something. □ *Your announcement raised havoc with the students.* □ *I didn't mean to play havoc with them.*

raise hell (with someone or something**)** Go to **raise the devil (with** someone or something**)**.

raise hob with someone or something AND **play hob with** someone or something to do something devilish to someone or something; to cause trouble for someone or something. (A *hob* is a hobgoblin, a wicked little elf.) □ *Your sudden arrival is going to play hob with my dinner plans.* □ *Sorry, I didn't mean to raise hob with you.*

raise one's **sights** to set higher goals for oneself. □ *When you're young, you tend to* *raise your sights too high.* ☐ *On the other hand, some people need to raise their sights.*

raise one's **voice (to** someone**)** to speak loudly or shout at someone in anger. ☐ *Don't you dare raise your voice to me!* ☐ *I'm sorry. I didn't mean to raise my voice.*

raise some eyebrows to shock or surprise people mildly (by doing or saying something). (*Some* can be replaced with *a few, someone's, a lot of,* etc.) ☐ *What you just said may raise some eyebrows, but it shouldn't make anyone really angry.* ☐ *John's sudden marriage to Ann raised a few eyebrows.*

raise the devil (with someone or something**)** AND **raise hell (with** someone or something**); raise cain (with** someone or something**); raise the dickens (with** someone or something**)** to act in some extreme manner; to make trouble; to behave wildly; to be very angry. (Informal. Use caution with *hell.*) ☐ *John was out all night raising the devil.* ☐ *Don't come around here and raise hell with everybody.* ☐ *That cheap gas I bought really raised the dickens with my car's engine.*

raise the dickens (with someone or something**)** Go to raise the devil (with someone or something).

raised in a barn brought up to behave like a barnyard animal; behaving crudely. (Folksy.) ☐ *Close the door behind you! Were you raised in a barn?* ☐ *Don't wipe your nose on your sleeve. Were you raised in a barn?*

rake someone **over the coals** AND **haul** someone **over the coals** to give someone a severe scolding. ☐ *My mother hauled me over the coals for coming in late last night.* ☐ *The manager raked me over the coals for being late again.*

rake something **off** to steal or embezzle a portion of a payment. (Also literal. Slang.) ☐ *They claimed that no one was raking anything off and that the money was only mislaid.* 🅃 *The county treasurer was caught raking off some of the tax money.*

rake something **up** AND **dredge** something **up** to uncover something unpleasant and remind people about it. (Also literal.) ☐ *The young journalist raked up the old scandal about the president.* 🅃 *The politician's opponents are trying to dredge up some unpleasant details about his past.*

rally (a)round someone or something to come together to support someone or something. ☐ *Everyone rallied around Jack when he lost his job.* ☐ *Former students rallied round their college when it was in danger of being closed.*

ram someone or something **down** someone's **throat** Go to shove someone or something down someone's throat.

ramble on (about someone or something**)** to talk aimlessly about someone or something. ☐ *John is so talkative. He's always rambling on about something.* ☐ *You're rambling on yourself.*

rank and file 1. regular soldiers, not the officers. ☐ *I think there is some trouble with the rank and file, sir.* ☐ *The rank and file usually do exactly as they are told.* **2.** the members of a group, not the leaders. ☐ *The rank and file will vote on the proposed contract tomorrow.* ☐ *The last contract was turned down by the rank and file last year.*

rant and rave (about someone or something**)** to shout angrily and wildly about someone or something. ☐ *Bob rants and raves when anything displeases him.* ☐ *Bob rants and raves about anything that displeases him.* ☐ *Father rants and raves if we arrive home late.*

rant (at someone**) about** someone or something to talk in a loud, violent way, about someone or something. ☐ *Anne ranted about the bad service she had received at the store.* ☐ *On the bus, someone was ranting at me about the end of the world.*

rap someone's **knuckles** to punish someone slightly. (Also literal.) ☐ *She rapped his knuckles for whispering too much.* ☐ *Don't rap my knuckles. I didn't do it.*

rap with someone to talk; to chat. (Slang.) ☐ *I rapped with the school counselor for* *half an hour.* ☐ *My neighbor rapped with me on my back porch all night.*

rarin' to go to be extremely eager to act or do something. (Informal.) ☐ *Jane can't wait to start her job. She's rarin' to go.* ☐ *Mary is rarin' to go and can't wait for her university term to start.*

rat on someone to report someone's bad behavior; to tattle on someone. (Slang.) ☐ *John ratted on me, and I got in trouble.* ☐ *If he rats on me, I'll hit him!*

rat race a fierce struggle for success, especially in one's career or business. ☐ *Bob got tired of the rat race. He's retired and gone to the country.* ☐ *The money market is a rat race, and many people who work in it die of the stress.*

rate with someone to be in someone's favor; to be thought of highly by someone. ☐ *Ann is great. She really rates with me.* ☐ *She doesn't rate with me at all.*

rattle something **off** AND **reel** something **off** to recite something quickly and accurately. ☐ *She can really reel them off.* 🅃 *Listen to Mary rattle off those numbers.*

ravished with delight made very happy or delighted; overcome with happiness or delight. (Men are less likely to be **ravished with delight.**) ☐ *Mary was ravished with delight by the dozen roses.* ☐ *My parents were ravished with delight when I graduated from college.*

reach a compromise to achieve a compromise; to make a compromise. ☐ *After many hours of discussion, we finally reached a compromise.* ☐ *We were unable to reach a compromise and quit trying.*

reach an agreement to achieve an agreement; to make an agreement. ☐ *We reached an agreement and signed a contract.* ☐ *We could not reach an agreement, so we stopped negotiating.*

reach an impasse to progress to the point that a barrier stops further progress. ☐ *When negotiations with management reached an impasse, the union went on strike.* ☐ *The discussion reached an impasse and no one was able to propose a compromise.*

reach first base (with someone or something**)** Go to **get to first base (with** someone or something**)**.

reach for the sky 1. to aspire to something; to set one's goals high. ☐ *It's a good idea to set high goals, but there is no point in reaching for the sky.* ☐ *Go ahead, you can do it! Reach for the sky!* **2.** <a command to put one's hands up, as in a robbery.> (Slang.) ☐ *Reach for the sky! This is a stickup!* ☐ *The sheriff told the bank robbers to reach for the sky.*

reach one's **stride** AND **hit** one's **stride** to do something at one's best level of ability. ☐ *When I reach my stride, things will go faster, and I'll be more efficient.* ☐ *Now that I've hit my stride, I can work more efficiently.*

read between the lines to infer something (from something). (Usually figurative. Does not necessarily refer to written or printed information.) ☐ *After listening to what she said, if you read between the lines, you can begin to see what she really means.* ☐ *Don't believe everything you hear. Learn to read between the lines.*

read one one's **rights** to make the required statement of legal rights to a person who has been arrested. ☐ *All right, read this guy his rights and book him on a charge of theft.* ☐ *You have to read them their rights before putting them in jail.*

read someone **like a(n open) book** to understand someone very well. ☐ *I've got John figured out. I can read him like a book.* ☐ *Of course I understand you. I read you like an open book.*

read someone **out of** something to expel someone from an organization, such as a political party. ☐ *Because of her statement, they read her out of the party.* ☐ *The officers tried to read me out of the society, but they didn't succeed.*

read someone's **mind** to guess what someone is thinking, as if one had special powers to sense someone else's thoughts. ☐ *You'll have to tell me what you want. I can't read your mind, you know.* ☐ *If I* *could read your mind, I'd know what you expect of me.*

read someone **the riot act** to give someone a severe scolding. □ *The manager read me the riot act for coming in late.* □ *The teacher read the students the riot act for their failure to do their assignments.*

read something **into** something to attach or attribute a new or different meaning to something. □ *This statement means exactly what it says. Don't try to read anything else into it.* □ *Am I reading too much into your comments?*

read something **over** to read something. □ *When you have a chance, read this over.* 🅃 *Also, read over this report.*

read something **through** to read all of something. □ *Take this home and read it through.* 🅃 *Read through this report and see if you can find any errors.*

read the handwriting on the wall to anticipate what is going to happen by observing small hints and clues. □ *I know I am going to be fired. I can read the handwriting on the wall.* □ *Can't you read the handwriting on the wall? Can't you see what they are planning?*

read up (on someone or something**)** to find and read some information about someone or something. □ *Please go to the library and read up on George Washington.* □ *I don't know anything about that. I guess I need to read up.*

ready to do something [of someone or some creature] prepared and willing. □ *Are you ready to leave for the airport?* □ *If you need me, I'm ready to help.*

ready, willing, and able eager or at least willing [to do something]. □ *If you need someone to help you move furniture, I'm ready, willing, and able.* □ *Fred is ready, willing, and able to do anything you ask him.*

the **real thing** something that is genuine and not an imitation. □ *I don't want frozen yogurt, I want the real thing! Yes, ice cream!* □ *She hates plastic that looks like wood. She wants the real thing.*

the **reality of the situation** the truth or actuality of the situation; the way the situation really is. □ *The reality of the situation is that we must act right now.* □ *Let's face the reality of the situation and go out and get jobs so we can buy food.*

rear its ugly head [for something unpleasant] to appear or become obvious after lying hidden. □ *Jealousy reared its ugly head and destroyed their marriage.* □ *The question of money always rears its ugly head in matters of business.*

receive someone **with open arms** AND **welcome** someone **with open arms** to greet someone eagerly. (Used literally or figuratively.) □ *I'm sure they wanted us to stay for dinner. They received us with open arms.* □ *When I came home from school, the whole family welcomed me with open arms.*

reckon with someone or something to deal with someone or something; to confront someone or something. □ *Eventually you will have to reckon with getting a job.* □ *I really don't want to have to reckon with the manager when she's mad.*

recognize one **for what** one **is** Go to recognize something for what it is.

recognize something **for what it is** AND **recognize** one **for what** one **is** to see and understand exactly what someone or something is or represents. □ *The disease represented a serious threat to all peoples, and Dr. Smith recognized it for what it was.* □ *I recognize you for what you are, you scoundrel!*

reconcile oneself **to** something to grow to feel comfortable with an undesirable or challenging situation. □ *John reconciled himself to living alone.* □ *Anne reconciled herself to having to wear glasses.*

red as a cherry Go to (as) red as a cherry.

red as a poppy Go to (as) red as a poppy.

red as a rose Go to (as) red as a rose.

red as a ruby Go to (as) red as a ruby.

red as blood Go to (as) red as blood.

red herring a piece of information or suggestion introduced to draw attention away from the real facts of a situation. (A red herring is a type of strong-smelling smoked fish that was once drawn across the trail of a scent to mislead hunting dogs and put them off the scent.) ☐ *The detectives were following a red herring, but they're on the right track now.* ☐ *Jack and Mary were hoping their friends would confuse their parents with a red herring so that they wouldn't realize that they had eloped.*

red in the face embarrassed. ☐ *After we found Ann hiding in the closet, she became red in the face.* ☐ *The speaker kept making errors and became red in the face.*

red tape over-strict attention to the wording and details of rules and regulations, especially by government workers. (From the color of the tape used by government departments in England to tie up bundles of documents.) ☐ *Because of red tape, Frank took weeks to get a visa.* ☐ *Red tape prevented Jack's wife from joining him abroad.*

reduced to something brought into a certain humble condition or state. ☐ *The grieving family was reduced to tears.* ☐ *The poor man was reduced to begging for food.*

reel something **off** Go to **rattle** something **off.**

refill a prescription sell a second or subsequent set of doses of a medicine upon a doctor's orders. ☐ *The pharmacy refused to refill my prescription because it has expired.* ☐ *If you want the drugstore to refill your prescription, just give them the prescription number over the telephone.*

regain one's **composure** to become calm and composed. ☐ *I found it difficult to regain my composure after the argument.* ☐ *Here, sit down and relax so that you can regain your composure.*

regain one's **feet 1.** to stand up again after falling or stumbling. ☐ *I fell on the ice and almost couldn't regain my feet.* ☐ *I helped my uncle regain his feet as he tried to get up from the chair.* **2.** to become independent after financial difficulties. ☐ *I lent Bill $400 to help him regain his feet.* ☐ *I'll be able to pay my bills when I regain my feet.*

regardless of something without considering something; at any rate; whatever is done; whatever option is chosen. ☐ *Regardless of what you say, I'm still going to the club tonight.* ☐ *I still have to pay the bill, regardless of the facts.*

regular as clockwork Go to (as) regular as clockwork.

relative to someone or something **1.** concerning someone or something. ☐ *I have something to say relative to Bill.* ☐ *Do you have any information relative to the situation in South America?* **2.** in proportion to someone or something. ☐ *My happiness is relative to yours.* ☐ *I can spend an amount of money relative to the amount of money I earn.*

reliance on someone or something trust and dependence on someone or something. ☐ *John's reliance on his family is holding him back.* ☐ *Reliance on sleeping pills is dangerous.*

religious about doing something strict about something; conscientious about something. ☐ *Bob is religious about paying his bills on time.* ☐ *Max tries to be religious about being polite to everyone.*

reluctance to do something a feeling of not wanting to do something; unwillingness to do something. ☐ *Mary showed great reluctance to go bowling with me.* ☐ *Because of John's reluctance to make friends, he was lonely.*

reminiscent of someone or something reminding someone about someone or something; seeming like or suggesting someone or something. ☐ *This fragrance is reminiscent of fresh flowers.* ☐ *Jane's dress is reminiscent of the style worn in the 1920s.*

reputed to be something AND **reputed to** do something**; reputed to have** something thought to do, be, or have something. ☐ *My boss is reputed to have cancer.* ☐ *My neighbor was reputed to have been a spy during the war.*

reputed to do something Go to reputed to be something.

reputed to have something Go to reputed to be something.

resign oneself **to** something to accept something reluctantly. □ *I finally resigned myself to going to Mexico even though I didn't want to.* □ *Mary resigned herself to her fate.*

resonate with someone [for an idea, issue, or concept] to appeal to someone or cause someone to relate to it. □ *The concept of buying CDs at a clothing store seems to resonate with young people.* □ *Your notion just doesn't resonate with the public in general.*

the **responsible party** the person or organization responsible or liable for something. □ *I intend to find the responsible party and get some answers to my questions.* □ *Mary sued the responsible party in the car crash.*

rest assured to be assured; to be certain. □ *Rest assured that you'll receive the best of care.* □ *Please rest assured that we will do everything possible to help.*

rest in peace to lie dead peacefully for eternity. □ *We prayed that the deceased would rest in peace.* □ *The bodies of the soldiers will rest in peace.*

rest on one's **laurels** to enjoy one's success and not try to achieve more. □ *Don't rest on your laurels. Try to continue to do great things!* □ *I think I'll rest on my laurels for a time before attempting anything new.*

result in something to cause something to happen. □ *The storm resulted in a lot of flooding.* □ *Her fall resulted in a broken leg.*

return someone's **compliment** Go to return the compliment.

return the compliment AND **return** someone's **compliment** to pay a compliment to someone who has paid you a compliment. (See also pay someone a compliment.) □ *Mary told me that my hair looked nice, so I returned her compliment and told her that her hair was lovely.* □ *When someone says something nice, it is polite to return the compliment.*

return the favor to do a good deed for someone who has done a good deed for you. □ *You helped me last week, so I'll return the favor and help you this week.* □ *There is no point in helping Bill. He'll never return the favor.*

rev something **up** to make an idling engine run very fast, in short bursts of speed. □ *Hey! Stop revving it up!* [T] *I wish that Tom wouldn't sit out in front of our house in his car and rev up his engine.*

rich in something having valuable resources, characteristics, traditions, or history. □ *The entire region is rich in historical churches.* □ *Our soil is rich in important nutrients.*

rich with something having a lot of something; not lacking; abundant. □ *The beautiful book was rich with color illustrations.* □ *The old town was rich with elegant Victorian houses.*

ride herd on someone or something to supervise someone or something. (Informal. Refers to a cowboy supervising cattle.) □ *I'm tired of having to ride herd on my kids all the time.* □ *My job is to ride herd on this project and make sure everything is done right.*

ride off in all directions to behave in a totally confused manner; to try to do everything at once. (Folksy. Can be said of one or more people.) □ *Bill has a tendency to ride off in all directions. He's not organized enough.* □ *Now, calm down. There is no sense in riding off in all directions.*

ride on someone's **coattails** AND **hang on** someone's **coattails** to make one's good fortune or success depend on another person. (Also with *else,* as in the examples below.) □ *Bill isn't very creative, so he rides on John's coattails.* □ *Some people just have to hang on somebody else's coattails.*

ride roughshod over someone or something to treat someone or something with disdain or scorn. □ *Tom seems to ride roughshod over his friends.* □ *You shouldn't have come into our town to ride roughshod over our laws and our traditions.*

ride something **out** to endure something unpleasant. (Originally referred to ships lasting out a storm.) □ *It was a nasty situation, but the mayor tried to ride it out.* 🅃 *The mayor decided to ride out the scandal.*

ride the gravy train to live in luxury. (Informal.) □ *If I had a million dollars, I sure could ride the gravy train.* □ *I wouldn't like loafing. I don't want to ride the gravy train.*

riding for a fall risking failure or an accident, usually due to overconfidence. □ *Tom drives too fast, and he seems too sure of himself. He's riding for a fall.* □ *Bill needs to eat better and get more sleep. He's riding for a fall.*

right and left AND **left and right** to both sides; on all sides; everywhere. □ *I dropped the tennis balls, and they rolled right and left.* □ *There were children everywhere—running right and left.*

right as rain Go to (as) right as rain.

right at a specific time exactly or precisely at [a specific place or time]. □ *Meet me at this corner right at noon.* □ *The restaurant is right at First and Main Streets.*

right away immediately. □ *Please do it right away!* □ *I'll be there right away. I'm leaving this instant.*

right down someone's **alley** AND **right up** someone's **alley** ideally suited to one's interests or abilities. (Informal.) □ *Skiing is right down my alley. I love it.* □ *This kind of thing is right up John's alley.*

right off the bat immediately; first thing. (Informal.) □ *When he was learning to ride a bicycle, he fell on his head right off the bat.* □ *The new manager demanded new office furniture right off the bat.*

right on time at the correct time; no later than the specified time. □ *Bill always shows up right on time.* □ *If you get there right on time, you'll get one of the free tickets.*

right side up with the correct side upwards, as with a box or some other container. □ *Keep this box right side up, or the contents will be crushed.* □ *Please set your coffee cup right side up so I can fill it.*

(right) under someone's **(very) nose 1.** right in front of someone. □ *I thought I'd lost my purse, but it was sitting on the table under my very nose.* □ *How did Mary fail to see the book? It was right under her nose.* **2.** in someone's presence. (Note the variation in the examples.) □ *The thief stole Jim's wallet right under his nose.* □ *The jewels were stolen from under the very noses of the security guards.*

right up someone's **alley** Go to right down someone's alley.

ring a bell [for something] to cause someone to remember something or for it to seem familiar. (Informal.) □ *I've never met John Franklin, but his name rings a bell.* □ *Whenever I see a bee, it rings a bell. I remember when I was stung by one.*

ring down the curtain (on something**)** AND **bring down the curtain (on** something**)** to bring something to an end; to declare something to be at an end. □ *It's time to ring down the curtain on our relationship. We have nothing in common anymore.* □ *We've tried our best to make this company a success, but it's time to ring down the curtain.* □ *After many years the old man brought down the curtain and closed the restaurant.*

ring in the New Year to celebrate the beginning of the new year at midnight on December 31. □ *We are planning a big party to ring in the New Year.* □ *How did you ring in the New Year?*

ring something **up** to record the cost of an item on a cash register. □ *Please ring this chewing gum up first, and I'll put it in my purse.* 🅃 *The cashier rang up each item and told me how much money I owed.*

ring true to sound or seem true or likely. (From testing the quality of metal or glass by striking it and evaluating the sound made.) □ *The student's excuse for being late doesn't ring true.* □ *Do you think that Mary's explanation for her absence rang true?*

rip into someone or something to attack someone or something, physically or verbally.

(Informal.) □ *The bear ripped into the deer.* □ *The angry teacher ripped into the student.*

rip someone or something **off 1.** [with *someone*] to cheat or deceive someone; to steal from someone. (Slang.) □ *That store operator ripped me off.* 🅃 *They shouldn't rip off people like that.* **2.** [with *something*] to steal something. (Slang.) □ *I bought it! I didn't rip it off!* 🅃 *The crooks ripped off a car in broad daylight.*

a **ripe old age** a very old age. □ *Mr. Smith died last night, but he lived to a ripe old age—99.* □ *All the Smiths seem to reach a ripe old age.*

a **ripple of excitement** a series of quiet but excited murmurs. □ *A ripple of excitement spread through the crowd.* □ *As the president came near, a ripple of excitement indicated that people could really see him.*

a **ripple of protest** a few quiet remarks protesting something; a small amount of subdued protest. □ *There was only a ripple of protest about the new tax law.* □ *The rude comedian hardly drew a ripple of protest.*

Rise and shine! Get out of bed and be lively and energetic! (Informal. Often a command.) □ *Come on, children! Rise and shine! We're going to the beach.* □ *Father always calls "Rise and shine!" in the morning when we want to go on sleeping.*

rise to the bait to be lured by some kind of bait. (Literal when referring to a fish.) □ *I threatened to take another job elsewhere, but the boss did not rise to the bait.* □ *When I said I was leaving, Ted rose to the bait and asked why.*

rise to the occasion to meet the challenge of an event; to try extra hard to do a task. □ *John was able to rise to the occasion and make the conference a success.* □ *It was a big challenge, but he rose to the occasion.*

risk of rain AND **risk of showers; risk of thunder(storms)** a chance of precipitation or rain. (Used only in weather forecasting. There is no "risk" of hazard or injury involved.) □ *And for tomorrow, there is a slight risk of showers in the morning.* □ *There is a 50 percent risk of rain tonight.*

risk of showers Go to risk of rain.

risk of thunder(storms) Go to risk of rain.

risk one's **neck (to** do something**)** to risk physical harm in order to accomplish something. (Informal.) □ *Look at that traffic! I refuse to risk my neck just to cross the street to buy a paper.* □ *I refuse to risk my neck at all.*

rivet someone's **attention** to keep someone's attention fixed [on something]. □ *The movie riveted the audience's attention.* □ *Professor Jones's lecture riveted the students' attention.*

road-hog someone who drives carelessly and selfishly. □ *Look at that road-hog driving in the middle of the road and stopping other drivers from passing him.* □ *That road-hog nearly knocked the children over. He was driving too fast.*

rob Peter to pay Paul to take from one in order to give to another. □ *Why borrow money to pay your bills? That's just robbing Peter to pay Paul.* □ *There's no point in robbing Peter to pay Paul. You will still be in debt.*

rob the cradle to marry or date someone who is much younger than you are. (Informal.) □ *I hear that Bill is dating Ann. Isn't that sort of robbing the cradle? She's much younger than he is.* □ *Uncle Bill—who is nearly eighty—married a thirty-year-old woman. That is really robbing the cradle.*

rock the boat to cause trouble where none is welcome; to disturb a situation that is otherwise stable and satisfactory. (Also literal. Often negative.) □ *Look, Tom, everything is going fine here. Don't rock the boat!* □ *You can depend on Tom to mess things up by rocking the boat.*

roll in to come in large numbers or amounts. (Informal.) □ *We didn't expect many people at the party, but they just kept rolling in.* □ *Money is simply rolling in for our charity appeal.*

roll one's **sleeves up** to get ready to do some work. (Also literal.) □ *Roll your* *sleeves up and get busy. This isn't a picnic. This is work!* 🅃 *Come on, you guys, get busy. Roll up your sleeves and go to work.*

roll out the red carpet for someone to provide special treatment for someone. (Literal when the special treatment actually includes a length of red carpeting.) □ *There's no need to roll out the red carpet for me.* □ *We rolled out the red carpet for the king and queen.*

roll (over) in one's **grave** Go to **turn (over) in** one's **grave.**

roll something **back** to reduce a price to a previous amount. (Also literal.) □ *The government forced the company to roll its prices back.* 🅃 *It wouldn't have rolled back its prices if the government hadn't forced it to.*

rolling in something having large amounts of something, usually money. (Informal.) □ *That family is rolling in money.* □ *Jack doesn't need to earn money. He's rolling in it.*

A **rolling stone gathers no moss.** A person who keeps changing jobs or residences and, therefore, accumulates no possessions or responsibilities. (Proverb.) □ *"John just can't seem to stay in one place," said Sally. "Oh, well, a rolling stone gathers no moss."* □ *Bill has no furniture to bother with because he keeps on the move. He keeps saying that a rolling stone gathers no moss.*

Rome wasn't built in a day. Important things don't happen overnight. (Proverb.) □ *Don't expect a lot to happen right away. Rome wasn't built in a day, you know.* □ *Don't be anxious about how fast you are growing. Rome wasn't built in a day.*

room and board food to eat and a place to live; the cost of food and lodging. □ *That college charges too much for room and board.* □ *How much is your room and board?*

root for someone or something to cheer and encourage someone or something. (Informal.) □ *Are you rooting for anyone in particular, or are you just shouting because you're excited?* □ *I'm rooting for the home team.*

root something **out** to get rid of something completely; to destroy something. □ *No government will ever root out crime completely.* □ *The headmaster wants to root troublemakers out at the local school.*

rooted in something based on something; connected to a source or cause. □ *The civil war was rooted in old ethnic hatred.* □ *This fictional book was rooted in actual events.*

rooted to the spot unable to move because of fear or surprise. □ *Joan stood rooted to the spot when she saw the ghostly figure.* □ *Mary was rooted to the spot as the mugger snatched her bag.*

rope someone **into** doing something to persuade or trick someone into doing something. (Informal.) □ *I don't know who roped me into this, but I don't want to do it.* □ *See if you can rope somebody into taking this to the post office.*

rotten to the core completely no good and worthless. (Also literal in reference to apples or other edible things.) □ *Fred is rotten to the core. He will never be a good member of society.* □ *I hope that just because I made one little mistake with my life that you don't think I am rotten to the core.*

rough-and-ready strong, active, and ready for anything. □ *John is not exactly rough-and-ready, but he is a moderately good athlete.* □ *Ralph is very rough-and-ready, but his table manners are very bad.*

rough-and-tumble [of physical activity] rough; [of living creatures] overly active. □ *The game got sort of rough-and-tumble, so I stopped playing.* □ *Jane runs with a rough-and-tumble crowd that's always involved in some sort of sport.*

rough it to live in discomfort; to live in uncomfortable conditions without the usual amenities, such as on a camping trip. (Informal.) □ *The students are roughing it in a shack with no running water.* □ *Bob and Jack had nowhere to live and so they had to rough it in a tent till they found somewhere.*

rough someone **up** to beat or physically harass someone. (Slang.) □ *The gangsters roughed their victim up.* 🅃 *The police roughed up the suspect, and they got in trouble for it.*

round out something Go to **round** something **off**.

round something **off 1.** to change a number to the next higher or lower whole number. □ *You should round 8.122 off.* 🅃 *I rounded off 8.789 to 9.* **2.** AND **round out** something to finish something by doing something special. □ *She rounded her schooling off with a trip to Europe.* 🅃 *I like to round out the day with a period of meditation.*

round something **off to** something AND **round** something **up to** something; **round** something **down to** something to express a number in the nearest whole amount or nearest group of 1, 10, 100, 1,000, $1/10$, $1/100$, $1/1,000$, etc. □ *When doing taxes, Anne rounded her figures off to the nearest dollar.* □ *These census figures are rounded up to the nearest million.*

round something **up to** something Go to **round** something **off to** something.

round the clock Go to **(a)round the clock**.

round-trip ticket a ticket (for a plane, train, bus, etc.) that allows one to go to a destination and return. □ *A round-trip ticket is usually cheaper than a one-way ticket.* □ *How much is a round-trip ticket to San Francisco?*

the **royal treatment** very good treatment; very good and thoughtful care of a person. □ *I was well cared for. They gave me the royal treatment.* □ *I had the royal treatment when I stayed at that expensive hotel.*

rub elbows (with someone**)** AND **rub shoulders with** someone to associate with someone; to work closely with someone. □ *I don't care to rub elbows with someone who acts like that!* □ *I rub shoulders with John at work. We are good friends.*

rub off (on someone**)** [for a characteristic of one person] to seem to transfer to someone else. (Also literal.) □ *I'll sit by Ann. She has been lucky all evening. Maybe it'll rub off on me.* □ *Sorry. I don't think that luck rubs off.*

rub salt in the wound deliberately to make someone's unhappiness, shame, or misfortune worse. (Also literal.) □ *Don't rub salt in the wound by telling me how enjoyable the party was.* □ *Jim is feeling miserable about losing his job, and Fred is rubbing salt into the wound by saying how good his replacement is.*

rub shoulders with someone Go to **rub elbows (with** someone**)**.

rub someone **out** to kill someone. (Slang.) □ *The crook said, "Bill is getting to be a problem. We're going to have to rub him out."* 🅃 *The gangsters tried to rub out the witness.*

rub someone**('s fur) the wrong way** to irritate someone. (From the rubbing of a cat's or dog's fur the wrong way.) □ *I'm sorry I rubbed your fur the wrong way. I didn't mean to upset you.* □ *Don't rub her the wrong way!*

rub someone's **nose in it** to remind one of something one has done wrong; to remind one of something bad or unfortunate that has happened. (From a method of housebreaking pets.) □ *When Bob failed his exam, his brother rubbed his nose in it.* □ *Mary knows she shouldn't have broken off her engagement. Don't rub her nose in it.*

rub something **in** to keep reminding one of one's failures; to nag someone about something. (Also literal. Informal.) □ *I like to rub it in. You deserve it!* 🅃 *Why do you have to rub in everything I do wrong?*

ruffle its feathers [for a bird] to point its feathers outward. □ *The bird ruffled its feathers when it was annoyed.* □ *My parrot ruffles its feathers whenever it is ready to preen itself.*

ruffle someone's **feathers** to upset or annoy someone. (See **ruffle its feathers** for an explanation.) □ *You certainly ruffled Mrs. Smith's feathers by criticizing her garden.* □ *Try to be tactful and not ruffle people's feathers.*

the **ruin of** someone or something the cause of destruction; a failure. ☐ *Your bad judgment will be the ruin of this company!* ☐ *The greedy politicians were the ruin of the old empire.*

a **rule of thumb** a rough or an inexact guide; a basic or accepted pattern or rule. (From the use of one's thumb to make quick and rough measurements.) ☐ *It's a rule of thumb that the bus will be late whenever I'm in a hurry.* ☐ *As a good rule of thumb, prepare two large potatoes for each person.*

rule someone or something **out** to prevent, disqualify, overrule, or cancel someone or something. ☐ *John's bad temper rules him out for the job.* 🅃 *The weather ruled out a picnic for the weekend.*

rule the roost to be the boss or manager, especially at home. (Informal.) ☐ *Who rules the roost at your house?* ☐ *Our new office manager really rules the roost.*

rump session a meeting held after a larger meeting. ☐ *A rump session continued after the meeting was adjourned.* ☐ *A lot of business was conducted in the rump session.*

run across someone or something Go to **come across** someone or something.

run a fever AND **run a temperature** to have a body temperature higher than normal; to have a fever. ☐ *I ran a fever when I had the flu.* ☐ *The baby is running a temperature and is grouchy.*

run afoul of someone or something Go to **fall afoul of** someone or something.

run after someone to chase someone of the opposite sex hoping for a date or some attention. (Also literal.) ☐ *Is John still running after Ann?* ☐ *No, Ann is running after John.*

run an errand AND **do an errand; go on an errand** to take a short trip to do a specific thing; to complete an errand. (The plural is with *some errands*.) ☐ *I've got to run an errand. I'll be back in a minute.* ☐ *John has gone on an errand. He'll be back shortly.*

run a risk (of something**)** AND **run the risk (of** something**)** to take a chance that something (bad) will happen. ☐ *I don't want to run the risk of losing my job.* ☐ *Don't worry. You won't have to run a risk.*

run (around) in circles Go to **run around like a chicken with its head cut off.**

run around like a chicken with its head cut off AND **run (around) in circles** to run around frantically and aimlessly; to be in a state of chaos. (See also **go (a)round in circles.**) ☐ *I spent all afternoon running around like a chicken with its head cut off.* ☐ *If you run around in circles, you'll never get anything done.* ☐ *Get organized and stop running in circles.*

run around with someone to be friends with someone; to go places with regular friends. ☐ *John and I were great friends. We used to run around with each other all the time.* ☐ *Mary ran around with June for about a year.*

run a taut ship Go to **run a tight ship.**

run a temperature Go to **run a fever.**

run a tight ship AND **run a taut ship** to run a ship or an organization in an orderly and disciplined manner. (*Taut* and *tight* mean the same thing. *Taut* is correct nautical use.) ☐ *The new office manager really runs a tight ship.* ☐ *Captain Jones is known for running a taut ship.*

run circles around someone AND **run rings around** someone to outrun or outdo someone. (Informal.) ☐ *John is a much better racer than Mary. He can run circles around her.* ☐ *Mary can run rings around Sally.*

run counter to something to be in opposition to something; to run against something. ☐ *Your proposal runs counter to what is required by the manager.* ☐ *His idea runs counter to good sense.*

run for it to try to escape by running. (Informal.) ☐ *The guard's not looking. Let's run for it!* ☐ *The convict tried to run for it, but the guard caught him.*

run for one's **life** to run away to save one's life. ☐ *The dam has burst! Run for your* *life!* □ *The captain told us all to run for our lives.*

run in the family for a characteristic to appear in all (or most) members of a family. □ *My grandparents lived well into their nineties, and it runs in the family.* □ *My brothers and I have red hair. It runs in the family.*

run into a stone wall to come to a barrier against further progress. (Also literal. Informal.) □ *We've run into a stone wall in our investigation.* □ *Algebra was hard for Tom, but he really ran into a stone wall with geometry.*

run into someone Go to **bump into** someone.

run like clockwork to run very well; to progress very well. □ *I want this office to run like clockwork—with everything on time and everything done right.* □ *The plans for the party were made and we knew that we could depend on Alice to make sure that everything ran like clockwork.*

run low (on something**)** to near the end of a supply of something. (See also **run short (of** something**)**.) □ *We are running low on salt. It's time to buy more.* □ *The car is running low on gas.*

run off at the mouth to talk excessively. (Slang.) □ *Shut up, John. You're always running off at the mouth.* □ *There is no need to run off at the mouth. Stop talking so much for so long.*

run off with someone or something **1.** to take something or someone away; to steal something or kidnap someone. □ *The thief ran off with the lady's purse.* □ *The kidnapper ran off with the baby.* **2.** [with *someone*] AND **run off** to run away with someone, as in an elopement. □ *Tom ran off with Ann.* □ *Tom and Ann ran off and got married.*

run-of-the-mill common or average; typical. □ *The restaurant we went to was nothing special—just run-of-the-mill.* □ *The service was good, but the food was run-of-the-mill or worse.*

run out of gas to use up all the gasoline in a car's tank. □ *I hope we don't run out of gas.* □ *I am sorry I am late. I ran out of gas.*

run out of patience to become annoyed after being patient for a while. □ *I finally ran out of patience and lost my temper.* □ *The boss ran out of patience with me and sent me back to my desk.*

run out of something to use up all of something and have no more. □ *We ran out of milk, so we will have to buy some more.* □ *I usually run out of money at the end of the month.*

run out of time to use up all the available time. □ *I ran out of time and couldn't finish.* □ *I hope she answers the question before she runs out of time.*

run rampant to run, develop, or grow out of control. □ *The children ran rampant through the house.* □ *Weeds have run rampant around the abandoned house.*

run rings around someone Go to **run circles around** someone.

run riot AND **run wild** to go out of control. □ *The dandelions have run riot in our lawn.* □ *The children ran wild at the birthday party and had to be taken home.*

run scared to behave as if one were going to fail. (Informal. Typically said of someone running for election.) □ *The mayor was running scared, but won anyway.* □ *When we lost that big contract, everyone in the office was running scared. We thought we'd be fired.*

run short (of something**)** to use up almost all of something; to have too little or few of something left. (See also **run low (on** something**)**.) □ *We are running short of milk. Please buy some on the way home.* □ *When it comes to money, we are always running short.*

run someone **in** to take someone to the police station and make an arrest. □ *"Don't run me in," cried the driver. "I'm innocent."* 🅃 *The police officer was angry and ran in the motorist.*

run someone or something **down 1.** to degrade physically or put wear on someone or something. □ *All these years of hard work have run Mrs. Brown down severely.* 🅃

Our neighbors ran down their house before they sold it. **2.** to say bad things about someone or something. ☐ *Why are you always running your friends down?* 🅃 *Don't run down my paintings! You just don't understand art!* **3.** to look for and finally find someone or something. ☐ *I finally ran John Smith down. He had moved to another town.* 🅃 *I will see if I can run down the book that you want.*

run someone or something **to earth** to find someone or something after a search. ☐ *Lisa finally ran her long-lost cousin to earth in Paris.* ☐ *After months of searching, I ran a copy of Jim's book to earth.*

run someone **ragged** to run someone hard and fast; to keep someone very busy. (Informal.) ☐ *This busy season is running us all ragged at the store.* ☐ *What a busy day. I ran myself ragged.*

run something **into the ground** AND **drive** something **into the ground** to carry something too far. (Informal.) ☐ *It was a good joke at first, Tom, but you've run it into the ground.* ☐ *Just because everyone laughed once, you don't have to drive it into the ground.*

run something **up 1.** to raise a flag. ☐ *I run it up every day except when it's raining.* 🅃 *We run up the flag every day.* **2.** to add to a bill; to add many charges to one's account. ☐ *He ran the bill up until they asked him to pay part of it.* 🅃 *Tom ran up a big tab at the hotel.*

run that by (someone**) again** say that again. (Slang.) ☐ *I didn't hear you. Could you run that by me again?* ☐ *Run that by again. I don't believe my ears.*

run the gamut to cover the range [from one thing to another]. ☐ *She wants to buy the house, but her requests run the gamut from expensive new carpeting to completely new landscaping.* ☐ *His hobbies run the gamut from piano repair to portrait painting.*

run the good race to do the best that one could; to live life as well and as fully as possible. (Also literal.) ☐ *He didn't get what he wanted, but he ran the good race.* ☐ *Joan ran the good race, and she will be remembered by all of us.*

run the risk (of something**)** Go to **run a risk (of** something**)**.

run through something **1.** to waste something; to use up something rapidly. (Also literal.) ☐ *Have you run through all those eggs already?* ☐ *I ran through my allowance in one day.* **2.** to read through something rapidly. ☐ *I ran through your report, and it looks okay.* ☐ *I didn't read the novel, I only ran through it.*

run to an amount of money to amount to a certain amount of money. ☐ *In the end, the bill ran to thousands of dollars.* ☐ *His account ran to more than I expected.*

run to seed AND **go to seed** to become worn-out and uncared for. (Said especially of a lawn that needs care.) ☐ *Look at that lawn. The whole thing has run to seed.* ☐ *Pick things up around here. This place is going to seed. What a mess!*

run wild Go to **run riot**.

running high [for feelings] to be in a state of excitement or anger. ☐ *Feelings were running high as the general election approached.* ☐ *The mood of the crowd was running high when they saw the mother slap her child.*

a **rush on** something a large demand for something. ☐ *There was a rush on bottled water during the drought.* ☐ *During the hot summer, there was a rush on air conditioners.*

rustle something **up** to find and prepare some food. (Folksy.) ☐ *I'm sure he can rustle something up.* 🅃 *Just go out into the kitchen and ask Bill to rustle up some food.*

S

sack out to go to bed; to go to sleep. (Slang. Compare this with **hit the sack** at **hit the hay**.) □ *Look at the clock. It's time to sack out.* □ *John sacks out at about nine o'clock.*

sacred cow something that is regarded by some people with such respect and veneration that they do not like it being criticized by anyone in any way. (From the fact that the cow is regarded as sacred in India and is not eaten or mistreated.) □ *A university education is a sacred cow in the Smith family. Fred is regarded as a failure because he quit school at 16.* □ *Don't talk about eating meat to Pam. Vegetarianism is one of her sacred cows.*

sadder but wiser unhappy but educated [about someone or something—after an unpleasant event]. □ *After the accident, I was sadder but wiser, and would never make the same mistake again.* □ *We left the meeting sadder but wiser, knowing that we could not ever come to an agreement with Becky's aunt.*

saddle someone **with** something to give someone something undesirable, annoying, or difficult to deal with. (Informal.) □ *Mary says she doesn't want to be saddled with a baby, but her husband would just love one.* □ *Jim saddled Eddie with the most boring jobs so that he would leave.*

safe and sound safe and whole or healthy. □ *It was a rough trip, but we got there safe and sound.* □ *I'm glad to see you here safe and sound.*

safety in numbers safety achieved by being concealed in large numbers of people or other creatures. □ *We stayed close together, thinking that there was safety in numbers.* □ *The elderly people went out together for a walk, knowing that there was safety in numbers.*

sage advice very good and wise advice. (Refers to a *sage* or wise man.) □ *My parents gave me some sage advice when I turned 18.* □ *I asked my uncle for some of his sage advice.*

sail (right) through something to finish something quickly and easily. (Informal.) □ *The test was not difficult. I sailed right through it.* □ *Bob sailed through his homework in a short amount of time.*

sail under false colors to pretend to be something that one is not. (Originally nautical, referring to a pirate ship disguised as an innocent merchant ship.) □ *John has been sailing under false colors. He's really a spy.* □ *I thought you were wearing that uniform because you worked here. You are sailing under false colors.*

the **salt of the earth** the most worthy of people; a very good or worthy person. (A biblical reference, *Matthew 5:13.*) □ *Mrs. Jones is the salt of the earth. She is the first to help anyone in trouble.* □ *Frank's mother is the salt of the earth. She has five children of her own and yet fosters three others.*

salt something **away** to store or save something. (Originally referred to preserving food and storing it.) □ *Mary salted some extra candy away for use during the holidays.* 🅃 *I salted away about $1,000 when I worked as a clerk in the grocery store.*

the **same as** someone or something identical to someone or something. □ *Can you build me a birdhouse the same as yours?* □ *Have you noticed that Mary looks the same as her mother?*

same here Me too!; I agree! (Informal.) □ *BOB: I'll have chocolate ice cream! BILL: Same here.* □ *MARY: I'll vote for the best candidate. TOM: Same here!*

the **same old story** something that occurs or has occurred in the same way often. □ *Jim's got no money. It's the same old story. He's spent it all on clothing.* □ *The company is getting rid of workers. It's the same old story—a shortage of orders.*

the **same to you** the same comment applies to you. (Informal. This can be a polite or a rude comment.) □ *BILL: Have a pleasant evening. BOB: Thank you. The same to you.* □ *MARY: You're the most horrible person I've ever met! JOHN: The same to you!*

the **sands of time** the accumulated tiny amounts of time; time represented by the sand in an hourglass. □ *The sands of time will make you grow old like everyone else.* □ *My only enemy is the sands of time.*

Save it. Stop talking.; Shut up!; Tell it to me later. (Informal.) □ *I've heard enough. Save it!* □ *Save it! You talk too much!*

save one's **breath** to refrain from talking, explaining, or arguing. □ *There is no sense in trying to convince her. Save your breath.* □ *Tell her to save her breath. He won't listen to her.*

save (one's) **face** to preserve one's good standing or high position (after a failure). □ *The ambassador was more interested in saving his face than winning the argument.* □ *Most diplomats are concerned with saving face.*

save someone's **neck** Go to **save** someone's skin.

save someone's **skin** AND **save** someone's **neck** to save someone from injury, embarrassment, or punishment. (Informal.) □ *I saved my skin by getting the job done on time.* □ *Thanks for saving my neck! I would have fallen down the stairs if you hadn't held my arm.*

save something **for a rainy day** to reserve something—usually money—for some future need. (Also literal. *Save something* can be replaced with *put something aside, hold something back, keep something,* etc.) □ *I've saved a little money for a rainy day.* □ *Keep some extra candy for a rainy day.*

save the day to produce a good result when a bad result was expected. □ *The team was expected to lose, but Sally made many points and saved the day.* □ *Your excellent speech saved the day.*

save up (for something**)** to save money in order to buy something. □ *I'm saving up for a bicycle.* □ *I'll have to save up for a long time. It costs a lot of money.*

saved by the bell rescued from a difficult or dangerous situation just in time by something that brings the situation to a sudden end. (From the sounding of a bell marking the end of a round in a boxing match.) □ *James didn't know the answer to the question but he was saved by the bell when the teacher was called away from the room.* □ *I couldn't think of anything to say to the woman at the bus stop, but I was saved by the bell when my bus arrived.*

saving grace the one thing that saves or redeems someone or something that would otherwise be a total disaster. □ *Her saving grace is that she has a lot of money.* □ *The saving grace for the whole evening was the good music played by the band.*

say a mouthful to say a lot; to say something very important or meaningful. (Folksy.) □ *When you said things were busy around here, you said a mouthful. It is terribly busy.* □ *You sure said a mouthful, Bob. Things are really busy.*

say grace to say a prayer of gratitude before or after a meal. □ *Grandfather always says grace at Thanksgiving.* □ *A local preacher said grace at the banquet.*

say something **in a roundabout way** to imply something without saying it; to say something indirectly; to speak using circumlocution. □ *Why don't you say what you mean? Why do you always say something in a roundabout way?* □ *What did she mean? Why did she say it in a roundabout way?*

say something **(right) to** someone's **face** to say something (unpleasant) directly to someone. □ *She knew I thought she was rude* *because I said it right to her face.* □ *I thought she felt that way about me, but I never thought she'd say it to my face.*

say something **under** one's **breath** to say something so softly that almost no one can hear it. □ *John was saying something under his breath, and I don't think it was very pleasant.* □ *I'm glad he said it under his breath. If he had said it out loud, it would have caused an argument.*

say that something is so to assume something; to suppose that something were so. □ *Say that x is equal to a whole number greater than 10.* □ *Say that two trains leave two different cities at the same time.*

say the word to give a signal to begin; to say yes or okay. □ *I'm ready to start any time you say the word.* □ *We'll all shout "Happy Birthday!" when I say the word.*

say uncle to surrender; to give in. (Informal.) □ *Ann held Bobby down on the ground until he said uncle.* □ *Why isn't it enough to win the argument? Why do you demand that I say uncle?*

scale something **down** to make something smaller by a certain amount or proportion. □ *I scaled down the guest list because I couldn't invite so many people.* □ *Jane's salary was scaled down by 10 percent last year.*

scarcely have time to breathe Go to hardly have time to breathe.

scarcer than hens' teeth Go to (as) scarce as hens' teeth.

scare one **out of** one's **wits** Go to frighten one out of one's wits.

scare someone or something **up** to search for and find someone or something. (Slang.) □ *Go out in the kitchen and scare some food up.* 🅃 *I'll see if I can scare up somebody to fix the broken chair.*

scare someone **stiff** to scare someone severely; to frighten someone to death. (See the explanation at scared stiff.) □ *That loud noise scared me stiff.* □ *The robber jumped out and scared us stiff.*

scare someone **to death** Go to frighten someone to death.

scare the living daylights out of someone Go to frighten the wits out of someone.

scare the wits out of someone Go to frighten the wits out of someone.

scared silly frightened very much. □ *I was scared silly by the loud explosion.* □ *We were scared silly to go into the park after dark.*

scared stiff badly frightened. (Frightened to the point of being petrified and unable to move.) □ *We were scared stiff by the robber.* □ *I was scared stiff when the dog growled at me.*

scared to death Go to frightened to death.

school of thought a particular philosophy or way of thinking about something. □ *One school of thought holds that cats cause allergic reactions.* □ *I come from the school of thought that believes people should always be polite.*

scout around for someone or something to search here and there for someone or something. □ *Tom is scouting around for a date for Friday night.* □ *Please scout around for some ideas on what to cook for dinner.*

scrape something **together** to assemble something quickly, usually from a small supply of components. □ *I'll try to scrape something together for dinner.* 🅃 *We really should try to have a party to celebrate the boss's birthday. Let's try to scrape together a little something.*

scrape the bottom of the barrel to select from among the worst; to choose from what is left over. □ *You've bought a bad-looking car. You really scraped the bottom of the barrel to get that one.* □ *The worker you sent over was the worst I've ever seen. Send me another—and don't scrape the bottom of the barrel.*

scratch around (for something**)** to look here and there for something. (Informal.) □ *Let me scratch around for a better bargain. Maybe I can come up with something you like.* □ *I'll scratch around for a week or two and see what I come up with.*

scratch someone's **back** to do a favor for someone in return for a favor done for you. (Also literal. Informal.) □ *You scratch my back, and I'll scratch yours.* □ *We believe that the mayor has been scratching the treasurer's back.*

scratch the surface to just begin to find out about something. □ *The investigation of the governor's staff revealed some suspicious dealing. It is thought that the investigators have just scratched the surface.* □ *We don't know how bad the problem is. We've only scratched the surface.*

scream bloody murder to complain bitterly; to complain unduly. (Slang. See also **cry bloody murder.**) □ *When we put him in an office without a window, he screamed bloody murder.* □ *There is something wrong next door. Everyone is screaming bloody murder.*

screw around (with someone or something**)** Go to **mess around (with** someone or something**)**.

screw someone or something **up** to cause trouble for someone or something. (Slang.) □ *Your advice about making a lot of money really screwed me up. Now I'm broke.* 🅃 *Your efforts screwed up the entire project.*

screw up one's **courage** to build up one's courage. □ *I guess I have to screw up my courage and go to the dentist.* □ *I spent all morning screwing up my courage to take my driver's test.*

scrimp and save to be very thrifty; to live on very little money, often in order to save up for something. □ *We had to scrimp and save in order to send the children to college.* □ *The Smiths scrimp and save all year in order to go on a Caribbean cruise.*

the **seamy side of life** the most unpleasant or roughest aspect of life. (Informal. Refers to the inside of a garment where the seams show. *Seamy* occurs only in this expression.) □ *Doctors in that area really see the seamy side of life.* □ *Mary saw the seamy side of life when she worked as a volunteer in the shelter.*

search high and low (for someone or something**)** Go to **hunt high and low (for** someone or something**)**.

search something **with a fine-tooth comb** Go to **go over** something **with a fine-tooth comb.**

second nature to someone easy and natural for someone. □ *Swimming is second nature to Jane.* □ *Driving is no problem for Bob. It's second nature to him.*

second-rate not of the best quality; inferior. □ *Bill's a second-rate tennis player compared with Bob.* □ *The government is building second-rate housing.*

second to none better than everything. □ *This is an excellent car—second to none.* □ *Her suggestion was second to none, and the manager accepted it eagerly.*

security against something something that keeps something safe; something that protects; a protection. □ *Insurance provides security against financial loss owing to theft, loss, or damage.* □ *A good education is a security against unemployment.*

see about something to ask about something; to check on something. □ *I'll have to see about your request to leave early.* □ *I must see about the cake I have in the oven.*

see a man about a dog to leave for some unmentioned purpose. (Informal. Often refers to going to the rest room.) □ *I don't know where Tom went. He said he had to see a man about a dog.* □ *When John said he was going to see a man about a dog, I thought he would be gone for only a minute.*

see double to see two of everything instead of one. □ *When I was driving, I saw two people on the road instead of one. I'm seeing double. There's something wrong with my eyes.* □ *Mike thought he was seeing double when he saw Mary with her twin sister. He didn't know she had a twin.*

see eye to eye (with someone**) (about** something**)** AND **see eye to eye (with** someone**) (on** something**)** to view something in the same way (as someone else). □ *John and Ann see eye to eye about the new law. Neither of them likes it.* □ *John sees eye to eye with Ann about it.* □ *That's interesting because they rarely see eye to eye.*

see eye to eye (with someone**) (on** something**)** Go to **see eye to eye (with** someone**) (about** something**)**.

see fit (to do something**)** to decide to do something. ☐ *If I see fit to return, I'll bring Bill with me.* ☐ *She'll do it if she sees fit.*

see into something Go to **look into** something.

see no objection (to something**)** AND **not see any objection (to** something**)** not to think of any objection to something. ☐ *I see no objection to your idea.* ☐ *Do you see any objection?* ☐ *I do not see any objection to anything you have done.*

see one's **way clear (to** do something**)** to find it possible to do something. ☐ *I'd be happy if you could see your way clear to attend our meeting.* ☐ *I wanted to be there, but I couldn't see my way clear.*

see red to be angry. (Informal.) ☐ *Whenever I think of the needless destruction of trees, I see red.* ☐ *Bill really saw red when the tax bill arrived.*

see someone or something **as** something to consider someone or something; to deem someone or something as something. ☐ *The manager saw the skilled employee as a godsend.* ☐ *John saw the new salesman as a threat to his territory.*

see someone **home** to accompany someone home. ☐ *Bill agreed to see his aunt home after the movie.* ☐ *You don't need to see me home. It's perfectly safe, and I can get there on my own.*

see someone **to** somewhere to escort someone to a place; to make sure that someone gets somewhere safely; to accompany someone to a place. ☐ *I saw Mary to her door, and then got back in my car and left.* ☐ *Bill saw his cousin to the train station, and then they parted.*

see someone **to the door** Go to **show** someone **(to) the door**.

see something **through** to follow through on something until it is completed. (Compare this with **see through** someone or something.) ☐ *Mary is prepared to see the project through.* ☐ *It's going to be an unpleasant experience, but I hope you'll see it through.*

see stars to see flashing lights after receiving a blow to the head. ☐ *I saw stars when I bumped my head on the attic ceiling.* ☐ *The little boy saw stars when he fell headfirst onto the concrete.*

see the color of someone's **money** to verify that someone has money or has enough money. (Slang.) ☐ *So, you want to make a bet? Not until I see the color of your money.* ☐ *I want to see the color of your money before we go any further with this business deal.*

see the (hand)writing on the wall to know that something is certain to happen. ☐ *If you don't improve your performance, they'll fire you. Can't you see the writing on the wall?* ☐ *I know I'll get fired. I can see the handwriting on the wall.*

see the last of someone or something to see someone or something for the last time. ☐ *I'm glad to see the last of that old car. It has a lot of problems.* ☐ *The people at my office were happy to see the last of John. He caused a lot of trouble before he left.*

see the light to understand something clearly at last. (Also literal. See also the following two entries.) ☐ *After a lot of studying and asking many questions, I finally saw the light.* ☐ *I know that geometry is difficult. Keep working at it. You'll see the light pretty soon.*

see the light (at the end of the tunnel) to foresee an end to something, such as a problem or a task, after a long period of time. ☐ *I had been horribly ill for two months before I began to see the light at the end of the tunnel.* ☐ *I began to see the light one day in early spring. At that moment, I knew I'd get well.* ☐ *When I got to the last chapter, I could see the light at the end of the tunnel.*

see the light (of day) to come to the end of a very busy time. ☐ *Finally, when the holiday season was over, we could see the light of day. We had been so busy!* ☐ *When business lets up for a while, we'll be able to see the light.*

see the sights to see the important things in a place; to see what tourists usually see. □ *We plan to visit Paris and see the sights.* □ *Everyone left the hotel early in the morning to see the sights.*

see through someone or something to understand or detect the true nature of someone or something. (Compare this with **see** something **through.**) □ *You can't fool me anymore. I can see through you and all your tricks.* □ *This plan is designed to make money for you, not to help people. I can see through it! I'm not a fool!*

see (to it) that something **is done** to make sure of something; to make certain of something; to be certain to do something. □ *The manager saw to it that everyone began working on time.* □ *The mayor should see that the potholes are repaired.*

see to someone or something to take care of someone or something. □ *Tom will see to the horses. Come to the house and freshen up.* □ *I hear the doorbell. Will someone please see to the door?* □ *This paper needs filling out. Will you please see to it?*

see which way the wind is blowing to determine what is the most expedient thing to do. □ *We studied the whole situation to see which way the wind was blowing and decided to avoid any conflict at that time.* □ *Sam failed to see which way the wind was blowing and got himself caught up in an argument.*

seeing is believing one must believe something that one sees. □ *I never would have thought that a cow could swim, but seeing is believing.* □ *I can hardly believe we are in Paris, but there's the Eiffel Tower, and seeing is believing.*

seeing things to imagine one sees someone or something that is not there. □ *Lisa says that she saw a ghost, but she was just seeing things.* □ *I thought I was seeing things when Bill walked into the room. Someone had told me he was dead.*

seize the bull by the horns Go to take the bull by the horns.

seize the opportunity to take advantage of an opportunity. □ *My uncle offered me a trip to Europe, so I seized the opportunity.* □ *Whenever you have a chance, you should seize the opportunity.*

seize (up)on something to (figuratively) take hold of something and make an issue of it. (Also literal.) □ *Whenever I mention money, you seize on it and turn it into an argument!* □ *The lawyer seized upon one point and asked many questions about it.*

sell like hotcakes [for something] to be sold very fast. □ *The delicious candy sold like hotcakes.* □ *The fancy new cars were selling like hotcakes.*

sell someone **a bill of goods** to get someone to believe something that isn't true; to deceive someone. (Informal.) □ *Don't pay any attention to what John says. He's just trying to sell you a bill of goods.* □ *I'm not selling you a bill of goods. What I say is true.*

sell someone **down the river** Go to sell (someone or something) out.

sell someone **on a plan or idea** to convince someone of something. (Informal.) □ *You don't have to sell me on the value of an education.* □ *Try to sell John on going to Mexico for a vacation.*

sell (someone or something**) out 1.** [with *someone*] AND **sell** someone **down the river** to betray someone; to reveal damaging information about someone. (Slang, especially criminal slang.) □ *Bill told everything he knew about Bob, and that sold Bob down the river.* □ *You'll be sorry if you sell me out.* 🅃 *Lefty sold out, and we'll all soon be arrested.* **2.** [with *something*] to sell all of something. □ *You've sold them all out?* 🅃 *We sold out all our red ones yesterday.*

sell someone or something **short** to underestimate someone or something; to fail to see the good qualities of someone or something. □ *This is a very good restaurant. Don't sell it short.* □ *When you say that John isn't interested in music, you're selling him short. Did you know he plays the violin quite well?*

sell something **for a song** to sell something for very little money. (As in trading something of value for the singing of a song.) □ *I had to sell my car for a song because I needed the money in a hurry.* □ *I have two geometry books and I would sell one of them for a song.*

sell something **off** to sell much or all of something. □ *Please try to sell these items off. We have too many of them.* 🅃 *I sold off all my books.*

sell something **on credit** to sell something now and let the purchaser pay for it later. (Compare this with **buy** something **on credit.**) □ *I'm sorry, we don't sell groceries on credit. It's strictly cash-and-carry.* □ *There is a shop around the corner that sells clothing on credit.*

send one **about** one's **business** to send someone away, usually in an unfriendly way. □ *Is that annoying man on the telephone again? Please send him about his business.* □ *Ann, I can't clean up the house with you running around. I'm going to have to send you about your business.*

send someone **into** something to cause someone to be in a certain state or condition. □ *The horrifying news sent our family into hysterics.* □ *The clerk's rude behavior sent the customer into a fit of anger.*

send someone **off** to participate in saying good-bye to someone who is leaving. □ *We had a party to send Tom off on his vacation.* □ *Bob's parents sent him off from the airport.*

send someone or something **up** to ridicule or make fun of someone or something; to satirize someone or something. (Informal.) □ *John is always sending Jane up by mocking the way she walks.* □ *The drama group sent their leaders up.*

send someone **(out) on an errand** to send someone out to do a specific task. □ *Mother sent Billy out on an errand.* □ *I'm late because Bill sent me on an errand.*

send someone **packing** to send someone away; to dismiss someone, possibly rudely. □ *I couldn't stand him anymore, so I sent him packing.* □ *The maid proved to be so incompetent that I had to send her packing.*

send someone **to the showers** to send a player out of the game and off the field, court, etc. (From sports.) □ *John played so badly that the coach sent him to the showers after the third quarter.* □ *After the fistfight, the coaches sent both players to the showers.*

send someone **up the river** to send someone to prison. (Slang.) □ *The judge sent Bill up the river for ten years.* □ *The same judge sent him up the river the last time.*

send something **C.O.D.** to send merchandise to someone who will pay for it when it is delivered. (*C.O.D.* means "cash on delivery" or "collect on delivery.") □ *I sent away for a special book and asked them to send it C.O.D.* □ *This person has ordered a copy of our record. Send the record C.O.D.*

send up a trial balloon to suggest something and see how people respond to it; to test public opinion. (Slang.) □ *Mary had an excellent idea, but when we sent up a trial balloon, the response was very negative.* □ *Don't start the whole project without sending up a trial balloon.*

separate but equal segregated but of equal value or quality. (A doctrine once sanctioned by the U.S. Supreme Court regarding racial segregation.) □ *The separate but equal doctrine was abandoned years ago.* □ *They were provided with facilities that were said to be separate but equal—but were really of a lower standard.*

separate the men from the boys to separate the competent from those who are less competent. □ *This is the kind of task that separates the men from the boys.* □ *This project requires a lot of thinking. It'll separate the men from the boys.*

separate the sheep from the goats to divide people into two groups. □ *Working in a place like this really separates the sheep from the goats.* □ *We can't go on with the game until we separate the sheep from the goats. Let's see who can jump the farthest.*

the **separation of church and state** the constitutional barrier that prevents government from establishing a state religion. (This refers to eliminating evidence of religion in connection with government as well as assuring that the U.S. government does not establish a state religion.) ☐ *The city council stopped beginning each meeting with a prayer because someone suggested that it violated the principle of the separation of church and state.* ☐ *Many countries do not have the separation of church and state.*

serve as a guinea pig [for someone] to be experimented on; to allow some sort of test to be performed on someone. (A guinea pig was once the quintessential experimental animal.) ☐ *Try it on someone else! I don't want to serve as a guinea pig!* ☐ *Jane agreed to serve as a guinea pig. She'll be the one to try out the new flavor of ice cream.*

serve notice (on someone**)** to announce (something) to someone. ☐ *John served notice on his fellow workers that he would not prepare the coffee anymore.* ☐ *I'm serving notice that I'll resign as secretary next month.*

serve someone **right** [for an act or event] to punish someone fairly [for doing something]. ☐ *John copied off my test paper. It would serve him right if he fails the test.* ☐ *It'd serve John right if he got arrested.*

serve someone's **purpose** Go to **answer** someone's **purpose.**

serve time to spend a certain amount of time imprisoned. ☐ *The criminal served ten years in jail.* ☐ *After the felon served his time, he was released from prison.*

set a precedent to establish a pattern; to set a policy that must be followed in future cases. ☐ *I'll do what you ask this time, but it doesn't set a precedent.* ☐ *We've already set a precedent in matters such as these.*

set a trap to adjust and prepare a trap to catch an animal. ☐ *Bill set a mousetrap and baited it with cheese.* ☐ *The old man set a trap to catch an annoying squirrel.*

set eyes on someone or something AND **lay eyes on** someone or something to see someone or something for the first time. ☐ *I knew when I set eyes on that car that it was the car for me.* ☐ *Have you ever laid eyes on such a beautiful flower?*

set fire to someone or something AND **set** someone or something **on fire** to ignite someone or something; to put someone or something to flames. ☐ *The thief set fire to the building.* ☐ *The poor man accidentally set himself on fire.*

set foot somewhere to go or enter somewhere. (Often in the negative.) ☐ *If I were you, I wouldn't set foot in that town.* ☐ *I wouldn't set foot in her house! Not after the way she spoke to me.*

set forth (on something**)** AND **launch forth (on** something**) 1.** to start out on something. (See also **take off (on** something**).**) ☐ *We intend to set forth on our journey very early in the morning.* ☐ *What time will you launch forth?* **2.** to begin presenting a speech or an explanation. ☐ *As soon as John set forth on his speech, three people walked out.* ☐ *Every time he launches forth, somebody walks out.*

set great store by someone or something to have positive expectations for someone or something; to have high hopes for someone or something. ☐ *I set great store by my computer and its ability to help me in my work.* ☐ *We set great store by John because of his quick mind.*

set in [for a kind of weather, especially winter] to begin. (Often said of weather or climatic conditions.) ☐ *Winter set in very early this year.* ☐ *We got the windows painted before winter set in.*

set in one's **ways** leading a fixed lifestyle; living according to one's own established patterns. ☐ *At her age, she's getting sort of set in her ways.* ☐ *If you weren't so set in your ways, you'd be able to understand young people better.*

set one **back on** one's **heels** to surprise, shock, or overwhelm someone. ☐ *Her sudden announcement set us all back on our heels.* ☐ *The manager scolded me, and that really set me back on my heels.*

set one's **heart against** something to turn against something; to become totally against something. (See also **have** one's

heart set against something.) □ *Jane set her heart against going to Australia.* □ *I set my heart against her departure.*

set one's **heart on** something to become determined about something. □ *Jane set her heart on going to London.* □ *Todd had set his heart on returning.*

set one's **sights on** something to select something as one's goal. □ *I set my sights on a master's degree from the state university.* □ *Don't set your sights on something you cannot possibly do.*

set sail (for somewhere**)** to depart in a boat for somewhere. (In a sailboat or powerboat.) □ *This ship sets sail for Japan in two days.* □ *When do you set sail?*

set someone **back (**some amount of money**)** to cost someone (an amount of money). (Informal.) □ *This coat set me back about $250.* □ *That dinner at the restaurant last night really set us back.*

set someone or something **free** to release someone or something; to allow someone or something to leave, go away, depart, escape. □ *Jimmy went outside and set his balloon free.* □ *The army set the political prisoners free.*

set someone or something **off 1.** [with *someone*] to get someone very excited and angry. □ *Whenever I see someone mistreating an animal, it really sets me off.* 🅃 *The tax bill set off Bob. He raved for an hour!* **2.** [with *something*] to start something. □ *Don't set another discussion off, please!* 🅃 *The question of taxes set off an argument.*

set someone or something **on fire** Go to **set fire to** someone or something.

set someone or something **straight 1.** [with *someone*] to explain (something) to someone. (See also **put** something **straight.**) □ *I don't think you understand about taxation. Let me set you straight.* □ *Ann was confused, so I set her straight.* **2.** [with *something*] to explain something (to someone). (See also **put** something **straight.**) □ *This is very confusing, but with a little explaining I can set it straight.* □ *We'll set this matter straight in a short time.*

set someone or something **up 1.** [with *someone*] to lead—by deception—a person to play a particular role in an event; to arrange an event—usually by deception—so that a specific person takes the consequences for the event; to frame someone. (Informal or slang.) □ *I had nothing to do with the robbery! I was just standing there. Somebody must have set me up!* 🅃 *John isn't the one who started the fight. Somebody set up the poor guy.* **2.** [with *something*] to put something together; to erect something. □ *My parents bought me a dollhouse, but I had to set it up myself.* 🅃 *It took nearly an hour to set up the tent.* **3.** [with *something*] to establish or found something. □ *We set up a fund to buy food for the needy.* □ *The business owners set a bank up in the small town.* **4.** [with *something*] to make plans for something. □ *John and Mary are hard at work setting something up for the meeting.* 🅃 *Sally and Tom set up a party for Saturday night.*

set someone's **teeth on edge 1.** [for a sour or bitter taste] to irritate one's mouth and make it feel funny. □ *Have you ever eaten a whole lemon? It'll set your teeth on edge.* □ *I can't stand food that sets my teeth on edge.* **2.** [for a person or a noise] to be irritating or get on one's nerves. □ *Please don't scrape your fingernails on the blackboard! It sets my teeth on edge!* □ *Here comes Bob. He's so annoying. He really sets my teeth on edge.*

set someone **up (as** something**)** to establish someone as something. (Compare this with **set** someone **up (in business)**.) □ *Bill set himself up as boss.* □ *When Mary got her degree, she set herself up as a consultant.* 🅃 *My father set up my sisters as co-owners of the family business.* □ *He set them up with the help of a lawyer.*

set someone **up (in business)** to help establish someone in business; to provide the money someone needs to start a business. □ *My father set my sisters up in business.* □ *He helped set them up so he could keep the business in the family.*

set something **down to** something Go to **put** something **down to** something.

set something **right** AND **put** something **right** to correct something; to alter a situation to make it more fair. (See also **make** something **good**.) ☐ *This is a very unfortunate situation. I'll ask the people responsible to set this matter right.* ☐ *I'm sorry that we overcharged you. We'll try to put it right.*

set something **straight** Go to **put** something **straight**.

set something **to music** to incorporate words into a piece of music; to write a piece of music to incorporate a set of words. ☐ *The musician set my lyrics to music.* ☐ *The rock band set the poem to music.*

set the ball rolling Go to **get the ball rolling**.

set the stage for something to prepare for something; to get all of the appropriate things in place for something. (Refers to arranging the scenery, properties, and lighting for a theater production.) ☐ *The events of the past week have set the stage for further negotiation with the other side.* ☐ *Your comments set the stage for the next step—which is the hard one.*

set the table to place plates, glasses, napkins, etc., on the table before a meal. (The opposite of **clear the table**.) ☐ *Jane, would you please set the table?* ☐ *I'm tired of setting the table. Ask someone else to do it.*

set the world on fire to do exciting things that bring fame and glory. ☐ *I'm not very ambitious. I don't want to set the world on fire.* ☐ *You don't have to set the world on fire. Just do a good job.*

set to do something Go to **(all) set to** do something.

set tongues (a)wagging to cause people to start gossiping. ☐ *The affair between the boss and her accountant set tongues awagging.* ☐ *If you don't get the lawn mowed soon, you will set tongues wagging in the neighborhood.*

set type to arrange type for printing, now usually on a computer. ☐ *Have you finished setting the type for page one yet?* ☐ *John sets type for a living.*

set upon someone or something to attack someone or something violently. ☐ *The dogs set upon the bear and chased it up a tree.* ☐ *Bill set upon Tom and struck him hard in the face.*

set up shop somewhere to establish one's place of work somewhere. (Informal.) ☐ *Mary set up shop in a small office building on Oak Street.* ☐ *The police officer said, "You can't set up shop right here on the sidewalk!"*

settle a score with someone AND **settle the score (with** someone**)** to clear up a problem with someone; to get even with someone. (Slang. See also **have a score to settle (with** someone**)**.) ☐ *John wants to settle a score with his neighbor.* ☐ *Tom, it's time you and I settled the score.*

settle down 1. to calm down. ☐ *Now, children, it's time to settle down and start class.* ☐ *If you don't settle down, I'll send you all home.* **2.** to settle into a stable way of life; to get married and settle into a stable way of life. ☐ *Tom, don't you think it's about time you settled down and stopped all of this running around?* ☐ *Bill and Ann decided to settle down and raise some children.*

settle for something to agree to accept something (even though something else would be better). ☐ *We wanted a red one, but settled for a blue one.* ☐ *Ask your grocer for Wilson's canned corn—the best corn in cans. Don't settle for less!*

settle on something to decide on something. ☐ *We've discussed the merits of all of them, and we've settled on this one.* ☐ *I can't settle on one or the other, so I'll buy both.*

settle someone's **affairs** to deal with one's business matters; to manage the business affairs of someone who can't. ☐ *When my uncle died, I had to settle his affairs.* ☐ *I have to settle my affairs before going to Mexico for a year.*

settle (something**) (out of court)** to end a disagreement and reach an agreement without having to go through a court of justice. ☐ *The plaintiff and defendant de-*

cided to settle before the trial. □ *Mary and Sue settled out of court before the trial.*

settle the score (with someone**)** Go to settle a score with someone.

settle up with someone to pay someone what one owes; to pay someone one's share of something. □ *I must settle up with Jim for the bike I bought for him.* □ *Fred paid the whole restaurant bill and we all settled up with him later.*

sever ties with someone to end a relationship or agreement suddenly. □ *The company severed its ties with the dishonest employee.* □ *John has severed all ties with his parents.*

sew something **up** to complete something; to secure something. (Also literal. Informal.) □ *The manager told me to sew the contract up, or else.* T *Let's sew up this contract today.*

shack up (with someone**) 1.** to have a one-night stand with someone; to copulate (with someone). (Informal.) □ *Those two just wanted to shack up for a while.* □ *He only wanted to shack up with me.* **2.** to move in with someone temporarily, presumably for sexual purposes. (Informal.) □ *They shacked up for over a year until her parents found out and stopped sending her money.*

shades of someone or something reminders of someone or something; reminiscent of someone or something. □ *When I met Jim's mother, I thought "shades of Aunt Mary."* □ *"Shades of grade school," said Jack as the university lecturer rebuked him for being late.*

shadow of itself Go to shadow of oneself.

shadow of oneself AND **shadow of itself** someone or something that is not as strong, healthy, full, or lively as before. □ *The sick man was a shadow of his former self.* □ *The redecorated house was merely a shadow of its old self.*

shake (hands) on something to clasp and shake the hand of someone as a sign of agreement about something. □ *The two people didn't sign a contract; they just shook hands on the terms of the agreement.* □ *I think it would be better to sign an agreement than shake on it.*

shake hands (with someone**)** to clasp and shake the hand of someone as a greeting. □ *His hands were full, and I didn't know whether to try to shake hands with him or not.* □ *He put down his packages, and we shook hands.*

shake in one's **boots** AND **quake in** one's **boots** to be afraid; to shake from fear. □ *I was shaking in my boots because I had to go see the manager.* □ *Stop quaking in your boots, Bob. I'm not going to fire you.*

shake someone or something **down 1.** [with *someone*] to extort money from someone; to blackmail someone. (Slang, especially criminal slang.) □ *The gang of criminals made a living from shaking people down.* T *Lefty was trying to shake down the storekeeper.* **2.** [with *something*] to try something out; to test something and give the flaws a chance to appear. (Informal.) □ *We took the new car out for a trip to shake it down.* T *You need to shake down a complicated piece of machinery when you first get it. Then any problems will show up while the guarantee is still in effect.*

shake someone or something **off 1.** [with *someone*] to get rid of someone; to get free of someone who is bothering you. (Slang.) □ *Stop bothering me! What do I have to do to shake you off?* T *I wish I could shake off John. He's such a pest!* **2.** [with *something*] to avoid getting a disease, such as a cold; to fight something off. (Informal.) □ *I thought I was catching a cold, but I guess I shook it off.* T *I hope I can shake off this cold pretty soon.*

shake someone or something **up 1.** [with *someone*] to shock or upset someone. (Slang. See also **shook up**.) □ *The sight of the injured man shook me up.* T *Your rude remark really shook up Tom.* **2.** to jostle or knock someone or something around; to toss someone or something back and forth. □ *We rode over a rough road, and that shook us up.* T *The accident shook up John quite a bit.* **3.** to reorganize something or a group of people. □ *The new manager shook the office up and made* *things run a lot better.* 🅃 *The coach shook the team up before the last game and made them better organized.*

shake something **off** Go to **toss** something **off.**

shake the lead out Go to **get the lead out.**

Shame on someone**.** What a shameful thing someone has done! ☐ *You've torn your shirt again, Billy! Shame on you!* ☐ *When Billy tore his shirt, his mother said, "Shame on you!"*

shape someone **up** to get someone into good physical shape; to make someone behave or perform better. (See also **shape up.**) ☐ *I've got to shape myself up to improve my health.* 🅃 *The trainer was told that he'd have to shape up the boxer before the fight.*

shape up to improve one's behavior or performance; to improve one's physical shape. ☐ *Look at this, John! What a poor job you've done! It's time you shaped up!* ☐ *If I'm going to run in the marathon, I'm going to have to shape up.*

Shape up or ship out. Either improve one's performance (or behavior) or leave. ☐ *Okay, Tom. That's the end. Shape up or ship out!* ☐ *John was late again, so I told him to shape up or ship out.*

share and share alike with equal shares. ☐ *I kept five and gave the other five to Mary—share and share alike.* ☐ *The two roommates agreed that they would divide expenses—share and share alike.*

share someone's **pain** to understand and sympathize with someone's pain or emotional discomfort. (Said in order to sound sympathetic.) ☐ *I am sorry about the loss of your home. I share your pain.* ☐ *We sympathize about the loss of your mother. We share your pain.*

share someone's **sorrow** to grieve as someone else grieves. ☐ *We all share your sorrow on this sad, sad day.* ☐ *I am sorry to hear about the death in your family. I share your sorrow.*

sharp as a razor Go to **(as) sharp as a razor.**

sharp as a tack Go to **(as) sharp as a tack.**

shed crocodile tears AND **cry crocodile tears** to shed false tears; to pretend that one is weeping. ☐ *The child wasn't hurt, but she shed crocodile tears anyway.* ☐ *He thought he could get his way if he cried crocodile tears.*

shed (some) light on something AND **throw (some) light on** something to reveal something about something; to clarify something. (Also with *any*.) ☐ *This discussion has shed some light on the problem.* ☐ *Let's see if Ann can throw any light on this question.*

shell something **out** to pay money (out). (Slang.) ☐ *You'll have to shell plenty out to settle this bill.* 🅃 *The traffic ticket turned out to be very expensive. I had to shell out $150.*

shift for oneself AND **fend for** oneself to get along by oneself; to support oneself. ☐ *I'm sorry, I can't pay your rent anymore. You'll just have to shift for yourself.* ☐ *When I became twenty years old, I left home and began to fend for myself.*

shine up to someone to try to gain someone's favor by being extra nice. ☐ *John is a nice guy, except that he's always trying to shine up to the professor.* ☐ *Mary never tries to shine up to the manager.*

shipping and handling the costs of handling a product and transporting it. (See also **postage and handling.**) ☐ *Shipping and handling charges were included in the price.* ☐ *The cost of the goods is low and shipping and handling added only a few cents.*

ships that pass in the night people who meet each other briefly by chance and who are unlikely to meet again. ☐ *Mary wanted to see Jim again, but to him, they were ships that passed in the night.* ☐ *When you travel a lot on business, you meet many ships that pass in the night.*

shirk one's **duty** to neglect one's job or task. ☐ *The guard was fired for shirking his duty.* ☐ *You cannot expect to continue shirking your duty without someone noticing.*

The **shoe is on the other foot.** One is experiencing the same things that one caused another person to experience. (Proverb. Note the variation in the examples. See also **have the shoe on the other foot.**) □ *The teacher is taking a course in summer school and is finding out what it's like when the shoe is on the other foot.* □ *When the policeman was arrested, he learned what it was like to have the shoe on the other foot.*

shook up upset; shocked. (Slang. See also **shake** someone or something **up.**) □ *Relax, man! Don't get shook up!* □ *I always get shook up when I see something like that.*

shoot for something to try to do something; to attempt to do something; to aim toward a goal. □ *The industrious student shot for success.* □ *The worker shot for a $2 per hour raise.*

shoot from the hip 1. to fire a gun that is held at one's side, against one's hip. (This increases one's speed in firing a gun.) □ *When I lived at home on the farm, my father taught me to shoot from the hip.* □ *I quickly shot the snake before it bit my horse. I'm glad I learned to shoot from the hip.* **2.** to speak directly and frankly. (Informal.) □ *John has a tendency to shoot from the hip, but he generally speaks the truth.* □ *Don't pay any attention to John. He means no harm. It's just his nature to shoot from the hip.*

shoot one's **mouth off** to boast or talk too much; to tell someone's secrets. (Slang.) □ *Don't pay any attention to Bob. He's always shooting his mouth off.* [T] *Oh, Sally! Stop shooting off your mouth! You don't know what you're talking about.*

shoot something **out 1.** to stick, throw, or thrust something outward. □ *The diamond shot bright shafts of light out when the sun fell on it.* [T] *The little girl shot out her tongue at the teacher.* **2.** to settle a matter by the use of guns. (Slang. Typical of gangster or western movies.) □ *Bill and the cowboy—with whom he had been arguing—went out in the street and shot it out.* [T] *Don't they know they can settle a problem by talking? They don't need to shoot out the problem when they can talk it over.*

shoot the breeze to spend time chatting. (Slang. See also the following entry.) □ *I went over to Bob's place and shot the breeze for about an hour.* □ *Don't spend so much time shooting the breeze. Get to work!*

shoot the bull to spend time chatting about one's accomplishments, especially with others who are doing the same. (Slang. See also the previous entry.) □ *Those guys out in the backyard are just sitting around shooting the bull.* □ *It was raining, so everybody spent the day indoors drinking beer and shooting the bull.*

shoot the works to do everything; to use up everything; to bet everything. (Slang.) □ *Shall I bet half our money, or shall I shoot the works?* □ *We shot the works at the carnival—spent every cent we brought with us.*

shop around (for something**)** to shop at different stores to find what you want at the best price. □ *I've been shopping around for a new car, but they are all priced too high.* □ *You can find a bargain, but you'll have to shop around.*

short and sweet brief (and pleasant because of briefness). □ *That was a good sermon—short and sweet.* □ *I don't care what you say, as long as you make it short and sweet.*

short for something <[of a word] being a shortened form of a word or phrase.> □ Photo *is short for* photograph. □ Dave *is short for* David.

short of something not having enough of something. □ *I wanted to bake a cake, but I was short of eggs.* □ *Usually at the end of the month, I'm short of money.*

a **shot in the arm** a boost; something that gives someone energy. (Informal.) □ *Thank you for cheering me up. It was a real shot in the arm.* □ *Your friendly greeting card was just what I needed—a real shot in the arm.*

a **shot in the dark** a random or wild guess or try. (Slang.) □ *I don't know how I guessed the right answer. It was just a shot in the dark.* □ *I was lucky to hire such a* *good worker as Sally. When I hired her, it was just a shot in the dark.*

shot through with something containing something; interwoven, intermixed, or filled with something. ☐ *The rose was a lovely pink shot through with streaks of white.* ☐ *John's comments are often shot through with sarcasm.* ☐ *I want a well-marbled steak—one shot through with fat.*

shot to hell Go to (all) shot to hell.

a **shotgun wedding** a forced wedding. (Informal. From imagery of the bride's father having threatened the bridegroom with a shotgun to force him to marry.) ☐ *Mary was six months pregnant when she married Bill. It was a real shotgun wedding.* ☐ *Bob would never have married Jane if she hadn't been pregnant. Jane's father saw to it that it was a shotgun wedding.*

should have stood in bed should have stayed in bed. ☐ *What a horrible day! I should have stood in bed.* ☐ *The minute I got up and heard the news this morning, I knew I should have stood in bed.*

shoulder to shoulder side by side; with a shared purpose. ☐ *The two armies fought shoulder to shoulder against the joint enemy.* ☐ *The strikers said they would stand shoulder to shoulder against the management.*

shove one's **way** somewhere to make a path through a crowd by pushing. ☐ *The impatient man shoved his way through the crowd.* ☐ *The reporter shoved her way to the front of the crowd.*

shove someone or something **down** someone's **throat** AND **ram** someone or something **down** someone's **throat; force** someone or something **down** someone's **throat** to force someone or something on someone. (Slang and a little rude.) ☐ *I don't want any more insurance, and I don't want anyone to shove any insurance down my throat.* ☐ *Mary isn't invited to my party, and I don't wish for anyone to ram her down my throat!* ☐ *Someone is always trying to force some stupid propaganda down my throat.*

show-and-tell a trivial presentation of something of little interest. (Refers to the name of a classroom period in the lower grades where children bring something interesting into the classroom and show it to the rest of the class.) ☐ *I wouldn't call that meeting useful. It was sort of a grown-up show-and-tell.* ☐ *After the show-and-tell session where the author talked about his book, we all went into the hall and had refreshments.*

show good faith to demonstrate good intentions or good will. ☐ *I'm certain that you showed good faith when you signed the contract.* ☐ *Do you doubt that she is showing good faith?*

show off to do things in a way that is meant to attract attention. ☐ *Please stop showing off! You embarrass me.* ☐ *John is always showing off to his girlfriend.*

a **show of hands** a display of raised hands [in a group of people] that can be counted for the purpose of votes or surveys. ☐ *We were asked to vote for the candidates for captain by a show of hands.* ☐ *Jack wanted us to vote on paper, not by a show of hands, so that we could have a secret ballot.*

show one's **hand** to reveal one's intentions to someone. (From card games.) ☐ *I don't know whether Jim is intending to marry Jane or not. He's not one to show his hand.* ☐ *If you want to get a raise, don't show the boss your hand too soon.*

show one's **(true) colors** to show what one is really like or what one is really thinking. ☐ *Whose side are you on, John? Come on. Show your colors.* ☐ *It's hard to tell what Mary is thinking. She never shows her true colors.*

show one **to** one's **seat** Go to **show** someone **to a seat.**

show signs of something to show hints or indications of something. ☐ *I let the horse run at full speed until it began to show signs of tiring.* ☐ *Sally is showing signs of going to sleep.*

show someone or something **off** to display someone or something so that the best features are apparent. 🅃 *Mrs. Williams* *was showing off her baby to the neighbors.* □ *Bill drove around all afternoon showing his new car off.*

show someone **the ropes** to tell or show someone how something is to be done. □ *Since this was my first day on the job, the manager spent a lot of time showing me the ropes.* □ *Take some time and show the new boy the ropes.*

show someone **to a seat** AND **show** one **to** one's **seat** to lead or direct someone to a place to sit. □ *May I show you to your seat, sir?* □ *The ushers showed us to our seats politely and efficiently.*

show someone **(to) the door** AND **see** someone **to the door** to lead or take someone to the door or exit. □ *After we finished our talk, she showed me to the door.* □ *Bill and I finished our chat as he saw me to the door.*

show someone **up** to make someone's faults or shortcomings apparent. 🆃 *John's excellent effort really showed up Bill, who didn't try very hard at all.* □ *John is always trying to show someone up to make himself look better.*

show someone **up as** something to reveal that someone is really something (else). □ *The investigation showed her up as a fraud.* □ *The test showed the banker up as unqualified.*

show something **to good advantage** to display the best features of something; to display something so that its best features are apparent. □ *Put the vase in the center of the table and show it to good advantage.* □ *Having and using a large vocabulary shows your intelligence to good advantage.*

shuffle off this mortal coil to die. (Often jocular or formal euphemism. Not often used in consoling someone.) □ *Cousin Fred shuffled off this mortal coil after drinking a jug full of rat poison.* □ *When I shuffle off this mortal coil, I want to go out in style—bells, flowers, and a long, boring funeral.*

shut someone **up** to silence someone. □ *Oh, shut yourself up!* 🆃 *Will you please shut up that crying baby!*

shut something **down** Go to **close** something **down.**

shut the door on someone or something AND **close the door on** someone or something **1.** to close the door in order to keep someone or something out. □ *Bob opened the door, and when he saw it was Mary, he closed the door on her.* □ *"Don't shut the door on me!" screamed Mary.* **2.** [with *something*] to terminate, exclude, or obstruct something. □ *Your bad attitude shuts the door on any future cooperation from me.* □ *The bad service at that store closes the door on any more business from my company.*

shuttle someone or something **from person to person** AND **shuttle** someone or something **from place to place** to move or pass someone or something from person to person; to move or pass someone or something from place to place. □ *My phone call was shuttled from person to person.* □ *Mary shuttled her children from home to school to practice.*

shuttle someone or something **from place to place** Go to **shuttle** someone or something **from person to person.**

shy away (from someone or something**)** to avoid someone or something. □ *The dog shies away from John since he kicked it.* □ *I can understand why the dog would shy away.* □ *I shy away from eating onions. I think I'm allergic to them.*

sick and tired of someone or something disgusted and annoyed with someone or something. □ *I'm sick and tired of Ann and her whistling.* □ *We are all sick and tired of this old car.*

sick as a dog Go to **(as) sick as a dog.**

sick in bed remaining in bed while (one is) ill. □ *Tom is sick in bed with the flu.* □ *He's been sick in bed for nearly a week.*

side against someone to be against someone; to take sides against someone. □ *I thought you were my friend! I never thought you would side against me!* □ *The two brothers were always siding against their sister.*

side with someone to join with someone; to take someone else's part; to be on someone's side. □ *Why is it that you always side with him when he and I argue?* □ *I never side with anybody. I form my own opinions.*

sight for sore eyes a welcome sight. (Folksy.) □ *Oh, am I glad to see you here! You're a sight for sore eyes.* □ *I'm sure hungry. This meal is a sight for sore eyes.*

a **sign of things to come** Go to a harbinger of things to come.

sign one's **own death warrant** to do something (knowingly) that will most likely result in severe trouble. (As if one were ordering one's own execution.) □ *I wouldn't ever gamble a large sum of money. That would be signing my own death warrant.* □ *The killer signed his own death warrant when he walked into the police station and gave himself up.*

sign on the dotted line to place one's signature on a contract or other important paper. (The line is usually straight and solid.) □ *This agreement isn't properly concluded until we both sign on the dotted line.* □ *Here are the papers for the purchase of your car. As soon as you sign on the dotted line, that beautiful, shiny automobile will be all yours!*

sign on (with someone**)** to sign an agreement to work with or for someone, especially on a ship. □ *The sailor signed on with Captain Smith.* □ *Hardly any other sailor was willing to sign on.*

signal (to) someone **to** do something [for someone] to give someone a command or instruction using a signal. □ *The traffic cop signaled me to stop.* □ *Bill signaled the other driver to pull over to the side of the road.*

signed, sealed, and delivered formally and officially signed; [for a formal document to be] executed. □ *Here is the deed to the property—signed, sealed, and delivered.* □ *I can't begin work on this project until I have the contract signed, sealed, and delivered.*

silent as the dead Go to (as) silent as the dead.

silent as the grave Go to (as) silent as the grave.

silly as a goose Go to (as) silly as a goose.

silly season the time of year, usually late in the summer, when there is a lack of important news and newspapers contain articles about unimportant or trivial things instead. □ *It must be the silly season. There's a story here about peculiarly shaped potatoes.* □ *There's a piece on the front page about people with big feet. Talk about the silly season!*

simmer down to get quiet or calm. (Informal.) □ *Hey, you guys! Simmer down! Stop all the noise and go to sleep!* □ *I'm very busy now. Please come back in a few hours when things have simmered down a bit.*

since time immemorial since a very long time ago. □ *My hometown has had a big parade on the Fourth of July since time immemorial.* □ *Since time immemorial, the trees have blossomed each spring.*

sing a different tune AND **sing another tune** to change one's manner, usually from bad to good. (Almost the same as dance to another tune.) □ *When she learned that I was a bank director, she began to sing a different tune.* □ *You will sing another tune as soon as you find out how right I am!*

sing another tune Go to sing a different tune.

sing someone's **praises** to praise someone highly and enthusiastically. □ *The boss is singing the praises of his new secretary.* □ *The theater critics are singing the praises of the young actor.*

single file Go to (in) single file.

sink in [for knowledge] to be understood. (Also literal. Informal.) □ *I heard what you said, but it took a while for it to sink in.* □ *I pay careful attention to everything I hear in class, but it usually doesn't sink in.*

sink into despair [for someone] to grieve or become depressed. □ *After losing all my money, I sank into despair.* □ *There is* *no need to sink into despair. Everything is going to be all right.*

sink one's **teeth into** something **1.** to take a bite of some kind of food, usually a special kind of food. □ *I can't wait to sink my teeth into a nice juicy steak.* □ *Look at that chocolate cake! Don't you want to sink your teeth into that?* **2.** to get a chance to do, learn, or control something. □ *That appears to be a very challenging assignment. I can't wait to sink my teeth into it.* □ *Being the manager of this department is a big task. I'm very eager to sink my teeth into it.*

sink or swim to fail or succeed. □ *After I've studied and learned all I can, I have to take the test and sink or swim.* □ *It's too late to help John now. It's sink or swim for him.*

sit around (somewhere**)** to sit somewhere and relax or do nothing; to sit idly somewhere. □ *Tom likes to sit around the house in shorts and a T-shirt on hot days.* □ *Too many people are just sitting around doing nothing at my office.*

sit at someone's **feet** to admire someone greatly; to be influenced by someone's teaching; to be taught by someone. □ *Jack sat at the feet of Picasso when he was studying in Europe.* □ *Tom would love to sit at the feet of the musician Yehudi Menuhin.*

sit back and let something happen to relax and not interfere with something; to let something happen without playing a part in it. □ *I can't just sit back and let you waste all our money!* □ *Don't worry. Just sit back and let things take care of themselves.*

sit bolt upright to sit up straight. □ *Tony sat bolt upright and listened to what the teacher was saying to him.* □ *After sitting bolt upright for almost an hour in that crowded airplane, I swore I would never travel again.*

sit (idly) by to remain inactive when other people are doing something; to ignore a situation that calls for help. □ *Bob sat idly by even though everyone else was hard at work.* □ *I can't sit by while all those people need food.*

sit in for someone to take someone's else's place in a specific activity. (The activity usually involves being seated.) □ *I can't be at the meeting Thursday. Will you sit in for me?* □ *Sorry, I can't sit in for you. John is also going to be absent, and I am sitting in for him.*

sit in (on something**)** to witness or observe something without participating. (Usually involves being seated.) □ *I can't sign up for the history class, but I have permission to sit in on it.* □ *I asked the professor if I could sit in.*

sit on its hands [for an audience] to refuse to applaud. □ *We saw a very poor performance of the play. The audience sat on its hands for the entire play.* □ *The audience just sat on its hands.*

sit on one's **hands** to do nothing; to fail to help. □ *When we needed help from Mary, she just sat on her hands.* □ *We need the cooperation of everyone. You can't sit on your hands!*

sit on someone or something to hold someone or something back; to delay someone or something. (Also literal. Informal.) □ *The project cannot be finished because the city council is sitting on the final approval.* □ *Ann deserves to be promoted, but the manager is sitting on her because of a disagreement.*

sit on the fence not to take sides in a dispute; not to make a clear choice between two possibilities. (Also literal.) □ *When Jane and Tom argue, it is well to sit on the fence and then you won't make either of them angry.* □ *No one knows which of the candidates Joan will vote for. She's sitting on the fence.*

sit something **out** not to participate in something; to wait until something is over before participating. □ *Oh, please play with us. Don't sit it out.* 🅃 *I'm tired of playing cards, so I think I'll sit out this game.*

sit through something to witness or endure all of something. □ *The performance was so bad that I could hardly sit through it.* □ *You can't expect small children to sit through a long movie.*

sit tight to wait; to wait patiently. (Informal. This does not necessarily refer to sitting.) ☐ *Just relax and sit tight. I'll be right with you.* ☐ *We were waiting in line for the gates to open when someone came out and told us to sit tight because it wouldn't be much longer before we could go in.*

sit up and take notice to become alert and pay attention. ☐ *A loud noise from the front of the room caused everyone to sit up and take notice.* ☐ *The company wouldn't pay any attention to my complaints. When I had my lawyer write them a letter, they sat up and took notice.*

sit up with someone to stay with someone through the night, especially with a sick or troubled person or with someone who is waiting for something. ☐ *I had to sit up with my younger sister when she was ill.* ☐ *I sat up with Bill while he waited for an overseas telephone call.*

sit with someone **1.** to stay with someone; to **sit up with** someone. ☐ *Sally was upset, so I sat with her for a while.* ☐ *My uncle sat with me my first day in the hospital.* **2.** to stay with and care for one or more children; to baby-sit for someone. ☐ *I hired Mrs. Wilson to sit with the children.* ☐ *We couldn't go out for dinner because we couldn't find anyone to sit with the kids.*

a **sitting duck** someone or something vulnerable to attack, physical or verbal. (Preceded by *be, become, seem like,* or *act like.* See also a **sitting target**.) ☐ *You are a sitting duck out there. Get in here where the enemy cannot fire at you.* ☐ *The senator was a sitting duck because of his position on school reform.*

sitting on a powder keg in a risky or explosive situation; in a situation where something serious or dangerous may happen at any time. (Informal. A *powder keg* is a keg of gunpowder.) ☐ *Things are very tense at work. The whole office is sitting on a powder keg.* ☐ *The fire at the oil field seems to be under control for now, but all the workers there are sitting on a powder keg.*

(sitting) on top of the world feeling wonderful; glorious; ecstatic. ☐ *Wow, I feel on top of the world.* ☐ *Since he got a new job, he's on top of the world.*

sitting pretty living in comfort or luxury; in a good situation. (Informal.) ☐ *My uncle died and left enough money for me to be sitting pretty for the rest of my life.* ☐ *Now that I have a good-paying job, I'm sitting pretty.*

a **sitting target** someone or something that is in a position that is easily attacked. (See also a **sitting duck**.) ☐ *The old man was a sitting target for the burglars. He lived alone and did not have a telephone.* ☐ *People recently hired will be sitting targets if the company needs to cut back.*

six of one and half a dozen of the other about the same one way or another. ☐ *It doesn't matter to me which way you do it. It's six of one and half a dozen of the other.* ☐ *What difference does it make? They're both the same—six of one and half a dozen of the other.*

sixth sense a supposed power to know or feel things that are not perceptible by the five senses of sight, hearing, smell, taste, and touch. ☐ *I have a sixth sense that told me to avoid going home by my usual route. Later I discovered there had been a fatal accident on it.* ☐ *Jane's sixth sense demanded that she not trust Tom, even though he seemed honest enough.*

size someone or something **up** to observe someone or something to get information; to **check** someone or something. ☐ *The comedian sized the audience up and decided not to use his new material.* 🅃 *I like to size up a situation before I act.*

skate on thin ice to be in a risky situation. (Also literal. See also **on thin ice**.) ☐ *I try to stay well informed so I don't end up skating on thin ice when the teacher asks me a question.* ☐ *You are skating on thin ice when you ask me that!*

a **skeleton in the closet** AND **skeletons in the closet** a hidden and shocking secret. ☐ *You can ask anyone about how reliable I am. I don't mind. I don't have any skeletons in the closet.* ☐ *My uncle was in jail for a day once. That's our family's skeleton in the closet.*

skin and bones Go to nothing but skin and bones.

skin someone **alive** to be very angry with someone; to scold someone severely. (Folksy.) □ *I was so mad at Jane that I could have skinned her alive.* □ *If I don't get home on time, my parents will skin me alive.*

skip bail Go to jump bail.

skip out (on someone or something**)** to sneak away from someone or some event; to leave someone or an event in secret. (Slang.) □ *I heard that Bill skipped out on his wife.* □ *I'm not surprised. I thought he should have skipped out long ago.*

skip rope to jump over an arc of rope that is passed beneath one's feet then over one's head, repeatedly. □ *The children skipped rope on the playground.* □ *The boxer skipped rope while training.*

The **sky's the limit.** There is no limit to the success that can be achieved or the money that can be gained or spent. □ *If you take a job with us, you'll find the promotion prospects very good. The sky's the limit, in fact.* □ *The insurance salesmen were told that the sky was the limit when it came to potential earnings.*

slack off 1. to taper off; to reduce gradually. □ *Business tends to slack off during the winter months.* □ *The storms begin to slack off in April.* **2.** to become less active; to become lazy or inefficient. □ *Near the end of the school year, Sally began to slack off, and her grades showed it.* □ *John got fired for slacking off during the busy season.*

a **slap in the face** an insult; an act that causes disappointment or discouragement. □ *Losing the election was a slap in the face for the club president.* □ *Failing to get into a good college was a slap in the face to Tim after his years of study.*

slap someone **down** to rebuke or rebuff someone, possibly with actual slapping. □ *You may disagree with her, but you needn't slap her down like that.* □ *I only asked you what time it was! There's no need to slap me down! What a rotten humor you're in!*

slap someone **on the wrist** Go to give someone a slap on the wrist.

slap someone's **wrist** Go to give someone a slap on the wrist.

slap something **together** Go to throw something together.

slated for something scheduled for something. (Refers to a schedule written on a slate.) □ *John was slated for Friday's game, but he couldn't play with the team.* □ *Ann is slated for promotion next year.*

slated to do something scheduled to do something. □ *John was slated to play ball Friday.* □ *Who is slated to work this weekend?*

a **slave to** something someone who is under the control of something; someone who is controlled by something. (Preceded by *be, become, seem like,* or *act like.*) □ *Mary is a slave to her job.* □ *Bill is a slave to his drug addiction.*

sleep in to oversleep; to sleep late in the morning. □ *If you sleep in again, you'll get fired.* □ *I really felt like sleeping in this morning.*

sleep like a baby Go to sleep like a log.

sleep like a log AND **sleep like a baby** to sleep very soundly. □ *Everyone in our family sleeps like a log, so no one heard the fire engines in the middle of the night.* □ *Nothing can wake me up. I usually sleep like a baby.*

sleep on something to think about something overnight; to weigh a decision overnight. □ *I don't know whether I agree to do it. Let me sleep on it.* □ *I slept on it, and I've decided to accept your offer.*

sleep something **off** to sleep while the effects of liquor or drugs pass away. □ *John drank too much and went home to sleep it off.* 🅃 *Bill is at home sleeping off the effects of the drug they gave him.*

sleep with someone **1.** to share a bed with someone. □ *Do I have to sleep with my little brother?* □ *Many little boys have to sleep with their brothers.* **2.** to copulate with someone. (Euphemistic.) □ *I hear*

Sam's sleeping with Sally now. ☐ *Whom did you say he slept with?*

a **slice of the cake** a share of something. (Also literal.) ☐ *There's not much work around and so everyone must get a slice of the cake.* ☐ *The company makes huge profits and the workers want a slice of the cake.*

slick as a whistle Go to (as) slick as a whistle.

slip away AND **slip off; slip out** to go away or escape quietly or in secret. ☐ *I slipped away when no one was looking.* ☐ *Let's slip off somewhere and have a little talk.* ☐ *I'll try to slip out for an hour or two when Tom is asleep.*

slip off Go to slip away.

a **slip of the tongue** an error in speaking where a word is pronounced incorrectly, or where something that the speaker did not mean to say is said. ☐ *I didn't mean to tell her that. It was a slip of the tongue.* ☐ *I failed to understand the instructions because the speaker made a slip of the tongue at an important point.*

slip one's **mind** [for something that was to be remembered] to be forgotten. ☐ *I meant to go to the grocery store on the way home, but it slipped my mind.* ☐ *My birthday slipped my mind. I guess I wanted to forget it.*

slip out 1. [for secret information] to be revealed. ☐ *I asked her to keep our engagement secret, but she let it slip out.* ☐ *I didn't mean to tell. It just slipped out.* **2.** Go to slip away.

slip through someone's **fingers** to get away from someone; for someone to lose track (of something or someone). (Also literal.) ☐ *I had a copy of the book you want, but somehow it slipped through my fingers.* ☐ *There was a detective following me, but I managed to slip through his fingers.*

slip up to make an error. (Informal. Also without *up*.) ☐ *Try as hard as you can to do it right and not slip up.* ☐ *Everything was going fine until the last minute when I slipped up.*

slippery as an eel Go to (as) slippery as an eel.

Slow and steady wins the race. Deliberateness and determination will lead to success, or (literally) a reasonable pace will win a race. (Proverb.) ☐ *I worked my way through college in six years. Now I know what they mean when they say, "Slow and steady wins the race."* ☐ *Ann won the race because she started off slowly and established a good pace. The other runners tried to sprint the whole distance, and they tired out before the final lap. Ann's trainer said, "You see! I told you! Slow and steady wins the race."*

slow as molasses in January Go to (as) slow as molasses in January.

slow going the rate of speed when one is making progress. ☐ *It was slow going at first, but I was able to finish the project by the weekend.* ☐ *Getting the heavy rocks out of the field is slow going.*

slow on the draw 1. slow in drawing a gun. (Slang. Compare this with **quick on the draw**. Cowboy and gangster talk.) ☐ *Bill got shot because he's so slow on the draw.* ☐ *The gunslinger said, "I have to be fast. If I'm slow on the draw, I'm dead."* **2.** AND **slow on the uptake** slow to figure something out; slow-thinking. (Slang. Compare this with **quick on the draw.**) ☐ *Sally didn't get the joke because she's sort of slow on the draw.* ☐ *Bill—who's slow on the uptake—didn't get the joke until it was explained to him.*

slow on the uptake Go to slow on the draw.

slow someone or something **down** Go to slow someone or something **up**.

slow someone or something **up** AND **slow** someone or something **down** to cause someone or something to reduce speed. (The phrases with *up* are informal.) ☐ *I'm in a hurry. Don't try to slow me down.* T *Please slow up the train. There are sheep near the track.*

slower and slower at a decreasing rate of speed; slow and then even slower. ☐ *The car is going slower and slower and will stop* *soon.* □ *The dog's breathing got slower and slower as it went to sleep.*

slower than molasses in January Go to (as) slow as molasses in January.

slow(ly) but sure(ly) slowly but with a purpose; slowly and deliberately. (The expression without the *-ly* is informal.) □ *Slowly but surely, the little train reached the top of the mountain.* □ *Progress was slow but sure. Someday we would be finished.*

sly as a fox Go to (as) sly as a fox.

smack-dab in the middle right in the middle. (Informal.) □ *I want a big helping of mashed potatoes with a glob of butter smack-dab in the middle.* □ *Tom and Sally were having a terrible argument, and I was trapped—smack-dab in the middle.*

small fry 1. unimportant people. (*Small fry* are small, juvenile fish.) □ *The police have only caught the small fry. The leader of the gang is still free.* □ *You people are just small fry! I want to talk to the boss.* **2.** children. □ *Peter's taking the small fry to the zoo.* □ *We should take the small fry to the pantomime.*

small hours (of the night) AND **wee hours (of the night)** the hours immediately after midnight. □ *The dance went on into the small hours of the night.* □ *Jim goes to bed in the wee hours and gets up at lunchtime.*

the **small print** AND the **fine print** the part of a document that is not easily noticed, often because of the smallness of the print, and that often contains important information. □ *You should have read the small print before signing the contract.* □ *You should always read the fine print in an insurance policy.*

small-time small; on a small scale. (Informal.) □ *Our business is small-time just now, but it's growing.* □ *He's a small-time crook.*

smear campaign (against someone**)** a campaign aimed at damaging someone's reputation by making accusations and spreading rumors. □ *The politician's opponents are engaging in a smear campaign against him.* □ *Jack started a smear campaign against Tom so that Tom wouldn't get the manager's job.*

smell a rat to suspect that something is wrong; to sense that someone has caused something wrong. (Slang.) □ *I don't think this was an accident. I smell a rat. Bob had something to do with this.* □ *The minute I came in, I smelled a rat. Sure enough, I had been robbed.*

smell to high heaven Go to stink to high heaven.

smile on someone or something to be favorable to someone or something. □ *Fate smiled on me and I got the job.* □ *Lady luck smiled on our venture and we made a profit.*

smoke and mirrors deception and confusion. (Said of statements or more complicated rhetoric used to mislead people rather than inform. Refers to the way a magician uses optical illusion to create believability while performing a trick.) □ *Most people know that the politician was just using smoke and mirrors to make things look better than they really were.* □ *Her report was little more than smoke and mirrors. No one will believe any of it.*

smoke someone or something **out** to force someone or something out (of something), perhaps with smoke. (In cowboy or gangster talk this refers to the smoke from gunfire.) □ *There was a mouse in the attic, but I smoked it out.* Ⓣ *The sheriff and the deputies smoked out the bank robbers.*

smooth as glass Go to (as) smooth as glass.

smooth as silk Go to (as) smooth as silk.

smooth something **out** Go to smooth something **over**.

smooth something **over** AND **smooth** something **out** to reduce the intensity of an argument or a misunderstanding; to try to make people feel better about something that has happened. (Also literal.) □ *Mary and John had a terrible argument, and they are both trying to smooth it over.* □ *Let's get everyone together and try to* *smooth things out. We can't keep on arguing with one another.* 🅃 *We can smooth over the whole affair.*

a **snake in the grass** a low and deceitful person. ☐ *Sally said that Bob couldn't be trusted because he was a snake in the grass.* ☐ *"You snake in the grass!" cried Sally. "You cheated me."*

snap at someone to speak sharply or angrily to someone. ☐ *Don't snap at me. What did I do?* ☐ *Why did you snap at me? What did I do?*

snap out of something to become suddenly freed from a state. (Informal. The state can be a depression, an illness, unconsciousness, etc.) ☐ *I was very depressed for a week, but this morning I snapped out of it.* ☐ *It isn't often that a cold gets me down. Usually I can snap out of it quickly.*

snap something **up 1.** to grab and buy something. ☐ *I always snap bargains up whenever I go shopping.* 🅃 *I went to the store, and they had soup on sale, so I snapped up plenty.* **2.** to make something go faster. ☐ *You're playing this music too slowly. Snap it up!* 🅃 *This performance is getting slow and dull. Let's snap up the whole thing!*

sniff someone or something **out** to locate someone or something. (Also literal.) 🅃 *I'll see if I can sniff out the correct stylus for your stereo.* ☐ *Billy was lost, but by looking around, we were able to sniff him out.*

snug as a bug in a rug Go to (as) snug as a bug in a rug.

so-and-so a despised person. (Informal. This expression is used in place of other very insulting terms. Often modified, as in the example below.) ☐ *You dirty so-and-so! I can't stand you!* ☐ *Don't you call me a so-and-so, you creep!*

So be it. This is the way it will be. ☐ *If you insist on running off and marrying her, so be it. Only don't say I didn't warn you!* ☐ *Mary has decided that this is what she wants. So be it.*

so clean you could eat off the floor [of a room or a house] very clean. ☐ *Her kitchen is so clean you could eat off the floor!* ☐ *It's so clean here you could eat off the floor. I prefer a little mess, myself.*

so far as anyone knows Go to (as) far as anyone knows.

so far as possible Go to as far as possible.

so far as someone or something **is concerned** Go to (as) far as someone or something is concerned.

so far as something **is concerned** Go to (as) far as something is concerned.

So far, so good. All is going well so far. ☐ *We are half finished with our project. So far, so good.* ☐ *The operation is proceeding quite nicely—so far, so good.*

So it goes. That is the kind of thing that happens.; That is life. ☐ *Too bad about John and his problems. So it goes.* ☐ *I just lost a twenty-dollar bill, and I can't find it anywhere. So it goes.*

so long good-bye. (Informal.) ☐ *So long, see you later.* ☐ *As John got out of the car, he said, "Thanks for the ride. So long."*

so long as Go to as long as.

so mad I could scream very mad. ☐ *I am just so mad I could scream! Why is he such a jerk?* ☐ *She makes me so made I could scream.*

so much for someone or something that is the last of someone or something; there is no need to consider someone or something anymore. ☐ *It just started raining. So much for our picnic this afternoon.* ☐ *So much for John. He just called in sick and can't come to work today.*

so much the better even better; all to the better. (Informal.) ☐ *Please come to the picnic. If you can bring a salad, so much the better.* ☐ *The flowers look lovely on the shelf. It would be so much the better if you put them on the table.*

so quiet you could hear a pin drop Go to so still you could hear a pin drop.

so-so not good and not bad; mediocre. (Informal.) ☐ *I didn't have a bad day. It was just so-so.* ☐ *The players put on a so-so performance.*

so soon early; before the regular time; ahead of schedule. □ *I got there early because my bus arrived so soon.* □ *Because the meeting ended so soon, I had some extra time.*

so still you could hear a pin drop AND **so quiet you could hear a pin drop** very quiet. (Also with *can.*) □ *When I came into the room, it was so still you could hear a pin drop. Then everyone shouted, "Happy birthday!"* □ *Please be quiet. Be so quiet you can hear a pin drop.*

so to speak as one might say; said a certain way, even though the words are not exactly accurate. □ *John helps me with my taxes. He's my accountant, so to speak.* □ *I just love my little poodle. She's my baby, so to speak.*

soaked to the skin with one's clothing wet clear through to the skin. □ *I was caught in the rain and got soaked to the skin.* □ *Oh, come in and dry off! You must be soaked to the skin.*

sober as a judge Go to (as) sober as a judge.

sock something **away** to store something in a safe place. (Informal.) □ *While I worked in the city, I was able to sock $100 away every month.* 🅃 *At the present time, I can't sock away that much.*

soft as a baby's bottom Go to (as) soft as a baby's bottom.

soft as down Go to (as) soft as down.

soft as silk Go to (as) soft as silk.

soft as velvet Go to (as) soft as velvet.

soil one's **diaper(s)** [for a baby] to excrete waste into its diaper. □ *The baby soiled his diapers.* □ *I detect that someone has soiled his diaper.*

soil one's **hands** Go to get one's hands dirty.

sold out [of a product] completely sold with no more items remaining; [of a store] having no more of a particular product. □ *The tickets were sold out so we couldn't go to the concert.* □ *I wanted new shoes like yours, but they were sold out.*

solid as a rock Go to (as) solid as a rock.

(some) new blood new personnel; new members brought into a group to revive it. □ *This company needs some new blood on its board to bring in new ideas.* □ *We're trying to get some new blood in the club. Our membership is falling.* □ *Our club needs new blood. It has become boring.* □ *The firm's management has at last got a little new blood. Things should improve now.*

someone or something **checks out** someone or something is verified or authenticated. (Informal.) □ *I spent all afternoon working with my checkbook, trying to get the figures to check out.* □ *The police wouldn't believe that I am who I say I am until they made a few telephone calls to see if my story checked out.*

someone **of note** a person who is famous. □ *We invited a speaker of note to lecture at the next meeting.* □ *The baseball player of note was inducted into the Hall of Fame.*

someone's **ace in the hole** something or someone held (secretly) in reserve; anything that can help in an emergency. (Slang. Refers to an ace dealt facedown in poker.) □ *The hostages served as the terrorists' ace in the hole for getting what they wanted.* □ *The twenty-dollar bill in my shoe is my ace in the hole.*

someone's **bread and butter** someone's income; someone's livelihood—the source of one's food. (Work or a job leads to a paycheck that will buy bread and butter.) □ *I can't miss another day of work. That's my bread and butter.* □ *I like to go to business conferences. That's good because that's my bread and butter.*

someone's **goose is cooked** one is finished; one has been found out and is in trouble. □ *It's over. His goose is cooked!* □ *If I get caught, my goose is cooked.*

someone's **last will and testament** a will; the last edition of someone's will. □ *The lawyer read Uncle Charles's last will and testament to a group of expectant relatives.* □ *Fred dictated his last will and testament on his deathbed.*

someone's **mission in life** one's purpose for living; the reason for which one lives on the earth. ☐ *Bob's mission in life is to make money.* ☐ *My mission in life is to help people live in peace.*

someone's **pet hate** something that is disliked intensely by someone and is a constant or repeated annoyance. ☐ *My pet hate is being put on hold on the telephone.* ☐ *Another pet hate of mine is having to stand in line.*

someone's **pet peeve** one's "favorite" or most often encountered annoyance. ☐ *My pet peeve is someone who always comes into the theater after the show has started.* ☐ *Drivers who don't signal are John's pet peeve.*

someone's **place of business** a place where business is done; a factory or office. ☐ *Our place of business opens at noon each day.* ☐ *You will have to come to our place of business to make a purchase.*

someone's **swan song** the last work or performance of a playwright, musician, actor, etc., before death or retirement. ☐ *His portrayal of Lear was the actor's swan song.* ☐ *We didn't know that her performance last night was the singer's swan song.*

someone's **train of thought** someone's pattern of thinking; someone's sequence of ideas; what one was just thinking about. (See also **lose** one's **train of thought**.) ☐ *My train of thought is probably not as clear as it should be.* ☐ *I cannot seem to follow your train of thought on this matter. Will you explain it a little more carefully, please?*

someone **wrote the book on** something to be very authoritative about something; to know enough about something to write the definitive book on it. (Also literal. Always in past tense.) ☐ *Ted wrote the book on unemployment. He's been looking for work in three states for two years.* ☐ *Do I know about misery? I wrote the book on misery!*

something about someone or something something strange, special, or curious about someone or something. ☐ *There is something about Jane. I just can't figure her out.* ☐ *I love Mexican food. There's just something about it.*

something else something wonderful; something extra special. (Also literal. Informal.) ☐ *Did you see her new car? That's really something else!* ☐ *John hit a ball yesterday that went out of the stadium and kept on going. He's something else!*

something else (again) something entirely different. (Informal.) ☐ *Borrowing is one thing, but stealing is something else.* ☐ *Skin diving is easy and fun, but scuba diving is something else again.*

something of the sort something of the kind just mentioned. ☐ *This is a spruce tree, or something of the sort.* ☐ *Jane has a cold or something of the sort.*

something or other something; one thing or another. (Informal.) ☐ *I can't remember what Ann said—something or other.* ☐ *A messenger came by and dropped off something or other at the front desk.*

something to that effect AND **words to that effect** something like what was just said. (Informal.) ☐ *She said she wouldn't be available until after three, or something to that effect.* ☐ *I was told to keep out of the house—or something to that effect.*

something's up something is going to happen; something is going on. (Slang.) ☐ *Everybody looks very nervous. I think something's up.* ☐ *From the looks of all the activity around here, I think something's up.*

(somewhere) in the neighborhood of an amount approximately a particular measurement. ☐ *I take somewhere in the neighborhood of ten pills a day for my various ailments.* ☐ *My rent is in the neighborhood of $700 per month.*

somewhere to hang (up) one's **hat** AND a **place to hang** one's **hat; a place to call** one's **own** a place to live; a place to call one's home. ☐ *What I need is somewhere to hang up my hat. I just can't stand all this traveling.* ☐ *A home is a lot more than a place to hang your hat.*

son of a bitch 1. a very horrible person. (Informal. Use with caution. Usually intended as a strong insult. Never used casually.) ☐ *Bill called Bob a son of a bitch, and Bob punched Bill in the face.* ☐ *This guy's a son of a bitch. He treats everybody rotten.* **2.** a useless annoyance; something worthless. ☐ *This car is a son of a bitch. It won't ever start when it's cold.* ☐ *This bumpy old road needs paving. It's a real son of a bitch.* **3.** a difficult task. (Informal.) ☐ *This job is a son of a bitch.* ☐ *I can't do this kind of thing. It's too hard—a real son of a bitch.*

son of a gun 1. a horrible person. (Informal. A euphemism for **son of a bitch.** Use with caution.) ☐ *When is that plumber going to show up and fix this leak? The stupid son of a gun!* ☐ *Bob is a rotten son of a gun if he thinks he can get away with that.* **2.** old (male) friend. (Informal. A friendly—male to male—way of referring to a friend. Use with caution.) ☐ *Why Bill, you old son of a gun, I haven't seen you in three or four years.* ☐ *When is that son of a gun John going to come visit us? He's neglecting his friends.*

son of a sea biscuit a person, usually a male. (Sometimes a substitute for **son of a bitch.**) ☐ *Why, good to see you, you old son of a sea biscuit.* ☐ *You son of a sea biscuit! You make me so mad I could slug you.*

soon as possible Go to (as) soon as possible.

sooner or later eventually; in the short term or in the long term. ☐ *He'll have to pay the bill sooner or later.* ☐ *She'll get what she deserves sooner or later.*

sorry Go to (I'm) sorry.

sort of something AND **kind of** something almost something; somewhat; somehow. (Informal.) ☐ *Isn't it sort of cold out?* ☐ *That was kind of a stupid thing to do, wasn't it?*

sort something **out** to clear up confusion; to straighten out something disorderly. (Also literal.) 🅃 *Now that things are settled down, I can sort out my life.* ☐ *This place is a mess. Let's sort things out before we do anything else.*

sound as a dollar Go to (as) sound as a dollar.

sound as if AND **sound like** to seem, from what has been said, as if something were so. (*Sound like* is colloquial.) ☐ *It sounds as if you had a good vacation.* ☐ *You sound like you are angry.*

sound like Go to sound as if.

sound like a broken record to say the same thing over and over again. (From an earlier age when a crack in a 78 rpm record would cause the needle (or stylus) to stay in the same groove and play it over and over.) ☐ *He's always complaining about the way she treats him. He sounds like a broken record!* ☐ *I hate to sound like a broken record, but we just don't have enough people on the payroll to work efficiently.*

sound like something to seem like something. ☐ *That sounds like a good idea.* ☐ *Your explanation sounds like an excuse!*

sound off (about something**)** to speak loudly and freely about something, especially when complaining. (Informal.) ☐ *The people at the bus stop were sounding off about the poor transportation services.* ☐ *Bob was sounding off about the government's economic policies.* ☐ *Sam sounds off every chance he gets.*

sound someone **out** to try to find out what someone thinks (about something). ☐ *I don't know what Jane thinks about your suggestion, but I'll sound her out.* 🅃 *Please sound out everyone in your department.*

soup something **up** to make something (especially a car) more powerful. (Slang.) ☐ *I wish someone would soup my car up. It'll hardly run.* 🅃 *Bill spent all summer souping up that old car he bought.*

sour as vinegar Go to (as) sour as vinegar.

sow one's **wild oats** to do wild and foolish things in one's youth. (Often assumed to have some sort of sexual meaning.) ☐ *Dale was out sowing his wild oats last night, and he's in jail this morning.* ☐ *Mrs. Smith told Mr. Smith that he was too old to be sowing his wild oats.*

spaced-out dopey; giddy. (Slang.) □ *I don't see how Sally can accomplish anything. She's so spaced-out!* □ *She's not really spaced-out. She acts that way on purpose.*

spare someone something to exempt someone from having to listen to or experience something. □ *I'll spare you the details and get to the point.* □ *Please, spare me the story and tell me what you want.*

speak for itself AND **speak for themselves** [for something] not to need explaining; [for things] to have an obvious meaning. □ *The evidence speaks for itself.* □ *The facts speak for themselves. Tom is guilty.* □ *Your results speak for themselves. You need to work harder.*

speak for themselves Go to speak for itself.

speak highly of someone or something to say good things about someone or something. (Note the variation in the examples. See also think a lot of someone or something.) □ *Ann speaks quite highly of Jane's work.* □ *Everyone speaks very highly of Jane.*

speak ill of someone to say something bad about someone. □ *I refuse to speak ill of any of my friends.* □ *Max speaks ill of no one and refuses to repeat gossip.*

speak off the cuff to speak in public without preparation. □ *I'm not too good at speaking off the cuff.* □ *I need to prepare a speech for Friday, although I speak off the cuff quite well.*

speak of the devil said when someone whose name has just been mentioned appears or is heard from. □ *Well, speak of the devil! Hello, Tom. We were just talking about you.* □ *I had just mentioned Sally when—speak of the devil—she walked in the door.*

speak one's **mind** to say frankly what one thinks (about something). (See also speak out (on something).) □ *Please let me speak my mind, and then you can do whatever you wish.* □ *You can always depend on John to speak his mind. He'll let you know what he really thinks.*

speak out of turn to say something unwise or imprudent; to say the right thing at the wrong time. □ *Excuse me if I'm speaking out of turn, but what you are proposing is quite wrong.* □ *Bob was quite honest, even if he was speaking out of turn.*

speak out (on something**)** to say something frankly and directly; to speak one's mind. (See also speak up.) □ *This law is wrong, and I intend to speak out on it until it is repealed.* □ *You must speak out. People need to know what you think.*

speak the same language [for people] to have similar ideas, tastes, etc. (Also literal.) □ *Jane and Jack get along very well. They really speak the same language about almost everything.* □ *Bob and his father didn't speak the same language when it comes to politics.*

speak up 1. to speak more loudly. □ *They can't hear you in the back of the room. Please speak up.* □ *What? Speak up, please. I'm hard of hearing.* **2.** to speak out (on something). □ *If you think that this is wrong, you must speak up and say so.* □ *I'm too shy to speak up.*

speak up for someone or something to speak in favor of someone or something; to speak in someone's defense. □ *If anybody says bad things about me, I hope you speak up for me.* □ *I want to speak up for the rights of students.*

speak with a forked tongue to tell lies; to try to deceive someone. □ *Jean's mother sounds very charming, but she speaks with a forked tongue.* □ *People tend to believe Fred because he seems plausible, but we know he speaks with a forked tongue.*

spell something **out 1.** to spell something (in letters). (Also without *out*.) □ *I can't understand your name. Can you spell it out?* 🅃 *Please spell out all the strange words so I can write them down correctly.* **2.** to give all the details of something. □ *I want you to understand this completely, so I'm going to spell it out very carefully.* 🅃 *The instruction book for my computer spells out everything very carefully.*

spell trouble to signify future trouble; to mean trouble. (Informal.) □ *This letter* *that came today spells trouble.* □ *The sky looks angry and dark. That spells trouble.*

spick-and-span very clean. (Informal.) □ *I have to clean up the house and get it spick-and-span for the party Friday night.* □ *I love to have everything around me spick-and-span.*

spill the beans Go to let the cat out of the bag.

spin a yarn to tell a tale. □ *Grandpa spun an unbelievable yarn for us.* □ *My uncle is always spinning yarns about his childhood.*

spin one's **wheels** to be in motion, but get nowhere. (Slang.) □ *This is a terrible job. I'm just spinning my wheels and not getting anywhere.* □ *Get organized and try to accomplish something. Stop spinning your wheels!*

spin something **off** to create something as a by-product of something else. □ *When the company reorganized, it spun its banking division off.* 🅃 *By spinning off part of its assets, a company gets needed capital.*

spit (something**) up** to throw something up; to vomit something. (A little gentler than throw (something) up.) □ *I guess that the food didn't agree with the dog, because he spit it up.* 🅃 *The baby has been spitting up all morning.* 🅃 *Bob spit up his whole dinner.*

split hairs to quibble; to try to make petty distinctions. □ *They don't have any serious differences. They are just splitting hairs.* □ *Don't waste time splitting hairs. Accept it the way it is.*

split one's **sides (with laughter)** to laugh so hard that one's sides almost split. (Always an exaggeration.) □ *The members of the audience almost split their sides with laughter.* □ *When I heard what happened to Patricia, I almost split my sides.*

split people up to separate two or more people (from one another). □ *If you two don't stop chattering, I'll have to split you up.* □ *The group of people grew too large, so we had to split them up.* 🅃 *I will have to split up that twosome in the corner.*

split something **fifty-fifty** Go to divide something fifty-fifty.

split the difference to divide the difference evenly (with someone else). □ *You want to sell for $120, and I want to buy for $100. Let's split the difference and close the deal at $110.* □ *I don't want to split the difference. I want $120.*

split up [for people] to separate or leave one another; [for a couple] to divorce or spearate. □ *I heard that Mr. and Mrs. Brown have split up.* □ *Our little club had to split up because everyone was too busy.*

spoken for taken; reserved (for someone). □ *I'm sorry, but this one is already spoken for.* □ *Pardon me. Can I sit here, or is this seat spoken for?*

spook someone or something to startle or disorient someone or something. (Folksy.) □ *A snake spooked my horse, and I nearly fell off.* □ *Your warning spooked me, and I was upset for the rest of the day.*

spoon-feed someone to treat someone with too much care or help; to teach someone with methods that are too easy and do not stimulate the learner to independent thinking. (Also literal.) □ *The teacher spoon-feeds the students by dictating notes on the novel instead of getting the children to read the books.* □ *You mustn't spoon-feed the new recruits by telling them what to do all the time. They must use their initiative.*

a **sporting chance** a reasonably good chance. (See also fighting chance.) □ *If you hurry, you have a sporting chance of catching the bus.* □ *The small company has only a sporting chance of getting the export order.*

spout off (about someone or something**)** to talk too much about someone or something. (Informal.) □ *Why do you always have to spout off about things that don't concern you?* □ *Everyone in our office spouts off about the boss.* □ *There is no need to spout off like that. Calm down and think about what you're saying.*

spread it on thick Go to lay it on thick.

spread like wildfire to spread rapidly and without control. □ *The epidemic is spreading like wildfire. Everyone is getting* *sick.* □ *John told a joke that was so funny it spread like wildfire.*

spread oneself **too thin** to do so many things that you can do none of them well. □ *It's a good idea to get involved in a lot of activities, but don't spread yourself too thin.* □ *I'm too busy these days. I'm afraid I've spread myself too thin.*

spring for something to treat (someone) to something. (Slang.) □ *John and I went out last night, and he sprang for dinner.* □ *At the park Bill usually springs for ice cream.*

spring something **on** someone to surprise someone with something. (Informal.) □ *I'm glad you told me now, rather than springing it on me at the last minute.* □ *I sprang the news on my parents last night. They were not glad to hear it.*

spruce someone or something **up** to make someone or something clean and orderly. □ *I'll be ready to go as soon as I spruce myself up a bit.* 🅃 *I have to spruce up the house for the party.*

square accounts (with someone**) 1.** to settle one's financial accounts with someone. □ *I have to square accounts with the bank this week, or it'll take back my car.* □ *I called the bank and said I needed to come in and square accounts.* **2.** to get even with someone; to straighten out a misunderstanding with someone. (Informal.) □ *I'm going to square accounts with Tom. He insulted me in public, and he owes me an apology.* □ *Tom, you and I are going to have to square accounts.*

square deal a fair and honest transaction; fair treatment. (Informal.) □ *All the workers want is a square deal, but their boss underpays them.* □ *You always get a square deal with that travel company.*

square meal a nourishing, filling meal. □ *All you've eaten today is junk food. You should sit down to a square meal.* □ *The poor old man hadn't had a square meal in weeks.*

square off (for something**)** to get ready for an argument or a fight. □ *John was angry and appeared to be squaring off for a fight.* □ *When those two square off, everyone gets out of the way.*

a **square peg in a round hole** a misfit. □ *John can't seem to get along with the people he works with. He's just a square peg in a round hole.* □ *I'm not a square peg in a round hole. It's just that no one understands me.*

square someone or something **away** to get someone or something arranged or properly taken care of. □ *See if you can square Bob away in his new office.* 🅃 *Please square away the problems we discussed earlier.*

square up to someone or something to face someone or something bravely; to tackle someone or something. □ *You'll have to square up to the bully or he'll make your life miserable.* □ *It's time to square up to your financial problems. You can't just ignore them.*

square up with someone to pay someone what one owes; to pay one's share of something to someone. (Informal.) □ *I'll square up with you later if you pay the whole bill now.* □ *Bob said he would square up with Tom for his share of the gas.*

squared away arranged or properly taken care of. □ *Is Ann squared away yet?* □ *I will talk to you when I am squared away.*

squeak by (someone or something**)** to just barely get by someone or something. (Informal.) □ *The guard was almost asleep, so I squeaked by him.* □ *I wasn't very well prepared for the test, and I just squeaked by.*

squirrel something **away** to hide or store something. (Folksy.) □ *Billy has been squirreling candy away in his top drawer.* 🅃 *I've been squirreling away a little money each week for years.*

stab someone **in the back** to betray someone. (Also literal. Informal.) □ *I thought we were friends! Why did you stab me in the back?* □ *You don't expect a person whom you trust to stab you in the back.*

stack something **up** to make a stack of things. (Also without the *up*.) □ *Where should I* *stack them up?* T *Please stack up these boxes.*

stack the cards (against someone or something**)** Go to **stack the deck (against** someone or something**)**.

stack the deck (against someone or something**)** AND **stack the cards (against** someone or something**)** to arrange things against someone or something. (Slang. Originally from card playing.) □ *I can't get ahead at my office. Someone has stacked the cards against me.* □ *Do you really think that someone has stacked the deck? Isn't it just fate?*

stake a claim (to something**)** to lay or make a claim for something. (Informal.) □ *I want to stake a claim to that last piece of pie.* □ *You don't need to stake a claim. Just ask politely.*

stall someone or something **off** to put off or delay someone or something. □ *The sheriff is at the door. I'll stall him off while you get out the back door.* T *You can stall off the sheriff, but you can't stall off justice.*

stamp someone or something **out 1.** [with *someone*] to get rid of or kill someone. (Slang.) □ *You just can't stamp somebody out on your own!* T *The victim wanted to stamp out the robbers without a trial.* **2.** [with *something*] to extinguish something. □ *Quick, stamp that fire out before it spreads.* T *Tom stamped out the sparks before they started a fire.* **3.** [with *something*] to eliminate something. □ *The doctors hope they can stamp cancer out.* T *Many people think that they can stamp out evil.*

stand a chance to have a chance. □ *Do you think I stand a chance of winning first place?* □ *Everyone stands a chance of catching the disease.*

stand and deliver to give up something to someone who demands it. (Originally used by highway robbers asking for passengers' valuables. Now used figuratively.) □ *And when the tax agent says "Stand and deliver" you have to be prepared to pay what is demanded.* □ *The robber stopped the coach and demanded of Lady Ellen, "Stand and deliver!"*

stand behind someone or something AND **stand (in) back of** someone or something to endorse or guarantee something or the actions of a person. (Also literal.) □ *Our company stands behind this product 100 percent.* □ *I stand behind Bill and everything he does.*

stand by to wait and remain ready. (Generally heard in communication, such as broadcasting, telephones, etc.) □ *Your transatlantic telephone call is almost ready. Please stand by.* □ *Is everyone ready for the telecast? Only ten seconds—stand by.*

stand by someone to support someone; to continue supporting someone even when things are bad. (Also literal. Compare this with **stick by** someone or something.) □ *Don't worry. I'll stand by you no matter what.* □ *I feel as though I have to stand by my brother even if he goes to jail.*

stand corrected to admit that one has been wrong. □ *I realize that I accused him wrongly. I stand corrected.* □ *We appreciate now that our conclusions were wrong. We stand corrected.*

stand for something **1.** to endure something. □ *The teacher won't stand for any whispering in class.* □ *We just can't stand for that kind of behavior.* **2.** to signify something. □ *In a traffic signal, the red light stands for "stop."* □ *The abbreviation* Dr. *stands for "doctor."* **3.** to endorse or support an ideal. □ *The mayor claims to stand for honesty in government and jobs for everyone.* □ *Every candidate for public office stands for all the good things in life.*

stand in awe (of someone or something**)** to be overwhelmed with respect for someone or something. □ *Many people stand in awe of the president.* □ *Bob says he stands in awe of a big juicy steak. I think he's exaggerating.* □ *When it comes to food, you can say that it's delicious, but one hardly stands in awe.*

stand (in) back of someone or something Go to **stand behind** someone or something.

stand in (for someone**)** to substitute for someone; to serve in someone's place. □ *The famous opera singer was ill, and an in-*

experienced singer had to stand in for her. □ *The new singer was grateful for the opportunity to stand in.*

stand in someone's **way** to be a barrier to someone's desires or intentions. (Also literal.) □ *I know you want a divorce so you can marry Ann. Well, I won't stand in your way. You can have the divorce.* □ *I know you want to leave home, and I don't want to stand in your way. You're free to go.*

stand on ceremony to hold rigidly to protocol or formal manners. (Often in the negative.) □ *Please help yourself to more. Don't stand on ceremony.* □ *We are very informal around here. Hardly anyone stands on ceremony.*

stand one's **ground** AND **hold** one's **ground** to stand up for one's rights; to resist an attack. □ *The lawyer tried to confuse me when I was giving testimony, but I managed to stand my ground.* □ *Some people were trying to crowd us off the beach, but we held our ground.*

stand on one's **own two feet** to be independent and self-sufficient. (Informal. Compare this with **get back on one's feet**.) □ *I'll be glad when I have a good job and can stand on my own two feet.* □ *When Jane gets out of debt, she'll be able to stand on her own two feet again.*

stand out to be uniquely visible or conspicuous. □ *This computer stands out as one of the best available.* □ *Because John is so tall, he really stands out in a crowd.*

stand over someone to monitor or watch over someone, possibly while actually standing near the person. □ *You don't have to stand over me. I can do it by myself.* □ *I know from previous experience that if I don't stand over you, you'll never finish.*

stand pat to remain as is; to preserve the status quo. (Informal.) □ *We can't just stand pat! We have to keep making progress!* □ *This company isn't increasing sales. It's just standing pat.*

stand someone **in good stead** to be useful or beneficial to someone. □ *This is a fine overcoat. I'm sure it'll stand you in good stead for many years.* □ *I did the mayor a favor that I'm sure will stand me in good stead.*

stand someone **to a treat** to pay for food or drink for someone as a special favor. □ *We went to the zoo, and my father stood us all to a treat. We had ice cream and soft drinks.* □ *We went to a nice restaurant and had a fine meal. It was even better when Mr. Williams told us he'd stand us to a treat, and he picked up the bill.*

stand someone **up** to fail to meet someone for a date or an appointment. □ *John and Jane were supposed to go out last night, but she stood him up.* 🅃 *If you stand up people very often, you'll find that you have no friends at all.*

stand still for something AND **hold still for** something to tolerate or endure something. (Often in the negative.) □ *I won't stand still for that kind of behavior!* □ *She won't hold still for that kind of talk.*

stand to reason to seem reasonable. □ *It stands to reason that it'll be colder in January than it is in November.* □ *It stands to reason that Bill left in a hurry, although no one saw him go.*

stand up and be counted to state one's support (for someone or something); to **come out for** someone or something. □ *If you believe in more government help for farmers, write your representative—stand up and be counted.* □ *I'm generally in favor of what you propose, but not enough to stand up and be counted.*

a **standing joke** a subject that regularly and over a period of time causes amusement whenever it is mentioned. □ *Uncle Jim's driving was a standing joke. He used to drive incredibly slowly.* □ *Their mother's inability to make a decision was a standing joke in the Smith family all their lives.*

stare someone **in the face** Go to **look** someone **in the face**.

stark raving mad totally insane; completely crazy; out of control. (Often an exaggeration.) □ *When she heard about what happened at the office, she went stark raving mad.* □ *You must be stark raving* *mad if you think I would trust you with my car!*

start from scratch to start from the beginning; to start from nothing. (Informal. Compare this with **make** something **from scratch.**) □ *Whenever I bake a cake, I start from scratch. I never use a cake mix in a box.* □ *I built every bit of my own house. I started from scratch and did everything with my own hands.*

start off on the wrong foot to begin [something] by doing something wrong. (Also literal. See also **be off on the wrong foot; get off on the wrong foot.**) □ *I don't want to start off on the wrong foot by saying something stupid. What should I say?* □ *Poor Donna started off on the wrong foot when she arrived forty minutes late.*

start (off) with a clean slate AND **start (over) with a clean slate** to start out again afresh; to ignore the past and start over again. (Refers to making marks on a [clean] slate with chalk.) □ *I plowed under all last year's flowers so I could start with a clean slate next spring.* □ *If I start off with a clean slate, then I'll know exactly what each plant is.* □ *When Bob got out of jail, he started over with a clean slate.*

start (over) with a clean slate Go to **start (off) with a clean slate.**

start someone **in (as** something**)** AND **start** someone **out (as** something**)** to start someone on a job as a certain kind of worker. □ *I got a job in a restaurant today. They started me in as a dishwasher.* □ *I now work for the telephone company. They started me out as a local operator.*

start someone **out (as** something**)** Go to **start** someone **in (as** something**).**

start something to start a fight or an argument. (Also literal. *Something* is *anything* or *nothing* in the negative.) □ *Hey, you! Better be careful unless you want to start something.* □ *I don't want to start anything. I'm just leaving.*

start something **up** to start something, such as a car or some procedure. (Also without *up*.) Ⓣ *It was cold, but I managed to start up the car without any difficulty.* □ *We can't start the project up until we have more money.*

start the ball rolling Go to **get the ball rolling.**

stay after someone Go to **keep after** someone.

stay in touch (with someone**)** Go to **keep in touch (with** someone**).**

stay put not to move; to stay where one is. (Informal.) □ *We've decided to stay put and not to move to Florida.* □ *If the children just stay put, their parents will come for them soon.*

steady as a rock Go to **(as) steady as a rock.**

steal a base to sneak from one base to another in baseball. □ *The runner stole second base, but he nearly got put out on the way.* □ *Tom runs so slowly that he never tries to steal a base.*

steal a march (on someone**)** to get some sort of an advantage over someone without being noticed. □ *I got the contract because I was able to steal a march on my competitor.* □ *You have to be clever and fast—not dishonest—to steal a march.*

steal someone's **thunder** to lessen someone's force or authority. □ *What do you mean by coming in here and stealing my thunder? I'm in charge here!* □ *Someone stole my thunder by leaking my announcement to the press.*

steal the show Go to **steal the spotlight.**

steal the spotlight AND **steal the show** to give the best performance in a show, play, or some other event; to get attention for oneself. □ *The lead in the play was very good, but the butler stole the show.* □ *Ann always tries to steal the spotlight when she and I make a presentation.*

steamed up angry. (Informal.) □ *What Bob said really got me steamed up.* □ *Why do you get so steamed up about nothing?*

steaming (mad) very angry; very mad; very upset. □ *The steaming coach yelled at the clumsy players.* □ *The principal was steaming mad when he found that his office had been vandalized.*

steer clear (of someone or something**)** to avoid someone or something. □ *John is mad at me, so I've been steering clear of him.* □ *Steer clear of that book. It has many errors in it.* □ *Good advice. I'll steer clear.*

step-by-step little by little, one step at a time. (Refers both to walking and following instructions.) □ *Just follow the instructions step-by-step, and everything will be fine.* □ *The old man slowly moved across the lawn step-by-step.*

step down (from something**)** to resign a job or a responsibility. (Also literal.) □ *The mayor stepped down from office last week.* □ *It's unusual for a mayor to step down.*

step into someone's **shoes** to take over a job or some role from someone. □ *I was prepared to step into the boss's shoes, so there was no disruption when he left for another job.* □ *There was no one who could step into Alice's shoes when she left, so everything came to a stop.*

step in(to the breach) to move into a space or vacancy; to assume the job of someone who has left it. □ *When Ann resigned as president, I stepped into the breach.* □ *A number of people asked me to step in and take her place.*

step on it Go to step on the gas.

step on someone's **toes** to interfere with or offend someone. (Also literal.) □ *When you're in public office, you have to avoid stepping on anyone's toes.* □ *Ann stepped on someone's toes during the last campaign and lost the election.*

step on the gas AND **step on it** hurry up. (Informal.) □ *I'm in a hurry, driver. Step on it!* □ *I can't step on the gas, mister. There's too much traffic.*

step out of line to misbehave; to do something offensive. (Also literal.) □ *I'm terribly sorry. I hope I didn't step out of line.* □ *John is a lot of fun to go out with, but he has a tendency to step out of line.*

step (right) up to move forward, toward someone. □ *Step up and get your mail when I call your name.* □ *Come on, everybody. Step right up and help yourself to supper.*

step something **up** to cause something to go faster. 🅃 *The factory was not making enough cars, so they stepped up production.* □ *The music was not fast enough, so the conductor told everyone to step it up.*

stew in one's **own juice** to be left alone to suffer one's anger or disappointment. (Informal.) □ *John has such a terrible temper. When he got mad at us, we just let him go away and stew in his own juice.* □ *After John stewed in his own juice for a while, he decided to come back and apologize to us.*

stick around [for a person] to remain in a place. (Informal.) □ *The kids stuck around for a time after the party was over.* □ *Oh, Ann. Please stick around for a while. I want to talk to you later.*

stick by someone or something AND **stick with** someone or something to support someone or something; to continue supporting someone or something when things are bad. (Informal. Compare this with **stand by** someone.) □ *Don't worry. I'll stick by you no matter what.* □ *I feel as if I have to stick by my brother even if he goes to jail.* □ *I'll stick by my ideas whether you like them or not.*

Stick 'em up! Go to **Hands up!**

stick-in-the-mud someone who is stubbornly old-fashioned. □ *Come on to the party with us and have some fun. Don't be an old stick-in-the-mud!* □ *Tom is no stick-in-the-mud. He's really up-to-date.*

stick one's **foot in** one's **mouth** Go to put one's **foot in** one's **mouth**.

stick one's **neck out (for** someone or something**)** to take a risk. (Informal.) □ *Why should I stick my neck out to do something for her? What's she ever done for me?* □ *He made a risky investment. He stuck his neck out for the deal because he thought he could make some money.*

stick one's **nose in(to** something**)** Go to poke one's **nose in(to** something).

stick out like a sore thumb to be very prominent or unsightly; to be obvious and visible. (Informal.) □ *Bob is so tall that he sticks out like a sore thumb in a* *crowd.* □ *The house next door needs painting. It sticks out like a sore thumb.*

stick someone or something **up 1.** [with *something*] to affix or attach something onto a wall, post, etc. □ *This notice ought to be on the bulletin board. Please stick it up.* 🆃 *I'm going to stick up this poster near the entrance.* **2.** to rob someone or something. □ *One robber stuck the cashier up first, but someone sounded the alarm before any money was taken.* 🆃 *The robbers came in and tried to stick up the bank, but they got caught first.*

stick someone **with** someone or something to burden someone with someone or something. (Informal.) □ *The dishonest merchant stuck me with a faulty television set.* □ *John stuck me with his talkative uncle and went off with his friends.*

stick something **out** to endure something. (Also literal.) □ *The play was terribly boring, but I managed to stick it out.* □ *College was very difficult for Bill, but he decided to stick it out.*

stick together to remain together as a group. (Also literal. Informal.) □ *Come on, you guys. Let's stick together. Otherwise somebody will get lost.* □ *Our group of friends has managed to stick together for almost twenty years.*

stick to one's **guns** to remain firm in one's convictions; to stand up for one's rights. (Informal. Compare this with **stand** one's **ground**.) □ *I'll stick to my guns on this matter. I'm sure I'm right.* □ *Bob can be persuaded to do it our way. He probably won't stick to his guns on this point.*

stick to one's **ribs** [for food] to last long and fortify one well; [for food] to sustain one even in the coldest weather. (Refers to the inside of one's ribs.) □ *This oatmeal ought to stick to your ribs. You need something hearty on a cold day like this.* □ *I don't want soup! I want something that will stick to my ribs.*

stick up for someone or something to support someone or something; to speak in favor of someone or something. □ *Everyone was making unpleasant remarks about John, but I stuck up for him.* □ *Our team was losing, but I stuck up for it anyway.*

stick with someone or something Go to **stick by** someone or something.

sticks and stones elements of harm [directed at someone]. (Part of a rhyme, "Sticks and stones may break my bones, but words will never hurt me.") □ *I have had enough of your sticks and stones. I have enough trouble without your adding to it.* □ *After the opposing candidate had used sticks and stones for a month, suddenly there were kind words heard.*

stiff as a poker Go to **(as) stiff as a poker.**

still as death Go to **(as) still as death.**

stink to high heaven AND **smell to high heaven** to smell very bad. □ *What happened? This place stinks to high heaven.* □ *This meat smells to high heaven. Throw it away!*

stir someone or something **up 1.** [with *someone*] to make someone angry or excited; to make someone get active. (Also literal.) □ *I need a cup of hot coffee to stir me up in the morning.* 🆃 *Reading the newspaper always stirs up my father.* **2.** [with *something*] to cause trouble; to foment disagreement and difficulty. 🆃 *They stirred up quite a commotion.* 🆃 *Who stirred up this matter?*

stir up a hornet's nest to create trouble or difficulties. (Also literal. Informal.) □ *What a mess you have made of things. You've really stirred up a hornet's nest.* □ *Bill stirred up a hornet's nest when he discovered the theft.*

stock up (on something**)** to build up a supply of something. □ *Before the first snow, we always stock up on firewood.* □ *John drinks a lot of milk, so we stock up when we know he's coming.*

a **stone's throw (away) (from** something**)** Go to **within a stone's throw (of** something**).**

stoop to doing something to degrade oneself or condescend to doing something; to do something that is beneath one. □ *Whoever thought that the manager of the de-*

partment would stoop to typing? □ *I never dreamed that Bill would stoop to stealing.*

stop-and-go halting repeatedly; stopping and continuing repeatedly. □ *This project has been stop-and-go since we began. Problems keep appearing.* □ *The traffic was stop-and-go for miles. I thought I would never get here!*

stop at nothing to do everything possible (to accomplish something); to be unscrupulous. □ *Bill would stop at nothing to get his way.* □ *Bob is completely determined to get promoted. He'll stop at nothing.*

stop by (somewhere) AND **stop in** (somewhere) to visit a place, usually briefly. □ *I was coming home, but I decided to stop by my aunt's on the way.* □ *She was very glad that I stopped in.*

stop in (somewhere) Go to **stop by** (somewhere).

stop, look, and listen to exercise caution at street corners and railroad crossings, by stopping, looking to the left and to the right, and listening for approaching vehicles or a train. □ *Sally's mother trained her to stop, look, and listen at every street corner.* □ *It is a good practice to stop, look, and listen at a railroad crossing.*

stop off (somewhere) to stop somewhere on the way to some other place. □ *I stopped off at the store to buy milk on the way home.* □ *We stopped off for a few minutes and chatted with my uncle.*

stop over (somewhere) to break one's journey somewhere, usually overnight or even longer. (Compare this with **lay over** (somewhere).) □ *On our way to New York, we stopped over in Philadelphia for the night.* □ *That's a good place to stop over. There are some nice hotels in Philadelphia.*

stop short of doing something not to go as far as doing something; not to go as far as something. □ *Fortunately Bob stopped short of hitting Tom.* □ *The boss criticized Jane's work, but stopped short of reprimanding her.* □ *Jack was furious but stopped short of hitting Tom.* □ *Jane wouldn't stop short of telling lies in order to get a job.*

A **storm is brewing. 1.** There is going to be a storm. □ *Look at the clouds. A storm is brewing.* □ *A storm is brewing in the west.* **2.** There is going to be trouble or emotional upset. □ *He looks angry. A storm is brewing.*

the **straight and narrow** a straight and law-abiding route through life. (Informal. From *straight and narrow pathway.*) □ *You should have no trouble with the police if you stick to the straight and narrow.* □ *Roger was the kind who followed the straight and narrow every day of his life.*

straight as an arrow Go to (as) straight as an arrow.

(straight) from the horse's mouth from an authoritative or dependable source. □ *I know it's true! I heard it straight from the horse's mouth!* □ *This comes from the horse's mouth, so it has to be believed.*

straight from the shoulder sincerely; frankly; holding nothing back. □ *Sally always speaks straight from the shoulder. You never have to guess what she really means.* □ *Bill gave a good presentation—straight from the shoulder and brief.*

straighten someone or something **out 1.** [with *someone*] to make someone understand something. (Also literal.) □ *Jane was confused about the date, so I straightened her out.* 🅃 *I took a few minutes and straightened out everyone.* **2.** [with *someone*] to reform someone. □ *Most people think that jail never straightens anybody out.* 🅃 *The judge felt that a few years at hard labor would straighten out the thief.* **3.** [with *something*] to make a situation less confused. □ *John made a mess of the contract, so I helped him straighten it out.* 🅃 *Please straighten out your checking account. It's all messed up.*

straighten someone or something **up 1.** to put someone or something into an upright position. □ *The fence is tilted. Please straighten up that post when you get a chance.* □ *Bill, you're slouching again. Straighten yourself up.* **2.** to tidy up someone or something. □ *John straightened himself up a little before going on stage.*

Ⓣ *This room is a mess. Let's straighten up this place, right now!*

straighten up 1. to sit or stand more straight. □ *Billy's mother told him to straighten up or he'd fall out of his chair.* □ *John straightened up so he'd look taller.* **2.** to behave better. □ *Bill was acting badly for a while; then he straightened up.* □ *Sally, straighten up, or I will punish you!*

stranger to something or somewhere someone who is new to an area or place. □ *Although John was no stranger to big cities, he did not enjoy visiting New York.* □ *You are a stranger to our town, and I hope you feel welcome.*

strapped (for something**)** very much in need of money. (Informal.) □ *I'm strapped for a few bucks. Can you loan me five dollars?* □ *Sorry, I'm strapped, too.*

stretch a point AND **stretch the point** to interpret a point flexibly and with great latitude. □ *Would it be stretching a point to suggest that everyone is invited to your picnic?* □ *To say that everyone is invited is stretching the point.*

stretch one's **legs** to walk around after sitting down or lying down for a time. □ *We wanted to stretch our legs during the theater intermission.* □ *After sitting in the car all day, the travelers decided to stretch their legs.*

stretch the point Go to stretch a point.

stretch the truth to exaggerate; to misrepresent the truth just a little bit. □ *She was stretching the truth when she said everything was ready for the party.* □ *I don't want to stretch the truth. Our town is probably the wealthiest around here.*

(strictly) on the level honest; dependably open and fair. □ *How can I be sure you're on the level?* □ *You can trust Sally. She's strictly on the level.*

(strictly) on the up-and-up honest; fair and straight. (Slang. Compare this with on the level.) □ *Do you think that the mayor is on the up-and-up?* □ *Yes, the mayor is strictly on the up-and-up.*

strike a balance (between two or more things**)** to find a satisfactory compromise between two extremes. □ *The political party must strike a balance between the right wing and the left wing.* □ *Jane is overdressed for the party and Sally is underdressed. What a pity they didn't strike a balance.*

strike a bargain to reach an agreement on a price (for something). □ *They argued for a while and finally struck a bargain.* □ *They were unable to strike a bargain, so they left.*

strike a chord (with someone**)** to cause someone to remember something; to remind someone or something; to be familiar. □ *The woman in the portrait struck a chord and I realized that it was my grandmother.* □ *His name strikes a chord with me, but I don't know why.*

strike a happy medium AND **hit a happy medium; find a happy medium.** to find a compromise position; to arrive at a position halfway between two unacceptable extremes. □ *Ann likes very spicy food, but Bob doesn't care for spicy food at all. We are trying to find a restaurant that strikes a happy medium.* □ *Tom is either very happy or very sad. He can't seem to hit a happy medium.*

strike a match to light a match. □ *Mary struck a match and lit a candle.* □ *When Sally struck a match to light a cigarette, Jane said quickly, "No smoking, please."*

strike a pose to position oneself in a certain posture. □ *Bob struck a pose in front of the mirror to see how much he had grown.* □ *Lisa walked into the room and struck a pose, hoping she would be noticed.*

strike a sour note AND **hit a sour note** to signify something unpleasant. (Informal.) □ *Jane's sad announcement struck a sour note at the annual banquet.* □ *News of the crime hit a sour note in our holiday celebration.*

strike home Go to hit home.

strike it rich to acquire wealth suddenly. (Informal.) □ *If I could strike it rich, I wouldn't have to work anymore.* □ *Sally ordered a dozen oysters and found a huge pearl in one of them. She struck it rich!*

strike out 1. [for a baseball batter] to be declared "out" after three strikes. (See also **strike** someone **out**.) □ *Bill almost never strikes out.* □ *John struck out at least once in every game this season.* **2.** to fail. (Slang.) □ *Ann did her best, but she struck out anyway.* □ *Give it another try. Just because you struck out once doesn't mean you can't do better now.*

strike out at someone or something to (figuratively or literally) hit at or attack someone or something. □ *She was so angry she struck out at the person she was arguing with.* □ *I was frantic. I wanted to strike out at everything and everybody.*

strike someone **as** something [for a thought or behavior] to affect someone a certain way. □ *John's rude behavior struck me as odd.* □ *Mary's attitude struck me as childish.*

strike someone **funny** to seem funny to someone. □ *Sally has a great sense of humor. Everything she says strikes me funny.* □ *Why are you laughing? Did something I said strike you funny?*

strike someone **out** [for a baseball pitcher] to get a batter declared "out" after three strikes. □ *I never thought he'd strike Tom out.* 🅃 *Bill struck out all our best players.*

strike someone's **fancy** to appeal to someone. (See also **tickle** someone's **fancy**.) □ *I'll have some ice cream, please. Chocolate strikes my fancy right now.* □ *Why don't you go to the store and buy a record album that strikes your fancy?*

strike the right note to achieve the desired effect; to do something suitable or pleasing. (A musical reference.) □ *Meg struck the right note when she wore a dark suit to the interview.* □ *The politician's speech failed to strike the right note with the crowd.*

strike up a conversation to start a conversation (with someone). □ *I struck up an interesting conversation with someone on the bus yesterday.* □ *It's easy to strike up a conversation with someone when you're traveling.*

strike up a friendship to become friends (with someone). □ *I struck up a friendship with John while we were on a business trip together.* □ *If you're lonely, you should go out and try to strike up a friendship with someone you like.*

strike while the iron is hot to do something at the best possible time; to do something when the time is ripe. □ *He was in a good mood, so I asked for a loan of $200. I thought I'd better strike while the iron was hot.* □ *Please go to the bank and settle this matter now! They are willing to be reasonable. You've got to strike while the iron is hot.*

string along (with someone**)** to accompany someone; to **run around with** someone. □ *Sally seemed to know where she was going, so I decided to string along with her.* □ *She said it was okay if I strung along.*

string something **out** to draw something out (in time); to make something last a long time. (Also literal.) □ *The meeting was long enough. There was no need to string it out further with all those speeches.* 🅃 *They tried to string out the meeting to make things seem more important.*

a **stroke of luck** a bit of luck; a lucky happening. □ *I had a stroke of luck and found Tom at home when I called. He's not usually there.* □ *Unless I have a stroke of luck, I'm not going to finish this report by tomorrow.*

strong as a horse Go to (as) strong as a horse.

strong as a lion Go to (as) strong as a lion.

strong as an ox Go to (as) strong as an ox.

a **struggle to the death** a bitter struggle either to success or failure. (Also literal.) □ *It was a struggle to the death, but I finally finished my report on time.* □ *I had a terrible time getting my car started. It was a struggle to the death, but it finally started.*

strung out 1. extended in time; overly long. □ *Why was that lecture so strung out? She talked and talked.* □ *It was strung out because there was very little to be said.* **2.** doped or drugged. (Slang.) □ *Bob acted very strangely—as if he were strung* *out or something.* □ *I've never seen Bob or any of his friends strung out.*

stubborn as a mule Go to (as) stubborn as a mule.

(stuck) in a rut kept in an established way of living that never changes. □ *David felt like he was stuck in a rut, so he went back to school.* □ *Anne was tired of being in a rut, so she moved to Los Angeles.*

stuck in traffic to be caught in a traffic jam. □ *I am sorry I am late. I was stuck in traffic.* □ *Our taxi was stuck in traffic, and I thought I would never get to the airport on time.*

stuck on someone or something **1.** [with *someone*] to be fond of or in love with someone. □ *John was stuck on Sally, but she didn't know it.* □ *He always is stuck on the wrong person.* **2.** [with *something*] to be locked into an idea, cause, or purpose. □ *Mary is really stuck on the idea of going to France this spring.* □ *You've proposed a good plan, Jane, but you're stuck on it. We may have to make some changes.*

stuck with someone or something burdened with someone or something; left having to care for someone or something. (Informal.) □ *Please don't leave me stuck with your aunt. She talks too much.* □ *My roommate quit school and left me stuck with the telephone bill.*

stuff and nonsense nonsense. (Informal.) □ *Come on! Don't give me all that stuff and nonsense!* □ *I don't understand this book. It's all stuff and nonsense as far as I am concerned.*

stuff the ballot box to put fraudulent ballots into a ballot box; to cheat in counting the votes in an election. □ *The election judge was caught stuffing the ballot box in the election yesterday.* □ *Election officials are supposed to guard against stuffing the ballot box.*

stumble across someone or something AND **stumble into** someone or something**; stumble (up)on** someone or something to find someone or something, usually by accident. □ *I stumbled across an interesting book yesterday when I was shopping.* □ *Guess who I stumbled into at the library yesterday?* □ *I stumbled on a real bargain at the bookstore last week.*

stumble into someone or something **1.** to bump into someone or something accidentally. □ *I stumbled into John, and I apologized. It was my fault.* □ *I stumbled into a post and hurt my arm.* **2.** Go to stumble across someone or something. **3.** [with *something*] to enter something or a place by stumbling. □ *I tripped on the curb and stumbled into the car.* □ *I stumbled into the house, exhausted and in need of a cool drink.*

stumble (up)on someone or something **1.** Go to stumble across someone or something. **2.** to trip over someone or something. □ *There were three of us sleeping in the small tent. Each of us would stumble on the others whenever we went out or came in.* □ *I stumbled on the curb and twisted my ankle.*

stumbling block something that prevents or obstructs progress. □ *We'd like to buy that house, but the high price is the stumbling block.* □ *Jim's age is a stumbling block to getting another job. He's over 60.*

subject to something **1.** likely to have something, such as a physical disorder. □ *The sick man was subject to dizzy spells.* □ *I am subject to frequent headaches.* **2.** tentative, depending on something; vulnerable to something. □ *I have made all the necessary plans, subject to your approval, of course.* □ *My remarks are, of course, subject to your criticisms.*

subscribe to something to have a standing order for a magazine or something similar. □ *I usually buy my monthly magazines at the newsstand. I don't subscribe to them.* □ *I subscribe to all the magazines I read because it's nice to have them delivered by mail.*

such and such someone or something whose name has been forgotten or should not be said. (Informal.) □ *Mary said that such and such was coming to her party, but I forgot their names.* □ *If you walk into a store and ask for such and such and they don't have it, you go to a different store.*

such as 1. of a particular kind; of the sort that is; like. ☐ *Where can I get a haircut such as yours?* ☐ *I'd like to buy a vase such as the one in your display case.* **2.** for example. ☐ *Bill enjoys many kinds of fruit, such as apples, pears, and plums.* ☐ *Mary has many hobbies, such as swimming, bowling, and running.*

such as it is in the imperfect state that one sees it; in the less-than-perfect condition in which one finds it. ☐ *This is where I live. This is my glorious home—such as it is.* ☐ *I've worked for days on this report, and I've done the best that I can do. It's my supreme effort—such as it is.*

Such is life! That is the way things happen, even it isn't the way I want it to be! ☐ *Oh, well. Everything can't be perfect. Such is life!* ☐ *So I failed my test. Such is life! I can take it again some time.*

suck someone **in** AND **take** someone **in** to deceive someone. (The expression with *suck* is slang.) ☐ *I try to shop carefully so that no one can take me in.* 🅃 *I think that someone sucked in both of them. I don't know why they bought this car.*

suggestive of something reminiscent of something; seeming to suggest something. ☐ *Bill's homemade soup is suggestive of his mother's.* ☐ *The new movie was suggestive of an old one I had seen on TV.*

suit oneself to do something one's own way; to do something to please oneself. ☐ *If he doesn't want to do it my way, he can suit himself.* ☐ *Take either of the books that you like. Suit yourself. I'll read the other one.*

suit someone **to a T** AND **fit** someone **to a T** to be very appropriate for someone. ☐ *This kind of job suits me to a T.* ☐ *This is Sally's kind of house. It fits her to a T.*

sum and substance a summary; the gist. (See also **form and substance**.) ☐ *Can you quickly tell me the sum and substance of your proposal?* ☐ *In trying to explain the sum and substance of the essay, Thomas failed to mention the middle name of the hero.*

sum something **up** to summarize something. (Literally, to figure out the total.) 🅃 *At the end of the lecture, Dr. Williams summed up the important points.* ☐ *He said when he finished, "Well, that about sums it up."*

Sunday-go-to-meeting clothes one's best clothes. (Folksy. See also **in** one's **Sunday best**.) ☐ *John was all dressed up in his Sunday-go-to-meeting clothes.* ☐ *I hate to be wearing my Sunday-go-to-meeting clothes when everyone else is casually dressed.*

supply and demand the availability of things or people as compared to the need to utilize the things or people; the availability of goods compared to the number of willing customers for the goods. ☐ *Sometimes you can find what you want by shopping around and other times almost no store carries the items you are looking for. It depends entirely on supply and demand.* ☐ *Sometimes customers ask for things we do not carry in stock and other times we have things in abundance that no one wants to buy. Whether or not we can make money off of a product depends entirely on supply and demand.*

supposed to do something expected or intended to do something; obliged or allowed to do something. ☐ *You're supposed to say "excuse me" when you burp.* ☐ *Mom says you're supposed to come inside for dinner now.*

sure as death Go to **(as) sure as death**.

surf and turf fish and beef; lobster and beef. (A type of meal incorporating both expensive seafood and an expensive cut of beef. Refers to the sea and to the pasture.) ☐ *Walter ordered the surf and turf, but Alice ordered only a tiny salad.* ☐ *No surf and turf for me. I want fish and fish alone.*

the **survival of the fittest** the idea that the most able or fit will survive (while the less able and less fit will perish). (This is used literally as a part of the theory of evolution.) ☐ *In college, it's the survival of the fittest. You have to keep working in order to survive and graduate.* ☐ *I don't give my houseplants very good care, but the* *ones I have are really flourishing. It's the survival of the fittest, I guess.*

susceptible to something **1.** easily persuaded; easily influenced. □ *The students were susceptible to the allure of drugs.* □ *The young revolutionaries were susceptible to propaganda.* **2.** likely to contract a sickness; likely to become sick. □ *People with AIDS are susceptible to pneumonia.* □ *Infants and the elderly are more susceptible to illness than other people.*

swallow one's **pride** to forget one's pride and accept something humiliating. □ *I had to swallow my pride and admit that I was wrong.* □ *When you're a student, you find yourself swallowing your pride quite often.*

swallow something**, hook, line, and sinker** to believe something completely. (Slang. These terms refer to fishing and fooling a fish into being caught.) □ *I made up a story about why I was so late. The boss swallowed it, hook, line, and sinker.* □ *I feel like a fool. I swallowed it, hook, line, and sinker.*

[swan song] Go to someone's swan song.

swear by someone or something **1.** to take an oath on someone or something. □ *My uncle is sort of old-fashioned. He makes promises by swearing by his "sainted mother."* □ *He sometimes swears by his foot!* **2.** to have complete faith and confidence in someone or something. □ *I'm willing to swear by John. He's completely dependable.* □ *This is an excellent brand of detergent. My sister swears by it.*

swear on a stack of Bibles AND **swear on** one's **mother's grave** to state something very earnestly, pledging to tell the truth. (*Stack of Bibles* refers to swearing to tell the truth in court by placing one's hand on a Bible.) □ *I swear on a stack of Bibles that I am telling the truth.* □ *Of course, I'm telling the truth. I swear on my mother's grave!*

swear on one's **mother's grave** Go to swear on a stack of Bibles.

sweat blood to be very anxious and tense. (Slang.) □ *What a terrible test! I was really sweating blood at the last.* □ *Bob is such a bad driver. I sweat blood every time I ride with him.*

sweat something **out** to endure or wait for something that causes tension or boredom. (Informal.) □ *I had to wait for her in the reception area. It was a long wait, but I managed to sweat it out.* 🅃 *I took the test and then spent a week sweating out the results.*

sweep one **off** one's **feet** AND **knock** one **off** one's **feet 1.** to knock someone down. □ *The wind swept me off my feet.* □ *Bill punched Bob playfully, and knocked him off his feet.* **2.** to overwhelm someone (figuratively). (Informal.) □ *Mary is madly in love with Bill. He swept her off her feet.* □ *The news was so exciting that it knocked me off my feet.*

sweep out of somewhere to move or leave in a flamboyant or theatrical way. □ *The insulted customer swept out of the store.* □ *The celebrity rose from his table and swept out of the restaurant.*

sweep something **under the carpet** AND **sweep** something **under the rug** to try to hide something unpleasant, shameful, etc., from the attention of others. □ *The boss said he couldn't sweep the theft under the carpet, that he'd have to call in the police.* □ *Roger had a tendency to sweep all the problems under the rug.*

sweep something **under the rug** Go to sweep something under the carpet.

sweet and low [of music] pleasing and quiet. □ *Play me something that is sweet and low.* □ *I like dance music that is sweet and low—not any of this rowdy, violent stuff.*

sweet and sour a combination of fruity sweet and sour, but not necessarily salty, flavors. (Often refers to certain Chinese-American foods.) □ *I prefer sweet and sour pork to anything else on the menu.* □ *Alice does not care for sweet and sour dishes, but she will usually eat whatever we serve her.*

sweet as honey Go to (as) sweet as honey.

sweet as sugar Go to (as) sweet as honey.

sweet nothings affectionate but unimportant or meaningless words spoken to a loved one. ☐ *Jack was whispering sweet nothings in Joan's ear when they were dancing.* ☐ *The two lovers sat in the cinema exchanging sweet nothings.*

sweet on someone fond of someone. (Folksy.) ☐ *Tom is sweet on Mary. He may ask her to marry him.* ☐ *Mary's sweet on him, too.*

sweet-talk someone to talk convincingly to someone with much flattery. (Folksy.) ☐ *I didn't want to help her, but she sweet-talked me into it.* ☐ *He sweet-talked her for a while, and she finally agreed to go to the dance with him.*

swift and sure fast and certain. (As with the flight of a well-aimed arrow.) ☐ *The response of the governor to the criticism by the opposing party was swift and sure.* ☐ *The boxer's punch was swift and sure and resulted in a quick knockout and a very short match.*

swift as an arrow Go to (as) swift as an arrow.

swift as the wind Go to (as) swift as the wind.

swift as thought Go to (as) swift as thought.

swim against the current Go to swim against the tide.

swim against the tide AND **swim against the current** to do the opposite of everyone else; to go against the trend. ☐ *Bob tends to do what everybody else does. He isn't likely to swim against the tide.* ☐ *Mary always swims against the current. She's a very contrary person.*

swing into action Go to go into action.

swing something to make something happen. (Slang.) ☐ *I hope I can swing a deal that will make us all a lot of money.* ☐ *We all hope you can swing it.*

T

table the motion to postpone the discussion of something during a meeting. □ *Mary suggested that they should table the motion.* 🅃 *The motion for a new policy was tabled until the next meeting.*

tag along to go along with or follow someone, often when uninvited or unwanted. □ *Lisa always tags along when Tim and Sally go out on a date.* □ *I took my children to the zoo and the neighbor's children tagged along.*

the **tail wagging the dog** a situation where a small part is controlling the whole thing. □ *John was just hired yesterday, and today he's bossing everyone around. It's a case of the tail wagging the dog.* □ *Why is this small matter so important? Now we see the tail wagging the dog!*

take a backseat (to someone**)** to defer to someone; to give control to someone. □ *I decided to take a backseat to Mary and let her manage the project.* □ *I had done the best I could, but it was time to take a backseat and let someone else run things.*

take a bath Go to take a shower.

take a bath (on something**)** to have large financial losses on an investment. (Slang.) □ *I took a bath on all my oil stock. I should have sold it sooner.* □ *I don't mind losing a little money now and then, but I really took a bath this time.*

take a bow to bow and receive credit for a good performance. □ *At the end of the concerto, the pianist rose and took a bow.* □ *The audience applauded wildly and demanded that the conductor come out and take a bow again.*

take a break AND **take** one's **break** to have a short rest period in one's work. □ *It's ten o'clock—time to take a break.* □ *I don't usually take my break until 10:30.*

take a chance AND **take a risk** to try something where failure or bad fortune is likely. □ *Come on, take a chance. You may lose, but it's worth trying.* □ *I'm not reckless, but I don't mind taking a risk now and then.*

take a course (in something**)** to enroll in a course and do the required work. □ *I decided to take a course in history.* □ *Bob drives into the city where he is taking a course.*

take a crack at something to have a try at something; to give something a try. (Informal.) □ *I don't think I can convince her to leave, but I'll take a crack at it.* □ *Someone had to try to rescue the child. Bill said he'd take a crack at it.*

take a dig at someone AND **take digs at** someone to insult someone; to say something that will irritate a person. (Slang.) □ *Jane took a dig at Bob for being late all the time.* □ *Jane is always taking digs at Bob, but she never really means any harm.*

take a dim view of something to regard something skeptically or pessimistically. □ *My aunt takes a dim view of most things that young people do.* □ *The manager took a dim view of my efforts on the project. I guess I didn't try hard enough.*

take advantage of someone or something **1.** [with *someone*] to cheat or deceive someone. □ *The store owner took advantage of me, and I'm angry.* □ *You must be alert when you shop to make sure that someone doesn't take advantage of you.* **2.** to utilize someone or something to one's own benefit. □ *Jane can be of great help to me, and I intend to take advantage of her.* □ *Try* *to take advantage of every opportunity that comes your way.*

take a fancy to someone or something AND **take a liking to** someone or something; **take a shine to** someone or something to develop a fondness or a preference for someone or something. (Folksy.) ☐ *John began to take a fancy to Sally late last August at the picnic.* ☐ *I've never taken a liking to cooked carrots.* ☐ *I think my teacher has taken a shine to me.*

take after someone to resemble a close, older relative. ☐ *Don't you think that Sally takes after her mother?* ☐ *No, Sally takes after her Aunt Ann.*

take a gander (at someone or something**)** to examine someone or something; to take a look (at someone or something). (Slang.) ☐ *Hey, will you take a gander at that fancy car!* ☐ *Drive it over here so I can take a gander.*

take a hand in something to help plan or do something. ☐ *I was glad to take a hand in planning the picnic.* ☐ *Jane refused to take a hand in any of the work.*

take a hard line (with someone**)** to be firm with someone; to have a firm policy for dealing with someone. ☐ *The manager takes a hard line with people who show up late.* ☐ *This is a serious matter. The police are likely to take a hard line.*

Take a hike! Go to Go climb a tree!

take a hint to understand a hint and behave accordingly. ☐ *I said I didn't want to see you anymore. Can't you take a hint? I don't like you.* ☐ *Sure I can take a hint, but I'd rather be told directly.*

take (a)hold of someone or something AND **get (a)hold of** someone or something to get in control of someone or something. (Also literal.) ☐ *Take hold of yourself! Calm down and relax.* ☐ *She took a few minutes to get hold of herself, and then she spoke.*

take aim (at someone or something**) 1.** to aim (something) at someone or something. ☐ *The hunter took aim at the deer and pulled the trigger.* ☐ *You must take aim carefully before you shoot.* **2.** to prepare to deal with someone or something. ☐ *Now we have to take aim at the problem and try to get it solved.* ☐ *He turned to me and took aim. I knew he was going to scold me severely.*

take a leaf out of someone's **book** to behave or to do something in the way that someone else would. ☐ *When you act like that, you're taking a leaf out of your sister's book, and I don't like it!* ☐ *You had better do it your way. Don't take a leaf out of my book. I don't do it well.*

take a licking Go to get a licking.

take a liking to someone or something Go to take a fancy to someone or something.

take a load off one's **feet** Go to get a load off one's feet.

Take a long walk off a short pier. AND **Go play in the traffic.** Get out of here!; Go do something that will get you permanently out of here! ☐ *Get out of here! Take a long walk off a short pier!* ☐ *You bother me. Go play in the traffic.*

take a look (at someone or something**)** to examine (briefly) someone or something. (Also with *have,* as in the example below.) ☐ *I asked the doctor to take a look at my ankle that has been hurting.* ☐ *"So your ankle's hurting," said the doctor. "Let's take a look."* ☐ *Please have a look at my car. It's not running well.*

take a look for someone or something AND **have a look for** someone or something to make a visual search for someone or something; to look for someone or something. ☐ *Please go to the library and have a look for a book about snakes.* ☐ *Take a look for a man in a black suit. He is your guide.*

take a nap to have a brief period of sleep. ☐ *I took a short nap just after lunch.* ☐ *The baby takes a long nap each afternoon.*

take a new turn [for something] to begin a new course or direction. ☐ *When I received the telegram with the exciting news, my life took a new turn.* ☐ *I began taking the medicine at noon, and by evening the disease had begun to take a new turn. I was getting better!*

take an interest (in something**)** to develop an interest in something. ☐ *I wish John would take an interest in his schoolwork.* ☐ *We hoped you'd take an interest and join our club.*

take an oath to make an oath; to swear to something. ☐ *You must take an oath that you will never tell anyone about this.* ☐ *When I was a witness in court, I had to take an oath that I would tell the truth.*

take a nosedive Go to go into a nosedive.

take a peep Go to have a peep.

take a potshot at someone or something to criticize someone or something; to include a criticism of someone or something in a broader or more general criticism. ☐ *Daily, the media took potshots at the foolish politician.* ☐ *John is taking potshots at me in his condemnation of office workers.*

take a powder to leave (a place); to sneak out or run out (of a place). (Slang.) ☐ *When the police came to the door, Tom decided it was time to take a powder. He left by the back door.* ☐ *When the party got a little dull, Bill and his friend took a powder.*

take a punch at someone to strike or strike at someone with one's fist. (Informal.) ☐ *Mary got so angry at Bob that she took a punch at him.* ☐ *She took a punch at him, but she missed.*

take a rain check (on something**)** Go to get a rain check (on something).

take a risk Go to take a chance.

take a shellacking Go to get a shellacking.

take a shine to someone or something Go to take a fancy to someone or something.

take a shot at something Go to give something a shot; take a try at something.

take a shower AND **take a bath** to bathe. ☐ *I take a shower every morning.* ☐ *John takes a hot bath to relax.*

take a spill to have a fall; to tip over. (Also with *bad, nasty, quite,* etc. Also with *have.*) ☐ *Ann tripped on the curb and took a nasty spill.* ☐ *John had quite a spill when he fell off his bicycle.*

take a stab at something Go to take a try at something.

take a stand (against someone or something**)** to take a position in opposition to someone or something; to oppose or resist someone or something. ☐ *The treasurer was forced to take a stand against the board because of its wasteful spending.* ☐ *The treasurer took a stand, and others agreed.*

take a toll the damage or wear that is caused by using something or by hard living. ☐ *Years of sunbathing took a toll on Mary's skin.* ☐ *Drug abuse takes a heavy toll on the lives of people.*

take a try at something AND **take a shot at** something**; take a stab at** something**; take a whack at** something to try to do something. (Also with *have;* see the variants at have a try at something. The second, third, and fourth entries can also be literal.) ☐ *I don't know if I can eat a whole pizza, but I'll be happy to take a shot at it.* ☐ *I can't seem to get this computer to work right. Would you like to take a try at it?* ☐ *Sure. Take a stab at it.* ☐ *I don't know if I can do it or not, but I'll take a whack at it.*

take attendance to make a record of persons attending something. ☐ *The teacher took attendance before starting the class.* ☐ *I will take attendance each day.*

take a turn for the better to start to improve; to start to get well. (The opposite of the following entry.) ☐ *She was very sick for a month; then suddenly she took a turn for the better.* ☐ *Things are taking a turn for the better at my store. I may make a profit this year.*

take a turn for the worse to start to get worse. (The opposite of the previous entry.) ☐ *It appeared that she was going to get well; then, unfortunately, she took a turn for the worse.* ☐ *My job was going quite well; then last week things took a turn for the worse.*

take a vacation to go somewhere for a vacation; to stop work to have a vacation. ☐ *Sue took a vacation at the Grand Canyon last year.* ☐ *I need to take a vacation and relax.*

Take a walk! Go to **Go climb a tree!**

take a whack at someone or something **1.** [with *someone*] (Slang. *Whack* is sometimes spelled *wack.* Also with *have,* as in the examples below.) to hit at someone; to hit someone. ☐ *He took a whack at me, so I punched him.* ☐ *Don't try to take a whack at me again!* ☐ *I'll have a wack at you!* **2.** [with *something*] Go to **take a try at** something.

take care of someone or something **1.** to deal with someone or something; to handle or manage someone or something. ☐ *Would you please take care of this little problem?* ☐ *This is an easy thing to take care of. I will fix it immediately.* **2.** to provide care for someone or something. ☐ *John and Mary took care of their aged grandmother.* ☐ *Please take care of my plants while I am on vacation.* **3.** [with *someone*] to tip someone. ☐ *I took care of the doorman as we left.* ☐ *Did you remember to take care of the waiter?* **4.** [with *someone*] to kill or dispose of someone. ☐ *Max said he was going to take care of Lefty once and for all.* ☐ *The crime king ordered Max to take care of a certain private detective.*

take charge (of someone or something**)** to take (over) control of someone or something. ☐ *The president came in late and took charge of the meeting.* ☐ *When the new manager took charge, things really began to happen.*

take cold Go to **catch cold.**

take digs at someone Go to **take a dig at** someone.

take effect Go to **go into effect.**

take exception (to something**)** to disagree with something (that someone has said). ☐ *I take exception to your remarks, and I would like to discuss them with you.* ☐ *I'm sorry you take exception. Let's discuss the matter.*

take five to take a five-minute rest period. (Slang.) ☐ *Okay, everybody. Take five!* ☐ *Hey, Bob. I'm tired. Can we take five?*

take forty winks Go to **catch forty winks.**

take (great) pains (to do something**)** to make a great effort to do something. ☐ *Tom took pains to decorate the room exactly right.* ☐ *We took pains to get there on time.*

take heart to be brave; to have courage. ☐ *Take heart, John. Things could be worse!* ☐ *I told her to take heart and try again next time.*

take heed to be cautious. ☐ *Take heed, and don't get involved with the wrong kind of people.* ☐ *Just take heed, and you'll be safe.*

take ill Go to **take sick.**

take inventory to make an inventory list. ☐ *They are taking inventory in the warehouse, counting each item and writing the number on a list.* ☐ *The hardware store closed once a year in order to take inventory.*

take issue (with someone**)** to argue with someone; to dispute a point with someone. ☐ *I hate to take issue with you on such a minor point, but I'm quite sure you're wrong.* ☐ *I don't mind if you take issue, but I'm sure I'm right.*

take it away to start up a performance. (Also literal. Typically a public announcement of the beginning of a musical performance. Slang.) ☐ *And now, here is the band playing "Song of Songs." Take it away!* ☐ *Sally will now sing us a song. Take it away, Sally!*

Take it easy. Good-bye and take care of yourself. (Informal.) ☐ *Bye, Tom. Take it easy.* ☐ *Take it easy. I'll see you later.*

take it easy (on someone or something**) 1.** to be gentle (with someone or something). (See also **go easy (on** someone or something**)**.) ☐ *Take it easy on Mary. She's been sick.* ☐ *Please take it easy on the furniture. It has to last us many years.* ☐ *Take it easy! You will break the chair!* **2.** [with *something*] to use less of something (rather than more). (Informal.) ☐ *Take it easy on the soup. There's just enough for one serving for each person.* ☐ *Please take it easy! There are hardly any left.*

take it on the chin to experience and endure a direct blow or assault. ☐ *The bad news was a real shock, and John took it on* *the chin.* □ *The worst luck comes my way, and I always end up taking it on the chin.*

take it or leave it to accept something (the way it is) or forget it. (Informal.) □ *This is my last offer. Take it or leave it.* □ *It's not much, but it's the only food we have. You can take it or leave it.*

take it slow to move or go slowly. (Informal.) □ *The road is rough, so take it slow.* □ *This book is very hard to read, and I have to take it slow.*

take it to one's **grave** to carry a secret with one until one dies. □ *I will never tell anyone. I'll take your secret to my grave.* □ *She took the answer to the mystery to her grave.*

take it (up)on oneself **(to** do something**)** to make something one's responsibility. □ *I took it upon myself to order more pencils since we were running out of them.* □ *I'm glad that you took it on yourself to do that.*

take kindly to something to be agreeable to something. □ *My father doesn't take kindly to anyone using his tools.* □ *I hope they'll take kindly to our request.*

take leave of one's **senses** to become irrational. (Often verbatim with *one's*.) □ *What are you doing? Have you taken leave of your senses?* □ *What a terrible situation! It's enough to make one take leave of one's senses.*

take liberties with someone or something AND **make free with** someone or something to use or abuse someone or something. □ *You are overly familiar with me, Mr. Jones. One might think you were taking liberties with me.* □ *I don't like it when you make free with my lawn mower. You should at least ask when you want to borrow it.*

take no stock in something AND **not take stock in** something to pay no attention to something; not to believe or accept something. □ *I take no stock in anything John has to say.* □ *He doesn't take stock in your opinions either.*

take note (of something**)** to observe and remember something. □ *Please take note of the point I'm about to make.* □ *Here is something else of which you should take note.*

take notice (of something**)** to observe something. □ *I didn't take notice of when he came in.* □ *They say he came in late, but I didn't take notice.*

take off 1. to leave the ground and begin to fly. (As with a bird or an airplane.) □ *When do we take off?* □ *The eagle took off and headed toward the mountains.* **2.** to become popular and successful. □ *Her book really took off after her television appearance.* □ *The idea took off, and soon everyone was talking about it.*

take off (after someone or something**)** AND **take out (after** someone or something**)** to begin to chase someone or something. □ *The bank guard took off after the robber.* □ *Did you see that police car take off?* □ *It took out after the bank robber's car.*

take offense (at someone or something**)** to become resentful of someone or something. □ *Bill took offense at Mary for her thoughtless remarks.* □ *Almost everyone took offense at Bill's new book.* □ *I'm sorry you took offense. I meant no harm.*

take off (from work) not to go to work (for a period of time). □ *I had to take off from work in order to renew my driver's license.* □ *I hate to take off for something like that.*

take office to begin serving as an elected or appointed official. □ *When did the mayor take office?* □ *All the elected officials took office just after the election.*

take off one's **hat (to** someone**)** to offer praise for someone's good accomplishments. (Refers to taking off one's hat to show deference to someone.) □ *I have to take off my hat to Mayor Johnson. She has done an excellent job.* □ *Yes, we all ought to take off our hats. She is our best mayor ever.*

take off (on something**)** AND **launch forth (on** something**)** to start out a lecture on something; to begin a discussion of something. (See also **set forth (on** something**)**.) □ *My father took off on the subject of taxes and talked for an hour.* □ *My uncle is always launching forth on the state* *of the economy.* □ *When he launches forth, I leave the room.*

take one **at** one's **word** to believe what someone says and act accordingly. □ *She told me to go jump in the lake, and I took her at her word.* □ *You shouldn't take her at her word. She frequently says things she doesn't really mean.*

take one's **break** Go to take a break.

take one's **cue from** someone to use someone else's behavior or reactions as a guide to one's own. (From the theatrical cue as a signal to speak, etc.) □ *If you don't know which spoons to use at the dinner, just take your cue from John.* □ *The other children took their cue from Tommy and ignored the new boy.*

take one's **death of cold** Go to catch one's death (of cold).

take (one's) **leave (of** someone**)** to say goodbye to someone and leave. □ *I took leave of the hostess at an early hour.* □ *One by one, the guests took their leave.*

take one's **medicine** to accept the punishment or the bad fortune that one deserves. (Also literal. Informal.) □ *I know I did wrong, and I know I have to take my medicine.* □ *Billy knew he was going to get spanked, and he didn't want to take his medicine.*

take one's **own life** to kill oneself; to commit suicide. □ *Bob tried to take his own life, but he was stopped in time.* □ *Later, he was sorry that he had tried to take his own life.*

take one's **time** to use as much time (to do something) as one wants. □ *There is no hurry. Please take your time.* □ *If you take your time, you'll be late.*

take out (after someone or something**)** Go to take off (after someone or something).

take out a loan to get a loan of money, especially from a bank. □ *Mary took out a loan to buy a car.* □ *We will have to take out a loan to pay the bills this month.*

take over to begin doing something that someone else was doing. □ *When you get tired of washing dishes, I'll take over.* □ *You have been playing the drums long enough. Let me take over.*

take part (in something**)** to participate in something. □ *They invited me to take part in their celebration.* □ *I was quite pleased to take part.*

take pity (on someone or something**)** to feel sorry for someone or something. □ *We took pity on the hungry people and gave them some warm food.* □ *She took pity on the little dog and brought it in to get warm.* □ *Please take pity! Please help us!*

take place to happen. □ *When will this party take place?* □ *It's taking place right now.*

take precedence over someone or something Go to have precedence over someone or something.

take pride in something to do something with pride; to have pride for or about something. □ *The union workers took pride in their work.* □ *The artist took pride in her paintings.*

take root to begin to take hold or have effect. (Refers to newly-planted plants.) □ *Things will begin to change when my new policies take root.* □ *My ideas began to take root and influence other people.*

take shape [for something, such as plans, writing, ideas, arguments, etc.] to begin to be organized and specific. □ *My plans are beginning to take shape.* □ *As my manuscript took shape, I started showing it to publishers.*

take sick AND **take ill** to become ill. (Folksy.) □ *I took sick with a bad cold last week.* □ *I hope I don't take ill before final exams.*

take sides to choose one side of an argument. □ *They were arguing, but I didn't want to take sides, so I left.* □ *I don't mind taking sides on important issues.*

take someone **apart** to beat someone up. (Slang.) □ *Don't talk to me that way, or I'll take you apart.* T *He was so mad that I thought he was going to take apart all of us.*

take someone **by surprise** to startle someone; to surprise someone with something unexpected. □ *Oh! You took me by surprise because I didn't hear you come in.* □ *Bill took his mother by surprise by coming to the door and pretending to be a solicitor.*

take someone **down a notch (or two)** Go to take someone down a peg (or two).

take someone **down a peg (or two)** AND **take** someone **down a notch (or two)** to reprimand someone who is acting too arrogant. □ *The teacher's scolding took Bob down a notch or two.* □ *He was so rude that someone was bound to take him down a peg or two.*

take someone **down (to size)** Go to cut someone down (to size).

take someone **for a fool** Go to take someone for an idiot.

take someone **for an idiot** AND **take** someone **for a fool** to assume that someone is stupid. □ *I wouldn't do anything like that! Do you take me for an idiot?* □ *I don't take you for a fool. I think you're very clever.*

take someone **for a ride** to trick or deceive someone. (Informal.) □ *Old people are being taken for a ride by bogus workmen.* □ *Whoever sold Tom that car took him for a ride. It needs a new engine.*

take someone **for** someone or something to mistake someone for someone or something. □ *I took Bill for his brother, Bob. They look so much alike!* □ *I took Mr. Brown for the gardener, and he was a little bit insulted.*

take someone **hostage** to kidnap or seize someone to be a hostage. □ *The terrorists planned to take the ambassador hostage.* □ *The entire family was taken hostage by the robber.*

take someone **in** Go to suck someone in.

take someone **into** one's **confidence** to trust someone with confidential information; to tell a secret to someone and trust the person to keep the secret. □ *We are good friends, but I didn't feel I could take her into my confidence.* □ *I know something very important about Jean. Can I take you into my confidence?*

take someone or something **at face value** to take someone or something by its outward appearance; to take someone or something as it first appears to be. □ *Don't just accept her offer at face value. Think of the implications.* □ *Jane tends to take people at face value and so she is always getting hurt.*

take someone or something **away** to remove someone or something. □ *I don't want any more soup. Please take it away.* 🅃 *Take away Bill and John. They are bothering me.*

take someone or something **by storm** to overwhelm someone or something; to attract a great deal of attention from someone or something. □ *Jane is madly in love with Tom. He took her by storm at the office party, and they've been together ever since.* □ *The singer took the world of opera by storm with her performance in* La Boheme.

take someone or something **by surprise** to startle or surprise someone or something. □ *She came into the room and took them by surprise.* □ *I took the little bird by surprise, and it flew away.*

take someone or something **for granted** to accept someone or something—without gratitude—as a matter of course. □ *We tend to take a lot of things for granted.* □ *Mrs. Franklin complained that Mr. Franklin takes her for granted.*

take someone or something **in 1.** to observe someone or something. (See also suck someone in.) □ *The zoo is too big to take in the whole thing in one day.* 🅃 *It takes two days to take in the museum.* **2.** to provide shelter for someone or something. □ *When I needed a place to live, my uncle took me in.* 🅃 *Mrs. Wilson took in the lonely little dog and gave it a warm home.* **3.** [with *something*] to inhale, drink, or eat something. 🅃 *I think I'll go for a walk and take in some fresh air.* 🅃 *Jane was very ill, but she managed to take in a little broth.*

take someone or something **into account** to remember to consider someone or something. □ *I hope you'll take Bill and Bob* *into account when you plan the party.* 🅃 *I'll try to take into account all the things that are important in a situation like this.*

take someone or something **on** to undertake to deal with someone or something. □ *Mrs. Smith is such a problem. I don't feel like taking her on just now.* 🅃 *I'm too busy to take on any new problems.*

take someone or something **out 1.** [with *someone*] to take someone out on the town on a date. (Also literal.) □ *I hear that Tom has been taking Ann out.* 🅃 *No, Tom has been taking out Mary.* **2.** [with *someone*] to remove someone who is acting as a barrier, especially in football. (Informal.) □ *Okay, Bill. Get in there and take the quarterback out.* 🅃 *Our player ran fast and took out the opposing player before he could tackle our runner.* **3.** [with *someone*] to kill someone. (Criminal slang.) □ *The thief who drove the car was afraid that the other thieves were going to take him out, too.* 🅃 *The crooks took out the witness to the crime.*

take someone or something **over** to take charge (of someone or something); to assume control of someone or something. □ *The new manager will take the office over next week.* 🅃 *Will you please take over your children? I can't seem to control them.*

take someone or something **wrong** to misunderstand someone or something. □ *Please don't take me wrong, but I believe that your socks don't match.* □ *You'll probably take this wrong, but I have to say that I've never seen you looking better.*

take someone's **breath away 1.** to cause someone to be out of breath due to a shock or hard exercise. □ *Walking this fast takes my breath away.* □ *Mary frightened me and took my breath away.* **2.** to overwhelm someone with beauty or grandeur. □ *The magnificent painting took my breath away.* □ *Ann looked so beautiful that she took my breath away.*

take someone's **part** to take a side in an argument; to support someone in an argument. □ *My sister took my mother's part in the family argument.* □ *You are always taking the part of underdog!*

take someone's **pulse** to measure the frequency of the beats of a person's pulse. □ *I can take my own pulse.* □ *The nurse took my pulse and said I was fine.*

take someone **to task** to scold or reprimand someone. □ *The teacher took John to task for his bad behavior.* □ *I lost a big contract, and the boss took me to task in front of everyone.*

take someone **to the cleaners** to abuse or damage someone. (Slang.) □ *There was a real rough guy there who threatened to take me to the cleaners if I didn't cooperate.* □ *The crook said he'd take anybody who interfered to the cleaners.*

take someone **under** one's **wing(s)** to take over and care for a person. □ *John wasn't doing well in geometry until the teacher took him under her wing.* □ *I took the new workers under my wings, and they learned the job in no time.*

take someone **up on** something to take advantage of someone's offer of something. (Informal.) □ *I'd like to take you up on your offer to help.* 🅃 *We took up the Browns on their invitation to come to dinner.*

take something to endure something; to survive something. (Also literal.) □ *I don't think I can take any more scolding today. I've been in trouble since I got up this morning.* □ *Mary was very insulting to Tom, but he can take it.*

take something **amiss** AND **take** something **the wrong way** to understand something as wrong or insulting. (Compare this with **take** someone or something **wrong.**) □ *Would you take it amiss if I told you I thought you look lovely?* □ *Why would anyone take such a nice compliment amiss?* □ *I was afraid you'd take it the wrong way.*

take something **at face value** to accept something exactly the way it appears to be. □ *I don't know whether I can take her story at face value, but I will assume that she is not lying.* □ *The committee took the report at face value and approved the suggested changes.*

take something **back** to withdraw or cancel one's statement. (Also literal, meaning "to return something.") □ *I heard what you said, and I'm very insulted. Please take it back.* 🅃 *Take back your words, or I'll never speak to you again!*

take something **home (with** oneself**) 1.** to carry something to one's home. □ *We took a lot of souvenirs home with us.* **2.** to take a thought, idea, or concept away [to one's home] from a meeting or conference. □ *Take this idea home with you. Think twice.*

take something **in stride** to accept something as natural or expected. □ *The argument surprised him, but he took it in stride.* □ *It was a very rude remark, but Mary took it in stride.*

take something **lying down** to endure something unpleasant without fighting back. □ *He insulted me publicly. You don't expect me to take that lying down, do you?* □ *I'm not the kind of person who'll take something like that lying down.*

take something **on faith** to accept or believe something on the basis of little or no evidence. □ *Please try to believe what I'm telling you. Just take it on faith.* □ *Surely you can't expect me to take a story like that on faith.*

take something **on the chin** to experience and endure a direct (figurative or literal) blow or assault. □ *The bad news was a real shock, but John took it on the chin.* □ *The worst luck comes my way, and I always end up taking it on the chin.*

take something **out on** someone or something to direct (or redirect) one's anger or fear onto someone or something. □ *I don't care if you're mad at your brother. Don't take it out on me!* □ *John took his anger out on the wall by kicking it.*

take something **personally** to interpret a remark as if it were mean or critical about oneself. □ *Don't take it personally, but you really need a haircut.* □ *I want to tell you something, but please don't take it personally.*

take something **the wrong way** Go to take something amiss.

take something **to heart** to take something very seriously. □ *John took the criticism to heart and made an honest effort to improve.* □ *I know Bob said a lot of cruel things to you, but he was angry. You shouldn't take those things to heart.*

take something **up 1.** to begin to deal with an issue. (See also take something up (with someone).) □ *That's too big a job for today. I'll take it up tomorrow.* 🅃 *Now we'll take up the task of the election of officers.* **2.** to make the bottom of a skirt or pants cuffs higher off the floor. □ *I'll have to take this skirt up. It's too long for me.* 🅃 *Please take up my pants cuffs. They are an inch too long.*

take something **up (with** someone**)** to raise and discuss a matter with someone. □ *This is a very complicated problem. I'll have to take it up with the office manager.* 🅃 *She'll take up this problem with the owner in the morning.*

take something **with a grain of salt** Go to take something with a pinch of salt.

take something **with a pinch of salt** AND **take** something **with a grain of salt** to listen to a story or an explanation with considerable doubt. □ *You must take anything she says with a grain of salt. She doesn't always tell the truth.* □ *They took my explanation with a pinch of salt. I was sure they didn't believe me.*

take steps (to prevent something**)** to do what is necessary to prevent something. □ *I took steps to prevent John from learning what we were talking about.* □ *I have to keep John from knowing what I've been doing. I can prevent it if I take steps.*

take stock (of something**)** to make an appraisal of resources and potentialities. □ *I spent some time yesterday taking stock of my good and bad qualities.* □ *We all need to take stock now and then.*

take the bit between the teeth Go to take the bit in one's teeth.

take the bit in one's **teeth** AND **take the bit between the teeth** to put oneself in charge. □ *Someone needed to direct the project, so I took the bit in my teeth.* □ *If you want to get something done, you've got* *to take the bit between your teeth and get to work.*

take the bitter with the sweet to accept the bad things along with the good things. □ *We all have disappointments. You have to learn to take the bitter with the sweet.* □ *There are good days and bad days, but every day you take the bitter with the sweet. That's life.*

take the bull by the horns AND **seize the bull by the horns** to meet a challenge directly. □ *If we are going to solve this problem, someone is going to have to take the bull by the horns.* □ *This threat isn't going to go away by itself. We are going to seize the bull by the horns and settle this matter once and for all.*

take the cake to win the prize; to be the best or the worst. (Folksy.) □ *Look at those fireworks. If they don't take the cake, I don't know what does.* □ *Well, Jane, this dinner really takes the cake! It's delicious.* □ *Tom really messed it up. What he did really takes the cake.*

take the day off to choose not to go to work for one day. (Compare this with **get the day off**.) □ *The sun was shining, and it was warm, so I took the day off and went fishing.* □ *Jane wasn't feeling well, so she took the day off.*

take the edge off (something**)** to remove the essence, power, or "bite" of something. □ *I had to tell her some very sad things, so I spoke slowly and softly to take the edge off the news.* □ *I put sugar in my coffee to take the edge off.*

take the initiative (to do something**)** to activate oneself to do something even if one has not been asked to do it. (See also **make it** one's **business to** do something.) □ *The door hinges squeak because no one will take the initiative to oil them.* □ *Sometimes, in order to get things done, you have to take the initiative.*

take the law into one's **own hands** to attempt to administer the law; to act as a judge and jury for someone who has done something wrong. □ *Citizens don't have the right to take the law into their own hands.* □ *The shopkeeper took the law into his own hands when he tried to arrest the thief.*

take the liberty of doing something to assume the right to do something. □ *Since I knew you were arriving late, I took the liberty of securing a hotel room for you.* □ *May I take the liberty of addressing you by your first name?*

take the rap (for someone or something**) 1.** [with *someone*] to take the blame (for something) for someone else. (Slang, especially criminal slang.) □ *I don't want to take the rap for you.* □ *John robbed the bank, but Tom took the rap for him.* **2.** [with *something*] to take the blame for (doing) something. (Slang, especially criminal slang.) □ *I won't take the rap for the crime. I wasn't even in town.* □ *Who'll take the rap for it? Who did it?*

take (the) roll Go to **call (the) roll**.

take the stand to go to and sit in the witness chair in a courtroom. □ *I was in court all day, waiting to take the stand.* □ *The lawyer asked the witness to take the stand.*

take the starch out of someone **1.** to make someone less arrogant or stiff. (Informal.) □ *I told a joke that made Mr. Jones laugh very hard. It really took the starch out of him.* □ *John is so arrogant. I'd really like to take the starch out of him!* **2.** to make someone tired and weak. (Informal.) □ *This hot weather really takes the starch out of me.* □ *What a long day! It sure took the starch out of me.*

take the trouble (to do something**)** to make an effort to do something (that one might not otherwise do). □ *I wish I had taken the trouble to study this matter more carefully.* □ *I just didn't have enough time to take the trouble.*

take the wind out of someone's **sails** to challenge someone's boasting or arrogance. (Informal.) □ *John was bragging about how much money he earned until he learned that most of us make more. That took the wind out of his sails.* □ *Learning that one has been totally wrong about something can really take the wind out of one's sails.*

take the words out of one's **mouth** [for someone else] to say what you were going to say. (Informal. Also with *right,* as in the example.) □ *John said exactly what I was going to say. He took the words out of my mouth.* □ *I agree with you, and I wanted to say the same thing. You took the words right out of my mouth.*

take time off not to work for a period of time—a few minutes or a longer period. (Compare this with **get time off.**) □ *I had to take time off to go to the dentist.* □ *Mary took time off to have a cup of coffee.*

take too much on to undertake to do too much work or too many tasks. □ *Don't take too much on, or you won't be able to do any of it well.* 🅃 *Ann tends to take on too much and get exhausted.*

take to one's **heels** to run away. □ *The little boy said hello and then took to his heels.* □ *The man took to his heels to try to get to the bus stop before the bus left.*

take to someone or something to become fond of or attracted to someone or something. (Informal.) □ *Mary didn't take to her new job, and she quit after two weeks.* □ *Mary seemed to take to John right away.*

take turns ((at) doing something**)** to do something, one (person) at a time (rather than everyone all at once). □ *Please take turns at reading the book.* □ *Everyone is taking turns looking at the picture.* □ *It's more orderly when everyone takes turns.*

take umbrage at something to feel that one has been insulted by something. □ *The employee took umbrage at not getting a raise.* □ *Mary took umbrage at the suggestion that she was being unreasonable.*

take up a collection to collect money for a specific project. □ *We wanted to send Bill some flowers, so we took up a collection.* □ *The office staff took up a collection to pay for the office party.*

take up arms (against someone or something**)** to prepare to fight against someone or something. □ *Everyone in the town took up arms against the enemy.* □ *They were all so angry that the leader convinced them to take up arms.*

take up one's **abode** somewhere to settle down and live somewhere. (Formal.) □ *I took up my abode downtown near my office.* □ *We decided to take up our abode in a warmer climate.*

take up room Go to take up space.

take up someone's **time** to require too much of someone else's time; to waste someone's time. (Also with *so much of* or *too much of,* as in the examples below.) □ *You're taking up my time. Please go away.* □ *I'm sorry. I didn't mean to take up so much of your time.* □ *This problem is taking up too much of my time.*

take up space AND **take up room** to fill or occupy space. (Note the variation in the examples.) □ *The piano is taking up too much room in our living room.* □ *John, you're not being any help at all. You're just taking up space.*

take up time to require or fill time. (Note the variation in the examples. Also without *up.*) □ *This project is taking up too much time.* □ *This kind of thing always takes up time.*

take up where one **left off** to start up again in the very place that one has stopped. □ *I had to leave the room for a minute, but when I got back, I took up where I left off.* □ *It's time to stop for lunch. After lunch, we will take up where we left off.*

take up with someone to become a friend or companion to someone. □ *Billy's mother was afraid that he was taking up with the wrong kind of people.* □ *John and Bob took up with each other and became close friends.*

taken aback surprised and confused. □ *When Mary told me the news, I was taken aback for a moment.* □ *When I told my parents I was married, they were completely taken aback.*

taken for dead appearing to be dead; assumed to be dead. □ *I was so ill with the flu that I was almost taken for dead.* □ *The accident victims were so seriously injured that they were taken for dead at first.*

talk a blue streak to talk very much and very rapidly. (Informal.) □ *Billy didn't talk until he was six, and then he started talking a blue streak.* □ *I can't understand anything Bob says. He talks a blue streak, and I can't follow his thinking.*

talk back (to someone**)** to respond (to a rebuke) rudely or impertinently. □ *John got in trouble for talking back to the teacher.* □ *A student never gains anything by talking back.*

talk big to brag or boast; to talk in an intimidating manner. (Slang.) □ *John is always talking big, but he hasn't really accomplished a lot in life.* □ *She talks big, but she's harmless.*

talk down to someone to speak to someone in a patronizing manner; to speak to someone in the simplest way. □ *The manager insulted everyone in the office by talking down to them.* □ *Please don't talk down to me. I can understand almost anything you have to say.*

talk in circles to talk in a confusing or roundabout manner. □ *I couldn't understand a thing he said. All he did was talk in circles.* □ *We argued for a long time and finally decided that we were talking in circles.*

the **talk of** somewhere someone or something who is the subject of a conversation somewhere, especially the town. □ *The handsome new teacher was the talk of the town.* □ *John's new car is the talk of the office.*

talk oneself **out** to talk until one can talk no more. □ *After nearly an hour, he had talked himself out. Then we began to ask questions.* □ *I talked myself out in the meeting, but no one would support my position.*

talk shop to talk about business matters at a social event (where business talk is out of place). (Informal.) □ *All right, everyone, we're not here to talk shop. Let's have a good time.* □ *Mary and Jane stood by the punch bowl, talking shop.*

talk someone **down 1.** to win out over someone in an argument; to convince someone by arguing. □ *She loves to argue. She takes pleasure in talking someone down.* □ *She tried to talk me down, but I held my ground.* **2.** to convince someone to lower the price. □ *She wanted $2,000 for the car, but I talked her down.* □ *This is my final offer. Don't try to talk me down.*

talk someone **into** (doing) something to overcome someone's objections to doing something; to convince someone to do something. □ *They talked me into going to the meeting, even though I didn't really have the time.* □ *No one can talk me into doing something illegal.*

talk someone or something **up** to promote or speak in support of someone or something. (Informal.) □ *I've been talking up the party all day, trying to get people to come.* □ *The mayor is running for reelection, and everyone at city hall is talking her up.*

talk someone **out of** (doing) something to convince someone not to do something. □ *I tried to talk her out of going, but she insisted.* □ *Don't try to talk me out of quitting school. My mind is made up.*

talk someone **out of** something to convince someone to give something up. □ *This is my candy, and you can't talk me out of it.* □ *I tried to talk her out of her property, but she didn't want to sell.*

talk someone's **ear off** Go to **talk** someone's **head off.**

talk someone's **head off 1.** [for someone] to speak too much. (Slang.) □ *Why does John always talk his head off? Doesn't he know he bores people?* □ *She talks her head off and doesn't seem to know what she's saying.* **2.** AND **talk** someone's **ear off** (Slang.) to talk to and bore someone. □ *John is very friendly, but watch out or he'll talk your head off.* □ *My uncle always talked my ear off whenever I went to visit him.*

talk something **out** to talk about all aspects of a problem or disagreement. □ *Ann and Sally had a problem, so they agreed to talk it out.* 🅃 *It's better to talk out a disagreement than to stay mad.*

talk something **over** to discuss something. □ *Come into my office so we can talk this* *over.* 🅃 *We talked over the plans for nearly an hour.*

talk through one's **hat** to talk nonsense; to brag and boast. (Informal.) □ *John isn't really as good as he says. He's just talking through his hat.* □ *Stop talking through your hat and start being sincere!*

talk turkey to talk business; to talk frankly. (Slang.) □ *Okay, Bob, we have business to discuss. Let's talk turkey.* □ *John wanted to talk turkey, but Jane just wanted to joke around.*

talk until one **is blue in the face** to talk until one is exhausted. (Informal.) □ *I talked until I was blue in the face, but I couldn't change her mind.* □ *She had to talk until she was blue in the face in order to convince him.*

talked out tired of talking; unable to talk more. (Folksy. See also **talk** oneself **out**.) □ *I can't go on. I'm all talked out.* □ *She was talked out in the first hour of discussion.*

tamper with something to attempt to alter or change something; to meddle with or damage something. □ *Someone has tampered with my door lock.* □ *Please don't tamper with my stereo.*

tan someone's **hide** to spank someone. (Folksy.) □ *Billy's mother said she'd tan Billy's hide if he ever did that again.* □ *"I'll tan your hide if you're late!" said Tom's father.*

taper off (doing something**)** to stop doing something gradually. □ *My doctor told me to taper off smoking cigarettes.* □ *I have to taper off because I can't stop all at once.*

tar and feather someone to chastise someone severely. (Also literal.) □ *They threatened to tar and feather me if I ever came back into their town.* □ *I don't believe that they'd really tar and feather me, but they could be very unpleasant.*

tarred with the same brush sharing the same characteristic(s); having the same good or bad points as someone else. □ *Jack and his brother are tarred with the same brush. They're both crooks.* □ *The Smith children are tarred with the same brush. They're all lazy.*

a **taste of** something an experience; an example. □ *Bill gave Sue a taste of her own rudeness.* □ *My friend used a parachute and got a taste of what it's like to be a bird.*

a **taste of things to come** Go to a harbinger of things to come.

tax-and-spend spending freely and taxing heavily. (Refers to a legislative body that repeatedly passes expensive new laws and keeps raising taxes to pay for the cost.) □ *I hope that people do not elect another tax-and-spend Congress this time.* □ *The only thing worse than a tax-and-spend legislature is one that spends and runs up a worsening deficit.*

tea and crumpets a fancy or fussy meeting or reception where refreshments, especially sweet and insubstantial refreshments, are served. (Alluding to a genteel appointment where tea and some light pastries are served.) □ *I don't have time to spend the afternoon having tea and crumpets with the office staff. I have work to do!* □ *Almost every one of my Sunday afternoons is taken up with tea and crumpets for this cause and tea and crumpets for that cause! My rest and relaxation is the only cause I am interested in this Sunday!*

teach one's **grandmother to suck eggs** to try to tell or show someone more knowledgeable or experienced than oneself how to do something. □ *Don't suggest showing Mary how to knit. It will be teaching your grandmother to suck eggs. She's an expert.* □ *Don't teach your grandmother to suck eggs. Bob has been playing tennis for years.*

teach someone **a lesson** to get even with someone for bad behavior. (Also literal.) □ *John tripped me, so I punched him. That ought to teach him a lesson.* □ *That taught me a lesson. I won't do it again.*

the **teacher's pet** the teacher's favorite student. (Preceded by *be, become, seem like,* or *act like.*) □ *Sally is the teacher's pet. She always gets special treatment.* □ *The other students don't like the teacher's pet.*

team up with someone to join with someone. □ *I teamed up with Jane to write the report.* □ *I had never teamed up with anyone else before. I had always worked alone.*

tear into someone or something **1.** [with *someone*] to criticize and scold someone. □ *Tom tore into John and yelled at him for an hour.* □ *Don't tear into me like that. You have no right to speak to me that way.* **2.** to attack or fight with someone or something. □ *The boxer tore into his opponent.* □ *The lion tore into the herd of zebras.*

tear off to leave or depart in a great hurry. (Informal.) □ *Well, excuse me. I have to tear off.* □ *Bob tore off down the street, chasing the fire engine.*

tear one's **hair (out)** to be anxious, frustrated, or angry. □ *I was so nervous, I was about to tear my hair.* □ *I had better get home. My parents will be tearing their hair out.*

tear someone or something **down 1.** to criticize or degrade someone or something. □ *Tom is always tearing Jane down. I guess he doesn't like her.* 🅃 *It's not nice to tear down the people who work in your office.* □ *Why are you always tearing my projects down?* **2.** [with *something*] to dismantle or destroy something. □ *They plan to tear the old building down and build a new one there.* 🅃 *They'll tear down the building in about two weeks.*

tear someone **up** to cause someone much grief. (Also literal. Slang.) □ *The news of Tom's death really tore Bill up.* 🅃 *Bad news tears up some people. Other people can take it calmly.*

tee someone **off** to make someone angry. (Slang.) □ *That kind of talk really tees me off!* □ *Don't let him tee you off. He doesn't mean any harm.*

teething troubles difficulties and problems experienced in the early stages of a project, activity, etc. □ *There have been a lot of teething troubles with the new computer system.* □ *We have finally gotten over the teething troubles connected with the new building complex.*

tell its own story AND **tell its own tale** [for the state of something] to indicate clearly what has happened. □ *The upturned boat told its own tale. The fisherman had drowned.* □ *The girl's tear-stained face told its own story.*

tell its own tale Go to tell its own story.

tell it to the marines I do not believe you (maybe the marines will). (Informal.) □ *That's silly. Tell it to the marines.* □ *I don't care how good you think your reason is. Tell it to the marines!*

tell one **to** one's **face** to tell (something) to someone directly. □ *I'm sorry that Sally feels that way about me. I wish she had told me to my face.* □ *I won't tell Tom that you're mad at him. You should tell him to his face.*

tell on someone to report someone's bad behavior; to tattle on someone. □ *If you do that again, I'll tell on you!* □ *Please don't tell on me. I'm in enough trouble as it is.*

tell people **apart** to distinguish one person or a group of people from another person or group of people. □ *Tom and John are brothers, and you can hardly tell them apart.* □ *Our team is wearing red, and the other team is wearing orange. I can't tell them apart.*

tell someone **a thing or two** AND **tell** someone **where to get off** to scold someone; to express one's anger to someone; to **tell** someone **off.** (Informal.) □ *Wait till I see Sally. I'll tell her a thing or two!* □ *She told me where to get off and then started in scolding Tom.*

tell someone **off** to scold someone; to attack someone verbally. (This has a sense of finality about it.) □ *I was so mad at Bob that I told him off.* 🅃 *By the end of the day, I had told off everyone else, too.*

tell someone **where to get off** Go to tell someone a thing or two.

tell tales out of school to tell secrets or spread rumors. □ *I wish that John would keep quiet. He's telling tales out of school again.* □ *If you tell tales out of school a lot, people won't know when to believe you.*

tell things **apart** to distinguish one thing or a group of things from another thing or group of things. □ *This one is gold, and the others are brass. Can you tell them apart?* □ *Without their labels, I can't tell them apart.*

tell time 1. to keep or report the correct time. □ *This clock doesn't tell time very accurately.* □ *My watch stopped telling time, so I had to have it repaired.* **2.** to be able to read time from a clock or watch. □ *Billy is only four. He can't tell time yet.* □ *They are teaching the children to tell time at school.*

tell which is which Go to know which is which.

a **tempest in a teapot** an uproar about practically nothing. □ *This isn't a serious problem—just a tempest in a teapot.* □ *Even a tempest in a teapot can take a lot of time to get settled.*

thank one's **lucky stars** to be thankful for one's luck. □ *You can thank your lucky stars that I was there to help you.* □ *I thank my lucky stars that I studied the right things for the test.*

Thank you for sharing. <a sarcastic remark made when someone tells something that is unpleasant, overly personal, disgusting, or otherwise annoying.> □ *Thank you for sharing. I really needed to hear about your operation.* □ *Thank you for sharing, Bob. I hope your parents' divorce goes well.*

thankful for small blessings grateful for any small benefits or advantages one has, especially in a generally difficult situation. (Preceded by *be, become,* or *seem.*) □ *We have very little money, but we must be thankful for small blessings. At least we have enough food.* □ *Bob was badly injured in the accident, but at least he's still alive. Let's be thankful for small blessings.*

thanks to someone or something owing to someone or something; because of someone or something. (This does not refer to gratitude.) □ *Thanks to the storm, we have no electricity.* □ *Thanks to Mary, we have tickets to the game. She bought them early before they were sold out.*

That ain't hay. That is not a small amount of money. (Folksy.) □ *I paid forty dollars for it, and that ain't hay!* □ *Bob lost his wallet with $200 in it—and that ain't hay.*

That does it! AND **That tears it!** That is the last thing that is needed to force me to take action! □ *That does it! I'm mad and I'm going home!* □ *Well, that tears it! I have never been so insulted!*

That makes two of us. The same is true for me. □ *So you're going to the football game? That makes two of us.* □ *BILL: I just passed my biology test. BOB: That makes two of us!*

That sucks. AND **It sucks.** That is worthless. (Slang. Use caution with *sucks.*) □ *Yuck! That sucks!* □ *This meat loaf is terrible. It sucks.*

That takes care of that. That is settled. □ *That takes care of that, and I'm glad it's over.* □ *I spent all morning dealing with this matter, and that takes care of that.*

That tears it! Go to That does it!

That'll be the day. I don't believe that the day will ever come (when something will happen). □ *Do you really think that John will pass geometry? That'll be the day.* □ *John graduate? That'll be the day!*

That's about the size of it. It is final and correct. (Slang.) □ *MARY: Do you mean that you aren't going? TOM: That's about the size of it.* □ *At the end of his speech Bob said, "That's about the size of it."*

That's all for someone. Someone will get no more chances to do things correctly. □ *That's all for you, Tom. I've had all I can take from you. One disappointment after another.* □ *You've gone too far, Mary. That's all for you. Good-bye!*

That's all she wrote. That is all. (Slang.) □ *At the end of his informal talk, Tom said, "That's all she wrote."* □ *Sally looked at the empty catsup bottle and said, "That's all she wrote."*

That's it! 1. That does it!; That's the last straw! (Informal.) □ *That's it! I'm leaving! I've had enough!* □ *Ok. That's it! I'm going to report you to human resources!*

2. That is the answer! ☐ *That's it! You are right.* ☐ *That's it! You got the right answer.*

That's that. It is permanently settled and need not be dealt with again. ☐ *I said no, and that's that.* ☐ *You can't come back. I told you to leave, and that's that.*

That's the ticket. That is exactly what is needed. ☐ *That's the ticket, John. You're doing it just the way it should be done.* ☐ *That's the ticket! I knew you could do it.*

That's the way the ball bounces. AND **That's the way the cookie crumbles.** That is too bad.; Those things happen. (Slang.) ☐ *Sorry to hear about your problems. That's the way the ball bounces.* ☐ *John wrecked his car and then lost his job. That's the way the cookie crumbles.*

That's the way the cookie crumbles. Go to That's the way the ball bounces.

[the] <Entries beginning with *a, an,* or *the* are alphabetized under the *second* word in the entry. That means that *a bed of roses* will appear in the *B*s.>

The jig is up. Go to The game is up.

Them's fighting words. Those are words that will start a fight. (Folksy. Note that *them is* is permissible in this expression.) ☐ *Better not talk like that around here. Them's fighting words.* ☐ *Them's fighting words, and you'd better be quiet unless you want trouble.*

then and there right then. ☐ *I asked him right then and there exactly what he meant.* ☐ *I decided to settle the matter then and there and not wait until Monday.*

There aren't enough hours in the day. There are too many things to do and not enough time. ☐ *I am behind in all my work. There aren't enough hours in the day!* ☐ *We can't handle all the problems that come our way. There aren't enough hours in the day.*

There are plenty of other fish in the sea. There are other choices. (Proverb. Used to refer to persons.) ☐ *When John broke up with Ann, I told her not to worry. There are plenty of other fish in the sea.* ☐ *It's too bad that your secretary quit, but there are plenty of other fish in the sea.*

there is no doing something one is not permitted to do something. (Informal.) ☐ *There is no arguing with Bill.* ☐ *There is no cigarette smoking here.*

There is trouble brewing. Go to Trouble is brewing.

There, now. Go to There, there.

There, there. AND **There, now.** <an expression used to comfort someone.> ☐ *There, there. You'll feel better after you take a nap.* ☐ *There, now. Everything will be all right.*

There will be the devil to pay. There will be lots of trouble. (Informal. See also have the devil to pay.) ☐ *If you damage my car, there will be the devil to pay.* ☐ *Bill broke a window, and now there will be the devil to pay.*

There you go. Go to Here you go.

There's more than one way to skin a cat. There is more than one way to do something. (Proverb.) ☐ *If that way won't work, try another way. There's more than one way to skin a cat.* ☐ *Don't worry, I'll figure out a way to get it done. There's more than one way to skin a cat.*

There's no accounting for taste. There is no explanation for people's preferences. (Proverb.) ☐ *Look at that purple and orange car! There's no accounting for taste.* ☐ *Some people seemed to like the music, although I thought it was worse than noise. There's no accounting for taste.*

They don't make them like they used to. goods are not as well made now as they were in the past. (Often used as a catch phrase. *Them* is often *'em.*) ☐ *Look at this flimsy door! They don't make 'em like they used to.* ☐ *Why don't cars last longer? They just don't make 'em like they used to.*

thick and fast in large numbers or amounts and at a rapid rate. ☐ *The enemy soldiers came thick and fast.* ☐ *New problems seem to come thick and fast.*

thick as pea soup Go to (as) thick as pea soup.

thick as thieves Go to (as) thick as thieves.

thick-skinned not easily upset or hurt; insensitive. (Also literal. The opposite of **thin-skinned**.) ☐ *Tom won't worry about your insults. He's completely thick-skinned.* ☐ *Jane's so thick-skinned she didn't realize Fred was being rude to her.*

thin on top balding. (Informal.) ☐ *James is wearing a hat because he's getting thin on top.* ☐ *Father got a little thin on top as he got older.*

thin-skinned easily upset or hurt; sensitive. (Also literal. The opposite of **thick-skinned**.) ☐ *You'll have to handle Mary's mother carefully. She's very thin-skinned.* ☐ *Jane weeps easily when people tease her. She's too thin-skinned.*

Things are looking up. Conditions are looking better. ☐ *Since I got a salary increase, things are looking up.* ☐ *Things are looking up at school. I'm doing better in all my classes.*

think a great deal of someone or something Go to **think a lot of** someone or something.

think a lot of someone or something AND **think a great deal of** someone or something; **think highly of** someone or something; **think much of** someone or something to think well of someone or something. (See also **speak highly of** someone or something.) ☐ *The teacher thinks a lot of Mary and her talents.* ☐ *No one really thinks a great deal of the new policies.* ☐ *I think highly of John.* ☐ *The manager doesn't think much of John and says so to everyone.*

think back (on someone or something**)** to remember and think about someone or something in one's past. ☐ *When I think back on Sally and the good times we had together, I get very sad.* ☐ *I like to think back on my childhood and try to remember what it was like.*

think better of something to reconsider something; to think again and decide not to do something. ☐ *Jack was going to escape, but he thought better of it.* ☐ *Jill had planned to resign, but thought better of it.*

think highly of someone or something Go to **think a lot of** someone or something.

think inside the box to think in traditional fashion, bound by old, nonfunctional, or limiting structures, rules, or practices. (As if thinking or creativity were confined or limited by a figurative box. See also **inside the box**. Compare this with **think outside the box**.) ☐ *You won't come up with good ideas if you think only inside the box.* ☐ *You guys only think inside the box and will never find a better solution.*

think little of someone or something AND **think nothing of** someone or something to have a low opinion of someone or something. ☐ *Most experts think little of Jane's theory.* ☐ *People may think nothing of it now, but in a few years everyone will praise it.* ☐ *The critics thought little of her latest book.*

think much of someone or something Go to **think a lot of** someone or something.

think nothing of someone or something Go to **think little of** someone or something.

think on one's **feet** to think, reason, and plan while one is talking. ☐ *If you want to be a successful teacher, you must be able to think on your feet.* ☐ *I have to write out everything I'm going to say, because I can't think on my feet too well.*

think out loud to say one's thoughts aloud. ☐ *Excuse me. I didn't really mean to say that. I was just thinking out loud.* ☐ *Mr. Johnson didn't prepare a speech. He just stood there and thought out loud. It was a terrible presentation.*

think outside the box to think freely, not bound by old, nonfunctional, or limiting structures, rules, or practices. (As if thinking or creativity were confined in or limited by a figurative box. See also **outside the box**. Compare this with **think inside the box**.) ☐ *You won't come up with good ideas until you think outside the box.* ☐ *Let's think outside the box for a minute and try to find a better solution.*

think someone or something **fit for** something to believe that someone or something is suitable for something. ☐ *I don't think John fit for the job.* ☐ *Do you think this car fit for a long trip?*

think something **out** to think through something; to prepare a plan or scheme. □ *This is an interesting problem. I'll have to take some time and think it out.* 🅃 *We spent all morning thinking out our plan.*

think something **over** to consider something; to think about something (before giving a decision). □ *Please think it over and give me your decision in the morning.* 🅃 *I need more time to think over your offer.*

think something **up** to contrive or invent something. □ *Don't worry. I'll find a way to do it. I can think something up in time to get it done.* 🅃 *John thought up a way to solve our problem.*

think the world of someone or something to be very fond of someone or something. □ *Mary thinks the world of her little sister.* □ *The old lady thinks the world of her cats.*

think twice (before doing something**)** to consider carefully whether one should do something; to be cautious about doing something. □ *You should think twice before quitting your job.* □ *That's a serious decision, and you should certainly think twice.*

thinking inside the box thinking traditionally, bound by old, nonfunctional, or limiting structures, rules, or practices. (Compare this with **thinking outside the box.**) □ *Thinking inside the box will seldom produce any creative solution for a serious problem.* □ *Thinking inside the box is what got us into this mess in the first place.*

thinking outside the box thinking freely, not being bound by old, nonfunctional, or limiting structures, rules, or practices. (Compare this with **thinking inside the box.**) □ *Thinking outside the box will often produce some creative solutions to a complex problem.* □ *Thinking outside the box is a popular way to encourage creative solutions, or it can waste a lot of valuable time.*

a **thirst for** something a craving or desire for something. (Also literal.) □ *The tyrant had an intense thirst for power.* □ *The actor's thirst for fame caused him to become unscrupulous.*

thirsty for something craving or desiring something. (Also literal.) □ *The students were thirsty for knowledge.* □ *That evil tyrant is thirsty for power.*

This is it. This is the time, place, or thing that we have been looking or waiting for. □ *This is it. This is the chance you've been waiting for!* □ *This is it. This is my stop. I have to get off the bus.*

thither and yon there and everywhere. (Archaic. See also **hither, thither, and yon.**) □ *I sent my résumé thither and yon, but no one responded.* □ *The children are all scattered thither and yon, and it is difficult for them to get home for the holidays.*

a **thorn in** someone's **side** a constant bother or annoyance to someone. (Preceded by *be, become, seem like,* or *act like.*) □ *This problem is a thorn in my side. I wish I had a solution to it.* □ *John was a thorn in my side for years before I finally got rid of him.*

Those were the days. The days we have been referring to were the greatest of times. □ *Ah, yes. The eighties. Those were the days!* □ *Those were the days. Back when people knew right from wrong.*

thrash something **out** to discuss something thoroughly and solve any problems. □ *The committee took hours to thrash the whole matter out.* 🅃 *Fred and Anne thrashed out the reasons for their constant disagreements.*

thread (one's **way) through** something to make a path for oneself through a crowded area; to make one's way through a crowded area. □ *The spy threaded his way through the crowd.* □ *The joggers threaded through the shoppers on the sidewalks.*

three sheets to the wind drunk. (These *sheets* are the ropes on a sailing vessel.) □ *I think that guy is three sheets to the wind. He can hardly stand up.* □ *Bob and Bill are three sheets to the wind. You know, drunk.*

thrill someone **to death** Go to **thrill** someone **to pieces.**

thrill someone **to pieces** AND **thrill** someone **to death** to please or excite someone very much. (Informal.) □ *John sent flowers to Ann and thrilled her to pieces.* □ *Your wonderful comments thrilled me to death.*

thrilled to death AND **thrilled to pieces** very excited; very pleased. □ *She was thrilled to death to get the flowers.* □ *I'm just thrilled to pieces to have you visit me.*

thrilled to pieces Go to thrilled to death.

through and through thoroughly; completely. □ *I've studied this report through and through trying to find the facts you've mentioned.* □ *I was angry through and through, and I had to sit and recover before I could talk to anyone.*

through hell and high water through all sorts of severe difficulties. (Use caution with *hell*.) □ *I came through hell and high water to get to this meeting on time. Why don't you start on time?* □ *You'll have to go through hell and high water to accomplish your goal, but it'll be worth it.*

through thick and thin through good times and bad times. □ *We've been together through thick and thin, and we won't desert each other now.* □ *Over the years, we went through thick and thin and enjoyed every minute of it.*

throw a fit to become very angry; to put on a display of anger. (Folksy.) □ *Sally threw a fit when I showed up without the things she asked me to buy.* □ *My dad threw a fit when I got home three hours late.*

throw a monkey wrench into the works to cause problems for someone's plans. (Informal.) □ *I don't want to throw a monkey wrench into the works, but have you checked your plans with a lawyer?* □ *When John suddenly refused to help us, he really threw a monkey wrench into the works.*

throw a party (for someone**)** to give or hold a party (for someone). □ *Mary was leaving town, so we threw a party for her.* □ *Fred is having a birthday. Do you know a place where we could throw a party?*

throw caution to the wind to become very careless. □ *Jane, who is usually cautious, threw caution to the wind and went windsurfing.* □ *I don't mind taking a little chance now and then, but I'm not the type of person who throws caution to the wind.*

throw cold water on something Go to pour cold water on something.

throw down the gauntlet to challenge (someone) to an argument or to (figurative) combat. □ *When Bob challenged my conclusions, he threw down the gauntlet. I was ready for an argument.* □ *Frowning at Bob is the same as throwing down the gauntlet. He loves to get into a fight about something.*

throw good money after bad to waste additional money after wasting money once. □ *I bought a used car and then had to spend $300 on repairs. That was throwing good money after bad.* □ *The Browns are always throwing good money after bad. They bought an acre of land that turned out to be swamp, and then had to pay to have it filled in.*

throw in the sponge Go to throw in the towel.

throw in the towel AND **throw in the sponge** to quit (doing something). (Informal.) □ *When John could stand no more of Mary's bad temper, he threw in the towel and left.* □ *Don't give up now! It's too soon to throw in the sponge.*

throw oneself **at** someone AND **fling** oneself **at** someone to give oneself willingly to someone else for romance. □ *I guess that Mary really likes John. She practically threw herself at him when he came into the room.* □ *Everyone could see by the way Tom flung himself at Jane that he was going to ask her for a date.*

throw oneself **at** someone's **feet** to behave in a very humble and contrite manner. (Refers to bowing down humbly at someone's feet.) □ *Do I have to throw myself at your feet in order to convince you that I'm sorry?* □ *I love you sincerely, Jane. I'll throw myself at your feet and await your command. I'm your slave!*

throw oneself **at the mercy of the court** Go to throw oneself on the mercy of the court.

throw oneself **on the mercy of the court** AND **throw** oneself **at the mercy of the court** to plead for mercy from a judge in a courtroom. □ *Your honor, please believe me, I didn't do it on purpose. I throw myself on the mercy of the court and beg for a light sentence.* □ *Jane threw herself at the mercy of the court and hoped for the best.*

throw one's **hands up in despair** to give up; to raise one's hands making a sign of giving up. □ *John threw his hands up in despair because they wouldn't let him see his brother in the hospital.* 🅃 *There was nothing I could do to help. I threw up my hands in despair and left.*

throw one's **hands up in horror** to be shocked; to raise one's hands as if one had been frightened. □ *When Bill heard the bad news, he threw his hands up in horror.* 🅃 *I could do no more. I had seen more than I could stand. I just threw up my hands in horror and screamed.*

throw one's **voice** to project one's voice so that it seems to be coming from some other place. □ *The ventriloquist threw his voice.* □ *Jane can throw her voice, so I thought she was standing behind me.*

throw one's **weight around** to attempt to boss people around; to give orders. (Informal.) □ *The district manager came to our office and tried to throw his weight around, but no one paid any attention to him.* □ *Don't try to throw your weight around in this office. We know who our boss is.*

throw (some) light on something Go to shed (some) light on something.

throw someone to confuse someone slightly. (See also throw someone **for a loop**.) □ *You threw me for a minute when you asked for my identification. I thought you recognized me.* □ *The question the teacher asked was so hard that it threw me, and I became very nervous.*

throw someone **a curve 1.** to pitch a curve ball to someone in baseball. □ *The pitcher threw John a curve, and John swung wildly against thin air.* □ *During that game, the pitcher threw everyone a curve at least once.* **2.** to confuse someone by doing something unexpected. □ *When you said "house" you threw me a curve. The password was supposed to be "home."* □ *John threw me a curve when we were making our presentation, and I forgot my speech.*

throw someone **for a loop** AND **knock** someone **for a loop** to confuse or shock someone. (Informal. This is more severe and upsetting than throw someone **a curve** or throw someone.) □ *When Bill heard the news, it threw him for a loop.* □ *The manager knocked Bob for a loop by firing him on the spot.*

throw someone **for a loss** to cause someone to be uncertain or confused. (Often passive.) □ *The stress of being in front of so many people threw Ann for a loss. She forgot her speech.* □ *It was a difficult problem. I was thrown for a loss for an answer.*

throw someone **off the track 1.** to cause one to lose one's place in the sequence of things. □ *The interruption threw me off the track for a moment, but I soon got started again with my presentation.* □ *Don't let little things throw you off the track. Concentrate on what you're doing.* **2.** AND **throw** someone **off the trail** to cause someone to lose the trail (when following someone or something). □ *The raccoon threw us off the track by running through the creek.* □ *The robber threw the police off the trail by leaving town.*

throw someone **off the trail** Go to throw someone off the track.

throw someone or something **off 1.** [with *someone*] to confuse someone; to mislead someone. □ *The interruption threw me off, and I lost my place in the speech.* □ *Little noises throw me off. Please try to be quiet.* □ *Your comment threw me off.* **2.** [with *something*] to resist or recover from a disease. □ *It was a bad cold, but I managed to throw it off in a few days.* 🅃 *I can't seem to throw off my cold. I've had it for weeks.* **3.** [with *something*] to emit or give off an odor. □ *The small animal threw a* *strong odor off.* 🅃 *The flowers threw off a heavy perfume.*

throw someone **out (of** something**)** to force a person to leave a place or an organization. (Also literal.) □ *John behaved so badly that they threw him out of the party.* □ *I was very loud, but they didn't throw me out.* □ *They threw Toni out of the club because she was so unpleasant.*

throw someone **over** to end a romance with someone. □ *Jane threw Bill over. I think she met someone she likes better.* □ *Bill was about ready to throw her over, so it's just as well.*

throw someone's **name around** to impress people by saying you know a famous or influential person. (Informal.) □ *You won't get anywhere around here by throwing the mayor's name around.* □ *When you get to the meeting, just throw my name around a bit, and people will pay attention to you.*

throw someone **to the wolves** to (figuratively) sacrifice someone. □ *The press was demanding an explanation, so the mayor blamed the mess on John and threw him to the wolves.* □ *I wouldn't let them throw me to the wolves! I did nothing wrong, and I won't take the blame for their errors.*

throw something **into the bargain** to include something in a deal. □ *To encourage me to buy a new car, the car dealer threw a free radio into the bargain.* □ *If you purchase three pounds of chocolates, I'll throw one pound of salted nuts into the bargain.*

throw something **together** AND **slap** something **together** to assemble or arrange something in haste. □ *Don't just slap something together! Use care and do it right.* □ *You assembled this device very badly. It seems that you just slapped it together.* 🅃 *John went into the kitchen to throw together something for dinner.*

throw (something**) up** to vomit something. (Compare this with **spit (**something**) up**.) □ *The meat was bad, and I threw it up.* 🅃 *I hate to throw up.* 🅃 *Billy threw up his dinner.*

throw something **up to** someone to mention a shortcoming to someone repeatedly. □ *I know I'm thoughtless. Why do you keep throwing it up to me?* □ *Bill was always throwing Jane's faults up to her.*

throw the baby out with the bath(water) to dispose of the good while eagerly trying to get rid of the bad. □ *In her haste to talk down the idea containing a few disagreeable points, she has thrown the baby out with the bathwater.* 🅃 *Hasty action will result in throwing out the baby with the bath.*

throw the book at someone to charge someone with, or convict someone of, as many crimes as is possible. (Slang.) □ *I made the police officer angry, so he took me to the station and threw the book at me.* □ *The judge threatened to throw the book at me if I didn't stop insulting the police officer.*

thrust and parry to enter into verbal combat [with someone]; to compete actively [with someone]. (Refers to movements in the sport of fencing.) □ *I spent the entire afternoon thrusting and parrying with a committee of so-called experts in the field of insurance.* □ *I do not intend to stand here and thrust and parry with you over a simple matter like this. Let's get someone else's opinion.*

thumb a ride AND **hitch a ride** to get a ride from a passing motorist; to make a sign with one's thumb that indicates to passing drivers that one is begging for a ride. □ *My car broke down on the highway, and I had to thumb a ride to get back to town.* □ *Sometimes it's dangerous to hitch a ride with a stranger.*

thumb one's **nose at** someone or something to (figuratively or literally) make a rude gesture of disgust with one's thumb and nose at someone or something. □ *The tramp thumbed his nose at the lady and walked away.* □ *You can't just thumb your nose at people who give you trouble. You've got to learn to get along.*

thumb through something AND **leaf through** something to look through a book, magazine, or newspaper, without reading it carefully. □ *I've only thumbed through this book, but it looks very interesting.* □ *I leafed through a magazine while waiting to see the doctor.*

a **thumbnail sketch** a short or small picture or description. □ *The manager gave a thumbnail sketch of her plans.* □ *The student wrote a thumbnail sketch of his project.*

thumbs down on someone or something opposed to someone or something. (See also **turn thumbs down (on** someone or something**)**.) □ *Bob is thumbs down on hiring anyone else.* □ *I had hoped that she'd agree with our plan, but she's thumbs down on it.*

thumbs up on someone or something in favor of someone or something. (See also **turn thumbs up (on** someone or something**)**.) □ *Bob is thumbs up on hiring Claude.* □ *I never hoped she'd agree with our plan, but she's totally thumbs up on it.*

thunder thunderstorms; thundershowers. (Used in weather forecasting.) □ *The forecast is for breezy conditions tonight, perhaps with some thunder later in the evening.* □ *There was a lot of thunder across the Midwest today, causing flooding in low-lying areas.*

tickle someone **pink** AND **tickle** someone **to death** to please or entertain someone very much. (Informal.) □ *Bill told a joke that really tickled us all pink.* □ *I know that these flowers will tickle her to death.*

tickle someone's **fancy** to interest someone; to make someone curious. (See also **strike** someone's **fancy**.) □ *I have an interesting problem here that I think will tickle your fancy.* □ *This doesn't tickle my fancy at all. This is dull and boring.*

tickle someone **to death** Go to **tickle** someone **pink**.

tickled pink AND **tickled to death** very much pleased or entertained. (Informal.) □ *I was tickled to death to have you visit us.* □ *We were tickled pink when your flowers arrived.*

tickled to death Go to **tickled pink**.

tide someone **over** [for a portion of something] to last until someone can get some more. □ *I don't get paid until next Wednesday. Could you lend me thirty dollars to tide me over?* □ *Could I borrow some coffee to tide me over until I can get to the store tomorrow?*

tie into something to connect to something. □ *I'm trying to get my home computer to tie in with the big one at the university.* □ *Could I tie into your water line while I'm waiting for mine to be repaired?* □ *What you just told me ties into John's version of the event.*

tie someone **down** to restrict or encumber someone. (Also literal.) □ *I'd like to go fishing every weekend, but my family ties me down.* □ *I don't want to tie you down, but you do have responsibilities here at home.*

tie someone or something **up 1.** [with *someone*] to keep someone busy or occupied. (Also literal.) □ *Sorry, this matter will tie me up for about an hour.* 🅃 *The same matter will tie up almost everyone in the office.* **2.** [with *something*] to conclude and finalize something. (Informal.) 🅃 *Let's try to tie up this deal by Thursday.* □ *We'll manage to tie our business up by Wednesday at the latest.*

tie someone's **hands** to prevent someone from doing something. (Also literal. See also **have** one's **hands tied**.) □ *I'd like to help you, but my boss has tied my hands.* □ *Please don't tie my hands with unnecessary restrictions. I'd like the freedom to do whatever is necessary.*

tie someone **(up) in knots** to become anxious or upset. (Informal.) □ *John tied himself in knots worrying about his wife during the operation.* □ *This waiting and worrying really ties me up in knots.*

tie the knot to get married. (Informal.) □ *Well, I hear that you and John are going to tie the knot.* □ *My parents tied the knot almost forty years ago.*

tie traffic up to cause road traffic to stop. □ *If you tie traffic up for too long, you'll get a traffic ticket.* 🅃 *Please don't stop on the roadway. It'll tie up traffic.*

tied down restricted by responsibilities. (Also literal.) □ *I love my home, but sometimes I don't like being tied down.* □ *I don't feel tied down, even though I have a lot of responsibility.*

tied to one's **mother's apron strings** dominated by one's mother; dependent on one's mother. □ *Tom is still tied to his mother's apron strings.* □ *Isn't he a little old to be tied to his mother's apron strings?*

tied up busy. (Also literal.) □ *How long will you be tied up?* □ *I will be tied up in a meeting for an hour.*

tight as a drum Go to (as) tight as a drum.

tight as a tick Go to (as) full as a tick.

tight as Dick's hatband Go to (as) tight as Dick's hatband.

tighten one's **belt** to manage to spend less money; to use less of something. □ *Things are beginning to cost more and more. It looks as if we'll all have to tighten our belts.* □ *Times are hard, and prices are high. I can tighten my belt for only so long.*

tightfisted (with money) AND **closefisted (with money)** very stingy with money. □ *The manager is very closefisted with expenditures.* □ *My parents are very tightfisted with money.*

till all hours (of the day and night) Go to until all hours (of the day and night).

till the cows come home Go to (un)til the cows come home.

tilt at windmills to fight battles with imaginary enemies; to fight against unimportant enemies or issues. (As with the fictional character, Don Quixote, who attacked windmills.) □ *Aren't you too smart to go around tilting at windmills?* □ *I'm not going to fight this issue. I've wasted too much of my life tilting at windmills.*

time after time AND **time and (time) again** repeatedly; over and over (again). □ *You've made the same error time after time! Please try to be more careful!* □ *I've told you time and again not to do that.* □ *You keep saying the same thing over and over, time and time again. Stop it!* □ *I have told you time and again: don't put wet garbage in the trash can!*

time and (time) again Go to time after time.

time flies time passes very quickly. (From the Latin *tempus fugit.*) □ *I didn't really think it was so late when the party ended. Doesn't time fly?* □ *Time simply flew while the old friends exchanged news.*

Time is money. (My) time is valuable, so don't waste it. □ *I can't afford to spend a lot of time standing here talking. Time is money, you know!* □ *People who keep saying that time is money may be working too hard.*

the **time is ripe** Exactly the right time has come. □ *I'll tell her the good news when the time is ripe.* □ *The time is ripe to ask the question again.*

Time is up. The allotted time has run out. □ *You must stop now. Your time is up.* □ *Time's up! Turn in your tests whether you're finished or not.*

time off a period of time during which one does not have to work; free time. □ *The next time I have some time off, I want to go to Miami.* □ *I don't have any time off until next week.*

time out 1. to record one's departure time. □ *Did you remember to time out when you left work?* □ *I timed out at the regular time.* **2.** stopping the clock in a sporting event that is played in a fixed time period. □ *The coach made a sign for time out, and the clock stopped and a buzzer sounded.* □ *After someone called time out, the players gathered around the coach.*

time to catch one's **breath** to find enough time to relax or behave normally. □ *When things slow down around here, I'll get time to catch my breath.* □ *Sally was so busy she didn't even have time to catch her breath.*

time was (when) there was a time when; at a time in the past. □ *Time was when old people were taken care of at home.* □ *Time was when people didn't travel around so much.*

Time will tell. Something will become known in the course of time. (Proverb.) □ *I don't know if things will improve. Time will tell.* □ *Who knows what the future will bring? Only time will tell.*

tip someone **off** to give someone a hint; to warn someone. (Slang.) □ *I tipped John off that there would be a test in his algebra class.* 🅃 *I didn't want to tip off everyone, so I only told John.*

tip the scales at something to weigh some amount. □ *Tom tips the scales at nearly 200 pounds.* □ *I'll be glad when I tip the scales at a few pounds less.*

tits and ass a public display of [the human female] breasts and buttocks. (Refers to television, film, and stage performances in which women exhibit prominent and well-formed breasts and buttocks or in which these body parts are emphasized or made prominent. Slang. Use caution with the expression.) □ *We have a really fine choice on television tonight. There is brutal violence on channel 2, bloody horror on channel 5, and tits and ass on channel 10.* □ *Without tits and ass, many Broadway musicals would flop.*

to a great extent mainly; largely. □ *To a great extent, Mary is the cause of her own problems.* □ *I've finished my work to a great extent. There is nothing important left to do.*

to and fro toward and away from (something). (Compare this with **back and forth**.) □ *The puppy was very active—running to and fro—wagging its tail.* □ *The lion in the cage moved to and fro, watching the people in front of the cage.*

to beat the band very much; very fast. (Folksy.) □ *The carpenter sawed and hammered to beat the band.* □ *They baked cookies and pies to beat the band.*

to be on the safe side to be safe; to be cautious; [to do something just] in case it is necessary; to be very well prepared. □ *To be on the safe side, carry some extra money in your shoe.* □ *I like to be on the safe side and stay in my hotel room at night.*

to be safe to be cautious; to be careful; [to do something just] in case it is necessary; to be very well prepared. □ *Just to be safe, you should take some clean water with you.* □ *Other people like to drive over the speed limit, but I prefer to be safe.*

to boot in addition; besides. (Informal.) □ *For breakfast I had my usual two eggs and a slice of ham to boot.* □ *When I left for school, my parents gave me an airplane ticket and fifty dollars to boot.*

to count heads to count people. □ *I'll tell you how many people are here after I count heads.* □ *Everyone is here. Let's count heads so we can order hamburgers.*

to date up to the present time. □ *How much have you accomplished to date?* □ *I've done everything I'm supposed to have done to date.*

to hell and gone very much gone; gone to hell. (Use caution with *hell.*) □ *All my hard work is to hell and gone.* □ *When you see everything you've planned to hell and gone, you get kind of angry.*

to no avail AND **of no avail** with no effect; unsuccessful. □ *All of my efforts were to no avail.* □ *Everything I did to help was of no avail. Nothing worked.*

to one's **heart's content** as much as one wants. □ *John wanted a week's vacation so he could go to the lake and fish to his heart's content.* □ *I just sat there, eating chocolate to my heart's content.*

to put it mildly to understate something; to say something politely. (Note the variation in the example below.) □ *She was angry at almost everyone—to put it mildly.* □ *To say she was angry is putting it mildly.* □ *To put it mildly, she was enraged.*

to say nothing of someone or something not to even mention the importance of someone or something. □ *John and Mary had to be taken care of, to say nothing of Bill, who would require even more attention.* □ *I'm having enough difficulty painting the house, to say nothing of the garage that is very much in need of paint.*

to say the least at the very least; without dwelling on the subject; **to put it mildly**.

☐ *We were not at all pleased with her work—to say the least.* ☐ *When they had an accident, they were upset to say the least.*

to some extent to some degree; in some amount; partly. ☐ *I've solved this problem to some extent.* ☐ *I can help you understand this to some extent.*

to someone's **liking** in a way that pleases someone. ☐ *I hope I've done the work to your liking.* ☐ *Sally didn't find the meal to her liking and didn't eat any of it.*

to someone's **way of thinking** in someone's opinion. ☐ *This isn't satisfactory to my way of thinking.* ☐ *To my way of thinking, this is the perfect kind of vacation.*

to the best of one's **ability** as well as one is able. ☐ *I did the work to the best of my ability.* ☐ *You should always work to the best of your ability.*

to the best of one's **knowledge** as far as one knows; from one's knowledge. ☐ *This is the true story to the best of my knowledge.* ☐ *To the best of my knowledge, John is the only person who can answer that question.*

to the bitter end to the very end. (Originally nautical. This originally had nothing to do with bitterness.) ☐ *I kept trying to the bitter end.* ☐ *It took me a long time to get through school, but I worked hard at it all the way to the bitter end.*

to the contrary as the opposite of what has been stated; contrary to what has been stated. (Compare this with **on the contrary**.) ☐ *The brown horse didn't beat the black horse. To the contrary, the black one won.* ☐ *Among spiders, the male is not the larger one. To the contrary, the female is larger.*

to the core all the way through; basically and essentially. (Usually with some negative sense, such as *evil, rotten,* etc.) ☐ *Bill said that John is evil to the core.* ☐ *This organization is rotten to the core.*

to the ends of the earth to the remotest and most inaccessible points on the earth. ☐ *I'll pursue him to the ends of the earth.* ☐ *We've explored almost the whole world. We've traveled to the ends of the earth trying to learn about our world.*

to the last to the end; to the conclusion. ☐ *All of us kept trying to the last.* ☐ *It was a very boring play, but I sat through it to the last.*

to the letter exactly as instructed; exactly as written. ☐ *I didn't make an error. I followed your instruction to the letter.* ☐ *We didn't prepare the recipe to the letter, but the cake still turned out very well.*

to the nth degree to the maximum amount. (Informal.) ☐ *Jane is a perfectionist and tries to be careful to the nth degree.* ☐ *This scientific instrument is accurate to the nth degree.*

to the tune of some amount of money a certain amount of money. (Informal.) ☐ *My checking account is overdrawn to the tune of $340.* ☐ *My wallet was stolen, and I'm short of money to the tune of seventy dollars.*

To the victors belong the spoils. AND **To the victor belongs the spoils.** The winners achieve power over people and property. (Proverb.) ☐ *The mayor took office and immediately fired many workers and hired new ones. Everyone said, "To the victors belong the spoils."* ☐ *The office of president includes the right to live in the White House and at Camp David. To the victors belong the spoils.*

to whom it may concern to the person to whom this applies. (A form of address used when you do not know the name of the person who handles the kind of business you are writing about.) ☐ *The letter started out, "To whom it may concern."* ☐ *When you don't know who to write to, just say, "To whom it may concern."*

to wit namely; that is; that is to say. ☐ *The criminal was punished; to wit, he received a 20-year sentence.* ☐ *Many students, to wit Mary, Bill, Sue, and Anne, complained about their teacher.*

toe the line Go to toe the mark.

toe the mark AND **toe the line** to do what one is expected to do; to follow the rules. ☐ *You'll get ahead, Sally. Don't worry. Just* *toe the mark, and everything will be okay.* ☐ *John finally got fired. He just couldn't learn to toe the line.*

toing and froing (on something**)** moving back and forth on an issue, first deciding one way and then changing to another. ☐ *The boss spent most of the afternoon toing and froing on the question of who was to handle the Wilson account.* ☐ *I wish you would stop toing and froing and make up your mind.*

Tom, Dick, and Harry Go to (every) Tom, Dick, and Harry.

tone something **down** to make something less extreme. ☐ *That yellow is too bright. Please try to tone it down.* 🅃 *Can you tone down your remarks? They seem quite strong for this situation.*

tongue-in-cheek mockingly; insincere; joking. ☐ *Ann made a tongue-in-cheek remark to John, and he got mad because he thought she was serious.* ☐ *The play seemed very serious at first, but then everyone saw that it was tongue-in-cheek, and they began laughing.*

too big for one's **britches** too haughty for one's status or age. (Also literal. Folksy or informal. *Britches* are trousers.) ☐ *Bill's getting a little too big for his britches, and somebody's going to straighten him out.* ☐ *You're too big for your britches, young man! You had better be more respectful.*

too close for comfort [for a misfortune or a threat] to be dangerously close. (See also close to home.) ☐ *That car nearly hit me! That was too close for comfort.* ☐ *When I was in the hospital, I nearly died from pneumonia. Believe me, that was too close for comfort.*

too good to be true almost unbelievable; so good as to be unbelievable. ☐ *The news was too good to be true.* ☐ *When I finally got a big raise, it was too good to be true.*

Too many cooks spoil the broth. Go to Too many cooks spoil the stew.

Too many cooks spoil the stew. AND **Too many cooks spoil the broth.** Too many people trying to manage something simply spoil it. (Proverb.) ☐ *Let's decide who is in charge around here. Too many cooks spoil the stew.* ☐ *Everyone is giving orders, but no one is following them! Too many cooks spoil the broth.*

too much of a good thing more of a good thing than is good or useful. ☐ *I usually take short vacations. I can't stand too much of a good thing.* ☐ *Too much of a good thing can make you sick, especially if the good thing is chocolate.*

toot one's **own horn** AND **blow** one's **own horn** to boast or praise oneself. ☐ *Tom is always tooting his own horn. Is he really as good as he says he is?* ☐ *I find it hard to blow my own horn, but I manage.*

top someone or something to do or be better than someone or something. (Informal.) ☐ *Ann has done very well, but I don't think she can top Jane.* ☐ *Do you think your car tops mine when it comes to gas mileage?*

top something **off** to add to the difficulty of something. ☐ *Jane lost her job, and to top that off, she caught the flu.* ☐ *I had a bad day, and to top it off, I have to go to a meeting tonight.*

top something **off (with** something**)** to end or terminate something with something; to put something on the top of something. ☐ *They topped the building off with a tall flagpole.* 🅃 *He topped off each piece of pie with a heap of whipped cream.* 🅃 *That's the way to top off a piece of pie!*

torn between bad choices Go to **torn between** choosing something or something else.

torn between choosing something or something else AND **torn between** bad choices troubled by a choice or dilemma. ☐ *Jane was torn between two bad choices.* ☐ *We were torn between telling our boss the bad news or keeping it a secret.*

toss a salad to mix the green of a salad together with dressing. ☐ *The chef tossed the salad.* ☐ *I tossed the salad just before my guests arrived.*

toss one's **cookies** to vomit. (Slang.) ☐ *Don't run too fast after you eat or you'll* *toss your cookies.* ☐ *Oh, I feel terrible. I think I'm going to toss my cookies.*

toss one's **hat into the ring** to announce that one is running for an elective office. (Informal.) ☐ *Jane wanted to run for treasurer, so she tossed her hat into the ring.* ☐ *The mayor never tossed his hat into the ring. Instead he announced his retirement.*

toss something **off** AND **shake** something **off** **1.** to throw something off (of oneself). ☐ *Bob coughed so hard he shook his blanket off.* 🅃 *Tom tossed off his jacket and sat down to watch television.* **2.** to ignore or resist the bad effects of something. ☐ *John insulted Bob, but Bob just tossed it off.* 🅃 *If I couldn't shake off insults, I'd be miserable.*

touch and go very uncertain or critical. ☐ *Things were touch and go at the office until a new manager was hired.* ☐ *Jane had a serious operation, and everything was touch and go for two days after her surgery.*

touch a sore point Go to touch a sore spot.

touch a sore spot AND **touch a sore point** to refer to a sensitive matter that will upset someone. (Also literal.) ☐ *I seem to have touched a sore spot. I'm sorry. I didn't mean to upset you.* ☐ *When you talk to him, avoid talking about money. It's best not to touch a sore point if possible.*

touch base (with someone**)** to talk to someone; to confer with someone. (Slang.) ☐ *I need to touch base with John on this matter.* ☐ *John and I touched base on this question yesterday, and we are in agreement.*

touch on something to mention something; to talk about something briefly. ☐ *In tomorrow's lecture I'd like to touch on the matter of taxation.* ☐ *The teacher only touched on the subject. There wasn't time to do more than that.*

touch someone **for** something to ask someone for a loan of something, usually a sum of money. (Informal.) ☐ *Fred's always trying to touch people for money.* ☐ *Jack touched John for ten dollars.*

touch someone or something **off** **1.** [with *someone*] to make someone very angry. ☐ *Your rude comments touched Mary off. She's very angry at you.* 🅃 *I didn't mean to touch off anyone. I was only being honest.* **2.** [with *something*] to ignite something; to start something. ☐ *A few sparks touched all the fireworks off at once.* 🅃 *The argument touched off a serious fight.*

touch something **up** to repair a paint job on something. ☐ *We don't need to paint the whole room. We can just touch the walls up.* 🅃 *You should touch up scratches on your car as soon as they occur.*

touched by someone or something emotionally affected or moved by someone or something. ☐ *Sally was very nice to me. I was very touched by her.* ☐ *I was really touched by your kind letter.*

touched (in the head) crazy. (Folksy or slang.) ☐ *Sometimes Bob acts like he's touched in the head.* ☐ *In fact, I thought he was touched.*

a **tough act to follow** a good presentation or performance that is difficult to follow with one's own performance. ☐ *Bill's speech was excellent. It was a tough act to follow, but my speech was good also.* ☐ *In spite of the fact that I had a tough act to follow, I did my best.*

tough as an old boot Go to (as) tough as an old boot.

tough break a bit of bad fortune. (Slang.) ☐ *I'm sorry to hear about your accident. Tough break.* ☐ *John had a lot of tough breaks when he was a kid, but he's doing okay now.*

tough it out to endure a difficult situation. (Slang.) ☐ *Geometry is very hard for John, but he managed to tough it out until the end of the year.* ☐ *This was a very bad day at the office. A few times, I was afraid I wouldn't be able to tough it out.*

tough nut to crack Go to hard nut to crack.

tough row to hoe a difficult task to undertake. ☐ *It was a tough row to hoe, but I finally got a college degree.* ☐ *Getting the contract signed is going to be a tough row to hoe, but I'm sure I can do it.*

a **tower of strength** Go to a pillar of strength.

town-and-gown the [poor] relations between a town and the university located within the town; the [poor] relations between university students and the nonstudents who live in a university town. □ *There is another town-and-gown dispute in Adamsville over the amount the university costs the city for police services.* □ *There was more town-and-gown strife reported at Larry's Bar and Grill last Saturday night.*

toy with someone or something **1.** [with *someone*] to tease someone; to deal lightly with someone's emotions. □ *Ann broke up with Tom because he was just toying with her. He was not serious at all.* □ *Don't toy with me! I won't have it!* **2.** [with *something*] to play or fiddle with something. □ *Stop toying with the radio, or you'll break it.* □ *John sat there toying with a pencil all through the meeting.*

trade on something to use a fact or a situation to one's advantage. □ *Tom was able to trade on the fact that he had once been in the Army.* □ *John traded on his poor eyesight to get a seat closer to the stage.*

[train of thought] Go to someone's **train of thought.**

train one's **sights on** something AND **have** one's **sights trained on** something to have something as a goal; to direct something or oneself toward a goal. □ *You should train your sights on getting a promotion in the next year.* □ *Lisa has her sights trained on a new car.*

a **travesty of justice** a miscarriage of justice; an act of the legal system that is an insult to the system of justice. □ *The jury's verdict was a travesty of justice.* □ *The lawyer complained that the judge's ruling was a travesty of justice.*

trial and error trying repeatedly for success. □ *I finally found the right key after lots of trial and error.* □ *Sometimes trial and error is the only way to get something done.*

trials and tribulations problems and tests of one's courage or perseverance. □ *I suppose I have the normal trials and tribulations for a person of my background, but some days are just a little too much for me.* □ *I promise not to tell you of the trials and tribulations of my day if you promise not to tell me yours!*

Trick or treat! Give me a treat of some kind or I will play a trick on you! (The formulaic expression said by children after they ring someone's doorbell and the door is answered on Halloween. It is now understood to mean simply that the child is requesting a treat of some kind—candy, fruit, popcorn, etc.) □ *"Trick or treat!" cried Jimmy when the door opened.* □ *Mr. Franklin opened the door to find four very small children dressed like flowers standing silently on his doorstep. After a moment, he said, "Isn't anyone going to say, 'Trick or treat'?"*

trick someone **into** doing something to fool someone; to deceive someone; to cheat someone. □ *The thief tricked John into giving him $10.* □ *Mary tricked her friends into paying for her dinner.*

tried-and-true tested by time and proven to be sound. □ *I have a tried-and-true remedy for poison ivy.* □ *All of her investment ideas are tried-and-true and you ought to be able to make money if you follow them.*

trip someone **up 1.** to trip someone. □ *Bob tripped himself up on his own feet.* 🆃 *The loose gravel beside the track tripped up Bob, and he fell.* **2.** to cause difficulty for someone; to cause someone to fail. □ *Bill tripped Tom up during the spelling contest, and Tom lost.* 🆃 *I didn't mean to trip up anyone. I'm sorry I caused trouble.*

trot something **out** to mention something regularly or habitually, without giving it much thought. (Informal.) □ *Jack always trots the same excuses out for being late.* 🆃 *When James disagreed with Mary, she simply trotted out her same old political arguments.*

Trouble is brewing. AND **There is trouble brewing.** Trouble is developing. □ *Trouble's brewing at the office. I have to get there early tomorrow.* □ *There is* *trouble brewing in the government. The prime minister may resign.*

trouble oneself **about** someone or something to worry oneself about someone or something. (Usually in the negative.) □ *Please don't trouble yourself about me. I'm doing fine.* □ *I can't take time to trouble myself about this matter. Do it yourself.*

trouble oneself **(to** do something**)** to bother oneself to do something. □ *He didn't even trouble himself to turn off the light when he left.* □ *No, thank you. I don't need any help. Please don't trouble yourself.*

trouble one's **head about** someone or something to worry about someone or something; to **trouble** oneself **about** someone or something that is none of one's business. (Folksy. Usually in the negative. Also with *pretty,* as in the example. Usually in the negative, meaning "to mind one's own business.") □ *Now, now, don't trouble your pretty head about all these things.* □ *You needn't trouble your head about Sally.*

trouble someone **for** something to ask someone to pass something or give something. (Usually a question.) □ *Could I trouble you for the salt?* □ *Could I trouble you for some advice?*

trouble someone **to** do something to ask someone to do something. (Usually a question.) □ *Could I trouble you to pass the salt?* □ *Could I trouble you to give me some advice?*

true as steel Go to (as) true as steel.

true to form exactly as expected; following the usual pattern. (Often with *running,* as in the example.) □ *As usual, John is late. At least he's true to form.* □ *And true to form, Mary left before the meeting was adjourned.* □ *This winter season is running true to form—miserable!*

true to one's **word** keeping one's promise. □ *True to his word, Tom showed up at exactly eight o'clock.* □ *We'll soon know if Jane is true to her word. We'll see if she does what she promised.*

trumped-up false; fraudulently devised. □ *They tried to have Tom arrested on a trumped-up charge.* □ *Bob gave some trumped-up excuse for not being at the meeting.*

The **truth will out.** eventually, the truth will become known; truth tends to become known, even when it is being concealed. □ *The truth will out! Some day my name will be cleared.* □ *We just found out about corruption in the mayor's office. Like they say, "The truth will out."*

try one's **hand (at** something**)** to take a try at something. □ *Someday I'd like to try my hand at flying a plane.* □ *Give me a chance. Let me try my hand!*

try one's **luck (at** something**)** to attempt to do something (where success requires luck). □ *My great-grandfather came to California to try his luck at finding gold.* □ *I went into a gambling casino to try my luck.*

try out (for something**)** to test one's fitness for a role in a play, a position on a sports team, etc. □ *I sing pretty well, so I thought I'd try out for the chorus.* □ *Hardly anyone else showed up to try out.*

try (out) one's **wings** to try to do something one has recently become qualified to do. (Like a young bird uses its wings to try to fly.) □ *John just got his driver's license and wants to borrow the car to try out his wings.* □ *I learned to skin-dive, and I want to go to the seaside to try my wings.* 🅃 *She was eager to try out her wings.*

try someone's **patience** to do something annoying that may cause someone to lose patience; to cause someone to be annoyed. □ *Stop whistling. You're trying my patience. Very soon I'm going to lose my temper.* □ *Some students think it's fun to try the teacher's patience.*

try something **out on** someone to test something on someone (to see how it works or if it is liked). □ *I found a recipe for oyster stew and tried it out on my roommate.* 🅃 *I'm glad you didn't try out that stuff on me!* □ *I have a tremendous idea! Let me try it out on you.* 🅃 *I want to try out my plan on you. Please give me your honest opinion.*

tuck into something to eat something with hunger and enjoyment. (Informal.) □

The children really tucked into the ice cream. □ *Jean would like to have tucked into the chocolate cake, but she's on a strict diet.*

tuckered out Go to (all) tuckered out.

tune someone or something **out** to ignore someone or something; to become unaware of someone or something. □ *Sally annoys me sometimes, so I just tune her out.* 🅃 *Your radio doesn't bother me. I just tune out the noise.*

tune (something) **in** to set a radio or television control so as to receive something. □ *Why don't you try to tune the ball game in?* 🅃 *This is a cheap radio, and I can't tune in distant stations.* □ *Please try to tune in.*

turn a blind eye to someone or something to ignore someone or something troublesome and pretend not to see it. □ *The usher turned a blind eye to the little boy who sneaked into the theater.* □ *How can you turn a blind eye to all those starving children?*

turn a deaf ear (to someone or something**)** to ignore what someone requests; to ignore a cry for help. □ *How can you just turn a deaf ear to their cries for food and shelter?* □ *The government has turned a deaf ear.*

turn in to go to bed. □ *It's late. I think I'll turn in.* □ *We usually turn in at about midnight.*

turn of the century the end of one century and the beginning of another. □ *It's just a few years until the turn of the century.* □ *People like to celebrate the turn of the century.*

turn on a dime to turn in a very tight turn. (Informal.) □ *This car handles very well. It can turn on a dime.* □ *The speeding car turned on a dime and headed in the other direction.*

turn one's **back (on** someone or something**)** to abandon or ignore someone or something. (Also literal.) □ *Don't turn your back on your old friends.* □ *Bob has a tendency to turn his back on serious problems.* □ *This matter needs your attention. Please don't just turn your back.*

turn one's **nose up at** someone or something to sneer at someone or something; to reject someone or something. □ *John turned his nose up at Ann, and that hurt her feelings.* 🅃 *I never turn up my nose at dessert, no matter what it is.*

turn on the waterworks to begin to cry. (Slang.) □ *Every time Billy got homesick, he turned on the waterworks.* □ *Sally hurt her knee and turned on the waterworks for about twenty minutes.*

turn out (all right) AND **pan out; work out (all right)** to end satisfactorily. (Compare this with **work out for the best**.) □ *I hope everything turns out all right.* □ *Oh, yes. It'll all pan out.* □ *Things usually work out, no matter how bad they seem.*

turn out (that) something is so to happen that; to end up that. □ *After it was all over, it turned out that both of us were pleased with the bargain.* □ *Have you heard how the game turned out?*

turn over AND **kick over** [for an engine] to start or to rotate. □ *My car engine was so cold that it wouldn't even turn over.* □ *The engine turned over a few times and then stopped for good.*

turn over a new leaf to start again with the intention of doing better; to begin again, ignoring past errors. (*Leaf* is a page. This refers to starting a new page.) □ *Tom promised to turn over a new leaf and do better from now on.* □ *After a minor accident, Sally decided to turn over a new leaf and drive more carefully.*

turn (over) in one's **grave** AND **roll (over) in** one's **grave** [for a dead person] to be shocked or horrified. (Refers to something that would be so shocking to a person who is actually dead, that the dead person would quicken enough to turn over.) □ *If Beethoven heard Mary play one of his sonatas, he'd turn over in his grave.* □ *If Aunt Jane knew what you were doing with her favorite chair, she would roll over in her grave.*

turn someone **off** to discourage or disgust someone. (Informal.) □ *His manner really turns me off.* 🅃 *That man has a way of turning off everyone he comes in contact with.*

turn someone **on** to excite someone; to excite someone sexually. (Informal. Often ambiguous.) □ *Sally said she preferred not to watch movies that attempted to turn people on.* 🅃 *The lecture was very good. It turned on the whole class.*

turn someone or something **down 1.** [with *someone*] to refuse or deny someone. □ *I applied for a job with the city, but they turned me down.* 🅃 *They turned down Mary who also applied.* **2.** to deny someone's request. □ *I offered her some help, but she turned it down.* 🅃 *She had turned down John's offer of help, too.* **3.** [with *something*] to fold part of something downward. □ *The hotel maid turned the bed down while I was at dinner.* 🅃 *In the mail-order catalog, I always turn down a page that interests me.* **4.** [with *something*] to lower the volume or amount of something, such as heat, sound, water, air pressure, etc. □ *It's hot in here. Please turn down the heat.* □ *Turn the stereo down. It's too loud.*

turn someone or something **out 1.** [with *someone*] to send someone out of somewhere. □ *I didn't pay my rent, so the manager turned me out.* 🅃 *I'm glad it's not winter. I'd hate to turn out someone in the snow.* **2.** [with *something*] to manufacture something; to produce something. □ *John wasn't turning enough work out, so the manager had a talk with him.* 🅃 *This machine can turn out two thousand items a day.*

turn someone or something **up** to search for and find someone or something. □ *Let me try to see if I can turn someone up who knows how to do the job.* 🅃 *I turned up a number of interesting items when I went through Aunt Jane's attic.*

turn someone's **head** [for flattery or success] to distract someone; to cause someone not to be sensible. (Also literal.) □ *Don't let our praise turn your head. You're not perfect!* □ *Her successes had turned her head. She was now quite arrogant.*

turn someone's **stomach** to disgust someone. (Refers to an attack of nausea.) □ *Your rude remarks simply turn my stomach.* □ *The play was so bad that it turned my stomach.*

turn something **to good account** to use something in such a way that it is to one's advantage; to make good use of a situation, experience, etc. □ *Pam turned her illness to good account and did a lot of reading.* □ *Many people turn their retirement time to good account and take up interesting hobbies.*

turn something **to** one's **advantage** to make an advantage for oneself out of something (which might otherwise be a disadvantage). □ *Sally found a way to turn the problem to her advantage.* □ *The ice cream store manager was able to turn the hot weather to her advantage.*

turn the clock back to try to return to the past. (Also literal.) □ *You are not facing up to the future. You are trying to turn the clock back to a time when you were more comfortable.* □ *Let us turn the clock back and pretend we are living at the turn of the century—the time that our story takes place.* 🅃 *No, you can't turn back the clock.*

turn the heat up (on someone**)** to use force to persuade someone to do something; to increase the pressure on someone to do something. (Informal.) □ *Management is turning the heat up to increase production.* 🅃 *The teacher really turned up the heat on the students by saying that everyone would be punished if the real culprit was not found.*

turn the other cheek to ignore abuse or an insult. □ *When Bob got mad at Mary and yelled at her, she just turned the other cheek.* □ *Usually I turn the other cheek when someone is rude to me.*

turn the tables (on someone**)** to cause a reversal in someone's plans; to make one's plans turn back on one. □ *I went to Jane's house to help get ready for a surprise party for Bob. It turned out that the surprise party was for me! Jane really turned the ta-*

bles on me! □ *Turning the tables like that requires a lot of planning and a lot of secrecy.*

turn the tide to cause a reversal in the direction of events; to cause a reversal in public opinion. □ *It looked as if the team was going to lose, but near the end of the game, our star player turned the tide.* □ *At first, people were opposed to our plan. After a lot of discussion, we were able to turn the tide.*

turn thumbs down (on someone or something**)** to veto someone or something; to reject someone or something. (See also **thumbs down on** someone or something.) □ *The board of directors turned thumbs down on my proposal.* □ *They turned thumbs down without even hearing my explanation.* □ *The committee turned thumbs down on Carl and we did not hire him after all.*

turn thumbs up (on someone or something**)** to accept someone or something; to approve someone or something. (See also **thumbs up on** someone or something.) □ *The board of directors turned thumbs up on my proposal and voted to fund the project.* □ *The committee turned thumbs up on Carl as the new manager.* □ *When the boss turned thumbs up, I knew everything was okay.*

turn to to begin to get busy. □ *Come on, you guys! Turn to! Let's get to work.* □ *If you people will turn to, we can finish this work in no time at all.*

turn to someone or something **(for** something**)** to seek something from someone or something. □ *I turned to Ann for help.* □ *Bill turned to aspirin for relief from his headache.*

turn turtle to turn upside down. (Slang.) □ *The sailboat turned turtle, but the sailors only got wet.* □ *The car ran off the road and turned turtle in the ditch.*

turn up to appear. □ *We'll send out invitations and see who turns up.* □ *Guess who turned up at my door last night?*

turn up one's **toes** to die. (Slang.) □ *When I turn up my toes, I want a big funeral with lots of flowers.* □ *Our cat turned up his toes during the night. He was nearly ten years old.*

twiddle one's **thumbs** to fill up time by playing with one's fingers. □ *What am I supposed to do while waiting for you? Sit here and twiddle my thumbs?* □ *Don't sit around twiddling your thumbs. Get busy!*

twist someone **around** one's **little finger** to manipulate and control someone. □ *Bob really fell for Jane. She can twist him around her little finger.* □ *Billy's mother has twisted him around her little finger. He's very dependent on her.*

twist someone's **arm** to force or persuade someone. □ *At first she refused, but after I twisted her arm a little, she agreed to help.* □ *I didn't want to run for mayor, but everyone twisted my arm.*

twist someone's **words (around)** to restate someone's words inaccurately when quoting them or trying to understand them. □ *Stop twisting my words around! Listen to what I am telling you!* □ *You are twisting my words again. That is not what I said!*

two bricks shy of a load Go to **a few cards shy of a full deck.**

two of a kind people or things of the same type or that are similar in character, attitude, etc. □ *Jack and Tom are two of a kind. They're both ambitious.* □ *The companies are two of a kind. They both pay their employees badly.*

two-time someone to cheat on or betray one's spouse or lover by dating or seeing someone else. (Slang.) □ *When Mrs. Franklin learned that Mr. Franklin was two-timing her, she left him.* □ *Ann told Bob that if he ever two-timed her, she would cause him a lot of trouble.*

Two's company(, three's a crowd). Two people want to be alone and a third person will be in the way. (Proverb.) □ *Two's company. I'm sure Tom and Jill won't want his sister to go to the movies with them.* □ *John has been invited to join Jane and Peter on their picnic, but he says, "Two's company, three's a crowd."*

U

ugly as a toad Go to (as) ugly as a toad.

ugly as sin Go to (as) ugly as sin.

unaccustomed to someone or something not used to someone or something. □ *The poor family was unaccustomed to going to fancy restaurants.* □ *Bill was unaccustomed to typing his own letters.*

under a cloud (of suspicion) to be suspected of (doing) something. □ *Someone stole some money at work, and now everyone is under a cloud of suspicion.* □ *Even the manager is under a cloud.*

under arrest being or having been arrested and in the care of the police in preparation for the filing of a charge. □ *Stop where you are! You are under arrest.* □ *Am I under arrest, officer? What did I do?*

under certain **circumstances** AND **under** certain **conditions** depending on or influenced by something; because of something. □ *Under certain conditions, you can see across the lake.* □ *Under no circumstances are you to leave the house tonight.*

under certain **conditions** Go to under certain circumstances.

under (close) scrutiny being watched or examined closely. □ *Under close scrutiny, the jeweler found a flaw in the diamond.* □ *The suspect was kept under scrutiny throughout the investigation.*

under construction being built or repaired. □ *We cannot travel on this road because it's under construction.* □ *Our new home has been under construction all summer. We hope to move in next month.*

under control manageable; restrained and controlled; not out of control. □ *We finally got things under control and functioning smoothly.* □ *The doctor felt she had the disease under control and that I would get well soon.*

under fire during an attack. □ *There was a scandal in city hall, and the mayor was forced to resign under fire.* □ *John is a good lawyer because he can think under fire.*

under oath bound by an oath; having taken an oath. □ *You must tell the truth because you are under oath.* □ *I was placed under oath before I could testify in the trial.*

under one's **own steam** by one's own power or effort. (Informal.) □ *I missed my ride to class, so I had to get there under my own steam.* □ *John will need some help with this project. He can't do it under his own steam.*

under someone's **(very) nose** Go to (right) under someone's (very) nose.

under (some) pressure experiencing something that causes an amount of stress or anxiety. □ *I have a headache because I'm under a lot of pressure at work.* □ *The professor's children were under pressure to do well in school.*

under the aegis of someone AND **under the auspices of** someone under the sponsorship of someone or some group; under the control or monitoring of someone or some group. □ *The entire project fell under the aegis of Thomas.* □ *The entire program is under the auspices of Acme-Global Paper Co., Inc.*

under the auspices of someone Go to under the aegis of someone.

under the circumstances in a particular situation; because of the circumstances.

□ *I'm sorry to hear that you're ill. Under the circumstances, you may take the day off.* □ *We won't expect you to come to work for a few days, under the circumstances.*

under the counter [bought or sold] in secret or illegally. (Also literal.) □ *The drugstore owner was arrested for selling liquor under the counter.* □ *The clerk sold dirty books under the counter.*

under the influence (of alcohol) drunk; nearly drunk; affected by alcohol. □ *She behaves quite rudely when under the influence of alcohol.* □ *Ed was stopped by a police officer for driving while under the influence.*

under the influence of something experiencing the effects of something such as alcohol, drugs, or any controlling power or person. (See also **under the influence (of alcohol)**.) □ *I think that guy is under the influence of drugs.* □ *Bill has lived under the influence of his mother for too long.*

under the sun anywhere on earth at all. □ *This is the largest cattle ranch under the sun.* □ *Isn't there anyone under the sun who can help me with this problem?*

under the table in secret, as with the giving of a bribe. (Also literal. Informal.) □ *The construction company had been paying money to the mayor under the table.* □ *Tom transferred the deed to the property to his wife under the table.*

under the weather ill. □ *I'm a bit under the weather today, so I can't go to the office.* □ *My head is aching, and I feel a little under the weather.*

under the wire just barely in time or on time. (Informal.) □ *I turned in my report just under the wire.* □ *Bill was the last person to get in the door. He got in under the wire.*

unfamiliar territory an area of knowledge unknown to the speaker. □ *We are in unfamiliar territory and I don't know the answer.* □ *Astronomy is unfamiliar territory, and I cannot answer any questions about the stars.*

an **unknown quantity** a person or thing about which no one is certain. (Preceded by *be, become, seem like,* or *act like.*) □ *John is an unknown quantity. We don't know how he's going to act.* □ *The new clerk is an unknown quantity. Things may not turn out all right.*

until all hours (of the day and night) until very late. □ *Mary is out until all hours, night after night.* □ *If I'm up until all hours two nights in a row, I'm just exhausted.*

until hell freezes over Go to when hell freezes over.

(un)til the cows come home until the last; until very late. (Folksy or informal. Refers to the end of the day, when the cows come home to be fed and milked.) □ *We were having so much fun that we decided to stay at school until the cows came home.* □ *Where've you been? Who said you could stay out 'til the cows come home?*

up a blind alley at a dead end; on a route that leads nowhere. (Informal.) □ *I have been trying to find out something about my ancestors, but I'm up a blind alley. I can't find anything.* □ *The police are up a blind alley in their investigation of the crime.*

up against something having trouble with something. (The *something* is often *it,* meaning facing trouble in general.) □ *Jane is up against a serious problem.* □ *Yes, she really looks as if she's up against it.*

up and about healthy and moving about—not sick in bed. □ *Mary is getting better. She should be up and about in a few days.* □ *She can't wait until she's up and about. She's tired of being in bed.*

up and around out of bed and moving about or able to move about. (Refers to a person who has just arisen for the day or to someone who has been sick in bed.) □ *When Tom is up and around, ask him to call me.* □ *The flu put Alice into bed for three days, but she was up and around on the fourth.*

up and at them to get up and go at people or things; to get active and get busy. (Informal. Usually *them* is *'em.*) □ *Come on, Bob—up and at 'em!* □ *There is a lot *of work to be done around here. Up and at 'em, everybody!*

up and away up into the air and into flight. (Said of a bird or an airplane.) □ *After a few seconds of speeding down the runway, our flight to Tucson was up and away.* □ *Just before the cat pounced on the sparrows, they were up and away and the cat was left with empty paws and jaws.*

up-and-coming new, but enterprising and alert. □ *Jane is a hard worker—really up-and-coming.* □ *Bob is also an up-and-coming youngster who is going to become well known.*

up a tree in a difficult situation and unable to get out; stymied and confused. (Slang.) □ *I'm really up a tree on this problem.* □ *Geometry is too hard for me. It's got me up a tree.*

up for grabs available to anyone. (Slang.) □ *Mary quit yesterday, and her job is up for grabs.* □ *Who's in charge around here? This whole organization is up for grabs.*

up for something enthusiastic about something. (Informal.) □ *Are you up for a hike through the woods?* □ *I'm really up for my job interview today.*

up-front 1. sincere and open. □ *Ann is a very up-front kind of person. Everyone feels easy around her.* □ *It's hard to tell what Tom is really thinking. He's not very up-front.* **2.** in advance. □ *I ordered a new car, and they wanted 20 percent up-front.* □ *I couldn't afford to pay that much up-front. I'd have to make a smaller deposit.*

up in arms rising up in anger; very angry. (Also literal when actual weapons are involved.) □ *My father was really up in arms when he got his tax bill this year.* □ *The citizens were up in arms, pounding on the gates of the palace, demanding justice.*

up in the air (about someone or something**)** undecided about someone or something; uncertain about someone or something. □ *I don't know what Sally plans to do. Things were sort of up in the air the last time we talked.* □ *Let's leave this question up in the air until next week.*

up in years AND **advanced in years; along in years; on in years** old; elderly. □ *My uncle is up in years and can't hear too well.* □ *Many people lose their hearing somewhat when they are along in years.*

up North to or at the northern part of the country or the world. (See also **back East**, **down South**, and **out West**.) □ *I don't like living up North. I want to move down South where it's warm.* □ *When you say "up North," do you mean where the polar bears live, or just in the northern states?*

up the creek (without a paddle) in a bad situation. (Slang. Use with caution. There is a taboo version of this phrase.) □ *What a mess I'm in. I'm really up the creek without a paddle.* □ *I tried to prevent it, but I seem to be up the creek, too.*

up-to-date modern; up to the current standards of fashion; with the latest information. □ *I'd like to see a more up-to-date report on Mr. Smith.* □ *This is not an up-to-date record of the construction project.* □ *I'm having my living room redecorated to bring it up-to-date.* □ *I don't care if my rooms are up-to-date. I just want them to be comfortable.*

up to doing something able to do something. □ *Do you feel up to going back to work today?* □ *She just isn't up to staying up all night.*

up to no good doing something bad. (Informal.) □ *I could tell from the look on Tom's face that he was up to no good.* □ *There are three boys in the front yard. I don't know what they are doing, but I think they are up to no good.*

up to one's **ears (in** something**)** Go to **up to** one's **neck (in** something**)**.

up to one's **eyeballs (in** something**)** Go to **up to** one's **neck (in** something**)**.

up to one's **neck (in** something**)** AND **up to** one's **ears (in** something**); up to** one's **eyeballs (in** something**)** having a lot of something; very much involved in something. (Informal.) □ *I can't come to the meeting. I'm up to my neck in these reports.* □ *Mary is up to her ears in her work.* □ *I am up* *to my eyeballs in things to do! I can't do any more!*

up to par as good as the standard or average; up to standard. □ *I'm just not feeling up to par today. I must be coming down with something.* □ *The manager said that the report was not up to par and gave it back to Mary to do over again.*

up to scratch Go to up to snuff.

up to snuff AND **up to scratch** as good as is required; meeting the minimum requirements. (Slang. Compare this with up to par.) □ *Sorry, Tom. Your performance isn't up to snuff. You'll have to improve or find another job.* □ *My paper wasn't up to scratch, so I got an F.*

up to someone [for a decision] to be someone's own choice. □ *She said I didn't have to go if I didn't want to. It's entirely up to me.* □ *It's up to Mary whether she takes the job or tries to find another one.*

up to something **1.** occupied in some activity, often something secret or wrong. □ *Those kids are up to something. They're too quiet.* □ *Goodness knows what that child will be up to next!* **2.** Go to **up to** doing something. **3.** to be as good as something; to be good enough for something. □ *This work's not up to the standard of the class.* □ *Your last essay was not up to your best.*

up-to-the-minute the very latest or most recent. □ *I want to hear some up-to-the-minute news on the hostage situation.* □ *I just got an up-to-the-minute report on Tom's health.*

(up)on impact at the place or time of making an impact. □ *The car crumpled upon impact with the brick wall.* □ *The man who fell from the top of the building died on impact.*

upper crust the higher levels of society; the upper class. (Informal. From the top, as opposed to the bottom, crust of a pie.) □ *Jane speaks like that because she pretends to be from the upper crust, but her father was a miner.* □ *James is from the upper crust, but he is penniless.*

ups and downs good fortune and bad fortune. □ *I've had my ups and downs, but in general life has been good to me.* □ *All people have their ups and downs.*

upset the apple cart to mess up or ruin something. □ *Tom really upset the apple cart by telling Mary the truth about Jane.* □ *I always knew he'd upset the apple cart.*

the **upshot of** something the result or outcome of something. □ *The upshot of my criticism was a change in policy.* □ *The upshot of the argument was an agreement to hire a new secretary.*

use every trick in the book to use every method possible. (Informal.) □ *I used every trick in the book, but I still couldn't manage to get a ticket to the game Saturday.* □ *Bob tried to use every trick in the book, but he still failed.*

use one's **head** AND **use** one's **noggin; use** one's **noodle** to use one's own intelligence. (*Noggin* and *noodle* are slang terms for "head.") □ *You can do better in math if you'll just use your head.* □ *Jane uses her noggin and gets things done correctly and on time.* □ *Yes, she sure knows how to use her noodle.*

use one's **noggin** Go to **use** one's **head**.

use one's **noodle** Go to **use** one's **head**.

use some elbow grease use some effort. (Slang. As if lubricating one's elbow would make one more efficient. Note the variation in the examples.) □ *Come on, Bill. You can do it. Just use some elbow grease.* □ *I tried elbow grease, but it doesn't help get the job done.*

use someone or something **as an excuse** to blame someone or something (for a failure). □ *John used his old car as an excuse for not going to the meeting.* □ *My husband was sick in bed, and I used him as an excuse.*

use strong language to swear, threaten, or use abusive language. □ *I wish you wouldn't use strong language in front of the children.* □ *If you feel that you have to use strong language with the manager, perhaps you had better let me do the talking.*

used to do something to have done something [customarily] in the past. □ *We used to go swimming in the lake before it became polluted.* □ *I used to eat nuts, but then I became allergic to them.*

used to someone or something accustomed to someone or something. □ *I'm not used to Jane yet. She's a bit hard to get along with.* □ *How long does it take to get used to this weather?*

V

vale of tears the earth; mortal life on earth. (A "valley" of tears.) ☐ *When it comes time for me to leave this vale of tears, I hope I can leave some worthwhile memories behind.* ☐ *Uncle Fred left this vale of tears early this morning.*

vanish into thin air to disappear without leaving a trace. ☐ *My money gets spent so fast. It seems to vanish into thin air.* ☐ *When I came back, my car was gone. I had locked it, and it couldn't have vanished into thin air!*

Variety is the spice of life. Differences and changes make life interesting. (Proverb.) ☐ *Mary reads all kinds of books. She says variety is the spice of life.* ☐ *The Franklins travel all over the world so they can learn how different people live. After all, variety is the spice of life.*

vent one's **spleen** to get rid of one's feelings of anger caused by someone or something by attacking someone or something else. ☐ *Jack vented his spleen at his wife whenever things went badly at work.* ☐ *Peter vented his spleen on his car by kicking it when he lost the race.*

verge on something to be almost something. ☐ *Your blouse is a lovely color. It seems to be blue verging on purple.* ☐ *Sally has a terrible case of the flu, and they are afraid it's verging on pneumonia.*

the **very last** the end; an absolute end of something. ☐ *At the very last of the movie, the hero gets killed.* ☐ *Bill stayed at the party until the very last.*

the **very thing** the exact thing that is required. ☐ *The vacuum cleaner is the very thing for cleaning the stairs.* ☐ *I have the very thing to remove that stain.*

the **villain of the piece** someone or something that is responsible for something bad or wrong. ☐ *I wondered who told the newspapers about the local scandal. I discovered that Joan was the villain of the piece.* ☐ *We couldn't think who had stolen the meat. The dog next door turned out to be the villain of the piece.*

vim and vigor energy and enthusiasm. ☐ *I just don't seem to have the vim and vigor that I had a few years ago.* ☐ *Alice appeared with all the vim and vigor of youth, and began to help carry in the packages.*

vote a split ticket to cast a ballot on which the votes are divided between two or more parties. ☐ *I always vote a spilt ticket since I detest both parties.* ☐ *Mary voted a split ticket for the first time in her life.*

vote a straight ticket to cast a ballot with all the votes for members of the same political party. ☐ *I'm not a member of any political party, so I never vote a straight ticket.* ☐ *I usually vote a straight ticket because I believe in the principles of one party and not in the other's.*

a **vote of confidence** a poll taken to discover whether or not a person, party, etc., still has the majority's support. ☐ *The government easily won the vote of confidence called for by the opposition.* ☐ *The president of the club resigned when one of the members called for a vote of confidence in his leadership.*

a **vote of thanks** a speech expressing appreciation and thanks to a speaker, lecturer, organizer, etc., and inviting the audience to applaud. ☐ *John gave a vote of thanks to Professor Jones for his talk.* ☐ *Mary was given a vote of thanks for organizing the dance.*

vote with one's **feet** to express one's dissatisfaction with something by leaving, especially by walking away. □ *I think that the play is a total flop. Most of the audience voted with its feet during the second act.* □ *I am prepared to vote with my feet if the meeting appears to be a waste of time.*

W

wade in(to something**)** to start in (doing) something immediately. (Also literal.) □ *I need some preparation. I can't just wade into the job and start doing things correctly.* □ *We don't expect you to wade in. We'll tell you what to do.*

wag one's **chin** to chatter or chat with someone. (Slang.) □ *We stood around and wagged our chins for almost an hour.* □ *Don't just wag your chin. Stop talking and get to work!*

wait-and-see attitude a skeptical attitude; an uncertain attitude where someone will just wait and see what happens. □ *John thought that Mary couldn't do it, but he took a wait-and-see attitude.* □ *His wait-and-see attitude didn't influence me at all.*

wait on someone **hand and foot** to serve someone very well, attending to all personal needs. □ *I don't mind bringing you your coffee, but I don't intend to wait on you hand and foot.* □ *I don't want anyone to wait on me hand and foot. I can take care of myself.*

wait up (for someone or something**)** **1.** to stay up late waiting for someone to arrive or something to happen. □ *I'll be home late. Don't wait up for me.* □ *We waited up for the coming of the new year, and then we went to bed.* **2.** AND **hold up (for** someone or something**)** to wait for someone or something to catch up. □ *Hey! Don't go so fast. Wait up for me.* □ *Hold up! You're going too fast.*

waiting in the wings ready or prepared to do something, especially to take over someone else's job or position. (Refers to a performer waiting at the side of the stage to go on.) □ *Mr. Smith retires as manager next year, and Mr. Jones is just waiting in the wings.* □ *Jane was waiting in the wings, hoping that a member of the hockey team would drop out and she would get a place on the team.*

wake the dead to be so loud as to wake those who are "sleeping" the most soundly: the dead. □ *You are making enough noise to wake the dead.* □ *Stop hollering! You'll wake the dead!*

walk all over someone to treat someone badly. (Also literal.) □ *She's so mean to her children. She walks all over them.* □ *The manager had walked all over Ann for months. Finally she quit.*

walk a tightrope to be in a situation where one must be very cautious. (Also literal.) □ *I've been walking a tightrope all day. I need to relax.* □ *Our business is about to fail. We've been walking a tightrope for three months.*

walk away with something AND **walk off with** something **1.** to win something easily. (Informal.) □ *John won the tennis match with no difficulty. He walked away with it.* □ *Our team walked away with first place.* **2.** to take or steal something. □ *I think somebody just walked off with my purse!* □ *Somebody walked off with my daughter's bicycle.*

walk off with something Go to walk away with something.

walk on air to be very happy; to be euphoric. □ *Ann was walking on air when she got the job.* □ *On the last day of school, all the children are walking on air.*

walk on eggs to be very cautious. (Informal.) □ *The manager is very hard to deal with. You really have to walk on eggs.*

☐ *I've been walking on eggs ever since I started working here.*

walk out (on someone or something**) 1.** [with *someone*] to abandon someone; to leave one's spouse. ☐ *Mr. Franklin walked out on Mrs. Franklin last week.* ☐ *Bob walked out on Jane without saying good-bye.* **2.** to leave a performance (of something by someone). ☐ *We didn't like the play at all, so we walked out.* ☐ *John was giving a very dull speech, and a few people even walked out on him.*

walk the floor to pace nervously while waiting. ☐ *While Bill waited for news of the operation, he walked the floor for hours on end.* ☐ *Walking the floor won't help. You might as well sit down and relax.*

walk the plank to suffer punishment at the hand of someone. (From the image of pirates making their blindfolded captives commit suicide by walking off the end of a plank jutting out over the open sea.) ☐ *Fred may think he can make the members of my department walk the plank, but we will fight back.* ☐ *Tom thought he could make John walk the plank, but John fought back.*

wall-to-wall with something covered with something in all places. (From *wall-to-wall carpeting.*) ☐ *The hallway is wall-to-wall with Jimmy's toys.* ☐ *The beach was wall-to-wall with tourists.*

Walls have ears. We may be overheard. (Proverb.) ☐ *Let's not discuss this matter here. Walls have ears, you know.* ☐ *Shhh. Walls have ears. Someone may be listening.*

want for nothing to lack nothing; to have everything one needs or wishes. ☐ *The Smiths don't have much money, but their children seem to want for nothing.* ☐ *Jean's husband spoils her. She wants for nothing.*

warm as toast Go to (as) warm as toast.

warm the bench [for a player] to remain out of play during a game—seated on a bench. ☐ *John spent the whole game warming the bench.* ☐ *Mary never warms the bench. She plays from the beginning to the end.*

warm the cockles of someone's **heart** to make someone feel warm and happy. ☐ *It warms the cockles of my heart to hear you say that.* ☐ *Hearing that old song again warmed the cockles of her heart.*

warm up to someone to become friendly with someone; to get used to a person and become friends. ☐ *It took a while before John warmed up to me, but then we became good friends.* ☐ *It's hard to warm up to Sally. She's very quiet and shy.*

warts and all including all the faults and disadvantages. ☐ *Jim has many faults, but Jean loves him, warts and all.* ☐ *The place where we went on vacation had some dismal aspects, but we liked it, warts and all.*

wash a few things out to do a little bit of laundry, such as socks and underclothing. ☐ *I'm sorry I can't go out tonight. I've got to wash a few things out.* 🅃 *I'll be ready to leave in just a minute. I've just got to wash out a few things.*

wash-and-wear referring to clothing made out of a kind of cloth that looks presentable after washing without ironing. ☐ *I always travel with wash-and-wear clothing.* ☐ *All his shirts are wash-and-wear, and this makes his life much easier since he used to burn them when he ironed them.*

wash one's **dirty linen in public** Go to air one's dirty linen in public.

wash one's **hands of** someone or something to end one's association with someone or something. ☐ *I washed my hands of Tom. I wanted no more to do with him.* ☐ *That car was a real headache. I washed my hands of it long ago.*

washed-out exhausted; lacking energy. (Informal.) ☐ *Pam was completely washed-out after the birth of the baby.* ☐ *I feel washed-out. I need a vacation.*

washed-up finished. (Informal.) ☐ *"You're through, Tom," said the manager, "fired—washed-up!"* ☐ *Max is washed-up as a bank teller.*

waste one's **breath** to waste one's time talking; to talk in vain. (Informal.) ☐ *Don't waste your breath talking to her. She won't* *listen.* ☐ *You can't persuade me. You're just wasting your breath.*

waste someone to kill someone. (Slang, especially criminal slang.) ☐ *The thief tried to waste the bank guard after the bank robbery.* ☐ *The crook said, "Try that again, and I'll waste you!"*

watch one's **step** to act with care and caution so as not to make a mistake or offend someone. (Also literal.) ☐ *John had better watch his step with the new boss. He won't put up with his lateness.* ☐ *Mary was told by the lecturer to watch her step and stop missing classes.*

watch out Go to **watch out for** someone or something.

watch out for someone or something AND **look out for** someone or something **1.** [with *someone*] to watch over and care for someone. ☐ *When I was a kid, my older brother always watched out for me.* ☐ *I really needed someone to look out for me then.* **2.** to be on guard for someone or something; to be on watch for the arrival or approach of someone or something. ☐ *Watch out for someone wearing a white carnation.* ☐ *Look out for John and his friends. They'll be coming this way very soon.* **3.** AND **look out; watch out** to try to avoid a confrontation with someone or something. ☐ *Watch out! That car nearly hit you!* ☐ *Look out for John. He's looking for you, and he's really mad.* ☐ *Thanks. I'd better look out.*

watch over someone or something to monitor or guard someone or something. ☐ *Please watch over my apartment while I am on vacation.* ☐ *I am looking for someone to watch over my grandmother during the day.*

watch someone or something **like a hawk** to watch someone very carefully. ☐ *The teacher watched the students like a hawk to make sure they did not cheat on the quiz.* ☐ *We have to watch our dog like a hawk in case he runs away.*

water something **down 1.** to dilute a liquid, usually with water. ☐ *The punch was good until someone watered it down.* ☐ *This is too strong! Water it down.* **2.** to make something milder or less intense. (Refers to diluting as in sense 1.) ☐ *The language in the script was rude but realistic until someone watered it down.* 🅃 *Professor Jones sometimes waters down his lectures so people can understand them better.*

water under the bridge [something] past and forgotten. (Refers to water that has already flowed under a bridge and has gone downstream.) ☐ *Please don't worry about it anymore. It's all water under the bridge.* ☐ *I can't change the past. It's water under the bridge.*

wax and wane to increase and then decrease, especially with reference to the phases of the moon. ☐ *As the moon waxes and wanes, so does the height of the tide change.* ☐ *Voter sentiment about the tax proposal waxes and wanes with each passing day.*

[way of life] Go to one's **way of life.**

(way) over there in a place some distance away. ☐ *I see a house way over there in the field.* ☐ *My hat is over there on the table.*

ways and means referring to the raising of money to pay for something. (Typically refers to a government committee or a committee of some organization charged with raising money.) ☐ *The suggestion was referred to the ways and means committee for discussion at the next meeting.* ☐ *The proposed legislation is stalled in ways and means.*

We aim to please. We really try to make people happy. ☐ *We aim to please because we want you to be our customer.* ☐ *I'm glad you like our food. We aim to please.*

weak as a baby Go to **(as) weak as a baby.**

weak as a kitten Go to **(as) weak as a kitten.**

a **wealth of** something a large amount of something. ☐ *There's a wealth of information on parrots at the library.* ☐ *The junkyard had a wealth of used car parts.*

wear and tear (on something**)** the process of wearing down or breaking down something. ☐ *Driving in freezing weather means lots of wear and tear on your car.*

☐ *I drive carefully and sensibly to avoid wear and tear.*

wear more than one hat to have more than one set of responsibilities; to hold more than one office. ☐ *The mayor is also the police chief. She wears more than one hat.* ☐ *I have too much to do to wear more than one hat.*

wear off to become less; to stop gradually. (Also literal.) ☐ *The effects of the painkiller wore off and my tooth began to hurt.* ☐ *I was annoyed at first, but my anger wore off.*

wear one's **heart on** one's **sleeve** AND **have** one's **heart on** one's **sleeve** to display one's feelings openly and habitually, rather than keep them private. ☐ *John always has his heart on his sleeve so that everyone knows how he feels.* ☐ *Because she wears her heart on her sleeve, it's easy to hurt her feelings.*

wear on someone to bother or annoy someone. ☐ *We stayed with them only a short time because my children seemed to wear on them.* ☐ *Always being short of money wears on a person after a while.*

wear out one's **welcome** to stay too long (at an event to which one has been invited); to visit somewhere too often. ☐ *Tom visited the Smiths so often that he wore out his welcome.* ☐ *At about midnight, I decided that I had worn out my welcome, so I went home.*

wear someone **down** to overcome someone's objections; to persist until someone has been persuaded. ☐ *John didn't want to go, but we finally wore him down.* 🅃 *We were unable to wear down John, and when we left, he was still insisting on running away from home.*

wear someone **out** to exhaust someone; to make someone tired. ☐ *The coach made the team practice until he wore them out.* 🅃 *If he wears out everybody on the team, nobody will be left to play in the game.*

weasel out (of something**)** to get out or sneak out of something. (Refers to the ability of a weasel to move through tiny openings. Informal.) ☐ *I don't want to go to the meeting. I think I'll try to weasel out of it.* ☐ *You had better be there! Don't try to weasel out!*

weather permitting if the weather allows it. ☐ *Weather permitting, we will be there on time.* ☐ *The plane lands at midnight, weather permitting.*

weave in and out (of something**)** to move, drive, or walk in and out of something, such as traffic, a line, etc. ☐ *The car was weaving in and out of traffic dangerously.* ☐ *The deer ran rapidly through the forest, weaving in and out of the trees.*

wed(ded) to someone married to someone. ☐ *The couple will have been wed to each other for fifty years next June.* ☐ *Anne is wed to one of my cousins.*

wedded to something mentally attached to something; firmly committed to something. ☐ *The manager was wedded to the idea of getting new computers.* ☐ *The mayor was wedded to the new budget plan.*

wee hours (of the night) Go to small hours (of the night).

weed someone or something **out** to remove someone or something unwanted or undesirable from a group or collection. ☐ *We had to weed them out one by one.* 🅃 *The auditions were held to weed out the actors with the least ability.* 🅃 *I'm going through my books to weed out those that I don't need anymore.*

week in, week out every week, week after week. (Informal.) ☐ *We have the same old food, week in, week out.* ☐ *I'm tired of this job. I've done the same thing—week in, week out—for three years.*

weeks running Go to days running.

weigh on someone's **mind** [for something] to be in a person's thoughts; [for something] to be bothering someone's thinking. ☐ *This problem has been weighing on my mind for many days now.* ☐ *I hate to have things weighing on my mind. I can't sleep when I'm worried.*

weigh someone **down** [for a thought or worry] to worry or depress someone. (Also literal.) ☐ *All these problems really weigh me down.* 🅃 *Financial problems* *have been weighing down our entire family.*

weigh someone's **words 1.** to consider carefully what someone says. ☐ *I listened to what he said, and I weighed his words very carefully.* ☐ *Everyone was weighing his words. None of us knew exactly what he meant.* **2.** to consider one's own words carefully when speaking. ☐ *I always weigh my words when I speak in public.* ☐ *John was weighing his words with great care because he didn't want to be misunderstood.*

welcome someone **with open arms** Go to receive someone with open arms.

welcome to do something to be free to do something. ☐ *You're welcome to leave whenever you wish.* ☐ *He's welcome to join the club whenever he feels he's ready.*

well and good Go to (all) well and good.

well-disposed toward someone or something feeling positively toward someone or something; favorable toward someone or something. ☐ *I do not think I will get a raise since the boss is not well-disposed toward me.* ☐ *The senators are well-disposed toward giving themselves a raise.*

well-fixed Go to well-heeled.

well-heeled AND **well-fixed; well-off** wealthy; with sufficient money. ☐ *My uncle can afford a new car. He's well-heeled.* ☐ *Everyone in his family is well-off.*

well-off Go to well-heeled.

well-to-do wealthy and of good social position. (Often with *quite,* as in the examples below.) ☐ *The Jones family is quite well-to-do.* ☐ *There is a gentleman waiting for you at the door. He appears quite well-to-do.*

well up in years aged; old. ☐ *Jane's husband is well up in years. He is nearly 75.* ☐ *Joan's well up in years but healthy.*

wet behind the ears AND **not dry behind the ears** young and inexperienced. ☐ *John's too young to take on a job like this! He's still wet behind the ears!* ☐ *He may be wet behind the ears, but he's well trained and totally competent.* ☐ *Tom is going into business by himself? Why, he's hardly dry behind the ears.* ☐ *That kid isn't dry behind the ears. He'll go broke in a month.*

wet blanket a dull or depressing person who spoils other people's enjoyment. ☐ *Jack's fun at parties, but his brother's a wet blanket.* ☐ *I was with Anne and she was being a real wet blanket.*

wet someone's **whistle** to take a drink of something. (Folksy.) ☐ *Wow, am I thirsty. I need something to wet my whistle.* ☐ *Hey, Sally! Give her something to wet her whistle.*

whale the tar out of someone Go to beat the living daylights out of someone.

What are you driving at? What are you implying?; What do you mean? (Informal.) ☐ *What are you driving at? What are you trying to say?* ☐ *Why are you asking me all these questions? What are you driving at?*

What can I say? I am at a loss for words. (Informal.) ☐ *I'm sorry. I'll pay for it. What can I say?* ☐ *What can I say? I never meant it to end like this.*

What do you want me to say? You caught me and I'm sorry, and I don't know what more to say. (Informal.) ☐ *What do you want me to say? I apologized. There is nothing more I can do.* ☐ *Okay, so I'm wrong. What do you want me to say?*

what for why?; for what reason? ☐ *"I want you to clean your room." "What for? It's clean enough."* ☐ *What did you do that for?*

What goes around, comes around. The results of things that one has done will someday have an effect on the person who started the events. (Proverb.) ☐ *So he finally gets to see the results of his activities. Whatever goes around, comes around.* ☐ *Now he is the victim of his own policies. Whatever goes around comes around.*

What have you been up to? I haven't seen you for a long time, so tell me what you have been doing? (Informal. In other persons also.) □ *Hi, Tom. Where have you been? What have you been up to?* □ *What have you been up to? Busy, I am sure.*

what if what would be the result if something were true? □ *What if you had all the money you want?* □ *What if everyone thought you were great?*

what makes someone **tick** something that motivates someone; something that makes someone behave in a certain way. (Informal.) □ *William is sort of strange. I don't know what makes him tick.* □ *When you get to know people, you find out what makes them tick.*

what makes something **tick** to cause something to run or function. □ *I don't know what makes it tick.* □ *I took apart the radio to find out what made it tick.*

What one **doesn't know won't hurt** one. Unknown facts cannot worry or upset a person. (Proverb.) □ *Don't tell me that I have made a mistake. What I don't know won't hurt me.* □ *Don't tell him the truth about his missing dog. What he doesn't know won't hurt him.*

Whatever will be, will be. Whatever will happen will just happen and there is little we can do about it. (Proverb.) □ *There is little I can do at this stage. Whatever will be, will be.* □ *The doctors have done all they can. Whatever will be, will be.*

What's done is done. It is final and in the past. (Proverb.) □ *It's too late to change it now. What's done is done.* □ *What's done is done. The past cannot be altered.*

What's keeping you? What is taking you so long?; Why are you still there and not here? □ *Dinner is ready, and you are still at work. I telephoned to ask what's keeping you.* □ *What's keeping you? I am ready to go and you are still in there dressing.*

What's new? How are you? Tell me what you have been doing. (Informal.) □ *Good to see you. What's new?* □ *What's new? How are things down your way?*

What's the good of something**?** What is the point of something?; Why bother with something? □ *What's the good of my going at all if I'll be late?* □ *There is no need to get there early. What's the good of that?*

What's up? Hello. What is happening? (Informal.) □ *What's up? How're you doing?* □ *Hey, Chuck! What's up?*

What's with someone**?** What is bothering or affecting someone? (Slang.) □ *John seems upset. What's with him?* □ *There's nothing wrong with me. What's with you?*

wheel and deal to take part in clever (but sometimes dishonest or immoral) business deals. □ *John loves to wheel and deal in the money markets.* □ *Jack got tired of all the wheeling and dealing of big business and retired to run a pub in the country.*

when all is said and done when everything is finished and settled; when everything is considered. (See also **after all is said and done**.) □ *When all is said and done, this isn't such a bad part of the country to live in after all.* □ *When all is said and done, I believe I had a very enjoyable time on my vacation.*

when hell freezes over AND **until hell freezes over** never. (The first entry is always affirmative and the second is always negative.) □ *I'll say I'm sorry to you when hell freezes over!* □ *I won't apologize until hell freezes over.*

When in Rome, do as the Romans do. One should behave in the same way that the local people behave. (Proverb.) □ *I don't usually eat lamb, but I did when I went to Australia. When in Rome, do as the Romans do.* □ *I always carry an umbrella when I visit London. When in Rome, do as the Romans do.*

when it comes right down to it all things considered; when one really thinks about something. □ *When it comes right down to it, I'd like to find a new job.* □ *When it comes right down to it, he can't really afford a new car.*

when it comes to something as for something; speaking about something. (Informal.) □ *When it comes to fishing, John is an expert.* □ *When it comes to trouble, Mary really knows how to cause it.*

when least expected when one does not expect (something). ☐ *An old car is likely to give you trouble when least expected.* ☐ *My pencil usually breaks when least expected.*

when one **is good and ready** when one is completely ready. (Informal.) ☐ *I'll be there when I'm good and ready.* ☐ *Ann will finish the job when she's good and ready and not a minute sooner.*

when push comes to shove when the situation becomes more difficult; when matters escalate. (See also **if push comes to shove**.) ☐ *When push comes to shove, I will take a stronger position.* ☐ *When push comes to shove, I will come up with the money you need.*

When the cat's away, the mice will play. Some people will get into mischief when they are not being watched. (Proverb.) ☐ *The students behaved very badly for the substitute teacher. When the cat's away, the mice will play.* ☐ *John had a wild party at his house when his parents were out of town. When the cat's away, the mice will play.*

when the chips are down at the final, critical moment; when things really get difficult. ☐ *When the chips are down, I know that I can depend on Jean to help out.* ☐ *I knew you would come and help when the chips were down.*

when the going gets rough Go to **when the going gets tough**.

when the going gets tough AND **when the going gets rough** when things get extremely difficult; when it becomes difficult to proceed. (Also literal when referring to travel. A second line is sometimes added to the main entry phrase: When the going gets tough, the tough get going. This means that when things become difficult, strong people began to work or move faster and harder.) ☐ *When the going gets tough, I will be there to help you.* ☐ *I appreciate the kind words you sent to us when the going got a little rough last month.*

when the time is ripe at exactly the right time. ☐ *I'll tell her the good news when the time is ripe.* ☐ *When the time is ripe, I'll bring up the subject again.*

where one **is coming from** one's point of view. (Slang.) ☐ *I think I know what you mean. I know where you're coming from.* ☐ *Man, you don't know where I'm coming from! You don't understand a single word I say.*

where one **lives** Go to **close to home**.

Where there's a will there's a way. One can do something if one really wants to. (Proverb.) ☐ *Don't give up, Ann. You can do it. Where there's a will there's a way.* ☐ *They told John he'd never walk again after his accident. He worked at it, and he was able to walk again! Where there's a will there's a way.*

Where there's smoke there's fire. Evidence of a problem probably indicates that there really is a problem. (Proverb.) ☐ *There is a lot of noise coming from the classroom. There is probably something wrong. Where there's smoke there's fire.* ☐ *I think there is something wrong at the old house on the corner. The police are there again. Where there's smoke there's fire.*

Where was I? Go to **(Now), where was I?**

Where've you been hiding yourself? Hello, I haven't seen you in a long time. (In other persons also.) ☐ *I haven't seen you in a long time. Where've you been hiding yourself?* ☐ *Where've you been hiding yourself? We missed you at the meeting.*

whet someone's **appetite** to cause someone to be interested in something and to be eager to have, know, learn, etc., more about it. ☐ *Seeing that film really whetted my sister's appetite for horror films. She now sees as many as possible.* ☐ *My appetite for theater was whetted when I was very young.*

whether or not either if something is the case or if something is not the case; one way or the other. ☐ *I'll drive to New York tomorrow whether or not it rains.* 🅃 *I'm going to the mall whether you come with me or not.*

while away the time to spend or waste time. ☐ *I like to read to while away the* *time.* 🅃 *Jane whiles the time away by daydreaming.*

whip something **into shape** Go to lick something into shape.

whip something **up** to prepare, create, or put something together quickly. (Informal.) □ *I haven't written my report yet, but I'll whip one up before the deadline.* 🅃 *Come in and sit down. I'll go whip up something to eat.*

white as a sheet Go to (as) white as a sheet.

white as the driven snow Go to (as) white as the driven snow.

white elephant something that is useless and which is either a nuisance or is expensive to keep up. (From the gift of a white elephant by the kings of Siam [Thailand] to courtiers who displeased them, knowing the cost of the upkeep would ruin them.) □ *Bob's father-in-law has given him an old Rolls-Royce, but it's a real white elephant. He has no place to park it and can't afford the maintenance on it.* □ *Those antique vases Aunt Mary gave me are white elephants. They're ugly and take ages to clean.*

Who do you think you're kidding? I don't believe you, and what makes you think you can deceive me? (In other persons also.) □ *Who does he think he's kidding? Nobody believes him.* □ *A: You are the finest batter I've ever seen. B: Who do you think you're kidding?*

Who do you think you're talking to? Do you know the importance of the person [me] you are talking to? (In other persons also.) □ *Who do you think you're talking to? I'm the boss here, you know!* □ *Don't talk to me that way! Who do you think you are talking to?*

Who would have thought? I would never have guessed that something so surprising could happen. □ *So he's run off with the maid. Who would have thought?* □ *It turns out she robbed a bank when she was 18. Who would have thought?*

the **whole ball of wax** AND the **whole shooting match** the whole thing; the whole matter or affair; the entire affair or organization. □ *John is not a good manager. Instead of delegating jobs to others, he runs the whole shooting match himself.* □ *There's not a hard worker in that whole shooting match.* □ *I will be glad to be finished with this project. I want to be done with the whole ball of wax.* □ *I am tired of this job. I am fed up with the whole ball of wax.*

(whole) new ball game a new set of circumstances. (Slang. Originally from sports.) □ *It's a whole new ball game since Jane took over the office.* □ *You can't do the things you used to do around here. It's a new ball game.*

the **whole shooting match** Go to the whole ball of wax.

whoop it up to enjoy oneself in a lively and noisy manner. (Informal.) □ *John's friends really whooped it up at his bachelor party.* □ *Jean wants to have a large party and whoop it up to celebrate her promotion.*

the **whys and wherefores of** something the reason or causes relating to something. □ *I refuse to discuss the whys and wherefores of my decision. It's final.* □ *Bob doesn't know the whys and wherefores of his contract. He just knows that it means he will get a lot of money when he finishes the work.*

wide-awake completely awake. □ *After the telephone rang, I was wide-awake for an hour.* □ *I'm not very wide-awake at six o'clock in the morning.*

wide of the mark 1. far from the target. □ *Tom's shot was wide of the mark.* □ *The pitch was quite fast, but wide of the mark.* **2.** inadequate; far from what is required or expected. □ *Jane's efforts were sincere, but wide of the mark.* □ *He failed the course because everything he did was wide of the mark.*

wild about someone or something enthusiastic about someone or something. □ *Bill is wild about chocolate ice cream.* □ *Sally is wild about Tom and his new car.*

a **wild-goose chase** a worthless hunt or chase; a futile pursuit. □ *I wasted all af-*

ternoon on a wild-goose chase. □ *John was angry because he was sent out on a wild-goose chase.*

Wild horses couldn't drag someone. nothing could force someone (to go somewhere). (Informal.) □ *I refuse to go to that meeting! Wild horses couldn't drag me.* □ *Wild horses couldn't drag her to that game.*

will not hear of something will not tolerate or permit something. □ *You mustn't drive home alone. I won't hear of it.* □ *My parents won't hear of my staying out that late.*

win by a nose to win by the slightest amount of difference. (Informal. As in a horse race where one horse wins with only its nose ahead of the horse that comes in second.) □ *I ran the fastest race I could, but I only won by a nose.* □ *Sally won the race, but she only won by a nose.*

win out (over someone or something**)** to beat someone or something in a race or a contest. □ *My horse won out over yours, so you lose your bet.* □ *I knew I could win out if I just kept trying.*

win someone **over** to succeed in gaining the support and sympathy of someone. □ *Jane's parents disapproved of her engagement at first, but she won them over.* □ *I'm trying to win the boss over and get him to give us the day off.*

win the day Go to carry the day.

wind down to decrease or diminish. □ *Things are very busy now, but they'll wind down in about an hour.* □ *I hope business winds down soon. I'm exhausted.*

wind something **up** to conclude something. (Also literal.) □ *Today we'll wind that deal up with the bank.* 🆃 *I have a few items of business to wind up; then I'll be with you.*

wind up doing something Go to **end up** doing something.

wind up somewhere Go to **end up** somewhere.

window-shopping the habit or practice of looking at goods in shop windows or stores without actually buying anything. □ *Mary and Jane do a lot of window-shopping in their lunch hour, looking for things to buy when they get paid.* □ *Jane said she was just window-shopping, but she bought a new coat.*

wine and dine someone to treat someone to an expensive meal of the type that includes fine wines; to entertain someone lavishly. □ *The lobbyists wined and dined the senators one by one in order to influence them.* □ *We were wined and dined every night and given the best hotel accommodations in town.*

wing it to do the best that one can in a situation, especially when one is not prepared. (Compare this with **play** something **by ear**.) □ *I lost my notes before my speech, and I had to wing it.* □ *The professor, it turned out, was winging it in every single lecture.*

wink at something to ignore something. (Informal.) □ *Billy caused me a little trouble, but I just winked at it.* □ *This is a serious matter, and you can't expect me just to wink at it.*

wipe someone or something **out 1.** to cause someone to be broke. (Slang.) □ *They wiped me out in the poker game.* 🆃 *The crop failure wiped out all the farmers.* **2.** to exterminate someone or something. (Slang.) □ *The hunters came and wiped all the deer out.* 🆃 *The crooks wiped out the two witnesses.*

wipe someone's **slate clean** to erase someone's (bad) record. (Figurative.) □ *I'd like to wipe my slate clean and start all over again.* □ *Bob did badly in high school, but he wiped his slate clean and did a good job in college.*

wipe something **off 1.** to remove something (from something else) by wiping or rubbing. □ *There is mud on your shirt. Please wipe it off.* 🆃 *My shirt has catsup on it. I must wipe off the catsup.* **2.** to tidy or clean something by wiping (something else) off. □ *Please wipe the table off. There's water on it.* 🆃 *Wipe off your shirt. There's catsup on it.*

wipe the floor up with someone to beat or physically abuse someone. (Slang. Usually said as a threat. See also **mop the**

floor up with someone.) □ *You say that to me one more time, and I'll wipe the floor up with you.* Ⓣ *Oh, yeah! You're not big enough to wipe up the floor with anybody!*

wise as an owl Go to (as) wise as an owl.

wise as Solomon Go to (as) wise as Solomon.

wise up (to someone or something**)** to begin to understand the truth about someone or something. (Slang.) □ *It was almost a week before I began to wise up to John. He's a total phony.* □ *You had better stay hidden for a while. The police are beginning to wise up.*

wish something **off on** someone to pass something off onto someone else. (Informal.) □ *I don't want to have to deal with your problems. Don't wish them off on me.* Ⓣ *The storekeeper wished off the defective watch on the very next customer who came in.*

wishful thinking believing that something is true or that something will happen just because one wishes that it were true or would happen. □ *Hoping for a car as a birthday present is just wishful thinking. Your parents can't afford it.* □ *Mary thinks that she is going to get a big rise, but that's wishful thinking. Her boss is so mean.*

with a heavy heart sadly. □ *With a heavy heart, she said good-bye.* □ *We left school on the last day with a heavy heart.*

with all one's **heart and soul** very sincerely. □ *Oh, Bill, I love you with all my heart and soul, and I always will!* □ *She thanked us with all her heart and soul for the gift.*

with all the fixings with all the condiments that accompany a certain kind of food. □ *For $5.99 you get a turkey dinner with all the fixings.* □ *Max likes his hamburgers with all the fixings.*

with an eye to doing something Go to with a view to doing something.

with a vengeance with determination and eagerness, as if angry. □ *The angry soldier attacked the enemy with a vengeance.* □ *Bill ate all his dinner and gobbled up his dessert with a vengeance.*

with a view to doing something AND **with an eye to** doing something with the intention of doing something. □ *I came to this school with a view to getting a degree.* □ *The mayor took office with an eye to improving the town.*

with a will with determination and enthusiasm. □ *The children worked with a will to finish the project on time.* □ *The workers set about manufacturing the new products with a will.*

with bells on (one's **toes)** eagerly, willingly, and on time. □ *Oh, yes! I'll meet you at the restaurant. I'll be there with bells on.* □ *All the smiling children were there waiting for me with bells on their toes.*

with both hands tied behind one's **back** Go to with one hand tied behind one's back.

with each passing day as days pass, one by one; day by day. □ *Things grow more expensive with each passing day.* □ *We are all growing older with each passing day.*

with ease without effort. □ *The smart student passed the test with ease.* □ *The gymnast did a back flip with ease.*

with every (other) breath [saying something] repeatedly or continually. □ *Bob was out in the yard, raking leaves and cursing with every other breath.* □ *The child was so grateful that she was thanking me with every breath.*

with everything (on it) [of a sandwich] ordered with everything available on it, such as ketchup, mustard, onions, cheese, peppers, chili, lettuce, tomato, etc., as appropriate. □ *Do you want it with everything?* □ *Give me a cheeseburger with everything on it.*

with flying colors easily and excellently. (*Flying colors* refers to ships' pennants.) □ *John passed his geometry test with flying colors.* □ *Sally qualified for the race with flying colors.*

(with) hat in hand with humility. (Also literal.) □ *She stormed off but came back with hat in hand when she ran out of money.* □ *We had to go hat in hand to the committee to get a grant for our proposal.*

with impunity without risk of punishment; with immunity from the negative consequences of an act; while being exempt from punishment. □ *The diplomat parked in illegal parking spaces with impunity.* □ *Bob used his brother's property with impunity.*

with it 1. alert and knowledgeable. (Slang.) □ *Jane isn't making any sense. She's not really with it tonight.* □ *Jean's mother is not really with it anymore. She's going senile.* □ *Peter's not with it yet. He's only just come round from the anesthetic.* **2.** up-to-date. (Slang.) □ *My parents are so old-fashioned. I'm sure they were never with it.* □ *Why do you wear those baggy old clothes? Why aren't you with it?*

with no strings attached AND **without any strings attached** unconditionally; with no obligations attached. □ *My parents gave me a computer without any strings attached.* □ *I want this only if it comes with no strings attached.*

with one hand tied behind one's **back** AND **with both hands tied behind** one's **back** even under a severe handicap; easily. □ *I could put an end to this argument with one hand tied behind my back.* □ *John could do this job with both hands tied behind his back.*

with one's **tail between** one's **legs** appearing frightened or cowardly, like a frightened or defeated dog; appearing threatened or humiliated. □ *John seems to lack courage. When people criticize him unjustly, he just goes away with his tail between his legs and doesn't tell them that they're wrong.* □ *The frightened dog ran away with its tail between its legs when the bigger dog growled.*

with regard to someone or something concerning someone or something. □ *What shall we do with regard to planning dinner?* □ *With regard to Bill, I think he is working too hard.*

with relish with pleasure or enjoyment. □ *John ate his juicy hamburger with great relish.* □ *We sampled the excellent food with relish.*

with respect to someone or something of or about someone or something. □ *With respect to radiation, this power plant is very safe.* □ *This article examines experiments with respect to ethical issues.*

with something **to spare** Go to and something to spare.

with the best will in the world however much one wishes to do something or however hard one tries to do something. □ *With the best will in the world, Jack won't be able to help Mary get the job.* □ *With the best will in the world, they won't finish the job in time.*

wither on the vine AND **die on the vine** [for something] to decline or fade away at an early stage of development. (Also literal in reference to grapes or other fruit.) □ *You have a great plan, Tom. Let's keep it alive. Don't let it wither on the vine.* □ *The whole project died on the vine when the contract was canceled.*

within an inch of one's **life** very close to taking one's life; almost to death. □ *The accident frightened me within an inch of my life.* □ *When Mary was seriously ill in the hospital, she came within an inch of her life.*

within a stone's throw (of something**)** AND **(just) a stone's throw (away) (from** something**)** very close (to something). (Possibly as close as the distance one could throw a stone. It usually refers to a distance much greater than one could throw a stone.) □ *The police department was located within a stone's throw of our house.* □ *We live in Carbondale, and that's just a stone's throw from the Mississippi River.* □ *Come visit. We live just a stone's throw away.* □ *John saw Mary across the street, just a stone's throw away.* □ *Philadelphia is a stone's throw from New York City.*

within bounds Go to within limits.

within calling distance Go to within hailing distance.

within hailing distance AND **within calling distance; within shouting distance** close enough to hear someone call out. □ *When the boat came within hailing distance, I asked if I could borrow* *some gasoline.* □ *We weren't within calling distance, so I couldn't hear what you said to me.*

within limits AND **within bounds** up to a certain point; with certain restrictions. □ *You're free to do what you want—within limits, of course.* □ *You must try to keep behavior at the party within bounds.*

within reason reasonable; reasonably. □ *You can do anything you want within reason.* □ *I'll pay any sum you ask—within reason.*

within shouting distance Go to within hailing distance.

within someone's **grasp** Go to within someone's reach.

within someone's **reach** AND **within** someone's **grasp** almost in the possession of someone. □ *My goals are almost within my reach, so I know I'll succeed.* □ *We almost had the contract within our grasp, but the deal fell through at the last minute.*

within walking distance close enough to walk to. □ *Is the train station within walking distance?* □ *My office is within walking distance from here.*

without a moment to spare Go to not a moment to spare.

without any strings attached Go to with no strings attached.

without batting an eye casually; without showing alarm or response. □ *I knew I had insulted her, but she turned to me and asked me to leave without batting an eye.* □ *Right in the middle of the speech—without batting an eye—the speaker walked off the stage.*

without fail for certain; absolutely. □ *I'll be there at noon without fail.* □ *The plane leaves on time every day without fail.*

without further ado without further talk. (An overworked phrase usually heard in public announcements.) □ *And without further ado, I would like to introduce Mr. Bill Franklin!* □ *The time has come to leave, so without further ado, good evening and good-bye.*

without question absolutely; certainly. □ *She agreed to help without question.* □ *She said, "I stand ready to support you without question."*

without rhyme or reason without purpose, order, or reason. □ *The teacher said my report was disorganized. My paragraphs seemed to be without rhyme or reason.* □ *Everything you do seems to be without rhyme or reason.* □ *This procedure is without rhyme or reason.*

without so much as doing something without even doing something. □ *Jane borrowed Bob's car without so much as asking his permission.* □ *Mary's husband walked out without so much as saying good-bye.*

Woe is me! I am unfortunate!; I am unhappy! (Usually humorous.) □ *Woe is me! I have to work when the rest of the office staff is off.* □ *Woe is me. I have the flu and my friends have gone to a party.*

a **wolf in sheep's clothing** someone or something threatening that is disguised as someone or something kind. □ *Beware of the police chief. He seems polite, but he's a wolf in sheep's clothing.* □ *This proposal seems harmless enough, but I think it's a wolf in sheep's clothing.*

woman to woman Go to man to man.

word by word one word at a time. □ *We examined the contract word by word to make sure everything was the way we wanted.* □ *We compared the stories word by word to see what made them different.*

word for word in the exact words; verbatim. □ *I memorized the speech, word for word.* □ *I can't recall word for word what she told us.*

a **word to the wise** a good piece of advice; a word of wisdom. □ *If I can give you a word to the wise, I would suggest going to the courthouse about an hour before your trial.* □ *Here is a word to the wise. Keep your eyes open and your mouth shut.*

words to that effect Go to something to that effect.

[work is cut out for one**]** Go to one's work is cut out for one.

work like a horse to work very hard. ☐ *I've been working like a horse all day, and I'm tired.* ☐ *I'm too old to work like a horse. I'd prefer to relax more.*

work one's **fingers to the bone** to work very hard. ☐ *I worked my fingers to the bone so you children could have everything you needed. Now look at the way you treat me!* ☐ *I spent the day working my fingers to the bone, and now I want to relax.*

work (one's **way) into** something to manage to join or become a member of something. (Refers to squeezing into something.) ☐ *Ann worked her way into the club, and now she's a member in good standing.* ☐ *Bob worked his way into the top management of the company.*

work one's **way through college** to hold a job that pays part of one's college expenses. ☐ *Tom couldn't get a loan, so he had to work his way through college.* ☐ *I worked my way through college, and that made college seem more valuable to me.*

work one's **way up** to advance in one's job or position, from the beginning level to a higher level. ☐ *I haven't always been president of this bank. I started as a teller and worked my way up.* ☐ *If I work my way up, can I be president of the bank?*

work on someone or something **1.** [with *someone*] to try to convince someone about something. (Informal.) ☐ *We worked on Tom for nearly an hour, but we couldn't get him to change his mind.* ☐ *I'll work on him for a while, and I'll change his mind.* **2.** [with *someone*] to give medical treatment to someone. ☐ *The dentist was working on Mary while I waited for her in the other room.* ☐ *The surgeon worked on the patient, trying to stop the bleeding.* **3.** [with *something*] to repair, build, or adjust something. ☐ *The carpenter worked on the fence for three hours.* ☐ *Bill is out working on his car engine.*

work out to do a program of exercise. ☐ *I have to work out every day in order to keep healthy.* ☐ *Working out a lot gives me a big appetite.*

work out (all right) Go to turn out (all right).

work out for the best to end up in the best possible way. ☐ *Don't worry. Things will work out for the best.* ☐ *It seems bad now, but it'll work out for the best.*

work someone or something **in** to insert someone or something (into a schedule or a line). ☐ *The doctor's schedule was very busy, but the nurse agreed to try to work me in.* ☐ *The mechanic had many cars to fix, but he said he'd work my car in.* 🅃 *I'm glad he could work in my car.*

work someone or something **up 1.** [with *someone*] to get someone ready for something, especially medical treatment. 🅃 *The coach worked up the whole team before the game.* ☐ *The doctor told the nurse to work Mr. Franklin up for surgery.* **2.** [with *something*] to create, cook, or arrange something. 🅃 *Bob is in the kitchen working up dinner.* ☐ *Is there something planned for Friday night, or should we work something up?*

work someone **over** to threaten, intimidate, or beat someone. (Slang, especially criminal slang.) ☐ *I thought they were really going to work me over, but they only asked a few questions.* 🅃 *The police worked over Bill until he told where the money was hidden.*

work something **into** something else to rub or knead something into something else. ☐ *You should work more butter into the dough before baking the bread.* ☐ *Work this lotion into your skin to make your sunburn stop hurting.*

work something **off** to get rid of something, such as fat, by doing physical exercise. ☐ *Bob put on weight on his vacation and is trying to work it off by swimming regularly.* 🅃 *Jane tried to work off her depression by playing a game of tennis.*

work something **out** to settle a problem. (Also literal.) ☐ *It was a serious problem, but we managed to work it out.* 🅃 *I'm glad we can work out our problems without fighting.*

work through channels to try to get something done by going through the proper procedures and persons. (See also go through channels.) ☐ *You can't ac-*

complish anything around here if you don't work through channels. ☐ *I tried working through channels, but it takes too long. This is an emergency.*

work wonders (with someone or something**)** to be surprisingly beneficial to someone or something; to be very helpful with someone or something. ☐ *This new medicine works wonders with my headaches.* ☐ *Jean was able to work wonders with the office staff. They improved their efficiency as soon as she took over.*

worked up (about something**)** Go to (all) worked up (over something).

worked up (over something**)** Go to (all) worked up (over something).

the **works** everything. (Informal.) ☐ *They gave me everything I could possibly want. They gave me the works!* ☐ *I want the works! Everything you have to offer!*

The **worm (has) turned.** Someone who is usually patient and humble has decided to stop being so. ☐ *Jane used to be treated badly by her husband and she just accepted it, but one day she hit him. The worm turned all right.* ☐ *Tom used to let the other boys bully him on the playground, but one day the worm turned and he's now leader of their gang.*

worm one's **way out of** something to squeeze or wiggle out of a problem or a responsibility. (Informal.) ☐ *This is your job, and you can't worm your way out of it!* ☐ *I'm not trying to worm my way out of anything!*

worm something **out of** someone to get some kind of information out of someone. (Informal.) ☐ *He didn't want to tell me the truth, but I finally wormed it out of him.* ☐ *She succeeded in worming the secret out of me. I didn't mean to tell it.*

worth its weight in gold very valuable. ☐ *This book is worth its weight in gold.* ☐ *Oh, Bill. You're wonderful. You're worth your weight in gold.*

worth one's **salt** worth one's salary. ☐ *Tom doesn't work very hard, and he's just barely worth his salt, but he's very easy to get along with.* ☐ *I think he's more than worth his salt. He's a good worker.*

worth someone's **while** worth one's time and trouble. (See also make it worth someone's while.) ☐ *The job pays so badly it's not worth your while even going for an interview.* ☐ *It's not worth Mary's while going all that way just for a one-hour meeting.*

worthy of the name deserving to be so called; good enough to enjoy a specific name. ☐ *There was not an actor worthy of the name in that play.* ☐ *Any art critic worthy of the name would know that painting to be a fake.*

would (just) as soon do something Go to had (just) as soon do something.

would give one's **right arm (for** someone or something**)** would be willing to give something of great value in exchange for someone or something. ☐ *I'd give my right arm for a nice cool drink.* ☐ *I'd give my right arm to be there.*

would like (to have) someone or something to want someone or something; to prefer someone or something. ☐ *I would like to have three cookies.* ☐ *I would like a piece of cake.*

would rather would prefer [something] more willingly; would prefer [something] more readily. ☐ *I would rather have an apple than a pear. I don't like pears.* ☐ *I'd rather live in the north than the south, because I like snow.*

wouldn't dream of doing something would not even consider doing something. (Informal.) ☐ *I wouldn't dream of taking your money!* ☐ *I'm sure that John wouldn't dream of complaining to the manager.*

wouldn't touch someone or something **with a ten-foot pole** would not be involved with something under any circumstances. ☐ *I know about the piece of vacant land for sale on Maple Street. I wouldn't touch it with a ten-foot pole because there used to be a gas station there and the soil is polluted.* ☐ *I wouldn't touch that book with a ten-foot pole. It is nothing but gossip and scandal.*

wrap something **up** to terminate something; to bring something to an end. (Also literal. Informal. See also **get** something **sewed up**.) □ *It's time to wrap this project up and move on to something else.* Ⓣ *Let's wrap up this discussion. It's time to go home.*

wrapped up in someone or something concerned and involved with someone or something. □ *Sally is wrapped up in her work.* □ *Ann is all wrapped up in her children and their activities.*

wreak havoc with something to cause a lot of trouble with something; to ruin or damage something. □ *Your attitude will wreak havoc with my project.* □ *The weather wreaked havoc with our picnic plans.*

wreak vengeance (up)on someone or something to seek and get revenge on someone by harming someone or something. □ *The thief wreaked his vengeance by destroying his rival's house.* □ *The general wanted to wreak vengeance on the opposing army for their recent successful attack.*

write someone or something **off 1.** [with *something*] to absorb a debt or a loss in accounting. □ *The bill couldn't be collected, so we had to write it off.* Ⓣ *The bill was too large, and we couldn't write off the amount. We decided to sue.* **2.** to drop someone or something from consideration. □ *The manager wrote Tom off for a promotion.* Ⓣ *I wrote off that piece of land as worthless. It can't be used for anything.*

write someone or something **up 1.** [with *something*] to prepare a bill, order, or statement. □ *Please write the order up and send me a copy.* Ⓣ *As soon as I finish writing up your check, I'll bring you some more coffee.* **2.** to write an article about someone or something. □ *A reporter wrote me up for the Sunday paper.* □ *I wrote up a local factory and sent the story to a magazine, but they didn't buy the story.*

write something **down** to write something; to make a note of something. (Also without *down*.) □ *If I write it down, I won't forget it.* Ⓣ *I wrote down everything she said.*

write something **out** to spell or write a number or an abbreviation. □ *Don't just write "7," write it out.* Ⓣ *Please write out all abbreviations, such as* Doctor *for* Dr.

the **wrong side of the tracks** the poor part of a town. (Often with *come from*, *be from*, or *live on*, as in the examples. Compare this with the **other side of the tracks**.) □ *They said that Bob was from the wrong side of the tracks, but that it didn't matter.* □ *We went to a school that was on the wrong side of the tracks, and we all got a fine education.*

[wrote the book on something**]** Go to someone **wrote the book on** something.

X

X marks the spot this is the exact spot. (Can be used literally when someone draws an X to mark an exact spot.) □ *This is where the rock struck my car—X marks the spot.* □ *Now, please move that table over here. Yes, right here—X marks the spot.*

Y

year after year for many years, one after another. ☐ *We go to the same place for our vacation year after year.* ☐ *I seem to earn the same salary year after year.*

year in, year out year after year, all year long. ☐ *I seem to have hay fever year in, year out. I never get over it.* ☐ *John wears the same old suit, year in, year out.*

year round Go to (all) year round.

years running Go to days running.

yield the right-of-way to give the right to turn or move forward to another person or vehicle. (See also have the right-of-way.) ☐ *When you're driving, it's better to yield the right-of-way than to have a wreck.* ☐ *You must always yield the right-of-way when you're making a left turn.*

a **yoke around** someone's **neck** something that oppresses people; a burden. ☐ *John's greedy children are a yoke around his neck.* ☐ *The Smiths have a huge mortgage that has become a yoke around their neck.*

You bet (your boots)! AND **You can bet on it!** Surely!; Absolutely! (Informal.) ☐ *BILL: Coming to the meeting next Saturday? BOB: You bet!* ☐ *You bet your boots I'll be there!*

You can bet on it! Go to You bet (your boots)!

You can say that again! AND **You said it!** That is true!; You are correct! (Informal. The word *that* is emphasized.) ☐ *MARY: It sure is hot today. JANE: You can say that again!* ☐ *BILL: This cake is yummy! BOB: You said it!*

You can't please everyone. It is not possible to make everyone happy. (Said when dismissing a complaint or when someone has pointed out a flaw that cannot be fixed.) ☐ *When Jean complained about the choices on the dinner menu, the waiter said, "Sorry. You can't please everyone."* ☐ *Jerry reported that many of his friends had noticed that the colors of the walls in the living room clashed. His mother said, "Oh, well. You can't please everyone."*

You can't take it with you. You should use your money now, because it is no good when you're dead. (Proverb.) ☐ *My uncle is a wealthy miser. I keep telling him, "You can't take it with you."* ☐ *If you have money, you should make out a will. You can't take it with you, you know!*

You can't teach an old dog new tricks. Old people cannot learn anything new. (Proverb. Also used literally of dogs.) ☐ *"Of course I can learn," bellowed Uncle John. "Who says you can't teach an old dog new tricks?"* ☐ *I'm sorry. I can't seem to learn to do it right. Oh, well. You can't teach an old dog new tricks.*

You got me there. I do not know the answer to your question. (In other persons also.) ☐ *You got me there. I don't know.* ☐ *You got me there. I have no idea what the answer is.*

You just don't get it! You really don't see what people are trying to tell you! (In other persons also.) ☐ *Everyone says that you are a bore, but you just don't get it!* ☐ *You just don't get it! People avoid you because you offend them.*

you know as you are aware, or should be aware. (Informal. This should not be overused.) ☐ *This is a very valuable book, you know.* ☐ *Goldfish can be overfed, you know.*

You said it! Go to You can say that again!

You scared me out of my wits. Go to You scared the hell out of me.

You scared the crap out of me. Go to You scared the hell out of me.

You scared the devil out of me. Go to You scared the hell out of me.

You scared the dickens out of me. Go to You scared the hell out of me.

You scared the hell out of me. AND **You scared the crap out of me.; You scared the dickens out of me.; You scared the devil out of me.; You scared me out of my wits.; You scared the pants off (of) me.** You frightened me very badly. (In other persons also.) □ *He scared the hell out of all of us.* □ *She really scared the pants off of me.*

You scared the pants off (of) me. Go to You scared the hell out of me.

You scratch my back and I'll scratch yours. You do a favor for me and I'll do a favor for you.; If you do something for me that I cannot do for myself, I will do something for you that you cannot do for yourself. (Also literal.) □ *I'll grab the box on the top shelf if you will creep under the table and pick up my pen. You scratch my back, and I'll scratch yours.* □ *Politicians are always saying to one another, "You scratch my back and I'll scratch yours."*

You think you're so smart! You act as if you knew far more than you do! (In other persons also.) □ *You think you're so smart! You don't know anything!* □ *Boy! He thinks he's so smart!*

Your guess is as good as mine. Your answer is likely to be as correct as mine. (Informal.) □ *I don't know where the scissors are. Your guess is as good as mine.* □ *Your guess is as good as mine as to when the train will arrive.*

Your secret is safe with me. I will not tell your secret to anyone. □ *Don't worry. I won't tell. Your secret's safe with me.* □ *Your secret is safe with me. I will carry it to my grave.*

yours truly 1. a polite closing phrase at the end of a letter, just before the signature. □ *Yours truly, Tom Jones* □ *Best wishes from yours truly, Bill Smith* **2.** oneself; I; me. (Informal.) □ *There's nobody here right now but yours truly.* □ *Everyone else got up and left the table leaving yours truly to pay the bill.*

Z

zero in on something to aim or focus directly on something. (Informal.) □ *"Now," said Mr. Smith, "I would like to zero in on another important point."* □ *Mary is very good about zeroing in on the most important and helpful ideas.*

zonk out to pass out; to fall asleep. (Slang.) □ *I was so tired after playing football that I almost zonked out on the floor.* □ *I had a cup of coffee before the test to keep from zonking out in the middle of it.*

zoom in (on someone or something**) 1.** to fly or move rapidly at someone or something. (Slang.) □ *The hawk zoomed in on the sparrow.* □ *The angry bees zoomed in on Jane and stung her.* □ *When the door opened, the cat zoomed in.* **2.** [for a photographer] to use a zoom lens to get a closer view of someone or something. □ *Bill zoomed in on Sally's face just as she grinned.* □ *On the next shot I'll zoom in for a close-up.*

Phrase-Finder Index

Use this index to find the form of a phrase that you want to look up in the dictionary. To use this index, pick out any major word in the phrase you are seeking, then look up that word in this index to find the form of the phrase that appears in the dictionary. Finally, look up the phrase in the main body of the dictionary. Words such as **someone or something** that are variable words in the dictionary entries are not indexed here.

aback **taken aback**
ABC (as) easy as ABC
ABC easy as ABC
ABCs know one's ABCs
abet aid and abet someone
abeyance in abeyance
abide abide by something
ability to the best of one's ability
able able to breathe (easily) again
able able to breathe (freely) again
able able to do something blindfolded
able able to do something standing on one's head
able able to do something with one's eyes closed
able able to fog a mirror
able able to make something
able able to take a joke
able able to take just so much
able able to take something
able not able to call one's time one's own
able not able to go on
able not able to help something
able not able to make anything out of someone or something
able not able to see the forest for the trees
able not able to stomach someone or something
able not able to wait
able ready, willing, and able
abode take up one's abode somewhere
about (all) at sea (about something)
about (all) worked up (about something)
about at sea (about something)
about be about something
about beat about the bush
about bring something about
about carry on (about someone or something)
about cast about for someone or something
about come about
about crazy about someone or something
about create a stink (about something)
about do an about-face
about fall out (with someone about something)
about fiddle about (with someone or something)
about get a rough idea (about something)
about get a thing about someone or something
about get one's wits about one
about get second thoughts about someone or something
about get worked up (about something)
about give someone a rough idea (about something)
about go about one's business
about go into one's song and dance (about something)
about halfhearted (about someone or something)
about have a clean conscience (about someone or something)
about have a clear conscience (about someone or something)
about have a clue (about something)
about have a feeling about something
about have a hunch about something
about have mixed feelings (about someone or something)
about have second thoughts about someone or something
about in a stew (about someone or something)
about in the dark (about someone or something)
about It's about time!
about keen about someone or something
about keep one's mouth shut (about someone or something)
about keep one's wits about one
about keep quiet (about someone or something)
about keep still (about someone or something)
about knock about (somewhere)
about knock someone or something about
about know a thing or two (about someone or something)
about know one's way about
about let someone know (about something)
about mad about someone or something
about make a big deal about something
about make a stink (about something)
about make cracks (about someone or something)
about Make no bones about it.
about make no mistake (about it)
about man-about-town
about mess about (with someone or something)
about millstone about one's neck
about much ado about nothing
about no buts about it
about no ifs, ands, or buts about it
about nose about
about not breathe a word (about someone or something)

about not care two hoots (about someone or something)
about not give a hang (about someone or something)
about not give a hoot (about someone or something)
about not give two hoots (about someone or something)
about nothing to complain about
about nothing to write home about
about not know beans (about someone or something)
about not know the first thing about someone or something
about no two ways about it
about nuts about someone or something
about on the fence (about something)
about order someone about
about out and about
about play about (with someone or something)
about poke about
about put one's foot down (about something)
about put out (about someone or something)
about rail at someone (about something)
about raise a stink (about something)
about ramble on (about someone or something)
about rant and rave (about someone or something)
about rant (at someone) about someone or something
about religious about doing something
about see about something
about see a man about a dog
about see eye to eye (with someone) (about something)
about send one about one's business
about something about someone or something
about sound off (about something)
about spout off (about someone or something)
about That's about the size of it.
about trouble oneself about someone or something
about trouble one's head about someone or something
about up and about
about up in the air (about someone or something)
about wild about someone or something
about worked up (about something)
above above and beyond (something)
above (above and) beyond the call of duty
above above average
above above par
above above reproach
above above suspicion
above get one's head above water
above head and shoulders above someone or something
above keep one's head above water
above over and above something
above a cut above someone or something
aboveboard aboveboard
aboveboard honest and aboveboard
aboveboard open and aboveboard
abreast keep abreast (of something)
absence conspicuous by one's absence
absence in the absence of someone or something
absent absent without leave
accident have an accident
accord of one's own accord
accordance in accordance with something
according according to all accounts
according according to Hoyle
according according to one's own lights
according according to someone or something
according according to something
account blow-by-blow account
account give a good account of oneself
account not on any account
account on account
account on any account
account on no account
account on someone's account
account take someone or something into account
account turn something to good account
accounting There's no accounting for taste.
accounts according to all accounts
accounts balance the accounts
accounts by all accounts
accounts cook the accounts
accounts square accounts (with someone)
accustomed accustomed to someone or something
ace ace in the hole
ace (as) black as the ace of spades
ace black as the ace of spades
ace come within an ace of doing something
ace have an ace up one's sleeve
ace someone's ace in the hole
aces hold all the aces
aching an aching heart
acid acid test
acknowledge acknowledge receipt (of something)
acknowledge acknowledge someone to be right
acquire acquire a taste for something
across across the board
across come across someone or something
across cut across something
across get someone or something across
across get something across (to someone)
across put someone or something across
across run across someone or something
across stumble across someone or something
act act as someone
act act high-and-mighty
act act one's age
act act something out
act act up
act catch someone in the act (of doing something)
act caught in the act
act clean up one's act
act get into the act
act get one's act together
act in the act (of doing something)
act keep up an act
act keep up one's act
act put on an act
act read someone the riot act
act an act of faith
act an act of God
act an act of war
act a tough act to follow
action all talk (and no action)
action course of action
action go into action
action swing into action
action a piece of the action

Actions Actions speak louder than words.
active on active duty
activity a hive of activity
Adam not know someone from Adam
add add fuel to the fire
add add fuel to the flame
add add insult to injury
add add up (to something)
addition in addition (to something)
address address someone as something
adieu bid adieu to someone or something
adieu bid someone or something adieu
ado much ado about nothing
ado without further ado
advance in advance
advance pay in advance
advanced advanced in years
advantage get the advantage of someone
advantage get the advantage over someone
advantage show something to good advantage
advantage take advantage of someone or something
advantage turn something to one's advantage
advice sage advice
advise advise against something
advise advise someone against doing something
advocate play (the) devil's advocate
aegis under the aegis of someone
affairs settle someone's affairs
affairs a fine state of affairs
affairs a pretty state of affairs
affinity an affinity for someone or something
affirmative in the affirmative
afire like a house afire
afoul fall afoul of someone or something
afoul run afoul of someone or something
afraid afraid of one's own shadow
aft fore and aft
after after a fashion
after after all
after after hours
after after the fact
after after the fashion of someone or something
after day after day
after get after someone
after keep after someone
after live happily ever after
after much sought after
after name someone after someone else
after one thing or person after another
after run after someone
after stay after someone
after take after someone
after take off (after someone or something)
after take out (after someone or something)
after throw good money after bad
after time after time
after year after year
after the morning after (the night before)
again able to breathe (easily) again
again able to breathe (freely) again
again again and again
again (all) over again
again at it again
again Come again.
again do something over (again)
again (every) now and again
again now and again
again off again, on again
again on again, off again
again oneself again
again over again
again over and over (again)
again run that by (someone) again
again something else (again)
again time and (time) again
again You can say that again!
against advise against something
against advise someone against doing something
against against someone's will
against against the clock
against assemble a case (against someone)
against bang one's head against a brick wall
against bear a grudge (against someone)
against beat one's head against the wall
against build a case (against someone)
against dead set against someone or something
against fight against time
against for the odds to be against one
against gather a case (against someone)
against get two strikes against one
against go against the grain
against guard against someone or something
against have a case (against someone)
against have a grudge (against someone)
against have one's heart set against something
against have something against someone or something
against have the cards stacked against one
against have the deck stacked against one
against have two strikes against one
against hold a grudge (against someone)
against hold something against someone
against hope against (all) hope
against lift a hand (against someone or something)
against nurse a grudge (against someone)
against one's heart is (dead) set against something
against pit someone or something against someone or something
against play both ends (against the middle)
against play someone off against someone else
against race against time
against raise a hand (against someone or something)
against security against something
against set one's heart against something
against side against someone
against smear campaign (against someone)
against stack the cards (against someone or something)
against stack the deck (against someone or something)
against swim against the current
against swim against the tide
against take a stand (against someone or something)
against take up arms (against someone or something)
against up against something
against the cards are stacked against one
age act one's age

age come of age
age in a coon's age
age in this day and age
age of age
age a ripe old age
agree not agree with someone
agreement in agreement
agreement reach an agreement
ahead ahead of one's time
ahead ahead of schedule
ahead ahead of the game
ahead ahead of time
ahead come out ahead
ahead dead ahead
ahead full steam ahead
ahead get ahead of oneself
ahead get the go-ahead
ahead give someone the go-ahead
ahead one jump ahead (of someone or something)
ahead one move ahead (of someone or something)
ahold get (a)hold of someone or something
ahold take (a)hold of someone or something
aid aid and abet someone
aim aim to do something
aim take aim (at someone or something)
aim We aim to please.
Ain't Ain't it the truth?
ain't That ain't hay.
air air one's dirty linen in public
air air one's grievances
air air something out
air (as) free as (the) air
air build castles in the air
air clear the air
air free as (the) air
air full of hot air
air get the air
air give someone the air
air gulp for air
air have one's nose in the air
air in the air
air off the air
air one's nose is in the air
air on the air
air out of thin air
air pull something out of thin air
air up in the air (about someone or something)
air vanish into thin air
air walk on air
air a breath of fresh air
airs put on airs
aisles have them rolling in the aisles
alcohol under the influence (of alcohol)
alert on the alert (for someone or something)
alike as alike as (two) peas in a pod
alike share and share alike
alive alive and kicking
alive alive and well
alive alive with someone or something
alive more dead than alive
alive skin someone alive
all according to all accounts
all after all
all (a little) new to (all) this
all all and sundry
all all around Robin Hood's barn
all all at once
all (all) at sea (about something)
all (all) balled up
all (all) beer and skittles
all all better now
all all day long
all all dressed up
all all for something
all (all) for the best
all all gone
all all in
all (all) in one breath
all (all) in the family
all (all) joking aside
all (all) kidding aside
all all kinds of someone or something
all all manner of someone or something
all all night long
all all of a sudden
all all or nothing
all all-out war
all all over
all (all) over again
all (all) over with
all all right
all all set
all (all) set to do something
all (all) shot to hell
all (all) skin and bones
all all sweetness and light
all all systems (are) go
all all talk (and no action)
All All that glitters is not gold.
all all the livelong day
all all the rage
all all the same
all all the time
all all the way
all all thumbs
all all told
all all to the good
all (all) tuckered out
all all walks of life
all (all) well and good
all all wet
all all wool and a yard wide
All All work and no play makes Jack a dull boy.
all (all) worked up (about something)
all (all) worked up (over something)
all (all) year round
all (as) bad as all that
all (as) big as all outdoors
all at all
all bad as all that
all be-all and (the) end-all
all be all ears
all be all eyes (and ears)
all be all things to all men

all be all things to all people
all big as all outdoors
all blow something out of all proportion
all by all accounts
all by all appearances
all by all means
all do not have all one's marbles
all downhill all the way
all fall (all) over oneself
all fall all over someone
all firing on all cylinders
all first of all
all for all I care
all for all I know
all for all intents and purposes
all for all it's worth
all for all practical purposes
all for all something
all for all the world
all free-for-all
all get (all) dolled up
all get away (from it all)
all get it (all) together
all go all out
all go all the way (with someone)
all have it all over someone or something
all hitting on all cylinders
all hold all the aces
all hope against (all) hope
all in (all) good conscience
all in all one's born days
all in all probability
all in no time (at all)
all It's (all) Greek to me.
all jump all over someone
all know (all) the tricks of the trade
all know where all the bodies are buried
all laugh all the way to the bank
all least of all
all let it all hang out
all make an all-out effort
all Money is the root of all evil.
all new to (all) this
all not all something is cracked up to be
all not all there
all not at all
all of all the nerve
all of all things
all on all fours
all once and for all
all one and all
all out of (all) proportion
all pull out all the stops
all put all one's eggs in one basket
all ride off in all directions
all That's all for someone.
all That's all she wrote.
all till all hours (of the day and night)
all turn out (all right)
all until all hours
all walk all over someone
all warts and all
all when all is said and done
all with all one's heart and soul
all with all the fixings
all work out (all right)
all an all-out effort
all a jack-of-all-trades
all the be-all and (the) end-all
alley right down someone's alley
alley right up someone's alley
alley up a blind alley
allow allow for someone or something
allowances make allowance(s) (for someone or something)
All's All's well that ends well.
almighty the almighty dollar
almost almost lost it
alone go it alone
alone leave well enough alone
alone let alone someone or something
alone let well enough alone
along along in years
along along with someone or something
along get along (in years)
along get along (on a shoestring)
along get along (without (someone or something))
along get along (with someone or something)
along go along for the ride
along go along (with someone or something)
along inch along (something)
along play along with someone or something
along string along (with someone)
along tag along
alongside alongside (of) someone or something
alpha alpha and omega
altogether in the altogether
amends make amends (for something)
amiss take something amiss
amount amount to something
amount amount to the same thing
amount down by some amount
amount run to an amount of money
amount set someone back (some amount of money)
amount (somewhere) in the neighborhood of an amount
amount to the tune of some amount of money
an give (an) ear to someone or something
an raise (an) objection (to someone or something)
an read someone like a(n open) book
analysis in the final analysis
analysis in the last analysis
and (above and) beyond the call of duty
and all talk (and no action)
and and change
and and so forth
and and something to spare
and and so on
and and the like
and and then some
and and what have you
and be all eyes (and ears)
and cross one's heart (and hope to die)
and pitch in (and help)

ands no ifs, ands, or buts about it
angels fools rush in (where angels fear to tread)
anger express one's anger
angry angry enough to chew nails
anon ever and anon
another another country heard from
another (another) nail in someone's or something's coffin
another dance to another tune
another get another guess coming
another get another think coming
another not give it another thought
another One good turn deserves another.
another One man's meat is another man's poison.
another One man's trash is another man's treasure.
another One thing leads to another.
another one thing or person after another
another one way or another
another sing another tune
another a horse of another color
answer answer for someone or something
answer answer someone's purpose
answer answer the door
answer answer to someone
answer not take no for an answer
ants get ants in one's pants
any any number of someone or something
Any Any port in a storm.
any at any cost
any at any rate
any by any means
any Don't let it go any further.
any go to any length
any in any case
any in any event
any not on any account
any not see any objection (to something)
any on any account
any without any strings attached
anyone (as) far as anyone knows
anyone far as anyone knows
anyone so far as anyone knows
anyone A little (hard) work never hurt anyone.
anyone A little (hard) work never killed anyone.
anything can't do anything with someone or something
anything not able to make anything out of someone or something
anything not for (anything in) the world
apart come apart at the seams
apart fall apart at the seams
apart poles apart
apart take someone apart
apart tell people apart
apart tell things apart
ape go ape (over someone or something)
appear appear as something
appear appear out of nowhere
appearance make an appearance
appearance put in an appearance
appearances by all appearances
appearances keep up appearances
appetite whet someone's appetite
apple (as) easy as (apple) pie
apple easy as (apple) pie
apple in apple-pie order
apple upset the apple cart
apple the apple of someone's eye
apples apples and oranges
appointed at the appointed time
appointment make an appointment (with someone)
approval on approval
apron tied to one's mother's apron strings
are all systems (are) go
are know where all the bodies are buried
are one's days are numbered
are one's ears are red
are one's ears are ringing
are One's eyes are bigger than one's stomach.
are There are plenty of other fish in the sea.
are Things are looking up.
are What are you driving at?
are when the chips are down
are Who do you think you're kidding?
are Who do you think you're talking to?
are You think you're so smart!
are A fool and his money are soon parted.
are the cards are stacked against one
area gray area
aren't There aren't enough hours in the day.
arguing arguing for the sake of arguing
arguing arguing for the sake of argument
argument arguing for the sake of argument
argument get into an argument (with someone)
arm arm in arm
arm cost an arm and a leg
arm pay an arm and a leg (for something)
arm put the arm on someone
arm twist someone's arm
arm would give one's right arm (for someone or something)
arm a shot in the arm
armed armed and dangerous
armed armed to the teeth
armed (as) busy as a one-armed paperhanger
armed busy as a one-armed paperhanger
armor chink in one's armor
arms receive someone with open arms
arms take up arms (against someone or something)
arms up in arms
arms welcome someone with open arms
around all around Robin Hood's barn
around (a)round the clock
around (a)round-the-clock
around beat around the bush
around blue around the gills
around boss someone around
around bring someone around
around bring something crashing down (around one)
around cast around for someone or something
around come (a)round
around drop around (sometime)
around enough to go (a)round
around every time one turns around
around fiddle around (with someone or something)
around find one's way (around)
around fool around (with someone or something)

around get around
around get (around) to something
around go (a)round in circles
around go (a)round the bend
around go around with someone
around green around the gills
around hang around (with someone)
around have been around
around hem and haw (around)
around horse around
around kick someone or something around
around kid around (with someone)
around knock someone or something around
around know one's way around
around mess around (with someone or something)
around monkey around (with someone or something)
around mope around
around nose around
around order someone around
around pal around (with someone)
around pale around the gills
around play around (with someone or something)
around poke around
around rally (a)round someone or something
around run (around) in circles
around run around like a chicken with its head cut off
around run around with someone
around run circles around someone
around run rings around someone
around scout around for someone or something
around scratch around (for something)
around screw around (with someone or something)
around shop around (for something)
around sit around (somewhere)
around stick around
around throw one's weight around
around throw someone's name around
around twist someone's words (around)
around twist someone around one's little finger
around up and around
around What goes around, comes around.
around a yoke around someone's neck
arrange arrange something with someone
arrange arrange to do something with someone
arrangements make arrangements (for someone or something)
arrears in arrears
arrest under arrest
arrive arrive in a body
arrive arrive on the scene
arrived have arrived
arrow (as) straight as an arrow
arrow (as) swift as an arrow
arrow straight as an arrow
arrow swift as an arrow
as act as someone
as address someone as something
as appear as something
as as a duck takes to water
as as a (general) rule
as as a last resort
as as alike as (two) peas in a pod
as as a matter of course
as as a matter of fact
as as an aside
as as a result of something
as as a token (of something)
as (as) awkward as a cow on a crutch
as (as) awkward as a cow on roller skates
as (as) bad as all that
as (as) bald as a baby's backside
as (as) bald as a coot
as (as) baleful as death
as (as) big as all outdoors
as (as) big as life
as (as) black as a skillet
as (as) black as a stack of black cats
as (as) black as a sweep
as (as) black as coal
as (as) black as night
as (as) black as one is painted
as (as) black as pitch
as (as) black as the ace of spades
as (as) blind as a bat
as (as) bold as brass
as (as) bright as a button
as (as) bright as a new pin
as (as) broad as a barn door
as (as) busy as a beaver
as (as) busy as a bee
as (as) busy as a cat on a hot tin roof
as (as) busy as a hibernating bear
as (as) busy as a one-armed paperhanger
as (as) busy as Grand Central Station
as (as) busy as popcorn on a skillet
as (as) calm as a toad in the sun
as (as) clean as a hound's tooth
as (as) clean as a whistle
as (as) clear as a bell
as (as) clear as crystal
as (as) clear as mud
as (as) clear as vodka
as (as) close as two coats of paint
as (as) cocky as the king of spades
as (as) cold as a witch's caress
as (as) cold as a witch's tit
as (as) cold as marble
as (as) comfortable as an old shoe
as (as) common as an old shoe
as (as) common as dirt
as (as) conceited as a barber's cat
as (as) cool as a cucumber
as (as) crazy as a betsy bug
as (as) crazy as a loon
as (as) crazy as a peach-orchard boar
as (as) crooked as a barrel of fishhooks
as (as) crooked as a dog's hind leg
as (as) crooked as a fishhook
as (as) dead as a dodo
as (as) dead as a doornail
as (as) deaf as a post
as (as) different as night and day
as (as) drunk as a lord

as (as) drunk as a skunk
as (as) dry as a bone
as (as) dry as dust
as (as) dull as dishwater
as (as) dull as ditchwater
as (as) easy as ABC
as (as) easy as (apple) pie
as (as) easy as duck soup
as (as) easy as falling off a log
as (as) easy as rolling off a log
as (as) exciting as watching (the) paint dry
as (as) far as anyone knows
as as far as it goes
as as far as possible
as (as) far as someone or something is concerned
as (as) fat as a pig
as (as) fit as a fiddle
as (as) flat as a board
as (as) flat as a pancake
as as for someone or something
as (as) free as a bird
as (as) free as (the) air
as (as) fresh as a daisy
as (as) full as a tick
as (as) funny as a barrel of monkeys
as (as) funny as a crutch
as (as) gaudy as a butterfly
as (as) gentle as a lamb
as (as) good as done
as (as) good as gold
as as good as one's word
as (as) graceful as a swan
as (as) gruff as a bear
as (as) happy as a clam
as (as) happy as a lark
as (as) happy as can be
as (as) hard as a rock
as (as) hard as nails
as (as) hard as stone
as (as) high as a kite
as (as) high as the sky
as (as) hoarse as a crow
as (as) hot as fire
as (as) hot as hell
as (as) hungry as a bear
as (as) hungry as a hunter
as as I expected
as (as) innocent as a lamb
as as it were
as (as) large as life
as (as) light as a feather
as (as) likely as not
as as long as
as as luck would have it
as (as) mad as a hatter
as (as) mad as a hornet
as (as) mad as a March hare
as (as) mad as a wet hen
as (as) mad as hell
as (as) meek as a lamb
as (as) merry as a cricket
as (as) merry as the day is long
as as much fun as a barrel of monkeys
as (as) naked as a jaybird
as (as) neat as a pin
as (as) nutty as a fruitcake
as (as) old as the hills
as as one
as as pale as a ghost
as (as) pale as death
as (as) patient as Job
as (as) phony as a three-dollar bill
as (as) plain as a pikestaff
as (as) plain as day
as (as) plain as the nose on one's face
as (as) pleased as punch
as (as) poor as a church mouse
as (as) pretty as a picture
as (as) proud as a peacock
as (as) pure as the driven snow
as (as) queer as a three-dollar bill
as (as) quick as a flash
as (as) quick as a wink
as (as) quick as greased lightning
as (as) quiet as a mouse
as (as) quiet as the grave
as (as) red as a cherry
as (as) red as a poppy
as (as) red as a rose
as (as) red as a ruby
as (as) red as blood
as (as) regular as clockwork
as (as) right as rain
as (as) scarce as hens' teeth
as (as) sharp as a razor
as (as) sharp as a tack
as (as) sick as a dog
as (as) silent as the dead
as (as) silent as the grave
as (as) silly as a goose
as (as) slick as a whistle
as (as) slippery as an eel
as (as) slow as molasses in January
as (as) sly as a fox
as (as) smooth as glass
as (as) smooth as silk
as (as) snug as a bug in a rug
as (as) sober as a judge
as (as) soft as a baby's bottom
as (as) soft as down
as (as) soft as silk
as (as) soft as velvet
as (as) solid as a rock
as as soon as
as (as) soon as possible
as (as) sound as a dollar
as (as) sour as vinegar
as (as) steady as a rock
as (as) stiff as a poker
as (as) still as death
as (as) straight as an arrow
as (as) strong as a horse
as (as) strong as a lion
as (as) strong as an ox

as (as) stubborn as a mule
as as such
as (as) sure as death
as (as) sweet as honey
as (as) sweet as sugar
as (as) swift as an arrow
as (as) swift as the wind
as (as) swift as thought
as as the crow flies
as (as) thick as pea soup
as (as) thick as thieves
as (as) tight as a drum
as (as) tight as a tick
as (as) tight as Dick's hatband
as as to someone or something
as (as) tough as an old boot
as (as) true as steel
as (as) ugly as a toad
as (as) ugly as sin
as as usual
as (as) warm as toast
as (as) weak as a baby
as (as) weak as a kitten
as as well
as (as) white as a ghost
as (as) white as a sheet
as (as) white as the driven snow
as (as) wise as an owl
as (as) wise as Solomon
as awkward as a cow on a crutch
as awkward as a cow on roller skates
as bad as all that
as bald as a baby's backside
as bald as a coot
as baleful as death
as be that as it may
as big as all outdoors
as big as life
as black as a skillet
as black as a stack of black cats
as black as a sweep
as black as coal
as black as night
as black as one is painted
as black as pitch
as black as the ace of spades
as blind as a bat
as bold as brass
as bright as a button
as bright as a new pin
as broad as a barn door
as business as usual
as busy as a beaver
as busy as a bee
as busy as a cat on a hot tin roof
as busy as a hibernating bear
as busy as a one-armed paperhanger
as busy as Grand Central Station
as busy as popcorn on a skillet
as calm as a toad in the sun
as catch-as-catch-can
as clean as a hound's tooth
as clean as a whistle
as clear as a bell
as clear as crystal
as clear as mud
as clear as vodka
as close as two coats of paint
as cocky as the king of spades
as cold as a witch's caress
as cold as a witch's tit
as cold as marble
as come as no surprise
as comfortable as an old shoe
as common as an old shoe
as common as dirt
as conceited as a barber's cat
as cool as a cucumber
as crazy as a betsy bug
as crazy as a loon
as crazy as a peach-orchard boar
as crooked as a barrel of fishhooks
as crooked as a dog's hind leg
as crooked as a fishhook
as dead as a dodo
as dead as a doornail
as deaf as a post
as different as night and day
as drunk as a lord
as drunk as a skunk
as dry as a bone
as dry as dust
as dull as dishwater
as dull as ditchwater
as easy as ABC
as easy as (apple) pie
as easy as duck soup
as easy as falling off a log
as easy as rolling off a log
as exciting as watching (the) paint dry
as far as anyone knows
as far as something is concerned
as fat as a pig
as fit as a fiddle
as flat as a board
as flat as a pancake
as free as a bird
as free as (the) air
as fresh as a daisy
as full as a tick
as funny as a barrel of monkeys
as funny as a crutch
as gaudy as a butterfly
as gentle as a lamb
as get a reputation (as a something)
as give as good as one gets
as give someone a reputation (as a something)
as good as done
as good as gold
as go so far as to say something
as graceful as a swan
as gruff as a bear
as had (just) as soon do something
as happy as a clam

as happy as a lark
as happy as can be
as hard as a rock
as hard as nails
as hard as stone
as have someone pegged as something
as high as a kite
as hoarse as a crow
as hold someone or something up (as an example)
as hot as fire
as hot as hell
as hungry as a bear
as hungry as a hunter
as innocent as a lamb
as in the same boat (as someone)
as (just) as I expected
as large as life
as light as a feather
as likely as not
as look as if butter wouldn't melt in one's mouth
as look on someone as something
as mad as a hatter
as mad as a hornet
as mad as a March hare
as mad as a wet hen
as mad as hell
as make as if to do something
as make good as something
as make it as far as something
as meek as a lamb
as merry as a cricket
as merry as the day is long
as naked as a jaybird
as neat as a pin
as nutty as a fruitcake
as old as the hills
as pale as death
as pass as someone or something
as patient as Job
as pay as you go
as peg someone as something
as phony as a three-dollar bill
as plain as a pikestaff
as plain as day
as plain as the nose on one's face
as pleased as punch
as poor as a church mouse
as pose as someone
as pretty as a picture
as Pretty is as pretty does.
as proud as a peacock
as pure as the driven snow
as put someone down as something bad
as queer as a three-dollar bill
as quick as a flash
as quick as a wink
as quick as greased lightning
as quiet as a mouse
as quiet as the grave
as red as a cherry
as red as a poppy
as red as a rose
as red as a ruby
as red as blood
as regular as clockwork
as right as rain
as see someone as something
as serve as a guinea pig
as set someone up (as something)
as sharp as a razor
as sharp as a tack
as show someone up as something
as sick as a dog
as silent as the dead
as silent as the grave
as silly as a goose
as slick as a whistle
as slippery as an eel
as slow as molasses in January
as sly as a fox
as smooth as glass
as smooth as silk
as snug as a bug in a rug
as sober as a judge
as so far as anyone knows
as so far as possible
as so far as someone or something is concerned
as so far as something is concerned
as soft as a baby's bottom
as soft as down
as soft as silk
as soft as velvet
as solid as a rock
as so long as
as soon as possible
as sound as a dollar
as sound as if
as sour as vinegar
as start someone in (as something)
as start someone out (as something)
as steady as a rock
as stiff as a poker
as still as death
as straight as an arrow
as strike someone as something
as strong as a horse
as strong as a lion
as strong as an ox
as stubborn as a mule
as such as
as sure as death
as sweet as honey
as sweet as sugar
as swift as an arrow
as swift as the wind
as swift as thought
as thick as pea soup
as thick as thieves
as tight as a drum
as tight as a tick
as tight as Dick's hatband
as tough as an old boot
as true as steel
as ugly as a toad

as ugly as sin
as use someone or something as an excuse
as warm as toast
as weak as a baby
as weak as a kitten
as When in Rome, do as the Romans do.
as white as a sheet
as white as the driven snow
as wise as an owl
as wise as Solomon
as without so much as doing something
as would as soon do something
as Your guess is as good as mine.
as the same as someone or something
aside (all) joking aside
aside (all) kidding aside
aside as an aside
aside aside from someone or something
aside joking aside
aside kidding aside
ask ask for something
ask ask for the moon
ask ask for trouble
ask ask someone out
asking one's for the asking
asleep asleep at the switch
asleep fall asleep
aspersions cast aspersions on someone
ass tits and ass
assault assault and battery
assault assault the ears
assemble assemble a case (against someone)
assume assume liability
assured rest assured
astray go astray
at all at once
at (all) at sea (about something)
at asleep at the switch
at at all
at at a loss (for words)
at at an early date
at at any cost
at at any rate
at at a premium
at at a set time
at at a sitting
at at a snail's pace
at at a stretch
at at bay
at at best
at at close range
at at cross-purposes
at at death's door
at at ease
at at every turn
at at face value
at at first
at (at) full blast
at at full speed
at at full tilt
at at half-mast
at at hand
at at hazard
at at home
at at it again
at at large
at at last
at at least
at at leisure
at at length
at at liberty
at at loggerheads (with someone)
at at (long) last
at at loose ends
at at most
at at night
at at odds (with someone)
at at once
at at one fell swoop
at at one's best
at at one's leisure
at at one's wit's end
at at peace
at at play
at at present
at at random
at at regular intervals
at at rest
at at risk
at at sea
at at sixes and sevens
at at some length
at at someone's beck and call
at at someone's doorstep
at at someone's earliest convenience
at at someone's mercy
at at someone's request
at at someone's service
at at some time sharp
at at stake
at at that rate
at at the appointed time
at at the bottom of the hour
at at the bottom of the ladder
at at the break of dawn
at at the crack of dawn
at at the drop of a hat
at at the eleventh hour
at at the end of nowhere
at at the end of one's rope
at at the end of one's tether
at at the end of the day
at at the expense of someone or something
at at the forefront (of something)
at at the height of something
at at the helm (of something)
at at the last gasp
at at the last minute
at at the latest
at at the mercy of someone
at at the outset
at at the point of doing something
at at the present time
at at the rear of something

at at the same time
at at the top of one's lungs
at at the top of one's voice
at at the top of the hour
at at the (very) outside
at at (the) worst
at at the zenith of something
at at this juncture
at at this point (in time)
at at this rate
at at this stage
at at times
at at will
at at work
at at worst
at blow up (at someone)
at burn someone at the stake
at burn the candle at both ends
at burst at the seams
at champ at the bit
at chomp at the bit
at close at hand
at clutch at straws
at come apart at the seams
at down-at-the-heels
at draw the line (at something)
at drive at something
at eat away at someone or something
at fall apart at the seams
at feel at home
at fire away at someone or something
at fling oneself at someone
at foam at the mouth
at get at someone or something
at get at the heart of the matter
at get back (at someone)
at get mad (at someone or something)
at go at it hammer and tongs
at go at it tooth and nail
at go at someone or something
at grasp at straws
at hammer away (at someone or something)
at have a crack at something
at have a go (at something)
at have a shot at something
at have a try at something
at have at someone or something
at have back at someone
at have something at hand
at have something at one's fingertips
at Here's looking at you.
at hold the line (at someone or something)
at hopeless at doing something
at hurl an insult (at someone)
at ill at ease
at I'm awful at names.
at I'm terrible at names.
at in at the kill
at in no time (at all)
at in the right place at the right time
at in the wrong place at the wrong time
at jump at something
at jump at the chance
at jump at the opportunity
at Keep at it!
at keep at someone or something
at leap at the opportunity
at level something at someone
at look at someone cross-eyed
at look daggers at someone
at look down one's nose at someone or something
at love at first sight
at make a face (at someone)
at make a pass at someone
at make eyes (at someone)
at make good (at something)
at make oneself at home
at more someone or something than one can shake a stick at
at near at hand
at not at all
at nothing to sneeze at
at one at a time
at peg away (at something)
at pick at someone or something
at plug away (at something)
at point the finger at someone
at poke fun (at someone)
at rail at someone (about something)
at rant (at someone) about someone or something
at right at a specific time
at run off at the mouth
at see the light (at the end of the tunnel)
at sit at someone's feet
at snap at someone
at stop at nothing
at strike out at someone or something
at take a crack at something
at take a dig at someone
at take a gander (at someone or something)
at take aim (at someone or something)
at take a look (at someone or something)
at take a potshot at someone or something
at take a punch at someone
at take a shot at something
at take a stab at something
at take a try at something
at take a whack at someone or something
at take digs at someone
at take offense (at someone or something)
at take one at one's word
at take someone or something at face value
at take something at face value
at take turns ((at) doing something)
at take umbrage at something
at throw oneself at someone's feet
at throw oneself at someone
at throw oneself at the mercy of the court
at throw the book at someone
at thumb one's nose at someone or something
at tilt at windmills
at tip the scales at something
at try one's hand (at something)

at try one's luck (at something)
at turn one's nose up at someone or something
at up and at them
at What are you driving at?
at wink at something
at an old hand at doing something
at a past master at something
attached attached to someone or something
attached with no strings attached
attached without any strings attached
attendance take attendance
attention attract someone's attention
attention bring something to someone's attention
attention grip someone's attention
attention hold someone's attention
attention pay attention (to someone or something)
attention rivet someone's attention
attitude devil-may-care attitude
attitude wait-and-see attitude
attract attract someone's attention
auction Dutch auction
augur augur well for someone or something
auspices under the auspices of someone
avail avail oneself of something
avail of no avail
avail to no avail
available make someone or something available to someone
avenue avenue of escape
average above average
average below average
average on the average
avoid avoid someone or something like the plague
awagging set tongues (a)wagging
awake wide-awake
away away from one's desk
away be a heartbeat away from something
away be a million miles away
away blow someone or something away
away carried away
away come away empty-handed
away do away with someone or something
away draw (someone's) fire (away from someone or something)
away eat away at someone or something
away explain something away
away far and away the best
away fire away at someone or something
away fritter something away
away get away (from it all)
away get away with something
away get carried away
away give the bride away
away give the game away
away go away empty-handed
away hammer away (at someone or something)
away (just) a stone's throw away (from something)
away lay someone away
away make away with someone or something
away pass away
away peg away (at something)
away plug away (at something)
away put someone away
away right away
away salt something away
away shy away (from someone or something)
away slip away
away sock something away
away squared away
away square someone or something away
away squirrel something away
away take it away
away take someone or something away
away take someone's breath away
away up and away
away walk away with something
away When the cat's away, the mice will play.
away while away the time
away a faraway look
away a stone's throw (away) (from something)
awe in awe (of someone or something)
awe stand in awe (of someone or something)
awful I'm awful at names.
awkward (as) awkward as a cow on a crutch
awkward (as) awkward as a cow on roller skates
awkward awkward as a cow on a crutch
awkward awkward as a cow on roller skates
awkwardness main strength and awkwardness
AWOL AWOL
AWOL go AWOL
ax get the ax
ax give someone the ax
ax have an ax to grind (with someone)
babe a babe in the woods
baby (as) weak as a baby
baby sleep like a baby
baby throw the baby out with the bath(water)
baby weak as a baby
baby's (as) bald as a baby's backside
baby's (as) soft as a baby's bottom
baby's bald as a baby's backside
baby's soft as a baby's bottom
back back and fill
back back and forth
back back down (from someone or something)
back back East
back back in circulation
back back off (from someone or something)
back back of the beyond
back back order something
back back out (of something)
back back someone or something up
back back the wrong horse
back back-to-back
back back to square one
back back to the drawing board
back back to the salt mines
back behind someone's back
back be the straw that broke the camel's back
back break one's back (to do something)
back break the back of something
back cut back (on something)
back date back (to sometime)
back double back (on someone or something)
back fall back on someone or something

back from way back
back get back (at someone)
back get back into circulation
back get back into harness
back get back on one's feet
back get back (to someone)
back Get off someone's back!
back get someone's back up
back give someone a pat on the back
back give someone the shirt off one's back
back go back on one's word
back hang back
back hark(en) back to something
back have back at someone
back have been to hell and back
back have eyes in the back of one's head
back have one's back to the wall
back knock something back
back know someone or something like the back of one's hand
back laid-back
back like water off a duck's back
back nurse someone back to health
back on someone's back
back pat someone on the back
back pay someone a back-handed compliment
back pin someone's ears back
back put one's back (in)to something
back put something on the back burner
back roll something back
back scratch someone's back
back set one back on one's heels
back set someone back (some amount of money)
back sit back and let something happen
back stab someone in the back
back stand (in) back of someone or something
back take something back
back talk back (to someone)
back think back (on someone or something)
back turn one's back (on someone or something)
back turn the clock back
back with both hands tied behind one's back
back with one hand tied behind one's back
back You scratch my back and I'll scratch yours.
back a crick in one's back
backseat take a backseat (to someone)
backside (as) bald as a baby's backside
backside bald as a baby's backside
backwards bend over backwards (to do something)
backwards fall over backwards (to do something)
backwards know something backwards and forwards
backwards know something forwards and backwards
backwards lean over backwards (to do something)
backyard in one's (own) backyard
bacon bring home the bacon
bad (as) bad as all that
bad bad as all that
bad bad blood (between people)
bad bad-mouth someone or something
bad be off to a bad start
bad come to a bad end
bad get off to a bad start
bad go bad
bad go from bad to worse
bad good riddance (to bad rubbish)
bad have a bad effect (on someone or something)
bad have a run of bad luck
bad in a bad mood
bad in a bad way
bad in bad faith
bad in bad sorts
bad in bad taste
bad in bad (with someone)
bad leave a bad taste in someone's mouth
bad not half bad
bad put someone down as something bad
bad throw good money after bad
bag bag and baggage
bag bag of tricks
bag leave someone holding the bag
bag let the cat out of the bag
bag put on the feed bag
bag a mixed bag
baggage bag and baggage
bail bail out (of something)
bail bail someone or something out
bail jump bail
bail out on bail
bail skip bail
bait bait and switch
bait fish or cut bait
bait rise to the bait
balance balance the accounts
balance balance the books
balance catch someone off-balance
balance hang in the balance
balance in the balance
balance strike a balance (between two or more things)
balances checks and balances
bald (as) bald as a baby's backside
bald (as) bald as a coot
bald bald as a baby's backside
bald bald as a coot
baleful (as) baleful as death
baleful baleful as death
ball ball and chain
ball ball of fire
ball behind the eight ball
ball carry the ball
ball drop the ball
ball get the ball rolling
ball have a ball
ball have something on the ball
ball have the ball in one's court
ball keep one's eye on the ball
ball keep the ball rolling
ball new ball game
ball on the ball
ball pitch someone a curve (ball)
ball play ball (with someone)
ball set the ball rolling
ball start the ball rolling
ball That's the way the ball bounces.
ball (whole) new ball game

ball the whole ball of wax
balled (all) balled up
balled balled up
balloon go over like a lead balloon
balloon send up a trial balloon
ballot stuff the ballot box
balls the balls of one's feet
bananas go bananas
band to beat the band
bandwagon climb on the bandwagon
bandwagon get on the bandwagon
bandwagon jump on the bandwagon
bang bang one's head against a brick wall
bang get a bang out of someone or something
bang give someone a bang
bang go over with a bang
bank bank on something
bank break the bank
bank can take it to the bank.
bank laugh all the way to the bank
baptism baptism of fire
barber's (as) conceited as a barber's cat
barber's conceited as a barber's cat
bare the bare something
bargain bargain for something
bargain bargain on something
bargain drive a hard bargain
bargain hold one's end (of the bargain) up
bargain in the bargain
bargain live up to one's end of the bargain
bargain strike a bargain
bargain throw something into the bargain
bargained more than someone bargained for
barge barge in (on someone or something)
bark bark up the wrong tree
bark One's bark is worse than one's bite.
barn all around Robin Hood's barn
barn (as) broad as a barn door
barn broad as a barn door
barn raised in a barn
barred no holds barred
barrel (as) crooked as a barrel of fishhooks
barrel (as) funny as a barrel of monkeys
barrel as much fun as a barrel of monkeys
barrel crooked as a barrel of fishhooks
barrel funny as a barrel of monkeys
barrel get someone over a barrel
barrel lock, stock, and barrel
barrel more fun than a barrel of monkeys
barrel scrape the bottom of the barrel
barrelhead cash on the barrelhead
barrels let someone have it (with both barrels)
base base one's opinion on something
base get to first base (with someone or something)
base off base
base reach first base (with someone or something)
base steal a base
base touch base (with someone)
basis on a first-name basis (with someone)
basket put all one's eggs in one basket
bat (as) blind as a bat
bat blind as a bat
bat go to bat for someone
bat like a bat out of hell
bat not bat an eyelid
bat right off the bat
bath take a bath
bathroom go to the bathroom
bathwater throw the baby out with the bath(water)
bats have bats in one's belfry
batten batten down the hatches
battery assault and battery
batting without batting an eye
battle battle something out
bawl bawl someone out
bay at bay
be acknowledge someone to be right
be (as) happy as can be
be be about something
be be a heartbeat away from something
be be-all and (the) end-all
be be all ears
be be all eyes (and ears)
be be all things to all men
be be all things to all people
be be a million miles away
be be a new one on someone
be be curtains for someone or something
be be death on something
be (be) easier said than done
be be flying high
be be friends with someone
be be from Missouri
be be game
be Beggars can't be choosers.
be be into something
be be off
be be of service (to someone)
be be of the persuasion that something is so
be be reluctant to do something
be be sick
be be so
be be swimming in something
be be that as it may
be be the case
be be the death of me (yet)
be be the last straw
be be the spit and image of someone
be be the spitting image of someone
be be the straw that broke the camel's back
be be to do something
be be too
be be used to doing something
be be used to something
be be with someone
be Boys will be boys.
be Could be better.
be Could be worse.
be couldn't be better
be couldn't be happier
be cut out to be something
be deem it (to be) necessary
be far be it from me to do something
be fit to be tied

be for the odds to be against one
be happy as can be
be leave a lot to be desired
be Let bygones be bygones.
be meant to be
be not all something is cracked up to be
be not what something is cracked up to be
be old enough to be someone's father
be old enough to be someone's mother
be prove to be something
be So be it.
be stand up and be counted
be That'll be the day.
be There will be the devil to pay.
be to be on the safe side
be to be safe
be too good to be true
be Whatever will be, will be.
be a force to be reckoned with
be the be-all and (the) end-all
be the powers that be
bead draw a bead on someone or something
beam broad in the beam
beam on the beam
beans full of beans
beans not know beans (about someone or something)
beans not worth a hill of beans
beans spill the beans
bear (as) busy as a hibernating bear
bear (as) gruff as a bear
bear (as) hungry as a bear
bear bear a grudge (against someone)
bear bear fruit
bear bear in mind that something is so
bear bear one's cross
bear bear someone or something in mind
bear bear something out
bear bear the brunt (of something)
bear bear watching
bear bear with someone or something
bear busy as a hibernating bear
bear grin and bear it
bear gruff as a bear
bear hungry as a bear
bear loaded for bear
bear more than one can bear
beard beard the lion in his den
bearing have bearing on something
bearings get one's bearings
beat beat about the bush
beat beat a dead horse
beat beat a (hasty) retreat
beat beat a path to someone's door
beat beat around the bush
beat beat one's brains out (to do something)
beat beat one's head against the wall
beat beat someone down (to size)
beat beat someone to the draw
beat beat someone to the punch
beat beat someone up
beat beat something into someone's head
beat beat the clock
beat beat the gun
beat beat the living daylights out of someone
beat beat the pants off someone
beat beat the rap
beat beat the stuffing out of someone
beat beat the tar out of someone
beat march to (the beat of) a different drummer
beat one's heart misses a beat
beat one's heart skips a beat
beat pound a beat
beat to beat the band
beaten off the (beaten) track
Beauty Beauty is only skin-deep.
beaver (as) busy as a beaver
beaver busy as a beaver
beaver an eager beaver
beck at someone's beck and call
becoming becoming on someone
becoming becoming to someone
bed Early to bed, early to rise(, makes a man healthy, wealthy, and wise.)
bed get out of the wrong side of the bed
bed get up on the wrong side of the bed
bed go to bed
bed make a bed
bed make someone's bed
bed make the bed
bed put someone or something to bed
bed put someone to bed with a shovel
bed should have stood in bed
bed sick in bed
bed a bed of roses
bee (as) busy as a bee
bee busy as a bee
bee get a bee in one's bonnet
bee have a bee in one's bonnet
bee put a bee in someone's bonnet
beef beef something up
beeline make a beeline for someone or something
been have been around
been have been had
been have been through the mill
been have been to hell and back
been Have you been keeping busy?
been How's the world (been) treating you?
been Life's been good (to me).
been What have you been up to?
been Where've you been hiding yourself?
been the moment everyone has been waiting for
beer (all) beer and skittles
beer beer and skittles
bees the birds and the bees
beeswax none of someone's beeswax
before before long
before before you can say Jack Robinson
before before you know it
before cast (one's) pearls before swine
before count one's chickens before they hatch
before cross a bridge before one comes to it
before cry before one is hurt
before Pride goes before a fall.
before put the cart before the horse

before think twice (before doing something)
before the calm before the storm
before the lull before the storm
before the morning after (the night before)
beg beg off (on something)
beg beg the question
beg beg to differ (with someone)
beggar beggar description
Beggars Beggars can't be choosers.
begging go begging
begin begin to see daylight
begin begin to see the light
beginning beginning of the end
behalf in behalf of someone
behalf in someone's behalf
behalf on behalf of someone
behalf on someone's behalf
behavior get time off for good behavior
behavior on one's best behavior
behind behind closed doors
behind behind in something
behind behind on something
behind behind schedule
behind behind someone's back
behind behind the eight ball
behind behind the scenes
behind behind the times
Behind Behind you!
behind burn one's bridges (behind one)
behind close ranks (behind someone or something)
behind driving force (behind someone or something)
behind not dry behind the ears
behind stand behind someone or something
behind wet behind the ears
behind with both hands tied behind one's back
behind with one hand tied behind one's back
behind the power behind the throne
behold a marvel to behold
behooves It behooves one to do something.
being for the time being
being into being
being other things being equal
belabor belabor the point
belfry have bats in one's belfry
believe believe it or not
believe lead someone to believe something
believe not believe one's eyes
believing seeing is believing
bell (as) clear as a bell
bell bell, book, and candle
bell clear as a bell
bell ring a bell
bell saved by the bell
bells with bells on (one's toes)
belong To the victors belong the spoils.
below below average
below below par
below hit (someone) below the belt
belt belt something out
belt get something under one's belt
belt hit (someone) below the belt
belt tighten one's belt
bench on the bench
bench warm the bench
bend bend over backwards (to do something)
bend bend someone's ear
bend go (a)round the bend
bended on bended knee
beneath feel it beneath one (to do something)
benefit get the benefit of the doubt
benefit give someone the benefit of the doubt
benefit of benefit (to someone)
bent bent on doing something
bent hell-bent for leather
berth give someone or something a wide berth
beside beside oneself (with something)
beside beside the point
beside beside the question
best (all) for the best
best at best
best at one's best
best best bib and tucker
best come off second-best
best do one's (level) best
best even in the best of times
best far and away the best
best for the best
best get the best of someone
best give something one's best shot
best had best do something
best have the best of both worlds
best He laughs best who laughs last.
best in one's (own) (best) interest(s)
best in one's Sunday best
best in the best of health
best make the best of something
best on one's best behavior
best put one's best foot forward
best to the best of one's ability
best to the best of one's knowledge
best with the best will in the world
best work out for the best
best the best-laid plans of mice and men
best the best-laid schemes of mice and men
best the best part of something
bet bet one's bottom dollar
bet bet one's life
bet You bet (your boots)!
bet You can bet on it!
bets hedge one's bets
betsy (as) crazy as a betsy bug
betsy crazy as a betsy bug
better all better now
better better late than never
better better off (doing something)
better better off (if one were somewhere else)
better better off (if something were done)
better better off (somewhere)
better Could be better.
better couldn't be better
better do someone one better
better for better or for worse
better for the better
better get better

better get the better of someone
better go on to a better land
better go someone one better
better had better do something
better Half a loaf is better than none.
better have seen better days
better know better (than to do something)
better one's better half
better so much the better
better take a turn for the better
better think better of something
between bad blood (between people)
between between a rock and a hard place
between between life and death
between between the devil and the deep blue sea
between between you, me, and the lamppost
between betwixt and between
between draw a line between something and something else
between fall between two stools
between few and far between
between hit someone (right) between the eyes
between in between
between in the interim (between things)
between no love lost (between someone and someone else)
between read between the lines
between strike a balance (between two or more things)
between take the bit between the teeth
between torn between bad choices
between torn between choosing something or something else
between with one's tail between one's legs
betwixt betwixt and between
beware Let the buyer beware.
beyond above and beyond (something)
beyond (above and) beyond the call of duty
beyond back of the beyond
beyond beyond a reasonable doubt
beyond beyond measure
beyond beyond one's depth
beyond beyond one's means
beyond beyond the call of duty
beyond beyond the pale
beyond beyond the shadow of a doubt
beyond beyond words
beyond can't see beyond the end of one's nose
beyond live beyond one's means
bias on a bias
bias on the bias
bib best bib and tucker
Bibles swear on a stack of Bibles
bid bid adieu to someone or something
bid bid someone or something adieu
bidding do someone's bidding
bide bide one's time
big (as) big as all outdoors
big (as) big as life
big big and bold
big big as all outdoors
big big as life
big big of someone
big cut a big swath
big get a big send-off
big give someone a big send-off
big go over big with someone
big have a big mouth
big Like it's such a big deal!
big make a big deal about something
big No big deal!
big talk big
big too big for one's britches
big a big frog in a small pond
big the big moment
bigger have bigger fish to fry
bigger have eyes bigger than one's stomach
bigger One's eyes are bigger than one's stomach.
bill (as) phony as a three-dollar bill
bill (as) queer as a three-dollar bill
bill fill the bill
bill fit the bill
bill foot the bill
bill get a clean bill of health
bill give someone a clean bill of health
bill pad the bill
bill phony as a three-dollar bill
bill queer as a three-dollar bill
bill sell someone a bill of goods
bind in a bind
binge binge and purge
binge go on a binge
bird (as) free as a bird
bird early bird
bird eat like a bird
bird free as a bird
bird A bird in the hand is worth two in the bush.
bird A little bird told me.
bird The early bird gets the worm.
Birds Birds of a feather flock together.
birds for the birds
birds kill two birds with one stone
bird's a bird's-eye view
birds the birds and the bees
birth give birth to someone or some creature
birth give birth to something
birthday in one's birthday suit
biscuit son of a sea biscuit
bit champ at the bit
bit chomp at the bit
bit do one's bit
bit in a little bit
bit not a bit
bit one little bit
bit quite a bit
bit take the bit between the teeth
bit take the bit in one's teeth
bit a little bit
bit the hair of the dog that bit one
bitch son of a bitch
bite bite off more than one can chew
bite bite one's nails
bite bite one's tongue
bite bite someone's head off
bite bite the bullet
bite bite the dust

bite bite the hand that feeds one
bite grab a bite (to eat)
bite One's bark is worse than one's bite.
bite put the bite on someone
bitter take the bitter with the sweet
bitter to the bitter end
bitter a bitter pill to swallow
black (as) black as a skillet
black (as) black as a stack of black cats
black (as) black as a sweep
black (as) black as coal
black (as) black as night
black (as) black as one is painted
black (as) black as pitch
black (as) black as the ace of spades
black black-and-blue
black black as a skillet
black black as a stack of black cats
black black as a sweep
black black as coal
black black as night
black black as one is painted
black black as pitch
black black as the ace of spades
black black out
black get a black eye
black give someone a black eye
black in black and white
black in the black
black pitch-black
black put something down in black and white
black the black sheep of the family
black the pot calling the kettle black
blame lay the blame on someone or something
blame place the blame on someone or something
blame put the blame on someone or something
blanche give carte blanche to someone
blanche give someone carte blanche
blank draw a blank
blank give a blank check to someone
blank give someone a blank check
blanket wet blanket
blast (at) full blast
blast blast off
blast full blast
blaze blaze a trail (in something)
bleep bleep something out
blessing a blessing in disguise
blessings thankful for small blessings
blind (as) blind as a bat
blind blind as a bat
blind turn a blind eye to someone or something
blind up a blind alley
blind the blind leading the blind
blindfolded able to do something blindfolded
blink on the blink
block knock someone's block off
block on the block
block put one's head on the block (for someone or something)
block stumbling block
block a chip off the old block
blood (as) red as blood
blood bad blood (between people)
Blood Blood is thicker than water.
Blood Blood runs thicker than water.
blood blood, sweat, and tears
blood blue blood
blood curdle someone's blood
blood draw blood
blood flesh and blood
blood have someone's blood on one's hands
blood in cold blood
blood in one's blood
blood in the blood
blood make someone's blood boil
blood make someone's blood run cold
blood new blood
blood red as blood
blood (some) new blood
blood sweat blood
bloody bloody but unbowed
bloody cry bloody murder
bloody scream bloody murder
bloom in bloom
blossom in blossom
blow blow a fuse
blow blow a gasket
blow blow-by-blow account
blow blow-by-blow description
blow blow hot and cold
blow blow off steam
blow blow one's cookies
blow blow one's cool
blow blow one's cork
blow blow one's lines
blow blow one's lunch
blow blow one's nose
blow blow one's own horn
blow blow one's stack
blow blow one's top
blow blow over
blow blow someone or something away
blow blow someone or something off
blow blow someone or something to smithereens
blow blow someone's cover
blow blow someone's mind
blow blow something
blow blow the lid off (something)
blow blow the whistle (on someone)
blow blow up
blowing see which way the wind is blowing
blowout have a blowout
blows come to blows (over something)
blue between the devil and the deep blue sea
blue black-and-blue
blue blue around the gills
blue blue blood
blue burn with a low blue flame
blue come out of the blue
blue like a bolt out of the blue
blue once in a blue moon
blue out of a clear blue sky
blue out of the blue

blue talk a blue streak
blue talk until one is blue in the face
blues get the blues
bluff call someone's bluff
blush at first blush
boar (as) crazy as a peach-orchard boar
boar crazy as a peach-orchard boar
board across the board
board (as) flat as a board
board back to the drawing board
board flat as a board
board go by the board
board on board
board room and board
boat in the same boat (as someone)
boat miss the boat
boat rock the boat
bodies know where all the bodies are buried
body arrive in a body
body come in a body
body go in a body
body keep body and soul together
body over my dead body
bog bog down
boggle boggle someone's mind
boil boil down to something
boil boil something down
boil make someone's blood boil
boiling have a low boiling point
bold (as) bold as brass
bold big and bold
bold bold as brass
bolt like a bolt out of the blue
bolt sit bolt upright
bolts the nuts and bolts (of something)
bombshell drop a bomb(shell)
bombshell explode a bombshell
bone (as) dry as a bone
bone bone of contention
bone bone up (on something)
bone chilled to the bone
bone cut someone or something to the bone
bone dry as a bone
bone have a bone to pick (with someone)
bone work one's fingers to the bone
boner pull a boner
bones (all) skin and bones
bones feel something in one's bones
bones know something in one's bones
bones Make no bones about it.
bones nothing but skin and bones
bones skin and bones
bonnet get a bee in one's bonnet
bonnet have a bee in one's bonnet
bonnet put a bee in someone's bonnet
book bell, book, and candle
book by the book
book coffee-table book
book crack a book
book go by the book
book have one's nose in a book
book in one's book
book know someone or something like a book
book (like) an open book
book make book on something
book read someone like a(n open) book
book someone wrote the book on something
book take a leaf out of someone's book
book throw the book at someone
book use every trick in the book
book an open book
books balance the books
books close the books (on someone or something)
books hit the books
books one for the (record) books
boom lower the boom on someone
boot (as) tough as an old boot
boot boot someone out
boot get the boot
boot give someone the boot
boot to boot
boot tough as an old boot
boots die in one's boots
boots die with one's boots on
boots quake in one's boots
boots shake in one's boots
boots You bet (your boots)!
bootstraps pull oneself up (by one's own bootstraps)
borderline on the borderline
bore bore someone stiff
bore bore someone to death
bored bored silly
bored bored stiff
bored bored to death
bored bored to distraction
bored bored to tears
boredom die of boredom
born born and bred
born born and raised
born born out of wedlock
born born with a silver spoon in one's mouth
born in all one's born days
born not born yesterday
borrow borrow trouble
borrowed live on borrowed time
boss boss someone around
both burn the candle at both ends
both cut both ways
both have a foot in both camps
both have it both ways
both have the best of both worlds
both land on both feet
both let someone have it (with both barrels)
both make (both) ends meet
both play both ends (against the middle)
both with both hands tied behind one's back
bothered hot and bothered
bottle bottle something up
bottle crack open a bottle
bottle hit the bottle
bottom (as) soft as a baby's bottom
bottom at the bottom of the hour
bottom at the bottom of the ladder
bottom bet one's bottom dollar

bottom bottom out
bottom from the bottom of one's heart
bottom from top to bottom
bottom get to the bottom of something
bottom hit bottom
bottom learn something from the bottom up
bottom scrape the bottom of the barrel
bottom soft as a baby's bottom
bottom the bottom line
Bottoms Bottoms up!
bounces That's the way the ball bounces.
bound bound and determined
bound bound for somewhere
bound bound hand and foot
bound bound to (do something)
bound duty bound (to do something)
bounds by leaps and bounds
bounds out of bounds
bounds within bounds
bow bow and scrape
bow bow out
bow take a bow
bowl bowl someone over
box inside the box
box open Pandora's box
box outside the box
box stuff the ballot box
box thinking inside the box
box thinking outside the box
box think inside the box
box think outside the box
boy All work and no play makes Jack a dull boy.
boy fair-haired boy
Boys Boys will be boys.
boys separate the men from the boys
brain brain someone
brain have something on the brain
brains beat one's brains out (to do something)
brains pick someone's brain(s)
brains rack one's brain(s)
branch hold out the olive branch
brass (as) bold as brass
brass bold as brass
brass double in brass
brass get down to brass tacks
brave put on a brave face
brave put on a (brave) front
brave put up a (brave) front
breach step in(to the breach)
bread bread-and-butter letter
bread bread and water
bread know which side one's bread is buttered on
bread someone's bread and butter
bread the greatest thing since sliced bread
breadth by a hair('s breadth)
break at the break of dawn
break break a code
break break a habit
break break a law
Break Break a leg!
break break a record
break break camp
break break down
break break even
break break ground (for something)
Break Break it up!
break break loose (from someone or something)
break break new ground
break break off (with someone)
break break one's back (to do something)
break break one's habit
break break one's neck (to do something)
break break one's word
break break out
break break (out) in(to) tears
break break someone or something down
break break someone or something in
break break someone or something up
break break someone's fall
break break someone's heart
break break something down (for someone)
break break something down (into something)
break break something to pieces
break break something to someone
break break the back of something
break break the bank
break break the habit
break break the ice
break break the law
break break the news (to someone)
break break through (something)
break break up (with someone)
break get a break
break give someone a break
break make a break for something or somewhere
break make or break someone
break take a break
break take one's break
break tough break
breaking breaking and entering
breast make a clean breast of something
breath (all) in one breath
breath catch one's breath
breath Don't hold your breath.
breath get time to catch one's breath
breath hold one's breath
breath in one breath
breath in the same breath
breath out of breath
breath save one's breath
breath say something under one's breath
breath take someone's breath away
breath time to catch one's breath
breath waste one's breath
breath with every (other) breath
breath a breath of fresh air
breathe able to breathe (easily) again
breathe able to breathe (freely) again
breathe breathe down someone's neck
breathe breathe easy
breathe breathe one's last
breathe hardly have time to breathe
breathe not breathe a word (about someone or something)

breathe not breathe a word of it
breathe scarcely have time to breathe
bred born and bred
breeds Familiarity breeds contempt.
breeze shoot the breeze
brew brew a plot
brewing There is trouble brewing.
brewing Trouble is brewing.
brewing A storm is brewing.
brick bang one's head against a brick wall
brick drop a brick
bricks bricks and mortar
bricks hit (someone) like a ton of bricks
bricks hit the bricks
bricks two bricks shy of a load
bride give the bride away
bridge cross a bridge before one comes to it
bridge cross a bridge when one comes to it
bridge water under the bridge
bridges burn one's bridges (behind one)
bridges burn one's bridges in front of one
brief hold no brief for someone or something
brief in brief
bright (as) bright as a button
bright (as) bright as a new pin
bright bright and early
bright bright as a button
bright bright as a new pin
bright bright-eyed and bushy-tailed
bright get a bright idea
bright give someone a bright idea
brim filled to the brim
brimming brimming with something
bring bring down the curtain (on something)
bring bring down the house
bring bring home the bacon
bring bring people or other creatures out in droves
bring bring someone or something up
bring bring someone around
bring bring someone to
bring bring someone up-to-date (on someone or something)
bring bring someone or something up-to-date
bring bring something about
bring bring something crashing down (around one)
bring bring something home to someone
bring bring something into question
bring bring something off
bring bring something to a head
bring bring something to light
bring bring something to someone's attention
bring bring up the rear
britches too big for one's britches
broad (as) broad as a barn door
broad broad as a barn door
broad broad in the beam
broad have broad shoulders
broad in broad daylight
Broadway on Broadway
broke be the straw that broke the camel's back
broke flat broke
broke go broke
broke go for broke
broken die of a broken heart
broken sound like a broken record
broth Too many cooks spoil the broth.
brother's one's brother's keeper
brow by the sweat of one's brow
brow knit one's brow
brown do something up brown
brunt bear the brunt (of something)
brush brush up (on something)
brush get the brush-off
brush give someone the brush-off
brush have a brush with something
brush tarred with the same brush
bubble burst someone's bubble
buck buck for something
buck buck up
buck make a fast buck
buck make a quick buck
buck pass the buck
bucket kick the bucket
bucket a drop in the bucket
buckle buckle down (to something)
bud nip something in the bud
buff in the buff
bug (as) crazy as a betsy bug
bug (as) snug as a bug in a rug
bug bug out
bug bug someone
bug crazy as a betsy bug
bug snug as a bug in a rug
buggy horse and buggy
build build a case (against someone)
build build a fire under someone
build build castles in Spain
build build castles in the air
build build (someone or something) up
build build something to order
build build up to something
building busy as a beaver (building a new dam)
built Rome wasn't built in a day.
bulk in bulk
bull cock-and-bull story
bull full of bull
bull seize the bull by the horns
bull shoot the bull
bull take the bull by the horns
bull a bull in a china shop
bullet bite the bullet
bullpen in the bullpen
bull's hit the bull's-eye
bum give someone a bum steer
bump bump into someone
bump bump someone off
bump like a bump on a log
bumps get goose bumps
bumps give someone goose bumps
bum's give someone the bum's rush
bundle make a bundle
bundle a bundle of nerves
burden groan under the burden of something
buried dead and buried
buried know where all the bodies are buried

burn burn (oneself) out
burn burn one's bridges (behind one)
burn burn one's bridges in front of one
burn burn out
burn burn someone or something to a crisp
burn burn someone at the stake
burn burn someone in effigy
burn burn someone up
burn burn the candle at both ends
burn burn the midnight oil
burn burn with a low blue flame
burn crash and burn
burn have money to burn
burned burned to a cinder
burned burned up
burned get one's fingers burned
burner put something on the back burner
burning keep the home fires burning
burns fiddle while Rome burns
burns Money burns a hole in someone's pocket.
burst burst at the seams
burst burst in on someone or something
burst burst into flames
burst burst into tears
burst burst onto the scene
burst burst out crying
burst burst out laughing
burst burst someone's bubble
burst burst with joy
burst burst with pride
bury bury one's head in the sand
bury bury the hatchet
bush beat about the bush
bush beat around the bush
bush A bird in the hand is worth two in the bush.
bushel hide one's light under a bushel
bushy bright-eyed and bushy-tailed
business business as usual
business do a land-office business
business drum some business up
business funny business
business get down to business
business get one's nose out of someone's business
business give someone the business
business go about one's business
business have no business doing something
business keep one's nose out of someone's business
business make it one's business to do something
business mean business
business mind one's own business
business monkey business
business none of someone's business
business open for business
business send one about one's business
business set someone up (in business)
business someone's place of business
business the business end of something
busman's a busman's holiday
bust bust a gut (to do something)
bustle hustle and bustle
busy (as) busy as a beaver
busy (as) busy as a bee
busy (as) busy as a cat on a hot tin roof
busy (as) busy as a hibernating bear
busy (as) busy as a one-armed paperhanger
busy (as) busy as Grand Central Station
busy (as) busy as popcorn on a skillet
busy busy as a beaver
busy busy as a bee
busy busy as a cat on a hot tin roof
busy busy as a hibernating bear
busy busy as a one-armed paperhanger
busy busy as Grand Central Station
busy busy as popcorn on a skillet
busy get busy
busy Have you been keeping busy?
but all over but the shouting
but bloody but unbowed
but but for someone or something
but can't help but do something
but everything but the kitchen sink
but gone but not forgotten
but It never rains but it pours.
but last but not least
but nothing but skin and bones
but nothing but something
but poor but clean
but sadder but wiser
but separate but equal
but slow(ly) but sure(ly)
buts no buts about it
buts no ifs, ands, or buts about it
butt butt in (on someone or something)
butter bread-and-butter letter
butter butter someone up
butter look as if butter wouldn't melt in one's mouth
butter someone's bread and butter
buttered know which side one's bread is buttered on
butterflies get butterflies in one's stomach
butterflies give one butterflies in one's stomach
butterfly (as) gaudy as a butterfly
butterfly gaudy as a butterfly
button (as) bright as a button
button bright as a button
button button one's lip
button on the button
button press the panic button
button push the panic button
buy buy a pig in a poke
buy buy someone off
buy buy something
buy not buy something
buyer Let the buyer beware.
buzz give someone a buzz
by abide by something
by blow-by-blow account
by blow-by-blow description
by by a hair('s breadth)
by by all accounts
by by all appearances
by by all means
by by a mile
by by and by
by by and large

by by any means
by by a show of hands
by by a whisker
by by chance
by by check
by by choice
by by coincidence
by by day
by by dint of something
by by fits and starts
by by guess and by golly
by by herself
by by himself
by by hook or (by) crook
by by itself
by by leaps and bounds
by by means of something
by by mistake
by by myself
by by night
by by no means
by by oneself
by by ourselves
by by return mail
by by shank's mare
by by the
by by virtue of something
by by way of something
by by word of mouth
by by yourself
by by yourselves
by cheek by jowl
by come by something
by conspicuous by one's absence
by crushed by something
by do somehow by someone
by do something by hand
by down by some amount
by drop by (sometime)
by drop by the wayside
by easy to come by
by end up by doing something
by fall by the wayside
by fly-by-night
by get by (on something)
by get by (with something)
by get the go-by
by give someone the go-by
by go by the board
by go by the book
by go (somewhere) by shank's mare
by hang by a hair
by hang by a thread
by hoist by one's own petard
by inch by inch
by judging by something
by know someone by sight
by know something by heart
by lay something by
by lead someone by the nose
by learn something by heart
by learn something by rote
by let something slide by
by let something slip by
by let the chance slip by
by little by little
by live by one's wits
by miss (something) by a mile
by not by a long shot
by one by one
by play by ear
by play something by ear
by possessed by something
by pull oneself up (by one's own bootstraps)
by put off by someone or something
by put something by
by put upon by someone
by run that by (someone) again
by saved by the bell
by seize the bull by the horns
by set great store by someone or something
by sit (idly) by
by squeak by (someone or something)
by stand by
by step-by-step
by stick by someone or something
by stop by (somewhere)
by swear by someone or something
by take someone or something by storm
by take someone or something by surprise
by take someone by surprise
by take the bull by the horns
by touched by someone or something
by win by a nose
by word by word
by a play-by-play description
bye kiss something good-bye
bygones Let bygones be bygones.
byways highways and byways
caboodle kit and caboodle
cahoots in cahoots (with someone)
cain raise cain (with someone or something)
cake eat one's cake and have it too
cake have one's cake and eat it too
cake piece of cake
cake take the cake
cake a slice of the cake
calf kill the fatted calf
call (above and) beyond the call of duty
call at someone's beck and call
call beyond the call of duty
call call a meeting
call call a spade a spade
call call for someone or something
call call it a day
call call it a night
call call it quits
call call of nature
call call on someone
call call out (to someone)
call call someone or something in
call call someone or something off
call call someone or something up
call call someone's bluff

call call someone down
call call someone names
call call someone on the carpet
call call the dogs off
call call the meeting to order
call call (the) roll
call call the shots
call call the tune
call have a close call
call issue a call for something
call not able to call one's time one's own
call on call
call pay a call on someone
call a place to call one's own
calling within calling distance
calling the pot calling the kettle black
calls He who pays the piper calls the tune.
calm (as) calm as a toad in the sun
calm calm as a toad in the sun
calm the calm before the storm
camel's be the straw that broke the camel's back
camp break camp
camp pitch camp
campaign smear campaign (against someone)
camps have a foot in both camps
campus off campus
campus on campus
can (as) happy as can be
can before you can say Jack Robinson
can bite off more than one can chew
can can take it to the bank.
Can Can you imagine?
can catch-as-catch-can
can happy as can be
can more someone or something than one can shake a stick at
can more than one can bear
can more than one can stand
can more than one can take
can No can do.
can open (up) a can of worms
can What can I say?
can You can bet on it!
can You can say that again!
can a game that two can play
canary look like the cat that swallowed the canary
cancel cancel something out
candle bell, book, and candle
candle burn the candle at both ends
candle can't hold a candle to someone
candle not hold a candle to someone or something
cannot cannot help doing something
cannot cannot stomach someone or something
canoe paddle one's own canoe
can't Beggars can't be choosers.
can't can't carry a tune
can't can't do anything with someone or something
can't can't help but do something
can't can't hold a candle to someone
can't can't make heads or tails (out) of someone or something
can't can't see beyond the end of one's nose
can't can't see one's hand in front of one's face
can't can't stand (the sight of) someone or something
can't can't stomach someone or something
can't can't wait (for something to happen)
can't can't wait (to do something)
can't You can't please everyone.
can't You can't take it with you.
can't You can't teach an old dog new tricks.
cap cap and gown
cap put a cap on something
cap put one's thinking cap on
cap a feather in one's cap
capable capable of doing something
card play one's trump card
card a card
cards have the cards stacked against one
cards in the cards
cards keep one's cards close to one's chest
cards keep one's cards close to one's vest
cards lay one's cards on the table
cards play one's cards close to one's vest
cards play one's cards close to the chest
cards play one's cards right
cards play one's cards well
cards put one's cards on the table
cards stack the cards (against someone or something)
cards a few cards short of a deck
cards a few cards shy of a full deck
cards the cards are stacked against one
care could(n't) care less
care devil-may-care attitude
care devil-may-care manner
care do not have a care in the world
care for all I care
care in care of someone
care in the care of someone
care not care two hoots (about someone or something)
care take care of someone or something
care That takes care of that.
caress (as) cold as a witch's caress
caress cold as a witch's caress
carpet call someone on the carpet
carpet get the red-carpet treatment
carpet give someone the red-carpet treatment
carpet roll out the red carpet for someone
carpet sweep something under the carpet
carriage horse and carriage
carried carried away
carried get carried away
carry can't carry a tune
carry carry (a lot of) weight (with someone or something)
carry carry a secret to one's grave
carry carry a secret to the grave
carry carry a torch (for someone)
carry carry coals to Newcastle
carry carry on (about someone or something)
carry carry one's cross
carry carry one's (own) weight
carry carry on somehow
carry carry on without someone or something
carry carry on (with someone or something)
carry carry over

carry carry *something* off
carry carry *something* out
carry carry *something* over
carry carry the ball
carry carry the day
carry carry the torch
carry carry the weight of the world on *one's* shoulders
carry carry through (on *something*)
carry cash-and-carry
cart put the cart before the horse
cart upset the apple cart
carte give carte blanche to *someone*
carte give *someone* carte blanche
case assemble a case (against *someone*)
case be the case
case build a case (against *someone*)
case gather a case (against *someone*)
case Get off *someone's* case!
case have a case (against *someone*)
case in any case
case in case
case in the case of *someone or something*
case just in case (*something happens*)
case make a federal case out of *something*
case on *someone's* case
case an open-and-shut case
case a case in point
case a case of mistaken identity
cases get down to cases
cash cash-and-carry
cash cash in *one's* chips
cash cash in (on *something*)
cash cash on the barrelhead
cash cash or credit
cash cash *something* in
cash cold, hard cash
cast cast about for *someone or something*
cast cast around for *someone or something*
cast cast aspersions on *someone*
cast cast doubt(s) (on *someone or something*)
cast cast in the same mold
cast cast *one's* lot in with *someone*
cast cast (*one's*) pearls before swine
cast cast *one's* vote
cast cast the first stone
cast The die is cast.
castles build castles in Spain
castles build castles in the air
cat (as) busy as a cat on a hot tin roof
cat (as) conceited as a barber's cat
cat busy as a cat on a hot tin roof
Cat Cat got your tongue?
cat conceited as a barber's cat
cat Curiosity killed the cat.
cat let the cat out of the bag
cat look like *something* the cat dragged in
cat look like the cat that swallowed the canary
cat not enough room to swing a cat
cat play cat and mouse (with *someone*)
cat There's more than one way to skin a cat.
catch catch-as-catch-can
catch catch a whiff of *something*
catch catch cold
catch catch fire
catch catch forty winks
catch catch hell
catch catch it
catch catch *one's* breath
catch catch *one's* death (of cold)
catch catch *one* off *one's* guard
catch catch *one* with *one's* pants down
catch catch (on) fire
catch catch on (to *someone or something*)
catch catch sight of *someone or something*
catch catch *someone's* eye
catch catch *someone* in the act (of *doing something*)
catch catch *someone* napping
catch catch *someone* off-balance
catch catch *someone* off guard
catch catch *someone* red-handed
catch catch some Zs
catch catch the devil
catch catch up (to *someone or something*)
catch catch up (with *someone or something*)
catch get time to catch *one's* breath
catch I didn't catch your name.
catch I'll (try to) catch you later.
catch not let *someone* catch *someone doing something*
catch not want to catch *someone doing something*
catch time to catch *one's* breath
cats (as) black as a stack of black cats
cats black as a stack of black cats
cats rain cats and dogs
cat's When the cat's away, the mice will play.
caught caught in the act
caught caught in the cross fire
caught caught in the middle
caught caught red-handed
caught caught short
caught caught unaware(s)
cause cause a commotion
cause cause a stir
cause cause (some) eyebrows to raise
cause cause (some) tongues to wag
cause a lost cause
caution throw caution to the wind
cave cave in (to *someone or something*)
cease cease and desist
ceiling hit the ceiling
cent not worth a red cent
center off-center
center on dead center
Central (as) busy as Grand Central Station
Central busy as Grand Central Station
cents' put *one's* two cents(' worth) in
century turn of the century
ceremony stand on ceremony
chain ball and chain
chair play first chair
chalk chalk *something* up to *something*
champ champ at the bit
chance by chance
chance chance *something*
chance chance (up)on *someone or something*

chance fat chance
chance have a snowball's chance in hell
chance jump at the chance
chance let the chance slip by
chance off chance
chance once-in-a-lifetime chance
chance on the off-chance
chance stand a chance
chance take a chance
chance a fighting chance
chance a ghost of a chance
chance a sporting chance
change and change
change change hands
change change horses in the middle of the stream
change change someone's mind
change change someone's tune
change change the subject
change have a change of heart
change a change of pace
change a change of scenery
changes go through the changes
channels go through channels
channels work through channels
chapter chapter and verse
character in character
character out of character
charge charge someone or something up
charge get a charge out of someone or something
charge give someone a charge
charge in the charge of someone
charge take charge (of someone or something)
charged charged up
charley get a charley horse
charm charm the pants off (of) someone
chase cut to the chase
chase give chase (to someone or something)
chase go chase oneself
chase lead someone on a merry chase
chase a wild-goose chase
cheap dirt cheap
cheat cheat on someone
check by check
check check in (on someone or something)
check check into something
check check out
check cut (someone) a check
check get a rain check (on something)
check give a blank check to someone
check give someone a blank check
check give someone a rain check (on something)
check hold someone or something in check
check honor someone's check
check keep someone or something in check
check make a check out (to someone)
check pick up the check
check take a rain check (on something)
checks checks and balances
checks someone or something checks out
checkup get a checkup
cheek cheek by jowl
cheek tongue-in-cheek
cheek turn the other cheek
cheer cheer someone on
cheer cheer someone up
cheer cheer up
cheesed cheesed off
cherry (as) red as a cherry
cherry red as a cherry
chest get something off one's chest
chest keep one's cards close to one's chest
chest play one's cards close to the chest
chew angry enough to chew nails
chew bite off more than one can chew
chew chew someone out
chew chew the fat
chew chew the rag
chew mad enough to chew nails
chicken chicken out (of something)
chicken for chicken feed
chicken no spring chicken
chicken run around like a chicken with its head cut off
chickens count one's chickens before they hatch
chickens go to bed with the chickens
chickens The chickens have come home to roost.
child expecting (a child)
childhood in one's second childhood
child's child's play
chilled chilled to the bone
chime chime in (with something)
chin keep one's chin up
chin make chin music
chin take it on the chin
chin take something on the chin
chin wag one's chin
china a bull in a china shop
chink chink in one's armor
chip chip in (on something)
chip chip in something on something
chip chip something in (on something)
chip have a chip on one's shoulder
chip a chip off the old block
chips cash in one's chips
chips chips and dip
chips in the chips
chips when the chips are down
chisel chisel someone out of something
choice by choice
choice Hobson's choice
choices torn between bad choices
choke choke someone up
choke choke something off
chomp chomp at the bit
choose choose up sides
choose nothing to choose from
choose pick and choose
choosers Beggars can't be choosers.
chops lick one's chops
chord strike a chord (with someone)
church (as) poor as a church mouse
church poor as a church mouse
church the separation of church and state
cinder burned to a cinder

circle come full circle
circle in a vicious circle
circles go (a)round in circles
circles run (around) in circles
circles run circles around someone
circles talk in circles
circulation back in circulation
circulation get back into circulation
circulation out of circulation
circumstances extenuating circumstances
circumstances under certain circumstances
circumstances under the circumstances
circus like a three-ring circus
civil keep a civil tongue (in one's head)
claim claim a life
claim stake a claim (to something)
clam (as) happy as a clam
clam clam up
clam happy as a clam
clamp clamp down (on someone or something)
clamps put the clamps on (someone)
clap clap eyes on someone or something
class cut class
clay have feet of clay
clean (as) clean as a hound's tooth
clean (as) clean as a whistle
clean clean as a hound's tooth
clean clean as a whistle
clean clean out (of something)
clean clean up
clean come clean (with someone)
clean get a clean bill of health
clean give someone a clean bill of health
clean have a clean conscience (about someone or something)
clean have clean hands
clean keep one's nose clean
clean make a clean breast of something
clean make a clean sweep
clean poor but clean
clean so clean you could eat off the floor
clean start (off) with a clean slate
clean start (over) with a clean slate
clean wipe someone's slate clean
cleaners take someone to the cleaners
clear (as) clear as a bell
clear (as) clear as crystal
clear (as) clear as mud
clear (as) clear as vodka
clear clear as a bell
clear clear as crystal
clear clear as mud
clear clear as vodka
clear clear of something
clear clear out
clear clear sailing
clear clear someone's name
clear clear something up
clear clear the air
clear clear the decks
clear clear the table
clear clear up
clear free and clear
clear have a clear conscience (about someone or something)
clear Have I made myself clear?
clear in the clear
clear loud and clear
clear make someone's position clear
clear out of a clear blue sky
clear see one's way clear (to do something)
clear steer clear (of someone or something)
clear The coast is clear.
climb climb on the bandwagon
climb climb the wall(s)
climb Go climb a tree!
clip clip someone's wings
cloak cloak-and-dagger
clock against the clock
clock (a)round the clock
clock (a)round-the-clock
clock beat the clock
clock round the clock
clock turn the clock back
clockwork (as) regular as clockwork
clockwork go like clockwork
clockwork regular as clockwork
clockwork run like clockwork
close (as) close as two coats of paint
close at close range
close close as two coats of paint
close close at hand
close close enough for government work
close close in (on someone or something)
close close one's eyes to something
close close ranks
close close something down
close close the books (on someone or something)
close close the door on someone or something
close close to home
close close to someone
close close up shop
close draw something to a close
close draw to a close
close get close (to someone or something)
close have a close call
close have a close shave
close hit one close to home
close keep a close rein on someone or something
close keep (close) watch (on someone or something)
close keep (close) watch (over someone or something)
close keep one's cards close to one's chest
close keep one's cards close to one's vest
close play one's cards close to one's vest
close play one's cards close to the chest
close too close for comfort
close under (close) scrutiny
closed able to do something with one's eyes closed
closed behind closed doors
closefisted closefisted (with money)
closet come out (of the closet)
closet a skeleton in the closet
cloth cut from the same cloth
cloth make something up out of whole cloth

clothes Sunday-go-to-meeting clothes
clothing a wolf in sheep's clothing
cloud cloud up
cloud Every cloud has a silver lining.
cloud on cloud nine
cloud under a cloud (of suspicion)
clouds have one's head in the clouds
clover in clover
club Join the club!
clue clue someone in (on something)
clue have a clue (about something)
clutch clutch at straws
clutches in(to) someone's clutches
coal (as) black as coal
coal black as coal
coals carry coals to Newcastle
coals haul someone over the coals
coals rake someone over the coals
coast coast-to-coast
coast The coast is clear.
coat coat and tie
coats (as) close as two coats of paint
coats close as two coats of paint
coattails hang on someone's coattails
coattails ride on someone's coattails
cock cock-and-bull story
cock cock of the walk
cocked go off half-cocked
cockles warm the cockles of someone's heart
cocky (as) cocky as the king of spades
cocky cocky as the king of spades
COD send something C.O.D.
code break a code
coffee coffee and Danish
coffee coffee-table book
coffee coffee, tea, or milk
coffin (another) nail in someone's or something's coffin
coffin nail in someone's or something's coffin
coil shuffle off this mortal coil
coincidence by coincidence
cold (as) cold as a witch's caress
cold (as) cold as a witch's tit
cold (as) cold as marble
cold blow hot and cold
cold break out in a cold sweat
cold catch cold
cold catch one's death (of cold)
cold cold as a witch's caress
cold cold as a witch's tit
cold cold as marble
cold cold comfort
cold cold, hard cash
cold dash cold water on something
cold get cold feet
cold get the cold shoulder
cold give someone the cold shoulder
cold go cold turkey
cold have cold feet
cold in cold blood
cold in cold storage
cold keep someone out in the cold
cold knock someone out (cold)
cold leave someone out in the cold
cold make someone's blood run cold
cold out cold
cold pour cold water on something
cold take cold
cold take one's death of cold
cold throw cold water on something
cold a cold fish
collar hot under the collar
collection take up a collection
college work one's way through college
color lend color to something
color off-color
color see the color of someone's money
color a horse of a different color
color a horse of another color
colors come through something with flying colors
colors sail under false colors
colors show one's (true) colors
colors with flying colors
coma lapse into a coma
comb go over something with a fine-tooth comb
comb search something with a fine-tooth comb
come come about
come come a cropper
come come across someone or something
Come Come again.
Come Come and get it!
come come and gone
come come apart at the seams
come come (a)round
come come as no surprise
come come away empty-handed
come come by something
come come clean (with someone)
come come down
come come from far and wide
come come from nowhere
come come full circle
come come hell or high water
come come home (to roost)
come come home to someone
come come in a body
come come in for something
come come in handy
come come in out of the rain
come come into its own
come come into one's own
come come into something
come come of age
come come off
come come on
come come out
come come over
come come someone's way
come come through
come come to
come come true
come come unglued
come come up
come come what may
come come within an ace of doing something

come come within an inch of doing something
come come with the territory
come easy come, easy go
come easy to come by
come First come, first served.
come have come a long way
come Johnny-come-lately
come not know enough to come in out of the rain
come till the cows come home
come (un)til the cows come home
come a dream come true
come a harbinger of things to come
come a portent of things to come
come a sign of things to come
come a taste of things to come
come The chickens have come home to roost.
comeback make a comeback
comes cross a bridge before one comes to it
comes cross a bridge when one comes to it
comes if push comes to shove
comes if worst comes to worst
comes What goes around, comes around.
comes when it comes right down to it
comes when it comes to something
comes when push comes to shove
comeuppance get one's comeuppance
comfort cold comfort
comfort too close for comfort
comfortable (as) comfortable as an old shoe
comfortable comfortable as an old shoe
comforts creature comforts
coming Everything's coming up roses.
coming get another guess coming
coming get another think coming
coming get what's coming to one
coming give one what's coming to one
coming (had) known it was coming
coming have something coming (to one)
coming knew it was coming
coming known it was coming
coming not know if one is coming or going
coming not know whether one is coming or going
coming up-and-coming
coming where one is coming from
command have a good command of something
comment No comment.
commission out of commission
commit commit something to memory
common (as) common as an old shoe
common (as) common as dirt
common common as an old shoe
common common as dirt
common have something in common (with someone or something)
commotion cause a commotion
company keep company (with someone)
company keep someone company
company part company (with someone)
company Two's company(, three's a crowd).
complain nothing to complain about
compliment fish for a compliment
compliment pay someone a back-handed compliment
compliment pay someone a compliment
compliment pay someone a left-handed compliment
compliment return someone's compliment
compliment return the compliment
composure regain one's composure
compromise reach a compromise
con con someone out of something
conceited (as) conceited as a barber's cat
conceited conceited as a barber's cat
concern to whom it may concern
concerned (as) far as someone or something is concerned
concerned far as something is concerned
concerned so far as someone or something is concerned
concerned so far as something is concerned
concert in concert (with someone)
conclusion a foregone conclusion
conclusions jump to conclusions
conclusions leap to conclusions
condition in condition
condition in good condition
condition in mint condition
condition in the pink (of condition)
condition out of condition
conditions under certain conditions
confide confide in someone
confidence take someone into one's confidence
confidence a vote of confidence
conk conk out
conniption have a conniption (fit)
conquer divide and conquer
conscience have a clean conscience (about someone or something)
conscience have a clear conscience (about someone or something)
conscience in (all) good conscience
consequence in consequence (of something)
consideration in consideration of something
consideration out of consideration (for someone or something)
consignment on consignment
conspicuous conspicuous by one's absence
conspicuous make oneself conspicuous
constant in a (constant) state of flux
construction under construction
contact have contact with someone
contempt Familiarity breeds contempt.
contempt in contempt (of court)
content to one's heart's content
contention bone of contention
context in the context of something
contradiction contradiction in terms
contrary contrary to something
contrary on the contrary
contrary to the contrary
control control the purse strings
control out of control
control under control
convenience at someone's earliest convenience
conversation open a conversation
conversation strike up a conversation
converted preach to the converted
convictions have the courage of one's convictions

cook cook someone's goose
cook cook something to perfection
cook cook something up
cook cook the accounts
cooked someone's goose is cooked
cookie That's the way the cookie crumbles.
cookies blow one's cookies
cookies juice and cookies
cookies toss one's cookies
cooking cooking with gas
cooks Too many cooks spoil the broth.
cooks Too many cooks spoil the stew.
cool (as) cool as a cucumber
cool blow one's cool
cool cool as a cucumber
cool cool down
Cool Cool it!
cool cool off
cool cool one's heels
cool cool someone down
cool cool someone off
cool keep cool
cool keep one's cool
cool lose one's cool
cool play it cool
coon's in a coon's age
coop fly the coop
coot (as) bald as a coot
coot bald as a coot
cop cop a plea
cop cop out
copycat a copycat
core rotten to the core
core to the core
cork blow one's cork
cork pop one's cork
corner have turned the corner
corner out of the corner of one's eye
corners cut corners
corrected stand corrected
cost at any cost
cost cost an arm and a leg
cost cost a pretty penny
costs at all costs
cough cough something up
Could Could be better.
Could Could be worse.
could could(n't) care less
could could do with someone or something
could if looks could kill
could so clean you could eat off the floor
could so mad I could scream
could so quiet you could hear a pin drop
could so still you could hear a pin drop
couldn't couldn't be better
couldn't couldn't be happier
couldn't could(n't) care less
couldn't Wild horses couldn't drag someone.
counsel keep one's own counsel
count count noses
count count one's chickens before they hatch
count count on someone or something
count count someone in (on something)
count count someone out (for something)
count down for the count
count to count heads
counted stand up and be counted
counter run counter to something
counter under the counter
country another country heard from
counts every minute counts
counts every moment counts
couple a couple of
courage Dutch courage
courage have the courage of one's convictions
courage muster (up) one's courage
courage pluck up one's courage
courage screw up one's courage
course as a matter of course
course course of action
course in due course
course in the course of time
course par for the course
course take a course (in something)
court have the ball in one's court
court in contempt (of court)
court laugh something out of court
court settle (something) (out of court)
court throw oneself at the mercy of the court
court throw oneself on the mercy of the court
courtesy out of courtesy (to someone)
cover blow someone's cover
cover cover a lot of ground
cover cover a lot of territory
cover cover for someone
cover cover someone's tracks (up)
cover cover something up
cover cover the territory
cover cover the waterfront
cover duck and cover
cow (as) awkward as a cow on a crutch
cow (as) awkward as a cow on roller skates
cow awkward as a cow on a crutch
cow awkward as a cow on roller skates
cow sacred cow
cows till the cows come home
cows (un)til the cows come home
cozy cozy up (to someone)
crack at the crack of dawn
crack crack a book
crack crack a joke
crack crack a smile
crack crack down (on someone or something)
crack crack open a bottle
crack crack someone or something up
crack crack something wide open
crack crack up
crack have a crack at something
crack take a crack at something
crack tough nut to crack
crack a hard nut to crack
cracked not all something is cracked up to be
cracked not what something is cracked up to be
cracking get cracking

cracks make cracks (about someone or something)
cracks paper over the cracks (in something)
cradle from the cradle to the grave
cradle rob the cradle
cramp cramp someone's style
crank crank something out
cranny every nook and cranny
crap You scared the crap out of me.
crash crash and burn
crashing bring something crashing down (around one)
craw have something stick in one's craw
crawl make someone's flesh crawl
crazy (as) crazy as a betsy bug
crazy (as) crazy as a loon
crazy (as) crazy as a peach-orchard boar
crazy crazy about someone or something
crazy crazy as a betsy bug
crazy crazy as a loon
crazy crazy as a peach-orchard boar
crazy crazy for someone or something
crazy drive someone crazy
crazy go crazy
crazy go stir-crazy
crazy like crazy
cream the cream of the crop
create create an uproar
create create a scene
create create a stink (about something)
creation in creation
creature creature comforts
creature give birth to someone or some creature
creature a match for someone, something, or some creature
creatures bring people or other creatures out in droves
credence give credence to something
credit buy something on credit
credit cash or credit
credit do credit to someone
credit do someone credit
credit extend credit (to someone)
credit extend someone credit
credit get credit (for something)
credit give credit where credit is due
credit give someone credit (for something)
credit on credit
credit sell something on credit
credit a credit to someone or something
creek up the creek (without a paddle)
creeps get the creeps
creeps give someone the creeps
crick a crick in one's back
crick a crick in one's neck
cricket (as) merry as a cricket
cricket merry as a cricket
crisp burn someone or something to a crisp
crocodile cry crocodile tears
crocodile shed crocodile tears
crook by hook or (by) crook
crooked (as) crooked as a barrel of fishhooks
crooked (as) crooked as a dog's hind leg
crooked (as) crooked as a fishhook
crooked crooked as a barrel of fishhooks
crooked crooked as a dog's hind leg
crooked crooked as a fishhook
crop the cream of the crop
cropper come a cropper
cross at cross-purposes
cross bear one's cross
cross carry one's cross
cross caught in the cross fire
cross cross a bridge before one comes to it
cross cross a bridge when one comes to it
cross cross-examine someone
cross cross one's fingers
cross cross one's heart (and hope to die)
cross cross someone's mind
cross cross someone's palm with silver
cross cross someone up
cross cross swords (with someone) (on something)
cross cross the Rubicon
cross double-cross someone
cross look at someone cross-eyed
crossed get one's wires crossed
crossed keep one's fingers crossed (for someone or something)
crow (as) hoarse as a crow
crow as the crow flies
crow hoarse as a crow
crow make someone eat crow
crowd follow the crowd
crowd Two's company(, three's a crowd).
crumbles That's the way the cookie crumbles.
crumpets tea and crumpets
crush get a crush on someone
crushed crushed by something
crust upper crust
crutch (as) awkward as a cow on a crutch
crutch (as) funny as a crutch
crutch awkward as a cow on a crutch
crutch funny as a crutch
crux the crux of the matter
cry cry before one is hurt
cry cry bloody murder
cry cry crocodile tears
cry cry one's eyes out
cry cry over spilled milk
cry cry wolf
cry a far cry from something
cry a hue and cry
crying burst out crying
crying crying need for someone or something
crying For crying out loud!
crying a crying shame
crystal (as) clear as crystal
crystal clear as crystal
cucumber (as) cool as a cucumber
cucumber cool as a cucumber
cue cue someone in
cue take one's cue from someone
cuff off-the-cuff
cuff put something on the cuff
cuff speak off the cuff
cup not someone's cup of tea
cups in one's cups

curdle curdle someone's blood
cure An ounce of prevention is worth a pound of cure.
Curiosity Curiosity killed the cat.
curiosity pique someone's curiosity
curl curl someone's hair
curl curl up and die
curl make someone's hair curl
current swim against the current
curry curry favor (with someone)
curtain bring down the curtain (on something)
curtain ring down the curtain (on something)
curtains be curtains for someone or something
curve pitch someone a curve (ball)
curve throw someone a curve
custody in custody of someone or something
custody in someone's or something's custody
customer one to a customer
cut cut a big swath
cut cut across something
cut cut a fine figure
cut cut-and-dried
cut cut and paste
cut cut and run
cut cut a wide swath
cut cut back (on something)
cut cut both ways
cut cut class
cut cut corners
cut cut from the same cloth
Cut Cut it out!
cut cut loose (from someone or something)
cut cut loose (with something)
cut cut no ice (with someone)
cut cut off
cut cut one's eyeteeth on something
cut cut one's losses
cut cut one's (own) throat
cut cut out for something
cut cut out the deadwood
cut cut out to be something
cut cut someone or something to the bone
cut cut someone or something up
cut cut (someone) a check
cut cut someone dead
cut cut someone down (to size)
cut cut someone in
cut cut someone off without a penny
cut cut someone to the quick
cut cut teeth
cut cut the ground out from under someone
cut cut to the chase
cut cut up
cut fish or cut bait
cut have one's work cut out for one
cut one's work is cut out for one
cut run around like a chicken with its head cut off
cut a cut above someone or something
cylinders firing on all cylinders
cylinders hitting on all cylinders
dab smack-dab in the middle
dagger cloak-and-dagger
daggers look daggers at someone
daily one's daily dozen
daily the daily grind
daisies pushing up daisies
daisy (as) fresh as a daisy
daisy fresh as a daisy
dam busy as a beaver (building a new dam)
damage do someone damage
damn damn someone or something with faint praise
damned I'm damned if I do and damned if I don't.
dance dance to another tune
dance dance with death
dance go into one's song and dance (about something)
dander get someone's dander up
dandy fine and dandy
danger fly into the face of danger
danger fraught with danger
dangerous armed and dangerous
dangerous A little knowledge is a dangerous thing.
Danish coffee and Danish
dare dare someone (to do something)
dark dark horse
dark in the dark (about someone or something)
dark pitch-dark
dark a shot in the dark
darken darken someone's door
dart dart in and out
dash dash cold water on something
dash dash something off
date at an early date
date bring someone or something up to date
date bring someone up to date (on someone or something)
date date back (to sometime)
date out-of-date
date to date
date up-to-date
Davy Davy Jones's locker
Davy go to Davy Jones's locker
dawn at the break of dawn
dawn at the crack of dawn
dawn dawn on someone
dawn from dawn to dusk
day all day long
day all the livelong day
day (as) different as night and day
day (as) merry as the day is long
day (as) plain as day
day at the end of the day
day by day
day by the day
day call it a day
day carry the day
day day after day
day day and night
day day in and day out
day day in, day out
day day-to-day
day different as night and day
day Don't quit your day job.
day Every dog has his day.
day Every dog has its day.
day forever and a day

day from day to day
day from this day forward
day from this day on
day get the day off
day have a field day
day have had its day
day in this day and age
day late in the day
day make a day of doing something
day make a day of it
day merry as the day is long
day night and day
day not give someone the time of day
day pass the time of day (with someone)
day plain as day
day Rome wasn't built in a day.
day save something for a rainy day
day save the day
day see the light (of day)
day take the day off
day That'll be the day.
day There aren't enough hours in the day.
day till all hours (of the day and night)
day win the day
day with each passing day
day the order of the day
daylight begin to see daylight
daylight daylight robbery
daylight in broad daylight
daylights beat the living daylights out of someone
daylights frighten the (living) daylights out of someone
daylights scare the living daylights out of someone
day's all in a day's work
days days running
days for days on end
days have seen better days
days in all one's born days
days in one's salad days
days one of these days
days one's days are numbered
days Those were the days.
days' a nine days' wonder
days the good old days
de a fine how-de-do
dead (as) dead as a dodo
dead (as) dead as a doornail
dead (as) silent as the dead
dead beat a dead horse
dead come to a dead end
dead cut someone dead
dead dead ahead
dead dead and buried
dead dead and gone
dead dead as a dodo
dead dead as a doornail
dead dead in someone's or something's tracks
dead dead letter
dead dead on its feet
dead dead on one's feet
dead dead set against someone or something
dead dead to the world
dead drop dead
dead have someone dead to rights
dead in a dead heat
dead knock someone dead
dead leave someone for dead
dead more dead than alive
dead on dead center
dead one's heart is (dead) set against something
dead over my dead body
dead silent as the dead
dead taken for dead
dead wake the dead
dead a dead duck
dead a dead loss
deadwood cut out the deadwood
deaf (as) deaf as a post
deaf deaf and dumb
deaf deaf as a post
deaf fall on deaf ears
deaf turn a deaf ear (to someone or something)
deal deal in something
deal get a raw deal
deal give someone a raw deal
deal Like it's such a big deal!
deal make a big deal about something
deal No big deal!
deal square deal
deal think a great deal of someone or something
deal wheel and deal
deal a great deal
death (as) baleful as death
death (as) pale as death
death (as) still as death
death (as) sure as death
death baleful as death
death be death on something
death be the death of me (yet)
death between life and death
death bored to death
death bore someone to death
death catch one's death (of cold)
death dance with death
death death and taxes
death death on someone or something
death die a natural death
death frightened to death
death frighten someone to death
death look like death warmed over
death meet one's death
death pale as death
death scared to death
death scare someone to death
death sign one's own death warrant
death still as death
death sure as death
death take one's death of cold
death thrilled to death
death thrill someone to death
death tickled to death
death tickle someone to death
death a matter of life and death
death a struggle to the death
death the kiss of death

death's at death's door
debt head over heels in debt
debt in debt
debt pay one's debt (to society)
decide decide in favor of someone or something
decision eleventh-hour decision
deck have the deck stacked against one
deck on deck
deck stack the deck (against someone or something)
deck a few cards short of a deck
deck a few cards shy of a full deck
decks clear the decks
deem deem it (to be) necessary
deem deem that it is necessary
deep Beauty is only skin-deep.
deep between the devil and the deep blue sea
deep deep-six someone or something
deep go off the deep end
deep in deep
deep jump off the deep end
deepest one's deepest sympathy
defensive on the defensive
defiance in defiance (of someone or something)
degree get the third degree
degree give someone the third degree
degree to the nth degree
delight ravished with delight
deliver stand and deliver
delivered signed, sealed, and delivered
demand in great demand
demand supply and demand
den beard the lion in his den
den a den of iniquity
denial in denial
dent make a dent in something
depth beyond one's depth
description beggar description
description blow-by-blow description
description a play-by-play description
desert desert a sinking ship
deserts get one's just deserts
deserves One good turn deserves another.
designs have designs on someone or something
desired leave a lot to be desired
desist cease and desist
desk away from one's desk
despair sink into despair
despair throw one's hands up in despair
detail down to the last detail
detail go into detail
detail in detail
determined bound and determined
devil between the devil and the deep blue sea
devil catch the devil
devil devil-may-care attitude
devil devil-may-care manner
devil for the devil of it
devil full of the devil
devil get the devil
devil give someone the devil
devil give the devil her due
devil give the devil his due
devil go to (the devil)
devil have the devil to pay
devil raise the devil (with someone or something)
devil speak of the devil
devil There will be the devil to pay.
devil You scared the devil out of me.
devil a devil of a job
devil's play (the) devil's advocate
devil's the devil's own job
diamond a diamond in the rough
diapers soil one's diaper(s)
dibs have dibs on something
dibs put (one's) dibs on something
Dick (every) Tom, Dick, and Harry
Dick Tom, Dick, and Harry
dickens raise the dickens (with someone or something)
dickens You scared the dickens out of me.
Dick's (as) tight as Dick's hatband
Dick's tight as Dick's hatband
didn't I didn't catch your name.
die cross one's heart (and hope to die)
die curl up and die
die die a natural death
die die in one's boots
die die laughing
die die of a broken heart
die die of boredom
die die on someone
die die on the vine
die die with one's boots on
die do or die
die Old habits die hard.
die The die is cast.
diet on a diet
differ beg to differ (with someone)
difference make no difference (to someone)
difference split the difference
different (as) different as night and day
different different as night and day
different march to (the beat of) a different drummer
different sing a different tune
different a horse of a different color
dig dig in
dig dig one's heels in
dig dig one's own grave
dig dig some dirt up on someone
dig dig someone or something
dig dig something out
dig take a dig at someone
digs take digs at someone
dilemma on the horns of a dilemma
dim take a dim view of something
dime nickel and dime someone
dime not worth a dime
dime turn on a dime
dime a dime a dozen
dine dine out
dine wine and dine someone
dint by dint of something
dip chips and dip
dip dip in(to something)
directions ride off in all directions

dirt (as) common as dirt
dirt common as dirt
dirt dig some dirt up on someone
dirt dirt cheap
dirt hit pay dirt
dirty air one's dirty linen in public
dirty dirty old man
dirty dirty one's hands
dirty dirty work
dirty down-and-dirty
dirty get a dirty look from someone
dirty get one's hands dirty
dirty give someone a dirty look
dirty quick and dirty
dirty wash one's dirty linen in public
disease down with some disease
disease have foot-in-mouth disease
disguise in disguise
disguise a blessing in disguise
dishes do the dishes
dishwater (as) dull as dishwater
dishwater dull as dishwater
disorderly drunk and disorderly
disposal put someone or something at someone's disposal
disposed ill-disposed to doing something
disposed well-disposed toward someone or something
distance go the distance
distance keep one's distance (from someone or something)
distance within calling distance
distance within hailing distance
distance within shouting distance
distance within walking distance
distraction bored to distraction
ditch a last-ditch effort
ditchwater (as) dull as ditchwater
ditchwater dull as ditchwater
divide divide and conquer
divide divide something fifty-fifty
do can't do anything with someone or something
do could do with someone or something
do do a double take
do do a flip-flop (on something)
do do a job on someone or something
do do a land-office business
do do an about-face
do do an errand
do do a number on someone or something
do do a snow job on someone
do do away with someone or something
do do credit to someone
Do Do I need to paint you a picture?
do do justice to something
do do not have a care in the world
do do not have a leg to stand on
do do not have all one's marbles
do do oneself proud
do do one's bit
do do one's duty
do do one's (level) best
do do one's (own) thing
do do one's part
do do or die
do do so
do do somehow by someone
do do someone or something in
do do someone or something over
do do someone's bidding
do do someone's heart good
do do someone a good turn
do do someone a kindness
do do someone credit
do do someone damage
do do someone good
do do someone one better
do do someone out of something
do do something by hand
do do something fair and square
do do something for a living
do do something hands down
do do something in a heartbeat
do do something in person
do do something in public
do do something in secret
do do something in vain
do do something on the fly
do do something on the run
do do something on the sly
do do something over (again)
do do something the hard way
do do something to excess
do do something up
do do the dishes
do do the honors
do do the trick
do do too
do do without (someone or something)
Do Do you read me?
do have nothing to do with someone or something
do have something to do with something
do have to do with someone or something
do I'm damned if I do and damned if I don't.
do Let's do lunch.
do make do (with someone or something)
do No can do.
do well-to-do
do What do you want me to say?
do When in Rome, do as the Romans do.
do Who do you think you're kidding?
do Who do you think you're talking to?
do a fine how-de-do
do a fine how-do-you-do
do the in thing (to do)
doctor just what the doctor ordered
dodo (as) dead as a dodo
dodo dead as a dodo
does Easy does it.
does Pretty is as pretty does.
does That does it!
doesn't What one doesn't know won't hurt one.
dog (as) sick as a dog
dog dog and pony show
dog dog-eat-dog
dog dog in the manger
dog Every dog has his day.

dog Every dog has its day.
dog put on the dog
dog see a man about a dog
dog sick as a dog
dog You can't teach an old dog new tricks.
dog the hair of the dog that bit one
dog the tail wagging the dog
doghouse in the doghouse
dog's (as) crooked as a dog's hind leg
dogs call the dogs off
dog's crooked as a dog's hind leg
dogs go to the dogs
dog's lead a dog's life
dogs Let sleeping dogs lie.
dog's live a dog's life
dogs rain cats and dogs
doing have something doing
doing nothing doing
doldrums in the doldrums
dollar (as) phony as a three-dollar bill
dollar (as) queer as a three-dollar bill
dollar (as) sound as a dollar
dollar bet one's bottom dollar
dollar dollar for dollar
dollar phony as a three-dollar bill
dollar queer as a three-dollar bill
dollar sound as a dollar
dollar the almighty dollar
dollars feel like a million (dollars)
dollars look like a million dollars
dolled get (all) dolled up
done after all is said and done
done (as) good as done
done (be) easier said than done
done better off (if something were done)
done done in
done done to a T
done easier said than done
done good as done
done No harm done.
done no sooner said than done
done over and done with
done see (to it) that something is done
done What's done is done.
done when all is said and done
Don't Don't hold your breath.
Don't Don't let it go any further.
Don't Don't let it out of this room.
Don't Don't let someone or something get you down.
Don't Don't quit your day job.
don't I'm damned if I do and damned if I don't.
don't They don't make them like they used to.
don't You just don't get it!
doomed doomed to failure
door answer the door
door (as) broad as a barn door
door at death's door
door beat a path to someone's door
door broad as a barn door
door close the door on someone or something
door darken someone's door
door door-to-door
door from door to door
door get one's foot in the door
door keep the wolf from the door
door next-door neighbor
door open the door to something
door see someone to the door
door show someone (to) the door
door shut the door on someone or something
doornail (as) dead as a doornail
doornail dead as a doornail
doors behind closed doors
doorstep at someone's doorstep
doorstep on someone's doorstep
dose a dose of one's own medicine
dot on the dot
dotted sign on the dotted line
double do a double take
double double back (on someone or something)
double double-cross someone
double double in brass
double double up (with someone)
double on the double
double see double
doubt beyond a reasonable doubt
doubt beyond the shadow of a doubt
doubt get the benefit of the doubt
doubt give someone the benefit of the doubt
doubt no doubt
doubting doubting Thomas
doubts cast doubt(s) (on someone or something)
down (as) soft as down
down back down (from someone or something)
down batten down the hatches
down beat someone down (to size)
down bog down
down boil down to something
down boil something down
down break down
down break someone or something down
down break something down (for someone)
down break something down (into something)
down breathe down someone's neck
down bring down the curtain (on something)
down bring down the house
down bring something crashing down (around one)
down buckle down (to something)
down call someone down
down catch one with one's pants down
down clamp down (on someone or something)
down close something down
down come down
down cool down
down cool someone down
down crack down (on someone or something)
down cut someone down (to size)
down Don't let someone or something get you down.
down do something hands down
down down-and-dirty
down down-and-out
down down-at-the-heels
down down by some amount
down down for the count

down down in the dumps
down down in the mouth
down down on one's luck
down down on someone or something
down down South
down down the drain
down down the hatch
down down the street
down down the tubes
down down-to-earth
down down to the last detail
down down to the wire
down down with some disease
down dress someone down
down face someone down
down fall down on the job
down force someone or something down someone's throat
down get down to brass tacks
down get down to business
down get down to cases
down get down to something
down get down to the facts
down get down to the nitty-gritty
down get down to work
down get someone or something down
down get someone down
down get the low-down (on someone or something)
down give someone a (good) dressing-down
down give someone the low-down (on someone or something)
down go down fighting
down go down in history
down hand-me-down
down hands down
down hand something down (to someone)
down have something down pat
down hold someone down
down jump down someone's throat
down keep something down
down knock-down-drag-out fight
down knock someone down (to size)
down knock something down
down knuckle down (to something)
down lay down one's life (for someone or something)
down lay down on the job
down lay down the law
down lead someone down the garden path
down let one's hair down
down let someone down
down lie down on the job
down live something down
down look down one's nose at someone or something
down look down on someone or something
down mark someone or something down
down nail someone or something down
down nothing down
down pin someone down
down pipe down
down play someone or something down
down pour money down the drain
down pull someone or something down
down put one's foot down (about something)
down put someone or something down
down put someone down as something bad
down put someone down (for something)
down put something down in black and white
down put something down to something
down ram someone or something down someone's throat
down right down someone's alley
down ring down the curtain (on something)
down run someone or something down
down scale something down
down sell someone down the river
down set something down to something
down settle down
down shake someone or something down
down shove someone or something down someone's throat
down shut something down
down simmer down
down slap someone down
down slow someone or something down
down soft as down
down step down (from something)
down take someone down a notch (or two)
down take someone down a peg (or two)
down take someone down (to size)
down take something lying down
down talk down to someone
down talk someone down
down tear someone or something down
down throw down the gauntlet
down thumbs down on someone or something
down tied down
down tie someone down
down tone something down
down turn someone or something down
down turn thumbs down (on someone or something)
down water something down
down wear someone down
down weigh someone down
down when it comes right down to it
down when the chips are down
down wind down
down write something down
downhill downhill all the way
downhill downhill from here on
downhill go downhill
downs ups and downs
dozen by the dozen
dozen one's daily dozen
dozen six of one and half a dozen of the other
dozen a dime a dozen
dozens by the dozens
drabs dribs and drabs
drag drag one's feet
drag in drag
drag knock-down-drag-out fight
drag Wild horses couldn't drag someone.
drag a drag (on someone)
dragged feel dragged out
dragged look like something the cat dragged in
drain down the drain
drain pour money down the drain
draw beat someone to the draw

draw draw a bead on someone or something
draw draw a blank
draw draw a line between something and something else
draw draw blood
draw draw interest
draw draw lots
draw draw someone or something out
draw draw (someone's) fire (away from someone or something)
draw draw something to a close
draw draw something up
draw draw straws
draw draw the line (at something)
draw draw the line between something and something else
draw draw to a close
draw quick on the draw
draw slow on the draw
drawing back to the drawing board
drawn drawn and quartered
Dream Dream on.
dream wouldn't dream of doing something
dream a dream come true
dream a pipe dream
dredge dredge something up
dress dress someone down
dressed all dressed up
dressed dressed to kill
dressed dressed to the nines
dressing give someone a (good) dressing-down
dribs dribs and drabs
dried cut-and-dried
drift get the drift of something
drink drink to excess
drink I'll drink to that!
drive drive a hard bargain
drive drive at something
drive drive someone crazy
drive drive someone mad
drive drive someone out (of office)
drive drive someone to the wall
drive drive someone up the wall
drive drive something home
drive drive something into the ground
driven (as) pure as the driven snow
driven (as) white as the driven snow
driven pure as the driven snow
driven white as the driven snow
driver's in the driver's seat
driving driving force (behind someone or something)
driving What are you driving at?
drop at the drop of a hat
drop drop a bomb(shell)
drop drop a brick
drop drop around (sometime)
drop drop by (sometime)
drop drop by the wayside
drop drop dead
drop drop everything
drop drop in one's tracks
drop drop in (on someone)
drop drop in (to say hello)
drop drop names
drop drop off (to sleep)
drop drop out (of something)
drop drop someone
drop drop the ball
drop drop the other shoe
drop drop the subject
drop so quiet you could hear a pin drop
drop so still you could hear a pin drop
drop a drop in the bucket
drop a drop in the ocean
droves bring people or other creatures out in droves
drown drown one's sorrows
drown drown one's troubles
drown drown someone or something out
drug drug on the market
drum (as) tight as a drum
drum drum some business up
drum drum someone out of something
drum drum something into someone('s head)
drum tight as a drum
drummer march to (the beat of) a different drummer
drunk (as) drunk as a lord
drunk (as) drunk as a skunk
drunk drunk and disorderly
drunk drunk as a lord
drunk drunk as a skunk
druthers have one's druthers
dry (as) dry as a bone
dry (as) dry as dust
dry (as) exciting as watching (the) paint dry
dry dry as a bone
dry dry as dust
dry dry run
dry dry someone out
dry dry up
dry exciting as watching (the) paint dry
dry high and dry
dry leave someone high and dry
dry not dry behind the ears
duck as a duck takes to water
duck (as) easy as duck soup
duck duck and cover
duck easy as duck soup
duck like a sitting duck
duck a dead duck
duck a sitting duck
ducks get one's ducks in a row
ducks like sitting ducks
duck's like water off a duck's back
ducks lovely weather for ducks
dudgeon in high dudgeon
due give credit where credit is due
due give the devil her due
due give the devil his due
due in due course
due in due time
dues pay one's dues
dull All work and no play makes Jack a dull boy.
dull (as) dull as dishwater
dull (as) dull as ditchwater

dull dull as dishwater
dull dull as ditchwater
dumb deaf and dumb
dumb play dumb
dumps down in the dumps
duration for the duration
dusk from dawn to dusk
dust (as) dry as dust
dust bite the dust
dust dry as dust
Dutch Dutch auction
Dutch Dutch courage
Dutch Dutch treat
Dutch Dutch uncle
Dutch go Dutch
Dutch in Dutch (with someone)
duty (above and) beyond the call of duty
duty beyond the call of duty
duty do one's duty
duty duty bound (to do something)
duty in the line of duty
duty off duty
duty on active duty
duty on duty
duty shirk one's duty
dyed dyed-in-the-wool
dying dying to do something
each made for each other
each with each passing day
eager an eager beaver
eagle an eagle eye
ear bend someone's ear
ear get someone's ear
ear give (an) ear to someone or something
ear give one's ear to someone or something
ear go in one ear and out the other
ear have an ear for something
ear have one's ear to the ground
ear in one ear and out (of) the other
ear keep one's ear to the ground
ear lend an ear (to someone)
ear make a silk purse out of a sow's ear
ear play by ear
ear play something by ear
ear talk someone's ear off
ear turn a deaf ear (to someone or something)
earful get an earful
earful give someone an earful
earliest at someone's earliest convenience
early at an early date
early bright and early
early early bird
early early on
Early Early to bed, early to rise(, makes a man healthy, wealthy, and wise.)
early The early bird gets the worm.
earn earn one's keep
earned A penny saved is a penny earned.
earnest in earnest
ears assault the ears
ears be all ears
ears be all eyes (and ears)
ears fall on deaf ears
ears not dry behind the ears
ears one's ears are red
ears one's ears are ringing
ears pin someone's ears back
ears prick up one's ears
ears up to one's ears (in something)
ears Walls have ears.
ears wet behind the ears
earshot out of earshot
earth all over the earth
earth come down to earth
earth down-to-earth
earth hell on earth
earth like nothing on earth
earth move heaven and earth to do something
earth on earth
earth run someone or something to earth
earth to the ends of the earth
earth a paradise (on earth)
earth the salt of the earth
ease at ease
ease ease off (on someone or something)
ease ease up (on someone or something)
ease ill at ease
ease with ease
easier (be) easier said than done
easier easier said than done
easily able to breathe (easily) again
East back East
easy (as) easy as ABC
easy (as) easy as (apple) pie
easy (as) easy as duck soup
easy (as) easy as falling off a log
easy (as) easy as rolling off a log
easy breathe easy
easy easy as ABC
easy easy as (apple) pie
easy easy as duck soup
easy easy as falling off a log
easy easy as rolling off a log
easy easy come, easy go
Easy Easy does it.
easy easy to come by
easy free and easy
easy get off easy
easy go easy (on someone or something)
easy let someone off easy
easy on easy street
easy Take it easy.
easy take it easy (on someone or something)
eat dog-eat-dog
eat eat (a meal) out
eat eat and run
eat eat away at someone or something
eat eat high on the hog
eat eat humble pie
eat eat like a bird
eat eat like a horse
eat eat one's cake and have it too
eat eat one's hat
eat eat one's heart out

eat eat one's words
eat eat out of someone's hands
eat eat someone out
eat eat something up
eat grab a bite (to eat)
eat have one's cake and eat it too
eat make someone eat crow
eat so clean you could eat off the floor
ebb ebb and flow
edge edge someone out
edge get the edge on someone
edge get the edge over someone
edge on edge
edge set someone's teeth on edge
edge take the edge off (something)
edgeways get a word in edgeways
edgewise get a word in edgewise
eel (as) slippery as an eel
eel slippery as an eel
effect go into effect
effect have a bad effect (on someone or something)
effect in effect
effect or words to that effect
effect something to that effect
effect take effect
effect words to that effect
effigy burn someone in effigy
effigy hang someone in effigy
effort make an all-out effort
effort an A for effort
effort an all-out effort
effort a last-ditch effort
egg egg someone on
egg Go fry an egg!
egg have egg on one's face
egg lay an egg
eggs put all one's eggs in one basket
eggs teach one's grandmother to suck eggs
eggs walk on eggs
eight behind the eight ball
either either feast or famine
elbow elbow someone out (of something)
elbow use some elbow grease
elbows rub elbows (with someone)
element in one's element
element out of one's element
elephant white elephant
eleventh at the eleventh hour
eleventh eleventh-hour decision
else better off (if one were somewhere else)
else draw a line between something and something else
else mistake someone for someone else
else mix someone up with someone else
else name someone after someone else
else name someone for someone else
else no love lost (between someone and someone else)
else or else
else play someone off against someone else
else something else
else torn between choosing something or something else
else work something into something else
else's in someone else's place
else's in someone else's shoes
else's put oneself in someone else's place
else's put oneself in someone else's shoes
'em Stick 'em up!
emotions let one's emotions show
empty come away empty-handed
empty go away empty-handed
end at one's wit's end
end at the end of nowhere
end at the end of one's rope
end at the end of one's tether
end at the end of the day
end be-all and (the) end-all
end beginning of the end
end can't see beyond the end of one's nose
end come to a bad end
end come to a dead end
end come to an end
end come to an untimely end
end end something up
end end up by doing something
end end up doing something
end end up (somehow)
end end up somewhere
end end up with the short end of the stick
end for days on end
end for hours on end
end get the short end of the stick
end go off the deep end
end hold one's end (of the bargain) up
end jump off the deep end
end live up to one's end of the bargain
end make someone's hair stand on end
end meet one's end
end no end of something
end not see farther than the end of one's nose
end not see past the end of one's nose
end put an end to something
end see the light (at the end of the tunnel)
end to the bitter end
end an end in itself
end the be-all and (the) end-all
end the business end of something
end the end of the line
end the end of the road
ends All's well that ends well.
ends at loose ends
ends burn the candle at both ends
ends make (both) ends meet
ends odds and ends
ends play both ends (against the middle)
ends to the ends of the earth
engage engage in small talk
English in plain English
Enjoy Enjoy your meal.
enough angry enough to chew nails
enough close enough for government work
Enough Enough is enough.
enough enough to go (a)round
enough get up enough nerve (to do something)
enough good enough for someone or something
enough have had enough

enough leave well enough alone
enough let well enough alone
enough mad enough to chew nails
enough not enough room to swing a cat
enough not know enough to come in out of the rain
enough old enough to be someone's father
enough old enough to be someone's mother
enough There aren't enough hours in the day.
enter enter one's mind
enter enter the fray
entering breaking and entering
entirety in its entirety
entirety in their entirety
envy green with envy
equal equal to someone or something
equal other things being equal
equal separate but equal
errand do an errand
errand go on an errand
errand on a fool's errand
errand run an errand
errand send someone (out) on an errand
error trial and error
escape avenue of escape
escape escape someone's notice
essence in essence
eve on the eve of something
even break even
even even in the best of times
even even steven
even get even (with someone)
even keep on an even keel
even keep something on an even keel
event in any event
event in the event of something
event in the unlikely event of something
event in the unlikely event that something happens
ever ever and anon
ever forever and ever
ever live happily ever after
every at every turn
Every Every cloud has a silver lining.
Every Every dog has his day.
Every Every dog has its day.
every every inch a something
every every inch the something
every every last one
every every living soul
every every minute counts
every every moment counts
every every nook and cranny
every (every) now and again
every (every) now and then
every (every) once in a while
every every other person or thing
every every time one turns around
every (every) Tom, Dick, and Harry
every every which way
every hang on someone's every word
every use every trick in the book
every with every (other) breath
everyone You can't please everyone.
everyone the moment everyone has been waiting for
everything drop everything
everything everything but the kitchen sink
everything everything from A to Z
everything everything from soup to nuts
everything everything humanly possible
everything with everything (on it)
Everything's Everything's coming up roses.
everywhere here, there, and everywhere
evidence much in evidence
evil Money is the root of all evil.
evils the lesser of two evils
examine cross-examine someone
example hold someone or something up (as an example)
example make an example of someone
exception make an exception (for someone)
exception take exception (to something)
exception the exception that proves the rule
excess do something to excess
excess drink to excess
exchange exchange more than some number of words with someone
exchange in exchange (for someone or something)
excitement a ripple of excitement
exciting (as) exciting as watching (the) paint dry
exciting exciting as watching (the) paint dry
excuse excuse oneself
excuse excuse someone
excuse use someone or something as an excuse
exhibition make an exhibition of oneself
existence in existence
expectations measure up (to someone's expectations)
expected as I expected
expected (just) as I expected
expected when least expected
expecting expecting (a child)
expedition go on a fishing expedition
expense at the expense of someone or something
expense expense is no object
expense go to the expense (of doing something)
expenses out-of-pocket expenses
explain explain oneself
explain explain something away
explode explode a bombshell
express express one's anger
extend extend credit (to someone)
extend extend one's sympathy (to someone)
extend extend someone credit
extent to a great extent
extent to some extent
extenuating extenuating circumstances
extra go the extra mile
eye catch someone's eye
eye get a black eye
eye get someone's eye
eye give someone a black eye
eye give someone the eye
eye have an eye for someone or something
eye have an eye on someone or something
eye have an eye out (for someone or something)
eye Here's mud in your eye.
eye hit the bull's-eye

eye in one's mind's eye
eye in the public eye
eye in the twinkling of an eye
eye keep an eye on someone or something
eye keep an eye out (for someone or something)
eye keep one's eye on the ball
eye keep one's weather eye open
eye look someone in the eye
eye more (to something) than meets the eye
eye out of the corner of one's eye
eye put someone's eye out
eye see eye to eye (with someone) (about something)
eye see eye to eye (with someone) (on something)
eye turn a blind eye to someone or something
eye with an eye to doing something
eye without batting an eye
eye an eagle eye
eye a bird's-eye view
eye the apple of someone's eye
eye the eye of the storm
eye the naked eye
eyeball eyeball-to-eyeball
eyeballs up to one's eyeballs (in something)
eyebrows cause (some) eyebrows to raise
eyebrows raise some eyebrows
eyed bright-eyed and bushy-tailed
eyed look at someone cross-eyed
eyeful get an eyeful (of someone or something)
eyelid not bat an eyelid
eyes able to do something with one's eyes closed
eyes be all eyes (and ears)
eyes clap eyes on someone or something
eyes close one's eyes to something
eyes cry one's eyes out
eyes feast one's eyes (on someone or something)
eyes get stars in one's eyes
eyes have eyes bigger than one's stomach
eyes have eyes in the back of one's head
eyes hit someone (right) between the eyes
eyes keep one's eyes open (for someone or something)
eyes keep one's eyes peeled (for someone or something)
eyes lay eyes on someone or something
eyes make eyes (at someone)
eyes not believe one's eyes
eyes One's eyes are bigger than one's stomach.
eyes only have eyes for someone
eyes open someone's eyes (to something)
eyes pull the wool over someone's eyes
eyes set eyes on someone or something
eyes sight for sore eyes
eyeteeth cut one's eyeteeth on something
face (as) plain as the nose on one's face
face at face value
face blow up in someone's face
face can't see one's hand in front of one's face
face cut off one's nose to spite one's face
face do an about-face
face face someone down
face face the music
face face-to-face
face fall flat (on its face)
face fall flat (on one's face)
face feed one's face
face fly in the face of someone or something
face fly into the face of danger
face have egg on one's face
face hide one's face in shame
face keep a straight face
face look someone in the face
face lose face
face make a face
face not show one's face
face on the face of it
face plain as the nose on one's face
face put on a brave face
face red in the face
face save (one's) face
face say something (right) to someone's face
face stare someone in the face
face take someone or something at face value
face take something at face value
face talk until one is blue in the face
face tell one to one's face
face a slap in the face
fact after the fact
fact as a matter of fact
fact grounded in fact
fact in fact
fact matter-of-fact
fact a known fact
facts get down to the facts
facts get the facts straight
facts the facts of life
fail without fail
failure doomed to failure
faint damn someone or something with faint praise
fair do something fair and square
fair fair and impartial
fair fair and square
fair fair game
fair fair-haired boy
fair fair to middling
fair fair-weather friend
fair give someone a fair shake
fair one's fair share
fair play fair
faith in bad faith
faith in good faith
faith pin one's faith on someone or something
faith show good faith
faith take something on faith
faith an act of faith
fall break someone's fall
fall fall afoul of someone or something
fall fall (all) over oneself
fall fall all over someone
fall fall apart at the seams
fall fall asleep
fall fall back on someone or something
fall fall between two stools
fall fall by the wayside
fall fall down on the job
fall fall flat (on its face)
fall fall flat (on one's face)

fall fall for someone or something
fall fall from grace
fall fall head over heels
fall fall ill
fall fall in
fall fall off
fall fall on deaf ears
fall fall out
fall fall over backwards (to do something)
fall fall short (of something)
fall fall through
fall fall to
fall fall (up)on someone or something
fall Pride goes before a fall.
fall riding for a fall
falling (as) easy as falling off a log
falling easy as falling off a log
fallow lie fallow
false lull someone into a false sense of security
false sail under false colors
familiar familiar with someone or something
familiar have a familiar ring
Familiarity Familiarity breeds contempt.
family (all) in the family
family in a family way
family in the family
family like one of the family
family run in the family
family the black sheep of the family
famine either feast or famine
fan fan the flames (of something)
fan a fan of someone
fancy flight of fancy
fancy footloose and fancy-free
fancy strike someone's fancy
fancy take a fancy to someone or something
fancy tickle someone's fancy
far (as) far as anyone knows
far as far as it goes
far as far as possible
far (as) far as someone or something is concerned
far come from far and wide
far far and away the best
far far as anyone knows
far far as something is concerned
far far be it from me to do something
far far from it
far far into the night
far far out
far few and far between
far from far and near
far from near and far
far go so far as to say something
far go too far
far make it as far as something
far so far as anyone knows
far so far as possible
far so far as someone or something is concerned
far so far as something is concerned
far So far, so good.
far a far-away look
far a far cry from something
far a far-off look
farm farm someone or something out
farther not see farther than the end of one's nose
fashion after a fashion
fashion after the fashion of someone or something
fashion go out of fashion
fashion in fashion
fashion out of fashion
fast fast and furious
fast get nowhere fast
fast hard-and-fast
fast make a fast buck
fast make fast work of someone or something
fast play fast and loose (with someone or something)
fast pull a fast one
fast thick and fast
faster faster and faster
fat (as) fat as a pig
fat chew the fat
fat fat and happy
fat fat as a pig
fat fat chance
fat live off the fat of the land
fate leave one to one's fate
father old enough to be someone's father
fatted kill the fatted calf
fault find fault (with someone or something)
fault generous to a fault
fauna flora and fauna
favor curry favor (with someone)
favor decide in favor of someone or something
favor favor someone or something with something
favor in favor of someone
favor in favor (of someone or something)
favor in someone's favor
favor out of favor (with someone)
favor return the favor
fear fools rush in (where angels fear to tread)
fear for fear of something
fear in fear and trembling
fear never fear
feast either feast or famine
feast feast one's eyes (on someone or something)
feather (as) light as a feather
feather Birds of a feather flock together.
feather feather one's (own) nest
feather in fine feather
feather knock someone over with a feather
feather light as a feather
feather tar and feather someone
feather a feather in one's cap
feathers make the feathers fly
feathers ruffle its feathers
feathers ruffle someone's feathers
fed fed up (to somewhere) (with someone or something)
federal make a federal case out of something
feed feed one's face
feed feed someone a line
feed feed the kitty
feed for chicken feed
feed put on the feed bag
feed spoon-feed someone

feeds bite the hand that feeds one
feel feel a glow of something
feel feel at home
feel feel dragged out
feel feel fit
feel feel free (to do something)
feel feel it beneath one (to do something)
feel feel like a million (dollars)
feel feel like a new person
feel feel like doing something
feel feel like (having) something
feel feel one's gorge rise
feel feel on top of the world
feel feel out of place
feel feel put-upon
feel feel someone out
feel feel something in one's bones
feel feel the pinch
feel feel up to something
feel get a feel for something
feel get the feel of something
feel have the feel of something
feelers put out (some) feelers
feeling feeling no pain
feeling gut feeling
feeling have a feeling about something
feeling have a feeling (that)
feeling I just have this feeling
feelings have mixed feelings (about someone or something)
feelings no hard feelings
feet dead on its feet
feet dead on one's feet
feet drag one's feet
feet find one's feet
feet get a load off one's feet
feet get back on one's feet
feet get cold feet
feet get one's feet on the ground
feet get one's feet wet
feet get to one's feet
feet have cold feet
feet have feet of clay
feet have one's feet on the ground
feet keep one's feet on the ground
feet knock one off one's feet
feet land on both feet
feet land on one's feet
feet let grass grow under one's feet
feet on one's feet
feet regain one's feet
feet sit at someone's feet
feet stand on one's own two feet
feet sweep one off one's feet
feet take a load off one's feet
feet think on one's feet
feet throw oneself at someone's feet
feet vote with one's feet
feet the balls of one's feet
fell at one fell swoop
fell in one fell swoop
fell a hush fell over someone or something
fellow hail-fellow-well-met
fence fence someone in
fence on the fence (about something)
fence sit on the fence
fences mend (one's) fences
fend fend for oneself
ferret ferret something out of someone or something
fever run a fever
few drop someone a few lines
few few and far between
few precious few
few quite a few
few wash a few things out
few a few cards short of a deck
few a few cards shy of a full deck
fiddle (as) fit as a fiddle
fiddle fiddle about (with someone or something)
fiddle fiddle around (with someone or something)
fiddle fiddle while Rome burns
fiddle fit as a fiddle
fiddle play second fiddle (to someone)
field come out of left field
field field questions
field have a field day
field out in left field
field play the field
fifty divide something fifty-fifty
fifty go fifty-fifty (on something)
fifty split something fifty-fifty
fight fight against time
fight fight someone or something hammer and tongs
fight fight someone or something tooth and nail
fight knock-down-drag-out fight
fight pick a fight with someone
fighting go down fighting
fighting Them's fighting words.
fighting a fighting chance
figure cut a fine figure
figure figure in something
figure figure on something
figure figure someone or something out
figures in round figures
file have something on file
file (in) single file
file rank and file
file single file
fill back and fill
fill fill someone's shoes
fill fill someone in (on someone or something)
fill fill the bill
fill get one's fill of someone or something
filled filled to the brim
final get the final word
final in the final analysis
final a final fling
find find a happy medium
find find fault (with someone or something)
find find it in one's heart (to do something)
find find it's way somewhere
find find oneself
find find one's feet
find find one's own level

find find one's tongue
find find one's way (around)
find find one's way somewhere
find find someone or something out
find find someone guilty
find find someone innocent
find find (something) out the hard way
Finders Finders keepers(, losers weepers).
fine cut a fine figure
fine fine and dandy
fine go over something with a fine-tooth comb
fine in fine feather
fine search something with a fine-tooth comb
fine a fine how-de-do
fine a fine how-do-you-do
fine a fine kettle of fish
fine a fine state of affairs
fine the fine print
finger have a finger in the pie
finger have one's finger in the pie
finger have one's finger in too may pies
finger lay a finger on someone or something
finger lay the finger on someone
finger not lift a finger (to help someone)
finger point the finger at someone
finger put one's finger on something
finger put the finger on someone
finger twist someone around one's little finger
fingers cross one's fingers
fingers get one's fingers burned
fingers have sticky fingers
fingers keep one's fingers crossed (for someone or something)
fingers slip through someone's fingers
fingers work one's fingers to the bone
fingertips have something at one's fingertips
finish from start to finish
fire add fuel to the fire
fire (as) hot as fire
fire ball of fire
fire baptism of fire
fire build a fire under someone
fire catch fire
fire catch (on) fire
fire caught in the cross fire
fire draw (someone's) fire (away from someone or something)
fire fire a gun
fire fire away at someone or something
fire hang fire
fire have too many irons in the fire
fire hold one's fire
fire hot as fire
fire like a house on fire
fire on fire
fire open fire (on someone)
fire out of the frying pan into the fire
fire play with fire
fire set fire to someone or something
fire set someone or something on fire
fire set the world on fire
fire under fire
fire Where there's smoke there's fire.
fires keep the home fires burning
firing firing on all cylinders
first at first
first cast the first stone
first first and foremost
first first and ten
First First come, first served.
first first of all
first first off
first first thing (in the morning)
first first things first
first get to first base (with someone or something)
first in the first instance
first in the first place
first love at first sight
first not know the first thing about someone or something
first of the first water
first on a first-name basis (with someone)
first play first chair
first reach first base (with someone or something)
fish (as) crooked as a barrel of fishhooks
fish (as) crooked as a fishhook
fish crooked as a barrel of fishhooks
fish crooked as a fishhook
fish fish for a compliment
fish fish for something
fish fish in troubled waters
fish fish or cut bait
fish have bigger fish to fry
fish have more important fish to fry
fish have other fish to fry
fish like a fish out of water
fish neither fish nor fowl
fish There are plenty of other fish in the sea.
fish a cold fish
fish a fine kettle of fish
fishing go on a fishing expedition
fist hand over fist
fit (as) fit as a fiddle
fit feel fit
fit fit and trim
fit fit as a fiddle
fit fit for a king
fit fit in someone
fit fit in (with someone or something)
fit fit like a glove
fit fit someone or something out (with something)
fit fit someone in(to something)
fit fit someone to a T
fit fit the bill
fit fit to be tied
fit fit to kill
fit have a conniption (fit)
fit have a fit
fit see fit (to do something)
fit think someone or something fit for something
fit throw a fit
fits by fits and starts
fits If the shoe fits, wear it.
fittest the survival of the fittest
five take five

five a nine-to-five job
fix fix *someone's* wagon
fix fix *someone* up (with *someone or something*)
fix get a fix on *something*
fix give *someone* a fix on *something*
fix in a fix
fixed well-fixed
fixings with all the fixings
fizzle fizzle out
flame add fuel to the flame
flame burn with a low blue flame
flames burst into flames
flames fan the flames (of *something*)
flames go up in flames
flare flare up
flash (as) quick as a flash
flash in a flash
flash quick as a flash
flash a flash in the pan
flat (as) flat as a board
flat (as) flat as a pancake
flat fall flat (on its face)
flat fall flat (on *one's* face)
flat flat as a board
flat flat as a pancake
flat flat broke
flat flat out
flat in nothing flat
flat leave *someone* flat
Flattery Flattery will get you nowhere.
flea not hurt a flea
flesh flesh and blood
flesh flesh *something* out
flesh in the flesh
flesh make *someone's* flesh crawl
flies as the crow flies
flies no flies on *someone*
flies time flies
flight flight of fancy
flight in flight
fling fling *oneself* at *someone*
fling a final fling
flip do a flip-flop (on *something*)
flip flip *one's* lid
flip flip *one's* wig
flirt flirt with the idea of *doing something*
float float a loan
flock Birds of a feather flock together.
floor get in (on the ground floor)
floor get the floor
floor mop the floor up with *someone*
floor so clean you could eat off the floor
floor walk the floor
floor wipe the floor up with *someone*
flop do a flip-flop (on *something*)
flora flora and fauna
flotsam flotsam and jetsam
flow ebb and flow
flow go with the flow
fluff fluff *one's* lines
flunk flunk out
flunk flunk *someone* out
flush flush with *something*
flux in a (constant) state of flux
flux in flux
fly do *something* on the fly
fly fly-by-night
fly fly in the face of *someone or something*
fly fly in the teeth of *someone or something*
fly fly into the face of danger
fly fly off the handle
fly fly the coop
fly Go fly a kite!
fly It'll never fly.
fly make the feathers fly
fly make the fur fly
fly a fly in the ointment
flying be flying high
flying come through *something* with flying colors
flying get off to a flying start
flying with flying colors
foam foam at the mouth
fob fob *something* off (on *someone*)
foe friend or foe
fog able to fog a mirror
fog in a fog
foist foist *something* (off) on *someone*
fold fold *one's* hands
fold fold *something* up
fold fold, spindle, or mutilate
fold fold up
follow follow in *someone's* footsteps
follow follow in *someone's* tracks
follow follow *one's* heart
follow follow *one's* nose
follow follow orders
follow follow *someone or something* up
follow follow *someone's* lead
follow follow suit
follow follow the crowd
follow follow through (on *something*)
follow follow up (on *someone or something*)
follow follow up (on *something*)
follow a tough act to follow
fond fond of *someone or something*
food food for thought
fool fool around (with *someone or something*)
fool make a fool out of *someone*
fool nobody's fool
fool play the fool
fool take *someone* for a fool
fool A fool and his money are soon parted.
foolish penny-wise and pound-foolish
fools fools rush in (where angels fear to tread)
fool's in a fool's paradise
fool's on a fool's errand
foot be off on the wrong foot
foot bound hand and foot
foot foot the bill
foot get off on the wrong foot
foot get *one's* foot in the door
foot have a foot in both camps
foot have foot-in-mouth disease
foot have one foot in the grave

foot have the shoe on the other foot
foot not set foot somewhere
foot on foot
foot put one's best foot forward
foot put one's foot down (about something)
foot put one's foot in it
foot put one's foot in one's mouth
foot set foot somewhere
foot start off on the wrong foot
foot stick one's foot in one's mouth
foot wait on someone hand and foot
foot wouldn't touch something with a ten-foot pole
foot The shoe is on the other foot.
foothold get a foothold (somewhere)
footloose footloose and fancy-free
footsie play footsie (with someone)
footsteps follow in someone's footsteps
for acquire a taste for something
for all for something
for (all) for the best
for allow for someone or something
for All right for you!
for answer for someone or something
for arguing for the sake of arguing
for arguing for the sake of argument
for as for someone or something
for ask for something
for ask for the moon
for ask for trouble
for at a loss (for words)
for augur well for someone or something
for bargain for something
for be curtains for someone or something
for bound for somewhere
for break ground (for something)
for break something down (for someone)
for buck for something
for but for someone or something
for buy something for a song
for call for someone or something
for can't wait (for something to happen)
for carry a torch (for someone)
for cast about for someone or something
for cast around for someone or something
for close enough for government work
for come in for something
for come out for someone or something
for count someone out (for something)
for cover for someone
for crazy for someone or something
for crying need for someone or something
for cut out for something
for dollar for dollar
for do something for a living
for down for the count
for fall for someone or something
for fall in for something
for fend for oneself
for fish for a compliment
for fish for something
for fit for a king
for food for thought
for for a lark
for for all I care
for for all I know
for for all intents and purposes
for for all it's worth
for for all practical purposes
for for all something
for for all the world
for for better or for worse
for for chicken feed
For For crying out loud!
for for days on end
for for fear of something
for for free
for for good
for for hours on end
for for instance
for for keeps
for for kicks
for fork money out (for something)
for for life
for for one's (own) part
for for one's (own) sake
for for openers
for for peanuts
for for real
for for safekeeping
for for sale
for for short
for for starters
for for sure
for for that matter
for for the best
for for the better
for for the birds
for for the devil of it
for for the duration
for for the good of someone or something
for for the heck of it
for for the hell of it
for for the life of one
for for the moment
for for the most part
for for the odds to be against one
for for the record
for for the sake of someone or something
for for the time being
for for what(ever) it's worth
for free-for-all
for gear (oneself) up (for something)
for get a feel for something
for get a reputation (for doing something)
for get a run for one's money
for get credit (for something)
for get time off for good behavior
for give one a run for one's money
for give someone a hand (for something)
for give someone a reputation (for doing something)
for give someone credit (for something)
for give someone tit for tat
for give someone what for
for glutton for punishment

for go along for the ride
for go for broke
for go for it
for go for someone or something
for go in for something
for good enough for someone or something
for good-for-nothing
for go out (for something)
for go to bat for someone
for grist for someone's mill
for grounds for something
for gulp for air
for gun for someone
for hard up (for something)
for have a head for something
for have a look for someone or something
for have a lot going (for one)
for have an ear for something
for have an eye for someone or something
for have an eye out (for someone or something)
for have an itch for something
for have a nose for something
for have a passion for someone or something
for have a penchant for doing something
for have a soft spot in one's heart for someone or something
for have a taste for something
for have a weakness for someone or something
for Have I got something for you!
for have it in for someone
for have one for the road
for have one's work cut out for one
for have something going (for oneself)
for have something in store (for someone)
for head for someone or something
for head for the last roundup
for hell-bent for leather
for hit someone up (for something)
for hold no brief for someone or something
for hold out for something
for hold still for something
for hold up (for someone or something)
for hunger for something
for hungry for something
for hunt high and low (for someone or something)
for in exchange (for someone or something)
for in for something
for in return for (someone or something)
for in the market (for something)
for in the mood for something
for issue a call for something
for jockey for position
for keep an eye out (for someone or something)
for keep one's eyes open (for someone or something)
for keep one's eyes peeled (for someone or something)
for keep one's fingers crossed (for someone or something)
for kick oneself (for doing something)
for knock someone for a loop
for lay down one's life (for someone or something)
for leave oneself wide open for something
for leave someone for dead
for lie in wait for someone or something
for light out (for somewhere)
for like looking for a needle in a haystack
for line someone up (for something)
for live for the moment
for loaded for bear
for look for trouble
for look high and low (for someone or something)
for look out for someone or something
for look to someone or something (for something)
for lovely weather for ducks
for made for each other
for mad for someone or something
for make a beeline for someone or something
for make a break for something or somewhere
for make allowance(s) (for someone or something)
for make amends (for something)
for make a name (for oneself)
for make an exception (for someone)
for make a pitch (for someone or something)
for make a play (for someone)
for make arrangements (for someone or something)
for make a run for it
for make for somewhere
for make it hot for someone
for make life miserable for someone
for make someone the scapegoat for something
for make time (for someone or something)
for make up for lost time
for make up for someone or something
for make way (for someone or something)
for mean for someone to do something
for meet the requirements (for something)
for milk someone for something
for mistake someone for someone else
for more than someone bargained for
for name someone for someone else
for none the worse for wear
for not able to see the forest for the trees
for not for a moment
for not for (anything in) the world
for not for hire
for not for love nor money
for not for publication
for not long for this world
for not take no for an answer
for once and for all
for one for the (record) books
for one's for the asking
for one's work is cut out for one
for only have eyes for someone
for on the alert (for someone or something)
for on the lookout (for someone or something)
for open for business
for out of consideration (for someone or something)
for par for the course
for pass for someone or something
for pave the way (for someone or something)
for pay a king's ransom (for something)
for pay an arm and a leg (for something)
for pay for something
for pay through the nose (for something)
for pinch-hit (for someone)

for play for keeps
for play someone for something
for poised for something
for pressed for time
for psyched up (for something)
for put in a good word (for someone)
for put one's head on the block (for someone or something)
for put someone down (for something)
for reach for the sky
for recognize one for what one is
for recognize something for what it is
for riding for a fall
for roll out the red carpet for someone
for root for someone or something
for run for it
for run for one's life
for save something for a rainy day
for save up (for something)
for scout around for someone or something
for scratch around (for something)
for search high and low (for someone or something)
for sell something for a song
for set sail (for somewhere)
for set the stage for something
for settle for something
for shift for oneself
for shoot for something
for shop around (for something)
for short for something
for sight for sore eyes
for sit in for someone
for slated for something
for so much for someone or something
for speak for itself
for speak for themselves
for speak up for someone or something
for spoken for
for spring for something
for square off (for something)
for stand for something
for stand in (for someone)
for stand still for something
for stick one's neck out (for someone or something)
for stick up for someone or something
for strapped (for something)
for take a look for someone or something
for take a turn for the better
for take a turn for the worse
for taken for dead
for take someone or something for granted
for take someone for a fool
for take someone for an idiot
for take someone for a ride
for take someone for someone or something
for take the rap (for someone or something)
for thankful for small blessings
for Thank you for sharing.
for That's all for someone.
for There's no accounting for taste.
for think someone or something fit for something
for thirsty for something
for throw a party (for someone)
for throw someone for a loop
for throw someone for a loss
for too big for one's britches
for too close for comfort
for touch someone for something
for trouble someone for something
for try out (for something)
for turn to someone or something (for something)
for up for grabs
for up for something
for wait up (for someone or something)
for want for nothing
for watch out for someone or something
for what for
for word for word
for work out for the best
for would give one's right arm (for someone or something)
for an affinity for someone or something
for an A for effort
for a match for someone, something, or some creature
for a Mecca for someone
for a thirst for something
for the moment everyone has been waiting for
forbidden forbidden fruit
force driving force (behind someone or something)
force force someone or something down someone's throat
force force someone's hand
force force someone out (of office)
force force someone to the wall
force in force
force out in force
force a force to be reckoned with
forces join forces (with someone)
fore come to the fore
fore fore and aft
forefront at the forefront (of something)
forefront in the forefront (of something)
foregone a foregone conclusion
foremost first and foremost
forest not able to see the forest for the trees
forever forever and a day
forever forever and ever
forever lost and gone forever
forget forget oneself
forget forgive and forget
forgive forgive and forget
forgotten gone but not forgotten
fork fork money out (for something)
fork fork something over
forked speak with a forked tongue
form form and substance
form form an opinion
form in top form
form true to form
fort hold the fort
forth and so forth
forth back and forth
forth hold forth (on something)
forth launch forth (on something)
forth set forth (on something)
forty catch forty winks

forty forty winks
forty take forty winks
forward from this day forward
forward look forward to something
forward put one's best foot forward
forward put something forward
forwards know something backwards and forwards
forwards know something forwards and backwards
foul foul one's own nest
foul foul play
foul foul someone or something up
foul foul up
fouled fouled up
found lost-and-found
fours on all fours
fowl neither fish nor fowl
fox (as) sly as a fox
fox sly as a fox
fraught fraught with danger
fray enter the fray
fray join the fray
fray jump into the fray
free (as) free as a bird
free (as) free as (the) air
free feel free (to do something)
free footloose and fancy-free
free for free
free free and clear
free free and easy
free free as a bird
free free as (the) air
free free-for-all
free free translation
free get a free hand (with someone or something)
free get off scot-free
free give free rein to someone
free give someone a free hand (with something)
free give someone free rein
free go scot-free
free make free with someone or something
free of one's own free will
free set someone or something free
freedom give one one's freedom
freely able to breathe (freely) again
freezes until hell freezes over
freezes when hell freezes over
French Pardon my French.
fresh (as) fresh as a daisy
fresh fresh as a daisy
fresh fresh out (of something)
fresh get fresh (with someone)
fresh a breath of fresh air
friend fair-weather friend
friend friend or foe
friend make a friend
friend A friend in need is a friend indeed.
friends be friends with someone
friends make friends
friendship strike up a friendship
frighten frighten one out of one's wits
frighten frighten someone to death
frighten frighten the (living) daylights out of someone
frighten frighten the wits out of someone
frightened frightened to death
fringe the lunatic fringe
fritter fritter something away
fritz on the fritz
fro to and fro
frog get a frog in one's throat
frog have a frog in one's throat
frog a big frog in a small pond
froing toing and froing (on something)
from another country heard from
from aside from someone or something
from away from one's desk
from back down (from someone or something)
from back off (from someone or something)
from be a heartbeat away from something
from be from Missouri
from break loose (from someone or something)
from come from far and wide
from come from nowhere
from cut from the same cloth
from cut loose (from someone or something)
from cut the ground out from under someone
from downhill from here on
from draw (someone's) fire (away from someone or something)
from everything from A to Z
from everything from soup to nuts
from fall from grace
from far be it from me to do something
from far from it
from from dawn to dusk
from from day to day
from from door to door
from from far and near
from from hand to hand
from from head to toe
from from near and far
from from overseas
from from pillar to post
from from rags to riches
from from side to side
from from start to finish
from from stem to stern
from from the bottom of one's heart
from from the cradle to the grave
from from the ground up
from from the heart
from from the horse's mouth
from from the old school
from from the outset
from from the top
from from the word *go*
from from this day forward
from from this day on
from from time to time
from from tip to toe
from from top to bottom
from from way back
from get a dirty look from someone
from get away (from it all)
from get out from under someone or something

from go from bad to worse
from hail from somewhere
from (just) a stone's throw away (from something)
from keep from doing something
from keep one's distance (from someone or something)
from keep someone from doing something
from keep the wolf from the door
from knock the props out from under someone
from know something from memory
from learn something from the bottom up
from live from hand to mouth
from made from the same mold
from make something from scratch
from nothing to choose from
from not know from nothing
from not know someone from Adam
from out from under (something)
from pull the rug out (from under someone)
from separate the men from the boys
from separate the sheep from the goats
from shoot from the hip
from shuttle someone or something from person to person
from shuttle someone or something from place to place
from shy away (from someone or something)
from start from scratch
from step down (from something)
from (straight) from the horse's mouth
from straight from the shoulder
from take off (from work)
from take one's cue from someone
from where one is coming from
from a far cry from something
from a stone's throw (away) (from something)
front burn one's bridges in front of one
front can't see one's hand in front of one's face
front out front
front put on a (brave) front
front put up a (brave) front
front up-front
fruit bear fruit
fruit forbidden fruit
fruitcake (as) nutty as a fruitcake
fruitcake nutty as a fruitcake
fruits fruit(s) of one's labor(s)
fry Go fry an egg!
fry have bigger fish to fry
fry have more important fish to fry
fry have other fish to fry
fry small fry
frying out of the frying pan into the fire
fuel add fuel to the fire
fuel add fuel to the flame
full (as) full as a tick
full (at) full blast
full at full speed
full at full tilt
full come full circle
full full as a tick
full full blast
full full of beans
full full of bull
full full of hot air
full full of it
full full of Old Nick
full full of oneself
full full of prunes
full full of the devil
full full steam ahead
full get into full swing
full have one's hands full (with someone or something)
full in full swing
full a few cards shy of a full deck
fun as much fun as a barrel of monkeys
fun fun and games
fun make fun (of someone or something)
fun more fun than a barrel of monkeys
fun poke fun (at someone)
funny (as) funny as a barrel of monkeys
funny (as) funny as a crutch
funny funny as a barrel of monkeys
funny funny as a crutch
funny funny business
funny funny ha-ha
funny funny peculiar
funny strike someone funny
fur make the fur fly
fur rub someone('s fur) the wrong way
furious fast and furious
further Don't let it go any further.
further without further ado
fuse blow a fuse
fuss kick up a fuss
fuss make a fuss (over someone or something)
future in the near future
gab have the gift of gab
gained Nothing ventured, nothing gained.
gains ill-gotten gains
gall have the gall to do something
gallery play to the gallery
gambit opening gambit
game ahead of the game
game at this stage of the game
game be game
game fair game
game give the game away
game new ball game
game (whole) new ball game
game a game that two can play
game The game is up.
game the name of the game
games fun and games
gamut run the gamut
gander take a gander (at someone or something)
gang gang up (on someone)
gangbusters come on like gangbusters
garden lead someone down the garden path
gas cooking with gas
gas gas up
gas out of gas
gas run out of gas
gas step on the gas
gas a gas
gasket blow a gasket

gasp at the last gasp
gate get the gate
gate give someone the gate
gather gather a case (against someone)
gathers A rolling stone gathers no moss.
gaudy (as) gaudy as a butterfly
gaudy gaudy as a butterfly
gauntlet throw down the gauntlet
gear gear (oneself) up (for something)
gear gear something to someone or something
gear get into high gear
gear in high gear
general as a (general) rule
general in general
generous generous to a fault
gentle (as) gentle as a lamb
gentle gentle as a lamb
get Come and get it!
get Don't let someone or something get you down.
get Flattery will get you nowhere.
get get a bang out of someone or something
get get a bee in one's bonnet
get get a big send-off
get get a black eye
get get a break
get get a bright idea
get get a charge out of someone or something
get get a charley horse
get get a checkup
get get a clean bill of health
get get a crush on someone
get get a dirty look from someone
get get a feel for something
get get a fix on something
get get a foothold (somewhere)
get get a free hand (with someone or something)
get get a frog in one's throat
get get after someone
get get a grasp of something
get get a handle on something
get get a hand with something
get get ahead of oneself
get get a head start (on someone or something)
get get (a)hold of someone or something
get get a hurry on
get get a jump(start)
get get a kick out of someone or something
get get a licking
Get Get a life!
get get a line on someone or something
get get (all) dolled up
get get a load off one's feet
get get a load off one's mind
get get a load of someone or something
get get along (in years)
get get along (on a shoestring)
get get along (without (someone or something))
get get along (with someone or something)
get get a lot of mileage out of something
get get a lump in one's throat
get get an earful
get get an eyeful (of someone or something)
get get an in (with someone)
get get another guess coming
get get another think coming
get get ants in one's pants
get get a rain check (on something)
get get a raw deal
get get a reputation (as a something)
get get a reputation (for doing something)
get get a rise out of someone
get get a rough idea (about something)
get get a rough idea (of something)
get get around
get get (around) to something
get get a run for one's money
get get a shellacking
get get a slap on the wrist
get get a start
get get a taste of one's own medicine
get get a thing about someone or something
get get a toehold (somewhere)
get get a tongue-lashing
get get at someone or something
get get at the heart of the matter
get get away (from it all)
get get away with something
get get a whiff of something
get get a word in edgeways
get get a word in edgewise
get get back (at someone)
get get back into circulation
get get back into harness
get get back on one's feet
get get back (to someone)
get get better
get get busy
get get butterflies in one's stomach
get get by (on something)
get get by (with something)
get get carried away
get get close (to someone or something)
get get cold feet
get get cracking
get get credit (for something)
get get down to brass tacks
get get down to business
get get down to cases
get get down to something
get get down to the facts
get get down to the nitty-gritty
get get down to work
get get even (with someone)
get get fresh (with someone)
get get goose bumps
get get goose pimples
get get gray hair(s)
get get hell
get get in on something
get get in (on the ground floor)
get get in someone's hair
get get into a jam
get get into a mess
get get into an argument (with someone)

get get into full swing
get get into high gear
get get in(to) hot water
get get into the act
get get into the swing of things
get get in touch (with someone)
get get involved (with someone)
get get it
get get lost
get get mad (at someone or something)
get get married
get get mixed-up
get get nowhere fast
get get off
get get (oneself) into a stew (over someone or something)
get get one's act together
get get one's bearings
get get one's comeuppance
get get one's ducks in a row
get get one's feet on the ground
get get one's feet wet
get get one's fill of someone or something
get get one's fingers burned
get get one's foot in the door
get get one's hands dirty
get get one's hands on someone or something
get get one's head above water
get get one's hooks into someone or something
get get one's just deserts
get get one's just reward(s)
get get one's knuckles rapped
get get one's money's worth
get get one's nose out of someone's business
get get one's (own) way (with someone or something)
get get one's say
get get one's sea legs
get get one's second wind
get get one's start
get get one's teeth into something
get get one's walking papers
get get one's wires crossed
get get one's wits about one
get get on someone
get get on the bandwagon
get get on the good side of someone
get get on (with someone or something)
get get out from under someone or something
get get out of a jam
get get out of a mess
get get out of someone's way
get get out of the way
get get out of the wrong side of the bed
get get out while the getting is good
get get over someone or something
get get physical (with someone)
get get ready (to do something)
get get religion
get get rid of someone or something
get get right on something
get get rolling
get get second thoughts about someone or something
get get set
get get sick
get get sidetracked
get get someone or something across
get get someone or something down
get get someone or something out of one's head
get get someone or something out of one's mind
get get someone or something out of the way
get get someone's back up
get get someone's dander up
get get someone's ear
get get someone's eye
get get someone's goat
get get someone's hackles up
get get someone's Irish up
get get someone's number
get get someone down
get get (someone) off the hook
get get someone out of a jam
get get someone over a barrel
get get someone under one's thumb
get get something
get get stars in one's eyes
get get the advantage of someone
get get the advantage over someone
get get the air
get get the ax
get get the ball rolling
get get the benefit of the doubt
get get the best of someone
get get the better of someone
get get the blues
get get the boot
get get the brush-off
get get the cold shoulder
get get the creeps
get get the day off
get get the devil
get get the drift of something
get get the edge on someone
get get the edge over someone
get get the facts straight
get get the feel of something
get get the final word
get get the floor
get get the gate
get get the glad hand
get get the go-ahead
get get the go-by
get get the goods on someone
get get the green light
get get the hang of something
get get the hard sell
get get the high sign
get get the inside track
get get the jump on someone
get get the last laugh
get get the last word
get get the lead out
get get the low-down (on someone or something)
get get the message
get get the nod
get get the (old) heave-ho

get get the once-over
get get the picture
get get the red-carpet treatment
get get the runaround
get get the sack
get get the shock of one's life
get get the short end of the stick
get get the show on the road
get get the slip
get get the third degree
get get the upper hand (on someone)
get get the willies
get get the word
get get the works
get get the worst of something
get get through something
get get through (to someone)
get get through with something
get get time off
get get time to catch one's breath
get get to first base (with someone or something)
get get to one's feet
get get to someone
get get to the bottom of something
get get to the heart of the matter
get get to the point
get get to the root of the problem
get get tough (with someone)
get get two strikes against one
get get under someone's skin
get get under way
get get-up-and-go
get get up enough nerve (to do something)
get get up on the wrong side of the bed
get get used to someone or something
get get well
get get wet
get get what's coming to one
get get wind of something
get get wise (to someone or something)
get get with something
get get worked up (about something)
get get worked up (over something)
get let something (get) out
get play hard to get
get tell someone where to get off
get You just don't get it!
gets give as good as one gets
gets when the going gets rough
gets when the going gets tough
gets The early bird gets the worm.
getting get out while the getting is good
getting It takes (some) getting used to.
ghost as pale as a ghost
ghost (as) white as a ghost
ghost give up the ghost
ghost a ghost of a chance
gift have the gift of gab
gild gild the lily
gills blue around the gills
gills green around the gills
gills pale around the gills
gird gird (up) one's loins
give give a blank check to someone
give give a good account of oneself
give give-and-take
give give (an) ear to someone or something
give give as good as one gets
give give birth to someone or some creature
give give birth to something
give give carte blanche to someone
give give chase (to someone or something)
give give credence to something
give give credit where credit is due
give give free rein to someone
give give ground
give give her the gun
give give in (to someone or something)
Give Give it a rest.
give give it the gun
Give Give it time.
give give it to someone (straight)
Give Give it up.
give give of oneself
give give one's ear to someone or something
Give Give one an inch, and one will take a mile.
give give one a run for one's money
give give one butterflies in one's stomach
give give one one's freedom
give give one one's walking papers
give give one what's coming to one
give give out
give give rise to something
give give someone or something a wide berth
give give someone or something the (old) heave-ho
give give someone a bang
give give someone a big send-off
give give someone a black eye
give give someone a blank check
give give someone a break
give give someone a bright idea
give give someone a bum steer
give give someone a buzz
give give someone a charge
give give someone a clean bill of health
give give someone a dirty look
give give someone a fair shake
give give someone a fix on something
give give someone a free hand (with something)
give give someone a (good) dressing-down
give give someone a hand (for something)
give give someone a hand (with someone or something)
give give someone a hard time
give give someone a head start (on someone or something)
give give someone a kick
give give someone a licking
give give someone a line
give give someone an earful
give give someone a pain
give give someone a pat on the back
give give someone a piece of one's mind
give give someone a rain check (on something)
give give someone a raw deal
give give someone a reputation (as a something)

give give someone a reputation (for doing something)
give give someone a ring
give give someone a rough idea (about something)
give give someone a rough idea (of something)
give give someone a shellacking
give give someone a slap on the wrist
give give someone a start
give give someone a swelled head
give give someone a tongue-lashing
give give someone carte blanche
give give someone credit (for something)
give give someone free rein
give give someone goose bumps
give give someone goose pimples
give give someone gray hair(s)
give give someone hell
give give someone pause
give give someone some skin
give give someone the air
give give someone the ax
give give someone the benefit of the doubt
give give someone the boot
give give someone the brush-off
give give someone the bum's rush
give give someone the business
give give someone the cold shoulder
give give someone the creeps
give give someone the devil
give give someone the eye
give give someone the gate
give give someone the glad hand
give give someone the go-ahead
give give someone the go-by
give give someone the green light
give give someone the hard sell
give give someone the high sign
give give someone the low-down (on someone or something)
give give someone the once-over
give give someone the red-carpet treatment
give give someone the runaround
give give someone the sack
give give someone the shirt off one's back
give give someone the slip
give give someone the third degree
give give someone the willies
give give someone the works
give give someone tit for tat
give give someone to understand something
give give someone what for
give give something a lick and a promise
give give something a shot
give give something a whirl
give give something one's best shot
give give the bride away
give give the devil her due
give give the devil his due
give give the game away
give give up the ghost
give give vent to something
give give voice to something
give not give a hang (about someone or something)
give not give a hoot (about someone or something)
give not give it another thought
give not give someone the time of day
give not give two hoots (about someone or something)
give would give one's right arm (for someone or something)
given given to doing something
given given to understand
given a given
glad get the glad hand
glad give someone the glad hand
glance at first glance
glass (as) smooth as glass
glass have a glass jaw
glass smooth as glass
glitters All that glitters is not gold.
glory in one's glory
gloss gloss something over
glove fit like a glove
glove hand in glove (with someone)
gloves handle someone with kid gloves
glow feel a glow of something
glutton glutton for punishment
gnash gnash one's teeth
go all systems (are) go
go buy something to go
go Don't let it go any further.
go easy come, easy go
go enough to go (a)round
go from the word *go*
go get something to go
go get the go-ahead
go get the go-by
go get-up-and-go
go give someone the go-ahead
go give someone the go-by
go go about one's business
go go against the grain
go go all out
go go all the way (with someone)
go go along for the ride
go go a long way in doing something
go go a long way toward doing something
go go along (with someone or something)
go go ape (over someone or something)
go go (a)round in circles
go go (a)round the bend
go go around with someone
go go astray
go go at it hammer and tongs
go go at it tooth and nail
go go at someone or something
go go away empty-handed
go go AWOL
go go back on one's word
go go bad
go go bananas
go go begging
go go broke
go go by the board
go go by the book
go go chase oneself
Go Go climb a tree!

go go cold turkey
go go crazy
go go down fighting
go go downhill
go go down in history
go go Dutch
go go easy (on someone or something)
go go fifty-fifty (on something)
Go Go fly a kite!
go go for broke
go go for it
go go for someone or something
go go from bad to worse
Go Go fry an egg!
go go great guns
go go haywire
go go hog-wild
go go in a body
go go in for something
go go in one ear and out the other
go go into action
go go into a nosedive
go go into a tailspin
go go into detail
go go into effect
go go into hiding
go go into hock
go go into one's song and dance (about something)
go go into orbit
go go into something
go go it alone
Go Go jump in the lake!
go go like clockwork
go good to go
go go off
go go on
go go out (for something)
go go out of fashion
go go out of one's way (to do something)
go go out of style
go go (out) on strike
go go out (with someone)
go go over
go go places
Go Go play in the traffic
go go right through someone
go go scot-free
go go sky-high
go go so far as to say something
go go someone one better
go go (somewhere) by shank's mare
go go stag
go go steady (with someone)
go go stir-crazy
go go straight
go go the distance
go go the extra mile
go go the limit
go go through
go go to any length
go go to bat for someone
go go to bed
go go to Davy Jones's locker
go go together
go go to (hell)
go go to hell in a handbasket
go go too far
go go to pieces
go go to pot
go go to rack and ruin
go go to seed
go go to someone's head
go go to the bathroom
go go to (the devil)
go go to the dogs
go go to the expense (of doing something)
go go to the lavatory
go go to the limit
go go to the toilet
go go to the trouble (of doing something)
go go to the trouble (to do something)
go go to the wall
go go to town
go go to waste
go go to wrack and ruin
go go under
go go up in flames
go go up in smoke
go go whole hog
go go window-shopping
go go without (something)
go go with something
go go with the flow
go go wrong
go have a go (at something)
go have one's heart go out to someone
go have something to go
go Here you go.
go let go of someone or something
go let go (with something)
go Let it go.
go let oneself go
go let someone go
go make a go of it
go not able to go on
go on the go
go order something to go
go pay as you go
go rarin' to go
go stop-and-go
go Sunday-go-to-meeting clothes
go There you go.
go touch and go
goat get someone's goat
goats separate the sheep from the goats
God Honest to God.
God an act of God
goes as far as it goes
goes goes to show you
goes goes without saying
goes Here goes nothing.
goes Here (it) goes.
goes How goes it (with you)?
goes off someone or something goes

goes one's heart goes out to someone
goes Pride goes before a fall.
goes So it goes.
goes What goes around, comes around.
going have a good thing going
going have a lot going (for one)
going have a thing going (with someone)
going have something going (for oneself)
going have something going (with someone)
going heavy going
going How's it going?
going not know if one is coming or going
going not know whether one is coming or going
going slow going
going when the going gets rough
going when the going gets tough
going the going
gold All that glitters is not gold.
gold (as) good as gold
gold good as gold
gold have a heart of gold
gold worth its weight in gold
gold a gold mine of information
golly by guess and by golly
gone all gone
gone come and gone
gone dead and gone
gone gone but not forgotten
gone gone goose
gone gone on
gone gone to meet one's Maker.
gone gone with the wind
gone lost and gone forever
gone to hell and gone
goner a goner
good all in good time
good all to the good
good (all) well and good
good (as) good as done
good (as) good as gold
good as good as one's word
good do someone's heart good
good do someone a good turn
good do someone good
good for good
good for the good of someone or something
good get on the good side of someone
good get out while the getting is good
good get time off for good behavior
good give a good account of oneself
good give as good as one gets
good give someone a (good) dressing-down
good good and something
good good as done
good good as gold
good good enough for someone or something
good good-for-nothing
good good riddance (to bad rubbish)
good good to go
good have a good command of something
good have a good head on one's shoulders
good have a (good) mind to do something
good have a good thing going
good (have) never had it so good
good in (all) good conscience
good in good condition
good in good faith
good in good hands
good in good repair
good in good shape
good in good spirits
good in good time
good in good (with someone)
good keep good time
good kiss something good-bye
good Life's been good (to me).
good look good on paper
good make good as something
good make good (at something)
good make good money
good make good on something
good make good time
good make someone look good
good make something good
good never had it so good
good No news is good news.
good One good turn deserves another.
good on good terms (with someone)
good put in a good word (for someone)
good put something to (good) use
good run the good race
good show good faith
good show something to good advantage
good So far, so good.
good stand someone in good stead
good throw good money after bad
good too good to be true
good too much of a good thing
good turn something to good account
good up to no good
good well and good
good What's the good of something?
good when one is good and ready
good Your guess is as good as mine.
good the good old days
goodness Honest to goodness.
goods get the goods on someone
goods sell someone a bill of goods
goof goof off
goose (as) silly as a goose
goose cook someone's goose
goose get goose bumps
goose get goose pimples
goose give someone goose bumps
goose give someone goose pimples
goose gone goose
goose silly as a goose
goose someone's goose is cooked
goose a wild-goose chase
gorge feel one's gorge rise
gorge make someone's gorge rise
gospel the gospel truth
got Cat got your tongue?
got Have I got something for you!

got You got me there.
gotten ill-gotten gains
government close enough for government work
gown cap and gown
gown town-and-gown
grab grab a bite (to eat)
grabs up for grabs
grace fall from grace
grace grace someone or something with one's presence
grace saving grace
grace say grace
graced graced with something
graceful (as) graceful as a swan
graceful graceful as a swan
grade make the grade
grain go against the grain
grain take something with a grain of salt
grain a grain of truth
Grand (as) busy as Grand Central Station
Grand busy as Grand Central Station
grandmother teach one's grandmother to suck eggs
granted take someone or something for granted
grasp get a grasp of something
grasp grasp at straws
grasp within someone's grasp
grass let grass grow under one's feet
grass a snake in the grass
grasshopper knee-high to a grasshopper
grate grate on someone('s nerves)
grave (as) quiet as the grave
grave (as) silent as the grave
grave carry a secret to one's grave
grave carry a secret to the grave
grave dig one's own grave
grave from the cradle to the grave
grave have one foot in the grave
grave quiet as the grave
grave roll (over) in one's grave
grave silent as the grave
grave swear on one's mother's grave
grave take it to one's grave
grave turn (over) in one's grave
gravy ride the gravy train
gray get gray hair(s)
gray give someone gray hair(s)
gray gray area
gray gray matter
grease grease someone's palm
grease use some elbow grease
greased (as) quick as greased lightning
greased like greased lightning
greased quick as greased lightning
great go great guns
great in great demand
great in great haste
great make a great show of something
great no great shakes
great set great store by someone or something
great take (great) pains (to do something)
great think a great deal of someone or something
great to a great extent
great a great deal
greatest the greatest thing since sliced bread
Greek Greek to me
Greek It's (all) Greek to me.
green get the green light
green give someone the green light
green green around the gills
green green with envy
green have a green thumb
grief come to grief
grievances air one's grievances
grin grin and bear it
grind grind to a halt
grind have an ax to grind (with someone)
grind the daily grind
grindstone keep one's nose to the grindstone
grindstone put one's nose to the grindstone
grip grip someone's attention
grip lose one's grip
grips come to grips with something
grist grist for someone's mill
grit grit one's teeth
gritty get down to the nitty-gritty
groan groan under the burden of something
gross gross someone out
ground break ground (for something)
ground break new ground
ground cover a lot of ground
ground cut the ground out from under someone
ground drive something into the ground
ground from the ground up
ground get in (on the ground floor)
ground get one's feet on the ground
ground get something off (the ground)
ground give ground
ground ground someone
ground have one's ear to the ground
ground have one's feet on the ground
ground hold one's ground
ground keep one's ear to the ground
ground keep one's feet on the ground
ground lose ground
ground one's old stamping ground
ground run something into the ground
ground stand one's ground
grounded grounded in fact
grounds grounds for something
grow grow on someone
grow grow out of something
grow grow to do something
grow let grass grow under one's feet
growing have growing pains
grudge bear a grudge (against someone)
grudge have a grudge (against someone)
grudge hold a grudge (against someone)
grudge nurse a grudge (against someone)
gruff (as) gruff as a bear
gruff gruff as a bear
grunt grunt work
guard catch one off one's guard
guard catch someone off guard
guard guard against someone or something
guard on (one's) guard

guess by guess and by golly
guess get another guess coming
guess hazard a guess
guess Your guess is as good as mine.
guessed never would have guessed
guest guest of honor
guilty find someone guilty
guinea serve as a guinea pig
gulp gulp for air
gum gum something up
gum gum up the works
gun beat the gun
gun fire a gun
gun give her the gun
gun give it the gun
gun gun for someone
gun jump the gun
gun pull a gun (on someone)
gun son of a gun
guns go great guns
guns stick to one's guns
gut bust a gut (to do something)
gut gut feeling
gut gut reaction
gut gut response
gut my gut tells me (that) something is so
guts hate someone's guts
gutter in the gutter
gyp gyp someone out of something
ha funny ha-ha
habit break a habit
habit break one's habit
habit break the habit
habit kick a habit
habit kick the habit
habits Old habits die hard.
hack hack something
hackles get someone's hackles up
had had best do something
had had better do something
had had (just) as soon do something
had (had) known it was coming
had had rather do something
had had sooner do something
had have been had
had have had enough
had have had its day
had have had it (up to here)
had (have) never had it so good
had never had it so good
hail hail-fellow-well-met
hail hail from somewhere
hailing within hailing distance
hair curl someone's hair
hair get in someone's hair
hair hang by a hair
hair let one's hair down
hair make someone's hair curl
hair make someone's hair stand on end
hair neither hide nor hair
hair part someone's hair
hair tear one's hair (out)
hair the hair of the dog that bit one
haired fair-haired boy
hair's by a hair('s breadth)
hairs get gray hair(s)
hairs give someone gray hair(s)
hairs split hairs
hale hale and hearty
half at half-mast
half go off half-cocked
Half Half a loaf is better than none.
half half-and-half
half have half a mind to do something
half have half a notion to do something
half not half bad
half one's better half
half six of one and half a dozen of the other
halfhearted halfhearted (about someone or something)
halfway meet someone halfway
halt grind to a halt
ham ham something up
hamburger make hamburger out of someone or something
hammer fight someone or something hammer and tongs
hammer go at it hammer and tongs
hammer hammer away (at someone or something)
hammer hammer something home
hammer hammer something out
hand at hand
hand bite the hand that feeds one
hand bound hand and foot
hand can't see one's hand in front of one's face
hand close at hand
hand do something by hand
hand force someone's hand
hand from hand to hand
hand get a free hand (with someone or something)
hand get a hand with something
hand get the glad hand
hand get the upper hand (on someone)
hand give someone a free hand (with something)
hand give someone a hand (for something)
hand give someone a hand (with someone or something)
hand give someone the glad hand
hand hand in glove (with someone)
hand hand in hand
Hand Hand it over.
hand hand it to someone
hand hand-me-down
hand hand over fist
hand hand over hand
hand hand something down (to someone)
hand hat in hand
hand have a hand in something
hand have one's hand in the till
hand have something at hand
hand have something in hand
hand in hand
hand keep one's hand in (something)
hand know someone or something like the back of one's hand
hand know someone or something like the palm of one's hand

hand lend a hand (to someone)
hand lend (someone) a hand
hand lift a hand (against someone or something)
hand live from hand to mouth
hand near at hand
hand not lift a hand (to help someone)
hand on (the) one hand
hand on the other hand
hand out of hand
hand put one's hand to the plow
hand raise a hand (against someone or something)
hand show one's hand
hand take a hand in something
hand try one's hand (at something)
hand wait on someone hand and foot
hand (with) hat in hand
hand with one hand tied behind one's back
hand an old hand at doing something
hand A bird in the hand is worth two in the bush.
handbasket go to hell in a handbasket
handed catch someone red-handed
handed caught red-handed
handed come away empty-handed
handed go away empty-handed
handed pay someone a back-handed compliment
handed pay someone a left-handed compliment
handful by the handful
handle fly off the handle
handle get a handle on something
handle handle someone with kid gloves
handle have a handle on something
handling postage and handling
handling shipping and handling
hands by a show of hands
hands change hands
hands dirty one's hands
hands do something hands down
hands eat out of someone's hands
hands fold one's hands
hands get one's hands dirty
hands get one's hands on someone or something
hands hands down
Hands Hands off!
Hands Hands up!
hands have clean hands
hands have one's hands full (with someone or something)
hands have one's hands tied
hands have someone or something in one's hands
hands have someone or something on one's hands
hands have someone's blood on one's hands
hands in good hands
hands join hands
hands keep one's hands off (someone or something)
hands lay one's hands on someone or something
hands leave someone or something in one's hands
hands Many hands make light work.
hands play into someone's hands
hands put one's hand(s) on something
hands putty in someone's hands
hands shake (hands) on something
hands shake hands (with someone)
hands sit on its hands
hands sit on one's hands
hands soil one's hands
hands take the law into one's own hands
hands throw one's hands up in despair
hands throw one's hands up in horror
hands tie someone's hands
hands wash one's hands of someone or something
hands with both hands tied behind one's back
hands a show of hands
handwriting read the handwriting on the wall
handwriting see the (hand)writing on the wall
handy come in handy
hang get the hang of something
hang hang a left
hang hang a right
hang hang around (with someone)
hang hang back
hang hang by a hair
hang hang by a thread
hang hang fire
hang hang in the balance
hang hang in there
hang hang loose
hang hang one's hat (up) somewhere
hang hang on someone's coattails
hang hang on someone's every word
hang hang on (to someone or something)
hang hang out (somewhere)
hang hang out (with someone)
hang hang someone in effigy
hang hang tough
hang hang up
hang let it all hang out
hang not give a hang (about someone or something)
hang somewhere to hang (up) one's hat
hang a place to hang one's hat
hanging have something hanging over one's head
hanging keep someone or something hanging in midair
hanging leave someone or something hanging in midair
happen can't wait (for something to happen)
happen happen (up)on someone or something
happen have a hunch (that) something will happen
happen sit back and let something happen
happens in case something happens
happens in the unlikely event that something happens
happens just in case (something happens)
happens no matter what happens
happens the minute something happens
happier couldn't be happier
happily live happily ever after
happy (as) happy as a clam
happy (as) happy as a lark
happy (as) happy as can be
happy fat and happy
happy find a happy medium
happy happy as a clam
happy happy as a lark
happy happy as can be
happy hit a happy medium
happy strike a happy medium
harbinger a harbinger of things to come
hard (as) hard as a rock

hard (as) hard as nails
hard (as) hard as stone
hard between a rock and a hard place
hard cold, hard cash
hard come down hard on someone or something
hard do something the hard way
hard drive a hard bargain
hard find (something) out the hard way
hard get the hard sell
hard give someone a hard time
hard give someone the hard sell
hard hard-and-fast
hard hard as a rock
hard hard as nails
hard hard as stone
hard hard of hearing
hard hard on someone's heels
hard hard pressed (to do something)
hard hard put (to do something)
hard hard up (for something)
hard have a hard time
hard hit someone hard
hard learn (something) the hard way
hard no hard feelings
hard Old habits die hard.
hard play hard to get
hard take a hard line (with someone)
hard a hard nut to crack
hard A little (hard) work never hurt anyone.
hard A little (hard) work never killed anyone.
hardly hardly have time to breathe
hardly hardly have time to think
hare (as) mad as a March hare
hare mad as a March hare
harken hark(en) back to something
harm No harm done.
harness get back into harness
harp harp on something
harping keep harping on something
Harry (every) Tom, Dick, and Harry
Harry Tom, Dick, and Harry
has Every cloud has a silver lining.
has Every dog has his day.
has Every dog has its day.
has the moment everyone has been waiting for
has The worm (has) turned.
hash hash something over
Haste Haste makes waste.
haste in great haste
hasty beat a (hasty) retreat
hat at the drop of a hat
hat eat one's hat
hat hang one's hat (up) somewhere
hat hat in hand
hat keep something under one's hat
hat old hat
hat pass the hat
hat pull something out of a hat
hat somewhere to hang (up) one's hat
hat take off one's hat (to someone)
hat talk through one's hat
hat toss one's hat into the ring
hat wear more than one hat
hat (with) hat in hand
hat a place to hang one's hat
hatband (as) tight as Dick's hatband
hatband tight as Dick's hatband
hatch count one's chickens before they hatch
hatch down the hatch
hatches batten down the hatches
hatchet bury the hatchet
hate hate someone's guts
hate someone's pet hate
hatter (as) mad as a hatter
hatter mad as a hatter
haul haul someone in
haul haul someone over the coals
haul haul up (somewhere)
haul over the long haul
haul over the short haul
have and what have you
have as luck would have it
have do not have a care in the world
have do not have a leg to stand on
have do not have all one's marbles
have eat one's cake and have it too
have hardly have time to breathe
have hardly have time to think
have have a bad effect (on someone or something)
have have a ball
have have a bee in one's bonnet
have have a big mouth
have have a blowout
have have a bone to pick (with someone)
have have a brush with something
have have a case (against someone)
have have a change of heart
have have a chip on one's shoulder
have have a clean conscience (about someone or something)
have have a clear conscience (about someone or something)
have have a close call
have have a close shave
have have a clue (about something)
have have a conniption (fit)
have have a crack at something
have have a familiar ring
have have a feeling about something
have have a feeling (that)
have have a field day
have have a finger in the pie
have have a fit
have have a foot in both camps
have have a frog in one's throat
have have a glass jaw
have have a go (at something)
have have a good command of something
have have a good head on one's shoulders
have have a (good) mind to do something
have have a good thing going
have have a green thumb
have have a grudge (against someone)
have have a hand in something

have have a handle on something
have have a hard time
have have a head for something
have have a heart
have have a hold on someone
have have a hunch about something
have have a hunch (that) something will happen
have have a keen interest in something
have have a look for someone or something
have have a lot going (for one)
have have a lot of promise
have have a lot on one's mind
have have a low boiling point
have have a mind like a steel trap
have have an accident
have have an ace up one's sleeve
have have an ax to grind (with someone)
have have an ear for something
have have a near miss
have have an eye for someone or something
have have an eye on someone or something
have have an eye out (for someone or something)
have have an in (with someone)
have have an itch for something
have have an itching palm
have have an itch to do something
have have an itchy palm
have have a nose for something
have have an out
have have a one-track mind
have have a passion for someone or something
have have a peep
have have a penchant for doing something
have have a pick-me-up
have have a price on one's head
have have a right to do something
have have a rough time (of it)
have have arrived
have have a run-in with someone
have have a run of bad luck
have have a run of something
have have a say (in something)
have have a score to settle (with someone)
have have a scrape (with someone or something)
have have a screw loose
have have a shot at something
have have a smoke
have have a snowball's chance in hell
have have a soft spot in one's heart for someone or something
have have a spaz
have have a stroke
have have a sweet tooth
have have a taste for something
have have a thing going (with someone)
have have a try at something
have have at someone or something
have have a vested interest in something
have have a voice (in something)
have have a way with someone or something
have have a weakness for someone or something
have have a whale of a time
have have a word with someone
have have back at someone
have have bats in one's belfry
have have bearing on something
have have been around
have have been had
have have been through the mill
have have been to hell and back
have have bigger fish to fry
have have broad shoulders
have have clean hands
have have cold feet
have have come a long way
have have contact with someone
have have designs on someone or something
have have dibs on something
have have egg on one's face
have have eyes bigger than one's stomach
have have eyes in the back of one's head
have have feet of clay
have have foot-in-mouth disease
have have growing pains
have have had enough
have have had its day
have have had it (up to here)
have have half a mind to do something
have have half a notion to do something
have have hell to pay
Have Have I got something for you!
Have Have I made myself clear?
have have it all over someone or something
have have it both ways
have have it in for someone
have have method in one's madness
have have mixed feelings (about someone or something)
have have money to burn
have have more important fish to fry
have (have) never had it so good
have have no business doing something
have have none of something
have have no staying power
have have nothing on someone or something
have have nothing to do with someone or something
have have one foot in the grave
have have one for the road
have have oneself something
have have one's back to the wall
have have one's cake and eat it too
have have one's druthers
have have one's ear to the ground
have have one's feet on the ground
have have one's finger in the pie
have have one's finger in too may pies
have have one's hand in the till
have have one's hands full (with someone or something)
have have one's hands tied
have have one's head in the clouds
have have one's heart go out to someone
have have one's heart in the right place
have have one's heart on one's sleeve
have have one's heart set against something
have have one's heart set on something

have have one's heart stand still
have have one's luck run out
have have one's nose in a book
have have one's nose in the air
have have one's sights trained on something
have have one's words stick in one's throat
have have one's work cut out for one
have have other fish to fry
have have precedence over someone or something;
have have pull with someone
have have rocks in one's head
have have second thoughts about someone or something
have have seen better days
have have so
have have someone or something in one's hands
have have someone or something in tow
have have someone or something on one's hands
have have someone or something on one's mind
have have someone's blood on one's hands
have have someone's hide
have have someone dead to rights
have have someone in one's pocket
have have someone on the string
have have someone over
have have someone pegged as something
have have something at hand
have have something at one's fingertips
have have something coming (to one)
have have something doing
have have something down pat
have have something going (for oneself)
have have something going (with someone)
have have something hanging over one's head
have have something in common (with someone or something)
have have something in hand
have have something in stock
have have something in store (for someone)
have have something made
have have something on
have have something out (with someone)
have have something stick in one's craw
have have something to go
have have something to spare
have have sticky fingers
have have the ball in one's court
have have the best of both worlds
have have the cards stacked against one
have have the courage of one's convictions
have have the deck stacked against one
have have the devil to pay
have have the feel of something
have have the gall to do something
have have the gift of gab
have have the makings of something
have have the Midas touch
have have them rolling in the aisles
have have the patience of a saint
have have the presence of mind to do something
have have the right-of-way
have have the right to do something
have have the shoe on the other foot
have have the time of one's life
have have the wherewithal (to do something)
have have to do with someone or something
have have to live with something
have have too
have have turned the corner
have have two strikes against one
have have what it takes
Have Have you been keeping busy?
have I just have this feeling
have let someone have it (with both barrels)
have never would have guessed
have only have eyes for someone
have scarcely have time to breathe
have should have stood in bed
have Walls have ears.
have What have you been up to?
have Who would have thought?
have would like (to have) someone or something
have The chickens have come home to roost.
having feel like (having) something
havoc play havoc with someone or something
havoc raise havoc with someone or something
havoc wreak havoc with something
haw hem and haw (around)
hawk watch someone or something like a hawk
hay hit the hay
hay That ain't hay.
haystack like looking for a needle in a haystack
haywire go haywire
hazard at hazard
hazard hazard a guess
hazard hazard an opinion
haze in a haze
He He laughs best who laughs last.
He He who laughs last, laughs longest.
He He who pays the piper calls the tune.
head able to do something standing on one's head
head bang one's head against a brick wall
head beat one's head against the wall
head beat something into someone's head
head bite someone's head off
head bring something to a head
head bury one's head in the sand
head come to a head
head drum something into someone('s head)
head fall head over heels
head from head to toe
head get a head start (on someone or something)
head get one's head above water
head get someone or something out of one's head
head get something into someone's thick head
head give someone a head start (on someone or something)
head give someone a swelled head
head go over someone's head
head go to someone's head
head have a good head on one's shoulders
head have a head for something
head have a price on one's head
head have eyes in the back of one's head
head have one's head in the clouds
head have rocks in one's head

head have *something* hanging over *one's* head
head head and shoulders above *someone or something*
head head for *someone or something*
head head for the last roundup
head head over heels in debt
head head over heels in love (with *someone*)
head head *someone or something* off
head head *something* up
head hide *one's* head in the sand
head hit the nail (right) on the head
head hold *one's* head up
head in over *one's* head
head keep a civil tongue (in *one's* head)
head keep *one's* head
head lose *one's* head (over *someone or something*)
head make *someone's* head spin
head make *someone's* head swim
head need *something* like a hole in the head
head off the top of *one's* head
head on *someone's* head
head out of *one's* head
head over *someone's* head
head per head
head put ideas into *someone's* head
head put *one's* head on the block (for *someone or something*)
head rear its ugly head
head run around like a chicken with its head cut off
head talk *someone's* head off
head touched (in the head)
head trouble *one's* head about *someone or something*
head turn *someone's* head
head use *one's* head
head a head
heads can't make heads or tails (out) of *someone or something*
heads heads or tails
Heads Heads up!
heads heads will roll
heads knock some heads together
heads to count heads
health get a clean bill of health
health give *someone* a clean bill of health
health in the best of health
health nurse *someone* back to health
healthy Early to bed, early to rise(, makes a man healthy, wealthy, and wise.)
hear hear a peep out of *someone*
hear hear of *something*
hear hear *someone* out
hear like to hear *oneself* talk
hear Now hear this!
hear so quiet you could hear a pin drop
hear so still you could hear a pin drop
hear will not hear of *something*
heard another country heard from
heard make *oneself* heard
hearing hard of hearing
heart break *someone's* heart
heart cross *one's* heart (and hope to die)
heart die of a broken heart
heart do *someone's* heart good
heart eat *one's* heart out
heart find it in *one's* heart (to *do something*)
heart follow *one's* heart
heart from the bottom of *one's* heart
heart from the heart
heart get at the heart of the matter
heart get to the heart of the matter
heart have a change of heart
heart have a heart
heart have a soft spot in *one's* heart for *someone or something*
heart have *one's* heart go out to *someone*
heart have *one's* heart in the right place
heart have *one's* heart on *one's* sleeve
heart have *one's* heart set against *something*
heart have *one's* heart set on *something*
heart have *one's* heart stand still
heart heart and soul
heart know *something* by heart
heart learn *something* by heart
heart lose heart
heart *one's* heart goes out to *someone*
heart *one's* heart is (dead) set against *something*
heart *one's* heart is in *one's* mouth
heart *one's* heart is in the right place
heart *one's* heart is set on *something*
heart *one's* heart misses a beat
heart *one's* heart skips a beat
heart *one's* heart stands still
heart open *one's* heart (to *someone*)
heart pour *one's* heart (out to *someone*)
heart set *one's* heart against *something*
heart set *one's* heart on *something*
heart take heart
heart take *something* to heart
heart warm the cockles of *someone's* heart
heart wear *one's* heart on *one's* sleeve
heart with a heavy heart
heart with all *one's* heart and soul
heart an aching heart
heartbeat be a heartbeat away from *something*
heartbeat do *something* in a heartbeat
heart's to *one's* heart's content
hearty hale and hearty
heat in a dead heat
heat in heat
heat put the heat on (*someone*)
heat turn the heat up (on *someone*)
heave get the (old) heave-ho
heave give *someone or something* the (old) heave-ho
heaven in heaven
heaven in seventh heaven
heaven move heaven and earth to *do something*
heaven smell to high heaven
heaven stink to high heaven
heavy heavy going
heavy hot and heavy
heavy with a heavy heart
heck for the heck of it
hedge hedge *one's* bets
heed take heed
heeled well-heeled

heels cool one's heels
heels dig one's heels in
heels down-at-the-heels
heels fall head over heels
heels hard on someone's heels
heels head over heels in debt
heels head over heels in love (with someone)
heels kick up one's heels
heels on the heels of something
heels set one back on one's heels
heels take to one's heels
height at the height of something
hell (all) shot to hell
hell (as) hot as hell
hell (as) mad as hell
hell catch hell
hell come hell or high water
hell for the hell of it
hell get hell
hell give someone hell
hell go to (hell)
hell go to hell in a handbasket
hell have a snowball's chance in hell
hell have been to hell and back
hell have hell to pay
hell hell-bent for leather
hell hell on earth
hell hot as hell
hell like a bat out of hell
hell mad as hell
hell raise hell (with someone or something)
hell shot to hell
hell through hell and high water
hell to hell and gone
hell until hell freezes over
hell when hell freezes over
hell You scared the hell out of me.
hello drop in (to say hello)
helm at the helm (of something)
help cannot help doing something
help can't help but do something
help help do something
help help oneself
help help (someone or something) out (with someone or something)
help not able to help something
help not lift a finger (to help someone)
help not lift a hand (to help someone)
help pitch in (and help)
hem hem and haw (around)
hem hem someone or something in
hen (as) mad as a wet hen
hen mad as a wet hen
hens' (as) scarce as hens' teeth
hens' scarcer than hens' teeth
her give her the gun
her give the devil her due
her let her rip
herd ride herd on someone or something
here downhill from here on
here have had it (up to here)
here here and there
Here Here goes nothing.
Here Here (it) goes.
here here, there, and everywhere
Here Here you go.
here neither here nor there
here same here
here the here and now
Here's Here's looking at you.
Here's Here's mud in your eye.
Here's Here's to someone or something.
herring red herring
herself by herself
hibernating (as) busy as a hibernating bear
hibernating busy as a hibernating bear
hide have someone's hide
hide hide-and-seek
hide hide one's face in shame
hide hide one's head in the sand
hide hide one's light under a bushel
hide neither hide nor hair
hide tan someone's hide
hiding go into hiding
hiding Where've you been hiding yourself?
high act high-and-mighty
high (as) high as a kite
high (as) high as the sky
high be flying high
high come hell or high water
high eat high on the hog
high get into high gear
high get off your high horse
high get the high sign
high give someone the high sign
high go sky-high
high high and dry
high high-and-mighty
high high as a kite
high high man on the totem pole
high high on something
high hit the high spots
high hold someone in high regard
high hunt high and low (for someone or something)
high in high dudgeon
high in high gear
high It's high time!
high knee-high to a grasshopper
high leave someone high and dry
high live high off the hog
high live high on the hog
high look high and low (for someone or something)
high running high
high search high and low (for someone or something)
high smell to high heaven
high stink to high heaven
high through hell and high water
highflier highflier
highly speak highly of someone or something
highly think highly of someone or something
hightail hightail it out of somewhere
highways highways and byways
hike Take a hike!
hill not worth a hill of beans

hill over the hill
hills (as) old as the hills
hills old as the hills
himself by himself
hind (as) crooked as a dog's hind leg
hind crooked as a dog's hind leg
hindsight in hindsight
hinge hinge on something
hint take a hint
hip shoot from the hip
hire new hire
hire not for hire
his beard the lion in his den
his Every dog has his day.
his give the devil his due
his A fool and his money are soon parted.
history go down in history
hit hit a happy medium
hit hit-and-miss
hit hit-and-run
hit hit a plateau
hit hit a snag
hit hit a sour note
hit hit bottom
hit hit home
hit hit it off (with someone)
hit hit one's stride
hit hit one close to home
hit hit one where one lives
hit hit-or-miss
hit hit pay dirt
hit hit (someone) below the belt
hit hit someone hard
hit hit (someone) like a ton of bricks
hit hit someone (right) between the eyes
hit hit someone up (for something)
hit hit the books
hit hit the bottle
hit hit the bricks
hit hit the bull's-eye
hit hit the ceiling
hit hit the hay
hit hit the high spots
hit hit the jackpot
hit hit the nail (right) on the head
hit hit the road
hit hit the sack
hit hit the skids
hit hit the spot
hit hit (up)on something
hit make a hit (with someone or something)
hit pinch-hit (for someone)
hitch hitch a ride
hither hither and thither
hither hither, thither, and yon
hitting hitting on all cylinders
hive a hive of activity
ho get the (old) heave-ho
ho give someone or something the (old) heave-ho
hoarse (as) hoarse as a crow
hoarse hoarse as a crow
hob play hob with someone or something
hob raise hob with someone or something
Hobson's Hobson's choice
hock go into hock
hock in hock
hoe tough row to hoe
hog eat high on the hog
hog go hog-wild
hog go whole hog
hog live high off the hog
hog live high on the hog
hog road-hog
hoist hoist by one's own petard
hoist hoist with one's own petard
hold can't hold a candle to someone
hold Don't hold your breath.
hold have a hold on someone
hold hold a grudge (against someone)
hold hold all the aces
hold hold a meeting
hold hold forth (on something)
hold hold no brief for someone or something
hold hold one's breath
hold hold one's end (of the bargain) up
hold hold one's fire
hold hold one's ground
hold hold one's head up
hold hold one's own
hold hold one's peace
hold hold one's temper
hold hold one's tongue
hold hold on (to someone or something)
hold hold out for something
hold hold out the olive branch
hold hold someone or something in check
hold hold someone or something over
hold hold someone or something still
hold hold someone or something up
hold hold someone's attention
hold hold someone down
hold hold someone hostage
hold hold someone in high regard
hold hold something against someone
hold hold still
hold hold the fort
hold hold the line (at someone or something)
hold hold true
hold hold up
hold hold with something
Hold Hold your horses!
Hold Hold your tongue!
hold lay hold of someone or something
hold not hold a candle to someone or something
hold not hold a stick to someone or something
hold not hold water
hold on hold
hold put a hold on something
hold put someone or something on hold
holding leave someone holding the bag
holds no holds barred
hole ace in the hole
hole hole up (somewhere)
hole in the hole

hole Money burns a hole in someone's pocket.
hole need something like a hole in the head
hole out of the hole
hole punch a hole in something
hole someone's ace in the hole
hole a hole in one
hole a square peg in a round hole
holes pick holes in something
holiday a busman's holiday
holier holier-than-thou
holler hoot and holler
homage pay homage to someone
home at home
home bring home the bacon
home bring something home to someone
home close to home
home come home (to roost)
home come home to someone
home drive something home
home eat someone out of house and home
home feel at home
home hammer something home
home hit home
home hit one close to home
home home in (on someone or something)
home keep the home fires burning
home make oneself at home
home nothing to write home about
home see someone home
home strike home
home take something home (with oneself)
home till the cows come home
home (un)til the cows come home
home The chickens have come home to roost.
honest honest and aboveboard
Honest Honest to God.
Honest Honest to goodness.
Honest Honest to Pete.
honestly come by something honestly
honey (as) sweet as honey
honey sweet as honey
honeymoon The honeymoon is over.
honor guest of honor
honor honor someone's check
honor in honor of someone or something
honor on one's honor
honors do the honors
hood look under the hood
Hood's all around Robin Hood's barn
hook (as) crooked as a fish hook
hook by hook or (by) crook
hook crooked as a fish hook
hook get off the hook
hook get (someone) off the hook
hook let someone off (the hook)
hook swallow something, hook, line, and sinker
hooked hooked (on something)
hooks (as) crooked as a barrel of fish hooks
hooks crooked as a barrel of fish hooks
hooks get one's hooks into someone or something
hooky play hooky
hoop jump through a hoop
hoops jump through hoops
hoot hoot and holler
hoot not give a hoot (about someone or something)
hoots not care two hoots (about someone or something)
hoots not give two hoots (about someone or something)
Hop Hop to it!
hop a hop, skip, and a jump
hope cross one's heart (and hope to die)
hope hope against (all) hope
hopeless hopeless at doing something
hopes in hopes of something
hopes pin one's hope(s) on someone or something
hopped hopped up
horizon loom large (on the horizon)
horizon on the horizon
horn blow one's own horn
horn horn in (on someone or something)
horn toot one's own horn
hornet (as) mad as a hornet
hornet mad as a hornet
hornet's stir up a hornet's nest
horns lock horns (with someone)
horns on the horns of a dilemma
horns seize the bull by the horns
horns take the bull by the horns
horror in horror
horror throw one's hands up in horror
horse (as) strong as a horse
horse back the wrong horse
horse beat a dead horse
horse dark horse
horse eat like a horse
horse get a charley horse
horse get off your high horse
horse horse and buggy
horse horse and carriage
horse horse around
horse horse sense
horse put the cart before the horse
horse strong as a horse
horse work like a horse
horse a horse of a different color
horse a horse of another color
horseback on horseback
horses change horses in the middle of the stream
horse's from the horse's mouth
horses Hold your horses!
horse's (straight) from the horse's mouth
horses Wild horses couldn't drag someone.
hostage hold someone hostage
hostage take someone hostage
hot (as) busy as a cat on a hot tin roof
hot (as) hot as fire
hot (as) hot as hell
hot blow hot and cold
hot busy as a cat on a hot tin roof
hot full of hot air
hot get in(to) hot water
hot hot and bothered
hot hot and heavy
hot hot as fire
hot hot as hell

hot hot on something
hot hot under the collar
hot in hot water
hot in the hot seat
hot make it hot for someone
hot on the hot seat
hot piping hot
hot strike while the iron is hot
hotcakes sell like hotcakes
hotfoot hotfoot it out of somewhere
hound's (as) clean as a hound's tooth
hound's clean as a hound's tooth
hour at the bottom of the hour
hour at the eleventh hour
hour at the top of the hour
hour by the hour
hour eleventh-hour decision
hour on the hour
hours after hours
hours for hours on end
hours keep late hours
hours small hours (of the night)
hours There aren't enough hours in the day.
hours till all hours (of the day and night)
hours until all hours
hours wee hours (of the night)
house bring down the house
house eat someone out of house and home
house keep house
house like a house afire
house like a house on fire
house on the house
house put one's house in order
How How goes it (with you)?
how know-how
how a fine how-de-do
how a fine how-do-you-do
How's How's it going?
How's How's the world (been) treating you?
Hoyle according to Hoyle
hue a hue and cry
huff huff and puff
huff in a huff
human milk of human kindness
humanly everything humanly possible
humble eat humble pie
hump over the hump
hunch have a hunch about something
hunch have a hunch (that) something will happen
hundred one in a hundred
hung hung up (on someone or something)
hunger hunger for something
hungry (as) hungry as a bear
hungry (as) hungry as a hunter
hungry hungry as a bear
hungry hungry as a hunter
hungry hungry for something
hunt hunt-and-peck
hunt hunt high and low (for someone or something)
hunt hunt someone or something up
hunter (as) hungry as a hunter
hunter hungry as a hunter
hurl hurl an insult (at someone)
hurry get a hurry on
hurt cry before one is hurt
hurt not hurt a flea
hurt What one doesn't know won't hurt one.
hurt A little (hard) work never hurt anyone.
hush hush money
Hush Hush your mouth!
hush a hush fell over someone or something
hustle hustle and bustle
Hyde Jekyll and Hyde
I as I expected
I Do I need to paint you a picture?
I for all I care
I for all I know
I Have I got something for you!
I Have I made myself clear?
I I didn't catch your name.
I I just have this feeling
I I'm damned if I do and damned if I don't.
I (just) as I expected
I (Now), where was I?
I so mad I could scream
I What can I say?
I Where was I?
ice break the ice
ice cut no ice (with someone)
ice on thin ice
ice put something on ice
ice skate on thin ice
idea flirt with the idea of doing something
idea get a bright idea
idea get a rough idea (about something)
idea get a rough idea (of something)
idea give someone a bright idea
idea give someone a rough idea (about something)
idea give someone a rough idea (of something)
idea sell someone on a plan or idea
ideas put ideas into someone's head
identity a case of mistaken identity
idiot take someone for an idiot
idly sit (idly) by
if better off (if one were somewhere else)
if better off (if something were done)
if if looks could kill
if if not
if if push comes to shove
if if so
If If the shoe fits, wear it.
if if worst comes to worst
if I'm damned if I do and damned if I don't.
if look as if butter wouldn't melt in one's mouth
if make as if to do something
if not know if one is coming or going
if sound as if
if what if
ifs no ifs, ands, or buts about it
ignorant play ignorant
ill fall ill
ill ill at ease
ill ill-disposed to doing something
I'll I'll drink to that!

ill ill-gotten gains
I'll I'll (try to) catch you later.
ill ill will
ill speak ill of someone
ill take ill
I'll You scratch my back and I'll scratch yours.
I'm I'm awful at names.
I'm I'm damned if I do and damned if I don't.
I'm (I'm) sorry.
I'm I'm terrible at names.
image be the spit and image of someone
image be the spitting image of someone
imagine Can you imagine?
Imagine Imagine that!
immediate immediate occupancy
immemorial since time immemorial
impact on impact
impact (up)on impact
impartial fair and impartial
impasse reach an impasse
implicate implicate someone (in something)
important have more important fish to fry
impression make an impression (on someone)
impulse on impulse
impunity with impunity
in ace in the hole
in advanced in years
in air one's dirty linen in public
in all in
in (all) in one breath
in (all) in the family
in along in years
in (another) nail in someone's or something's coffin
in Any port in a storm.
in arm in arm
in arrive in a body
in as alike as (two) peas in a pod
in (as) calm as a toad in the sun
in (as) slow as molasses in January
in (as) snug as a bug in a rug
in at this point (in time)
in back in circulation
in barge in (on someone or something)
in beard the lion in his den
in bear in mind that something is so
in bear someone or something in mind
in behind in something
in be swimming in something
in blaze a trail (in something)
in blow up in someone's face
in born with a silver spoon in one's mouth
in break out in a cold sweat
in break out (in something)
in break someone or something in
in bring people or other creatures out in droves
in broad in the beam
in build castles in Spain
in build castles in the air
in burn one's bridges in front of one
in burn someone in effigy
in burst in on someone or something
in bury one's head in the sand
in butt in (on someone or something)
in buy a pig in a poke
in call someone or something in
in calm as a toad in the sun
in can't see one's hand in front of one's face
in cash in one's chips
in cash in (on something)
in cash something in
in cast in the same mold
in cast one's lot in with someone
in catch someone in the act (of doing something)
in caught in the act
in caught in the cross fire
in caught in the middle
in cave in (to someone or something)
in change horses in the middle of the stream
in check in (on someone or something)
in chime in (with something)
in chink in one's armor
in chip in (on something)
in chip in something on something
in chip something in (on something)
in close in (on someone or something)
in clue someone in (on something)
in come down in the world
in come in a body
in come in for something
in come in handy
in come in out of the rain
in come out in the wash
in come up in the world
in confide in someone
in contradiction in terms
in count someone in (on something)
in cue someone in
in cut someone in
in dart in and out
in day in and day out
in day in, day out
in dead in someone's or something's tracks
in deal in something
in decide in favor of someone or something
in die in one's boots
in dig in
in dig one's heels in
in dog in the manger
in done in
in do not have a care in the world
in do someone or something in
in do something in a heartbeat
in do something in person
in do something in public
in do something in secret
in do something in vain
in double in brass
in down in the dumps
in down in the mouth
in drop in one's tracks
in drop in (on someone)
in drop in (to say hello)
in dyed-in-the-wool
in engage in small talk

in even in the best of times
in (every) once in a while
in fall head over heels in love (with someone)
in fall in
in feel something in one's bones
in fence someone in
in figure in something
in fill someone in (on someone or something)
in find it in one's heart (to do something)
in first thing (in the morning)
in fish in troubled waters
in fit in someone
in fit in (with someone or something)
in fly in the face of someone or something
in fly in the teeth of someone or something
in follow in someone's footsteps
in follow in someone's tracks
in fools rush in (where angels fear to tread)
in get a bee in one's bonnet
in get a frog in one's throat
in get along (in years)
in get a lump in one's throat
in get an in (with someone)
in get ants in one's pants
in get a word in edgeways
in get a word in edgewise
in get butterflies in one's stomach
in get in on something
in get in (on the ground floor)
in get in someone's hair
in get in touch (with someone)
in get it in the neck
in get one's ducks in a row
in get one's foot in the door
in get something out in the open
in get stars in one's eyes
in give in (to someone or something)
in give one butterflies in one's stomach
in go a long way in doing something
in go (a)round in circles
in go down in history
in go in a body
in go in for something
in go in one ear and out the other
in Go jump in the lake!
in Go play in the traffic!
in go to hell in a handbasket!
in go up in flames
in go up in smoke
in grounded in fact
in hand in glove (with someone)
in hand in hand
in hang in the balance
in hang in there
in hang someone in effigy
in hat in hand
in haul someone in
in have a bee in one's bonnet
in have a finger in the pie
in have a foot in both camps
in have a frog in one's throat
in have a hand in something
in have a keen interest in something
in have an in (with someone)
in have a run-in with someone
in have a say (in something)
in have a snowball's chance in hell
in have a soft spot in one's heart for someone or something
in have a vested interest in something
in have a voice (in something)
in have bats in one's belfry
in have eyes in the back of one's head
in have foot-in-mouth disease
in have it in for someone
in have method in one's madness
in have one foot in the grave
in have one's finger in the pie
in have one's finger in too may pies
in have one's hand in the till
in have one's head in the clouds
in have one's heart in the right place
in have one's nose in a book
in have one's nose in the air
in have one's words stick in one's throat
in have rocks in one's head
in have someone or something in one's hands
in have someone or something in tow
in have someone in one's pocket
in have something in mind
in have something in common (with someone or something)
in have something in hand
in have something in stock
in have something in store (for someone)
in have something stick in one's craw
in have the ball in one's court
in have them rolling in the aisles
in have too many irons in the fire
in head over heels in debt
in head over heels in love (with someone)
in hem someone or something in
in Here's mud in your eye.
in hide one's face in shame
in hide one's head in the sand
in hold someone or something in check
in hold someone in high regard
in home in (on someone or something)
in horn in (on someone or something)
in implicate someone (in something)
in in a bad mood
in in a bad way
in in abeyance
in in a bind
in in accordance with something
in in a (constant) state of flux
in in a coon's age
in in addition (to something)
in in a dead heat
in in advance
in in a family way
in in a fix
in in a flash
in in a fog
in in a fool's paradise
in in agreement

in in a haze
in in a huff
in in a jam
in in a jiffy
in in a lather
in in a little bit
in in (all) good conscience
in in all one's born days
in in all probability
in in a mad rush
in in a month of Sundays
in in and of itself
in in a nutshell
in in any case
in in any event
in in a pinch
in in apple-pie order
in in a (pretty) pickle
in in a quandary
in in a real pickle
in in arrears
in in a rut
in in a sense
in in a snit
in in a split second
in in a stage whisper
in in a stew (about someone or something)
in in a stupor
in in a (tight) spot
in in a tizzy
in in at the kill
in in a vicious circle
in in awe (of someone or something)
in in a word
in in a world of one's own
in in bad faith
in in bad sorts
in in bad taste
in in bad (with someone)
in in behalf of someone
in in between
in in black and white
in in bloom
in in blossom
in in brief
in in broad daylight
in in bulk
in in cahoots (with someone)
in in care of someone
in in case
in in character
in in clover
in in cold blood
in in cold storage
in in concert (with someone)
in in condition
in in consequence (of something)
in in consideration of something
in in contempt (of court)
in in creation
in in custody of someone or something
in in debt
in in deep
in in defiance (of someone or something)
in in denial
in in detail
in in disguise
in in drag
in in due course
in in due time
in in Dutch (with someone)
in in earnest
in in effect
in in essence
in in exchange (for someone or something)
in in existence
in in fact
in in fashion
in in favor of someone
in in favor (of someone or something)
in in fear and trembling
in in fine feather
in in flight
in in flux
in in force
in in for something
in in full swing
in in general
in in good condition
in in good faith
in in good hands
in in good repair
in in good shape
in in good spirits
in in good time
in in good (with someone)
in in great demand
in in great haste
in in hand
in in heat
in in heaven
in in high dudgeon
in in high gear
in in hindsight
in in hock
in in honor of someone or something
in in hopes of something
in in horror
in in hot water
in in ink
in in its entirety
in in its prime
in in jeopardy
in in (just) a minute
in in (just) a second
in in keeping (with something)
in in kind
in in labor
in in league (with someone)
in in less than no time
in in lieu of something
in in light of something
in in limbo
in in line

in in love (with someone or something)
in in luck
in in many respects
in in memory of someone
in in midair
in in mint condition
in in name only
in in need
in in neutral
in in no mood to do something
in in nothing flat
in in no time (at all)
in in no uncertain terms
in in one breath
in in one ear and out (of) the other
in in one fell swoop
in in one's birthday suit
in in one's blood
in in one's book
in in one's cups
in in one's element
in in one's glory
in in one's mind's eye
in in one's opinion
in in one's (own) backyard
in in one's (own) (best) interest(s)
in in one's prime
in in one's right mind
in in one's salad days
in in one's second childhood
in in one's spare time
in in one's Sunday best
in in on the kill
in in orbit
in in order to do something
in in other words
in in over one's head
in in park
in in part
in in passing
in in pencil
in in perpetuity
in in person
in in place
in in plain English
in in plain language
in in poor taste
in in practice
in in print
in in private
in in progress
in in proportion
in in public
in in pursuit of something
in in quest of someone or something
in in rags
in in reality
in in receipt of something
in in recent memory
in in rehearsal
in in remission
in in retrospect
in in return for (someone or something)
in in round figures
in in round numbers
in in ruin
in in search of someone or something
in in season
in in secret
in in session
in in seventh heaven
in in shambles
in in shape
in in short
in in sight
in (in) single file
in in so many words
in in someone else's place
in in someone else's shoes
in in someone's or something's custody
in in someone's behalf
in in someone's favor
in in someone's name
in in someone's prayers
in in some respects
in in some neck of the woods
in in spite of someone or something
in in step (with someone or something)
in in stock
in in storage
in instrumental in doing something
in in style
in in surgery
in in tandem
in in tatters
in in terms of something
in in the absence of someone or something
in in the act (of doing something)
in in the affirmative
in in the air
in in the altogether
in in the balance
in in the bargain
in in the best of health
in in the black
in in the blood
in in the buff
in in the bullpen
in in the cards
in in the care of someone
in in the case of someone or something
in in the charge of someone
in in the chips
in in the clear
in in the context of something
in in the course of time
in in the dark (about someone or something)
in in the doghouse
in in the doldrums
in in the driver's seat
in in the event of something
in in the family
in in the final analysis
in in the first instance

in in the first place
in in the flesh
in in the forefront (of *something*)
in in the gutter
in in the hole
in in the hot seat
in in the interest of *someone or something*
in in the interim (between *things*)
in in their entirety
in in the know
in in the lap of luxury
in in the last analysis
in in the laundry
in in the limelight
in in the line of duty
in in the long run
in in the mainstream (of *something*)
in in the market (for *something*)
in in the meantime
in in the middle of nowhere
in in the money
in in the mood for *something*
in in the mood to *do something*
in in the near future
in in the neighborhood of *something*
in in the nick of time
in in the nude
in in the offing
in in the open
in in theory
in in the pink (of condition)
in in the prime of life
in in the public eye
in in the raw
in in the rear
in in the red
in in there pitching
in in the right
in in the running
in in the same boat (as *someone*)
in in the same breath
in in the second place
in in the short run
in in the soup
in in the spotlight
in in the swim of things
in in the trust of *someone*
in in the twinkling of an eye
in in the unlikely event of *something*
in in the unlikely event that *something happens*
in in the (very) nick of time
in in the wake of *something*
in in the way of *something*
in in the wind
in in the works
in in the world
in in the worst way
in in the wrong
in in this day and age
in in time
in in top form
in in tow
in in transit
in in triplicate
in in trouble
in in tune
in in turn
in in two shakes of a lamb's tail
in in unison
in invest *someone's* time in *something*
in invest *something* in *someone or something*
in in view of *something*
in in with *someone*
in just in case (*something happens*)
in keep a civil tongue (in *one's* head)
in keep in touch (with *someone*)
in keep *one's* hand in (*something*)
in keep *someone or something* hanging in midair
in keep *someone or something* in check
in keep *someone or something* in mind
in keep *someone* in line
in keep *someone* in stitches
in keep *someone* out in the cold
in kick *something* in
in know *something* in *one's* bones
in late in life
in late in the day
in lay *something* in
in leave a bad taste in *someone's* mouth
in leave *someone or something* hanging in midair
in leave *someone or something* in *one's* hands
in leave *someone* in peace
in leave *someone* in the lurch
in leave *someone* out in the cold
in let *someone* in on *something*
in lie in state
in lie in wait for *someone or something*
in Lightning never strikes twice (in the same place).
in like looking for a needle in a haystack
in like (two) peas in a pod
in live in
in lock *something* in
in look as if butter wouldn't melt in *one's* mouth
in look in (on *someone or something*)
in look like *something* the cat dragged in
in look *someone* in the eye
in look *someone* in the face
in lose *oneself* (in *something*)
in lost in thought
in make a dent in *something*
in melt in *one's* mouth
in mention *someone or something* in passing
in milestone in *someone's* life
in misplace *one's* trust (in *someone*)
in Money burns a hole in *someone's* pocket.
in move in (on *someone or something*)
in move up (in the world)
in much in evidence
in muscle in (on *someone or something*)
in nail in *someone's or something's* coffin
in need *something* like a hole in the head
in never in *one's* life
in nip *something* in the bud
in no point in *something*

in not for (anything in) the world
in not in the same league with *someone or something*
in not know enough to come in out of the rain
in not take stock in *something*
in once in a blue moon
in once-in-a-lifetime chance
in once in a while
in one in a hundred
in one in a million
in one in a thousand
in *one's* heart is in *one's* mouth
in *one's* heart is in the right place
in *one's* nose is in the air
in on in years
in out in force
in out in left field
in packed (in) like sardines
in pack them in
in paper over the cracks (in *something*)
in pay in advance
in persist in *doing something*
in pick holes in *something*
in pie in the sky
in pitch in (and help)
in plug *something* in
in pride *oneself* in *something*
in punch a hole in *something*
in put a bee in *someone's* bonnet
in put all *one's* eggs in one basket
in put in a good word (for *someone*)
in put in an appearance
in put *oneself* in *someone else's* place
in put *oneself* in *someone else's* shoes
in put *one's* foot in it
in put *one's* foot in *one's* mouth
in put *one's* house in order
in put *one's* oar in
in put *one's* two cents(' worth) in
in put *one* in *one's* place
in put *someone* in the picture
in put *something* down in black and white
in put *something* in
in Put that in your pipe and smoke it!
in putty in *someone's* hands
in quake in *one's* boots
in raised in a barn
in red in the face
in rest in peace
in result in *something*
in rich in *something*
in ride off in all directions
in ring in the New Year
in roll in
in rolling in *something*
in roll (over) in *one's* grave
in Rome wasn't built in a day.
in rooted in *something*
in rub salt in the wound
in rub *someone's* nose in it
in rub *something* in
in run (around) in circles
in run in the family
in run *someone* in
in safety in numbers
in say *something* in a roundabout way
in set in
in set *someone* up (in business)
in shake in *one's* boots
in ships that pass in the night
in should have stood in bed
in sick in bed
in sink in
in sit in for *someone*
in sit in (on *something*)
in sleep in
in slow as molasses in January
in slower than molasses in January
in smack-dab in the middle
in snug as a bug in a rug
in *someone's* ace in the hole
in *someone's* mission in life
in (somewhere) in the neighborhood of *an amount*
in stab *someone* in the back
in stand in awe (of *someone or something*)
in stand (in) back of *someone or something*
in stand in (for *someone*)
in stand in *someone's* way
in stand *someone* in good stead
in stare *someone* in the face
in start *someone* in (as *something*)
in stay in touch (with *someone*)
in stew in *one's* own juice
in stick-in-the-mud
in stick *one's* foot in *one's* mouth
in stop in (*somewhere*)
in (stuck) in a rut
in stuck in traffic
in suck *someone* in
in take a course (in *something*)
in take a hand in *something*
in take an interest (in *something*)
in take no stock in *something*
in take part (in *something*)
in take pride in *something*
in take *someone or something* in
in take *someone* in
in take *something* in stride
in take the bit in *one's* teeth
in talk in circles
in talk until *one* is blue in the face
in There aren't enough hours in the day.
in There are plenty of other fish in the sea.
in throw in the sponge
in throw in the towel
in throw *one's* hands up in despair
in throw *one's* hands up in horror
in tie *someone* (up) in knots
in tongue-in-cheek
in touched (in the head)
in tune (*something*) in
in turn in
in turn (over) in *one's* grave
in up in arms
in up in the air (about *someone or something*)

in up in years
in up to one's ears (in something)
in up to one's eyeballs (in something)
in up to one's neck (in something)
in use every trick in the book
in waiting in the wings
in wash one's dirty linen in public
in weave in and out (of something)
in week in, week out
in well up in years
in When in Rome, do as the Romans do.
in (with) hat in hand
in with the best will in the world
in work someone or something in
in worth its weight in gold
in wrapped up in someone or something
in year in, year out
in zero in on something
in zoom in (on someone or something)
in an end in itself
in a babe in the woods
in a big frog in a small pond
in A bird in the hand is worth two in the bush.
in a blessing in disguise
in a bull in a china shop
in a case in point
in a crick in one's back
in a crick in one's neck
in a diamond in the rough
in a drop in the bucket
in a drop in the ocean
in a feather in one's cap
in a flash in the pan
in a fly in the ointment
in A friend in need is a friend indeed.
in a hole in one
in a kink in my neck
in a pain in the neck
in a shot in the arm
in a shot in the dark
in a skeleton in the closet
in a slap in the face
in a snake in the grass
in a square peg in a round hole
in a tempest in a teapot
in a thorn in someone's side
in a wolf in sheep's clothing
in the in thing (to do)
in the man in the street
inch come within an inch of doing something
inch every inch a something
inch every inch the something
inch Give one an inch, and one will take a mile.
inch inch along (something)
inch inch by inch
inch within an inch of one's life
inclined inclined to do something
incumbent incumbent upon someone to do something
indeed A friend in need is a friend indeed.
influence under the influence (of alcohol)
influence under the influence of something
information a gold mine of information
information a mine of information
iniquity a den of iniquity
initiative take the initiative (to do something)
injury add insult to injury
ink in ink
innocent (as) innocent as a lamb
innocent find someone innocent
innocent innocent as a lamb
innocent play innocent
ins ins and outs of something
inside get the inside track
inside inside the box
inside know something inside out
inside thinking inside the box
inside think inside the box
instance for instance
instance in the first instance
instrumental instrumental in doing something
insult add insult to injury
insult hurl an insult (at someone)
intent intent on doing something
intents for all intents and purposes
interest draw interest
interest have a keen interest in something
interest have a vested interest in something
interest in the interest of someone or something
interest of interest (to someone)
interest pique someone's interest
interest take an interest (in something)
interests in one's (own) (best) interest(s)
interim in the interim (between things)
intervals at regular intervals
into beat something into someone's head
into be into something
into break (out) in(to) tears
into break something down (into something)
into bring something into question
into bump into someone
into burst into flames
into burst into tears
into call someone or something into question
into check into something
into come into its own
into come into one's own
into come into something
into dip in(to something)
into drive something into the ground
into drum something into someone('s head)
into fall into a trap
into fall in(to) line
into fall in(to) place
into fall into someone's trap
into fall into the trap
into far into the night
into fit someone in(to something)
into fly into the face of danger
into get back into circulation
into get back into harness
into get into a jam
into get into a mess
into get into an argument (with someone)
into get into full swing

into get into high gear
into get in(to) hot water
into get into the act
into get into the swing of things
into get (oneself) into a stew (over someone or something)
into get one's hooks into someone or something
into get one's teeth into something
into get something into someone's thick head
into go into action
into go into a nosedive
into go into a tailspin
into go into detail
into go into effect
into go into hiding
into go into hock
into go into one's song and dance (about something)
into go into orbit
into go into something
into in(to) a jam
into into being
into in(to) someone's clutches
into jump into the fray
into lace into someone or something
into lapse into a coma
into lay into someone or something
into lick something into shape
into light into someone or something
into look into something
into lull someone into a false sense of security
into move into something
into nose in(to something)
into out of the frying pan into the fire
into pile in(to something)
into play into someone's hands
into plow into someone or something
into poke one's nose in(to something)
into put ideas into someone's head
into put one's back (in)to something
into put some teeth into something
into put something into practice
into put something into print
into put something into words
into put words into someone's mouth
into read something into something
into rip into someone or something
into rope someone into doing something
into run into a stone wall
into run into someone
into run something into the ground
into see into something
into send someone into something
into sink into despair
into sink one's teeth into something
into step into someone's shoes
into step in(to the breach)
into stick one's nose in(to something)
into stumble into someone or something
into swing into action
into take someone or something into account
into take someone into one's confidence
into take the law into one's own hands
into talk someone into (doing) something
into tear into someone or something
into throw a monkey wrench into the works
into throw something into the bargain
into tie into something
into toss one's hat into the ring
into trick someone into doing something
into tuck into something
into vanish into thin air
into wade in(to something)
into whip something into shape
into work (one's way) into something
into work something into something else
invasion invasion of (someone's) privacy
inventory take inventory
invest invest someone's time in something
invest invest someone with something
invest invest something in someone or something
involved get involved (with someone)
iota not one iota
Irish get someone's Irish up
iron iron something out
iron strike while the iron is hot
irons have too many irons in the fire
is after all is said and done
is All that glitters is not gold.
is (as) black as one is painted
is (as) far as someone or something is concerned
is (as) merry as the day is long
is bear in mind that something is so
is Beauty is only skin-deep.
is be of the persuasion that something is so
is black as one is painted
is Blood is thicker than water.
is cry before one is hurt
is deem that it is necessary
is Enough is enough.
is expense is no object
is far as something is concerned
is get out while the getting is good
is give credit where credit is due
is Half a loaf is better than none.
is know when one is not wanted
is know which is which
is know which side one's bread is buttered on
is life is too short
is many is the time
is merry as the day is long
is Money is no object.
is Money is the root of all evil.
is my gut tells me (that) something is so
is No news is good news.
is not all something is cracked up to be
is not know if one is coming or going
is not know whether one is coming or going
is not what something is cracked up to be
is One man's meat is another man's poison.
is One man's trash is another man's treasure.
is One's bark is worse than one's bite.
is one's heart is (dead) set against something
is one's heart is in one's mouth
is one's heart is in the right place
is one's heart is set on something

is one's name is mud
is one's nose is in the air
is one's number is up
is one's work is cut out for one
is Pretty is as pretty does.
is provided that something is so
is Put your money where your mouth is!
is recognize one for what one is
is recognize something for what it is
is say that something is so
is seeing is believing
is see (to it) that something is done
is see which way the wind is blowing
is so far as someone or something is concerned
is so far as something is concerned
is someone's goose is cooked
is strike while the iron is hot
is such as it is
is Such is life!
is talk until one is blue in the face
is tell which is which
is The jig is up.
is there is no doing something
is There is trouble brewing.
is This is it.
is Time is money.
is Time is up.
is Trouble is brewing.
is turn out (that) something is so
is Variety is the spice of life.
is What's done is done.
is when all is said and done
is when one is good and ready
is when the time is ripe
is where one is coming from
is Woe is me!
is Your guess is as good as mine.
is Your secret is safe with me.
is An ounce of prevention is worth a pound of cure.
is A bird in the hand is worth two in the bush.
is A friend in need is a friend indeed.
is A little knowledge is a dangerous thing.
is A penny saved is a penny earned.
is A storm is brewing.
is The coast is clear.
is The die is cast.
is The game is up.
is The honeymoon is over.
is The jig is up.
is The jury is still out (on someone or something).
is The shoe is on the other foot.
is the time is ripe
issue issue a call for something
issue make an issue of someone or something
issue take issue (with someone)
it Ain't it the truth?
it almost lost it
it as far as it goes
it as it were
it as luck would have it
it at it again
it before you know it
it believe it or not
it be that as it may
it Break it up!
it call it a day
it call it a night
it call it quits
it can take it to the bank.
it catch it
it Come and get it!
it Come off it!
it come to think of it
it Cool it!
it cross a bridge before one comes to it
it cross a bridge when one comes to it
it Cut it out!
it deem it (to be) necessary
it deem that it is necessary
it Don't let it go any further.
it Don't let it out of this room
it Easy does it.
it eat one's cake and have it too
it far be it from me to do something
it far from it
it feel it beneath one (to do something)
it find it in one's heart (to do something)
it for the devil of it
it for the heck of it
it for the hell of it
it full of it
it get away (from it all)
it get it
it Get off it!
it Give it a rest.
it give it the gun
it Give it time.
it give it to someone (straight)
it Give it up.
it go at it hammer and tongs
it go at it tooth and nail
it go for it
it go it alone
it grin and bear it
it (had) known it was coming
it Hand it over.
it hand it to someone
it have a rough time (of it)
it have had it (up to here)
it have it all over someone or something
it have it both ways
it have it in for someone
it (have) never had it so good
it have one's cake and eat it too
it have what it takes
it Here (it) goes.
it hightail it out of somewhere
it hit it off (with someone)
it Hop to it!
it hotfoot it out of somewhere
it How goes it (with you)?
it How's it going?
it If the shoe fits, wear it.
It It behooves one to do something.

It It never rains but it pours.
It It (only) stands to reason.
It It sucks.
It It takes (some) getting used to.
it Keep at it!
it knew it was coming
it knock it off
it known it was coming
it lay it on thick
it lay it on with a trowel
it let it all hang out
it Let it go.
it let it roll
it let someone have it (with both barrels)
it like it or lump it
it live it up
it long and (the) short of it
it lord it over someone
it make a day of it
it make a go of it
it make a run for it
it make it
it Make no bones about it.
it make no mistake (about it)
it mix it up
it never had it so good
it no buts about it
it no ifs, ands, or buts about it
it not breathe a word of it
it not give it another thought
it nothing to it
it not with it
it no two ways about it
it on the face of it
it out of it
it play it cool
it play it safe
it pour it on thick
it put one's foot in it
it Put that in your pipe and smoke it!
it put to it
it recognize something for what it is
it rough it
it rub someone's nose in it
it run for it
it Save it.
it see (to it) that something is done
it So be it.
it So it goes.
it spread it on thick
it step on it
it strike it rich
it such as it is
it take it away
it Take it easy.
it take it easy (on someone or something)
it take it on the chin
it take it or leave it
it take it slow
it take it to one's grave
it take it upon oneself to do something
it take it (up)on oneself (to do something)
it tell it to the marines
it That does it!
it That's about the size of it.
it That's it!
it That tears it!
it This is it.
it to put it mildly
it tough it out
it to whom it may concern
it when it comes right down to it
it when it comes to something
it whoop it up
it wing it
it with everything (on it)
it with it
it You can bet on it!
it You can't take it with you.
it You just don't get it!
it You said it!
itch have an itch for something
itch have an itch to do something
itching have an itching palm
itchy have an itchy palm
It'll It'll never fly.
its come into its own
its dead on its feet
its Every dog has its day.
its fall flat (on its face)
it's for all it's worth
it's for what(ever) it's worth
its have had its day
its in its entirety
its in its prime
It's It's about time!
It's It's (all) Greek to me.
It's It's high time!
It's It's not over 'til it's over.
It's It's no use (doing something).
its judge something on its own merit(s)
it's Like it's such a big deal!
its put something through its paces
its rear its ugly head
its ruffle its feathers
its run around like a chicken with its head cut off
its sit on its hands
its tell its own story
its tell its own tale
its worth its weight in gold
itself by itself
itself in and of itself
itself lend oneself or itself to something
itself shadow of itself
itself speak for itself
itself an end in itself
ivory live in an ivory tower
Jack All work and no play makes Jack a dull boy.
Jack before you can say Jack Robinson
jack jack someone up
jack jack something up
jack a jack-of-all-trades
jackpot hit the jackpot
jam get into a jam

jam get out of a jam
jam get someone out of a jam
jam in a jam
jam in(to) a jam
January (as) slow as molasses in January
January slow as molasses in January
January slower than molasses in January
jaw have a glass jaw
jaybird (as) naked as a jaybird
jaybird naked as a jaybird
jazz jazz something up
Jekyll Jekyll and Hyde
jeopardy in jeopardy
jetsam flotsam and jetsam
jiffy in a jiffy
jig The jig is up.
jig The jig is up.
Job (as) patient as Job
job do a job on someone or something
job do a snow job on someone
job Don't quit your day job.
job fall down on the job
job lay down on the job
job lie down on the job
job on the job
Job patient as Job
job a devil of a job
job a nine-to-five job
job the devil's own job
jockey jockey for position
jog jog someone's memory
Johnny Johnny-come-lately
Johnny Johnny-on-the-spot
join join forces (with someone)
join join hands
Join Join the club!
join join the fray
joint put someone's nose out of joint
joke able to take a joke
joke crack a joke
joke no joke
joke play a joke on someone
joke a standing joke
joking (all) joking aside
joking joking aside
jolt jolt to a start
jolt jolt to a stop
Joneses keep up (with the Joneses)
Jones's Davy Jones's locker
Jones's go to Davy Jones's locker
jowl cheek by jowl
joy burst with joy
joy pride and joy
judge (as) sober as a judge
judge judge one on one's own merit(s)
judge judge something on its own merit(s)
judge sober as a judge
judging judging by something
juice juice and cookies
juice stew in one's own juice
jump get the jump on someone
jump Go jump in the lake!
jump jump all over someone
jump jump at something
jump jump at the chance
jump jump at the opportunity
jump jump bail
jump jump down someone's throat
jump jump into the fray
jump jump off the deep end
jump jump on someone
jump jump on the bandwagon
jump jump out of one's skin
jump jump the gun
jump jump the track
jump jump through a hoop
jump jump through hoops
jump jump to conclusions
jump one jump ahead (of someone or something)
jump a hop, skip, and a jump
jumping jumping-off place
jumping jumping-off point
jumpstart get a jump(start)
juncture at this juncture
jury The jury is still out (on someone or something).
just able to take just so much
just get one's just deserts
just get one's just reward(s)
just had (just) as soon do something
just I just have this feeling
just in (just) a minute
just in (just) a second
just (just) as I expected
just (just) a stone's throw away (from something)
just just in case (something happens)
just just one of those things
just just so
just just the same
just just what the doctor ordered
just You just don't get it!
justice do justice to something
justice poetic justice
justice a miscarriage of justice
justice a travesty of justice
keel keel over
keel keep on an even keel
keel keep something on an even keel
keen have a keen interest in something
keen keen about someone or something
keen keen on doing something
keen keen on someone or something
keep earn one's keep
keep keep abreast (of something)
keep keep a civil tongue (in one's head)
keep keep a close rein on someone or something
keep keep after someone
keep keep an eye on someone or something
keep keep an eye out (for someone or something)
keep keep a secret
keep keep a stiff upper lip
keep keep a straight face
keep keep a tight rein on someone or something
Keep Keep at it!
keep keep at someone or something

keep keep body and soul together
keep keep (close) watch (on someone or something)
keep keep (close) watch (over someone or something)
keep keep company (with someone)
keep keep cool
keep keep from doing something
keep keep good time
keep keep harping on something
keep keep house
keep keep in touch (with someone)
keep keep late hours
keep keep off (something)
keep keep on an even keel
keep keep one's cards close to one's chest
keep keep one's cards close to one's vest
keep keep one's chin up
keep keep one's cool
keep keep one's distance (from someone or something)
keep keep one's ear to the ground
keep keep one's eye on the ball
keep keep one's eyes open (for someone or something)
keep keep one's eyes peeled (for someone or something)
keep keep one's feet on the ground
keep keep one's fingers crossed (for someone or something)
keep keep one's hand in (something)
keep keep one's hands off (someone or something)
keep keep one's head
keep keep one's mouth shut (about someone or something)
keep keep one's nose clean
keep keep one's nose out of someone's business
keep keep one's nose to the grindstone
keep keep one's opinions to oneself
keep keep one's own counsel
keep keep one's place
keep keep one's temper
keep keep one's weather eye open
keep keep one's wits about one
keep keep one's word
keep keep on one's toes
keep keep on someone
keep keep pace (with someone or something)
keep keep quiet (about someone or something)
keep keep someone or something hanging in midair
keep keep someone or something in check
keep keep someone or something in mind
keep keep someone or something quiet
keep keep someone or something still
keep keep someone or something up
keep keep someone company
keep keep someone from doing something
keep keep someone in line
keep keep someone in stitches
keep keep someone on tenterhooks
keep keep someone out in the cold
keep keep someone posted
keep keep something down
keep keep something on an even keel
keep keep something quiet
keep keep something to oneself
keep keep something under one's hat
keep keep something under wraps
keep keep still
keep keep tab(s) (on someone or something)
keep keep the ball rolling
keep keep the home fires burning
keep keep the lid on something
keep keep the wolf from the door
keep keep time
keep keep to oneself
keep keep track (of someone or something)
keep keep up an act
keep keep up appearances
keep keep up one's act
keep keep up (with someone or something)
keep keep up (with the Joneses)
keep keep up (with the times)
Keep Keep your shirt on!
keeper one's brother's keeper
keepers Finders keepers(, losers weepers).
keeping Have you been keeping busy?
keeping in keeping (with something)
keeping out of keeping (with something)
keeping What's keeping you?
keeps for keeps
keeps play for keeps
keg sitting on a powder keg
kettle a fine kettle of fish
kettle the pot calling the kettle black
keyed keyed up
kibosh put the kibosh on something
kick get a kick out of someone or something
kick give someone a kick
kick kick a habit
kick kick off
kick kick oneself (for doing something)
kick kick over
kick kick someone or something around
kick kick someone out
kick kick something in
kick kick something off
kick kick the bucket
kick kick the habit
kick kick up
kicking alive and kicking
kicks for kicks
kid handle someone with kid gloves
kid kid around (with someone)
kidding (all) kidding aside
kidding kidding aside
kidding no kidding
kidding Who do you think you're kidding?
kid's kid('s) stuff
kill dressed to kill
kill fit to kill
kill if looks could kill
kill in at the kill
kill in on the kill
kill kill the fatted calf
kill kill time
kill kill two birds with one stone
killed Curiosity killed the cat.
killed killed outright
killed A little (hard) work never killed anyone.

killing make a killing
kilter out of kilter
kin kith and kin
kin next of kin
kind in kind
kind kind of something
kind let out some kind of sound
kind nothing of the kind
kind two of a kind
kind a kind of (a) something
kindly take kindly to something
kindness do someone a kindness
kindness milk of human kindness
kinds all kinds of someone or something
king (as) cocky as the king of spades
king cocky as the king of spades
king fit for a king
king's pay a king's ransom (for something)
kink a kink in my neck
kiss kiss and make up
kiss kiss and tell
kiss kiss something good-bye
kiss the kiss of death
kit kit and caboodle
kitchen everything but the kitchen sink
kite (as) high as a kite
kite Go fly a kite!
kite high as a kite
kith kith and kin
kitten (as) weak as a kitten
kitten weak as a kitten
kitty feed the kitty
knee knee-high to a grasshopper
knee on bended knee
knew knew it was coming
knife go under the knife
knife pull a knife (on someone)
knit knit one's brow
knock knock about (somewhere)
knock knock-down-drag-out fight
knock knock it off
knock knock off work
knock knock oneself out (to do something)
knock knock one off one's feet
knock knock on wood
knock knock some heads together
knock knock someone or something about
knock knock someone or something around
knock knock someone's block off
knock knock someone dead
knock knock someone down (to size)
knock knock someone for a loop
knock knock someone off
knock knock someone out (cold)
knock knock someone over with a feather
knock knock something back
knock knock something down
knock knock something off
knock knock the props out from under someone
knot tie the knot
knots tie someone (up) in knots
know before you know it
know for all I know
know in the know
know know (all) the tricks of the trade
know know a thing or two (about someone or something)
know know a trick or two
know know better (than to do something)
know know-how
know know one's ABCs
know know one's onions
know know one's place
know know one's stuff
know know one's way about
know know one's way around
know know someone or something like a book
know know someone or something like the back of one's hand
know know someone or something like the palm of one's hand
know know someone by sight
know know something backwards and forwards
know know something by heart
know know something forwards and backwards
know know something from memory
know know something in one's bones
know know something inside out
know know something only too well
know know the ropes
know know the score
know know what's what
know know when one is not wanted
know know where all the bodies are buried
know know whereof one speaks
know know where someone stands (on someone or something)
know know which is which
know know which side one's bread is buttered on
know let someone know (about something)
know not know beans (about someone or something)
know not know enough to come in out of the rain
know not know from nothing
know not know if one is coming or going
know not know one's own strength
know not know someone from Adam
know not know the first thing about someone or something
know not know where to turn
know not know whether one is coming or going
know not know which way to turn
know What one doesn't know won't hurt one.
know you know
knowledge to the best of one's knowledge
knowledge A little knowledge is a dangerous thing.
known (had) known it was coming
known known it was coming
known a known fact
known a known quantity
knows (as) far as anyone knows
knows far as anyone knows
knows so far as anyone knows
knuckle knuckle down (to something)
knuckle knuckle under (to someone or something)
knuckles get one's knuckles rapped

knuckles rap someone's knuckles
labor in labor
labor a labor of love
labors fruit(s) of one's labor(s)
lace lace into someone or something
ladder at the bottom of the ladder
laid laid-back
laid laid up
laid the best-laid plans of mice and men
laid the best-laid schemes of mice and men
lake Go jump in the lake!
lamb (as) gentle as a lamb
lamb (as) innocent as a lamb
lamb (as) meek as a lamb
lamb gentle as a lamb
lamb innocent as a lamb
lamb meek as a lamb
lamb's in two shakes of a lamb's tail
lambs like lambs to the slaughter
lamppost between you, me, and the lamppost
land do a land-office business
land go on to a better land
land land on both feet
land land on one's feet
land land up somehow or somewhere
land live off the fat of the land
land on land
land the land of Nod
land the lay of the land
landslide a landslide victory
language in plain language
language speak the same language
language use strong language
lap in the lap of luxury
lap lap something up
lapse lapse into a coma
large (as) large as life
large at large
large by and large
large large as life
large loom large (on the horizon)
lark (as) happy as a lark
lark for a lark
lark happy as a lark
lark on a lark
lashing get a tongue-lashing
lashing give someone a tongue-lashing
last as a last resort
last at last
last at (long) last
last at the last gasp
last at the last minute
last be the last straw
last breathe one's last
last down to the last detail
last every last one
last get the last laugh
last get the last word
last head for the last roundup
last He laughs best who laughs last.
last He who laughs last, laughs longest.
last in the last analysis
last last but not least
last last will and testament
last on someone's or something's last legs
last pay one's last respects
last see the last of someone or something
last someone's last will and testament
last to the last
last a last-ditch effort
last the last person
last the very last
late better late than never
late keep late hours
late late in life
late late in the day
late of late
lately Johnny-come-lately
later I'll (try to) catch you later.
later sooner or later
latest at the latest
lather in a lather
laugh get the last laugh
laugh laugh all the way to the bank
laugh laugh out of the other side of one's mouth
laugh laugh something off
laugh laugh something out of court
laugh laugh up one's sleeve
laughing burst out laughing
laughing die laughing
laughing no laughing matter
laughingstock make a laughingstock of oneself or something
laughingstock make oneself or something a laughingstock
laughs He laughs best who laughs last.
laughs He who laughs last, laughs longest.
laughter split one's sides (with laughter)
launch launch forth (on something)
laundry in the laundry
laurels look to one's laurels
laurels rest on one's laurels
lavatory go to the lavatory
law break a law
law break the law
law law unto oneself
law lay down the law
law take the law into one's own hands
lay lay a finger on someone or something
lay lay an egg
lay lay down one's life (for someone or something)
lay lay down on the job
lay lay down the law
lay lay eyes on someone or something
lay lay hold of someone or something
lay lay into someone or something
lay lay it on thick
lay lay it on with a trowel
lay lay low
lay lay off (someone or something)
lay lay one's cards on the table
lay lay one's hands on someone or something
lay lay over (somewhere)
lay lay someone away

lay lay someone off
lay lay someone up
lay lay something by
lay lay something in
lay lay something on someone
lay lay something on the line
lay lay something to rest
lay lay something to waste
lay lay the blame on someone or something
lay lay the finger on someone
lay lay waste to something
lay the lay of the land
lead follow someone's lead
lead get the lead out
lead go over like a lead balloon
lead lead a dog's life
lead lead off
lead lead someone by the nose
lead lead someone down the garden path
lead lead someone on a merry chase
lead lead someone to believe something
lead lead someone to do something
lead lead the life of Riley
lead lead up to something
lead shake the lead out
leading a leading question
leading the blind leading the blind
leads One thing leads to another.
leaf leaf through something
leaf take a leaf out of someone's book
leaf turn over a new leaf
league in league (with someone)
league not in the same league with someone or something
leak leak something (out)
lean lean on someone
lean lean over backwards (to do something)
lean lean toward doing something
leap leap at the opportunity
leap leap to conclusions
leaps by leaps and bounds
learn learn something by heart
learn learn something by rote
learn learn something from the bottom up
learn learn (something) the hard way
learn learn the ropes
learn learn to live with something
learn live and learn
lease a new lease on life
least at least
least last but not least
least least of all
least to say the least
least when least expected
least the line of least resistance
least the path of least resistance
leather hell-bent for leather
leave absent without leave
leave leave a bad taste in someone's mouth
leave leave a lot to be desired
leave leave a sinking ship
leave leave no stone unturned
leave leave oneself wide open for something
leave leave oneself wide open to something
leave leave one's mark on someone
leave leave one to one's fate
leave leave someone or something hanging in midair
leave leave someone or something in one's hands
leave leave someone flat
leave leave someone for dead
leave leave someone high and dry
leave leave someone holding the bag
leave leave someone in peace
leave leave someone in the lurch
leave leave someone out in the cold
leave leave something on
leave leave something open
leave leave well enough alone
leave leave word (with someone)
leave take it or leave it
leave take leave of one's senses
leave take (one's) leave (of someone)
left come out of left field
left hang a left
left left and right
left out in left field
left pay someone a left-handed compliment
left right and left
left take up where one left off
leg (as) crooked as a dog's hind leg
leg Break a leg!
leg cost an arm and a leg
leg crooked as a dog's hind leg
leg do not have a leg to stand on
leg pay an arm and a leg (for something)
leg pull someone's leg
legs get one's sea legs
legs on someone's or something's last legs
legs stretch one's legs
legs with one's tail between one's legs
leisure at leisure
leisure at one's leisure
lend lend a hand (to someone)
lend lend an ear (to someone)
lend lend color to something
lend lend oneself or itself to something
lend lend (someone) a hand
length at length
length at some length
length go to any length
less could(n't) care less
less in less than no time
less less than pleased
less more or less
lesser the lesser (of the two)
lesser the lesser of two evils
lesson teach someone a lesson
let Don't let it go any further.
let Don't let it out of this room.
let Don't let someone or something get you down.
let let alone someone or something
Let Let bygones be bygones.
let let go of someone or something
let let go (with something)
let let grass grow under one's feet

let let her rip
let let it all hang out
Let Let it go.
let let it roll
let let loose (with something)
let let off steam
let let oneself go
let let one's emotions show
let let one's hair down
let let out some kind of sound
Let Let sleeping dogs lie.
let let someone or something off
let let someone down
let let someone go
let let someone have it (with both barrels)
let let someone in on something
let let someone know (about something)
let let someone off easy
let let someone off (the hook)
let let something (get) out
let let something pass
let let something ride
let let something slide
let let something slip by
let let something slip (out)
Let Let the buyer beware.
let let the cat out of the bag
let let the chance slip by
let let things slide
let let up (on someone or something)
let let us do something
let let well enough alone
let live and let live
let not let someone catch someone doing something
let sit back and let something happen
Let's Let's do lunch.
letter bread-and-butter letter
letter dead letter
letter to the letter
level at sea level
level do one's (level) best
level find one's own level
level level something at someone
level level with someone
level lower oneself to some level
level on the level
level (strictly) on the level
liability assume liability
liberties take liberties with someone or something
liberty at liberty
liberty take the liberty of doing something
license license to do something
lick give something a lick and a promise
lick lick one's chops
lick lick one's lips
lick lick something into shape
lick a lick of work
licking get a licking
licking give someone a licking
licking take a licking
lid blow the lid off (something)
lid flip one's lid
lid keep the lid on something
lie Let sleeping dogs lie.
lie lie down on the job
lie lie fallow
lie lie in state
lie lie in wait for someone or something
lie lie low
lie lie through one's teeth
lies a pack of lies
lieu in lieu of something
life all walks of life
life (as) big as life
life (as) large as life
life bet one's life
life between life and death
life big as life
life claim a life
life come to life
life for life
life for the life of one
life Get a life!
life get the shock of one's life
life have the time of one's life
life in the prime of life
life large as life
life late in life
life lay down one's life (for someone or something)
life lead a dog's life
life lead the life of Riley
life life is too short
life live a dog's life
life live a life of something
life make life miserable for someone
life milestone in someone's life
life never in one's life
life not on your life
life one's way of life
life run for one's life
life someone's mission in life
life Such is life!
life take one's own life
life Variety is the spice of life.
life within an inch of one's life
life a matter of life and death
life a new lease on life
life the facts of life
life the life of the party
life the seamy side of life
Life's Life's been good (to me).
lifetime once-in-a-lifetime chance
lift lift a hand (against someone or something)
lift not lift a finger (to help someone)
lift not lift a hand (to help someone)
light all sweetness and light
light (as) light as a feather
light begin to see the light
light bring something to light
light come to light
light get the green light
light give someone the green light
light hide one's light under a bushel
light in light of something

light light as a feather
light light into someone or something
light light out (for somewhere)
light light out (of somewhere)
light make light of something
light Many hands make light work.
light out like a light
light see the light
light shed (some) light on something
light throw (some) light on something
lightly get off lightly
lightly once-over-lightly
lightning (as) quick as greased lightning
Lightning Lightning never strikes twice (in the same place).
lightning like greased lightning
lightning quick as greased lightning
lights according to one's own lights
like and the like
like avoid someone or something like the plague
like come on like gangbusters
like come up smelling like roses
like eat like a bird
like eat like a horse
like feel like a million (dollars)
like feel like a new person
like feel like doing something
like feel like (having) something
like fit like a glove
like go like clockwork
like go over like a lead balloon
like have a mind like a steel trap
like hit (someone) like a ton of bricks
like know someone or something like a book
like know someone or something like the back of one's hand
like know someone or something like the palm of one's hand
like like a bat out of hell
like like a bolt out of the blue
like like a bump on a log
like like a fish out of water
like like a house afire
like like a house on fire
like (like) an open book
like like a sitting duck
like like a three-ring circus
like like crazy
like like greased lightning
like like it or lump it
Like Like it's such a big deal!
like like lambs to the slaughter
like like looking for a needle in a haystack
like like mad
like like nothing on earth
like like one of the family
like like sitting ducks
like like to hear oneself talk
like like (two) peas in a pod
like like water off a duck's back
like look like a million dollars
like look like death warmed over
like look like something
like look like the cat that swallowed the canary
like need something like a hole in the head
like off like a shot
like out like a light
like packed (in) like sardines
like read someone like a(n open) book
like run around like a chicken with its head cut off
like run like clockwork
like sell like hotcakes
like sleep like a baby
like sleep like a log
like sound like
like spread like wildfire
like stick out like a sore thumb
like They don't make them like they used to.
like watch someone or something like a hawk
like work like a horse
like would like (to have) someone or something
likely (as) likely as not
likely likely as not
likes the likes of someone
liking take a liking to someone or something
liking to someone's liking
lily gild the lily
limb out on a limb
limbo in limbo
limelight in the limelight
limit go the limit
limit go to the limit
limit The sky's the limit.
limits off limits
limits within limits
line draw a line between something and something else
line draw the line (at something)
line drop someone a line
line fall in(to) line
line feed someone a line
line get a line on someone or something
line give someone a line
line hold the line (at someone or something)
line in line
line in the line of duty
line keep someone in line
line lay something on the line
line line one's own pockets
line line someone or something up with something
line line someone up (for something)
line line someone up with someone
line on line
line out of line
line put something on the line
line sign on the dotted line
line step out of line
line swallow something, hook, line, and sinker
line take a hard line (with someone)
line toe the line
line the bottom line
line the end of the line
line the line of least resistance
line the party line
linen air one's dirty linen in public

linen wash one's dirty linen in public
lines blow one's lines
lines drop someone a few lines
lines fluff one's lines
lines muff one's lines
lines read between the lines
lining Every cloud has a silver lining.
lion (as) strong as a lion
lion beard the lion in his den
lion strong as a lion
lion's the lion's share (of something)
lip button one's lip
lip keep a stiff upper lip
lip pay lip service (to something)
lips lick one's lips
list on a waiting list
listen listen to reason
listen stop, look, and listen
litmus litmus test
little (a little) new to (all) this
little in a little bit
little little by little
little make little of someone or something
little one little bit
little precious little
little quite a little
little think little of someone or something
little twist someone around one's little finger
little A little bird told me.
little a little bit
little A little (hard) work never hurt anyone.
little A little (hard) work never killed anyone.
little A little knowledge is a dangerous thing.
live have to live with something
live learn to live with something
live live a dog's life
live live a life of something
live live and learn
live live and let live
live live beyond one's means
live live by one's wits
live live for the moment
live live from hand to mouth
live live happily ever after
live live high off the hog
live live high on the hog
live live in
live live it up
live live off the fat of the land
live live on borrowed time
live live out of a suitcase
live live something down
live live through something
live live up to one's end of the bargain
live live up to something
live live within one's means
livelong all the livelong day
lives hit one where one lives
lives where one lives
living beat the living daylights out of someone
living do something for a living
living every living soul
living frighten the (living) daylights out of someone
living make a living
living not a living soul
living not tell a (living) soul
living scare the living daylights out of someone
load get a load off one's feet
load get a load off one's mind
load get a load of someone or something
load take a load off one's feet
load two bricks shy of a load
loaded loaded for bear
loaf Half a loaf is better than none.
loan float a loan
loan take out a loan
location on location
lock lock horns (with someone)
lock lock something in
lock lock, stock, and barrel
lock pick a lock
locker Davy Jones's locker
locker go to Davy Jones's locker
loco plumb loco
log (as) easy as falling off a log
log (as) easy as rolling off a log
log easy as falling off a log
log easy as rolling off a log
log like a bump on a log
log sleep like a log
loggerheads at loggerheads (with someone)
loins gird (up) one's loins
long all day long
long all night long
long as long as
long (as) merry as the day is long
long at (long) last
long before long
long go a long way in doing something
long go a long way toward doing something
long have come a long way
long in the long run
long long and (the) short of it
Long Long time no see.
long make a long story short
long merry as the day is long
long not by a long shot
long not long for this world
long over the long haul
long so long
long Take a long walk off a short pier.
longest He who laughs last, laughs longest.
look get a dirty look from someone
look give someone a dirty look
look have a look for someone or something
look look as if butter wouldn't melt in one's mouth
look look at someone cross-eyed
look look daggers at someone
look look down one's nose at someone or something
look look down on someone or something
look look for trouble
look look forward to something
look look good on paper
look look high and low (for someone or something)

look look in (on someone or something)
look look into something
look look like a million dollars
look look like death warmed over
look look like something
look look like the cat that swallowed the canary
look look on someone as something
look look out
look look someone or something over
look look someone or something up
look look someone in the eye
look look someone in the face
look look the other way
look look to one's laurels
look look to someone or something (for something)
look look under the hood
look look up to someone
look make someone look good
look make someone look ridiculous
look stop, look, and listen
look take a look (at someone or something)
look take a look for someone or something
look a faraway look
look a far-off look
looking Here's looking at you.
looking like looking for a needle in a haystack
looking Things are looking up.
lookout on the lookout (for someone or something)
looks if looks could kill
loom loom large (on the horizon)
loon (as) crazy as a loon
loon crazy as a loon
loop knock someone for a loop
loop throw someone for a loop
loose at loose ends
loose break loose (from someone or something)
loose cut loose (from someone or something)
loose cut loose (with something)
loose hang loose
loose have a screw loose
loose let loose (with something)
loose on the loose
loose play fast and loose (with someone or something)
lord (as) drunk as a lord
lord drunk as a lord
lord lord it over someone
lose lose face
lose lose ground
lose lose heart
lose lose oneself (in something)
lose lose one's cool
lose lose one's grip
lose lose one's head (over someone or something)
lose lose one's marbles
lose lose one's mind
lose lose one's reason
lose lose one's shirt
lose lose one's temper
lose lose one's touch (with someone or something)
lose lose one's train of thought
lose lose out (on something)
lose lose out to someone or something
lose lose sleep (over someone or something)
lose lose touch (with someone or something)
lose lose track (of someone or something)
losers Finders keepers(, losers weepers).
loss at a loss (for words)
loss throw someone for a loss
loss a dead loss
losses cut one's losses
lost almost lost it
lost get lost
lost lost-and-found
lost lost and gone forever
lost lost in thought
lost lost on someone
lost make up for lost time
lost no love lost (between someone and someone else)
lost a lost cause
lot carry (a lot of) weight (with someone or something)
lot cast one's lot in with someone
lot cover a lot of ground
lot cover a lot of territory
lot get a lot of mileage out of something
lot have a lot going (for one)
lot have a lot of promise
lot have a lot on one's mind
lot leave a lot to be desired
lot quite a lot
lot think a lot of someone or something
lot a lot of someone or something
lots draw lots
lots lots of people or things
loud For crying out loud!
loud loud and clear
loud think out loud
louder Actions speak louder than words.
louse louse something up
lousy lousy with something
love fall head over heels in love (with someone)
love fall in love (with someone)
love head over heels in love (with someone)
love in love (with someone or something)
love love at first sight
love make love (to someone)
love no love lost (between someone and someone else)
love not for love nor money
love a labor of love
lovely lovely weather for ducks
low burn with a low blue flame
low get the low-down (on someone or something)
low give someone the low-down (on someone or something)
low have a low boiling point
low hunt high and low (for someone or something)
low lay low
low lie low
low look high and low (for someone or something)
low low man on the totem pole
low run low (on something)
low search high and low (for someone or something)
low sweet and low
lower lower oneself to some level
lower lower one's sights

lower lower one's voice
lower lower the boom on someone
luck as luck would have it
luck down on one's luck
luck have a run of bad luck
luck have one's luck run out
luck in luck
luck luck out
luck one's luck runs out
luck out of luck
luck press one's luck
luck push one's luck
luck try one's luck (at something)
luck a stroke of luck
lucky thank one's lucky stars
lull lull someone into a false sense of security
lull lull someone to sleep
lull the lull before the storm
lump get a lump in one's throat
lump like it or lump it
lunatic the lunatic fringe
lunch blow one's lunch
lunch Let's do lunch.
lunch out to lunch
lungs at the top of one's lungs
lurch leave someone in the lurch
luxury in the lap of luxury
lying take something lying down
mad (as) mad as a hatter
mad (as) mad as a hornet
mad (as) mad as a March hare
mad (as) mad as a wet hen
mad (as) mad as hell
mad drive someone mad
mad get mad (at someone or something)
mad in a mad rush
mad like mad
mad mad about someone or something
mad mad as a hatter
mad mad as a hornet
mad mad as a March hare
mad mad as a wet hen
mad mad as hell
mad mad enough to chew nails
mad mad for someone or something
mad so mad I could scream
mad stark raving mad
mad steaming (mad)
made Have I made myself clear?
made have something made
made made for each other
made made from the same mold
made made to measure
made made to order
made not made of money
madness have method in one's madness
maiden maiden voyage
mail by return mail
main main strength and awkwardness
main might and main
mainstream in the mainstream (of something)
make able to make something
make can't make heads or tails (out) of someone or something
make kiss and make up
make make a bed
make make a beeline for someone or something
make make a big deal about something
make make a break for something or somewhere
make make a bundle
make make a check out (to someone)
make make a clean breast of something
make make a clean sweep
make make a comeback
make make a day of doing something
make make a day of it
make make a dent in something
make make a face
make make a fast buck
make make a federal case out of something
make make a fool out of someone
make make a friend
make make a fuss (over someone or something)
make make a go of it
make make a great show of something
make make a hit (with someone or something)
make make a killing
make make a laughingstock of oneself or something
make make a living
make make allowance(s) (for someone or something)
make make a long story short
make make a meal of something
make make amends (for something)
make make a monkey out of someone
make make a mountain out of a molehill
make make an all-out effort
make make a name (for oneself)
make make an appearance
make make an appointment (with someone)
make make an example of someone
make make an exception (for someone)
make make an exhibition of oneself
make make a night of doing something
make make an impression (on someone)
make make an issue of someone or something
make make a note of something
make make a nuisance of oneself
make make an uproar
make make a pass at someone
make make a pile
make make a pitch (for someone or something)
make make a play (for someone)
make make a point
make make a practice of something
make make a quick buck
make make a reservation
make make arrangements (for someone or something)
make make a run for it
make make a scene
make make as if to do something
make make a silk purse out of a sow's ear
make make a stink (about something)
make make away with someone or something
make make book on something

make make (both) ends meet
make make chin music
make make cracks (about someone or something)
make make do (with someone or something)
make make eyes (at someone)
make make fast work of someone or something
make make for somewhere
make make free with someone or something
make make friends
make make fun (of someone or something)
make make good as something
make make good (at something)
make make good money
make make good on something
make make good time
make make hamburger out of someone or something
make make it
make make life miserable for someone
make make light of something
make make little of someone or something
make make love (to someone)
make make merry
make make mincemeat out of someone or something
make make mischief
Make Make no bones about it.
make make no difference (to someone)
make make no mistake (about it)
make make nothing of something
make make off with someone or something
make make oneself at home
make make oneself conspicuous
make make oneself heard
make make oneself or something a laughingstock
make make oneself scarce
make make (oneself) up
make make one's mind up
make make one's way through something
make make or break someone
make make out (with someone or something)
make make over someone or something
make make overtures
make make peace (with someone)
make make points (with someone)
make make reservations
make make sense
make make short work of someone or something
make make someone or something available to someone
make make someone or something over
make make someone sick
make make someone's bed
make make someone's blood boil
make make someone's blood run cold
make make someone's flesh crawl
make make someone's gorge rise
make make someone's hair curl
make make someone's hair stand on end
make make someone's head spin
make make someone's head swim
make make someone's mouth water
make make someone's position clear
make make someone eat crow
make make someone look good
make make someone look ridiculous
make make someone the scapegoat for something
make make someone up
make make something
make make the bed
make make the best of something
make make the feathers fly
make make the fur fly
make make the grade
make make the most of something
make make the scene
make make time (for someone or something)
make make time (with someone)
make make up for lost time
make make up for someone or something
make make up (with someone)
make make use of someone or something
make make waves
make make way
make Many hands make light work.
make not able to make anything out of someone or something
make on the make
make They don't make them like they used to.
Maker gone to meet one's Maker.
makes All work and no play makes Jack a dull boy.
makes Early to bed, early to rise(, makes a man healthy, wealthy, and wise.)
makes Haste makes waste.
makes That makes two of us.
makes what makes someone tick
makes what makes something tick
makings have the makings of something
man dirty old man
man Early to bed, early to rise(, makes a man healthy, wealthy, and wise.)
man high man on the totem pole
man low man on the totem pole
man man-about-town
man man to man
man odd man out
man see a man about a dog
man the man in the street
manger dog in the manger
manner all manner of someone or something
manner devil-may-care manner
manners mind your manners
man's One man's meat is another man's poison.
man's One man's trash is another man's treasure.
many have too many irons in the fire
many in many respects
many in so many words
Many Many hands make light work.
many many is the time
many Too many cooks spoil the broth.
many Too many cooks spoil the stew.
marble (as) cold as marble
marble cold as marble
marbles do not have all one's marbles
marbles lose one's marbles
March (as) mad as a March hare
March mad as a March hare

march march to (the beat of) a different drummer
march steal a march (on someone)
mare by shank's mare
mare go (somewhere) by shank's mare
marines tell it to the marines
mark leave one's mark on someone
mark mark my word(s)
mark mark someone or something down
mark mark something up
mark off the mark
mark toe the mark
mark wide of the mark
market drug on the market
market in the market (for something)
market on the market
market play the market
marks X marks the spot
married get married
marvel a marvel to behold
mast at half-mast
master a past master at something
match meet one's match
match mix and match
match strike a match
match a match for someone, something, or some creature
match the whole shooting match
matter as a matter of course
matter as a matter of fact
matter for that matter
matter get at the heart of the matter
matter get to the heart of the matter
matter gray matter
matter matter-of-fact
matter no laughing matter
matter no matter what happens
matter a matter of life and death
matter a matter of opinion
matter the crux of the matter
may be that as it may
may come what may
may devil-may-care attitude
may devil-may-care manner
may have one's finger in too may pies
may to whom it may concern
me be the death of me (yet)
me between you, me, and the lamppost
me Do you read me?
me far be it from me to do something
me Greek to me
me hand-me-down
me have a pick-me-up
me It's (all) Greek to me.
me Life's been good (to me).
me my gut tells me (that) something is so
me What do you want me to say?
me Woe is me!
me You got me there.
me Your secret is safe with me.
me You scared me out of my wits.
me You scared the crap out of me.
me You scared the devil out of me.
me You scared the dickens out of me.
me You scared the hell out of me.
me You scared the pants off (of) me.
me A little bird told me.
meal eat (a meal) out
meal Enjoy your meal.
meal make a meal of something
meal square meal
mean mean business
mean mean for someone to do something
mean mean nothing (to someone)
mean mean something (to someone)
mean mean to (do something)
means beyond one's means
means by all means
means by any means
means by means of something
means by no means
means live beyond one's means
means live within one's means
means ways and means
meant meant to be
meantime in the meantime
measure beyond measure
measure for good measure
measure made to measure
measure measure up (to someone or something)
measure measure up (to someone's expectations)
meat measure up to someone's standards
meat meat-and-potatoes
meat One man's meat is another man's poison.
Mecca a Mecca for someone
medication on medication
medicine get a taste of one's own medicine
medicine take one's medicine
medicine a dose of one's own medicine
medium find a happy medium
medium hit a happy medium
medium strike a happy medium
meek (as) meek as a lamb
meek meek as a lamb
meet gone to meet one's Maker.
meet make (both) ends meet
meet meet one's death
meet meet one's end
meet meet one's match
meet meet one's Waterloo
meet meet someone halfway
meet meet the requirements (for something)
meeting call a meeting
meeting call the meeting to order
meeting hold a meeting
meeting Sunday-go-to-meeting clothes
meeting a meeting of minds
meets more (to something) than meets the eye
melt look as if butter wouldn't melt in one's mouth
melt melt in one's mouth
memory commit something to memory
memory in memory of someone
memory in recent memory
memory jog someone's memory
memory know something from memory
men be all things to all men

men separate the men from the boys
men the best-laid plans of mice and men
men the best-laid schemes of mice and men
mend mend (one's) fences
mend mend one's ways
mend on the mend
mention mention someone or something in passing
mentioning not worth mentioning
mercy at someone's mercy
mercy at the mercy of someone
mercy throw oneself at the mercy of the court
mercy throw oneself on the mercy of the court
merits judge one on one's own merit(s)
merits judge something on its own merit(s)
merrier the more the merrier
merry (as) merry as a cricket
merry (as) merry as the day is long
merry lead someone on a merry chase
merry make merry
merry merry as a cricket
merry merry as the day is long
mess get into a mess
mess get out of a mess
mess mess about (with someone or something)
mess mess around (with someone or something)
mess mess someone or something up
message get the message
met hail-fellow-well-met
method have method in one's madness
mice When the cat's away, the mice will play.
mice the best-laid plans of mice and men
mice the best-laid schemes of mice and men
midair in midair
midair keep someone or something hanging in midair
midair leave someone or something hanging in midair
Midas have the Midas touch
middle caught in the middle
middle change horses in the middle of the stream
middle in the middle of nowhere
middle middle-of-the-road
middle play both ends (against the middle)
middle smack-dab in the middle
middling fair to middling
midnight burn the midnight oil
might might and main
mighty act high-and-mighty
mighty high-and-mighty
mildly to put it mildly
mile by a mile
mile Give one an inch, and one will take a mile.
mile go the extra mile
mile miss (something) by a mile
mileage get a lot of mileage out of something
miles be a million miles away
milestone milestone in someone's life
milk coffee, tea, or milk
milk cry over spilled milk
milk milk of human kindness
milk milk someone for something
mill grist for someone's mill
mill have been through the mill
mill run-of-the-mill
million be a million miles away
million feel like a million (dollars)
million look like a million dollars
million one in a million
millstone millstone about one's neck
mince mince (one's) words
mincemeat make mincemeat out of someone or something
mind bear in mind that something is so
mind bear someone or something in mind
mind blow someone's mind
mind boggle someone's mind
mind change someone's mind
mind come to mind
mind cross someone's mind
mind enter one's mind
mind get a load off one's mind
mind get someone or something out of one's mind
mind give someone a piece of one's mind
mind have a (good) mind to do something
mind have a lot on one's mind
mind have a mind like a steel trap
mind have a one-track mind
mind have half a mind to do something
mind have someone or something on one's mind
mind have something in mind
mind have the presence of mind to do something
mind in one's right mind
mind keep someone or something in mind
mind lose one's mind
mind make one's mind up
mind mind one's own business
mind mind one's p's and q's
mind mind the store
mind mind you
mind never mind
mind on one's mind
mind out of one's mind
mind Out of sight, out of mind.
mind pass through someone's mind
mind put one's mind to something
mind put someone or something out of one's mind
mind read someone's mind
mind slip one's mind
mind speak one's mind
mind weigh on someone's mind
mind's in one's mind's eye
minds a meeting of minds
mine Your guess is as good as mine.
mine a gold mine of information
mine a mine of information
mines back to the salt mines
mint in mint condition
minute at the last minute
minute every minute counts
minute in (just) a minute
minute up-to-the-minute
minute the minute something happens
mirror able to fog a mirror
mirrors smoke and mirrors
miscarriage a miscarriage of justice
mischief make mischief

miserable make life miserable for someone
misplace misplace one's trust (in someone)
miss have a near miss
miss hit-and-miss
miss hit-or-miss
miss miss out (on something)
miss miss (something) by a mile
miss miss the boat
miss miss the point
miss not miss a thing
miss not miss much
misses one's heart misses a beat
mission someone's mission in life
Missouri be from Missouri
mistake by mistake
mistake make no mistake (about it)
mistake mistake someone for someone else
mistaken a case of mistaken identity
mix mix and match
mix mix it up
mix mix someone or something up
mix mix someone up with someone else
mixed get mixed-up
mixed have mixed feelings (about someone or something)
mixed a mixed bag
molasses (as) slow as molasses in January
molasses slow as molasses in January
molasses slower than molasses in January
mold cast in the same mold
mold made from the same mold
molehill make a mountain out of a molehill
moment every moment counts
moment for the moment
moment live for the moment
moment not a moment to spare
moment not for a moment
moment on the spur of the moment
moment without a moment to spare
moment the big moment
moment the moment everyone has been waiting for
moment the moment of truth
money closefisted (with money)
money fork money out (for something)
money get a run for one's money
money give one a run for one's money
money have money to burn
money hush money
money in the money
money make good money
Money Money burns a hole in someone's pocket.
Money Money is no object.
Money Money is the root of all evil.
money money talks
money not for love nor money
money not made of money
money on the money
money pour money down the drain
money Put your money where your mouth is!
money run to an amount of money
money see the color of someone's money
money set someone back (some amount of money)
money throw good money after bad
money tightfisted (with money)
money Time is money.
money to the tune of some amount of money
money A fool and his money are soon parted.
money's get one's money's worth
monkey make a monkey out of someone
monkey monkey around (with someone or something)
monkey monkey business
monkey monkey suit
monkey throw a monkey wrench into the works
monkeys (as) funny as a barrel of monkeys
monkeys as much fun as a barrel of monkeys
monkeys funny as a barrel of monkeys
monkeys more fun than a barrel of monkeys
month by the month
month in a month of Sundays
months months running
mood in a bad mood
mood in no mood to do something
mood in the mood for something
mood in the mood to do something
moon ask for the moon
moon once in a blue moon
moon promise someone the moon
moon promise the moon (to someone)
mop mop the floor up with someone
mope mope around
more bite off more than one can chew
more exchange more than some number of words with someone
more have more important fish to fry
more more and more
more more dead than alive
more more fun than a barrel of monkeys
more more often than not
more more or less
more more someone or something than one can shake a stick at
more more than one can bear
more more than one can stand
more more than one can take
more more than someone bargained for
more more (to something) than meets the eye
more strike a balance (between two or more things)
more There's more than one way to skin a cat.
more wear more than one hat
more the more the merrier
morning first thing (in the morning)
morning the morning after (the night before)
mortal shuffle off this mortal coil
mortar bricks and mortar
moss A rolling stone gathers no moss.
most at most
most for the most part
most make the most of something
mothballs put something in mothballs
mother old enough to be someone's mother
mother's swear on one's mother's grave
mother's tied to one's mother's apron strings
motion table a motion
motions go through the motions
mountain make a mountain out of a molehill

mouse (as) poor as a church mouse
mouse (as) quiet as a mouse
mouse play cat and mouse (with someone)
mouse poor as a church mouse
mouse quiet as a mouse
mouth bad-mouth someone or something
mouth born with a silver spoon in one's mouth
mouth by word of mouth
mouth down in the mouth
mouth foam at the mouth
mouth from the horse's mouth
mouth have a big mouth
mouth have foot-in-mouth disease
mouth Hush your mouth!
mouth keep one's mouth shut (about someone or something)
mouth laugh out of the other side of one's mouth
mouth leave a bad taste in someone's mouth
mouth live from hand to mouth
mouth look as if butter wouldn't melt in one's mouth
mouth make someone's mouth water
mouth melt in one's mouth
mouth not open one's mouth
mouth one's heart is in one's mouth
mouth put one's foot in one's mouth
mouth put words into someone's mouth
mouth Put your money where your mouth is!
mouth run off at the mouth
mouth shoot one's mouth off
mouth stick one's foot in one's mouth
mouth (straight) from the horse's mouth
mouth take the words out of one's mouth
mouthful say a mouthful
move move heaven and earth to do something
move move in (on someone or something)
move move into something
move move up (in the world)
move not move a muscle
move one move ahead (of someone or something)
move on the move
mover prime mover
movers movers and shakers
much able to take just so much
much as much fun as a barrel of monkeys
much much ado about nothing
much much in evidence
much much sought after
much not miss much
much so much for someone or something
much so much the better
much take too much on
much think much of someone or something
much too much of a good thing
much without so much as doing something
mud (as) clear as mud
mud clear as mud
mud Here's mud in your eye.
mud one's name is mud
mud stick-in-the-mud
muddy muddy the water
muff muff one's lines
mule (as) stubborn as a mule
mule stubborn as a mule
mull mull something over
mum's mum's the word
murder cry bloody murder
murder murder on something
murder scream bloody murder
muscle muscle in (on someone or something)
muscle not move a muscle
music face the music
music make chin music
music set something to music
must a must
muster muster (up) one's courage
muster pass muster
mutilate fold, spindle, or mutilate
my mark my word(s)
my my gut tells me (that) something is so
my my one and only
my over my dead body
my Pardon my French.
my You scared me out of my wits.
my You scratch my back and I'll scratch yours.
my a kink in my neck
myself by myself
myself Have I made myself clear?
nail (another) nail in someone's or something's coffin
nail fight someone or something tooth and nail
nail go at it tooth and nail
nail hit the nail (right) on the head
nail nail in someone's or something's coffin
nail nail someone or something down
nails angry enough to chew nails
nails (as) hard as nails
nails bite one's nails
nails hard as nails
nails mad enough to chew nails
naked (as) naked as a jaybird
naked naked as a jaybird
naked the naked eye
name clear someone's name
name drop someone's name
name I didn't catch your name.
name in name only
name in someone's name
name make a name (for oneself)
name name someone after someone else
name name someone for someone else
name on a first-name basis (with someone)
name one's name is mud
name throw someone's name around
name worthy of the name
name the name of the game
names call someone names
names drop names
names I'm awful at names.
names I'm terrible at names.
nap take a nap
nape by the nape of the neck
napping catch someone napping
narrow the straight and narrow
natural die a natural death
nature call of nature

nature second nature to someone
naught come to naught
near from far and near
near from near and far
near have a near miss
near in the near future
near near at hand
near nowhere near
neat (as) neat as a pin
neat neat as a pin
necessary deem it (to be) necessary
necessary deem that it is necessary
necessity out of necessity
neck break one's neck (to do something)
neck breathe down someone's neck
neck by the nape of the neck
neck get it in the neck
neck in some neck of the woods
neck millstone about one's neck
neck neck and neck
neck risk one's neck (to do something)
neck save someone's neck
neck stick one's neck out (for someone or something)
neck up to one's neck (in something)
neck a crick in one's neck
neck a kink in my neck
neck a pain in the neck
neck a yoke around someone's neck
need crying need for someone or something
need Do I need to paint you a picture?
need in need
need need something like a hole in the head
need need something yesterday
need A friend in need is a friend indeed.
needle like looking for a needle in a haystack
needles on pins and needles
needles pins and needles
neighbor next-door neighbor
neighborhood in the neighborhood of something
neighborhood (somewhere) in the neighborhood of an amount
neither neither fish nor fowl
neither neither here nor there
neither neither hide nor hair
nerve get up enough nerve (to do something)
nerve of all the nerve
nerves get on someone's nerves
nerves grate on someone('s nerves)
nerves a bundle of nerves
nest feather one's (own) nest
nest foul one's own nest
nest stir up a hornet's nest
neutral in neutral
never better late than never
never (have) never had it so good
never It'll never fly.
never It never rains but it pours.
never Lightning never strikes twice (in the same place).
never never fear
never never had it so good
never never in one's life
never never mind
never never would have guessed
never now or never
never A little (hard) work never hurt anyone.
never A little (hard) work never killed anyone.
new (a little) new to (all) this
new (as) bright as a new pin
new be a new one on someone
new break new ground
new bright as a new pin
new busy as a beaver (building a new dam)
new feel like a new person
new new ball game
new new blood
new new hire
new new to (all) this
New ring in the New Year
new (some) new blood
new take a new turn
new turn over a new leaf
new What's new?
new (whole) new ball game
new You can't teach an old dog new tricks.
new a new lease on life
Newcastle carry coals to Newcastle
news break the news (to someone)
news No news is good news.
next next-door neighbor
next next of kin
next next to nothing
next next to someone or something
nice nice and some quality
Nick full of Old Nick
nick in the nick of time
nick in the (very) nick of time
nickel nickel and dime someone
nickel not worth a plugged nickel
night all night long
night (as) black as night
night (as) different as night and day
night at night
night black as night
night by night
night call it a night
night day and night
night different as night and day
night far into the night
night fly-by-night
night make a night of doing something
night night and day
night night owl
night one-night stand
night ships that pass in the night
night small hours (of the night)
night till all hours (of the day and night)
night wee hours (of the night)
night a night on the town
night the morning after (the night before)
nine on cloud nine
nine a nine days' wonder
nine a nine-to-five job
nines dressed to the nines

nip nip and tuck
nip nip something in the bud
nitty get down to the nitty-gritty
no all talk (and no action)
no All work and no play makes Jack a dull boy.
no by no means
no come as no surprise
no cut no ice (with someone)
no expense is no object
no feeling no pain
no have no business doing something
no have no staying power
no hold no brief for someone or something
no in less than no time
no in no mood to do something
no in no time (at all)
no in no uncertain terms
no It's no use (doing something).
no leave no stone unturned
no Long time no see.
no Make no bones about it.
no make no difference (to someone)
no make no mistake (about it)
no Money is no object.
No No big deal!
no no buts about it
No No can do.
No No comment.
no no doubt
no no end of something
no no flies on someone
no no great shakes
no no hard feelings
No No harm done.
no no holds barred
no no ifs, ands, or buts about it
no no joke
no no kidding
no no laughing matter
no no love lost (between someone and someone else)
no no matter what happens
No No news is good news.
no no point in something
no no problem
no no skin off someone's nose
no no skin off someone's teeth
no no sooner said than done
no no spring chicken
no no sweat
no no trespassing
no not take no for an answer
no no two ways about it
no no-win situation
no no wonder
no of no avail
no on no account
no see no objection (to something)
no take no stock in something
no there is no doing something
no There's no accounting for taste.
no to no avail
no up to no good
no with no strings attached
no A rolling stone gathers no moss.
no the point of no return
nobody's nobody's fool
nod get the nod
nod nod off
Nod the land of Nod
noggin use one's noggin
none Half a loaf is better than none.
none have none of something
none none of someone's beeswax
none none of someone's business
none none other than someone
none none the wiser
none none the worse for wear
none none too something
none second to none
nonsense stuff and nonsense
noodle use one's noodle
nook every nook and cranny
nor neither fish nor fowl
nor neither here nor there
nor neither hide nor hair
nor not for love nor money
North up North
nose (as) plain as the nose on one's face
nose blow one's nose
nose can't see beyond the end of one's nose
nose cut off one's nose to spite one's face
nose follow one's nose
nose get one's nose out of someone's business
nose have a nose for something
nose have one's nose in a book
nose have one's nose in the air
nose keep one's nose clean
nose keep one's nose out of someone's business
nose keep one's nose to the grindstone
nose lead someone by the nose
nose look down one's nose at someone or something
nose nose about
nose nose around
nose nose in(to something)
nose nose someone out
nose no skin off someone's nose
nose not see farther than the end of one's nose
nose not see past the end of one's nose
nose one's nose is in the air
nose on the nose
nose pay through the nose (for something)
nose plain as the nose on one's face
nose poke one's nose in(to something)
nose put one's nose to the grindstone
nose put someone's nose out of joint
nose (right) under someone's (very) nose
nose rub someone's nose in it
nose stick one's nose in(to something)
nose thumb one's nose at someone or something
nose turn one's nose up at someone or something
nose under someone's (very) nose
nose win by a nose
nosedive go into a nosedive
nosedive take a nosedive

noses count noses
not All that glitters is not gold.
not (as) likely as not
not believe it or not
not do not have a care in the world
not do not have a leg to stand on
not do not have all one's marbles
not gone but not forgotten
not if not
not It's not over 'til it's over.
not know when one is not wanted
not last but not least
not likely as not
not more often than not
not not a bit
not not able to call one's time one's own
not not able to go on
not not able to help something
not not able to make anything out of someone or something
not not able to see the forest for the trees
not not able to stomach someone or something
not not able to wait
not not agree with someone
not not a living soul
not not all something is cracked up to be
not not all there
not not a moment to spare
not not at all
not not bat an eyelid
not not believe one's eyes
not not born yesterday
not not breathe a word (about someone or something)
not not breathe a word of it
not not buy something
not not by a long shot
not not care two hoots (about someone or something)
not not dry behind the ears
not not enough room to swing a cat
not not for a moment
not not for (anything in) the world
not not for hire
not not for love nor money
not not for publication
not not give a hang (about someone or something)
not not give a hoot (about someone or something)
not not give it another thought
not not give someone the time of day
not not give two hoots (about someone or something)
not not half bad
not not hold a candle to someone or something
not not hold a stick to someone or something
not not hold water
not not hurt a flea
not not in the same league with someone or something
not not know beans (about someone or something)
not not know enough to come in out of the rain
not not know from nothing
not not know if one is coming or going
not not know one's own strength
not not know someone from Adam
not not know the first thing about someone or something
not not know where to turn
not not know whether one is coming or going
not not know which way to turn
not not let someone catch someone doing something
not not lift a finger (to help someone)
not not lift a hand (to help someone)
not not long for this world
not not made of money
not not miss a thing
not not miss much
not not move a muscle
not not on any account
not not one iota
not not one's place
not not on your life
not not open one's mouth
not not see any objection (to something)
not not see farther than the end of one's nose
not not see past the end of one's nose
not not set foot somewhere
not not show one's face
not not sleep a wink
not not someone's cup of tea
not not take no for an answer
not not take stock in something
not not tell a (living) soul
not not up to scratch
not not up to snuff
not not utter a word
not not want to catch someone doing something
not not what something is cracked up to be
not not with it
not not worth a dime
not not worth a hill of beans
not not worth a plugged nickel
not not worth a red cent
not not worth mentioning
not not worth one's while
not not worth the trouble
not whether or not
not will not hear of something
notch take someone down a notch (or two)
note hit a sour note
note make a note of something
note someone of note
note strike a sour note
note strike the right note
note take note (of something)
nothing all or nothing
nothing come to nothing
nothing good-for-nothing
nothing have nothing on someone or something
nothing have nothing to do with someone or something
nothing Here goes nothing.
nothing in nothing flat
nothing like nothing on earth
nothing make nothing of something
nothing make something out of nothing
nothing mean nothing (to someone)
nothing much ado about nothing
nothing next to nothing
nothing nothing but skin and bones

nothing nothing but something
nothing nothing doing
nothing nothing down
nothing nothing of the kind
nothing nothing short of something
nothing nothing to choose from
nothing nothing to complain about
nothing nothing to it
nothing nothing to sneeze at
nothing nothing to speak of
nothing nothing to write home about
Nothing Nothing ventured, nothing gained.
nothing not know from nothing
nothing stop at nothing
nothing think nothing of someone or something
nothing to say nothing of someone or something
nothing want for nothing
nothings sweet nothings
notice escape someone's notice
notice serve notice (on someone)
notice sit up and take notice
notice take notice (of something)
notion have half a notion to do something
now all better now
now (every) now and again
now (every) now and then
now now and again
now now and then
Now Now hear this!
now now or never
Now (Now), where was I?
now There, now.
now the here and now
nowhere appear out of nowhere
nowhere at the end of nowhere
nowhere come from nowhere
nowhere come out of nowhere
nowhere Flattery will get you nowhere.
nowhere get nowhere fast
nowhere in the middle of nowhere
nowhere nowhere near
nth to the nth degree
nude in the nude
nuisance make a nuisance of oneself
null null and void
number any number of someone or something
number do a number on someone or something
number exchange more than some number of words with someone
number get someone's number
number one's number is up
number quite a number
number a number of things or people
numbered one's days are numbered
numbers by the numbers
numbers in round numbers
numbers safety in numbers
nurse nurse a grudge (against someone)
nurse nurse someone back to health
nut off one's nut
nut tough nut to crack
nut a hard nut to crack
nuts everything from soup to nuts
nuts nuts about someone or something
nuts the nuts and bolts (of something)
nutshell in a nutshell
nutty (as) nutty as a fruitcake
nutty nutty as a fruitcake
nuzzle nuzzle up to someone or something
oar put one's oar in
oath take an oath
oath under oath
oats sow one's wild oats
object expense is no object
object Money is no object.
objection not see any objection (to something)
objection raise (an) objection (to someone or something)
objection see no objection (to something)
occasion on occasion
occasion rise to the occasion
occupancy immediate occupancy
occur occur to someone
ocean an ocean of someone or something
ocean a drop in the ocean
oceans oceans of someone or something
odd odd man out
odd the odd something
odds at odds (with someone)
odds for the odds to be against one
odds odds and ends
odor odor of sanctity
of (above and) beyond the call of duty
of acknowledge receipt (of something)
of afraid of one's own shadow
of after the fashion of someone or something
of ahead of one's time
of ahead of schedule
of ahead of the game
of ahead of time
of all kinds of someone or something
of all manner of someone or something
of all of a sudden
of all walks of life
of alongside (of) someone or something
of any number of someone or something
of appear out of nowhere
of arguing for the sake of arguing
of arguing for the sake of argument
of as a matter of course
of as a matter of fact
of as a result of something
of as a token (of something)
of (as) black as a stack of black cats
of (as) black as the ace of spades
of (as) close as two coats of paint
of (as) cocky as the king of spades
of (as) crooked as a barrel of fish hooks
of (as) funny as a barrel of monkeys
of as much fun as a barrel of monkeys
of at the bottom of the hour
of at the bottom of the ladder
of at the break of dawn
of at the crack of dawn
of at the drop of a hat

of at the end of nowhere
of at the end of one's rope
of at the end of one's tether
of at the end of the day
of at the expense of someone or something
of at the forefront (of something)
of at the height of something
of at the helm (of something)
of at the mercy of someone
of at the point of doing something
of at the rear of something
of at the top of one's lungs
of at the top of one's voice
of at the top of the hour
of at the zenith of something
of at this stage of the game
of avail oneself of something
of avenue of escape
of back of the beyond
of back out (of something)
of bag of tricks
of bail out (of something)
of ball of fire
of baptism of fire
of bear the brunt (of something)
of beat the living daylights out of someone
of beat the stuffing out of someone
of beat the tar out of someone
of beginning of the end
of be of service (to someone)
of be of the persuasion that something is so
of be the death of me (yet)
of be the spit and image of someone
of be the spitting image of someone
of beyond the call of duty
of beyond the shadow of a doubt
of big of someone
of Birds of a feather flock together.
of black as a stack of black cats
of black as the ace of spades
of blow something out of all proportion
of bone of contention
of born out of wedlock
of break out (of something)
of break the back of something
of burn one's bridges in front of one
of by all means of something
of by a show of hands
of by dint of something
of by means of something
of by the nape of the neck
of by the seat of one's pants
of by the skin of one's teeth
of by the sweat of one's brow
of by virtue of something
of by way of something
of by word of mouth
of call of nature
of can't make heads or tails (out) of someone or something
of can't see beyond the end of one's nose
of can't see one's hand in front of one's face
of can't stand (the sight of) someone or something
of capable of doing something
of carry (a lot of) weight (with someone or something)
of carry the weight of the world on one's shoulders
of catch a whiff of something
of catch one's death (of cold)
of catch sight of someone or something
of catch someone in the act (of doing something)
of change horses in the middle of the stream
of charm the pants off (of) someone
of chicken out (of something)
of chisel someone out of something
of clean out (of something)
of clear of something
of close as two coats of paint
of cock of the walk
of cocky as the king of spades
of come in out of the rain
of come of age
of come out of left field
of come out of nowhere
of come out of one's shell
of come out of the blue
of come out (of the closet)
of come to think of it
of come within an ace of doing something
of come within an inch of doing something
of con someone out of something
of course of action
of cover a lot of ground
of cover a lot of territory
of crooked as a barrel of fish hooks
of decide in favor of someone or something
of die of a broken heart
of die of boredom
of Don't let it out of this room.
of do someone out of something
of drive someone out (of office)
of drop out (of something)
of drum someone out of something
of eat out of someone's hands
of eat someone out of house and home
of elbow someone out (of something)
of end up with the short end of the stick
of even in the best of times
of exchange more than some number of words with someone
of fall afoul of someone or something
of fall short (of something)
of fan the flames (of something)
of feel a glow of something
of feel on top of the world
of feel out of place
of ferret something out of someone or something
of first of all
of flight of fancy
of flirt with the idea of doing something
of fly in the face of someone or something
of fly in the teeth of someone or something
of fly into the face of danger
of fond of someone or something
of force someone out (of office)

of for fear of something
of for the devil of it
of for the good of someone or something
of for the heck of it
of for the hell of it
of for the life of one
of for the sake of someone or something
of fresh out (of something)
of frighten one out of one's wits
of frighten the (living) daylights out of someone
of frighten the wits out of someone
of from the bottom of one's heart
of fruit(s) of one's labor(s)
of full of beans
of full of bull
of full of hot air
of full of it
of full of Old Nick
of full of oneself
of full of prunes
of full of the devil
of funny as a barrel of monkeys
of get a bang out of someone or something
of get a charge out of someone or something
of get a clean bill of health
of get a grasp of something
of get ahead of oneself
of get (a)hold of someone or something
of get a kick out of someone or something
of get a load of someone or something
of get a lot of mileage out of something
of get an eyeful (of someone or something)
of get a rise out of someone
of get a rough idea (of something)
of get a taste of one's own medicine
of get at the heart of the matter
of get a whiff of something
of get into the swing of things
of get one's fill of someone or something
of get one's nose out of someone's business
of get on the good side of someone
of get out of a jam
of get out of a mess
of get out of someone's way
of get out of the way
of get out of the wrong side of the bed
of get rid of someone or something
of get someone or something out of one's head
of get someone or something out of one's mind
of get someone or something out of the way
of get someone out of a jam
of get something out of one's system
of get something out of something
of get the advantage of someone
of get the benefit of the doubt
of get the best of someone
of get the better of someone
of get the drift of something
of get the feel of something
of get the hang of something
of get the shock of one's life
of get the short end of the stick
of get the worst of something
of get to the bottom of something
of get to the heart of the matter
of get to the root of the problem
of get up on the wrong side of the bed
of get wind of something
of give a good account of oneself
of give of oneself
of give someone a clean bill of health
of give someone a piece of one's mind
of give someone a rough idea (of something)
of give someone the benefit of the doubt
of go out of fashion
of go out of one's way (to do something)
of go out of style
of go to the expense (of doing something)
of go to the trouble (of doing something)
of groan under the burden of something
of grow out of something
of guest of honor
of gyp someone out of something
of hard of hearing
of have a change of heart
of have a good command of something
of have a heart of gold
of have a heart of stone
of have a lot of promise
of have a rough time (of it)
of have a run of bad luck
of have a run of something
of have a whale of a time
of have eyes in the back of one's head
of have feet of clay
of have none of something
of have something on the tip of one's tongue
of have the best of both worlds
of have the courage of one's convictions
of have the feel of something
of have the gift of gab
of have the makings of something
of have the patience of a saint
of have the presence of mind to do something
of have the right-of-way
of have the time of one's life
of hear a peep out of someone
of hear of something
of hightail it out of somewhere
of hit (someone) like a ton of bricks
of hold one's end (of the bargain) up
of hotfoot it out of somewhere
of in a (constant) state of flux
of in a month of Sundays
of in and of itself
of in awe (of someone or something)
of in a world of one's own
of in behalf of someone
of in care of someone
of in case of something
of in consequence (of something)
of in consideration of something
of in contempt (of court)
of in custody of someone or something

of in defiance (of someone or something)
of in favor of someone
of in favor (of someone or something)
of in honor of someone or something
of in hopes of something
of in lieu of something
of in light of something
of in memory of someone
of in need of something
of in one ear and out (of) the other
of in place of someone or something
of in pursuit of something
of in quest of someone or something
of in receipt of something
of ins and outs of something
of in search of someone or something
of in some neck of the woods
of in spite of someone or something
of in terms of something
of in the absence of someone or something
of in the act (of doing something)
of in the best of health
of in the care of someone
of in the case of someone or something
of in the charge of someone
of in the context of something
of in the course of time
of in the event of something
of in the forefront (of something)
of in the interest of someone or something
of in the lap of luxury
of in the line of duty
of in the mainstream (of something)
of in the middle of nowhere
of in the neighborhood of something
of in the nick of time
of in the pink (of condition)
of in the prime of life
of in the swim of things
of in the trust of someone
of in the twinkling of an eye
of in the unlikely event of something
of in the (very) nick of time
of in the wake of something
of in the way of something
of in two shakes of a lamb's tail
of invasion of (someone's) privacy
of in view of something
of jump out of one's skin
of just one of those things
of keep abreast (of something)
of keep one's nose out of someone's business
of keep track (of someone or something)
of kind of something
of know (all) the tricks of the trade
of know someone or something like the back of one's hand
of know someone or something like the palm of one's hand
of laugh out of the other side of one's mouth
of laugh something out of court
of lay hold of someone or something
of lead the life of Riley
of least of all
of let go of someone or something
of let out some kind of sound
of let the cat out of the bag
of light out (of somewhere)
of like a bat out of hell
of like a bolt out of the blue
of like a fish out of water
of like one of the family
of live a life of something
of live off the fat of the land
of live out of a suitcase
of live up to one's end of the bargain
of long and (the) short of it
of lose one's train of thought
of lose track (of someone or something)
of lots of people or things
of lull someone into a false sense of security
of make a clean breast of something
of make a day of doing something
of make a day of it
of make a federal case out of something
of make a fool out of someone
of make a go of it
of make a great show of something
of make a laughingstock of oneself or something
of make a meal of something
of make a monkey out of someone
of make a mountain out of a molehill
of make an example of someone
of make an exhibition of oneself
of make a night of doing something
of make an issue of someone or something
of make a note of something
of make a nuisance of oneself
of make a point of doing something
of make a point of someone or something
of make a practice of something
of make a silk purse out of a sow's ear
of make fast work of someone or something
of make fun (of someone or something)
of make hamburger out of someone or something
of make light of something
of make little of someone or something
of make mincemeat out of someone or something
of make nothing of something
of make sense out of someone or something
of make short work of someone or something
of make something out of nothing
of make something (out) of something
of make something up out of whole cloth
of make the best of something
of make the most of something
of make use of someone or something
of march to (the beat of) a different drummer
of matter-of-fact
of middle-of-the-road
of milk of human kindness
of Money is the root of all evil.
of more fun than a barrel of monkeys
of next of kin
of no end of something
of none of someone's beeswax

of none of someone's business
of not able to make anything out of someone or something
of not breathe a word of it
of not give someone the time of day
of nothing of the kind
of nothing short of something
of nothing to speak of
of not know enough to come in out of the rain
of not made of money
of not see farther than the end of one's nose
of not see past the end of one's nose
of not someone's cup of tea
of not worth a hill of beans
of oceans of someone or something
of odor of sanctity
of of age
of of all the nerve
of of all things
of of benefit (to someone)
of off the top of one's head
of of interest (to someone)
of of late
of of no avail
of of one's own accord
of of one's own free will
of of the first water
of of the old school
of on behalf of someone
of one jump ahead (of someone or something)
of one move ahead (of someone or something)
of one of these days
of one sandwich short of a picnic
of one's way of life
of on the eve of something
of on the face of it
of on the heels of something
of on the horns of a dilemma
of on the point of doing something
of on the spur of the moment
of on the strength of something
of on the tip of one's tongue
of on the track of someone or something
of on the trail of someone or something
of on the verge (of doing something)
of on top of something
of on top of the world
of open (up) a can of worms
of out of a clear blue sky
of out of (all) proportion
of out of bounds
of out of breath
of out of character
of out of circulation
of out of commission
of out of condition
of out of consideration (for someone or something)
of out of control
of out of courtesy (to someone)
of out-of-date
of out of earshot
of out of fashion
of out of favor (with someone)
of out of gas
of out of hand
of out of it
of out of keeping (with something)
of out of kilter
of out of line
of out of luck
of out of necessity
of out of one's element
of out of one's head
of out of one's mind
of out of one's senses
of out of one's way
of out of order
of out of place
of out-of-pocket expenses
of out of practice
of out of print
of out of proportion
of out of reach
of out of season
of out of service
of out of shape
of out of sight
of out of sorts
of out of spite
of out of step (with someone or something)
of out of stock
of out of style
of out of the blue
of out of the corner of one's eye
of out of the frying pan into the fire
of out of the hole
of out of the ordinary
of out of the question
of out of the red
of out of the running
of out of the swim of things
of out-of-the-way
of out of the woods
of out of thin air
of out of this world
of out of time (with someone or something)
of out of touch (with someone or something)
of out of town
of out of tune (with someone or something)
of out of turn
of out of w(h)ack
of out of work
of outside of something
of partake of something
of part and parcel (of something)
of parting of the ways
of pass the time of day (with someone)
of piece of cake
of pile out (of something)
of plenty of something
of point of view
of possessed of something
of pull something out of a hat
of pull something out of thin air
of put someone or something out of one's mind

of put someone's **nose out of joint**
of read someone **out of** something
of regardless **of** something
of reminiscent **of** someone or something
of risk of rain
of risk of showers
of risk of thunder(storms)
of run afoul **of** someone or something
of run a risk (of something)
of run-of-the-mill
of run out of gas
of run out of patience
of run out of something
of run out of time
of run short (of something)
of run the risk (of something)
of run to an amount of money
of scare one out of one's wits
of scare the living daylights out of someone
of scare the wits out of someone
of school of thought
of scrape the bottom of the barrel
of see the color of someone's money
of see the last of someone or something
of see the light (at the end of the tunnel)
of see the light (of day)
of sell someone a bill of goods
of set someone back (some amount of money)
of settle (something) (out of court)
of shades of someone or something
of shadow of itself
of shadow of oneself
of short of something
of show signs of something
of sick and tired of someone or something
of (sitting) on top of the world
of six of one and half a dozen of the other
of small hours (of the night)
of snap out of something
of someone's place of business
of someone's train of thought
of someone of note
of something of the sort
of (somewhere) in the neighborhood of an amount
of son of a bitch
of son of a gun
of son of a sea biscuit
of sort of something
of speak highly of someone or something
of speak ill of someone
of speak of the devil
of speak out of turn
of stand in awe (of someone or something)
of stand (in) back of someone or something
of steer clear (of someone or something)
of step out of line
of stop short of doing something
of suggestive of something
of swear on a stack of Bibles
of sweep out of somewhere
of take a dim view of something
of take advantage of someone or something
of take (a)hold of someone or something
of take a leaf out of someone's book
of take care of someone or something
of take charge (of someone or something)
of take leave of one's senses
of take note (of something)
of take notice (of something)
of take one's death of cold
of take (one's) leave (of someone)
of take something with a grain of salt
of take something with a pinch of salt
of take stock (of something)
of take the liberty of doing something
of take the starch out of someone
of take the wind out of someone's sails
of take the words out of one's mouth
of talk someone out of (doing) something
of talk someone out of something
of tell tales out of school
of That makes two of us.
of That's about the size of it.
of That takes care of that.
of There are plenty of other fish in the sea.
of think a great deal of someone or something
of think a lot of someone or something
of think better of something
of think highly of someone or something
of think little of someone or something
of think much of someone or something
of think nothing of someone or something
of think the world of someone or something
of throw oneself at the mercy of the court
of throw oneself on the mercy of the court
of throw someone out (of something)
of till all hours (of the day and night)
of too much of a good thing
of to say nothing of someone or something
of to someone's way of thinking
of to the best of one's ability
of to the best of one's knowledge
of to the ends of the earth
of to the tune of some amount of money
of turn of the century
of two bricks shy of a load
of two of a kind
of under a cloud (of suspicion)
of under the aegis of someone
of under the auspices of someone
of under the influence (of alcohol)
of under the influence of something
of vale of tears
of Variety is the spice of life.
of warm the cockles of someone's heart
of wash one's hands of someone or something
of weasel out (of something)
of weave in and out (of something)
of wee hours (of the night)
of whale the tar out of someone
of What's the good of something?
of wide of the mark
of will not hear of something
of within an inch of one's life

of within a stone's throw (of something)
of worm one's way out of something
of worm something out of someone
of worthy of the name
of wouldn't dream of doing something
of yield the right-of-way
of You scared me out of my wits.
of You scared the crap out of me.
of You scared the devil out of me.
of You scared the dickens out of me.
of You scared the hell out of me.
of You scared the pants off (of) me.
of an act of faith
of an act of God
of an act of war
of an ocean of someone or something
of An ounce of prevention is worth a pound of cure.
of a bed of roses
of a breath of fresh air
of a bundle of nerves
of a case of mistaken identity
of a change of pace
of a change of scenery
of a couple of
of a den of iniquity
of a devil of a job
of a dose of one's own medicine
of a fan of someone
of a few cards short of a deck
of a few cards shy of a full deck
of a fine kettle of fish
of a fine state of affairs
of a ghost of a chance
of a gold mine of information
of a grain of truth
of a harbinger of things to come
of a hive of activity
of a horse of a different color
of a horse of another color
of a jack-of-all-trades
of a kind of (a) something
of a labor of love
of a lick of work
of a lot of someone or something
of a matter of life and death
of a matter of opinion
of a meeting of minds
of a mine of information
of a miscarriage of justice
of a number of things or people
of a pack of lies
of a piece of the action
of a pillar of strength
of a pillar of support
of a portent of things to come
of a pretty state of affairs
of a ripple of excitement
of a ripple of protest
of a rule of thumb
of a show of hands
of a sign of things to come
of a slice of the cake
of a slip of the tongue
of a stroke of luck
of a taste of something
of a taste of things to come
of a tower of strength
of a travesty of justice
of a vote of confidence
of a vote of thanks
of a wealth of something
of the apple of someone's eye
of the balls of one's feet
of the best-laid plans of mice and men
of the best-laid schemes of mice and men
of the best part of something
of the black sheep of the family
of the business end of something
of the cream of the crop
of the crux of the matter
of the end of the line
of the end of the road
of the eye of the storm
of the facts of life
of the hair of the dog that bit one
of the kiss of death
of the land of Nod
of the lay of the land
of the lesser (of the two)
of the lesser of two evils
of the life of the party
of the likes of someone
of the line of least resistance
of the lion's share (of something)
of the moment of truth
of the name of the game
of the nuts and bolts (of something)
of the order of the day
of the other side of the tracks
of the particulars of something
of the path of least resistance
of the pick of something
of the picture of something
of the point of no return
of the reality of the situation
of the ruin of someone or something
of the salt of the earth
of the sands of time
of the seamy side of life
of the separation of church and state
of the survival of the fittest
of the talk of somewhere
of the upshot of something
of the villain of the piece
of the whole ball of wax
of the whys and wherefores of something
of the wrong side of the tracks
off (as) easy as falling off a log
off (as) easy as rolling off a log
off back off (from someone or something)
off beat the pants off someone
off beg off (on something)
off be off
off better off (doing something)

off better off (if one were somewhere else)
off better off (if something were done)
off better off (somewhere)
off bite off more than one can chew
off bite someone's head off
off blast off
off blow off steam
off blow someone or something off
off blow the lid off (something)
off break off (with someone)
off bring something off
off bump someone off
off buy someone off
off call someone or something off
off call the dogs off
off carry something off
off catch one off one's guard
off catch someone off balance
off catch someone off guard
off charm the pants off (of) someone
off cheesed off
off choke something off
off come off
off cool off
off cool someone off
off cut off
off cut someone off without a penny
off dash something off
off drop off (to sleep)
off ease off (on someone or something)
off easy as falling off a log
off easy as rolling off a log
off fall off
off first off
off fly off the handle
off fob something off (on someone)
off foist something (off) on someone
off get a big send-off
off get a load off one's feet
off get a load off one's mind
off get off
off get (someone) off the hook
off get something off one's chest
off get something off (the ground)
off get the brush-off
off get the day off
off get time off
off give someone a big send-off
off give someone the brush-off
off give someone the shirt off one's back
off go off
off goof off
off Hands off!
off head someone or something off
off hit it off (with someone)
off jumping-off place
off jumping-off point
off jump off the deep end
off keep off (something)
off keep one's hands off (someone or something)
off kick off
off kick something off
off knock it off
off knock off work
off knock one off one's feet
off knock someone's block off
off knock someone off
off knock something off
off laugh something off
off lay off (someone or something)
off lay someone off
off lead off
off let off steam
off let someone or something off
off let someone off easy
off let someone off (the hook)
off like water off a duck's back
off live high off the hog
off live off the fat of the land
off make off with someone or something
off nod off
off no skin off someone's nose
off no skin off someone's teeth
off off again, on again
off off and on
off off and running
off off base
off off campus
off off-center
off off chance
off off-color
off off duty
off off like a shot
off off limits
off off one's nut
off off one's rocker
off off one's trolley
off off season
off off someone or something goes
off off the air
off off the (beaten) track
off off-the-cuff
off off the mark
off off the record
off off the subject
off off the top of one's head
off off the track
off off-the-wall
off off to a running start
off off to one side
off on again, off again
off on and off
off on the off-chance
off palm something off (on someone)
off pay someone or something off
off pick someone or something off
off play someone off against someone else
off polish something off
off pop off
off pull something off
off push off
off put off by someone or something
off put someone or something off
off put someone off

off put something off
off rake something off
off rattle something off
off reel something off
off ride off in all directions
off right off the bat
off rip someone or something off
off round something off
off rub off (on someone)
off run around like a chicken with its head cut off
off run off at the mouth
off run off with someone or something
off sell something off
off send someone off
off set someone or something off
off shake someone or something off
off shake something off
off shoot one's mouth off
off show off
off show someone or something off
off shuffle off this mortal coil
off slack off
off sleep something off
off slip off
off so clean you could eat off the floor
off sound off (about something)
off speak off the cuff
off spin something off
off spout off (about someone or something)
off square off (for something)
off stall someone or something off
off start off on the wrong foot
off start (off) with a clean slate
off stop off (somewhere)
off sweep one off one's feet
off take a load off one's feet
off Take a long walk off a short pier.
off take off
off take the day off
off take the edge off (something)
off take time off
off take up where one left off
off talk someone's ear off
off talk someone's head off
off taper off (doing something)
off tear off
off tee someone off
off tell someone off
off tell someone where to get off
off throw someone or something off
off throw someone off the track
off throw someone off the trail
off time off
off tip someone off
off top something off
off toss something off
off touch someone or something off
off turn someone off
off walk off with something
off wear off
off well-off
off wipe something off
off wish something off on someone
off work something off
off write someone or something off
off You scared the pants off (of) me.
off a chip off the old block
off a far-off look
offense take offense (at someone or something)
office do a land-office business
office drive someone out (of office)
office force someone out (of office)
office take office
offing in the offing
often more often than not
oil burn the midnight oil
oil oil someone's palm
oil pour oil on troubled water(s)
ointment a fly in the ointment
old (as) comfortable as an old shoe
old (as) common as an old shoe
old (as) old as the hills
old (as) tough as an old boot
old comfortable as an old shoe
old common as an old shoe
old dirty old man
old from the old school
Old full of Old Nick
old get the (old) heave-ho
old give someone or something the (old) heave-ho
old of the old school
old old as the hills
old old enough to be someone's father
old old enough to be someone's mother
Old Old habits die hard.
old old hat
old one's old stamping ground
old tough as an old boot
old You can't teach an old dog new tricks.
old an old hand at doing something
old a chip off the old block
old a ripe old age
old the good old days
old the same old story
olive hold out the olive branch
omega alpha and omega
on able to do something standing on one's head
on and so on
on arrive on the scene
on (as) awkward as a cow on a crutch
on (as) awkward as a cow on roller skates
on (as) busy as a cat on a hot tin roof
on (as) busy as popcorn on a skillet
on (as) plain as the nose on one's face
on awkward as a cow on a crutch
on awkward as a cow on roller skates
on bank on something
on bargain on something
on barge in (on someone or something)
on base one's opinion on something
on be a new one on someone
on becoming on someone
on be death on something
on beg off (on something)

on behind **on** something
on bent **on** doing something
on be off **on** the wrong foot
on blow the whistle (**on** someone)
on bone up (**on** something)
on bring down the curtain (**on** something)
on bring someone up to date (**on** someone or something)
on brush up (**on** something)
on burst in **on** someone or something
on busy as a cat **on** a hot tin roof
on busy as popcorn **on** a skillet
on butt in (**on** someone or something)
on buy something **on** credit
on call **on** someone
on call someone **on** the carpet
on carry **on** (about someone or something)
on carry **on** somehow
on carry **on** without someone or something
on carry **on** (with someone or something)
on carry the weight of the world **on** one's shoulders
on carry through (**on** something)
on cash in (**on** something)
on cash **on** the barrelhead
on cast aspersions **on** someone
on cast doubt(s) (**on** someone or something)
on catch (**on**) fire
on catch **on** (to someone or something)
on cheat **on** someone
on check in (**on** someone or something)
on cheer someone **on**
on chip in (**on** something)
on chip in something **on** something
on chip something in (**on** something)
on clamp down (**on** someone or something)
on clap eyes **on** someone or something
on climb **on** the bandwagon
on close in (**on** someone or something)
on close the books (**on** someone or something)
on close the door **on** someone or something
on clue someone in (**on** something)
on come down hard **on** someone or something
on come **on**
on count **on** someone or something
on count someone in (**on** something)
on crack down (**on** someone or something)
on cross swords (with someone) (**on** something)
on cut back (**on** something)
on cut one's eyeteeth **on** something
on dash cold water **on** something
on dawn **on** someone
on dead **on** its feet
on dead **on** one's feet
on death **on** someone or something
on die **on** someone
on die **on** the vine
on die with one's boots **on**
on dig some dirt up **on** someone
on do a flip-flop (**on** something)
on do a job **on** someone or something
on do a number **on** someone or something
on do a snow job **on** someone
on do not have a leg to stand **on**
on do something **on** the fly
on do something **on** the run
on do something **on** the sly
on double back (**on** someone or something)
on downhill from here **on**
on down **on** one's luck
on down **on** someone or something
on draw a bead **on** someone or something
on Dream **on**.
on drop in (**on** someone)
on drug **on** the market
on early **on**
on ease off (**on** someone or something)
on ease up (**on** someone or something)
on eat high **on** the hog
on egg someone **on**
on fall back **on** someone or something
on fall down **on** the job
on fall flat (**on** its face)
on fall flat (**on** one's face)
on fall **on** deaf ears
on feast one's eyes (**on** someone or something)
on feel **on** top of the world
on figure **on** something
on fill someone in (**on** someone or something)
on firing **on** all cylinders
on fob something off (**on** someone)
on foist something (off) **on** someone
on follow through (**on** something)
on follow up (**on** someone or something)
on follow up (**on** something)
on for days **on** end
on for hours **on** end
on from this day **on**
on gang up (**on** someone)
on get a crush **on** someone
on get a fix **on** something
on get a handle **on** something
on get a head start (**on** someone or something)
on get a hurry **on**
on get a line **on** someone or something
on get along (**on** a shoestring)
on get a rain check (**on** something)
on get a slap **on** the wrist
on get back **on** one's feet
on get by (**on** something)
on get in **on** something
on get in (**on** the ground floor)
on get off **on** the wrong foot
on get one's feet **on** the ground
on get one's hands **on** someone or something
on get **on** someone
on get **on** the bandwagon
on get **on** the good side of someone
on get **on** (with someone or something)
on get right **on** something
on get something **on** someone
on get the edge **on** someone
on get the goods **on** someone
on get the jump **on** someone
on get the low-down (**on** someone or something)
on get the show **on** the road

on get the upper hand (on someone)
on get up on the wrong side of the bed
on give someone a fix on something
on give someone a head start (on someone or something)
on give someone a pat on the back
on give someone a rain check (on something)
on give someone a slap on the wrist
on give someone the low-down (on someone or something)
on go back on one's word
on go easy (on someone or something)
on go fifty-fifty (on something)
on gone on
on go off on a tangent
on go on
on go (out) on strike
on grate on someone('s nerves)
on grow on someone
on hang on someone's coattails
on hang on someone's every word
on hang on (to someone or something)
on hard on someone's heels
on harp on something
on have a bad effect (on someone or something)
on have a chip on one's shoulder
on have a good head on one's shoulders
on have a handle on something
on have a hold on someone
on have a lot on one's mind
on have an eye on someone or something
on have a price on one's head
on have bearing on something
on have designs on someone or something
on have dibs on something
on have egg on one's face
on have nothing on someone or something
on have one's feet on the ground
on have one's heart on one's sleeve
on have one's heart set on something
on have one's sights trained on something
on have someone or something on one's hands
on have someone or something on one's mind
on have someone's blood on one's hands
on have someone on the string
on have something on
on have the shoe on the other foot
on hell on earth
on high man on the totem pole
on high on something
on hinge on something
on hit the nail (right) on the head
on hitting on all cylinders
on hold forth (on something)
on hold on (to someone or something)
on hold up on something
on home in (on someone or something)
on hooked (on something)
on horn in (on someone or something)
on hot on something
on hung up (on someone or something)
on in on the kill
on intent on doing something
on Johnny-on-the-spot
on judge one on one's own merit(s)
on judge something on its own merit(s)
on jump on someone
on jump on the bandwagon
on keen on doing something
on keen on someone or something
on keep a close rein on someone or something
on keep an eye on someone or something
on keep a tight rein on someone or something
on keep (close) watch (on someone or something)
on keep harping on something
on keep on an even keel
on keep one's eye on the ball
on keep one's feet on the ground
on keep on one's toes
on keep on someone
on keep someone on tenterhooks
on keep something on an even keel
on keep tab(s) (on someone or something)
on keep the lid on something
on Keep your shirt on!
on knock on wood
on know where someone stands (on someone or something)
on know which side one's bread is buttered on
on land on both feet
on land on one's feet
on launch forth (on something)
on lay a finger on someone or something
on lay down on the job
on lay eyes on someone or something
on lay it on thick
on lay it on with a trowel
on lay one's cards on the table
on lay one's hands on someone or something
on lay something on someone
on lay something on the line
on lay the blame on someone or something
on lay the finger on someone
on lead someone on a merry chase
on lean on someone
on leave one's mark on someone
on leave something on
on let someone in on something
on let up (on someone or something)
on lie down on the job
on like a bump on a log
on like a house on fire
on like nothing on earth
on live high on the hog
on live on borrowed time
on look down on someone or something
on look good on paper
on look in (on someone or something)
on look on someone as something
on loom large (on the horizon)
on lose out (on something)
on lost on someone
on lower the boom on someone
on low man on the totem pole
on make an impression (on someone)
on make book on something
on make good on something

on make someone's **hair stand on end**
on miss out (on something)
on move in (on someone or something)
on murder on something
on muscle in (on someone or something)
on no flies on someone
on not able to go on
on not on any account
on not on your life
on off again, on again
on off and on
on on a bias
on on account
on on active duty
on on a diet
on on a first-name basis (with someone)
on on a fool's errand
on on again, off again
on on a lark
on on all fours
on on and off
on on any account
on on approval
on on a shoestring
on on a splurge
on on a waiting list
on on behalf of someone
on on bended knee
on on board
on on Broadway
on on call
on on campus
on on cloud nine
on on consignment
on on credit
on on dead center
on on deck
on on duty
on on earth
on on easy street
on on edge
on one's heart is set on something
on one up (on someone)
on on fire
on on foot
on on good terms (with someone)
on on hold
on on horseback
on on impact
on on impulse
on on in years
on on land
on on line
on on location
on on medication
on on no account
on on occasion
on on one's best behavior
on on one's feet
on on (one's) guard
on on one's honor
on on one's mind
on on one's own
on on one's person
on on one's toes
on on one's way to doing something
on on order
on on par (with someone or something)
on on patrol
on on pins and needles
on on probation
on on purpose
on on sale
on on schedule
on on second thought
on on someone's or something's last legs
on on someone's account
on on someone's back
on on someone's behalf
on on someone's case
on on someone's doorstep
on on someone's head
on on someone's say-so
on on someone's shoulders
on on someone's way (somewhere)
on on speaking terms (with someone)
on on standby
on on target
on on the air
on on the alert (for someone or something)
on on the average
on on the ball
on on the beam
on on the bench
on on the bias
on on the blink
on on the block
on on the borderline
on on the button
on on the contrary
on on the defensive
on on the dot
on on the double
on on the eve of something
on on the face of it
on on the fence (about something)
on on the fritz
on on the go
on on the heels of something
on on the horizon
on on the horns of a dilemma
on on the hot seat
on on the hour
on on the house
on on the job
on on the level
on on the lookout (for someone or something)
on on the loose
on on the make
on on the market
on on the mend
on on the money
on on the move
on on the nose

on on the off-chance
on on (the) one hand
on on the other hand
on on the point of doing something
on on the QT
on on the right track
on on the rocks
on on the spot
on on the spur of the moment
on on the strength of something
on on the take
on on the tip of one's tongue
on on the track of someone or something
on on the trail of someone or something
on on the up-and-up
on on the verge (of doing something)
on on the wagon
on on the warpath
on on the way (somewhere)
on on the way to doing something
on on the whole
on on the wing
on on the wrong track
on on thin ice
on on time
on on tiptoe
on on top
on on trial
on on vacation
on on view
on open fire (on someone)
on open season (on someone or something)
on open up (on someone or something)
on out on a limb
on out on bail
on out on parole
on (out) on patrol
on out on the town
on palm something off (on someone)
on pass on
on pat someone on the back
on pay a call on someone
on perspective on something
on pick on somebody your own size
on pick on someone or something
on pick on someone your own size
on pin one's faith on someone or something
on pin one's hope(s) on someone or something
on pin someone down (on something)
on pin something on someone
on place the blame on someone or something
on plain as the nose on one's face
on play a joke on someone
on play a trick on someone
on play on something
on play tricks (on someone)
on pour cold water on something
on pour it on thick
on pour oil on troubled water(s)
on pride oneself on something
on pull a gun (on someone)
on pull a knife (on someone)
on pull a stunt (on someone)
on pull a trick (on someone)
on pull rank (on someone)
on pull something on someone
on pull the plug (on someone or something)
on put a cap on something
on put a hold on something
on put a spin on something
on put on
on put one's cards on the table
on put (one's) dibs on something
on put one's finger on something
on put one's hand(s) on something
on put one's head on the block (for someone or something)
on put one's thinking cap on
on put someone or something on hold
on put someone on
on put something on
on put something over (on someone)
on put the arm on someone
on put the bite on someone
on put the blame on someone or something
on put the clamps on (someone)
on put the finger on someone
on put the heat on (someone)
on put the kibosh on something
on put the screws on (someone)
on put the skids on (something)
on put the squeeze on (someone)
on put the touch on someone
on put weight on
on quick on the draw
on quick on the trigger
on quick on the uptake
on rain on someone's parade
on ramble on (about someone or something)
on rat on someone
on read the handwriting on the wall
on read up (on someone or something)
on reliance on someone or something
on rest on one's laurels
on ride herd on someone or something
on ride on someone's coattails
on right on time
on ring down the curtain (on something)
on rub off (on someone)
on run low (on something)
on see eye to eye (with someone) (on something)
on see the (hand)writing on the wall
on sell someone on a plan or idea
on sell something on credit
on send someone (out) on an errand
on serve notice (on someone)
on set eyes on someone or something
on set forth (on something)
on set one's heart on something
on set one's sights on something
on set one back on one's heels
on set someone or something on fire
on set someone's teeth on edge
on set the world on fire
on settle on something

on shake (hands) on *something*
on Shame on *someone.*
on shed (some) light on *something*
on shut the door on *someone or something*
on sign on the dotted line
on sign on (with *someone*)
on sit in (on *something*)
on sit on its hands
on sit on *one's* hands
on sit on *someone or something*
on sit on the fence
on sitting on a powder keg
on (sitting) on top of the world
on skate on thin ice
on skip out (on *someone or something*)
on slap *someone* on the wrist
on sleep on *something*
on slow on the draw
on slow on the uptake
on smile on *someone or something*
on *someone* wrote the book on *something*
on speak out (on *something*)
on spread it on thick
on spring *something* on *someone*
on stand on ceremony
on stand on *one's* own two feet
on start off on the wrong foot
on steal a march (on *someone*)
on step on it
on step on *someone's* toes
on step on the gas
on stock up (on *something*)
on (strictly) on the level
on (strictly) on the up-and-up
on stuck on *someone or something*
on swear on a stack of Bibles
on swear on *one's* mother's grave
on sweet on *someone*
on take a bath (on *something*)
on take a rain check (on *something*)
on take it easy (on *someone or something*)
on take it on the chin
on take off (on *something*)
on take pity (on *someone or something*)
on take *someone or something* on
on take *someone* up on *something*
on take *something* on faith
on take *something* on the chin
on take *something* out on *someone or something*
on take too much on
on tell on *someone*
on think back (on *someone or something*)
on think on *one's* feet
on thin on top
on throw cold water on *something*
on throw *oneself* on the mercy of the court
on throw (some) light on *something*
on thumbs down on *someone or something*
on thumbs up on *someone or something*
on to be on the safe side
on toing and froing (on *something*)
on touch on *something*
on trade on *something*
on train *one's* sights on *something*
on try *something* out on *someone*
on turn on a dime
on turn *one's* back (on *someone or something*)
on turn on the waterworks
on turn *someone* on
on turn the heat up (on *someone*)
on turn the tables (on *someone*)
on turn thumbs down (on *someone or something*)
on turn thumbs up (on *someone or something*)
on verge on *something*
on wait on *someone* hand and foot
on walk on air
on walk on eggs
on walk out (on *someone or something*)
on wear and tear (on *something*)
on wear *one's* heart on *one's* sleeve
on wear on *someone*
on weigh on *someone's* mind
on wish *something* off on *someone*
on with bells on (*one's* toes)
on wither on the vine
on with everything (on it)
on work on *someone or something*
on You can bet on it!
on zero in on *something*
on zoom in (on *someone or something*)
on a drag (on *someone*)
on a new lease on life
on a night on the town
on a paradise (on earth)
on a rush on *something*
on The jury is still out (on *someone or something*).
on The shoe is on the other foot.
once all at once
once at once
once (every) once in a while
once get the once-over
once give *someone* the once-over
once once and for all
once once in a blue moon
once once-in-a-lifetime chance
once once in a while
once once-over-lightly
once once upon a time
one (all) in one breath
one all in one piece
one (as) busy as a one-armed paperhanger
one as one
one at one fell swoop
one back to square one
one be a new one on *someone*
one busy as a one-armed paperhanger
one do *someone* one better
one every last one
one go in one ear and out the other
one go *someone* one better
one have a lot going (for one)
one have a one-track mind
one have one foot in the grave
one have one for the road

one in one breath
one in one ear and out (of) the other
one in one fell swoop
one just one of those things
one kill two birds with one stone
one like one of the family
one my one and only
one not one iota
one off to one side
one one and all
one one and the same
one one at a time
one one by one
one one for the (record) books
One One good turn deserves another.
one one in a hundred
one one in a million
one one in a thousand
one one jump ahead (of someone or something)
one one little bit
One One man's meat is another man's poison.
One One man's trash is another man's treasure.
one one move ahead (of someone or something)
one one-night stand
one one of these days
one one sandwich short of a picnic
One One thing leads to another.
one one to a customer
one one up (on someone)
one one way or another
one on (the) one hand
one pull a fast one
one put all one's eggs in one basket
one six of one and half a dozen of the other
one There's more than one way to skin a cat.
one wear more than one hat
one with one hand tied behind one's back
one a hole in one
one the one and only
oneself suit oneself
onions know one's onions
only Beauty is only skin-deep.
only in name only
only It (only) stands to reason.
only know something only too well
only my one and only
only only have eyes for someone
only the one and only
onto burst onto the scene
onto onto someone or something
open crack open a bottle
open crack something wide open
open get something out in the open
open in the open
open keep one's eyes open (for someone or something)
open keep one's weather eye open
open leave oneself wide open for something
open leave oneself wide open to something
open leave something open
open (like) an open book
open not open one's mouth
open open a conversation
open open and aboveboard
open open fire (on someone)
open open for business
open open one's heart (to someone)
open open Pandora's box
open open season (on someone or something)
open open secret
open open someone's eyes (to something)
open open something up
open open the door to something
open open to something
open open up
open open (up) a can of worms
open open with something
open read someone like a(n open) book
open receive someone with open arms
open welcome someone with open arms
open an open-and-shut case
open an open book
openers for openers
opening opening gambit
opinion base one's opinion on something
opinion form an opinion
opinion hazard an opinion
opinion in one's opinion
opinion a matter of opinion
opinions keep one's opinions to oneself
opportunity jump at the opportunity
opportunity leap at the opportunity
opportunity seize the opportunity
opposite the opposite sex
or all or nothing
or believe it or not
or by hook or (by) crook
or cash or credit
or coffee, tea, or milk
or come hell or high water
or do or die
or either feast or famine
or fish or cut bait
or fold, spindle, or mutilate
or for better or for worse
or friend or foe
or heads or tails
or hit-or-miss
or know a trick or two
or land up somehow or somewhere
or lend oneself or itself to something
or like it or lump it
or lots of people or things
or make oneself or something a laughingstock
or make or break someone
or more or less
or no ifs, ands, or buts about it
or not know if one is coming or going
or not know whether one is coming or going
or now or never
or one way or another
or or else
or or words to that effect
or publish or perish
or Put up or shut up!

or rain or shine
or sell someone on a plan or idea
or Shape up or ship out.
or sink or swim
or something or other
or sooner or later
or take it or leave it
or take someone down a notch (or two)
or take someone down a peg (or two)
or tell someone a thing or two
or Trick or treat!
or whether or not
or without rhyme or reason
or a number of things or people
oranges apples and oranges
orbit go into orbit
orbit in orbit
orchard (as) crazy as a peach-orchard boar
orchard crazy as a peach-orchard boar
order back order something
order build something to order
order call the meeting to order
order in apple-pie order
order in order to do something
order in short order
order made to order
order make something to order
order on order
order order someone about
order order someone around
order order something to go
order out of order
order place an order
order put one's house in order
order the order of the day
ordered just what the doctor ordered
orders follow orders
ordinary out of the ordinary
other bring people or other creatures out in droves
other drop the other shoe
other every other person or thing
other go in one ear and out the other
other have other fish to fry
other have the shoe on the other foot
other in one ear and out (of) the other
other in other words
other laugh out of the other side of one's mouth
other look the other way
other made for each other
other none other than someone
other on the other hand
other other things being equal
other six of one and half a dozen of the other
other something or other
other There are plenty of other fish in the sea.
other turn the other cheek
other with every (other) breath
other the other side of the tracks
other the other way round
other The shoe is on the other foot.
ounce An ounce of prevention is worth a pound of cure.
ourselves by ourselves
out act something out
out air something out
out all-out war
out (all) tuckered out
out appear out of nowhere
out ask someone out
out back out (of something)
out bail out (of something)
out bail someone or something out
out battle something out
out bawl someone out
out bear something out
out beat one's brains out (to do something)
out beat the living daylights out of someone
out beat the stuffing out of someone
out beat the tar out of someone
out belt something out
out black out
out bleep something out
out blow something out of all proportion
out boot someone out
out born out of wedlock
out bottom out
out bow out
out break out
out break (out) in(to) tears
out bring people or other creatures out in droves
out bug out
out burn (oneself) out
out burn out
out burst out crying
out burst out laughing
out call out (to someone)
out cancel something out
out can't make heads or tails (out) of someone or something
out carry something out
out check out
out chew someone out
out chicken out (of something)
out chisel someone out of something
out clean out (of something)
out clear out
out come in out of the rain
out come out
out conk out
out con someone out of something
out cop out
out count someone out (for something)
out crank something out
out cry one's eyes out
out Cut it out!
out cut out for something
out cut out the deadwood
out cut out to be something
out cut the ground out from under someone
out dart in and out
out day in and day out
out day in, day out
out dig something out
out dine out

out Don't let it out of this room.
out do someone out of something
out down-and-out
out draw someone or something out
out drive someone out (of office)
out drop out (of something)
out drown someone or something out
out drum someone out of something
out dry someone out
out eat (a meal) out
out eat one's heart out
out eat out of someone's hands
out eat someone out
out edge someone out
out elbow someone out (of something)
out fall out
out farm someone or something out
out far out
out feel dragged out
out feel out of place
out feel someone out
out ferret something out of someone or something
out figure someone or something out
out find someone or something out
out find (something) out the hard way
out fit someone or something out (with something)
out fizzle out
out flat out
out flesh something out
out flunk out
out flunk someone out
out force someone out (of office)
out For crying out loud!
out fork money out (for something)
out fresh out (of something)
out frighten one out of one's wits
out frighten the (living) daylights out of someone
out frighten the wits out of someone
out get a bang out of someone or something
out get a charge out of someone or something
out get a kick out of someone or something
out get a lot of mileage out of something
out get a rise out of someone
out get one's nose out of someone's business
out get out from under someone or something
out get out of a jam
out get out of a mess
out get out of someone's way
out get out of the way
out get out of the wrong side of the bed
out get out while the getting is good
out get someone or something out of one's head
out get someone or something out of one's mind
out get someone or something out of the way
out get someone out of a jam
out get something out in the open
out get something out of one's system
out get something out of something
out get the lead out
out give out
out go all out
out go in one ear and out the other
out go out (for something)
out go out of fashion
out go out of one's way (to do something)
out go out of style
out go (out) on strike
out go out (with someone)
out gross someone out
out grow out of something
out gyp someone out of something
out hammer something out
out hang out (somewhere)
out hang out (with someone)
out have an eye out (for someone or something)
out have an out
out have one's heart go out to someone
out have one's luck run out
out have one's work cut out for one
out have something out (with someone)
out hear a peep out of someone
out hear someone out
out help (someone or something) out (with someone or something)
out hightail it out of somewhere
out hold out for something
out hold out the olive branch
out hotfoot it out of somewhere
out in one ear and out (of) the other
out iron something out
out jump out of one's skin
out keep an eye out (for someone or something)
out keep one's nose out of someone's business
out keep someone out in the cold
out kick someone out
out knock-down-drag-out fight
out knock oneself out (to do something)
out knock someone out (cold)
out knock the props out from under someone
out know something inside out
out laugh out of the other side of one's mouth
out laugh something out of court
out leak something (out)
out leave someone out in the cold
out let it all hang out
out let out some kind of sound
out let something (get) out
out let something slip (out)
out let the cat out of the bag
out light out (for somewhere)
out light out (of somewhere)
out like a bat out of hell
out like a bolt out of the blue
out like a fish out of water
out live out of a suitcase
out look out
out lose out (on something)
out lose out to someone or something
out luck out
out make a check out (to someone)
out make a federal case out of something
out make a fool out of someone
out make a monkey out of someone
out make a mountain out of a molehill

out make an all-out effort
out make a silk purse out of a sow's ear
out make hamburger out of someone or something
out make mincemeat out of someone or something
out make out (with someone or something)
out make sense out of someone or something
out make something out of nothing
out make something (out) of something
out make something up out of whole cloth
out miss out (on something)
out nose someone out
out not able to make anything out of someone or something
out not know enough to come in out of the rain
out odd man out
out one's heart goes out to someone
out one's luck runs out
out one's work is cut out for one
out out and about
out out cold
out out from under (something)
out out front
out out in force
out out in left field
out out like a light
out out of a clear blue sky
out out of (all) proportion
out out of bounds
out out of breath
out out of character
out out of circulation
out out of commission
out out of condition
out out of consideration (for someone or something)
out out of control
out out of courtesy (to someone)
out out-of-date
out out of earshot
out out of fashion
out out of favor (with someone)
out out of gas
out out of hand
out out of it
out out of keeping (with something)
out out of kilter
out out of line
out out of luck
out out of necessity
out out of one's element
out out of one's head
out out of one's mind
out out of one's senses
out out of order
out out of place
out out-of-pocket expenses
out out of practice
out out of print
out out of proportion
out out of reach
out out of season
out out of service
out out of shape
out out of sight
out out of sorts
out out of spite
out out of step (with someone or something)
out out of stock
out out of style
out out of the blue
out out of the corner of one's eye
out out of the frying pan into the fire
out out of the hole
out out of the ordinary
out out of the question
out out of the red
out out of the running
out out of the swim of things
out out-of-the-way
out out of the woods
out out of thin air
out out of this world
out out of time (with someone or something)
out out of touch (with someone or something)
out out of town
out out of tune (with someone or something)
out out of turn
out out of w(h)ack
out out of work
out out on a limb
out out on bail
out out on parole
out (out) on patrol
out out on the town
out out to lunch
out out West
out pan out
out pass out
out peter out
out pile out (of something)
out played out
out point someone or something out
out pooped out
out poop out
out pound something out
out pour one's heart (out to someone)
out psyched out
out psyche out
out psyche someone out
out pull out all the stops
out pull something out of a hat
out pull something out of thin air
out pull the rug out (from under someone)
out put out (about someone or something)
out put out (some) feelers
out put someone or something out
out put someone's eye out
out put someone's nose out of joint
out puzzle something out
out rain something out
out read someone out of something
out ride something out
out roll out the red carpet for someone
out root something out
out round out something

out rub someone out
out rule someone or something out
out run out of gas
out run out of patience
out run out of something
out run out of time
out sack out
out scare one out of one's wits
out scare the living daylights out of someone
out scare the wits out of someone
out sell (someone or something) out
out send someone (out) on an errand
out settle (something) (out of court)
out shake the lead out
out Shape up or ship out.
out shell something out
out shoot something out
out sit something out
out skip out (on someone or something)
out slip out
out smoke someone or something out
out smooth something out
out snap out of something
out sniff someone or something out
out sold out
out someone or something checks out
out sort something out
out sound someone out
out spaced-out
out speak out of turn
out speak out (on something)
out spell something out
out stamp someone or something out
out stand out
out start someone out (as something)
out step out of line
out stick one's neck out (for someone or something)
out stick out like a sore thumb
out stick something out
out straighten someone or something out
out strike out
out strike someone out
out string something out
out strung out
out sweat something out
out sweep out of somewhere
out take a leaf out of someone's book
out take out (after someone or something)
out take out a loan
out take someone or something out
out take something out on someone or something
out take the starch out of someone
out take the wind out of someone's sails
out take the words out of one's mouth
out talked out
out talk oneself out
out talk someone out of (doing) something
out talk someone out of something
out talk something out
out tear one's hair (out)
out tell tales out of school
out think out loud
out think something out
out thrash something out
out throw someone out (of something)
out throw the baby out with the bath(water)
out time out
out tough it out
out trot something out
out try out (for something)
out try (out) one's wings
out try something out on someone
out tuckered out
out tune someone or something out
out turn out (all right)
out turn out (that) something is so
out turn someone or something out
out walk out (on someone or something)
out wash a few things out
out washed-out
out watch out
out wear out one's welcome
out wear someone out
out weasel out (of something)
out weave in and out (of something)
out weed someone or something out
out week in, week out
out whale the tar out of someone
out win out (over someone or something)
out wipe someone or something out
out work out
out work something out
out worm one's way out of something
out worm something out of someone
out write something out
out year in, year out
out You scared me out of my wits.
out You scared the crap out of me.
out You scared the devil out of me.
out You scared the dickens out of me.
out You scared the hell out of me.
out zonk out
out an all-out effort
out an out-and-out something
out The jury is still out (on someone or something).
out The truth will out.
outdoors (as) big as all outdoors
outdoors big as all outdoors
outgrow outgrow something
outguess outguess someone
outright killed outright
outs ins and outs of something
outset at the outset
outset from the outset
outside at the (very) outside
outside outside of something
outside outside the box
outside thinking outside the box
outside think outside the box
over all over
over (all) over again
over (all) over with
over (all) worked up (over something)
over bend over backwards (to do something)

over blow over
over bowl someone over
over carry over
over carry something over
over come over
over come to blows (over something)
over cry over spilled milk
over do someone or something over
over do something over (again)
over fall (all) over oneself
over fall all over someone
over fall head over heels
over fall out (with someone over something)
over fall over backwards (to do something)
over fork something over
over get (oneself) into a stew (over someone or something)
over get over someone or something
over get someone over a barrel
over get something over (with)
over get the advantage over someone
over get the once-over
over get worked up (over something)
over give someone the once-over
over gloss something over
over go ape (over someone or something)
over go over
over Hand it over.
over hand over fist
over hand over hand
over hash something over
over haul someone over the coals
over have it all over someone or something
over have precedence over someone or something;
over have someone over
over have something hanging over one's head
over head over heels in debt
over head over heels in love (with someone)
over hold someone or something over
over in over one's head
over It's not over 'til it's over.
over jump all over someone
over keel over
over keep (close) watch (over someone or something)
over kick over
over knock someone over with a feather
over lay over (somewhere)
over lean over backwards (to do something)
over look like death warmed over
over look someone or something over
over lord it over someone
over lose one's head (over someone or something)
over lose sleep (over someone or something)
over make a fuss (over someone or something)
over make over someone or something
over make someone or something over
over mull something over
over once-over-lightly
over over again
over over and above something
over over and done with
over over and over (again)
over over my dead body
over over someone's head
over over the hill
over over the hump
over over the long haul
over over there
over over the short haul
over over the top
over over with
over paper over the cracks (in something)
over picked over
over pick something over
over pull the wool over someone's eyes
over put something over
over rake someone over the coals
over read something over
over ride roughshod over someone or something
over roll (over) in one's grave
over smooth something over
over stand over someone
over start (over) with a clean slate
over stop over (somewhere)
over take over
over take someone or something over
over talk something over
over think something over
over throw someone over
over tide someone over
over turn over
over turn (over) in one's grave
over until hell freezes over
over walk all over someone
over watch over someone or something
over (way) over there
over when hell freezes over
over win out (over someone or something)
over win someone over
over worked up (over something)
over work someone over
over a hush fell over someone or something
over take precedence over someone or something
over The honeymoon is over.
over The party's over.
overboard go overboard
overseas from overseas
overtures make overtures
owing owing to
owl (as) wise as an owl
owl night owl
owl wise as an owl
own according to one's own lights
own afraid of one's own shadow
own blow one's own horn
own carry one's (own) weight
own come into its own
own come into one's own
own cut one's (own) throat
own dig one's own grave
own do one's (own) thing
own feather one's (own) nest
own find one's own level
own for one's (own) part
own for one's (own) sake

own foul one's own nest
own get a taste of one's own medicine
own get one's (own) way (with someone or something)
own hoist by one's own petard
own hoist with one's own petard
own hold one's own
own in a world of one's own
own in one's (own) backyard
own in one's (own) (best) interest(s)
own judge one on one's own merit(s)
own judge something on its own merit(s)
own keep one's own counsel
own line one's own pockets
own mind one's own business
own not able to call one's time one's own
own not know one's own strength
own of one's own accord
own of one's own free will
own on one's own
own own up (to something)
own paddle one's own canoe
own pay someone's (own) way
own pick on somebody your own size
own pick on someone your own size
own pull oneself up (by one's own bootstraps)
own pull one's (own) weight
own sign one's own death warrant
own stand on one's own two feet
own stew in one's own juice
own take one's own life
own take the law into one's own hands
own tell its own story
own tell its own tale
own toot one's own horn
own under one's own steam
own a dose of one's own medicine
own a place to call one's own
own the devil's own job
ox (as) strong as an ox
ox strong as an ox
pace at a snail's pace
pace keep pace (with someone or something)
pace a change of pace
paces put one through one's paces
paces put something through its paces
pack pack a punch
pack pack a wallop
pack pack them in
pack a pack of lies
packed packed (in) like sardines
packing send someone packing
pad pad the bill
paddle paddle one's own canoe
paddle up the creek (without a paddle)
pain feeling no pain
pain give someone a pain
pain racked with pain
pain share someone's pain
pain a pain in the neck
pains have growing pains
pains take (great) pains (to do something)
paint (as) close as two coats of paint
paint (as) exciting as watching (the) paint dry
paint close as two coats of paint
paint Do I need to paint you a picture?
paint exciting as watching (the) paint dry
paint paint the town red
painted (as) black as one is painted
painted black as one is painted
pal pal around (with someone)
pale as pale as a ghost
pale (as) pale as death
pale beyond the pale
pale pale around the gills
pale pale as death
palm cross someone's palm with silver
palm grease someone's palm
palm have an itching palm
palm have an itchy palm
palm know someone or something like the palm of one's hand
palm oil someone's palm
palm palm something off (on someone)
pan out of the frying pan into the fire
pan pan out
pan a flash in the pan
pancake (as) flat as a pancake
pancake flat as a pancake
Pandora's open Pandora's box
panic press the panic button
panic push the panic button
pants beat the pants off someone
pants by the seat of one's pants
pants catch one with one's pants down
pants charm the pants off (of) someone
pants get ants in one's pants
pants You scared the pants off (of) me.
paper look good on paper
paper paper over the cracks (in something)
paper put something on paper
paperhanger (as) busy as a one-armed paperhanger
paperhanger busy as a one-armed paperhanger
papers get one's walking papers
papers give one one's walking papers
par above par
par below par
par on par (with someone or something)
par par for the course
par up to par
parade rain on someone's parade
paradise in a fool's paradise
paradise a paradise (on earth)
parcel part and parcel (of something)
Pardon Pardon my French.
park in park
parole out on parole
parry thrust and parry
part do one's part
part for one's (own) part
part for the most part
part in part
part part and parcel (of something)
part part company (with someone)
part part someone's hair

part take part (in something)
part take someone's part
part the best part of something
partake partake of something
parted A fool and his money are soon parted.
partial partial to someone or something
particular in particular
particulars the particulars of something
parting parting of the ways
party throw a party (for someone)
party the life of the party
party the party line
party the responsible party
party's The party's over.
pass come to a pretty pass
pass come to pass
pass let something pass
pass make a pass at someone
pass pass as someone or something
pass pass away
pass pass for someone or something
pass pass muster
pass pass on
pass pass out
pass pass the buck
pass pass the hat
pass pass the time
pass pass through someone's mind
pass ships that pass in the night
passing in passing
passing mention someone or something in passing
passing with each passing day
passion have a passion for someone or something
passport passport to something
past in times past
past not see past the end of one's nose
past past someone's or something's prime
past a past master at something
paste cut and paste
pasture put someone or something out to pasture
pat give someone a pat on the back
pat have something down pat
pat pat someone on the back
pat stand pat
patch patch someone or something up
path beat a path to someone's door
path lead someone down the garden path
path the path of least resistance
patience have the patience of a saint
patience run out of patience
patience try someone's patience
patient (as) patient as Job
patient patient as Job
patrol on patrol
patrol (out) on patrol
Paul rob Peter to pay Paul
pause give someone pause
pave pave the way (for someone or something)
pavement pound the pavement
pay have hell to pay
pay have the devil to pay
pay hit pay dirt
pay pay a call on someone
pay pay a king's ransom (for something)
pay pay an arm and a leg (for something)
pay pay as you go
pay pay attention (to someone or something)
pay pay a visit to someone or something
pay pay for something
pay pay homage to someone
pay pay in advance
pay pay lip service (to something)
pay pay one's debt (to society)
pay pay one's dues
pay pay one's last respects
pay pay (someone or something) a visit
pay pay someone or something off
pay pay someone's (own) way
pay pay someone a back-handed compliment
pay pay someone a compliment
pay pay someone a left-handed compliment
pay pay someone respect
pay pay the piper
pay pay through the nose (for something)
pay pay to do something
pay pay up
pay rob Peter to pay Paul
pay There will be the devil to pay.
pays He who pays the piper calls the tune.
pea (as) thick as pea soup
pea thick as pea soup
peace at peace
peace hold one's peace
peace leave someone in peace
peace make peace (with someone)
peace rest in peace
peach (as) crazy as a peach-orchard boar
peach crazy as a peach-orchard boar
peacock (as) proud as a peacock
peacock proud as a peacock
peanuts for peanuts
pearls cast (one's) pearls before swine
peas as alike as (two) peas in a pod
peas like (two) peas in a pod
peck hunt-and-peck
peculiar funny peculiar
pedestal put someone on a pedestal
peeled keep one's eyes peeled (for someone or something)
peep have a peep
peep hear a peep out of someone
peep take a peep
peeve someone's pet peeve
peg peg away (at something)
peg peg someone as something
peg take someone down a peg (or two)
peg a square peg in a round hole
pegged have someone pegged as something
penchant have a penchant for doing something
pencil in pencil
penny cost a pretty penny
penny cut someone off without a penny
penny penny-wise and pound-foolish
penny A penny saved is a penny earned.
people be all things to all people

people split people up
people a number of things or people
pep pep *someone or something* up
per per head
perfection cook *something* to perfection
Perish Perish the thought.
perish publish or perish
perk perk *someone or something* up
permitting weather permitting
perpetuity in perpetuity
persist persist in *doing something*
persist persist with *something*
person do *something* in person
person feel like a new person
person in person
person on *one's* person
person shuttle *someone or something* from person to person
person the last person
personally take *something* personally
perspective perspective on *something*
persuasion be of the persuasion that *something is so*
pet *someone's* pet hate
pet *someone's* pet peeve
pet the teacher's pet
petard hoist by *one's* own petard
petard hoist with *one's* own petard
Pete Honest to Pete.
peter peter out
Peter rob Peter to pay Paul
phony (as) phony as a three-dollar bill
phony phony as a three-dollar bill
physical get physical (with *someone*)
pick have a bone to pick (with *someone*)
pick have a pick-me-up
pick pick a fight with *someone*
pick pick a lock
pick pick and choose
pick pick a quarrel (with *someone*)
pick pick at *someone or something*
pick pick holes in *something*
pick pick *one's* way through *something*
pick pick on somebody your own size
pick pick on *someone or something*
pick pick on someone your own size
pick pick *someone or something* off
pick pick *someone or something* up
pick pick *someone's* brain(s)
pick pick *something* over
pick pick *something* to pieces
pick pick up
pick the pick of *something*
picked picked over
pickle in a (pretty) pickle
pickle in a real pickle
picnic one sandwich short of a picnic
picture (as) pretty as a picture
picture Do I need to paint you a picture?
picture get the picture
picture pretty as a picture
picture put *someone* in the picture
picture the picture of *something*
pie (as) easy as (apple) pie
pie easy as (apple) pie
pie eat humble pie
pie have a finger in the pie
pie have *one's* finger in the pie
pie in apple-pie order
pie pie in the sky
piece all in one piece
piece give *someone* a piece of *one's* mind
piece piece of cake
piece a piece of the action
piece the villain of the piece
pieces break *something* to pieces
pieces go to pieces
pieces pick *something* to pieces
pieces thrilled to pieces
pieces thrill *someone* to pieces
pier Take a long walk off a short pier.
piercing a piercing scream
pies have *one's* finger in too may pies
pig (as) fat as a pig
pig buy a pig in a poke
pig fat as a pig
pig serve as a guinea pig
pikestaff (as) plain as a pikestaff
pikestaff plain as a pikestaff
pile make a pile
pile pile in(to *something*)
pile pile out (of *something*)
pile pile *something* up
pile pile up
pill a bitter pill to swallow
pillar from pillar to post
pillar a pillar of strength
pillar a pillar of support
pimples get goose pimples
pimples give *someone* goose pimples
pin (as) bright as a new pin
pin (as) neat as a pin
pin bright as a new pin
pin neat as a pin
pin pin *one's* faith on *someone or something*
pin pin *one's* hope(s) on *someone or something*
pin pin *someone's* ears back
pin pin *someone* down
pin pin *something* on *someone*
pin so quiet you could hear a pin drop
pin so still you could hear a pin drop
pinch feel the pinch
pinch in a pinch
pinch pinch-hit (for *someone*)
pinch take *something* with a pinch of salt
pink in the pink (of condition)
pink tickled pink
pink tickle *someone* pink
pins on pins and needles
pins pins and needles
pipe pipe down
pipe pipe up with *something*
pipe Put that in your pipe and smoke it!
pipe a pipe dream
piper He who pays the piper calls the tune.

piper pay the piper
piping piping hot
pique pique someone's curiosity
pique pique someone's interest
pit pit someone or something against someone or something
pitch (as) black as pitch
pitch black as pitch
pitch make a pitch (for someone or something)
pitch pitch a tent
pitch pitch-black
pitch pitch camp
pitch pitch-dark
pitch pitch in (and help)
pitch pitch someone a curve (ball)
pitching in there pitching
pits the pits
pity take pity (on someone or something)
place all over the place
place between a rock and a hard place
place fall in(to) place
place feel out of place
place have one's heart in the right place
place in place
place in someone else's place
place in the first place
place in the right place at the right time
place in the second place
place in the wrong place at the wrong time
place jumping-off place
place keep one's place
place know one's place
place Lightning never strikes twice (in the same place).
place not one's place
place one's heart is in the right place
place out of place
place place an order
place place someone
place place the blame on someone or something
place put oneself in someone else's place
place put one in one's place
place shuttle someone or something from place to place
place someone's place of business
place take place
place a place to call one's own
place a place to hang one's hat
places go places
plague avoid someone or something like the plague
plain (as) plain as a pikestaff
plain (as) plain as day
plain (as) plain as the nose on one's face
plain in plain English
plain in plain language
plain plain and simple
plain plain as a pikestaff
plain plain as day
plain plain as the nose on one's face
plainly put something plainly
plan sell someone on a plan or idea
plank walk the plank
plans the best-laid plans of mice and men
plateau hit a plateau
play All work and no play makes Jack a dull boy.
play at play
play child's play
play foul play
play Go play in the traffic
play make a play (for someone)
play play about (with someone or something)
play play a joke on someone
play play along with someone or something
play play around (with someone or something)
play play a trick on someone
play play ball (with someone)
play play both ends (against the middle)
play play by ear
play play cat and mouse (with someone)
play play dumb
play play fair
play play fast and loose (with someone or something)
play play first chair
play play footsie (with someone)
play play for keeps
play play hard to get
play play havoc with someone or something
play play hob with someone or something
play play hooky
play play ignorant
play play innocent
play play into someone's hands
play play it cool
play play it safe
play play one's cards close to one's vest
play play one's cards close to the chest
play play one's cards right
play play one's cards well
play play one's trump card
play play on something
play play politics
play play possum
play play second fiddle (to someone)
play play someone or something down
play play someone or something up
play play someone for something
play play someone off against someone else
play play something by ear
play play (the) devil's advocate
play play the field
play play the fool
play play the market
play play to the gallery
play play tricks (on someone)
play play up to someone
play play with fire
play When the cat's away, the mice will play.
play a game that two can play
play a play-by-play description
played played out
plea cop a plea
please We aim to please.
please You can't please everyone.
pleased (as) pleased as punch
pleased less than pleased
pleased pleased as punch

plenty plenty of something
plenty There are plenty of other fish in the sea.
plot brew a plot
plot The plot thickens.
plow plow into someone or something
plow plow through something
plow put one's hand to the plow
pluck pluck up one's courage
plug plug away (at something)
plug plug something in
plug plug something up
plug pull the plug (on someone or something)
plugged not worth a plugged nickel
plumb plumb loco
pocket have someone in one's pocket
pocket Money burns a hole in someone's pocket.
pocket out-of-pocket expenses
pockets line one's own pockets
pod as alike as (two) peas in a pod
pod like (two) peas in a pod
poetic poetic justice
point at the point of doing something
point at this point (in time)
point belabor the point
point beside the point
point come to the point
point get to the point
point have a low boiling point
point jumping-off point
point make a point
point miss the point
point no point in something
point on the point of doing something
point point of view
point point someone or something out
point point something up
point point the finger at someone
point stretch a point
point stretch the point
point touch a sore point
point a case in point
point the point of no return
points make points (with someone)
poised poised for something
poised poised to do something
poison One man's meat is another man's poison.
poke buy a pig in a poke
poke poke about
poke poke around
poke poke fun (at someone)
poke poke one's nose in(to something)
poker (as) stiff as a poker
poker stiff as a poker
pole high man on the totem pole
pole low man on the totem pole
pole wouldn't touch something with a ten-foot pole
poles poles apart
polish polish something off
politics play politics
pond a big frog in a small pond
pony dog and pony show
poop poop out
pooped pooped out
poor (as) poor as a church mouse
poor in poor taste
poor poor as a church mouse
poor poor but clean
pop pop off
pop pop one's cork
pop pop the question
pop pop up
popcorn (as) busy as popcorn on a skillet
popcorn busy as popcorn on a skillet
poppy (as) red as a poppy
poppy red as a poppy
port Any port in a storm.
portent a portent of things to come
pose pose a question
pose pose as someone
pose strike a pose
position jockey for position
position make someone's position clear
possessed possessed by something
possessed possessed of something
possible as far as possible
possible (as) soon as possible
possible everything humanly possible
possible so far as possible
possible soon as possible
possum play possum
post (as) deaf as a post
post deaf as a post
post from pillar to post
postage postage and handling
posted keep someone posted
pot go to pot
pot the pot calling the kettle black
potatoes meat-and-potatoes
potshot take a potshot at someone or something
pound penny-wise and pound-foolish
pound pound a beat
pound pound something out
pound pound the pavement
pound An ounce of prevention is worth a pound of cure.
pour pour cold water on something
pour pour it on thick
pour pour money down the drain
pour pour oil on troubled water(s)
pour pour one's heart (out to someone)
pouring pouring rain
pours It never rains but it pours.
powder sitting on a powder keg
powder take a powder
power have no staying power
power the power behind the throne
powers the powers that be
practical for all practical purposes
practice in practice
practice make a practice of something
practice make something a practice
practice out of practice
practice put something into practice
praise damn someone or something with faint praise

praise praise someone or something to the skies
praises sing someone's praises
prayers in someone's prayers
preach preach to the converted
precedence have precedence over someone or something
precedence take precedence over someone or something
precedent set a precedent
precious precious few
precious precious little
prelude a prelude to something
premium at a premium
prescription refill a prescription
presence grace someone or something with one's presence
presence have the presence of mind to do something
present at present
present at the present time
press press one's luck
press press someone to the wall
press press the panic button
pressed hard pressed (to do something)
pressed pressed for time
pressure under (some) pressure
pretty (as) pretty as a picture
pretty come to a pretty pass
pretty cost a pretty penny
pretty in a (pretty) pickle
pretty pretty as a picture
Pretty Pretty is as pretty does.
pretty sitting pretty
pretty a pretty state of affairs
prevail prevail (up)on someone
prevent take steps (to prevent something)
prevention An ounce of prevention is worth a pound of cure.
price have a price on one's head
price quote a price
prick prick up one's ears
pride burst with pride
pride pride and joy
Pride Pride goes before a fall.
pride pride oneself in something
pride pride oneself on something
pride swallow one's pride
pride take pride in something
prime in its prime
prime in one's prime
prime in the prime of life
prime past someone's or something's prime
prime prime mover
print in print
print out of print
print put something into print
print the fine print
print the small print
privacy invasion of (someone's) privacy
private in private
privy privy to something
probability in all probability
probation on probation
problem get to the root of the problem
problem no problem
progress in progress
promise give something a lick and a promise
promise have a lot of promise
promise promise someone the moon
promise promise the moon (to someone)
prone prone to something
proportion blow something out of all proportion
proportion in proportion
proportion out of (all) proportion
proportion out of proportion
propose propose a toast
props knock the props out from under someone
protest a ripple of protest
proud (as) proud as a peacock
proud do oneself proud
proud proud as a peacock
prove prove to be something
proves the exception that proves the rule
provided provided that something is so
prunes full of prunes
p's mind one's p's and q's
psyche psyche out
psyche psyche someone out
psyche psyche someone up
psyched psyched out
psyched psyched up (for something)
public air one's dirty linen in public
public do something in public
public in public
public in the public eye
public wash one's dirty linen in public
publication not for publication
publish publish or perish
puff huff and puff
pull have pull with someone
pull pull a boner
pull pull a fast one
pull pull a gun (on someone)
pull pull a knife (on someone)
pull pull a stunt (on someone)
pull pull a trick (on someone)
pull pull oneself together
pull pull oneself up (by one's own bootstraps)
pull pull one's (own) weight
pull pull one's punches
pull pull out all the stops
pull pull rank (on someone)
pull pull someone or something down
pull pull someone's or something's teeth
pull pull someone's leg
pull pull someone through (something)
pull pull something on someone
pull pull something off
pull pull something out of a hat
pull pull something out of thin air
pull pull something together
pull pull strings
pull pull the plug (on someone or something)
pull pull the rug out (from under someone)
pull pull the wool over someone's eyes
pull pull through
pull pull up (somewhere)
pull pull up stakes

pulse take someone's pulse
punch (as) pleased as punch
punch beat someone to the punch
punch pack a punch
punch pleased as punch
punch punch a hole in something
punch take a punch at someone
punches pull one's punches
punishment glutton for punishment
pure (as) pure as the driven snow
pure pure and simple
pure pure as the driven snow
purge binge and purge
purpose answer someone's purpose
purpose on purpose
purpose serve someone's purpose
purposes at cross-purposes
purposes for all intents and purposes
purposes for all practical purposes
purse control the purse strings
purse make a silk purse out of a sow's ear
pursuit in pursuit of something
push if push comes to shove
push push off
push push one's luck
push push someone to the wall
push push the panic button
push when push comes to shove
pushing pushing up daisies
put feel put-upon
put hard put (to do something)
put put a bee in someone's bonnet
put put a cap on something
put put a hold on something
put put all one's eggs in one basket
put put an end to something
put put a spin on something
put put a stop to something
put put ideas into someone's head
put put in a good word (for someone)
put put in an appearance
put put off by someone or something
put put on
put put oneself in someone else's place
put put oneself in someone else's shoes
put put one's back (in)to something
put put one's best foot forward
put put one's cards on the table
put put (one's) dibs on something
put put one's finger on something
put put one's foot down (about something)
put put one's foot in it
put put one's foot in one's mouth
put put one's hand(s) on something
put put one's hand to the plow
put put one's head on the block (for someone or something)
put put one's house in order
put put one's mind to something
put put one's nose to the grindstone
put put one's oar in
put put one's shoulder to the wheel
put put one's thinking cap on
put put one's two cents(' worth) in
put put one in one's place
put put one through one's paces
put put out (about someone or something)
put put out (some) feelers
put put someone or something across
put put someone or something at someone's disposal
put put someone or something down
put put someone or something off
put put someone or something on hold
put put someone or something out
put put someone or something to bed
put put someone or something to sleep
put put someone or something to the test
put put someone or something up
put put someone's eye out
put put someone's nose out of joint
put put someone away
put put someone down as something bad
put put someone down (for something)
put put someone in the picture
put put someone off
put put someone on
put put someone through the wringer
put put someone to bed with a shovel
put put someone to shame
put put someone up to something
put put someone wise to someone or something
put put some teeth into something
put put something by
put put something down in black and white
put put something down to something
put put something forward
put put something in
put put something off
put put something on
put put something over
put put something plainly
put put something right
put put something straight
put put something through its paces
put put something together
put put something to (good) use
put put something to rest
Put Put that in your pipe and smoke it!
put put the arm on someone
put put the bite on someone
put put the blame on someone or something
put put the cart before the horse
put put the clamps on (someone)
put put the finger on someone
put put the heat on (someone)
put put the kibosh on something
put put the screws on (someone)
put put the skids on (something)
put put the squeeze on (someone)
put put the touch on someone
put put to it
put put two and two together
put put up a (brave) front
put put upon by someone

Put Put up or shut up!
put put up with someone or something
put put weight on
put put words into someone's mouth
Put Put your money where your mouth is!
put stay put
put to put it mildly
putty putty in someone's hands
puzzle puzzle something out
q's mind one's p's and q's
QT on the QT
quake quake in one's boots
quality nice and some quality
quandary in a quandary
quantity an unknown quantity
quantity a known quantity
quarrel pick a quarrel (with someone)
quartered drawn and quartered
queer (as) queer as a three-dollar bill
queer queer as a three-dollar bill
quest in quest of someone or something
question beg the question
question beside the question
question bring something into question
question call someone or something into question
question out of the question
question pop the question
question pose a question
question without question
question a leading question
questions field questions
quick (as) quick as a flash
quick (as) quick as a wink
quick (as) quick as greased lightning
quick cut someone to the quick
quick make a quick buck
quick quick and dirty
quick quick as a flash
quick quick as a wink
quick quick as greased lightning
quick quick on the draw
quick quick on the trigger
quick quick on the uptake
quiet (as) quiet as a mouse
quiet (as) quiet as the grave
quiet keep quiet (about someone or something)
quiet keep someone or something quiet
quiet keep something quiet
quiet quiet as a mouse
quiet quiet as the grave
quiet so quiet you could hear a pin drop
quit Don't quit your day job.
quite quite a bit
quite quite a few
quite quite a little
quite quite a lot
quite quite a number
quite quite a something
quits call it quits
quote quote a price
race race against time
race rat race
race run the good race
race Slow and steady wins the race.
rack go to rack and ruin
rack rack one's brain(s)
racked racked with pain
rag chew the rag
rage all the rage
ragged run someone ragged
rags from rags to riches
rags in rags
rail rail at someone (about something)
rain (as) right as rain
rain come in out of the rain
rain get a rain check (on something)
rain give someone a rain check (on something)
rain not know enough to come in out of the rain
rain pouring rain
rain rain cats and dogs
rain rain on someone's parade
rain rain or shine
rain rain something out
rain right as rain
rain risk of rain
rain take a rain check (on something)
rains It never rains but it pours.
rainy save something for a rainy day
raise cause (some) eyebrows to raise
raise raise a hand (against someone or something)
raise raise (an) objection (to someone or something)
raise raise a stink (about something)
raise raise cain (with someone or something)
raise raise havoc with someone or something
raise raise hell (with someone or something)
raise raise hob with someone or something
raise raise one's sights
raise raise one's voice (to someone)
raise raise some eyebrows
raise raise the devil (with someone or something)
raise raise the dickens (with someone or something)
raised born and raised
raised raised in a barn
rake rake someone over the coals
rake rake something off
rake rake something up
rally rally (a)round someone or something
ram ram someone or something down someone's throat
ramble ramble on (about someone or something)
rampage go on a rampage
rampant run rampant
random at random
range at close range
rank pull rank (on someone)
rank rank and file
ranks close ranks
ransom pay a king's ransom (for something)
rant rant and rave (about someone or something)
rant rant (at someone) about someone or something
rap beat the rap
rap rap someone's knuckles
rap rap with someone
rap take the rap (for someone or something)
rapped get one's knuckles rapped

rarin' rarin' to go
rat rat on someone
rat rat race
rat smell a rat
rate at any rate
rate at that rate
rate at this rate
rate rate with someone
rate second-rate
rate the going rate
rather had rather do something
rather would rather
rattle rattle something off
rave rant and rave (about someone or something)
raving stark raving mad
ravished ravished with delight
raw get a raw deal
raw give someone a raw deal
raw in the raw
razor (as) sharp as a razor
razor sharp as a razor
reach out of reach
reach reach a compromise
reach reach an agreement
reach reach an impasse
reach reach first base (with someone or something)
reach reach for the sky
reach reach one's stride
reach within someone's reach
reaction gut reaction
read Do you read me?
read read between the lines
read read one one's rights
read read someone's mind
read read someone like a(n open) book
read read someone out of something
read read someone the riot act
read read something into something
read read something over
read read something through
read read the handwriting on the wall
read read up (on someone or something)
ready get ready (to do something)
ready ready to do something
ready ready, willing, and able
ready rough-and-ready
ready when one is good and ready
real for real
real in a real pickle
real the real thing
reality in reality
reality the reality of the situation
rear at the rear of something
rear bring up the rear
rear in the rear
rear rear its ugly head
reason It (only) stands to reason.
reason listen to reason
reason lose one's reason
reason stand to reason
reason within reason
reason without rhyme or reason
reasonable beyond a reasonable doubt
receipt acknowledge receipt (of something)
receipt in receipt of something
receive receive someone with open arms
recent in recent memory
reckon reckon with someone or something
reckoned a force to be reckoned with
recognize recognize one for what one is
recognize recognize something for what it is
reconcile reconcile oneself to something
record break a record
record for the record
record off the record
record one for the (record) books
record sound like a broken record
red (as) red as a cherry
red (as) red as a poppy
red (as) red as a rose
red (as) red as a ruby
red (as) red as blood
red catch someone red-handed
red caught red-handed
red get the red-carpet treatment
red give someone the red-carpet treatment
red in the red
red not worth a red cent
red one's ears are red
red out of the red
red paint the town red
red red as a cherry
red red as a poppy
red red as a rose
red red as a ruby
red red as blood
red red herring
red red in the face
red red tape
red roll out the red carpet for someone
red see red
reduced reduced to something
reel reel something off
refill refill a prescription
regain regain one's composure
regain regain one's feet
regard hold someone in high regard
regard with regard to someone or something
regardless regardless of something
regular (as) regular as clockwork
regular at regular intervals
regular regular as clockwork
rehearsal in rehearsal
rein give free rein to someone
rein give someone free rein
rein keep a close rein on someone or something
rein keep a tight rein on someone or something
relative relative to someone or something
reliance reliance on someone or something
religion get religion
religious religious about doing something
relish with relish
reluctance reluctance to do something
reluctant be reluctant to do something

reminiscent reminiscent of someone or something
remission in remission
repair in good repair
reproach above reproach
reputation get a reputation (as a something)
reputation get a reputation (for doing something)
reputation give someone a reputation (as a something)
reputation give someone a reputation (for doing something)
reputed reputed to do something
reputed reputed to have something
request at someone's request
requirements meet the requirements (for something)
reservation make a reservation
reservations make reservations
resign resign oneself to something
resistance the line of least resistance
resistance the path of least resistance
resonate resonate with someone
resort as a last resort
respect pay someone respect
respect with respect to someone or something
respects in many respects
respects in some respects
respects pay one's last respects
response gut response
responsible the responsible party
rest at rest
rest come to rest
rest Give it a rest.
rest lay something to rest
rest put something to rest
rest rest assured
rest rest in peace
rest rest on one's laurels
result as a result of something
result result in something
retreat beat a (hasty) retreat
retrospect in retrospect
return by return mail
return in return for (someone or something)
return return someone's compliment
return return the compliment
return return the favor
return the point of no return
rev rev something up
rewards get one's just reward(s)
rhyme without rhyme or reason
ribs stick to one's ribs
rich rich in something
rich rich with something
rich strike it rich
riches from rags to riches
rid get rid of someone or something
riddance good riddance (to bad rubbish)
ride go along for the ride
ride hitch a ride
ride let something ride
ride ride herd on someone or something
ride ride off in all directions
ride ride on someone's coattails
ride ride roughshod over someone or something
ride ride something out
ride ride the gravy train
ride take someone for a ride
ride thumb a ride
ridiculous make someone look ridiculous
riding riding for a fall
right acknowledge someone to be right
right all right
right (as) right as rain
right get right on something
right go right through someone
right hang a right
right have a right to do something
right have one's heart in the right place
right have the right-of-way
right have the right to do something
right hit someone (right) between the eyes
right hit the nail (right) on the head
right in one's right mind
right in the right
right left and right
right make something right
right one's heart is in the right place
right on the right track
right play one's cards right
right put something right
right right and left
right right as rain
right right at a specific time
right right away
right right down someone's alley
right right off the bat
right right on time
right right side up
right (right) under someone's (very) nose
right right up someone's alley
right sail (right) through something
right say something (right) to someone's face
right serve someone right
right set something right
right step (right) up
right strike the right note
right turn out (all right)
right when it comes right down to it
right work out (all right)
right would give one's right arm (for someone or something)
right yield the right-of-way
rights have someone dead to rights
rights read one one's rights
Riley lead the life of Riley
ring give someone a ring
ring have a familiar ring
ring like a three-ring circus
ring ring a bell
ring ring down the curtain (on something)
ring ring in the New Year
ring ring something up
ring ring true
ring toss one's hat into the ring
ringing one's ears are ringing
rings run rings around someone

riot read someone the riot act
riot run riot
rip let her rip
rip rip into someone or something
rip rip someone or something off
ripe when the time is ripe
ripe a ripe old age
ripe the time is ripe
ripple a ripple of excitement
ripple a ripple of protest
rise Early to bed, early to rise(, makes a man healthy, wealthy, and wise.)
rise feel one's gorge rise
rise get a rise out of someone
rise give rise to something
rise make someone's gorge rise
Rise Rise and shine!
rise rise to the bait
rise rise to the occasion
risk at risk
risk risk of rain
risk risk of showers
risk risk of thunder(storms)
risk risk one's neck (to do something)
risk run a risk (of something)
risk run the risk (of something)
risk take a risk
river sell someone down the river
river send someone up the river
rivet rivet someone's attention
road get the show on the road
road have one for the road
road hit the road
road middle-of-the-road
road road-hog
road the end of the road
rob rob Peter to pay Paul
rob rob the cradle
robbery daylight robbery
Robin all around Robin Hood's barn
Robinson before you can say Jack Robinson
rock (as) hard as a rock
rock (as) solid as a rock
rock (as) steady as a rock
rock between a rock and a hard place
rock hard as a rock
rock rock the boat
rock solid as a rock
rock steady as a rock
rocker off one's rocker
rocks have rocks in one's head
rocks on the rocks
roll call (the) roll
roll heads will roll
roll let it roll
roll roll in
roll roll one's sleeves up
roll roll out the red carpet for someone
roll roll (over) in one's grave
roll roll something back
roll take (the) roll
roller (as) awkward as a cow on roller skates
roller awkward as a cow on roller skates
rolling (as) easy as rolling off a log
rolling easy as rolling off a log
rolling get rolling
rolling get the ball rolling
rolling have them rolling in the aisles
rolling keep the ball rolling
rolling rolling in something
rolling set the ball rolling
rolling start the ball rolling
rolling A rolling stone gathers no moss.
Romans When in Rome, do as the Romans do.
Rome fiddle while Rome burns
Rome Rome wasn't built in a day.
Rome When in Rome, do as the Romans do.
roof (as) busy as a cat on a hot tin roof
roof busy as a cat on a hot tin roof
roof go through the roof
room Don't let it out of this room.
room not enough room to swing a cat
room room and board
room take up room
roost come home (to roost)
roost rule the roost
roost The chickens have come home to roost.
root get to the root of the problem
root Money is the root of all evil.
root root for someone or something
root root something out
root take root
rooted rooted in something
rooted rooted to the spot
rope at the end of one's rope
rope rope someone into doing something
rope skip rope
ropes know the ropes
ropes learn the ropes
ropes show someone the ropes
rose (as) red as a rose
rose red as a rose
roses come up smelling like roses
roses Everything's coming up roses.
roses a bed of roses
rote learn something by rote
rotten rotten to the core
rough get a rough idea (about something)
rough get a rough idea (of something)
rough give someone a rough idea (about something)
rough give someone a rough idea (of something)
rough have a rough time (of it)
rough rough-and-ready
rough rough-and-tumble
rough rough it
rough rough someone up
rough when the going gets rough
rough a diamond in the rough
roughshod ride roughshod over someone or something
round (all) year round
round in round figures
round in round numbers
round round out something
round round something off

round round *something* up to *something*
round round the clock
round round-trip ticket
round year round
round a square peg in a round hole
round the other way round
roundabout say *something* in a roundabout way
roundup head for the last roundup
row get *one's* ducks in a row
row kick up a row
row tough row to hoe
royal the royal treatment
rub rub elbows (with *someone*)
rub rub off (on *someone*)
rub rub salt in the wound
rub rub shoulders with *someone*
rub rub *someone's* nose in it
rub rub *someone* out
rub rub *someone*('s fur) the wrong way
rub rub *something* in
rubbish good riddance (to bad rubbish)
Rubicon cross the Rubicon
ruby (as) red as a ruby
ruby red as a ruby
ruffle ruffle its feathers
ruffle ruffle *someone's* feathers
rug (as) snug as a bug in a rug
rug pull the rug out (from under *someone*)
rug snug as a bug in a rug
rug sweep *something* under the rug
ruin go to rack and ruin
ruin go to wrack and ruin
ruin in ruin
ruin the ruin of *someone or something*
rule as a (general) rule
rule rule *someone or something* out
rule rule the roost
rule a rule of thumb
rule the exception that proves the rule
rump rump session
run cut and run
run do *something* on the run
run dry run
run eat and run
run get a run for *one's* money
run give *one* a run for *one's* money
run have a run-in with *someone*
run have a run of bad luck
run have a run of *something*
run have *one's* luck run out
run hit-and-run
run in the long run
run in the short run
run make a run for it
run make *someone's* blood run cold
run run across *someone or something*
run run a fever
run run afoul of *someone or something*
run run after *someone*
run run an errand
run run a risk (of *something*)
run run (around) in circles
run run around like a chicken with its head cut off
run run around with *someone*
run run a taut ship
run run a temperature
run run a tight ship
run run circles around *someone*
run run counter to *something*
run run for it
run run for *one's* life
run run in the family
run run into a stone wall
run run into *someone*
run run like clockwork
run run low (on *something*)
run run off at the mouth
run run off with *someone or something*
run run-of-the-mill
run run out of gas
run run out of patience
run run out of *something*
run run out of time
run run rampant
run run rings around *someone*
run run riot
run run scared
run run short (of *something*)
run run *someone or something* down
run run *someone or something* to earth
run run *someone* in
run run *someone* ragged
run run *something* into the ground
run run *something* up
run run that by (*someone*) again
run run the gamut
run run the good race
run run the risk (of *something*)
run run through *something*
run run to *an amount of money*
run run to seed
run run wild
runaround get the runaround
runaround give *someone* the runaround
running days running
running in the running
running months running
running off and running
running off to a running start
running out of the running
running running high
running weeks running
running years running
runs Blood runs thicker than water.
runs *one's* luck runs out
rush fools rush in (where angels fear to tread)
rush give *someone* the bum's rush
rush in a mad rush
rush a rush on *something*
rustle rustle *something* up
rut in a rut
rut (stuck) in a rut
sack get the sack
sack give *someone* the sack

sack hit the sack
sack sack out
sacred sacred cow
sadder sadder but wiser
saddle saddle someone with something
safe play it safe
safe safe and sound
safe to be on the safe side
safe to be safe
safe Your secret is safe with me.
safekeeping for safekeeping
safety safety in numbers
sage sage advice
said after all is said and done
said (be) easier said than done
said easier said than done
said no sooner said than done
said when all is said and done
said You said it!
sail sail (right) through something
sail sail under false colors
sail set sail (for somewhere)
sailing clear sailing
sails take the wind out of someone's sails
saint have the patience of a saint
sake arguing for the sake of arguing
sake arguing for the sake of argument
sake for one's (own) sake
sake for the sake of someone or something
salad in one's salad days
salad toss a salad
sale for sale
sale on sale
salt back to the salt mines
salt rub salt in the wound
salt salt something away
salt take something with a grain of salt
salt take something with a pinch of salt
salt worth one's salt
salt the salt of the earth
same all the same
same amount to the same thing
same at the same time
same by the same token
same cast in the same mold
same come to the same thing
same cut from the same cloth
same in the same boat (as someone)
same in the same breath
same just the same
same Lightning never strikes twice (in the same place).
same made from the same mold
same not in the same league with someone or something
same one and the same
same same here
same speak the same language
same tarred with the same brush
same the same as someone or something
same the same old story
same the same to you
sanctity odor of sanctity
sand bury one's head in the sand
sand hide one's head in the sand
sands the sands of time
sandwich one sandwich short of a picnic
sardines packed (in) like sardines
Save Save it.
save save one's breath
save save (one's) face
save save someone's neck
save save someone's skin
save save something for a rainy day
save save the day
save save up (for something)
save scrimp and save
saved saved by the bell
saved A penny saved is a penny earned.
saving saving grace
say before you can say Jack Robinson
say drop in (to say hello)
say get one's say
say go so far as to say something
say have a say (in something)
say on someone's say-so
say say a mouthful
say say grace
say say something in a roundabout way
say say something (right) to someone's face
say say something under one's breath
say say that something is so
say say the word
say say uncle
say to say nothing of someone or something
say to say the least
say What can I say?
say What do you want me to say?
say You can say that again!
saying goes without saying
scale scale something down
scales tip the scales at something
scapegoat make someone the scapegoat for something
scarce (as) scarce as hens' teeth
scarce make oneself scarce
scarcely scarcely have time to breathe
scarcer scarcer than hens' teeth
scare scare one out of one's wits
scare scare someone or something up
scare scare someone stiff
scare scare someone to death
scare scare the living daylights out of someone
scare scare the wits out of someone
scared run scared
scared scared silly
scared scared stiff
scared scared to death
scared You scared me out of my wits.
scared You scared the crap out of me.
scared You scared the devil out of me.
scared You scared the dickens out of me.
scared You scared the hell out of me.
scared You scared the pants off (of) me.
scene arrive on the scene
scene burst onto the scene

scene come on the scene
scene create a scene
scene make a scene
scene make the scene
scenery a change of scenery
scenes behind the scenes
schedule ahead of schedule
schedule behind schedule
schedule on schedule
schemes the best-laid schemes of mice and men
school from the old school
school of the old school
school school of thought
school tell tales out of school
score have a score to settle (with someone)
score know the score
score settle a score with someone
score settle the score (with someone)
scot get off scot-free
scot go scot-free
scout scout around for someone or something
scrape bow and scrape
scrape have a scrape (with someone or something)
scrape scrape something together
scrape scrape the bottom of the barrel
scratch make something from scratch
scratch not up to scratch
scratch scratch around (for something)
scratch scratch someone's back
scratch scratch the surface
scratch start from scratch
scratch up to scratch
scratch You scratch my back and I'll scratch yours.
scream scream bloody murder
scream so mad I could scream
scream a piercing scream
screw have a screw loose
screw screw around (with someone or something)
screw screw someone or something up
screw screw up one's courage
screws put the screws on (someone)
scrimp scrimp and save
scrutiny under (close) scrutiny
sea (all) at sea (about something)
sea at sea
sea between the devil and the deep blue sea
sea get one's sea legs
sea son of a sea biscuit
sea There are plenty of other fish in the sea.
sealed signed, sealed, and delivered
seams burst at the seams
seams come apart at the seams
seams fall apart at the seams
seamy the seamy side of life
search in search of someone or something
search search high and low (for someone or something)
search search something with a fine-tooth comb
season in season
season off season
season open season (on someone or something)
season out of season
season silly season
seat by the seat of one's pants
seat in the driver's seat
seat in the hot seat
seat on the hot seat
seat show one to one's seat
seat show someone to a seat
second come off second-best
second get one's second wind
second get second thoughts about someone or something
second have second thoughts about someone or something
second in a split second
second in (just) a second
second in one's second childhood
second in the second place
second on second thought
second play second fiddle (to someone)
second second nature to someone
second second-rate
second second to none
secret carry a secret to one's grave
secret carry a secret to the grave
secret do something in secret
secret in secret
secret keep a secret
secret open secret
secret Your secret is safe with me.
security lull someone into a false sense of security
security security against something
see begin to see daylight
see begin to see the light
see can't see beyond the end of one's nose
see can't see one's hand in front of one's face
see Long time no see.
see not able to see the forest for the trees
see not see any objection (to something)
see not see farther than the end of one's nose
see not see past the end of one's nose
see see about something
see see a man about a dog
see see double
see see eye to eye (with someone) (about something)
see see eye to eye (with someone) (on something)
see see fit (to do something)
see see into something
see see no objection (to something)
see see one's way clear (to do something)
see see red
see see someone as something
see see someone home
see see someone to somewhere
see see someone to the door
see see something through
see see stars
see see the color of someone's money
see see the (hand)writing on the wall
see see the last of someone or something
see see the light
see see the sights
see see through someone or something
see see (to it) that something is done
see see to someone or something

see see which way the wind is blowing
see wait-and-see attitude
seed go to seed
seed run to seed
seeing seeing is believing
seeing seeing things
seek hide-and-seek
seen have seen better days
seize seize the bull by the horns
seize seize the opportunity
seize seize (up)on something
sell get the hard sell
sell give someone the hard sell
sell sell like hotcakes
sell sell (someone or something) out
sell sell someone or something short
sell sell someone a bill of goods
sell sell someone down the river
sell sell someone on a plan or idea
sell sell something for a song
sell sell something off
sell sell something on credit
send get a big send-off
send give someone a big send-off
send send one about one's business
send send someone or something up
send send someone into something
send send someone off
send send someone (out) on an errand
send send someone packing
send send someone to the showers
send send someone up the river
send send something C.O.D.
send send up a trial balloon
sense horse sense
sense in a sense
sense lull someone into a false sense of security
sense make sense
sense sixth sense
senses come to one's senses
senses out of one's senses
senses take leave of one's senses
separate separate but equal
separate separate the men from the boys
separate separate the sheep from the goats
separation the separation of church and state
serve serve as a guinea pig
serve serve notice (on someone)
serve serve someone's purpose
serve serve someone right
serve serve time
served First come, first served.
service at someone's service
service be of service (to someone)
service out of service
service pay lip service (to something)
session in session
session rump session
set all set
set (all) set to do something
set at a set time
set dead set against someone or something
set get set
set have one's heart set against something
set have one's heart set on something
set not set foot somewhere
set one's heart is (dead) set against something
set one's heart is set on something
set set a precedent
set set a trap
set set eyes on someone or something
set set fire to someone or something
set set foot somewhere
set set forth (on something)
set set great store by someone or something
set set in
set set one's heart against something
set set one's heart on something
set set one's sights on something
set set one back on one's heels
set set sail (for somewhere)
set set someone or something free
set set someone or something off
set set someone or something on fire
set set someone or something straight
set set someone or something up
set set someone's teeth on edge
set set someone back (some amount of money)
set set someone up (as something)
set set someone up (in business)
set set something down to something
set set something right
set set something straight
set set something to music
set set the ball rolling
set set the stage for something
set set the table
set set the world on fire
set set to do something
set set tongues (a)wagging
set set type
set set upon someone or something
set set up shop somewhere
settle have a score to settle (with someone)
settle settle a score with someone
settle settle down
settle settle for something
settle settle on something
settle settle someone's affairs
settle settle (something) (out of court)
settle settle the score (with someone)
settle settle up with someone
sevens at sixes and sevens
seventh in seventh heaven
sever sever ties with someone
sew sew something up
sewed get something sewed up
sex the opposite sex
shack shack up (with someone)
shades shades of someone or something
shadow afraid of one's own shadow
shadow beyond the shadow of a doubt
shadow shadow of itself
shadow shadow of oneself

shake give someone a fair shake
shake more someone or something than one can shake a stick at
shake shake (hands) on something
shake shake hands (with someone)
shake shake in one's boots
shake shake someone or something down
shake shake someone or something off
shake shake someone or something up
shake shake something off
shake shake the lead out
shakers movers and shakers
shakes in two shakes of a lamb's tail
shakes no great shakes
shambles in shambles
shame hide one's face in shame
shame put someone to shame
Shame Shame on someone.
shame a crying shame
shank's by shank's mare
shank's go (somewhere) by shank's mare
shape in good shape
shape in shape
shape lick something into shape
shape out of shape
shape shape someone up
shape shape up
shape take shape
shape whip something into shape
share one's fair share
share share and share alike
share share someone's pain
share share someone's sorrow
share the lion's share (of something)
sharing Thank you for sharing.
sharp (as) sharp as a razor
sharp (as) sharp as a tack
sharp at some time sharp
sharp sharp as a razor
sharp sharp as a tack
shave have a close shave
she That's all she wrote.
shed shed crocodile tears
shed shed (some) light on something
sheep separate the sheep from the goats
sheep the black sheep of the family
sheep's a wolf in sheep's clothing
sheet (as) white as a sheet
sheet white as a sheet
sheets three sheets to the wind
shell come out of one's shell
shell shell something out
shellacking get a shellacking
shellacking give someone a shellacking
shellacking take a shellacking
shift shift for oneself
shine rain or shine
shine Rise and shine!
shine shine up to someone
shine take a shine to someone or something
ship desert a sinking ship
ship leave a sinking ship
ship run a taut ship
ship run a tight ship
ship Shape up or ship out.
shipping shipping and handling
ships ships that pass in the night
shirk shirk one's duty
shirt give someone the shirt off one's back
shirt Keep your shirt on!
shirt lose one's shirt
shock get the shock of one's life
shoe (as) comfortable as an old shoe
shoe (as) common as an old shoe
shoe comfortable as an old shoe
shoe common as an old shoe
shoe drop the other shoe
shoe have the shoe on the other foot
shoe If the shoe fits, wear it.
shoe The shoe is on the other foot.
shoes fill someone's shoes
shoes in someone else's shoes
shoes put oneself in someone else's shoes
shoes step into someone's shoes
shoestring get along (on a shoestring)
shoestring on a shoestring
shook shook up
shoot shoot for something
shoot shoot from the hip
shoot shoot one's mouth off
shoot shoot something out
shoot shoot the breeze
shoot shoot the bull
shoot shoot the works
shooting the whole shooting match
shop close up shop
shop set up shop somewhere
shop shop around (for something)
shop talk shop
shop a bull in a china shop
shopping go window-shopping
shopping window-shopping
short caught short
short end up with the short end of the stick
short fall short (of something)
short for short
short get the short end of the stick
short in short
short in the short run
short life is too short
short long and (the) short of it
short make a long story short
short make short work of someone or something
short nothing short of something
short one sandwich short of a picnic
short over the short haul
short run short (of something)
short sell someone or something short
short short and sweet
short short for something
short short of something
short stop short of doing something
short Take a long walk off a short pier.
short a few cards short of a deck

shot (all) shot to hell
shot give something a shot
shot give something one's best shot
shot have a shot at something
shot not by a long shot
shot off like a shot
shot shot through with something
shot shot to hell
shot take a shot at something
shot a shot in the arm
shot a shot in the dark
shotgun a shotgun wedding
shots call the shots
should should have stood in bed
shoulder get the cold shoulder
shoulder give someone the cold shoulder
shoulder have a chip on one's shoulder
shoulder put one's shoulder to the wheel
shoulder shoulder to shoulder
shoulder straight from the shoulder
shoulders carry the weight of the world on one's shoulders
shoulders have a good head on one's shoulders
shoulders have broad shoulders
shoulders head and shoulders above someone or something
shoulders on someone's shoulders
shoulders rub shoulders with someone
shouting all over but the shouting
shouting within shouting distance
shove if push comes to shove
shove shove one's way somewhere
shove shove someone or something down someone's throat
shove when push comes to shove
shovel put someone to bed with a shovel
show by a show of hands
show dog and pony show
show get the show on the road
show goes to show you
show let one's emotions show
show make a great show of something
show not show one's face
show show-and-tell
show show good faith
show show off
show show one's hand
show show one's (true) colors
show show one to one's seat
show show signs of something
show show someone or something off
show show someone the ropes
show show someone to a seat
show show someone (to) the door
show show someone up
show show something to good advantage
show steal the show
show a show of hands
shower take a shower
showers risk of showers
showers send someone to the showers
shuffle shuffle off this mortal coil
shut keep one's mouth shut (about someone or something)
shut Put up or shut up!
shut shut someone up
shut shut something down
shut shut the door on someone or something
shut an open-and-shut case
shuttle shuttle someone or something from person to person
shuttle shuttle someone or something from place to place
shy shy away (from someone or something)
shy two bricks shy of a load
shy a few cards shy of a full deck
sick (as) sick as a dog
sick be sick
sick get sick
sick make someone sick
sick sick and tired of someone or something
sick sick as a dog
sick sick in bed
sick take sick
side from side to side
side get on the good side of someone
side get out of the wrong side of the bed
side get up on the wrong side of the bed
side know which side one's bread is buttered on
side laugh out of the other side of one's mouth
side off to one side
side right side up
side side against someone
side side with someone
side to be on the safe side
side a thorn in someone's side
side the other side of the tracks
side the seamy side of life
side the wrong side of the tracks
sides choose up sides
sides split one's sides (with laughter)
sides take sides
sidetracked get sidetracked
sight buy something sight unseen
sight can't stand (the sight of) someone or something
sight catch sight of someone or something
sight in sight
sight know someone by sight
sight love at first sight
sight out of sight
sight sight for sore eyes
sights have one's sights trained on something
sights lower one's sights
sights raise one's sights
sights see the sights
sights set one's sights on something
sights train one's sights on something
sign get the high sign
sign give someone the high sign
sign sign one's own death warrant
sign sign on the dotted line
sign sign on (with someone)
sign a sign of things to come
signal signal (to) someone to do something
signed signed, sealed, and delivered
signs show signs of something
silent (as) silent as the dead

silent (as) silent as the grave
silent silent as the dead
silent silent as the grave
silk (as) smooth as silk
silk (as) soft as silk
silk make a silk purse out of a sow's ear
silk smooth as silk
silk soft as silk
silly (as) silly as a goose
silly bored silly
silly scared silly
silly silly as a goose
silly silly season
silver born with a silver spoon in one's mouth
silver cross someone's palm with silver
silver Every cloud has a silver lining.
simmer simmer down
simple plain and simple
simple pure and simple
sin (as) ugly as sin
sin ugly as sin
since since time immemorial
since the greatest thing since sliced bread
sing sing a different tune
sing sing another tune
sing sing someone's praises
single (in) single file
single single file
sink everything but the kitchen sink
sink sink in
sink sink one's teeth into something
sink sink or swim
sinker swallow something, hook, line, and sinker
sinking desert a sinking ship
sinking leave a sinking ship
sit sit around (somewhere)
sit sit at someone's feet
sit sit back and let something happen
sit sit bolt upright
sit sit (idly) by
sit sit in for someone
sit sit in (on something)
sit sit on its hands
sit sit on one's hands
sit sit on someone or something
sit sit on the fence
sit sit something out
sit sit through something
sit sit tight
sit sit up and take notice
sit sit up with someone
sit sit with someone
sitting at a sitting
sitting like a sitting duck
sitting like sitting ducks
sitting sitting on a powder keg
sitting (sitting) on top of the world
sitting sitting pretty
sitting a sitting duck
sitting a sitting target
situation no-win situation
situation the reality of the situation
six deep-six someone or something
six six of one and half a dozen of the other
sixes at sixes and sevens
sixth sixth sense
size beat someone down (to size)
size cut someone down (to size)
size knock someone down (to size)
size pick on somebody your own size
size pick on someone your own size
size size someone or something up
size take someone down (to size)
size That's about the size of it.
skate skate on thin ice
skates (as) awkward as a cow on roller skates
skates awkward as a cow on roller skates
skeleton a skeleton in the closet
sketch a thumbnail sketch
skids hit the skids
skids put the skids on (something)
skies praise someone or something to the skies
skillet (as) black as a skillet
skillet (as) busy as popcorn on a skillet
skillet black as a skillet
skillet busy as popcorn on a skillet
skin (all) skin and bones
skin Beauty is only skin-deep.
skin by the skin of one's teeth
skin get under someone's skin
skin give someone some skin
skin jump out of one's skin
skin no skin off someone's nose
skin no skin off someone's teeth
skin nothing but skin and bones
skin save someone's skin
skin skin and bones
skin skin someone alive
skin soaked to the skin
skin There's more than one way to skin a cat.
skinned thick-skinned
skinned thin-skinned
skip skip bail
skip skip out (on someone or something)
skip skip rope
skip a hop, skip, and a jump
skips one's heart skips a beat
skittles (all) beer and skittles
skittles beer and skittles
skull get something through someone's thick skull
skunk (as) drunk as a skunk
skunk drunk as a skunk
sky (as) high as the sky
sky go sky-high
sky out of a clear blue sky
sky pie in the sky
sky reach for the sky
sky's The sky's the limit.
slack slack off
slap get a slap on the wrist
slap give someone a slap on the wrist
slap slap someone's wrist
slap slap someone down
slap slap someone on the wrist

slap slap something together
slap a slap in the face
slate start (off) with a clean slate
slate start (over) with a clean slate
slate wipe someone's slate clean
slated slated for something
slated slated to do something
slaughter like lambs to the slaughter
slave a slave to something
sleep drop off (to sleep)
sleep lose sleep (over someone or something)
sleep lull someone to sleep
sleep not sleep a wink
sleep put someone or something to sleep
sleep sleep in
sleep sleep like a baby
sleep sleep like a log
sleep sleep on something
sleep sleep something off
sleep sleep with someone
sleeping Let sleeping dogs lie.
sleeve have an ace up one's sleeve
sleeve have one's heart on one's sleeve
sleeve have something up one's sleeve
sleeve laugh up one's sleeve
sleeve wear one's heart on one's sleeve
sleeves roll one's sleeves up
slice a slice of the cake
sliced the greatest thing since sliced bread
slick (as) slick as a whistle
slick slick as a whistle
slide let something slide
slide let things slide
slip get the slip
slip give someone the slip
slip let something slip by
slip let something slip (out)
slip let the chance slip by
slip slip away
slip slip off
slip slip one's mind
slip slip out
slip slip through someone's fingers
slip slip up
slip a slip of the tongue
slippery (as) slippery as an eel
slippery slippery as an eel
slow (as) slow as molasses in January
Slow Slow and steady wins the race.
slow slow as molasses in January
slow slow going
slow slow on the draw
slow slow on the uptake
slow slow someone or something down
slow slow someone or something up
slow take it slow
slower slower and slower
slower slower than molasses in January
slowly slow(ly) but sure(ly)
sly (as) sly as a fox
sly do something on the sly
sly sly as a fox
smack smack-dab in the middle
small engage in small talk
small small fry
small small hours (of the night)
small small-time
small thankful for small blessings
small a big frog in a small pond
small the small print
smart You think you're so smart!
smear smear campaign (against someone)
smell smell a rat
smell smell to high heaven
smelling come up smelling like roses
smile crack a smile
smile smile on someone or something
smithereens blow someone or something to smithereens
smoke go up in smoke
smoke have a smoke
smoke Put that in your pipe and smoke it!
smoke smoke and mirrors
smoke smoke someone or something out
smoke Where there's smoke there's fire.
smooth (as) smooth as glass
smooth (as) smooth as silk
smooth smooth as glass
smooth smooth as silk
smooth smooth something out
smooth smooth something over
snag hit a snag
snail's at a snail's pace
snake a snake in the grass
snap snap at someone
snap snap out of something
snap snap something up
sneeze nothing to sneeze at
sniff sniff someone or something out
snit in a snit
snow (as) pure as the driven snow
snow (as) white as the driven snow
snow do a snow job on someone
snow pure as the driven snow
snow white as the driven snow
snowball's have a snowball's chance in hell
snuff not up to snuff
snuff up to snuff
snug (as) snug as a bug in a rug
snug snug as a bug in a rug
so able to take just so much
so and so forth
so and so on
so bear in mind that something is so
so be of the persuasion that something is so
so be so
so do so
so go so far as to say something
so (have) never had it so good
so have so
so if so
so in so many words
so just so
so my gut tells me (that) something is so
so never had it so good

so on someone's say-so
so provided that something is so
so say that something is so
so so-and-so
So So be it.
so so clean you could eat off the floor
so so far as anyone knows
so so far as possible
so so far as someone or something is concerned
so so far as something is concerned
So So far, so good.
So So it goes.
so so long
so so mad I could scream
so so much for someone or something
so so much the better
so so quiet you could hear a pin drop
so so-so
so so soon
so so still you could hear a pin drop
so so to speak
so turn out (that) something is so
so without so much as doing something
so You think you're so smart!
soaked soaked to the skin
sober (as) sober as a judge
sober sober as a judge
society pay one's debt (to society)
sock sock something away
soft (as) soft as a baby's bottom
soft (as) soft as down
soft (as) soft as silk
soft (as) soft as velvet
soft have a soft spot in one's heart for someone or something
soft soft as a baby's bottom
soft soft as down
soft soft as silk
soft soft as velvet
soil soil one's diaper(s)
soil soil one's hands
sold sold out
solid (as) solid as a rock
solid solid as a rock
Solomon (as) wise as Solomon
Solomon wise as Solomon
some and then some
some at some length
some catch some Zs
some cause (some) eyebrows to raise
some cause (some) tongues to wag
some dig some dirt up on someone
some drum some business up
some give birth to someone or some creature
some give someone some skin
some in some respects
some It takes (some) getting used to.
some knock some heads together
some put out (some) feelers
some put some teeth into something
some raise some eyebrows
some shed (some) light on something
some (some) new blood
some throw (some) light on something
some to some extent
some use some elbow grease
some a match for someone, something, or some creature
somebody pick on somebody your own size
somehow carry on somehow
someone make someone sick
someone pick on someone your own size
someone's get out of someone's way
something have something in mind
something have something to do with something
something have something up one's sleeve
something pull something on someone
something something else
something something of the sort
something something or other
something something to that effect
something's something's up
sometime date back (to sometime)
somewhere (somewhere) in the neighborhood of an amount
somewhere somewhere to hang (up) one's hat
somewhere stranger to something or somewhere
son son of a bitch
son son of a gun
son son of a sea biscuit
song buy something for a song
song go into one's song and dance (about something)
song sell something for a song
song someone's swan song
soon as soon as
soon (as) soon as possible
soon had (just) as soon do something
soon soon as possible
soon so soon
soon would as soon do something
soon A fool and his money are soon parted.
sooner had sooner do something
sooner no sooner said than done
sooner sooner or later
sore sight for sore eyes
sore stick out like a sore thumb
sore touch a sore point
sore touch a sore spot
sorrow share someone's sorrow
sorrows drown one's sorrows
sorry (I'm) sorry.
sorry sorry
sort something of the sort
sort sort of something
sort sort something out
sorts in bad sorts
sorts out of sorts
sought much sought after
soul every living soul
soul heart and soul
soul keep body and soul together
soul not a living soul
soul not tell a (living) soul
soul with all one's heart and soul
sound (as) sound as a dollar

sound let out some kind of sound
sound safe and sound
sound sound as a dollar
sound sound as if
sound sound like
sound sound off (about something)
sound sound someone out
soup (as) easy as duck soup
soup (as) thick as pea soup
soup easy as duck soup
soup everything from soup to nuts
soup in the soup
soup soup something up
soup thick as pea soup
sour (as) sour as vinegar
sour hit a sour note
sour sour as vinegar
sour strike a sour note
sour sweet and sour
South down South
sow sow one's wild oats
sow's make a silk purse out of a sow's ear
space take up space
spaced spaced-out
spade call a spade a spade
spades (as) black as the ace of spades
spades (as) cocky as the king of spades
spades black as the ace of spades
spades cocky as the king of spades
Spain build castles in Spain
span spick-and-span
spare and something to spare
spare have something to spare
spare in one's spare time
spare not a moment to spare
spare spare someone something
spare without a moment to spare
spare with something to spare
spaz have a spaz
speak Actions speak louder than words.
speak nothing to speak of
speak so to speak
speak speak for itself
speak speak for themselves
speak speak highly of someone or something
speak speak ill of someone
speak speak off the cuff
speak speak of the devil
speak speak one's mind
speak speak out of turn
speak speak out (on something)
speak speak the same language
speak speak up
speak speak with a forked tongue
speaking on speaking terms (with someone)
speaks know whereof one speaks
specific right at a specific time
speed at full speed
spell spell something out
spell spell trouble
spend tax-and-spend
spice Variety is the spice of life.
spick spick-and-span
spill spill the beans
spill take a spill
spilled cry over spilled milk
spin make someone's head spin
spin put a spin on something
spin spin a yarn
spin spin one's wheels
spin spin something off
spindle fold, spindle, or mutilate
spirits in good spirits
spit be the spit and image of someone
spit spit (something) up
spite cut off one's nose to spite one's face
spite in spite of someone or something
spite out of spite
spitting be the spitting image of someone
spleen vent one's spleen
split in a split second
split split hairs
split split one's sides (with laughter)
split split people up
split split something fifty-fifty
split split the difference
split split up
split vote a split ticket
splurge on a splurge
spoil Too many cooks spoil the broth.
spoil Too many cooks spoil the stew.
spoils To the victors belong the spoils.
spoken spoken for
sponge throw in the sponge
spook spook someone or something
spoon born with a silver spoon in one's mouth
spoon spoon-feed someone
sporting a sporting chance
spot have a soft spot in one's heart for someone or something
spot hit the spot
spot in a (tight) spot
spot Johnny-on-the-spot
spot on the spot
spot put someone on the spot
spot rooted to the spot
spot touch a sore spot
spot X marks the spot
spotlight in the spotlight
spotlight steal the spotlight
spots hit the high spots
spout spout off (about someone or something)
spread spread it on thick
spread spread like wildfire
spread spread oneself too thin
spring no spring chicken
spring spring for something
spring spring something on someone
spruce spruce someone or something up
spur on the spur of the moment
square back to square one
square do something fair and square
square fair and square
square square accounts (with someone)

square square deal
square square meal
square square off (for something)
square square someone or something away
square square up to someone or something
square square up with someone
square a square peg in a round hole
squared squared away
squeak squeak by (someone or something)
squeeze put the squeeze on (someone)
squirrel squirrel something away
stab stab someone in the back
stab take a stab at something
stack (as) black as a stack of black cats
stack black as a stack of black cats
stack blow one's stack
stack stack something up
stack stack the cards (against someone or something)
stack stack the deck (against someone or something)
stack swear on a stack of Bibles
stacked have the cards stacked against one
stacked have the deck stacked against one
stacked the cards are stacked against one
stag go stag
stage at this stage
stage in a stage whisper
stage set the stage for something
stake at stake
stake burn someone at the stake
stake stake a claim (to something)
stakes pull up stakes
stall stall someone or something off
stamp stamp someone or something out
stamping one's old stamping ground
stand can't stand (the sight of) someone or something
stand do not have a leg to stand on
stand have one's heart stand still
stand make someone's hair stand on end
stand more than one can stand
stand one-night stand
stand stand a chance
stand stand and deliver
stand stand behind someone or something
stand stand by
stand stand corrected
stand stand for something
stand stand in awe (of someone or something)
stand stand (in) back of someone or something
stand stand in (for someone)
stand stand in someone's way
stand stand on ceremony
stand stand one's ground
stand stand on one's own two feet
stand stand out
stand stand over someone
stand stand pat
stand stand someone in good stead
stand stand someone to a treat
stand stand someone up
stand stand still for something
stand stand to reason
stand stand up and be counted
stand take a stand (against someone or something)
stand take the stand
standards measure up to someone's standards
standby on standby
standing able to do something standing on one's head
standing a standing joke
stands It (only) stands to reason.
stands know where someone stands (on someone or something)
stands one's heart stands still
standstill come to a standstill
starch take the starch out of someone
stare stare someone in the face
stark stark raving mad
stars get stars in one's eyes
stars see stars
stars thank one's lucky stars
start be off to a bad start
start from start to finish
start get a head start (on someone or something)
start get a start
start get off to a bad start
start get off to a flying start
start get one's start
start give someone a head start (on someone or something)
start give someone a start
start jolt to a start
start off to a running start
start start from scratch
start start off on the wrong foot
start start (off) with a clean slate
start start (over) with a clean slate
start start someone in (as something)
start start someone out (as something)
start start something
start start the ball rolling
starters for starters
starts by fits and starts
state in a (constant) state of flux
state lie in state
state a fine state of affairs
state a pretty state of affairs
state the separation of church and state
Station (as) busy as Grand Central Station
Station busy as Grand Central Station
stay stay after someone
stay stay in touch (with someone)
stay stay put
staying have no staying power
stead stand someone in good stead
steady (as) steady as a rock
steady go steady (with someone)
steady Slow and steady wins the race.
steady steady as a rock
steal steal a base
steal steal a march (on someone)
steal steal someone's thunder
steal steal the show
steal steal the spotlight
steam blow off steam
steam full steam ahead
steam let off steam

steam under one's own steam
steamed steamed up
steaming steaming (mad)
steel (as) true as steel
steel have a mind like a steel trap
steel true as steel
steer give someone a bum steer
steer steer clear (of someone or something)
stem from stem to stern
step in step (with someone or something)
step out of step (with someone or something)
step step-by-step
step step down (from something)
step step into someone's shoes
step step in(to the breach)
step step on it
step step on someone's toes
step step on the gas
step step out of line
step step (right) up
step step something up
step watch one's step
steps take steps (to prevent something)
stern from stem to stern
steven even steven
stew get (oneself) into a stew (over someone or something)
stew in a stew (about someone or something)
stew stew in one's own juice
stew Too many cooks spoil the stew.
stick end up with the short end of the stick
stick get the short end of the stick
stick have one's words stick in one's throat
stick have something stick in one's craw
stick more someone or something than one can shake a stick at
stick not hold a stick to someone or something
stick stick around
stick stick by someone or something
Stick Stick 'em up!
stick stick-in-the-mud
stick stick one's foot in one's mouth
stick stick one's neck out (for someone or something)
stick stick one's nose in(to something)
stick stick out like a sore thumb
stick stick someone or something up
stick stick someone with someone or something
stick stick something out
stick stick together
stick stick to one's guns
stick stick to one's ribs
stick stick up for someone or something
stick stick with someone or something
sticks sticks and stones
sticky have sticky fingers
stiff (as) stiff as a poker
stiff bored stiff
stiff bore someone stiff
stiff keep a stiff upper lip
stiff scared stiff
stiff scare someone stiff
stiff stiff as a poker
still (as) still as death
still have one's heart stand still
still hold someone or something still
still hold still
still keep someone or something still
still keep still
still one's heart stands still
still so still you could hear a pin drop
still stand still for something
still still as death
still The jury is still out (on someone or something).
stink create a stink (about something)
stink make a stink (about something)
stink raise a stink (about something)
stink stink to high heaven
stir cause a stir
stir go stir-crazy
stir stir someone or something up
stir stir up a hornet's nest
stitches keep someone in stitches
stock have something in stock
stock in stock
stock lock, stock, and barrel
stock not take stock in something
stock out of stock
stock stock up (on something)
stock take no stock in something
stock take stock (of something)
stomach cannot stomach someone or something
stomach can't stomach someone or something
stomach get butterflies in one's stomach
stomach give one butterflies in one's stomach
stomach have eyes bigger than one's stomach
stomach not able to stomach someone or something
stomach One's eyes are bigger than one's stomach.
stomach turn someone's stomach
stone (as) hard as stone
stone cast the first stone
stone hard as stone
stone have a heart of stone
stone kill two birds with one stone
stone leave no stone unturned
stone run into a stone wall
stone A rolling stone gathers no moss.
stone's (just) a stone's throw away (from something)
stones sticks and stones
stone's within a stone's throw (of something)
stone's a stone's throw (away) (from something)
stood should have stood in bed
stools fall between two stools
stoop stoop to doing something
stop come to a stop
stop jolt to a stop
stop put a stop to something
stop stop-and-go
stop stop at nothing
stop stop by (somewhere)
stop stop in (somewhere)
stop stop, look, and listen
stop stop off (somewhere)
stop stop over (somewhere)
stop stop short of doing something
stops pull out all the stops

storage in cold storage
storage in storage
store have something in store (for someone)
store mind the store
store set great store by someone or something
storm Any port in a storm.
storm kick up a storm
storm take someone or something by storm
storm A storm is brewing.
storm the calm before the storm
storm the eye of the storm
storm the lull before the storm
story cock-and-bull story
story make a long story short
story tell its own story
story the same old story
straight (as) straight as an arrow
straight get something straight
straight get the facts straight
straight give it to someone (straight)
straight go straight
straight keep a straight face
straight put something straight
straight set someone or something straight
straight set something straight
straight straight as an arrow
straight (straight) from the horse's mouth
straight straight from the shoulder
straight vote a straight ticket
straight the straight and narrow
straighten straighten someone or something out
straighten straighten someone or something up
straighten straighten up
stranger stranger to something or somewhere
strapped strapped (for something)
straw be the last straw
straw be the straw that broke the camel's back
straws clutch at straws
straws draw straws
straws grasp at straws
streak talk a blue streak
stream change horses in the middle of the stream
street down the street
street on easy street
street the man in the street
strength main strength and awkwardness
strength not know one's own strength
strength on the strength of something
strength a pillar of strength
strength a tower of strength
stretch at a stretch
stretch stretch a point
stretch stretch one's legs
stretch stretch the point
stretch stretch the truth
strictly (strictly) on the level
strictly (strictly) on the up-and-up
stride hit one's stride
stride reach one's stride
stride take something in stride
strike go (out) on strike
strike strike a balance (between two or more things)
strike strike a bargain
strike strike a chord (with someone)
strike strike a happy medium
strike strike a match
strike strike a pose
strike strike a sour note
strike strike home
strike strike it rich
strike strike out
strike strike someone's fancy
strike strike someone as something
strike strike someone funny
strike strike someone out
strike strike the right note
strike strike up a conversation
strike strike up a friendship
strike strike while the iron is hot
strikes get two strikes against one
strikes have two strikes against one
strikes Lightning never strikes twice (in the same place).
string have someone on the string
string string along (with someone)
string string something out
strings control the purse strings
strings pull strings
strings tied to one's mother's apron strings
strings with no strings attached
strings without any strings attached
stroke have a stroke
stroke a stroke of luck
strong (as) strong as a horse
strong (as) strong as a lion
strong (as) strong as an ox
strong strong as a horse
strong strong as a lion
strong strong as an ox
strong use strong language
struggle a struggle to the death
strung strung out
stubborn (as) stubborn as a mule
stubborn stubborn as a mule
stuck (stuck) in a rut
stuck stuck in traffic
stuck stuck on someone or something
stuck stuck with someone or something
stuff kid('s) stuff
stuff know one's stuff
stuff stuff and nonsense
stuff stuff the ballot box
stuffing beat the stuffing out of someone
stumble stumble across someone or something
stumble stumble into someone or something
stumble stumble (up)on someone or something
stumbling stumbling block
stunt pull a stunt (on someone)
stupor in a stupor
style cramp someone's style
style go out of style
style in style
style out of style
subject change the subject

subject drop the subject
subject off the subject
subject subject to something
subscribe subscribe to something
substance form and substance
substance sum and substance
such as such
such Like it's such a big deal!
such such and such
such such as
Such Such is life!
suck suck someone in
suck teach one's grandmother to suck eggs
sucks It sucks.
sucks That sucks.
sudden all of a sudden
sugar (as) sweet as sugar
sugar sweet as sugar
suggestive suggestive of something
suit follow suit
suit in one's birthday suit
suit monkey suit
suit suit oneself
suit suit someone to a T
suitcase live out of a suitcase
sum sum and substance
sum sum something up
sun (as) calm as a toad in the sun
sun calm as a toad in the sun
sun under the sun
Sunday in one's Sunday best
Sunday Sunday-go-to-meeting clothes
Sundays in a month of Sundays
sundry all and sundry
supply in short supply
supply supply and demand
support a pillar of support
supposed supposed to do something
sure (as) sure as death
sure for sure
sure sure as death
sure swift and sure
surely slow(ly) but sure(ly)
surf surf and turf
surface scratch the surface
surgery in surgery
surprise come as no surprise
surprise take someone or something by surprise
surprise take someone by surprise
survival the survival of the fittest
susceptible susceptible to something
suspicion above suspicion
suspicion under a cloud (of suspicion)
swallow swallow one's pride
swallow swallow something, hook, line, and sinker
swallow a bitter pill to swallow
swallowed look like the cat that swallowed the canary
swan (as) graceful as a swan
swan graceful as a swan
swan someone's swan song
swath cut a big swath
swath cut a wide swath
swear swear by someone or something
swear swear on a stack of Bibles
swear swear on one's mother's grave
sweat blood, sweat, and tears
sweat break out in a cold sweat
sweat by the sweat of one's brow
sweat no sweat
sweat sweat blood
sweat sweat something out
sweep (as) black as a sweep
sweep black as a sweep
sweep make a clean sweep
sweep sweep one off one's feet
sweep sweep out of somewhere
sweep sweep something under the carpet
sweep sweep something under the rug
sweet (as) sweet as honey
sweet (as) sweet as sugar
sweet have a sweet tooth
sweet short and sweet
sweet sweet and low
sweet sweet and sour
sweet sweet as honey
sweet sweet as sugar
sweet sweet nothings
sweet sweet on someone
sweet sweet-talk someone
sweet take the bitter with the sweet
sweetness all sweetness and light
swelled give someone a swelled head
swift (as) swift as an arrow
swift (as) swift as the wind
swift (as) swift as thought
swift swift and sure
swift swift as an arrow
swift swift as the wind
swift swift as thought
swim in the swim of things
swim make someone's head swim
swim out of the swim of things
swim sink or swim
swim swim against the current
swim swim against the tide
swimming be swimming in something
swine cast (one's) pearls before swine
swing get into full swing
swing get into the swing of things
swing in full swing
swing not enough room to swing a cat
swing swing into action
swing swing something
switch asleep at the switch
switch bait and switch
swoop at one fell swoop
swoop in one fell swoop
swords cross swords (with someone) (on something)
sympathy extend one's sympathy (to someone)
sympathy one's deepest sympathy
system get something out of one's system
systems all systems (are) go
T done to a T

T fit someone to a T
T suit someone to a T
tab pick up the tab
table clear the table
table coffee-table book
table lay one's cards on the table
table put one's cards on the table
table set the table
table table a motion
table under the table
tables turn the tables (on someone)
tabs keep tab(s) (on someone or something)
tack (as) sharp as a tack
tack sharp as a tack
tacks get down to brass tacks
tag tag along
tail Get off someone's tail!
tail in two shakes of a lamb's tail
tail with one's tail between one's legs
tail the tail wagging the dog
tailed bright eyed and bushy tailed
tails can't make heads or tails (out) of someone or something
tails heads or tails
tailspin go into a tailspin
take able to take a joke
take able to take just so much
take able to take something
take can take it to the bank.
take do a double take
take give-and-take
take Give one an inch, and one will take a mile.
take more than one can take
take not take no for an answer
take not take stock in something
take on the take
take sit up and take notice
take take a backseat (to someone)
take take a bath
take take a bow
take take a break
take take a chance
take take a course (in something)
take take a crack at something
take take a dig at someone
take take a dim view of something
take take advantage of someone or something
take take a fancy to someone or something
take take after someone
take take a gander (at someone or something)
take take a hand in something
take take a hard line (with someone)
Take Take a hike!
take take a hint
take take (a)hold of someone or something
take take aim (at someone or something)
take take a leaf out of someone's book
take take a licking
take take a liking to someone or something
take take a load off one's feet
Take Take a long walk off a short pier.
take take a look (at someone or something)
take take a look for someone or something
take take a nap
take take a new turn
take take an interest (in something)
take take an oath
take take a nosedive
take take a peep
take take a potshot at someone or something
take take a powder
take take a punch at someone
take take a rain check (on something)
take take a risk
take take a shellacking
take take a shine to someone or something
take take a shot at something
take take a shower
take take a spill
take take a stab at something
take take a stand (against someone or something)
take take a toll
take take a try at something
take take attendance
take take a turn for the better
take take a turn for the worse
take take a vacation
Take Take a walk!
take take a whack at someone or something
take take care of someone or something
take take charge (of someone or something)
take take cold
take take digs at someone
take take effect
take take exception (to something)
take take five
take take forty winks
take take (great) pains (to do something)
take take heart
take take heed
take take ill
take take inventory
take take issue (with someone)
take take it away
Take Take it easy.
take take it easy (on someone or something)
take take it on the chin
take take it or leave it
take take it slow
take take it to one's grave
take take it upon oneself to do something
take take it (up)on oneself (to do something)
take take kindly to something
take take leave of one's senses
take take liberties with someone or something
take take no stock in something
take take note (of something)
take take notice (of something)
take take off
take take one's break
take take one's cue from someone
take take one's death of cold
take take (one's) leave (of someone)
take take one's medicine

take take one's own life
take take one's time
take take one at one's word
take take out (after someone or something)
take take out a loan
take take over
take take part (in something)
take take pity (on someone or something)
take take place
take take precedence over someone or something
take take pride in something
take take root
take take shape
take take sick
take take sides
take take someone or something at face value
take take someone or something away
take take someone or something by storm
take take someone or something by surprise
take take someone or something for granted
take take someone or something in
take take someone or something on
take take someone or something out
take take someone or something over
take take someone or something wrong
take take someone's breath away
take take someone's part
take take someone's pulse
take take someone apart
take take someone by surprise
take take someone down a notch (or two)
take take someone down a peg (or two)
take take someone down (to size)
take take someone for a fool
take take someone for an idiot
take take someone for a ride
take take someone for someone or something
take take someone hostage
take take someone in
take take someone to task
take take someone to the cleaners
take take someone under one's wing(s)
take take someone up on something
take take something
take take steps (to prevent something)
take take stock (of something)
take take the bit between the teeth
take take the bit in one's teeth
take take the bitter with the sweet
take take the bull by the horns
take take the cake
take take the day off
take take the edge off (something)
take take the initiative (to do something)
take take the law into one's own hands
take take the liberty of doing something
take take the rap (for someone or something)
take take (the) roll
take take the stand
take take the starch out of someone
take take the trouble (to do something)
take take the wind out of someone's sails
take take the words out of one's mouth
take take time off
take take too much on
take take to one's heels
take take to someone or something
take take turns ((at) doing something)
take take umbrage at something
take take up a collection
take take up arms (against someone or something)
take take up one's abode somewhere
take take up room
take take up someone's time
take take up space
take take up time
take take up where one left off
take take up with someone
take You can't take it with you.
taken taken aback
taken taken for dead
takes as a duck takes to water
takes have what it takes
takes It takes (some) getting used to.
takes That takes care of that.
tale tell its own tale
tales tell tales out of school
talk all talk (and no action)
talk engage in small talk
talk have a heart-to-heart (talk)
talk like to hear oneself talk
talk sweet-talk someone
talk talk a blue streak
talk talk back (to someone)
talk talk big
talk talk down to someone
talk talk in circles
talk talk oneself out
talk talk shop
talk talk someone or something up
talk talk someone's ear off
talk talk someone's head off
talk talk someone down
talk talk someone into (doing) something
talk talk someone out of (doing) something
talk talk someone out of something
talk talk something out
talk talk something over
talk talk through one's hat
talk talk turkey
talk talk until one is blue in the face
talk the talk of somewhere
talked talked out
talking Who do you think you're talking to?
talks money talks
tamper tamper with something
tan tan someone's hide
tandem in tandem
tangent go off on a tangent
tape red tape
taper taper off (doing something)
tar beat the tar out of someone
tar tar and feather someone
tar whale the tar out of someone

target on target
target a sitting target
tarred tarred with the same brush
task take someone to task
taste acquire a taste for something
taste get a taste of one's own medicine
taste have a taste for something
taste in bad taste
taste in poor taste
taste leave a bad taste in someone's mouth
taste There's no accounting for taste.
taste a taste of something
taste a taste of things to come
tat give someone tit for tat
tatters in tatters
taut run a taut ship
tax tax-and-spend
taxes death and taxes
tea coffee, tea, or milk
tea not someone's cup of tea
tea tea and crumpets
teach teach one's grandmother to suck eggs
teach teach someone a lesson
teach You can't teach an old dog new tricks.
teacher's the teacher's pet
team team up with someone
teapot a tempest in a teapot
tear tear into someone or something
tear tear off
tear tear one's hair (out)
tear tear someone or something down
tear tear someone up
tear wear and tear (on something)
tears blood, sweat, and tears
tears bored to tears
tears break (out) in(to) tears
tears burst into tears
tears cry crocodile tears
tears shed crocodile tears
tears That tears it!
tears vale of tears
tee tee someone off
teeth armed to the teeth
teeth (as) scarce as hens' teeth
teeth by the skin of one's teeth
teeth cut teeth
teeth fly in the teeth of someone or something
teeth get one's teeth into something
teeth gnash one's teeth
teeth grit one's teeth
teeth lie through one's teeth
teeth no skin off someone's teeth
teeth pull someone's or something's teeth
teeth put some teeth into something
teeth scarcer than hens' teeth
teeth set someone's teeth on edge
teeth sink one's teeth into something
teeth take the bit between the teeth
teeth take the bit in one's teeth
teething teething troubles
tell kiss and tell
tell not tell a (living) soul
tell show-and-tell
tell tell its own story
tell tell its own tale
tell tell it to the marines
tell tell one to one's face
tell tell on someone
tell tell people apart
tell tell someone a thing or two
tell tell someone off
tell tell someone where to get off
tell tell tales out of school
tell tell things apart
tell tell time
tell tell which is which
tell Time will tell.
tells my gut tells me (that) something is so
temper hold one's temper
temper keep one's temper
temper lose one's temper
temperature run a temperature
tempest a tempest in a teapot
ten first and ten
ten wouldn't touch something with a ten-foot pole
tent pitch a tent
tenterhooks keep someone on tenterhooks
terms come to terms with someone or something
terms contradiction in terms
terms in no uncertain terms
terms in terms of something
terms on good terms (with someone)
terms on speaking terms (with someone)
terrible I'm terrible at names.
territory come with the territory
territory cover a lot of territory
territory cover the territory
territory unfamiliar territory
test acid test
test litmus test
test put someone or something to the test
testament last will and testament
testament someone's last will and testament
tether at the end of one's tether
than Actions speak louder than words.
than (be) easier said than done
than better late than never
than bite off more than one can chew
than Blood is thicker than water.
than Blood runs thicker than water.
than easier said than done
than exchange more than some number of words with someone
than Half a loaf is better than none.
than have eyes bigger than one's stomach
than holier-than-thou
than in less than no time
than know better (than to do something)
than less than pleased
than more dead than alive
than more fun than a barrel of monkeys
than more often than not
than more someone or something than one can shake a stick at

than more than one can bear
than more than one can stand
than more than one can take
than more than someone bargained for
than more (to something) than meets the eye
than none other than someone
than no sooner said than done
than not see farther than the end of one's nose
than One's bark is worse than one's bite.
than One's eyes are bigger than one's stomach.
than scarcer than hens' teeth
than slower than molasses in January
than There's more than one way to skin a cat.
than wear more than one hat
thank thank one's lucky stars
Thank Thank you for sharing.
thankful thankful for small blessings
thanks thanks to someone or something
thanks a vote of thanks
that All's well that ends well.
that All that glitters is not gold.
that (as) bad as all that
that at that rate
that bad as all that
that bear in mind that something is so
that be of the persuasion that something is so
that be that as it may
that be the straw that broke the camel's back
that bite the hand that feeds one
that deem that it is necessary
that for that matter
that have a feeling (that)
that have a hunch (that) something will happen
that I'll drink to that!
that Imagine that!
that in the unlikely event that something happens
that look like the cat that swallowed the canary
that my gut tells me (that) something is so
that or words to that effect
that provided that something is so
that Put that in your pipe and smoke it!
that run that by (someone) again
that say that something is so
that see (to it) that something is done
that ships that pass in the night
that something to that effect
That That ain't hay.
That That does it!
That That makes two of us.
that That's that.
That That sucks.
That That takes care of that.
That That tears it!
that turn out (that) something is so
that words to that effect
that You can say that again!
that a game that two can play
that the exception that proves the rule
that the hair of the dog that bit one
that the powers that be
That'll That'll be the day.
That's That's about the size of it.
That's That's all for someone.
That's That's all she wrote.
That's That's it!
That's That's that.
That's That's the ticket.
That's That's the way the ball bounces.
That's That's the way the cookie crumbles.
the (as) exciting as watching (the) paint dry
the (as) free as (the) air
the at (the) worst
the be-all and (the) end-all
the call (the) roll
the can't stand (the sight of) someone or something
the exciting as watching (the) paint dry
the free as (the) air
the get something off (the ground)
the go to (the devil)
the let someone off (the hook)
the long and (the) short of it
the march to (the beat of) a different drummer
the on (the) one hand
the play (the) devil's advocate
the take (the) roll
The The jig is up.
the the be-all and (the) end-all
the the morning after (the night before)
their in their entirety
them have them rolling in the aisles
them pack them in
them They don't make them like they used to.
them up and at them
Them's Them's fighting words.
themselves by themselves
themselves speak for themselves
then and then some
then (every) now and then
then now and then
then then and there
theory in theory
there hang in there
there here and there
there here, there, and everywhere
there in there pitching
there neither here nor there
there not all there
there over there
there then and there
There There aren't enough hours in the day.
There There are plenty of other fish in the sea.
there there is no doing something
There There is trouble brewing.
There There, now.
There There, there.
There There will be the devil to pay.
There There you go.
there (way) over there
there You got me there.
There's There's more than one way to skin a cat.
There's There's no accounting for taste.
there's Where there's a will there's a way.
there's Where there's smoke there's fire.
these one of these days

they count one's chickens before they hatch
They They don't make them like they used to.
thick (as) thick as pea soup
thick (as) thick as thieves
thick get something into someone's thick head
thick get something through someone's thick skull
thick lay it on thick
thick pour it on thick
thick spread it on thick
thick thick and fast
thick thick as pea soup
thick thick as thieves
thick thick-skinned
thick through thick and thin
thickens The plot thickens.
thicker Blood is thicker than water.
thicker Blood runs thicker than water.
thieves (as) thick as thieves
thieves thick as thieves
thin on thin ice
thin out of thin air
thin pull something out of thin air
thin skate on thin ice
thin spread oneself too thin
thin thin on top
thin thin-skinned
thin through thick and thin
thin vanish into thin air
thing amount to the same thing
thing come to the same thing
thing do one's (own) thing
thing every other person or thing
thing first thing (in the morning)
thing get a thing about someone or something
thing have a good thing going
thing have a thing going (with someone)
thing know a thing or two (about someone or something)
thing not know the first thing about someone or something
thing not miss a thing
thing One thing leads to another.
thing one thing or person after another
thing tell someone a thing or two
thing too much of a good thing
thing A little knowledge is a dangerous thing.
thing the greatest thing since sliced bread
thing the in thing (to do)
thing the real thing
thing the very thing
things be all things to all men
things be all things to all people
things first things first
things get into the swing of things
things in the swim of things
things just one of those things
things let things slide
things lots of people or things
things of all things
things other things being equal
things out of the swim of things
things seeing things
Things Things are looking up.
things wash a few things out
things a harbinger of things to come
things a number of things or people
things a portent of things to come
things a sign of things to come
things a taste of things to come
think come to think of it
think get another think coming
think hardly have time to think
think think a great deal of someone or something
think think a lot of someone or something
think think back (on someone or something)
think think better of something
think think highly of someone or something
think think inside the box
think think little of someone or something
think think much of someone or something
think think nothing of someone or something
think think on one's feet
think think out loud
think think outside the box
think think someone or something fit for something
think think something out
think think something over
think think something up
think think the world of someone or something
think think twice (before doing something)
think Who do you think you're kidding?
think Who do you think you're talking to?
think You think you're so smart!
thinking put one's thinking cap on
thinking thinking inside the box
thinking thinking outside the box
thinking to someone's way of thinking
thinking wishful thinking
third get the third degree
third give someone the third degree
thirst a thirst for something
thirsty thirsty for something
this (a little) new to (all) this
this at this juncture
this at this point (in time)
this at this rate
this at this stage
this Don't let it out of this room.
this from this day forward
this from this day on
this I just have this feeling
this in this day and age
this new to (all) this
this not long for this world
this Now hear this!
this out of this world
this shuffle off this mortal coil
This This is it.
thither hither and thither
thither hither, thither, and yon
thither thither and yon
Thomas doubting Thomas
thorn a thorn in someone's side
those just one of those things
Those Those were the days.

thou holier-than-thou
thought (as) swift as thought
thought food for thought
thought lose one's train of thought
thought lost in thought
thought not give it another thought
thought on second thought
thought Perish the thought.
thought school of thought
thought someone's train of thought
thought swift as thought
thought Who would have thought?
thoughts get second thoughts about someone or something
thoughts have second thoughts about someone or something
thousand one in a thousand
thrash thrash something out
thread hang by a thread
thread thread (one's way) through something
three (as) phony as a three-dollar bill
three (as) queer as a three-dollar bill
three like a three-ring circus
three phony as a three-dollar bill
three queer as a three-dollar bill
three three sheets to the wind
three's Two's company(, three's a crowd).
thrill thrill someone to death
thrill thrill someone to pieces
thrilled thrilled to death
thrilled thrilled to pieces
throat cut one's (own) throat
throat force someone or something down someone's throat
throat get a frog in one's throat
throat get a lump in one's throat
throat have a frog in one's throat
throat have one's words stick in one's throat
throat jump down someone's throat
throat ram someone or something down someone's throat
throat shove someone or something down someone's throat
throne the power behind the throne
through break through (something)
through carry through (on something)
through come through
through fall through
through follow through (on something)
through get something through someone's thick skull
through get through something
through get through (to someone)
through get through with something
through go right through someone
through go through
through have been through the mill
through jump through a hoop
through jump through hoops
through leaf through something
through lie through one's teeth
through live through something
through make one's way through something
through pass through someone's mind
through pay through the nose (for something)
through pick one's way through something
through plow through something
through pull someone through (something)
through pull through
through put one through one's paces
through put someone through the wringer
through put something through its paces
through read something through
through run through something
through sail (right) through something
through see something through
through see through someone or something
through shot through with something
through sit through something
through slip through someone's fingers
through talk through one's hat
through thread (one's way) through something
through through and through
through through hell and high water
through through thick and thin
through thumb through something
through work one's way through college
through work through channels
throw (just) a stone's throw away (from something)
throw throw a fit
throw throw a monkey wrench into the works
throw throw a party (for someone)
throw throw caution to the wind
throw throw cold water on something
throw throw down the gauntlet
throw throw good money after bad
throw throw in the sponge
throw throw in the towel
throw throw oneself at someone's feet
throw throw oneself at someone
throw throw oneself at the mercy of the court
throw throw oneself on the mercy of the court
throw throw one's hands up in despair
throw throw one's hands up in horror
throw throw one's voice
throw throw one's weight around
throw throw (some) light on something
throw throw someone
throw throw something into the bargain
throw throw something together
throw throw (something) up
throw throw something up to someone
throw throw the baby out with the bath(water)
throw throw the book at someone
throw within a stone's throw (of something)
throw a stone's throw (away) (from something)
thrust thrust and parry
thumb get someone under one's thumb
thumb have a green thumb
thumb stick out like a sore thumb
thumb thumb a ride
thumb thumb one's nose at someone or something
thumb thumb through something
thumb a rule of thumb
thumbnail a thumbnail sketch
thumbs all thumbs
thumbs thumbs down on someone or something
thumbs thumbs up on someone or something

thumbs turn thumbs down (on someone or something)
thumbs turn thumbs up (on someone or something)
thumbs twiddle one's thumbs
thunder steal someone's thunder
thunder thunder
thunderstorms risk of thunder(storms)
tick (as) full as a tick
tick (as) tight as a tick
tick full as a tick
tick tight as a tick
tick what makes someone tick
tick what makes something tick
ticket round-trip ticket
ticket That's the ticket.
ticket vote a split ticket
ticket vote a straight ticket
tickle tickle someone's fancy
tickle tickle someone pink
tickle tickle someone to death
tickled tickled pink
tickled tickled to death
tide swim against the tide
tide tide someone over
tide turn the tide
tie coat and tie
tie tie into something
tie tie someone or something up
tie tie someone's hands
tie tie someone down
tie tie someone (up) in knots
tie tie the knot
tie tie traffic up
tied fit to be tied
tied have one's hands tied
tied tied down
tied tied to one's mother's apron strings
tied tied up
tied with both hands tied behind one's back
tied with one hand tied behind one's back
ties sever ties with someone
tight (as) tight as a drum
tight (as) tight as a tick
tight (as) tight as Dick's hatband
tight in a (tight) spot
tight keep a tight rein on someone or something
tight run a tight ship
tight sit tight
tight tight as a drum
tight tight as a tick
tight tight as Dick's hatband
tighten tighten one's belt
tightfisted tightfisted (with money)
tightrope walk a tightrope
till have one's hand in the till
till It's not over till it's over.
till till all hours (of the day and night)
till till the cows come home
tilt at full tilt
tilt tilt at windmills
time ahead of one's time
time ahead of time
time all in good time
time all the time
time at a set time
time at the appointed time
time at the present time
time at the same time
time at this point (in time)
time bide one's time
time every time one turns around
time fight against time
time for the time being
time from time to time
time get time off
time get time to catch one's breath
time Give it time.
time give someone a hard time
time hardly have time to breathe
time hardly have time to think
time have a hard time
time have a rough time (of it)
time have a whale of a time
time have the time of one's life
time in due time
time in good time
time in less than no time
time in no time (at all)
time in one's spare time
time in the course of time
time in the nick of time
time in the right place at the right time
time in the (very) nick of time
time in the wrong place at the wrong time
time in time
time invest someone's time in something
time It's about time!
time It's high time!
time keep good time
time keep time
time kill time
time live on borrowed time
time Long time no see.
time make good time
time make time (for someone or something)
time make time (with someone)
time make up for lost time
time many is the time
time not able to call one's time one's own
time not give someone the time of day
time once upon a time
time one at a time
time on one's own time
time on time
time out of time (with someone or something)
time pass the time
time pressed for time
time race against time
time right at a specific time
time right on time
time run out of time
time scarcely have time to breathe
time serve time
time since time immemorial
time small-time

time take one's time
time take time off
time take up someone's time
time take up time
time tell time
time time after time
time time and (time) again
time time flies
Time Time is money.
Time Time is up.
time time off
time time out
time time to catch one's breath
time time was (when)
Time Time will tell.
time two-time someone
time when the time is ripe
time while away the time
time the sands of time
time the time is ripe
times at all times
times at times
times behind the times
times even in the best of times
times in times past
times keep up (with the times)
tin (as) busy as a cat on a hot tin roof
tin busy as a cat on a hot tin roof
tip from tip to toe
tip have something on the tip of one's tongue
tip on the tip of one's tongue
tip tip someone off
tip tip the scales at something
tiptoe on tiptoe
tired sick and tired of someone or something
tit (as) cold as a witch's tit
tit cold as a witch's tit
tit give someone tit for tat
tits tits and ass
tizzy in a tizzy
to able to breathe (easily) again
to able to breathe (freely) again
to able to do something blindfolded
to able to do something standing on one's head
to able to do something with one's eyes closed
to able to fog a mirror
to able to make something
to able to take a joke
to able to take just so much
to able to take something
to according to all accounts
to according to Hoyle
to according to one's own lights
to according to someone or something
to according to something
to accustomed to someone or something
to acknowledge someone to be right
to add fuel to the fire
to add fuel to the flame
to add insult to injury
to add up (to something)
to aim to do something
to (a little) new to (all) this
to (all) set to do something
to (all) shot to hell
to all the same (to someone)
to all to the good
to amount to something
to amount to the same thing
to and something to spare
to angry enough to chew nails
to answer to someone
to armed to the teeth
to arrange to do something with someone
to as a duck takes to water
to as to someone or something
to attached to someone or something
to back-to-back
to back to square one
to back to the drawing board
to back to the salt mines
to be all things to all men
to be all things to all people
to beat a path to someone's door
to beat one's brains out (to do something)
to beat someone down (to size)
to beat someone to the draw
to beat someone to the punch
to becoming to someone
to begin to see daylight
to begin to see the light
to beg to differ (with someone)
to bend over backwards (to do something)
to be off to a bad start
to be of service (to someone)
to be reluctant to do something
to be to do something
to be used to doing something
to be used to something
to bid adieu to someone or something
to blow someone or something to smithereens
to boil down to something
to bored to death
to bored to distraction
to bored to tears
to bore someone to death
to bound to (do something)
to break one's back (to do something)
to break one's neck (to do something)
to break something to pieces
to break something to someone
to break the news (to someone)
to bring someone or something up to date
to bring someone to
to bring someone up to date (on someone or something)
to bring something home to someone
to bring something to a head
to bring something to light
to bring something to someone's attention
to buckle down (to something)
to build something to order
to build up to something
to burned to a cinder
to burn someone or something to a crisp

to bust a gut (to do something)
to buy something to go
to call out (to someone)
to call the meeting to order
to can take it to the bank.
to can't hold a candle to someone
to can't wait (for something to happen)
to can't wait (to do something)
to carry a secret to one's grave
to carry a secret to the grave
to carry coals to Newcastle
to catch on (to someone or something)
to catch up (to someone or something)
to cause (some) eyebrows to raise
to cause (some) tongues to wag
to cave in (to someone or something)
to chalk something up to something
to chilled to the bone
to close one's eyes to something
to close to home
to close to someone
to coast-to-coast
to come down to earth
to come down to something
to come home (to roost)
to come home to someone
to come to
to commit something to memory
to contrary to something
to cook something to perfection
to cozy up (to someone)
to cross a bridge before one comes to it
to cross a bridge when one comes to it
to cross one's heart (and hope to die)
to cut off one's nose to spite one's face
to cut out to be something
to cut someone or something to the bone
to cut someone down (to size)
to cut someone to the quick
to cut to the chase
to dance to another tune
to dare someone (to do something)
to date back (to sometime)
to day-to-day
to dead to the world
to deem it (to be) necessary
to do credit to someone
to Do I need to paint you a picture?
to do justice to something
to done to a T
to do not have a leg to stand on
to doomed to failure
to door-to-door
to do something to excess
to down-to-earth
to down to the last detail
to down to the wire
to draw something to a close
to draw to a close
to dressed to kill
to dressed to the nines
to drink to excess
to drive someone to the wall
to drop in (to say hello)
to drop off (to sleep)
to duty bound (to do something)
to dying to do something
to Early to bed, early to rise(, makes a man healthy, wealthy, and wise.)
to easy to come by
to enough to go (a)round
to equal to someone or something
to everything from A to Z
to everything from soup to nuts
to extend credit (to someone)
to extend one's sympathy (to someone)
to eyeball-to-eyeball
to face-to-face
to fair to middling
to fall over backwards (to do something)
to fall to
to far be it from me to do something
to fed up (to somewhere) (with someone or something)
to feel free (to do something)
to feel it beneath one (to do something)
to feel up to something
to filled to the brim
to find it in one's heart (to do something)
to fit someone to a T
to fit to be tied
to fit to kill
to fools rush in (where angels fear to tread)
to force someone to the wall
to for the odds to be against one
to frightened to death
to frighten someone to death
to from dawn to dusk
to from day to day
to from door to door
to from hand to hand
to from head to toe
to from pillar to post
to from rags to riches
to from side to side
to from start to finish
to from stem to stern
to from the cradle to the grave
to from time to time
to from tip to toe
to from top to bottom
to gear something to someone or something
to generous to a fault
to get around to doing something
to get (around) to something
to get back (to someone)
to get close (to someone or something)
to get down to brass tacks
to get down to business
to get down to cases
to get down to something
to get down to the facts
to get down to the nitty-gritty
to get down to work
to get off to a bad start

to get off to a flying start
to get ready (to do something)
to get something across (to someone)
to get something to go
to get through (to someone)
to get time to catch one's breath
to get to first base (with someone or something)
to get to one's feet
to get to someone
to get to the bottom of something
to get to the heart of the matter
to get to the point
to get to the root of the problem
to get up enough nerve (to do something)
to get used to someone or something
to get what's coming to one
to get wise (to someone or something)
to give a blank check to someone
to give (an) ear to someone or something
to give birth to someone or some creature
to give birth to something
to give carte blanche to someone
to give chase (to someone or something)
to give credence to something
to give free rein to someone
to give in (to someone or something)
to give it to someone (straight)
to given to doing something
to given to understand
to give one's ear to someone or something
to give one what's coming to one
to give rise to something
to give someone to understand something
to give vent to something
to give voice to something
to goes to show you
to go from bad to worse
to gone to meet one's Maker
to good riddance (to bad rubbish)
to good to go
to go on to a better land
to go out of one's way (to do something)
to go so far as to say something
to go to any length
to go to bat for someone
to go to bed
to go to Davy Jones's locker
to go to (hell)
to go to hell in a handbasket
to go to pieces
to go to pot
to go to rack and ruin
to go to seed
to go to someone's head
to go to the bathroom
to go to (the devil)
to go to the dogs
to go to the expense (of doing something)
to go to the lavatory
to go to the limit
to go to the toilet
to go to the trouble (of doing something)
to go to the trouble (to do something)
to go to the wall
to go to town
to go to waste
to go to wrack and ruin
to grab a bite (to eat)
to Greek to me
to grind to a halt
to grow to do something
to hand it to someone
to hand something down (to someone)
to hang on (to someone or something)
to hardly have time to breathe
to hardly have time to think
to hard-pressed (to do something)
to hard put (to do something)
to hark(en) back to something
to have a bone to pick (with someone)
to have a (good) mind to do something
to have a heart-to-heart (talk)
to have an ax to grind (with someone)
to have an itch to do something
to have a right to do something
to have a score to settle (with someone)
to have been to hell and back
to have bigger fish to fry
to have had it (up to here)
to have half a mind to do something
to have half a notion to do something
to have hell to pay
to have money to burn
to have more important fish to fry
to have nothing to do with someone or something
to have one's back to the wall
to have one's ear to the ground
to have one's heart go out to someone
to have other fish to fry
to have someone dead to rights
to have something to do with something
to have something coming (to one)
to have something to go
to have something to spare
to have the devil to pay
to have the gall to do something
to have the presence of mind to do something
to have the right to do something
to have the wherewithal (to do something)
to have to do with someone or something
to have to live with something
to Here's to someone or something.
to hit one close to home
to hold on (to someone or something)
to Honest to God.
to Honest to goodness.
to Honest to Pete.
to Hop to it!
to if push comes to shove
to if worst comes to worst
to ill-disposed to doing something
to I'll drink to that!
to I'll (try to) catch you later.
to in addition (to something)

to inclined to do something
to incumbent upon someone to do something
to in no mood to do something
to in order to do something
to in the mood to do something
to It behooves one to do something.
to It (only) stands to reason.
to It's (all) Greek to me.
to It takes (some) getting used to.
to jolt to a start
to jolt to a stop
to jump to conclusions
to just the same (to someone)
to keep one's cards close to one's chest
to keep one's cards close to one's vest
to keep one's ear to the ground
to keep one's nose to the grindstone
to keep one's opinions to oneself
to keep something to oneself
to keep to oneself
to knee-high to a grasshopper
to knock oneself out (to do something)
to knock someone down (to size)
to know better (than to do something)
to knuckle down (to something)
to knuckle under (to someone or something)
to laugh all the way to the bank
to lay something to rest
to lay something to waste
to lay waste to something
to lead someone to believe something
to lead someone to do something
to lead up to something
to lean over backwards (to do something)
to leap to conclusions
to learn to live with something
to leave a lot to be desired
to leave oneself wide open to something
to leave one to one's fate
to lend a hand (to someone)
to lend an ear (to someone)
to lend color to something
to lend oneself or itself to something
to license to do something
to Life's been good (to me).
to like lambs to the slaughter
to like to hear oneself talk
to listen to reason
to live from hand to mouth
to live up to one's end of the bargain
to live up to something
to look forward to something
to look to one's laurels
to look to someone or something (for something)
to look up to someone
to lose out to someone or something
to lower oneself to some level
to lull someone to sleep
to mad enough to chew nails
to made to measure
to made to order
to make a check out (to someone)
to make as if to do something
to make it one's business to do something
to make it to something
to make love (to someone)
to make no difference (to someone)
to make someone or something available to someone
to make something to order
to make something up to someone
to man to man
to march to (the beat of) a different drummer
to mean for someone to do something
to mean nothing (to someone)
to mean something (to someone)
to mean to (do something)
to meant to be
to measure up (to someone or something)
to measure up (to someone's expectations)
to more (to something) than meets the eye
to move heaven and earth to do something
to new to (all) this
to next to nothing
to next to someone or something
to not able to call one's time one's own
to not able to go on
to not able to help something
to not able to make anything out of someone or something
to not able to see the forest for the trees
to not able to stomach someone or something
to not able to wait
to not all something is cracked up to be
to not a moment to spare
to not enough room to swing a cat
to nothing to choose from
to nothing to complain about
to nothing to it
to nothing to sneeze at
to nothing to speak of
to nothing to write home about
to not hold a candle to someone or something
to not hold a stick to someone or something
to not know enough to come in out of the rain
to not know where to turn
to not know which way to turn
to not lift a finger (to help someone)
to not lift a hand (to help someone)
to not see any objection (to something)
to not up to scratch
to not up to snuff
to not want to catch someone doing something
to not what something is cracked up to be
to nurse someone back to health
to nuzzle up to someone or something
to occur to someone
to of benefit (to someone)
to off to a running start
to off to one side
to of interest (to someone)
to old enough to be someone's father
to old enough to be someone's mother
to one's heart goes out to someone
to One thing leads to another.
to one to a customer

to on one's **way to** doing something
to on **the way to** doing something
to open one's **heart** (**to** someone)
to open someone's **eyes** (**to** something)
to open **the door to** something
to open **to** something
to open **up** (**to** someone)
to order something **to go**
to or **words to that effect**
to out **of courtesy** (**to** someone)
to out **to lunch**
to owing **to**
to own **up** (**to** something)
to partial **to** someone or something
to passport **to** something
to pay **attention** (**to** someone or something)
to pay **a visit to** someone or something
to pay **homage to** someone
to pay **lip service** (**to** something)
to pay one's **debt** (**to society**)
to pay **to** do something
to pick something **to pieces**
to play **hard to get**
to play one's **cards close to** one's **vest**
to play one's **cards close to the chest**
to play **second fiddle** (**to** someone)
to play **to the gallery**
to play **up to** someone
to poised **to** do something
to pour one's **heart** (**out to** someone)
to praise someone or something **to the skies**
to preach **to the converted**
to press someone **to the wall**
to privy **to** something
to promise **the moon** (**to** someone)
to prone **to** something
to prove **to be** something
to push someone **to the wall**
to put **an end to** something
to put **a stop to** something
to put one's **hand to the plow**
to put one's **mind to** something
to put one's **nose to the grindstone**
to put one's **shoulder to the wheel**
to put someone or something **out to pasture**
to put someone or something **to bed**
to put someone or something **to sleep**
to put someone or something **to the test**
to put someone **to bed with a shovel**
to put someone **to shame**
to put someone **up to** something
to put someone **wise to** someone or something
to put something **down to** something
to put something **to** (**good**) **use**
to put something **to rest**
to put **to it**
to raise (**an**) **objection** (**to** someone or something)
to raise one's **voice** (**to** someone)
to rarin' **to go**
to ready **to** do something
to reconcile oneself **to** something
to reduced **to** something
to relative **to** someone or something
to reluctance **to** do something
to reputed **to** do something
to reputed **to have** something
to resign oneself **to** something
to rise **to the bait**
to rise **to the occasion**
to risk one's **neck** (**to** do something)
to rob **Peter to pay Paul**
to rooted **to the spot**
to rotten **to the core**
to round something **off to** something
to round something **up to** something
to run **counter to** something
to run someone or something **to earth**
to run **to** an amount of money
to run **to seed**
to say something (**right**) **to** someone's **face**
to scarcely **have time to breathe**
to scared **to death**
to scare someone **to death**
to second **nature to** someone
to second **to none**
to see **eye to eye** (**with** someone) (**about** something)
to see **eye to eye** (**with** someone) (**on** something)
to see **fit** (**to** do something)
to see **no objection** (**to** something)
to see one's **way clear** (**to** do something)
to see someone **to** somewhere
to see someone **to the door**
to see (**to it**) **that** something **is done**
to see **to** someone or something
to send someone **to the showers**
to set **fire to** someone or something
to set something **down to** something
to set something **to music**
to set **to** do something
to shine **up to** someone
to shot **to hell**
to shoulder **to shoulder**
to show one **to** one's **seat**
to show someone **to a seat**
to show someone (**to**) **the door**
to show something **to good advantage**
to shuttle someone or something **from person to person**
to shuttle someone or something **from place to place**
to signal (**to**) someone **to** do something
to slated **to** do something
to smell **to high heaven**
to soaked **to the skin**
to something **to that effect**
to somewhere **to hang** (**up**) one's **hat**
to so **to speak**
to square **up to** someone or something
to stake **a claim** (**to** something)
to stand someone **to a treat**
to stand **to reason**
to stick **to** one's **guns**
to stick **to** one's **ribs**
to stink **to high heaven**
to stoop **to** doing something
to stranger **to** something or somewhere

to subject to something
to subscribe to something
to suit someone to a T
to Sunday-go-to-meeting clothes
to supposed to do something
to susceptible to something
to take a backseat (to someone)
to take a fancy to someone or something
to take a liking to someone or something
to take a shine to someone or something
to take exception (to something)
to take (great) pains (to do something)
to take it to one's grave
to take it upon oneself to do something
to take it (up)on oneself (to do something)
to take kindly to something
to take off one's hat (to someone)
to take someone down (to size)
to take someone to task
to take someone to the cleaners
to take something to heart
to take steps (to prevent something)
to take the initiative (to do something)
to take the trouble (to do something)
to take to one's heels
to take to someone or something
to talk back (to someone)
to talk down to someone
to teach one's grandmother to suck eggs
to tell it to the marines
to tell one to one's face
to tell someone where to get off
to thanks to someone or something
to There's more than one way to skin a cat.
to There will be the devil to pay.
to They don't make them like they used to.
to three sheets to the wind
to thrilled to death
to thrilled to pieces
to thrill someone to death
to thrill someone to pieces
to throw caution to the wind
to throw someone to the wolves
to throw something up to someone
to tickled to death
to tickle someone to death
to tied to one's mother's apron strings
to time to catch one's breath
to to a great extent
to to and fro
to to beat the band
to to be on the safe side
to to be safe
to to boot
to to count heads
to to date
to to hell and gone
to to no avail
to too good to be true
to to one's heart's content
to to put it mildly
to to say nothing of someone or something
to to say the least
to to some extent
to to someone's liking
to to someone's way of thinking
to to the best of one's ability
to to the best of one's knowledge
to to the bitter end
to to the contrary
to to the core
to to the ends of the earth
to to the last
to to the letter
to to the nth degree
to to the tune of some amount of money
To To the victors belong the spoils.
to tough nut to crack
to tough row to hoe
to to whom it may concern
to to wit
to trouble oneself (to do something)
to trouble someone to do something
to true to form
to true to one's word
to turn a blind eye to someone or something
to turn a deaf ear (to someone or something)
to turn something to good account
to turn something to one's advantage
to turn to
to unaccustomed to someone or something
to up-to-date
to up to doing something
to up to no good
to up to one's ears (in something)
to up to one's eyeballs (in something)
to up to one's neck (in something)
to up to par
to up to scratch
to up to snuff
to up to someone
to up to something
to up-to-the-minute
to used to do something
to used to someone or something
to wall-to-wall with something
to warm up to someone
to We aim to please.
to wed(ded) to someone
to wedded to something
to welcome to do something
to well-to-do
to What do you want me to say?
to What have you been up to?
to when it comes right down to it
to when it comes to something
to when push comes to shove
to Who do you think you're talking to?
to wise up (to someone or something)
to with an eye to doing something
to with a view to doing something
to without a moment to spare
to with regard to someone or something
to with respect to someone or something

to with *something* to spare
to woman to woman
to words to that effect
to work *one's* fingers to the bone
to would like (to have) *someone or something*
to a bitter pill to swallow
to a credit to *someone or something*
to a force to be reckoned with
to a harbinger of things to come
to a hard nut to crack
to a marvel to behold
to a nine-to-five job
to a place to call *one's* own
to a place to hang *one's* hat
to a portent of things to come
to a prelude to *something*
to a sign of things to come
to a slave to *something*
to a struggle to the death
to a taste of things to come
to a tough act to follow
to a word to the wise
to The chickens have come home to roost.
to the in thing (to do)
to the same to you
toad (as) calm as a toad in the sun
toad (as) ugly as a toad
toad calm as a toad in the sun
toad ugly as a toad
toast (as) warm as toast
toast propose a toast
toast warm as toast
toe from head to toe
toe from tip to toe
toe toe the line
toe toe the mark
toehold get a toehold (*somewhere*)
toes keep on *one's* toes
toes on *one's* toes
toes step on *someone's* toes
toes turn up *one's* toes
toes with bells on (*one's* toes)
together Birds of a feather flock together.
together get it (all) together
together get *one's* act together
together go together
together keep body and soul together
together knock some heads together
together pull *oneself* together
together pull *something* together
together put *something* together
together put two and two together
together scrape *something* together
together slap *something* together
together stick together
together throw *something* together
toilet go to the toilet
toing toing and froing (on *something*)
token as a token (of *something*)
token by the same token
told all told
told A little bird told me.
toll take a toll
Tom (every) Tom, Dick, and Harry
Tom Tom, Dick, and Harry
ton hit (*someone*) like a ton of bricks
tone tone *something* down
tongs fight *someone or something* hammer and tongs
tongs go at it hammer and tongs
tongue bite *one's* tongue
tongue Cat got your tongue?
tongue find *one's* tongue
tongue get a tongue-lashing
tongue give *someone* a tongue-lashing
tongue have *something* on the tip of *one's* tongue
tongue hold *one's* tongue
tongue Hold your tongue!
tongue keep a civil tongue (in *one's* head)
tongue on the tip of *one's* tongue
tongue speak with a forked tongue
tongue tongue-in-cheek
tongue a slip of the tongue
tongues cause (some) tongues to wag
tongues set tongues (a)wagging
too be too
too do too
too eat *one's* cake and have it too
too go too far
too have *one's* cake and eat it too
too have *one's* finger in too may pies
too have too
too know *something* only too well
too life is too short
too none too *something*
too spread *oneself* too thin
too take too much on
too too big for *one's* britches
too too close for comfort
too too good to be true
Too Too many cooks spoil the broth.
Too Too many cooks spoil the stew.
too too much of a good thing
toot toot *one's* own horn
tooth (as) clean as a hound's tooth
tooth clean as a hound's tooth
tooth fight *someone or something* tooth and nail
tooth go at it tooth and nail
tooth go over *something* with a fine-tooth comb
tooth have a sweet tooth
tooth search *something* with a fine-tooth comb
top at the top of *one's* lungs
top at the top of *one's* voice
top at the top of the hour
top blow *one's* top
top feel on top of the world
top from the top
top from top to bottom
top in top form
top off the top of *one's* head
top on top
top over the top
top (sitting) on top of the world
top thin on top
top top *someone or something*

top top something off
torch carry a torch (for someone)
torch carry the torch
torn torn between bad choices
torn torn between choosing something or something else
toss toss a salad
toss toss one's cookies
toss toss one's hat into the ring
toss toss something off
totem high man on the totem pole
totem low man on the totem pole
touch get in touch (with someone)
touch have the Midas touch
touch keep in touch (with someone)
touch lose one's touch (with someone or something)
touch lose touch (with someone or something)
touch out of touch (with someone or something)
touch put the touch on someone
touch stay in touch (with someone)
touch touch and go
touch touch a sore point
touch touch a sore spot
touch touch base (with someone)
touch touch on something
touch touch someone or something off
touch touch someone for something
touch touch something up
touch wouldn't touch something with a ten-foot pole
touched touched by someone or something
touched touched (in the head)
tough (as) tough as an old boot
tough get tough (with someone)
tough hang tough
tough tough as an old boot
tough tough break
tough tough it out
tough tough nut to crack
tough tough row to hoe
tough when the going gets tough
tough a tough act to follow
tow have someone or something in tow
tow in tow
toward go a long way toward doing something
toward lean toward doing something
toward well-disposed toward someone or something
towel throw in the towel
tower live in an ivory tower
tower a tower of strength
town all over town
town go to town
town man-about-town
town out of town
town out on the town
town paint the town red
town town-and-gown
town a night on the town
toy toy with someone or something
track get the inside track
track have a one-track mind
track jump the track
track keep track (of someone or something)
track lose track (of someone or something)
track off the (beaten) track
track off the track
track on the right track
track on the track of someone or something
track on the wrong track
track throw someone off the track
tracks cover someone's tracks (up)
tracks dead in someone's or something's tracks
tracks drop in one's tracks
tracks follow in someone's tracks
tracks the other side of the tracks
tracks the wrong side of the tracks
trade know (all) the tricks of the trade
trade trade on something
trades a jack-of-all-trades
traffic Go play in the traffic
traffic stuck in traffic
traffic tie traffic up
trail blaze a trail (in something)
trail on the trail of someone or something
trail throw someone off the trail
train lose one's train of thought
train ride the gravy train
train someone's train of thought
train train one's sights on something
trained have one's sights trained on something
transit in transit
translation free translation
trap fall into a trap
trap fall into someone's trap
trap fall into the trap
trap have a mind like a steel trap
trap set a trap
trash One man's trash is another man's treasure.
travesty a travesty of justice
tread fools rush in (where angels fear to tread)
treasure One man's trash is another man's treasure.
treat Dutch treat
treat stand someone to a treat
treat Trick or treat!
treating How's the world (been) treating you?
treatment get the red-carpet treatment
treatment give someone the red-carpet treatment
treatment the royal treatment
tree bark up the wrong tree
tree Go climb a tree!
tree up a tree
trees not able to see the forest for the trees
trembling in fear and trembling
trespassing no trespassing
trial on trial
trial send up a trial balloon
trial trial and error
trials trials and tribulations
tribulations trials and tribulations
trick do the trick
trick know a trick or two
trick play a trick on someone
trick pull a trick (on someone)
Trick Trick or treat!
trick trick someone into doing something
trick use every trick in the book

tricks bag of tricks
tricks know (all) the tricks of the trade
tricks play tricks (on someone)
tricks You can't teach an old dog new tricks.
tried tried-and-true
trigger quick on the trigger
trim fit and trim
trip round-trip ticket
trip trip someone up
triplicate in triplicate
trolley off one's trolley
trot trot something out
trouble ask for trouble
trouble borrow trouble
trouble go to the trouble (of doing something)
trouble go to the trouble (to do something)
trouble in trouble
trouble look for trouble
trouble not worth the trouble
trouble spell trouble
trouble take the trouble (to do something)
trouble There is trouble brewing.
Trouble Trouble is brewing.
trouble trouble oneself about someone or something
trouble trouble oneself (to do something)
trouble trouble one's head about someone or something
trouble trouble someone for something
trouble trouble someone to do something
troubled fish in troubled waters
troubled pour oil on troubled water(s)
troubles drown one's troubles
troubles teething troubles
trowel lay it on with a trowel
true (as) true as steel
true come true
true hold true
true ring true
true show one's (true) colors
true too good to be true
true tried-and-true
true true as steel
true true to form
true true to one's word
true a dream come true
truly yours truly
trump play one's trump card
trumped trumped-up
trust in the trust of someone
trust misplace one's trust (in someone)
truth Ain't it the truth?
truth stretch the truth
truth a grain of truth
truth the gospel truth
truth the moment of truth
truth The truth will out.
try have a try at something
try I'll (try to) catch you later.
try take a try at something
try try one's hand (at something)
try try one's luck (at something)
try try out (for something)
try try (out) one's wings
try try someone's patience
try try something out on someone
tubes down the tubes
tuck nip and tuck
tuck tuck into something
tucker best bib and tucker
tuckered (all) tuckered out
tuckered tuckered out
tumble rough-and-tumble
tune call the tune
tune can't carry a tune
tune change someone's tune
tune dance to another tune
tune He who pays the piper calls the tune.
tune in tune
tune out of tune (with someone or something)
tune sing a different tune
tune sing another tune
tune to the tune of some amount of money
tune tune someone or something out
tune tune (something) in
tunnel see the light (at the end of the tunnel)
turf surf and turf
turkey go cold turkey
turkey talk turkey
turn at every turn
turn done to a turn
turn do someone a good turn
turn in turn
turn not know where to turn
turn not know which way to turn
turn One good turn deserves another.
turn out of turn
turn speak out of turn
turn take a new turn
turn take a turn for the better
turn take a turn for the worse
turn turn a blind eye to someone or something
turn turn a deaf ear (to someone or something)
turn turn in
turn turn of the century
turn turn on a dime
turn turn one's back (on someone or something)
turn turn one's nose up at someone or something
turn turn on the waterworks
turn turn out (all right)
turn turn out (that) something is so
turn turn over
turn turn (over) in one's grave
turn turn someone or something down
turn turn someone or something out
turn turn someone or something up
turn turn someone's head
turn turn someone's stomach
turn turn someone off
turn turn someone on
turn turn something to good account
turn turn something to one's advantage
turn turn the clock back
turn turn the heat up (on someone)
turn turn the other cheek
turn turn the tables (on someone)

turn turn the tide
turn turn thumbs down (on someone or something)
turn turn thumbs up (on someone or something)
turn turn to
turn turn turtle
turn turn up
turned have turned the corner
turned The worm (has) turned.
turns every time one turns around
turns take turns ((at) doing something)
turtle turn turtle
twice (as) big as life and twice as ugly
twice big as life and twice as ugly
twice Lightning never strikes twice (in the same place).
twice think twice (before doing something)
twiddle twiddle one's thumbs
twinkling in the twinkling of an eye
twist twist someone's arm
twist twist someone's words (around)
twist twist someone around one's little finger
two as alike as (two) peas in a pod
two (as) close as two coats of paint
two close as two coats of paint
two fall between two stools
two get two strikes against one
two have two strikes against one
two in two shakes of a lamb's tail
two kill two birds with one stone
two know a thing or two (about someone or something)
two know a trick or two
two like (two) peas in a pod
two not care two hoots (about someone or something)
two not give two hoots (about someone or something)
two no two ways about it
two put one's two cents(' worth) in
two put two and two together
two stand on one's own two feet
two take someone down a notch (or two)
two take someone down a peg (or two)
two tell someone a thing or two
two That makes two of us.
two two bricks shy of a load
two two of a kind
two two-time someone
two A bird in the hand is worth two in the bush.
two a game that two can play
two the lesser (of the two)
two the lesser of two evils
Two's Two's company(, three's a crowd).
type set type
ugly (as) big as life and twice as ugly
ugly (as) ugly as a toad
ugly (as) ugly as sin
ugly big as life and twice as ugly
ugly rear its ugly head
ugly ugly as a toad
ugly ugly as sin
umbrage take umbrage at something
unaccustomed unaccustomed to someone or something
unawares caught unaware(s)
unbowed bloody but unbowed
uncertain in no uncertain terms
uncle Dutch uncle
uncle say uncle
under build a fire under someone
under cut the ground out from under someone
under get out from under someone or something
under get someone under one's thumb
under get something under one's belt
under get something under way
under get under someone's skin
under get under way
under go under
under groan under the burden of something
under hide one's light under a bushel
under hot under the collar
under keep something under one's hat
under keep something under wraps
under knock the props out from under someone
under knuckle under (to someone or something)
under let grass grow under one's feet
under look under the hood
under out from under (something)
under pull the rug out (from under someone)
under (right) under someone's (very) nose
under sail under false colors
under say something under one's breath
under sweep something under the carpet
under sweep something under the rug
under take someone under one's wing(s)
under under a cloud (of suspicion)
under under arrest
under under certain circumstances
under under certain conditions
under under (close) scrutiny
under under construction
under under control
under under fire
under under oath
under under one's own steam
under under someone's (very) nose
under under (some) pressure
under under the aegis of someone
under under the auspices of someone
under under the circumstances
under under the counter
under under the influence (of alcohol)
under under the influence of something
under under the sun
under under the table
under under the weather
under under the wire
under water under the bridge
understand given to understand
understand give someone to understand something
unfamiliar unfamiliar territory
unglued come unglued
unison in unison
unknown an unknown quantity
unlikely in the unlikely event of something
unlikely in the unlikely event that something happens
unseen buy something sight unseen
until make it (until something)

until talk until one is blue in the face
until until all hours
until until hell freezes over
until (un)til the cows come home
untimely come to an untimely end
unto law unto oneself
unturned leave no stone unturned
up act up
up add up (to something)
up (all) balled up
up all dressed up
up (all) worked up (about something)
up (all) worked up (over something)
up back someone or something up
up balled up
up bark up the wrong tree
up beat someone up
up beef something up
up blow up
up bone up (on something)
up bottle something up
up Bottoms up!
up Break it up!
up break someone or something up
up break up (with someone)
up bring someone or something up
up bring someone up to date (on someone or something)
up bring up the rear
up brush up (on something)
up buck up
up build (someone or something) up
up build up to something
up burned up
up burn someone up
up butter someone up
up call someone or something up
up catch up (to someone or something)
up catch up (with someone or something)
up chalk something up to something
up charged up
up charge someone or something up
up cheer someone up
up cheer up
up choke someone up
up choose up sides
up clam up
up clean up
up clear something up
up clear up
up close up shop
up cloud up
up come up
up cook something up
up cough something up
up cover someone's tracks (up)
up cover something up
up cozy up (to someone)
up crack someone or something up
up crack up
up cross someone up
up curl up and die
up cut someone or something up
up cut up
up dig some dirt up on someone
up dig someone or something up
up do something up
up double up (with someone)
up draw something up
up dredge something up
up drive someone up the wall
up drum some business up
up dry up
up ease up (on someone or something)
up eat something up
up end something up
up end up by doing something
up end up doing something
up end up (somehow)
up end up somewhere
up end up with the short end of the stick
up Everything's coming up roses.
up fed up (to somewhere) (with someone or something)
up feel up to something
up fix someone up (with someone or something)
up flare up
up fold something up
up fold up
up follow someone or something up
up follow up (on someone or something)
up follow up (on something)
up fouled up
up foul someone or something up
up foul up
up from the ground up
up gang up (on someone)
up gas up
up gear (oneself) up (for something)
up get (all) dolled up
up get mixed-up
up get someone's back up
up get someone's dander up
up get someone's hackles up
up get someone's Irish up
up get something sewed up
up get something wrapped up
up get-up-and-go
up get up enough nerve (to do something)
up get up on the wrong side of the bed
up get worked up (about something)
up get worked up (over something)
up gird (up) one's loins
up Give it up.
up give up the ghost
up go up in flames
up go up in smoke
up gum something up
up gum up the works
up ham something up
up Hands up!
up hang one's hat (up) somewhere
up hang up
up hard up (for something)
up haul up (somewhere)
up have an ace up one's sleeve

up have a pick-me-up
up have had it (up to here)
up have something up one's sleeve
up head something up
up Heads up!
up hit someone up (for something)
up hold one's end (of the bargain) up
up hold one's head up
up hold someone or something up
up hold up
up hole up (somewhere)
up hopped up
up hung up (on someone or something)
up hunt someone or something up
up jack someone up
up jack something up
up jazz something up
up keep one's chin up
up keep someone or something up
up keep up an act
up keep up appearances
up keep up one's act
up keep up (with someone or something)
up keep up (with the Joneses)
up keep up (with the times)
up keyed up
up kick up
up kiss and make up
up laid up
up land up somehow or somewhere
up lap something up
up laugh up one's sleeve
up lay someone up
up lead up to something
up learn something from the bottom up
up let up (on someone or something)
up line someone or something up with something
up line someone up (for something)
up line someone up with someone
up live it up
up live up to one's end of the bargain
up live up to something
up look someone or something up
up look up to someone
up louse something up
up make (oneself) up
up make one's mind up
up make someone up
up make something up
up make up for lost time
up make up for someone or something
up make up (with someone)
up mark something up
up measure up (to someone or something)
up measure up (to someone's expectations)
up mess someone or something up
up mix it up
up mix someone or something up
up mix someone up with someone else
up mop the floor up with someone
up move up (in the world)
up muster (up) one's courage
up not all something is cracked up to be
up not up to scratch
up not up to snuff
up not what something is cracked up to be
up nuzzle up to someone or something
up one's number is up
up one up (on someone)
up on the up-and-up
up open something up
up open up
up open (up) a can of worms
up own up (to something)
up patch someone or something up
up pay up
up pep someone or something up
up perk someone or something up
up pick someone or something up
up pick up
up pile something up
up pile up
up pipe up with something
up play someone or something up
up play up to someone
up pluck up one's courage
up plug something up
up point something up
up pop up
up prick up one's ears
up psyched up (for something)
up psyche someone up
up pull oneself up (by one's own bootstraps)
up pull up (somewhere)
up pull up stakes
up pushing up daisies
up put someone or something up
up put someone up to something
up put up a (brave) front
up Put up or shut up!
up put up with someone or something
up rake something up
up read up (on someone or something)
up rev something up
up right side up
up right up someone's alley
up ring something up
up roll one's sleeves up
up rough someone up
up round something up to something
up run something up
up rustle something up
up save up (for something)
up scare someone or something up
up screw someone or something up
up screw up one's courage
up send someone or something up
up send someone up the river
up send up a trial balloon
up set someone or something up
up set someone up (as something)
up set someone up (in business)
up settle up with someone
up set up shop somewhere

up sew something up
up shack up (with someone)
up shake someone or something up
up shape someone up
up shape up
up shine up to someone
up shook up
up show someone up
up shut someone up
up sit up and take notice
up sit up with someone
up size someone or something up
up slip up
up slow someone or something up
up snap something up
up something's up
up somewhere to hang (up) one's hat
up soup something up
up speak up
up spit (something) up
up split people up
up split up
up spruce someone or something up
up square up to someone or something
up square up with someone
up stack something up
up stand someone up
up stand up and be counted
up start something up
up steamed up
up step (right) up
up step something up
up Stick 'em up!
up stick someone or something up
up stick up for someone or something
up stir someone or something up
up stir up a hornet's nest
up stock up (on something)
up straighten someone or something up
up straighten up
up (strictly) on the up-and-up
up strike up a conversation
up strike up a friendship
up sum something up
up take someone up on something
up take something up
up take up a collection
up take up arms (against someone or something)
up take up one's abode somewhere
up take up room
up take up someone's time
up take up space
up take up time
up take up where one left off
up take up with someone
up talk someone or something up
up team up with someone
up tear someone up
up The jig is up.
up Things are looking up.
up think something up
up throw one's hands up in despair
up throw one's hands up in horror
up throw (something) up
up throw something up to someone
up thumbs up on someone or something
up tied up
up tie someone or something up
up tie someone (up) in knots
up tie traffic up
up Time is up.
up touch something up
up trip someone up
up trumped-up
up turn one's nose up at someone or something
up turn someone or something up
up turn the heat up (on someone)
up turn thumbs up (on someone or something)
up turn up
up up a blind alley
up up against something
up up and about
up up and around
up up and at them
up up and away
up up-and-coming
up up a tree
up up for grabs
up up for something
up up-front
up up in arms
up up in the air (about someone or something)
up up in years
up up North
up up the creek (without a paddle)
up up-to-date
up up to doing something
up up to no good
up up to one's ears (in something)
up up to one's eyeballs (in something)
up up to one's neck (in something)
up up to par
up up to scratch
up up to snuff
up up to someone
up up to something
up up-to-the-minute
up wait up (for someone or something)
up warm up to someone
up washed-up
up well up in years
up What have you been up to?
up What's up?
up whip something up
up whoop it up
up wind something up
up wind up doing something
up wind up somewhere
up wipe the floor up with someone
up wise up (to someone or something)
up worked up (about something)
up worked up (over something)
up work one's way up
up work someone or something up

up wrapped up in someone or something
up wrap something up
up write someone or something up
up The game is up.
up The jig is up.
upon chance (up)on someone or something
upon fall (up)on someone or something
upon feel put-upon
upon happen (up)on someone or something
upon hit (up)on something
upon incumbent upon someone to do something
upon once upon a time
upon prevail (up)on someone
upon put upon by someone
upon seize (up)on something
upon set upon someone or something
upon stumble (up)on someone or something
upon take it upon oneself to do something
upon take it (up)on oneself (to do something)
upon (up)on impact
upon wreak vengeance (up)on someone or something
upper get the upper hand (on someone)
upper keep a stiff upper lip
upper upper crust
upright sit bolt upright
uproar create an uproar
uproar make an uproar
ups ups and downs
upset upset the apple cart
upshot the upshot of something
uptake quick on the uptake
uptake slow on the uptake
us let us do something
us That makes two of us.
use It's no use (doing something).
use make use of someone or something
use put something to (good) use
use use every trick in the book
use use one's head
use use one's noggin
use use one's noodle
use use some elbow grease
use use someone or something as an excuse
use use strong language
used be used to doing something
used be used to something
used get used to someone or something
used It takes (some) getting used to.
used They don't make them like they used to.
used used to do something
used used to someone or something
usual as usual
usual business as usual
utter not utter a word
vacation on vacation
vacation take a vacation
vain do something in vain
vale vale of tears
value at face value
value take someone or something at face value
value take something at face value
vanish vanish into thin air
Variety Variety is the spice of life.
velvet (as) soft as velvet
velvet soft as velvet
vengeance do something with a vengeance
vengeance with a vengeance
vengeance wreak vengeance (up)on someone or something
vent give vent to something
vent vent one's spleen
ventured Nothing ventured, nothing gained.
verge on the verge (of doing something)
verge verge on something
verse chapter and verse
very at the (very) outside
very in the (very) nick of time
very (right) under someone's (very) nose
very under someone's (very) nose
very the very last
very the very thing
vest keep one's cards close to one's vest
vest play one's cards close to one's vest
vested have a vested interest in something
vicious in a vicious circle
victors To the victors belong the spoils.
victory a landslide victory
view in view of something
view on view
view point of view
view take a dim view of something
view with a view to doing something
view a bird's-eye view
vigor vim and vigor
villain the villain of the piece
vim vim and vigor
vine die on the vine
vine wither on the vine
vinegar (as) sour as vinegar
vinegar sour as vinegar
virtue by virtue of something
visit pay a visit to someone or something
visit pay (someone or something) a visit
vodka (as) clear as vodka
vodka clear as vodka
voice at the top of one's voice
voice give voice to something
voice have a voice (in something)
voice lower one's voice
voice raise one's voice (to someone)
voice throw one's voice
void null and void
vote cast one's vote
vote vote a split ticket
vote vote a straight ticket
vote vote with one's feet
vote a vote of confidence
vote a vote of thanks
voyage maiden voyage
wade wade in(to something)
wag cause (some) tongues to wag
wag wag one's chin
wagging the tail wagging the dog
wagon fix someone's wagon

wagon on the wagon
wait can't wait (for something to happen)
wait can't wait (to do something)
wait lie in wait for someone or something
wait not able to wait
wait wait-and-see attitude
wait wait on someone hand and foot
wait wait up (for someone or something)
waiting on a waiting list
waiting waiting in the wings
waiting the moment everyone has been waiting for
wake in the wake of something
wake wake the dead
walk cock of the walk
walk Take a long walk off a short pier.
walk Take a walk!
walk walk all over someone
walk walk a tightrope
walk walk away with something
walk walk off with something
walk walk on air
walk walk on eggs
walk walk out (on someone or something)
walk walk the floor
walk walk the plank
walking get one's walking papers
walking give one one's walking papers
walking within walking distance
walks all walks of life
wall bang one's head against a brick wall
wall beat one's head against the wall
wall drive someone to the wall
wall drive someone up the wall
wall force someone to the wall
wall go to the wall
wall have one's back to the wall
wall off-the-wall
wall press someone to the wall
wall push someone to the wall
wall read the handwriting on the wall
wall run into a stone wall
wall see the (hand)writing on the wall
wall wall-to-wall with something
wallop pack a wallop
walls climb the wall(s)
Walls Walls have ears.
wane wax and wane
want not want to catch someone doing something
want want for nothing
want What do you want me to say?
wanted know when one is not wanted
war all-out war
war an act of war
warm (as) warm as toast
warm warm as toast
warm warm the bench
warm warm the cockles of someone's heart
warm warm up to someone
warmed look like death warmed over
warpath on the warpath
warrant sign one's own death warrant
warts warts and all
was (had) known it was coming
was knew it was coming
was known it was coming
was (Now), where was I?
was time was (when)
was Where was I?
wash come out in the wash
wash wash a few things out
wash wash-and-wear
wash wash one's dirty linen in public
wash wash one's hands of someone or something
washed washed-out
washed washed-up
wasn't Rome wasn't built in a day.
waste go to waste
waste Haste makes waste.
waste lay something to waste
waste lay waste to something
waste waste one's breath
waste waste someone
watch keep (close) watch (on someone or something)
watch keep (close) watch (over someone or something)
watch watch one's step
watch watch out
watch watch over someone or something
watch watch someone or something like a hawk
watching (as) exciting as watching (the) paint dry
watching bear watching
watching exciting as watching (the) paint dry
water as a duck takes to water
water Blood is thicker than water.
water Blood runs thicker than water.
water bread and water
water come hell or high water
water dash cold water on something
water get in(to) hot water
water get one's head above water
water in deep water
water in hot water
water keep one's head above water
water like a fish out of water
water like water off a duck's back
water make someone's mouth water
water muddy the water
water not hold water
water of the first water
water pour cold water on something
water through hell and high water
water throw cold water on something
water water something down
water water under the bridge
waterfront cover the waterfront
Waterloo meet one's Waterloo
waters fish in troubled waters
waters pour oil on troubled water(s)
waterworks turn on the waterworks
waves make waves
wax wax and wane
wax the whole ball of wax
way all the way
way by the way
way by way of something

way come someone's way
way do something the hard way
way downhill all the way
way every which way
way find it's way somewhere
way find one's way (around)
way find one's way somewhere
way find (something) out the hard way
way from way back
way get one's (own) way (with someone or something)
way get out of someone's way
way get out of the way
way get someone or something out of the way
way get something under way
way get under way
way go all the way (with someone)
way go a long way in doing something
way go a long way toward doing something
way go out of one's way (to do something)
way have a way with someone or something
way have come a long way
way have the right-of-way
way in a bad way
way in a family way
way in the family way
way in the way of something
way in the worst way
way know one's way about
way know one's way around
way laugh all the way to the bank
way learn (something) the hard way
way look the other way
way make one's way through something
way make way
way not know which way to turn
way one's way of life
way one way or another
way on one's way to doing something
way on someone's way (somewhere)
way on the way (somewhere)
way on the way to doing something
way out of one's way
way out-of-the-way
way pave the way (for someone or something)
way pay someone's (own) way
way pick one's way through something
way rub someone('s fur) the wrong way
way say something in a roundabout way
way see one's way clear (to do something)
way see which way the wind is blowing
way shove one's way somewhere
way stand in someone's way
way take something the wrong way
way That's the way the ball bounces.
way That's the way the cookie crumbles.
way There's more than one way to skin a cat.
way thread (one's way) through something
way to someone's way of thinking
way (way) over there
way Where there's a will there's a way.
way work (one's way) into something
way work one's way through college
way work one's way up
way worm one's way out of something
way yield the right-of-way
way the other way round
ways cut both ways
ways have it both ways
ways mend one's ways
ways no two ways about it
ways parting of the ways
ways set in one's ways
ways ways and means
wayside drop by the wayside
wayside fall by the wayside
We We aim to please.
weak (as) weak as a baby
weak (as) weak as a kitten
weak weak as a baby
weak weak as a kitten
weakness have a weakness for someone or something
wealth a wealth of something
wealthy Early to bed, early to rise(, makes a man healthy, wealthy, and wise.)
wear If the shoe fits, wear it.
wear none the worse for wear
wear wash-and-wear
wear wear and tear (on something)
wear wear more than one hat
wear wear off
wear wear one's heart on one's sleeve
wear wear on someone
wear wear out one's welcome
wear wear someone down
wear wear someone out
weasel weasel out (of something)
weather fair-weather friend
weather keep one's weather eye open
weather lovely weather for ducks
weather under the weather
weather weather permitting
weave weave in and out (of something)
wedded wed(ded) to someone
wedded wedded to something
wedding a shotgun wedding
wedlock born out of wedlock
wee wee hours (of the night)
weed weed someone or something out
week by the week
week week in, week out
weeks weeks running
weepers Finders keepers(, losers weepers).
weigh weigh on someone's mind
weigh weigh someone's words
weigh weigh someone down
weight carry (a lot of) weight (with someone or something)
weight carry one's (own) weight
weight carry the weight of the world on one's shoulders
weight pull one's (own) weight
weight put weight on
weight throw one's weight around
weight worth its weight in gold

welcome wear out one's welcome
welcome welcome someone with open arms
welcome welcome to do something
well alive and well
well All's well that ends well.
well (all) well and good
well as well
well augur well for someone or something
well get well
well hail-fellow-well-met
well know something only too well
well leave well enough alone
well let well enough alone
well play one's cards well
well well and good
well well-disposed toward someone or something
well well-fixed
well well-heeled
well well-off
well well-to-do
well well up in years
were as it were
were better off (if one were somewhere else)
were better off (if something were done)
were Those were the days.
West out West
wet all wet
wet (as) mad as a wet hen
wet get one's feet wet
wet get wet
wet mad as a wet hen
wet wet behind the ears
wet wet blanket
wet wet someone's whistle
whack out of w(h)ack
whack take a whack at someone or something
whale have a whale of a time
whale whale the tar out of someone
what and what have you
what come what may
what give someone what for
what have what it takes
what just what the doctor ordered
what know what's what
what no matter what happens
what not what something is cracked up to be
what recognize one for what one is
what recognize something for what it is
What What are you driving at?
What What can I say?
What What do you want me to say?
what what for
What What goes around, comes around.
What What have you been up to?
what what if
what what makes someone tick
what what makes something tick
What What one doesn't know won't hurt one.
whatever for what(ever) it's worth
Whatever Whatever will be, will be.
what's get what's coming to one
what's give one what's coming to one
what's know what's what
What's What's done is done.
What's What's keeping you?
What's What's new?
What's What's the good of something?
What's What's up?
What's What's with someone?
wheel put one's shoulder to the wheel
wheel wheel and deal
wheels spin one's wheels
when cross a bridge when one comes to it
when know when one is not wanted
when time was (when)
when when all is said and done
when when hell freezes over
When When in Rome, do as the Romans do.
when when it comes right down to it
when when it comes to something
when when least expected
when when one is good and ready
when when push comes to shove
When When the cat's away, the mice will play.
when when the chips are down
when when the going gets rough
when when the going gets tough
when when the time is ripe
where fools rush in (where angels fear to tread)
where give credit where credit is due
where hit one where one lives
where know where all the bodies are buried
where know where someone stands (on someone or something)
where not know where to turn
where (Now), where was I?
where Put your money where your mouth is!
where take up where one left off
where tell someone where to get off
where where one is coming from
where where one lives
Where Where there's a will there's a way.
Where Where there's smoke there's fire.
Where Where was I?
wherefores the whys and wherefores of something
whereof know whereof one speaks
Where've Where've you been hiding yourself?
wherewithal have the wherewithal (to do something)
whet whet someone's appetite
whether not know whether one is coming or going
whether whether or not
which every which way
which know which is which
which know which side one's bread is buttered on
which not know which way to turn
which see which way the wind is blowing
which tell which is which
whiff catch a whiff of something
whiff get a whiff of something
while (every) once in a while
while fiddle while Rome burns
while get out while the getting is good
while make it worth someone's while
while make something worth someone's while

while not worth one's while
while once in a while
while strike while the iron is hot
while while away the time
while worth someone's while
whip whip something into shape
whip whip something up
whirl give something a whirl
whisker by a whisker
whisper in a stage whisper
whistle (as) clean as a whistle
whistle (as) slick as a whistle
whistle blow the whistle (on someone)
whistle clean as a whistle
whistle slick as a whistle
whistle wet someone's whistle
white (as) white as a ghost
white (as) white as a sheet
white (as) white as the driven snow
white in black and white
white put something down in black and white
white white as a sheet
white white as the driven snow
white white elephant
who He laughs best who laughs last.
who He who laughs last, laughs longest.
who He who pays the piper calls the tune.
Who Who do you think you're kidding?
Who Who do you think you're talking to?
Who Who would have thought?
whole go whole hog
whole make something up out of whole cloth
whole on the whole
whole (whole) new ball game
whole the whole ball of wax
whole the whole shooting match
whom to whom it may concern
whoop whoop it up
whys the whys and wherefores of something
wide all wool and a yard wide
wide come from far and wide
wide crack something wide open
wide cut a wide swath
wide give someone or something a wide berth
wide leave oneself wide open for something
wide leave oneself wide open to something
wide wide-awake
wide wide of the mark
wig flip one's wig
wild go hog-wild
wild run wild
wild sow one's wild oats
wild wild about someone or something
Wild Wild horses couldn't drag someone.
wild a wild-goose chase
wildfire spread like wildfire
will against someone's will
will at will
will Boys will be boys.
will Flattery will get you nowhere.
will Give one an inch, and one will take a mile.
will have a hunch (that) something will happen
will heads will roll
will ill will
will last will and testament
will of one's own free will
will someone's last will and testament
will There will be the devil to pay.
will Time will tell.
will Whatever will be, will be.
will When the cat's away, the mice will play.
will Where there's a will there's a way.
will will not hear of something
will with a will
will with the best will in the world
will The truth will out.
willies get the willies
willies give someone the willies
willing ready, willing, and able
win no-win situation
win win by a nose
win win out (over someone or something)
win win someone over
win win the day
wind (as) swift as the wind
wind get one's second wind
wind get wind of something
wind gone with the wind
wind in the wind
wind see which way the wind is blowing
wind swift as the wind
wind take the wind out of someone's sails
wind three sheets to the wind
wind throw caution to the wind
wind wind down
wind wind something up
wind wind up doing something
wind wind up somewhere
windmills tilt at windmills
window go window-shopping
window window-shopping
wine wine and dine someone
wing on the wing
wing wing it
wings clip someone's wings
wings take someone under one's wing(s)
wings try (out) one's wings
wings waiting in the wings
wink (as) quick as a wink
wink not sleep a wink
wink quick as a wink
wink wink at something
winks catch forty winks
winks forty winks
winks take forty winks
wins Slow and steady wins the race.
wipe wipe someone or something out
wipe wipe someone's slate clean
wipe wipe something off
wipe wipe the floor up with someone
wire down to the wire
wire under the wire
wires get one's wires crossed
wise (as) wise as an owl

wise (as) wise as Solomon
wise Early to bed, early to rise(, makes a man healthy, wealthy, and wise.)
wise get wise (to someone or something)
wise penny-wise and pound-foolish
wise put someone wise to someone or something
wise wise as an owl
wise wise as Solomon
wise wise up (to someone or something)
wise a word to the wise
wiser none the wiser
wiser sadder but wiser
wish wish something off on someone
wishful wishful thinking
wit to wit
witch's (as) cold as a witch's caress
witch's (as) cold as a witch's tit
witch's cold as a witch's caress
witch's cold as a witch's tit
with able to do something with one's eyes closed
with alive with someone or something
with (all) over with
with all right with someone
with along with someone or something
with arrange something with someone
with arrange to do something with someone
with at home with someone or something
with at loggerheads (with someone)
with at odds (with someone)
with bear with someone or something
with be friends with someone
with beg to differ (with someone)
with beside oneself (with something)
with be with someone
with born with a silver spoon in one's mouth
with break off (with someone)
with break up (with someone)
with brimming with something
with burn with a low blue flame
with burst with joy
with burst with pride
with can't do anything with someone or something
with carry (a lot of) weight (with someone or something)
with carry on (with someone or something)
with cast one's lot in with someone
with catch one with one's pants down
with catch up (with someone or something)
with chime in (with something)
with closefisted (with money)
with close ranks (with someone)
with come clean (with someone)
with come down with something
with come out with something
with come through something with flying colors
with come to grips with something
with come to terms with someone or something
with come up with someone or something
with come with the territory
with cooking with gas
with could do with someone or something
with cross someone's palm with silver
with cross swords (with someone) (on something)
with curry favor (with someone)
with cut loose (with something)
with cut no ice (with someone)
with damn someone or something with faint praise
with dance with death
with die with one's boots on
with do away with someone or something
with do something with a vengeance
with double up (with someone)
with down with some disease
with end up with the short end of the stick
with exchange more than some number of words with someone
with fall head over heels in love (with someone)
with fall in love (with someone)
with fall in with someone or something
with fall out (with someone about something)
with fall out (with someone over something)
with familiar with someone or something
with favor someone or something with something
with fed up (to somewhere) (with someone or something)
with fiddle about (with someone or something)
with fiddle around (with someone or something)
with find fault (with someone or something)
with fit in (with someone or something)
with fit someone or something out (with something)
with fix someone up (with someone or something)
with flirt with the idea of doing something
with flush with something
with fool around (with someone or something)
with fraught with danger
with get a free hand (with someone or something)
with get a hand with something
with get along (with someone or something)
with get an in (with someone)
with get away with something
with get by (with something)
with get even (with someone)
with get fresh (with someone)
with get into an argument (with someone)
with get in touch (with someone)
with get involved (with someone)
with get one's (own) way (with someone or something)
with get on (with someone or something)
with get physical (with someone)
with get something over (with)
with get through with something
with get to first base (with someone or something)
with get tough (with someone)
with get with something
with give out with something
with give someone a free hand (with something)
with give someone a hand (with someone or something)
with go all the way (with someone)
with go along (with someone or something)
with go around with someone
with gone with the wind
with go out (with someone)
with go over big with someone
with go over something with a fine-tooth comb
with go over with a bang
with go steady (with someone)

with go through with something
with go to bed (with someone)
with go to bed with the chickens
with go with something
with go with the flow
with graced with something
with grace someone or something with one's presence
with green with envy
with hand in glove (with someone)
with handle someone with kid gloves
with hang around (with someone)
with hang out (with someone)
with have a bone to pick (with someone)
with have a brush with something
with have an ax to grind (with someone)
with have an in (with someone)
with have a run-in with someone
with have a score to settle (with someone)
with have a scrape (with someone or something)
with have a thing going (with someone)
with have a way with someone or something
with have a word with someone
with have contact with someone
with have nothing to do with someone or something
with have one's hands full (with someone or something)
with have pull with someone
with have something to do with something
with have something going (with someone)
with have something in common (with someone or something)
with have something out (with someone)
with have to do with someone or something
with have to live with something
with head over heels in love (with someone)
with help (someone or something) out (with someone or something)
with hit it off (with someone)
with hoist with one's own petard
with hold with something
with How goes it (with you)?
with in accordance with something
with in bad (with someone)
with in cahoots (with someone)
with in concert (with someone)
with in Dutch (with someone)
with in good (with someone)
with in keeping (with something)
with in league (with someone)
with in line with something
with in love (with someone or something)
with in step (with someone or something)
with in tune with someone or something
with invest someone with something
with in with someone
with join forces (with someone)
with keep company (with someone)
with keep in touch (with someone)
with keep pace (with someone or something)
with keep up (with someone or something)
with keep up (with the Joneses)
with keep up (with the times)
with kid around (with someone)
with kill two birds with one stone
with knock someone over with a feather
with lay it on with a trowel
with learn to live with something
with leave word (with someone)
with let go (with something)
with let loose (with something)
with let someone have it (with both barrels)
with level with someone
with line someone or something up with something
with line someone up with someone
with lock horns (with someone)
with lose one's touch (with someone or something)
with lose touch (with someone or something)
with lousy with something
with make a hit (with someone or something)
with make an appointment (with someone)
with make away with someone or something
with make do (with someone or something)
with make free with someone or something
with make off with someone or something
with make out (with someone or something)
with make peace (with someone)
with make points (with someone)
with make time (with someone)
with make up (with someone)
with mess about (with someone or something)
with mess around (with someone or something)
with mix someone up with someone else
with monkey around (with someone or something)
with mop the floor up with someone
with not agree with someone
with not in the same league with someone or something
with not with it
with on a first-name basis (with someone)
with on good terms (with someone)
with on par (with someone or something)
with on speaking terms (with someone)
with open up (with someone)
with open with something
with out of favor (with someone)
with out of keeping (with something)
with out of line (with something)
with out of step (with someone or something)
with out of time (with someone or something)
with out of touch (with someone or something)
with out of tune (with someone or something)
with over and done with
with over with
with pal around (with someone)
with part company (with someone)
with pass the time of day (with someone)
with persist with something
with pick a fight with someone
with pick a quarrel (with someone)
with pipe up with something
with play about (with someone or something)
with play along with someone or something
with play around (with someone or something)
with play ball (with someone)
with play cat and mouse (with someone)
with play fast and loose (with someone or something)

with play footsie (with someone)
with play havoc with someone or something
with play hob with someone or something
with play with fire
with put someone to bed with a shovel
with put up with someone or something
with racked with pain
with raise cain (with someone or something)
with raise havoc with someone or something
with raise hell (with someone or something)
with raise hob with someone or something
with raise the devil (with someone or something)
with raise the dickens (with someone or something)
with rap with someone
with rate with someone
with ravished with delight
with reach first base (with someone or something)
with receive someone with open arms
with reckon with someone or something
with resonate with someone
with rich with something
with rub elbows (with someone)
with rub shoulders with someone
with run around like a chicken with its head cut off
with run around with someone
with run off with someone or something
with saddle someone with something
with screw around (with someone or something)
with search something with a fine-tooth comb
with see eye to eye (with someone) (about something)
with see eye to eye (with someone) (on something)
with settle a score with someone
with settle the score (with someone)
with settle up with someone
with sever ties with someone
with shack up (with someone)
with shake hands (with someone)
with shot through with something
with side with someone
with sign on (with someone)
with sit up with someone
with sit with someone
with sleep with someone
with speak with a forked tongue
with split one's sides (with laughter)
with square accounts (with someone)
with square up with someone
with start (off) with a clean slate
with start (over) with a clean slate
with stay in touch (with someone)
with stick someone with someone or something
with stick with someone or something
with strike a chord (with someone)
with string along (with someone)
with stuck with someone or something
with take a hard line (with someone)
with take issue (with someone)
with take liberties with someone or something
with take something home (with oneself)
with take something up (with someone)
with take something with a grain of salt
with take something with a pinch of salt
with take the bitter with the sweet
with take up with someone
with tamper with something
with tarred with the same brush
with team up with someone
with throw the baby out with the bath(water)
with tightfisted (with money)
with top something off (with something)
with touch base (with someone)
with toy with someone or something
with vote with one's feet
with walk away with something
with walk off with something
with wall-to-wall with something
with welcome someone with open arms
with What's with someone?
with wipe the floor up with someone
with with a heavy heart
with with all one's heart and soul
with with all the fixings
with with an eye to doing something
with with a vengeance
with with a view to doing something
with with a will
with with bells on (one's toes)
with with both hands tied behind one's back
with with each passing day
with with ease
with with every (other) breath
with with everything (on it)
with with flying colors
with (with) hat in hand
with with impunity
with with it
with with no strings attached
with with one hand tied behind one's back
with with one's tail between one's legs
with with regard to someone or something
with with relish
with with respect to someone or something
with with something to spare
with with the best will in the world
with work wonders (with someone or something)
with wouldn't touch something with a ten-foot pole
with wreak havoc with something
with You can't take it with you.
with Your secret is safe with me.
with a force to be reckoned with
wither wither on the vine
within come within an ace of doing something
within come within an inch of doing something
within live within one's means
within within an inch of one's life
within within a stone's throw (of something)
within within bounds
within within calling distance
within within hailing distance
within within limits
within within reason
within within shouting distance
within within someone's grasp
within within someone's reach

within within walking distance
without absent without leave
without carry on without someone or something
without cut someone off without a penny
without do without (someone or something)
without get along (without (someone or something))
without goes without saying
without go without (something)
without up the creek (without a paddle)
without without a moment to spare
without without any strings attached
without without batting an eye
without without fail
without without further ado
without without question
without without rhyme or reason
without without so much as doing something
wit's at one's wit's end
wits frighten one out of one's wits
wits frighten the wits out of someone
wits get one's wits about one
wits keep one's wits about one
wits live by one's wits
wits scare one out of one's wits
wits scare the wits out of someone
wits You scared me out of my wits.
Woe Woe is me!
wolf cry wolf
wolf keep the wolf from the door
wolf a wolf in sheep's clothing
wolves throw someone to the wolves
woman woman to woman
wonder no wonder
wonder a nine days' wonder
wonders work wonders (with someone or something)
won't What one doesn't know won't hurt one.
wood knock on wood
woods in some neck of the woods
woods out of the woods
woods a babe in the woods
wool all wool and a yard wide
wool dyed-in-the-wool
wool pull the wool over someone's eyes
word as good as one's word
word break one's word
word by word of mouth
word from the word go
word get a word in edgeways
word get a word in edgewise
word get the final word
word get the last word
word get the word
word go back on one's word
word hang on someone's every word
word have a word with someone
word in a word
word keep one's word
word leave word (with someone)
word mum's the word
word not breathe a word (about someone or something)
word not breathe a word of it
word not utter a word
word put in a good word (for someone)
word say the word
word take one at one's word
word true to one's word
word word by word
word word for word
word a word to the wise
words Actions speak louder than words.
words at a loss (for words)
words beyond words
words eat one's words
words exchange more than some number of words with someone
words have one's words stick in one's throat
words in other words
words in so many words
words mark my word(s)
words mince (one's) words
words or words to that effect
words put something into words
words put words into someone's mouth
words take the words out of one's mouth
words Them's fighting words.
words twist someone's words (around)
words weigh someone's words
words words to that effect
work all in a day's work
work All work and no play makes Jack a dull boy.
work at work
work close enough for government work
work dirty work
work get down to work
work grunt work
work have one's work cut out for one
work knock off work
work make fast work of someone or something
work make short work of someone or something
work Many hands make light work.
work one's work is cut out for one
work out of work
work take off (from work)
work work like a horse
work work one's fingers to the bone
work work (one's way) into something
work work one's way through college
work work one's way up
work work on someone or something
work work out
work work someone or something in
work work someone or something up
work work someone over
work work something into something else
work work something off
work work something out
work work through channels
work work wonders (with someone or something)
work a lick of work
work A little (hard) work never hurt anyone.
work A little (hard) work never killed anyone.
worked (all) worked up (about something)
worked (all) worked up (over something)
worked get worked up (about something)

worked get worked up (over something)
worked worked up (about something)
worked worked up (over something)
works get the works
works give someone the works
works gum up the works
works in the works
works shoot the works
works throw a monkey wrench into the works
works the works
world all over the world
world carry the weight of the world on one's shoulders
world come down in the world
world come up in the world
world dead to the world
world do not have a care in the world
world feel on top of the world
world for all the world
world How's the world (been) treating you?
world in a world of one's own
world in the world
world move up (in the world)
world not for (anything in) the world
world not long for this world
world on top of the world
world out of this world
world set the world on fire
world (sitting) on top of the world
world think the world of someone or something
world with the best will in the world
worlds have the best of both worlds
worm worm one's way out of something
worm worm something out of someone
worm The early bird gets the worm.
worm The worm (has) turned.
worms open (up) a can of worms
worse Could be worse.
worse for better or for worse
worse go from bad to worse
worse none the worse for wear
worse One's bark is worse than one's bite.
worse take a turn for the worse
worst at (the) worst
worst at worst
worst get the worst of something
worst if worst comes to worst
worst in the worst way
worth for all it's worth
worth for what(ever) it's worth
worth get one's money's worth
worth make it worth someone's while
worth make something worth someone's while
worth not worth a dime
worth not worth a hill of beans
worth not worth a plugged nickel
worth not worth a red cent
worth not worth mentioning
worth not worth one's while
worth not worth the trouble
worth put one's two cents(' worth) in
worth worth its weight in gold
worth worth one's salt
worth worth someone's while
worth An ounce of prevention is worth a pound of cure.
worth A bird in the hand is worth two in the bush.
worthy worthy of the name
would as luck would have it
would never would have guessed
would Who would have thought?
would would as soon do something
would would give one's right arm (for someone or something)
would would like (to have) someone or something
would would rather
wouldn't look as if butter wouldn't melt in one's mouth
wouldn't wouldn't dream of doing something
wouldn't wouldn't touch something with a ten-foot pole
wound rub salt in the wound
wrack go to wrack and ruin
wrap wrap something up
wrapped get something wrapped up
wrapped wrapped up in someone or something
wraps keep something under wraps
wreak wreak havoc with something
wreak wreak vengeance (up)on someone or something
wrench throw a monkey wrench into the works
wringer put someone through the wringer
wrist get a slap on the wrist
wrist give someone a slap on the wrist
wrist slap someone's wrist
wrist slap someone on the wrist
write nothing to write home about
write write someone or something off
write write someone or something up
write write something down
write write something out
wrong back the wrong horse
wrong bark up the wrong tree
wrong be off on the wrong foot
wrong get off on the wrong foot
wrong get out of the wrong side of the bed
wrong get up on the wrong side of the bed
wrong go wrong
wrong in the wrong
wrong on the wrong track
wrong rub someone('s fur) the wrong way
wrong start off on the wrong foot
wrong take someone or something wrong
wrong take something the wrong way
wrong the wrong side of the tracks
wrote someone wrote the book on something
wrote That's all she wrote.
X X marks the spot
yard all wool and a yard wide
yarn spin a yarn
year (all) year round
year by the year
Year ring in the New Year
year year after year
year year in, year out

year year round
years advanced in years
years along in years
years get along (in years)
years on in years
years up in years
years well up in years
years years running
yesterday need *something* yesterday
yesterday not born yesterday
yet be the death of me (yet)
yield yield the right-of-way
yoke a yoke around *someone's* neck
yon hither, thither, and yon
yon thither and yon
you All right for you!
you and what have you
you before you can say Jack Robinson
you before you know it
you Behind you!
you between you, me, and the lamppost
you Can you imagine?
you Do I need to paint you a picture?
you Don't let *someone or something* get you down.
you Do you read me?
you Flattery will get you nowhere.
you goes to show you
you Have I got *something* for you!
you Have you been keeping busy?
you Here's looking at you.
you Here you go.
you How goes it (with you)?
you How's the world (been) treating you?
you I'll (try to) catch you later.
you mind you
you pay as you go
you so clean you could eat off the floor
you so quiet you could hear a pin drop
you so still you could hear a pin drop
you Thank you for sharing.
you There you go.
you What are you driving at?
you What do you want me to say?
you What have you been up to?
you What's keeping you?
you Where've you been hiding yourself?
you Who do you think you're kidding?
you Who do you think you're talking to?
You You bet (your boots)!
You You can bet on it!
You You can say that again!
You You can't please everyone.
You You can't take it with you.
You You can't teach an old dog new tricks.
You You got me there.
You You just don't get it!
you you know
You You said it!
You You scared me out of my wits.
You You scared the crap out of me.
You You scared the devil out of me.
You You scared the dickens out of me.
You You scared the hell out of me.
You You scared the pants off (of) me.
You You scratch my back and I'll scratch yours.
You You think you're so smart!
you a fine how-do-you-do
you the same to you
your Cat got your tongue?
your Don't hold your breath.
your Don't quit your day job.
your Enjoy your meal.
your get off your high horse
your Here's mud in your eye.
your Hold your horses!
your Hold your tongue!
your Hush your mouth!
your I didn't catch your name.
your Keep your shirt on!
your mind your manners
your not on your life
your pick on somebody your own size
your pick on someone your own size
your Put that in your pipe and smoke it!
your Put your money where your mouth is!
your You bet (your boots)!
Your Your guess is as good as mine.
Your Your secret is safe with me.
you're Who do you think you're kidding?
you're Who do you think you're talking to?
you're You think you're so smart!
yours yours truly
yours You scratch my back and I'll scratch yours.
yourself by yourself
yourself Where've you been hiding yourself?
yourselves by yourselves
Z everything from A to Z
zenith at the zenith of *something*
zero zero in on *something*
zonk zonk out
zoom zoom in (on *someone or something*)
Zs catch some Zs

Appendix

Irreversible Binomials and Trinomials

Irreversible binomials and trinomials are sequences of two or three words that are in a fixed order, such as *fast and furious*, but not *furious and fast*. The following sequences of words are joined by *and*, *or*, *but*, or some type of implied conjunction. The words are found only in the sequences shown here and cannot be reordered. Those marked with an asterisk (*) are entries in this dictionary.

above and beyond* See above and beyond something.
Adam and Eve
alive and kicking*
again and again
aid and abet* See aid and abet someone.
alive and well*
all and sundry*
all or nothing*
all work and no play* See All work and no play makes Jack a dull boy.
alpha and omega*
apples and oranges*
arm and a leg* See cost an arm and a leg.
armed and dangerous*
arts and letters
(a division of a university)
arts and sciences
(a division of a university)
assault and battery*
back and fill*
back and forth*
backwards and forwards* See know something backwards and forwards.
bacon and eggs
bacon, lettuce, and tomato [sandwich]
bag and baggage*
bait and switch*
ball and chain*
bar and grill
beck and call* See at someone's beck and call.
bed-and-breakfast
beer and pretzels
beer and skittles* See (all) beer and skittles.
before and after
bell, book, and candle*
betwixt and between*
bib and tucker* See best bib and tucker.
big and bold*
binge and purge*
birds and the bees*
biscuits and gravy
black and blue
black and white* See in black and white.
blood and gore
blood and guts
blood, sweat, and tears*
bloody but unbowed*
body and soul* See keep body and soul together.
born and bred*
born and raised*
bound and determined*
bound and gagged
bourbon and water
bow and scrape*
bread and butter*
bread and water
breaking and entering*
bricks and mortar*
bride and groom
bright and early*
bright-eyed and bushy-tailed*
business or pleasure
by and by*

by and large*
by guess and by golly*
cap and gown*
cash-and-carry*
cash or credit*
cat and mouse* See play cat and mouse (with someone).
cats and dogs* See rain cats and dogs.
cause and effect
cease and desist*
chapter and verse*
checks and balances*
cheese and crackers
chips and dip*
church and state*
clip and save
cloak-and-dagger*
coat and tie*
cock and bull* See cock-and-bull story.
coffee and Danish*
coffee and doughnuts
coffee, tea, or milk*
come and gone*
coming or going* See not know if one is coming or going.
country and western [music]
crash and burn*
cream and sugar
crime and punishment
cup and saucer
curds and whey
cut-and-dried*
cut and paste*
cut and run*
cute and cuddly
dark and stormy
day and age* See in this day and age.
day in and day out*
dead and buried*
dead and gone*
dead or alive
deaf and dumb*
death and destruction
death and taxes*
decline and fall
dilation and curettage
divide and conquer*
do or die*
dog and pony show*
doom and gloom
down-and-dirty*
down-and-out*
drawn and quartered*
dribs and drabs*
drum and bugle
drunk and disorderly*
duck and cover*
duck and drake
easy come, easy go*
eat and run*
ebb and flow*
ever and anon*
fad and fashion
fair and impartial*
fair and square*
faith, hope, and charity
far and away* See far and away the best.
far and wide* See come from far and wide.
fast and furious*
fast and loose* See play fast and loose (with someone or something).
fat and happy*
Father, Son, and Holy Ghost
fear and loathing
fear and trembling* See in fear and trembling.
feast or famine* See either feast or famine.
fin and feather
few and far between*
field and stream
fight or flight
Finders keepers(, losers weepers).*
fine and dandy*
first and foremost*
first and last
first and ten*
first come, first served*
first, last, and always
fish and chips
fish or fowl* See neither fish nor fowl.
fish or cut bait*
fit and trim*
fits and starts* See by fits and starts.
flesh and blood*
flora and fauna*
flotsam and jetsam*
fold, spindle, or mutilate*
food and drink
food and water
footloose and fancy-free*
for better or for worse*
fore and aft*
forever and a day*
forever and always
forgive and forget*
form and substance*
franks and beans (frankfurters and beans)
free and clear*
free and easy*
friend or foe*
fries and a shake (French fries and a milkshake)
front and center
fun and games*
give-and-take*
God and country
gone but not forgotten*
good and ready* See when one is good and ready.
goose and gander
grin and bear it*
hale and hearty*
half-and-half*
ham and eggs
hammer and nails
hammer and sickle

hammer and tongs* See go at it hammer and tongs.
hand and foot* See bound hand and foot.
hard-and-fast*
hat and gloves
have and to hold
haves and have-nots
head and shoulders* See head and shoulders above someone or something.
head over heels* See head over heels in debt; head over heels in love (with someone).
head to toe* See from head to toe.
heads or tails*
health and welfare
heart and soul*
heating and air-conditioning
heaven and earth* See move heaven and earth to do something.
hellfire and damnation
hell or high water* See come hell or high water.
hem and haw* See hem and haw (around).
hen and chicken
here and there*
here, there, and everywhere
hide-and-seek*
hide nor hair* See neither hide nor hair.
high and dry* See leave someone high and dry.
high-and-mighty*
highways and byways*
hill and dale
hit-and-miss*
hit-and-run*
hit-or-miss*
hither and thither*
hither, thither, and yon*
honest and aboveboard*
hook, line, and sinker* See swallow something hook, line, and sinker.
hook or crook* See by hook or (by) crook.
hoot and holler*
hop, skip, and a jump*
horse and buggy*
horse and carriage*
hot and bothered*
hot and cold* See blow hot and cold.
hot and heavy*
hot and humid
house and home* See eat someone out of house and home.
hue and cry*
hunt-and-peck*
husband and wife
hustle and bustle*
ice-cream and cake
in and of itself*
in and out
in sickness and in health
ins and outs* See ins and outs of something.
intents and purposes* See for all intents and purposes.
jack and jill
Jekyll and Hyde*
Jesus, Mary, and Joseph
joint and several
jot and tittle
juice and cookies*
king and queen
kiss and tell*
kit and caboodle*
kith and kin*
knife and fork
knife, fork, and spoon
ladies and gentlemen
last but not least*
last will and testament*
law and order
leaps and bounds* See by leaps and bounds.
lick and a promise* See give something a lick and a promise.
lie, cheat, and steal
life and death* See matter of life and death.
life or death
like it or lump it*
live and learn*
live and let live*
liver and onions
lock and key
lock, stock, and barrel*
long and (the) short it*
lost-and-found*
lost and gone forever*
loud and clear*
love and marriage
love nor money* See not for love nor money.
make or break* See make or break someone.
main strength and awkwardness*
man and wife
master and servant
meat and drink
meat-and-potatoes*
meek and mild
mergers and acquisitions
mice and men* See best-laid plans of mice and men.
might and main*
milk and honey
mind and body
mix and match*
more or less*
mortar and pestle
mother and child
motherhood and apple pie
movers and shakers*
Mr. and Mrs.
name and address
needle and thread
new and improved
nice and easy
nickel and dime* See nickel and dime (someone)
nip and tuck*
nook and cranny*
nothing ventured, nothing gained*
now and again*
now and then*

now or never*
null and void*
nuts and bolts* See nuts and bolts (of something).
odds and ends*
off and running*
old and gray
once and for all*
one and all*
one and only*
one and the same*
open-and-shut case*
out and about*
Out of sight, out of mind.*
over and above* See over and above something.
over and done with*
over and over* See over and over (again).
over and under
pain and suffering
part and parcel* See part and parcel (of something).
past and present
peaches and cream
peanut butter and jelly
pen and ink
pen and pencil
penny-wise and pound-foolish*
pick and choose*
pickles and onions
pins and needles* See on pins and needles.
plain and simple*
pomp and circumstance
poor but clean*
pork and beans
postage and handling*
potatoes and gravy
pots and pans
power and might
pride and joy*
pride and prejudice
principal and interest
profit and loss
pros and cons
p's and q's* See mind one's p's and q's.
publish or perish*
pure and simple*
Put up or shut up!*
question and answer
quick and dirty*
rack and pinion
rain or shine*
rank and file*
rant and rave* See rant and rave (about someone or something).
rape and pillage
read and write
reading and writing
ready and able
ready and willing
ready, get set, go
ready, willing, and able*
red, white, and blue
research and development
rest and recreation
rest and relaxation
rhyme or reason* See without rhyme or reason.
rice and beans
rice and peas
right and wrong
right or wrong
rise and fall
Rise and shine!*
rock and a hard place* See between a rock and a hard place.
rock and roll
rocks and rills
rod and reel
rod and staff
room and board*
root and branch
rough-and-ready*
rough-and-tumble*
rum and coke
rhythm and blues
sackcloth and ashes
sadder but wiser*
sadism and masochism
safe and sound*
said and done* See after all is said and done.
salt and pepper
sand and sea
sane and sober
sausage and eggs
savings and loan
scotch and soda
scotch and water
search and destroy
seek and destroy
separate but equal*
sex and violence
Shape up or ship out.*
shave and shower
shipping and handling*
shirt and tie
shoes and socks
short and fat
short and sassy
short and stout
short and sweet
show-and-tell*
sick and tired* See sick and tired of someone or something.
signed, sealed, and delivered*
sink or swim*
sir or madam
six of one and half a dozen of another*
sixes and sevens* See at sixes and sevens.
skin and bones* See (all) skin and bones.
skull and crossbones
slim and trim
slings and arrows "... of outrageous fortune." (Shakespeare)
slip and slide
slow and sure
slow(ly) but sure(ly)*

smoke and mirrors*
So far, so good.*
soap and water
Sodom and Gomorrah
song and dance* See go into one's song and dance (about something).
sooner or later*
sound and fury
soup and salad
soup and sandwich
spick-and-span*
spit and image* See be the spit and image of someone.
stand and deliver*
stars and stripes
start and stop
stem to stern* See from stem to stern.
sticks and stones*
stop-and-go*
stop, look, and listen*
straight and narrow*
strawberries and cream
stuff and nonsense*
sugar and spice
suit and tie
sum and substance*
supply and demand*
surf and turf*
sweet and low*
sweet and sour*
sweetness and light* See all sweetness and light.
swift and sure*
take it or leave it*
tall and thin
tar and feather* See tar and feather someone.
tax-and-spend*
tea and crumpets*
then and there*
thick and thin* See through thick and thin.
thither and yon*
thrust and parry*
thunder and lightning
time and (time) again*
time and space
tip to toe* See from tip to toe.
tits and ass*
to and fro*
toing and froing* See toing and froing (on something).
Tom, Dick, and Harry* See (every) Tom, Dick, and Harry.
tool and die
tooth and nail* See fight someone or something tooth and nail.
touch and go*
town-and-gown*
town and country
trial and error*
trials and tribulations*
Trick or treat!*
tried-and-true*
twist and shout
two's company(, three's a crowd)*
up and around*
up-and-coming*
up and at them*
up and away*
up and down
ups and downs*
vim and vigor*
vinegar and oil
waifs and strays
wait and see* See wait-and-see attitude.
war and peace
wash-and-wear*
wax and wane*
ways and means*
weak and weary
wear and tear* See wear and tear (on something).
week in, week out*
weights and measures
well and good* See (all) well and good.
wiggle and squirm
wine and cheese
wine and dine* See wine and dine someone.
wit and wisdom
wrack and ruin* See go to wrack and ruin.
year in, year out*
you, me, and the lamppost* See between you, me, and the lamppost.